Principles and practice of marketing

4th edition

David Jobber

The McGraw·Hill Companies

London · Boston · Burr Ridge, IL · Dubuque, IA · Madison, WI · New York · San Francisco · St. Louis
Bangkok · Bogotá · Caracas · Kuala Lumpur · Lisbon · Madrid · Mexico City · Milan · Montreal · New Delhi
Santiago · Seoul · Singapore · Sydney · Taipei · Toronto

Principles and Practice of Marketing, fourth edition
David Jobber
ISBN 0-07-710708-X

Published by McGraw-Hill International (UK) Ltd
Shoppenhangers Road
Maidenhead
Berkshire
SL6 2QL
Telephone: 44 (0) 1628 502 500
Fax: 44 (0) 1628 770 224
Website: www.mcgraw-hill.co.uk

British Library Cataloguing in Publication Data
A catalogue record for this book is available from the British Library

Library of Congress Cataloging in Publication Data
The Library of Congress data for this book has been applied for from the Library of Congress

Senior Development Editor: Caroline Howell
Associate Development Editor: Deborah Newcombe
Marketing Director: Petra Skytte
Senior Production Manager: Max Elvey
Senior Production Editor: Eleanor Hayes
Permissions Manager: Judith Spencer

Project management by Cambridge Publishing Management Limited
Picture research by Caroline Thompson
Text design by Claire Brodmann
Cover design by Ego Creative
Printed in Singapore

Published by McGraw-Hill International (UK) Limited an imprint of The McGraw-Hill Companies, Inc., 1221 Avenue of the Americas, New York, NY 10020. Copyright © 2004 by McGraw-Hill Education (UK) Limited. All rights reserved. No part of this publication may be reproduced or distributed in any form or by any means, or stored in a database or retrieval system, without the prior written consent of The McGraw-Hill Companies, Inc., including, but not limited to, in any network or other electronic storage or transmission, or broadcast for distance learning.

ISBN 0-07-710708-X
© 2004. Exclusive rights by The McGraw-Hill Companies, Inc. for manufacture and export. This book cannot be re-exported from the country to which it is sold by McGraw-Hill.

❝These guys say I'm crazy—crazy in the head like a sheep: But I'm as happy as if I had good sense.❞

DAMON RUNYON, *Two Men Named Collins*

❝It is not the critic who counts, not the one who points out how the strong man stumbled or how the doer of deeds might have done them better. The credit belongs to the man who is in the arena; whose face is marred with sweat and dust and blood; who strives valiantly; who errs and comes short again and again; who knows the great enthusiasms, the great devotions and spends himself in worthy cause and who, if he fails, at least fails while bearing greatly so that his place shall never be with those cold and timid souls who know neither victory nor defeat.❞

THEODORE ROOSEVELT

About the author

David Jobber is an internationally recognized marketing academic. He is Professor of Marketing at the University of Bradford School of Management. He holds an honours degree in Economics from the University of Manchester, a masters degree from the University of Warwick and a doctorate from the University of Bradford.

Before joining the faculty at the Bradford Management School, David worked for the TI Group in marketing and sales, and was Senior Lecturer in Marketing at the University of Huddersfield. He has wide experience of teaching core marketing courses at undergraduate, postgraduate and post-experience levels. His specialisms are industrial marketing, sales management and marketing research. He has a proven, ratings-based record of teaching achievements at all levels. His competence in teaching is reflected in visiting appointments at the universities of Aston, Lancaster, Loughborough and Warwick. He has taught marketing to executives of such international companies as Allied Domecq, the BBC, Bass, Croda International, Kalamazoo, Royal and Sun Alliance, Rolls Royce and RTZ.

Supporting his teaching is a record of achievement in academic research. David has over 100 publications in the marketing area in such journals as the *International Journal of Research in Marketing*, *MIS Quarterly*, *Strategic Management Journal*, *Journal of International Business Studies*, *Journal of Business Research*, *Journal of Product Innovation Management* and the *Journal of Personal Selling and Sales Management*. David has served on the editorial boards of the *International Journal of Research in Marketing*, *Journal of Personal Selling and Sales Management*, *European Journal of Marketing* and the *Journal of Marketing Management*.

In 2001, David was appointed Special Advisor to the Research Assessment Exercise panel that rated research output from business and management schools throughout the UK.

Brief table of contents

About the Author	iv
Case Contributors	xvi
List of Vignettes	xviii
Preface to the Fourth Edition	xxi
Acknowledgements	xxvi
Guided Tour	xxix
Technology to Enhance Learning and Teaching	xxxii
Currency Conversion Table	xxxiv

1 Fundamentals of Modern Marketing Thought

1	Marketing in the Modern Firm	3
2	Marketing Planning: an Overview of Marketing	35
3	Understanding Consumer Behaviour	65
4	Understanding Organizational Buying Behaviour	99
5	The Marketing Environment	131
6	Marketing Research and Information Systems	169
7	Market Segmentation and Positioning	209

2 Marketing Mix Decisions

8	Managing Products: Brand and Corporate Identity Management	259
9	Managing Products: Product Life Cycle, Portfolio Planning and Product Growth Strategies	307
10	Developing New Products	337
11	Pricing Strategy	375
12	Advertising	413
13	Personal Selling and Sales Management	461
14	Direct Marketing	505
15	Internet Marketing	549
16	Other Promotional Mix Methods	593
17	Distribution	633

3 Competition and Marketing

18	Analysing Competitors and Creating a Competitive Advantage	677
19	Competitive Marketing Strategy	711

4 Marketing Implementation and Application

20	Managing Marketing Implementation, Organization and Control	751
21	Marketing Services	791
22	International Marketing	843

References	883
Glossary	905
Companies and Brands Index	917
Subject Index	922

Contents

About the Author	iv
Case Contributors	xvi
List of Vignettes	xviii
Preface to the Fourth Edition	xxi
Acknowledgements	xxvi
Guided Tour	xxix
Technology to Enhance Learning and Teaching	xxxii
Currency Conversion Table	xxxiv

1 Fundamentals of Modern Marketing Thought

1 Marketing in the modern firm — 3
- Learning objectives — 3
- The marketing concept — 4
- Marketing versus production orientation — 5
- Efficiency versus effectiveness — 7
- Market-driven versus internally orientated businesses — 8
- Limitations of the marketing concept — 10
- Creating customer value and satisfaction — 13
- Developing an effective marketing mix — 16
- Key characteristics of an effective marketing mix — 19
- Criticisms of the 4-Ps approach to marketing management — 21
- Marketing and business performance — 22
- Review — 25
- Key terms — 26
- Internet exercise — 27
- Study questions — 27
- Case 1 H&M Gets Hot — 28
- Case 2 Legoland and the Millennium Dome: a Tale of the Launch of Two London Visitor Attractions — 31

2 Marketing planning: an overview of marketing — 35
- Learning objectives — 35
- The fundamentals of planning — 36
- The process of marketing planning — 37
- Marketing objectives — 46
- Core strategy — 48
- The rewards of marketing planning — 52
- Problems in making planning work — 53
- How to handle marketing planning problems — 54
- Review — 55
- Key terms — 57
- Internet exercise — 58
- Study questions — 58

	Case 3 Heron Engineering	59
	Case 4 Weatherpruf Shoe Waxes	62
3	**Understanding consumer behaviour**	**65**
	Learning objectives	65
	The dimensions of buyer behaviour	66
	Consumer behaviour	67
	Influences on consumer behaviour	77
	Review	90
	Key terms	92
	Internet exercise	93
	Study questions	94
	Case 5 Cappuccino Wars	95
	Case 6 Ethical Consumer Decision-making	97
4	**Understanding organizational buying behaviour**	**99**
	Learning objectives	99
	Characteristics of organizational buying	100
	The dimensions of organizational buying behaviour	102
	Influences on organizational buying behaviour	110
	Developments in purchasing practice	113
	Relationship management	117
	How to build relationships	122
	Review	125
	Key terms	127
	Internet exercise	127
	Study questions	128
	Case 7 Winters Company	129
	Case 8 Morris Services	130
5	**The marketing environment**	**131**
	Learning objectives	131
	Economic forces	132
	Social/cultural forces	138
	Political/legal forces	145
	Ecological/physical forces	148
	Technological forces	151
	Environmental scanning	153
	Responses to environmental change	155
	Ethical dilemma	157
	Review	157
	Key terms	158
	Internet exercise	159
	Study questions	159
	Case 9 Marks & Spencer: Responding to Environmental Change	160
	Case 10 Fiat's Fall From Grace—Can Fiat Turn it Around?	163

6	**Marketing research and information systems**	**169**
	Learning objectives	169
	Marketing information systems	170
	The importance of marketing research	172
	Approaches to conducting marketing research	174
	Types of marketing research	175
	Stages in the marketing research process	178
	The use of marketing information systems and marketing research	195
	Ethical issues in marketing research	196
	Ethical dilemma	198
	Review	198
	Key terms	200
	Internet exercise	201
	Study questions	201
	Case 11 Carbery: Developing New Products in a Mature Market	202
	Case 12 Air Catering Enterprises	206
7	**Market segmentation and positioning**	**209**
	Learning objectives	209
	Why bother to segment markets?	210
	The process of market segmentation and target marketing	212
	Segmenting consumer markets	212
	Segmenting organizational markets	225
	Target marketing	228
	Positioning	236
	Review	242
	Key terms	244
	Internet exercise	244
	Study questions	245
	Case 13 Positioning Budweiser	246
	Case 14 Corus Engineering Steels	253

2 Marketing Mix Decisions

8	**Managing products: brand and corporate identity management**	**259**
	Learning objectives	259
	Products and brands	260
	The product line and product mix	262
	Brand types	262
	Why strong brands are important	264
	Brand building	266
	Key branding decisions	273
	Rebranding	276
	Brand extension and stretching	279
	Co-branding	281

	Global and pan European branding	285
	Corporate identity management	288
	Ethical issues concerning products	293
	Ethical dilemma	295
	Review	296
	Key terms	299
	Internet exercise	300
	Study questions	300
	Case 15 Levi's Jeans: Re-engaging the Youth Market	301
	Case 16 Reinventing Burberry	304
9	**Managing products: product life cycle, portfolio planning and product growth strategies**	**307**
	Learning objectives	307
	Managing product lines and brands over time: the product life cycle	308
	Uses of the product life cycle	310
	Limitations of the product life cycle	314
	Managing brand and product line portfolios	317
	Product strategies for growth	325
	Review	328
	Key terms	330
	Internet exercise	330
	Study questions	330
	Case 17 Microsoft Xbox Live!: Who will Win the Gaming Battle in the Latest Games Console Wars?	331
	Case 18 Unilever Culls for Growth	335
10	**Developing new products**	**337**
	Learning objectives	337
	What is a new product?	339
	Creating and nurturing an innovative culture	340
	Organizing effectively for new product development	341
	Managing the new product development process	346
	Competitive reaction to new product introductions	363
	Review	364
	Key terms	366
	Internet exercise	366
	Study questions	367
	Case 19 The Development of a Motoring Icon: The Launch of the New Mini	368
	Case 20 The UK National Lottery	371
11	**Pricing strategy**	**375**
	Learning objectives	375
	Economists' approach to pricing	376
	Cost-orientated pricing	378
	Competitor-orientated pricing	380
	Marketing-orientated pricing	382

Initiating price changes	397
Reacting to competitors' price changes	400
Ethical issues in pricing	401
Ethical dilemma	404
Review	405
Key terms	406
Internet exercise	407
Study questions	407
Case 21 easyJet and Ryanair: Flying High with Low Prices	408
Case 22 Hansen Bathrooms (a)	411

12 Advertising — 413
Learning objectives	413
Integrated marketing communications	416
The communication process	418
Strong and weak theories of how advertising works	421
Developing an advertising strategy	422
Organizing for campaign development	440
Ethical issues in advertising	444
Ethical dilemma	446
Review	446
Key terms	448
Internet exercise	449
Study questions	449
Case 23 The Repositioning of White Horse Whisky	450
Case 24 NFO MarketMind: Brand Tracking and the 'Lettuseat' Advertising Campaign	453

13 Personal selling and sales management — 461
Learning objectives	461
Environmental and managerial forces affecting sales	462
Types of seller	466
Sales responsibilities	469
Personal selling skills	472
Sales management	479
Ethical issues in personal selling and sales management	495
Ethical dilemma	497
Review	498
Key terms	500
Internet exercise	500
Study questions	501
Case 25 Glaztex	502
Case 26 Selling Exercise	504

14 Direct marketing — 505
Learning objectives	505
Defining direct marketing	507

	Growth in direct marketing activity	508
	Database marketing	509
	Customer relationship management	514
	Managing a direct marketing campaign	519
	Media decisions	522
	Ethical issues in direct marketing	538
	Ethical dilemma	539
	Review	540
	Key terms	542
	Internet exercise	543
	Study questions	543
	Case 27 The Launch of Nectar: Will the Nectar Loyalty Scheme Reap Rewards?	544
	Case 28 Customer Relationship Management and Value Creation	548
15	**Internet marketing**	**549**
	Learning objectives	549
	More than just a website	550
	Internet marketing and e-commerce	553
	E-commerce market exchanges	556
	Factors affecting the adoption of Internet marketing	557
	The benefits and limitations of the Internet and e-commerce	558
	Assessing online competence	563
	Competitive online advantage and strategy	566
	Selecting an e-commerce marketing mix	569
	Ethical issues in Internet marketing	575
	Ethical dilemma	578
	Review	578
	Key terms	580
	Internet exercise	581
	Study questions	582
	Case 29 Google: a Victim of its own Success?	583
	Case 30 Thin Red Line	586
16	**Other promotional mix methods**	**593**
	Learning objectives	593
	Sales promotion	594
	Public relations and publicity	603
	Sponsorship	607
	Exhibitions	613
	Product placement	616
	Ethical issues in sales promotion and public relations	618
	Ethical dilemma	619
	Review	620
	Key terms	622
	Internet exercise	623

	Study questions	623
	Case 31 Community Relations: Building Masts for 3G Phones	624
	Case 32 Movie Marketing: How Studios Make and Spend Fortunes, Creating Hype for their Blockbusters	626
17	**Distribution**	**633**
	Learning objectives	633
	Functions of channel intermediaries	635
	Types of distribution channel	637
	Channel strategy	641
	Channel management	647
	Physical distribution	652
	The physical distribution system	655
	Ethical issues in distribution	662
	Ethical dilemma	664
	Review	665
	Key terms	667
	Internet exercise	667
	Study questions	668
	Case 33 The Trouble with TopUps: Vodafone Causes a Stir by Lowering the Margins of Retailers	669
	Case 34 Avon and L'Oréal: Keep Young and Beautiful!	673

3 Competition and Marketing

18	**Analysing competitors and creating a competitive advantage**	**677**
	Learning objectives	677
	Analysing competitive industry structure	678
	Competitor analysis	681
	Competitive advantage	687
	Creating a differential advantage	691
	Creating cost leadership	697
	Review	700
	Key terms	701
	Internet exercise	702
	Study questions	702
	Case 35 Wal-Mart Grows Asda	703
	Case 36 StoraEnso: using an Ethics Code to Create a Competitive Advantage	706
19	**Competitive marketing strategy**	**711**
	Learning objectives	711
	Competitive behaviour	712
	Developing competitive marketing strategies	714
	Build objectives	714
	Hold objectives	725
	Niche objectives	729

		Harvest objectives	730
		Divest objectives	731
		Review	731
		Key terms	733
		Internet exercise	734
		Study questions	734
		Case 37 The Battle over Safeway	735
		Case 38 Mitsubishi Ireland: Building the Black Diamond Brand	740

4 Marketing Implementation and Application

	20	**Managing marketing implementation, organization and control**	**751**
		Learning objectives	751
		Marketing strategy, implementation and performance	753
		Implementation and the management of change	754
		Objectives of marketing implementation and change	757
		Barriers to the implementation of the marketing concept	758
		Forms of resistance to marketing implementation and change	761
		Developing implementation strategies	762
		Marketing organization	773
		Marketing control	779
		Strategic control	781
		Operational control	781
		Review	783
		Key terms	785
		Internet exercise	786
		Study questions	786
		Case 39 Jambo Records	787
		Case 40 Hansen Bathrooms (b)	790
	21	**Marketing services**	**791**
		Learning objectives	791
		The nature of services	792
		Managing services	796
		Retailing	817
		Marketing in non-profit organizations	826
		Review	829
		Key terms	831
		Internet exercise	832
		Study questions	832
		Case 41 The Leith Agency	833
		Case 42 Hope Community Resources, Inc.	837
	22	**International marketing**	**843**
		Learning objectives	843
		Deciding whether to go international	844
		Deciding which markets to enter	846

Deciding how to enter a foreign market	850
Developing international marketing strategy	856
Organizing for international operations	869
Centralization vs decentralization	870
Review	873
Key terms	874
Internet exercises	875
Study questions	875
Case 43 Going International: the Case of McDonald's	876
Case 44 British Airways World Cargo	879

References	883
Glossary	905
Companies and Brands Index	917
Subject Index	922

Case contributors

Case 1 **H&M Gets Hot** DAVID JOBBER, *Professor of Marketing, University of Bradford*

Case 2 **Legoland and the Millennium Dome: a Tale of the Launch of Two London Visitor Attractions** JULIAN RAWEL, *Managing Director, The Julian Rawel Consultancy Ltd and Visiting Fellow in Strategic Management, Bradford University School of Management*

Case 3 **Heron Engineering** DAVID SHIPLEY, *Professor of Marketing, Trinity College, University of Dublin, Ireland*

Case 4 **Weatherpruf Shoe Waxes** GRAHAM HOOLEY, *Professor of Marketing, Aston University*

Case 5 **Cappuccino Wars** DAVID JOBBER, *Professor of Marketing, University of Bradford*

Case 6 **Ethical Consumer Decision-making** DR DEIRDRE SHAW, *Division of Marketing, Glasgow Caledonian University, and* DR TERRY NEWHOLM, *Manchester School of Management, UMIST*

Case 7 **Winters Company** DAVID JOBBER, *Professor of Marketing, University of Bradford*

Case 8 **Morris Services** DAVID JOBBER, *Professor of Marketing, University of Bradford*

Case 9 **Marks & Spencer: Responding to Environmental Change** DAVID COOK, *Senior Lecturer in Marketing, University of Leeds, and* DAVID JOBBER, *Professor of Marketing, University of Bradford*

Case 10 **Fiat's Fall From Grace—Can Fiat Turn it Around?** CONOR CARROLL, *Lecturer in Marketing, University of Limerick, Ireland*

Case 11 **Carbery: Developing New Products in a Mature Market** BREDA MCCARTHY, *College Lecturer in Marketing at University College Cork, Ireland*

Case 12 **Air Catering Enterprises** RAVI CHANDRAN, *Operating Manager at a major airline and* DARAGH O'REILLY, *Lecturer in Marketing, University of Leeds*

Case 13 **Positioning Budweiser** SUE BRIDGEWATER, *Lecturer in Marketing and Strategy, University of Warwick*

Case 14 **Corus Engineering Steels** BRIDGET ROWE, *Researcher,* GARY REED, *Lecturer, and* JIM SAKER, *Professor in Retail Management, Loughborough University Business School*

Case 15 **Levi's Jeans: Re-engaging the Youth Market** DAVID JOBBER, *Professor of Marketing, University of Bradford*

Case 16 **Reinventing Burberry** DAVID JOBBER, *Professor of Marketing, University of Bradford*

Case 17 **Microsoft Xbox Live!: Who will Win the Gaming Battle in the Latest Games Console Wars?** CONOR CARROLL, *Lecturer in Marketing, University of Limerick, Ireland*

Case 18 **Unilever Culls for Growth** DAVID JOBBER, *Professor of Marketing, University of Bradford*

Case 19 **The Development of a Motoring Icon: Launch of the New Mini** COLIN GILLIGAN, *Professor of Marketing, Sheffield Hallam University*

Case 20 **The UK National Lottery** DR CLARE BRINDLEY, *Department of Business and Management Studies, Crewe and Alsager Faculty, Manchester Metropolitan University*

Case 21 **easyJet and Ryanair: Flying High with Low Prices** DAVID JOBBER, *Professor of Marketing, University of Bradford*

Case 22 **Hansen Bathrooms (a)** DAVID JOBBER, *Professor of Marketing, University of Bradford*

Case 23 **The Repositioning of White Horse Whisky** ANN MURRAY CHATTERTON, *Director of Training and Development, Institute of Practitioners in Advertising (IPA)*

Case 24 **NFO MarketMind: Brand Tracking and the 'Lettuseat' Advertising Campaign** CLIVE NANCARROW, *Professor of Marketing Research, University of the West of England, Bristol;* LEN TIU WRIGHT, *Professor of Marketing, De Montfort University, Leicester;* IAN BRACE, *Director, NFO WorldGroup*

Case 25 **Glaztex** DAVID JOBBER, *Professor of Marketing, University of Bradford*

Case contributors

Case 26 Selling Exercise ROBERT EDWARDS, *Zeneca*

Case 27 The Launch of Nectar: Will the Nectar Loyalty Scheme Reap Rewards? CONOR CARROLL, *Lecturer in Marketing, University of Limerick, Ireland*

Case 28 Customer Relationship Management and Value Creation TRACY HARWOOD, *Senior Lecturer in Marketing, De Montfort University, and* MICHAEL STARKEY *Senior Lecturer in Marketing, De Montfort University*

Case 29 Google: a Victim of its own Success? DR FIONA ELLIS-CHADWICK, *Lecturer in Marketing and e-Commerce, Loughborough University*

Case 30 Thin Red Line DAVID HARMSTON, JILL SCHWABL *and* RIAN VAN DER MERWE, *graduate students, and* LEYLAND PITT *Professor of Marketing, School of Marketing, Curtin University of Technology, Perth, Australia*

Case 31 Community Relations: Building Masts for 3G Phones ALAN RAWEL, *Head of Education and Training, Institute of Public Relations, London*

Case 32 Movie Marketing: How Studios Make and Spend Fortunes, Creating Hype for their Blockbusters CONOR CARROLL, *Lecturer in Marketing, University of Limerick, Ireland*

Case 33 The Trouble with TopUps: Vodafone causes a Stir by Lowering the Margins of Retailers CONOR CARROLL, *Lecturer in Marketing, University of Limerick, Ireland*

Case 34 Avon and L'Oréal: Keep Young and Beautiful! JIM BLYTHE, *Reader in Marketing, Glamorgan University*

Case 35 Wal-Mart Grows Asda DAVID JOBBER, *Professor of Marketing, University of Bradford*

Case 36 StoraEnso: Using an Ethics Code to Create a Competitive Advantage LISE-LOTTE LINDFELT MBA, *Doctoral Researcher, Department of Business Administration, Åbo Akademi University, Finland*

Case 37 The Battle over Safeway CONOR CARROLL, *Lecturer in Marketing, University of Limerick, Ireland*

Case 38 Mitsubishi Ireland: Building the Black Diamond Brand JOHN FAHY, *Professor of Marketing, University of Limerick*

Case 39 Jambo Records KEN PEATTIE, *Professor of Marketing, Cardiff University;* JAMES ROBERTS, *Informed Sources International*

Case 40 Hansen Bathrooms (b) DAVID JOBBER, *Professor of Marketing, University of Bradford*

Case 41 The Leith Agency CHRISTINE BAND, *Lecturer in Marketing, Napier University*

Case 42 Hope Community Resources, Inc. MARIE O'DWYER, *Lecturer in Marketing, Waterford Institute of Technology, Ireland*

Case 43 Going International: the Case of McDonald's JUSTIN O'BRIEN, *Manager Global Selling, British Airways;* ELEANOR HAMILTON, *Director of the Entrepreneurship Unit, Lancaster University Management School*

Case 44 British Airways World Cargo ELEANOR HAMILTON, *Director of the Entrepreneurship Unit, Lancaster University Management School, and* SION O'CONNOR, *Brand Manager, British Airways World Cargo*

Vignettes

Marketing in Action

1.1	Toyota Changes to a Marketing Orientation for Long-term Success	7
1.2	Listening to Customers	16
1.3	Creating a Competitive Advantage	20
2.1	Corporate Vision at Nokia	40
2.2	Core Competences at Canon	43
2.3	Matching Strengths to Opportunities	46
3.1	Emotions and Consumer Behaviour	76
3.2	Customer Psychology and Retailing	81
3.3	'On-the-go' Consumption	85
3.4	Young Consumers	87
4.1	Business-to-Business Marketing Communications	104
4.2	Orange Talks to Business Customers	110
4.3	Changes in Buyer–Seller Relationships	123
5.1	Central and Eastern European Movement to the EU	138
5.2	Bosses Beware: Cartels Under Fire	148
5.3	Going 3G?	152
6.1	Validity in Marketing Research	173
6.2	Achieving Close Client–Agency Relationships	176
6.3	Sources of Marketing Information	183
6.4	Understanding Consumers through Ethnographic Research	186
7.1	Lifestyle Segmentation of Chinese Consumers	219
7.2	Understanding the Youth Market	221
7.3	Segmentation with Geographic Information Systems	224
7.4	Targeting the Grey Market	235
7.5	Positioning in the Imported Premium Bottled Lager Market	239
7.6	Tangible Repositioning at Skoda	241
8.1	Own-label Copycatting	263
8.2	Strong Brand Names Affect Consumer Perceptions and Preferences	265
8.3	Putting Quality into Brand Building	269
8.4	Naming Egg	275
8.5	Corporate Identity Misalignment at Hilton Hotels	291
9.1	Surviving a Shakeout	309
9.2	Mobile Marketing Strategies in a Mature Market	312
9.3	Turnaround Strategies in the Decline Stage	316
9.4	Portfolio Planning to the Core	317
10.1	Keys to Innovation Success	339
10.2	Creative Leadership and Innovation	342
10.3	Launching the Latin Spirit	348
10.4	Innovation at the Speed of Light	363
11.1	Price Drivers in the Twenty-first Century	377
11.2	Pricing a German Car using Trade-off Analysis	391
11.3	Parallel Importing and Pricing	395
11.4	Information Technology Aids Price Setting	397
12.1	The Opportunities and Challenges of Media-neutral Planning	418
12.2	Positioning against Competitors	426
12.3	Developments in Poster Advertising	435
12.4	Cinema Renaissance	436
12.5	Managing the Client–Agency Relationship	442
13.1	Personal Selling and the Chinese Culture	479
13.2	Motivating an International Salesforce	492
14.1	Using a Marketing Database in Retailing	513
14.2	Toyota Targets the Responsive Car Buyer	525
14.3	Mobile Marketing at Cadbury and Kiss	531
14.4	Niche Marketing with Catalogues	534
16.1	Sampling for Success	599
16.2	Integrated Public Relations	608
16.3	Sports Sponsorship	611
17.1	International Franchising: the Case of Benetton	646
17.2	Managing the Supply Chain the Zara Way	653
17.3	The Human Element in Distribution	654
17.4	Smart Warehouses at Lever Fabergé	661
18.1	Differentiation at Dyson	687
18.2	Using Style to Differentiate Products	694
19.1	Browser Wars	718
19.2	Counting the Cost of Mergers and Acquisitions	722
19.3	Building through Strategic Alliances	724
20.1	Ten Ways of Blocking a Marketing Report	762

20.2	A Master of Change at Xerox	763
20.3	Good Ideas Mean Successful Implementation	770
20.4	The Growth of the Category Manager	776
20.5	What Marketing Managers Really Do	779
21.1	Complaint Handling at Virgin Trains	804
21.2	Trade Marketing	818
21.3	Retail Positioning in Asia	823
21.4	Locating Stores Using Geographic Information Systems	824
21.5	Sponsoring the Arts	829
22.1	Classic Communications Faux Pas	848
22.2	Barriers to Developing Standardized Global Brands	859
22.3	Marketing to China	861
22.4	Global Advertising Taboos	863
22.5	Levi's versus Tesco: the Case of 'Grey' Jeans	868
22.6	Managing the Process of Globalization	871

e-Marketing

1.1	Fast Food Served up Online	14
2.1	Planning Your Online Activity	51
3.1	Online Consumer Research	67
4.1	Pooling Organizational Buying within the Automobile Industry	115
4.2	Integrated Internet Business-to-Business Marketing at Cisco	118
5.1	Social Responsibility and the Effect on Online Communities	142
5.2	Building an Environment for e-Business	146
6.1	Using Website Analysis to Improve Online Performance	178
6.2	Using the Internet as a Survey Tool	191
7.1	Segmenting Consumers using Database Technology	217
7.2	BMW Targets using Technology	229
8.1	Branding by Association	261
9.1	The Internet Extends the Product Life Cycle Curve	314
10.1	The Internet as a Tool for New Product Development	343
10.2	Online Product Development	344
10.3	Creating Radical Innovation	350
10.4	Linux: the Ultimate in Product Development	354
11.1	The Internet: where Customers set the Price	386
12.1	Interactive Television Advertising	434
12.2	New Models in Internet Advertising	437
13.1	The Impact of the Internet on Personal Selling and Sales Management	465
13.2	Technology and the Salesperson's Job	473
14.1	Customer Relationship Management in Business-to-Business Markets	516
14.2	The Successful Implementation of CRM Programmes	518
14.3	Telemarketing Versus the Web	530
15.1	Early Entry into E-commerce	551
15.2	Technology-driven Success at Wal-Mart	554
15.3	Successful E-procurement Systems	555
15.4	Internet Geography	560
15.5	Network Communities	562
15.6	Online Service at Amazon	565
15.7	E-commerce Productivity	566
15.8	E-mail Marketing	573
16.1	Exhibition Promotion through Viral Marketing	615
17.1	Express Delivery Companies: Leaders in Online Support and Service	635
17.2	The Internet: Making the Music Industry Rethink Distribution	638
18.1	Measuring Competitiveness: the Purpose of a Website Audit	691
18.2	Low-cost Airlines: Using the Internet to Build Competitive Advantage	696
19.1	Building in Growth Markets: the Case of Cisco	715
19.2	Guerrilla Marketing: an Online Concept	721
20.1	The Internet as a Change Agent: the Case of Reuters	752
21.1	Online Financial Services	805
21.2	E-business in the Hotel Industry	808
21.3	Information Technology in Retailing	821
22.1	Considerations in Using the Internet to Export	852

Vignettes

Ethical Marketing in Action

1.1	Social Marketing or Social Engineering?	11
5.1	Social Reporting	143
6.1	Ethics in Marketing Research: the Case of the Femidom	197
8.1	What's in a Name: are Brands Divisive?	295
11.1	Penetration Pricing: Should Fast-food Companies take the Blame for Youth Obesity?	403
12.1	Controlling Misleading Advertising	445
13.1	Nurse Knows Best: the Inappropriate Selling of Infant Formula	496
14.1	Consumer Protection in Direct Marketing	539
15.1	Marketing to 'Cybertots': Online or Out of Line?	577
16.1	Happy Hours: Sad Results?	619
17.1	Fair Trade Expansion	664

Preface to the fourth edition

Marketing is a vibrant, challenging activity that requires an understanding of both principles and how they can be applied in practice. The fourth edition of my book attempts to capture both aspects of the multidiscipline. Marketing concepts and principles are supported by examples of international practice to crystallize those ideas in the minds of students who may have little personal experience of real-life marketing.

My objective, then, was to produce a tightly written textbook supported by a range of international examples and case studies. The third edition placed a great emphasis on the use of the case study as a teaching method. In my experience, all types of students enjoy applying principles to real-life marketing problems. This is natural, as marketing does not exist in a vacuum; it is through application that students gain a richer understanding of marketing.

Becoming a successful marketing practitioner requires an understanding of the principles of marketing together with practical experience of implementing marketing ideas, processes and techniques in the marketplace. This book provides a framework for understanding important marketing issues such as understanding the customer, marketing segmentation and targeting, brand building, pricing, innovation and marketing implementation, which form the backbone of marketing practice.

Marketing, as I have already said, does not exist in a vacuum: it is a vibrant, sometimes energy-sapping profession that is full of exciting examples of success and failure. Moreover, marketing practitioners need to understand the changes that are taking place in the environment. As the quotation that heads Chapter 5 says, 'Change is the only constant.' Marketing-orientated companies are undergoing fundamental readjustments to their structure to cope with the accelerating rate of change. If you wish to enter the marketing profession then an acceptance of change and a willingness to work long hours are essential prerequisites.

Marketing in Europe has never looked stronger. International conferences organized by the European Marketing Academy and national organizations such as the Academy of Marketing in the UK make being a marketing academic challenging, rewarding and enjoyable. We should always value the companionship and pleasure that meeting fellow marketing academics brings. The growth in the number of students wishing to study marketing has brought with it a rise in the number of marketing academics in Europe. Their youth and enthusiasm bode well for the future of marketing as a major social science.

Most students enjoy studying marketing; they find it relevant and interesting. I hope that this book enhances your enjoyment, understanding and skills.

The structure of the book

The book comprises 22 chapters organized into four parts, as outlined below.

Part 1: Fundamentals of Modern Marketing Thought summarizes core marketing theory including the marketing concept and marketing planning, consumer and organizational buyer behaviour, marketing research and segmentation, and positioning. The emphasis throughout is on the strategic development of a market-driven company committed to exceeding the expectations of its customers.

Part 2: Marketing Mix Decisions focuses on the development of effective strategies for pricing, promotion, product development and distribution. The text emphasizes that each element of the marketing mix should be developed within the context of the overall marketing strategy.

Part 3: Competition and Marketing discusses the issues of competitive strategy, competitive advantage and the nature of competitive behaviour.

Part 4: Marketing Implementation and Application provides in-depth coverage of how to overcome resistance to marketing-led change, and analyses the various forms of marketing organization. This part also covers the special characteristics of service industries and their implications for marketing strategy, and particular issues associated with marketing in the global marketplace.

Taking into account its European readership, foreign currency conversion rates are given in appropriate places. Figures were accurate at the time of writing (2003). Obviously, changes since then may need to be taken into account.

New to this edition

As always, recent events are reflected throughout this book and all changes have been updated with new conceptual and research material, illustrative examples and case studies. Here follows a summary of the key content and learning feature changes for this edition.

Brand and corporate identity management

A major feature of this fourth edition is a new chapter entitled 'Managing products: brand and corporate identity management'. This reflects the most recent developments in creating and managing successful brands. Contemporary issues such as rebranding, co-branding, global branding and managing corporate brands are covered in-depth.

Ethical marketing

The fourth edition places a greater emphasis on social responsibility and ethical marketing issues, which are of increasing concern to companies. These are introduced in the chapter entitled 'The marketing environment' and appropriate chapters conclude with a discussion of ethical issues in marketing. Unique 'Ethical dilemmas' ask students to ponder the ethics of real-life marketing decisions. New 'Ethical Marketing in Action' vignettes focus specifically on ethical issues in practice.

Relationship marketing

Relationship marketing issues are given greater coverage with new sections throughout the book. For example, relationship building with advertising and marketing research agencies is discussed, as is developing and managing relationships with suppliers, distributors and customers. The emergence of customer relationship management (CRM) systems and the impact of technology on the human element of CRM are discussed in Chapter 14.

Internet marketing and the new media

This fourth edition contains an extensively revised and updated chapter on Internet marketing with a new Glossary, 'e-Marketing' vignettes (which appear in this chapter and throughout the book), and new sections on the analysis of factors affecting the adoption of Internet marketing, the benefits and limitations of Internet marketing to consumers and organizations, viral marketing and website design. The development and impact of new media, such as mobile marketing (Chapter 14) and interactive television advertising (Chapter 12), are also discussed in the appropriate chapters.

Marketing research

The 'Marketing research and information systems' chapter has been revised to provide a 'roadmap' that leads students through the research process with clear figures, diagrams and explanations. The 'roadmap' can be used as a guide by students when embarking on research-based projects so that they have a clear understanding of the stages and activities involved in carrying out such exercises.

Chapter reviews

A major learning feature innovation is the provision of 'Review' sections at the end of each chapter. The key learning points associated with each chapter are summarized under the chapter's objectives. This allows students to check the knowledge and understanding gained by reading a chapter, and to revise and review any shortfalls. Nearer examination time, students can use these Reviews as an aid to revision. They can test their knowledge and understanding of chapter fundamentals by reference to the key points found within the Reviews.

How to study using this book

This book has been designed to help you to learn and understand the important principles behind successful marketing. To check that you really understand the new concepts you are reading about, work through the case studies, exercises and questions at the end of each chapter.

Case studies

An innovation associated with the fourth edition was a case study competition, sponsored by McGraw-Hill, designed to attract Europe's top case study writers. This was very successful and 13 new cases were accepted for publication as a result of the competition. First prize was won by Conor Carroll from Limerick University with 'The Trouble with TopUps: Vodafone Causes a Stir by Lowering the Margins of Retailers'; second prize was claimed by Marie O'Dwyer from Waterford Institute of Technology with 'Hope Community Resources, Inc.'; and there were three third prize winners: 'Legoland and the Millennium Dome' by Julian Rawel from the University of Bradford, 'Corus Engineering Steels' by Bridget Rowe, Gary Reed and Jim Saker from Loughborough University, and 'Carbery: Developing New Products in a Mature Market' by Breda McCarthy from University College, Cork.

This new edition contains 44 cases as support material for classroom teaching; 30 are new to this edition and others have been revised and updated. The new cases often feature well-known brands such as Burberry, Microsoft Xbox, the Mini, easyJet, Nectar, Google, Vodafone, Hutchison 3g, H&M, Fiat, Safeway, Starbucks, Unilever and McDonald's. Popular cases such as Levi's jeans, Marks & Spencer, Budweiser and Wal-Mart/Asda have been revised and updated.

Each chapter ends with two case studies. To cater for all requirements, there is a mixture of short, medium and long cases.

Case study analysis

The aim of this book is not to tell you what marketing is about. Rather, I hope that the book will develop the skills you need to analyse marketing situations and make sensible recommendations. Your lecturers and tutors will select cases, which they feel are particularly relevant to the principles they are teaching. At first the prospect of case analysis can seem daunting, particularly when a case is long and full of unfamiliar facts and statistics. A sensible approach is to read the case fairly quickly to get an understanding of the broad situation and major issues covered. Follow this with a slower, more in-depth reading to extract the key details of the case.

The figures and discussion in each chapter can be useful in providing a framework for case analysis. Key questions to ask are: What are the important customer characteristics and behaviour patterns? How is the market segmented? How well is the company matching or exceeding customer expectations? Who are the competitors, and what are their strengths and weaknesses? These are fundamental to understanding marketing situations.

To guide your thinking, most of the case studies end with questions. Above all, remember that marketing is an inexact science: there are no unambiguously right answers. Marketing decisions are fraught with risk. For example, the success of a strategy may depend on how competitors react. Predictions of reactions should be built in to the decision-making phase, but ultimately competitor response is uncontrollable and hence there can be no guarantee that a strategy will work in the marketplace. The best that can be asked of you is that you justify your strategy choice based upon a clear understanding of the major marketing issues that impinge on the decisions.

Internet exercises

The Internet exercises have been fully revised for this new edition. They are designed to support your learning by providing short exercises, which will help you develop a clearer understanding of marketing principles and practice. They should also help to make you aware of the richness of marketing information available on the Internet. Finally, they should help you relate the organizations, products and services you will encounter to your own experience as a consumer. I hope you find them interesting and useful.

Study questions

Study questions appear at the end of each chapter. These may be used by your tutors as essay subjects or as the basis for tutorial questions. Their aim is to test knowledge and understanding of marketing principles. Whether or not your tutor uses them as a formal part of his or her marketing teaching, you can use them to check how well you have assimilated the information and procedures discussed in each chapter. Allocate some time after reading each chapter to answering these questions. If you make notes you may find them useful when the time for revision comes.

To assist you in working through this text, we have developed a number of distinctive study and design features. To familiarize yourself with these features, please turn to the 'Guided tour' on pages xxix–xxxi.

Indexes and Glossary

For ease of reference and to help you in revising, towards the end of the text we have provided the following:

Glossary—a full list of all key terms used in the text, with accompanying definitions
Companies and brands index—all brands and companies featured in the text
Subject index—all concepts discussed in the text.

Preface to the fourth edition

Additional teaching and learning resources

We are always trying to improve the quality of this text and the supplementary resources that accompany it. For this edition, we have significantly expanded the range, quality and delivery of online resources both to support students in their studying and lecturers in their teaching of marketing on the Online Learning Centre (OLC) at www.mcgraw-hill.co.uk/textbooks/jobber.

PowerWeb

New to this edition, students and lecturers have access to a PowerWeb, a range of refereed articles and daily news feeds about marketing topics. This exciting innovation allows free access to up-to-the-minute marketing stories. These can be used as an aid to essay and project work.

Inside this book you will find a unique password card. To access the PowerWeb resources, go to www.mcgraw-hill.co.uk/textbooks/jobber and follow the instructions on the card to register.

Integration of technology

For this edition, the book also integrates the website resources in several ways.

- Students can attempt to answer the 'Ethical dilemmas' within the text, and go to the website to check if their answers reflect the issues of corporate responsibility.
- At the end of each chapter, students are directed to the online quizzes to test their knowledge and to explore other extra support available. These online quizzes are graded and also give feedback to the student with references to the text.
- Internet exercises encourage students to go online and explore marketing through the Internet.
- Crossword puzzles on the OLC test students' understanding of the key terms listed at the end of the chapters.

For more details of the technology to enhance learning and teaching, go to pages xxxii–xxxiii.

Acknowledgements

I should like to thank my colleagues (past and present) at the University of Bradford School of Management for their stimulating insights and discussions. I would particularly like to thank Conor Carroll from Limerick University for his outstanding contribution to the new edition. Not only did Conor win the case competition with Vodafone, he also wrote five other new cases (Movie Marketing, Safeway, Nectar, Fiat and Microsoft Xbox) for the book. As if that were not enough, Conor agreed to produce the new set of Internet exercises that appear at the end of each chapter. I also wish to thank Fiona Ellis-Chadwick for displaying her e-marketing talents by revising and updating the Internet chapter, Alan Stevenson from Strathclyde University for providing most of the e-Marketing in Action vignettes, Deirdre Shaw from Glasgow Caledonian University for supplying the 'Ethical dilemmas', and Gerard Hastings from Strathclyde University for writing most of the Ethical Marketing in Action vignettes.

I shall never forget the work of the tireless Chris Barkby, Dee Dwyer, Lynne Lancaster, Jo Cousins and Carole Zajac from Bradford School of Management, and Irene Andrew from McGraw-Hill for their secretarial and administrative support. Many thanks to all of the case contributors for providing such a varied selection of cases and to all those of you who have reviewed previous editions of my book. I am also indebted to Ann Murray Chatterton at the Institute of Practitioners in Advertising and Alan Rawal at the Institute of Public Relations for supplying case material. Finally, my thanks go to Janet, Paul and Matthew who have had to endure my weekends of toil.

The publishers would also like to thank the following lecturers, whose comments, reviews and contributions assisted in the development of the text and Online Learning Centre website:

Samar Baddar, *Middlesex University*
Jeanette Baker, *Sheffield Hallam University*
John Balmer, *Bradford University*
Christine Band, *Napier University*
Jose Bloemer, *Nijmegen University*
Claire Brindley, *Manchester Metropolitan University*
Conor Carroll, *University of Limerick*
Declan Doyle, *Institute of Technology, Carlow*
Fiona Ellis-Chadwick, *Loughborough University*
James Fitchett, *University of Exeter*
Hans Haans, *University of Tilburg*
Jim Hammil, *Hammil Associates*
Aileen Harrison, *Oxford Brookes University*
Tracy Harwood, *De Montfort University*
Gerard Hastings, *University of Strathclyde*
Thomas Helgesson *University of Halmstad*
Lise-Lotte Lindfelt, *Åbo Akademi University*
David Longbottom, *University of Derby*
Danielle McCartan Quinn, *University of Ulster at Jordanstown*
Breda McCarthy, *University College Cork*
Clive Nancarrow, *University of the West of England*
Cariona Neary, *Marketing Institute*
Terry Newholm, *UMIST*
Marie O'Dwyer, *Waterford Institute of Technology*
Daragh O'Reilly, *University of Bradford*

Acknowledgements

Piet Pauwels, *Maastricht University*
Tony Pyne, *University of Luton*
Julian Rawel, *Julian Rawel Consultancy and University of Bradford*
Gary Reed, *Loughborough University*
Jill Ross, *University of Teesside*
Deirdre Shaw, *Glasgow Caledonian*
Graeme Stephen, *Robert Gordon University*
Noreen Siddiqui, *Glasgow Caledonian University*
Nikolaos Tzokas, *University of East Anglia*
Cleopatra Veloutsou, *University of Glasgow*
Len Tiu Wright, *De Montfort University*
Martin Wetzels, *University of Eindhoven*

Finally, thanks to the companies and organizations who granted us permission to reproduce material in the text. Every effort has been made to trace and acknowledge ownership of copyright. The publishers would be pleased to make suitable arrangements to clear permission with any copyright holders whom it has not been possible to contact.

Picture Credits

The publishers would like to thank the following for permission to reproduce photographs: (T = Top, B = Bottom, C = Centre, L= Left, R = Right):

Absolut, 76
The Advertising Archives, 305, 331, 432, 673, 674, 759
Air Products, 108
Anheuser-Busch Europe Ltd, 246, 247, 248, 612
Apple iMac, 695
Archibald Ingall Stretton, 523
Bacardi, 220, 349
BBH, 301
Anthony Blake Photo Library/*Martin Brigdale*, 95, *David Marsden*, 96
Bluetooth, 553
EHS Brann and Tesco, 521
British Airways, 794
Britvic Tango, 75
Burkitt DDB, 425
Campbell Doyle Dye and Mercedes-Benz, 826
Canon, 218, 362
Cathay Pacific Airways Ltd, 313
Martyn Chillmaid, 336, 597R, 598T, L, R
Coors Brewers, 555, 611
DHL, 656
Drambuie International Ltd, 430
Dyson, 325, 634
eBay, 557
Emirates, 424
FCB, 270

Acknowledgements

France Télécom, 551
Erik Freeland/CORBIS SABA, 28
Lucozade, 597
Bananabix, 598
Friends Reunited, 562
Guardian, 271
GeoPost UK, 103
Getty Images, 163, 194, 256, 472, 368, 378, 435, 583, 629
Grey Worldwide and Nokia, 9, 801
Guinness, 436 *The GUINNESS word, the HARP device and ARTHUR GUINNESS signature are trademarks and are reproduced together with the "Eskimo" advertisement (Faiyaz Jafri www.unit.nl and Jeremy Carr; Agency: AMV BBDO) with the kind permission of Guinness & Co. All rights reserved.*
Hope Community Resources, 837, 838
Interbrew UK and Bartle Bogle Hegarty Ltd, 270, 424
Landrover, 260
Legoland Windsor, 34
The Leith Agency, 833
Little Chef, 600
Lowe Worldwide and Reebok, 18; and Tesco, 69; and HSBC, 872
Mars, 432 *Reproduced with permission of Masterfoods. MARS is a registered trademark.*
MG Rover, 238
Mitsubishi Black Diamond, 744, 745, 746
National Lottery, 371
Nectar Group, 514, 544
The Norwegian Tourist Board, 814
PA Photos, 150, 408, 409, 703, 705
P&O and MCDB, 812
Panasonic UK Ltd, 695
PeopleSoft, 657
PriMetrica, 560
Royal Dutch Airlines, 522
Royal Dutch Shell, 151
Saab Great Britain, 17, 524
Safeway, 735 *Reproduced with permission of Safeway Stores PLC.*
The Samaritans, 826
Samsung Electronics, 310
Science Photo Library/Cordelia Molloy, 625
Scottish Courage, 239
Seiko UK, 720
Siemens, 106
Stora Enso Oyj, 706
Team Saatchi and Sony, 268
Tesco, 521
The Thin Red Line, 586, 590
Toshiba/Intel, 282
Toyota Europe, 150
UPS, 107
Virgin Atlantic, 693
Vodafone Ltd, 669
Volkswagen UK, 74
ZDNet, 572

Guided tour

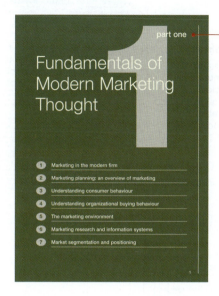

Part openings
Part openings set the scene for each main area of study, giving a brief overview of the topics to be covered.

Key terms
Key terms are highlighted and explained in the text where they first appear.

Learning objectives
This page identifies the main learning objectives you should acquire after studying each chapter.

Colour advertisements
Colour advertisements and illustrations throughout the book demonstrate how marketers have presented their products in real promotions and campaigns.

xxix

Guided tour

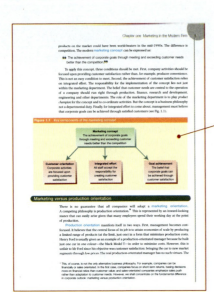

Graphs and tables
Improved graphs and tables are presented in a simple and clear design to help you to understand and absorb key data and concepts.

e-Marketing
e-Marketing examples demonstrate how organizations have used new technologies in their marketing strategies.

Web address
URLs (Internet addresses) point you towards the Internet sites of organizations mentioned in the text.

Marketing in action and ethical marketing in action
Marketing in action boxes provide additional practical examples to highlight the application of concepts, and encourage you to critically analyse and discuss real-world issues, including marketing ethics.

xxx

Guided tour

Review
Expanded chapter review briefly reinforces the main topics you will have covered in each chapter.

Key terms
The Key terms list at the end of each chapter collates all the key terms from the chapter.

Internet exercise
The Internet exercise provides an opportunity to test out your marketing knowledge on the Internet.

Ethical dilemmas
New ethical dilemmas question the responsibilities of marketers and organisations.

Study questions
Study questions encourage you to review and apply the knowledge you have acquired from each chapter.

Case studies
Each chapter concludes with two case studies. These up-to-date examples encourage you to apply what you have learned in each chapter to a real-life marketing problem.

References
There is a full list of references for each chapter so that if you wish, you can continue to research in greater depth after reading the chapter.

xxxi

Technology to enhance learning and teaching

Visit www.mcgraw-hill.co.uk/textbooks/jobber today

Online Learning Centre (OLC)

After completing each chapter, log on to the supporting Online Learning Centre website. Take advantage of the study tools offered to reinforce the material you have read in the text, and to develop your knowledge of marketing in a fun and effective way.

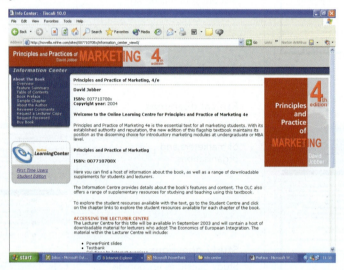

Resources for students include:

- Multiple Choice Questions (with feedback) to test your knowledge
- Online Marketing Research Project to develop your research skills
- A guide to writing a Marketing Plan
- Extra Case studies exploring brands and organizations
- Crosswords, Internet Exercises, Glossary of marketing terms, web links and more

Also available for lecturers:

- PowerPoint slides for lecture presentations
- Case Study Teaching Notes and Summary Slides
- Test bank of questions for marketing assessments
- Guide Notes to the end of chapter study questions
- Guide Solutions to Internet Exercises
- Artwork and Ads from the book

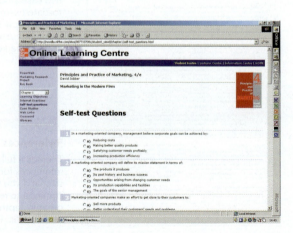

Technology to enhance learning and teaching

PowerWeb

Free with this book, you will be able to access a subject-specific online database containing carefully refereed articles and daily news feeds about marketing topics.

PowerWeb is ideal for researching essays and projects, keeping in touch with marketing current affairs, and seeing how the topics you've learnt in class apply to real-life marketing practice.

Visit the OLC at www.mcgraw-hill.co.uk/textbooks/jobber to access PowerWeb and use the card in this book to register.

Study skills

Open University Press publishes guides to study, research and exam skills, to help undergraduate and postgraduate students through their university studies.

Visit www.openup.co.uk/ss/ to see the full selection.

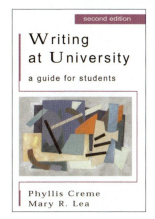
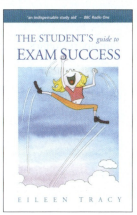

Computing skills

If you'd like to brush up on your Computing skills, we have a range of titles covering MS Office applications such as Word, Excel, PowerPoint, Access and more.

Get a £2 discount off these titles by entering the promotional code "cit" when ordering online at www.mcgraw-hill.co.uk/cit

For lecturers: Primis Content Centre

If you need to supplement your course with additional cases or content, create a personalised e-Book for your students. Visit www.primiscontentcenter.com or e-mail primis_euro@mcgraw-hill.com for more information.

xxxiii

Currency Conversion Table

The value of one pound sterling at the time of going to press was:

2.43	Australian dollars
2.24	Canadian dollars
10.72	Danish kroner
1.44	Euros
12.94	Hong Kong dollars
183.79	Japanese yen
6.35	Malaysian ringgits
2.81	New Zealand dollars
11.84	Norwegian kroner
2.90	Singapore dollars
12.85	Swedish kronor
2.22	Swiss francs
1.67	US dollars

Fundamentals of Modern Marketing Thought

part one

1. Marketing in the modern firm
2. Marketing planning: an overview of marketing
3. Understanding consumer behaviour
4. Understanding organizational buying behaviour
5. The marketing environment
6. Marketing research and information systems
7. Market segmentation and positioning

Part one Fundamentals of Modern Marketing Thought

chapter one

Marketing in the modern firm

> Management must think of itself not as producing products, but as providing customer-creating value satisfactions. It must push this idea (and everything it means and requires) into every nook and cranny of the organization. It has to do this continuously and with the kind of flair that excites and stimulates the people in it.
>
> THEODORE LEVITT

Learning Objectives

This chapter explains:

1. The marketing concept: an understanding of the nature of marketing, its key components and limitations

2. The difference between a production orientation and marketing orientation

3. The differing roles of efficiency and effectiveness in achieving corporate success

4. The differences between market-driven and internally driven businesses

5. How to create customer value and satisfaction

6. How an effective marketing mix is designed, and the criticisms of the 4-Ps approach to marketing management

7. The relationship between marketing characteristics, market orientation, adoption of a marketing philosophy, and business performance

In general, marketing has a bad press. Phrases like 'marketing gimmicks', 'marketing ploys' and 'marketing tricks' abound. The result is that marketing is condemned by association. Yet this is unfortunate and unfair because the essence of marketing is value not trickery. Successful companies rely on customers returning to repurchase; the goal of marketing is long-term satisfaction, not short-term deception. This theme is reinforced by the writings of top management consultant Peter Drucker, who stated:[1]

> Because the purpose of business is to create and keep customers, it has only two central functions—marketing and innovation. The basic function of marketing is to attract and retain customers at a profit.

What can we learn from this statement? First, it places marketing in a central role for business success since it is concerned with the creation and retention of customers. Second, it implies that the purpose of marketing is not to chase any customer at any price. Drucker used profit as a criterion. While profit may be used by many commercial organizations, in the non-profit sector other criteria might be used such as social deprivation or hunger. Many of the concepts, principles and techniques described in this book are as applicable to Action Aid as to Renault.

Third, it is a reality of commercial life that it is much more expensive to attract new customers than to retain existing ones. Indeed, the costs of attracting a new customer have been found to be up to six times higher than the costs of retaining old ones.[2] Consequently marketing-orientated companies recognize the importance of building relationships with customers by providing satisfaction and attracting new customers by creating added value. Grönroos has stressed the importance of relationship building in his definition of marketing in which he describes the objective of marketing as to establish, develop and commercialize long-term customer relationships so that the objectives of the parties involved are met.[3] Finally, since most markets are characterized by strong competition, the statement also suggests the need to monitor and understand competitors, since it is to rivals that customers will turn if their needs are not being met.

Marketing exists through exchanges. Exchange is the act or process of receiving something from someone by giving something in return. The 'something' could be a physical good, service, idea or money. Money facilitates exchanges so that people can concentrate on working at things they are good at, earn money (itself an exchange) and spend it on products that someone else has supplied. The objective is for all parties in the exchange to feel satisfied so each party exchanges something of less value to them than that which is received. The idea of satisfaction is particularly important to suppliers of products because satisfied customers are more likely to return to buy more products than dissatisfied ones. Hence, the notion of customer satisfaction as the central pillar of marketing is fundamental to the creation of a stream of exchanges upon which commercial success depends.

The rest of this chapter will examine some of these ideas in more detail and provide an introduction to how marketing can create customer value and satisfaction.

The marketing concept

The above discussion introduces the notion of the marketing concept—that is, that companies achieve their profit and other objectives by satisfying (even delighting) customers.[4] This is the traditional idea underlying marketing. However, it neglects a fundamental aspect of commercial life: competition. The traditional marketing concept is a necessary but not a sufficient condition for corporate achievement. To achieve success, companies must go further than mere customer satisfaction; they must do better than the competition. Many also-ran products on the market could have been world-beaters in the mid-1990s. The difference is competition. The modern marketing concept can be expressed as:

> ❝ The achievement of corporate goals through meeting and exceeding customer needs better than the competition. ❞

To apply this concept, three conditions should be met. First, company activities should be focused upon providing customer satisfaction rather than, for example, producer convenience. This is not an easy condition to meet. Second, the achievement of customer satisfaction relies on integrated effort. The responsibility for the implementation of the concept lies not just within the marketing department. The belief that customer needs are central to the operation of a company should run right through production, finance, research and development, engineering and other departments. The role of the marketing department is to play *product champion* for the concept and to co-ordinate activities. But the concept is a business philosophy not a departmental duty. Finally, for integrated effort to come about, management must believe that corporate goals can be achieved through satisfied customers (see Fig. 1.1).

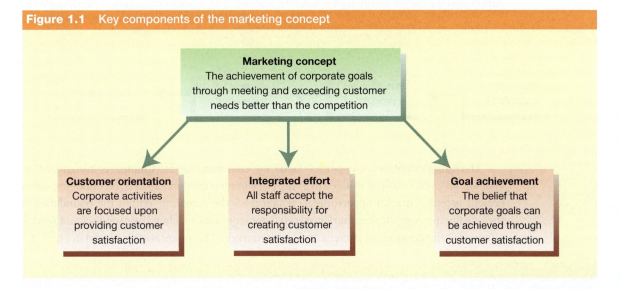

Figure 1.1 Key components of the marketing concept

Marketing versus production orientation

There is no guarantee that all companies will adopt a marketing orientation. A competing philosophy is production orientation.* This is represented by an inward-looking stance that can easily arise given that many employees spend their working day at the point of production.

Production orientation manifests itself in two ways. First, management becomes cost-focused. It believes that the central focus of its job is to attain economies of scale by producing a limited range of products (at the limit, just one) in a form that minimizes production costs. Henry Ford is usually given as an example of a production-orientated manager because he built just one car in one colour—the black Model T—in order to minimize costs. However, this is unfair to Mr Ford since his objective was customer satisfaction: bringing the car to new market segments through low prices. The real production-orientated manager has no such virtues. The

---

* This, of course, is not the only alternative business philosophy. For example, companies can be financially or sales orientated. In the first case, companies focus on short-term returns, basing decisions more on financial ratios than customer value; and sales-orientated companies emphasize sales push rather than adaptation to customer needs. However, we shall concentrate on the fundamental difference in corporate outlook: marketing versus production orientation.

objective is cost reduction for its own sake, an objective at least partially fuelled by the greater comfort and convenience that comes from producing a narrow product range.

The second way in which production orientation reveals itself is in the belief that the business should be defined in terms of its production facilities. Levitt has cited the example of film companies defining their business in terms of the product produced, which meant they were slow to respond when the demand to watch cinema films declined in the face of increasing competition for people's leisure time.[5] Had they defined their business in marketing terms—entertainment—they may have perceived television as an opportunity rather than a threat.

Figure 1.2 illustrates production orientation in its crudest form. The focus is on current production capabilities that define the business mission. The purpose of the organization is to manufacture products and aggressively sell them to unsuspecting customers. A classic example of the catastrophe that can happen when this philosophy drives a company is that of Pollitt and Wigsell, a steam engine producer that sold its products to the textile industry. It made the finest steam engine available and the company grew to employ over 1000 people on a 30-acre (12-hectare) site. Its focus was on steam engine production, so when the electric motor superseded the earlier technology it failed to respond. The 30-acre site is now a housing estate.

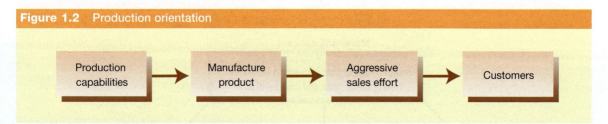

Figure 1.2 Production orientation

Marketing-orientated companies focus on customer needs. Change is recognized as endemic and adaptation considered to be the Darwinian condition for survival. Changing needs present potential market opportunities, which drive the company. Within the boundaries of their distinctive competences market-driven companies seek to adapt their product and service offerings to the demands of current and latent markets. This orientation is shown in Fig. 1.3.

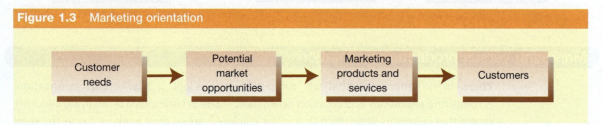

Figure 1.3 Marketing orientation

Marketing-orientated companies get close to their customers so that they understand their needs and problems. When personal contact is insufficient or not feasible, formal marketing research is commissioned to understand customer motivations and behaviour.

Part of the success of German machine tool manufacturers can be attributed to their willingness to develop new products with lead customers: those companies who themselves are innovative.[6] This contrasts sharply with the attitude of UK machine tool manufacturers, who have seen marketing research as merely a tactic to delay new product proposals and who feared that involving customers in new product design would have adverse effects on the sales of current products. Marketing orientation is related to the strategic orientation of companies. Marketing-orientated firms adopt a proactive search for market opportunities, use market information as a base for analysis and organizational learning, and adopt a long-term strategic perspective on markets and brands.[7]

Marketing in Action 1.1 describes how a move to a marketing orientation has laid the foundations for success at Toyota.

1.1 marketing in action

Toyota Changes to a Marketing Orientation for Long-Term Success

Toyota GB is the national sales and marketing company responsible for sales and after-sales service for Toyota cars and commercial vehicles in the UK. Its success is reflected in sales growth from 47,500 in 1992 to over 130,000 cars in 2002. Despite a consistent upward trend, the decade has seen the implementation of two fundamentally different philosophies. From 1992 to 1997, Toyota's market share grew from 2.6 per cent to 3.3 per cent as a result of a 'push' strategy fuelled by the achievement of short-term sales targets and focused on selling low-cost Japanese-designed cars. The approach was supported by a major tactical incentive programme but with little marketing or brand investment.

Despite this short-term success, Toyota GB management considered the strategy unsustainable as low-price competitors began to match its offer, resulting in lower profit margins.

Based on a major customer research survey, the company began to be marketing led. The brand values of Toyota cars were mapped out, and the emphasis moved from the aggressive selling of cars to understanding what the Toyota brand meant to customers and how the company could better meet their needs. The marketing research budget was increased by a factor of four and the company worked much more closely with its Japanese parent and European cousin to ensure that new models were aligned more effectively to the requirements of the European customer. Other aspects of marketing changed too: expenditure was moved from tactical incentives to media advertising ('The Car in Front is a Toyota') and Toyota GB worked with its dealers to transfer the new values and culture to the car showroom.

The result is that customer perception of Toyota cars has moved from 'cheap and reliable' to 'a quality car at competitive prices'. Market share has risen to 4.7 per cent over the past five years, together with a healthy rise in profit margins.

Paul Philpott, marketing director of Toyota GB, says there are four key learning points from this story: (i) make marketing the number one priority in your company; (ii) put the views of your customers before your own; (iii) invest for the future; and (iv) be patient.

Based on: Simms (2002)[8]

Efficiency versus effectiveness

Another perspective on business philosophy can be gained by understanding the distinction between efficiency and effectiveness.[9] **Efficiency** is concerned with inputs and outputs. An efficient firm produces goods economically: it does things right. The benefit is that the cost per unit of output is low and, therefore, the potential for offering low prices to gain market share, or charging medium to high prices and achieving high profit margins, is present. However, to be successful, a company needs to be more than just efficient—it needs to be effective as well. **Effectiveness** means doing the right things. This implies operating in attractive markets and making products that consumers want to buy. Conversely, companies that operate in unattractive markets or are not producing what consumers want to buy will go out of business; the only question is one of timing.

The link between performance and combinations of efficiency and effectiveness can be conceived as shown in Fig. 1.4. A company that is both inefficient and ineffective will go out of business quickly because it is a high-cost producer of products that consumers do not want to buy. One company that went out of business because it was inefficient and ineffective was boo.com. The company spent lavishly while trying to persuade consumers to buy sports clothing online via its extremely slow website. It became clear that shoppers preferred to try on these products rather than view a rotating 3D image.[10]

Figure 1.4 Efficiency and effectiveness

	Ineffective	Effective
Inefficient	Goes out of business quickly	Survives
Efficient	Dies slowly	Does well Thrives

A company that is efficient and ineffective may last a little longer because its low cost base may generate more profits from the dwindling sales volume it is achieving. Firms that are effective but inefficient are likely to survive because they are operating in attractive markets and are marketing products that people want to buy. The problem is that their inefficiency is preventing them from reaping the maximum profits from their endeavours. It is the combination of both efficiency and effectiveness that leads to optimum business success. Such firms do well and thrive because they are operating in attractive markets, are supplying products that consumers want to buy and are benefiting from a low cost base.

One company that set out to establish itself as both efficient and effective is Virgin Atlantic. Innovations in service delivery (for instance, personal televisions built into the seating) and low costs (for example, promotional expenditures kept low by Richard Branson's capacity to generate publicity for the airline) mean that both objectives are achieved. Direct Line, the UK insurance company, has also achieved efficiency by eliminating the broker through its direct marketing operation, while becoming highly effective through its service excellence (for example, convenient motor repairs through its nationwide dealer network, which eliminates the need to 'get two quotes'; a fast telephone response facility, which removes the need to fill in forms; and a car return service).

The essential difference between efficiency and effectiveness, then, is that the former is cost focused while the latter is customer focused. An effective company has the ability to attract and retain customers.

Market-driven versus internally orientated businesses

A deeper understanding of the marketing concept can be gained by contrasting in detail a market-driven business with one that is internally orientated. Table 1.1 summarizes the key differences.

Market-driven companies display customer concern throughout the business. All departments recognize the importance of the customer to the success of the business. In internally focused businesses convenience comes first. If what the customer wants is inconvenient to produce, excuses are made to avoid giving it.

Market-driven businesses know how their products and services are being evaluated against the competition. They understand the choice criteria that customers are using and ensure that their marketing mix matches those criteria better than that of the competition. The advertisement for the Nokia 7250 illustrates that Nokia understand that a key choice criterion for their customers is fashion. Internally driven companies assume that certain criteria—perhaps price and performance if the company is supplying industrial goods—are uppermost in all customers' minds. They fail to understand the real concerns of customers.

Mobile phones are not simply devices for talking to people on the telephone, but fashion statements.

Businesses that are driven by the market base their segmentation analyses on customer differences that have implications for marketing strategy. Businesses that are focused internally, segment by product (e.g. large bulldozers versus small bulldozers) and consequently are vulnerable when customers' requirements change.

A key feature of market-driven businesses is their recognition that marketing research expenditure is an investment that can yield rich rewards through better customer understanding. Internally driven businesses see marketing research as a non-productive intangible and prefer to rely on anecdotes and received wisdom. Market-orientated businesses welcome the organizational changes that are bound to occur as an organization moves to maintain strategic fit between its environment and its strategies. In contrast, internally orientated businesses cherish the status quo and resist change.

Attitudes towards competition also differ. Market-driven businesses try to understand competitive objectives and strategies, and anticipate competitive actions. Internally driven companies are content to ignore the competition. Marketing spend is regarded as an investment that has long-term consequences in market-driven businesses. The alternative view is that marketing expenditure is viewed as a luxury that never appears to produce benefits.

In marketing-orientated companies those employees who take risks and are innovative are rewarded. Recognition of the fact that most new products fail is reflected in a reluctance to

Table 1.1 Marketing-orientated businesses

Market-driven businesses	Internally orientated businesses
Customer concern throughout business	Convenience comes first
Know customer choice criteria and match with marketing mix	Assume price and product performance key to most sales
Segment by customer differences	Segment by product
Invest in market research (MR) and track market changes	Rely on anecdotes and received wisdom
Welcome change	Cherish status quo
Try to understand competition	Ignore competition
Marketing spend regarded as an investment	Marketing spend regarded as a luxury
Innovation rewarded	Innovation punished
Search for latent markets	Stick with the same
Being fast	Why rush?
Strive for competitive advantage	Happy to be me-too

punish those people who risk their career championing a new product idea. Internally orientated businesses reward time-serving and the ability not to make mistakes. This results in risk avoidance and the continuance of the status quo. Market-driven businesses search for latent markets: markets that no other company has exploited. 3M's Post-it product filled a latent need for a quick, temporary attachment to documents, for example. The radio station Classic FM has become successful by filling the latent need for accessible classical music among people who wished to aspire to this type of music but were somewhat intimidated by the music and style of presentation offered by Radio 3. A third example is the retailer Next, which initially built a business by meeting the latent need for smart women's clothing among 20–35 year olds who could not find what they wanted in department stores and were unwilling to pay designer-label prices. Internally driven businesses are happy to stick with their existing products and markets.

Intensive competition means that companies need to be fast to succeed. Market-driven companies are fast to respond to latent markets, innovate, manufacture and distribute their products and services. They realize that strategic windows soon close.[11] Dallmer, chief executive of a major European company, told a story that symbolizes the importance of speed to competitive success.[12] Two people were walking through the Black Forest where it was rumoured a very dangerous lion lurked. They took a break and were sitting in the sun when one of them changed out of his hiking boots and in to his jogging shoes. The other one smiled and, laughing, asked, 'You don't think you can run away from the lion with those jogging shoes?' 'No,' he replied, 'I just need to be faster than you!' Internally driven companies when they spot an opportunity take their time. 'Why rush?' is their epitaph.

Finally, marketing-orientated companies strive for competitive advantage. They seek to serve customers better than the competition. Internally orientated companies are happy to produce me-too copies of offerings already on the market.

Limitations of the marketing concept

A number of academics have raised important questions regarding the value of the marketing concept. Four issues—the marketing concept as an ideology, marketing and society, marketing as a constraint on innovation, and marketing as a source of dullness—will now be explored.

The marketing concept as an ideology

Brownlie and Saren argue that the marketing concept has assumed many of the characteristics of an ideology or an article of faith that should dominate the thinking of organizations.[13] They recognize the importance of a consumer orientation for companies but ask why, after 40 years of trying, the concept has not been fully implemented. They argue that there are other valid considerations that companies must take into account when making decisions (e.g. economies of scale) apart from giving customers exactly what they want. Marketers' attention should therefore be focused not only on propagation of the ideology but also on its integration with the demands of other core business functions in order to achieve a compromise between the satisfaction of consumers and the achievement of other company requirements.

Marketing and society

A second limitation of the marketing concept concerns its focus on individual market transactions. Since many individuals weigh heavily their personal benefits while discounting the societal impact of their purchases, the adoption of the marketing concept will result in the production of goods and services that do not adequately correspond to societal welfare. Providing customer satisfaction is simply a means to achieve a company's profit objective and does not guarantee protection of the consumer's welfare. This view is supported by Wensley, who regards consumerism as a challenge to the adequacy of the atomistic and individual view of market transactions.[14] An alternative view is presented by Bloom and Greyser, who regard consumerism as the ultimate expression of the marketing concept compelling marketers to

1.1 ethical marketing in action

Social Marketing or Social Engineering?

Marketing is essentially a means of influencing human behaviour—typically consumer behaviour. It can, for example, encourage us to buy more of a particular product, switch brands or try something entirely new. This capacity to influence behaviour can also be used to tackle social and health problems. 'Social marketing' campaigns have, for example, attempted to reduce illicit drug use among teenagers, encouraged the uptake of immunization, and promoted water fluoridation schemes. In each case key marketing principles such as consumer orientation, the marketing mix and strategic planning have been brought to bear on the problem. As with commercial marketing, there is a lot of evidence that social marketing is effective.

Although such campaigns are well intentioned and aim to bring about socially desirable outcomes, they also present ethical challenges. Most fundamentally, if marketing provides a powerful means of influencing behaviour, who decides which behaviour should be addressed? Stopping teens using drugs seems self-evidently desirable, but how would you feel about a social marketing campaign designed to promote harm minimization, perhaps through needle exchanges, rather than abstinence? Similarly, does the social marketing of safer sex actually encourage earlier sexual experimentation? Beyond the behaviour they choose to target, social marketers also face dilemmas about the sort of tactics they use—for example, the danger of 'collateral' when mass-mediated messages hit the wrong target (for example, during the UK's high-profile advertising about HIV/AIDS in the early 1990s some children became very anxious that they were at risk from the disease) and the potential for stigmatizing certain groups, such as the overweight, through segmentation and targeting.

consider consumer needs and wants that hitherto may have been overlooked:[15] 'The resourceful manager will look for the positive opportunities created by consumerism rather than brood over its restraints.'

Marketing can be used in a positive way in society to influence behaviour regarding social problems. Such social marketing campaigns have been used to address behavioural problems such as drug abuse and to promote health projects in developing countries. Ethical Marketing in Action 1.1 discusses some issues.

Marketing as a constraint on innovation

In an influential article Tauber showed how marketing research discouraged major innovation.[16] The thrust of his argument was that relying on customers to guide the development of new products has severe limitations. This is because customers have difficulty articulating needs beyond the realm of their own experience. This suggests that the ideas gained from marketing research will be modest compared to those coming from the 'science push' of the research and development laboratory. Brownlie and Saren agree that, particularly for discontinuous innovations (e.g. Xerox, penicillin), the role of product development ought to be far more proactive than this.[17] Indeed technological innovation is the process that 'realizes' market demands that were previously unknown. Thus the effective exploitation and utilization of technology in developing new products is at least as important as market-needs analysis.

However, McGee and Spiro point out that these criticisms are not actually directed at the marketing concept itself but towards its faulty implementation: an overdependence on customers as a source of new product ideas.[18] They state that the marketing concept does not suggest that companies must depend solely on the customer for new product ideas; rather the concept implies that new product development should be based on sound interfacing between perceived customer needs and technological research. Project SAPPHO, which investigated innovation in the chemical and scientific instrument industries, found that successful innovations were based on a good understanding of user needs.[19] Unsuccessful innovations, on the other hand, were characterized by little or no attention to user needs.

Marketing as a source of dullness

A fourth criticism of marketing is that its focus on analysing customers and developing offerings that reflect their needs leads to dull marketing campaigns, me-too products, copycat promotion and marketplace stagnation. Instead, marketing should create demand rather than reflect demand. As Brown states, consumers should be 'teased, tantalized and tormented by deliciously insatiable desire'.[20] This approach he terms 'retromarketing', and says that it is built on five principles: exclusivity, secrecy, amplification, entertainment and tricksterism.

Exclusivity is created by deliberately holding back supplies and threatening gratification. Consumers are encouraged to 'buy now while stocks last'. The lucky ones are happy in the knowledge that they are the select few, the discerning elite. Short supply of brands like Harley-Davidson (motorcycles), certain models of Mercedes cars and even the BMW Mini has created an aura of exclusivity.

The second principle of retromarketing—secrecy—has the intention of teasing would-be purchasers. An example is the pre-launch of the blockbuster *Harry Potter and the Goblet of Fire*, which involved a complete blackout of advance information. The book's title, price and review copies were withheld, and only certain interesting plot details were drip-fed to the press. The result was heightened interest, fed on a diet of mystery and intrigue.

Even exclusive products and secrets need promotion, which leads to the third retromarketing principle of amplification. This is designed to get consumers talking about the 'cool' motorbike or the 'hot' film. Where promotional budgets are limited, this can be achieved by creating outrage (e.g. the controversial Benetton ads, including one showing a dying AIDS victim and his family) or surprise (e.g. the placing of a Pizza Hut logo on the side of a Russian rocket).

Entertainment is the fourth principle, so that marketing engages consumers. This, claims Brown, is 'modern marketing's greatest failure' with marketing losing its sense of fun in its quest to be rigorous and analytical. The final principle of retromarketing is tricksterism. This should be done with panache and audacity as when Britvic bought advertising time to make what appeared to be a public service announcement. Viewers were told that some rogue grocery stores were selling an imitation of their brand, Tango. The difference could be detected because it was not fizzy and they were asked to call a freefone number to name the outlets. Around 30,000 people rang, only to be informed that they had been tricked ('Tango'd') as part of the company's promotion for a new, non-carbonated version of the drink. Despite attracting censure for abusing the public information service format the promotion had succeeded in amplifying the brand extension launch and reinforcing Tango's irreverent image.

Creating customer value and satisfaction

Customer value

Marketing-orientated companies attempt to create **customer value** in order to attract and retain customers. Their aim is to deliver superior value to their target customers. In doing so, they implement the marketing concept by meeting and exceeding customer needs better than the competition. For example, the global success of McDonald's has been based on creating added value for its customers, which is based not only on the food products it sells but on the complete delivery system that goes to make up a fast-food restaurant. It sets high standards in quality, service, cleanliness and value (termed QSCV). Customers can be sure that the same high standards will be found in all of the McDonald's outlets around the world. This example shows that customer value can be derived from many aspects of what the company delivers to its customers—not just the basic product.

Customer value is dependent on how the customer perceives the benefits of an offering and the sacrifice that is associated with its purchase. Therefore:

$$\text{Customer value} = \text{perceived benefits} - \text{perceived sacrifice}$$

Perceived benefits can be derived from the product (for example, the taste of the hamburger), the associated service (for example, how quickly customers are served and the cleanliness of the outlet) and the image of the company (for example, is the image of the company/product favourable?). E-Marketing 1.1 discusses how Pizza Magic raised perceived benefits through improved customer service using the Internet.

A further source of perceived benefits is the relationship between customer and supplier. Customers may enjoy working with suppliers with whom they have developed close relationships. They may have developed close personal and professional friendships, and value the convenience of working with trusted partners.

Perceived sacrifice is the total cost associated with buying a product. This consists of not just monetary cost but the time and energy involved in purchase. For example, with fast-food restaurants, good location can reduce the time and energy required to find a suitable eating place. But marketers need to be aware of another critical sacrifice in some buying situations.

1.1 e-marketing

Fast Food Served up Online

Pizza Magic (www.pizza-magic.co.uk) is a small, fast-food company based in Glasgow. It sells pizzas, fried meals and a range of homemade desserts and ice-creams. Already offering a phone delivery service, it decided a number of years ago to sell its products online to customers in the local area. Through its website, customers can peruse the menu, select options from a drop-down list and pay for their order online. Importantly, there is now a choice of direct ordering methods (by phone or website), both of which avoid the hassle of waiting for an order to be prepared.

For Pizza Magic, although demand has increased, its shop is less hectic than before—reducing pressure on staff during traditionally busy periods. Also, managers can now analyse the order information; the ability to assess fast-moving items at particular times of the day or week now informs the planning and scheduling of resources and activities.

The company's website also provides an ongoing marketing resource and communication tool. With the information collected online, Pizza Magic can e-mail its customers special offers and advise on important caveats to the service (for example, to maintain quality of service it decided that only those customers within a specific postcode area could receive home delivery).

Pizza Magic is a small business that has successfully expanded its operations, retaining the same levels of staff and size of premises, while improving customer service. All this has been enabled through imaginative use of the Internet.

This is the potential psychological cost of not making the right decision. Uncertainty means that people perceive risk when purchasing. McDonald's attempts to reduce perceived risk by standardizing its complete offer so that customers can be confident of what they will receive before entering its outlets. In organizational markets, companies offer guarantees to reduce the risk of purchase. Figure 1.5 illustrates how perceived benefits and sacrifice affect customer value. It provides a framework for considering ways of maximizing value. The objective is to find ways of raising perceived benefits and reducing perceived sacrifice.

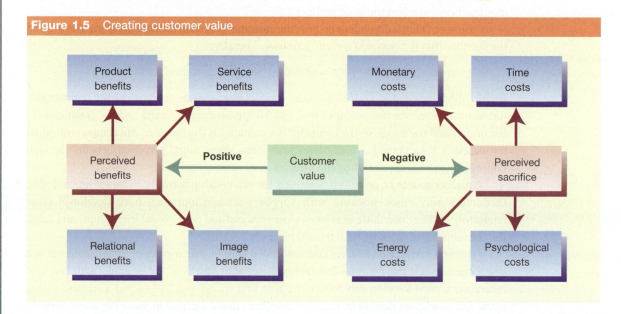

Figure 1.5 Creating customer value

Customer satisfaction

Exceeding the value offered by competitors is key to marketing success. Consumers decide upon purchases on the basis of judgements about the values offered by suppliers. Once a product has been bought, customer satisfaction depends upon its perceived performance compared to the buyer's expectations. Customer satisfaction occurs when perceived performance matches or exceeds expectations.

Expectations are formed through post-buying experiences, discussions with other people, and suppliers' marketing activities. Companies need to avoid the mistake of setting customer expectations too high through exaggerated promotional claims, since this can lead to dissatisfaction if performance falls short of expectations.

Customer satisfaction is taken so seriously by some companies that financial bonuses are tied to it. For example, two days after taking delivery of a new car, BMW (and Mini) customers receive a telephone call to check on how well they were treated in the dealership. The customer is asked 15 questions, with each question scored out of 5. The franchised dealership only receives a financial bonus from BMW if the average score across all questions is 92 or better (5 is equivalent to 100, 4 to 80, and so on). Customer satisfaction with after-sales service is similarly researched. Aspiring dealerships have to be capable of achieving such scores, and existing dealerships that consistently fail to meet these standards are under threat of franchise termination.

In today's competitive climate, it is often not enough to match performance and expectations. Expectations need to be exceeded for commercial success so that customers are delighted with the outcome. In order to understand the concept of customer satisfaction the so-called 'Kano model' (see Fig. 1.6) helps to separate characteristics that cause dissatisfaction, satisfaction and delight. Three characteristics underlie the model: 'Must be', 'More is better' and 'Delighters'.

'Must be' characteristics are expected to be present and are taken for granted. For example, in a hotel, customers expect service at reception and a clean room. Lack of these characteristics causes annoyance but their presence only brings dissatisfaction up to a neutral level. 'More is better' characteristics can take satisfaction past neutral into the positive satisfaction range. For example, no response to a telephone call can cause dissatisfaction, but a fast response may cause positive satisfaction or even delight. 'Delighters' are the unexpected characteristics that surprise the customer. Their absence does not cause dissatisfaction but their presence delights the customer. For example, a UK hotel chain provides free measures of brandy in the rooms of its adult guests. This delights many of its customers, who were not expecting this treat. Another way to delight the customer is to under-promise and over-deliver (for example, by saying that a repair will take about five hours but getting it done in two).[21]

A problem for marketers is that, over time, delighters become expected. For example, some car manufacturers provided small unexpected delighters such as pen holders and delay mechanisms on interior lights so that there is time to find the ignition socket at night. These are standard on most cars now and have become 'Must

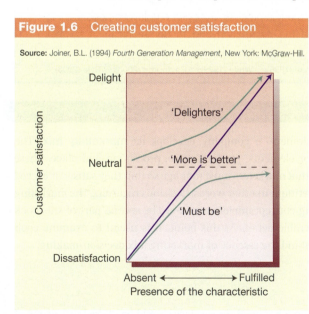

Figure 1.6 Creating customer satisfaction

Source: Joiner, B.L. (1994) *Fourth Generation Management*, New York: McGraw-Hill.

be' characteristics as customers expect them. This means that marketers must constantly strive to find new ways of delighting. Innovative thinking and listening to customers are key ingredients in this. Marketing in Action 1.2 explains how to listen to customers.

1.2 marketing in action

Listening to Customers

Top companies recognize the importance of listening to their customers as part of their strategy to manage satisfaction. Customer satisfaction indices are based on surveys of customers, and the results plotted over time to reveal changes in satisfaction levels. The first stage is to identify those characteristics (choice criteria) that are important to customers when evaluating competing products. The second stage involves the development of measure scales (often statements followed by strongly agree/strongly disagree response boxes) to quantitatively assess satisfaction. Customer satisfaction data should be collected over a period of time to measure change. Only long-term measurement of satisfaction ratings will provide a clear picture of what is going on in the marketplace.

The critical role of listening to customers in marketing success was emphasized by Tom Leahy, chief executive of Tesco, the successful UK supermarket chain, when talking to a group of businesspeople. 'Let me tell you a secret,' he said, 'the secret of successful retailing. Are you ready? It's this: never stop listening to customers, and giving them what they want. I'm sorry if that is a bit of an anticlimax … but it is that simple.'

Marketing research can also be used to question new customers about why they first bought, and lost customers (defectors) on why they have ceased buying. In the latter case, a second objective would be to stage a last-ditch attempt to keep the customer. One bank found that a quarter of its defecting customers would have stayed had the bank attempted to rescue the situation.

One company that places listening to customers high on its list of priorities is Kwik-Fit, the car repair group. Customer satisfaction is monitored by its customer survey unit, which telephones 5000 customers a day within 72 hours of their visit to a Kwik-Fit centre.

A strategy also needs to be put in place to manage customer complaints, comments and questions. A system needs to be set up that solicits feedback on product and service quality, and feeds the information to the appropriate employees. To facilitate this process, front-line employees need training to ask questions, to listen effectively, to capture the information and to communicate it so that corrective action can be taken.

Based on: Jones and Sasser Jr (1995);[22] Morgan (1996);[23] White (1999);[24] Roythorne (2003);[25] Ryle (2003)[26]

Developing an effective marketing mix

Based on its understanding of customers, a company develops its marketing mix. The marketing mix consists of four major elements: product, price, promotion and place. These '4-Ps' are the four key decision areas that marketers must manage so that they satisfy or exceed customer needs better than the competition. In other words, decisions regarding the marketing mix form a major aspect of marketing concept implementation. The second part of this book looks at each of the 4-Ps in considerable detail. At this point, it is useful to examine each element briefly so that we can understand the essence of marketing mix decision-making.

Product

The product decision involves deciding what goods or services should be offered to a group of customers. An important element is new product development. As technology and tastes change, products become out of date and inferior to those of the competition, so companies must replace them with features that customers value. The launch of the £40,000 (€57,600) Range Rover Vogue incorporated a new suspension system based upon 10 litres of microprocessed air.[27] Four air springs are operated by an electronic control unit under the right front seat, which reads height sensors, road and engine speed, foot and handbrake, autotransmission level and door-closing switches. The air springs offer five different height settings varying by 13 cm: high profile for wading or off-road; standard for normal road use; low, which automatically engages under 50 mph; extended to regain traction when the bottom is grounded; and access for getting into and out of the vehicle. Sensors read each wheel 100 times a second for a ride of remarkable smoothness. These features have been built in to the Range Rover because they confer customer benefits. For example, the new lower level for access was incorporated into the design because marketing research had discovered that women occasionally found it embarrassing to climb into the old version. Some motoring journalists have christened this the 'modesty' level. The illustration for the Saab 9-3 communicates the benefit of driver enjoyment.

This press advertisement for the Saab 9-3 communicates the key benefit of the car as 'pure driver enjoyment' using the exhilarated sketchman image.

Product decisions also involve choices regarding brand names, guarantees, packaging and the services that should accompany the product offering. Guarantees can be an important component of the product offering. For example, the operators of the AVE, Spain's high-speed train, capable of travelling at 300 kph, are so confident of its performance that they guarantee to give customers a full refund of their fare if they are more than five minutes late.

Price

Price is a key element of the marketing mix because it represents on a unit basis what the company receives for the product or service that is being marketed. All of the other elements represent costs—for example, expenditure on product design (product), advertising and salespeople (promotion), and transportation and distribution (place). Marketers, therefore, need to be very clear about pricing objectives, methods and the factors that influence price setting. They must also take into account the necessity to discount and give allowances in some transactions. These requirements can influence the level of list price chosen, perhaps with an element of negotiation margin built in. Payment periods and credit terms also affect the real price received in any transaction. These kinds of decisions can affect the perceived value of a product or service offering.

Promotion

Decisions have to be made with respect to the promotional mix: advertising, personal selling, sales promotions, public relations, direct marketing, and Internet and online promotion. By these means the target audience is made aware of the existence of a product or service, and the benefits (both economic and psychological) it confers to customers. Each element of the promotional mix has its own set of strengths and weakness, and these will be explored in the second part of this book. Advertising, for example, has the property of being able to reach wide audiences very quickly. Procter & Gamble used advertising to reach the emerging market of 290 million Russian consumers. It ran a 12-minute commercial on Russian television as its first promotional venture in order to introduce the company and its range of products.[28] The illustration for Reebok shows how advertising can convey a simple but powerful message. A growing form of promotion is the use of the Internet as a promotional tool. A great advantage of the Internet is its global reach. This means that companies that did not have the resources to promote overseas can reach consumers worldwide by creating a website. In business-to-business markets, suppliers

This poster advertisement conveys the power and 'street cred' of Reebok Strikezone boots.

and customers can communicate using the Internet and purchases can be made using e-marketplaces.

Place

Place involves decisions concerning the distribution channels to be used and their management, the locations of outlets, methods of transportation and inventory levels to be held. The objective is to ensure that products and services are available in the proper quantities, at the right time and place. Distribution channels consist of organizations such as retailers or wholesalers through which goods pass on their way to customers. Producers need to manage their relationships with these organizations well because they may provide the only cost-effective access to the marketplace.

Key characteristics of an effective marketing mix

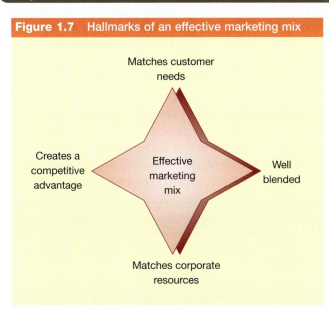

Figure 1.7 Hallmarks of an effective marketing mix

There are four hallmarks of an effective marketing mix (see Fig. 1.7).

The marketing mix matches customer needs

Sensible marketing mix decisions can be made only when the target customer is understood. Choosing customer groups to target will be discussed in Chapter 7, which examines the process of market segmentation and target marketing. Once the decision about the target market(s) is taken, marketing management needs to understand how customers choose between rival offerings. They need to look at the product or service through customers' eyes and understand, among other factors, the choice criteria they use.

Figure 1.8 illustrates the link between customer choice criteria and the marketing mix. The starting point is the realization that customers evaluate products on economic and psychological criteria. Economic criteria include factors such as performance, availability, reliability, durability and productivity gains to be made by using the product. Examples of psychological criteria are self-image, a desire for a quiet life, pleasure, convenience and risk reduction. These will be discussed in detail in Chapter 3. The important point at this stage is to note that an analysis of customer choice criteria will reveal a set of key customer requirements that must be met in order to succeed in the marketplace. Meeting or exceeding these requirements better than the competition leads to the creation of a competitive advantage.

The marketing mix creates a competitive advantage

A competitive advantage may be derived from decisions about the 4-Ps. A competitive advantage is a clear performance differential over the competition on factors that are important to customers. The example of the Range Rover Vogue launch is an example of a company using

Figure 1.8 Matching the marketing mix to customer needs

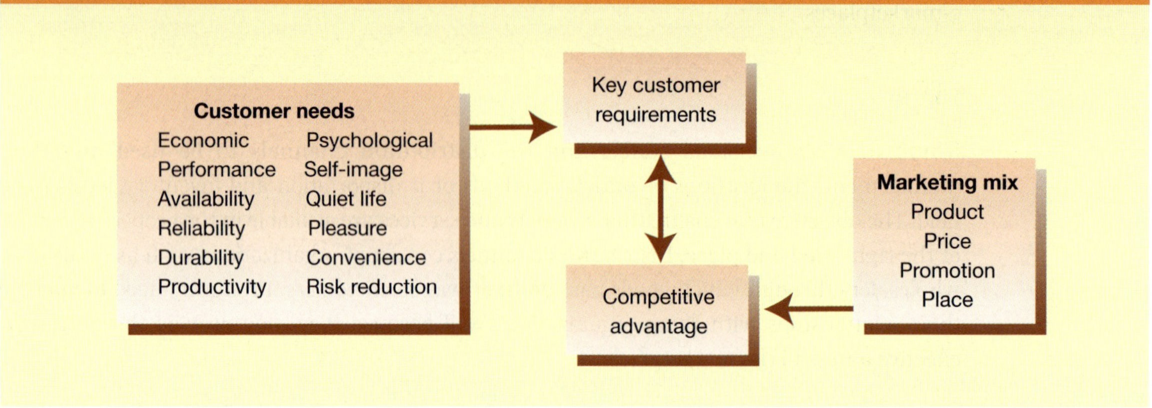

Customer needs
- Economic
- Performance
- Availability
- Reliability
- Durability
- Productivity
- Psychological
- Self-image
- Quiet life
- Pleasure
- Convenience
- Risk reduction

Key customer requirements ↔ Competitive advantage

Marketing mix
- Product
- Price
- Promotion
- Place

product features to convey customer benefits in excess of what the competition is offering. Variable height adjustment can therefore be regarded as an attempt to establish a competitive advantage through product decisions. Aldi, the German supermarket chain, is attempting to establish a competitive advantage in the UK by low prices, a key customer requirement of its chosen target group of customers.

The strategy of using advertising as a tool for competitive advantage is often employed when product benefits are particularly subjective and amorphous in nature. Thus the advertising for perfumes such as those produced by Chanel, Givenchy and Yves St Laurent is critical in preserving the exclusive image established by such brands. The size and quality of the salesforce can act as a competitive advantage. A problem that a company such as Rolls-Royce faces is the relatively small size of its salesforce compared to those of its giant competitors Boeing and General Electric. Finally, distribution decisions need to be made with the customer

1.3 marketing in action

Creating a Competitive Advantage

Launched with a marketing budget of £5 million (€6.5 million), and targeting women in their twenties, *Glamour* entered the intensely competitive women's magazine market. Leading this sector was *Cosmopolitan*, the 30-year-old glitzy, best-selling monthly. Many had tried to dislodge *Cosmopolitan* from its perch and many had failed. *Glamour* had one unique advantage, though: its size.

Condé Nast, the magazine's publishers, decided that instead of being the normal magazine size, *Glamour* would be small enough to fit into a woman's handbag—approximately two-thirds of the size of *Cosmopolitan*. Condé Nast believed that this would create a competitive advantage for *Glamour*. Women would value the convenience of carrying the magazine in their handbag to browse through it when they were waiting in queues, on public transport, at the hairdresser, and so on.

This decision was not based on intuition but marketing research. Condé Nast had previously launched an Italian version of the magazine. It tested two formats: normal (*Cosmopolitan*) size and A5 size (the smaller version). The smaller version outsold the normal size at a rate of two to one. Its print run quickly jumped from 130,000 to 240,000 per month.

Glamour's sales in the UK exceeded those of *Cosmopolitan* within a year—a remarkable achievement that highlights the importance of seeking competitive advantage to attain marketing success.

Based on: Anonymous (2001);[29] Singh (2002);[30] Anonymous (2002)[31]

in mind, not only in terms of availability but also with respect to service levels, image and customer convenience. The Radisson SAS hotel at Manchester Airport is an example of creating a competitive advantage through customer convenience. It is situated five minutes' walk from the airport terminals, which are reached by covered walkways. Guests at rival hotels have to rely on taxis or transit buses to reach the airport.

Although some competitive advantages rely on technology-based benefits, this need not be the case. The essential ingredient is knowledge of what customers value and the means to satisfy them better than the competition, as Marketing in Action 1.3 explains.

The marketing mix should be well blended

The third characteristic of an effective marketing mix is that the four elements—product, price, promotion and place—should be well blended to form a consistent theme. If a product gives superior benefits to customers, price, which may send cues to customers regarding quality, should reflect those extra benefits. All of the promotional mix should be designed with the objective of communicating a consistent message to the target audience about these benefits, and distribution decisions should be consistent with the overall strategic position of the product in the marketplace. The use of exclusive outlets for upmarket fashion and cosmetic brands—Armani, Christian Dior and Calvin Klein, for example—is consistent with their strategic position.

The marketing mix should match corporate resources

The choice of marketing mix strategy may be constrained by the financial resources of the company. Laker Airlines used price as a competitive advantage to attack British Airways and TWA in transatlantic flights. When they retaliated by cutting their airfares, Laker's financial resources were insufficient to win the price war. Certain media—for example, television advertising—require a minimum threshold investment before they are regarded as feasible. In the UK a rule of thumb is that at least £1 million (€1.44 million) per year is required to achieve impact in a national advertising campaign. Clearly those brands that cannot afford such a promotional budget must use other less expensive media—for example, posters or sales promotion—to attract and hold customers.

A second internal resource constraint may be the internal competences of the company. A marketing mix strategy may be too ambitious for the limited marketing skills of personnel to implement effectively. While an objective may be to reduce or eliminate this problem in the medium to long term, in the short term marketing management may have to heed the fact that strategy must take account of competences. An area where this may manifest itself is within the place dimension of the 4-Ps. A company lacking the personal selling skills to market a product directly to end users may have to use intermediaries (distributors or sales agents) to perform that function.

Criticisms of the 4-Ps approach to marketing management

Some critics of the 4-Ps approach to the marketing mix argue that it oversimplifies the reality of marketing management. Booms and Bitner, for example, argue for a 7-Ps approach to services marketing.[32] Their argument, which will be discussed in some detail in Chapter 21 on services marketing, is that the 4-Ps do not take sufficient account of people, process and physical evidence. In services, people often *are* the service itself; the process or how the service is delivered to the customer is usually a key part of the service, and the physical evidence—the décor of the restaurant or shop, for example—is so critical to success that it should be considered as a separate element in the services marketing mix.

Rafiq and Ahmed argue that this criticism of the 4-Ps can be extended to include industrial marketing.[33] The interaction approach to understanding industrial marketing stresses that success does not come solely from manipulation of the marketing mix components but long-term relationship building, whereby the bond between buyer and seller becomes so strong that it effectively acts as a barrier to entry for out-suppliers.[34] This phenomenon undoubtedly exists to such an extent that industrial buyers are now increasingly seeking long-term supply relationships with suppliers. Lucas (a UK components producer), as part of its Strategic Sources Review, sought such partnerships with preferred suppliers. Lucas helps investment with such suppliers who, in turn, allow Lucas to understand their costs. Bosch, the German producer of industrial and consumer goods, conducts quality audits of its suppliers. These kinds of activities are not captured in the 4-Ps approach, it is claimed.

Nevertheless, there is no absolute reason why these extensions cannot be incorporated within the 4-Ps framework.[35] People, process and physical evidence can be discussed under 'product', and long-term relationship building under 'promotion', for example. The important issue is not to neglect them, whether the 4-Ps approach or some other method is used to conceptualize the decision-making areas of marketing. The strength of the 4-Ps approach is that it represents a memorable and practical framework for marketing decision-making and has proved useful for case study analysis in business schools for many years.

Marketing and business performance

The basic premise of the marketing concept is that its adoption will improve business performance. Marketing is not an abstract concept: its acid test is the effect that its use has on key corporate indices such as profitability and market share. Fortunately, in recent years, three quantitative studies in both Europe and North America have sought to examine the relationship between marketing and performance. The results suggest that the relationship is positive. We will now examine each of the three studies in turn.

Marketing characteristics and business performance

In a study of 1700 senior marketing executives, Hooley and Lynch reported the marketing characteristics of high- versus low-performing companies.[36] The approach that they adopted was to isolate the top 10 per cent of companies (based on such measures as profit margin, return on investment and market share) and to compare their marketing practices with the remainder of the sample. The 'high fliers' differed from the 'also-rans' as follows:

- more committed to marketing research
- more likely to be found in new, emerging or growth markets
- adopted a more proactive approach to marketing planning
- more likely to use strategic planning tools
- placed more emphasis on product performance and design, rather than price, for achieving a competitive advantage
- worked more closely with the finance department
- placed greater emphasis on market share as a method of evaluating marketing performance.

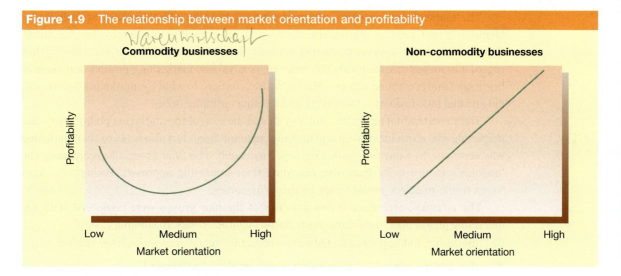

Figure 1.9 The relationship between market orientation and profitability

Marketing orientation and business performance

Narver and Slater studied the relationship between marketing orientation and business performance.[37] Marketing orientation was based on three measures: customer orientation, competitor orientation, and degree of inter-functional co-ordination. They collected data from 113 strategic business units (SBUs) of a major US corporation.

The businesses comprised 36 commodity businesses (forestry products) and 77 non-commodity businesses (speciality products and distribution businesses). They related each SBU's profitability, as measured by return on assets in relation to competitors over the last year in the SBU's principal served market, to their three-component measure of market orientation.

Figure 1.9 shows the results of their study. For commodity businesses the relationship was U-shaped, with low and high market-orientation businesses showing higher profitability than the businesses in the mid-range of market orientation. Businesses with the highest market orientation had the highest profitability and those with the lowest market orientation had the second highest profitability. Narver and Slater explained this result by suggesting that the businesses lowest in market orientation may achieve some profit success through a low cost strategy, though not the profit levels of the high market-orientation businesses, an explanation supported by the fact that they were the largest companies of the three groups.

For the non-commodity businesses the relationship was linear, with the businesses displaying the highest level of market orientation achieving the highest levels of profitability and those with the lowest scores on market orientation having the lowest profitability figures. As the authors state, 'The findings give marketing scholars and practitioners a basis beyond mere intuition for recommending the superiority of a market orientation.'

A number of more recent studies have also found a positive relationship between market orientation and business performance. Market orientation has been found to have a positive effect on sales growth, market share and profitability,[38] sales growth,[39] sales growth and new product success,[40] perception of product quality[41] and overall business performance.[42]

The marketing philosophy and business performance

A study published in 1990 by Hooley, Lynch and Shepherd sought to develop a typology of approaches to marketing and to relate those approaches to business performance.[43] Based on a sample of over 1000 companies, they identified four distinct groups of companies, as shown in Fig. 1.10.

The 'marketing philosophers' saw marketing as a function with the prime responsibility for identifying and meeting customers' needs and as a guiding philosophy for the whole organization; they did not see marketing as confined to the marketing department, nor did they regard it as merely sales support. The 'sales supporters' saw marketing's primary functions as being sales and promotion support. Marketing was confined to what the marketing department did and had little to do with identifying and meeting customer needs.

The 'departmental marketers' not only shared the view of the marketing philosophers that marketing was about identifying and meeting customer needs but also believed that marketing was restricted to what the marketing department did. The final group of companies—the 'unsures'—tended to be indecisive regarding their marketing approach. Perhaps the term 'stuck-in-the-middlers' would be apt for these companies.

The attitudes, organization and practices of the four groups were compared, with the marketing philosophers exhibiting many distinct characteristics. In summary:

- marketing philosophers adopted a more proactive, aggressive approach towards the future
- they had a more proactive approach to new product development
- they placed a higher importance on marketing training
- they adopted longer time horizons for marketing planning
- marketing had a higher status within the company
- marketing had a higher chance of being represented at board level
- marketing had more chance of working closely with other functional areas
- marketing made a greater input into strategic plans.

The performance of the four groups was also compared using two criteria: a subjectively reported return on investment (ROI) figure, and performance relative to major competitors. The marketing philosophers achieved a significantly higher ROI than the remainder of the sample. The departmental marketers performed at the sample average, while the unsures and sales supporters performed significantly worse. The marketing philosophers performed significantly better than each of the other groups. Using the performance relative to competitors' criteria, the marketing philosophers again came out on top, followed by the departmental marketers.

Hooley *et al.*'s conclusion was that marketing should be viewed not merely as a departmental function but as a guiding philosophy for the whole organization: 'Our evidence

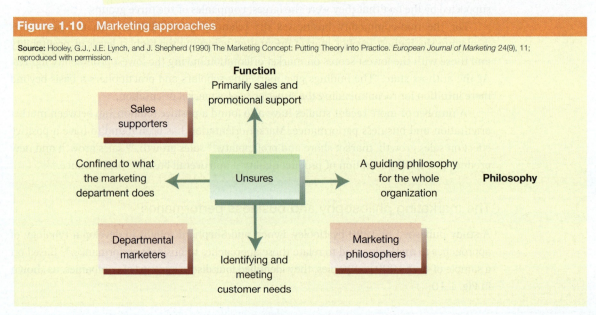

Figure 1.10 Marketing approaches

Source: Hooley, G.J., J.E. Lynch, and J. Shepherd (1990) The Marketing Concept: Putting Theory into Practice. *European Journal of Marketing* 24(9), 11; reproduced with permission.

points to improved performance among companies that adopt this wider approach to business.'[44]

What overall conclusions can be drawn from these three studies? In order to make a balanced judgement their limitations must be recognized. They were all cross-sectional studies based on self-reported data. With any such survey there is the question of the direction of causality. Perhaps some respondents inferred their degree of marketing orientation by reference to their performance level. However, this clearly did not occur with the commodity sample in the Narver and Slater study.[45] What these three separate studies have consistently and unambiguously shown is a strong association between marketing and business performance. As one condition for establishing causality, this is an encouraging result for those people concerned with promoting the marketing concept as a guiding philosophy for business.

Review

1. The marketing concept: an understanding of the nature of marketing, its key components and limitations

- The marketing concept is the achievement of corporate goals through meeting and exceeding customer needs better than the competition.
- It exists through exchanges where the objective is for all parties in the exchange to feel satisfied.
- Its key components are customer orientation, integrated effort and goal achievement (e.g. profits).
- The limitations of the concept are that the pursuit of customer satisfaction is only one objective companies should consider (others, such as achieving economies of scale, are equally valid), the adoption of the marketing concept may result in a focus on short-term personal satisfaction rather than longer-term societal welfare, the focus on customers to guide the development of new products may lead to only modest improvements compared to the innovations resulting from technological push, and the emphasis on reflecting rather than creating demand can lead to dull marketing campaigns and me-too products.

2. The difference between a production orientation and marketing orientation

- Marketing orientation focuses on customer needs to identify potential market opportunities, leading to the creation of products that create customer satisfaction.
- Production orientation focuses on production capabilities, which defines the business mission and the products that are manufactured. These are then sold aggressively to customers.

3. The differing roles of efficiency and effectiveness in achieving corporate success

- Efficiency is concerned with inputs and outputs. Business processes are managed to a high standard so that cost per unit of output is low. Its role is to 'do things right'—that is, use processes that result in low cost production.
- Effectiveness is concerned with making the correct strategic choice regarding which products to make for which markets. Its role is to 'do the right things'—that is, make the right products for attractive markets.

4. The differences between market-driven and internally orientated businesses

- Customer concern vs convenience.
- Know customer choice criteria and match with marketing mix vs the assumption that price and performance are key.

- Segment by customer differences vs segment by product.
- Marketing research vs anecdotes and received wisdom.
- Welcome change vs cherish status quo.
- Understand competition vs ignore competition.
- Marketing spend is an investment vs marketing spend is a luxury.
- Innovation rewarded and reluctance to punish failure vs avoidance of mistakes rewarded and failure to innovate conspicuously punished.
- Search for latent markets vs stick with the same.
- Recognize the importance of being fast vs content to move slowly.
- Strive for competitive advantage vs happy to be me-too.

5 How to create customer value and satisfaction

- Customer value is created by maximizing perceived benefits (e.g. product or image benefits) and minimizing perceived sacrifice (e.g. monetary or time costs).
- Customer satisfaction once a product is bought is created by maximizing perceived performance compared to the customer's expectations. Customer satisfaction occurs when perceived performance matches or exceeds expectations.

6 How an effective marketing mix is designed, and the criticisms of the 4-Ps approach to marketing management

- The classical marketing mix consists of product, price, promotion and place (the '4-Ps').
- An effective marketing mix is designed by ensuring that it matches customer needs, creates a competitive advantage, is well blended and matches corporate resources.
- Criticisms of the 4-Ps approach to marketing management are that it oversimplifies reality. For example, for services marketing three further Ps—people, process and physical evidence—should be added and, for industrial (business-to-business) marketing, the marketing mix approach neglects the importance of long-term relationship building.

7 The relationship between marketing characteristics, market orientation, adoption of a marketing philosophy and business performance

- Research has shown a positive relationship between business performance and marketing characteristics, market orientation (although for commodity businesses the relationship was U-shaped) and the adoption of a marketing philosophy.

Key terms

competitive advantage a clear performance differential over competition on factors that are important to target customers

customer satisfaction the fulfilment of customers' requirements or needs

customer value perceived benefits minus perceived sacrifice

effectiveness doing the right thing, making the correct strategic choice

efficiency a way of managing business processes to a high standard, usually concerned with cost reduction; also called 'doing things right'

exchange the act or process of receiving something from someone by giving something in return

marketing concept the achievement of corporate goals through meeting and exceeding customer needs better than the competition

marketing mix a framework for the tactical management of the customer relationship, including

- **product, place, price, promotion (the 4-Ps);** in the case of services three other elements to be taken into account are process, people and physical evidence

marketing orientation companies with a marketing orientation focus on customer needs as the primary drivers of organizational performance

place the distribution channels to be used, outlet locations, methods of transportation

price (1) the amount of money paid for a product; (2) the agreed value placed on the exchange by a buyer and seller

product a good or service offered or performed by an organization or individual, which is capable of satisfying customer needs

production orientation a business approach that is inwardly focused either on costs or on a definition of a company in terms of its production facilities

promotional mix advertising, personal selling, sales promotions, public relations, direct marketing, and Internet and online promotion

Internet exercise

Northern Foods is a leading food producer in the UK and Ireland. The company owns a number of brands, such as Goodfellas, Batchelors, Green Isles and Fox's Biscuits. The company has produced a number of position statements regarding its policies on genetically modified (GM) foods, environmental policy and the sourcing of raw materials. Visit http://www.northern-foods.co.uk/company/position.html to explore Northern Foods' policy statements.

Visit: www.northern-foods.co.uk

Questions

(a) Why do companies need to publish such policy statements?
(b) How can marketing improve the corporate image of organizations?
(c) Can you name any companies that have generated controversy due to their marketing activities? What can be done by companies to avoid a consumer backlash?

Visit the Online Learning Centre at www.mcgraw-hill.co.uk/textbooks/jobber for more Internet exercises.

Study questions

1. What are the essential characteristics of a marketing-orientated company?
2. Are there any situations where marketing orientation is not the most appropriate business philosophy?
3. Explain how the desire to become efficient may conflict with being effective.
4. How far do you agree or disagree with the criticism that marketing is a source of dullness? Are there any ethical issues relevant to the five principles of 'retromarketing'?
5. To what extent do you agree with the criticisms of the marketing concept and the 4-Ps approach to marketing decision-making?

When you have read this chapter log on to the Online Learning Centre at www.mcgraw-hill.co.uk/textbooks/jobber to explore chapter-by-chapter test questions, links and further online study tools for marketing.

case one

H&M Gets Hot

Stefan Persson, chairman of Swedish retailer Hennes & Mauritz (H&M), vividly remembers his company's first attempt at international expansion. It was 1976, the year H&M opened its London store in Oxford Circus. 'I stood outside trying to lure in customers by handing out Abba albums,' he recalls with a wry laugh. Persson, then 29, and son of the company's founder, waited for the crowds. And waited. 'I still have most of those albums,' he says.

But Stefan is not crying over that unsold vinyl. In a slowing global economy, with lacklustre consumer spending and retailers across Europe struggling to make a profit, H&M's pre-tax profits hit $833 million in 2002, a 34 per cent increase on the previous year, on sales of $5.8 billion. The growth is

Table C1.1	The clash of the clothing titans			
	Style	**Strategy**	**Global reach**	**Financials**
H&M	Motto is 'fashion and quality at the best price'. Translates into cutting-edge clothes.	Production outsourced to suppliers in Europe and Asia. Some lead times are just three weeks.	Has 809 stores in 14 countries. More than 88 per cent of sales come from outside Sweden.	Estimated 2002 pre-tax profit of $833 million on sales of $5.8 billion.
Gap, Inc.	Built its name on wardrobe basics such as denim, combats and T-shirts.	Outsources all production. An average of nine months for turnaround.	Operates 656 stores in the US, Canada, Japan and Europe, which produce 8 per cent of sales.	Estimated 2002 pre-tax profit of $554 million on sales of $13.8 billion.
Zara	Billed as 'Armani on a budget' for its Euro-style clothing for women and men.	Bulk of production is handled by company's own manufacturing facilities in Spain.	Runs 507 outlets in 30 countries, but Spain still accounts for 50 per cent of sales.	Parent Inditex does not break out sales.

Data: company reports, Santander Central Hispano, BNP Paribas, Goldman, Sachs & Co.

being fuelled not only by expansion: same-store sales were up between 4 per cent and 5 per cent in 2002. H&M has $1 billion in cash. Its market capitalization of $15 billion outstrips that of Gap, Inc. and Zara International, its closest competitors (see Table C1.1). And at current sales levels, the chain is the largest apparel retailer in Europe. This is not just a store chain—it is a money-making machine.

Marketing at H&M

If you stop by its Fifth Avenue location in New York or check out the mothership at the corner of Regeringsgatan and Hamngatan in Stockholm, it's easy to see what's powering H&M's success. The prices are as low as the fashion is trendy, turning each location into a temple of 'cheap chic'. At the Manhattan flagship, mirrored disco balls hang from the ceiling, and banks of televisions broadcast videos of the body-pierced, belly-baring pop princesses of the moment. On a cool afternoon in October, teenage girls in flared jeans and two-toned hair mill around the ground floor, hoisting piles of velour hoodies, Indian-print blouses and patchwork denim skirts—each $30 or under. (The average price of an H&M item is just $18.) This is not Gap's brand of classic casuals or the more grown-up Euro-chic of Zara. It's exuberant, it's over-the-top and it's working. 'Everything is really nice—and cheap,' says Sabrina Farhi, 22, as she clutches a suede trenchcoat she has been eyeing for weeks.

The H&M approach also appeals to Erin Yuill, a 20-year-old part-time employee from New Jersey who explains, 'Things go out of style fast. Sometimes, I'll wear a dress or top a few times, and that's it. But I'm still in school and I don't have a lot of money. For me this is heaven.'

H&M is also shrewdly tailoring its strategy to fit the US market. In Europe, H&M is more like a department store—selling a range of merchandise from edgy street fashion to casual basics for the whole family. Its US stores are geared to younger, more fashion-conscious females. H&M's menswear line, a strong seller in Europe, hasn't proved popular with the less-fashion-conscious American male. So a number of US outlets have either cut back the selection or eliminated the line. And while the pricing is cheap, the branding isn't. H&M spends a hefty 4 per cent of revenues on marketing. This year's photo ad campaign was shot by fashion-world legend Richard Avedon.

Behind this stylish image is a company so buttoned-down and frugal that you can't imagine its executives tuning into a soft-rock station, let alone getting inside a teenager's head. Stefan Persson, whose late father founded the company, looks and talks more like a financier than a merchant prince. A penny-pinching financier, at that. 'H&M is run on a shoestring,' says Nathan Cockrell, a retail analyst at Credit Suisse First Boston in London. 'They buy as cheaply as possible and keep overheads low.' Fly business class? Only in emergencies. Taking cabs? Definitely frowned upon. To rein in costs, Persson even took away all employees' mobile phones in the 1990s. Today, only a few key employees have cell-phone privileges.

But that gimlet eye is just what a retailer needs to stay on its game—especially the kind of high-risk game H&M is playing. Not since IKEA set out to conquer the world one modular wall unit at a time has a Swedish retailer displayed such bold international ambition. H&M is pressing full steam ahead on a programme that brought its total number of stores to 844 by the end of 2002, an almost 75 per cent increase in the past six years.

Yet H&M is pursuing a strategy that has undone a number of rivals. Benetton tried to become the world's fashion retailer but retreated after a disastrous experience in the USA in the 1980s. Gap, once the hottest chain in the States, has lately been choking on its mismanaged inventory and has never taken off abroad. Body Shop and Sephora had similar misadventures.

Nevertheless, Persson and his crew are undaunted. 'When I joined in 1972, H&M was all about price,' he says. 'Then we added quality fashion to the equation, but everyone said you could never combine [them] successfully. But we were passionate that we could.' Persson is just as passionate that he can apply the H&M formula internationally.

What's that formula, exactly? Treat fashion as if it were perishable product: keep it fresh, and keep it moving. That means spotting the trends even before the trendoids do, turning the ideas into affordable clothes, and making the apparel fly off the racks. 'We hate inventory,' says H&M's head of buying, Karl Gunnar Fagerlin, whose job it is to make sure the merchandise doesn't pile up at the company's warehouses. Not an easy task, considering H&M stores sell 550 million items per year.

Although H&M sells a range of clothing for women, men and children, its cheap-chic formula goes down particularly well with the 15-to-30 set. Lusting after that Dolce & Gabbana corduroy trenchcoat but unwilling to cough up $1000-plus? At $60, H&M's version is too good to pass up. It's more Lycra than luxe and won't last forever. But if you're trying to keep *au courant*, one season is sufficient. 'At least half my wardrobe comes from H&M,' says Emma Mackie, a 19-year-old student from London. 'It's really good value for money.'

H&M's high-fashion, low-price concept distinguishes it from Gap, Inc., with its all-basics-at-all-price-points, and chains such as bebe and Club Monaco, whose fashions are of the moment but by no means inexpensive. It offers an alternative for consumers who may be bored with chinos and cargo pants, but not able—or willing—to trade up for more fashion. H&M has seized on the fact that what's in today will not be in tomorrow. Shoppers at the flagship store agreed, particularly the younger ones that the retailer caters to.

Design at H&M

H&M's design process is as dynamic as its clothes. The 95-person design group is encouraged to draw inspiration not from fashion runways but from real life. 'We travel a lot,' says designer Ann-Sofie Johansson, whose recent trip to Marrakech inspired a host of creations worthy of the bazaars. 'You need to get out, look at people, new places. See colours. Smell smells.' When at home, Johansson admits to following people off the subway in Stockholm to ask where they picked up a particular top or unusual scarf. Call it stalking for style's sake.

The team includes designers from Sweden, the Netherlands, Britain, South Africa and the USA. The average age is 30. Johansson is part of the design group for 15 to 25 year olds, and the style they are marketing this autumn is Bohemian: long crinkled cotton skirts with matching blouses and sequinned sweaters for a bit of night-time glamour. Johansson and Emneryd aren't pushing a whole look. They know H&M's customers ad-lib, pairing up one of its new off-the-shoulder chiffon tops with last year's khaki cargo pants, for instance. The goal is to keep young shoppers coming into H&M's stores on a regular basis, even if they're spending less than $30 a pop. If they get hooked they'll stay loyal later on, when they become more affluent.

Not all designs are brand new: many are based on proven sellers such as washed denim and casual skirts, with a slight twist to freshen them up. The trick is striking the right balance between cutting-edge designs and commercially viable clothes.

To deliver 500 new designs to the stores for a typical season, designers may do twice as many finished sketches. H&M also has merchandise managers in each country, who talk with customers about the clothes and accessories on offer. When they travel, buyers and designers spend time with store managers to find out why certain items in each country have or haven't worked. In Stockholm, they stay close to the customers by working regularly in H&M's stores. Still, Johansson and her crew won't chase after every fad: 'There are some things I could never wear, no matter how trendy,' she says. Hot pants are high on that list. It's safe to say they won't be popping up at H&M any time soon.

H&M's young designers find inspiration in everything from street trends to films to flea markets. Despite the similarity between haute couture and some of H&M's trendier pieces, copying the catwalk is not allowed, swears Margareta van den Bosch, who heads the H&M design team. 'Whether it's Donna Karan, Prada or H&M, we all work on the same time frames,' she says. 'But we can add garments during the season.'

Cutting lead times and costs

Working hand in glove with suppliers, H&M's 21 local production offices have compressed lead times—meaning how long it takes for a garment to travel from design table to store floor—to as little as three weeks. Only Zara has a faster turnaround. But Zara has nearly 300 fewer stores. In addition, Zara's parent, Inditex, owns it own production facilities in Galicia, Spain, allowing Zara to shrink lead time to a mere two weeks. Gap, Inc. operates on a nine-month cycle, a factor analysts say is to blame for its chronic overstock problem.

H&M's speed maximizes its ability to churn out more hot items during any season, while minimizing its fashion faux pas. Every day, Fagerlin and his team tap into the company's database for itemized sales reports by country, store and type of merchandise. Stores are restocked daily. Items that do not sell are quickly marked down in price to make room for the next styles. Faster turnaround means higher sales, which helps H&M charge low prices and still log gross profit margins of 53 per cent.

All major fashion retailers aim for fast turnaround these days, but H&M is one of the few in the winners' circle. To keep costs down, the company outsources all manufacturing to a huge network of 900 garment shops located in 21 mostly low-wage countries, primarily Bangladesh, China and Turkey. 'They are constantly shifting production to get the best deal,' says John Tisell, an analyst at Enskilda Securities in Stockholm.

Questions

1. To what extent is H&M marketing orientated? What evidence is there in the case to support your view?
2. Into which cell of the efficiency/effectiveness matrix does H&M fall? Justify your answer.
3. What is the basis of the customer value H&M provides for its customers?
4. What future challenges are likely to face H&M in the future?
5. Do you consider the marketing of disposable clothes contrary to societal welfare? Justify your opinion.

This case was compiled by Professor David Jobber and is almost completely based on Capell, K., G. Khermouch and A. Sains (2002) How H&M Got Hot, *Business Week*, 11 November, 37–42, with additional material from M. Wilson (2000) Disposable Chic at H&M, *Chain Store Age*, May, 64–6.

case two

Legoland and the Millennium Dome: a Tale of the Launch of Two London Visitor Attractions

At Easter 1996, a new theme park, Legoland, opened in Windsor, some 40 kilometres to the west of central London. By the end of its first operating season (it closed during the winter), it had attracted over 1.4 million visitors, making it one of Britain's top ten most visited admission-charging attractions. It was considered by many to be an unqualified success. On New Year's Day 2000, another new attraction, the Millennium Dome, opened in Greenwich some 15 kilometres to the east of central London. By the end of its first and (as planned) only operating year it had attracted 6.5 million visitors, making it by some way the country's most visited admission-charging attraction. Yet, it was considered by most people to be an unqualified failure. What lay behind such different perceptions of success and failure?

Purpose and description of the two attractions

Legoland was designed as a theme park for children, aged 3–13. Based on the original, and then only, Legoland theme park at Billund, Denmark, its aim was fun, learning, stimulation and family interaction. According to Christina Majgaard, then vice president of Lego, it was a 'family park' rather than a theme park.[1]

The park was sited on a 150-acre, wooded site and included a number of 'areas', each related to a Lego theme, including Beginning, Imagination Centre, Miniland, Lego Exploreland, Lego Traffic and My Town. Within these was a product mix of rides, attractions and shows. The rides were 'pink knuckle' (enjoyable but not frightening), attractions included walk-through humour areas (at child height), a role-play circus where children were trained to be clowns and acrobats, and a 'driving school'. Five live shows were put on each day in three auditoria.

Legoland was very much a full-day-out attraction and prices were set accordingly, at £15 (€22) for adults, £12 (€17) for children and £11 (€16) for senior citizens. For motorists, the park was conveniently situated, within easy reach of the M3, M4 and M25 motorways, and with free onsite parking. By rail, Windsor was just an hour by train from central London.

The Millennium Dome was created to celebrate the new millennium and Britain's place within it. Sited in a massive, temporary, weatherproof tent-like structure, the Dome was to be an attraction for everyone, young and old and from all socio-economic groups. The Dome was developed around eight 'zones': Body, Learning, Money, Mind, Faith, Talk, Home Planet and Living Island. Each showed an appropriate theme. The Body, for example, allowed visitors to walk though a huge, model body complete with visual and audio representation of the workings of internal organs. Faith described the world's principal religions and Living Island addressed issues of litter and pollution. There would be a cinema showing a specially produced comedy film, based on the popular British *Blackadder* series, and a spectacular live acrobatic show would be performed daily in the Dome's massive central arena. Admission to the attraction, which was to be open for one year only, was to be priced at £20 (€29) for an adult or £57 (€82) for a family.

Access to the Dome was exclusively by tube (metro) with a 20-minute Jubilee Line journey from central London. Car access was discouraged and no parking facilities were provided.

The philosophy behind the attractions

Corporate philosophy played a big part in the development of both attractions.

Legoland was very much based on the business philosophy of parent company Lego. Founded in 1932, its name derived from the Danish words *leg godt* (play well), the company, still private and family owned, reflected the values of its founder Ole Kirk Christiansen: creativity, fun, development, play and teaching as well as a strict adherence to quality—'only the best is good enough'.[2] It is estimated that more than 300 million adults and children have played with Lego bricks. In 1996, Lego was recognized as the fifth strongest brand in Europe and the 13th strongest worldwide. For Lego, its theme parks provided a natural opportunity for all the family to share the company's vision and philosophy. As Legoland's managing director, Robert Montgomery said, 'we are not a park for everyone, we are specifically a good, family day out'.[3]

The Millennium Dome's philosophy was somewhat different, and had in fact developed through circumstance rather than vision. It all started in 1992 when one of

America's leading television networks enquired about buying up the rights to broadcast London's millennium celebrations. What celebrations? None had been planned. However, seeing an opportunity through funding from the newly announced National Lottery for an ambitious project that could also contribute to urban regeneration, the then Conservative Deputy Prime Minister Michael Heseltine championed the Dome concept for the eastern fringes of central London. Though the Conservative's lost power in 1997, their successors, 'New' Labour, adopted the project, promising that its success would be a leading inclusion in their next election manifesto. Adoption was not without opposition, however. A number of ministers, including the Chancellor of the Exchequer, were against the project and Deputy Prime Minister John Prescott queried whether it was supposed to be Alton Towers (Britain's leading all-purpose theme park) or a more traditional expo. Philosophy was now very much political and presentational. According to new Prime Minister Tony Blair, 'this is Britain's opportunity to greet the world with a celebration that is so bold, so beautiful, that it embodies at once the spirit of the future in the world'.[4] He appointed close cabinet colleague, Minister Without Portfolio Peter Mandelson to lead the project. Mandelson enthused, 'I want it to be fun; I want it to be entertaining; but I also want it to be an opportunity for people to reflect on who we are, what sort of society we live in and where we are going as a country.'[5]

Pre-opening and launch

Lego's decision to choose London as the location for its second theme park was strongly research based. The research had examined two factors: number of children aged between 2 and 13 and the popularity of Lego toys. London and the surrounding area scored well on both, with a two-hours' travelling time catchment of some 20 million potential users. However, the company believed that it was targeting a niche family market, rather than the traditional north European mass one of theme-park thrill-seeking, C1/C2, 18–24 year olds. Accordingly, an ambitious but manageable £85 million (€122 million), funded entirely from within the company, was invested in the project.

Focus was the watchword for Lego. From core philosophy to design and build, everything had to reflect the values of the company—otherwise there was a risk of product and ultimately brand dilution. A team of designers worked to pre-set plans. Everything was designed to be cheerful and safe, and to blend in to the woodland surroundings. Layouts were produced to minimize queuing and to allow parents to watch over their children from safe and comfortable vantage points. Catering was treated in the same way, with an emphasis on fresh food, wide choice and low-level food service counters. Even park sponsorship was handled in a brand-responsible manner. Lego wanted sponsors with criteria that included the environment, corporate citizenship, market leadership and a reputation for high quality.

Ten days before opening, 250,000 tickets had been sold, representing nearly 20 per cent of the projected first-year visitors.

Launch PR was handled calmly and effectively. Regular information culminated in a themed launch press day with children acting out the key Legoland parts to some 600 journalists, photographers and broadcast crews. As with the whole pre-opening period, everything was done in a relaxed, sensible manner. After all, according to Michael Moore, press relations manager of Lego UK, 'there was no need to deviate from the brand position as it was already well known'.[6]

The pre-opening and launch of the Millennium Dome were somewhat more exciting. The massive £758 million (€1092 million) that was to be invested in the project was matched with equally bold projections and statements. A total of 12 million paying visitors would go through the turnstiles, two million more than Disneyland, Paris. Rhetoric from organizers and politicians included statements such as 'the world's most ambitious project' or 'we are constructing the most famous building in the world' or 'an achievement that the rest of the world is looking on with envy and admiration'. Research was hardly conclusive, but projections were at the very top of expectations. Yet, as early as 1996, the man in charge of the project, Barry Hartop, had warned of a potential worst-case scenario; he was quickly removed from office and eventually replaced by Jennie Page, a civil servant with heritage but not visitor attraction experience.

Reality did not match rhetoric. To start with, there was confusion as to what the attraction was going to stand for. The religious meaning of the millennium took second place to more populist themes such as play, rest and talk. A £500,000 (€720,000) research survey was commissioned to ask the British public what they thought was meant by British national identity, with questionable results. Original champion Michael Heseltine summed up the confusion in 1998, two years before opening: 'it's a fantastic site and it's going to be quite wonderful but don't ask me how'.[7]

From confusion of purpose came confusion of operation. Specialist attraction design company Imagination resigned as sole agency to be replaced by 11 separate ones and a team of specially, some say politically, appointed 'godparents' to the Dome from the world of arts and the media. Creative director Stephen Bayley resigned, citing political interference in the design process. According to him, 'If Mandy [Peter Mandelson, government minister in charge of the project] went to a voodoo sacrifice in Brixton [south London suburb] tonight, he'd come back tomorrow saying we must have a voodoo sacrifice in the Dome.'[8] One contractor employed 30 designers for a year to create the Body Zone, only to see the blueprints scrapped and a new design team appointed. According to one insider, 'it was like trying to compose a symphony by committee'.[9] This confusion was not kept 'in house' but constantly leaked to the media. As early as the summer of 1997, a survey by the BBC (the British Broadcasting Corporation) found that 95 per cent of those polled were opposed to the project.

With confusion growing, the opening deadline loomed ever nearer and getting things done became more important than what those things actually were. By way of example, the Body Zone was completed on 30 December, just one day before launch. The opening ceremony was, however, to mark the beginning of the end, rather than the end of the beginning. The NMEC (New Millennium Experience Company) had not only left completion of the attraction until the last minute, it had also omitted to send out 3000 tickets for the opening-night celebrations and guests arriving to claim their tickets were met with a single security screen, which meant that people from all walks of life—from newspaper editors to children in wheelchairs, were subject to a queue of up to three hours. The story was the opening fiasco not the opening itself. And the press were out for blood—the government had insisted that the Dome's contents were kept secret until millennium night, and once on display they were but a distraction from the 'real' story.

Open and operating

Legoland opened on time and with little fuss. Positive publicity followed and by the time it had closed for the winter it had attracted just under 1.5 million visitors, in line with expectations. Visitors appeared to be happy, and word of mouth recommendations spread. Though some days were exceptionally busy, the experience was overall a pleasurable one. An interesting comment came from a corporate financier who had been briefed at the very beginning of the project: 'I was ... unprepared for the reality of Legoland ... and the integrity with which the promise of a child-centred park has been carried out'.[10]

For the Dome, life was not so smooth. The last-minute rush for completion had resulted in many of the attractions lacking proper testing. In the early part of January every zone was showing faults, from the bouncy castle banned to children in the Living Island to a whirling tornado model coming off its hinges in the Home Planet: 'Like medic teams in an emergency ward faced with a catastrophe, the staff at the Dome last week seemed not to know what had hit them. After working flat out for weeks, their creation was already taking a battering.'[11]

An early visitor poll, conducted by *The Sunday Times*, showed that while many of those visiting enjoyed the experience, few thought it was worth its £758 million cost, many perceiving Lottery funds as little different from the public purse. Then there was a problem with the actual number of visitors. The attraction needed 35,000 visitors a day for 365 days of the year to meet its targets, but even its respectable first week of operation only attracted 100,000, less than half of what was needed, and by the middle of January visitor numbers were falling to less than 10,000 a day. The promotion budget had been fixed at a relatively modest £7 million (€10 million), relying on word of mouth and use of Lottery outlets to sell tickets. But word of mouth became second to an avalanche of poor press coverage ('The Dome that fell to earth', 'Dome was doomed from the start', 'the Disaster Zone') and most Lottery outlets registered no interest whatsoever.

By the end of 2000, the Dome had recorded 6.5 million visitors, by no means all paying ones. An additional £179 million (€258 million) of Lottery funds had been paid to the Dome, resulting in an overall 'subsidy' of around £100 (€144) per visitor. The original chief executive and chairman had been dismissed, replaced by an operator from Disney and a well-known company doctor. According to *The Times*, 'after half a decade of anguish, uncertainty, sweat and paranoia, the team's reward is humiliation'.[12]

[1] *Management Today*, September 1995.
[2] *Leisure Management*, April 1996.
[3] *Marketing Week*, 29 March 1996.
[4] *Sunday Times*, 9 January 2000.
[5] *Sunday Times*, 9 January 2000.
[6] *Marketing Week*, 14 May 1998.
[7] *Economist*, 17 January 1998.
[8] *Times*, 8 November 2000.
[9] *Times*, 8 November 2000.
[10] *Leisure Management*, April 1996.
[11] *Sunday Times*, 9 January 2000.
[12] *Times*, 8 November 2000.

Questions

1. Outline the differences in approach to marketing orientation taken by the two attractions.
2. In what ways could the Millennium Dome have managed the concept/launch/operation in a way to avoid such perceptions of failure?
3. Can political leadership and the marketing concept co-exist?

This case was prepared by Julian Rawel, managing director, The Julian Rawel Consultancy Ltd, and Visiting Fellow in Strategic Management at Bradford University School of Management.

The building blocks for success: the launch of Legoland in Windsor saw it become one of Britain's top ten most visited admission-charging attractions in its opening season.

chapter two

Marketing planning: an overview of marketing

❝Life is what happens to you while you're busy making other plans.❞ **JOHN LENNON ('Beautiful Boy')**

❝I'm patient of this plan, as humble as I am
I'll wait another day, before I turn away.❞ **THE WHITE STRIPES ('Offend in Every Way')**

Learning Objectives

This chapter explains:

1. The role of marketing planning within businesses
2. The key planning questions
3. The process of marketing planning
4. The concept of the business mission
5. The nature of the marketing audit and SWOT analysis
6. The nature of marketing objectives
7. The components of core strategy and the criteria for testing its effectiveness
8. Where marketing mix decisions are placed within the marketing planning process
9. The importance of organization, implementation and control within the marketing planning process
10. The rewards and problems associated with marketing planning
11. Recommendations for overcoming marketing planning problems

In Chapter 1 we saw that commercial success follows companies that can create and retain customers by providing better value than the competition. But this begs the question 'Which customers?' The choice of which customer groups to serve is a major decision that managers have to make. Furthermore the question 'How should value be created?' also needs to be addressed. This involves choices regarding technology, competitive strategies and the creation of competitive advantages. As the environment changes, so businesses must adapt in order to maintain strategic fit between their capabilities and the marketplace. The process by which businesses analyse the environment and their capabilities, decide upon courses of marketing action and implement those decisions is called **marketing planning**.

Marketing planning is part of a broader concept known as *strategic planning*, which involves not only marketing, but also the fit between production, finance and personnel strategies and the environment. The aim of strategic planning is to shape and reshape a company so that its business and products continue to meet corporate objectives (e.g. profit or sales growth). Because marketing management is charged with the responsibility of managing the interface between the company and its environment, it has a key role to play in strategic planning.

In trying to understand the role of marketing planning in strategy development the situation is complicated somewhat by the nature of companies. At the simplest level a company may market only one product in one market. The role of marketing planning would be to ensure that the marketing mix for the product matches (changing) customer needs, as well as seeking opportunities to use the companies' strengths to market other products in new markets. Many companies, however, market a range of products in numerous markets. The contribution that marketing planning can make in this situation is similar to the first case. However, there is an additional function: the determination of the allocation of resources to each product. Inasmuch as resource allocation should be dependent, in part, on the attractiveness of the market for each product, marketing is inevitably involved in this decision.

Finally a company may comprise a number of businesses (often equating to divisions) each of which serves distinct groups of customers and has a distinct set of competitors.[1] Each business may be strategically autonomous and thus form a **strategic business unit** (SBU). A major component of a corporate plan will be the allocation of resources to each SBU. Strategic decisions at the corporate level are normally concerned with acquisition, divestment and diversification.[2] Here, too, marketing can play a part through the identification of opportunities and threats in the environment as they relate to current and prospective businesses.

Despite these complications, the essential questions that need to be asked are similar in each situation. These questions will now be discussed.

The fundamentals of planning

Planning can focus on many personal as well as business issues. We can produce a career plan, we can plan our use of leisure time or we can plan for our retirement. In each case the framework for the planning process is similar and can be understood by asking the questions posed in Table 2.1. Let us first examine planning in the context of a person developing a career plan. Then the process of planning in a business context will be explained.

Table 2.1 Key planning questions

1	Where are we now?
2	How did we get here?
3	Where are we heading? *(anstreben)*
4	Where would we like to be?
5	How do we get there?
6	Are we on course?

The starting point is asking the basic question 'Where are we now?' This may involve a factual statement and a value judgement as to the degree of success achieved against expectations. The answer will depend upon 'facts' as perceived by the individual. The next question, 'How did we get here?', focuses on an analysis of significant events that had a bearing on the achievements and shortcomings identified earlier. To illustrate the process so far, the answer to the first question could be 'assistant brand manager in a fast-moving consumer goods company for five years with experience in developing advertising, sales promotion and new product variations'. Our self-assessment of this situation may be negative: five years is too long in this position. Our assessment of how we got there might include the gaining of academic (degree) and professional qualifications, and the use and development of personal skills, which we assess are communicational and analytical.

The next question, 'Where are we heading?', focuses on the future, given that we make no significant changes in our actions. If we proceed as we have done in the past, what are the likely outcomes? Our assessment of this may be that we proceed to brand manager status at our company in three years' time and product manager in ten. But 'Where would we like to be?' This question allows us to compare our prediction of the future with our aspirations. It is a key planning question. If our aspirations match our predictions based on current behaviour, we shall proceed as before. We are satisfied that we shall achieve brand manager status in three years and become a product manager in ten.

However, if we want to become a brand manager in one year and a product manager in five, we need to change our behaviour. Our assessment of the situation is that current actions are insufficient to achieve where we would like to be. So we need to ask 'How do we get there?' We begin thinking creatively; we identify options that make sense in the light of our aspirations; we consider changing jobs; we ponder working more effectively; we assess the likely impact of working longer hours; we look at the methods of successful people in our company and analyse the reasons for their success. Out of this process we decide on courses of action that give us a better chance of achieving our aspirations than current behaviour. Thus answering the question 'How do we get there?' provides us with our strategy. Finally, after putting into practice our new actions, we periodically check our position by asking 'Are we on course?' If we are, then the plan remains unaltered; if not, then we modify our plan.

In business the process is essentially the same in theory. However, the practice is much more complex. Businesses are comprised of individuals who may have very differing views on the answers to these questions. Furthermore, the outcome of the planning process may have fundamental implications for their jobs. Planning is therefore a political activity and vested interests may view it from a narrow departmental view rather than a business-wide perspective. A key issue in getting planning systems to work is tackling such behavioural problems.[3] However, at this point in the chapter it is important to understand the process of marketing planning. A common approach to the analysis of the marketing planning process is at the business unit level (see, for example, Day)[4] and this is the level adopted here.

The process of marketing planning

The process of marketing planning is outlined in Fig. 2.1. It provides a well-defined path from generating a business mission to implementing and controlling the resultant plans. In real life, planning is rarely so straightforward and logical. Different people may be involved at various stages of the planning process, and the degree to which they accept and are influenced by the outcomes of earlier planning stages is variable.

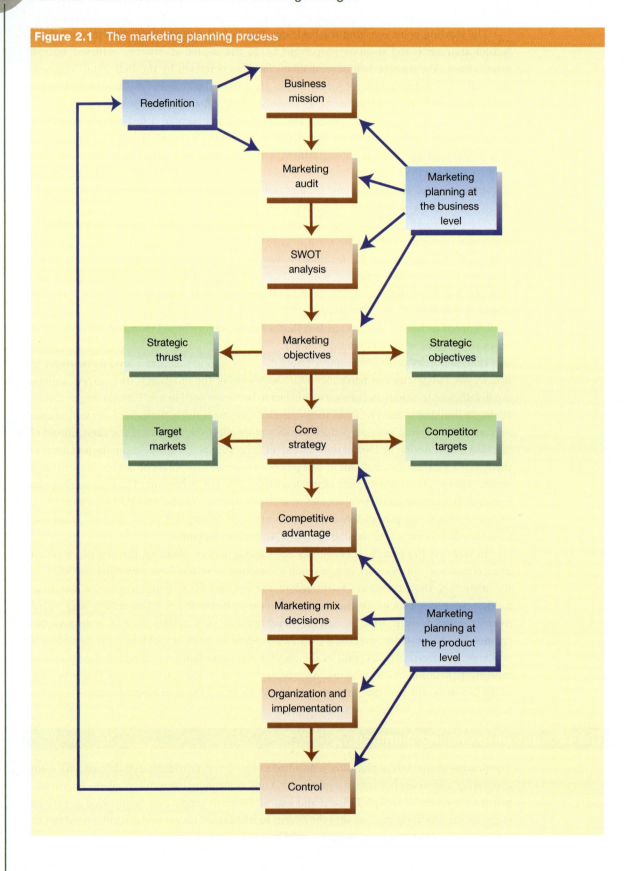

Figure 2.1 The marketing planning process

However, the presentation of the planning process in Fig. 2.1 serves two purposes. First, it provides a systematic framework for understanding the analysis and decision-making processes involved in marketing planning and, second, it provides a framework for understanding how the key elements of marketing discussed in subsequent chapters of this book relate to each other. The stages in marketing planning will now be discussed in some detail, and finally they will be related to the basic planning questions listed in Table 2.1.

Business mission

Ackoff defined **business mission** as:

> ❝ A broadly defined, enduring statement of purpose that distinguishes a business from others of its type.[5] ❞

This definition captures two essential ingredients in mission statements: they are enduring and specific to the individual organization.[6] Two fundamental questions that need to be addressed are 'What business are we in?' and 'What business do we want to be in?' The answers define the scope and activities of the company. The business mission explains the reason for its existence. As such it may include a statement of market, needs and technology.[7] The market reflects the customer groups being served; needs refer to the customer needs being satisfied, and technology describes the process by which a customer need can be satisfied, or a function performed.

The inclusion of market and needs ensures that the business definition is market focused rather than product based. Thus the purpose of a company such as IBM is not to manufacture computers but to solve customers' information problems. The reason for ensuring that a business definition is market focused is that products are transient but basic needs such as transportation, entertainment and eating are lasting. Thus Levitt argued that a business should be viewed as a customer-satisfying process not a goods-producing process.[8] By adopting a customer perspective, new opportunities are more likely to be seen.

While this advice has merit in advocating the avoidance of a narrow business definition, management must be wary of a definition that is too wide. Levitt suggested that railroad companies would have survived had they defined their business as transportation and moved into the airline business. But this ignores the limits of the business competence of the railroads. Did they possess the necessary skills and resources to run an airline? Clearly a key constraint on a business definition can be the competences (both actual and potential) of management, and the resources at their disposal. Conversely, competences can act as the motivator for widening a business mission. Asda (Associated Dairies) redefined its business mission as a producer and distributor of milk to a retailer of fast-moving consumer goods partly on the basis of its distribution skills, which it rightly believed could be extended to products beyond milk.

A second influence on business mission is environmental change. Change provides opportunities and threats that influence mission definition. Asda saw that changes in retail practice from corner shops to high-volume supermarkets presented an opportunity that could be exploited by its skills. Its move redefined its business. Imperial Tobacco redefined its business (manufacturing and marketing cigarettes) in the early 1960s partly as a result of the threat of the anti-smoking lobby.

The final determinants of business mission are the background of the company and the personalities of its senior management. Businesses that have established themselves in the marketplace over many years, and that have a clear position in the minds of the customer, may ignore opportunities that are at variance with that position. The personalities and beliefs of the people who run businesses also shape the business mission. This last factor emphasizes the judgemental nature of business definition. There is no right or wrong business mission in abstract. The mission should be based on the vision that top management and its subordinates have of the future of the business. This vision is a coherent and powerful statement of what the business should aim to become.[9]

Four characteristics are associated with an effective mission statement.[10] First, it should be based on a solid understanding of the business, and the vision to foresee how the forces acting on its operations will change in the future. A major factor in the success of Perrier was the understanding that its business was natural beverages (rather than water or soft drinks). This subtle distinction was missed by major competitors such as Nestlé, with grave marketing consequences. The vision of the future plays a major role in delivering a business mission, as Marketing in Action 2.1 explains.

2.1 marketing in action

Corporate Vision at Nokia

Nokia was established in 1865 when Finnish mining engineer Fredrik Idestam established a wood pulp mill to manufacture paper. The company expanded into a conglomerate operating in industries such as paper, chemicals and rubber.

The vision of management in the early 1990s transformed the company by redefining its mission. Nokia abandoned life as a conglomerate to concentrate on mobile phone technology, a strategic decision that provided the foundation for its future success. Nokia is now the world leader in mobile phones with over $14 billion in assets.

Strategic vision provides the basis for answering 'Where are we going?' in the long term. As such it is the cornerstone of the business mission. Vision provides a picture of a long-term destination five to twenty years in the future. Values answer the question 'What beliefs will guide us on the journey?' Vision matters because, without it, a company is rudderless in the long run. Values must support the vision and be embodied in the company's practices.

By changing its business mission, based on a new vision of the future, and by creating the right set of values through the right kinds of actions, signals and words, Nokia has become one of Europe's most successful companies.

Based on: Davidson (2002);[11] Maitland (2003);[12] Mitchell (2002)[13]

Second, the mission should be based upon the strong personal conviction and motivation of the leader, who has the ability to make their vision contagious. It must be shared throughout the organization. Third, powerful mission statements should create the strategic intent of winning throughout the organization. This helps to build a sense of common purpose, and stresses the need to create competitive advantages rather than settle for imitative moves. Finally, mission statements should be enabling. Managers must believe they have the latitude to make decisions about strategy without being second-guessed by top management. The mission statement provides the framework within which managers decide which opportunities and threats to address, and which to disregard.

A well-defined mission statement, then, is a key element in the marketing planning process by defining boundaries within which new opportunities are sought and by motivating staff to succeed in the implementation of marketing strategy.

Marketing audit

The marketing audit is a systematic examination of a business's marketing environment, objectives, strategies and activities, with a view to identifying key strategic issues, problem areas and opportunities. The marketing audit is therefore the basis upon which a plan of action to improve marketing performance can be built. The marketing audit provides answers to the following questions.

1. Where are we now?
2. How did we get here?
3. Where are we heading?

Answers to these questions depend upon an analysis of the internal and external environment of a business. This analysis benefits from a clear mission statement since the latter defines the boundaries of the environmental scan and helps decisions regarding which strategic issues and opportunities are important.

The internal audit focuses on those areas that are under the control of marketing management, whereas the external audit is concerned with those forces over which management has no control. The results of the marketing audit are a key determinant of the future direction of the business and may give rise to a redefined business mission statement. Alongside the marketing audit, a business may conduct audits of other functional areas such as production, finance and personnel. The co-ordination and integration of these audits produces a composite business plan in which marketing issues play a central role since they concern decisions about which products to manufacture for which markets. These decisions clearly have production, financial and personnel implications, and successful implementation depends upon each functional area acting in concert.

A checklist of areas that are likely to be examined in a marketing audit is given in Tables 2.2 and 2.3. External analysis covers the macroenvironment, the market and competition. The macroenvironment consists of broad environmental issues that may impinge on the business. These include the economy, social/cultural issues, technological changes, political/legal factors and ecological/physical concerns.

Table 2.2 External marketing auditing checklist
Macroenvironment
Economic: inflation, interest rates, unemployment
Social/cultural: age distribution, lifestyle changes, values, attitudes
Technological: new product and process technologies, materials
Political/legal: monopoly control, new laws, regulations
Ecological/physical: conservation, pollution, energy
The market
Market size, growth rates, trends and developments
Customers: who they are, their choice criteria, how, when and where they buy, how they rate us vis-à-vis competition on product, promotion, price and distribution
Market segmentation: how customers group, what benefits each group seeks
Distribution: power changes, channel attractiveness, growth potential, physical distribution methods, decision-makers and influencers
Suppliers: who and where they are, their competences and shortcomings, the trends affecting them, the future outlook for suppliers

Table 2.2 External marketing auditing checklist (continued)

Competition

Who are the major competitors (actual and potential)?

What are their objectives and strategies?

What are their strengths (distinctive competences) and weaknesses (vulnerability analysis)?

Market share and size of competitors

Profitability analysis

Entry barriers

Table 2.3 Internal marketing audit checklist

Operating results (by product, customer, geographic region)	Marketing mix effectiveness
	Product
Sales	Price
Market share	Promotion
Profit margins	Distribution
Costs	**Marketing structures**
Strategic issues analysis	Marketing organization
Marketing objectives	Marketing training
Market segmentation	Intra- and interdepartmental communication
Competitive advantage	**Marketing systems**
Core competences	Marketing information systems
Positioning	Marketing planning system
Portfolio analysis	Marketing control system

The market consists of statistical analyses of market size, growth rates and trends, and customer analysis including who they are, what choice criteria they use, how they rate competitive offerings and market segmentation bases; distribution analysis covers significant movements in power bases, channel attractiveness studies, an identification of physical distribution methods, and understanding the role and interests of decision-makers and influencers within distributors; finally, supplier analysis examines who and where they are located, what their competences and shortcomings are, what trends are affecting them and what the future outlook for suppliers appears to be.

Competitor analysis examines the nature of actual and potential competitors, and their objectives and strategies. It would also seek to identify their strengths (distinctive competences), weaknesses (vulnerability analysis), market shares and size. Profitability analysis examines industry profitability and the comparative performance of competitors. Finally, entry barrier analysis identifies the key financial and non-financial barriers that protect the industry from competitor attack.

The internal audit allows the performance and activities of the business to be assessed in the light of environmental developments. Operating results form a basis of assessment through analysis of sales, market share, profit margins and costs. Strategic issues analysis examines the suitability of marketing objectives and segmentation bases in the light of changes in the marketplace. Competitive advantages and the core competences on which they are based would be reassessed and the positioning of products in the market critically reviewed. Core competences are the principal distinctive capabilities possessed by a company, and which define what it really is good at. Marketing in Action 2.2 describes how Canon uses and develops its core competences to succeed in highly competitive markets.

2.2 marketing in action

Core Competences at Canon

Canon is a consistently high performer in the highly competitive camera and office equipment markets. While ever alert to the need to control costs, its success is built upon succeeding in high-margin businesses by continually winning technology battles.

It does this by ploughing money into R&D (which is currently 8 per cent of sales revenues) to support and develop its core competences. In doing so it has improved on the core technologies that give it a competitive advantage in printers and copiers. This has resulted in high market share and economies of scale, which together with the company's technological edge provide it with the muscle to develop rapidly upgraded products ahead of its rivals.

This approach has led to Canon's core engine technology gaining and holding almost 60 per cent of the laser printer market (including machines sold through an alliance with Hewlett Packard). Products such as high-margin toner cartridges provide a steady flow of profits off the back of its printer business.

While Xerox focused on financial matters, Canon continued to develop its core competences by investing in new technologies to gain share in the copier market. Innovations in the printing of multiple colours and finer, more efficient inks have given it a competitive edge.

Based on: Anonymous (2002);[14] Desmond (1998)[15]

Finally, product portfolios should be analysed to determine future strategic objectives.

Each element of the marketing mix is reviewed in the light of changing customer requirements and competitor activity. The marketing structures on which marketing activities are based should be analysed. Marketing structure consists of the marketing organization, training, and intra- and interdepartmental communication that takes place within an organization. Marketing organization is reviewed to determine fit with strategy and the market, and marketing training requirements are examined. Finally, communications and the relationship within the marketing department and between marketing and other functions (e.g. R&D, engineering, production) need to be appraised.

Marketing systems are audited for effectiveness. These consist of the marketing information, planning and control systems that support marketing activities. Shortfalls in information provision are analysed; the marketing planning system is critically appraised for cost effectiveness, and the marketing control system is assessed in the light of accuracy, timeliness (Does it provide evaluations when managers require them?) and coverage (Does the system evaluate the key variables affecting company performance?).

This checklist provides the basis for deciding on the topics to be included in the marketing audit. However, to give the same amount of attention and detailed analysis to every item would grind the audit to a halt under a mass of data and issues. In practice, the judgement of those conducting the audit is critical in deciding the key items to focus upon. Those factors that are considered of crucial importance to the company's performance will merit most attention. One by-product of the marketing audit may be a realization that information about key environmental issues is lacking.

All assumptions should be made explicit as an ongoing part of the marketing audit. For example, key assumptions might be:
- inflation will average 3 per cent during the planning period
- VAT levels will not be changed
- worldwide overcapacity will remain at 150 per cent
- no new entrants into the market will emerge.

Figure 2.2 Strengths, weaknesses, opportunities and threats (SWOT) analysis

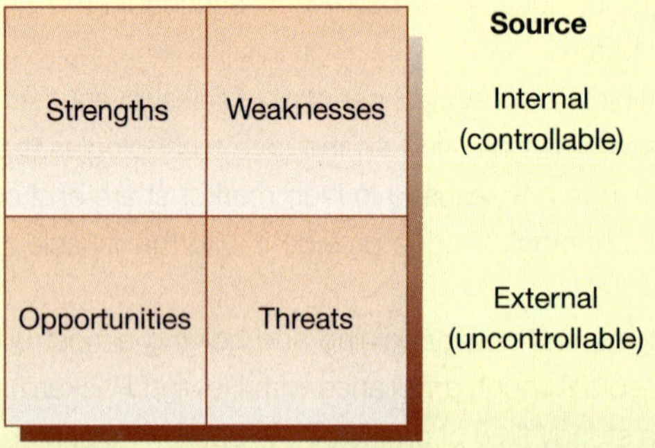

		Source
Strengths	Weaknesses	Internal (controllable)
Opportunities	Threats	External (uncontrollable)

The marketing audit should be an ongoing activity, not a desperate attempt to turn round an ailing business. Some companies conduct an annual audit as part of their annual planning system; others operating in less turbulent environments may consider two or three years an adequate period between audits. Some companies may feel that the use of an outside consultant to co-ordinate activities and provide an objective, outside view is beneficial, while others may believe that their own managers are best equipped to conduct the analyses. Clearly there is no set formula for deciding when and by whom the audit is conducted. The decision ultimately rests on the preferences and situation facing the management team.

Figure 2.3 A SWOT chart

Strengths	Weaknesses
1 Reliable products	1 Production limited to 20 cars per week, resulting in six-month waiting lists
2 Well-respected brand name worldwide	2 Out-dated production methods
3 Competitive prices	3 Lack of marketing expertise
4 Tightly focused on a specialist niche market	4 Limited marketing research information
	5 Only distributed in UK (mainly) and USA
	6 Low profit margin
Opportunities	**Threats**
1 Growing marketing in USA	1 Volume manufacturers could target specialist niche market
2 High market potential in Germany, France, Benelux and Scandinavia	2 Increasing number of specialist car manufacturers setting up in Europe
3 Untapped market potential in UK	3 Tough European legislation on exhaust emission standards likely

SWOT analysis

A SWOT analysis is a structured approach to evaluating the strategic position of a business by identifying its strengths, weaknesses, opportunities and threats. It provides a simple method of synthesizing the results of the marketing audit. Internal strengths and weaknesses are summarized as they relate to external opportunities and threats (see Fig. 2.2).

Figure 2.4 SWOT analysis and strategy development

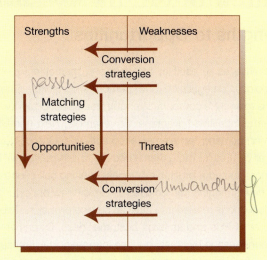

When evaluating strengths and weaknesses, only those resources or capabilities that would be valued by the customer should be included.[16] Thus strengths such as 'We are an old established firm', 'We are a large supplier' and 'We are technologically advanced' should be questioned for their impact on customer satisfaction. It is conceivable that such bland generalizations confer as many weaknesses as strengths. Also, opportunities and threats should be listed as anticipated events or trends *outside* the business that have implications for performance. Figure 2.3 shows an example of a SWOT chart for a specialist, low-volume US sports car manufacturer.

Once a SWOT analysis has been completed, thought can be given to how to turn weaknesses into strengths and threats into opportunities. For example, a perceived weakness in customer care might suggest the need for staff training to create a new strength. A threat posed by a new entrant might call for a strategic alliance to combine the strengths of both parties to exploit a new opportunity. Because these activities are designed to convert weaknesses into strengths and threats into opportunities they are called conversion strategies (see Fig. 2.4). Another way to use a SWOT analysis is to match strengths with opportunities. These are called matching strategies and are discussed in Marketing in Action 2.3.

Using the SWOT chart for the specialist sports car manufacturer (Fig. 2.3), conversion strategies might include building a new manufacturing facility to raise production levels to 50 cars per week and to incorporate more modern production methods, establishing a marketing function and (if marketing research supports it) raising price levels. The company could also seek to eliminate the threat of tougher European standards on exhaust emissions by redesigning its engines to meet them. Matching strategies might include building on the company's strengths in producing reliable products and possessing a well-respected global brand name to establish distribution in Germany, France, Benelux and Scandinavia, while building sales in the USA and UK (opportunities). Given the company's lack of marketing expertise, the geographic expansion would need to be carefully planned (with full input from the newly created marketing department) at a rate of growth compatible with its managerial capabilities and production capacity. International marketing research would be conducted to establish the relative attractiveness of the new European markets to decide the order of entry. Such a phased entry strategy would enable the company to learn progressively about what is needed to market successfully in Europe.

2.3 marketing in action

Matching Strengths to Opportunities

New opportunities can arise as a result of the changing market environment—for example, those created by new technology, deregulation and demographic shifts. One way of choosing which opportunities to exploit is to analyse company strengths and select opportunities where those strengths can be used to create a competitive advantage. For example, Next (the UK clothing retailer) saw an opportunity in the growing demand for telemarketing activities. One of Next's strengths was the fact that it had run its own call centres for more than a decade to service its own home shopping operation. The result is that Next has created a profitable business running call centres for other businesses.

Another example of how strengths can be used to exploit new opportunities is the move by Dixons (the UK's leading electrical goods retailer) into Internet service provision. Two of Dixons' strengths were its credibility as a supplier of PCs and its large customer base. Dixons leveraged these strengths to exploit the growth in Internet usage by creating a free Internet portal, Freeserve. There was no need to advertise its service at huge expense because a large traffic of PC users already passed through its stores. All Dixons had to do was stick up posters in its stores and hand out a free CD-Rom to anyone who was interested. A measure of the value of this approach is given by the fact that Dixons sold Freeserve in December 2000, at the height of the dotcom boom, for £1.6 billion (€2.3 billion) to French Internet service provider Wanadoo.

The skill of both Next and Dixons was to identify things they were already good at that could be exploited in new ways. By matching strengths to new opportunities, both companies succeeded in creating attractive new businesses.

Based on: Jackson (1999);[17] Barker (2000)[18]

Marketing objectives

The results of the marketing audit and SWOT analysis lead to the definition of **marketing objectives**. Two types of objective need to be considered: strategic thrust and strategic objectives.

Strategic thrust

Objectives should be set in terms of which products to sell in which markets.[19] This describes the **strategic thrust** of the business. The strategic thrust defines the future direction of the business. The alternatives comprise:

- existing products in existing markets (market penetration or expansion)
- new/related products for existing markets (product development)
- existing products in new/related markets (market development)
- new/related products for new/related markets (entry into new markets).

Figure 2.5 shows these alternatives in diagram form.

Market penetration

This strategy is to take the existing product in the existing market and to attempt increased penetration. Existing customers may become more brand loyal (brand-switch less often) and/or new customers in the same market may begin to buy the brand. Other tactics to increase

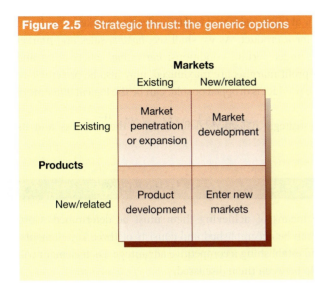

Figure 2.5 Strategic thrust: the generic options

penetration include getting existing customers to use the brand more often (e.g. wash their hair more frequently) and to use a greater quantity when they use it (e.g. two spoonsful of tea instead of one). The latter tactic would also have the effect of expanding the market.

Product development

This strategy involves increasing sales by improving present products or developing new products for current markets. The Ford Mondeo, which replaced the Ford Sierra, is an example of a product development strategy. By improving style, performance and comfort, the aim is to gain higher sales and market share among its present market (especially fleet buyers).

Market development

This strategy is used when current products are sold in new markets. This may involve moving into new geographical markets, as Marks & Spencer has done in Europe, or moving into new market segments, as Apple did when it expanded its market (high penetration of the educational sector) to desktop publishing.

Entry into new markets

This strategy occurs when new products are developed for new markets. This is the most risky strategy but may be necessary when a company's current products and markets offer few prospects for future growth. When there is synergy between the existing and new products, this strategy is more likely to work. For example, Heinz developed a new service, Weight Watchers, to support a new range of low-calorie brands targeted at dieters. This has proved very successful in both Europe and the USA in expanding sales beyond Heinz's traditional product lines of baked beans and soups.

Strategic objectives

Alongside objectives for product/market direction, strategic objectives for each product need to be agreed. This begins the process of planning at the product level. There are four alternatives:

1. build
2. hold
3. harvest
4. divest.

For new products, the strategic objective will inevitably be to build sales and market share. For existing products, the appropriate strategic objective will depend on the particular situation associated with the product. This will be determined in the marketing audit, SWOT analysis and evaluation of the strategic options outlined earlier. In particular, product portfolio planning tools such as the Boston Consulting Group Growth–Share Matrix, the General Electric Market Attractiveness–Competitive Position Model and the Shell Directional Policy Matrix may be used to aid this analysis. These will be discussed in detail in Chapter 9, on managing products.

The important point to remember at this stage is that *building* sales and market share is not the only sensible strategic objective for a product. As we shall see, *holding* sales and market share may make commercial sense under certain conditions; *harvesting*, where sales and market share are allowed to fall but profit margins are maximized, may also be preferable to building; finally, *divestment*, where the product is dropped or sold, can be the logical outcome of the situation analysis.

Together, strategic thrust and strategic objectives define where the business and its products intend to go in the future.

Core strategy

Once objectives have been set, the means of achieving them must be determined. Core strategy focuses on how objectives can be accomplished and consists of three key elements: target markets, competitor targets and establishing a competitive advantage. Each element will now be examined and the relationship between them discussed.

Target markets

A central plank of core strategy is the choice of target market(s). Marketing is not about chasing any customer at any price. A decision has to be made regarding those groups of customers (segments) that are attractive to the business and match its supply capabilities. The illustration for *The Economist* shows how it targets professionals that aspire to be thought of as knowledgeable and intelligent. To varying degrees the choice of target market to serve will be considered during SWOT analysis, and the setting of marketing objectives. For example, when considering the strategic thrust of the business, decisions regarding which markets to serve must be made. However, this may be defined in broad terms—for example, 'enter the business personal computer market'. Within that market there will be a number of segments (customer groups) of varying attractiveness and a choice has to be made regarding which segments to serve.

One way of segmenting such a market is into large, medium and small customers. Information regarding size, growth potential, level of competitor activity, customer requirements and key factors for success is needed to assess the attractiveness of each segment. This may have been compiled during the marketing audit and should be considered in the light of the capabilities of the business to compete effectively in each specific target market. The marketing audit and SWOT analysis will provide the basis for judging capabilities.

For existing products, management should consider its current target markets. If the needs of customers have changed, this should be recognized so that the marketing mix can be adapted to match the new requirements. In other cases, current target markets may have fallen in attractiveness and so products will need to be repositioned to target different market segments. The process of market segmentation and targeting is examined in depth in Chapter 7.

An important part of marketing planning is target marketing: *The Economist* targets professionals that wish to be perceived as knowledgeable and intelligent.

Competitor targets

Alongside decisions regarding markets lie judgements about competitor targets. These are the organizations against which the company chooses to compete directly. Weak competitors may be viewed as easy prey and resources channelled to attack them. The importance of understanding competitors and strategies for attacking and defending against competitors is discussed in Chapters 18 and 19, which examine in detail the areas of competitor analysis and competitive strategy.

Competitive advantage

The link between target markets and competitor targets is the establishment of a competitive advantage. For major success, businesses need to achieve a clear performance differential over competition on factors that are important to target customers. The most successful methods are built upon some combination of three advantages:[20]

1. *being better*—superior quality or service
2. *being faster*—anticipate or respond to customer needs faster than the competition
3. *being closer*—establishing close long-term relationships with customers.

Another route to competitive advantage is achieving the lowest relative rate cost position of all competitors.[21] Methods of achieving high profitability through cost control will have been discussed under 'generation and evaluation of strategic options'. Lowest cost can be translated into a competitive advantage through low prices, or by producing standard items at price parity when comparative success may be achieved through higher profit margins than those of competitors. Achieving a highly differentiated product is not incompatible with a low cost position, however.[22] Inasmuch as high-quality products suffer lower rejection rates through quality control and lower repair costs through their warranty period, they may incur lower total costs than their inferior rivals. Methods of achieving competitive advantages and their sources are analysed in Chapter 18.

Tests of an effective core strategy

The six tests of an effective core strategy are given in Fig. 2.6. First, the strategy must be based upon a *clear definition of target customers and their needs*. Second, an understanding of competitors is required so that the core strategy can be based on a *competitive advantage*. Third, the strategy must *incur acceptable risk*. Challenging a strong competitor with a weak competitive advantage and a low resource base would not incur acceptable risk. Fourth, the strategy should be *resource and managerially supportable*. The strategy should match the resource capabilities and managerial competences of the business. Fifth, core strategy should be derived from the *product and marketing objectives* established as part of the planning process. A strategy (e.g. heavy promotion) that makes commercial logic following a build objective may make no sense when a harvesting objective has been decided. Finally, the strategy should be *internally consistent*. The elements should blend to form a coherent whole.

Many companies are considering use of the Internet to enhance their core strategy. Care must be taken to ensure that its use as a promotional tool does not conflict with other elements of marketing. E-marketing 2.1 discusses how Sunderland of Scotland avoided possible conflict between establishing a website and its sales activities. The result was a coherent strategy that was internally consistent.

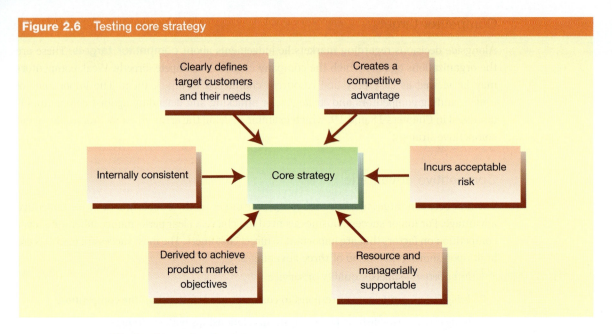

Figure 2.6 Testing core strategy

Marketing mix decisions

Marketing managers have at their disposal four broad tools with which they can match their offerings to customers' requirements. These marketing mix decisions consist of judgements about price levels, the blend of promotional techniques to employ, the distribution channels and service levels to use, and the types of products to manufacture. Where promotional, distribution and product standards surpass those of the competition, competitive advantage may be gained. Alternatively, a judgement may be made only to match, or even undershoot, the competition on some elements of the marketing mix. To outgun the competition on everything is normally not feasible. Choices have to be made about how the marketing mix can be achieved to provide a superior offering to the customer at reasonable cost.

A common failing is to keep the marketing mix the same when moving from one target segment to another. If needs and buying behaviour differ, then the marketing mix must change to match the new requirements. The temptation, for example, to use the same distribution outlets may be great but, if customers prefer to buy elsewhere, a new distribution system, with its associated extra costs, must be established.

Organization and implementation

No marketing plan will succeed unless it 'degenerates into work'.[23] Consequently the business must design an organization that has the capability of implementing the plan. Indeed, organizational weaknesses discovered as part of the SWOT analysis may restrict the feasible range of strategic options. Reorganization could mean the establishment of a marketing organization or department in the business. A study of manufacturing organizations by Piercy found that 55 per cent did not have a marketing department.[24] In some cases marketing was done by the chief executive, in others the sales department dealt with customers and no need for other marketing inputs was perceived. In other situations, environmental change may cause strategy change and this may imply reorganization of marketing and sales. The growth of large corporate customers with enormous buying power has resulted in businesses focusing their resources more firmly on meeting their needs (strategy change), which in turn has led

2.1 e-marketing

Planning Your Online Activity

Sunderland of Scotland (www.sunderlandgolf.com) is involved in the highly competitive and international market for quality golf rainwear. Some will recognize the brand through its promotion by such well-known names as Seve Ballesteros. A number of years ago, Sunderland decided that it needed a web presence to supplement its existing sales and marketing channels (these included agents in sports outlets and professional golf shops worldwide).

Before the website was developed, Sunderland carefully planned its marketing activities, discussing the possibilities of Internet technology for expanding its business and any potential negative impact that may occur. It soon became clear to Sunderland that a website, properly marketed, had the potential to sell factory products direct to huge numbers of golfers worldwide, without the need for agents. Rather than seizing this as an opportunity, Sunderland felt that this could be a disaster for its existing business; it would be perceived to take sales from the agents, many of whom were golf pros heavily involved in selling to the end customer.

Because of this, Sunderland now routes enquiries through to individual agents in international markets, using a sophisticated database system on the website. Consequently, it maintains a good relationship with its agents, generates new sales leads from its website activity (the site receives more than half a million visits per annum) and has further developed its international brand. Through careful marketing planning the website has benefited all parties.

---

to dedicated marketing and sales teams being organized to service these accounts (reorganization). Organizational issues are explored in Chapter 20.

Because strategy change and reorganization affects the balance of power in businesses, and the daily life and workloads of people, resistance may occur. Consequently marketing personnel need to understand the barriers to change, the process of change management and the techniques of persuasion that can be used to affect the implementation of the marketing plan. These issues are dealt with in Chapter 20.

Control

The final stage in the marketing planning process is control. The aim of control systems is to evaluate the results of the marketing plan so that corrective actions can be taken if performance does not match objectives. Short-term control systems can plot results against objectives on a weekly, monthly, quarterly and/or annual basis. Measures include sales, profits, costs and cash flow. Strategic control systems are more long term. Managers need to stand back from week-by-week and month-by-month results to critically reassess whether their plans are in line with their capabilities and the environment.

Lack of this long-term control perspective may result in the pursuit of plans that have lost strategic credibility. New competition, changes in technology and moving customer requirements may have rendered old plans obsolete. This, of course, returns the planning process to the beginning since this kind of fundamental review is conducted in the marketing audit. It is the activity of assessing internal capabilities and external opportunities and threats that results in a SWOT analysis. This outcome may be a redefinition of the business mission, and, as we have seen, changes in marketing objectives and strategies to realign the business with its environment.

So how do the stages of marketing planning relate to the fundamental planning questions stated earlier in this chapter? Table 2.4 illustrates this relationship. The question 'Where are we now and how did we get here?' is answered by the business mission definition, the marketing audit and SWOT analysis.

Table 2.4 Key questions and the process of marketing planning

Key questions	Stages in marketing planning
Where are we now and how did we get here?	Business mission
	Marketing audit
	SWOT analysis
Where are we heading?	Marketing audit
	SWOT analysis
Where would we like to be?	Marketing objectives
How do we get there?	Core strategy
	Marketing mix decisions
	Organization
	Implementation
Are we on course?	Control

'Where are we heading?' is forecast by reference to the marketing audit and SWOT analysis. 'Where would we like to be?' is determined by the setting of marketing objectives. 'How do we get there?' refers to core strategy, marketing mix decisions, organization and implementation. Finally 'Are we on course?' is answered by the establishment of a control system.

The rewards of marketing planning

Various authors have attributed the following benefits to marketing planning.[25,26,27]

1. *Consistency:* the plan provides a focal point for decisions and actions. By reference to a common plan, decisions by the same manager over time, and by different managers, should be more consistent and actions better co-ordinated.

2. *Encourages the monitoring of change*: the planning process forces managers to step away from day-to-day problems and review the impact of change on the business from a strategic perspective.

3. *Encourages organizational adaptation*: the underlying premise of planning is that the organization should adapt to match its environment. Marketing planning, therefore, promotes the necessity to accept the inevitability of change. This is an important consideration since adaptive capability has been shown to be linked to superior performance.[28]

4. *Stimulates achievement:* the planning process focuses on objectives, strategies and results. It encourages people to ask, 'What can we achieve given our capabilities?' As such it motivates people to set new horizons for objectives when they otherwise might be content to accept much lower standards of performance.

5. *Resource allocation*: the planning process asks fundamental questions about resource allocation. For example, which products should receive high investment (build), which

should be maintained (hold), which should have resources withdrawn slowly (harvest) and which should have resources withdrawn immediately (divest)?

6) *Competitive advantage*: planning promotes the search for sources of competitive advantage.

However, it should be realized that this logical planning process, sometimes called *synoptic* planning, may be at variance with the culture of the business, which may plan effectively using an *incremental approach*.[29] The style of planning must match business culture.[30] Saker and Speed argue that the considerable demands on managers in terms of time and effort implied by the synoptic marketing planning process may mean that alternative planning schemes are more appropriate, particularly for small companies.[31]

Incremental planning is more problem-focused in that the process begins with the realization of a problem (for example, a fall-off in orders) and continues with an attempt to identify a solution. As solutions to problems form, so strategy emerges. However, little attempt is made to integrate consciously the individual decisions that could possibly affect one another. Strategy is viewed as a loosely linked group of decisions that are handled individually. Nevertheless, its effect may be to attune the business to its environment through its problem-solving nature. Its drawback is that the lack of a broad situation analysis and strategy option generation renders the incremental approach less comprehensive. For some companies, however, its inherent practicality may support its use rather than its rationality.[32]

Problems in making planning work

Empirical work into the marketing planning practices of commercial organizations has found that most companies did not practise the kinds of systematic planning procedures described in this chapter and, of those that did, many did not enjoy the rewards described in the previous section.[33] However, others have shown that there is a relationship between planning and commercial success (see, for example, Armstrong and McDonald).[34,35] The problem is that the *contextual difficulties* associated with the process of marketing planning are substantial and need to be understood. Inasmuch as forewarned is forearmed, the following is a checklist of potential problems that have to be faced by those charged with making marketing planning work.

Political

Marketing planning is a resource allocation process. The outcome of the process is an allocation of more funds to some products and departments, the same or less to others. Since power bases, career opportunities and salaries are often tied to whether an area is fast or slow growing, it is not surprising that managers view planning as a highly political activity. An example is a European bank, whose planning process resulted in the decision to insist that its retail branch managers divert certain types of loan application to the industrial/merchant banking arm of the group where the return was greater. This was required because the plan was designed to optimize the return to the group as a whole. However, the consequence was considerable friction between the divisions concerned because the decision lowered the performance of the retail branch.

Opportunity cost

Some busy managers view marketing planning as a time-wasting ritual that conflicts with the need to deal with day-to-day problems. They view the opportunity cost of spending two or three days away at a hotel thrashing out long-term plans as too high. This difficulty may be compounded by the fact that people who are attracted to the hectic pace of managerial life may be the type who prefer to live that way.[36] Hence they may be ill at ease with the thought of a long period of sedate contemplation.

Reward systems

The reward systems of many businesses are geared to the short term. Incentives and bonuses may be linked to quarterly or annual results. Managers may thus overweight short-term issues and underweight medium- and long-term concerns if there is a conflict of time. Thus marketing planning may be viewed as of secondary importance.

Information

To function effectively a systematic marketing planning system needs informational inputs. Market share, size and growth rates are basic inputs into the marketing audit but may be unavailable. More perversely, information may be wilfully withheld by vested interests who, recognizing that knowledge is power, distort the true situation to protect their position in the planning process.

Culture

The establishment of a systematic marketing planning process may be at variance with the culture of the organization. As has already been stated, businesses may 'plan' by making incremental decisions. Hence the strategic planning system may challenge the status quo and be seen as a threat. In other cases, the values and beliefs of some managers may be hostile to a planning system altogether.

Personalities

Marketing planning usually involves a discussion between managers about the strategic choices facing the business and the likely outcomes. This can be a highly charged affair where personality clashes and pent-up antagonisms can surface. The result can be that the process degenerates into abusive argument and sets up deep chasms within the management team.

Lack of knowledge and skills

Another problem that can arise when setting up a marketing planning system is that the management team does not have the knowledge and skills to perform the tasks adequately.[37] Basic marketing knowledge about market segmentation, competitive advantage and the nature of strategic objectives may be lacking. Similarly, skills in analysing competitive situations and defining core strategies may be inadequate.

How to handle marketing planning problems

Some of the problems revealed during the market planning process may be deep-seated managerial inadequacies rather than being intrinsic to the planning process itself. As such the attempt to establish the planning system may be seen as a benefit to the business by revealing the nature of these problems. However, various authors have proposed recommendations (as follows) for minimizing the impact of such problems.[38,39]

(1) *Senior management support*: top management must be committed to planning and be seen by middle management to give it total support. This should be ongoing support, not a short-term fad.

(2) *Match the planning system to the culture of the business*: how the marketing planning process is managed should be consistent with the culture of the organization. For example, in

some organizations the top-down/bottom-up balance will move towards top-down; in other less directive cultures the balance will move towards a more bottom-up planning style.

(3) *The reward system*: this should reward the achievement of longer-term objectives rather than exclusively focus on short-term results.

(4) *Depoliticize outcomes*: less emphasis should be placed on rewarding managers associated with build (growth) strategies. Recognition of the skills involved in defending share and harvesting products should be made. At General Electric, managers are classified as 'growers', 'caretakers' and 'undertakers', and matched to products that are being built, defended or harvested in recognition of the fact that the skills involved differ according to the strategic objective. No stigma is attached to caretaking or undertaking; each is acknowledged as contributing to the success of the organization.

(5) *Clear communication*: plans should be communicated to those charged with implementation.

(6) *Training:* marketing personnel should be trained in the necessary marketing knowledge and skills to perform the planning job. Ideally the management team should attend the same training course so that they each share a common understanding of the concepts and tools involved and can communicate using the same terminology.

Review

1 **The role of marketing planning within business**
- Marketing planning is part of a broader concept known as strategic planning.
- For one-product companies, its role is to ensure that the product continues to meet customers' needs as well as seeking new opportunities.
- For companies marketing a range of products in a number of markets, marketing planning's role is as above plus the allocation of resources to each product.
- For companies comprising a number of businesses (SBUs), marketing planning's role is as above plus a contribution to the allocation of resources to each business.

2 **The key planning questions**
- These are: 'Where are we now?', 'How did we get there?', 'Where are we heading?', 'Where would we like to be?', 'How do we get there?' and 'Are we on course?'

3 **The process of marketing planning**
- The steps in the process are: deciding the business mission, conducting a marketing audit, producing a SWOT analysis, setting marketing objectives (strategic thrust and strategic objectives), deciding core strategy (target markets, competitive advantage and competitor targets), making marketing mix decisions, organizing and implementing, and control.

4 **The concept of the business mission**
- A business mission is a broadly defined, enduring statement of purpose that distinguishes a business from others of its type.
- A business mission should answer two questions: 'What business are we in?' and 'What business do we want to be in?'

5 The nature of the marketing audit and SWOT analysis

- The marketing audit is a systematic examination of a business's marketing environment, objectives, strategies and activities, with a view to identifying key strategic issues, problem areas and opportunities.
- It consists of an examination of a company's external and internal environments. The external environment is made up of the macroenvironment, the market and competition. The internal environmental audit consists of operating results, strategic issues analysis, marketing mix effectiveness, marketing structures and systems.
- A SWOT analysis provides a simple method of summarizing the results of the marketing audit. Internal issues are summarized under strengths and weaknesses, and external issues are summarized under opportunities and threats.

6 The nature of marketing objectives

- There are two types of marketing objective: (i) strategic thrust, which defines the future direction of the business in terms of which products to sell in which markets; and (ii) strategic objectives, which are product-level objectives relating to the decision to build, hold, harvest or divest products.

7 The components of core strategy and the criteria for testing its effectiveness

- The components are target markets, competitor targets and competitive advantage.
- The criteria for testing its effectiveness are that core strategy clearly defines target customers and their needs, creates a competitive advantage, incurs acceptable risk, is resource and managerially supportable, is derived to achieve product–market objectives and is internally consistent.

8 Where marketing mix decisions are placed within the marketing planning process

- Marketing mix decisions follow those of core strategy as they are based on an understanding of target customers' needs and the competition so that a competitive advantage can be created.

9 The importance of organization, implementation and control within the marketing planning process

- Organization is needed to support the strategies decided upon. Strategies are unlikely to be effective without attention to implementation issues. For example, techniques to overcome resistance to change and the training of staff who are required to implement strategic decisions are likely to be required.
- Control systems are important so that the results of the marketing plan can be evaluated and corrective action taken if performance does not match objectives.

10 The rewards and problems associated with marketing planning

- The rewards are consistency of decision-making, encouragement of the monitoring of change, encouragement of organizational adaptation, stimulation of achievement, aiding resource allocation and promotion of the creation of a competitive advantage.
- The potential problems with marketing planning revolve around the context in which it takes place and are political, high opportunity cost, lack of reward systems tied to longer-term results, lack of relevant information, cultural and personality clashes, and lack of managerial knowledge and skills.

▶ **11 Recommendations for overcoming marketing planning problems**
● Recommendations for minimizing the impact of marketing planning problems are: attaining senior management support, matching the planning system to the culture of the business, creating a reward system that is focused on longer-term performance, depoliticizing outcomes, communicating clearly to those responsible for implementation, and training in the necessary marketing knowledge and skills to conduct marketing planning.

Key terms

business mission the organization's purpose, usually setting out its competitive domain, which distinguishes the business from others of its type

competitor analysis an examination of the nature of actual and potential competitors, and their objectives and strategies

competitor targets the organizations against which a company chooses to compete directly

control the stage in the marketing planning process or cycle when the performance against plan is monitored so that corrective action, if necessary, can be taken

core strategy the means of achieving marketing objectives, including target markets, competitor targets and competitive advantage

customer analysis a survey of who the customers are, what choice criteria they use, how they rate competitive offerings and on what variables they can be segmented

distribution analysis an examination of movements in power bases, channel attractiveness, physical distribution and distribution behaviour

macroenvironment a number of broader forces that affect not only the company but the other actors in the environment, e.g. social, political, technological and economic

marketing audit a systematic examination of a business's marketing environment, objectives, strategies, and activities with a view to identifying key strategic issues, problem areas and opportunities

marketing objectives there are two types of marketing objective: strategic thrust, which dictates which products should be sold in which markets, and strategic objectives, i.e. product-level objectives, such as build, hold, harvest and divest

marketing planning the process by which businesses analyse the environment and their capabilities, decide upon courses of marketing action and implement those decisions

marketing structures the marketing frameworks (organization, training and internal communications) upon which marketing activities are based

marketing systems sets of connected parts (information, planning and control) that support the marketing function

product portfolio the total range of products offered by the company

strategic business unit a business or company division serving a distinct group of customers and with a distinct set of competitors, usually strategically autonomous

strategic issues analysis an examination of the suitability of marketing objectives and segmentation bases in the light of changes in the marketplace

strategic objectives product-level objectives relating to the decision to build, hold, harvest or divest products

strategic thrust the decision concerning which products to sell in which markets

SWOT analysis a structured approach to evaluating the strategic position of a business by identifying its strengths, weaknesses, opportunities and threats

target market a segment that has been selected as a focus for the company's offering or communications

Internet exercise

Firebox is a website that specializes in selling gadgets, games and boys' toys through the Internet.

Visit: www.firebox.com

Questions

(a) Conduct a SWOT analysis of Firebox's operations.
(b) Critically analyse the SWOT technique as an approach in evaluating the strategic position of a business.

Visit the Online Learning Centre at www.mcgraw-hill.co.uk/textbooks/jobber for more Internet exercises.

Study questions

1. Is a company that forecasts future sales and develops a budget on the basis of these forecasts conducting marketing planning?

2. Explain how each stage of the marketing planning process links with the fundamental planning questions identified in Table 2.1.

3. Under what circumstances may *incremental* planning be preferable to *synoptic* marketing planning, and vice versa?

4. Why is a clear business mission statement a help to marketing planners?

5. What is meant by core strategy? What role does it play in the process of marketing planning?

6. Distinguish between strategic thrust and strategic objectives.

When you have read this chapter log on to the Online Learning Centre at www.mcgraw-hill.co.uk/textbooks/jobber to explore chapter-by-chapter test questions, links and further online study tools for marketing.

case three

Heron Engineering

Established in 1899 and based in Manchester, Heron was the global market leader in the industrial stacking and storage business when John Toft was appointed marketing director for its European division. The European market alone was estimated to be worth around £275 million (€396 million) and Heron had generated some £100 million (€144 million) sales revenue and £24 million (€35 million) gross profits in it during the financial year to March 1999. However, the market had changed markedly and Toft's first responsibility was to review the overall marketing situation and, if necessary, to propose a new long-term marketing plan for the European region.

To help with his review, Toft had held a briefing meeting in February 2000 with his predecessor, Peter Box, who had retired the week before. Box had begun by explaining that Heron had divided the market geographically into the Western European (WE) region and the Central and Eastern European (CEE) region, and that in each geography it served a low-technology storage products sector and a high-technology storage systems sector.

The low-technology sector consisted of customers for shelving brackets and simple storage units into which trays and small pallets could be placed by hand. The latter products were often used by supermarkets to stock and display bread and other items in-store. However, the vast majority of customers in this sector were in the manufacturing, wholesaling and distribution industries. The prime customer choice criterion in this sector in both WE and CEE was price, while product availability was very important. Product functionality was also important to customers although minimum acceptable standards for this were met by all suppliers in the market.

The high-technology sector was made up of customers seeking to buy high-value sophisticated storage and materials handling systems. These consisted of advanced mechanical storage units, conveyor systems, overhead lifting and carrying technologies, and so on, for use in factories, airports, docks, warehouses and other large facilities. Customers in WE applied product functionality and systems customization as their prime supplier selection criteria. However, they also valued having close relationships with suppliers and the benefits these provide, such as easy contact, empathy, trust, advice, training in systems usage and help in crises. In many CEE countries, customers faced difficulties in being able to pay for the high-cost sophisticated storage systems due to hard currency shortages and inaccessibility to international credit. Consequently, the main choice criteria among these customers were attractive financing and systems functionality. Customers also regarded price as important, as well as customization and local contact with suppliers.

Approximately 65 per cent of Heron's 1999 European revenue had been generated in WE with the remainder in CEE. Around 65 per cent of the WE revenue was gained from sales of high-technology systems whereas some 65 per cent of CEE revenue was for sales of the low-technology products. There had been a marked inter-regional contrast in market growth rates, and Heron's market share performance during the 1990s. In WE, market growth had been negligible and as competition had intensified Heron's share had fallen from over 50 per cent in 1990 to around 40 per cent in 1999 in both the high- and low-technology sectors. Conversely, demand for storage technologies had grown strongly in CEE during the decade following the collapse of the former communist regimes in the region. Moreover, Heron had been among the first western firms to enter the CEE market, and had achieved an approximately 50 per cent market share in both technologies by 1995. After that time, however, Heron's sales volume had stabilized and, as the market continued to grow, the company's market shares had fallen to about 30 per cent in both the high- and low-technology sectors.

Peter Box explained to John Toft that he had been neither surprised nor alarmed by the changes in Heron's market shares in CEE. Numerous local producers of the low-technology products had emerged after 1992. These firms had achieved much lower costs and prices than Heron, and it had to be expected that they would win some market share in this very price-sensitive market. Also, from 1995 several other WE companies had been offering high-technology systems in CEE and it had been inevitable that they would gain some success. Even so, Box had felt content that Heron remained the market leader in both technologies in CEE and was the only firm in that region offering the full range of high- and low-technology products.

Peter Box had expressed some concern about the reduction of Heron's market shares and profits in the mature WE market as this had always been the company's main business. However, he had also felt that the demise was understandable. He had admitted that Heron had been focusing most of its attention on achieving growth in CEE during the 1990s and had perhaps been slow to react to changing competitive conditions in WE. Throughout the decade, WE-based rivals had been attacking aggressively in the high-technology sector, while rivals in CEE had been exporting low-technology products into WE at very low prices. Nevertheless, Box had contended that the division was in better shape at the end of the decade than it had been at the beginning. Heron had become firmly established in CEE. Moreover, with the right strategy, the company would be able to re-establish its former position in WE.

In summarizing Heron's competitors, Peter Box had noted that whereas WE rivals were strong in high-technology systems, they were weak in low-technology products. Conversely, CEE competitors were strong in the low-technology sectors but lacked the technological capability needed to produce the high-technology systems. Box then opined that he did not anticipate any further shrinkage of Heron's market shares and that, indeed, the share trends could easily be reversed. The low-technology competitors produced only crude, simple products with far less functionality than Heron's range. The CEE rivals' low-cost situation did enable them to produce what he described as 'cheap and nasty' products, which might be of interest to some customers and distributors. Nevertheless, although these firms were price-sensitive, Box was confident that Heron's global reputation, extensive and high-quality product range, and its own wide distribution network provided the necessary basis for a market share recovery exercise in both CEE and WE.

Box had been similarly optimistic about Heron's potential for rebuilding high-technology market shares in both regions. The company's high-quality products offered more functionality and productivity than those of other WE firms. Allied to Heron's outstanding reputation and other competences this provided a strong competitive base. Most of the WE rivals were more willing than Heron to customize their offerings to meet customer requirements. Further, they each had a wide network of sales offices throughout Europe, which they had used in 'going to extraordinary lengths to buy their way into customers' favours' by forming local relationships with them. They had started to offer very generous financial terms, systems training and a host of other 'customer bribes to ingratiate themselves'. However, these were very costly activities, Box had noted, and Heron had been able to undercut its rivals' prices in the high-technology sector in both geographic regions.

In line with industry convention, Heron used distributors for sales of low-technology products in both WE and CEE. Distributors had been selected on the basis of being financially sound and having storage products experience, established customer contacts, stocking facilities and service capabilities. Heron offered slightly smaller distributor margins than its rivals. However, Heron endeavoured to keep distributors motivated by providing company information, product training, catalogues and advertising support in the English, German and French languages, two months' trade credit and other supports. However, many of the distributors were often difficult to communicate with and did not appear to push sales energetically.

All of the distributors were independent companies and all had exclusive rights to distribute Heron's products in their local areas. A problem was that many distributors had often sold products at prices above or below those stipulated by Heron. Also some of them had been violating their neighbours' exclusivity rights by attacking their territories. Further, many of Heron's distributors had started to carry competitor products and some others had switched their loyalties to rivals entirely. Due to this, local producers had collectively established wider market coverage than Heron in CEE although Heron had managed to retain the widest coverage in WE.

Heron handled its high-technology business directly. For this purpose, the company had established sales offices in Paris, Brussels, Frankfurt, Milan, Vienna, Warsaw and Moscow to build and maintain customer contacts. These offices were staffed by indigenous technological salespeople who provided customers with technical assistance and advice about storage systems design. Heron had three technically qualified key account managers, based in Manchester, to make sales calls throughout Europe and to assist personnel in the regional sales offices as required. Heron's headquarters also accommodated an effective research and development department, and a department responsible for tendering and financing.

Heron maintained a continuous product innovation policy to preserve its strong reputation for product functionality and quality. The company also utilized a cost-plus pricing method. Sales personnel were allowed some freedom to adjust prices to meet local demand and competitive conditions. However, company policy precluded acceptance of any orders for sales with profit margins less than 12 per cent above full average costs.

After his meeting with Peter Box, John Toft felt very dispirited. Despite the optimism that had been displayed by his predecessor, Toft wondered whether his division of the company was in dire trouble. He also wondered about what, if anything, he could do to remedy the situation.

Question

(1) Propose a long-term marketing plan for Heron's high-technology and low-technology businesses in the two European regions.

This case was prepared by David Shipley, Professor of Marketing, Trinity College, University of Dublin. The name of the company, financial data, market characteristics and other matters have been disguised. Copyright © David Shipley 2000.

case four

Weatherpruf Shoe Waxes

Peter Smith, sales director at Weatherpruf Shoe Waxes, was asked by the company chairman and sole owner, Austin Thomas, to prepare a forecast of expected sales during the coming year. The last few years had seen some dramatic changes in the market for shoe waxes, in particular the introduction by a major competitor of liquid polishes in plastic bottles with foam-pad applicators. The whole market seemed in a state of flux, and Mr Thomas was concerned that the company should predict, and therefore be in a better position to meet, market demand.

At the time, Weatherpruf Shoe Waxes was a manufacturer of high-quality men's and women's solid shoe waxes, marketed under the Weatherpruf brand name. The waxes were produced in a range of colours—black, light tan and dark tan—and sold in half-inch-deep, two-inch-diameter, resealable tins. The company has been in the market since the 1930s when it was started by Mortimer Thomas, father of the current chairman. Since its inception, the company has built, without recourse to media advertising, an enviable reputation for high-quality products that both protect (especially from water) and enhance the appearance of the leather to which they are applied. The majority of sales had been achieved through high-street speciality shoe shops, although the product was also available through multiple grocery stores.

Margins on solid shoe waxes were good. Accumulated experience of producing waxes had seen unit variable costs fall consistently to the then current level of 15p (€0.22). An average selling price to retailers of 20p (€0.29) per unit gave Weatherpruf an annual gross contribution to selling expenses, overheads and profit of £5 million (€7.2 million). Mr Thomas was well pleased.

The market and competition

The total market for shoe polish (both solid waxes and liquids) had been static, in volume, for the past five years. Liquid polishes were, however, growing at about 20 per cent per year. The market currently stood at around 300 million per year with a total value of £100 million (€144 million). Waxes accounted for two-thirds of the market by volume and half by value.

Weatherpruf was market leader in solid shoe waxes. Its market dominance of the 1950s (80 per cent by volume) had, however, been affected by a major competitor brand, Bloom. Bloom, launched three years previously, and manufactured and marketed by Smart Shoe Co, now held approximately 30 per cent of the solid shoe-wax market compared to the 50 per cent held by Weatherpruf.

The remainder of the market was made up of smaller, speciality application waxes (e.g. 'Everest' for climbing boots). The success of Bloom was believed to lie in aggressive selling to gain distribution in grocery multiples, extensive advertising to create customer brand awareness and a wider range of colours in the waxes marketed. Smart Shoe had a declared aim of dominating the shoe polish market within five years.

Market developments

The major market development of recent years had been the introduction of liquid shoe polishes. These were not wax based, but offered a quick, clean method of improving shoe appearance. With a built-in applicator (a sponge at the top of the plastic bottle) the liquid was easily spread on the shoe and left to dry to a glossy shine. This development was particularly welcomed by parents as it helped to make scuffed and worn children's shoes look respectable again. Scuffer, a product of Smart Shoe, had developed the liquid polish market and commanded approximately 70 per cent market share by volume. The only other competitor was Patent, manufactured and marketed by the Patent Leather Company (PLC). PLC also manufactured patent leather for shoes, handbags, briefcases, and so on.

Weatherpruf estimated that unit costs for liquid shoe polishes (including the plastic bottle and applicator) were approximately twice those of solid waxes. They were sold into multiple grocery stores at around 40p per unit.

Uses of shoe polishes

Most shoe polishes were bought as household items during supermarket shopping trips. Around 80 per cent of sales were through the major grocery multiples. A trade survey conducted by an independent marketing research agency had identified three main uses of shoe polish.

1. Approximately one-third of all polish bought was used primarily to protect the shoes or boots to which it was applied. For this use, solid waxes were considered far superior to liquid polishes as

the wax filled the pores of the leather and stitch holes, making the footwear more water resistant. Weatherpruf dominated this use on the basis of high brand awareness built over a considerable period of time and a reputation for quality second to none. This use was not expected to show any growth in the foreseeable future.

(2) A further one-third of purchases were primarily to enhance the appearance of adults' shoes. For this application a good-quality wax was preferred, although 25 per cent of this market (predicted to rise to 30 per cent in the next year) was now accounted for by liquid polishes. A disturbing trend for solid wax manufacturers was the growth in sales of non-leather footwear. This footwear required less polishing; even when it was polished this was better accomplished by liquid polish rather than by waxing. This use was thought to be in long-term decline at an annual rate of about 15 per cent.

(3) The remainder of purchases were made by parents wishing to improve the appearance of children's shoes, especially after rough treatment during play. For this purpose, liquid polishes had achieved significant inroads, accounting for three-quarters of sales. This use was growing at around 15 per cent per year.

The research report also revealed that the usage of solid waxes and liquids differed. On average, a solid wax lasted 50 per cent longer than an equivalent bottle of liquid polish.

Question

(1) Peter Smith is not a marketing specialist, but he realizes that the preparation of merely a sales forecast is a woefully inadequate response to the recent worrying developments. He has hired you as a marketing consultant to develop an effective marketing plan for the company's salvation. What would your plan entail?

This case was prepared by Graham Hooley, Professor of Marketing, Aston University. Company names, financial data and market characteristics have been disguised.

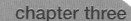

Understanding consumer behaviour

> **❝**You can be through with the past, but the past isn't through with you.**❞**
>
> PAUL THOMAS ANDERSON (from the film *Magnolia*)

> **❝**The things you own end up owning you.**❞**
>
> JIM UHLS (from the film *Fight Club*)

Learning Objectives

This chapter explains:

1. The dimensions of buyer behaviour
2. The role of the buying centre: who buys
3. The consumer decision-making process: how people buy
4. The marketing implications of need recognition, information search, evaluation of alternatives, purchase and post-purchase evaluation stages
5. The differences in evaluation of high versus low involvement situations
6. The nature of choice criteria: what are used
7. The influences on consumer behaviour—the buying situation, personal and social influences—and their marketing implications

In Chapter 2 we saw that a fundamental marketing decision was the choice of target customer. Marketing-orientated companies make clear decisions about the type of customer to whom they wish to aim their product offerings. Thus an in-depth knowledge of customers is a prerequisite of successful marketing—it influences the choice of target market and the nature of the marketing mix developed to serve it. Indeed, understanding customers is the cornerstone upon which the marketing concept is built.

In this chapter we will explore the nature of consumer behaviour and, in Chapter 4, organizational buying behaviour will be analysed. We shall see that the frameworks and concepts used to understand each type of customer are similar although not identical. Furthermore, we shall gain an understanding of the dimensions we need to consider in order to grasp the nuances of buyer behaviour and the influences on it.

Understanding consumer behaviour is important because European consumers are changing. While average incomes rise, income distribution is more uneven in most nations, household size is gradually decreasing in all EU nations, more women have jobs outside the home, the consumption of services is rising at the expense of consumer durables and demand for (and supply of) health, green (ecological), fun/luxury and convenience products is increasing. Examples of luxury or fun goods are 'gourmet', exotic and ethnic food, especially in Denmark, the UK and Germany, expensive off-roaders and two-seater cars, and other expensive brands such as Rolex, Cartier and Armani. Concern for the environment and European legislation has led to an increase in recyclable and reusable packaging, while concern for value for money and increasing retailer concentration has led to an increase in market share for private-label (own-label) brands.[1]

The dimensions of buyer behaviour

Consumers are individuals who buy products or services for personal consumption. Organizational buying, on the other hand, focuses on the purchase of products and services for use in an organization's activities. Sometimes it is difficult to classify a product as being either a consumer or an organizational good. Cars, for example, sell to consumers for personal consumption and organizations for use in carrying out their activities (e.g. to provide transport for a sales executive). For both types of buyer, an understanding of customers can be gained only by answering the following questions (see also Fig. 3.1).

Figure 3.1 Understanding consumers: the key questions

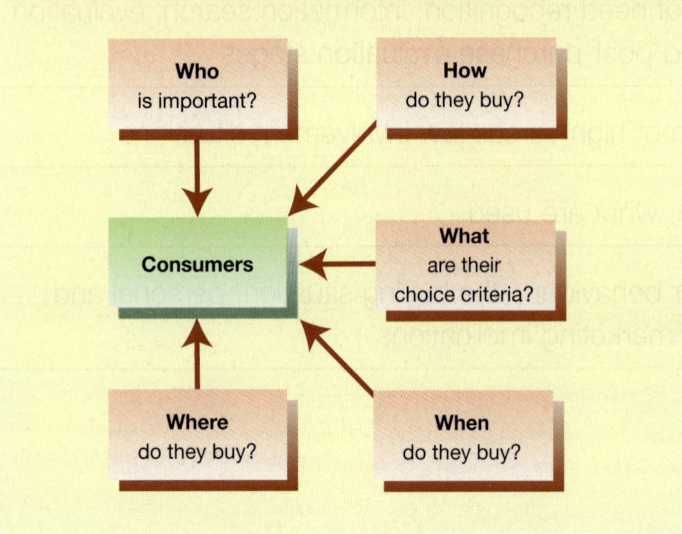

(1) *Who* is important in the buying decision?

(2) *How* do they buy?

(3) *What* are their choice criteria?

(4) *Where* do they buy?

(5) *When* do they buy?

These questions define the five key dimensions of buyer behaviour.

Answers to these questions can be provided by personal contact with customers and, increasingly, by the use of marketing research. Chapter 6 examines the role and techniques of marketing research. An important source of consumer information is the Internet, as e-Marketing 3.1 explains.

3.1 e-marketing

Online Consumer Research

The Internet is a fantastic source of consumer research; using search engines like Google (www.google.com) can provide links to articles or web pages that provide important consumer statistics. For example, there are sites, like Trendwatching (www.trendwatching.com), that specialize in identifying emerging global consumer and marketing trends. In addition, all major research companies, like IDC and Gartner, have an Internet presence, and although many are fee-based, most provide a level of information free of charge (particularly through newsletters).

Among the best free online source for information on Internet demographics and trends is Nua (www.nua.ie). Started in 1997, this Irish company now provides online news and analysis to over 200,000 people in 140 countries every week. For the Internet marketer it is the first stop for online consumer intelligence: to predict e-commerce trends, new technology adoption, application use by sector, and much more. Do you know how many people in each region of the world access the Internet? According to Nua figures from September 2002 there were 605 million Internet users worldwide and, of those, 191 million were European.

There is a clear lesson from the online marketer: you need to start exploring online to understand what consumers are doing online.

Buyer behaviour as it relates to consumers will now be examined. The structure of this analysis will be based upon the first three questions listed above: who, how and what. These are often the most intractable aspects of buyer behaviour; certainly, answering the questions where and when do customers buy is usually much more straightforward.

Consumer behaviour

Who buys?

Many consumer purchases are individual. When purchasing a Mars bar a person may make an impulse purchase upon seeing an array of confectionery at a newsagent's counter. However, decision-making can also be made by a group such as a household. In such a situation a number of individuals may interact to influence the purchase decision. Each person may assume a role in the decision-making process. Blackwell, Miniard and Engel describe five roles, as outlined below.[2] Each may be taken by parents, children or other members of the **buying centre**.

1. *Initiator*: the person who begins the process of considering a purchase. Information may be gathered by this person to help the decision.
2. *Influencer*: the person who attempts to persuade others in the group concerning the outcome of the decision. Influencers typically gather information and attempt to impose their choice criteria on the decision.
3. *Decider*: the individual with the power and/or financial authority to make the ultimate choice regarding which product to buy.
4. *Buyer*: the person who conducts the transaction. The buyer calls the supplier, visits the store, makes the payment and effects delivery.
5. *User*: the actual consumer/user of the product.

One person may assume multiple roles in the buying group. In a toy purchase, for example, a girl may be the *initiator*, and attempt to *influence* her parents, who are the *deciders*. The girl may be *influenced* by her sister to buy a different brand. The *buyer* may be one of the parents, who visits the store to purchase the toy and brings it back to the home. Finally, both children may be *users* of the toy. Although the purchase was for one person, in this example marketers have four opportunities—two children and two parents—to affect the outcome of the purchase decision.

Much of the research into the roles of household members has been carried out in the USA. Woodside and Mote, for example, found that roles differed according to product type, with the woman's influence stronger for carpets and washing machines while the man's influence was stronger for television sets.[3] Also the respective roles may change as the purchasing process progresses. In general, one or other partner will tend to dominate the early stages, then joint decision-making tends to occur as the process moves towards final purchase. Joint decision-making is more common when the household consists of two income-earners.

As roles change within households so do purchasing activities. Men now make more than half of their family's purchase decisions in food categories such as cereals, food and soft drinks.[4] Women, however, still purchase the majority of men's sweaters, socks and sports shirts in the USA.[5] Working-woman families spend more on eating out and childcare.[6] However, they do not spend more on time-saving appliances, convenience foods or spend less time on shopping when income and life-cycle stage are held constant.[7] Working women are forming a growing market segment for cars. Teenagers also play an important role in an increasing range of products, including cars and household appliances, and may be seen as the household experts when considering high-technology products such as video recorders and compact disc players.[8]

The marketing implications of understanding who buys lie within the areas of marketing communications and segmentation. An identification of the roles played within the buying centre is a prerequisite for targeting persuasive communications. As the previous discussion has demonstrated, the person who actually uses or consumes the product may not be the most influential member of the buying centre, nor the decision-maker. Even when the user does play the predominant role, communication with other members of the buying centre can make sense when their knowledge and opinions may act as persuasive forces during the decision-making process. The second implication is that the changing roles and influences within the family buying centre are providing new opportunities to creatively segment hitherto stable markets (e.g. cars).

How they buy

How consumers buy may be regarded as a decision-making process beginning with the recognition that a problem exists. For example, a personal computer may be bought to solve a perceived problem, e.g. slowness or inaccuracy in calculations. Problem-solving may thus be considered a thoughtful reasoned action undertaken to bring about need satisfaction. In this example, the need was fast and accurate calculations. Blackwell, Miniard and Engel define a series of steps a consumer may pass through before choosing a brand.[9] Figure 3.2 shows these stages, which form the consumer decision-making process.

Need recognition/problem awareness

In the computer example, *need recognition* is essentially *functional*, and recognition may take place over a period of time. Other problems may occur as a result of routine depletion (e.g. petrol, food) or unpredictably (e.g. the breakdown of a television set or video recorder). In other situations consumer purchasing may be initiated by more *emotional* or *psychological* needs.

For example, the purchase of Chanel perfume is likely to be motivated by status needs rather than any marginal functional superiority over other perfumes. The advertisement for Cherokee recognizes the need for 'cool' fashionable clothing.

The degree to which the consumer intends to resolve the problem depends on two issues: the magnitude of the discrepancy between the desired and present situation, and the relative importance of the problem.[10] A problem may be perceived but if the difference between the *current and desired situation* is small then the consumer may not be sufficiently motivated to move to the next step in the decision-making process. For example, a person may be considering upgrading their personal computer from a Pentium III to a Pentium IV model. The Pentium IV model may be viewed as desirable but if the individual considers the difference in benefits to be small then no further purchase activity may take place.

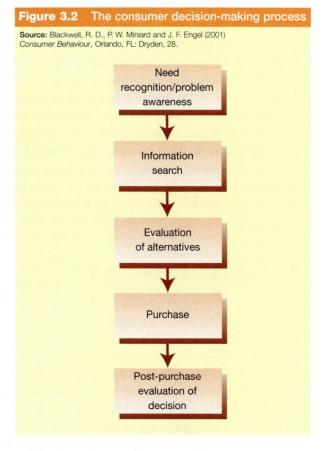

Figure 3.2 The consumer decision-making process

Source: Blackwell, R. D., P. W. Miniard and J. F. Engel (2001) *Consumer Behaviour*, Orlando, FL: Dryden, 28.

Need recognition/problem awareness → Information search → Evaluation of alternatives → Purchase → Post-purchase evaluation of decision

Cherokee recognizes the need to be considered fashionable and 'cool' by consumers. *Photograph by Geof Kern*

Conversely, a large discrepancy may be perceived but the person may not proceed to information search because the *relative importance* of the problem is small. A person may feel that a Pentium IV has significant advantages over a Pentium III computer but that the relative importance of these advantages compared with other purchase needs (for example, the mortgage or a holiday) are small.

The existence of a need, however, may not activate the decision-making process in all cases. This is due to the existence of *need inhibitors*.[11] For example, someone running a small business may feel the need for a personal computer to replace a manual accounting system but be inhibited from carrying out search activities because of concerns about not being able to master a computer and its cost. In such circumstances the need remains passive.

There are a number of marketing implications of the need-recognition stage. First, marketing managers must be *aware of the needs* of consumers and the problems that they face. By being more attuned to customers' needs, companies have the opportunity to create a competitive advantage. This may be accomplished by intuition. For example, intuitively, a marketing manager of a washing machine company may believe that consumers would value a silent machine. Alternatively, marketing research could be used to assess customer problems or needs. For example, group discussions could be carried out among people who use washing machines, to assess their dissatisfaction with current models, what problems they encountered and what their ideal machine would be. This could be followed by a large-scale survey to determine how representative the views of the group members were. The results of such research can have significant effects on product redesign. Second, marketers should be *aware of need inhibitors*. In the personal computer example, fears of not being able to use a computer might suggest offering easy hands-on opportunities to use a computer. Apple Computer provided such opportunities through its 'Test-drive a Mac' dealer promotion when it launched its Macintosh.

Third, marketing managers should be aware that needs may arise because of *stimulation*. Their activities, such as developing advertising campaigns and training salespeople to sell product benefits, may act as cues to needs arousal. For example, an advertisement displaying the features and benefits of a Pentium computer may stimulate customers to regard their lack of a computer, or the limitations of their current model, to be a problem that warrants action. As we have seen, activating problem recognition depends on the size of the discrepancy between the current and desired situation, and the relative importance of the problem. The advertisement could therefore focus on the advantages of a Pentium IV over a Pentium III to create awareness of a large discrepancy, and also stress the importance of owning a top-of-the-range model as a symbol of innovativeness and professionalism (thereby increasing the relative importance of purchasing a computer relative to other products).

Not all consumer needs are readily apparent. Consumers often engage in exploratory consumer behaviour such as being early adopters of new products and retail outlets, taking risks in making product choices, recreational shopping and seeking variety in purchasing products. Such activities can satisfy the need for novel purchase experiences, offer a change of pace and relief from boredom, and satisfy a thirst for knowledge and the urge of curiosity.[12]

Information search

If problem recognition is sufficiently strong the second stage in the consumer decision-making process will begin. **Information search** involves the identification of alternative ways of problem solution. The search may be internal or external. *Internal search* involves a review of relevant information from memory. This review would include potential solutions, methods of comparing solutions, reference to personal experiences and marketing communications. If a satisfactory solution is not found, then *external search* begins. This involves *personal sources* such as friends, the family, work colleagues and neighbours, and *commercial sources* such as advertisements and salespeople. *Third-party reports*, such as *Which?* reports and product-testing reports in newspapers and magazines, may provide unbiased information, and *personal experiences* may be sought such as asking for demonstrations and viewing, touching or tasting the product.

The objective of information search is to build up the awareness set—that is, the array of brands that may provide a solution to the problem. Using the computer example again, an advertisement may not only stimulate a search for more unbiased information regarding the advertised computer, but also stimulate an external search for information about rival brands.

Information search by consumers is facilitated by the growth of Internet usage and companies that provide search facilities, such as Yahoo! and Google.

Evaluation of alternatives and the purchase

The first step in *evaluation* is to reduce the awareness set to a smaller set of brands for serious consideration. The awareness set of brands passes through a screening filter to produce an evoked set: those brands that the consumer seriously considers before making a purchase. In a sense, the evoked set is a shortlist of brands for careful evaluation. The screening process may use different choice criteria from those used when making the final choice, and the number of choice criteria used is often fewer.[13] One choice criteria used for screening may be price. Those Pentium III computers priced below a certain level may form the evoked set. Final choice may then depend on such choice criteria as reliability, storage capacity and physical size. The range of choice criteria used by consumers will be examined in more detail later in this chapter.

Although brands may be perceived as similar, this does not necessarily mean they will be equally preferred. This is because different product attributes (e.g. benefits, imagery) may be used by people when making similarity and preference judgements. For example two brands may be perceived as similar because they provide similar functional benefits, yet one may be preferred over the other because of distinctive imagery.[14]

A key determinant of the extent to which consumers evaluate a brand is their level of *involvement*. Involvement is the degree of perceived relevance and personal importance accompanying the brand choice.[15] When a purchase is highly involving, the consumer is more likely to carry out extensive evaluation. High-involvement purchases are likely to include those incurring high expenditure or personal risk, such as car or home buying. In contrast, low-involvement situations are characterized by simple evaluations about purchases. Consumers use simple choice tactics to reduce time and effort rather than maximize the consequences of the purchase.[16] For example, when purchasing baked beans or breakfast cereal, consumers are likely to make quick choices rather than agonize over the decision.

This distinction between high- and low-involvement situations implies different evaluative processes. For high-involvement purchases the Fishbein and Ajzen theory of reasoned action[17] has proven robust in predicting purchase behaviour,[18] while in low-involvement situations work by Ehrenberg and Goodhart has shown how simple evaluation and decision-making can be.[19] Each of these models will now be examined.

Fishbein and Ajzen model: this model suggests that an attitude towards a brand is based upon a set of beliefs about the brand's attributes (e.g. value for money, durability). These are the perceived consequences resulting from buying the brand. Each attribute is weighted by how good or bad the consumer believes the attribute to be. Those attributes that are weighted highly will be that person's choice criteria and have a large influence in the formation of attitude. Attitude is the degree to which someone likes or dislikes the brand overall. The link between personal beliefs and attitudes is shown in Fig. 3.3a. However, evaluation of a brand is not limited to personal beliefs about the consequences of buying a brand. Outside influences also play a part. Individuals will thus evaluate the extent to which *important others* believe that they should or should not buy the brand. These beliefs may conflict with their personal beliefs. People may personally believe that buying a sports car may have positive consequences (providing fun driving, being more attractive to other people) but refrain from doing so if they believe that important others (e.g. parents, boss) would disapprove of the purchase. This collection of *normative beliefs* forms an overall evaluation of the degree to which these outside influences approve or disapprove of the purchase (*subjective norms*). The link between normative beliefs and subjective norms is shown in Fig. 3.3a. This clearly is a *theory of reasoned action*. Consumers are highly involved in the purchase to the extent that they evaluate the consequences of the purchase and what others will think about it. Only after these considerations have taken place does purchase intention and the ultimate purchase result.

Ehrenberg and Goodhart model: in low-involvement situations the amount of information processing implicit in the earlier model may not be worthwhile or sensible. A typical low-involvement situation is the *repeat purchase* of fast-moving consumer goods. The work of Ehrenberg and Goodhart suggests that a very simple process may explain purchase behaviour (see Fig. 3.3b). According to this model, awareness precedes trial, which, if satisfactory, leads to repeat purchase. This is an example of a behavioural model of consumer behaviour: the behaviour becomes *habitual* with little conscious thought or formation of attitudes preceding behaviour. The limited importance of the purchase simply does not warrant the reasoned evaluation of alternatives implied in the Fishbein and Ajzen model. The notion of low involvement suggests that awareness precedes behaviour and behaviour precedes attitude. In this situation the consumer does not actively seek information but is a passive recipient. Furthermore, since the decision is not inherently involving, the consumer is likely to satisfice, i.e. search for a satisfactory solution rather than the best one.[20] Consequently any of several brands that lie in the evoked set may be considered adequate.

Distinguishing between high- and low-involvement situations: the distinction between these two purchasing situations is important because the variations in how consumers evaluate products and brands lead to contrasting marketing implications. The complex evaluation outlined in the high-involvement situation suggests that marketing managers need to provide

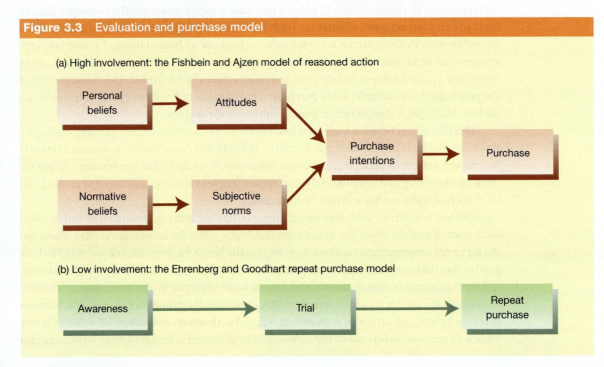

Figure 3.3 Evaluation and purchase model

a good deal of information about the positive consequences of buying. Messages with *high information content* would enhance knowledge about the brand; because the consumer is actively seeking information, high levels of repetition are not needed.[21] Print media may be appropriate in the high-involvement case since they allow detailed and repeated scrutiny of information. Car advertisements often provide information about the comfort, reliability and performance of the model, and also appeal to status considerations. All of these appeals may influence the consumer's beliefs about the consequences of buying the model. However, persuasive communications should also focus on how the consumer views the influence of important others. This is an area that is underdeveloped in marketing and provides avenues for further development of communications for high-involvement products.

The salesforce also has an important role to play in the high-involvement situation by ensuring that the customer is aware of the important attributes of the product and correctly evaluates their consequences. For example, if the differential advantage of a particular model of a car is fuel economy the salesperson would raise fuel economy as a salient product attribute and explain the cost benefits of buying that model vis-à-vis the competition.

For low-involvement situations, as we have seen, the evaluation of alternatives is much more rudimentary, and attitude change is likely to follow purchase. In this case, attempting to gain *top-of-mind awareness* through advertising and providing positive *reinforcement* (e.g. through sales promotion) to gain trial may be more important than providing masses of information about the consequences of buying the brand. Furthermore, as this is of little interest, the consumer is not actively seeking information but is a passive receiver. Consequently advertising messages should be *short* with a small number of key points but with high repetition to enhance learning.[22] Television may be the best medium since it allows passive reception to messages while the medium actively transmits them. Also, it is ideal for the transmission of short, highly repetitive messages. Much soap powder advertising follows this format.[23]

Marketers must be aware of the role of emotion in consumer evaluation of alternatives. A major source of high emotion is when a product is high in symbolic meaning. Consumers believe that the product helps them to construct and maintain their self-concept and sense of identity. Furthermore, ownership of the product will help them communicate the desired image to other people. In such cases, non-rational preferences may form and information search is confined to providing objective justification for an emotionally based decision. Studies have shown the effects of emotion on judgement to be less thought, less information-seeking, less analytical reasoning and less attention to negative factors that might contradict the decision.[24] Instead, consumers consult their feelings for information about a decision: 'How do I feel about it?' Consequently, many marketers attempt to create a feeling of warmth about their brands. The mere exposure to a brand name over time, and the use of humour in advertisements, can create such feelings.

Impulse buying is another area that can be associated with emotions. Consumers have described a compelling feeling that was 'thrilling', 'wild', 'a tingling sensation', 'a surge of energy', and 'like turning up the volume'.[25]

Post-purchase evaluation of the decision

The art of effective marketing is to create customer satisfaction. This is true in both high- and low-involvement situations. Marketing managers want to create positive experiences from the purchase of their products or services. Nevertheless, it is common for customers to experience some post-purchase concerns; this is called cognitive dissonance. These concerns arise because of uncertainty about making the right decision. This is because the choice of one product often means the rejection of the attractive features of the alternatives.

Dissonance is likely to increase in four ways: with the *expense* of purchase; when the decision is *difficult* (e.g. many alternatives, many choice criteria and each alternative offering benefits not available with the others); when the decision is *irrevocable*; and when the purchaser has a tendency *to experience anxiety*.[26] Thus it is often associated with high-involvement purchases. Shortly after purchase, car buyers may attempt to reduce dissonance by looking at advertisements and brochures for their model, and seeking reassurance from owners of the same model. Rover buyers are more likely to look at Rover advertisements and avoid Renault or Ford ads. Clearly, advertisements can act as positive reinforcers in such situations, and follow-up sales efforts can act similarly. Car dealers can reduce *buyer remorse* by contacting recent purchasers by letter to reinforce the wisdom of their decision and to confirm the quality of their after-sales service.

However, the outcome of post-purchase evaluation is dependent on many factors besides this kind of reassurance. The quality of the product or service is obviously a key determinant, and the role of the salesperson acting as a problem-solver for the customer rather than simply pushing the highest-profit-margin product can also help create customer satisfaction, and thereby reduce cognitive dissonance.

Choice criteria

Choice criteria are the various attributes (and benefits) a consumer uses when evaluating products and services. They provide the grounds for deciding to purchase one brand or another. Different members of the buying centre may use different choice criteria. For example, a child may use the criterion of self-image when choosing shoes, whereas a parent may use price. The same criterion may be used differently. For example, a child may want the most expensive video game while the parent may want a less expensive alternative. Choice criteria can change over time due to changes in income through the family life cycle. As disposable income rises, so price may no longer be the key criterion but is replaced by considerations of status or social belonging.

Table 3.1 lists four types of choice criteria and gives examples of each. Technical criteria are related to the performance of the product or service and include reliability, durability,

VW highlights the durability and toughness of its Polo model.

Chapter three Understanding Consumer Behaviour

Table 3.1	Choice criteria used when evaluating alternatives		
Type of criteria	Examples	Type of criteria	Examples
Technical	Reliability	Social	Status
	Durability		Social belonging
	Performance		Convention
	Style/looks		Fashion
	Comfort	Personal	Self-image
	Delivery		Risk reduction
	Convenience		Ethics
	Taste		Emotions
Economic	Price		
	Value for money		
	Running costs		
	Residual value		
	Life-cycle costs		

This poster advertising Tango relies on evoking emotions to sell a soft drink. *Photograph by Andy Green*

comfort and convenience. The importance of durability is stressed in the illustration for the VW Polo. Economic criteria concern the cost aspects of purchase and include price, running costs and residual values (e.g. the trade-in value of a car). Social criteria concern the impact that the purchase makes on the person's perceived relationships with other people, and the influence of social norms on the person. The purchase of a BMW car may be due to status considerations as much as any technical advantages over its rivals. Choosing a brand of trainer may be determined by the need for social belonging. Nike and Reebok recognize the need for their trainers to have 'street cred'. The need to project success gives rise to celebrity endorsements where a product is associated with a high-flying sportsman, film star, television personality or team. That is why Nike paid £300 million (€432 million) to ensure that Manchester United wears its shirts and shorts for 13 years.[27] Social norms such as convention and fashion can also be important choice criteria, with some brands being rejected as too unconventional (e.g. fluorescent spectacles) or out of fashion (e.g. Mackeson stout).

Personal criteria concern how the product or service relates to the individual psychologically. Self-image is our personal view of ourselves. Some people might view themselves as 'cool' and successful, and only buy fashion items such as Hugo Boss or Burberry clothes which reflect that perception of themselves. Risk reduction can affect choice decisions since some people are risk averse and prefer to choose 'safe' brands; the IBM advertising campaign that used the slogan 'No one ever got the sack for buying IBM' reflected its importance. Ethical criteria can also be employed. For example, brands may be rejected because they are manufactured by companies that have offended a person's ethical code of behaviour. Research has shown that

3.1 marketing in action

Emotions and Consumer Behaviour

In a world where many rival brands possess similar functional benefits, the role of emotional criteria has never been more important. The new marketing approach is to build a brand to appeal to emotions, which is a much harder task than simply describing the functional virtues of a product.

An example of a brand that has been successful in achieving this is Absolut Vodka, one of the world's biggest spirits brands. Its clever, simple ads, featuring its now famous clear bottle and taglines such as 'Absolut Bangkok', have appealed to consumers' sense of fun (see illustration). Gorun Lundquist, the Swedish company's president, claims that it is Absolut's wit rather than its taste that is the reason for the brand's success: 'Absolut is a personality,' he says. 'We like certain people, but some people are just more fun and interesting.'

Absolut Vodka is not the only brand that has built success by touching emotions. The Ben & Jerry's ice-cream brand was built on the trendiness of its ethical stance, and the Harley-Davidson motorbike brand evokes feelings of love from its owners. Even the computer industry is beginning to log in to the importance of emotion. Apple's iMac computer, with its radical shape, recognizes the emotional power of design.

The importance of emotion is also shown by a survey of consumers, which revealed that 31 per cent of those surveyed claimed that many of their purchases were motivated by a desire to 'cheer themselves up'. In today's turbulent and high-pressure world such behaviour is hardly surprising.

Photography by Andy Glass — Under permission by V&S Vin & Sprit AB
Absolut Vodka captures a sense of fun in its advertising.

Absolut Country of Sweden Vodka and logo, Absolut, Absolut bottle design and Absolut calligraphy are trademarks owned by V&S Vin & Sprit AB. ©2003 V&S Vin & Sprit AB.

Based on: Anonymous (2002);[32] Carter (2002);[33] Dwek (2002)[34]

consumers weigh up the ethical arguments for buying products against other more personal criteria.[28] For example, for many young consumers the importance of image, fashion and price outweighs ethical issues as an influence on purchase behaviour.[29]

Emotional criteria can be important in decision-making. The rejection of new-formula Coca-Cola in 1985 despite product tests that showed it to be preferred on taste criteria to traditional Coca-Cola has been explained in part by emotional reactions to the withdrawal of an old, well-loved brand.[30] Many purchase decisions are experiential in that they evoke feelings such as fun, pride, pleasure, boredom or sadness. Research by Elliot and Hamilton showed that a decision about out-of-home leisure activities such as going for a drink, a meal, to the cinema, a disco, or to play sport is affected by the desire to 'do something different for a change' and 'do what I'm in the mood to do', both of which reflect emotional criteria.[31] The illustration featuring Tango (see page 75) shows how emotion can be generated by advertising. Concern about store design and ambience at shops such as Next, Principles and Marks & Spencer reflect the importance of creating the right feeling or atmosphere when shopping for clothes. Saab ran a two-page advertising campaign that combined technical and economic appeals with an emotional one. The first page was headlined '21 Logical Reasons to Buy a Saab'. The second page ran the headline 'One Emotional Reason'. The first page supported the headline with detailed body copy explaining the technical and economic rationale for purchase. The second page showed a Saab powering through a rain-drenched road.

Marketing in Action 3.1 discusses some further issues relating to emotions.

Marketing managers need to understand the choice criteria that are being used by customers to evaluate their products and services. Such knowledge has implications for priorities in product design and the appeals to use in advertising and personal selling.

Influences on consumer behaviour

As we saw when discussing the evaluation of alternatives, not all decisions follow the same decision-making process. Nor do all decisions involve the same buying centre or use identical choice criteria. The following is a discussion of the major influences on the process, buying centre and choice criteria in consumer behaviour. They are classified into three groups: the buying situation, personal influences and social influences (see Fig. 3.4).

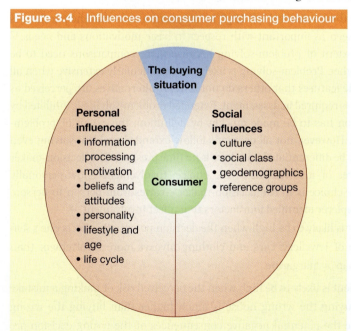

Figure 3.4 Influences on consumer purchasing behaviour

The buying situation

Three types of buying situation can be identified: extended problem-solving, limited problem-solving, and habitual problem-solving.

Extended problem-solving

Extended problem-solving involves a high degree of information search, and close examination of alternative solutions using many choice criteria.[35] It is commonly seen in the purchase of cars, video and audio equipment, houses and expensive clothing, where it is important to make the right choice. Information search and evaluation may focus not only on which brand/model to buy but also on where to make the purchase. The potential for cognitive dissonance is greatest in this buying situation.

Extended problem-solving is usually associated with three conditions: the alternatives are differentiated and numerous; there is an adequate amount of time available for deliberation; and the purchase has a high degree of involvement.[36]

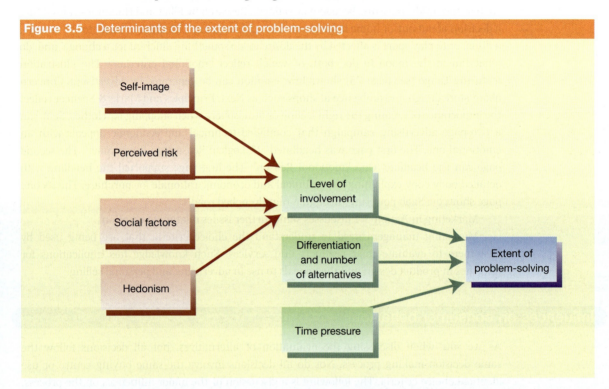

Figure 3.5 Determinants of the extent of problem-solving

Figure 3.5 summarizes these relationships. High involvement means that the purchase is personally relevant and is seen as important with respect to basic motivations and needs.[37] Differentiation affects the extent of problem-solving because more comparisons need to be made and uncertainty is higher. Problem-solving is likely to be particularly extensive when all alternatives possess desirable features that others do not have. If alternatives are perceived as being similar, then less time is required in assessment. Extended problem-solving is inhibited by time pressure. If the decision has to be made quickly, by definition, the extent of problem-solving activity is curtailed. However, not all decisions follow extended problem-solving even though the alternatives may be differentiated and there is no time pressure. The decision-maker must also feel a high degree of involvement in the choice. Involvement—how personally relevant and important the choice is to the decision-maker—varies from person to person. Research by Laurent and Kapferer identified four factors that affect involvement.[38]

1. *Self-image*: involvement is likely to be high when the decision potentially affects one's self-image. Thus purchase of jewellery, cars and clothing invokes more involvement than choosing a brand of soap or margarine.

2. *Perceived risk*: involvement is likely to be high when the perceived risk of making a mistake is high. The risk of buying the wrong house is much higher than buying the wrong chewing gum, because the potential negative consequences of the wrong decision are higher. Risk usually increases with the price of the purchase.

3. *Social factors*: when social acceptance is dependent upon making a correct choice, involvement is likely to be high. The purchase of golf clubs may be highly involving because the correct decision may affect social standing among fellow golfers.

4. *Hedonistic influences*: when the purchase is capable of providing a high degree of pleasure, involvement is usually high. The choice of restaurant when on holiday can be highly involving since the difference between making the right or wrong choice can severely affect the amount of pleasure associated with the experience.

Marketers can help in this buying situation by providing information-rich communications via advertising and the salesforce. Table 3.2 shows how the consumer decision-making process changes between high- and low-involvement purchases.

Table 3.2 The consumer decision-making process and level of purchase involvement		
Stage	Low involvement	High involvement
Need recognition/problem awareness	Minor	Major, personally important
Information search	Limited search	Extensive search
Evaluation of alternatives and the purchase	Few alternatives evaluated on few choice criteria	Many alternatives evaluated on many choice criteria
Post-purchase evaluation of the decision	Limited evaluation	Extensive evaluation including media search

Salespeople should be trained to adopt a problem–solution approach to selling. This involves identifying customer needs and acting as an information provider to help the customer evaluate alternatives. This approach will be discussed in Chapter 13 on personal selling.

Limited problem-solving

Many consumer purchases fall into the limited problem-solving category. The consumer has some experience with the product in question so that an information search may be mainly internal, through memory. However, a certain amount of external search and evaluation may take place (e.g. checking prices) before purchase is made. This situation provides marketers with some opportunity to affect purchase by stimulating the need to conduct search (e.g. advertising) and reducing the risk of brand switching (e.g. warranties).

Habitual problem-solving

Habitual problem-solving occurs when a consumer repeat-buys the same product with little or no evaluation of alternatives. The consumer may recall the satisfaction gained by purchasing a brand and automatically buy it again. Advertising may be effective in keeping the brand name in the consumer's mind and reinforcing already favourable attitudes towards it.

Personal influences

There are six personal influences on consumer behaviour: information processing, motivation, beliefs and attitudes, personality, lifestyle, and life cycle.

Information processing

Information processing refers to the process by which a stimulus is received, interpreted, stored in memory and later retrieved.[39] It is therefore the link between external influences, including marketing activities and the consumer's decision-making process. Two key aspects of information processing are perception and learning.

Perception is the complex process by which people select, organize and interpret sensory stimulation into a meaningful picture of the world.[40] Three processes may be used to sort out the masses of stimuli that could be perceived into a manageable amount. These are selective attention, selective distortion and selective retention. **Selective attention** is the process by which we screen out those stimuli that are neither meaningful to us nor consistent with our experiences and beliefs. On entering a supermarket there are thousands of potential stimuli (brands, point-of-sale displays, prices, etc.) to which we could pay attention. To do so would be unrealistic in terms of time and effort. Consequently we are selective in attending to these messages. Selective attention has obvious implications for advertising considering that studies have shown that consumers consciously attend to only 5–25 per cent of the advertisements to which they are exposed.[41] A number of factors influence attention. We pay more attention to stimuli that contrast with their background than to stimuli that blend with it. The name Apple Computer is regarded as an attention-getting brand name because it contrasts with the technologically orientated names usually associated with computers. The size, colour and movement of a stimulus also affect attention. Position is critical too. Objects placed near the centre of the visual range are more likely to be noticed than those on the periphery. This is why there is intense competition to obtain eye-level positions on supermarket shelves. We are also more likely to notice those messages that relate to our needs (benefits sought)[42] and those that provide surprises (for example, large price reductions).

Selective distortion occurs when consumers distort the information they receive according to their existing beliefs and attitudes. We may distort information that is not in accord with our existing views. Methods of doing this include thinking that we misheard the message, and discounting the message source. Consequently it is very important to present messages clearly without the possibility of ambiguity and to use a highly credible source. In a classic experiment a class of students was presented with a lecturer who was introduced as an expert in the area. To another comparable group of students the same lecturer was presented without such an introduction. The ratings of the same lecture were significantly higher in the former group. Another important implication of selective distortion is always to present evidence of a sales message whenever possible. This again reduces the scope for selective distortion of the message on the part of the recipient.

Distortion can occur because people interpret the same information differently. Interpretation is a process whereby messages are placed into existing categories of meaning. A cheaper price, for example, may be categorized not only as providing better value for money but also as implying lower quality. **Information framing** can affect interpretation. Framing refers to ways in which information is presented to people. Levin and Gaeth asked people to taste minced beef after telling half the sample that it was 70 per cent lean and the other half that it was 30 per cent fat.[43] Despite the fact that the two statements are equivalent, the sample that had the information framed positively (70 per cent lean) recorded higher levels of taste satisfaction.

Information framing has obvious implications for advertising and sales messages. The weight of evidence suggests that messages should be positively framed. Colour is another important influence on interpretation. Blue and green are viewed as cool, and evoke feelings of security. Red and yellow are regarded as warm and cheerful. Black is seen as an indication of strength. By using the appropriate colour in pack design it is possible to affect the consumer's feelings about the product. The packaging of full-strength cigarettes is usually black. The complete branding concept may also be based on colour. For example, mobile phone company Orange has achieved success with the 'colour as brand' approach. The colour orange is distinctive in its sector and conveys feelings of energy and warmth.[44]

Selective retention refers to the fact that only a selection of messages may be retained in memory. We tend to remember messages that are in line with existing beliefs and attitudes. In another experiment, 12 statements were given to a group of Labour and Conservative supporters. Six of the statements were favourable to Labour and six to the Conservatives. The group members were asked to remember the statements and to return after seven days. The result was that Labour supporters remembered the statements that were favourable to Labour and Conservative supporters remembered the pro-Conservative statements. Selective retention has a role to play in reducing cognitive dissonance: when reading reviews of a recently purchased car, positive messages are more likely to be remembered than negative ones.

Retailers understand how the senses affect perception. Marketing in Action 3.2 illustrates how they are used.

3.2 marketing in action

Customer Psychology and Retailing

How people perceive and respond to messages is vitally important to marketers. Retailers recognize that psychological devices can be used to influence consumer behaviour in this way. Aroma can provoke an emotional response, whether it is the smell of cakes baking or of disinfectant that is reminiscent of school. Luxury car manufacturers are believed to spray their cars and showrooms with essence of leather to convey the perception of luxury.

Lighting can also have a psychological impact. Red-toned lighting is used in areas of impulse purchases. For example, one stationer uses red tones at the front of its stores for impulse buys such as pens and stationery.

Sound also needs to be managed. Research has shown that consumers regard quiet stores as intimidating. In such cases, retailers may consider the use of 'white noise'—a dull hum like that of a refrigerator, which is barely discernible but eliminates the awkwardness of silence.

The gestalt (the perceived whole) is also important in a retail environment. Sales of the components of a snack lunch—sandwiches, crisps, fruit and drinks, etc.—are believed to have increased by 39 per cent in Marks & Spencer when stand-alone sandwich shops were introduced in its food halls, because of the convenience of buying them in one place rather than having to wander around to try and find them. This grouping together of products is called 'consumer preference layout' and works for supermarkets too. This is why fruit may be grouped together—fresh, tinned and dried—because consumers think in terms of fruit rather than, say, fresh food and tinned food.

Packaging of brands is also critical. Research has shown that the average consumer spends just 11 seconds deciding which brand to buy. This means that the time factor is paramount; if a brand does not seem to be there or fails to attract consumers, they will simply buy a rival brand. It was these issues that influenced the design of the packaging for Ski yoghurt, which uses a strikingly simple and bold design.

The time factor also affected the design of point-of-sale material for Schweppes tonic water, which was created to catch consumers' attention quickly and remind them instantly of the brand's core values. It used yellow-paper shelf stripes impregnated with lemon scent, with the intention not only of refreshing weary shoppers with thoughts of a cool gin and tonic, but also to reflect the distinctive yellow packaging of Schweppes tonic water in the overcrowded supermarket shelf environment.

Based on: Jones (1996);[45] Kemp (2000)[46]

Learning is any change in the content or organization of long-term memory, and is the result of information processing.47 There are numerous ways in which learning can take place. These include *conditioning* and *cognitive learning*. Classical conditioning is the process of using an established relationship between a stimulus and response to cause the learning of the same response to a different stimulus. Thus, in advertising, humour, which is known to elicit a pleasurable response, may be used in the belief that these favourable feelings will carry over to the product. The promotion of Labbatt's lager on the body of racing cars generates the feeling of excitement for the brand by association. Similarly, the use of heavy metal music in advertising Irn-Bru, a soft drink, imbues the brand with connotations of youthfulness and strength.

Operant conditioning differs from classical conditioning by way of the role and timing of the reinforcement. In this case, reinforcement results from rewards: the more rewarding the response, the stronger the likelihood of the purchase being repeated. Operant conditioning occurs as a result of product trial. The use of free samples is based on the principles of operant conditioning. For example, free samples of a new shampoo are distributed to a large number of households. Because the use of the shampoo is costless, it is used (desired response), and because it has desirable properties it is liked (reinforcement) and the likelihood of it being bought is increased. Thus the sequence of events is different between classical and operant conditioning. In the former, by association, liking precedes trial; in the latter, trial precedes liking. A series of rewards (reinforcements) may be used over time to encourage repeat buying of a product. Thus the free sample may be accompanied by a coupon to buy the shampoo at a discounted rate (reinforcement). On the pack may be another discount coupon to encourage repeat buying. Only after this purchase does the shampoo rely on its own intrinsic reward— product performance—to encourage purchase. This process is known as *shaping*. Repeat purchase behaviour will have been shaped by the application of repeated reinforcers so that the consumer will have learned that buying the shampoo is associated with pleasurable experiences.

Cognitive learning involves the learning of knowledge and development of beliefs and attitudes without direct reinforcement. Rote learning involves the learning of two or more concepts without conditioning. Having seen the headline 'Lemsip is for 'flu attacks' the consumer may remember that Lemsip is a remedy for 'flu attacks without the kinds of conditioning and reinforcement previously discussed.

Vicarious learning involves learning from others without direct experience or reward. It is the promise of the reward that motivates. Thus we may learn the type of clothes that attract potential admirers by observing other people. In advertising, the 'admiring glance' can be used to signal approval of the type of clothing being worn. We imagine that the same may happen to us if we dress in a similar way.

Reasoning is a more complex form of cognitive learning and is usually associated with high-involvement situations. For example, some advertising messages rely on the recipient to draw their own conclusions, through reasoning. An anti-Richard Nixon ad campaign in the USA used a photograph of Nixon under the tag-line 'Would You Buy a Used Car From This Man?' to dissuade people from voting for him in the presidential election.

Whichever type of learning has taken place, the result of the learning process is the creation of *product positioning*. The market objective is to create a clear and favourable position in the mind of the consumer.48

Motivation

An understanding of motivation lies in the relationship between needs, drives and goals.49 The basic process involves needs (deprivations) that set drives in motion (deprivations with direction) to accomplish goals (anything that alleviates a need and reduces a drive). Motives can be grouped into five categories as proposed by Maslow[50] (see Fig. 3.6).

1. *Physiological*: the fundamentals of survival, e.g. hunger or thirst.
2. *Safety*: protection from the unpredictable happening in life, e.g. accidents, ill-health.
3. *Belongingness and love*: striving to be accepted by those to whom we feel close, and to be an important person to them.
4. *Esteem and status*: striving to achieve a high standing relative to other people; a desire for prestige and a high reputation.
5. *Self-actualization*: the desire for self-fulfilment in achieving what one is capable of for one's own sake.

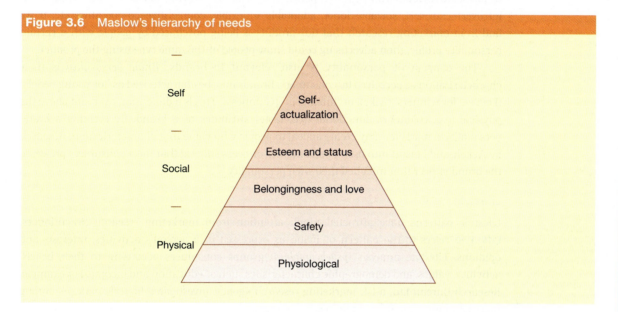

Figure 3.6 Maslow's hierarchy of needs

It is important to understand the motives that drive consumers because they determine choice criteria. For example, a consumer who is driven by the esteem and status motive may use self-image as a key choice criterion when considering the purchase of a car, clothes, shoes or other visible accessories.

Variety-seeking is an important consumer motive. Consumers seek variety to satisfy their need to experiment with different brands, seek new experiences and to explore a product category. Usually, this can be explained by experiential or hedonistic motives rather than by utilitarian aspects of consumption.[51]

Beliefs and attitudes

A *belief* is a thought that a person holds about something. In a marketing context, it is a thought about a product or service on one or more choice criteria. Beliefs about a Volvo car might be that it is safe, reliable and high status. Marketing people are very interested in consumer beliefs because they are related to attitudes. In particular, misconceptions about products can be harmful to brand sales. Duracell batteries were believed by consumers to last three times as long as Ever Ready batteries but in continuous use they lasted over six times as long. This promoted Duracell to launch an advertising campaign to correct this misconception.

An *attitude* is an overall favourable or unfavourable evaluation of a product or service. The consequence of a set of beliefs may be a positive or negative attitude towards the product or service. As we have seen, beliefs and attitudes play an important part in the evaluation of alternatives in the consumer decision-making process. They may be developed as part of the information search activity and/or as a result of product use. As such they play an important role in product design (matching product attributes to beliefs and attitudes), persuasive communications (reinforcing existing positive beliefs and attitudes, correcting misconceptions, and establishing new beliefs—for example 'Radion kills odours') and pricing (matching price with customers' beliefs about what a 'good' product would cost).

Personality

Our everyday dealings with people tell us that they differ enormously in their personalities. Personality is the inner psychological characteristics of individuals that lead to consistent responses to their environment.[52] A person may tend to be warm–cold, dominant–subservient, introvert–extrovert, sociable–loner, adaptable–inflexible, competitive–co-operative, etc. If we find from marketing research that our product is being purchased by people with a certain personality profile, then advertising could show people of the same type using the product.

The concept of personality is also relevant to brands. Brand personality is their characterization as perceived by consumers. Brands may be characterized as 'for young people' (Levi's), 'for winners' (Nike), or 'intelligent' (Guinness). This is a dimension over and above the physical (e.g. colour) or functional (e.g. taste) attributes of a brand. By creating a brand personality, a marketer may create appeal to people who value that characterization. Research by Ackoff and Emsott into brand personalities of beers showed that most consumers preferred the brand of beer that matched their own personality.[53]

Lifestyle

Lifestyle patterns have attracted much attention from marketing research practitioners. Lifestyle refers to the pattern of living as expressed in a person's activities, interests and opinions. Lifestyle analysis (*psychographics*) groups consumers according to their beliefs, activities, values, and demographic characteristics such as education and income. For example, Research Bureau Ltd, a UK marketing research agency, investigated lifestyle patterns among married women and found eight distinct groups.[54]

1. *The young sophisticates:* extravagant, experimental, non-traditional; young, ABC1 social class, well educated, affluent, owner-occupiers, full-time employed; interested in new products; sociable, cultural interests.

2. *The home-centred:* conservative, less quality conscious, demographically average, middle class, average income and education; lowest interest in new products; very home-centred; little entertaining.

3. *Traditional working class:* traditional, quality conscious, unexperimental in food, enjoy cooking; middle-aged, DE social group, less education, lower income, council house tenants; sociable; husband and wife share activities, like betting.

4. *Middle-aged sophisticates:* experimental, not traditional; middle-aged, ABC1 social class, well educated, affluent, owner-occupiers, full-time housewives, interested in new products; sociable with cultural interests.

5. *Coronation Street housewives:* quality conscious, conservative, traditional; DE social class, tend to live in Lancashire and Yorkshire TV areas, less educated, lower incomes, part-time employment; low level of interest in new products; not sociable.

6. *The self-confident:* self-confident, quality conscious, not extravagant; young, well educated, owner-occupier, average income.

⑦ *The homely:* bargain seekers, not self-confident, houseproud, C1C2 social class, tend to live in Tyne Tees and Scotland TV areas; left school at an early age; part-time employed; average level of entertainment.

⑧ *The penny-pinchers:* self-confident, house-proud, traditional, not quality conscious; 25–34 years, C2DE social class, part-time employment, less education, average income; betting, saving, husband and wife share activities, sociable.

Lifestyle analysis has implications for marketing since lifestyles have been found to correlate with purchasing behaviour.[55] A company may choose to target a particular lifestyle group (e.g. the 'Middle-aged sophisticates') with a product offering, and use advertising that is in line with the values and beliefs of this group. As information on the readership/viewership habits of lifestyle groups becomes more widely known, so media selection may be influenced by lifestyle research.

An example of how changing lifestyles affect consumer behaviour is the move to 'on-the-go' products by people who live very busy lives, as Marketing in Action 3.3 explains.

3.3 marketing in action

'On-the-go' Consumption

As people work longer hours and with consumers living in densely populated urban areas, the demand for on-the-go products continues to rise. Consumer choice in terms of on-the-go products is expanding as manufacturers target the out-of-home market. On-the-go drinks, such as bottled water or take-away coffee, and on-the-go food, such as cereal-based breakfast snack bars, are finding favour among time-pressured consumers.

The availability of on-the-go products is also expanding, with 'instant' foods and drinks available in a larger number of vending machines, kiosks and convenience stores. The supermarket chains Tesco and Sainsbury have begun to develop smaller urban formats, which target affluent consumers in urban areas 24 hours a day.

Food outlets such as Little Chef and McDonald's are appearing on a growing number of petrol forecourts. In addition, some petrol stations are catering for the on-the-go market by providing hot snacks through the use of self-serve microwave ovens for consumers with busy lifestyles.

The growth in coffee bars such as Starbucks is also partly being fuelled by the demand for leisure activities that can fit into the work schedule. They provide the opportunity to spend half an hour during lunch or after work with friends or colleagues.

Based on: Singh (2001)[56]

Life cycle and age

Consumer behaviour may also depend on the stage that people have reached during their life. Of particular relevance is a person's *life-cycle stage* (shown in Fig. 3.7) since disposable income and purchase requirements may vary according to stage. For example, young couples with no children may have high disposable income if both work, and may be heavy purchasers of home furnishings and appliances since they may be setting up home. When they have children, disposable income may fall, particularly if they become a single-income family and the purchase of baby- and child-related products increases. At the empty-nester stage, disposable income may rise due to the absence of dependent children, low mortgage repayments and high personal income. This type of person may be a high-potential target for financial services and holidays.

It is important to note, however, that not all people follow the classic family life-cycle stages. Figure 3.7 also shows alternative paths that may have consumer behaviour and market segmentation implications.

Age is also an effective discriminator of consumer behaviour. For example, young people have very different tastes in product categories such as clothing, drinks, holidays and television viewing compared to older people. The young have always been a prime target for marketers because of their capacity to spend. Marketing in Action 3.4 describes some characteristics of young consumers.

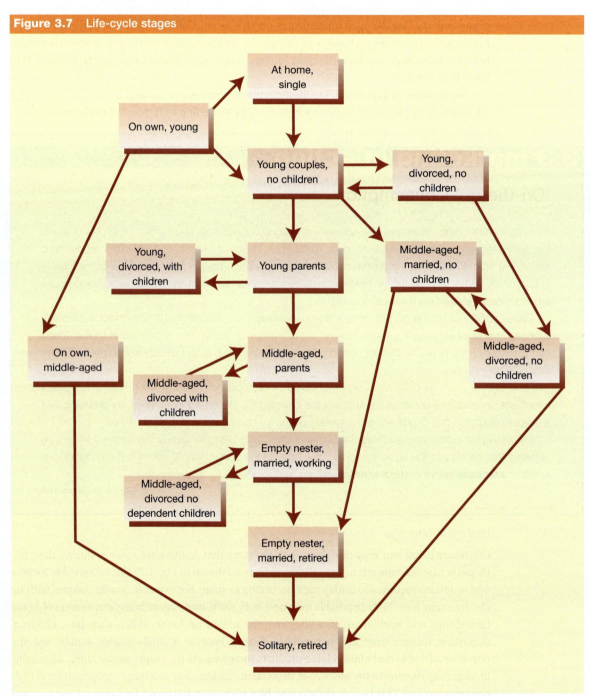

Figure 3.7 Life-cycle stages

3.4 marketing in action

Young Consumers

The teenage–early twentysomethings have always been a key target for marketers. Surveys have shown, however, that they are not an easy group to attract. One study of 20- to 22-year-old European consumers found that they are sceptical about conventional aspirational brand advertising. Many reject the dream that 'Nikeworld' is a world of success. They recognize it is a good trainer but then ask about the company's stance on child labour in developing-world countries.

They like their advertising to be entertaining. They deeply dislike sameness, preferring advertising to be quirky, different and relevant.

'European' was not a concept that appealed to them: they preferred to celebrate their national differences. Nor was it something they valued in brands. Even IKEA was only perceived as European through its distribution. As a brand it was praised for its Scandinavian values.

Young consumers were found to be inconsistent between their actions and beliefs, and were comfortable with this. For example, they may not agree with McDonald's but still eat there; they rate a brand like Benetton highly but do not necessarily buy its products.

Young consumers like the Internet. Today's teenagers are the first generation to have grown up with the Internet as part of their everyday lives, and they see it in the same way as previous generations saw television. European teenagers represent 12 per cent of the European online population and spend long periods online, e-mailing their friends about information they have found on the web. There are clear implications for viral marketing campaigns where brand messages are spread through the target audience by e-mail. Young consumers also treasure mobile phones, another medium for sending SMS messages with the potential for a viral-type spread if the message taps into the values and interests of today's young.

Based on: Carter (2002);[57] Murphy (2001)[58]

Social influences

There are four social influences on consumer behaviour: culture, social class, geodemographics and reference groups.

Culture

Culture refers to the traditions, taboos, values and basic attitudes of the whole society within which an individual lives. It provides the framework within which individuals and their lifestyles develop. Cultural norms are the rules that govern behaviour, and are based upon values: beliefs about what attitudes and behaviour are desirable. Conformity to norms is created by reward-giving (e.g. smiling) and sanctioning (e.g. criticism). Cultural values affect how business is conducted. In the UK people are expected to arrive on time for a business appointment; in Spain this norm is not so deeply adhered to. In Arabian countries it is not unusual for a salesperson to conduct a sales presentation in the company of a competitor's salesperson. Culture also affects consumption behaviour. In France, for example, chocolate is sometimes eaten between slices of bread.

In a comparative study of materialism and life satisfaction in the Netherlands and the USA, Bamossy and Dawson found that the Dutch displayed higher levels of possessiveness than Americans, but no overall differences in envy, generosity or general materialism were found.[59] The 'possessiveness' of the Dutch is reflected in their reluctance to partake in second-hand markets; car boot sales and flea markets, for example, are virtually non-existent in the Netherlands. Another notable difference was that lower-income Americans were more envious than their Dutch counterparts. The higher level of social welfare spending in the Netherlands may have accounted for this result. The greatest difference, however, was found in the levels of life satisfaction, with the Dutch being significantly more satisfied with life. Thus, even in countries that are very similar in economic development, cultural variations can be seen that have implications for consumption behaviour.

Social class

Social class has been regarded as an important determinant of consumer behaviour for many years. In the UK it is based upon occupation (often that of the chief income earner). This is one way in which respondents in marketing research surveys are categorized, and it is usual for advertising media (e.g. newspapers) to give readership figures broken down by social class groupings. Indeed, one of the most widely used classifications is based on the National Readership Survey, which was designed to measure readership of certain magazines and newspapers. Each occupation is placed in one of the six social classes shown in Table 3.3.

Table 3.3 Social class categorization

Social grade	Social status	Occupation	Percentage in UK population (all adults over 15 years old)
A	Upper middle class	Higher managerial, administrative or professional	3.2
B	Middle class	Intermediate managerial, administrative or professional	20.5
C1	Lower middle class	Supervisory or clerical, and junior managerial, administrative or professional	27.7
C2	Skilled working class	Skilled manual workers	20.9
D	Working class	Semi-skilled or unskilled manual workers	17.6
E	Those at lowest level of subsistence	State pensioners or widows (no other earner), casual or lowest-grade workers	10

Based upon grades of the chief income earner
Source: National Readership Survey, July 2001–June 2002.

Recently, however, the use of social class to explain differences in consumer behaviour has been criticized. Certainly, social class categories may not relate to differences in disposable income; it is perfectly possible for a household in the C2 or D category to have more disposable income than an AB household (after the latter's mortgage and private education payments, say). Also within the C2 group (skilled manual workers) it has been found that some people spend a high proportion of their income on buying their own house, furniture, carpets and in-home entertainment, while others prefer to spend their money on more transitory pleasures such as drinking, smoking and playing bingo. Clearly social class fails to distinguish between these contrasting consumption patterns. Nevertheless, two important studies, by the Market Research Society and by O'Brien and Ford, have produced similar conclusions (as listed below) when measuring the discriminatory power of social class compared to other methods such as lifestyle and life-stage analysis.[60,61]

① Social class provides satisfactory power to discriminate between consumption patterns (e.g. owning a dishwasher, having central heating, privatization share ownership).

② No alternative classification provides consistently better discriminatory power.

③ No one classification system works best across all product fields.

To which O'Brien and Ford added a fourth conclusion, as follows.

④ Sometimes other classifications discriminate better and often are just as powerful as social class.

The implication is that social class as a predictive measure of consumption differences is not dead but can usefully be supplemented by other measures such as life stage and lifestyle.

Geodemographics

An alternative method of classifying households is based on their geographic location. This analysis—called **geodemographics**—is based on population census data. Households are grouped into geographic clusters based on information such as type of accommodation, car ownership, age, occupation, number and age of children, and (since 1991) ethnic background. These clusters can be identified by means of their postcodes so that targeting households by mail is easy. There are a number of systems in use in the UK, including PINPOINT and MOSAIC, but the best known is ACORN (A Classification Of Residential Neighbourhoods), which has identified 11 neighbourhood types. These are discussed in more detail in Chapter 7 on market segmentation and positioning, as they form an effective method of segmenting many markets, including financial services and retailing. ACORN has proved to be a powerful discriminator between different lifestyles, purchasing patterns and media exposure.[62]

Reference groups

The term **reference group** is used to indicate a group of people that influences an individual's attitude or behaviour. Where a product is conspicuous—for example, clothing or cars—the brand or model chosen may have been strongly influenced by what buyers perceive as acceptable to their reference group. This group may consist of family members, a group of friends or work colleagues. Some reference groups may be formal (e.g. members of a club or society), while others may be informal (friends with similar interests). Reference groups influence their members by the roles and norms expected of them. For example, students may have to play several roles: to lecturers, students' role may be that of learner; to other students, their role may vary from peer to social companion. Depending on the role, various behaviours may be expected based upon group norms. To the extent that group norms influence values and attitudes, these reference groups may be seen as an important determinant of behaviour. Sometimes reference group norms can conflict, as when reference to the learning role suggests different patterns of behaviour from that of social companion. In terms of consumption, reference group influence can affect student purchasing of clothing, beverages, social events and textbooks, for example. The more conspicuous the choice is to the reference group, the stronger its influence.

An opinion leader is someone in a reference group from whom other members seek guidance on a particular topic. As such, opinion leaders can exert enormous influence on purchase decisions. In terms of the type of off-road, four-wheel-drive vehicle to buy, the British royal family acts as significant opinion leader. The sight of members of royalty driving Range Rovers on television, and in newspapers and magazines is invaluable publicity, indicating the 'right' model to buy.

Review

1 **The dimensions of buyer behaviour**
- The dimensions are who is important in the buying decision, how they buy, what their choice criteria are, where they buy and when they buy.

2 **The role of the buying centre: who buys**
- Some consumer purchase decisions are made by a group such as a household. A decision may be in the hands of a buying centre with up to five roles: initiator, influencer, decider, buyer and user. It is the interaction of the people playing these roles that determines which purchase will be made.

3 **The consumer decision-making process: how people buy**
- The decision to purchase a consumer product may pass through a number of stages: need recognition/problem awareness, information search, evaluation of alternatives, purchase, and post-purchase evaluation of the decision.

4 **The marketing implications of need recognition, information search, evaluation of alternatives, purchase and post-purchase evaluation stages**
- Need recognition: marketing managers need to be aware of the needs of consumers so that needs can be met and the opportunity of building a competitive advantage is created; aware of need inhibitors so that strategies can be designed to overcome them; and alert to the benefits of stimulating need recognition (for example, through advertisements and the efforts of salespeople) to start the process off.
- Information search: marketing managers need to know where consumers look for information to help solve their decision-making. Communication can then be directed to consumers through those sources. One objective is to ensure that the company's brand appears in the consumer's awareness set.
- Evaluation of alternatives: for decisions where the consumer is highly involved, marketing managers need to provide a lot of information about the positive consequences of buying. The print media may be suitable because these allow detailed and repeated scrutiny of information. Salespeople may also be important in ensuring the consumer is aware of product attributes (features) and benefits. For low-involvement decisions, marketing managers should seek top-of-mind awareness through repetitive advertising, and trial (e.g. through sales promotion). For all consumer decisions, marketing managers must understand the choice criteria used to evaluate brands, including the importance of emotion.
- Post-purchase evaluation of the decision: marketing managers need to dispel cognitive dissonance by using advertisements, direct mail or telephone calls to act as positive reinforcers. However, besides this kind of reassurance, marketing managers need to market products that meet and exceed the needs and expectations of customers so that this stage is associated with high levels of customer satisfaction.

5 **The differences in evaluation of high- versus low-involvement situations**
- High-involvement situations: the consumer is more likely to carry out extensive evaluation and take into account beliefs about the perceived consequences of buying the brand, the extent to which important others believe they should or should not buy the brand, attitudes (which are the degree to which the consumer likes or dislikes the brand overall), and subjective norms (which form an overall evaluation of the degree to which

important others approve or disapprove of the purchase). All of this means that a considerable amount of information processing takes place.
- Low-involvement situations: the consumer carries out a simple evaluation and uses simple choice tactics to reduce time and effort. Awareness precedes trial, which, if satisfactory, leads to repeat purchase. The behaviour may become habitual, with little conscious thought or formation of attitudes before purchase.

6 The nature of choice criteria: what are used

- Choice criteria are the various attributes (and benefits) a consumer uses when evaluating products and services. These may be technical (e.g. reliability), economic (e.g. price), social (e.g. status) or personal (e.g. self-image).

7 The influences on consumer behaviour—the buying situation, personal and social influences—and their marketing implications

- Buying situation: the three types are extended problem-solving, limited problem-solving and habitual problem-solving. The marketing implications are that for extended problem-solving marketers should provide information-rich communication and salespeople should adopt the problem–solution approach to selling; for limited problem-solving, marketers should stimulate the need to conduct a search (when their brand is not currently bought) or reduce the risk of brand switching by, for example, giving warranties (when their brand is currently being bought); and for habitual problem-solving, repetitive advertising should be used to create awareness and reinforce already favourable attitudes.
- Personal influences: the six types are information processing, motivation, beliefs and attitudes, personality, lifestyle, and life cycle and age.
- Information processing has two key aspects: perception and learning. Three processes may be used to sort out the masses of stimuli that can be perceived into a manageable amount: (i) selective attention, which implies that advertisements, logos and packaging need to be attention-getting, and explains why there is intense competition to obtain eye-level positions on supermarket shelves; (ii) selective distortion, which implies that messages should be presented clearly, using a credible source and with supporting evidence whenever possible; and (iii) selective retention, which implies that messages that are in line with existing beliefs and attitudes are more likely to be remembered.
- Two ways in which learning takes place are conditioning and cognitive learning. Conditioning suggests that associating a brand with humour (e.g. in advertisements) or excitement (e.g. motor racing sponsorship) will carry over to the brand, and also that the use of free samples and coupons (reinforcers) can encourage sales by inducing trial and repeat buying. Through the reinforcers the consumer will have learnt to associate the brand with pleasurable experiences.
- Cognitive learning suggests that statements in an advertisement may be remembered, the promise of a reward may influence behaviour, as may communications that allow the recipient to draw his/her own conclusions. The result of the learning process is the creation of product positioning.
- Motives influence choice criteria and include physiological, safety, belongingness and love, esteem and status, and self-actualization.
- Beliefs and attitudes are linked in that the consequence of a set of beliefs may be a positive or negative attitude. Marketers attempt to match product attributes to desired beliefs and attitudes, and use communications to influence these and establish new beliefs.

- The personality of the type of person who buys a brand may be reflected in the type of person used in its advertisements. Brand personality is used to appeal to people who identify with that characterization.
- Lifestyles have been shown to be linked to purchase behaviour. Lifestyle groups can be used for market segmentation and targeting purposes.
- Life-cycle stage may affect consumer behaviour as the level of disposable income and purchase requirements (needs) may depend on the stage that people have reached during their life. For similar reasons, age may affect consumer behaviour.
- The four types of social influence are culture, social class, geodemographics and reference groups.
- Culture affects how business is conducted and consumption behaviour. Marketers have to adjust their behaviour and the marketing mix to accommodate different cultures.
- Social class can predict some consumption patterns, and so can be used for market segmentation and targeting purposes.
- Geodemographics classifies consumers according to their location, and is used for market segmentation and targeting purposes.
- Reference groups influence their members by the roles and norms expected of them. Marketers attempt to make their brands acceptable to reference groups, and target opinion leaders to gain brand acceptability.

Key terms

attitude the degree to which a customer or prospect likes or dislikes a brand

awareness set the set of brands that the consumer is aware may provide a solution to the problem

beliefs descriptive thoughts that a person holds about something

buying centre a group that is involved in the buying decision (also known as a decision-making unit)

choice criteria the various attributes (and benefits) people use when evaluating products and services

classical conditioning the process of using an established relationship between a stimulus and a response to cause the learning of the same response to a different stimulus

cognitive dissonance post-purchase concerns of a consumer arising from uncertainty as to whether a decision to purchase was the correct one

cognitive learning the learning of knowledge, and development of beliefs and attitudes without direct reinforcement

consumer decision-making process the stages a consumer goes through when buying something—namely, problem awareness, information search, evaluation of alternatives, purchase and post-purchase evaluation

culture the traditions, taboos, values and basic attitudes of the whole society in which an individual lives

evoked set the set of brands that the consumer seriously evaluates before making a purchase

geodemographics the process of grouping households into geographic clusters based on information such as type of accommodation, occupation, number and age of children, and ethnic background

information framing the way in which information is presented to people

information processing the process by which a stimulus is received, interpreted, stored in memory and later retrieved

information search the identification of alternative ways of problem-solving

lifestyle the pattern of living as expressed in a person's activities, interests and opinions

motivation the process involving needs that set drives in motion to accomplish goals

operant conditioning the use of rewards to generate reinforcement of response

perception the process by which people select, organize and interpret sensory stimulation into a meaningful picture of the world

personality the inner psychological characteristics of individuals that lead to consistent responses to their environment

reasoning a more complex form of cognitive learning where conclusions are reached by connected thought

reference group a group of people that influences an individual's attitude or behaviour

rote learning the learning of two or more concepts without conditioning

selective attention the process by which people screen out those stimuli that are neither meaningful to them nor consistent with their experiences and beliefs

selective distortion the distortion of information received by people according to their existing beliefs and attitudes

selective retention the process by which people only retain a selection of messages in memory

vicarious learning learning from others without direct experience or reward

Internet exercise

Magazine stands are awash with publications that try to help their readers make sense of everyday products, giving countless reviews of what to buy and what not to buy (e.g. *What Car?* and *What Hi-Fi?*). These product-review magazines are numerous and make up a lucrative market niche for magazine publishers. Examine the following websites, assessing their impact on the consumer decision-making process for buying a home cinema system.

Visit: www.homecinemachoice.com
www.home-entertainment.co.uk
www.t3.co.uk

Questions

(a) What role do these product-review magazines have on the consumer decision-making process?
(b) What are the marketing implications, due to these types of review magazines, for marketers?
(c) In your opinion, are magazine reviews used only in a buying situation involving large economic outlay? Explain, giving reasons for your answer.
(d) What was the last purchase you made that involved an extensive decision-making process? What sources of information did you use?
(e) When making a purchase decision, which sources of information do you use to reach a final decision? Furthermore, which source has the most impact on that decision?

Visit the Online Learning Centre at www.mcgraw-hill.co.uk/textbooks/jobber for more Internet exercises.

Study questions

1. Choose a recent purchase that involved not only yourself but other people in making the decision. What role(s) did you play in the buying centre? What roles did these other people play and how did they influence your choice?

2. What decision-making process did you go through? At each stage (need recognition, information search, etc.), try to remember what you were thinking about and what activities took place.

3. What choice criteria did you use? Did they change between drawing up a shortlist and making the final choice?

4. Think of the last time you made an impulse purchase. What stimulated you to buy? Have you bought the brand again? Why or why not? Did your thoughts and actions resemble those suggested by the Ehrenberg and Goodhart model?

5. Can you think of a brand that has used the principles of classical conditioning in its advertising?

6. Are there any brands that you buy (e.g. beer, perfume) that have personalities that match your own?

7. To what kind of lifestyle do you aspire? How does this affect the types of product (particularly visible ones) you buy now and in the future?

8. Are you influenced by any reference groups? How do these groups influence what you buy?

When you have read this chapter log on to the Online Learning Centre at www.mcgraw-hill.co.uk/textbooks/jobber to explore chapter-by-chapter test questions, links and further online study tools for marketing.

case five

Cappuccino Wars

Coffee shops have become big business—and new coffee variants are aimed at high-earning professionals.

The UK has come a long way from the days when a request for coffee would bring a cup of uniformly grey, unappealing liquid, sometimes served in polystyrene cups, which bore no relation to the rich, flavoursome coffee experienced on trips to continental Europe. The origin of this change was not Europe, however, but the USA, where the coffee bar culture was grounded.

Recent years have seen an explosion of coffee bars on UK high streets with over 5 million lattés, cappuccinos and espressos served each week. The market is dominated by US-owned Starbucks with 330 coffee bars, Costa Coffee (backed by Whitbread) with over 300 and two independents: Caffé Nero and Coffee Republic, each with around 100 bars. In total the UK has over 1800 coffee shops, all charging over £2 (€2.90) for a small coffee. Often three or more bars will be located within a hundred yards of each other.

The first US west coast-style coffee shop was opened in the UK in 1995 and was called the Seattle Coffee Company. The owners were Americans who saw an opportunity to serve the British with good-quality coffee in relaxed surroundings just like they experienced in the USA. The concept was a huge success and by 1997 the company had 49 coffee outlets. It was joined by Coffee Republic and Caffé Nero, which also grew rapidly. But in 1997 the coffee market in the UK was to change dramatically with the arrival of the US-based Starbucks coffee bar giant, which bought the Seattle Coffee Company.

Its strategy was to gain market share through fast roll-out. For the first five years, Starbucks opened an average of five stores a month in the UK: in 1999, it had 95 stores, by 2001 this had increased to 250. Today, Starbucks is in the *Fortune* Top 500 US companies and has over 6000 stores in more than 30 countries, with three new stores opening every day. Its approach is simple: blanket an area completely, even if the shops cannibalize one another's business. A new coffee bar will often capture about 30 per cent of the sales of a nearby Starbucks but the company considers this more than offset by lower delivery and management costs (per store), shorter queues at individual shops and increased foot traffic for all the stores in an area as new shops take custom from competitors too. Some 20 million people buy coffee at Starbucks every week, with the average Starbucks' customer visiting 18 times a month. Sales have climbed an average of 20 per cent a year since it went public.

One of its strengths is the quality of its coffee. Starbucks has its own roasting plant, from which the media are banned lest its secrets be revealed. In its coffee shops, coffee is mixed with a lot of milk and offered in hundreds of flavours. Its Frappuccino is positioned as a midday break in advertisements where a narrator explains 'Starbucks Frappuccino coffee drink is a delicious blend of coffee and milk to smooth out your day'. The tag-line is 'Smooth out your day, everyday'.

A key problem is that Starbucks' major competitors—Costa Coffee, Caffé Nero and Coffee Republic—have also followed a fast roll-out strategy, causing rental prices to spiral upwards. For example, Starbucks' Leicester Square coffee shop in London was part of a £1.5 million (€2.2 million) two-store rental deal. Many coffee shops are not profitable and, with Starbucks continuing to operate them, it has been accused of

Cappuccino, Frappuccino or tall skinny latté? The choice of coffees—and coffee bars—is burgeoning.

unfairly trying to squeeze out the competition. In fact, none of the four major players achieves positive pre-tax profits. For example, in 2002 Coffee Republic lost £7.5 million (€11 million) and Caffé Nero had debts of £7 million (€10 million); Coffee Republic's response was to get rid of unprofitable bars, reducing their number from 100 to 65.

The typical consumer at these coffee bars is young, single and a high earner. They are likely to be professionals, and senior or middle managers with company cars. Students also are an important part of the market. Coffee bars are seen as a 'little bit of heaven', a refuge where consumers can lounge on sofas, read broadsheet newspapers and view new age poetry on the walls. They provide an oasis of calm for people between their homes and offices. They are regarded as a sign of social mobility for people who may be moving out of an ordinary café or low-end department store into something more classy. Even the language is important for these consumers, where terms such as latté, cappuccino and espresso allow them to demonstrate connoisseurship.

Coffee bars also cater for the different moods of consumers. For example, Sahar Hashemi, a founding partner of Coffee Republic, explains: 'If I'm in my routine, I'll have a tall, skinny latté. But if I'm feeling in a celebratory mood or like spoiling myself, it's a grand vanilla mocha with whip and marshmallows. The whole idea behind Coffee Republic was that you could get the right coffee to suit your mood at the moment.'

Coffee Republic also designs its coffee bars using a 'zoning' principle. The front zone of the store is a 'high-paced' area where people on the go can order and drink their coffee quickly. In the middle of the bar are tables and chairs arranged for meetings and larger groups, while at the back are sofas. The objective is to position Coffee Republic as a retreat where the design communicates the ideas of socializing and gatherings.

Questions

1. Why have coffee bars been so popular with consumers in the UK?

2. You are considering visiting a coffee bar for the first time. What would influence your choice of coffee bar to visit? Is this likely to be a high- or low-involvement decision?

3. The marketing concept states that corporate goals (e.g. profits) can be achieved through meeting and exceeding customer needs better than the competition. All major coffee bar chains appear to be meeting customer needs, as evidenced by their popularity, yet none is making a profit. Explain this situation.

4. Coffee bars are mainly located in the centres of towns and cities. Are there other locations where they could satisfy customer needs?

Based on: Anonymous (2001) Coffee Republic Revamps Stores for Social Focus, *Marketing*, 15 March, 4; BBC (2003) Cappuccino Kings, *The Money Programme*; Cree, R. (2003) Sahar Hashemi, *The Director*, January, 44–7; Daniels, C. (2003) Mr Coffee, *Fortune*, 14 April, 139–40; Hedburg, A. and M. Rowe (2001) UK Goes Coffee House Crazy, *Marketing Week*, 4 January, 28–9; Sutter, S. (2003) Staff the Key to Marketing Success, *Marketing*, 19 May, 4.
This case was written by David Jobber, Professor of Marketing, University of Bradford.

case six

Ethical Consumer Decision-making

The growing awareness among consumers of the environmental and social impact of their own consumption has led to an increased demand for more 'ethical' product alternatives. Studies have confirmed the existence and continued growth of 'ethical consumers'.[1] Pressure groups and selected media, such as the UK magazine *Ethical Consumer*, inform consumers on issues that are of concern. These are environmental issues, including company environmental reporting policies, pollution, genetic engineering and nuclear power. They also report on animal issues, including testing and factory farming, and social issues, including oppressive regimes, workers' rights, companies' codes of conduct and irresponsible marketing. They alert consumers to globalization issues, boycott calls and recommended 'buycotts' of best ethical buys.

Ethical concerns, therefore, are very wide and in some way are applicable to every product or service. They are often highly emotive too. Taking the example of a typically low-involvement product like a banana, choice criteria might include the 'people' issue of whether the banana is fairly traded, the health and/or environmental issue of organic production and the environmental concern of excess packaging. The consumer may consider the issue of country of origin and transportation, and wish to purchase a locally produced alternative product. This must also be coupled with traditional choice criteria such as price, quality, convenience and availability, and a consideration of the preferences of others in the buying centre. Conflict can arise between choice criteria, whereby, for example, a concern to trade fairly with poorer countries in order to promote their economies can run counter to the environmental problems of excessive transportation. Or the lack of availability of non-packaged organic produce may conflict with environmental concerns, forcing the consumer to seek alternative outlets or to compromise on their choice criteria. In such a situation, a traditionally low-involvement product can require substantially more effort on the part of the consumer in terms of decision-making.

In ethical consumption contexts, therefore, the concepts of 'perfect' and 'rational choice' appear hard to support. In reality it is likely that ethical consumers find themselves confronted by uncertainty in terms of information and the consequences of their actions. Uncertainty stems from the complex interaction between the multiple ethical concerns they wish to satisfy, in a context of changeable circumstances where consumer-decision rules need to be re-evaluated in light of new information. Information is, therefore, vital to the ethical consumer, and there is evidence of individuals demanding more information, which can come from labels, pressure groups or selected media. While this demand might not be surprising given the complex nature of ethical concerns, the ability of individuals to digest and act upon this information must be limited. In some ways information adds to the complexity of their decisions.

Although consumers may voice concern for a varying number of issues at different times, their attention is often confined to a limited number of those they consider they can 'cope' with when making consumption choices.[2] An individual might consciously decide to assiduously avoid animal-based products but do nothing about trade inequities despite being disposed to the arguments underpinning fair trade.

Many 'ethical' product sectors are now well established with their own certification marks that aid consumer decision-making. Examples are the fair trade movement, managed forest products, the RSPCA's Freedom Foods range, environmental reporting on some white goods and the organics movement. Consumer concern in other product sectors—notably fashion and clothing, where child labour and workers' rights are strong issues—is exerting pressure for similar action. As yet, consumer decision-making clues, such as labelling, are not as readily available in this sector.

In essence, for ethical consumers a purchase may not be governed solely by self-interest but, rather, may be strongly influenced by an 'obligation' to consume ethically. Thus, while many consumers acting in a rational self-motivated manner may select coffee on the basis of factors such as price and taste, those concerned about ethical issues may be guided by a sense of obligation to others and identification with ethical issues. Concerns such as providing a fair price for producers can take priority in the evaluation of product alternatives.[3]

[1] Doane, D. (2001) *Taking Flight: The Rapid Growth of Ethical Consumerism*, New Economics Foundation.
[2] Newholm, T. (2000) Consumer Exit, Voice and Loyalty: Indicative, Legitimation and Regulatory Role in Agricultural and Food Ethics, *Journal of Agricultural and Environmental Ethics* 12(2), 153–64.
[3] Shaw, D. S. and I. Clarke (1999) Belief Formation in Ethical Consumer Groups: An Exploratory Study. *Marketing Intelligence & Planning* 17(2), 109–19.

Questions

1. List six issues about which an ethical consumer may be concerned. Discuss how these issues may be related to two different products and one service.

2. Describing each stage of the consumer decision-making process, illustrate with examples how in an ethical consumption context consumer decision-making could move from low involvement to high involvement.

3. Examine the potential influences on ethical consumer behaviour, considering situational, personal and external influences.

This case was prepared by Dr Deirdre Shaw, Division of Marketing, Glasgow Caledonian University, and Dr Terry Newholm, Manchester School of Management, UMIST.

chapter four

Understanding organizational buying behaviour

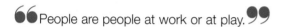
People are people at work or at play. ANONYMOUS

Learning Objectives

This chapter explains:

1 The characteristics of organizational buying

2 The dimensions of organizational buying

3 The nature and marketing implications of who buys, how organizations buy and the choice criteria used to evaluate products

4 The influences on organizational buying behaviour—the buy class, product type and purchase importance—and their marketing implications

5 The developments in purchasing practice: just-in-time and centralized purchasing, reverse marketing and leasing

6 The nature of relationship marketing and how to build customer relationships

7 The development of buyer–seller relationships

Organizational buying concerns the purchase of products and services for use in an organization's activities. There are three types of organizational market. First, the *industrial market* concerns those companies that buy products and services to help them produce other goods and services. Industrial goods include raw materials, components and capital goods such as machinery. Second, the *reseller market* comprises organizations that buy products and services to resell. Mail-order companies, retailers and supermarkets are examples of resellers. Manufacturers of consumer goods such as toys, groceries and furniture require an understanding of the reseller market since success depends on persuading resellers to stock their products. Third, the *government market* consists of government agencies that buy products and services to help them carry out their activities. Purchases for local authorities and defence are examples. The activities concerned with marketing to such organizations are sometimes called business-to-business marketing.

An understanding of organizational buying behaviour in all of these markets is a prerequisite for marketing success. One of the fascinating aspects of marketing to organizations is that different players in the buying company may be evaluating suppliers' offerings along totally different choice criteria. The key is to be able to satisfy these diverse requirements in a single offering. A product that gives engineers the performance characteristics they demand, production managers the delivery reliability they need, purchasing managers the value for money they seek and shopfloor workers the ease of installation they desire is likely to be highly successful. This complexity of organizational buying makes marketing an extremely interesting task.

This chapter examines some characteristics of organizational buying and marketing before examining the three key elements of buying identified in Chapter 3: who buys, how they buy and what choice criteria they use. For each element, the marketing implications will be addressed. Finally, some recent developments in purchasing practice—just-in-time purchasing, centralized purchasing, online purchasing and reverse marketing—will be discussed and their implications for marketing explored.

Characteristics of organizational buying

Nature and size of customers

Typically the number of customers in organizational markets will be small. The Pareto rule often applies, with 80 per cent of output being sold to 20 per cent of customers who may number fewer than 12. The reseller market is a case in point where Tesco, Sainsbury's and Asda account for the dominant share of supermarket sales in the UK. Similarly in the industrial market, component suppliers to the UK motor car industry sell to a small number of large car manufacturers: Ford, Vauxhall, Rover, Nissan, Toyota and Honda. Clearly the importance of one customer is paramount. If a component supplier loses the Ford account, or Kellogg's, say, loses the Tesco account this would have a serious impact on sales (and careers). Because such order sizes are large it becomes economic to sell directly from manufacturer to organizational customer, dispensing with the services of middlemen. Also, the importance of large customers makes it sensible to invest in close, long-term relationships with them. Dedicated sales and marketing teams are sometimes used to service large accounts.

Complexity of buying

Often, organizational purchases, notably those that involve large sums of money and that are new to the company, involve many people at different levels of the organization. The managing director, product engineers, production managers, purchasing managers and operatives may influence the decision as to which expensive machine to purchase. The sales task may be to influence as many of these people as possible and may involve multilevel selling by means of a sales team, rather than an individual salesperson.[1]

Economic and technical choice criteria

Although organizational buyers, being people, are affected by emotional factors, such as like or dislike of a salesperson, organizational buying decisions are often made on economic and technical criteria. This is because organizational buyers have to justify their decisions to other members of their organization.[2] Also the formalization of the buying function through the establishment of purchasing departments leads to the use of economic rather than emotional choice criteria. As purchasing becomes more sophisticated, economic criteria came to the fore with techniques such as life-cycle cost and value-in-use analysis. British Rail, for example, calculated life-cycle costs including purchase price, running and maintenance costs when commissioning a new diesel locomotive.

Risks

Industrial markets are sometimes characterized by a contract being agreed before the product is made. Further, the product itself may be highly technical and the seller may be faced with unforeseen problems once work has started. Thus, Scott-Lithgow won an order to build an oil rig for British Petroleum, but the price proved uneconomic given the nature of the problems associated with its construction. In the government market, GEC won the contract to develop the Nimrod surveillance system for the Ministry of Defence, but technical problems caused the project to be terminated, with much money wasted. British Rail had technical problems with the commissioning of the Class 60 diesel locomotive built by Brush Traction although these were eventually resolved.

Buying to specific requirements

Because of the large sums of money involved organizational buyers sometimes draw up product specifications and ask suppliers to design their products to meet them. Services, too, are often conducted to specific customer requirements, marketing research and advertising services being examples. This is much less a feature of consumer marketing, where a product offering may be developed to meet a need of a market segment but, beyond that, meeting individual needs would prove uneconomic.

Reciprocal buying

Because an industrial buyer may be in a powerful negotiating position with a seller, it may be possible to demand concessions in return for placing an order. In some situations, buyers may demand that sellers buy some of their products in return for securing the order. For example, in negotiating to buy computers a company like Volvo might persuade a supplier to buy a fleet of Volvo company cars.

Derived demand

The demand for many organizational goods is derived from the demand for consumer goods. If the demand for compact discs increases, the demand for the raw materials and machinery used to make the discs will also expand. Clearly raw material and machinery suppliers would be wise to monitor consumer trends and buying characteristics as well as their immediate organizational customers. A further factor based upon the derived demand issue is the tendency for demand for some industrial goods and services to be more volatile than that for consumer goods and services. For example, a small fall in demand for compact discs may mean the complete cessation of orders for the machinery to make them. Similarly a small increase in demand if manufacturers are working at full capacity may mean a massive increase in demand for machinery as investment to meet the extra demand is made. This is known as the *accelerator principle*.[3]

Negotiations

Because of the existence of professional buyers and sellers, and the size and complexity of organizational buying, negotiation is often important. Thus supermarkets will negotiate with manufacturers about price since their buying power allows them to obtain discounts. Car manufacturers will negotiate attractive prices from tyre manufacturers such as Pirelli and Michelin since the replacement brand may be dependent upon the tyre fitted to the new car. The supplier's list price may be regarded as the starting point for negotiation and the profit margin ultimately achieved will be heavily influenced by the negotiating skills of the seller. The implication is that sales and marketing personnel need to be conversant with negotiating skills and tactics.

The dimensions of organizational buying behaviour

As with consumer behaviour, the dimensions of organizational buying behaviour cover who buys, how they buy, the choice criteria used, and where and when they buy. We will examine the first three of these issues in detail.

Who buys?

An important point to understand in organizational buying is that the buyer, or purchasing officer, is often not the only person that influences the decision, or actually has the authority to make the ultimate decision. Rather, the decision is in the hands of a decision-making unit (DMU), or buying centre as it is sometimes called. This is not necessarily a fixed entity. Members of the DMU may change as the decision-making process continues. Thus a managing director may be involved in the decision that new equipment should be purchased, but not in the decision as to which manufacturer to buy it from. Six roles have been identified in the structure of the DMU, as follows.[4]

1. *Initiators*: those who begin the purchase process, e.g. maintenance contracts.
2. *Users*: those who actually use the product, e.g. welders.
3. *Deciders*: those who have authority to select the supplier/model, e.g. production managers.
4. *Influencers*: those who provide information and add decision criteria throughout the process, e.g. accountants.
5. *Buyers*: those who have authority to execute the contractual arrangements, e.g. purchasing.
6. *Gatekeepers*: those who control the flow of information, e.g. secretaries who may allow or prevent access to a DMU member, or a buyer whose agreement must be sought before a supplier can contact other members of the DMU.

For very important decisions the structure of the DMU will be complex, involving numerous people within the buying organization. The marketing task is to identify and reach the key members in order to convince them of the product's worth. Often communicating only to the purchasing officer will be insufficient, as this person may be only a minor influence on supplier choice. Relationship management (discussed later in this chapter) is of key importance in many organizational markets.

When the problem to be solved is highly technical, suppliers may work with engineers in the buying organization in order to solve problems and secure the order. One example where this approach was highly successful involved a small company that won a large order from a major car company owing to its ability to work with the car company in solving the technical problems associated with the development of an exhaust gas recirculation valve.[5] In this case, the small company's policy was to work with the major company's engineers and to keep the purchasing department out of the decision until the last possible moment, by which time it alone would be qualified to supply the part.

Often, organizational purchases are made in committees where the salesperson will not be present. The salesperson's task is to identify a person from within the decision-making unit who is a positive advocate and champion of the supplier's product. This person (or 'coach') should be given all the information needed to win the arguments that may take place within the decision-making unit. For example, even though the advocate may be a technical person, he or she should be given the financial information that may be necessary to justify buying the most technologically superior product.

Where DMU members are inaccessible to salespeople, advertising, the Internet or direct marketing tools may be used as alternatives. The illustration for Parceline is an example of business-to-business direct mail. Also where users are an important influence and the product is relatively inexpensive and consumable, free samples may be effective in generating preference.

Parceline wanted to demonstrate the benefits of its DPD (Europe by road) service, and set up face-to-face meetings with targeted prospects. The direct mail package comprised a stopwatch and a bespoke brochure incorporating timed Polaroids of the prospect's parcel being processed through the DPD system from pick up to delivery. The award-winning campaign paid for itself 80 times over.

4.1 marketing in action

Business-to-Business Marketing Communications

Marketing communications in business-to-business markets are usually associated with personal selling, as salespeople can develop relationships with customers and provide tailored answers to customers' questions. The size of a typical order also justifies their expense.

However, suppliers also use a range of non-personal communications tools to reach organizational customers. Advertising in trade magazines is the traditional way to reach members of the DMU who are not accessible to salespeople, and to build up company and product credibility in their eyes.

Direct marketing techniques such as direct mail or telemarketing are also used, often as a means of contacting those customers whose value does not render a salesperson's call viable. While a personal visit might cost £50 (€72), a telephone call might cost less than £5 (€7.20) and a mailing less than £1 (€1.44). The low cost of a direct mailing makes a large-scale campaign look tempting. If 1000 people are mailed and a 2 per cent response rate is elicited, that is still 20 replies, which might encourage the company to keep doing it. The danger, though, is that a good proportion of the non-responders have been annoyed at receiving the direct mailing.

A practical consideration when response to a mailing requires a follow-up call from salespeople is to phase the mailings to allow them time to make such a call. Direct marketing campaigns need to understand fully the nature of the DMU. For example, a campaign for the train operator GNER that focused on trying to encourage business people to travel first class was directed not at the travellers themselves but rather the accounts departments that have to authorize the expense.

An alternative is to use the Internet. This usually means setting up a website and/or conducting e-mail campaigns. As with direct mail, a poor website or a badly executed e-mail marketing campaign could have a very negative impact on the image of a brand or company. A well-designed website, however, can provide a wealth of valuable information to customers and allow online purchasing (Dell Computers' site is a good example).

E-mail marketing should maintain respect for customers' privacy. Best practice is to employ 'opt-in' or 'permission-based' campaigns. Executed well, e-mail campaigns can be effective, with companies such as Lucent Technology and Apple Computer recording response rates 50–70 per cent higher than those for direct mail.

Based on: Benady (2001);[6] Reed (2001);[7] Thatcher (2001)[8]

Marketing in Action 4.1 discusses how such focus on non-personal communication can be used in organizational (business-to-business) markets.

How they buy

Figure 4.1 describes the decision-making process for an organizational product.[9] The exact nature of the process will depend on the buying situation. In some situations some stages will be omitted. For example, in a routine rebuy situation the purchasing officer is unlikely to pass through the third, fourth and fifth stages (search for suppliers, and analysis and evaluation of their proposals). These stages will be bypassed, as the buyer, recognizing a need—perhaps shortage of stationery—routinely reorders from an existing supplier. In general, the more complex the decision and the more expensive the item, the more likely it is that each stage will be passed through and that the process will take more time.

Recognition of a problem (need)

Needs and problems may be recognized through either *internal or external factors*.[10] An example of an internal factor would be the realization of undercapacity leading to the decision to purchase plant or equipment. Thus, internal recognition leads to active behaviour (internal/active). Some problems that are recognized internally may not be acted upon. This condition may be termed internal/passive. A production manager may realize that there is a problem with a machine but, given more pressing problems, decide to put up with it.

Other potential problems may not be recognized internally, and become problems only because of external cues. Production managers may be quite satisfied with their production process until they are made aware of another, more efficient, method.

Clearly, these different problems have important implications for marketing and sales. The internal/passive condition implies that there is an opportunity for a salesperson, having identified the condition, to highlight the problem by careful analysis of cost inefficiencies and other symptoms, so that the problem is perceived to be pressing and in need of solution (internal/active). The internal/active situation requires the supplier to demonstrate a differential advantage of its products over those of the competition. In this situation problem stimulation is unnecessary, but where internal recognition is absent, the marketer can provide the necessary external cues. A fork-lift truck sales representative might stimulate problem recognition by showing how the truck can save the customer money, due to lower maintenance costs, and lead to more efficient use of warehouse space through higher lifting capabilities. Advertising or direct mail could also be used to good effect. The illustration featuring Siemens (overleaf) shows how advertising was used to create awareness of its ability to provide solutions using its Totally Integrated Automation system.

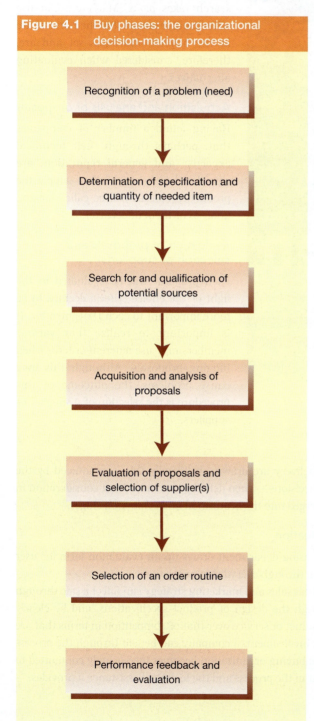

Figure 4.1 Buy phases: the organizational decision-making process

- Recognition of a problem (need)
- Determination of specification and quantity of needed item
- Search for and qualification of potential sources
- Acquisition and analysis of proposals
- Evaluation of proposals and selection of supplier(s)
- Selection of an order routine
- Performance feedback and evaluation

Determination of specification and quantity of needed item

At this stage of the decision-making process the DMU will draw up a description of what is required. For example, it might decide that five lathes are required to meet certain specifications. The ability of marketers to influence the specification can give their company an advantage at later stages of the process. By persuading the buying company to specify features that only the marketer's own product possesses, the sale may be virtually closed at this stage. This is the process of setting up *lock-out criteria*.

Search for and qualification of potential sources

A great deal of variation in the degree of search takes place in industrial buying. Generally speaking, the cheaper and less important the item, and the more information the buyer possesses, the less search takes place. Marketers can use advertising to ensure that their brands are in the buyers' awareness set and are, therefore, considered when evaluating alternatives.

Acquisition and analysis of proposals

Having found a number of companies that, perhaps through their technical expertise and general reputation, are considered to be qualified to supply the product, proposals will be called for and analysis of them undertaken.

Evaluation of proposals and selection of supplier(s)

Each proposal will be evaluated in the light of the choice criteria deemed to be more important to each DMU member. It is important to realize that various members may use different criteria when judging proposals. Although this may cause problems, the outcome of this procedure is the selection of a supplier or suppliers.

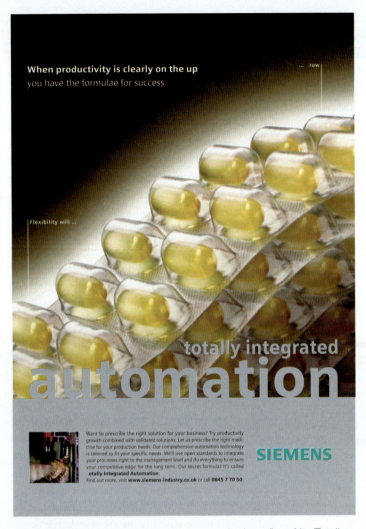

Siemens creates awareness and presents the benefits of its Totally Integrated Automation approach to productivity solutions.

Selection of an order routine

Next, the details of payment and delivery are drawn up. Usually this is conducted by the purchasing officer. In some buying decisions—when delivery is an important consideration in selecting a supplier—this stage is merged into the acquisition and evaluation stages.

Performance feedback and evaluation

This may be formal, where a purchasing department draws up an evaluation form for user departments to complete, or informal through everyday conversations.

The implications of all this are that sales and marketing strategy can affect a sale through influencing need recognition, through the design of product specifications, and by clearly presenting the advantages of the product or service over that of competition in terms that are relevant to DMU members. By early involvement, a company can benefit through the process of *creeping commitment*, whereby the buying organization becomes increasingly committed to one supplier through its involvement in the process and the technical assistance it provides.

Choice criteria

This aspect of industrial buyer behaviour refers to the criteria used by members of the DMU to evaluate supplier proposals. These criteria are likely to be determined by the performance criteria used to evaluate the members themselves.[11] Thus purchasing managers who are judged by the extent to which they reduce purchase expenditure are likely to be more cost conscious than production engineers, who are evaluated in terms of the technical efficiency of the production process they design.

As with consumers, organizational buying is characterized by *technical*, *economic*, *social* (organizational) and *personal criteria*. Key considerations may be, for plant and equipment, return on investment, while for materials and components parts they may be cost savings, together with delivery reliability, quality and technical assistance. Because of the high costs associated with production downtime, a key concern of many purchasing departments is the long-run development of the organization's supply system. Personal factors may also be important, particularly when suppliers' product offerings are essentially similar. In this situation the final decision may rest upon the relative liking for the supplier's salesperson. The UPS advertisement illustrates the importance of economic criteria in organizational buying.

Customers' choice criteria can change in different regions of the world. For example, Xerox is generally known as a company that provides solutions for creating documents. In the West, when choosing a printer, a consumer considers the print quality and how easy the machine is to network and update. In eastern Europe other choice criteria prevail. Networking and servicing are not issues that are considered very much, rather value for money is the key. The consumer attitude is: 'I can buy a Xerox, or I can buy a Canon and a car.' The marketing task for Xerox is to reduce the consumer's price sensitivity by stressing its reliability, quality, after-sales service, wide range of suppliers and medium- to long-term value for money.[12]

UPS recognizes the importance of economic criteria (supply chain efficiency) in organizational buying.

What are the range of motives that key players in organizations use to compare supplier offerings? Economic considerations play a part because commercial firms have profit objectives and work within budgetary constraints. Emotional factors should not be ignored, however, as decisions are made by people who do not suddenly lose their personalities, personal likes and dislikes and prejudices simply because they are at work. Let us examine a number of important technical and economic motives (quality, price and life-cycle costs, and continuity of supply) and then some organizational and personal factors (perceived risk, office politics, and personal liking/disliking).

Quality

The emergence of **total quality management** as a key aspect of organizational life reflects the important of quality in evaluating suppliers' products and services. Many buying organizations are unwilling to trade quality for price. In particular, buyers are looking for consistency of product or service quality so that end products (e.g. motor cars) are reliable, inspection costs are reduced and production processes run smoothly. They are installing just-in-time delivery systems, which rely upon incoming supplies being quality guaranteed. The important part people have to play in creating quality products is illustrated in the advertisement for Air Products.

Air Products promotes the competences of its people as creators of quality products.

Price and life-cycle costs

For materials and components of similar specification and quality, price becomes a key consideration. For standard items such as ball-bearings, price may be critical to making a sale given that a number of suppliers can meet delivery and specification requirements. However, it should not be forgotten that price is only one component of cost for many buying organizations. Increasingly buyers take into account life-cycle costs, which may include productivity savings, maintenance costs and residual values as well as initial purchase price when evaluating products. Marketers can use life-cycle costs analysis to break into an account. By calculating life-cycle costs with a buyer, new perceptions of value may be achieved.

Continuity of supply

Another major cost to a company is disruption of a production run. Delays of this kind can mean costly machine downtime and even lost sales. Continuity of supply is, therefore, a prime consideration in many purchase situations. Companies that perform badly on this criteria lose out even if the price is competitive because a small percentage price edge does not compare with the costs of unreliable delivery. Supplier companies that can guarantee deliveries and realize their promises can achieve a significant differential advantage in the marketplace. Organizational customers are demanding close relationships with *accredited suppliers* that can guarantee reliable supply, perhaps on a just-in-time basis.

Perceived risk

Perceived risk can come in two forms: *functional risk* such as uncertainty with respect to product or supplier performance, and *psychological risk* such as criticism from work colleagues.[13] This latter risk—fear of upsetting the boss, losing status, being ridiculed by others in the department, or, indeed, losing one's job—can play a determining role in purchase decisions. Buyers often reduce uncertainty by gathering information about competing suppliers, checking the opinions of important others in the buying company, buying only from familiar and/or reputable suppliers and by spreading risk through multiple sourcing.

Office politics

Political factions within the buying company may also influence the outcome of a purchase decision. Interdepartmental conflict may manifest itself in the formation of competing camps over the purchase of a product or service. Because department X favours supplier 1, department Y automatically favours supplier 2. The outcome not only has purchasing implications but also political implications for the departments and individuals concerned.

Personal liking/disliking

A buyer may personally like one salesperson more than another and this may influence supplier choice, particularly when competing products are very similar. Even when supplier selection is on the basis of competitive bidding, it is known for purchasers to help salespeople they like to be competitive.[14] Obviously perception is important in all organizational purchases as how someone behaves depends upon the perception of the situation. One buyer may perceive a salesperson as being honest, truthful and likeable while another may not. As with consumer behaviour, three selective processes may be at work on buyers.

1. *Selective attention:* only certain information sources may be sought.
2. *Selective distortion:* information from those sources may be distorted.
3. *Selective retention:* only some information may be remembered.

In general, people tend to distort, avoid and forget messages that are substantially different to their existing beliefs and attitudes.

Implications

The implications of understanding the content of the decision are that appeals may need to change when communicating to different DMU members: discussion with a production engineer may centre on the technical superiority of the product offering, while much more emphasis on cost factors may prove effective when talking to the purchasing officer. Furthermore, the criteria used by buying organizations change over time as circumstances change. Price may be relatively unimportant to a company when trying to solve a highly visible technical problem, and the order will be placed with the supplier that provides the necessary technical assistance. Later, after the problem has been solved and other suppliers become qualified, price may be of crucial significance.

An illustration of how appeals (messages) may need to change when talking to different members of the DMU is given in Marketing in Action 4.2.

4.2 marketing in action

Orange Talks to Business Customers

The mobile phone operator Orange is a major consumer brand with over 39 million customers worldwide. Orange wants to expand on this base, but not just in consumer markets: the company is targeting businesses as well. Orange is offering a complete portfolio of voice and data solutions to allow companies to have a fully wire-free environment that allows customers to take their office with them wherever they are. To meet business requirements the technology has to be robust enough to handle the demands of business networks.

Success in this market is not just about technology, however. Orange recognizes that talking to the customer means that the choice criteria of the different members of the DMU need to be taken into account. One group of DMU members is the information technologists. Here Orange talks technology because that is what the IT person expects. Another group is composed of non-technical people, such as accountants and users of the equipment. For them Orange keeps its message much simpler and focuses on how more effective phone use can boost productivity.

By varying the message, Orange can keep its messages relevant and appealing to the people in the DMU whose interests and priorities, and the criteria upon which they base their choice, vary.

Based on: Mazur (2002)[15]

Influences on organizational buying behaviour

Figure 4.2 shows the three factors that influence how organizations buy, who buys and the choice criteria they use: the product type, the buy class and the importance of purchase.[16]

The buy class

Organizational purchases may be distinguished between a new task, a straight rebuy and a modified rebuy.[17] A **new task** occurs when the need for the product has not arisen previously so that there is little or no relevant experience in the company, and a great deal of information is required. A **straight rebuy** occurs where an organization buys previously purchased items from suppliers already judged acceptable. Routine purchasing procedures are set up to facilitate straight rebuys. The **modified rebuy** lies between the two extremes. A regular requirement for the type of product exists, and the buying alternatives are known, but sufficient change (e.g. a delivery problem) has occurred to require some alteration to the normal supply procedure.

Figure 4.2 Influences on organizational purchasing behaviour

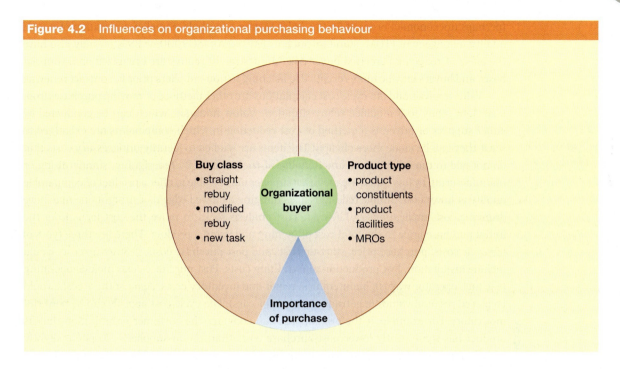

The buy classes affect organizational buying in the following ways. First, the membership of the DMU changes. For a straight rebuy possibly only the purchasing officer is involved, whereas for a new buy senior management, engineers, production managers and purchasing officers may be involved. Modified rebuys often involve engineers, production managers and purchasing officers, but senior management, except when the purchase is critical to the company, is unlikely to be involved. Second, the decision-making process may be much longer as the buy class changes from a straight rebuy to a modified rebuy and to a new task. Third, in terms of influencing DMU members, they are likely to be much more receptive to new task and modified rebuy situations than straight rebuys. In the latter case, the purchasing manager has already solved the purchasing problem and has other problems to deal with. So why make it a problem again?

The first implication of this buy class analysis is that there are big gains to be made if a company can enter the new task at the start of the decision-making process. By providing information and helping with any technical problems that can arise, the company may be able to create goodwill and creeping commitment, which secures the order when the final decision is made. The second implication is that since the decision process is likely to be long, and many people are involved in the new task, supplier companies need to invest heavily in sales personnel for a considerable period of time. Some firms employ missionary sales teams, comprising their best salespeople, to help secure big new-task orders.

Companies in straight rebuy situations must ensure that no change occurs when they are in the position of the supplier. Regular contact to ensure that the customer has no complaints may be necessary, and the buyer may be encouraged to use automatic reordering systems. For the out-supplier (i.e. a new potential supplier) the task can be difficult unless poor service or some other factor has caused the buyer to become dissatisfied with the present supplier. The obvious objective of the out-supplier in this situation is to change the buy class from a straight rebuy to a modified rebuy. Price alone may not be enough since changing supplier represents a large personal risk to the purchasing officer. The new supplier's products might be less reliable, and delivery might be unpredictable. In order to reduce this risk, the company may offer delivery guarantees with penalty clauses and be very willing to accept a small (perhaps uneconomic) order at first in order to gain a foothold. Supplier acquisition of a total quality management (TQM) standard such as EM29000, ISO9000 or BS5750 may also have the effect of reducing perceived buyer risk. Many straight rebuys are organized on a contract basis, and buyers may be more receptive to listening to non-suppliers prior to contract renewal.

Value analysis and life-cycle cost calculations are other methods of moving purchases from a straight rebuy to a modified rebuy situation. Value analysis, which can be conducted by either supplier or buyer, is a method of cost reduction in which components are examined to see if they can be made more cheaply. The items are studied to identify unnecessary costs that do not add to the reliability or functionality of the product. By redesigning, standardizing or manufacturing by less expensive means, a supplier may be able to offer a product of comparable quality at lower cost. Simple redesigns like changing a curved edge to a straight one may have dramatic cost implications.[18] Life-cycle cost analysis seeks to move the cost focus from the initial purchase price to the total cost of owning and using a product. There are three types of life-cycle costs: purchase price, start-up costs and post-purchase costs.[19] Start-up costs would include installation, lost production and training costs. Post-purchase costs include operating (e.g. fuel, operator wages), maintenance, repair and inventory costs. Against these costs would be placed residual values (e.g. trade-in values of cars). Life-cycle cost appeals can be powerful motivators. For example, if the out-supplier can convince the customer organization that its product has significantly lower post-purchase costs than the in-supplier's, despite a slightly higher purchase price, it may win the order. This is because it will be delivering a higher economic value to the customer. This can be a powerful competitive advantage and, at the same time, justify the premium price.

The product type

Products can be classified according to four types: materials, components, plant and equipment, and MROs (maintenance repair and operation), as follows:

1. materials to be used in the production process, e.g. aluminium
2. components to be incorporated in the finished product, e.g. headlights
3. plant and equipment, e.g. bulldozer
4. products and services for maintenance repair and operation (MRO), e.g. spanners, welding equipment and lubricants.

This classification is based upon a customer perspective—how the product is used—and may be employed to identify differences in organizational buyer behaviour. First, the people who take part in the decision-making process tend to change according to product type. For example, senior management tend to get involved in the purchase of plant and equipment or, occasionally, when new materials are purchased if the change is of fundamental importance to company operations, e.g. if a move from aluminium to plastic is being considered. Rarely do they involve themselves in component or MRO supply. Similarly, design engineers tend to be involved in buying components and materials but not normally MRO and plant equipment. Second, the decision-making process tends to be slower and more complex as product type moves from:

MRO → components → materials → plant and equipment

For MRO items, *blanket contracts* rather than periodic purchase orders are increasingly being used. The supplier agrees to resupply the buyer on agreed price terms over a period of time. Stock is held by the seller and orders are automatically printed out by the buyer's computer when stock falls below a minimum level. This has the advantage to the supplying company of effectively blocking the effort of the competitors for long periods of time.

Classification of suppliers' offerings by product type gives clues as to who is likely to be influenced in the purchase decision. The marketing task is then to confirm this in particular situations and attempt to reach those people involved. A company selling MROs is likely to be wasting effort attempting to communicate with design engineers, whereas attempts to reach operating management are likely to prove fruitful.

The importance of purchase

A purchase is likely to be perceived as being important to the buying organization when it involves large sums of money, when the cost of making the wrong decision, e.g. in production downtime, is high and when there is considerable uncertainty about the outcome of alternative offerings. In such situations, many people at different organizational levels are likely to be involved in the decision and the process will be long, with extensive search and analysis of information. Thus extensive marketing effort is likely to be required, but great opportunities present themselves to those sales teams that work with buying organizations to convince them that their offering has the best pay-off; this may involve acceptance trials, e.g. private diesel manufacturers supply railway companies with prototypes for testing, engineering support and testimonials from other users. Additionally, guarantees of delivery dates and after-sales service may be necessary when buyer uncertainty regarding these factors is high. An example of the time and effort that may be required to win very important purchases is the order secured by GEC to supply £250 million (€360 million) worth of equipment for China's largest nuclear power station. The contract was won after six years of negotiation, 33 GEC missions to China and 4000 person-days of work.

Developments in purchasing practice

Several trends have taken place within the purchasing function that have marketing implications for supplier firms. The advent of just-in-time purchasing and the increased tendency towards centralized purchasing, reverse marketing and leasing have all changed the nature of purchasing and altered the way in which suppliers compete.

Just-in-time purchasing

The just-in-time concept aims to minimize stocks by organizing a supply system that provides materials and components as they are required.[20] Stockholding costs are significantly reduced or eliminated, thus profits are increased. Furthermore, since the holding of stocks is a hedge against machine breakdowns, faulty parts and human error they may be seen as a cushion that acts as a disincentive to management to eliminate such inefficiencies.

A number of just-in-time (JIT) practices are also associated with improved quality. Suppliers are evaluated on their ability to provide high-quality products. The effect of this is that suppliers may place more emphasis on product quality. Buyers are encouraged to specify only essential product characteristics, which means that suppliers have more discretion in product design and manufacturing methods. Also, the emphasis is on the supplier certifying quality—which means that quality inspection at the buyer company is reduced and overall costs are minimized, since quality control at source is more effective than further down the supply chain.

The total effects of JIT can be enormous. Purchasing, inventory and inspection costs can be reduced, product design can be improved, delivery streamlined, production downtime reduced, and the quality of the finished item enhanced.

However, the implementation of JIT requires integration into both purchasing and production operations. Since the system requires the delivery of the exact amount of materials or components to the production line as they are required, delivery schedules must be very reliable and suppliers must be prepared to make deliveries on a regular basis, perhaps even daily. Lead times for ordering must be short and the number of defects very low. An attraction for suppliers is that it is usual for long-term purchasing agreements to be drawn up. The marketing implication of the JIT concept is that to be competitive in many industrial markets—for example, motor cars—suppliers must be able to meet the requirements of this fast-growing system.

An example of a company that employs just-in-time is the Nissan car assembly plant at Sunderland in the UK. The importance of JIT to its operations has meant that the number of component suppliers in the north-east of England has increased from three when Nissan arrived in 1986 to 27 in 1992.[21] Nissan has adopted what it terms synchronous supply: parts are delivered only minutes before they are needed. For example, carpets are delivered by Sommer Allibert, a French supplier, from its facility close to the Nissan assembly line in sequence for fitting to the correct model. Only 42 minutes elapse between the carpet being ordered and fitted to the car. The stockholding of carpets for the Nissan Micra is now only 10 minutes. Just-in-time practices do carry risks, however, if labour stability cannot be guaranteed. Renault discovered this to its cost when a strike at its engine and gearbox plant caused its entire French and Belgian car production lines to close in only 10 days.

Centralized purchasing

Where several operating units within a company have common requirements, and where there is an opportunity to strengthen a negotiating position by bulk buying, centralized purchasing is an attractive option. Centralization encourages purchasing specialists to concentrate their energies on a small group of products, thus enabling them to develop an extensive knowledge of cost factors and the operation of suppliers.[22] The move from local to centralized buying has important marketing implications. Localized buying tends to focus on short-term cost and profit considerations, whereas centralized purchasing places more emphasis on long-term supply relationships. Outside influences—for example, engineers—play a greater role in supplier choice in local purchasing organizations since less specialized buyers often lack the expertise and status to question the recommendations of technical people. The type of purchasing organization can therefore give clues to suppliers regarding the important people in the decision-making unit and their respective power positions.

Online purchasing

While many people relate the Internet to consumer online shopping, the reality is that business-to-business e-procurement is of a much greater size. Companies not only post their own websites on the Internet but also develop extranets for buyers to send out requests for bids to suppliers. Electronic marketplaces take many forms, as described below.[23]

- Catalogue sites: companies can order items through electronic catalogues.
- Vertical markets: companies buying industrial products such as steel, chemicals or plastic, or buying services such as logistics (distribution) or media can use specialized websites (called e-hubs). For instance, Plastics.com permits thousands of plastics buyers to search for the lowest prices from thousands of plastics sellers.
- Auction sites: suppliers can place industrial products on auction sites where purchasers can bid for them.

- Exchange (or spot) markets: many commodities are sold on electronic exchange markets where prices can change by the minute. CheMatch.com is a spot market for buyers and sellers of bulk chemicals such as benzine.
- Buying alliances: companies in the same market for products join together to gain bigger discounts on higher volumes. E-Marketing 4.1 describes how three car manufacturers formed an alliance to obtain lower prices for auto parts.

The main benefits of online purchasing are reduced buying costs, more rapid supply, the identification of new suppliers, the ability to share information between buyers and sellers, reduced paperwork and closer working relationships between suppliers and customers. However, the ability to source large numbers of suppliers and price quotes means that supplier–buyer loyalty may be eroded.

4.1 e-marketing

Pooling Organizational Buying within the Automobile Industry

A few years ago the top three car manufacturers in the world—General Motors, Daimler Chrysler and Ford—got together and realized that there were huge annual cost savings to be made by pooling their individual e-business procurement activities. Projected savings were in the region of $250 billion per year.

The way to attain these cost savings, they believed, was to standardize the way in which manufacturers and suppliers transacted (until this point each manufacturer had a different system for doing this).

One solution was to put standards in place to which both the manufacturer and supplier would adhere—this would be difficult, though, as it would take time for companies to develop new procurement systems. A more favourable solution was to develop a business-to-business marketplace for the automobile industry and, in 2000, the Covisint online marketplace was launched.

Since then, more auto manufacturers (including Renault-Nissan and Peugeot-Citroën) have joined and over 5000 suppliers now trade globally with these manufacturers through Covisint. It is estimated that between 15 and 25 per cent of all auto-maker purchasing is now made through this marketplace; activities include e-auctions, online proposals, catalogue purchases, information exchange, and so on.

Perhaps Covisint proves that competitors that are able to collaborate through e-business technology can increase their own efficiency and the efficiency of the industry as a whole. However, other manufacturers believe there is too much emphasis on standard-setting over relationship-building, and it is significant that Volkswagen Group, Honda and Toyota have yet to join.

Based on: Moffat (2003)[24]

Reverse marketing

The traditional view of marketing is that supplier firms will actively seek the requirements of customers and attempt to meet those needs better than the competition. This model places the initiative with the supplier. Purchasers could assume a passive dimension relying on their suppliers' sensitivity to their needs, and on technological capabilities to provide them with solutions to their problems. However, this trusting relationship is at odds with a new corporate purchasing situation that developed during the 1980s and is gaining momentum. Purchasing is taking on a more proactive, aggressive stance in acquiring the products and services needed to compete. This process, whereby the buyer attempts to persuade the supplier to provide exactly what the organization wants, is called reverse marketing.[25] Zeneca, an international supplier of chemicals, uses reverse marketing very effectively to target suppliers with a customized list of requirements concerning delivery times, delivery success rates and how often sales visits should occur. Figure 4.3 shows the difference between the traditional model and this new concept.

Figure 4.3 Reverse marketing

The essence of reverse marketing is that the purchaser takes the initiative in approaching new or existing suppliers and persuading them to meet their supply requirements. The implications of reverse marketing are that it may pose serious threats to in-suppliers that are not co-operative but offer major opportunities to responsive in- and out-suppliers. The growth of reverse marketing presents two key benefits to those suppliers willing to listen to the buyer's proposition and carefully consider its merits. First, it provides the opportunity to develop a stronger and longer-lasting relationship with the customer and, second, it may be a source of new product opportunities that may be developed to a broader customer base later on.

Leasing

A lease is a contract by which the owner of an asset (e.g. a car) grants the right to another party to use the asset for a period of time in exchange for payment of rent.[26] The benefits to the customer are that a leasing arrangement avoids the need to pay the cash purchase price of the product or service, is a hedge against fast product obsolescence, may have tax advantages, avoids the problem of equipment disposal and, with certain types of leasing contract, avoids some maintenance costs. These benefits need to be weighed against the costs of leasing, which may be higher than outright buying.

There are two main types of leases: financial (or full payment) leases and operating leases (sometimes called rental agreements). A *financial lease* is a longer-term arrangement that is fully amortized over the term of the contract. Lease payments, in total, usually exceed the purchase price of the item. The terms and conditions of the lease vary according to convention and competitive conditions. Sometimes the supplier will agree to pay maintenance costs over the leasing period. This is common when leasing photocopiers, for example. The lessee may also be given the option of buying the equipment at the end of the period. An *operating lease* is for a shorter period of time, is cancellable and is not completely amortized.[27] Operating lease rates are usually higher than financial lease rates since they run for a shorter term. When equipment is required intermittently this form of acquisition can be attractive because it avoids the need to let plant lie idle. Many types of equipment, such as diggers, bulldozers and skips, may be available for short-term hire, as may storage facilities.

Leasing may be advantageous to suppliers because it provides customer benefits that may differentiate product and service offerings. As such it may attract customers who might otherwise find the product unaffordable or uneconomic. The importance of leasing in such industries as cars, photocopiers and data processing has led an increasing number of companies to employ leasing consultants to work with customers on leasing arrangements and benefits. A crucial marketing decision is the setting of leasing rates. These should be set with the following factors in mind:

① the desired relative attractiveness of leasing vs buying (the supplier may wish to promote/discourage buying compared with leasing)

② the net present value of lease payments vs outright purchase

③ the tax advantages of leasing vs buying to the customer

④ the rates being charged by competition

⑤ the perceived advantages of spreading payments to customers

⑥ any other perceived customer benefits, e.g. maintenance and insurance costs being assumed by the supplier.

Relationship management

Four types of relationship have been identified.[28] The first two are market relationships between suppliers and customers. They make up the core of relationship marketing and are externally orientated. The first of these is classic market relationships concerning supplier–customer, supplier–customer–competitor and the physical distribution network. These types of relationship are discussed in this chapter. The second type is special market relationships such as the customer as a member of a loyalty programme and the interaction in the service encounter. These are examined in the direct marketing and marketing services chapters (Chapters 14 and 21).

The third type of relationship is the mega-relationship, and concerns the economy and society in general. Examples of such relationships are mega-marketing (lobbying, public opinion and political power), mega-alliances (the European Union, which forms a stage for marketing) and social relationships (friendships and ethnic bonds). These issues are covered in the consumer behaviour and marketing environment chapters (Chapters 3 and 5). Finally, nano-relationships concern the internal operations of an organization, such as relationships between internal customers, internal markets, divisions and business areas inside organizations. Such relationships are discussed within the managing products (portfolio planning) and marketing implementation organization and control chapters (Chapters 9 and 20).

Managing relationships is a key ingredient in successful organizational marketing. Relationship marketing concerns the shifting from activities of attracting customers to activities concerned with current customers and how to retain them. Customer retention is critical since small changes in retention rates have significant effects on future revenues.[29] At its core is the maintenance of relations between a company and its suppliers, channel intermediaries, the public and its customers. The key idea is to create customer loyalty so that a stable, mutually profitable and long-term relationship is developed.[30] The idea of relationship marketing implies at least two essential conditions. First, a relationship is a mutually rewarding connection between the parties so that they expect to obtain benefits from it. Second, the parties have a commitment to the relationship over time and are, therefore, willing to make adaptations to their own behaviour to maintain its continuity.[31] An absolutely central feature of relationship marketing is the role that trust plays in creating satisfaction between parties in the relationship. Building trust is a very effective way to increase satisfaction and develop long-term relationships.[32]

The discussion of reverse marketing has given examples of buyers adopting a proactive stance in their dealings with suppliers, and has introduced the importance of buyer–seller relationships in marketing between organizations. The Industrial Marketing and Purchasing Group developed the interaction approach to explain the complexity of buyer–seller relationships.33 This approach views these relationships as taking place between two active parties. Thus reverse marketing is one manifestation of the interaction perspective. Both parties may be involved in adaptations to their own process or product technologies to accommodate each other, and changes in the activities of one party are unlikely without consideration of or consultation with the other party. In such circumstances a key objective of industrial markets will be to manage customer relationships. This means considering not only formal organizational arrangements such as the use of distributors, salespeople and sales subsidiaries, but also the informal network consisting of the personal contacts and relationships between supplier and customer staff. Marks & Spencer's senior directors meet the boards of each of its major suppliers twice a year for frank discussions. When Marks & Spencer personnel visit a supplier it is referred to as a 'royal visit'. Factories may be repainted, new uniforms issued and machinery cleaned: this reflects the exacting standards that the company demands from its suppliers and the power it wields in its relationship with them.34

The development of technology is facilitating the improvement of buyer–seller relationships. Developments in the use of the Internet to strengthen such relationships are gathering pace. E-Marketing 4.2 describes how the Cisco Corporation uses the Internet in its business-to-business marketing.

4.2 e-marketing

Integrated Internet Business-to-Business Marketing at Cisco

One of the world leaders in developing integrated information exchange systems based around the Internet is Cisco Corporation, an $8 billion manufacturer of network routers and switches. As a leading producer of the electronic components that provide the infrastructure that underpins the World Wide Web, it is understandable that the company has sought to exploit technology to improve the management of customer relationships. Features of its system include:

- an online customer enquiry and order placement system that handles over 80 per cent of all orders received by the company
- a website that allows customers to configure and price their router, and switch product orders online
- an online customer care service that permits the customer to identify a solution from Cisco's data warehouse of technical information and then to download relevant data or computer software; the firm estimates that this facility has saved $250 million per year in the cost of distributing software and an additional $75 million in the staffing of its customer care operation. The service allows 80 per cent of queries to be solved online. As well as forums and an array of interactive problem-solving tools, Cisco Live allows customers to have 'text chats' with engineers who can, if necessary, take control of visitors' browsers to point them to the relevant information.

Based on: Pollack (1999);35 Bowen (2002)36

A key aspect of the work of the IMP group is an understanding of how relationships are established and developed over time. Ford37 has modelled the development of buyer–seller relationships as a five-stage process (see Fig. 4.4).

Stage 1: the pre-relationship stage

Something has caused the customer to evaluate a potential new supplier. Perhaps a price rise or a decline in service standards of the current supplier has triggered the need to consider a change. The customer will be concerned about the perceived risk of change and the distance that is perceived to exist between itself and the potential supplier. Distance has five dimensions, as follows.

- *Social distance*: the extent to which both the individuals and organizations in a relationship are unfamiliar with each other's ways of working.
- *Cultural distance*: the degree to which the norms and values, or working methods, between two companies differ because of their separate national characteristics.
- *Technological distance*: the differences between the two companies' product and process technologies.
- *Time distance*: the time that must elapse between establishing contact or placing an order, and the actual transfer of the product or service involved.
- *Geographical distance*: the physical distance between the two companies.

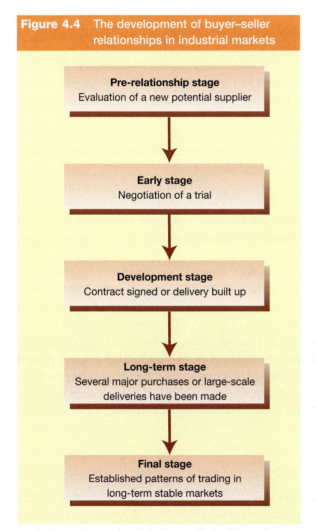

Figure 4.4 The development of buyer–seller relationships in industrial markets

Stage 2: the early stage

At this stage, potential suppliers are in contact with buyers to negotiate trial deliveries for frequently purchased supplies or components, or to develop a specification for a capital good purchase. Much uncertainty will exist and the supplier will be working to reduce perceived risk of change. The reputation of the potential supplier is likely to be important and the lack of social relationships may mean a lack of trust on the part of both supplier and buyer. The supplier may believe that it is being used as a source of information and that the buyer has no intention of placing an order. The buyer may fear that the supplier is promising things it cannot deliver in order to make a sale. Both companies will have little or no evidence on which to judge their partner's commitment to the relationship.

Stage 3: the development stage

This stage occurs as deliveries of frequently purchased products increase, or after contract signing for major capital purchases. The development stage is marked by increasing experience between the companies of the operations of each other's organizations, and greater knowledge of each other's norms and values. As this occurs, uncertainty and distance reduce. A key element in the evaluation of a supplier or customer at this stage of their relationship depends on perceptions of the degree of commitment to its development. Commitment can be shown by:

- reducing social distance through familiarization with each other's way of working
- making formal adaptations that are contractually agreed methods of meeting the needs of the other company by incurring costs or by management involvement

- making informal adaptations beyond the terms of the contract to cope with particular issues and problems that arise as the relationship develops.

This stage is characterized by an increasing level of business between the companies. Many of the difficulties experienced in the early stages of the relationship are overcome through the processes at work in the development stage.

Stage 4: the long-term stage

By this stage both companies share mutual dependence. It is reached after large-scale deliveries of continuously purchased products have occurred, or after several purchases of major capital products. Experience of the operations of each party and trust are high, with the accompanying low levels of uncertainty and distance. The reduction in uncertainty can cause problems in that routine ways of dealing with the partner may cease to be questioned by this stage. This can happen even though these routines may no longer relate well to either party's needs. This is called 'institutionalization'. For example, the seller may be providing greater product variety (and incurring higher production costs) than the buyer really needs. Since no one questions the arrangements, these inefficiencies continue. Institutionalized practices may make a supplier appear less responsive to a customer or exploit the customer by taking advantage of its lack of awareness of changes in market conditions (for example, by not passing on cost savings) or by accepting annual price rises without question. Strong personal relationships will have developed between individuals in the two companies and mutual problem-solving and informal adaptations will occur. In extreme cases, problems arising from 'side changing' can arise where individuals act in the interests of the other company and against their own on the strength of their personal allegiances.

Extensive formal adaptations resulting from successive contracts and agreements narrow the technological distance between the companies. Close integration of the operations of the companies is motivated by cost reductions and increased control of the other partner. For example, automatic reordering systems based on information technology may act as a barrier to the entry of other supplier companies.

Commitment to the relationship will have been shown by the extensive adaptations that have occurred. However, the supplier has to be aware of two difficulties. First, the need to demonstrate commitment to a customer must be balanced by the danger of becoming too dependent on that customer. The supplier may feel the need to make the customer feel it is important yet does not wield too much power in the relationship. Second, there is a danger that the customer's perception of a supplier's commitment to the relationship is lower than it actually is. This is because the peak of investment of resources has taken place before the long-term stage has been reached. And so, ironically, when a supplier is at its most committed to a long-term and important customer, it may appear less committed than during the development stage.

Stage 5: the final stage

This stage is reached in stable markets over long time periods. The institutionalization process that started during the long-term stage continues to the point where the conduct of business may be based upon industry codes of practice. These may stipulate the 'right way to do business', such as the avoidance of price cutting. Often, attempts to break out of institutionalized patterns of trading will be met by sanctions from other trading partners.

This model of how buyer–seller relationships develop highlights some of the dangers that can occur during the process. Furthermore, suppliers can segment their customers according to the stage of development. Each stage requires differing actions based on the differing requirements of customers. The market for a supplier can be seen as a network of relationships. Each must be assessed according to the opportunity it represents, the threats posed by competitive challenges and the costs of developing the relationship. The marketing task is the establishment, development and maintenance of these relationships. They also need to be managed strategically. Decisions need to be made regarding the relative importance of a portfolio of relationships, and resources allocated to each of them based on their stage of development and likely return.

The reality of organizational marketing is that many suppliers and buying organizations have been conducting business between themselves for many years. For example, Lucas has been supplying components to Rover (and its antecedents) for over 50 years. Marks & Spencer has trading relationships with suppliers that stretch back almost 100 years. Such long-term relationships can have significant advantages for both buyer and seller. Risk is reduced for buyers as they get to know people in the supplier organization, and know whom to contact when problems arise. Communication is thus improved and joint problem-solving and design management can take place. Sellers gain through closer knowledge of buyer requirements, and by gaining the trust of the buyer an effective barrier to entry for competing firms may be established. New product development can benefit from such close relationships. The development of machine-washable lambs' wool fabrics and easy-iron cotton shirts came about because of Marks & Spencer's close relationship with UK manufacturers.[38]

Closer relationships in organizational markets are inevitable as changing technology, shorter product life cycles and increased foreign competition places marketing and purchasing departments in key strategic roles. Buyers are increasingly treating trusted suppliers as *strategic partners*, sharing information and drawing on their expertise when developing cost-efficient, quality-based new products. The marketing implication is that successful organizational marketing is more than the traditional manipulation of the 4-Ps (product, price, promotion and place). Its foundation rests upon the skilful handling of customer relationships. This had led some companies to appoint customer relationship managers to oversee the partnership and act in a communicational and co-ordinated role to ensure customer satisfaction. Still more companies have reorganized their salesforces to reflect the importance of managing key customer relationships effectively. This process is called key or national account management.

The term 'national account' is generally used to refer to large and important customers that may have centralized purchasing departments that buy or co-ordinate buying for decentralized, geographically dispersed business units. Selling to such firms involves:

- obtaining acceptance of the company's products at the buyer's headquarters
- negotiating long-term supply contracts
- maintaining favourable buyer–seller relationships at various levels in the buying organization
- establishing first-class customer service.

This depth of selling activity frequently calls for the expertise of a range of personnel in the supplying company in addition to the salesperson. It is for this reason that many companies serving national accounts employ team selling.

Team selling involves the combined efforts of salespeople, product specialists, engineers, sales managers and even directors if the buyer's decision-making unit includes personnel of equivalent rank. Team selling provides a method of responding to the various commercial, technical and psychological requirements of large buying organizations.

Companies are increasingly structuring both external and internal staff on the basis of specific responsibility for accounts. Examples of such companies are those in the electronics industry, where internal desk staff are teamed up with outside staff around key customers. An in-depth understanding of the buyer's decision-making unit is developed by the salesperson being able to develop a relationship with a large number of individual decision-makers. In this way, marketing staff can be kept informed of customer requirements, enabling them to improve products and services, and plan effective communications.

Where companies offer similar high levels of product quality, the quality of an ongoing relationship becomes a means of gaining a competitive advantage. Putting resources into the development and continuation of a relationship with customers is most appropriate where purchases involve a high level of risk, where a stream of product and service benefits is produced and consumed over a period of time or where the costs associated with repeat purchase can be reduced by close relationships.[39] The success of the German machine tool industry is attributable not only to excellent product quality but also its capability and willingness to engage in long-term relationship building through first-rate after-sales service.[40]

How to build relationships

A key decision that marketers have to make is the degree of effort to put into relationship building.[41] Some organizations' customers may desire more distant contact because they prefer to buy on price and do not perceive major benefits accruing to closer ties. A supplier that attempts a relationship-building programme may be wasting resources in this situation. However, in most situations there is some potential benefit to be gained from relationship development. Indeed, as Marketing in Action 4.3 describes, there has been a movement towards the establishment of buyer–supplier partnerships and a concomitant reduction in the number of accredited suppliers.

Some features of close partnership relationships are that the parties adapt their processes and products to achieve a better match with each other, and share information and experience, which reduces insecurity and uncertainty. Sharing information and experience demonstrates commitment leading to trust and a better atmosphere for future business.[45] Some companies are using the Internet to allow their customers to share information. For example, John Deere, the agricultural machinery manufacturer, has promoted virtual communities among farmers with similar interests.[46]

A key method of building relationships and goodwill is the provision of *customer services*. The supplier—at zero or nominal cost to the customer—gives the latter help in carrying out its operations. This help can take a number of forms, as described below.[47]

Technical support

This can take the form of research and development co-operation, before-sales or after-sales service, and providing training to the customer's staff. The supplier is thus enhancing the customer's know-how and productivity.

Expertise

Suppliers can provide expertise to their customers. Examples include the offer of design and engineering consultancies, and dual selling, where the customer's salesforce is supplemented by the supplier. The customer benefits through acquiring extra skills at low cost.

4.3 marketing in action

Changes in Buyer–Seller Relationships

The ability to blend technology with customer requirements is an important success factor for many business-to-business companies, but managing customer relationships is also critical. Increasingly, suppliers have been focusing on improving customer relationships as a method of differentiating themselves from their rivals. To do so they must recognize and take advantage of changes in the environment that have an impact on such relationships. For example, new technology is facilitating electronic business-to-business commerce by allowing much easier and cheaper communications between companies. Web services technology provides a powerful glue that unifies databases and applications across organizations into a single smart information system. Dell Computers Corporation, for example, has saved up to £130 million (€187 million) by using web services to improve co-ordination between its factories and its parts suppliers. Inventories have been significantly reduced and speed of delivery accelerated.

Many companies, including ICL, are introducing a system of *accredited vendor status* to suppliers that pass the buyer's test of 'supply-worthiness'. Toyota UK, for example, assess supplier capabilities on four criteria:

1. the attitude and capability of management
2. the quality of manufacturing facilities and the level of investment in technology
3. the system for quality control
4. capability in research and development.

The chosen suppliers are left in no doubt about the standards expected of them and the necessity to earn long-term relationships. To aid the relationship-building process Toyota UK has set up *technology help teams* to help suppliers understand what its requirements are and how to go about meeting them.

Peugeot and Renault run joint audits to maintain quality at component suppliers. Suppliers are graded according to their ability to conduct their own quality control. Suppliers are also expected to deliver more frequently to meet just-in-time control requirements in both groups' factories.

A trend in buyer–seller relationships is to reduce the number of suppliers so that close relationships can be built. Rank Xerox, for example, reduced its number of suppliers from 5000 to 500 when it found that it used nine times more suppliers than Japanese rivals like Canon. Similarly, Nissan has reduced its number of suppliers from 1145 to 600. It buys only from firms that can supply on a global basis, be cost efficient and work closely with its engineers to develop new models.

Lean and flexible manufacturing has also meant changes in buyer–seller relationships. The maturing of the market for high-tech products such as video recorders has meant that production and delivery processes can be stabilized, with resultant cost savings. Sony UK, for example, replaced the practice of keeping a month's supply of stock with a 48-hour ordering system, and reduced by two-thirds the time taken to assemble a video recorder. Lean production requires product cycles to be long to allow integration of production processes and co-ordination among component suppliers, but marketing benefits can accrue. Sony UK had problems in the past when a particular colour television set had sold out. With shorter production times and fast parts supply, however, Sony can now quickly change its production plans to counter such occurrences.

Just-in-time manufacturing was once seen as a Japanese innovation which gave that country's car manufacturers a competitive edge. Now 'supplier parks'—where component makers are grouped around car plants—are commonplace worldwide, reducing delivery costs and giving the geographical proximity that aids the building of buyer–seller relationships.

Based on: Bannister (1999);[42] Milne and Bannister (1999);[43] Hayward (2002)[44]

Resource support

Suppliers can support the resource base of customers by extending credit facilities, giving low-interest loans, agreeing to co-operative promotion and accepting reciprocal buying practices where the supplier agrees to buy goods from the customer. The net effect of all of these activities is a reduced financial burden for the customer.

Service levels

Suppliers can improve their relationships with customers by improving the level of service offered to them. This can involve providing more reliable delivery, fast or just-in-time delivery, setting up computerized reorder systems, offering fast, accurate quotes and reducing defect levels. In so doing the customer gains by lower inventory costs, smoother production runs and lower warranty costs. By creating systems that link the customer to the supplier—for example, through recorder systems or just-in-time delivery—*switching costs* may be built, making it more expensive to change supplier.[48]

Advances in technology are providing opportunities to improve service levels. E-Marketing 4.1 describes how the use of electronic data interchange (EDI) and the Internet offers the potential to enhance service provision.

Risk reduction

This may involve free demonstrations, the offer of products for trial at zero or low cost to the customer, product and delivery guarantees, preventative maintenance contracts, swift complaint handling and proactive follow-ups. These activities are designed to provide customers with reassurance.

Review

1 **The characteristics of organizational buying**
- The characteristics are based on the nature and size of customers, the complexity of buying, the use of economic and technical choice criteria, the risky nature of selling and buying, buying to specific requirements, reciprocal buying, derived demand and negotiations.

2 **The dimensions of organizational buying**
- The dimensions are who buys, how they buy, the choice criteria used, and where and when they buy.

3 **The nature and marketing implications of who buys, how organizations buy and the choice criteria used to evaluate products**
- Who buys: there are six roles in the decision-making unit—initiators, users, deciders, influencers, buyers and gatekeepers. Marketers need to identify who plays each role, target communication at them and develop products to satisfy their needs.
- How organizations buy: the decision-making process has up to seven stages— recognition of problem (need), determination of specification and quantity of needed item, search for and qualification of potential sources, acquisition and analysis of proposals, evaluation of proposals and selection of supplier(s), selection of an order routine, and performance feedback and evaluation. Marketers can influence need recognition and gain competitive advantage by entering the process early.
- Choice criteria can be technical, economic, social (organizational) and personal. Marketers need to understand the choice criteria of the different members of the decision-making unit and target communications accordingly. Other marketing mix decisions such as product design will also depend on an understanding of choice criteria. Choice criteria can change over time necessitating a change in the marketing mix.

4 **The influences on organizational buying behaviour—the buy class, product type and purchase importance—and their marketing implications**
- The buy class consists of three types: new task, straight rebuy and modified rebuy. For new task, there can be large gains for suppliers entering the decision process early, but heavy investment is usually needed. For straight rebuys, the in-supplier should build a defensible position to keep out new potential suppliers. For out-suppliers, a key task is to reduce the risk of change for the buyers so that a modified rebuy will result.
- Product types consist of materials, components, plant and equipment, and maintenance items. Marketers need to recognize that the people who take part in the purchase decision usually change according to product type, and channel communications accordingly.
- The importance of purchase depends on the costs involved and the uncertainty (risk) regarding the decision. For very important decisions, heavy investment is likely to be required on the part of suppliers, and risk-reduction strategies (e.g. guarantees) may be needed to reduce uncertainty.

5 **The developments in purchasing practice: just-in-time and centralized purchasing, reverse marketing and leasing**

- Just-in-time practices aim to minimize stocks by organizing a supply system that provides materials and components as they are required. Potential gains are reduced purchasing, inventory and inspection costs, improved product design, streamlined delivery, reduced production downtime and improved quality.
- Centralized purchasing encourages purchasing specialists to concentrate on a small group of products. This often increases the power of the purchasing department and results in a move to long-term relationships with suppliers.
- Reverse marketing places the initiative with the buyer, who attempts to persuade the supplier to produce exactly what the buyer wants. Suppliers need to be responsive to buyers and provide for them an opportunity to build long-term relationships and develop new products.
- Leasing may give financial benefits to customers and may attract customers that otherwise could not afford the product.

6 **The nature of relationship marketing and how to build customer relationships**

- Relationship marketing concerns the shift from activities associated with attracting customers to activities concerned with current customers and how to retain them. A key element is the building of trust between buyers and sellers.
- Relationship building can be enhanced by the provision of customer services including giving technical support, expertise, resource support, improving service levels and using risk-reduction strategies.

7 **The development of buyer–seller relationships**

- Relationships are established and developed through a five-stage process: pre-relationship stage, early stage, development stage, long-term stage and final stage.
- The pre-relationship stage is characterized by customer concern about the risk of change and the distance between itself and the potential supplier.
- The early stage is characterized by potential suppliers attempting to reduce risk of change and to build trust.
- The development stage is characterized by the reduction of uncertainty and distance.
- The long-term stage is characterized by shared mutual dependence and high levels of commitment.
- The final stage is characterized by industry codes of practice that stipulate 'the right way to do business'. Processes have become 'institutionalized'.
- Each stage requires different actions by suppliers based on the different requirements of customers.

Key terms

decision-making process the stages that organizations and people pass through when purchasing a physical product or service

decision-making unit (DMU) a group of people within an organization who are involved in the buying decision (also known as the buying centre)

interaction approach an approach to buyer–seller relations that treats the relationships as taking place between two active parties

just-in-time (JIT) this concept aims to minimize stocks by organizing a supply system that provides materials and components as they are required

life-cycle costs all the components of costs associated with buying, owning and using a physical product or service

modified rebuy where a regular requirement for the type of product exists and the buying alternatives are known but sufficient change (e.g. a delivery problem) has occurred to require some alteration to the normal supply procedure

new task refers to the first time purchase of a product or input by an organization

relationship marketing the process of creating, maintaining and enhancing strong relationships with customers and other stakeholders

reverse marketing the process whereby the buyer attempts to persuade the supplier to provide exactly what the organization wants

straight rebuy refers to a purchase by an organization from a previously approved supplier of a previously purchased item

team selling the use of the combined efforts of salespeople, product specialists, engineers, sales managers and even directors to sell products

total quality management the set of programmes designed to constantly improve the quality of physical products, services and processes

value analysis a method of cost reduction in which components are examined to see if they can be made more cheaply

Internet exercise

Buying aircraft is an expensive business. In some cases, airlines can only afford to lease aircraft instead. Visit some of the following websites to assess the organizational buying behaviour of airlines when purchasing aircraft.

Visit: www.airbus.com
www.boeing.com
www.bombardier.com

Questions

(a) Identify the types of factor that may influence airlines' buying behaviour.
(b) Which of these factors do you believe is the strongest influencer of airlines' purchase behaviour?
(c) Do you believe that aircraft manufacturers need to advertise? Why?

Visit the Online Learning Centre at www.mcgraw-hill.co.uk/textbooks/jobber for more Internet exercises.

Study questions

1. What are the six roles that form the decision-making unit (DMU) for the purchase of an organizational purchase? What are the marketing implications of the DMU?

2. Why do the choice criteria used by different members of the DMU often change with the varying roles?

3. What are creeping commitment and lockout criteria? Why are they important factors in the choice of supplier?

4. Explain the difference between a straight rebuy, a modified rebuy and a new task purchasing situation. What implications do these concepts have for the marketing of industrial products?

5. Why is relationship management important in many supplier–customer interactions? How can suppliers build close relationships with organizational customers?

6. Explain the meaning of reverse marketing. What implications does it have for suppliers?

When you have read this chapter log on to the Online Learning Centre at www.mcgraw-hill.co.uk/textbooks/jobber to explore chapter-by-chapter test questions, links and further online study tools for marketing.

case seven

Winters Company

Mr J. Herbert, a trainee salesman with Winters Company Ltd, observed the following incident while spending part of his introductory tour of the company in the purchasing department.

Mr Jones, the purchasing officer of Winters, received a request from his company's R&D department to order 100 fluidic drives from the Gillis Company. The attached documentation indicated that the R&D department had recently had a lot of contact with representatives of Gillis; in fact, a price and delivery date had been quoted for this order by Gillis. In effect, Mr Jones was being asked only to rubber-stamp the company's approval of an arrangement arrived at between R&D and Gillis.

Mr Jones phoned the R&D department on the pretext that the information on the requisition was incomplete, but in fact he did so in order to establish whether or not the drives were, as he believed, standard ones also made by several other well-known companies. The information gained from R&D confirmed his opinion that the drives were standard items, but he also learned that a Gillis representative had given R&D a lot of help with technical problems associated with the installation of the drives, and that Mr Smith, head of R&D, therefore felt that Gillis was entitled to the order. However, instead of ordering the components from Gillis, Mr Jones asked three other companies, who also listed these drives in their catalogues, to quote price and delivery dates for a batch of 100.

At about this time, Mr Scott, the production manager of Winters, was discussing with Mr Jones the difficulties he was having in keeping production up to schedule because of late deliveries of some plastic components from a supplier whose products he considered were of above-average quality. In the course of this discussion Mr Scott commented, 'The situation reminds me of the problem we had with Gillis Company about two years ago when they were about four weeks late.'

When the quotations from the three other companies arrived, Mr Jones assembled them and compared them with the Gillis figures (see Table C7.1). His assessment of the situation was that the order should go to the Richards Company. The fact that the total cost of the order would then be less than £5000 (€7200), and thus within the limits in which he was allowed to operate without higher authority, was an added incentive for him to make this choice as it saved him having to prepare a special report to explain his decision.

Mr Herbert, who was kept fully informed of all the above developments by Mr Jones, wondered what this situation could teach him about the problems he might face when selling to industrial customers.

Table C7.1 Competing quotations

Company	Price per unit (£)	Delivery (from date of order)
Gillis	51.00	2 months
Herman	49.50	3 months
Richards	48.00	10 weeks
Satilmatic	51.50	9 weeks

Questions

1. Identify the decision-making unit (DMU), the roles played and the choice criteria of each player.

2. Why did different decision-making unit players use different choice criteria when evaluating potential suppliers?

This case was prepared by David Jobber, Professor of Marketing, University of Bradford.

case eight

Morris Services

Claire Morris, managing director of Morris Services, a small company providing cleaning services to industry, had reluctantly come to the conclusion that a personal computer was needed for her business. Her immediate problem was cash-flow monitoring; a year ago she had fallen into cash-flow difficulties because, for a variety of reasons, her short-term expenditures exceeded her receipts. Consequently she was looking for a computer that would store information on outgoings and receipts so that, at the touch of a button, she could monitor cash flow at any time. Also, she felt that a computer would be useful for her secretary, who was forever complaining of not having word-processing facilities.

She viewed her visit to a local computer outlet with trepidation, as she knew little about computers. For support she invited along her secretary, Helen Berry, although she didn't know much about computers either. They approached a salesperson seated behind a desk.

Claire: Good morning, I'm looking for a personal computer for my business.

Salesperson: I think we can help here. We have a wide range of computers, as you can see. I have to go to the storeroom for a few minutes but here are some brochures. Have a look around and see if there is one that you like.

The salesperson hands over the brochures, and leaves Claire and Helen alone in the shop.

Helen: These look really complicated. Why are some bigger than others?

Claire: I don't know. Perhaps the bigger they are, the more they can do. What worries me are all these buttons. I don't know what half of them mean.

After five minutes the salesperson returns.

Salesperson: Sorry about that, but I had to sort out a delivery problem. Have you seen anything you like?

Claire: No. They all look alike to me.

Salesperson: Don't worry. You say you want a computer for work. I have just the one for you. If you come this way I would like to show it to you.

Claire and Helen follow.

Salesperson: This incorporates the latest technology. This machine is based on the Intel 1.8 GHz Pentium IV processor. It has 256 megabytes of SD RAM and a 20 Gb hard drive. It contains ATI's mobility Radeon graphics card and the latest DVD-ROM drive. The machine comes with nine software applications to cover all business requirements.

Claire: I bet it's expensive. How much will it cost?

Salesperson: Not as much as you think. The price of this machine is £1000, which is good value given its high-tech specification.

Claire: I have seen advertisements in newspapers for computers for a lot less than that.

Salesperson: Yes, but do they have hi-spec graphic facilities and Pentium IV technology?

Claire: I have no idea but they looked fairly good to me.

Helen: It looks quite complicated to use.

Salesperson: No problem at all. My 10-year-old daughter uses one of these. But I've left the best until last: if you buy this month we are giving an extra 10 per cent discount reducing the price to only £900. What a bargain!

Claire: Actually my business is quite small. I only employ 10 people. I do not think it is ready for a computer yet. Perhaps when we grow a little we'll be ready. Anyway, thanks for your time.

Claire and Helen retired to a nearby snack bar for coffee. They discussed their reactions to the sales encounter. Undismayed, they decided to visit another computer shop to give themselves one last chance to buy a computer.

Questions

1. What choice criteria were important to Claire and Helen?

2. Did the salesperson understand what was important to the customers? If not, why not? Did the salesperson make any other mistakes? Why do you think the salesperson chose that particular computer model?

3. You are the salesperson in the second shop they are about to visit. Based on your knowledge of buyer behaviour, plan how you would conduct the sales interview.

This case was prepared by David Jobber, Professor of Marketing, University of Bradford.

chapter five

The marketing environment

> **"** Change is the only constant. **"** A. TOFFLER

Learning Objectives

This chapter explains:

1 The nature of the marketing environment

2 The distinction between the microenvironment and the macroenvironment

3 The impact of economic, social, political and legal, physical and technological forces on marketing decisions

4 Social responsibility and marketing ethics

5 How to conduct environmental scanning

6 How companies respond to environmental change

A marketing-orientated firm looks outwards to the environment in which it operates, adapting to take advantage of emerging opportunities and to minimize potential threats. In this chapter we will examine the marketing environment and how to monitor it. In particular we will look at some of the major forces acting on companies, such as the economic, social, legal, physical and technological issues that affect corporate activities. Attention will be given to two recent developments that have implications for marketing management into the twenty-first century: the establishment of the single European market and the opportunities posed by the transition to market economics of central and eastern European countries such as Poland, Hungary and the former USSR.

The marketing environment consists of the actors and forces that affect a company's capability to operate effectively in providing products and services to its customers. It is useful to classify these forces into the microenvironment and the macroenvironment (see Fig. 5.1). The microenvironment consists of the actors in the firm's immediate environment that affect its capabilities to operate effectively in its chosen markets. The key actors are suppliers, distributors, customers and competitors. The macroenvironment consists of a number of broader forces that affect not only the company but also the other actors in the microenvironment. These can be grouped under economic, social/cultural, political/legal, ecological/physical and technological forces. These shape the character of the opportunities and threats facing a company, and yet are largely uncontrollable.

We have already examined the changes taking place between suppliers and their customers (Chapter 4) and the nature of the influences on customers (Chapters 3 and 4). Distribution and competitive factors will be examined in Chapters 17 and 18. Consequently this chapter will focus on the major macroeconomic forces that affect marketing decisions: economic, social/cultural, political/legal, ecological/physical and technological.

Economic forces

The *economic environment* can have a critical impact on the success of companies through its effect on supply and demand. Companies must choose those economic influences that are relevant to their business and monitor them. We will examine three major economic influences on the marketing environment of companies: economic growth and unemployment, the development and implications of the single European market, and the economic changes that are accompanying the transition to market economies of eastern bloc countries.

Economic growth and unemployment

The general state of a nation's and the world economy can have a profound effect on a company's prosperity. Economies tend to fluctuate according to the business cycle. The UK economy was depressed during the early 1980s, with low annual growth rates, but gathered momentum during the late 1980s only to be followed by a further spell of low growth and high unemployment during the early 1990s. The fortunes of many retail organizations, such as Body Shop and Next, closely mirrored this economic pattern. This was followed by a period of sustained growth since the late 1990s, with the worst excesses of boom and slump largely avoided. Nevertheless, by 2002, economic growth forecasts were revised downwards as the business cycle ran its course. A major marketing problem is predicting the next boom or slump. Investments made during periods of high growth can become huge cash drains if consumer spending suddenly falls. The problems facing many of the world's leading technology companies, such as Cisco Systems, Compaq and Intel, in the early 2000s were partly caused by this trap.

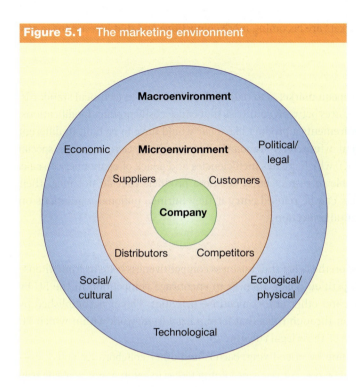

Figure 5.1 The marketing environment

Low growth rates are reflected in high unemployment levels, which in turn affect consumer spending power. As governments grapple with managing economies, unemployment levels in the European Union (EU) tend to be low, ranging from 2.4 per cent in Luxembourg to 11.4 per cent in Spain, with an average of 7.6 per cent across all countries in 2002.[1]

When times are good consumers tend to spend more heavily because of higher disposable income and greater job security. Luxury items such as upmarket cars, fashion items, consumer durables and houses benefit, and consumers spend more on services such as overseas holidays and restaurant meals. In times of economic recession, consumers tend to postpone discretionary spending and become more cost-conscious, shifting more of their spending to discount stores.

Development of the single European market

The Single European Act 1986 provided the foundation for a free internal market in the EU. The intention was to create a massive deregulated market of 320 million consumers by abolishing barriers to the free flow of products, services, capital and people among the member states. More recently, the Maastricht Treaty (1992), the Nice Treaty (2000) and the introduction of the Euro (2002) are all additional steps towards the development of full economic union. Clearly this development has the potential for creating opportunities and threats, and the changes it brings need to be monitored closely by marketers.

One objective was to improve economic performance by lowering the costs of operating throughout Europe. Barriers to competition are being reduced by removing physical, fiscal and technical barriers, and by establishing a strict competition policy.

Physical barriers

The single European market has reduced the number of barriers that restrict the movement of products and people. Transportation in the EU has been overburdened with regulations and excessive amounts of documentation. For example, a lorry travelling from Glasgow to Athens, a distance of 2368 miles, and crossing five national boundaries, including a sea crossing, would travel at an average of only eight miles per hour.[2] On average, lorry drivers spent 30 per cent of their time at border crossings just waiting or filling in as many as 200 forms. The European Commission estimated that such delays increased overall prices by 2 per cent and cut EU firms' profits by 25 per cent. Although border controls cannot be eliminated completely, the introduction in 1988 of the Single Administrative Document enabled 70 pieces of paperwork to be replaced by a single form.[3]

Fiscal barriers

Although differences in tax rates—e.g. value added tax (VAT)—still exist between member countries, the single European market has created greater freedom of capital movements.

This means that financial markets are becoming more competitive and that investment in any EU country is easier.

Technical barriers

An objective of the single European market is to reduce the differences in technical standards, testing and certification procedures between countries that cause costly product modifications. To comply with national requirements a product like a car would have to be built in different versions (e.g. to meet different windscreen standards in France and Germany, and special wiring requirements in the UK), which creates inefficiencies and a lack of economies of scale. However, countries are still able to restrict entry to those products that do not meet their *essential requirements*. Products can be refused entry if they infringe national regulations on health, safety and environmental protection.

Competition policy

EU competition policy is based on the belief that business competitiveness benefits from intense competition. The role of competition policy, then, is to encourage competition in the EU by removing restrictive practices and other anti-competitive activities. This is accomplished by tackling barriers to competition through rules that form a legal framework within which EU firms must operate. The objects of these legal rules are to:[4]

- prevent firms from colluding by price-fixing, cartels and other collaborative activities—competition is encouraged by preventing firms joining forces to act in a monopolistic way

- prevent firms from abusing a position of market dominance—firms are discouraged from taking such actions as monopoly and discriminatory pricing, which could harm small buyers with little bargaining power

- control the size that firms grow to through acquisition and merger—the objective is to prevent firms acquiring excessive market power through acquiring, or merging with, other firms within defined markets, and thereby reaping monopolistic profits

- restrict state aid to firms—it can be in a nation's interest for its government to give state aid to ailing firms within its boundaries; on a broader scale this can give artificial competitive advantages to recipient firms that may, for example, be able to charge lower prices than their unsupported rivals. Recipients may, also, be unfairly shielded from the full force of the competitive pressures affecting their markets.

The European Commission has been successful in disbanding and fining cartels. For example, cartel partners ABB Løgstør, Henss/Isoplus, Sigma and six other firms were fined for price-fixing, market-sharing and bid-rigging in the European insulated heating pipe market. Market dominance has also been successfully challenged, as when Italian cigarette producer and distributor AAMS was found to be abusing its dominant position for the wholesale distribution of cigarettes in Italy. AAMS was protecting its own sales by imposing restrictive distribution contracts on foreign manufacturers that limited the access of foreign cigarettes to the Italian market.[5]

Regarding mergers and acquisitions, some proposed mergers/acquisitions have been dropped while under EU investigation but before a final decision had been made (for example, the proposed merger between publishers Reed Elsevier and Wolters Kluwer). Some mergers have been blocked, such as the merger between UK tour operators Airtours and First Choice, and the proposed merger between Swedish truck, bus and coach builders Scania and Volvo. Other mergers/acquisitions have been approved but only with strict conditions. For example, Nestlé's acquisition of Perrier was approved subject to Nestlé selling a number of Perrier brands to encourage a third force to emerge in the French mineral market to compete with Nestlé and BSN.

EC approval of state aid is usually given as part of a restructuring or rescue package for ailing firms. The general principle is that such payments should be 'one-offs' to prevent uncompetitive firms being repeatedly bailed out by their governments. This has not always applied, however, with Air France being given financial assistance several times.[6] Overall, though, the level of state aid given to firms in most of the EU member states is declining.

Implications of the single European market

Although the full impact of the single European market is far from clear, there are a number of likely implications: scale building, reorganization, pan-European marketing, foreign investment by Japanese companies, and foreign investment by US companies.

Scale building

The single European market has created an internal market of 320 million consumers, compared with 220 million in the United States and 120 million in Japan.[7] This gives European industry an opportunity to organize on a scale large enough to compete with its main rivals in the USA and Japan. Many European high-technology industries suffer from a fragmented structure, making it difficult for them to keep pace with the research and development expenditures of foreign competitors. For example, in 1990 there were 11 companies battling for the $8 billion European market for central-office telephone exchanges, compared with only four in the USA.[8] In order to compete, European companies are forming strategic alliances to reduce the effects of market fragmentation. For example, Olivetti acquired Telecom Italia in 2001 in a deal worth almost $12 billion. Other European companies that wish to become world leaders are building scale (e.g. Unilever, Electrolux, Nestlé, Lufthansa and Deutsche Bank).

The period before 1993 saw a wave of mergers and acquisitions. Nestlé acquired Rowntree, the British chocolate company, and Buitoni, the Italian food company. Pearson and Elsevier have joined forces in the publishing industry. Banco de Bilbao and Banco Vizcaya have combined to become the only Spanish bank to rank among the top 30 in Europe. In consumer electronics, Philips acquired Grundig, the German television producer, and France's Thompson bought Thorn EMI's British television manufacturing arm. Mergers are not confined to the EU, however, with countries of the European Free Trade Association (EFTA) also feeling the effects. For example, Nokia of Finland has taken over a number of poor-performing consumer electronics companies in the EU, and consolidations in the Swedish paper industry have led to the establishment of producer groups like Stora Kopparbergs Bergslags and Svenska Cellulosa.

Reorganization

A second feature is the move towards new organization structures.[9] For example, Philips reorganized its consumer electronics business by replacing its 60-year-old structure of autonomous national subsidiaries—a Dutch Philips, a British Philips, etc.—with Europe-wide product-based businesses. Pilkington, Europe's second largest glass manufacturer, relocated its headquarters from St Helens in north-west England to Brussels, and at the same time reduced its head office staff from 500 to 130.[10] BSN, the French food giant, has aggressively rationalized its production of yoghurt to one plant near Lyon that supplies the entire European market. Jacobs Suchard, the Swiss packaged-foods manufacturer, has consolidated production of individual brands to specific factories to gain economies of scale. Electrolux rationalized its production of white goods, manufacturing all front-loading washing machines in Pordenone, Italy, all top loaders in Revin, France, and all microwave ovens in Luton, England.[11]

Pan-European marketing

There has been considerable debate about the extent to which the single European market will advance the cause of pan-European marketing. On the one hand, the increasing mobility of European consumers, the accelerating flow of information across borders and the publicity surrounding the introduction of the Euro has promoted a pan-European marketing approach; on the other, the persistence of local tastes and preferences means that the elimination of formal trade barriers may not bring about the standardization of marketing strategies between countries. Standardization appears to depend on product type. In the case of many industrial goods, consumer durables (such as cameras, toasters, watches and radios) and clothing (Gucci shoes, Benetton sweaters, Levi's jeans) standardization is well advanced. However, for fast-moving consumer goods such as food, standardization of products is more difficult to achieve because of local tastes. Even a global brand like McDonald's has to make concessions to national tastes—for example, in Norway, customers are offered a salmon sandwich invented to cater for Norwegian tastes, and in Italy, where demand for fresh foods is strong, there are salad bars.

Each element of the marketing mix may be affected by the changes accompanying the single European market, as outlined below.[12]

1. *Product*: as standards, testing and certification procedures harmonize, manufacturers should benefit by avoiding expensive product modifications and market entry delays (e.g. pharmaceuticals) due to different country-specific requirements. For example, Philips no longer has to produce seven types of television set to cope with different national standards in Europe. As cross-border segmentation of markets develops, new Euro-brands may be launched targeted at newly identified pan-European consumer segments. Patenting of products may become even more important because of the larger potential market.

2. *Price*: the European Commission has estimated that the price of goods and services throughout the EU could decrease by as much as 8 per cent. Quelch and Buzzell argue that the downward pressure on prices is caused by decreased costs, the opening up of public procurement contracts on broader competition, foreign investment that raises production capacity, more vigorous enforcement of anti-monopoly measures, and the general intensified competition resulting from the lowering of barriers.[13] The introduction of the Euro has raised levels of price transparency, enabling consumers to easily and accurately compare prices across the countries that have adopted the currency. The potential for parallel importing, whereby goods sold in different countries at varying prices are exported from low- to high-price countries may also depress price levels. A countervailing force may be that as European consumers become wealthier, quality rather than price becomes the major strategic weapon for producers.

3. *Promotion*: despite the attraction of a common advertising campaign (with different voice-overs) directed at 320 million Europeans, variations in tastes, attitudes and perceptions restrict its application. Even Coca-Cola, the ultimate 'one sight, one sound, one sell' global brand modifies the advertising of its other drinks, such as Fanta, to national markets. A study of advertising standardization practices by Whitelock and Kalpaxoglou concluded that many fast-moving consumer goods do not lend themselves readily to standardization, except for products that are not culture bound—for example, cosmetics.[14]

Also, a variation in business culture affects the behaviour of salespeople: the relaxed attitude to timekeeping at meetings in Spain contrasts sharply with German punctuality.

Furthermore, difficulties in sales promotional regulations mean that premiums (gifts), given as promotional items with products, and money-off vouchers are not allowed in Denmark but are perfectly acceptable in the UK or France.

(4) *Place*: Franchising is likely to increase as global companies link with local franchises, combining buying and marketing muscle with local know-how. European-wide competition between supermarkets is likely to increase. For example, companies like Ahold (the Netherlands), Aldi (Germany), Netto (Denmark) and Carrefour (France) have expanded across Europe.

In spite of these implications, the impact of the single European Market has not given rise to the anticipated tidal wave of change. For example, the restructuring of business has not take place at the pace that was expected across Europe.[15] It appears that the transformation of European industry will be a relatively slow and gradual process.

Foreign investment

The trade restrictions implicit in the creation of the single European market have encouraged foreign companies, notably from Japan and the USA to invest in EU countries. For example, major investments have been made by Japanese car manufacturers such as Nissan, Toyota and Honda (UK), Mitsubishi (the Netherlands), Suzuki (Spain) and Hewlett Packard (Ireland). These investments have added to the competitive rivalry within Europe.

Central and eastern Europe

Another major economic change that has far-reaching marketing implications is the move from centrally planned to market-driven economies by central and eastern European countries. The most obvious implication is the opening up of vast potential markets. The population of central and eastern Europe, including the former USSR—now the Confederation of Independent States (CIS)—is over 400 million, which is larger than the USA (220 million) and the EU (320 million). This opportunity needs to be tempered, of course, by the lower living standards, the low or negative economic growth rates and the political instability of some of these countries.

Nevertheless, with these central and eastern European countries accounting for around 15 per cent of world gross national product (GNP) and wage rates that are much lower than in Spain, Portugal and Greece, it represents not only an important market but also a major low-cost manufacturing opportunity.[16]

The result of such economic (and political) changes is the move by many central and eastern European countries to join the EU. Marketing in Action 5.1 discusses some of the implications for companies in such countries.

A key marketing question is the relative attractiveness of the former eastern bloc countries. These can be divided into two groups. The first includes Hungary, the Czech Republic, Poland and Slovenia, which are adjusting more rapidly to a market economy, and are the first countries in line to join an enlarged EU. They are also proving very attractive markets for foreign investment. The second group contains countries like Slovakia, Bulgaria, Romania, the Baltic States (Estonia, Latvia and Lithuania), Croatia, Bosnia and Yugoslavia. These are facing a range of difficulties and progressing more slowly.

Clearly the changes taking place in eastern bloc countries are having a major effect on supply and demand conditions. For many companies, monitoring the opportunities and threats that result may be a critical factor for long-term corporate survival.

5.1 marketing in action

Central and Eastern European Movement to the EU

The movement of such central and eastern European countries as Poland, the Czech Republic, Hungary, Lithuania, Latvia, Slovakia, Estonia and Slovenia to join the EU will add over 20 per cent to the EU's land mass and bring in over 70 million additional citizens, creating a market of over 450 million people. Its economy of £6 trillion (€8.6 trillion) will approach that of the USA.

One likely consequence is a rush of investment into countries like Poland, the Czech Republic, Hungary and the Baltic states, fuelled by low-cost manufacturing opportunities. For these countries, Ireland and Spain are models for what can be achieved by joining the EU. When Ireland enlisted in 1973, its GDP per capita was less than 70 per cent of the European average and unemployment was about 17 per cent. Now the country has a labour shortage and living standards are about average. 'It was joining the EU that ... made Ireland rich,' says Noreen Aher, an Irish dairy farmer. Spain, once under-developed, is now one of Europe's most vibrant regions. 'EU membership underpinned Spain's success,' claims Polish finance minister Grzegorz Kolodko, 'We want to do the same for Poland.'

Many central and eastern European businesses are welcoming the freedom that will come as the trade barriers come down. Kovinoplastika, a Slovenian manufacturer of sheet metal tool sets, casting machines and CAD-CAM equipment is anticipating rising sales. Its production costs are 10 to 15 per cent lower than those of its competitors in Germany and Austria, and new distributors in western Europe have already been established. Another company that is relishing taking advantage of the new market opportunities is Media Meru, an Estonian information technology company focused on Internet-based solutions. It can undercut the prices of its EU competitors because its labour costs are one-sixth of those in the EU.

Not every company will be a winner, though. Western manufacturers may have higher labour costs but their productivity levels are higher too. They also have better-developed distribution skills and are likely to continue to make inroads into central and eastern European markets.

Based on: Fairlamb and Rossant (2002)[17]

Social/cultural forces

Four key *social/cultural forces* that have implications for marketing are the changes in the demographic profile of the population, cultural differences within and between nations, social responsibility and marketing ethics, and the influence of the consumer movement. Each will now be examined.

Demographic forces

Demographic forces concern changes in population. Three major forces are world population growth, the changing age distribution and the rise in the number of two-income households.

World population growth

The population in developed economies is expected to be stable or shrinking, whereas countries of Africa, India, 'Other Asia' and Latin America are expected to account for over 90 per cent of the projected population increase during the twenty-first century (see Fig. 5.2).[18] As these countries grow more youthful, the developed countries will play host to an ageing population. In 2025, half the population of Europe will be over 45 years old. For the next decade, the world population is expected to grow by an average of 97 million per year.

Figure 5.2 World population growth

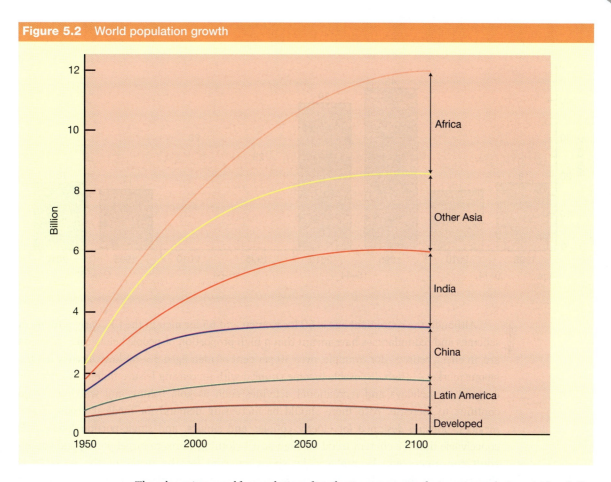

The changing world population distribution suggests that new markets outside of the developed economies may provide attractive opportunities, although the extent to which this force progresses will depend on a concomitant rise in income levels in the less developed world. The problem is that the major growth is predicted to be in countries that are already poor. Concern for their well-being is growing among people in the developed world. One response is the social marketing of family planning and birth control.[19] Companies such as Hewlett Packard and Citibank are increasingly focusing their attention on these so-called 'pre-markets' (i.e. those not yet sufficiently developed to be considered consumer markets). For example, Hewlett Packard aims to sell, lease or donate a billion dollars worth of computer equipment and services to these under-served markets.[20]

Age distribution

A major demographic change that will continue to affect the demand for products and services is the rising proportion of people over the age of 45 in the EU, and the decline in the younger age group. Figure 5.3 gives age distribution trends in the EU between 1995 and 2010. The fall in the 15–44-year-old group suggests a slowdown in sales of such products as CDs, denim jeans and housing. However, the rise in over-45s creates substantial marketing opportunities because of their high level of per capita income. They have much lower commitments on mortgage repayments than younger people, tend to benefit from inheritance wealth, are healthier than ever before, and hold the highest proportion of building society funds in the UK. In France, for example, the average per capita disposable income for households headed by a retired person is now higher than the average for all households, and people over 60 who constitute 18 per cent of the population consume more than 22 per cent of the French gross domestic product (GCP).[21]

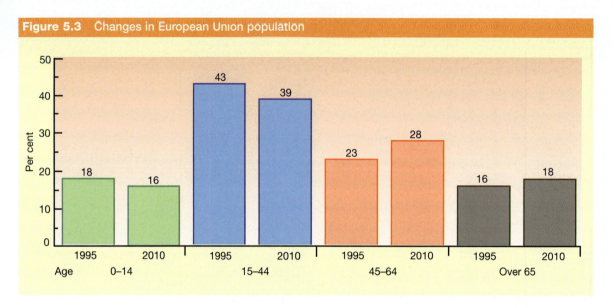

Figure 5.3 Changes in European Union population

Although the retirement age is 60 for women and 65 for men in the UK, early retirement schemes and redundancies have meant that a high proportion of people below this age group are, in effect, retired—for example, over 30 per cent of men aged 55–64 have already left the labour market.[22] High disposable income coupled with increasing leisure time mean that the demand for holidays and recreational activities such as golf, fishing and walking should continue to increase. Also there should be increasing demand for medical products and services, housing designed for elderly couples and singles, and single-portion foods. It is conceivable that the current trend for high-street clothing stores to target young and young-adult consumers will be replaced by shops catering for the tastes of the over-50s.[23] Understanding the needs of the over-45s presents a huge marketing opportunity, so that products and services can be created that possess the differential advantages valued by these people. In reality it is likely that there are a number of subgroups according to age band, which will allow market segmentation to be used. The overall implication of these trends is that many consumer companies may need to reposition their product and service offerings to take account of the rise in 'grey' purchasing power.

Two-income households

Over half of the couples with dependent children in the UK are dual-earner families. This is very different from the time when women were supported to work in the home, and only men engaged in paid employment. The rise of two-income households among professional and middle-class households means that this market segment has high disposal income, leading to reduced price sensitivity and the capacity to buy luxury furniture and clothing products (e.g. upmarket furniture and clothing) and expensive services (e.g. foreign holidays, restaurant meals). Also the combination of high income and busy lives has seen a boom in connoisseur convenience foods. Marks & Spencer, in particular, has catered for this market very successfully. Demand for childcare and homecare facilities has also risen.

Cultural forces

Culture is the combination of traditions, taboos, values and basic attitudes of the whole society in which an individual lives. A number of distinctive subcultures in the UK provide a rich tapestry of lifestyles and the creation of new markets. The Asian population, for example, has provided restaurants and stores supplying food from that part of the world. This influence is now seen in supermarkets, where Asian foods are readily available and multinationals such as Campbell Foods market 'Tastes of the World' products such as its premium-priced Indian chicken korma soup.

Within Europe, *cultural differences* have implications for the way in which business is conducted. Humour in business life is acceptable in the UK, Italy, Greece, the Netherlands and Spain but less commonplace in France and Germany. These facts of business life need to be recognized when interacting with European customers.

A study by Mole examined business culture in the EU and the USA.[24] Management styles were analysed using two dimensions: type of leadership and organization. Figure 5.4 shows the position of each of the 14 nations according to these two characteristics. Individual leadership (autocratic, directive) is to be found in Spain and France, whereas organic leadership style (democratic, equalitarian) tends to be found in Italy and the Netherlands. Systematic organization (formal, mechanistic) is found in Germany, Denmark and the Netherlands, while organic companies (informal, social) are more likely to exist in Spain, Portugal and Greece.

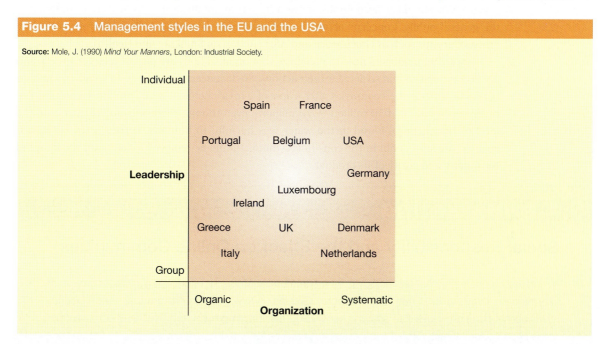

Figure 5.4 Management styles in the EU and the USA

Source: Mole, J. (1990) *Mind Your Manners*, London: Industrial Society.

Based on the Mole survey, Wolfe describes business life in Italy, Spain and the Netherlands.[25] As Fig. 5.4 shows, Italian organizations tend to be informal, with democratic leadership. Decisions are taken informally, usually after considerable personal contact and discussion. Italian managers are flexible improvisers who have a temperamental aversion to forecasting and planning. Interpersonal contact with deciders and influencers in the decision-making unit (DMU) is crucial for suppliers. Finding the correct person to talk to is not easy since DMUs tend to be complex, with authority vested in trusted individuals outside of the apparent organizational structure. Suppliers must demonstrate commitment to a common purpose with their Italian customers.

In Spain, on the other hand, business is typified by the family firm where the leadership style is autocratic and the organizational system informal. Communications tend to be vertical, with little real teamwork. Important purchasing decisions are likely to be passed to top management for final approval, but good personal relationships with middle management are vital to prevent them blocking approaches.

Leadership in the Netherlands is more democratic, although organizational style tends to be systematic, with rigorous management systems designed to involve multilevel consensus decision-making. Buying is, therefore, characterized by large DMUs and long decision-making processes as members attempt to reach agreement without conflict or one-sided outcomes.

Cultural differences between European consumers must also be appreciated. The German preference for locally brewed beer has proved a major barrier to entry for foreign brewers, such as Guinness, which have attempted to penetrate that market. The slower-than-expected take-off of the Euro-Disney complex near Paris was partly attributed to the French consumer's reluctance to accede to the US concept of spending a lot of money on a one-day trip to a single site. Once there, the French person, being an individualist, 'hates being taken by the hand and led around'.[26]

Social responsibility and marketing ethics

Companies need to be aware that they have a responsibility to society that is beyond their legal responsibilities. **Social responsibility** refers to the ethical principle that a person or organization should be accountable for how its acts might affect the physical environment and the general public. Concerns about the environment and public welfare are represented by pressure groups such as Greenpeace and ASH (Action on Smoking and Health).

Marketing managers need to recognize that organizations are part of a larger society and are accountable to that society for their actions. Such concerns led Perrier to recall 160 million bottles of water in 120 countries after traces of a toxic chemical were found in 13 bottles. The recall cost a total of £50 million (€72 million), even though there was no evidence that the level of the chemical found in the water was harmful to humans. Perrier acted because it believed the least doubt in the consumers' minds should be removed to maintain the image of the quality and purity of its product.

5.1 e-marketing

Social Responsibility and the Effect on Online Communities

An interesting use of Internet technology is as a communication medium for communities or groups of like-minded individuals. Sites like Google Groups (www.google.com/groups) and Usenet (www.usenet.com) allow users to search over 30,000 discussion groups and post their comments in areas of particular interest. Almost every subject is catered for and, if it is not, it is simple to set up your own interest group—why not try it?

Companies are conscious of the power of online communities. America Online (AOL) had accumulated so many disgruntled users at one point that these users set up their own site called AOL Sucks (www.aolsucks.com). Its main objective was to spread the 'bad word' about AOL. Bad news travels seven times faster than good news, and the presence of AOL Sucks soon became a major cause for concern for the AOL management team. So much so that AOL spent a long time on AOL Sucks to 'learn' what it should do better. A search on a well-known company more often than not results in finding a prominent site of dissenters.

Online discussion groups and e-mail were two of the main methods used to organize anti-globalization rallies with devastating effect in Seattle, and at other World Trade Organization and G7 meetings. Much to the chagrin of the authorities this style of organization was quick, effective and almost impossible to monitor.

Companies are increasingly conscious of the need to communicate their socially responsible activities. The term 'green marketing' is used to describe marketing efforts to produce, promote and reclaim environmentally sensitive products.[27]

Online communities of like-minded people can foster social responsibility. E-marketing 5.1 considers the relationship between social responsibility and the use of Internet technology.

Social responsibility is no longer an optional extra but a key part of business strategy that comes under close scrutiny from pressure groups, private shareholders and institutional investors, some of whom manage ethical investment funds. Companies are increasingly producing corporate social responsibility reports to communicate their activities to these key audiences. Ethical Marketing in Action 5.1 examines the practice of social reporting.

5.1 ethical marketing in action

Social Reporting

No longer are companies judged solely by their financial success. The interest taken by such groups as environmental agencies, journalists, private and institutional investors, government bodies and employees in the social performance of companies means that the need for a well-presented social report has moved up the corporate agenda. Some companies employ consultants such as PricewaterhouseCoopers or KPMG to conduct independent audits of their social performance. Such an audit often includes surveys of employees and other stakeholders, and can throw up some surprising results, as when a Body Shop survey showed 8 per cent of suppliers 'strongly disagreed' with the statement that they had never encountered unethical behaviour from Body Shop employees. This has resulted in the introduction of a code of conduct for Body Shop purchasers.

A growing number of European companies are providing information about how well they are performing on issues relating to employees, local communities and society at large. The upswing in social reporting has been driven by the FTSE4Good and Dow Jones Sustainability indices, and the emergence of 'ethical oscars'. Recent winners include the Co-op Bank, Novo Nordisk, BAA, British Telecom, Rio Tinto, Shell and BP.

Social audits normally take the form of printed reports, but observers believe that these will be replaced by the Internet as the main communication medium. The EMI Group has already moved in this direction, using a bi-media approach: a short printed summary report allows readers access to key points but also acts as a signpost for more detailed information to be found on EMI's website. The advantages of the Internet are that it is easy to update, cost effective to distribute, searchable, swiftly produced and environmentally friendly.

Whatever the medium used, there are a few key guidelines that can enhance the quality of a social report:

- gain credibility by providing hard evidence, full facts and open disclosure
- hard evidence should be verified independently
- trust should be sought by honestly presenting both the good and the bad
- design should be uncluttered and should reflect the company's personality and style
- presentation should not rely on dull facts—these need inspiration and character to engage the reader and add credibility
- social reporting should be placed within the context of the overall business strategy
- an action plan should be presented, and feedback encouraged and listened to.

Based on: Buxton (2000);[28] Slavin (2000);[29] Anonymous (2002);[30] Crowe (2001)[31]

Cause-related marketing works well when the business and charity have a similar target audience. For example, Nambarrie Tea Company, a Northern Ireland winner of the annual Business in the Community award for excellence in cause-related marketing, chose to sponsor the breast cancer agency Action Cancer. The company and the charity targeted women aged 16–60. In a two-month period, Nambarrie released 100,000 specially designed packs promoting its sponsorship of Action Cancer and covered media costs for a TV advertising campaign. This generated income of over £200,000 (€288,000).[32]

Companies are becoming more proactive in this acceptance of social responsibility through the practice of cause-related marketing. This is a commercial activity by which businesses and charities or causes form a partnership with each other to market an image, good or service for mutual benefit. As consumers increasingly demand greater accountability and responsibility from businesses so companies such as Procter & Gamble, Tesco, Cadbury, Schweppes, Barclays, Diageo and Lever Brothers have all incorporated major cause-related marketing programmes into their marketing activities.

A set of cause-related marketing principles has been developed by Business in the Community, as listed below.[33]

(1) Integrity: behaving honestly and ethically.

(2) Transparency: misleading information could cast doubt on the equity of the partnership.

(3) Sincerity: consumers need to be convinced about the strength and depth of a cause-related marketing partnership.

(4) Mutual respect: the partner and its values must be appreciated and respected.

(5) Partnership: each partner needs to recognize the opportunities and threats the relationship presents.

(6) Mutual benefit: for the relationship to be sustainable, both sides must benefit.

Cause-related marketing is often focused on consumers, but social responsibility also concerns the environment. Six environmental issues will be discussed later in this chapter when examining physical forces on companies; these are the use of environmentally friendly ingredients in products, recyclable and non-wasteful packaging, protection of the ozone layer, animal testing of new products, pollution, and energy conservation. We will now turn our attention to a related issue: marketing ethics.

Ethics are the moral principles and values that govern the actions and decisions of an individual or group.[34] They involve values about right and wrong conduct. There can be a distinction between the legality and ethicality of marketing decisions. Ethics concern personal moral principles and values, while laws reflect society's principles and standards that are enforceable in the courts.

Not all unethical practices are illegal. For example, it is not illegal to include genetically modified (GM) ingredients in products sold in supermarkets. However, some organizations, such as Greenpeace, believe it is unethical to sell GM products when their effect on health has not been scientifically proven. Such concerns have led supermarket chains such as Iceland and Sainsbury's to remove GM foods from their own-brand products.

Ethical principles reflect the cultural values and norms of society. Norms guide what ought to be done in a particular situation. For example, being truthful is regarded as good. This societal norm may influence marketing behaviour. Hence, since it is good to be truthful, deceptive, untruthful advertising should be avoided. Often unethical behaviour may be clear-cut but, in other cases deciding what is ethical is highly debatable. Ethical dilemmas arise when two principles or values conflict. For example, Ben & Jerry's, the US ice-cream firm was a leading member of the Social Venture Network in San Francisco, a group that promotes ethical standards in business. A consortium, Meadowbrook Lane Capital, was part of this group and was formed to raise enough capital to make Ben & Jerry's a private company again. However, its bid was lower than that made by the Anglo-Dutch food multinational Unilever NV. If Ben & Jerry's stayed true to its ethical beliefs it would have accepted the Meadowbrook bid. On the other hand, if the company wished to do the best financially for its shareholders it would accept the Unilever bid. It faced an ethical dilemma because one of its values and preferences inhibited the achievement of the other. Financial considerations won the day: the Unilever bid was accepted.[35]

Many ethical dilemmas derive from a conflict between profits and business actions. For example, by using child labour, the cost of producing products is kept low and profit margins are raised. Nevertheless, this has not stopped companies such as Reebok from monitoring their overseas production of sporting goods to ensure that no child labour is used.

Because of the importance of marketing ethics, many of the chapters in the book end with a discussion of ethical issues. For example, Chapter 8, on managing products, finishes with an examination of product safety and planned obsolescence issues.

The consumer movement

The *consumer movement* is a collection of individuals, organizations and groups whose objective is to protect the rights of consumers. For example, the Consumers' Association in the UK campaigns for consumers and provides information about products, often on a comparative basis that allows consumers to make more informed choices between products and services. This information is published in *Which?*, the association's magazine.

Besides providing unbiased product testing and campaigning against unfair business practices, the consumer movement has been active in areas such as product quality and safety, and information accuracy. Notable successes have been the campaign for real ale, improvements in car safety, the stipulation that advertisements for credit facilities must display the true interest charges (annual percentage rate, APR), and health warnings on cigarette packets and advertisements.

Consumer groups can influence production processes. For example, pressure from environmental movements in both Finland and Germany on UPM-Kymmene, Finland's largest company and Europe's biggest paper-making firm, ensured that replanting of new trees matches felling. German customers (which constitute the firm's biggest market) such as Springer write clauses on forest sustainability and biodiversity in their contracts with paper companies.[36]

Marketing management should not consider the consumer movement a threat to business but an opportunity to create new product and service offerings to meet the needs of emerging market segments. For example, in the detergent market brands have been launched that are more environmentally friendly (this issue will be explored in more detail when we examine the physical environment later in this chapter).

Political/legal forces

Political and legal forces can influence marketing decisions by determining the rules by which business can be conducted. Close relationships with politicians are often cultivated by organizations both to monitor political moods and also to influence them. The cigarette industry, for example, has a vested interest in maintaining close ties with government to counter proposals from pressure groups such as ASH (Action on Smoking and Health), which demand that cigarette advertising is banned. Companies sometimes make sizeable contributions to the funds of political parties in an attempt to maintain favourable relationships.

The relationships between government and business organizations can have major implications not only for the respective parties, but also other companies. An example was the alleged corruption connected with a large order given to the Swedish firm Bofors by the Indian Defence Ministry. Not only was Bofors affected (it has since withdrawn from the market), but other Swedish firms in India (Ericsson, ABB and Uri Civil) faced serious problems because of the scandal.[37]

Political action, then, through legislation and less formal directives, can have a profound influence on business conduct. As we saw in Chapter 4, the government and its agencies form a massive market for producers and services, and so they can exert economic influence on company actions.

Government and its agencies can also influence and provide information on the marketing environment. E-marketing 5.2 illustrates the role the UK government is taking to improve and understand the e-business environment.

5.2 e-marketing

Building an Environment for e-Business

Government steps in the UK to improve the e-business environment include: putting public services online through e-government initiatives; supporting private companies in making broadband Internet connections accessible to all; and encouraging more sophisticated use of e-business within individual companies, through focused training, advice and other support.

The Economist Intelligence Unit (www.ebusinessforum.com) takes into account over 70 environmental factors (political-legal, economic, socio-cultural and technological) to assess and compare e-business environments across 60 of the world's largest economies. These 'e-readiness' rankings provide an interesting e-business league table for: marketers (a first step in finding the best markets for a product or service); foreign investors (e.g. helping to assess the best location for a new multinational); and governments (highlighting key areas of improvement).

By accessing the most recent 'e-readiness' results, you can predict where countries will rank and then check to find out if you are right. For example, Scandinavia and South-east Asia have for the last few years been among the best Internet- and wireless-connected countries (remember that Nokia and Ericsson are both Scandinavian companies). The UK, in contrast, has lagged behind in terms of connectivity, but does the UK rank higher or lower overall?

The 'e-readiness' rankings provide a useful insight into the environmental conditions that are important for carrying out e-business within and across countries—critical information for the marketer.

National laws governing advertising across Europe mean that what is acceptable in one country is banned in another. For example, toys cannot be advertised in Greece, tobacco advertising is illegal in Scandinavia and Italy, alcohol advertising is banned on television in France and at sports grounds, and in Germany any advertisement believed to be in bad taste can be prohibited. This patchwork of national advertising regulations means that companies attempting to create a brand image across Europe often need to make substantial changes to advertising strategy on a national basis.

We will now review some of the more important legal influences on marketing activities.

Monopolies and mergers

Control of monopolies in Europe was made possible through Article 86 of the Treaty of Rome, which was aimed at preventing the 'abuse' of a dominant market position. However, control was increased in 1990 when the EU introduced its first direct mechanism for dealing with mergers and take-overs: the Merger Regulation. This gave the Competition Directorate of the European Commission jurisdiction over 'concentrations with a European dimension'.

The Commission found against a joint bid for de Havilland, a Canadian aircraft producer, by two state-owned concerns, Aérospatiale of France and Alenia of Italy. The reason was that the acquisition would have given the enlarged group half of the world market and three-quarters of the EU market for commuter aircraft of 20–70 seats. In the Commission's view this constituted an unacceptable degree of concentration with the proposed group facing only limited competition from other EU manufacturers, such as British Aerospace and Fokker of the Netherlands, and from American and Japanese producers.[38] As noted earlier, the Commission also intervened to force Nestlé to sell a number of Perrier brands to another company as a condition for allowing the acquisition.

European regulations are often supplemented by national bodies—for example, the Competition Commission in the UK. This body has the authority to investigate monopolies and mergers that are thought to be anti-competitive.

Restrictive practices

In Europe, Article 85 of the Treaty of Rome was designed to ban practices 'preventing, restricting or distorting competition' except where these contribute to efficiency without inhibiting consumers' 'fair share of the resulting benefit' and without eliminating competition. A notable success for the Commission was the breaking of the plastics cartel involving Britain (ICI), France (Atochem), Germany (BASF) and Italy (Montedison), among others. Since 2000, the European Commission has crusaded with renewed vigour against cartels, as Marketing in Action 5.2 explains.

In addition to the work of the European Commission, organizations such as the Bundeskartellamt in Germany and the Competition Council in France provide national protection against anti-competitive practices. Many countries in Europe supplement cross-border regulations with their own national laws.

Codes of practice

In addition to laws, various industries have drawn up codes of practice to protect consumer interests, sometimes as a result of political pressure. The UK advertising industry, for example, has drawn up a self-regulatory Code of Advertising Standards and Practice designed to keep advertising 'legal, decent, honest and truthful'. Similarly the marketing research industry has drawn up a code of practice to protect people from unethical activities such as using marketing research as a pretext for selling.

Marketing management must be aware of the constraints on its activities made by the political and legal environment. Such staff must assess the extent to which they feel the need to influence political decisions that may affect their operations, and the degree to which industry practice needs to be self-regulated in order to maintain high standards of customer satisfaction and service.

5.2 marketing in action

Bosses Beware: Cartels Under Fire

Both in the USA and the EU the battle against price-fixing cartels has never been so strongly fought. In the USA, auction houses Sotheby's and Christie's were convicted of fixing the prices they charge clients. For many years America has been obsessed by bringing down price-fixing cartels but the message is now spreading, with new measures against anti-competitive cartel behaviour such as bid-rigging and deals to carve up market share being adopted from Sweden to South Korea.

In the EU, anti-competitive behaviour has been stamped on with large fines being imposed since 2000 on cartels in the vitamins, carbonless paper, graphide electrodes, citric acid, amino acid and banking industries. In the vitamins case, manufacturers from France, Germany, Japan and Switzerland, including Aventis, BASF and Roche were fined €855 million by the European Commission for fixing prices and setting sales quotas. In another recent decision, the games console maker Nintendo was fined for anti-competitive behaviour down the distribution chain rather than horizontally with competitors. Its offence was to demand that its retailers sell its products at differential prices across the EU. This meant that German consumers paid up to two-thirds more than their UK counterparts for the same product.

One of the driving forces behind the EC's efforts to drive out anti-competitive behaviour is the desire to create a genuine single market in Europe, where geographic 'market sharing' is seen as highly damaging. Companies are responding by educating themselves. Roche, for example, has put thousands of its managers through training to teach them to follow the law.

Based on: Anonymous (2002);[39] Ritson (2002)[40]

Ecological/physical forces

Whereas the consumer movement attempts to protect the rights of consumers, environmentalists attempt to protect the *physical environment* from the costs associated with producing and marketing products and services. They are concerned with the social costs of consumption, not just the personal costs to the consumer. Six environmental issues are of particular concern. These are the use of environmentally friendly ingredients in products, recyclable and non-wasteful packaging, protection of the ozone layer, animal testing of new products, pollution, and energy conservation. Marketers need to be aware of the threats and opportunities associated with each of these issues.

Use of environmentally friendly ingredients

Environmentalists favour the use of biodegradable and natural ingredients when practicable. For example, Smith & Vandiver introduced in the UK the Botanical range of skincare, soap and bath products based on essential oils and herbs; this marked them out as both environmentally and animal friendly. In Germany, Estée Lauder introduced the Origins skincare and cosmetics range of vegetable-based products containing no animal ingredients.[41] ICI, the UK chemical group, has developed Biopol, which it claims is the first fully biodegradable commercial plastic. They state that its applications include disposable nappies, rubbish bags, and paper plates and cups coated with a thin plastic film. Already it is being used in Germany to make bottles for Wella's Sanara shampoo, in the USA for Brocato International's Evanesce shampoo and in Japan for Ishizawa Kenkyujo's Earthic Alga shampoos and conditioners.[42]

Recyclable and non-wasteful packaging

Germany took the lead in the recycling of packaging when it introduced the Verpackvo, a law that allows shoppers to return packaging to retailers and retailers to pass it back to suppliers. In response, suppliers promised to assume responsibility for the management of packaging waste. Over 400 companies have created a mechanism called the Dual System Deutschland (DSD). Consumers are asked to return glass bottles and waste paper to recycling bins and are also encouraged to separate other recyclable materials such as plastics, composite packaging and metals, and place them in yellow bags and bins supplied by the DSD. Collection is every month and is, together with separation of the refuse, paid for by the DSD and the cost eventually absorbed by the packaging manufacturers.[43]

In Austria, used batteries, PCs, refrigerators and other products containing potentially dangerous wastes have to be returned by consumers; they are then gathered by retailers and are recycled or treated centrally. Household waste is sorted into materials to be recycled: biological waste and the non-reusable rest. Because Austrians are particularly environmentally conscious, this has led to an oversupply of recycled material, raising the price of waste disposal. As a result, consumers have put pressure on retailers and manufacturers to avoid overpackaging.[44] Recycling is also important in Sweden, where industry has established a special company to organize the collection and sorting of waste for recycling, and in Finland where 35 per cent of packaging is recycled.[45]

Not only is cutting out waste in packaging environmentally friendly, it also makes commercial sense. Thus companies have introduced concentrated detergents and refill packs, and removed the cardboard around some brands of toothpaste, for example. The savings can be substantial: in Germany, Lever GmbH saved 15 per cent paper, carton and corrugated board, 30 per cent by introducing concentrated detergents, 20 per cent by using lightweight plastic bottles, and the introduction of refills for concentrated liquids reduced the weight of packaging materials by half. Henkel has introduced special 22-gram 'light packs', which are polyethylene bottles that save 270 tons of plastic a year.[46] Environmental concern is being taken seriously by retailers in the UK. Sainsbury, for example, employs an environment affairs manager.

Protection of the ozone layer

This issue has had a dramatic effect on the production of chlorofluorocarbons (CFCs), which are used in refrigerators and aerosols but are a major contributor to the breakdown of the ozone layer, allowing harmful radiation to pass through. The Montreal Protocol Conference in 1990 ruled that production of CFCs should be completely phased out by 2000, though this target was not achieved.

Animal testing of new products

Many potential new products, such as shampoos and cosmetics, are first tested on animals before launch to reduce the risk that they will be harmful to humans. This has aroused much opposition. One of the major concepts underlining the initial success of the Body Shop, the UK retailer, was that its products were not subject to animal testing. This is an example of the Body Shop's ethical approach to business. This extends to its suppliers too. Other larger stores, responding to the Body Shop's success, have introduced their own range of animal-friendly products.

Pollution

The manufacture, use and disposal of products can have a harmful effect on the quality of the physical environment. The production of chemicals that pollute the atmosphere, the use of nitrates as a fertilizer that pollutes rivers, and the disposal of by-products into the sea have caused considerable public concern. In recent years the introduction of lead-free petrol and catalytic converters has reduced the level of harmful exhaust emissions.

Denmark has introduced a series of anti-pollution measures including a charge on pesticides and a CFC tax. In the Netherlands higher taxes on pesticides, fertilizers and carbon monoxide emissions are proposed. Not all of the activity is simply cost raising, however. In Germany one of the marketing benefits of its involvement in green technology has been a thriving export business in pollution-control equipment.

Consumer groups can exert enormous pressure on companies by influencing public opinion. For example, environmentalist protests convinced Shell to abandon its plans to dump its obsolete North Sea oil installation, *Brent Spar*, at sea. The company now plans to consult environmental groups about any sensitive projects it may be considering. The advertisement shows how Toyota is attempting to reduce pollution from exhaust emissions.

Energy conservation

The finite nature of the world's energy resources has stimulated the drive to conserve energy. This is reflected in the demand for energy efficient housing and fuel-efficient motor cars, for example. In Europe, Sweden has taken the lead in developing an energy policy based on domestic and renewable resources. The tax system penalizes the use of polluting energy sources like coal and oil, while less polluting and domestic sources such as peat and woodchip receive favourable tax treatment. In addition, nuclear power is to be phased out by 2010. More efficient use of energy and the development of energy-efficient products (backed by an energy technology fund) will compensate for the shortfall in nuclear energy capacity. The illustration featuring Shell (opposite) explains how the company is attempting to pursue renewable resources like solar and wind energy.

Toyota describes how it is aiming to reduce the pollution caused by exhaust emissions.

Shell International Renewables was set up to develop new renewable resource opportunities.

Technological forces

Technology can have a substantial impact on people's lives and companies' fortunes. Technological breakthroughs have given us body scanners, robotics, camcorders, computers and many other products that have contributed to our quality of life. Many technological breakthroughs change the rules of the competitive game: the launch of the calculator made slide rules obsolete; the growth of television spelt the decline of the film industry; and the rise of the motor car and lorry has threatened rail transport.

Monitoring the technological environment may result in the spotting of opportunities and major investments in new areas. ICI, for example, invested heavily in the biotechnology area, and is leader in the market for the equipment used for genetic fingerprinting. Japanese companies are investing heavily in such areas as microelectronics, biotechnology, new materials and telecommunications. The key to successful technological investment is market potential, however, not technological sophistication for its own sake. The classic example of a high-technology initiative driven by technologists rather than pulled by the market is Concorde. Although technologically sophisticated, management knew before its launch that it never had any chance of being commercially viable.

Technological advances do not always go smoothly and, when they do, a knowledge of consumers is still an advantage to securing success, as Marketing in Action 5.3 explains.

5.3 marketing in action

Going 3G?

As the market for mobile phones reaches saturation point (over two-thirds of consumers in the UK own one), the need to develop new technologies that provide additional benefits has become apparent to mobile phone suppliers and operators. The answer is 3G technology, which has seen operators such as Vodafone spend £6 billion on a UK licence. Unfortunately, the launch of 3G services has repeatedly been delayed because of technical problems, the most usual being that the handsets would not work on both the new 3G networks and the existing 2G systems, and that European operators have encountered problems with internal trials of their 3G network equipment.

So why all the hype surrounding 3G? Its supporters claim that the new technology offers revolutionary services including unprecedented high-speed data communications, full multimedia messaging with sound and colour, live video streaming and video conference calls, high-quality voice calls, the downloading of music and video, and a more comprehensive, faster 'always on' wireless Internet service.

Despite these potential benefits, suppliers and operators need to understand their consumers. A study by Detica, a mobile phone consultancy, has highlighted the need to develop a range of 3G services tailored to specific consumer groups (segments). Its key finding is that consumers can be segmented by their willingness to adopt and use advanced technology. Around 12 per cent of consumers are *early adopters*, whose outlook is 'if it's technology, I want it'. A further 46 per cent—the *majority*—will use the technology but only with much encouragement and support. The remaining 42 per cent—the *laggards*—only want mobile technology at its simplest level—voice calls but not data services. Such people are unlikely to embrace 3G technology for the foreseeable future.

This means that around 58 per cent of consumers are susceptible to the 3G message. But their needs differ. The early adopters want a rich menu of service offerings, while the majority seek simplicity. Entertainment, finance and travel, in that order, are the most appealing services across the board. Even here there were differences: for example, younger consumers said they would use 3G financial services mainly to check their bank balances, while older consumers said they would be able to use them to pay bills.

By conducting studies such as this, marketers are better placed to take advantage of new technology by offering tailored services to those consumer groups whose differing requirements they most closely meet.

Based on: Cane (2002);[47] McCartney (2002);[48] Nakamoto (2001)[49]

Technological change can also pose threats to those companies that gradually find they cannot compete effectively with their more advanced rivals. The technological gap between Europe and the USA/Japan has widened since the early 1980s. With the exception of a small number of areas, such as computer-aided manufacturing, Europe trails the USA and Japan. This is despite the fact that Europe has an enviable record in science. Between 1940 and 1990, Europeans won 86 Nobel Prizes (in medicine, physics and chemistry); the USA won 143 and the Japanese five. While expenditure on research and development is somewhat lower as a percentage of GDP (Europe 2 per cent, USA 2.8 per cent, Japan 2.9 per cent) the high-technology gap can probably be explained more in terms of US and Japanese firms being better at using the results of scientific research; the links between scientists and businesspeople are stronger.[50]

An example of how technological change can act as a threat is the case of Psion, the inventor of the handheld personal electronic organizer. The development of smart phones by companies such as Nokia, which combined the functions of a personal organizer with a phone meant that Psion could not compete as it lacked the scale and competences to compete with global mobile phone manufacturers. Thus the pioneer of electronic handheld organizers was forced to leave the business.[51]

A major technological change that is affecting marketing is the developments in information technology. The Internet is revolutionizing how companies conduct business. Computer firm Dell, for example, was one of the first businesses to implement e-commerce, combining marketing and sales opportunities into one electronic experience. Dell is also using the Internet as a direct marketing tool. It has a database of addresses to which it sends e-mail, targeting only those people who have requested it. It can do this at a fraction of the price of a paper-based campaign because print and postage costs are eliminated. Sophisticated database software is also used to segment customers for its more traditional direct marketing campaigns. Clearly, technological advances can also create opportunities for companies to improve their marketing systems.[52]

Environmental scanning

The process of monitoring and analysing the marketing environment of a company is called *environmental scanning*. Two key decisions that management need to make are what to scan and how to organize the activity. Clearly, in theory, every event in the world has the potential to affect a company's operations but to establish a scanning system that covers every conceivable force would be unmanageable. The first task, then, is to define a feasible range of forces that require monitoring. These are the *potentially relevant environmental forces* that have the most likelihood of affecting future business prospects. The second prerequisite for an effective scanning system is to design a system that provides a fast response to events that are only partially predictable, emerge as surprises and grow very rapidly. This is essential because of the increasing turbulence of the marketing environment. Ansoff proposes that environmental scanning monitors the company's environment for signals of the development of *strategic issues* that can have an influence on company performance.[53]

Figure 5.5 provides the framework for corporate response, which is dependent on an analysis of the perceived impact, signal strength and urgency of the strategic issue.

There are four approaches to the organization of environmental scanning, as follows.[54]

1. *Line management*: functional managers (e.g. sales, marketing, purchasing) can be required to conduct environmental scanning in addition to their existing duties. This approach can falter because of line management resistance to the imposition of additional duties, and a lack of the specialist research and analytical skills required of scanners.

Figure 5.5 A framework for analysing and responding to environmental (strategic) issues

Source: Ansoff, H.I. (1991) *Implementing Strategic Management*, Englewood Cliffs, NJ: Prentice-Hall, 396; reproduced with permission.

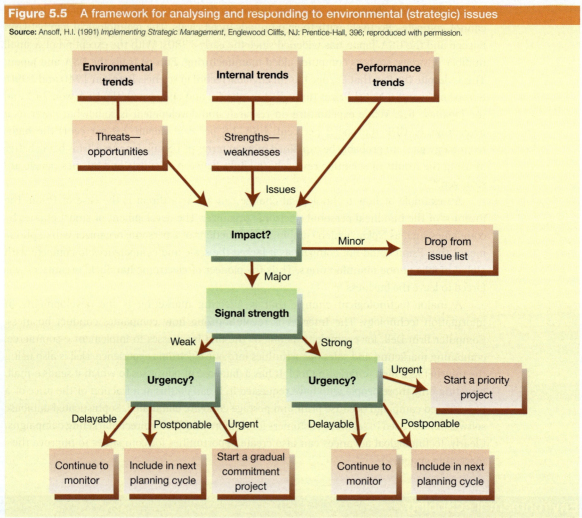

(2) *Strategic planner*: environmental scanning is made part of the strategic planner's job. The drawback of this approach is that a head office planner may not have the depth of understanding of a business unit's operations to be able to do the job effectively.

(3) *Separate organizational unit*: regular and ad hoc scanning is conducted by a separate organizational unit and is responsible for disseminating relevant information to managers. General Electric uses such a system with the unit's operations funded by the information recipients. The advantage is that there is a dedicated team concentrating its efforts on this important task. The disadvantage is that it is very costly and unlikely to be feasible except for large, profitable companies.

(4) *Joint line/general management teams*: a temporary planning team consisting of line and general (corporate) management may be set up to identify trends and issues that may have an impact on the business. Alternatively, an environmental trend or issue may have emerged that requires closer scrutiny. A joint team may be set up to study its implications.

The most appropriate organizational arrangement for scanning will depend on the unique circumstances facing a firm. A judgement needs to be made regarding the costs and benefits of each alternative. The size and profitability of the company and the perceived degree of environmental turbulence will be factors that impinge on this decision.

Brownlie suggests that a complete environmental scanning system would perform the following tasks:[55]

- monitor trends, issues and events, and study their implications
- develop forecasts, scenarios and issues analysis as input to strategic decision-making
- provide a focal point for the interpretation and analysis of environmental information identified by other people in the company
- establish a library or database for environmental information
- provide a group of internal experts on environmental affairs
- disseminate information on the business environment through newsletters, reports and lectures
- evaluate and revise the scanning system itself by applying new tools and procedures.

Formal environmental scanning was researched by Diffenbach, who found that practitioners believed it provided the following benefits:[56]

- better general awareness of, and responsiveness to, environmental changes
- better strategic planning and decision-making
- greater effectiveness in dealing with government
- improved industry and market analysis
- better foreign investment and international marketing
- improved resource allocation and diversification decisions
- superior energy planning.

Environmental scanning provides the essential informational input to create strategic fit between strategy, organization and the environment (see Fig. 5.6). Marketing strategy should reflect the environment even if this means a fundamental reorganization of operations.

Responses to environmental change

Companies respond in various ways to environmental change (see Fig. 5.7).

Figure 5.6 Strategic marketing fit

Ignorance

Because of poor environmental scanning, companies may not realize that salient forces are affecting their future prospects. They therefore continue as normal, ignorant of the environmental issues that are threatening their existence, or opportunities that could be seized. No change is made.

Delay

The second response is to delay action once the force is understood. This can be caused by *bureaucratic decision processes* that stifle swift action. The slow response by Swiss watch manufacturers to the introduction of digital watches was thought, in part, to be caused by the bureaucratic nature of their decision-making. *Marketing myopia* can slow response through management being product rather than

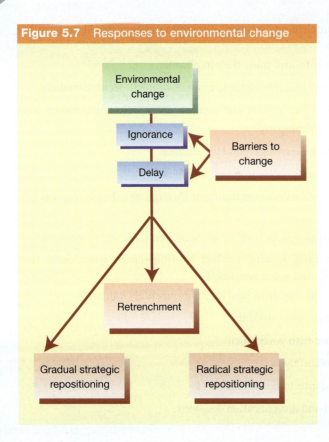

Figure 5.7 Responses to environmental change

customer focused. Management believes that there will always be a need for made-to-measure suits, for example, and delays responding to the growth in casual wear. A third source of delay is *technological myopia*, where a company fails to respond to technological change. The example of Pollitt and Wigsell, a steam engine manufacturer, which were slow to respond to the emergence of electrical power, is an example of technological myopia. The fourth reason for delay is *psychological recoil* by managers who see change as a threat and thus defend the status quo. These are four powerful contributors to inertia.

Retrenchment

This response tackles efficiency problems but ignores effectiveness issues. As sales and profits decline, management cuts costs; this leads to a period of higher profits but does nothing to stem declining sales. Costs (and capacity) are reduced once more but the fundamental strategic problems remain. Retrenchment policies only delay the inevitable.

Gradual strategic repositioning

This involves a gradual, planned and continuous adaptation to the changing marketing environment. Marks & Spencer is a company that has continually repositioned itself in response to changing demographic and economic trends (connoisseur convenience foods, financial services and European expansion, for example) in order to maintain a fit between the organization, its strategies and the environment. If, occasionally, a strategic move fails (e.g. moving into North America) the organization can cope and survive because of earlier successful repositionings.

Radical strategic repositioning

When procrastination leads to a crisis, companies may have to consider a radical shift in strategic positioning: the direction of the entire business is fundamentally changed. An example was Burtons, the UK clothing retailer, which moved out of made-to-measure suits and into casual wear. Another UK clothing retailer, Hepworths, was radically repositioned as Next, a more upmarket outlet for women's wear targeted at working women aged 25 to 35. Radical strategic repositioning is much riskier than gradual repositioning because, if unsuccessful, the company is likely to fold.

This chapter has explored a number of major events that are occurring in the marketing environment and has discussed methods of scanning for these and other changes that may fundamentally reshape the fortunes of companies. Failure to respond to a changing environment would have the same effect on companies that lack of adaptation had on animals: extinction.

Ethical dilemma

Ethical principles reflect the cultural values and norms of society. The increase in globalization has resulted in exposure to other cultural values and norms, which can result in ethical conflict and dilemma. For example, where cases of child labour have been uncovered in the manufacture of products made for our consumption, this may result in a consumer response to stop purchasing from the company(s) concerned. Would this be the most socially responsible decision?

Review

1 The nature of the marketing environment

- The marketing environment consists of the microenvironment (customers, competitors, distributors and suppliers) and the macroenvironment (economic, social, political, legal, physical and technological forces). These shape the character of the opportunities and threats facing a company and yet are largely uncontrollable.

2 The distinction between the microenvironment and the macroenvironment

- As can be seen above, the microenvironment consists of those actors in the firm's immediate environment that affect its capabilities to operate effectively in its chosen markets.
- The macroenvironment consists of a number of broader forces that affect not only the company but also the other actors in the microenvironment.

3 The impact of economic, social, political and legal, physical and technological forces on marketing decisions

- Economic forces can impact marketing decisions through their effect on supply and demand. Three major influences are economic growth and unemployment, the development of the single European market, and changes in the economies of eastern bloc countries.
- Social forces can have an impact on marketing decisions by changing demand patterns (e.g. the growth of the over-50s market) and the need to take into account social responsibility and ethics when making decisions. Four major influences are demographics, culture, social responsibility and marketing ethics, as well as the influence of the consumer movement.
- Political and legal forces can influence marketing decisions by determining the rules by which business can be conducted.
- Physical forces are concerned with the physical environment and relate to the environmental costs of consumption. Six issues are the use of environmentally friendly ingredients in products, recyclable and non-wasteful packaging, protection of the ozone layer, animal testing of new products, pollution, and energy conservation. Marketers need to be aware of the threats and opportunities associated with these issues.
- Technological forces can change the rules of the competitive game. Technological change can provide major opportunities and also pose enormous threats to companies. Marketers need to monitor the technological environment closely because of this.

4 Social responsibility and marketing ethics

- Social responsibility refers to the ethical principle that a person or an organization should be accountable for how its acts might affect the physical environment and the general public.
- Marketing ethics are the moral principles and values that govern the actions and decisions of people involved in marketing decision-making.
- Marketing managers need to recognize that organizations are part of a larger society and are accountable to that society for their actions. This realization should influence their decision-making.

5 How to conduct environmental scanning

- Two key decisions are what to scan and how to organize the activity.
- Four approaches to the organization of environmental scanning are line management, the strategic planner, a separate organizational unit and joint line/general management teams.
- The system should monitor trends, develop forecasts, interpret and analyse internally produced information, establish a database, provide environmental experts, disseminate information, and evaluate and revise the system.

6 How companies respond to environmental change

- Response comes in five forms, which are: ignorance, delay, retrenchment, gradual strategic repositioning and radical strategic repositioning.

Key terms

cause-related marketing the commercial activity by which businesses and charities or causes form a partnership with each other to market an image, good or service for mutual benefit

environmental scanning the process of monitoring and analysing the marketing environment of a company

ethics the moral principles and values that govern the actions and decisions of an individual or group

marketing environment the actors and forces that affect a company's capability to operate effectively in providing products and services to its customers

microenvironment the actors in the firm's immediate environment that affect its capability to operate effectively in its chosen markets—namely, suppliers, distributors, customers and competitors

social responsibility the ethical principle that a person or organization should be accountable for how its acts might affect the physical environment and general public

Internet exercise

Health and beauty retailer the Body Shop employs a variety of corporate social responsibility programmes. Visit its website and explore its activities.

Visit: www.thebodyshop.com

Questions

(a) What macroenvironment variables are affecting the Body Shop at present?
(b) Why is the Body Shop adopting these corporate social responsibility programmes? Furthermore, analyse the effectiveness of these.
(c) Debate whether all publicly quoted companies can ever be truly socially conscious.
(d) Find examples of other companies that are adopting corporate social responsibility programmes.

Visit the Online Learning Centre at www.mcgraw-hill.co.uk/textbooks/jobber for more Internet exercises.

Study questions

1. Choose an organization (if you are in paid employment use your own organization) and identify the major forces in the environment that are likely to affect its prospects in the next five to ten years.

2. Assess the impact of the single European market on the prospects for a motor car manufacturer such as the Rover Group.

3. What are the major opportunities and threats to EU businesses arising from the move to market-driven economies of eastern bloc countries?

4. Generate two lists of products and services. The first list will identify those products and services that are likely to be associated with falling demand as a result of changes in the age structure in Europe. The second list will consist of those that are likely to increase in demand. What are the marketing implications for their providers?

5. Discuss how you would approach the task of selling to German buyers.

6. Evaluate the marketing opportunities and threats posed by the growing importance of the socially conscious consumer.

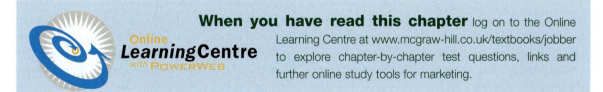

When you have read this chapter log on to the Online Learning Centre at www.mcgraw-hill.co.uk/textbooks/jobber to explore chapter-by-chapter test questions, links and further online study tools for marketing.

case nine

Marks & Spencer: Responding to Environmental Change

Luc Vandevelde, Chairman & Chief Executive of High Street giant M&S. At the Marks & Spencer's Annual General Meeting 2001 at the Royal Festival Hall, London, Mr Vandevelde offered a trading statement and an update on corporate restructuring.

Marks & Spencer, founded in a Leeds market in 1884, had grown, some 100-plus years later, to become a major international retailer. By the end of the 1990s it operated stores in 718 locations across 34 countries. For example, in the USA the company owned the upmarket preppy clothing retailer Brooks Brothers and the King's supermarket chain.

All Marks & Spencer goods are manufactured to the company's specifications and before 2000 were sold under the exclusive St Michael brand name. The company differentiated itself by 'serving the mass market with innovative, high-quality goods at competitive prices'. Its range of goods included clothing (outerwear and underwear), food products, financial services and homewares.

Annus horribilis

Throughout the 1980s and 1990s, Marks & Spencer showed steadily improving levels of sales and profitability. It is true that particular difficulties had been experienced in France and, more generally, Canada, but overall progress was achieved in a broad range of fields. This state of affairs came to a halt in 1999 sending a shock through both the retail trade and the financial community. Compared to 1998 figures, sales in 1999 were stagnant at £8224 million (€11,843 million) while profit before tax halved from £1155 million (€1663 million) to £546 million (€786 million). The company share price collapsed too, falling 50 per cent to the £2.30–£2.40 (€3.30–3.45) bracket.

In his review of the year's trading the company chairman, Sir Richard Greenbury, recognized 1999 as a major reversal of company fortunes, drawing particular attention to flat sales in the peak Christmas trading period, the need for heavy price reductions to shift large quantities of fashion merchandise, a cyclical downturn in housewares, overseas economic turmoil (e.g. riots in Indonesia, and currency problems in Thailand, Malaysia and Indonesia), adverse trading conditions in the Far East, together with the strength of the pound sterling and difficulties in supply-chain sourcing from relatively high-cost UK-based manufacturers.

When asked the almost polemical question 'What went wrong?' the company chief executive, Peter Salsbury, responded, 'the answer is simple ... we have not kept pace with the tremendous changes taking place in the retail market'.

Anecdotal evidence

To some extent the fall in the share price, dramatic though it was, was not as great as it might have been as the anticipated bad news had already been built in to the share price as the stock market listened to press, analyst and trade comment, which had suggested that all was not well. A broad spectrum of comments had been aired, hinting that M&S was not only becoming increasingly out of touch with its retail market but also, and more importantly, losing touch with both its more general macroenvironment and microenvironment.

Despite its problems, M&S was still regarded as a well-known and trusted store with a strong high-street presence. Also, it possessed an excellent reputation for underwear and food. Furthermore, changes in consumer demographics and behaviour meant that part of its core market—the traditional older shopper—was growing in numbers, more consumers were involved in aspirational shopping, both for clothing and home furnishings, and busier lifestyles meant that consumers were increasingly buying and consuming food 'on the go'.

In no particular order, the kinds of comment that were being voiced as possible explanations for M&S's demise in the late 1990s included the following.

- Its merchandise—especially ladies outerwear (e.g. trousers, skirts, suits, jackets and knitwear)—was not of modern design and cut.

Indeed, the offering was of staid fashion with little category breadth or depth. The colours, too, it was often said, were dreary and monotonous.
- The attempt to satisfy in one store a broad array of age groups from, say, teenage daughter via mother and aunt to grandmother, was proving difficult.
- Resistance, especially on the part of the younger age group, to shop in a store selling M&S-labelled merchandise. Clearly for such a group there were brand perception problems surrounding the ego-intensive fashion clothing sector.
- A lack of flair, cut, style and colour for the older female age group. Famously, one fiftysomething female shareholder berated the board at the 1999 AGM. She explained she had visited a major M&S store to buy a series of items for her wardrobe prior to going on a summer holiday. Failing to find anything at M&S she had bought all her requirements from competitive outlets. She challenged the mainly male board to understand the physiological and psychological needs of the older woman!
- Problems of being out of stock of the more popular, better-selling clothing items.
- The non-performance of the home delivery/shopping service, even sometimes involving wedding lists. Customers were told items were out of stock, no longer available (although they were still listed in the home shopping catalogue) and that china patterns had been withdrawn, meaning it was not possible to replace broken items.
- A refusal to accept credit cards. The company would only accept three forms of payment: cash/direct debit, cheque or the M&S chargecard.
- Increasingly the company was offering poor value for money, full prices being combined with deteriorating quality, i.e. in terms of wear, wash and care. This comment was often made with regard to lingerie, a product class in which M&S had once been pre-eminent.
- The high prices charged for food, especially the convenience value-added items.
- Political and planning constraints on out-of-town shopping developments and encouragement of the use of brownfield as compared to greenfield sites. Brownfield sites, though, often have significant preparation costs (clearance and possibly pollution) and, more importantly, are rarely in preferred locations.
- The emergence of shopping over the Internet. Some customers in particular seek out opportunities to buy from the USA where branded clothing prices are regularly lower than those in the UK.
- Aspiration purchasing of brand labels by affluent younger consumers/executives, e.g. Paul Smith; Hugo Boss, etc.
- Competition from specialist, trendy, niche retailers (often American), e.g. Gap, Warehouse, Next and Benetton.
- The success of specialist mail-order operations, e.g. Lands End, Cotton Traders and James Meade.
- In the financial services sector concerns about charges for savings plans—PEPs (personal equity plans), ISAs (individual savings accounts), and so on—for management, entry and exit. As a result, a number of companies and brokers are offering low-cost options, e.g. Virgin, Legal & General and David Aaron.
- The increasing acceptance by consumers of discounters, e.g. What Everyone Wants, TM Hughes, Peacocks and Matalan.
- The practice of dressing down on Fridays.
- Problems of the stretchability of St Michael brand values, e.g. to golf and sportswear.
- A general strengthening of M&S's mainstream competitors: in food, Tesco and Sainsbury's (especially in value-added 'designer-boutiqued' convenience food); in clothing, a spectrum of competitors, ranging from discounters to Harvey Nichols and niche operators.
- Recession in the Far East.
- The relative over-reliance by M&S, compared to its main-line clothing competitors, on high-cost UK-based suppliers. Often the relationship with such suppliers stretched back 100 years.
- An ageing UK population, often with high disposable income, i.e. empty nesters with no mortgage.
- The high cost of IT investment.
- General problems of product design and delivery in the supply chain.
- The general decline of the department store sector in the UK.
- The fact that a large number of stores in the M&S portfolio are located in cities/town centres where cars are discouraged and where

conveniently located. Inexpensive parking is scarce.
- The strength of the pound sterling working to the disadvantage of those UK retailers sourcing at home with markets in both the UK and overseas, and to the advantage of those sourcing predominately overseas with markets particularly in the UK.
- General problems forecasting next season's strong sellers in the fashion industry and maintaining purchasing flexibility to stock 'hot'-selling items.
- Boardroom debate and argument as to the successor to Sir Richard Greenbury (M&S chairman throughout the 1990s).
- Lack of success of some overseas operations, e.g. in the USA and Europe.

Marks & Spencer's strategic responses

In response to these problems M&S made a series of significant strategy changes in the early years of the new millennium, including the following.

- The retirement of Richard Greenbury, replaced by Luc Vandevelde, who became chairman and chief executive.
- The replacement of the entire board by Vandevelde.
- The commissioning of George Davies, the successful fashion entrepreneur, to develop the Per Una clothing range targeting 18- to 35-year-old fashion-conscious women. The range would be displayed in a distinct, branded area of the store.
- The commissioning of Jasim Yusuf from Warehouse to improve the menswear and childrenswear ranges.
- The development of a new clothing range called Perfect, designed to give what the more traditional M&S customer (middle income, 35-plus) wants: classic, stylish basics in high-quality fabrics at reasonable prices (e.g. well-cut white shirts, soft black jumpers that will go through the wash, and jeans that never lose their shape). These are exactly what M&S was known for at the height of its success. The Perfect positioning statement was 'good quality clothes that flatter'.
- The development of the more upmarket, fashionable Autograph range to compete with designer labels.
- More extensive use of advertising featuring high-profile celebrities, tailored to appeal to distinct target segments. There was DJ Zoë Ball for the aspirational, trendy twenties and thirties, actress Honor Blackman for the older, traditional female shopper, Sir Steve Redgrave and George Best for the straight men and Julian Clary for the pink pound.
- Major nationwide revamps to improve store ambience.
- The opening of smaller food and clothing stores (e.g. Simply Food) on the high street and at railway stations.
- The selling of Brooks Brothers and King's in the USA, and the closing of 38 European stores.
- The closure of M&S Direct, its mail-order operation.
- The sourcing of a higher proportion of clothing from abroad.
- The setting up of a new chain of stand-alone M&S homeware stores to be run by Vittorio Radice, the highly regarded ex-chief executive of Selfridges.
- The dropping of the St Michael brand, which was replaced with the Marks & Spencer brand name.
- The acceptance of credit cards.
- The investment in IT and distribution systems to improve stock control.

The results of these activities were significant improvements in profits and share price.

Questions

1. As a marketing consultant, you are asked to analyse M&S's macroenvironment and microenvironment for the period 1995–99. Summarize your analysis as a SWOT chart.

2. Relate M&S's strategic responses to your SWOT chart, identifying conversion and matching strategies (see Chapter 2).

This case was prepared by David Cook, Senior Lecturer in Marketing, University of Leeds, and Professor David Jobber, University of Bradford.

case ten

Fiat's Fall From Grace—Can Fiat Turn it Around?

Times have changed for Fiat (www.fiat.co.uk), once the icon of Italian industry. The company literally drove much of the Italian economy for decades, at one stage accounting for 5 per cent of its GDP. The car company is over a century old and is dominated by the Agnelli family dynasty, which still controls 34 per cent of Fiat's shares. The company was once seen as Europe's leading automotive player, however it now faces mounting debts, which threaten its very survival. Fiat, during the course of its lifetime, evolved into an unwieldy conglomerate, diversifying into a wide range of industries such as insurance and pharmaceuticals. Nevertheless, Fiat Auto still accounts for 40 per cent of the Fiat business. The car manufacturing operations were seen as the very essence of the Fiat brand. Yet, the Fiat Auto division is haemorrhaging cash at an enormous rate. The brand has lost much of its lustre due to its market share for both the Italian and European car markets being halved in recent years. Fiat has failed to keep pace with leaner and meaner competitors and the changing needs of the market. So, how could a company that made profits of €1.8 billion in 1987 now be making losses of nearly €4,000,000,000 only 15 years on? What went wrong?

The car manufacturing giant has been facing enormous difficulties since the late 1990s: falling sales, falling share price (its share price hit a 20-year low in 2002), erosion of market share, disgruntled workers, countless management reshuffles, poor sales of new models, economic problems in key overseas markets, retrenchment of foreign expansion, investor discontent, and operating losses running into billions of Euros. Its bosses and investors are trying to come up with strategies to halt the decline. The firm has focused primarily on cutting costs and selling off assets. The Fiat group has attempted to raise cash by selling off non-core businesses and is considering splitting up the company into separate entities. In addition, setting up Fiat Auto as a totally separate entity from the rest of the group is seen as a viable alternative. In the past, the Italian government would have intervened to help out the beleaguered company, but due to European Union competition laws it cannot inject cash from government coffers to protect the Italian colossus. The company seems destined to fall into total foreign ownership or face collapse.

Three years ago, Fiat Group sold 20 per cent of its auto unit to American giant General Motors (GM). GM is the world's biggest car firm. Furthermore, Fiat has the option to sell GM the remainder of the business, starting in 2004. This arrangement could prove to be Fiat's only viable lifeline for survival. Now GM wants to cancel this purchase option as it has problems of its own and does not want to be burdened with an ailing company. GM bought 20 per cent of Fiat Auto, with the option to buy the entire company, originally as a defensive measure. At the time of the deal, Fiat and BMW were planning to merge, yet this fell through. As a result, Daimler-Benz wanted to buy Fiat outright. Fearing this combination would be detrimental to GM's European operations, GM approached Fiat with its attractive offer. This 'put' option lasts from January 2004 to July 2009. If the two firms cannot agree a price, three independent investment banks will decide the price for the remaining 80 per cent of Fiat Auto.

GM lost €500 million in its European car markets in 2002. A reluctant GM has written down the original investment of $2.4 billion it paid to just $220 million. Both Fiat and GM are heavily involved in manufacturing strategic alliances, sharing car platforms for particular models and parts sharing. Fiat Auto has a wide array of automotive brands (see Table C10.1). Other car manufacturers are waiting in the wings to purchase Fiat's premium brands, such as Ferrari, Alfa Romeo and Maserati, during a credit crunch. Fiat's bankers are putting pressure on Fiat to either sell or fix its auto business or no further financing will be forthcoming. Fiat is desperately trying to bail water out of a sinking ship, offloading assets to remain an independent Italian car manufacturer.

Table C10.1 Fiat's main automotive brands

Cars	Light commercial vehicles	Heavy trucks	Buses and coaches	Tractors and agricultural equipment	Construction equipment
Alfa Romeo	Fiat	Iveco	Iveco	New Holland	Fiat Hitachi
Ferrari	Iveco	Iveco-Ford	Iveco-Ford	Braud	Fiat Allis
Fiat	Iveco-Pegaso	Iveco-Pegaso	Iveco-Pegaso	Flexi-Coil	O&K
Lancia		Astra	Orlandi	Bizon	New Holland
Maserati		Iveco-Magirus			
		Seddon Atkinson			

Fiat has survived past crises during its eventful life—such as crippling debts, labour unrest, even terrorist attacks—but this crisis may be terminal for the proud Italian company. Gianni Agnelli, the Fiat patriarch died on 24 January 2003, aged 81. Gianni had been one of Italy's leading industrialists for nearly 60 years. On his death the leading Italian newspaper devoted 19 pages to his life. Over 100,000 people went to see Gianni's body as it lay in state in Turin. Italy's president and prime minister, who arrived in upmarket Audis at his funeral, were roundly booed by the crowds for not arriving in Fiat cars. In his early years, Gianni was seen as an Italian playboy, living off his family's fortune and enjoying the high life. The Agnellis nearly lost control of their empire after the Second World War, due to Fiat founder Giovanni Agnelli's connections with the Italian fascist regime. The playboy stepped into the breach, convincing the Americans that Fiat would be better in private hands and represented a bastion of free enterprise. As the young playboy grew older he gradually accepted his dynastic responsibilities. Fiat grew steadily during Italy's post-war economic boom as Italians bought small cars in their droves. By the mid-1960s, the company was producing a million cars a year, diversifying into trucks, planes and tractors, and expanding to further pastures such as the then Soviet Union, Turkey and South America. Fiat acquired Italian automaker Lancia in 1968.

In the late 1980s, Fiat was a sprawling conglomerate, due to its diversification strategy. The group was involved in a myriad of enterprises, ranging from trains, telecoms and newspapers to pharmaceuticals, even investing in football. The Agnellis owned European soccer giant Juventus, a Turin-based team. In 1976, Giovanni Agnelli controversially sold almost 10 per cent of Fiat to the Libyan government, before eventually buying it back. During this time the other large car manufacturers continually tried to woo Fiat Auto with offers. Agnelli was courted by the likes of Ford, Volkswagen, BMW, Toyota and Daimler Chrysler. In 1986, Fiat bought the Alfa Romeo brand. Fiat relied heavily on its own domestic market. The removal of Italian protectionist policies left it uncompetitive in terms of global market forces, and its share of the Italian auto market fell from 60 per cent to 39 per cent during the 1990s.

Mounting troubles

Fiat has always over relied on a few popular car models to be the main earner for the division. On numerous occasions in the past, the company has been saved due to the sales performance of particular small-car models such as the Punto, Panda, Uno and the famous 186. The Fiat Uno saved the company in the 1980s, as did the Punto in the 1990s. Fiat is forever seen as a small-car specialist. Fiat always prided itself on the performance of its models in this 'subcompact' category. In 2001, Fiat launched its next great hope for the future, the Stilo, the replacement for the Bravo/Brava model. The Stilo was Fiat's attempt to capture the lucrative mid-size hatchback market, popular with families and fleet buyers. It was seen as Fiat's attempt to move into the middle-range category of the market.

The car flopped with poor sales, failing to emulate past Fiat success stories. A first-year sales target of 400,000 units was set for the Stilo, yet only 300,000 were sold. The Stilo was full of accessories for which consumers did not want to pay extra. Now the company has launched a cheaper and more basic version of the car. The car that came with all the accessories was seen as too expensive a purchase for 'normal' Fiat buyers. In addition, competitors successfully undertook price cuts on their competing car models. Table C10.2 shows how Fiat's market share fell between 2001 and 2002 and as Table C10.3 illustrates, Fiat Auto is experiencing decline in the majority of car categories in which it competes. The company has found it difficult to stretch its brand to bigger cars, unlike its industry rivals.

Table C10.2 New car registrations for EU and EFTA countries, 2002

	% share 02	% share 01	Units 02	Units 01	% chg 02/01
All brands			14,390,163	14,817,679	−2.9
VW Group	18.4	18.9	2,653,104	2,794,576	−5.1
Volkswagen	10.4	10.8	1,490,602	1,603,708	−7.1
Seat	2.6	2.7	375,841	403,998	−7.0
Skoda	1.7	1.7	238,303	246,356	−3.3
PSA Group	15.0	14.4	2,163,181	2,139,747	+1.1
Peugeot	8.9	8.6	1,277,262	1,278,840	−0.1
Citroën	6.2	5.8	885,919	860,907	+2.9
Japanese	11.4	10.4	1,646,730	1,544,732	+6.6
Toyota and Lexus	4.4	3.7	627,052	550,720	+13.9
Nissan	2.5	2.5	354,423	365,712	−3.1
Mazda	1.1	0.9	157,934	139,393	+13.3
Honda	1.3	1.0	180,385	154,731	+16.6
Ford Group	11.4	11.1	1,635,561	1,649,002	−0.8
Renault	10.7	10.6	1,543,228	1,575,264	−2.0
GM Group	10.0	10.8	1,433,953	1,600,190	−10.4
Fiat Group	8.2	9.6	1,177,355	1,415,932	−16.8
Fiat	6.2	7.2	894,616	1,062,455	−15.8
Lancia	0.8	1.0	109,410	148,482	−26.3
Alfa Romeo	1.2	1.4	169,183	201,306	−16.0
Others	0.0	0.0	4,146	3,689	+12.4
Daimler Chrysler	6.6	6.3	947,003	938,823	+0.9
Mercedes	5.1	5.0	736,757	736,234	+0.1
Smart	0.8	0.7	110,233	104,217	+5.8
BMW Group	4.3	3.7	618,394	543,271	+13.8
BMW	3.6	3.5	513,028	517,778	−0.9
Mini	0.7	0.2	105,366	25,493	+313.3
Korean	2.7	2.8	389,222	410,706	−5.2
Hyundai	1.6	1.5	224,697	218,900	+2.6
Others	1.1	1.3	164,525	191,806	−14.2
MG Rover Group	1.0	1.1	143,745	160,400	−10.4

Source: Association des Constructeurs Européens d'Automobiles, 2003

Fiat relied heavily on growth from export countries. The group put in place manufacturing capacity that could produce nearly four million cars per year. It felt that countries such as Brazil and Poland, where Fiat had a strong presence, would help the group meet these ambitious targets. However, due to the economic crisis in Brazil in 1998, Brazilian demand was shattered. Fiat was also obliterated by low-cost Korean competition in Poland. When valuable cash flow dried up from cash-strapped countries such as Brazil and Argentina, this left a large hole in the company's finances to be filled. Even the group's stalwart, the Italian market, faced problems and Fiat's market share plunged. As a result Fiat Auto had huge excess capacity, which was an enormous drain on the group's financial resources. The European car market has approximately 30 per cent overcapacity.

Table C10.3	Fiat's sales performance by sector from 1995 to 2001 (automobiles)						
	1995	1996	1997	1998	1999	2000	2001
City subcompact	333,087	328,464	385,237	375,797	404,852	333,339	256,877
Subcompact	1,081,345	1,117,172	1,266,949	1,041,878	945,144	1,072,576	949,907
Intermediate/compact	378,170	431,430	490,492	450,835	380,500	331,395	349,303
Intermediate	162,837	138,968	220,379	230,071	245,669	252,377	165,569
Full-size	58,658	35,364	23,852	28,090	39,246	26,130	11,497
Sports cars	38,973	38,301	34,519	26,860	22,013	12,681	8,998
Minivans	20,321	17,387	15,418	19,716	60,960	59,582	91,478
TOTAL CARS	2,073,391	2,107,086	2,436,846	2,173,247	2,098,384	2,088,080	1,833,629

The firm had become over-reliant on its domestic Italian market. Years of protectionist policy had helped stave off competitors for decades. The Italian market accounts for over 40 per cent of Fiat Auto sales—however, its market share is now rapidly diminishing. In 2002, the company had a market share of 27.3 per cent. A very respectable figure in the vast majority of industries—however, this figure is half the market share Fiat enjoyed during the 1980s. Fiat is experiencing strong competition, particularly from French, Japanese and Korean manufacturers, in its key market segments. Boardroom battles have not helped to alleviate the situation. On the death of the family patriarch, Gianni, there have been succession difficulties among the Agnelli family as to who will take control of the group. Complicating the matter further, two external investors are vying for control of the group, vowing to inject much-needed capital into the company in return for full control and the transfer of ownership of valuable assets. The Agnelli family appointed a Turin outsider, Giuseppe Morchio, as the new Fiat Auto CEO. Morchio worked with Italian tyre manufacturer Pirelli and is Fiat's fourth chief executive in nine months. Fiat desperately needs success in key European markets like France, Germany and the UK. For example, in the key UK market, in 2002, Fiat was the 11th most popular car manufacturer with a market share of only 3.23 per cent. However, its sales have tumbled dramatically, falling by nearly 15,000 units (15.3 per cent) on the previous year, whereas sales in the entire UK market rose by 4.26 per cent. Worryingly for the Fiat group too, Alfa Romeo sales fell by over 30 per cent.

Fiat has committed some cardinal sins, which may have exacerbated its fall from grace. First, the company had a minuscule research and development budget in comparison to those of its industry rivals during the 1990s. During the period 1995–2001, the firm spent €4.5 billion on R&D, whereas Renault and Mercedes spent €9 billion, and Volkswagen €20 billion. The Fiat company once prided itself on using state-of-the-art robotic technology, and glorified this by encapsulating its use of this technology in a famous ad campaign during the 1980s. The company, however, was clearly losing the R&D race. For example, it did not have any new product launches for over 18 months—from January 2002 to September 2003 when the Gingo was launched. Fiat's lack of innovation can be seen in the fact that it was the last major car manufacturer to install catalytic converters or offer free airbags in its cars.

Fiat has been dogged by a reputation for poor quality, which has been hard to shake off. This can clearly be seen by the scores the Fiat brand achieved in the annual JD Power survey. Fiat cars scored abysmally. The 2003 JD Power Customer Satisfaction Index is based on feedback from 24,255 car owners in the UK. Only owners of cars registered within a one-year timeframe are invited to complete the survey. Every owner completes an eight-page survey, containing over 100 questions, covering what goes wrong and how often, what drivers like and dislike about their car, the service from dealers and the car's running costs. The survey highlighted huge problems with Fiat's dealership network, giving the car marque dreadful scores as a result. Of 138 car models tested, the scores for some of the Fiat range were as follows: the Fiat Multipla came in 113th, the Fiat Seicento came in 120th, the Fiat Brava and Marea were joint 124th, the Fiat Bravo was 131st and the Fiat Punto 132nd. In addition, the Alfa Romeo 156 model received the ignominy of being third last in the survey. No Fiat cars were in the top 25. In essence, customers were rating their Fiat cars as abysmal. The Fiat name has also inherited the unfortunate acronym 'Fix It Again Tomorrow', due to its poor image. The company only began to offer the industry norm of a two-year product guarantee in 2002. Other competitors are offering impressive five-year warranties with their cars. Moreover, some commentators believe that Fiat failed in some Asian markets like Singapore, due to its failure to offer a 'tropicalization pack' for its Punto, which would typically include coating the undercarriage with a special sealant to protect against rust, and having an air-conditioning system customized for Singapore's climate.

The turnaround strategy

The group has launched a three-pronged strategy in order to reverse its declining fortunes: gaining access to fresh capital, reducing surplus capacity, and revitalizing a weak product offering. Fiat outlined its restructuring plan, which involves cutting costs by €1.1 billion, increasing R&D spending by €100 million to €1.2 billion, reducing European capacity to 1.6 million vehicles a year, trying to boost sales in Europe by 9 per cent with the launch of new models and, finally, investing €150 million a year through 2005 to expand its dealer network. The group plans to reduce its cost base by €1.1 billion in 2003. The main savings are: €500 million derived from a 3.5 per cent price cut requested from suppliers, €200 million from cutting warranty costs by 20 per cent and reducing other distribution costs, and €200 million from a capacity reduction in Italy. Since late 2001, Fiat has reduced inventory from an equivalent of 1.9 months of sales to 1.3 months. Fiat's base recovery plan relies on investing more than €8.1 billion in the next three years to launch 20 new models. Fiat plans to sharply reduce unprofitable sales such as rental cars and demos. In addition, Fiat's new CEO is halting the group's diversification plans and trying to salvage Fiat's auto business by selling off particular group assets. The company laid off 8100 of its car workers in 2002, more than one-fifth of its national workforce.

This restructuring plan is facing huge opposition from labour unions and Italian prime minister and media mogul Silvio Berlusconi. Fiat Auto's car brands—such as Fiat, Ferrari, Alfa Romeo and Lancia—are a source of national pride for Italians. The planned job cuts led to strikes and street protests, leading to the direct involvement of Berlusconi in rescue talks. Unsurprisingly, commentators suggest that he is simply vying for ownership of Fiat's publishing empire. The government has said that it is willing to step in only if Fiat rejects its right to sell 80 per cent of the group to GM and agrees not to close down car plants in Italy. GM is not in favour of governmental support, as it fears this will lead to interference with management. Some members of the ruling government coalition have strongly advocated the nationalization of Fiat Auto. The government has even introduced incentives for people trading in their old cars to buy new cars, yet this has benefited all car marques, not just Fiat. The group is toying with the idea of floating the successful Iveco brand and its much beloved Ferrari brand as separate listed companies, in order to stem the tide.

For 2004, Fiat says it plans to sell between 180,000 and 200,000 units of the Fiat Gingo, the replacement for the Seicento and Panda. The Gingo, which is built in Poland, went on sale in September 2003. Fiat also plans to sell 100,000–120,000 units of the Fiat Idea, the Punto-based compact MPV, which went on sale in November 2003. These new models seem to suggest that Fiat is refocusing on what it is best known for: small, city cars. The company is investing €450 million to overhaul its distribution network. In addition, Fiat is buying out some of its distributors. Fiat UK has begun restructuring around separate Fiat and Alfa Romeo brands, each with separate managing and marketing directors. Fiat has also decided to slash its global marketing budget by €152 million. The company flew out hundreds of its dealers to Milan to update them on brand positioning for Fiat. The car company is also offering aggressive price promotions in order to boost flagging sales volume, including initiatives such as 0 per cent finance, scrapping schemes, trade-in bonuses and cash rebates.

The successful rejuvenation of the Alfa brand has led optimists to believe that the same turnaround can be achieved by the Fiat brand. But can the magic work second time around for Fiat? Fiat now has debts totalling €5.8 billion. Some potential car buyers are realizing that Fiat is in severe financial difficulties and are defecting to other car brands as a result. So, will these turnaround strategies described above work or will Fiat simply jettison its car business on to GM?

Questions

(1) Outline and discuss the macroenvironmental and microenvironmental factors that are influencing Fiat's strategy.

(2) Conduct a SWOT analysis on the Fiat Auto division.

(3) Outline the strategic options available to Fiat Auto division, recommending what you believe to be the best option available, and giving reasons for your answer.

This case was written by Conor Carroll, Lecturer in Marketing, University of Limerick. Copyright © Conor Carroll (2003). The material in the case has been drawn from a variety of published sources and research reports.

chapter six

Marketing research and information systems

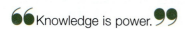
Knowledge is power.   MACHIAVELLI

Learning Objectives

This chapter explains:

1. The nature and purpose of marketing information systems, and the role of marketing research within such systems
2. The types of marketing research
3. The approaches to conducting marketing research
4. The stages in the marketing research process
5. How to prepare a research brief and proposal
6. The nature and role of exploratory research
7. Quantitative research design decisions: sampling, survey method and questionnaire design issues
8. Analysis and interpretation of data
9. Report writing and presentation
10. The factors that affect the usage of marketing information systems and marketing research reports
11. Ethical issues in marketing research

What kinds of people buy my products? What do they value? Where do they buy? What kinds of new products would they like to see on the market? These and other related questions are the key to informed marketing decision-making. As we have seen, a prerequisite for the adoption of a marketing orientation is knowledge about customers and other aspects of the marketing environment that affect company operations. Managers obtain this information by informal and formal means. Casual discussions with customers at exhibitions or through sales calls can provide valuable informal information about their requirements, competitor activities and future happenings in the industry. Some companies, particularly those who have few customers, rely on this type of interaction gathering to keep abreast of market changes.

As the customer base grows, such methods may be inadequate to provide the necessary in-depth market knowledge to compete effectively. A more formal approach is needed to supply information systematically to managers. This chapter focuses on this formal method of information provision. First, we will describe the nature of a marketing information system and its relationship to marketing research. Then we look at the process of marketing research and its uses in more detail. Finally, we will examine the influences on information system and marketing research use. Marketing information system design is important since the quality of a marketing information system has been shown to have an impact on the effectiveness of decision-making.[1]

Marketing information systems

A **marketing information system** has been defined as:[2]

> A system in which marketing information is formally gathered, stored, analysed and distributed to managers in accord with their informational needs on a regular planned basis.

The system is built on an understanding of the information needs of marketing management, and supplies that information when, where and how the manager requires it. Data are derived from the marketing environment and transferred into information that marketing managers can use in their decision-making. The difference between data and information is as follows.

- **Data** is the most basic form of knowledge, e.g. the brand of butter sold to a particular customer in a certain town; this statistic is of little worth in itself but may become meaningful when combined with other data.

- **Information** is a combination of data that provide decision-relevant knowledge, e.g. the brand preferences of customers in a certain age category in a particular geographic region.

An insight into the nature of marketing information systems (MkIS) is given in Fig. 6.1. The MkIS comprises four elements: internal continuous data, internal ad hoc data, environmental scanning, and marketing research.

Internal continuous data

Companies possess an enormous amount of marketing and financial data that may never be used for marketing decision-making unless organized by means of an MkIS. One advantage of setting up an MkIS is the conversion of financial data into a form usable by marketing

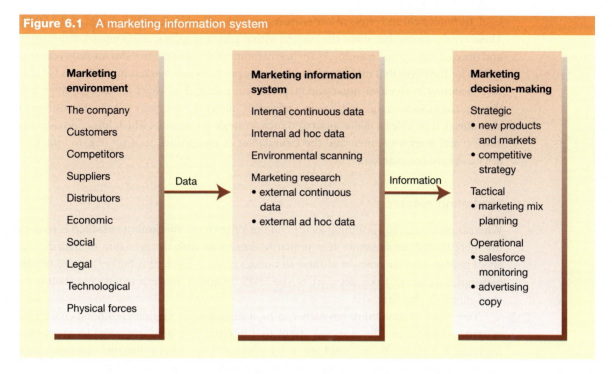

Figure 6.1 A marketing information system

management. Traditionally, profitability figures have been calculated for accounting and financial reporting purposes. This has led to two problems. First, the figures may be too aggregated (e.g. profitability by division (SBU)) to be of much use for marketing decisions at a product level, and, second, arbitrary allocations of marketing expenditures to products may obscure their real profitability.

The setting up of an MkIS may stimulate the provision of information that marketing managers can use, e.g. profitability of a particular product, customer or distribution channel, or even the profitability of a particular product to an individual customer.

Another application of the MkIS concept to internal continuous data is within the area of salesforce management. As part of the sales management function, many salesforces are monitored by means of recording sales achieved, number of calls made, size of orders, number of new accounts opened, etc. This can be recorded in total or broken down by product or customer/customer type. The establishment of an MkIS where these data are stored and analysed over time can provide information on salesforce effectiveness. For example, a fall-off in performance of a salesperson can quickly be identified and remedial action taken.

Internal ad hoc data

Company data can also be used for a specific (ad hoc) purpose. For example, management may look at how sales have reacted to a price increase or a change in advertising copy. Although this could be part of a continuous monitoring programme, specific one-off analyses are inevitably required from time to time. Capturing the data on the MkIS allows specific analyses to be conducted when needed.

Environmental scanning

The environmental scanning procedures discussed in Chapter 5 also form part of the MkIS. Although often amorphous in nature, environmental analysis—whereby the economic, social, legal, technological and physical forces are monitored—should be considered part of the MkIS. These are the forces that shape the context within which suppliers, the company, distributors and the competition do business. As such, environmental scanning provides an early warning system for the forces that may impact a company's products and markets in the future.[3] In this way, scanning enables an organization to act on, rather than react to, opportunities and threats. The focus is on the longer-term perspective, allowing a company to be in the position to plan ahead. It provides a major input into such strategic decisions as which future products to develop and market to enter, and the formulation of competitive strategy (e.g. to attack or defend against competition).

Marketing research

Whereas environmental scanning focuses on the longer term, marketing research considers the more immediate situation. It is primarily concerned with the provision of information about markets and the reaction of these to various product, price, distribution and promotion decisions.[4] As such, it is a key part of the MkIS because it make a major contribution to marketing mix planning.

Two types of marketing research can be distinguished: external continuous data and external ad hoc data. This does not mean that internal data are never used by marketing researchers, but usually the emphasis is on external data sources. *External continuous data sources* include television audience monitoring and consumer panels where household purchases are recorded over time. Loyalty cards are also a source of continuous data, providing information on customer purchasing patterns and responses to promotions. The growth of e-commerce has led to new forms of continuous data collection—for example, the measurement of visits to websites ('hits'). *External ad hoc data* are often gathered by means of surveys into specific marketing issues, including usage and attitude studies, advertising and product testing, and corporate image research. The rest of this chapter will examine the process of marketing research and the factors that affect the use of research information.

The importance of marketing research

The importance of marketing research was highlighted in a study of the factors that were significant in the selection of an industrial goods supplier.[5] The company, as part of its marketing audit (see Chapter 2), wanted to know what were the main considerations its customers took into account when deciding to do business with it or its competitors. Before conducting marketing research, it asked its marketing staff; they said that the two main factors were price and product quality. Next the sales staff were asked the same question and their response was that customers mainly considered company reputation and quick response to customer needs (see Table 6.1). When marketing research was carried out, however, the results were very different. Customers explained that, to them, the key issues were technical support services and prompt delivery. Clearly the viewpoints within and outside the company were at odds with each other. The lesson is that it is dangerous to rely solely on the internal views of managers. Only when this company really understood what its customers wanted could it put into action marketing initiatives that improved technical and delivery services. The result was improved customer satisfaction, which led to increased sales and profits.

Marketing research is used by political parties as well as commercial organizations. In the 1996 US presidential election, the winner Bill Clinton was reported to be awash with marketing research findings.[6] The pollsters told him to be a father figure with a powerful red tie, and suggested how he should spend his holidays. 'Can I golf?' asked Clinton sarcastically, 'Maybe if I wear a baseball cap?' 'No sir', came the reply, 'Go rafting.'

Table 6.1	Factors in the selection of a manufacturer*		
Factor	Users	Salespeople	Marketing
Reputation	5	①	4
Credit	9	11	9
Sales reps	8	5	7
Technical support services	①	3	6
Literature	11	10	11
Prompt delivery	②	4	5
Quick response to customer needs	3	②	3
Price	6	6	①
Personal relationships	10	7	8
Complete product line	7	9	10
Product quality	4	8	②

*Factors are rated in order of importance from 1 to 11. First and second positions are circled for ease of reference.
Source: Kotler, P., W. McGregor and W. Rodgers (1977) The Marketing Audit Comes of Age, *Sloan Management Review*, Winter, 30. Reprinted with permission. Copyright © 1977 by the Sloan Management Review Association. All rights reserved.

The value of marketing research information is reflected in a European market size of over €7000 million (£4860 million). Figure 6.2 shows how the European market is divided between countries.[7] The importance of marketing research means that data must be accurate, otherwise incorrect decisions are likely to be made. Unfortunately, several problems have arisen in recent times, which means that great care is needed to ensure valid survey findings. Marketing in Action 6.1 discusses these issues.

6.1 marketing in action

Validity in Marketing Research

In most advanced economies there are few manufacturers, advertising agencies, government departments, public bodies, universities and service providers who do not integrate research into their decision-making processes. Yet, despite its widespread acceptance, marketing researchers are concerned about three trends.

First, some members of the public actually enjoy taking part in research surveys and focus groups. The paid interviewers know who they are and some may be tempted to return to them again and again, leading to biased results. In other cases, so keen are these so-called 'research groupies' to take part that they change identity. In one interview they will be married with no children; in the next they will be divorced with teenage children. So concerned is the industry that the Association of Qualitative Research Practitioners has introduced measures to protect the validity of focus group members. In future, focus group participants will have to provide proof of identity each time they attend a group, and will be warned that they could face criminal prosecution for deception if they deliberately mislead researchers. Second, other people are fed up with marketing research and refuse to take part. In Britain, over 15 million interviews are conducted and 100 million questionnaires mailed every year. The result is lower response rates. For example, the National Readership Survey achieves just over a 60 per cent response rate after eight calls. In 1954, when it began, 85 per cent was reached after only six calls to respondents. So concerned are marketing researchers in Europe that they are considering following the USA and making it standard practice to pay respondents.

Finally, as respondents become more accustomed to research they have begun to play games with market researchers. They understand the process and consciously manipulate their responses. For example, many know that questions about an acceptable price for a new brand will influence its launch price and so respond with low figures. It takes only a small percentage of such respondents to invalidate findings. So important is this problem that at a recent Association of Market Survey Organizations conference, several of the key papers addressed the issue of the increasingly uncertain relationship between market researchers and the public.

Based on: Cook (1999);[8] Hemsley (1999);[9] Flack (2002)[10]

Figure 6.2 European marketing research markets 2001 (total = €7058 million)

Source: ESOMAR Annual Study on the Market Research Industry 2001. Copyright ESOMAR © 2003. Permission for using this material has been granted by ESOMAR®, Amsterdam, Netherlands. website: www.esomar.org.

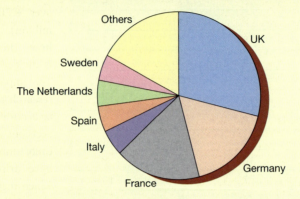

Approaches to conducting marketing research

Depending on the situation facing a company, particularly the resources allocated to marketing research, there are four ways of carrying out marketing research, described below.

Do it yourself—personally

Where a company has marketing staff but a low or non-existent marketing research budget, the only option may be for marketing staff to carry out the marketing research task themselves. This is particularly feasible when the study is small scale, perhaps involving data-gathering from libraries. Where sample sizes are small—for example, in some industrial marketing research studies involving interviews with a small number of organizational customers—this option may also be feasible. Training in research techniques may be necessary. Fortunately there are many good courses available from professional organizations such as the Market Research Society.

Do it yourself—using a marketing research department

By hiring a marketing research executive, a company would benefit from professional specialist skills. It could be possible for the executive to design, implement and present marketing research surveys to marketing management. If the outside services of a marketing research agency are used, the executive would act as the link between company and agency.

Do it yourself—using a fieldwork agency

Where the design of the study can be done in-company but interviewing by internal staff is not possible, the fieldwork could be conducted by a marketing research agency. These organizations provide a wide range of services, which include fieldwork services; indeed, some specialize in fieldwork only. One possibility would be for the survey design, questionnaire design and analysis of results to be done in-company but the administration of the questionnaire to be handled by fieldwork staff employed by the marketing research agency.

Table 6.2	Top global marketing research agencies	
Agency	Parent country	Global research revenues (Euro millions)
VNU NV	Netherlands	2688
IMS Health, Inc.	USA	1312
WPP plc	UK	1131
Taylor Nelson Sofres plc	UK	911
Information Resources, Inc.	USA	627
GFK Group	Germany	538
NFO WorldGroup Inc	USA	507
Ipsos Group SA	France	482
NOP World	UK	364
Westat, Inc.	USA	320

Source: ESOMAR Annual Study on the Market Research Industry 2001. Copyright ESOMAR © 2001, Amsterdam, Netherlands. website www.esomar.org.

Use the full services of a marketing research agency

Where resources permit, a company (client) could use the full range of skills offered by marketing research agencies. The company would brief the agency about its marketing research requirements and the agency would do the rest. A complete service would mean that the agency would:

- prepare a research proposal stating the survey design and costs
- conduct exploratory research
- design the questionnaire
- select the sample
- choose the survey method (telephone, postal or face to face)
- conduct the interviewing
- analyse and interpret the results
- prepare a report
- make a presentation.

Table 6.2 lists the top global marketing research agencies.[11]

A key to successful marketing research is close, effective relationships between client and agency. Marketing in Action 6.2 discusses how these can be achieved.

Types of marketing research

A major distinction is between **ad hoc research** and **continuous research**.

Ad hoc research

An *ad hoc study* focuses on a specific marketing problem and collects data at one point in time from one sample of respondents. Examples of *ad hoc* studies are usage and attitude surveys, product and concept tests, advertising development and evaluation studies, corporate image

6.2 marketing in action

Achieving Close Client–Agency Relationships

Two companies that have worked closely together to produce effective marketing research are British Telecom and the NOP Research Group. Crispin Beale, head of customer satisfaction and competitor intelligence, BT, and Phyllis MacFarlane, client executive officer, NOP, explain how their relationship works.

'I've noticed that I talk to the team at NOP almost as much as I talk to my own team here at BT,' says Beale. 'Today our key agencies are receiving a briefing about what we're doing on broadband. They know as much about what we're doing in certain areas as we do and will be able to make suggestions. We have encouraged NOP to develop a "can do" attitude, whereby they find solutions rather than problems. This involves an investment of time up-front—to create service-level agreements and manage expectations. Yet only by setting up such processes can both parties deliver actionable and insightful intelligence to the business on a timely basis.'

'Our relationship with BT began more than 20 years ago,' explains MacFarlane. 'We've been working together on a wide and growing range of research projects ever since. Now our relationship has evolved into a real partnership. We work closely with BT people across the business and at the highest levels of BT management. We strive to keep ourselves informed so that we can identify opportunities for insight.'

So what are the essentials for making a relationship last?

- Issue a clear brief and agree objectives, outputs and costs.
- Remove any ambiguity—this means personal contact rather than relying on e-mail alone.
- Ensure regular exchange of information.
- Communicate any changes that might affect the research project.
- Encourage honest, open, two-way constructive communication.
- Work as a team—the agency should be empowered to make decisions.
- Work with agencies that adopt a 'can do' attitude and are not afraid to challenge preconceptions.

Based on: Miles (2002)[12]

---

surveys, and customer satisfaction surveys. *ad hoc* surveys are either custom-designed or omnibus studies.

Custom-designed studies

Custom-designed studies are based on the specific needs of the client. The research design is based on the research brief given to the marketing research agency or internal marketing researcher. Because they are tailor-made, such surveys can be expensive.

Omnibus studies

The alternative is to use an **omnibus survey** in which space is bought on questionnaires for face-to-face or telephone interviews. The interview may cover many topics as the questionnaire space is bought by a number of clients who benefit from cost sharing. Usually the type of information sought is relatively simple (e.g. awareness levels and ownership data). Often the survey will be based on demographically balanced samples of 1000–2000 adults. However, more specialist surveys covering the markets for children, young adults, mothers and babies, the 'grey' market and motorists exist.

Continuous research

Continuous research gathers information from external sources on an ongoing basis. Major types of continuous research are consumer panels, retail audits, television viewership panels, marketing databases, customer relationship management systems and website analysis.

Consumer panels

Consumer panels are formed by recruiting large numbers of households, which provide information on their purchases over time. For example, a grocery panel would record the brands, pack sizes, prices and stores used for a wide range of supermarket brands. By using the same households over a period of time, measures of brand loyalty and switching can be achieved, together with a demographic profile of the type of person who buys particular brands.

Retail audits

Retail audits are a second type of continuous research. By gaining the cooperation of retail outlets (e.g. supermarkets) sales of brands can be measured by means of laser scans of barcodes on packaging, which are read at the checkout. Although brand loyalty and switching cannot be measured, retail audits can provide accurate assessment of sales achieved by store. A major provider of retail audit data is the ACNielsen Corp.

Television viewership panels

Television viewership panels measure audience sizes minute by minute. Commercial breaks can be allocated *ratings points* (the proportion of the target audience watching), which are the currency by which television advertising is bought and judged. In the UK the system is controlled by the Broadcasters' Audience Research Board (BARB), and run by AGB and RSMB. AGB handles the measurement process and uses *peoplemeters* that record whether a TV set is on/off, which channel is being watched and, by means of a hand console, who is watching.

Marketing databases

Companies collect data on customers on an ongoing basis. The data are stored on marketing databases, which contain each customer's name, address, telephone number, past transactions and, sometimes, demographic and lifestyle data. Information on the types of purchase, frequency of purchase, purchase value and responsiveness to promotional offers may be held.

Retailers are encouraging the collection of such data by introducing loyalty card schemes such as the Nectar card, which allows customers to collect points that can be redeemed for cashback or gifts at a group of retailers including Sainsbury, Barclays Bank and Debenhams. The card, which is swiped through the cash machine at the checkout, contains information about the cardholder, such as name and address, so that purchasing data including expenditure per visit, types of brands purchased, how often the customer shops and when, and at which branch, can be linked to individuals.

Customer relationship management systems

A potential problem with the growth of marketing databases is that separate ones are created in different departments of the company. For example, the sales department may have an account management database containing information on customers, while call centre staff may use a different database created at a different time also containing information on customers. This fragmented approach can lead to problems when, for example, a customer transaction is recorded on one but not the other database.

Issues like this have led to the development of customer relationship management systems, where a single database is created from customer information to inform all staff who deal with customers. Customer relationship management is a term for the methodologies, technologies and e-commerce capabilities used by companies to manage customer relationships.[13]

Data is collected, stored, analysed and used in a way that provides information to customer-contact staff in a way that conforms to the way they work and the way customers want to access the company (e.g. via the salesforce, telephone, e-mail or websites).

Website analysis

Continuous data can also be provided by analysing consumers' use of websites. Measurements of the areas of the site most frequently visited, how long each visitor spends seeking out information, which products are purchased and the payment method used can be made. Other measurements include how well the site loads on browsers, how well it downloads, whether it ranks within the top three pages on major search engines and the number of sites to which it is linked. These measurement issues and their importance are discussed in e-Marketing 6.1.

Online retailers can get valuable information through website analysis. For example, an online camera store can track sales by time of day, or they can be related to promotional campaigns or even sporting events. The retailer can analyse a customer's behaviour to build a profile of their habits. For example, if a shopper visits the website but does not buy, a promotional voucher discount might be sent to persuade them to try again.[14]

6.1 e-marketing

Using Website Analysis to Improve Online Performance

Website analysis is an invaluable means of assessing the current performance of a site and can identify key areas for improvement. Using Netmechanic (www.netmechanic.com), individual pages of a website can be assessed on issues such as browser compatibility (if the site fails to load properly on particular browsers, e.g. Internet Explorer versions 5 and 6, this could prevent between 80 per cent and 90 per cent of the potential audience from viewing the site properly) and download time (if the site takes too long to download customers will move on).

Using MarketLeap (www.marketleap.com), and in particular the key word verification tool, a site can again be tested on whether it ranks within the top three pages on major search engines. If the site does not rank within the top few pages of returns, then over 90 per cent of potential customers will not look any further. In addition, using the link popularity tool, it is possible to tell the number of sites on the Internet on which the website address appears as a link; the more sites it can be found on, the more popular it is and the greater the marketing effect. These online tools provide the base level of online marketing research that any online organization should attempt to conduct and act on.

Stages in the marketing research process

Each ad hoc marketing research project may be different in order to fit the particular requirements and resources of various clients. For example, one study may focus on *qualitative research* using small numbers of respondents while another may be largely quantitative, involving interviewing hundreds or thousands of consumers. Nevertheless, a useful framework for understanding the steps involved in the marketing research process is provided in Fig. 6.3. This provides a 'road map' of what is involved in a major marketing research study covering both qualitative and quantitative research. It is used by marketing

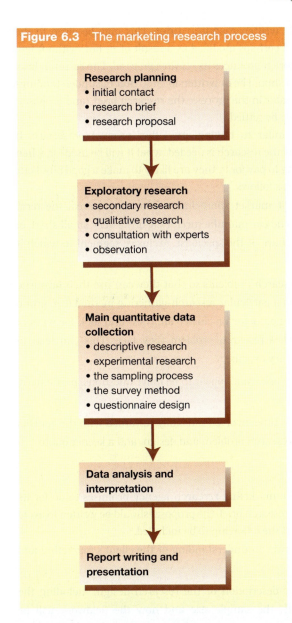

Figure 6.3 The marketing research process

research practitioners and can form the structure for a student marketing research project. Each of the stages in this process will now be discussed.

Research planning

Considerable thought needs to go into a marketing research project before data is gathered. Decisions made at the research planning stage will fundamentally affect what is done later. A commercial marketing research project is likely to involve marketing management at the client company, internal marketing research staff and, usually, research staff at an outside marketing research agency. The following discussion assumes this is the situation. Student projects are usually conducted in small groups. In this case the module leader or tutor takes on the role of the client, and the group becomes the research team responsible for drawing up a research proposal that meets the requirements of the research project brief and for conducting the research.

Initial contact

The start of the process is usually the realization that a marketing problem (e.g. a new product development or advertising decision) requires information to help its solution. Marketing management may contact internal marketing research staff or an outside agency. Let us assume that the research requires the assistance of a marketing research agency. A meeting will be arranged to discuss the nature of the problem and the client's research needs. If the client and its markets are new to the agency, some rudimentary exploratory research (e.g. a quick library search for information about the client and its markets) may be conducted prior to the meeting.

Research brief

At the meeting, the client will explain the marketing problem and outline the research objectives. The marketing problem might be to attract new customers to a product line, and the research objectives could be to identify groups of customers (market segments) that might have a use for the product, and the characteristics of the product that appeal to them most.[15]

Other information that should be provided for the research agency includes the following.[16]

1. *Background information*: the product's history and the competitive situation.
2. *Sources of information*: the client may have a list of industries that might be potential users of the product. This helps the researchers to define the scope of the research.
3. *The scale of the project*: is the client looking for a 'cheap and cheerful' job or a major study? This has implications for the research design and survey costs.
4. *The timetable*: when is the information required?

The client should produce a specific written **research brief**. This may be given to the research agency prior to the meeting and perhaps modified as a result of it, but, without fail, should be in the hands of the agency before it produces its *research proposal*. The research brief should state the client's requirements and should be in written form so that misunderstandings are minimized. In the event of a dispute later in the process, the research brief (and proposal) form the benchmarks against which it can be settled.

Commissioning good research is similar to buying any other product or service. If marketing management can agree on why the research is needed, what it will be used for, when it is needed and how much they are willing to pay for it, they are likely to make a good buy. Four suggestions for buying good research are as follows.

1. Define terms clearly. For example, if market share information is required, the term 'market' should clearly be defined. The car manufacturer TVR has a very small share of the car market but a much higher share of the specialist, exclusive segment in which it markets.

2. Beware of researchers who bend research problems so that they can use their favourite technique. They may be specialists in a particular research-gathering method (e.g. group discussion) or statistical technique (e.g. factor or cluster analysis) and look for ways of using these methods no matter what research problem they face. This can lead to irrelevant information and unnecessary expense.

3. Do not be put off by researchers who ask what appear to be naive questions, particularly if they are new to the client's industry.

4. Brief two or three agencies. The extra time involved is usually rewarded with the benefits of more than one viewpoint on the research problem and design, and a keener quote.

Research proposal

The **research proposal** defines what the marketing research agency promises to do for its client, and how much it will cost. Like the research brief, the proposal should be written to avoid misunderstandings. A client should expect the following to be included.

1. *A statement of objectives*: to demonstrate an understanding of the client's marketing and research problems.

2. *What will be done*: an unambiguous description of the research design, including the survey method, the type of sample, the sample size and how the fieldwork will be controlled.

3. *Timetable*: if and when a report will be produced.

4. *Costs*: how much the research will cost and what, specifically, is/is not being included in those costs.

When assessing proposals a client might usefully check the following points.

1. *Beware of vagueness*: if the proposal is vague, assume that the report is also likely to be vague. If the agency does not state what is going to be done, why, who is doing it and when, assume that it is not clear in its own mind about these important issues.

2. *Beware of jargon*: there is no excuse for jargon-ridden proposals. Marketing research terminology can be explained in non-expert language, so it is the responsibility of the agency to make the proposal understandable to the client.

3. *Beware of omissions*: assume that anything not specified will not be provided. For example, if no mention of a presentation is made in the proposal, assume it will not take place. If in doubt, ask the agency.

Exploratory research

Exploratory research involves the preliminary exploration of a research area prior to the main quantitative data-collection stage. It usually occurs between acceptance of the research proposal and the main data-collection stage, but can also take place prior to the client–agency briefing meeting (as we have seen) and before submission of the research proposal, as an aid to its construction. The discussion that follows assumes that the proposal has been accepted and that exploratory research is being used as the basis for survey design.

A major purpose of exploratory research is to guard against the sins of omission and admission.[17]

- *Sin of omission*: not researching a topic in enough detail, or failing to provide sufficient respondents in a group to allow meaningful analysis.

- *Sin of admission*: collecting data that are irrelevant to the marketing problem, or using too many groups for analysis purposes and thereby unnecessarily increasing the sample size.

Exploratory research techniques allow the research to understand the people who are to be interviewed in the main data-collection stage, and the market that is being researched. The main survey stage can thus be designed with this knowledge in mind rather than being based on the researcher's ill-informed prejudices and guesswork.

Figure 6.4 displays the four exploratory research activities. An individual research project may involve all or some of them.

Secondary research

Secondary research is so called because the data come to the researcher 'second-hand' (other people have compiled the data). When the researcher actively collects new data—for example, by interviewing respondents—this is called primary research.

Secondary data can be found by examination of internal records and reports of research previously carried out for the company. External sources include government and European Union statistics, publishers of reports and directories on markets, countries and industries, trade associations, banks, newspapers, magazines and journals. The development of search engines, for example, means that secondary information searches on newspapers and journals

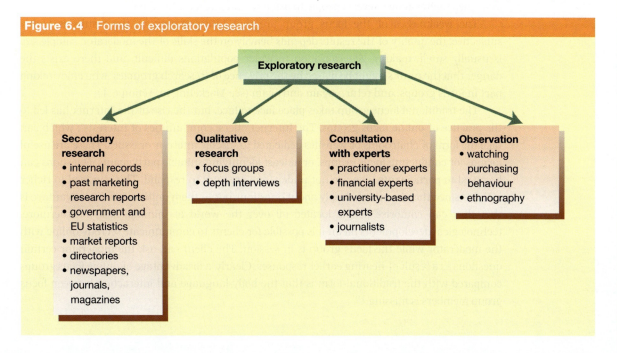

Figure 6.4 Forms of exploratory research

can be quickly and simply accomplished. By typing in the appropriate keywords the computer searches the relevant publications and can provide a printout of the article. The European Community is well blessed with secondary sources of data, and Marketing in Action 6.3 lists some of the major sources of marketing information classified by research questions.

Secondary research should be carried out before primary research. Without the former, an expensive primary research survey might be commissioned to provide information that is already available from secondary sources. Furthermore, directories such as *Kompass* can be invaluable when selecting a sample in an industrial marketing research project.

Qualitative research

The main forms of qualitative research are group discussions and depth interviews. Qualitative research aims to establish customers' attitudes, values, behaviour and beliefs. It attempts to understand consumers in a way that traditional methods of interviewing people using questionnaires cannot. Qualitative research seeks to understand the 'why' and 'how' of consumer behaviour.[18]

Focus groups involve unstructured or semi-structured discussions between a *moderator*, or group leader, who is often a psychologist, and a group of consumers. The moderator has a list of areas to cover within the topic but allows the group considerable freedom to discuss the issues that are important to them. The topic might be coffee drinking, do-it-yourself car mechanics or holiday pursuits. By arranging groups of 6–12 people to discuss their beliefs, attitudes, motivation, behaviour and preferences a good deal of knowledge may be gained about the consumer. This can be helpful when planning questionnaires, which can then be designed to focus on what is important to the respondent (as opposed to the researcher) and worded in language that the respondent uses and understands.

A further advantage of the focus group is that the findings in themselves may provide rich insights into consumer motivations and behaviour because of the group dynamics where group members 'feed off' each other and reveal ideas that would not have arisen on a one-to-one basis. Such findings may be used as food for thought for marketers without the need for quantitative follow-up. Also, the use of two-way mirrors allows marketers and other people from the client organization to view the focus group session without themselves being viewed, and video taping allows several people to listen to and interpret the data.

The weaknesses of the focus group are that interpretation of the results is highly subjective, the quality of the results depends heavily on the skills of the moderator, sample size is usually small, making generalization to wider populations difficult, and there exists the danger that the results might be biased by the presence of 'research groupies' who enjoy taking part in focus groups, and return again and again (see Marketing in Action 6.1).

The traditional focus group takes place face to face, but the rise of the Internet has led to the practice of online focus groups. The Internet offers 'communities of interests', which can take the form of chatrooms or websites dedicated to specific interests or issues. These are useful forums for conducting focus groups, or at least identifying suitable participants. Questions can be posed to participants who are not under time pressure to respond. This can lead to richer insights since they can think deeply about questions put to them online. Another advantage is that they can comprise people located all over the world at minimal cost. Furthermore, technological developments mean it is possible for clients to communicate secretly online with the moderator while the focus group is in session. The client can ask the moderator certain questions as a result of hearing earlier responses. Clearly, a disadvantage of online focus groups compared with the traditional form is that the body language and interaction between focus group members is missing.[19]

6.3 marketing in action

Sources of Marketing Information

Is there a survey of the industry?

Euromonitor GMID Database has in-depth analysis and current market information in the key areas of country data, consumer lifestyles, market sizes, forecasts, brand and company information, business information sources and marketing profiles.

Reuters Business Insight Reports are full text reports available online in the sectors of healthcare, financial services, consumer goods, energy, and e-commerce and technology.

Key Note Reports cover size of market, economic trends, prospects and company performance.

Snapshots on CD-Rom The 'Snapshots' CD series is a complete library of market research reports, providing coverage of consumer, business-to-business and industrial markets. Containing 2000 market reports, this series provides incisive data and analysis on over 8000 market segments for the UK, Europe and the United States.

Index to Business Reports is an index to reports on markets, products and industries.

British Library Market Research is a guide to British Library Holdings. It lists titles of reports arranged by industries. Some items are available on inter-library loan; others may be seen at the British Library in London.

Marketsearch: International Directory of Published Market Research

How large is the market?

European Marketing Data and Statistics Now available on the Euromonitor GMID database.
International Marketing Data and Statistics Now available on the Euromonitor GMID database.
European Marketing Pocket Book
The Asia Pacific Marketing Pocket Book
The Americas Marketing Pocket Book

Where is the market?

Regional Marketing Pocket Book
Regional Trends gives the main economic and social statistics for UK regions.
Geodemographic Pocket Book

Who are the competitors?

British companies can be identified using any of the following:
Kompass (most European countries have their own edition).
Key British Enterprises
Quarterly Review—KPMG
Sell's Products and Services Directory (Gen Ref E 380.02542 SEL)

For more detailed company information consult:
Companies Annual Reports Collection
Carol—Company Annual Reports Online at www.carol.co.uk
Fame DVD (CD-Rom service)
Business Ratio Reports
Retail Rankings

▶

▶ Overseas companies' sources include:
   Asia's 7,500 Largest Companies
   D&B Europa
   Dun's Asia Pacific Key Business Enterprises
   Europe's 15,000 Largest Companies
   Major Companies of the Arab World
   Million Dollar Directory (US)
   Principal International Businesses

What are the trends?
Possible sources to consider are:
Consumer Europe Now available on the Euromonitor GMID database.
Consumer Goods Europe
Economic Trends
Family Expenditure Survey
Social Trends
The Book of European Forecasts Now available on the Euromonitor GMID database.
Lifestyle Pocket Book
World Drink Trends
Marketing Pocket Book
Media Pocket Book
Asia Pacific Marketing Pocket Book
Americas Marketing Pocket Book

EU statistical and information sources

Eurostat is a series of publications that provide a detailed picture of the EU. They can be obtained by visiting European Documentation Centres (often in university libraries) in all EU countries. Themes include general statistics, economy and finance, and population/social conditions.

European Access is a bulletin on issues, policies, activities and events concerning EU member states.

European Report is a twice-weekly news publication from Brussels on industrial, economic and political issues.

Guides to marketing information
World Directory of Marketing Information Sources
Croner's A–Z of Business Information Sources

Abstracts and indices
BPO (Business Periodicals On Disc) ABI and Proquest Direct
Elsevier Science Direct
Emerald
Web of Science
Wiley Interscience and Boldideas

Statistics
Guide to Official Statistics
Sources of Non-Official UK Statistics
Annual Abstract of Statistics

▶

▶ *Key Data*
World Directory of Non-Official Statistical Sources Also available on the Euromonitor GMID database.

Online sources
BIZ/ED (http://www.bized.ac.uk) provides a range of resources for students of business and economics. Materials include study skills, advice, glossaries, notes and databases of resources.

Directory of Business Information Websites provides details of a wealth of business information sources that are available on the net. Coverage includes nearly 1400 websites providing access to statistics, market and company information. Also available on the Euromonitor GMID database.

World Business Resources.com

Business Information on the Internet (compiled by Karen Blakeman) is a useful portal for business information on the web, with links to sites covering company and market information, country and news sources and much more: http://www.rba.co.uk/sources/

Mintel market research reports: http://reports.mintel.com
Euromonitor market reports: www.euromonitor.com
Department of Trade and Industry trade and market information: www.dt.gov.uk
Competition Commission reports: www.competition-commission.org.uk
Company information on companies in 30 European countries: www.europager.com
Company financial information in the UK: http://fame.bvdep.com
Key Note summary reports: www.keynote.co.uk
CIM marketing research reports: www.marketingportal.co.uk
Business journal contents: http://proquest.umi.com/pqdweb

Note: some of these sites require passwords, which can be obtained from libraries.
Source: the author thanks Jenny Finder of Bradford University School of Management Library for her help in compiling this list.

Depth interviews involve the interviewing of consumers individually for perhaps one or two hours about a topic. The aims are broadly similar to those of group discussion but are used when the presence of other people could inhibit honest answers and viewpoints, when the topic requires individual treatment, as when discussing an individual's decision-making process, and where the organization of a group is not feasible (for example, it might prove impossible to arrange for six busy purchasing managers to come together for a group discussion).

Care has to be taken when interpreting the results of qualitative research in that the findings are usually based on small sample sizes, and the more interesting or surprising viewpoints may be disproportionately reported. This is particularly significant when qualitative research is not followed by a quantitative study.

Qualitative research accounts for 10 per cent of all European expenditure on marketing research, of which 60 per cent is spent on group discussions, 30 per cent on depth interviews and 10 per cent on other qualitative techniques. Because of its ability to provide in-depth understanding it is of growing importance within the field of consumer research.[20]

Consultation with experts

Qualitative research is based on discussions and interviews with actual and potential buyers of a brand or service. However, consultation with experts involves interviewing people who may not form part of the target market but who, nevertheless, can provide important marketing-related insights. Many industries have their experts in universities, financial institutions and the press who may be willing to share their knowledge. They can provide invaluable background information and can be useful for predicting future trends and developments.

Observation

Observation can also help in exploratory research when the product field is unfamiliar. Watching people buy wine in a supermarket or paint in a DIY store may provide useful background knowledge when planning a survey in these markets, for example.

A form of observation that involves detailed and prolonged observation of consumers is called ethnography. Its origins are in social anthropology, where researchers live in a studied society for months or years. Consumer researchers usually make their observations more quickly and use a range of methods, including direct observations, interviews and video and audio recordings.[21] Marketing in Action 6.4 illustrates its use in marketing research.

6.4 marketing in action

Understanding Consumers through Ethnographic Research

The growing demand for getting closer to consumers and understanding their behaviour has given rise to the increasing use of ethnographic research. Such research investigates ways in which people behave in their own environment and how they interact with the world around them. Unlike focus groups, where consumers are brought to the researcher, ethnography takes the researcher to the consumer. Advocates of this form of research argue that focus groups only provide part of the story and do not yield the kinds of 'consumer insights' that ethnography can.

One company that has embraced ethnographic research is Procter & Gamble. Twenty families in the UK and a further 20 in Italy were chosen to take part in a study that involved the recording of their daily household behaviour by video camera. The idea was that by studying people who buy P&G products—such as Max Factor cosmetics, Ariel washing powder and Pampers nappies—the company could gain valuable insights into people's consumer habits. The findings have had implications for its approach to product design, packaging and advertising. A P&G spokesman pointed out that ethnography will not replace other forms of research and that ethical issues concerning privacy are dealt with by getting full permission beforehand and giving the families complete editorial control over what is eventually shown to the marketing team.

The objective of ethnographic research is to bridge the gap between what people say they do and what they actually do. Its usefulness is reflected in the fact that companies such as Nokia, Toyota, Land Rover, Intel, Van den Berghs, Adidas and Nike have used this genre of research. It has been used in the technology field to understand how electronic products are really used. The findings showed that people will use technology in ways its inventors never imagined. For example, one family used broadband technology to pipe sound from the local mosque into their home. Another had two Sony PlayStations: one to play games on, the other for only playing CDs. Of ten families studied, two left their televisions on all day even when they went out—something they were unlikely to admit in a focus group.

Based on: Cozens (2001);[22] Earnshaw (2001);[23] Gofton (2001);[24] James (2002);[25] Ritson (2002);[26] Singh (2001)[27]

The objective of exploratory research, then, is not to collect quantitative data and form conclusions but to get better acquainted with the market and its customers. This allows the researcher to base the quantitative survey on *informed assumptions* rather than guesswork.

The main quantitative data-collection stage

Following careful exploratory research, the design of the main quantitative data-collection procedures will be made. Two alternative approaches are descriptive and experimental research.

Assuming the main data-collection stage requires interviewing, the research design will be based on the following factors:

- who and how many people to interview (the sampling process)
- how to interview them (the survey method)
- what questions to ask (questionnaire design).

Figure 6.5 displays the two types and three research design methods associated with the main quantitative data-collection stage. These research approaches and methods will now be examined.

Descriptive research

Descriptive research may be undertaken to describe consumers' beliefs, attitudes, preferences, behaviour, etc. For example, a survey into advertising effectiveness might measure awareness of the brand, recall of the advertisement and knowledge about its content.

Experimental research

The aim of experimental research is to establish cause and effect. **Experimental research** involves the setting up of control procedures to isolate the impact of a factor (e.g. a money-off sales promotion) on a dependent variable (e.g. sales). The key to successful experimental design is the elimination of other explanations of changes in the dependent variable. One way of doing this is to use random sampling. For example, the sales promotion might be applied in a random selection of stores with the remaining stores selling the brand without the money-off offer. Statistical significance testing can be used to test whether differences in sales are likely to be caused by the sales promotion or are simply random variations. The effects of other influences on sales are assumed to impact randomly on both the sales promotion and the no promotion alternatives.

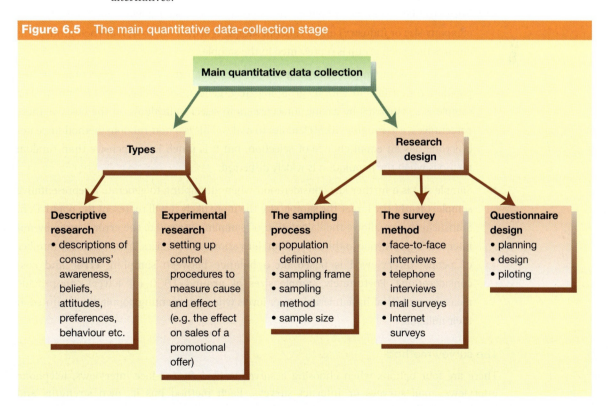

Figure 6.5 The main quantitative data-collection stage

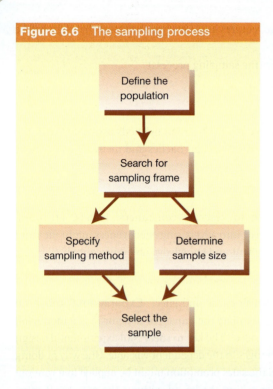

Figure 6.6 The sampling process

The sampling process

Figure 6.6 outlines the **sampling process**. It begins by *defining the population*—that is, the group that forms the subject of study in a particular survey. The survey objective will be to provide results that are representative of this group. Sampling planners, for example, must ask questions like: 'Do we interview all people over the age of 18 or restrict it to those of the population aged 18–60?', 'Do we interview purchasing managers in all textile companies or only those that employ more than 200 people?'

Once the population has been defined, the next step is to search for a *sampling frame*—that is, a list or other record of the chosen population from which a sample can be selected. Examples include a register of electors, or the *Kompass* directory of companies. The result determines whether a random or non-random sample can be chosen. A random sample requires an accurate sampling frame; without one, the researcher is restricted to non-random methods.

Three major *sampling methods* are simple random sampling, stratified random sampling and quota sampling. It is also important to determine *sample size*.

- With simple random sampling, each individual (or company) in the sampling frame is given a number, and numbers are drawn at random (by chance) until the sample is complete. The sample is random because everyone on the list has an equal chance of selection.

- With stratified random sampling, the population is broken down into groups (e.g. by company size or industry) and a random sample is drawn (as above) for each group. This ensures that each group is represented in the sample.

- With quota sampling, a sampling frame does not exist but the percentage of the population that falls in various groupings (e.g. gender, social class, age) is known. The sample is constructed by asking interviewers to select individuals on the basis of these percentages, e.g. roughly 50:50 females to males. This is a non-random method since not everyone has an equal chance of selection, but it is much less expensive than random methods when the population is widely dispersed.

- Sample size is a further key consideration when attempting to generate a representative sample. Clearly, the larger the sample size the more likely it will represent the population. Statistical theory allows the calculation of sampling error (i.e. the error caused by not interviewing everyone in the population) for various sample sizes. In practice, the number of people interviewed is based on a balance between sampling error and cost considerations. Fortunately sample sizes of around 1000 (or fewer) can provide measurements that have tolerable error levels when representing populations counted in their millions.

The survey method

There are four options when choosing a *survey method*: face-to-face interviews, telephone interviews, mail surveys or Internet surveys. Each method has its own strengths and limitations; Table 6.3 gives an overview of these.

Table 6.3 A comparison of face-to-face, telephone, mail and Internet surveys				
	Face to face	Telephone	Mail	Internet
Questionnaire				
Use of open-ended questions	High	Medium	Low	Low
Ability to probe	High	Medium	Low	Low
Use of visual aids	High	Poor	High	High
Sensitive questions	Medium	Low	High	Low
Resources				
Cost	High	Medium	Low	Low
Sampling				
Widely dispersed populations	Low	Medium	High	High
Response rates	High	Medium	Low	Low
Experimental control	High	Medium	Low	Low
Interviewing				
Control of who completes questionnaire	High	High	Low	Low/high
Interviewer bias	Possible	Possible	Low	Low

A major advantage of *face-to-face interviews* is that response rates are generally higher than for telephone interviews or mail surveys.[28] Seemingly the personal element in the contact makes refusal less likely. This is an important factor when considering how representative the sample is of the population and when using experimental designs. Testing the effectiveness of a stimulus would normally be conducted by face-to-face interview rather than a mail survey where high non-response rates and the lack of control over who completes the questionnaire would invalidate the results. Face-to-face interviews are more versatile than telephone and mail surveys.

The use of many open-ended questions on a mail survey would lower response rates,[29] and time restrictions for a telephone interview limit their use. Probing is easier with face-to-face interviews. Two types of probes are *clarifying probes* (e.g. 'Can you explain what you mean by …?'), which help the interviewer understand exactly what the interviewee is saying, and *exploratory probes*, which stimulate the interviewee to give a full answer (e.g. 'Are there any other reasons why …?'). A certain degree of probing can be achieved with a telephone interview, but time pressure and the less personalized situation will inevitably limit its use. Visual aids (e.g. a drawing of a new product concept) can be used where clearly they cannot with a telephone interview.

However, face-to-face interviews have their drawbacks. They are more expensive than telephone and mail questionnaires. Telephone and mail surveys are cheaper because the cost of contacting respondents is much less expensive, unless the population is very concentrated (face-to-face interviewing of students on a business studies course, for instance, would be relatively inexpensive). The presence of an interviewer can cause bias (e.g. socially desirable answers) and lead to the misreporting of sensitive information. For example, O'Dell found that only 17 per cent of respondents admitted borrowing money from a bank in a face-to-face interview compared to 42 per cent in a comparable mail survey.[30]

In some ways *telephone interviews* are a halfway house between face-to-face and mail surveys. They generally have a higher response rate than mail questionnaires but lower than face-to-face interviews; their cost is usually less than face-to-face but higher than for mail surveys; and they allow a degree of flexibility when interviewing. However, the use of visual aids is not possible and there are limits to the number of questions that can be asked before

Table 6.4 Methods of improving mail survey response rates	
Activity	Effect on response rate
Prior notification by mail	Increase in consumer research but not for commercial populations
Prior notification by telephone	Increased response rate
Monetary and non-monetary incentives	Increased response rate
Type of postage	Higher response rates for stamped return envelopes
Personalization	The effect varies: it cannot be assumed that personalization always increases response
Granting anonymity to respondents	Higher response rate when issue is sensitive
Coloured questionnaire	No effect on response rate
Deadline	No effect on response rate
Types of question	Closed-ended questions get higher response than open-ended
Follow-ups	Follow-up telephone calls and mailing increase response rates

respondents either terminate the interview or give quick (invalid) answers to speed up the process. The use of computer-aided telephone interviewing (CATI) is growing. Centrally located interviewers read questions from a computer monitor and input answers via the keyboard. *Routing* through the questionnaire is computer-controlled, helping the process of interviewing.

Mail surveys given a reasonable response rate; mail survey research normally is the least expensive of the first three options. A low research budget, combined with a widely dispersed population, may mean that there is no alternative to the mail survey. However, the major problem is the potential of low response rates and the accompanying danger of an unrepresentative sample. Much research has focused on ways of improving response rates to mail surveys and Table 6.4 gives a summary of the results.[31]

Mail questionnaires must be fully structured, so there is no opportunity to probe further. Control over who completes the questionnaire is low; for example, a marketing manager may pass the questionnaire to a subordinate for completion. However, visual aids can be supplied with the questionnaire and because of self-completion, interviewer bias is low although there may still be a source effect (e.g. whether the questionnaire was sent from a commercial or non-commercial source).

The Internet is a new medium for conducting survey research. With *Internet surveys*, the questionnaire is usually administered by e-mail, or signals its presence on a website by registering key words, or appears in banner advertising on search engines such as Yahoo! or Google which drive people to the questionnaire. E-Marketing 6.2 describes how the Internet can be used as a survey tool.

The major advantage of the Internet as a marketing research vehicle is its low cost, since printing and postal costs are eliminated, making it even cheaper than mail surveys. In other ways its characteristics are similar to those of mail surveys: the use of open-ended questions is limited (as these will reduce response rates) and its impersonal nature limits the ability to probe further on some questions. Visual aids can be supplied with the questionnaire and response rates are likely to be lower than face-to-face and telephone interviews. Experimental control is low since there is not complete control over who responds to the questionnaire, but interviewer bias is likely to be lower than for face-to-face and telephone interviews because of the impersonal administration of the questionnaire. A strength of the Internet survey is its ability to cover global populations at low cost, although sampling problems can arise because of the skewed nature of Internet users. These tend to be from the younger and more affluent groups in society. For surveys requiring a cross-sectional sample, this can be severely restricting.

6.2 e-marketing

Using the Internet as a Survey Tool

Survey Monkey (http://www.surveymonkey.com) is a website that allows users to develop a professional marketing research survey and to analyse the results. Usually this type of development falls within the realm of the professional market research company (at great expense). However, through use of online forms and drop-down options, a fully customized questionnaire, which meets the highest standards, can easily be formed.

Once a questionnaire has been developed, it can be sent to potential respondents as part of an e-mail, or the questionnaire can be highlighted through a link on the website—in this way it can provide, for example, valuable customer feedback about the site. As the questionnaire is already in digital format the market researcher is not required to re-type information from written results—this means that data collation is much quicker and less prone to human error.

Survey Monkey is a revolution in market research as it allows non-professionals access to sophisticated market research tools, in many cases free of charge. The free version is limited only by the number of questions that can be set (10) and the number of responses that can be collated (100) but offers the same levels of design and analysis sophistication as the paid version. Survey Monkey is an ideal starting point for business professionals and marketing students alike to develop their own online marketing research survey.

When response is by e-mail the identity of the respondent will automatically be sent to the survey company. This lack of anonymity may restrict the respondent's willingness to answer sensitive questions honestly. However, for e-mail surveys, control over who completes the questionnaire is fairly high, although for Internet surveys that invite anyone to complete the questionnaire, using registration or banner advertising with search engines, control is low.

A problem when using e-mail to survey populations is the absence of accurate lists. Even when lists can be found researchers need to tread very carefully as 'spamming'—sending junk mail—is seen as very offensive by most e-mail users.

Another approach is to recruit a panel of respondents from which members can be selected to take part in a particular survey. This panel-based approach has been popular in the USA for several years and is growing in popularity in Europe.[32]

Surveys of consumer discussions of the web are also taking place. For example, Audi commissioned research which monitors consumer discussions across a range of over 20 websites. Audi receives a stream of information—500 to 800 individual messages a week. This information is analysed so that the company can see who has been saying what about which model and dealership.[33]

Questionnaire design

Three conditions are necessary to get a true response to a question. First, respondents must *understand* the question; second, respondents must be *able to provide* the information; and, third, they must be *willing* to provide it. Researchers must remember these conditions when designing questionnaires. Questions need to be phrased in language the respondent understands. This can prove problematical with some types of respondents, however. A psychological survey of footballers called upon club managers to pass on questionnaires to their players.[34] One manager replied, 'Please feel free to send your questionnaires to me. I shall be happy to distribute them to the two or three players who can read or write, and have an attention span of longer than two minutes.'

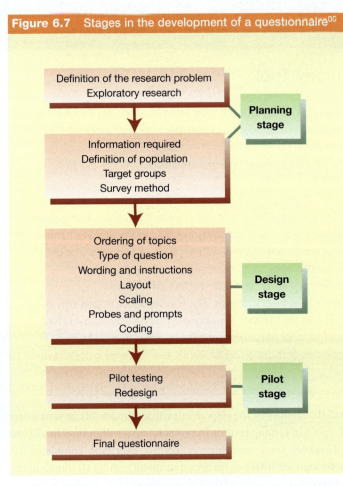

Figure 6.7 Stages in the development of a questionnaire[06]

Equally, researchers must not ask about issues that respondents cannot remember or that are outside their experience. For example, it would be invalid to ask about attitudes towards a brand of which the respondent is unaware. Finally, researchers need to consider the best way to elicit sensitive or personal information. As we have already seen, willingness to provide such information depends on the survey method employed.

Figure 6.7 shows the three stages in the development of the questionnaire: planning, design and pilot.

The *planning stage* involves the types of decision discussed so far in this chapter. It provides a firm foundation for designing a questionnaire that provides relevant information for the marketing problem that is being addressed.

The *design stage* involves a number of interrelated issues, as described below.

1. *Ordering of topics*: an effective questionnaire has a logical flow. It is sensible to start with easy-to-answer questions. This helps to build the confidence of respondents and allows them to relax. Respondents are often anxious at the beginning of an interview, concerned that they might show their ignorance. Other rules of thumb are simply common sense: for example, it would be logical to ask awareness questions before attitude measurement questions, and not vice versa. Unaided awareness questions must be asked before aided ones. Classificatory questions that ask for personal information such as age and occupation are usually asked last.

2. *Types of question*: closed-ended questions specify the range of answers that will be recorded. If there are only two possible answers (e.g. 'Did you visit a cinema within the last seven days?' YES/NO) the question is *dichotomous* (either/or). If there are more than two possible answers, then the question is *multiple choice* (e.g. 'Which, if any, of the following cinemas have you visited within the last seven days?' ODEON, SHOWCASE, CANNON, NONE). *Open-ended questions* allow respondents to answer the question in their own words (e.g. 'Please tell me what you liked about the cinema you visited?'). The interviewer then writes the answer in a space on the questionnaire.

3. *Wording and instructions*: great care needs to be taken in the wording of questions. Questionnaire designers need to guard against ambiguity, leading questions, asking two-questions-in-one and using unfamiliar words. Table 6.5 gives some examples of poorly worded questions and suggests remedies. Instructions should be printed in capital letters or underlined so that they are easily distinguishable from questions.

Table 6.5 Poorly worded questions and how to avoid them	
Question	Problem and solution
What type of wine do you prefer?	'Type' is ambiguous: respondents could say 'French', 'red', 'claret' depending on their interpretation. Showing the respondent a list and asking 'from this list ...' would avoid the problem.
Do you think that prices are cheaper at Asda than at Aldi?	Leading question favouring Asda: a better question would be 'Do you think that prices at Asda are higher, lower or about the same as at Aldi?' Names should be reversed for half the sample.
Which is more powerful and kind to your hands: Ariel or Bold?	Two questions in one: Ariel may be more powerful but Bold may be kinder to the hands. Ask the two questions separately.
Do you find it paradoxical that X lasts longer and yet is cheaper than Y?	Unfamiliar word: a study has shown that less than a quarter of the population understand such words as paradoxical, chronological or facility. Test understanding before use.

(4) *Layout*: the questionnaire should not appear cluttered. If possible, answers and codes should each form a column so that they are easy to identify. In mail questionnaires, it is a mistake to squeeze too many questions on to one page so that the questionnaire length (in pages) is shortened. Response is more likely to be lower if the questionnaire appears heavy than if its page length is extended.[36]

(5) *Scaling*: careful exploratory research may allow attitudes and beliefs to be measured by means of scales. Respondents are given lists of statements (e.g. 'My company's marketing information system allows me to make better decisions') followed by a choice of five positions on a scale ranging from 'strongly agree' to 'strongly disagree'.

Exploratory research identifies statements, and a structured questionnaire is used to provide quantification.

(6) *Probes and prompts*: probes seek to explore or clarify what a respondent has said. Following a question about awareness of brand names, the *exploratory probe* 'Any others?' would seek to identify further names. Sometimes respondents use vague words or phrases like 'I like going on holiday because it is nice.' A *clarifying probe* such as, 'In what way is it nice?' would seek a more meaningful response. *Prompts*, on the other hand, aid responses to a question. For example, in an aided-recall question, a list of brand names would be provided for the respondent.

(7) *Coding*: by using closed questions the interviewer merely has to ring the code number next to the respondent's choice of answer. In computer-assisted telephone interviewing and with the increasing use of laptop computers for face-to-face interviewing, the appropriate code number can be keyed directly into the computer's memory. Such questionnaires are *pre-coded*, making the process of interviewing and data analysis much simpler. Open-ended questions, however, require the interviewer to write down the answer verbatim. This necessitates *post-coding*, whereby answers are categorized after the interview. This can be a time-consuming and laborious task.

Once the preliminary questionnaire has been designed, it should be piloted with a representative sub-sample, to test for faults. The *pilot stage* is not the same as exploratory research. Exploratory research helps to decide upon the research design; piloting tests the questionnaire design and helps to estimate costs. Face-to-face piloting, where respondents are asked to answer questions and comment on any problems concerning a questionnaire read out

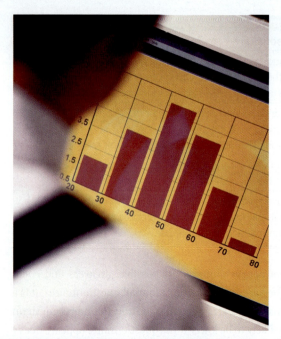

A computer-generated histogram displaying marketing research information.

by an interviewer, is preferable to impersonal piloting, where the questionnaire is given to respondents for self-completion and they are asked to write down any problems found.[37] If desired, several kinds of question on the same topic can be asked in order to assess the effects of the wording on respondents.[38] Once the pilot work proves satisfactory the final questionnaire can be administered to the chosen sample.

Data analysis and interpretation

Quantitative analysis of questionnaire data will invariably be carried out by computer. Basic marketing analyses can be carried out using such software-analysis packages as SNAP or MARQUIS on a personal computer. More sophisticated analyses can be conducted using a package such as SPSS-PC.

Basic analysis may be at the descriptive level (e.g. means, standard deviations and frequency tables) or on a comparative basis (e.g. cross tabulations and t-tests). The illustration shows a computer-generated histogram. More sophisticated analysis may search for relationships (e.g. regression analysis), group respondents (e.g. cluster analysis) or establish cause and effect (e.g. analysis of variance techniques used on experimental data). Computer-aided analysis of marketing research data is not limited to quantitative data. The analysis of vast volumes of qualitative data can be aided by the use of a software package called NUD.IST, where data can be filed, accessed and organized in more sophisticated ways than manual analysis.

Great care is required when interpreting marketing research results. One common failing is to infer cause and effect when only association has been established. For example, establishing a relationship that sales rise when advertising levels increase does not necessarily mean that raising advertising expenditure will lead to an increase in sales. Other marketing variables—for example, salesforce effect—may have increased at the same time as the increase in advertising, or the advertising budget may have been dependent on sales levels. Either explanation would invalidate the claim that advertising causes sales to rise.

A second cautionary note concerns the interpretation of means and percentages. Given that a sample has been taken, any mean or percentage is an estimate subject to *sampling error*—that is, the error in an estimate due to taking a sample rather than interviewing the entire population. A market research survey which estimates that 50 per cent of males but only 45 per cent of females smoke does not necessarily suggest that smoking is more prevalent among males. Given the sampling error associated with each estimate, the true conclusion might be that there is no difference between males and females. Statistical hypothesis testing allows sample differences to be evaluated in the light of sampling error to establish whether they are likely to be real differences (statistically significant) or likely to be a result of taking a sample (rather than interviewing the entire population).

Report writing and presentation

Crouch suggests that the key elements in a research report are as follows:[39]

① title page

② list of contents

(3) preface (outline of agreed brief, statement of objectives, scope and methods of research)

(4) summary of conclusions and recommendations

(5) previous related research (how previous research has had a bearing on this research)

(6) research method

(7) research findings

(8) conclusions

(9) appendices.

Sections 1–4 provide a concise description of the nature and outcomes of the research for busy managers. Sections 5–9 provide the level of detail necessary if any particular issue (e.g. the basis of a finding, or the analytical technique used) needs checking. The report should be written in language the reader will understand; jargon should be avoided.

Software packages such as PowerPoint considerably ease the production of pie charts, histograms, graphs, and so on, for use in the report or for presentational purposes (such as the production of acetates for overhead projection).

The emergence of inexpensive colour printers means that colour graphics can be used.

The use of marketing information systems and marketing research

A key issue is an understanding of the factors that affect the use of marketing information systems and marketing research. Systems and marketing research reports that remain unused are valueless in decision-making. So what factors are likely to bring about increased usage? Two studies of MkIS have examined the factors that affect usage. Systems are used more when:

- the system is sophisticated and confers prestige to its users
- other departments view the system as a threat
- there is pressure from top management to use the system
- users are more involved in automation.

The system takes more of the marketing executive's time when:

- it provides information indiscriminately
- it provides less assistance
- it is changed without consultation.

These results have implications for the design of MkIS. Sophisticated systems should be designed that provide information on a selective basis (for example, by means of a direct, interactive capability).[40] Senior management should conspicuously support use of the system. These recommendations are in line with Ackoff's view that a prime task of an information system is to eliminate irrelevant information by tailoring information flows to individual manager's needs.[41] It also supports the prescription of Piercy and Evans that the system should be seen to have top management support.[42]

Research into the use of marketing research has shown that use is higher if:[43]

- results conform to the client's prior beliefs
- the research is technically competent
- the presentation of results is clear
- the findings are politically acceptable
- the status quo is not challenged.

These findings suggest that marketing researchers need to appreciate not only the technical aspects of research and the need for clarity in report presentation but also the political dimension of information provision: it is unlikely that marketing research reports will be used in decision-making if the results threaten the status quo or are likely to have adverse political repercussions. As Machiavelli said, 'Knowledge is power.' The sad fact is that perfectly valid and useful information may be ignored in decision-making for reasons that are outside the technical competence of the research.

Ethical issues in marketing research

The intention of marketing research is to benefit both the sponsoring company and its consumers. The company learns about the needs and buyer behaviour of consumers with the objective of better satisfying their needs. Despite these good intentions there are four ethical concerns about marketing research. These are intrusions on privacy, the misuse of marketing research findings, competitive information gathering, and the use of marketing research surveys as a guise for selling.

Intrusions on privacy

While many consumers recognize the positive role marketing research plays in the provision of goods and services, some resent the intrusive nature of some marketing research surveys. Most consumer surveys ask for classificatory data such as age, occupation and income. While most surveys ask respondents to indicate an age and income band rather than request specifics, some people feel that this is an intrusion on privacy. Other people object to receiving unsolicited telephone calls or mail surveys, and dislike being stopped in the street to be asked to complete a face-to-face survey. As the use of the Internet as a marketing research tool grows, ethical issues regarding the unsolicited receipt of e-mail questionnaires may arise. The right of individuals to privacy is incorporated in the guidelines of many research associations. For example, a code of conduct of the European Society for Opinion and Marketing Research (ESOMAR) states that 'no information which could be used to identify informants, either directly or indirectly, shall be revealed other than to research personnel within the researchers' own organization who require this knowledge for the administration and checking of interviews and data processing'.[44] Under no circumstances should the information from a survey combined with the address/telephone number of the respondent be supplied to a salesperson.

Some intrusions on privacy involve questioning about personal issues, as Ethical Marketing in Action 6.1 explains.

Misuse of marketing research findings

Where the findings of marketing research are to be used in an advertising campaign or as part of a sales pitch there can be a temptation to bias the results in favour of the desired outcome. Respondents could be chosen who are more likely to give a favourable response. For example, a study comparing a domestic versus foreign brand of car could be biased by only choosing people that own domestic-made cars. Another source of bias would be using leading questions—for example, 'In a world that is becoming increasingly environmentally aware, would you prefer more or less recyclable packaging?'

Another potential source of bias in the use of marketing research findings is where the client explicitly or implicitly communicates to the researcher the preferred research result. For example, a product champion for a new product may have a vested interest in the product being

6.1 ethical marketing in action

Ethics in Marketing Research: the Case of the Femidom

All market research makes demands of the consumer and hence has the potential to do harm by wasting their time, raising worrying issues or presenting spurious needs; but good research can also bring consumer benefits by ironing out product faults or clarifying marketing communications. Researchers therefore have two fundamental obligations: on the one hand to ensure that their research does no harm to respondents and, on the other, that their data is reliable. Unsound research is, by definition, also unethical. The former demands attention to such principles as confidentiality and respondent comfort, the latter highlights the need for rigour and scientific method.

Consider for example, the female condom, or Femidom. This is the only barrier contraceptive that women can control, and therefore brings important health benefits. Women can use the product to give themselves protection against pregnancy and disease even when their partners are uncooperative. Marketing research has a crucial role to play in ensuring, for instance, that women understand instruction leaflets on how to use the Femidom, and the benefits the product can bring. However, pre-testing such a leaflet will require women to discuss very intimate and possibly upsetting aspects of their lives. It may raise disturbing issues like sexual abuse or molestation. Researchers, therefore, have to tread a careful line; their methods do need to be rigorous—responses have to be probed and embarrassment overcome—but this thoroughness has to be matched with consideration for the respondent. Supportive sex education material may be distributed, or access to appropriate counselling provided, for example.

Remember, there will always be an ethical risk in marketing research. The researcher's job is to minimize it.

---

launched. For it to be ditched at the later stages of the new product development process may represent a political defeat for the product champion, who may have spent the last six months pushing it through a series of internal committees. In such circumstances, there is the potential for the most favoured outcome to be communicated to the research agency. Where the product champion is influential in the choice of agency, the latter may recognize that giving bad news to the client may sour their relationship and jeopardize future business. While most marketing researchers accept the need for objective studies where there is room for more than one interpretation of study findings, for example, the temptation to present the more favourable representation could be overpowering.

Competitive information gathering

The modern marketing concept stresses the need to understand both customers and competitors in order to build a competitive advantage. However, the methods that may be required to gather competitor intelligence can raise ethical questions. Questionable practices include using student projects to gather information without the student revealing the sponsor of the research, pretending to be a potential supplier who is conducting a telephone survey to understand the market, posing as a potential customer at an exhibition, bribing a competitor's employee to pass on proprietary information, and covert surveillance such as through the use of hidden cameras. Procter & Gamble was embarrassed by a scandal that arose when it emerged that the company had hired 'corporate intelligence agents', who searched through bins outside Unilever's Chicago new product development headquarters in an attempt to spy on the company's plans for the haircare market.[45] Thankfully, competitive information gathering does not exclusively depend on such methods since much useful information can be gathered by reading trade journals and newspapers, searching the Internet, analysing databases and acquiring financial statements.

Selling under the guise of marketing research

This practice, commonly known as 'sugging', is a real danger to the reputation of marketing research. Despite the fact that it is not usually practised by bona fide marketing research agencies but unscrupulous selling companies who use marketing research as a means of gaining compliance to their requests to ask people questions, it is the marketing research industry that suffers from its aftermath. Usually, the questions begin innocently enough but move towards the real purpose of the exercise. Often this is to qualify prospects and ask whether they would be interested in buying the product or have a salesperson call.

In Europe, ESOMAR encourages research agencies to adopt codes of practice to prevent this, and national bodies such as the Market Research Society in the UK draw up strict guidelines. However, the problem remains that the organizations that practise sugging are unlikely to be members of such bodies. The ultimate deterrent is the realization on the part of 'suggers' that the method is no longer effective.

Ethical dilemma

An individual approaches you saying they are conducting market research into health and longevity for an important project they are conducting. Considering this a critical societal issue you agree. As the questions progress and you are asked to trial a product you realize this data collection is for the development and marketing of a new low-alcohol drink. Has the company acted ethically in obtaining its market research?

Review

1 **The nature and purpose of marketing information systems, and the role of marketing research within such systems**

- A marketing information system provides the information required for marketing decision-making and comprises internal continuous data, internal ad hoc data and environmental scanning.
- Marketing research is one component of a marketing information system and is primarily concerned with the provision of information about markets and the reaction of these to various product, price, distribution and promotion decisions.

2 **The types of marketing research**

- There are two types of marketing research, which are ad hoc research (custom-designed and omnibus studies) and continuous research (consumer panels, retail audits, television viewership panels, marketing databases, customer relationship management systems and website analysis).

3 **The approaches to conducting marketing research**

- The options are to do it yourself personally, do it yourself using a marketing research department, do it yourself using a fieldwork agency, or use the full services of a marketing research agency.

4 The stages in the marketing research process

- The stages in the marketing research process are research planning (research brief and proposal), exploratory research (secondary research, qualitative research, consultation with experts, and observation), the main (quantitative) data-collection stage (descriptive and experimental research, sampling, survey method, questionnaire design), data analysis and interpretation, and report writing and presentation.

5 How to prepare a research brief and proposal

- A research brief should explain the marketing problem and outline the research objectives. Other useful information would be background information, possible sources of information, the proposed scale of the project and a timetable.
- A research proposal should provide a statement of objectives, what will be done (research design), a timetable and costs.

6 The nature and role of exploratory research

- Exploratory research involves the preliminary exploration of a research area prior to the quantitative data-collection stage. Its major purpose is to avoid the sins of omission and admission. By providing an understanding of the people who are to be interviewed later, the quantitative survey is more likely to collect valid and reliable information.
- It comprises secondary research, qualitative research, consultation with experts and observation.

7 Quantitative research design decisions: sampling, survey method and questionnaire design issues

- Sampling decisions cover who and how many people to interview. The stages are population definition, sampling frame search, sampling method specification, sample size determination and sample selection.
- Survey method decisions relate to how to interview people. The options are face to face, telephone, mail and the Internet.
- Questionnaire design decisions cover what questions to ask. Questionnaires should be planned, designed and piloted before administering to the main sample.

8 Analysis and interpretation of data

- Qualitative data analysis can be facilitated by software packages such as NUD.IST.
- Quantitative data analysis is conducted by software packages such as SPSS.
- Care should be taken when interpreting marketing research results. One common failing is inferring cause and effect when only association has been established.

9 Report writing and presentation

- The contents of a marketing research report should be title page, list of contents, preface, summary, previous related research, research method, research findings, conclusions and appendices.
- Software packages such as PowerPoint can be used to make professional presentations.

▶ **10** **The factors that affect the usage of marketing information systems and marketing research reports**
- Usage of marketing information systems has been shown to be higher when the system is sophisticated and confers prestige to its users, other departments view it as a threat, there is pressure from top management to use the system and users are more involved.
- Usage of marketing research is higher if results conform to the client's prior beliefs, the research is technically competent, the presentation of results is clear, the findings are politically acceptable and the status quo is not challenged.

11 **Ethical issues in marketing research**
- These are potential problems relating to intrusions on privacy, misuse of marketing research findings, competitive information gathering, and selling under the guise of marketing research.

Key terms

ad hoc research a research project that focuses on a specific problem, collecting data at one point in time with one sample of respondents

consumer panel household consumers who provide information on their purchases over time

continuous research repeated interviewing of the same sample of people

data the most basic form of knowledge, the result of observations

depth interviews the interviewing of consumers individually for perhaps one or two hours, with the aim of understanding their attitudes, values, behaviour and/or beliefs

descriptive research research undertaken to describe customers' beliefs, attitudes, preferences and behaviour

experimental research research undertaken in order to establish cause and effect

exploratory research the preliminary exploration of a research area prior to the main data-collection stage

focus group a group normally of six to eight consumers brought together for a discussion focusing on an aspect of a company's marketing

information combinations of data that provide decision-relevant knowledge

marketing information system a system in which marketing information is formally gathered, stored, analysed and distributed to managers in accordance with their informational needs on a regular, planned basis

marketing research the gathering of data and information on the market

omnibus survey a regular survey, usually operated by a marketing research specialist company, which asks questions of respondents for several clients on the same questionnaire

qualitative research exploratory research that aims to understand consumers' attitudes, values, behaviour and beliefs

research brief a written document stating the client's requirements

research proposal a document defining what the marketing research agency promises to do for its client and how much it will cost

retail audit a type of continuous research tracking the sales of products through retail outlets

sampling process a term used in research to denote the selection of a sub-set of the total population in order to interview them

secondary research data that has already been collected by another researcher for another purpose

Internet exercise

Envirosell and Kahn Research are research agencies. Their research tries to capture customer behaviour patterns, by combining traditional market research techniques, anthropological observation methodologies and video taping. They have developed research systems to document and analyse people's behaviour as they shop in retail centres. Explore their websites and examine their research methodologies.

Visit: www.envirosell.com
www.kahnresearch.com

Questions

(a) Describe the research methodologies used by these companies.
(b) Discuss the weaknesses associated with observational research techniques.
(c) Discuss the ethical implications associated with video taping consumers while they shop.
(d) What other research methodologies may be used to analyse consumer behaviour?

Visit the Online Learning Centre at www.mcgraw-hill.co.uk/textbooks/jobber for more Internet exercises.

Study questions

1. What are the essential differences between a marketing information system and marketing research?

2. What are secondary and primary data? Why should secondary data be collected before primary data?

3. What is the difference between a research brief and proposal? What advice would you give a marketing research agency when making a research proposal?

4. Mail surveys should be used only as a last resort. Do you agree?

5. Discuss the problems of conducting a multi-country marketing research survey in the EU. How can these problems be minimized?

6. Why are marketing research reports more likely to be used if they conform to the prior beliefs of the client? Does this raise any ethical questions regarding the interpretation and presentation of findings?

7. What are the strengths and limitations of using the Internet as a data-collection instrument?

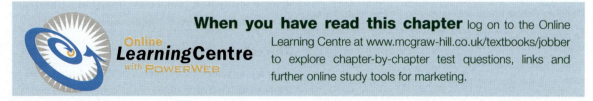

When you have read this chapter log on to the Online Learning Centre at www.mcgraw-hill.co.uk/textbooks/jobber to explore chapter-by-chapter test questions, links and further online study tools for marketing.

case eleven

Carbery: Developing New Products in a Mature Market

The challenge of developing new products in a traditional food category

Carbery, the West Cork-based company, is a key player in the Irish cheese sector. Carbery has been making cheddar cheese since 1968 and, today, it is Ireland's largest exporter of cheese. In Ireland, cheese-making benefits from the abundant supply of natural raw materials—for instance, the mild climate and the good condition of the grassland lead to high-quality cows' milk, which in turn results in well-flavoured cheddar.

Up until the 1980s, the Irish dairy processing sector was strongly orientated towards the production of commodities such as cheddar cheese, milk and butter. In the late 1980s, Carbery made a decision to reduce its dependency on cheddar and to diversify into new valued-added cheeses and food ingredients. Carbery recently made a major investment in its cheese manufacture and ingredient-processing facilities. It is estimated that total cheese production will surpass 30,000 tonnes in the years ahead. This will make Carbery one of the largest cheese plants in Europe and it expects that investment in site specialization and scale will enable it to provide a world-class, efficient service to its customers.

Carbery employs 195 people both in Ireland and overseas, and its output will represent some 30 per cent of national cheese production once the new facility is fully on-stream.

This is the story of Carbery's route to market leadership in Ireland and the role it played in transforming the Irish cheese market. By looking back over what has happened in the cheese market over the past ten years, a clear picture of how Carbery achieved success emerges.

Carbery: the cheese-maker

Following eight years of research and development, the Dubliner cheese brand was launched on the Irish market in 1996. The product was a great success for Carbery, winning numerous awards at national and international level. Dubliner was a novel product, being a mature cheese with a distinctive flavour and a hint of sweetness. As a result, it was more expensively priced than mild cheddar.

Research showed that the imagery of the new product would play an important role in its success. The brand was positioned as a distinctly Irish product, and it embodied values such as quality, tradition, heritage and craftsmanship. The art of cheese-making was emphasized in commercials. In one advertising campaign, a traditional musician, Ronnie Drew (a member of the renowned folk group, the Dubliners), was used to endorse the product. Due to the popularity of the folk group at that time, awareness grew dramatically.

Research showed that packaging could also create a 'difference'. In general, the objectives of cheese packaging are to:

- protect the cheese against physical, chemical or microbial contamination
- reduce loss of moisture from the surface of the cheese
- prevent physical deformation of the cheese and facilitate stacking during ripening, transport, retailing
- allow for product labelling and brand identification.[1]

Carbery was the first company in Ireland to introduce parchment wrapping to the cheese market. This packaging helped differentiate the new product and carried connotations of quality.

Carbery continues to invest in new product development and its range of products includes:

- cheddar (mild red and white cheddar, full-flavour cheese)
- low-fat cheddar (Carbery Light)
- vegetarian cheddar
- mozzarella cheese
- Dubliner Irish cheese.

The food-service sector, pizza and burger chains in particular, are important customers. The company supplies own-label products to retailers as well as branded products. Carbery's products are sold in the UK, Europe and the United States, and the Dubliner brand has coast-to-coast distribution in the USA through the Irish Dairy Board's comprehensive distribution network.

The cheese consumer

In order to prosper, the players in the industry need to adapt to the changing needs of the consumer. Cheese is a dairy product and forms an important part of people's diets. Studies on nutrition and health have found that saturated fat is connected with coronary heart disease and consumers have been advised to lower their saturated fat intake. This factor has led to the development of cheeses with a lower fat content. Research conducted with Irish consumers[2] shows that cheese still has a healthy image, although the high fat content of cheese is perceived to be a negative factor. There has been a change in the way the product is used. It is surprisingly versatile and is used by consumers as a snack, in sandwiches, in contemporary dishes, and also on cheese boards. Research shows that consumers exhibit strong loyalty towards local dairy processors. They tend to be brand conscious rather than price conscious, and the most important purchasing criteria are taste, packaging and convenience. Research found the ability of the packaging to seal and accept adhesive was important to customers. Many cheese producers have introduced new forms of packaging such as resealable packs to keep the cheese fresh for longer.

One demographic trend that has the potential to change consumer preferences is the increasing number of women in paid employment, a development that creates time pressure on families, making them more inclined to buy convenience products (for example, grated cheese). Traditionally, Irish consumers have a taste for cheddar cheese. However, research shows that consumers have become more adventurous in their buying habits and more discerning in terms of products that offer good quality and taste. In-store tastings have a significant influence on consumers and encourage trial of a new product. Irish consumers have become more familiar with non-cheddar varieties. There is growing demand for speciality cheeses; the target market for speciality cheese is female, 20–55 years old, middle to upper class, married, and in full-time employment. Blue vein cheese is the fastest-growing type of speciality cheese, with a growth rate of around 10 per cent per annum.[3]

The Irish cheese market is valued at approximately €99 million (£69 million).[4] It has strong growth potential, given that Irish consumption levels of 6.5 kg is well below the European average. Due to competition between the major supermarket chains and rivalry between multinational food companies, the food choices available to consumers have become more sophisticated and refined. Table C11.1 illustrates the wide variety of cheeses available in the Irish marketplace.

Table C11.1 Cheese varieties available in the Irish market

Type of cheese	Examples
Hard cheeses	Mild Cheddar, Mature and Extra Mature Cheddar, Edam, Gouda, Cheshire, Red Leicester, etc.
Soft cheeses	Danish Blue Cheese, Cream Cheese, Cottage Cheese
Speciality and farmhouse cheeses	These cheeses are treated and have added ingredients such as herbs, garlic or peppercorns
Industrial cheeses	Mozzarella cheese used mainly by pizza manufacturers
Processed cheeses, spreads and portion packs	Cavita and Galtee brands
Cheese snacks	Cheeses sold with dips and snacks, such as Golden Vale's Cheese Strings, which is aimed at the children's market
Vegetarian cheese	Carbery Vegetarian Cheese
Reduced-fat cheese	Carbery Light
Other varieties	Goat's Cheese, Feta Cheese, Parmesan Cheese, etc.

Source: FactFinder

The challenge of developing a new cheese product

Carbery is committed to the development of new products. Ideas come from a wide variety of sources, such as in-house marketing and research personnel, competitors, and contacts with retailers, industrial customers, research institutes, state agencies, market research reports, and so forth. Carbery has a strong relationship with the Irish Dairy Board, which markets Irish cheese overseas. One of the key challenges faced by Carbery is the screening of ideas. There is the risk that good ideas may be dropped or that poor ideas may be developed. The company appraises each idea from a financial, commercial and marketing perspective. The major questions to be answered are as follows.

Production capabilities

- Can the new product be produced at the existing plant?

- Will it have an adverse impact on the production of other cheese products?
- Is significant investment in existing plant required?
- Can it be produced off-site?

Compatibility with existing product range
- Does the new product have synergies or 'fit' with the existing product portfolio?
- Can the same raw materials be used?

Marketing issues and performance of similar products in the marketplace
- What are the market trends?
- Will it appeal to consumers?
- What is the predicted rate of return on the product?
- Is the market growing?
- Is it a me-too product or is there a high level of newness?
- Is there a need to educate the consumers through advertising and promotion?
- Are there well-established competitor brands in the marketplace?
- What are its advantages over similar products?
- Is it competitively priced?

The product concepts are assessed by a team of top, middle and junior management, who are drawn from the R&D, marketing and financial departments. Samples of the product are normally developed in a pilot laboratory plant and focus-group research is conducted with customers in order to test their reaction to the product. Table C11.2 describes various product concepts, along with their advantages and disadvantages.

Table C11.2 Produce concepts			
Cheese type	**Description**	**Positive factors**	**Negative factors**
Blue Brie	Soft cream cheese with blue veins.	Good flavour and texture. Attractive appearance.	Very expensive to make. Production problems: risk of blue mould contaminating cheddar cheese. Well-established competitors.
Semi-hard round cheese	Mild taste, close to the flavour and texture of Gouda.	Good flavour and texture. Existing plant facilities can be used.	Cheese lacks distinctive characteristics. Investment in plant needed.
Soft cheese	Soft cheese, with pungent flavour and creamy texture.	Well liked by cheese connoisseurs. Strong flavour and texture. Distinctive. Unique appearance.	Expensive to make. Not a mainstream product, a niche product.
Probiotic cheese	Cheddar cheese with live, probiotic cultures that survive in the digestive system and benefit the immune system.	Good flavour. Healthy image. Easily made at Carbery.	Similar product failed in the UK. High advertising costs: need to educate consumer about probiotic concept. Must eat a large amount of cheese to obtain benefit. Not a low-fat product.

The marketing department decided that a phase of focus-group research was required in order to explore the reactions of consumers to the various product concepts. Market research could help the company select one product concept, deal with adverse comments, fine-tune the product before launch, and explore ideas for a market entry strategy. The research objectives were to:
- evaluate customers' attitudes towards new product concepts
- identify market segments and develop a demographic profile of the target customer
- obtain information on how best to promote the product.

[1] Fox, P. F., T. P. Guinee, T. M. Cogan and P. L. H. McSweeney (2000) *Fundamentals of Cheese Science*, Gaithersburg, MD: Aspen Publishers.
[2] Focus group research conducted by the Department of Food Business and Development, University College Cork, 1999.
[3] Study by Gira Cheese Europe (1998).
[4] Anonymous (2001) Dairy Success, *Retail Magazine*, 31 January.

Questions

1. What are the strengths and weaknesses of focus-group marketing research?

2. This company chose to commission a programme of focus groups. Given the aims of the company, what other research tools might it have used? Explain your selection(s).

3. Design a guide for the moderator/focus group interviewer.

Appendix 1 Website

www.carbery.com

Appendix 2 Awards

Carbery Milk Products won three gold medals at the International Cheese Competition staged on 11 June 2000, held by the International Food and Drinks show, IFEX in Dublin. Its Dubliner Irish Cheese won the Speciality Hard Cheese Award. Carbery's low-fat cheese took the Lowfat Cheese Award and the company was awarded the Best Overall Hard Cheese Award. During the 2001 World Cheese Awards, held in London, Dubliner Irish Cheese was awarded a Bronze medal and Mature Carbery Cheddar was named Joint World Supreme Champion.

This case was written by Breda McCarthy, College Lecturer in Marketing at UCC. It is intended to be used as a basis for class discussion rather than to illustrate either effective or ineffective handling of an administrative situation.

case twelve

Air Catering Enterprises

Background

Ashish Narayan has recently been promoted to the job of catering manager, responsible for his company's five catering outlets at Gulf International Airport (GIA). Competition to get these concessionary facilities is intense. Operators who succeed in getting the concessionary outlets then face severe competition from other catering concessionaires at the airport, as GIA believes in keeping all of the catering providers on their toes.

Narayan reports to the commercial director of Air Catering Enterprises (ACE), a company with airline and airport catering operations throughout the Gulf area. When he took on the job, his boss said to him, 'We need to hold on to our outlets at GIA and, if possible, expand them in the next concession review by displacing some of our competitors.' The difficulty of doing this was brought home to Narayan shortly after he started. There was no information available to indicate how ACE outlets performed relative to customer expectations or relative to the competition.

He decided to do a customer survey in order to gather some insight into customer satisfaction. Having studied competitor examples, he developed a questionnaire (see Appendix 1) and arranged for it to be given by the counter staff to customers when they purchased their food and beverages.

The outlets

The following is a brief description of the five ACE outlets at Gulf International Airport.

Hi-Flite Restaurant

This food service outlet is very busy, catering to transit passengers. On average, 650 customers eat at this outlet every day, generating an average daily total revenue of US$5200.

Airport Staff Bar

This food service outlet caters to staff at all levels working at GIA. On average, about 400 customers eat at this outlet every day, yielding an average daily total revenue of US$520.

Airlines Training Café

As the name implies, this outlet serves the catering needs of all categories of staff attending GIA's International Training Facility, which is used by a number of different airlines. On average, 250 customers eat at this outlet with an average daily total revenue of US$750.

Departure Snack Bar

This outlet caters for passengers departing on all international flights. On average, about 2000 customers eat here every day, generating an average total daily revenue of US$8000 per day.

Technical Workers' Canteen

This food service outlet caters to the technical staff working in the airline hangars and workshops. On an average 500 customers dine at this outlet every day with an average daily total revenue of $750.

Survey results

Altogether over 750 questionnaires were completed, and Narayan analysed the results, curious to find out for the first time what the customers thought of ACE's catering outlets. Table C12.1 shows a summary of the average scores for all five outlets.

Table C12.1 Summary of the average scores for ACE's five food service outlets

Comparison of mean scores among five catering outlets (n = 752) (maximum score = 5)

Category	Hi-Flite Restaurant	Airport Staff Bar	Airlines Training Café	Departure Snack Bar	Technical Workers' Canteen
Food	4.21	3.23	4.25	4.08	3.45
Menu	3.90	2.97	4.20	3.86	3.07
Service	4.52	4.07	4.09	3.52	3.87
Staff	4.59	3.90	4.16	4.24	3.94
Cleanliness	3.82	3.23	4.34	4.22	3.33

Questions

1. In Narayan's position, what questions should he be asking himself about this data?

2. What management action should he take as a result of this survey?

3. Comment on the method used to develop the questionnaire shown on the following page.

This case was written by Ravi Chandran, Operations Manager at a major airline, and Daragh O'Reilly, Lecturer in Marketing, University of Leeds.

Appendix 1 Customer Satisfaction Survey

PLEASE RATE THE PERFORMANCE BY PUTTING A X FOR EACH OF THE FOLLOWING QUESTIONS.

	Very good	Good	Average	Poor	Very poor

1 FOOD
How do we rate for:
- 1.1 Taste of Food?
- 1.2 Quantity of Food?
- 1.3 OVERALL QUALITY OF FOOD?

2 MENU
How do we rate for:
- 2.1 Range and variety of food?
- 2.2 Range and variety of drinks?

3 SERVICE
How satisfied were you with:
- 3.1 Being able to order quickly?
- 3.2 Our speed of service?
- 3.3 OVERALL QUALITY OF SERVICE?

4 PERSONNEL
How satisfied were you with our staff:
- 4.1 Being friendly smiling and courteous?
- 4.2 Suggesting to buy our food and drinks?

5. CLEANLINESS
How satisfied were you with:
- 5.1 Cleanliness inside the restaurant?
- 5.2 Cleanliness outside the restaurant?

HOW DO YOU RATE YOUR VISIT TO THIS FOOD SERVICE OUTLET OVERALL?

SUGGESTIONS/COMMENTS

What do you think we should be concentrating on most to improve our operation?
Further comments

Name: Nationality:

Age: Occupation: Date: Time:

Your favourite food: Your favourite drink:

Thank you very much for your help.

chapter seven

Market segmentation and positioning

❝Finding the most revealing way to segment a market is more an art than a science. ... Any useful segmentation scheme will be based around the needs of customers and should be effective in revealing new business opportunities.❞

PETER DOYLE, *Value-Based Marketing*

Learning Objectives

This chapter explains:

1. The concepts of market segmentation and target marketing, and their use in developing marketing strategy

2. The methods of segmenting consumer and organizational markets

3. The factors that can be used to evaluate market segments

4. Four target market strategies: undifferentiated, differentiated, focused and customized marketing

5. The concept of positioning and the keys to successful positioning

6. Positioning and repositioning strategies

Very few products or services can satisfy all customers in a market. Not all customers want or are prepared to pay for the same things. For example, airlines such as British Airways, KLM and SAS recognize that business and pleasure travellers are different in terms of their price sensitivity and the level of service required. In the watch market, the type of person that buys a Swatch is very different from the type of person that buys a Rolex: their reasons for purchase are different (fashion vs status) and the type of watch they want is different in terms of appearance and materials. Therefore to implement the marketing concept and successfully satisfy customer needs, different product and service offerings must be made to the diverse customer groups that typically comprise a market.

The technique that is used by marketers to get to grips with the diverse nature of markets is called **market segmentation**. Market segmentation may be defined as 'the identification of individuals or organizations with similar characteristics that have significant implications for the determination of marketing strategy'.

Market segmentation, then, consists of dividing a diverse market into a number of smaller, more similar, sub-markets. The objective is to identify groups of customers with similar requirements so that they can be served effectively while being of a sufficient size for the product or service to be supplied efficiently. Usually, particularly in consumer markets, it is not possible to create a marketing mix that satisfies every individual's particular requirements exactly. Market segmentation, by grouping together customers with *similar* needs, provides a commercially viable method of serving these customers. It is therefore at the heart of strategic marketing since it forms the basis by which marketers understand their markets and develop strategies for serving their chosen customers better than the competition.

For the process of market segmentation and targeting to be implemented successfully all relevant people in the organization should be made aware of the reasons for segmentation and its importance, and be involved in the process as much as is practicable. By gaining involvement, staff will be more committed to the results, leading to better implementation in the later stages.

Why bother to segment markets?

Why go to the trouble of segmenting markets? What are the gains to be made? Figure 7.1 identifies four benefits, which will now be discussed.

Figure 7.1 The advantages of market segmentation

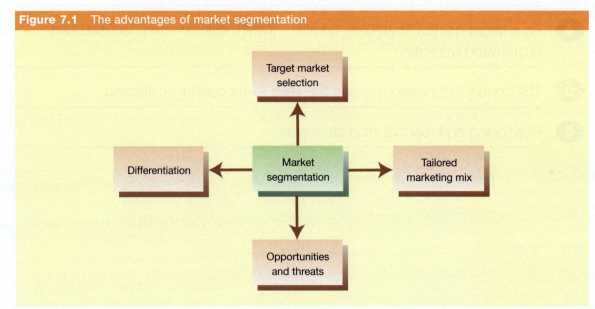

Target market selection

Market segmentation provides the basis for the *selection of target markets*. A *target market* is a chosen segment of market that a company has decided to serve. As customers in the target market segment have similar characteristics, a single marketing mix strategy can be developed to match those requirements. Creative segmentation may result in the identification of new segments that have not been served adequately hitherto and may form attractive target markets to attack. For example, the success of Carphone Warehouse, which supplies mobile phones, was originally based on the founder Charles Dunstone's realization that a key market segment—self-employed tradesmen, such as builders, plumbers and roofers—was not being catered for. The main suppliers were targeting large corporate clients. His vision was to be the first to allow customers to visit a shop and see what mobile phones were available. His staff were trained to help customers decide which combination of rental and call charges best met their needs.[1] Later in this chapter we will explore methods of segmenting markets so that new insight may be gained.

Tailored marketing mix

Market segmentation allows the grouping of customers based upon similarities (e.g. benefits sought) that are important when designing marketing strategies. Consequently this allows marketers to understand in-depth the requirements of a segment and *tailor a marketing mix package* that meets their needs. This is a fundamental step in the implementation of the marketing concept: segmentation promotes the notion of customer satisfaction by viewing markets as diverse sets of needs that must be understood and met by suppliers.

Differentiation

Market segmentation allows the development of differential marketing strategies. By breaking a market into its constituent sub-segments a company may differentiate its offerings between segments (if it chooses to target more than one segment), and within each segment it can differentiate its offering from the competition. By creating a differential advantage over the competition, a company is giving the customer a reason to buy from it rather than the competition.

Opportunities and threats

Market segmentation is useful when attempting to spot *opportunities and threats*. Markets are rarely static. As customers become more affluent, seek new experiences and develop new values, new segments emerge. The company that first spots a new under-served market segment and meets its needs better than the competition can find itself on a sales and profit growth trajectory. The success of Next, the UK clothing retailer, was founded on its identification of a new market segment: working women who wanted smart fashionable clothing at affordable prices. Similarly the neglect of a market segment can pose a threat if competition use it as a gateway to market entry. The Japanese manufacturers exploited British companies' lack of interest in the low-powered motorcycle segment, and the reluctance of US motor car producers to make small cars allowed Japanese companies to form a beachhead from which they swiftly achieved market-wide penetration. The lesson is that market segments may need to be targeted by established competitors, even though in short-term commercial terms they do not appear attractive, if there is a threat that they might be used by new entrants to establish a foothold in the market.

The process of market segmentation and target marketing

The selection of a target market or markets is a three-step process, as shown in Fig. 7.2. First, the requirements and characteristics of the individuals and/or organizations that comprise the market are understood. Marketing research has an important role to play here. Second, customers are grouped according to these requirements and characteristics into segments that have implications for developing marketing strategies. Note that a given market can be segmented in various ways depending on the choice of criteria at this stage. For example, the market for motor cars could be broken down according to type of buyer (individual or organizational), by major benefit sought in a car (e.g. functionality or status) or by family size (empty nester vs family with children). The choice of the most appropriate basis for segmenting a market is a creative act. There are no rules that lay down how a market should be segmented. Using a new criterion, or using a combination of well-known criteria in a novel way, may give fresh insights into a market. Marketing personnel should be alert to the necessity of visualizing markets from fresh perspectives. In this way they may locate attractive, under-exploited market segments, and be the first to serve their needs.

Finally, one or more market segments are chosen for targeting. A marketing mix is developed, founded on a deep understanding of what target-market customers value. The aim is to design a mix that is distinctive from competitors' offerings. This theme of creating a *differential advantage* will be discussed in more detail when we examine how to position a product in the marketplace.

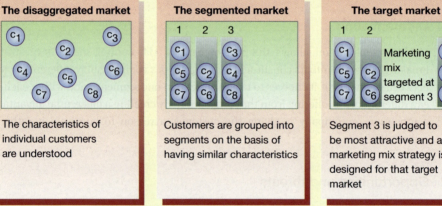

Figure 7.2 The process of market segmentation and target marketing

Segmenting consumer markets

As we have noted, markets can be segmented in many ways. Segmentation variables are the criteria that are used for dividing a market into segments. When examining criteria, the marketer is trying to identify good predictors of differences in buyer behaviour. There is an array of options and no single, prescribed way of segmenting a market.[2] Here, we shall examine the possible ways of segmenting consumer markets; in the next section we shall look at segmentation of organizational markets.

There are three broad groups of consumer segmentation criteria: *behavioural*, *psychographic* and *profile* variables. Since the purpose of segmentation is to identify differences in behaviour that have implications for marketing decisions, *behavioural variables* such as benefits sought from the product and buying patterns may be considered the ultimate bases for segmentation. Psychographic variables are used when researchers believe that purchasing behaviour is correlated with the personality or lifestyle of consumers: consumers with different personalities or lifestyles have varying product or service preferences and may respond differently to marketing mix offerings. Having found these differences, the marketer needs to describe the people who exhibit them, and this is where profile variables such as socio-economic group or geographic location are valuable.[3] For example, a marketer may see whether there are groups of people who value low calories in soft drinks and then attempt to profile them in terms of their age, socio-economic groupings, and so on.

In practice, however, segmentation may not follow this logical sequence. Often, profile variables will be identified first and then the segments so described will be examined to see if they show different behavioural responses. For example, differing age or income groups may be examined to see if they show different attitudes and requirements towards cars. Figure 7.3 shows the major segmentation variables used in consumer markets and Table 7.1 describes each of these variables in greater detail.

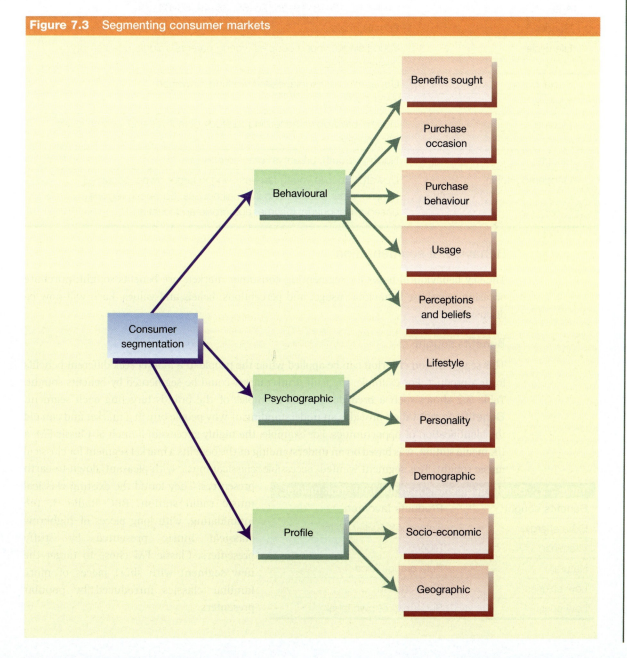

Figure 7.3 Segmenting consumer markets

Table 7.1	Consumer segmentation methods
Variable	**Examples**
Behavioural	
Benefits sought	Convenience, status, performance
Purchase occasion	Self-buy, gift
Purchase behaviour	Solus buying, brand switching, innovators
Usage	Heavy, light
Perceptions and beliefs	Favourable, unfavourable
Psychographic	
Lifestyle	Trendsetter, conservatives, sophisticates
Personality	Extroverts, introverts, aggressive, submissive
Profile	
Age	Under 12, 12–18, 19–25, 26–35, 36–49, 50–64, 65+
Gender	Female, male
Life cycle	Young single, young couples, young parents, middle-aged empty nesters, retired
Social class	Upper middle, middle, skilled working, unwaged
Terminal education age	16, 18, 21 years
Income	Income breakdown according to study objectives and income levels per country
Geographic	North vs South, urban vs rural, country
Geodemographic	Upwardly mobile young families living in larger owner-occupied houses; older people living in small houses; European regions based on language, income, age profile and location.

Behavioural segmentation

The key behavioural bases for segmenting consumer markets are benefits sought; purchase occasion; purchase behaviour; usage; and perceptions, beliefs and values. Each will now be discussed.

Benefits sought

This segmentation criterion can be applied when the people in a market seek different benefits from a product. For example, the fruit drink market could be segmented by benefits sought. Table 7.2 shows such a breakdown with examples of the brands targeting each segment. Benefit segmentation provides an understanding of why people buy in a market and can aid the identification of opportunities. For example, the highly successful launch of Classic FM, a UK media station, was based on an understanding of the benefits a market segment for classical music sought. This segment wanted 'accessible' classical music with pleasant, down-to-earth presenters. They found the existing classical music radio station, BBC Radio 3, too intimidating, with long pieces of highbrow classical music presented by stuffy presenters. Classic FM chose to target the new segment with short pieces of more familiar classics introduced by popular presenters.

Table 7.2	Benefit segmentation in the fruit drink market
Benefits sought	**Products favoured**
Extra energy	Robinson's Barley Water
Vitamins	Ribena
Natural	Pure orange juice
Low calories	'Diet' squash
Low cost	Supermarket own label

Based upon psychological research across Europe, Sampson has shown how the benefits sought from a car can predict car and motor accessory/consumables buying.[4]

- *Pleasure seekers*: driving is all about pleasure (freedom, enjoyment and well-being).
- *Image seekers*: driving is all about self-image. The car provides feelings of power, prestige, status and self-enhancement. Driving is important too, but secondary.
- *Functionality seekers*: driving is only a means of getting from A to B. They enjoy the convenience afforded by the car rather than the act of driving.

Benefit segmentation is a fundamental method of segmentation because the objective of marketing is to provide customers with benefits they value. Knowing the various benefits people value is therefore a basic prerequisite of understanding markets. Benefit segmentation provides the framework for classifying individuals based upon this knowledge. Profile analyses can then be performed to identify the type of people (e.g. by age, gender, socio-economic grouping) in each benefit segment so that targeting can take place.

Purchase occasion

Customers can be distinguished according to the occasions when they purchase a product. For example, a product (e.g. tyres) or service (e.g. plumbing) may be purchased as a result of an emergency or as a routine unpressurized buy. Price sensitivity, for example, is likely to be much lower in the former case than the latter. Some products (e.g. electric shavers) may be bought as gifts or as self-purchases. These differing occasions can have implications for marketing mix and targeting decisions. If it is found that the gift market is concentrated at Christmas, advertising budgets will be concentrated in the pre-Christmas period. Package design may differ for the gift vs personal-buy segment also. Some brands, such as Black Magic chocolates, are targeted at the gift segment of the confectionery market.

Often, special occasions such as Easter and Christmas are associated with higher prices. For example, the prices of chocolate Easter eggs fall dramatically after Easter Sunday. Also marketers have to be aware that the price of a gift can be too low to make it acceptable as a present. Gift occasions, then, pose very interesting marketing problems and opportunities.

Purchase behaviour

Differences in purchase behaviour can be based on the time of purchase relative to the launch of the product or on patterns of purchase. When a new product is launched, a key task is to identify the innovator segment of the market. These people (or organizations) may have distinct characteristics that allow communication to be targeted specifically at them (e.g. young, middle class). Innovators are more likely to be willing to buy the product soon after launch. Other segments of the market may need more time to assess the benefits, and delay purchase until after the innovators have taken the early risks of purchase. An example is the highly successful launch of Boddingtons draught beer. To build the credentials of the brand, Campaign for Real Ale (CamRA) members and beer connoisseurs were initially targeted to gain acceptance first. Only when the credential had been established among these 'innovators' was the brand moved to a wider target audience.

The degree of *brand loyalty* in a market may also be a useful basis for segmenting customers. Solus buyers are totally brand loyal, buying only one brand in the product group. For example, a person might buy Ariel washing powder invariably. Most customers brand-switch, however. Some may have a tendency to buy Ariel but also buy two or three other brands; others might show no loyalty to any individual brand but switch brands on the basis of special offers (e.g. money-off) or because they are variety seekers who look to buy a different brand each time. By profiling the characteristics of each group, a company can target each segment accordingly. By knowing the type of person (e.g. by age, socio-economic group, media habits) who is brand loyal, a company can channel persuasive communications to defend this segment. By knowing the characteristics and shopping habits of the offer seekers, sales promotions can be targeted correctly.

In the consumer durables market, brand loyalty can be used as a segment variable to good purpose. For example, Volkswagen has divided its customers into first-time buyers, replacement buyers (model-loyal replacers and company-loyal replacers) and switch replacers. These segments are used to measure performance and market trends, and for forecasting purposes.[5]

In services, too, brand loyalty has been used to segment and target customers. For example, British Airways identified a new segment that it wanted to target: 'weakly loyals'. These were people who flew BA but would also use any other airline. Using the BA customer database, the 'weakly loyals' were identified and contacted to ask questions about their media habits. This research revealed that they were light and selective television viewers. This led to an advertising campaign using channels such as Channel 4, Eurosport and Sky One, which were popular among this segment. The result was a 15 per cent increase in revenue.[6]

A recent trend in retailing has been towards biographics. This is the linking of actual purchase behaviour to individuals. The growth in loyalty schemes in supermarkets has provided the mechanism for gathering this information. Customers are given cards that are swiped through an electronic machine at the checkout so that points can be accumulated towards discounts and vouchers. The more loyal the shopper, the higher the number of points gained. The supermarket also benefits by knowing what a named individual purchases and where. Such biographic data can be used to segment and target customers very precisely. For example, it would be easy to identify a group of customers that are 'ground coffee' purchasers and target them through direct mail. Analysis of the data allows supermarkets to stock products in each of their stores that are most relevant to their customers' age, lifestyle and expenditure.

Database technology can also be used to segment consumers by purchasing behaviour. E-Marketing 7.1 explains how websites can be analysed using this technology to reveal, among other things, purchasing behaviour, which then allows personalized e-mail offers to be made.

Usage

Customers can also be segmented on the basis of heavy users, light users and non-users of a product category. The profiling of heavy users allows this group to receive most marketing attention (particularly promotion efforts) on the assumption that creating brand loyalty among these people will pay heavy dividends. Sometimes the 80:20 rule applies, where about 80 per cent of a product's sales come from 20 per cent of its customers. Beer is a market where this rule often applies.[7] However, attacking the heavy user segment can have drawbacks if all of the competition are following this strategy. Analysing the light (and non-user) category may provide insights that permit the development of appeals that are not being mimicked by the competition. The identity of heavy, light and non-user categories, and their accompanying profiles for many consumer goods can be accomplished by using survey information provided by the Target Group Index (TGI). This is a large-scale annual survey of buying and media habits in the UK.

Segmenting by use highlights an important issue in market segmentation. Some observers of markets have noted that an individual may buy product offerings that appear to appeal to different people in the market.[8] For example, the same person may buy shredded wheat and cornflakes, cheap wine and chateau-bottled wine, and an economy-class and a business-class air ticket. These critics argue that markets are not made up of segments with different requirements because buyers of one brand buy other brands as well. However, the fact that an

7.1 e-marketing

Segmenting Consumers using Database Technology

Perhaps the biggest advantage that websites have over other forms of marketing communication is their ability to draw information from a database. This may not sound like much, but if used properly, this technology can segment the target audience, giving each customer a very different view of the same website.

In a database, information is organized under headings and categories; the more information that is collected the greater the number of categories that are used to organize it and the more specific the information that can be searched on. Some websites store content (the text that appears on the site) in a database, this means that the information the user sees on the website depends on the information the user requests. The Clarks shoes website (www.clarks.co.uk) demonstrates this concept simply: each choice the user makes presents more specific categories that help them to narrow their search further.

This type of site can be compared to browsing a high-street store with the help of a shop assistant: the more information the prospect provides, the more help the assistant can give. The power of database technology is almost limitless: as the company learns more about the user, it can begin to offer products and services designed specifically for them. For example, Amazon (www.amazon.com) tracks purchases through its database and offers customers similar new products by e-mail newsletter.

---

individual may purchase two completely different product offerings does not in itself imply the absence of meaningful segments.[9] The purchases may reflect different use occasions, purchases for different family members or for variety. For example, the purchase of shredded wheat and cornflakes may reflect variety-seeking behaviour or purchases for different family members. Cheap wine may be bought as a family drink and chateau-bottled wine for a dinner party with friends. Finally, someone may purchase an economy-class air ticket when going on holiday and a business-class ticket when on a business trip. Both the wine and air-ticket examples reflect purchasing behaviour that is dependent on use occasion.

Use occasion can also provide insights into new opportunities. For example, Walkers carried out extensive research of the consumption of snacks. It identified in-home evening snacking as an under-exploited occasion. Further qualitative research identified a 'chill-out' position for a snack that could be shared with friends or partners. Walkers' response was to launch the successful Doritos Dippas snack.[10]

The key issue to remember is that market segmentation concerns the grouping of individuals or organizations with similar characteristics that have implications for the determination of marketing strategy. The fact that an individual may have differing requirements at different points in time (e.g. use occasions) does not mean that segmentation is not warranted. For example, it is still worthwhile targeting businesspeople through the media they read to sell business-class tickets, and charging a higher price, and the leisure traveller through different media with a lower price to sell economy flights. The fact that there will be some overlap on an individual basis does not deny the sense in formulating a different marketing strategy for each of the two segments.

Perceptions, beliefs and values

The final behavioural base for segmenting consumer markets is by studying perceptions, beliefs and values. This is classified as a behaviour variable because perceptions, beliefs and values are often strongly linked to behaviour. Consumers are grouped by identifying those people who view the products in a market in a similar way (perceptual segmentation) and have similar beliefs (belief segmentation). These kinds of segmentation analyses provide an understanding of how groups of customers view the marketplace. To the extent that their perceptions and beliefs are different, opportunities to target specific groups more effectively may arise.

Values-based segmentation is based on the principles and standards that people use to judge what is important in life. Values are relatively consistent and underpin behaviour. Values form the basis of attitudes and lifestyles, which in turn manifest as behaviour. One research company has developed seven value groups: self-explorers, experimentalists, conspicuous consumers, belongers, social resisters, survivors, and the aimless.[11] Marketers have recognized the importance of identifying the values that trigger purchase for many years, but now it is possible to link value groups to profiling systems that make targeting feasible (see the section on page 224 on 'Combining segmentation variables').

Consumers buy brands not only for their functional characteristics but to reflect the lifestyle to which they aspire.

Psychographic segmentation

Psychographic segmentation involves grouping people according to their lifestyle and personality characteristics.

Lifestyle

This form of segmentation attempts to group people according to their way of living, as reflected in their activities, interests and opinions. As we saw in Chapter 3, marketing researchers attempt to identify groups of people with similar patterns of living. The question that arises with lifestyle segmentation is the extent to which general lifestyle patterns are predictive of purchasing behaviour in specific markets.[12] Nevertheless, lifestyle segmentation has proved popular among advertising agencies, which have attempted to relate brands (e.g. Hugo Boss) to a particular lifestyle (e.g. aspirational). The illustration featuring the Canon Ixus 400 is an example of a lifestyle-based product. Lifestyle segmentation can also help marketers to understand consumers in overseas markets, as Marketing in Action 7.1 explains.

7.1 marketing in action

Lifestyle Segmentation of Chinese Consumers

For many years, western businesspeople have been excited about China. If there is one thing multinationals cannot resist it is the opportunity to market to a developing economy of 1.3 billion people. As with all markets, the key is understanding consumers. In the case of China, a research study into consumer lifestyles has revealed eight segments, as outlined below.

1. *Individualists* (17 per cent): these are confident, self-centred risk-takers, with few traditional Chinese values. They tend to be city dwellers with an attraction to money.
2. *Followers* (14 per cent): these come from smaller cities and are early adopters of new products. Money is important to them and they are motivated by novelty. Enthusiastic shoppers, they are more likely to buy products they have seen advertised on television.
3. *Amiable neighbours* (13 per cent): these tend to live in big cities and exhibit strong community values. They are careful with their money, tend to save and not take risks.
4. *Sophisticates* (12 per cent): these tend to be twenty- or thirtysomething males from a high-income background. They value image and designer brands as well as working hard to get what they want. They are self-confident, sociable and early adopters of new products.
5. *Traditionalists* (12 per cent): they tend to come from smaller cities and lower-income backgrounds. They take marriage seriously and are careful with their money. They are unlikely to purchase branded goods and are unreceptive to television ads.
6. *Explorers* (12 per cent): these are mainly female, in their teens or early twenties. They are carefree, spontaneous and image-conscious with active social lives. They like foreign TV shows and regard technology as an important part of their lives.
7. *Custodians* (10 per cent): these are mostly female, brand loyal and love watching television. They tend to stay at home, with high priorities being placed on traditional values and their family.
8. *Pessimists* (10 per cent): they are in their early thirties, come from low-income backgrounds and are not receptive to advertising, being likely to switch channels to avoid commercial breaks. They are late adopters of new products.

Segmentation studies like this help marketers to understand consumers and avoid stereotyping people from overseas countries.

Based on: Lord (2002);[13] Oliver (2002)[14]

Personality

The idea that brand choice may be related to personality is intuitively appealing. Indeed, as we saw in Chapter 3, there is a relationship between the brand personality of beers and the personality of the buyer.[15] However, the usefulness of personality as a segmentation variable is likely to depend on the product category. Buyer and brand personalities are likely to match where brand choice is a direct manifestation of personal values but for most fast-moving consumer goods (e.g. detergents, tea, cereals), the reality is that people buy a repertoire of brands.[16] Personality (and lifestyle) segmentation is more likely to work when brand choice is a reflection of self-expression; the brand becomes a *badge* that makes public an aspect of personality: 'I choose this brand to say this about me and this is how I would like you to see me.' It is not surprising, then, that successful personality segmentation has been found in the areas of cosmetics, alcoholic drinks and cigarettes.[17]

Profile segmentation

Profile segmentation variables allow consumer groups to be classified in such a way that they can be reached by the communications media (e.g. advertising, direct mail). Even if behaviour and/or psychographic segmentation have successfully distinguished between buyer preferences, there is often a need to analyse the resulting segments in terms of profile variables such as age and socio-economic group to communicate to them. The reason is that readership and viewership profiles of newspapers, magazines and television programmes tend to be expressed in that way.

We shall now examine a number of demographic, socio-economic and geographic segmentation variables.

Demographic variables

The demographic variables we shall look at are age, gender and life cycle.

- *Age* has been used to segment many consumer markets.[18] For example, children receive their own television programmes; cereals, computer games, and confectionery are other examples of markets where products are formulated with children in mind. The sweeter tooth of children is reflected in sugared cereal brands targeted at children (e.g. Kellogg's Frosties). Lego, the Danish construction toy manufacturer, segments the children's market by age: in broad terms, Explore targets the up to six year olds; the Lego range aims at the 5–12 year olds and the Technics range caters for the 8–16 age group. Age is also an important segmentation variable in services. The holiday market is heavily age segmented with offerings targeted at the under-30s and the over-60s segments, for example. This reflects the differing requirements of these age groups when on holiday. As noted in Chapter 3, age distribution changes within the European Union are having profound effects on the attractiveness of various age segments. Many companies covet the youth

BACARDI and the Bat Device are registered trademarks of Bacard & Company Ltd.
Bacardi Rum captures a feeling of excitement when targeting the youth market.

segment, who are major purchasers of items such as clothing, consumer electronics, drinks, personal care products and magazines. An example is Bacardi, as illustrated in the advertisement (left), which targets the youth market. Marketing in Action 7.2 explores some of the issues relating to understanding this key market segment.

7.2 marketing in action

Understanding the Youth Market

Today's young people have experienced very different technologies to their parents. Whereas older people may be described as the television generation, the current crop of young people have grown up with VCRs, cable, satellite and digital TV choices. They will have learnt from an early age how to use computers, the Internet and games consoles. But they are not just observers of the media explosion, they are learning how to control that media. They are growing up wise to marketing and media messages. For example, research into men's style magazines shows that boys use them almost as cultural catalogues.

The importance of the youth market has promoted the growth of research into their behaviour and attitudes. This has shown that stereotypical viewpoints can be misleading. For example, the notion that young people spend hours on the Internet is misguided. As one young person said, 'I used to think that the Internet was really cool, I really pestered my Mum to get me a computer but people don't really think it is cool now. I'd much rather be out playing football or computer games, but not on my computer; they are better on PlayStation.'

Research into the youth market does not always take the form of standard questionnaire or focus-group approaches. In order to understand their customers, the marketing executives for Unilever's Lynx (known as Axe outside the UK) deodorant for males, and Impulse body spray for females hang out once a month in the coolest clubs and check out the hottest bands. The company has formed a 'youth board' to get closer to the consumers for whom the two products are part of teenage rites of passage. Made up of brand and marketing managers, advertising executives and PR people, it operates through all-day immersion events away from head office. A day's programme might include examining in detail youth brands such as Sony's PlayStation or the energy drink Red Bull to see how they promote themselves through channels such as the Internet or dance clubs. One outcome was the realization that advertising executions (versions of the advert) needed to be changed very frequently. They observed that PlayStation had 19 different advertising executions in one year because Sony knew young people get bored quickly. Their response was to raise the number of Lynx executions from three to ten a year.

One thing that is known about those in the youth market is that they spend a lot of time out and about. This has led to the use of posters to reach them. Research has shown that 15 to 24 years olds are 35 per cent more likely to notice bus shelter advertising and posters at the sides of roads than other age groups. Based on this knowledge, Coca-Cola launched a new drink, Fanta Icy Lemon, using 3000 Adshel bus shelter panels to target 15 to 24 year olds. The campaign reached 40 per cent of them, with unprompted awareness rising from 17 per cent to 40 per cent. Levi's also used bus shelter advertising as part of its campaign to target young consumers for its Engineered Jeans and Type 1 brands. Posters are also used on university campuses to reach the student population.

Based on: Considine (1999);[19] Green (1999);[20] Willman (1999);[21] Bosworth (2002);[22] Ray (2002)[23]

- Differing tastes and customs between men and women are reflected in specialist products aimed at these market segments. Magazines, clothing, hairdressing and cosmetics are product categories that have used segmentation based on *gender*. More recently, the car market has segmented by gender: the Corsa range of cars from General Motors in Europe is specifically targeted at women.

- The classic family *life cycle* stages were described in Chapter 3. To briefly recap, disposable income and purchase requirements may vary according to life-cycle stage (e.g. young single vs married with two children). Consumer durable purchases may be dependent on life-cycle stage, with young couples without children being a prime target market for furnishings and appliances as they set up home. The use of life-cycle analysis may give better precision in segmenting markets than age because family responsibilities and the presence of children may have a greater bearing than age on what people buy. The consumption pattern of a single 28 year old is likely to be very different from that of a married 28 year old with three children.

Socio-economic variables

Socio-economic variables include social class, terminal education age and income. Here we shall look at social class as a predictor of buyer behaviour. *Social class* is measured in varying ways across Europe; in the UK occupation is used, whereas in other European centres a combination of variables is used. Like the demographic variables discussed earlier, social class has the advantage of being fairly easy to measure and is used for media readership and viewership profiles. The extent to which social class is a predictor of buyer behaviour, however, has been open to question. Clearly many people who hold similar occupations have very dissimilar lifestyles, values and purchasing patterns. Nevertheless, social class has proved useful in discriminating between owning a dishwasher, having central heating, and privatization share ownership, for example, and therefore should not be discounted as a segmentation variable.[24]

Geographic variables

The final set of segmentation variables is based on geographic differences. A marketer can use pure geographic segmentation or a hybrid of geographic and demographic variables called geodemographics.

The *geographic* segmentation method is useful where there are geographic locational differences in consumption patterns and preferences. For example, in the UK beer drinkers in the north of England prefer a frothy head on their beer, whereas in some parts of the south, local taste dictates that beer should not have a head. In Germany, local tastes for beer are reflected in numerous local brewers. In Europe, differences between countries may form geographic segments. For example, variations in food preferences may form the basis of geographic segments: France, Spain and Italy are oil-based cooking markets, while Germany and the UK are margarine and butter orientated.[25] Differences in national advertising expectations may also form geographic segments for communicational purposes. Germans expect a great deal of factual information in their advertisements, to an extent that would bore French or British audiences. France, with its more relaxed attitudes to nudity, broadcasts commercials that would be banned in the UK. In the highly competitive Asian car market both Honda and Toyota have launched their first 'Asia-specific' cars, designed and marketed solely for Asian consumers.

Geodemographic: in countries that produce population census data the potential for classifying consumers on the combined basis of location and certain demographic (and socio-economic) information exists. Households are classified into groups according to a wide range of factors, depending on what is asked for on census returns. In the UK variables such as household size, number of cars, occupation, family size and ethnic background are used to group small geographic areas (known as enumeration districts) into segments that share similar characteristics. A number of research companies (e.g. Pinpoint and CNN) provide such analyses but the best known is that produced by CACI Market Analysis and is known as ACORN (A Classification Of Residential Neighbourhoods). The main groups and their characteristics are shown in Table 7.3.

Table 7.3 The ACORN targeting classification

Categories	% in population	Groups	% in population
A Thriving	20	1. Wealthy achievers, suburban areas	15
		2. Affluent greys, rural communities	2
		3. Prosperous pensioners, retirement areas	3
B Expanding	12	4. Affluent executives, family areas	4
		5. Well-off workers, family areas	8
C Rising	7	6. Affluent urbanites, town and city areas	2
		7. Prosperous professionals, metropolitan areas	2
		8. Better-off executives, inner-city areas	3
D Settling	24	9. Comfortable middle-agers, mature home-owning areas	13
		10. Skilled workers, home-owning areas	11
E Aspiring	14	11. New home owners, mature communities	10
		12. White-collar workers, better-off multi-ethnic areas	4
F Striving	23	13. Older people, less prosperous areas	4
		14. Council estate residents, better-off homes	12
		15. Council estate residents, high unemployment	3
		16. Council estate residents, greatest hardship	3
		17. People in multi-ethnic, low-income areas	2

Source: © CACI Limited (data source BMRB and OPCS/GRO(S)). © Crown Copyright. All rights reserved. ACORN is a registered trademark of CACI Limited; reproduced with permission.

Such information has been used to select recipients of direct mail campaigns, to identify the best locations for stores and to find the best poster sites. This is possible because consumers in each group can be identified by means of their postcodes. Another area where census data are employed is in buying advertising spots on television. Agencies depend upon information from viewership panels, which record their viewing habits so that advertisers have an insight into who watches what. In the UK, census analyses performed by Pinpoint are combined with viewership data via the postcodes of panellists.[26] This means that advertisers who wish to reach a particular geodemographic group can discover the type of programme they prefer to watch and buy television spots accordingly.

A major strength of geodemographics is to link buyer behaviour to customer groups. Buying habits can be determined by large-scale syndicated surveys (for example, the TGI and MORI Financial Services) or from panel data (for example, the grocery and toiletries markets are covered by Superpanel from AGB). By 'geocoding' respondents, those ACORN groups most likely to purchase a product or brand can be determined. This can be useful for branch location since many service providers use a country-wide branch network and need to match the market segments to which they most appeal to the type of customer in their catchment area. Merchandise mix decisions of retailers can also be affected by customer profile data. Media selections can be made more precise by linking buying habits to geodemographic data.[27]

Marketing in Action 7.3 gives other examples of how information systems based on geography, demographics and other variables are used for segmentation and targeting.

7.3 marketing in action

Segmentation with Geographic Information Systems

Segmentation using geographic information systems (GIS) has been widespread since the early 1990s. Central governments and local authorities use birth and death data to plan for hospitals, school, transport facilities and nursing homes. Retailers use GIS to decide where to locate stores to target specific segments of the population. Marketers also use the information to decide where to buy advertising space, from magazines to posters, based on where they are likely to be seen by their target market. The main variable is geography: what works in one area may not in another.

GIS software is used by Marks & Spencer to find out more about its customers. The key inputs are data from its three million active chargecard holders, point-of-purchase information and data from external sources. Such information has allowed the company to stock stores according to detailed profiles of its customers; previously, stocking was based on store size. Segmentation analysis based on GIS also enables it to tailor in-store sales promotions according to customer profile.

The most common use of GIS assumes a static, residential customer base. M&S's new outlets at railway stations require a different type of analysis, as the resident population around a station is often negligible. Modern GIS software, however, has the ability to predict sales based on the flow of people through the station.

This combination of data capture and sophisticated, analytical software is enabling marketers to segment, target and tailor marketing mixes in a fashion unheard of before its invention.

Based on: Hayward (2002)[28]

Combining segmentation variables

We have seen that there is a wide range of variables that can be used to segment consumer markets. Often a combination of variables will be used to identify groups of consumers that respond in the same way to marketing mix strategies. For example, Research Services Ltd, a UK marketing research company, has developed SAGACITY, a market segmentation scheme based on a combination of life cycle, occupation and income; 12 distinct consumer groupings are formed with differing aspirations and behaviour patterns.

Research companies are also combining lifestyle and values-based segmentation schemes with geodemographic data. For example, CACI's Census Lifestyle system classifies segments using lifestyle and geodemographic data. Also, CCN has produced Consumer Surveys, which combines social value groups with geodemographic data. In both cases the link to geodemographic data, which contains household address information, means that targeting of people with similar lifestyles or values is feasible.

Flexibility and creativity are the hallmarks of effective segmentation analyses; for example, one study of Europeans used a combination of demographic, psychographic and socio-economic variables to identify those segments that appeared to be ready for a pan-European marketing approach.[29] Segment 1 comprised young people across Europe who had more unified tastes in music, sports and cultural activities than was the case in previous generations.

Trendsetters (intelligent pleasure seekers longing for a rich and full life) and social climbers formed the second segment. The third segment was Europe's businesspeople, totalling over 6 million people (mostly male) who regularly travel abroad and have a taste for luxury goods.

Segmenting organizational markets

While the consumer goods marketer is interested in grouping individuals into marketing-relevant segments, the business-to-business marketer profiles organizations and organizational buyers. The organizational market can be segmented on several factors broadly classified into two major categories: macrosegmentation and microsegmentation.[30]

Macrosegmentation focuses on the characteristics of the buying organization such as size, industry and geographic location. *Microsegmentation* requires a more detailed level of market knowledge as it concerns the characteristics of decision-making within each macrosegment, based on such factors as choice criteria, decision-making unit structure, decision-making process, buy class, purchasing organization and organizational innovativeness. Often, organizational markets are first grouped on a macrosegment basis and then finer sub-segments are identified through microsegmentation.[31]

Figure 7.4 shows how this two-stage process works. The choice of the appropriate macrosegmentation and microsegmentation criteria is based on the marketer's evaluation of which criteria are most useful in predicting buyer behaviour differences that have implications for developing marketing strategies. Figure 7.5 shows the criteria that can be used.

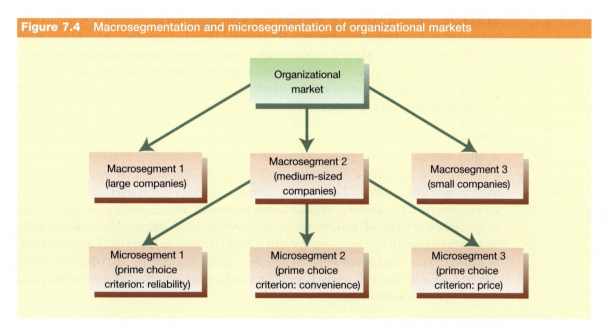

Figure 7.4 Macrosegmentation and microsegmentation of organizational markets

Macrosegmentation

The key macrosegmentation criteria of organizational size, industry and geographic location will now be discussed.

Organizational size

The size of buying organizations may be used to segment markets. Large organizations differ from medium-sized and small organizations in having greater order potential, more formalized buying and management processes, increased specialization of function, and special needs (e.g.

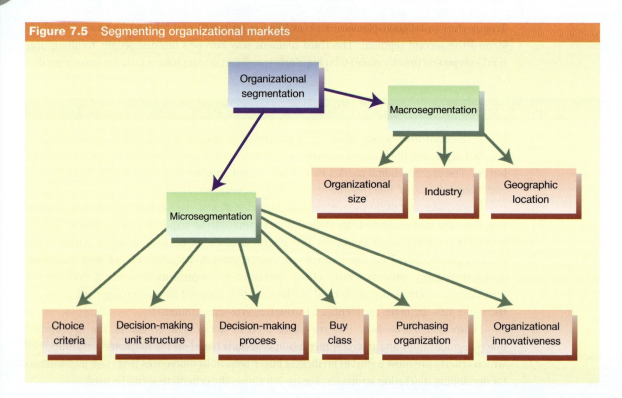

Figure 7.5 Segmenting organizational markets

quantity discounts). The result is that they may form important target market segments and require tailored marketing mix strategies. For example, the salesforce may need to be organized on a key account basis, where a dedicated sales team is used to service important industrial accounts. List pricing of products and services may need to take into account the inevitable demand for volume discounts from large purchasers, and the salesforce team will need to be well versed in the art of negotiation.

Industry

Another common macrosegmentation variable is industry sector, sometimes identified by using Standard Industrial Classification (SIC) codes. Different industries may have unique requirements from products. For example, computer suppliers can market their products to various sectors such as banking, manufacturing, healthcare, and education, each of which has unique needs in terms of software programs, servicing price and purchasing practice. By understanding each industry's needs in depth, a more effective marketing mix can be designed. In some instances further segmentation may be required. For example, the education sector may be further divided into primary, secondary and further education as their product and service requirements may differ.

Geographic location

Regional variations in purchasing practice and needs may imply the use of geographic location as a basis for differentiating marketing strategies. The purchasing practices and expectations of companies in central and eastern Europe are likely to differ markedly from those in western Europe. Their more bureaucratic structures may imply a fundamentally different approach to doing business that needs to be recognized by companies attempting to enter these emerging industrial markets. In Chapter 5, we saw how different cultural factors affect the purchasing practices in European countries. These differences, in effect, imply regional segments since marketing needs to reflect these variations.

Microsegmentation

Marketers may find it useful to divide each macrosegment into smaller microsegments on the basis of the buyer's choice criteria, decision-making unit structure, decision-making process, buy class, purchasing organization, and organizational innovativeness.

Choice criteria

This factor segments the organizational market on the basis of the key choice criteria used by buyers when evaluating supplier offering. One group of customers may rate price as the key choice criterion, another segment may favour productivity, while a third segment may be service-orientated. These varying preferences mean that marketing and sales strategies need to be adapted to cater for each segment's needs. Three different marketing mixes would be needed to cover the three segments, and salespeople would have to stress different benefits when talking to customers in each segment. Variations in key choice criteria can be powerful predictors of buyer behaviour. For example, Moriarty found differences in choice criteria in the computer market.[32] One segment used software support and breadth of product line as key criteria and bought IBM equipment. Another segment was more concerned with price and the willingness of suppliers to negotiate lower prices; these buyers favoured non-IBM machines.

Decision-making unit structure

Another way of segmenting organizational markets is based on decision-making unit (DMU) composition: members of the DMU and its size may vary between buying organizations. As discussed in Chapter 4, the DMU consists of all those people in a buying organization who have an effect on supplier choice. One segment might be characterized by the influence of top management on the decision; another by the role played by engineers; and a third segment might comprise organizations where the purchasing manager plays the key role. DMU size can also vary considerably: one segment might feature large, complex units, while another might comprise single-member DMUs.

Decision-making process

As we saw in Chapter 4, the decision-making process can take a long time or be relatively short in duration. The length of time is often correlated with DMU composition. Long processes are associated with large DMUs. Where the decision time is long, high levels of marketing expenditure may be needed, with considerable effort placed on personal selling. Much less effort is needed when the buy process is relatively short and where, perhaps, only the purchasing manager is involved.

Buy class

Organizational purchases can be categorized into straight rebuy, modified rebuy and new task. As we discussed in Chapter 4, the buy class affects the length of the decision-making process, the complexity of the DMU and the number of choice criteria that are used in supplier selection. It can therefore be used as a predictor of different forms of buyer behaviour, and hence is useful as a segmentation variable.

Purchasing organization

Decentralized versus centralized purchasing is another microsegmentation variable because of its influence on the purchase decision.[33] Centralized purchasing is associated with purchasing specialists who become experts in buying a range of products. Specialization means that they become more familiar with cost factors, and the strengths and weaknesses of suppliers than decentralized generalists. Furthermore, the opportunity for volume buying means that their power base to demand price concessions from suppliers is enhanced. They have also been found to have greater power within the DMU vis-à-vis technical people, like engineers, than decentralized buyers, who often lack the specialist expertise and status to challenge their preferences. For these reasons, purchasing organization provides a good base for distinguishing between buyer behaviour and can have implications for marketing activities. For example, the centralized purchasing segment could be served by a national account salesforce, whereas the decentralized purchasing segment might be covered by territory representatives.

Organizational innovativeness

A key segmentation variable when launching new products is the degree of innovativeness of potential buyers. In Chapter 9 we will discuss some general characteristics of innovator firms but marketers need to identify the specific characteristics of the innovator segment since these are the companies that should be targeted first when new products are launched. Follower firms may be willing to buy the product but only after the innovators have approved it. Although categorized here as a microsegmentation variable it should be borne in mind that organizational size (a macrosegmentation variable) may be a predictor of innovativeness too.

Table 7.4 summarizes the methods of segmenting organizational markets, and provides examples of how each variable can be used to form segments.

Table 7.4   Organizational segmentation methods

Variable	Examples
Macrosegmentation	
Organizational size	Large, medium, small
Industry	Engineering, textiles, banking
Geographic location	Local, national, European, global
Microsegmentation	
Choice criteria	Value in use, delivery, price, status
Decision-making unit structure	Complex, simple
Decision-making process	Long, short
Buy class	Straight rebuy, modified rebuy, new task
Purchasing organization	Centralized, decentralized
Organizational innovativeness	Innovator, follower, laggard

Target marketing

Market segmentation is a means to an end: *target marketing*. This is the choice of specific segments to serve and is a key element in marketing strategy. A firm needs to evaluate the segments and decide which ones to serve. For example, CNN targets its news programmes to what are known as 'influentials'. This is why CNN has, globally, focused so much of its distribution effort into gaining access to hotel rooms. Businesspeople know that wherever they are in the world they can see international news on CNN in their hotel. Its sports programming is also targeted, with plenty of coverage of upmarket sports such as golf and tennis.

An innovative approach to targeting is discussed in e-Marketing 7.2. BMW uses technology to target a distinct segment of consumers.

7.2 e-marketing

BMW Targets using Technology

BMW makes innovative use of technology to market its cars to its target market. Through the website BMW films (www.bmwfilms.com), the company has assembled some of the best action-film directors in the world, including Guy Ritchie, Ang Lee and John Woo. These directors have each developed a short film that can be viewed only through the website, which involves one- or two-star actors and, of course, a BMW car.

These action movies show some of the best aspects of BMW cars: their speed, handling and solid build, and associate the brand with Hollywood excitement and glamour. Downloading and playing these movies requires a large broadband Internet connection (512 kbits/second and above is preferable). Use of a dial-up connection (56 kbits/second) is, at least, ten times as slow and involves severe degradation of film quality.

Given that broadband Internet connections are still used by only a small minority of the population, does the move to display BMW films only through a website make sense for the company? In a word, yes. BMW figures that the next generation of BMW owners are highly literate in IT and from middle-income families (in many ways they are, and can afford to be, early adopters of the latest connections and technologies). In this way BMW has made a conscious decision to make more sophisticated use of technology, to capture the minds of a small percentage of individuals, rather than using more basic technology with a wider impact. BMW has used technology to target a distinct group of consumers.

We shall first examine how to evaluate market segments, and then how to make a balanced choice about which ones to serve.

Evaluating market segments

When evaluating market segments, a company should examine two broad issues: market attractiveness and the company's capability to compete in the segment. Market attractiveness can be assessed by looking at market factors, competitive factors, and political, social and environmental factors.[34] Figures 7.6 and 7.7 illustrate the factors that need to be examined when evaluating market segments.

Market factors

Segment size: generally, large-sized segments are more attractive than small ones since sales potential is greater, and the chance of achieving economies of scale is improved. However, large segments are often highly competitive since other companies are realizing their attraction, too. Furthermore, smaller companies may not have the resources to compete in large segments, and so may find smaller segments more attractive.

Segment growth rate: growing segments are usually regarded as more attractive than stagnant or declining segments, as new business opportunities will be greater. However, growth markets are often associated with heavy competition (e.g. the personal computer market during the late 1980s). Therefore an analysis of growth rate should always be accompanied by an examination of the state of competition.

Segment profitability: the potential to make profits is an important factor in market attractiveness.

Figure 7.6 Factors used to assess market attractiveness

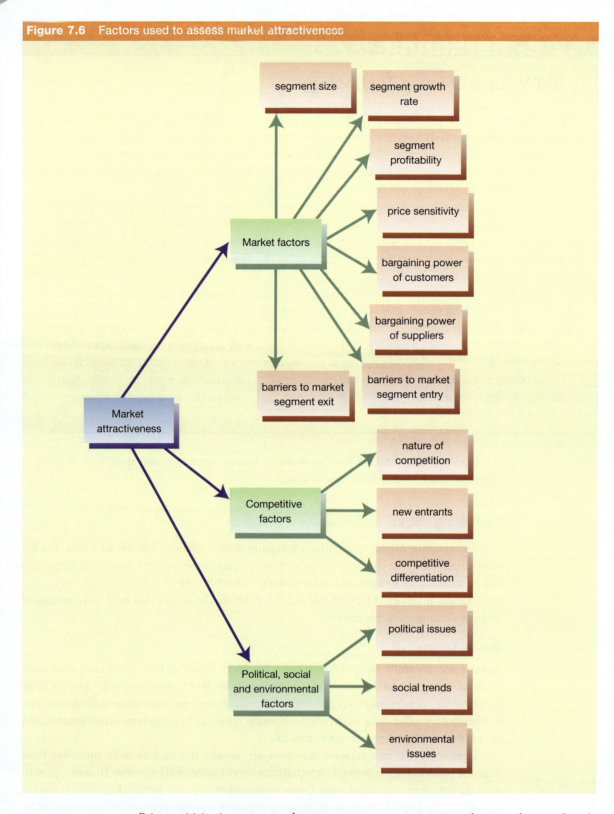

Price sensitivity: in segments where customers are price sensitive there is a danger of profit margins being eroded by price competition. Low price-sensitive segments are usually more attractive since margins can be maintained. Competition may be based more on quality and other non-price factors.

Figure 7.7 Factors used to assess the company's capability to compete

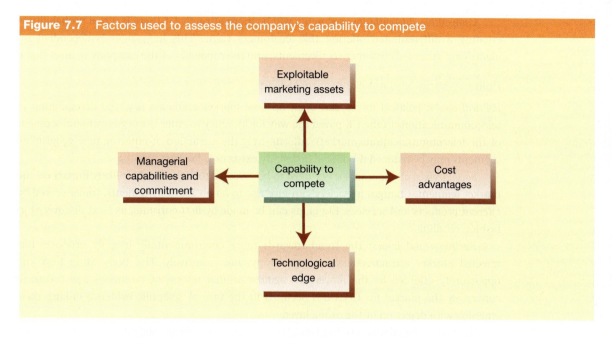

Bargaining power of customers: both end and intermediate customers (e.g. distributors) can reduce the attraction of a market segment if they can exert high bargaining pressure on suppliers. The result is usually a reduction in profit margins as customers (e.g. supermarket chains) negotiate lower prices in return for placing large orders.

Bargaining power of suppliers: a company must assess not only the negotiating muscle of its customers but also its potential suppliers in the new segment. Where supply is in the hands of a few dominant companies, the segment will be less attractive than when served by a large number of competing suppliers.

Barriers to market segment entry: for companies considering entering a new segment there may be substantial entry barriers that reduce its attractiveness. Barriers can take the form of the high marketing expenditures necessary to compete, patents, or high switching costs for customers. However, if a company judges that it can afford or overcome barriers to entry, their existence may raise segment attractiveness if the company judges that the barriers will deter new rivals from entering.

Barriers to market segment exit: a segment may be regarded as less attractive if there are high barriers to exit. Exit barriers may take the form of specialized production facilities that cannot easily be liquidated, or agreements to provide spare parts to customers. Their presence may make exit extremely expensive and therefore segment entry more risky.

Competitive factors

Nature of competition: segments that are characterized by strong aggressive competition are less attractive than where competition is weak. The weakness of European and North American car manufacturers made the Japanese entry into a seemingly highly competitive (in terms of number of manufacturers) market segment relatively easy. The quality of the competition is far more significant than the number of companies operating in a market segment.

New entrants: a segment may seem superficially attractive because of the lack of current competition, but care must be taken to assess the dynamics of the market. A judgement must be made regarding the likelihood of new entrants, possibly with new technology, which might change the rules of the competitive game.

Competitive differentiation: segments will be more attractive if there is a real probability of creating a differentiated offering that customers value. This judgement is dependent on identifying unserved customer requirements, and the capability of the company to meet them.

Political, social and environmental factors

Political issues: political forces can open up new market segments (e.g. the deregulation of telecommunications in the UK paved the way for Mercury to enter the organizational segment of the telecommunications market). Alternatively the attraction of entering new geographic segments may be reduced if political instability exists or is forecast.

Social trends: changes in society need to be assessed to measure their likely impact on the market segment. Changes in society can give rise to latent market segments, under-served by current products and services. Big gains can be made by first entrants, as Next discovered in fashion retailing.

Environmental issues: the trend towards more environmentally friendly products has affected market attractiveness both positively and negatively. The Body Shop took the opportunity afforded by the movement against animal testing of cosmetics and toiletries; conversely the market for CFCs has declined in the face of scientific evidence linking their emission with depletion of the ozone layer.

In organizational markets, individual customers may be evaluated on such criteria as sales volume, profitability, growth potential, financial strength and their fit with market and product strategy. The allocation to a segment will be based on these factors.

Capability

Against the market attractiveness factors must be placed the firm's *capability to serve the market segment*. The market segment may be attractive but outside the resources of the company. Capability may be assessed by analysing exploitable marketing assets, cost advantages, technological edge, and managerial capabilities and commitment.

Exploitable marketing assets: does the market segment allow the firm to exploit its current marketing strengths? For example, is segment entry consonant with the image of its brands, or does it provide distribution synergies? However, where new segment entry is inconsistent with image, a new brand name may be created. For example, Toyota developed the Lexus model name when entering the upper-middle executive car segment.

Cost advantages: companies that can exploit cheaper material, labour or technological cost advantages to achieve a low cost position compared to the competition may be in a strong position, particularly if the segment is price sensitive.

Technological edge: strength may also be derived by superior technology, which is the source of differential advantage in the market segment. Patent protection (e.g. in pharmaceuticals) can form the basis of a strong defensible position, leading to high profitability. For some companies, segment entry may be deferred if they do not possess the resources to invest in technological leadership.

Managerial capabilities and commitment: a segment may look attractive but a realistic assessment of managerial capabilities and skills may lead to rejection of entry. The technical and judgemental skills of management may be insufficient to compete against strong competitors. Furthermore, the segment needs to be assessed from the viewpoint of managerial objectives. Successful marketing depends on implementation. Without the commitment of management, segment entry will fail on the altar of neglect.

Target marketing strategies

The purpose of evaluating market segments is to choose one or more segments to enter. Target market selection is the choice of which and how many market segments in which to compete. There are four generic **target marketing** strategies from which to choose: undifferentiated marketing, differentiated marketing, focused marketing, and customized marketing (see Fig. 7.8). Each option will now be examined.

Undifferentiated marketing

Occasionally, a market analysis will show no strong differences in customer characteristics that have implications for marketing strategy. Alternatively, the cost in developing a separate market mix for separate segments may outweigh the potential gains of meeting customer needs more exactly. Under these circumstances a company may decide to develop a single marketing mix for the whole market. This absence of segmentation is called **undifferentiated marketing**. Unfortunately this strategy can occur by default. For example, companies that lack a marketing orientation may practise undifferentiated marketing through lack of customer knowledge. Furthermore, undifferentiated marketing is more convenient for managers since they have to develop only a single product. Finding out that customers have diverse needs that can be met only by products with different characteristics means that managers have to go to the trouble and expense of developing new products, designing new promotional campaigns, training the salesforce to sell the new products and developing new distribution channels. Moving into new segments also means that salespeople have to start prospecting for new customers. This is not such a pleasant activity as calling on existing customers who are well known and liked.

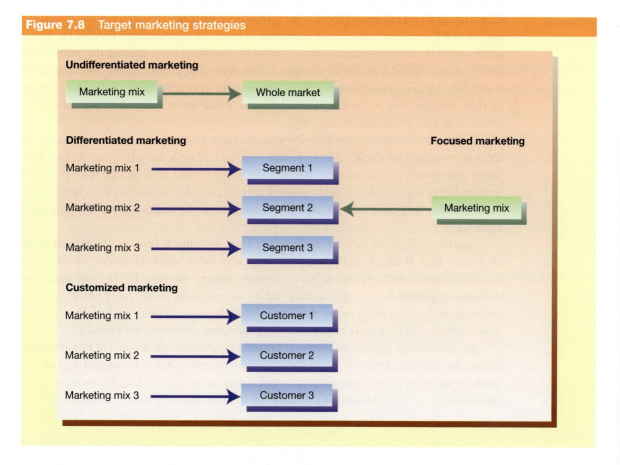

Figure 7.8 Target marketing strategies

The process of market segmentation, then, is normally the motivator to move such companies from practising undifferentiated marketing to one of the next three target marketing strategies.

Differentiated marketing

When market segmentation reveals several potential targets, specific marketing mixes can be developed to appeal to all or some of the segments. This is called **differentiated marketing**. For example, Walters and Knee showed how differentiated marketing was applied by the Burton Group.[35] Segmentation of the fashion market revealed distinct customer groups for which a specific marketing mix (including shop name, style of clothing, décor and ambience of the shop) was developed—for example, the style market (Next) and young women's market (Dorothy Perkins), the larger women's market (Evans) and the family market (Debenhams). A differentiated target marketing strategy exploits the differences between marketing segments by designing a specific marketing mix for each segment.

One potential disadvantage of a differentiated compared to an undifferentiated marketing strategy is the loss of cost economies. However, the use of flexible manufacturing systems can minimize such problems.

Focused marketing

The identification of several segments in a market does not imply that a company should serve all of them. Some may be unattractive or out of line with business strengths. Perhaps the most sensible route would be to serve just one of the market segments. When a company develops a single marketing mix aimed at one target market (*niche*) it is practising **focused marketing**. This strategy is particularly appropriate for companies with limited resources. Small companies may stretch their resources too far by competing in more than one segment. Focused marketing allows research and development expenditure to be concentrated on meeting the needs of one set of customers, and managerial activities can be devoted to understanding and catering for their needs. Large organizations may not be interested in serving the needs of this one segment, or their energies may be so dissipated across the whole market that they pay insufficient attention to their requirements.

The exclusive high-performance car manufacturer TVR is an example of a successful focused marketer. One danger that such niche marketers face is attracting competition from larger organizations in the industry. In the UK, for example, Sock Shop and Tie Rack grew very quickly during the 1980s and were conspicuously successful. The reaction from larger stores such as Marks & Spencer was to jazz up their range of socks and ties to key into this niche segment.[36]

Another example of focused marketing is given by Bang & Olufsen, the Danish audio electronics firm. It targets upmarket consumers who value self-development, pleasure and open-mindedness, with its stylish music systems. Anders Kwitsen, B&O's chief executive, describes its positioning as 'high quality but we are not Rolls-Royce; more BMW'. Focused targeting and cost control mean that B&O defies the conventional wisdom that a small manufacturer could not make profits marketing consumer electronics in Denmark.[37]

Another form of focused marketing is to target a particular age group. For example, Saga targets the over-50s. Originally a specialist holiday company, it has broadened its range of products marketed to this age group to include financial services such as an award-winning share-dealing service.[38] Marketing in Action 7.4 discusses the targeting of the over-55s.

7.4 marketing in action

Targeting the Grey Market

The grey market is a general term for anyone aged 55 or over. In industrialized countries it already accounts for 25 per cent of the population compared to around 15 per cent in 1950, and is set to double by 2020. Not only that, these people are wealthier and healthier than ever. The over-50s account for three-quarters of all financial assets and for half of all discretionary spending in developed countries. They also live longer: most of them can look forward to 15 to 20 years of free time after they retire and, with medical advances, remain active for most of it.

For most market segments, this would indicate an extremely attractive target market with heavy investment to tap into it. Yet companies still spend 95 per cent of their marketing and advertising budgets on the under-50s. The reasons are that most marketing and advertising staff are relatively young and there is a belief that older people are set in their ways and unresponsive to new products and advertising. Indeed, many advertisements caricature older people in order to make the young laugh—as in the soft drinks advertisement that portrayed a teenager using his grandfather's trembling hand to shake a can.

What do companies need to do to target the grey market?
As with any market, they need to understand consumers, and this means segmentation. One study segmented the elderly into four groups: 'healthy hermits', 'ailing outgoers', 'healthy indulgers' and 'frail reclusives'. Another used lifestyle segmentation to classify them into 'empty nesters', 'grandparents' and (sometimes) 'single again'. Travel companies such as Grandtravel and Family Hostel have used such research to develop packages tailored for older travellers and their grandchildren.

Great care has to go into targeting the grey market. When Gerber, a maker of baby food, realized that many older people with dental and stomach problems were buying its products for themselves, it decided to launch a similar product called Senior Citizen. The product failed because grey consumers were unwilling to turn up at the cashpoint with a product that branded them old. Glaxo SmithKline learnt this lesson when branding a toothpaste targeting the over-50s: it called it Macleans 40+.

There is evidence of companies starting to take the grey market seriously. Here are some examples.

- L'Oréal has launched grey-specific brands such as Age Perfect and Plenitude.
- Estée Lauder has used Karen Graham, its star model in the 1970s, to promote a face cream, and L'Oréal recruited the 57-year-old French actress Catherine Deneuve to promote its haircare products.
- Unilever used happy consumers, who were mostly over 50, to advertise its cholesterol-reducing Proactive spread.
- Danone, a food and beverage company, took great care over the packaging of its calcium-rich Talians mineral water. The label was designed to be clear and readable, and the cap was large and easy to grip.
- NTTDoCoMo, a Japanese telecoms company, launched its new mobile phone—Raku-Raku, which means Easy-Easy—with larger buttons and easier-to-read figures.
- Ford car designers wear a 'third age suit', which is designed to replicate stiffened knees, elbows, ankles and wrists to simulate what it is like for some older people to get into and out of a car.
- EMAP, the publishing company, has successfully launched *Yours*, a women's monthly magazine targeted at the over-60s, which outsells *Elle*, *New Woman* and *Red*.

Based on: Anonymous (2002);[39] Anonymous (2002);[40] Curtis (2002)[41]

One form of focused marketing is to concentrate efforts on the relatively small percentage of customers that account for a disproportionately large share of sales of a product (the heavy buyers). For example, in some markets 20 per cent of customers account for 80 per cent of sales. Some companies aim at such a segment because it is so superficially attractive. Unfortunately, they may be committing the *majority fallacy*.[42] The majority fallacy is the name given to the blind pursuit of the largest, most easily identified, market segment. It is a fallacy because that segment is the one that everyone in the past has recognized as the best segment and, therefore, it attracts the most intense competition. The result is likely to be high marketing expenditures, price cutting and low profitability. A more sensible strategy may be to target a small, seemingly less attractive, segment rather than choose the same customers that everyone else is after.

Customized marketing

In some markets the requirements of individual customers are unique and their purchasing power sufficient to make designing a separate marketing mix for each customer viable. Segmentation at this disaggregated level leads to the use of **customized marketing**. Many service providers, such as advertising and marketing research agencies, architects and solicitors, vary their offerings on a customer-to-customer basis. They will discuss face to face with each customer their requirements and tailor their services accordingly. Customized marketing is also found within organizational markets because of the high value of orders and the special needs of customers. Locomotive manufacturers will design and build products to specifications given to them by individual rail transport providers. Customized marketing is often associated with close relationships between supplier and customer in these circumstances because the value of the order justifies large marketing and sales efforts being focused on each buyer.

A fascinating development in marketing in recent years has been the introduction of *mass customization* in consumer markets. This is the marketing of highly individual products on a mass scale. Car companies such as Audi, BMW, Mercedes and Renault have the capacity to build to order where cars are manufactured only when there is an order specification from a customer. Dell Computers will also build customized products, often ordered on the Internet. Such flexible manufacturing processes allow customers to specify their own individual products from an extensive range of optional equipment.[43] For example, promotional material for the BMW Mini claims that there is only a 1 in 10,000 chance that any two Minis are the same. Even trainers can be customized, with both Nike and Adidas offering this service.[44]

Positioning

Figure 7.9 Key tasks in positioning

1. Market segmentation
2. Target market
3. Differential advantage
} Positioning

Where and *how* we compete

So far our discussion has taken us through market segmentation and on to target market selection. The next step in developing an effective marketing strategy is to clearly position a product or service offering in the marketplace. Figure 7.9 summarizes the key tasks involved, and shows where **positioning** fits into the process.

Positioning is the choice of:

- *target market*—*where* we want to compete
- *differential advantage*—*how* we wish to compete.

The objective is to create and maintain a distinctive place in the market for a company and/or its products.

Target market selection, then, has accomplished part of the positioning job already. But to compete successfully in a target market involves providing the customer with a differential advantage. This involves giving the target customer something better than the competition is offering. Creating a differential advantage will be discussed in detail in Chapter 18. Briefly, it involves using the marketing mix to create something special for the customer. Product differentiation may result from added features that give customers benefits that rivals cannot match. Promotional differentiation may stem from unique, valued images created by advertising, or superior service provided by salespeople. Distribution differentiation may arise through making the buy situation more convenient for customers. Finally, price differentiation may involve giving superior value for money through lower prices.

A landmark book by Ries and Trout suggested that marketers are involved in a battle for the minds of target customers.[45] Successful positioning is often associated with products and services possessing favourable connotations in the minds of customers. For example, McDonald's is associated with cleanliness, consistency of product, fast service and value for money. These add up to a differential advantage in the minds of its target customers whether they be in London, Amsterdam or Moscow. Such positioning is hard won and relies on four factors, as shown in Fig. 7.10.

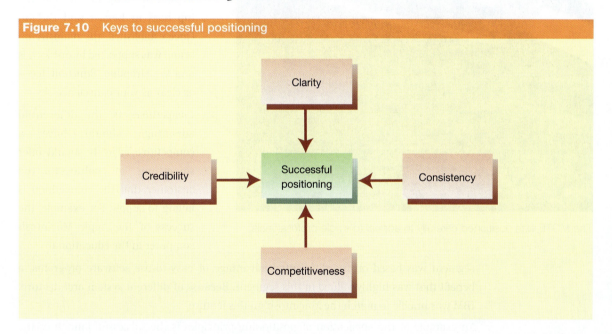

Figure 7.10 Keys to successful positioning

(1) *Clarity*: the positioning idea must be clear in terms of both target market and differential advantage. Complicated positioning statements are unlikely to be remembered. Simple messages such as 'BMW, The Ultimate Driving Machine', 'Asda Price' and 'Good Food Costs Less at Sainsbury's' are clear and memorable.

(2) *Consistency*: people are bombarded with messages daily. To break through this noise a consistent message is required. Confusion will arise if this year we position on 'quality of service', then next year we change it to 'superior product performance'.

(3) *Credibility*: the differential advantage that is chosen must be credible in the minds of the target customer. Attempting to position roll-your-own cigarette tobacco as an upmarket

The MGTF was positioned carefully to appeal to single professionals.

exclusive product failed because of lack of credibility. Similarly, the attempt to position Lada as an exciting, sporty car by showing it in ads charging through dirt tracks in Africa failed because of the lack of consonance between image and reality. In order to establish credibility, brands sometimes have to build their credentials early in their life. We saw earlier in this chapter how the Boddingtons beer brand was targeted initially at CAMRA members and beer connoisseurs. Smirnoff Ice, the pre-mixed vodka drink, also built its credentials in Ireland by being sold in only the top bars in Belfast and Dublin. Once established, the mainstream brand was supported by quirky ads and the strapline 'Smirnoff Ice—as clear as your conscience'.[46]

(4) *Competitiveness*: the differential advantage should have a competitive edge. It should offer something of value to the customer that the competition is failing to supply. For example, the success of the Apple Macintosh computer in the educational segment was based on the differential advantage of easy-to-use software programs, a benefit that was highly valued in this segment. Because of different system architecture, IBM was unable to match the Macintosh on this feature.

An example of the application of positioning principles is the successful launch of the MGTF (see illustration). The MGTF was positioned as the ultimate escape route for single professionals. By identifying the places that these professionals go when they are working, the car was promoted using appropriate media such as postcards in pubs and bars, posters and postcards at the gym, posters at airports, ferry ports and Eurostar, together with bespoke 'escape' supplements in the weekend press and leisure magazines such as *Time Out*. The award-winning campaign helped to build the MGTF into the biggest-selling two-seat-open-top car in the UK.

Marketing in Action 7.5 describes how the four brands of imported premium lagers—Budweiser, Grolsch, Holsten Pils and Beck's—have used positioning to achieve market domination. In their market segment, both image and product quality are vital ingredients in the race to be the brand to be seen with.

7.5 marketing in action

Positioning in the Imported Premium Bottled Lager Market

Since the growth years of the early 1990s the premium bottled lager market has stagnated due to the rise of draught equivalents in pubs and bars. The dominant brands are Budweiser from the USA, Grolsch from the Netherlands, and Holsten Pils and Beck's from Germany. Together, these four brands account for over 80 per cent of the imported premium bottled lager market. The key to success is clear positioning through advertising and packaging.

Budweiser emphasizes its quality (with the 'King of Beers' and 'True' advertising campaigns) and its US heritage (the 'Real American Heroes' campaign), and supports its positioning with humour (the 'frogs and lizard' and 'Whassup' campaigns). Grolsch gains distinctiveness with its swing-top embossed bottle. Its ads stress the Dutch heritage of the lager and its distinctive taste, ensured by being brewed for longer than other beers. Holsten Pils positions itself as tough, honest and down to earth, featuring Ray Winstone, the British movie hardman, in its advertising. The ads end with the line 'Who is the daddy of all bottled beers?' Beck's positioning is based on a humorous, arty ad campaign featuring the bottle. One version shows the state of the bottle reflecting the state of the drinker—for example, a shrink-wrapped bottle was accompanied by the strapline 'paranoid' (see illustration). Another uses visual puns to relate how different character types might customize their bottles of beer. For 'fashion victim', a bottle is left with only the CK letters on it, the rest having been picked away from the foil wrapper; for the 'tight-fisted', a chalk line has been drawn to the mark the point the drink was left at when last sipped. Beck's also donates prizes for modern art and student film-making.

Beck's positioning is based on humorous arty advertisements.

Positioning in this segment is critical for brand legitimacy. The aim is to make Budweiser, Grolsch, Holsten Pils and Beck's the brands to be seen with. To do this, two factors are vital: first, a fashionable and stylish image and, second, a track record of product quality (emphasized in the brand's promotion) that sustains its attraction after the novelty has worn off.

Based on: Anonymous (2002);[47] Anonymous (2001);[48] Clark (2001);[49] Hedburg (2001);[50] Smith (2002)[51]

Perceptual mapping

A useful tool for determining the position of a brand in the marketplace is the *perceptual map*. This is a visual representation of consumer perceptions of the brand and its competitors using attributes (dimensions) that are important to consumers. The key steps in developing a perceptual map are as follows.

1. Identify a set of competing brands.
2. Identify important attributes that consumers use when choosing between brands using qualitative research (e.g. group discussions).
3. Conduct quantitative marketing research where consumers score each brand on all key attributes.
4. Plot brands on a two-dimensional map(s).

Figure 7.11 shows a perceptual map for seven supermarket chains. Qualitative marketing research has shown that consumers evaluate supermarkets on two key dimensions: price and width of product range. Quantitative marketing research is then carried out using scales that measure consumers' perception of each supermarket on these dimensions. Average scores are then plotted on a perceptual map.

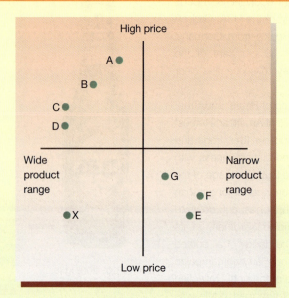

Figure 7.11 A perceptual map of supermarkets

The results show that the supermarkets are grouped into two clusters: the high price, wide product range group; and the low price, narrow price range group. These are indicative of two market segments and show that supermarkets C and D are close rivals, as measured by consumers' perceptions, and have very distinct perceptual positions in the marketplace compared with E, F and G. Perceptual maps are useful in considering strategic moves. For example, an opportunity may exist to create a differential advantage based on a combination of wide product range and low prices (as shown by the theoretical position at X).

Perceptual maps can also be valuable in identifying the strengths and weaknesses of brands as perceived by consumers. Such findings can be very revealing to managers, whose own perceptions may be very different from those of consumers. Consumers can also be asked to score their ideal position on each of the attributes so that actual and ideal positions can be compared.

Repositioning

Occasionally a product or service will need to be repositioned because of changing customer tastes or poor sales performance. Repositioning involves changing the target markets, the differential advantage, or both. A useful framework for analysing repositioning options is given in Fig. 7.12. Using product differentiation and target market as the key variables, four generic repositioning strategies are shown.

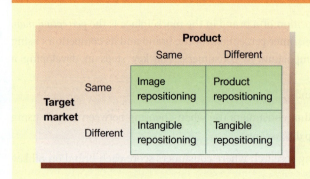

Figure 7.12 Repositioning strategies

Image repositioning

The first option is to keep product and target market the same but to change the image of the product. In markets where products act as a form of self-expression, the product may be acceptable in functional terms but fail because it lacks the required image. The move to humorous, arty advertising for Beck's is an example of image repositioning (Marketing in Action 7.5).

Product repositioning

With this strategy the product is modified to make it more acceptable to its present target

7.6 marketing in action

Tangible Repositioning at Skoda

When Volkswagen AG acquired Skoda Auto in 1991 it knew it had a major marketing task on its hands. The butt of countless jokes, the brand suffered from serious negative images in western European countries. VW's first task was to improve the quality of the cars to bring them up to the standards consumers expected. As early as 1994 the fruits of the VW investment were being seen with the launch of the Felicia, which received six consecutive 'Budget Car of the Year' awards from *Auto Express* magazine.

However, by the late 1990s despite wide acknowledgement in the UK motoring press that Skoda cars had improved beyond recognition, deep-seated brand prejudice remained and only 1 per cent of the market had been captured. Conventional approaches to marketing the brand were not working. For example, the 1998 launch of the Octavia highlighted the car's features and suggested a serious, confident tone with the strapline 'The New Octavia. The Way Things Should Be.' The campaign targeted existing owners (product repositioning) but, despite Skoda UK's largest marketing budget ever, achieved an increase in sales of only 6 per cent and only minimal change in perception.

Skoda's response was to tackle the perception problem head-on. Rather than aim at existing owners, the new marketing campaign would target a different segment—rejectors—those who said they would not consider buying a Skoda. This meant that Skoda was moving from a product repositioning strategy (different, improved products targeted at the same target market) to tangible repositioning (different, improved products targeted at a different target market). Key to the new strategy's success was a series of self-deprecating, humorous ads to win the right to gain consumers' re-evaluation. One TV ad featured a pompous English dignitary on a tour of a Skoda factory, showering praise on the new plant as well as the unbranded cars on the production line. At the end of the tour, he whispers to the guide, 'I hear you make those funny little Skoda cars, too.' Each new ad ended with the strapline 'It's a Skoda. Honest!' The results were dramatic. The ads got noticed (50 per cent awareness), perception improved (the percentage of UK consumers who said they would consider buying a Skoda rose from 14 per cent to 21 per cent) and Skoda sales ended the year up 34 per cent.

This case history illustrates how effective tangible repositioning, backed up with an advertising campaign that effectively communicates the new improved brand values, can be in revitalizing an ailing brand.

Based on: Anonymous (2002);[54] Jobber and Fahy (2003)[55]

---

market. For example, the BMW Mini did not have a compartment under the dashboard, in an attempt to be true to it predecessor: the original 1960s Mini. Customers complained that there was nowhere secure to store CDs and other items, so BMW responded by modifying the car to include a secure compartment. An example of product repositioning in services is the successful rebranding of Talk Radio, a generalist speech-based radio station, as talkSPORT. The target market of 25–44-year-old males remains the same but the product has changed its focus to sport.[52]

Intangible repositioning

This strategy involves targeting a different market segment with the same product. Lucozade, a carbonated drink, was initially targeted by Beecham's Foods at sick children. Marketing research found that mothers were drinking it as a midday pick-me-up and the brand was consequently repositioned to aim at this new segment. Subsequently the energy-giving attributes of Lucozade were used to appeal to a wider target market—young adults—by means of advertisements featuring the athletes Daley Thompson and, more recently, Linford Christie. The history of Lucozade shows how a combination of repositioning strategies over time has been necessary for successful brand building.

Pharmaceutical companies practise intangible repositioning when patents on their prescription drugs expire. Rather than fight against generic competition by price-cutting in the prescription segment they often switch to the over-the-counter (OTC) sector where they can fight by investing in brand equity. Market leaders benefit by being able to claim 'the product most often prescribed by doctors'. An example is Tagamet, SmithKline Beecham's indigestion drug, which by switching to the OTC sector was able to transfer to the new segment the value the consumer associated with the brand name developed through doctors' prescriptions.[53]

Tangible repositioning

When both product and target market are changed, a company is practising tangible repositioning. For example, a company may decide to move up- or downmarket by introducing a new range of products to meet the needs of the new target customers. Tangible repositioning with the help of an innovative advertising campaign has been used to successfully revitalize the Skoda brand, as Marketing in Action 7.6 explains.

Mercedes-Benz found it necessary to use tangible and product repositioning in the face of Japanese competition. Tangible repositioning took the form of developing new products (e.g. a city car) to appeal to new target customers. Product repositioning was also required in its current market segments to bring down the cost of development and manufacture in the face of lower-priced rivals such as Toyota's Lexus.

Review

1 **The concepts of market segmentation and target marketing, and their use in developing marketing strategy**
- Market segmentation is the identification of individuals or organizations with similar characteristics that have significant implications for the determination of marketing strategy.
- Its use aids target market selection, the ability to design a tailored marketing mix, the development of differential marketing strategies, and the identification of opportunities and threats.
- Target marketing is the choice of specific segment(s) to serve. It concerns the decision where to compete.
- Its use is focusing company resources on those segments it is best able to serve in terms of company resources and segment attractiveness. Once chosen, a tailored marketing mix that creates a differential advantage can be designed based on an in-depth understanding of target customers.

2 **The methods of segmenting consumer and organizational markets**
- Consumer markets can be segmented by behavioural (benefits sought, purchase occasion, purchase behaviour, usage, and perceptions and beliefs), psychographic (lifestyle and personality), and profile (demographic, socio-economic and geographic) methods.
- Organizational markets can be segmented by macrosegmentation (organizational size, industry and geographic location) and microsegmentation (choice criteria, decision-making unit structure, decision-making process, buy class, purchasing organization, and organizational effectiveness) methods.

▶ **3** **The factors that can be used to evaluate market segments**
- Two broad issues should be used: market attractiveness and the company's capability to compete.
- Market attractiveness can be assessed by examining market factors (segment size, segment growth rate, price sensitivity, bargaining power of customers, bargaining power of suppliers, barriers to market segment entry and barriers to market segment exit), competitive factors (nature of competition, the likelihood of new entrants, and competitive differentiation), and political, social and environmental factors (political issues, social trends, and environmental issues).
- Capability to compete can be assessed by analysing exploitable marketing assets, cost advantages, technological edge, and managerial capabilities and commitments.

4 **Four target market strategies: undifferentiated, differentiated, focused and customized marketing**
- Undifferentiated marketing occurs where a company does not segment but applies a single marketing mix to the whole market.
- Differentiated marketing occurs where a company segments the market and applies separate marketing mixes to appeal to all or some of the segments (target markets).
- Focused marketing occurs where a company segments the market and develops one specific marketing mix to one segment (target market).
- Customized marketing occurs where a company designs a separate marketing mix for each customer.

5 **The concept of positioning and the keys to successful positioning**
- There are two aspects of positioning: the choice of target market (where to compete) and the creation of a differential advantage (how to compete).
- The objective is to create and maintain a distinctive place in the market for a company and/or its products.
- The four keys to successful positioning are: clarity, consistency, credibility and competitiveness.

6 **Positioning and repositioning strategies**
- A useful tool for determining the position of a brand in the marketplace is the perceptual map.
- Positioning strategy should be based on a clear choice of target market based on market segment attractiveness and company capability, and the creation of a differential advantage (based on an understanding of the attributes—choice criteria—that consumers use when choosing between brands).
- Repositioning strategies can be based on changes to the product and/or target market. Four strategies are image repositioning, product repositioning, intangible repositioning and tangible repositioning.

Key terms

benefit segmentation the grouping of people based on the different benefits they seek from a product

customized marketing the market coverage strategy where a company decides to target individual customers and develops separate marketing mixes for each

differentiated marketing a market coverage strategy where a company decides to target several market segments and develops separate marketing mixes for each

differential marketing strategies market coverage strategies where a company decides to target several market segments and develops separate marketing mixes for each

focused marketing a market coverage strategy where a company decides to target one market segment with a single marketing mix

lifestyle segmentation the grouping of people according to their pattern of living as expressed in their activities, interests and opinions

macrosegmentation the segmentation of organizational markets by size, industry and location

market segmentation the process of identifying individuals or organizations with similar characteristics that have significant implications for the determination of marketing strategy

microsegmentation segmentation according to choice criteria, DMU structure, decision-making process, buy class, purchasing structure and organizational innovativeness

positioning the choice of target market (where the company wishes to compete) and differential advantage (how the company wishes to compete)

profile segmentation the grouping of people in terms of profile variables, such as age and socio-economic group, so that marketers can communicate to them

psychographic segmentation the grouping of people according to their lifestyle and personality characteristics

repositioning changing the target market or differential advantage, or both

target marketing selecting a segment as a focus for the company's offering or communications

undifferentiated marketing a market coverage strategy where a company decides to ignore market segment differences and develops a single marketing mix for the whole market

Internet exercise

Vertu produces the world's most expensive mobile phones. The company sees the mobile phone as a jewellery item, rather than a clunky piece of cheap plastic. It produces platinum, gold and stainless-steel mobile phones. These phones do come at a price, however, with only multimillionaires or celebrities being able to afford such luxuries. The starting price of a Vertu phone is £3750 (€5400) and they are priced up to £15,280 (€22,000). Customers include Madonna and Jennifer Lopez. The real luxury is the free personal concierge service (which lasts for only one year) that comes with the phone. The concierge can book restaurants, get concert tickets and make travel arrangements. See what the rich spend their money on: visit Vertu's website and examine this unique business.

Visit: www.vertu.com

Questions

(a) Using the segmentation bases described in this chapter, describe the potential market segment for the Vertu.

(b) Apart from the price tag, what marketing strategies are employed by Vertu to target the world's super-rich?

(c) Recommend what marketing strategies you would adopt in targeting this market.

Visit the Online Learning Centre at www.mcgraw-hill.co.uk/textbooks/jobber for more Internet exercises.

Study questions

1. What are the advantages of market segmentation? Can you see any advantages of mass marketing, i.e. treating a market as homogeneous and marketing to the whole market with one marketing mix?

2. Choose a market you are familiar with and use benefit segmentation to identify market segments. What are the likely profiles of the resulting segments?

3. In what kind of markets is psychographic segmentation likely to prove useful? Why?

4. How might segmentation be of use when marketing in Europe?

5. One way of segmenting organizational markets is to begin with macrosegmentation variables and then develop sub-segments using microsegmentation criteria. Does this seem sensible to you? Are there any circumstances where the process should be reversed?

6. Why is *buy class* a potentially useful method of segmenting organizational markets? (Use both this chapter and Chapter 4 when answering this question.)

7. What is the majority fallacy? Why should it be taken into account when evaluating market segments?

8. What is the difference between positioning and repositioning? Choose three products and services and describe how they are positioned in the marketplace, i.e. what is their target market and differential advantage?

When you have read this chapter log on to the Online Learning Centre at www.mcgraw-hill.co.uk/textbooks/jobber to explore chapter-by-chapter test questions, links and further online study tools for marketing.

case thirteen

Positioning Budweiser

Budweiser in the USA

Anheuser-Busch is the biggest brewer not only in America but also globally. The US beer market had been tough for Anheuser-Busch in the mid-1990s: number-two brewer Miller (owned by Philip Morris) was growing in strength; the US beer market was static; and Anheuser-Busch had to contend with ongoing legal battles globally with Czech brewer Budvar for the rights to the Budweiser brand name.

Yet the late 1990s witnessed a number of changes. First, the US beer market began to grow. In 1998, it grew by 1.5 per cent and analysts attributed this sales growth to Anheuser-Busch, the largest player in the US market.[1] Second, Anheuser-Busch saw its Bud Light brand overhauling Budweiser, or 'Big Red': volume of Bud Light doubled between 1994 and 2001. Market share in 2001 was heading for 20 per cent—more than that of Budweiser itself and less than 20 years after the launch of Bud Light. Finally, and largely in consequence of the growth of Bud Light, Anheuser's share of the US market topped 50 per cent for the first time in its 123-year history and barrelage exceeded 100 million.[2]

The changing fortunes of Anheuser-Busch are even more dramatic when considered in relation to its nearest US competitor, Miller. Miller Brewing Co. had been a close competitor of Anheuser-Busch until the late 1990s but, by 2002, analysts commented, 'Their position is untenable. Anheuser-Busch Co. basically punches them in the face every day.'[3] In 2001, Miller saw its market share drop below 20 per cent for the first time since the mid-1980s.

So how has Anheuser-Busch transformed the fortunes of Budweiser and its family of brands? Brands that, in the mid-1990s, looked to have a positioning that was no longer appropriate to the target market?

The Budweiser brand

The core US market for Anheuser-Busch's Budweiser is 18- to 24-year-old blue-collar males. There is strong association between the brand and its American origins. Brand analysts describe Budweiser as the 'safe back-up buy for hosts uncertain what guests will want'. This positioning as the brand for everybody, however, may run counter to the needs and wants of the target market it describes as its core.

Yet by the mid-1990s, Budweiser seemed to have become a victim of its own success. The brand had grown so strong that it was institutionalized, established, difficult to move. There is strong identification with the classic brown bottle and busy label (see the illustration, left). Says AB, 'Our customers say, whatever you do, don't change that.'

However, so great is the tradition surrounding Big Red that it may be viewed by today's youngsters as 'Dad's beer'.[4]

Researchers into the beer market suggest that its ongoing success depends on a continual inflow of drinkers in their early twenties. If the younger age group associates Budweiser with its parents' generation, then the beer may be less attractive to them. The challenge for Anheuser-Busch coming to the end of the century was to freshen up the image of the brand. To this end, AB replaced long-standing agency D'Arcy, Masius, Benton and Bowles (DMB&B) with DDB Needham, and continued to pump marketing money into creative advertising of the brand.[5]

Budweiser: 'Big Red'

Bud Light—new kid on the block

Since its launch in 1981, the growth of Bud Light (see the illustration opposite) has been dramatic. Apart from one blip around its eighth or ninth year (1990), Bud Light has been 'the hottest beer in the USA'.[6] Dry beers, ice beers and micro-beers have largely come and gone, but Bud Light has continued to grow. Even Budweiser, the original AB branded beer has been eclipsed by the new arrival. Volume has doubled since 1994. Even in 2001, despite a growing number of competitors, Bud Light sales in the USA grew by 8.2 per cent. Bud Light has used humorous ads; Budweiser has mixed humour—using lizards, frogs, quail and creativity to attract younger consumers—with messages about the freshness and taste of its products. AB spent US$64 million advertising Budweiser in 2001 and a further US$59.7 million on Bud Light. Even competing distributors comment, 'They're able to put out ads that don't give you a reason to drink the products, but entertain you and give you a pleasant memory of the products.'[7]

The US beer market

In the early 1990s, the US beer market underwent significant upheaval. For ten years, the size of the market had been relatively static, with a small decline in the total market in 1992 and 1993. At the same time, established beer brands were under attack from all sides. Imports had risen significantly, and comprised almost 5 per cent of the market. The regional and micro-brewing segments of the market had become a significant force, claiming 4.6 per cent of the market in 1994.[8] In addition, niche products like ice beer, dry beer and red beer, and a host of new non-alcoholic beverages were are all growing at the expense of large, established beer brands. Anheuser-Busch employed several strategies to deal with this competitive situation in the domestic market. First, it pursued new, innovative products. This led to the launch of its own ice beer and dry beer products. It also pursued a number of freshness and taste initiatives. Innovation in the brewing industry, though, can only go so far. AB, therefore, began to acquire equity stakes in micro-breweries and regional breweries to tap into the surge in consumer interest in these beers. It also began to focus intensively on new markets abroad.[9]

By the late 1990s, a new trend dominated the US beer market. Consumers were increasingly concerned at their belt size. This calorie-conscious trend—at first dominated by Miller Lite—is seemingly here to stay. Commentators agree:

> Tull-calorie[10] premium beers are not the consumer preference right now. ... Since it was the No. 1 brand, Budweiser had the most to lose as consumers switched to light beer. A competing beer distributor in the West said the movement toward light beers is so pronounced that not even AB can reverse it. With domestic beers it's the wave of the future. The wave of drinking people.[11]

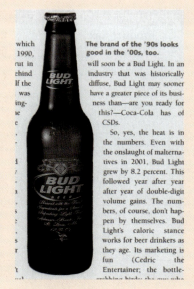

Bud Light: dramatic growth

AB's international marketing strategy

Anheuser-Busch first launched itself seriously on to the international scene in 1981, with the formation of its international division. In the period from 1981–94, international sales climbed from a paltry 900,000 barrels to 4.5 million barrels in 1994.[12] This growth in sales was achieved through a combination of exporting, licensing and contracting-out production of AB's beer. While AB sold some Michelob and Busch brands of beer abroad, Budweiser remains its primary international brand. Interestingly, while Budweiser is positioned domestically as a mainstream, and to some extent working man's beer, internationally it is positioned as a premium product with a premium price attached.

While AB initially concentrated on developing a foothold in established beer markets like Canada and Europe, it now sees greater profits in equity stakes and acquisitions in developing markets. AB has established a number of equity links to support this strategy. It has a 50 per cent stake in Mexico's Grupo Modelo, Mexico's leading brewer. Modelo has a 56.9 per cent share of the Mexican market and holds the number-one position in the US import market with Corona beer. In 2002, AB also struck a deal to take 27 per cent equity in China's Tsingtao Brewery Co. China became the world's largest beer market and AB sees it has having 'enormous potential'.[13] AB also has a 20 per cent stake in Chilean Brewer, Compania Cervecerias Unidas (CCU). Latin America is considered attractive because it has low beer consumption rates with a growing population and a large segment of 21–27 year olds.

By 2001, Anheuser-Busch stood at number three in the global rankings of beverage companies, with total sales worth US$12,911 million (see Table C13.1). Budweiser was sold in 80 countries, with total international sales of more than 8 million barrels. Growth from international sales is accelerating. Net income from international markets was up by 25 per cent in 2001, with profits increasing by 76 per cent (this shows the higher margins to be gained in international markets compared with tough price competition in the domestic market).

While AB has focused on the fast-growing beer markets of the developing world, it is still interested in

Table C13.1	Beverage companies: global rankings, 2001			
Rank	Company and location	Product mix	2000 sales (in US$m)	2001 sales (in US$m)
1	Coca-Cola Co. Atlanta, Georgia, USA	soft drinks, water, sports drinks	20,458	20,092
2	Nestlé S.A. Vevey, Switzerland	coffee, water, juice, dairy, mixes, beer	12,969	16,128
3	Anheuser-Busch, Inc. St Louis, Missouri, USA	beer	12,262	12,911
4	PepsiCo Inc. Purchase, New York, USA	soft drinks, water, juice, sports drinks	7,488	10,440
5	Suntory Int. Group	water, spirits	NA	8,726
6	Heineken NV Amsterdam, Netherlands	beer, wine, spirits	6,981	8,515
7	Interbrew Leuwen, Belgium	beer	7,690	6,791
12	Miller Brewing Co. Milwaukee, USA	beer	4,375	4,244
14	South African Breweries	beer, wine, spirits, fruit drinks	5,424	4,184

Source: Cosgrove, 2002[14]

developing its profile in Europe. The United Kingdom accounts for most of the premium beer sold outside the USA. Ireland, Spain and Italy also represent primary beer markets for AB. Despite significant sales volumes in Europe, Anheuser-Busch's marketing is seriously constrained by its trademark dispute with Budvar (see Appendix C13.1). AB can sell under the Budweiser name in Cyprus, Denmark, Finland, Iceland, Ireland, Malta, Sweden and the United Kingdom, having won lawsuits against Budvar in these countries. However, AB is restricted to using the Bud name in Belgium, France, Greece, Italy, Luxemburg, the Netherlands, Portugal, Spain, Switzerland, the Canary Islands and Gibraltar due to the trademark dispute. Legal cases are ongoing to win the rights to the use of the Budweiser name in more international markets. In a recent landmark case[15] Budvar also won the rights to use the Budweiser name, making UK the only market where the two brands will go head to head.

The illustration (right) shows the different brand names, and the similarities in identity and positioning adopted for these by Budweiser.

Building a global brand

AB's drive to globalize the Budweiser brand is partly influenced by what the competition is doing. It now has sales in approximately 80 countries[16] and has made strides towards matching its international competitors. Table C13.1 shows AB as larger than Heineken, Interbrew

Budweiser brand names

and South African Breweries, its largest rivals. This is largely based on its success in domestic markets. In international terms, AB is a relative newcomer. The other major international brewers have been busy far longer building an international presence. The Dutch brewer Heineken has been very active internationally since the early part of the century and now sells in approximately 160 countries. Similarly, Carlsberg currently sells in over 140 countries, and has 80 per cent of sales outside its home market of Denmark.[17] Guinness also has successfully been building a global presence in the past decade.

While industry analysts once thought that the brewing industry would remain dominated by regional and national brewing companies, Carlsberg, Heineken and Guinness have proven that beer has global branding potential. The omens for AB are good. International sales and profit continue to grow strongly. International sales of $399 million in 2002 represent a 29.3 per cent growth on 2001. This is now 21 per cent of AB's total earnings. Resolution of the trademark dispute with Budvar, however, is crucial for Anheuser-Busch's effort to build a global beer brand out of *Budweiser*. Without unrestricted access to the European market, AB will not be able to utilize a unified branding strategy, and will not be able to freely pursue new opportunities for Budweiser.

Attempts to resolve the trademark dispute

The end of Communism opened a new chapter in relations between Anheuser-Busch and Budvar. Anheuser-Busch saw its golden opportunity to settle the dispute once and for all when privatization of Czech industries got under way in 1991. Anheuser-Busch approached Budvar, and the two firms agreed to a moratorium on legal action, under the assumption that they would attempt to resolve the dispute. However, Anheuser-Busch refused to discuss the trademark dispute until talks got under way regarding the purchase of a stake in Budvar. This was the ideal opportunity to end the dispute forever.

Stephen J. Burrows, vice president of Anheuser-Busch International, was quoted as implying that AB would employ a carrot-and-stick approach with Budvar. He suggested that if AB could invest in Budvar, resolution of the dispute could be quick and painless, but that if Budvar was sold to another party, settling the dispute might be far more difficult.[18] In early 1993, AB suggested a 'strategic alliance' that would ensure co-existence in the world market between Budvar's and AB's Budweiser brands. AB's proposal included providing Budvar access to Anheuser-Busch's formidable marketing and distribution network, and gave guarantees of continuous investment in the Budejovice brewery. AB also promised that it would not tamper with Budvar's taste, production process or ingredients. The only changes that would be necessary, according to AB, were 'appropriate name and label modifications to avoid confusion wherever necessary'.[19]

Full-scale public relations campaign

Anheuser-Busch recognized that its proposal would be greeted with suspicion by the Czech public. In early 1993, AB started a massive public relations campaign explaining why it wanted to buy a stake in Budvar. AB took out full-page advertisements in several national daily newspapers discussing its intentions and giving promises to maintain the distinctive quality of the beer and the centuries-old brewing traditions. Anheuser-Busch promised to uphold 'Eight Principles' if it bought a stake in Budvar.

AB also spent over a million dollars on building the St Louis Cultural Centre in Ceske Budejovice. The centre offers English language classes and a library, and sponsors events. Some residents of Ceske Budejovice believe the centre serves as a thinly veiled public relations arm for AB in Budvar's hometown, and the centre has been compared to a Trojan horse.[20] Despite its extensive public relations campaign, the Czech government made it clear that AB would need to follow the normal procedures of the Czech privatization process, and would not receive special treatment. AB would need to put in its bid along with any other interested parties when, and if, the government decided that a stake in Budvar should be sold to a foreign investor.

Back to the negotiating table

The government's indecision over the Budvar privatization situation endured until July 1995, when the prime minister suddenly announced publicly that privatization would definitely not proceed until the trademark dispute with AB was resolved. Anheuser-Busch had little choice but to agree to meet Budvar for a fresh attempt at negotiations to resolve the trademark dispute.

Anheuser-Busch's final offer included a 10-year agreement to purchase Czech hops worth US$76 million and a down-payment of US$20 million on the future purchase of shares in Budvar by Anheuser-Busch. But Budvar general manager Jiri Bocek was concerned that the final offer 'would [leave] his company playing second fiddle to US Budweiser in European markets'. Bocek said the offer was unacceptable to Budvar and the government: 'I believe the decision was rational and based on pragmatic considerations. Budvar is capable of developing itself without becoming a vassal of Anheuser-Busch.'[21]

Budvar's uncertain future was hindering other privatizations. The UK's Bass, Denmark's Carlsberg and Anheuser-Busch were bidding for a minority stake in Jihoceske Pivovary (South Bohemian Breweries), a regional Czech brewery. As there was a simultaneous plan to merge SBB with Budvar, this plan was suspended by the Czech government until the outcome of the SBB privatization was clear: 'If SBB selected Anheuser-Busch, any merger with Budvar would be abandoned.'[22] Finally, in September 1996, Anheuser-Busch pulled out of the talks when the Czech government finally decided to privatize Budvar, but indicated that it would remain in domestic hands.[23]

Anheuser-Busch recently won court rulings allowing it to use the Budweiser name in Spain and the Bud name in Norway. It has had nine wins in European countries—five in the past year—and has 27 under way.[24] Anheuser-Busch believes it has achieved 'undisputed access' to Europe, with sales of 2.2 hectolitres of beer in Europe, an increase of 25 per cent. However, each legal battle involves both time and expense, and hinders its expansion strategy. Anheuser-Busch recently pulled out of a US$145-million Vietnamese brewing joint venture because Budvar registered the name there in 1960.

Repositioning the Budweiser brand

The trademark dispute notwithstanding, AB has a number of positioning issues to consider for its brand. First, in the USA, AB has to face a reality in which Bud Light has eclipsed the longer-established Budweiser brand. AB has to put its efforts into creative marketing for Budweiser so that it remains static—or at least, as at present, declines only slowly. Second, AB must consider the new market leadership of its Bud Light brand and create strategies to manage the rising star. In international markets, AB has to consider the difference in positioning of Budweiser as a mass-market beer in the USA and as a premium beer in international markets. It also has a growing portfolio of brands to manage (including the Corona and Tsingtao brands, which are well known in their own right).

Appendix C13.1 Background to the trademark dispute

Use of the *Budweiser* name in connection with beer dates back to as early as 1531. In that year, the German king Ferdinand, whose royal court was in the town of Ceske Budejovice (then called Budweis) gave the city the right to brew beer for his court. This beer was identified as Budweiser, literally meaning beer 'from the town of Budweis'. Budweiser beer became known as the 'Beer of Kings' due to its link with Ferdinand's court.[25]

Several centuries later, in the mid-1860s, a German immigrant named Adolphus Busch established a small brewery in St Louis, USA, called the Bavarian Brewery. In 1876, in searching for a name for a new beer that would appeal to the many German immigrants living in and around St Louis, Busch appropriated the name 'Budweiser' from the beer long produced in the Bohemian town of Budweis. Busch also borrowed the old slogan of Budweiser beer, 'Beer of Kings', but inverted it, calling American Budweiser the 'King of Beers'.[26] In 1879 Busch's brewery merged with another brewery and changed its name to Anheuser-Busch.

Two decades later, in 1895, a group of Czech investors founded Budejovicky Budvar (also called Budweiser Budvar) and also laid claim to the name Budweiser. The Czechs cited historical precedent for using the name, dating back to the early sixteenth century. Moreover, they claimed the right to the name as it properly identified the origin of their beer.

The 1911 agreement

As Budvar and Anheuser-Busch grew, it was inevitable that they would eventually run into conflict over use of the Budweiser name. In 1911, the two breweries came together and signed an agreement which, they hoped, would end the dispute. The agreement recognized AB's right to the name Budweiser, as it was a registered trademark of AB in the United States. However, the agreement also acknowledged Budvar's legal right to the Budweiser name. AB was thus given the right to use the Budweiser name in the USA and all other non-European countries. AB could use the Budweiser name in any way it chose—however, it had to stop using the words 'original' in combination with its product, in order to avoid giving the impression to the consumer that this was the first beer to be known as Budweiser.

The 1939 agreement

By the late 1930s, Budvar was selling significant quantities of Czech Budweiser in the USA. Anheuser-Busch clearly felt that Budvar was overstepping its bounds in AB's home market. AB charged that the US public associated the Budweiser and Bud names with AB products. Since Budvar was exporting its beer to the USA under the name Budweiser, Budvar was confusing the customer, and unfairly using the brand name that AB had built.[27] In the settlement proposed by AB, Budvar agreed to surrender all rights to the Budweiser, Budweis and Bud names, and all other names containing 'Bud', in all territories north of Panama, as well as all US colonies and territories. In addition, Budvar could not market other beer brands in these markets using the word 'manufactured in Budweis'. Instead, it had to use the words 'manufactured in Ceske Budejovice'. In return, Anheuser-Busch agreed to pay US$50,000 to Budvar and US$15,000 to Budvar's American distributor, provided that Budvar's Budweiser was removed from the North American market within six months.[28] A few days after the agreement was signed, the Nazis invaded what remained of Czechoslovakia. The Czechs later claimed that the 1939 agreement was signed under duress and declared it invalid.

AB's attempt to buy rights to Budweiser

Legal battles

After failing to buy the right to the Budweiser name in Europe, Anheuser-Busch attempted an attack from a different angle. AB launched legal challenges to Budvar's right to the Budweiser name in 15 countries throughout Europe.[29] In 1984, AB won a decisive victory in its battle to enter the European market when a UK court judged that AB's Budweiser should be allowed to co-exist with Budvar's Budweiser brand. The court ruled that the co-existence should be reinforced by the two firms using their respective names in different ways.[30] In Finland and Sweden, Anheuser-Busch also succeeded in legal battles, and was able to market Budweiser. However, in France, Italy, Portugal and a number of other markets, AB's legal offensives failed. In these markets, AB was able, however, to sell its beer under the name 'Bud'.

The appellation of origin issue

AB's legal defeat in the 1980s in a number of European countries was ultimately the result of the development of a new concept in intellectual property law called the 'appellation of origin'. An appellation of origin is a name that serves to identify the geographic origin of a product. If registered, the appellation of origin cannot be used by a producer from outside that town or region. The names Champagne, Cognac and Bordeaux are three of the best-known examples of protected appellations of origin. Over the past several decades, the appellation of origin has emerged as a strongly protected element of intellectual property in many European countries, as well as in a group of non-European countries that have signed on to a special multilateral convention on intellectual property called the Lisbon Agreement.[31]

Budvar had registered and uses a number of appellations of origin. Most importantly, 'Budweiser' is a registered appellation of origin, designating Budvar's beer as a product of Budweis. For the European countries that recognized the appellation of origin, it was an infringement of Budvar's rights for Anheuser-Busch to use the name Budweiser.

Post-1989

After the velvet revolution in 1989, the dispute over the rights to the Budweiser name intensified. AB attempted to buy a stake in Budvar but the Czech government decided not to sell the firm, which it considered to be 'part of the family silver'. AB and Budvar continue to battle for the rights to the Budweiser name on a market-by-market basis.

---

[1] Rekha Balu (1999) Anheuser-Busch Enjoying Upturn in Domestic Beer Business, *Wall Street Journal*, 20 May, B6.

[2] Greg Prince (2001) Top 10 Beer: Solid Ground, *Beverage World*, 15 April, Vol. 120, Issue 1701, 45–9.

[3] Robert Frank and Gordon Fairclough (2002) Miller Brewing Co. has Discussed Deals with Several Rivals, *Wall Street Journal*, 28 Jan., B2.

[4] Richard Gibson and Marj Charlier (1994) Corporate Focus: Fresher Bud Image Requires Light Touch, *Wall Street Journal*, 25 November, 1.

[5] Greg Prince (2002) Eternal Flame, *Beverage World*, 15 October, Vol. 121, Issue 1719, 42.

[6] Greg Prince (2002) op. cit.

[7] Greg Prince (2002) op. cit.

[8] Gibson and Charlier (1994) op. cit.

[9] Anheuser-Busch (1993, 1994) Annual Reports.

[10] 'Tull calorie' is a play on words with 'null calorie' or 'low calorie'. 'Tull' equals the opposite—high-calorie beers.

[11] Greg Prince (2002) op. cit.

[12] Anheuser-Busch public relations materials, July 1995.

[13] Anheuser-Busch (2002) Annual Report.

[14] Joanna Cosgrove (2002) The Top 100 Beverage Companies: The List, *Beverage Industry*, July, 28.

[15] T. Mason (2003) Bud Superstrong in UK Debut after Budvar Legal Win, *Marketing*, 20 Feb., 1.

[16] Anheuser-Busch (2002) Annual Report.

[17] Robert J. Guttman (1995) Danish Business Goes Global, *Europe*, 10.

[18] Janet Guyon, (1993) Row Over Budweiser Brand Name Highlights the Value of Brands, *Wall Street Journal Europe*, 16 September.

[19] J.S. Newton (1993) Stalking Budvar, Disregarding Heritage, *Prognosis* 14–27 May, 11.

[20] Newton (1993) op. cit.

[21] Vincent Boland (1996) Budvar takes lid off US Rival's Offer, *Financial Times* (Companies and Finance: International), 20 December.

[22] Vincent Boland (1996) Brewing Bid Battle may Affect Budvar, *Financial Times* (International Company News), 5 March.

[23] Vincent Boland (1996) Anheuser-Busch Pulls Out of Budweiser Name Talks, *Financial Times* (back page, first section), 23 September.

[24] Vincent Boland and Roderick Oram (1996) US Brewer Leaves Budvar Fighting for Identity: Czech Group Faces Marketing Challenge after Collapse of Brand Right Talks with Anheuser-Busch, *Financial Times* (Companies and Finance: Europe), 1 November.

[25] Ivan Masek (1993) Jiri Bocek: Anheuser-Busch je pouze jednim ze zajemcu!, *Magazin Uspech*, September, 19.

[26] Ivan Masek (1993) op. cit.

[27] Original mutual restraint agreement between Budvar and Anheuser-Busch, 7 March 1939.

[28] Mutual restraint agreement, 1939.

[29] Mutual restraint agreement, 1939, 20.

[30] F. Gever, trademark attorney (1995) Conflict Between Appellation of Origin and Trademark, Preliminary Answers, June.

[31] A very prominent legal case involving appellations of origin concerned the champagne makers of the Champagne region of France. French champagne makers were able to force producers from outside the Champagne region to cease calling their products 'Champagne', as this word had been a registered appellation of origin and served to identify the origin of the product. Producers outside the Champagne region were instead to call their products 'sparkling wine'.

Questions

1. What are the major challenges facing AB in the US beer market?

2. Analyse the positioning of Budweiser and of Bud Light. What are the similarities and differences in their positioning?

3. What are the implications for Budweiser's international marketing strategy of its different positioning in the USA and other international markets?

4. What are the advantages and disadvantages for AB of managing both global beer brands (Budweiser, Bud Light) alongside local or regionally adapted brands (Corona and Tsingtao)?

This case was written by Sue Bridgewater, Lecturer in Marketing and Strategy, University of Warwick, UK.

personnel to determine what factors should be used to score customers. A list of factors was agreed upon and weighted. This was presented to the commercial managers responsible for implementing the new service level agreements, and their feedback was sought. In addition, the views of more senior personnel were canvassed, and all responses were discussed and considered when calculating the final list of factors and their weightings. The commercial director had the final input before the factors were agreed.

The factors contained in the programme were as follows.

Profitability to CES
CES's business strategy was to grow its business with its most profitable customers. This factor was given the heaviest weighting, thus the segmentation would align itself with the business strategy.

All other factors were given similar weighting.

Financial strength
Assesses the creditworthiness/credit risk associated with dealing with a customer.

Total contribution
Considers the revenue generated from a customer.

Total volume
Considers the volume of steel a customer has purchased over the previous year.

Growth potential
Predicts the amount of additional profitable/desirable business which CES could target with the customer.

Share of business
Examines the proportion of steel the customer purchases from CES.

Fit with market strategy
Considers the customer fit with CES's market strategy. For example, one CES strategy is to sell more added-value processing, e.g. pre-painted panels.

Fit with product strategy
Examines the customer fit with CES's product strategy. For example, the HSSP scoring system gave more points to customers buying products that are within its product strategy.

Future prospects
Evaluates the customer's standing in its marketplace, its future prospects and its connections. The category was examining the potential sales of CES products by forecasting whether the customer was likely to grow, remain static or decline in size.

Cost to serve
This factor combines a number of issues: the level of commercial and technical support demanded by the customer, transport demands, the degree of difficulty in getting the product to the customer, and ease of order progress. The category is intended to reflect the additional service costs CES incurs in dealing with the customer and that are not included in the selling price.

Current relationship
Considers the current customer relationship and its loyalty towards CES as a supplier.

Cultural fit
Similar to relationship, this is intended to look at the similarities between the two businesses in the way that they do business.

Stability of ordering
Reflects the number of changes a customer makes to an order once it has been processed. Any changes require administrative time, production programme changes and changes to transportation requirements. All create additional cost to CES.

Outcome
Once the array of data was collected from various departments for all the factors, and had been processed and weighted using computer software, CES's customers were re-categorized into the three segments. The proportions in each segment were as follows:
- 10 per cent platinum customers
- 50 per cent gold customers
- 40 per cent silver customers.

The segmentation strategy was successful and implemented successfully. However, it must be kept under constant review in terms of checking customer status, but also periodically ensuring that the factors and their weightings are still applicable. The involvement of a number of managers in developing the categorization was a key aspect of aiding implementation.

The additional stages in the segmentation process to 'catch' customers likely to experience a reduced service, as a result of the re-categorization, proved prudent. Two of CES's largest customers were categorized as silver. Neither company is profitable for CES, but their large-volume purchases provide significant contribution to the business, which is, to an extent, still dependent on large-volume orders to keep the steel mills employed. To ensure these customers stayed with CES, they were moved up a service category, but with the expectation that the commercial managers responsible for these accounts would work with them to improve profitability to CES.

Questions

1. Why was the Hoogovens Special Strip Products (HSSP) customer-classification segmentation considered better than the Corus Engineering Steels (CES) needs-based segmentation?

2. What are the benefits to Corus Engineering Services (CES) of segmenting its customers using the customer scoring system?

3. Why were so many managers involved in developing the customer scoring system? What were the advantages/disadvantages of this?

References and further reading

Dibb, S. and L. Simkin (1994) Implementation Problems in Industrial Market Segmentation, *Industrial Marketing Management* 23, 55–63.

Fiocca, R. (1982) Account Portfolio Analysis for Strategy Development, *Industrial Marketing Management* 11, 53–62.

Sarabia, F. J. (1996), Model for Market Segments Evaluation and Selection, *European Journal of Marketing* 30, 58–74.

Yorke, D. A. and G. Droussiotis (1994) The Use of Customer Portfolio Theory—an Empirical Survey, *Journal of Business and Industrial Marketing* 9, 6–18.

This case study was written by Bridget Rowe, Researcher, Gary Reed, Lecturer, and Jim Saker, Professor in Retail Management, Loughborough University Business School.

The merger of British Steel and Hoogovens to form Corus called for creative ideas on marketing segmentation.

Marketing Mix Decisions

part two

8. Managing products: brand and corporate identity management
9. Managing products: product life cycle, portfolio planning and growth strategies
10. Developing new products
11. Pricing strategy
12. Advertising
13. Personal selling and sales management
14. Direct marketing
15. Internet marketing
16. Other promotional mix methods
17. Distribution

chapter eight

Managing products: brand and corporate identity management

> ❝... a rose
> By any other name would smell as sweet.❞
> — SHAKESPEARE, *Romeo and Juliet*

> ❝Or would it?❞
> — ANONYMOUS

Learning Objectives

This chapter explains:

1. The concept of a product, brand, product line and product mix
2. The difference between manufacturer and own-label brands
3. The difference between a core and an augmented product (the brand)
4. Why strong brands are important
5. How to build strong brands
6. The differences between family, individual and combined brand names, and the characteristics of an effective brand name
7. Why companies rebrand, and how to manage the process
8. The concepts of brand extension and stretching, their uses and limitations
9. The two major forms of co-branding, and their advantages and risks
10. The arguments for and against global and pan-European branding, and the strategic options for building such brands
11. The dimensions of corporate identity
12. The management of corporate identity programmes
13. Ethical issues concerning products

Part two Marketing Mix Decisions

The core element in the marketing mix is the company's product because this provides the functional requirements sought by customers. For example, a watch that does not tell the time or a car that does not start in the morning will rapidly be rejected by consumers. Marketing managers develop their products into brands that help to create a unique position (see Chapter 7) in the minds of customers. Brand superiority leads to high sales, the ability to charge price premiums and the power to resist distributor power. Firms attempt to retain their current customers through brand loyalty. Loyal customers are typically less price sensitive, and the presence of a loyal customer base provides the firm with valuable time to respond to competitive actions.[1] The management of products and brands is therefore a key factor in marketing success.

This chapter will explore the nature of products and brands, and the importance of strong brands. Given that importance, the ways in which successful brands are built will be revealed. Then a series of key branding decisions will be examined: brand name strategies and choices, rebranding, brand extension and stretching, and co-branding. Next, the special issues relating to global and pan-European branding will be analysed. Finally, corporate identity management, an area that is gaining increasing attention among corporate brand managers, is discussed.

Products and brands

A product is anything that is capable of satisfying customer needs. In everyday speech we often distinguish between products and services, with products being tangible (e.g. a car) and services mainly intangible (e.g. a medical examination). However, when we look at what the customer is buying, it is essentially a service whether the means is tangible or intangible. For example, a car provides the service of transportation; a medical examination provides the service of a health check. Consequently, it is logical to include services within the definition of the product. Hence, there are *physical products* such as a watch, car or gas turbine, or *service*

This award-winning advertisement for Land Rover associates the brand with toughness and durability.

8.1 e-marketing

Branding by Association

British Telecom (BT) is one of the major suppliers of broadband connections in the United Kingdom. In fact, to receive the main broadband technology (ADSL, which stands for Asynchronous Digital Subscriber Line), and regardless of the company that supplies the broadband service, BT must first enable the nearest telephone exchange to the user base. BT is integral to broadband deployment in the UK and has made a huge investment in broadband technology, including promoting the use of broadband to the public through some high-profile television advertising.

BT (through the BT Openworld network) has recently sponsored and/or developed some important content websites, including Games Domain (www.gamesdomain.co.uk) and DotMusic (www.dotmusic.com)—review sites in games and pop music, respectively. Why should a telecommunications company become involved in content areas where it has little or no prior experience?

The reason is simple. Through associating BT with key broadband uses, the company should benefit from greater uptake and associate the BT brand with use and connection. Both games and music or, more importantly, online gaming and mp3 downloading are still the strongest reasons for many to get broadband.

Can you think of other websites with which BT or other broadband suppliers will associate in the future? To help you in this task, remember that other key features of broadband include the transfer of large files, the use of remote software applications, an always-on connection, videoconferencing, online chatting and e-learning; think of key sites in these areas.

products such as medical services, insurance or banking. All of these products satisfy customer needs—for example, a gas turbine provides power and insurance reduces financial risk. The principles discussed in this chapter apply equally to physical and service products. However, because there are special considerations associated with service products (e.g. intangibility) and as service industries (e.g. fast-food restaurants, tourism and the public sector) form an important and growing sector within the EU, Chapter 21 is dedicated to examining services marketing in detail.

Branding is the process by which companies distinguish their product offerings from the competition. By developing a distinctive name, packaging and design, a **brand** is created. Some brands are supported by logos—for example, the Nike 'swoosh' and the prancing horse of Ferrari. By developing an individual identity, branding permits customers to develop associations with the brand (e.g. prestige, economy) and eases the purchase decision.[2] The illustration featuring Land Rover shows how the company associates the brand with toughness and durability. The marketing task is to ensure that the associations made are positive and in line with the chosen positioning objectives (see Chapter 7). The importance of creating positive associations for a brand is illustrated in e-Marketing 8.1, which explains how BT is attempting to associate its brand with being the first name in broadband Internet connection.

Branding affects perceptions since it is well known that in blind product testing consumers often fail to distinguish between brands in each product category, hence the questioning of Shakespeare's famous statement at the start of this chapter.

The word 'brand' is derived from the Old Norse word 'brandr', which means 'to burn' as brands were and still are the means by which livestock owners mark their animals to identify ownership.[3]

The product line and product mix

Brands are not often developed in isolation. They normally fall within a company's product line and mix. A product line is a group of brands that are closely related in terms of their functions and the benefits they provide (e.g. Dell's range of personal computers or Philips Consumer Electronics line of television sets). The *depth* of the product line depends upon the pattern of customer requirements (e.g. the number of segments to be found in the market), the product depth being offered by competitors, and company resources. For example, although customers may require wide product variations, a small company may decide to focus on a narrow product line serving only sub-segments of the market.

A product mix is the total set of brands marketed in a company. It is the sum of the product lines offered. Thus, the *width* of the product mix can be gauged by the number of product lines an organization offers. Philips, for example, offers a wide product mix comprising the brands found within its product lines of television, audio equipment, video recorders, camcorders, and so on. Other companies have a much narrower product mix comprising just one product line, such as TVR, which produces high-performance cars.

The management of brands and product lines is a key element of product strategy. First, we shall examine the major decisions involved in managing brands—namely the type of brand to market (manufacturer vs own-label), how to build brands, brand name strategies, brand extension and stretching, and the brand acquisition decision. Then we shall look at how to manage brands and product lines over time using the product life cycle concept. Finally, managing brand and product line portfolios will be discussed.

Brand types

The two alternatives regarding brand type are manufacturer and own-label brands. Manufacturer brands are created by producers and bear their own chosen brand name. The responsibility for marketing the brand lies in the hands of the producer. Examples include Kellogg's Cornflakes, Gillette Sensor razors and Ariel washing powder. The value of the brand lies with the producer and, by building major brands, producers can gain distribution and customer loyalty.

A fundamental distinction that needs to be made is between category, brands and variants (see Fig. 8.1). A category (or product field) is divided into brands, which in turn may be divided into variants based on flavour, formulation or other feature.[4] For example, Heinz Tomato Soup is the tomato variant of the Heinz brand of the category 'soup'.

Own-label brands (sometimes called distributor brands) are created and owned by distributors. Sometimes the entire product mix of a distributor may be own-label (e.g. Marks & Spencer's original brand name St Michael) or only part of the mix may be own-label as is the case with many supermarket chains. Own-label branding, if associated with tight quality control of suppliers, can provide consistent high value for customers, and be a source of retail power as suppliers vie to fill excess productive capacity with manufacturing products for own-label branding. The power of low-price supermarket own-label brands has focused many producers of manufacturer brands to introduce so-called fighter brands (i.e. their own low-price alternative).

A major decision that producers have to face is whether to agree to supply own-label products for distributors. The danger is that, should customers find out, they may believe that there is no difference between the manufacturer brand and its own-label equivalent. This led some companies, such as Kellogg's, to refuse to supply own-label products for many years. For

Figure 8.1 Categories, brands and variants

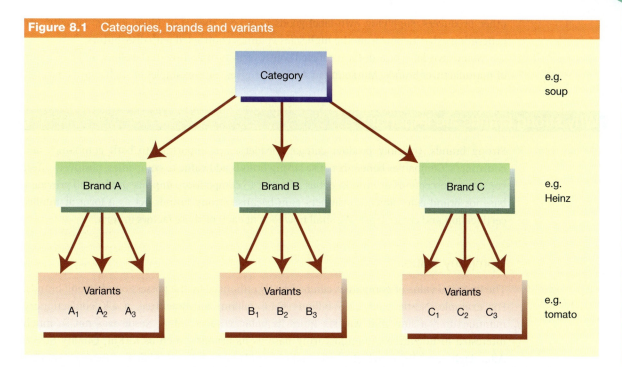

8.1 marketing in action

Own-label Copycatting

It is what every owner of a manufacturer's brand dreads. The brand has been thoroughly researched, the marketing team has sweated over the right product, advertising and direct marketing strategy, and the launch has been successful, with high distribution and sales levels. The brand is a hit with consumers, and the board is well pleased. Until, that is, an own-label brand bearing an uncanny resemblance to the successful new brand suddenly appears on the supermarket shelves—at a cheaper price. This was the situation facing Walkers when its successful Sensations premium crisp brand, which took 18 months to develop at a cost of £2 million (€2.9 million) with a further £9 million (€13 million) being spent on a marketing campaign, suddenly found itself competing with an own-label supermarket brand, Tesco Temptations, with similar packaging.

Such threats to manufacturers' brands are not taken lightly. McVitie's took the supermarket chain Asda to court claiming that the latter's Puffin chocolate bar was an illegal copycat of its own Penguin brand in both name and package design. The judge ruled that the image of a puffin must be removed from the packaging but stopped short of forcing Asda to change the brand name.

Coca-Cola was also threatened by Sainsbury's, which launched its own-label brand Classic Cola in a can coloured red and white with a swirling logo that bore a close resemblance to the Coca-Cola design. In this instance commercial pressure rather than the courts forced Sainsbury's to redesign its can and restore Coke's share of shelf space, which had been halved to make way for Classic.

If a manufacturer resorts to the legal system to protect a brand, it needs to show that three conditions have been met:

① that the brand has built up a reputation with consumers
② that misrepresentation has taken place in that one trader is presenting its goods as being the goods of another trader
③ that the misrepresentation has resulted in damage or loss of sales.

Based on: Benady (2002);[5] Charles (2003);[6] Smith (2002)[7] other producers, supplying own label goods may be a means of filling excess capacity and generating extra income from the high sales volumes contracted with distributors.

Some own-label brands have courted controversy by imitating the labelling and packaging of manufacturer brands. Marketing in Action 8.1 gives some examples of such copycat brands.

Why strong brands are important

Strong brands, typically product category leaders, are important to both companies and consumers. Companies benefit because strong brands add value to companies, positively affect consumer perceptions of brands, act as a barrier to competition, improve profits and provide a base for brand extensions. Consumers gain because strong brands act as a form of quality certification and create trust. We shall now look at each of these factors in turn.

Company value

The financial value of companies can be greatly enhanced by the possession of strong brands. For example, Nestlé paid £2.5 billion (€3.6 billion) for Rowntree, a UK confectionery manufacturer, a sum that was six times its balance sheet value. Nestlé was not so much interested in Rowntree's manufacturing base as its brands—such as KitKat, Quality Street, After Eight and Polo—which were major brands with brand-building potential. Another example is Coca-Cola, which attributes only 7 per cent of its value to its plants and machinery—its real value lies in its brands.[8]

Consumer perceptions and preferences

Strong brand names can have positive effects on consumer perceptions and preferences. Marketing in Action 8.2 describes evidence from the soft drinks and car markets, which shows how strong brands can influence perception and preference. Clearly, the strength of Diet Coke and Toyota as powerful brand names influenced perception and preference in both markets.

Barrier to competition

The impact of the strong, positive perceptions held by consumers about top brands means it is difficult for new brands to compete. Even if the new brand performs well on blind taste testing, as we have seen, this may be insufficient to knock the market leader off the top spot. This may be one of the reasons Virgin Coke failed to dent Coca-Cola's domination of the cola market. The reputation of strong brands, then, may be a powerful barrier to competition.

High profits

Strong, market-leading brands are rarely the cheapest. Brands such as Heinz, Kellogg's, Coca-Cola, Mercedes, Nokia and Microsoft are all associated with premium prices. This is because their superior brand equity means that consumers receive added value over their less powerful rivals. Strong brands also achieve distribution more readily and are in a better position to resist retailer demands for price discounts. These forces feed through to profitability. A major study of the factors that lead to high profitability (the Profit Impact of Marketing Strategy project) shows that return on investment is related to a brand's share of the market: bigger brands yield higher returns than smaller brands.[11] For example, brands with a market share of 40 per cent

8.2 marketing in action

Strong Brand Names Affect Consumer Perceptions and Preferences

Two matched samples of consumers were asked to taste Diet Coke, the market leader in diet colas, and Diet Pepsi. The first group tasted the drinks 'blind' (i.e. the brand identities were concealed) and were asked to state a preference. The procedure was repeated for the second group, except that the test was 'open' (i.e. the brand identities were shown). The results are presented below.

	Blind %	Open %
Prefer Diet Pepsi	51	23
Prefer Diet Coke	44	65
Equal/can't say	5	12

This test clearly shows the power of strong brand names in influencing perceptions and preferences towards Diet Coke.

A second example comes from the car industry. A joint venture between Toyota and General Motors (GM) resulted in two virtually identical cars being produced from the same manufacturing plant in the USA. One was branded the Toyota Corolla, and the other GM's Chevrolet Prizm. Although the production costs were the same, the Toyota was priced higher than the Chevrolet Prizm. Despite the price difference, the Toyota achieved twice the market share of its near identical twin. The reason was that the Toyota brand enjoyed an excellent reputation for reliable cars whereas GM's reputation had been tarnished by a succession of unreliable cars. Despite the fact that the cars were virtually the same, consumers' perceptions and preferences were strongly affected by the brand names attached to each model.

Based on: De Chernatony and McDonald (1998);[9] Doyle (1998)[10]

---

generate, on average, three times the return on investment of brands with only 10 per cent market share. These findings are supported by research into return on investment for US food brands. The category leader's average return was 18 per cent, number two achieved 6 per cent, number three returned 1 per cent, while the number four position was associated with a –6 per cent average return on investment.[12]

Base for brand extensions

A strong brand provides the foundation for leveraging positive perceptions and goodwill from the core brand to brand extensions. Examples include Diet Coke, Pepsi Max, Lucozade Sport, Smirnoff Ice, Microsoft Internet Explorer and Lego Spybotics. The new brand benefits from the added value that the brand equity of the core brand bestows on the extension. There is a full discussion of brand extensions later in this chapter.

Quality certification

Strong brands also benefit consumers in that they provide quality certification, which can aid decision-making. The following example illustrates the lengths consumers will go to when using strong brands as a form of quality certification. In the old Soviet Russia all television sets were made in two manufacturing plants. The sets were apparently unbranded and were made to the same design. The problem was that some of these sets were unreliable, causing a lot of customer annoyance. Consumers learnt that the problems were arising from television sets made by one of the plants, while the other made reliable sets. The question was how to tell whether a particular set was made by the reliable or unreliable manufacturer. Although they looked the same, consumers discovered that each set had a code printed on the back that identified its source. In effect the code was acting as a brand identifier and consumers were using it as a form of quality certification.

Trust

Consumers tend to trust strong brands. The Henley Forecasting Centre found that consumers are increasingly turning to 'trusted guides' to manage choice. A key 'trusted guide' is the brand name and its perceptual associations. When consumers stop trusting a brand, the fallout can be catastrophic as when the once strong Marks & Spencer brand lost the trust of many of its customers. Happily, the brand is regaining that trust under new management. The lesson is never to do anything that might compromise the trust held by consumers towards a brand. Europe's most trusted brands in 12 product categories are shown in Table 8.1.

Table 8.1 Europe's most trusted brands

Product category	Brand	Countries where it leads its sector*
Mobile phone	Nokia	18
Credit card	Visa	16
Skincare	Nivea	16
Hi-fi/audio equipment	Sony	14
Cameras	Canon	14
Toothpaste	Colgate	12
Personal computers	IBM	10
Soap powder	Ariel	7
Haircare	Pantene	5
	L'Oréal	5
Automotive	Mercedes	5
Vitamins	Centrum	4
Airline	SAS	3

* Respondents in 18 European countries were asked to name their most trusted brand in each product category.
Based on: Reader's Digest Trusted Brands 2002 report

Brand building

The importance of strong brands means that brand building is an essential marketing activity. Successful brand building can reap benefits in terms of premium prices, achieving distribution more readily, and sustaining high and stable sales and profits through brand loyalty.[13]

A brand is created by augmenting a core product with distinctive values that distinguish it from the competition. To understand the notion of brand values we first need to understand the difference between features and benefits. A feature is an aspect of a brand that may or may

Figure 8.2 Creating a brand

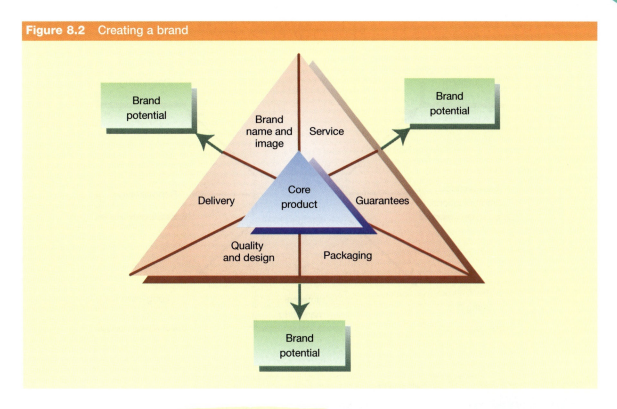

not confer a customer benefit. For example, adding fluoride (*feature*) to a toothpaste confers the customer *benefits* of added protection against tooth decay and decreased dental charges. Not all features necessarily confer benefits: a cigarette lighter (*feature*) in a car confers no *benefit* to non-smokers, for example.

Core benefits derive from the core product (see Fig. 8.2). Toothpaste, for example, cleans teeth and therefore protects against tooth decay. But all toothpastes achieve that. Branding allows marketers to create added values that distinguish one brand from another. Successful brands are those that create a set of brand values that are superior to other rival brands. So brand building involves a deep understanding of both the functional (e.g. ease of use) and emotional (e.g. confidence) values that customers use when choosing between brands, and the ability to combine them in a unique way to create an augmented *product* that customers prefer. This unique, **augmented product** is what marketers call the *brand*. The success of the Swatch brand was founded on the recognition that watches could be marketed as fashion items to younger age groups. By using colour and design, Swatch successfully augmented a basic product—a watch—to create appeal for its target market. The advertisement featuring Sony (overleaf) shows how that company augments the brand through superior service. Unsuccessful brands provide no added values over the competition; they possess no differential advantage and, therefore, no reason for customers to purchase them in preference to a competitive brand.

Managing brands involves a constant search for ways of achieving the full brand potential. To do so usually means the creation of major global brands. Leading brands such as Coca-Cola, Microsoft, IBM, General Electric and Ford have achieved this. But how are successful brands built? A combination of some or all of seven factors can be important.[14] These are shown in Fig. 8.3 and described overleaf.

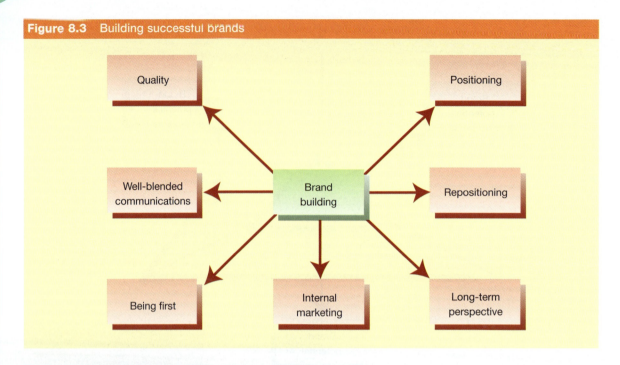

Figure 8.3 Building successful brands

Service is one way of augmenting a brand, as this advertisement for Sony demonstrates.

Quality

It is vital to build quality into the core product: a major reason for brand failure is the inability to get the basics right. Marketing a computer that overheats, a car that refuses to start or a garden fork that breaks is courting disaster. The core product must achieve the basic functional requirements expected of it. A major study of factors that affect success has shown statistically that higher-quality brands achieve greater market share and higher profitability than their inferior rivals.[15] Total quality management techniques (see Chapter 4) are increasingly being employed to raise quality standards. Product quality improvements have been shown to mainly be driven by market pull (changing customer tastes and expectations), organizational push (changes in the technical potential and resources of a company) and competitor actions.[16]

Marketing in Action 8.3 discusses the role of quality in building the Pret A Manger, Dyson and Dell brands.

Positioning

Creating a unique position in the marketplace involves a careful choice of target market and establishing a clear differential advantage in the

8.3 marketing in action

Putting Quality into Brand Building

People in advertising tend to equate brand building with advertising. But advertising is simply a way of communicating brand values. Brand building begins before advertising by building quality into the brand. Successful brands such as Pret A Manger, Dyson and Dell built their success on a quality focus.

Pret A Manger built its reputation on its excellent product (based on a 'green' theme) and service, and used its sandwich boxes, bags, paper cups and staff to promote itself to its customers. Pret's core customers work within 500 yards of the shops and typically buy lunch there three or four times a week. It is a quality- and location- rather than an advertising-driven business.

Dyson, the bagless vacuum cleaner business, ploughed its money into research and development to provide a high-quality product that performed better than its bag rivals. Within two years of its launch it became the best-selling vacuum cleaner without advertising. Even now, 70 per cent of the cleaners are bought on word-of-mouth recommendation. Although some money has been spent on advertising as competition has intensified, this is focused around product launches. Most of the company's resources are still directed at improving quality through enhanced technology.

Computer supplier Dell sells direct to customers with little brand advertising. Instead, Dell invests in providing value, performance and service. Its philosophy is that investing in quality leads to giving customers real value, which will encourage them to buy again and again. Dell also invests heavily in public relations, ensuring the company is represented at key IT events and that its products are frequently reviewed in the trade press.

Based on Brierley (2002);[17] Simms (2002)[18]

---

minds of those people. This can be achieved through brand names and image, service, design, guarantees, packaging and delivery. In today's highly competitive global marketplace, unique positioning will normally rely on combinations of these factors. For example, the success of BMW is founded on a quality, well-designed product, targeted at distinct customer segments and supported by a carefully nurtured exclusive brand name and image. Viewing markets in novel ways can create unique positioning concepts. For example, Swatch, as mentioned earlier, was built on the realization that watches could be marketed as fashion items to younger age groups.

An analytical framework that can be used to dissect the current position of a brand in the marketplace and form the basis of a new brand positioning strategy is given in Fig. 8.4. The strength of a brand's position in the marketplace is built on six elements: brand domain, brand heritage, brand values, brand assets, brand personality and brand reflection. The first element, brand domain, corresponds to the choice of target market (where the brand competes); the other five elements provide avenues for creating a clear differential advantage with these target consumers. Each will now be explained.

(1) *Brand domain*: the brand's target market, i.e. where it competes in the marketplace. For example, the brand domain for Alpen bars (see illustration overleaf) is young, busy people, who eat at least part of their breakfast 'on the go'.

(2) *Brand heritage*: the background to the brand and its culture. How it has achieved success (and failure) over its life. The advertisement for Boddingtons (overleaf) shows how brand heritage can be used in advertising.

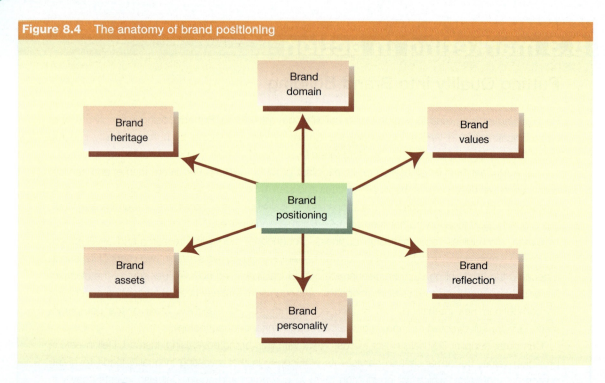

Figure 8.4 The anatomy of brand positioning

(3) *Brand values*: the core *values* and characteristics of the brand.

(4) *Brand assets*: what makes the brand distinctive from other competing brands such as symbols, features, images and relationships.

(5) *Brand personality*: the character of the brand described in terms of other entities such as people, animals or objects.

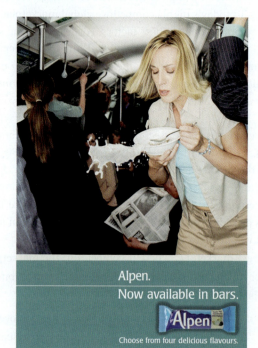

Young, busy, people form the brand domain for Alpen bars.

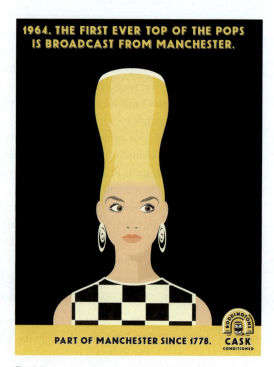

Boddingtons advertises its brand heritage.

Chapter eight Managing Products: Brand and Corporate Identity Management

Illustrator: © Daniel Hanson at The Organisation

Consumers use brands to reflect their self-identity and project it to other people.

6 *Brand reflection*: how the brand relates to self-identity; how the customer perceives him/herself as a result of buying/using the brand. The branding illustration visualizes how people use brands to reflect and project their self-identity.

By analysing each element, brand managers can form an accurate portrait of how brands are positioned in the marketplace. From there, thought can be given to whether and how the brand can be repositioned to improve performance.

Repositioning

As markets change and opportunities arise, repositioning may be needed to build brands from their initial base. Lucozade was first built as a brand providing energy to children who were ill. When market research found that mothers were drinking Lucozade as a midday pick-me-up it was repositioned accordingly. More recently it has been repositioned as a mass-market energy drink, using the athletes Daley Thompson and Linford Christie. Johnson's baby lotion brand was also built through repositioning when it was found that women were using it themselves. In the popular music industry Elvis Presley and Cliff Richard maintained their success by repositioning themselves from rock'n'roll artists to middle-of-the-road singers as their target audience matured.

Well-blended communications

Brand positioning is based on customer perception. To create a clear position in the minds of a target audience requires considerable thought and effort regarding advertising, selling and other promotional activities. Awareness needs to be built, the brand personality projected and favourable attitudes reinforced. Advertising is often the major communication medium for many classic leaders, such as:[19]

- Esso—the tiger (grace and power)
- Andrex—the puppy (soft and durable)
- Persil—mother love (metaphor for taking care of clothes).

These themes need to be reinforced by salespeople, public relations and sales promotion campaigns.

Marketers can make their brands more noticeable through attractive display or package design, and also through generating customer familiarity with brand names, brand logos and a brand's visual appearance. A well-blended communications strategy is necessary to achieve these objectives.[20]

Being first

Research has shown that pioneer brands are more likely to be successful than follower brands.[21] Being first gives a brand the opportunity to create a clear position in the minds of target customers before the competition enters the market. It also gives the pioneer the opportunity to build customer and distributor loyalty. Nevertheless, being first into a market with a unique marketing proposition does not guarantee success; it requires sustained marketing effort and the strength to withstand competitor attacks. Being first into a niche market, as achieved by the Body Shop and Tie Rack, usually guarantees short-term profits but the acid test arrives when competitors (sometimes with greater resources) enter with similar products.

Being first into a market can also bring the potential advantages of technological leadership, cost advantages through the experience curve effect, the acquisition and control of scarce resources and the creation of switching costs to later entrants (for example, the costs of switching from one computer system to another may be considerable).[22] Late entry can be costly: one study showed that a delay of one year in launching the Sierra after GM's Cavalier cost Ford $1 billion in lost profits over five years.[23]

Companies are, therefore, speeding up their new product development processes, even if it means being over budget.[24] A McKinsey & Co study showed that being 50 per cent over NPD budget and on time can lead to a 4 per cent reduction in profits. However, being on budget and six months late to launch can lead to a 33 per cent reduction in profits.[25]

Being first does not necessarily mean pioneering the technology. Bigger returns may come to those who are first to enter the mass market. For example, America's Ampex pioneered video recorder technology in the mid-1950s but its machines sold for $50,000. It made little effort to cut costs and expand its market. It was left to Sony, JVC and Matsushita, who had the vision to see the potential for mass-market sales. They embarked on a research and development programme to make a video recorder that could be sold for $500—a goal that took them 20 years to achieve.[26]

Long-term perspective

Brand building is a long-term activity. There are many demands on people's attention. Consequently, generating awareness, communicating brand values and building customer loyalty usually takes many years. Management must be prepared to provide a consistently high level of brand investment to establish and maintain the position of a brand in the marketplace. Unfortunately, it can be tempting to cut back on expenditure in the short term. Cutting advertising spend by £0.5 million (€0.72 million) immediately cuts costs and increases profits. Conversely, for a well-established brand, sales are unlikely to fall substantially in the short term because of the effects of past advertising. The result is higher short-term profits. This may be an attractive proposition for brand managers who are often in charge of a brand for less than two years. One way of overcoming this danger is to measure brand manager (and brand) performance by measuring brand equity in terms of awareness levels, brand associations, intentions to buy, and so on, and being vigilant in resisting short-term actions that may harm it. To underline the importance of consistent brand investment Sir Adrian Cadbury (then chairman of Cadbury's Schweppes) wrote:

> ❝For brands to endure they have to be maintained properly and imaginatively. Brands are extremely valuable properties and, like other forms of property, they need to be kept in good repair, renewed from time to time and defended against squatters.[27] ❞

Internal marketing

Many brands are corporate in the sense that the marketing focus is on building the company brand.[28] This is particularly the case in services, with banks, supermarkets, insurance companies, airlines and restaurant chains attempting to build awareness and loyalty to the services they offer. A key feature in the success of such efforts is internal marketing—that is, training and communicating with internal staff. Training of staff is crucial because service companies rely on face-to-face contact between service provider (e.g. waiter) and service user (e.g. diner). Also, brand strategies must be communicated to staff so that they understand the company ethos on which the company brand is built. Investment in staff training is required to achieve the service levels required for the brand strategy. Top service companies like McDonald's, Sainsbury and British Airways make training a central element in their company brand building plans.

Key branding decisions

Besides the branding decisions so far discussed, marketers face four further key branding decisions: brand name strategies and choices, rebranding, brand extension and stretching, and co-branding.

Brand name strategies and choices

Another key decision area is the choice of brand name. Three brand name strategies can be identified: family, individual and combination.

Family brand names

A family brand name is used for all products (e.g. Philips, Campbell's, Heinz, Del Monte). The goodwill attached to the family brand name benefits all brands, and the use of the name in advertising helps the promotion of all of the brands carrying the family name. The risk is that if one of the brands receives unfavourable publicity or is unsuccessful, the reputation of the whole range of brands can be tarnished. This is also called umbrella branding. Some companies create umbrella brands for part of their brand portfolios to give coherence to their range of products. For example, Cadbury created the umbrella brand of Cadburyland for its range of children's chocolate confectionery.[29]

Individual brand names

An individual brand name does not identify a brand with a particular company (e.g. Procter & Gamble does not use the company name on brands such as Ariel, Fairy Liquid, Daz and Pampers). This may be necessary when it is believed that each brand requires a separate, unrelated identity. In some instances, the use of a family brand name when moving into a new market segment may harm the image of the new product line. An example was the decision to use the Levi's family brand name on a new product line—Levi's Tailored Classics—despite marketing research information which showed that target customers associated the name Levi's with casual clothes, which was incompatible with the smart suits it was launching. This mistake was not repeated by Toyota, which abandoned its family brand name when it launched its upmarket executive car, which was simply called the Lexus. BMW also chose not to attach its family brand name to the Mini since it would have detracted from the car's sense of 'Britishness'.

Nevertheless, the lack of company association can prove risky. For example, Sainsbury's, a UK supermarket chain, launched a successful own-label detergent, Novon, after extensive research found that since consumers did not care whether Ariel, Daz or Persil was made by Procter & Gamble or Lever Brothers, why should they worry that Novon was 'made' by Sainsbury's.

Combination brand names

A *combination of family and individual brand names* capitalizes on the reputation of the company while allowing the individual brands to be distinguished and identified (e.g. Kellogg's All Bran, Rover 400, Microsoft Windows).

Criteria for choosing brand names

The choice of brand name should be carefully thought out since names convey images. For example, Renault chose the brand name Safrane for one of its executive saloons because research showed that the brand name conveyed the image of luxury, exotica, high technology and style. The brand name Pepsi Max was chosen for Pepsi's diet cola targeted at men as it conveyed a masculine image in a product category that was associated with women. So one criterion for deciding on a good brand name is that it evokes *positive associations*.

A second criterion is that the brand name should be easy to *pronounce and remember*. Short names such as Esso, Shell, Daz, Ariel, Novon and Mini fall into this category. There are exceptions to this general rule, as in the case of Häagen-Dazs, which was designed to sound European in the USA where it was first launched. A brand name may suggest *product benefits*, such as Right Guard (deodorant), Alpine Glade (air and fabric freshener), Head & Shoulders (anti-dandruff shampoo), Compaq (portable computer), or express what the brand is offering in a *distinctive way* such as Toys 'Я' Us. Technological products may benefit from *numerical* brand naming (e.g. BMW 300, Porsche 911) or *alphanumeric* brand names (e.g. Audi A4, WD40). This also overcomes the need to change brand names when marketing in different countries.

The question of brand *transferability* is another brand name consideration. With the growth of global brands, names increasingly need to be able to cross geographical boundaries. Companies that do not check the meaning of a brand name in other languages can be caught out, as when General Motors launched its Nova car in Spain only to discover later that the word meant 'it does not go' in Spanish. The lesson is that brand names must be researched for cultural meaning before being introduced into a new geographic market. One advantage of non-meaningful names such as Diageo and Exxon is that they transfer well across national boundaries.

Table 8.2	Brand name considerations
A good brand name should:	
1	evoke positive associations
2	be easy to pronounce and remember
3	suggest product benefits
4	be distinctive
5	use numerals or alphanumerics when emphasizing technology
6	be transferable
7	not infringe an existing registered brand name.

Specialist companies have established themselves as brand name consultants. Market research is used to test associations, memorability, pronunciation and preferences. One such consultancy is Mastername, which has an international team of name creation specialists, linguists and legal experts. Legal advice is important so that a brand name *does not infringe an existing brand name*. Table 8.2 summarizes the issues that are important when choosing a brand name.

A considerable amount of research goes into choosing a brand name. One successful financial services brand in the UK is Egg, a savings account launched by Prudential. Marketing in Action 8.4 describes the work that went into its selection.

Brand names can also be categorized, as shown in Table 8.3.

8.4 marketing in action

Naming Egg

Egg, the financial services brand launched by Prudential, reached its five-year target of savers in just six months. It has closed its offerings to new telephone customers and is now focusing on its Internet services. Competitive interest rates are a major factor in its attraction, but the name has clearly captured the imagination of the consumer.

The work on the name began by briefing a corporate naming agency. Prudential wanted something genuinely new and distinctive. It wanted to challenge the idiom of a marketplace where many corporate names are names of people or places, such as Barclays or Halifax.

Consumer research was used, beginning with the testing of 'marker' names that were not serious contenders but types of names that made clear the limits consumers would accept. The research showed that the name could be radical but consumers would not accept frivolity. The second stage was to work on a range of names from the straight descriptive to the more adventurous. At the final stage, the options included: 360°, suggesting all of the consumer's financial services taken care of; Oxygen, suggesting a breath of fresh air (but also slightly colder than Egg and rather scientific); and ID, suggesting identity and individuality.

The name had to convey the notion of having a relationship with the customer, and it had to be contemporary and be reassuring. The name Egg was chosen because it is a reassuring word with cosy, warm connotations. The success of the Egg brand is reflected in the fact that it had gained over 2 million customers by 2002.

Based on: Miller (1999);[30] Anonymous (2002)[31]

Table 8.3	Brand name categories
People	Cadbury, Mars, Heinz
Places	National Westminster, Halifax Building Society
Descriptive	I Can't Believe It's Not Butter, The Body Shop, Going Places
Abstract	KitKat, Kodak, Prozac
Evocative	Egg, Orange, Fuse
Brand extensions	Dove Deodorant, Virgin Direct, Playtex Affinity
Foreign meanings	Lego (from 'play well' in Danish), Thermos (meaning 'heat' in Greek)

Adapted from: Miller, R. (1999) Science Joins Art in Brand Naming, *Marketing*, 27 May, 31–2.

Rebranding

The act of changing a brand name is called **rebranding**. It can occur at the product level (e.g. Treets to M&Ms) and the corporate level (e.g. One2One to T-mobile). Table 8.4 gives some examples of name changes. Rebranding is risky and the decision should not be taken lightly. The abandonment of a well-known and, for some, favourite brand runs the risk of customer confusion and resentment, and loss of market share. When Coca-Cola was rebranded (and reformulated) as New Coke, negative customer reaction forced the company to withdraw the new brand and reinstate the original brand.[32] Similarly, the move to rebrand the Post Office as Consignia was met with objections from consumers, employees and the media. The result was a reversal of the decision, with the Royal Mail Group corporate name chosen instead.

Table 8.4 Brand name changes

Product level		Corporate level	
Old name	New name	Old name	New name
Treets/Bonitos	M&Ms	One2One	T-mobile
Marathon	Snickers	BT Wireless	mmO$_2$
Pal	Pedigree	Grand Metropolitan/ Guinness	Diageo
Duplo	Lego Explore	Post Office	Royal Mail Group
Jif/Cif/Vif/Vim	Cif	Airtours	MyTravel
Raider	Twix	Ciba-Geigy/Sandoz	Novartis
Virgin One	The One Account		

Why rebrand?

Despite such well-publicized problems, rebranding is a common activity. The reasons are as follows.[33]

Merger or acquisition

When a merger or acquisition takes place a new name may be chosen to identify the new company. Sometimes a combination of the original corporate names may be chosen (e.g. when Glaxo Wellcome and SmithKline Beecham formed Glaxo SmithKline), a completely new name may be preferred (e.g. when Grand Metropolitan and Guinness became Diageo) or the stronger corporate brand name may be chosen (e.g. when Nestlé acquired Rowntree Mackintosh).

Desire to create a new image/position in the marketplace

Some brand names are associated with negative or old-fashioned images. The move by BT Wireless to drop its corporate brand name was because it had acquired an old fashioned, bureaucratic image. The new brand name mmO$_2$ was chosen because it sounded scientific and modern, and because focus groups saw their mobile phones as an essential part of their lives (like oxygen).[34] The negative image caused by Gerald Ratner describing the products sold in his stores as 'crap' forced the name change of his jewellery stores from Ratners to Signet. Also the negative association of the word 'fried' in Kentucky Fried Chicken stimulated the move to change the name to KFC. Lego has rebranded its Duplo range as Lego Explore to place greater emphasis on the relationship between the product and learning. The brand has been repositioned in the marketplace by focusing on four 'playworlds': explore being me, explore together, explore imagination and explore logic. Previously, Duplo was only associated with the 'imagination' dimension.[35]

The sale or acquisition of parts of a business

The sale of the agricultural equipment operations of the farm equipment maker International Harvester prompted the need to change its name to Navistar. The acquisition of the Virgin One financial services brand by the Royal Bank of Scotland from the Virgin Group necessitated the dropping of the Virgin name. The new brand is called The One Account.

Corporate strategy changes

When a company diversifies out of its original product category, the original corporate brand name may be considered too limiting. This is why Esso (Standard Oil) changed its name to Exxon as its product portfolio extended beyond oil. Also British Steel has become Corus as the company widens its products beyond steel.

Brand familiarity

Sometimes the name of a major product brand owned by a company becomes so familiar to customers that it supersedes the corporate brand. In these circumstances the company may decide to discard the unfamiliar name in favour of the familiar. That is why Consolidated Foods became Sara Lee and BSN became Danone.

International marketing considerations

A major driver for rebranding is the desire to harmonize a brand name across national boundaries in order to create a global brand. This was the motivation for the change of the Marathon chocolate bar name in the UK to Snickers, which was used in continental Europe, the dropping of the Treets and Bonitos names in favour of M&Ms, the move from Raider to Twix chocolate bars, the consolidation of the Unilever cleaning agent Jif/Cif/Vif/Vim to Cif, and the One2One brand in the UK to T-mobile, which is used by its parent company Deutsche Telecom in Germany. Companies may also change brand names to discourage parallel importing. When sales of a premium-priced brand in some countries are threatened by re-imports of the same brand from countries where the brand is sold at lower prices, rebranding may be used to differentiate the product. This is why the Italian cleaning agent Viakal was rebranded in some European countries as Antikal.

Consolidation of brands within a national boundary

When a company has a number of brand names in one country there is a temptation to consolidate them all under one brand. This motivated the creation of the MyTravel brand to cover the travel operator Airtours, and the travel agents Going Places, Travelworld and Holiday World. The rebranding meant that the new name could be used on all travel agents, aircraft, cruise ships and the company's website, although the Airtours brand was retained for its travel brochures as rival travel agents Thomas Cook and Lunn Poly would be uncomfortable selling MyTravel-branded holidays once the name appeared on travel agents' shops.[36]

Legal problems

A brand name may contravene an existing legal restriction on its use. For example, the Yves St Laurent perfume brand Champagne required a name change because the brand name was protected for use only with the sparkling wine from the Champagne region of France.

Managing the rebranding process

Rebranding is usually an expensive, time-consuming and risky activity, and should only be undertaken when there is a clear marketing and financial case in its favour and a strong marketing plan in place to support its implementation.[37] Management should recognize that a rebranding exercise cannot of itself rectify more deep-seated marketing problems.

Once the decision to rebrand has been made, two key decisions remain: choosing the new name and implementing the name change.

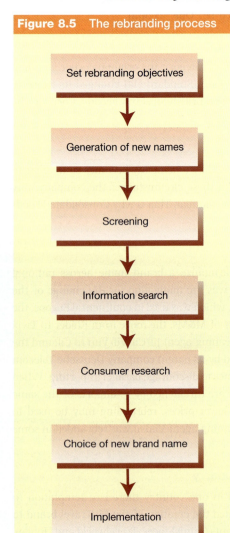

Figure 8.5 The rebranding process

Choosing the new brand name

The issues discussed earlier in this chapter regarding choosing brand names are relevant when changing an existing name. These are that the new brand name should evoke positive associations, be easy to pronounce and remember, suggest positive benefits, be distinctive, be transferable, not infringe an existing registered brand name, and consideration should be given to the use of numerals when emphasizing technology. These issues should form the basis of the first step, setting the rebranding objectives (see Fig. 8.5). For example, a key objective of the new name might be that it should be easily remembered, evoke positive associations and be transferable across national boundaries.

The second step is to generate as many brand names as possible. Potential sources of names include consumers, employees, distributors, specialist brand name consultants and advertising agencies.

The third step is to screen the names to remove any with obvious flaws, such as those that are difficult to pronounce, too close to an existing name, have adverse double meanings and do not fit with the rebranding objectives. The objective is to reduce the names to a shortlist of around 6–12. The fourth step, an information search is carried out to check that each name does not infringe an existing registered brand name in each country where the brand is, or may be, marketed.

The fifth step is to test the remaining names through consumer research. The key criteria, such as memorability, associations and distinctiveness, chosen in step one (rebranding objectives) will be used to assess the performance of the new names. Finally, management will assess the virtues of each of the shortlisted brand names and come to a conclusion about which one should be chosen and registered.

Implementing the name change

Name changes can meet considerable resistance from consumers, employees and distributors. All three groups can feel that their loyalty to a brand has been betrayed. Attention also has to be paid to the media and financial institutions, particularly for corporate name changes. It was such resistance that reversed the mooted renaming of the Post Office as Consignia. Careful thought needs to be given to how the name change should be implemented so that all interested parties understand the logic behind the change and support it. Implementation requires attention to five key issues, as described below.[38]

1. *Co-ordination*: the delicacy of the name change requires harmonious working between the company departments and those groups most involved—marketing, production, the salesforce, logistics and general management. All must work together to avoid problems and solve any that may arise.

(2) *Communication*: consumers, employees and distributors need to be targeted with communications that notify them early and with a full explanation. When the chocolate bar known as Raider in continental Europe changed its name to Twix, which was the name used everywhere else, consumers in Europe were informed by a massive advertising campaign (two years' advertising budget was spent in three weeks). Retailers were told of the name change well in advance by a salesforce whose top priority was the Twix brand. Trial was encouraged by promotional activities at retail outlets. The result was a highly successful name change and the creation of a global brand.

(3) *Understanding what the consumer identifies with the brand*: consumer research is required to fully understand what consumers identify as the key characteristics of the brand. Shell made the mistake of failing to include the new colour (yellow) of the rebranded Shell Helix Standard in its advertising, which stressed only the name change from Puissance 7 in France. Unfortunately customers, when looking for their favourite brand of oil, paid most attention to the colour of the can. When they could not find their usual brown can of Puissance 7 they did not realize it had been changed to a yellow can with a name they were not familiar with. The lesson is that advertising for a rebrand should have shown consumers that the colour of the can had changed as well as focusing on the name change from Puissance to Helix.

(4) *Providing assistance to distributors/retailers*: to avoid confusion at distributors/retailers, manufacturers should avoid double-stocking of the old and new brand. Mars management took great care to ensure that on the day of the transfer from Raider to Twix, no stocks of Raider would be found in the shops, even if this meant buying back stock. The barcode should be kept the same so that no problems occur at optical checkouts. If a new code is used there is the chance it might not be registered correctly in the store's computer system.

(5) *Speed of change*: consideration should be given to whether the change should be immediate (as with Twix) or subject to a transitional phase where, for example, the old name is retained (perhaps in small letters) on the packaging after the rebrand (the Philips name was retained on all Whirlpool household appliances, which were branded Philips Whirlpool in Europe for seven years after the companies joined to form the world's largest household appliance group). Old names are retained during a transitional period when the old name has high awareness and positive associations among consumers. Retaining an old brand name following a takeover may be wise for political reasons, as when Nestlé retained the Rowntree name on its brands for a few years after its takeover of the UK confectionery company.

Brand extension and stretching

The goodwill that is associated with a brand name adds tangible value to a company through the higher sales and profits that result. This higher financial value is called **brand equity**. Brand names with high brand equity are candidates to be used on other new brands since their presence has the potential to enhance their attractiveness. A **brand extension** is the use of an established brand name on a new brand within the same broad market or product category. For example, the Anadin brand name has been extended to related brands: Anadin Extra, Maximum Strength, Soluble, Paracetamol and Ibuprofen. The Lucozade brand has undergone a very successful brand extension with the introduction of Lucozade Sport, with isotonic properties that help to rehydrate people more quickly than other drinks, and replace the minerals lost through perspiration. Unilever has successfully expanded its Dove soap brand into deodorants, shower gel, liquid soap and body-wash.[39] Brand stretching is when an established brand name is used for brands in unrelated markets or product categories, such as the use of the Yamaha motorcycle brand name on hi-fi equipment, skis and pianos. The Tommy Hilfiger brand has also been extended from clothing to fragrances, footwear and home furnishings.[40] Table 8.5 gives some examples of brand extensions and stretching.

Table 8.5 Brand extensions and stretching	
Brand extensions	**Brand stretching**
Anadin brand name used for Anadin Extra, Maximum Strength, Soluble, Paracetamol and Ibuprofen	Cadbury (confectionery) launched Cadbury's Cream Liqueur
Guinness launched Guinness draught beer in a can and Guinness Extra Cold	Yamaha (motor cycles) brand name used on hi-fi, skis, pianos and summerhouses
Lucozade extends to Lucozade Sport, Energy, Hydroactive and Carbo Gel	Pierre Cardin (clothing) brand name used on toiletries, cosmetics, etc.
United Distillers used Johnnie Walker brand name for liqueur	Bic (disposable pens) brand name used on lighters, razors, perfumes and women's tights
Unilever used Dove brand name for deodorants, shower gel, liquid soap and body-wash	Tommy Hilfiger brand name used on fragrances, footwear and home furnishings
Diageo used Smirnoff brand name for the premium packaged spirit sector (Smirnoff Ice and Black Ice)	fcuk (fashion retailer) brand name used on flavoured alcoholic drinks

Some companies have used brand extensions and stretching very successfully. Richard Branson's Virgin company is a classic example. Beginning in 1970 as Virgin Records the company grew through Virgin Music (music publishing), Megastores (music retailing), Radio, Vodka, Cola, Atlantic Airways (long-haul routes), Express (short-haul routes), Rail, Direct (direct marketing of financial services) and One (one-stop banking). Others have been less successful, such as Levi's move into suits, the Penguin ice-cream bar and Timotei facial care products.

Brand extension is an important marketing tactic. A study by Nielsen showed that brand extensions account for approximately 40 per cent of new grocery launches.[41] Two key advantages of brand extension in releasing new products are that it reduces risk and is less costly than alternative launch strategies.[42] Both distributors and consumers may perceive less risk if the new brand comes with an established brand name. Distributors may be reassured about the 'saleability' of the new brand and therefore be more willing to stock it. Consumers appear to attribute the quality associations they have of the original brand to the new one.[43] An established name enhances consumer interest and willingness to try the new brand.[44] Consumer attitudes towards brand extensions are more favourable when the perceived quality of the parent brand is high.[45]

Launch costs can also be reduced by using brand extension. Since the established brand name is already well known, the task of building awareness of the new brand is eased. Consequently, advertising, selling and promotional costs are reduced. Furthermore, there is the likelihood of achieving advertising economies of scale since advertisements for the original brand and its extensions reinforce each other.[46]

A further advantage of brand extensions is that the introduction of the extension can benefit the core brand because of the effects of the accompanying marketing expenditure. Sales of the core brand can rise due to the enhancement of consumers' perception of brand values and image through increased communication.[47]

However, these arguments can be taken too far. Brand extensions that offer no functional, psychological or price advantage over rival brands often fail.[48] Consumers shop around, and brand extensions that fail to meet expectations will be rejected. There is also the danger that marketing management underfunds the launch believing that the spin-off effects from the original brand name will compensate. This can lead to low awareness and trial. *Cannibalization*, which refers to a situation where the new brand gains sales at the expense of the established brand, can also occur. Anadin Extra, for example, could cannibalize the sales of the original Anadin brand. Further, brand extension has been criticized as leading to a managerial focus on minor modifications, packaging changes and advertising rather than the development of real innovations.[49] There is also the danger that bad publicity for one brand affects the reputation of other brands under the same name. An example was the problem of the sudden, sharp acceleration of the Audi 5000, which affected sales of both the Audi 4000 and the Audi Quattro even though they did not suffer from the problem.[50] A related difficulty is the danger of the new brand failing or generating connotations that damage the reputation of the core brand. Both of these risks were faced by Guinness, whose core brand is stout, when it launched its canned beer under the Guinness brand name, and Mars when it extended the Mars brand name into ice cream.

A major test of any brand extension opportunity is to ask if the new brand concept is compatible with the values inherent in the core brand. Mention has already been made of the failure to extend the Levi's brand name to suits in the USA partly as a result of consumers refusing to accept the casual, denim image of Levi's as being suitable for smart, exclusive clothing. Another example is Bic's attempt to stretch the brand into perfume. Bic misunderstood the choice criteria that drive perfume sales and how these clashed with its own brand image of being a cheap and disposable pen.[51]

Brand extensions, therefore, are not viable when a new brand is being developed for a target group that holds different values and aspirations from those in the original market segment. When this occurs the use of the brand extension tactic would detract from the new brand. The answer is to develop a separate brand name, as did Toyota with the Lexus, and Seiko with its Pulsar brand name developed for the lower-priced mass market for watches.

Finally, management needs to guard against the loss of credibility if a brand name is extended too far. This is particularly relevant when brand stretching. The use of the Pierre Cardin name for such disparate products as clothing, toiletries and cosmetics has diluted the brand name's credibility.[52]

Brand extensions are likely to be successful if they make sense to the consumer. If the values and aspirations of the new target segment(s) match those of the original segment, and the qualities of the brand name are likewise highly prized, then success is likely. The prime example is Marks & Spencer, which successfully extended its original brand name, St Michael, from clothing to food based on its core values of quality and reliability.

Co-branding

There are two major forms of co-branding: product-based and communications-based co-branding (see Fig. 8.6 overleaf).

Product-based co-branding

Product-based co-branding involves the linking of two or more existing brands from different companies or business units to form a product in which the brand names are visible to

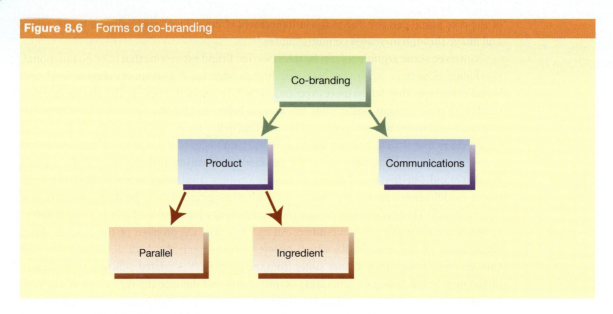

Figure 8.6 Forms of co-branding

consumers. There are two variants: parallel and ingredient co-branding. Parallel co-branding occurs when two or more independent brands join forces to produce a combined brand. An example is Häagen-Dazs ice cream and Baileys liqueur combining to form Häagen-Dazs with Baileys flavour ice cream.

Ingredient co-branding is found when one supplier explicitly chooses to position its brand as an ingredient of a product. Intel is an ingredient brand. It markets itself as a key component (ingredient) of computers. The ingredient co-brand is formed by the combination of the ingredient brand and the manufacturer brand—for example, Hewlett Packard or Toshiba

This advertisement depicts Intel as an ingredient brand linked to Toshiba's multi-media products.

(see the illustration on the opposite page). Usually the names and logos of both brands appear on the computer. Although Baileys liqueur may at first sight seem to be an ingredient brand it is not since its main market positioning is as an independent brand (a liqueur) not as an ingredient of ice cream.[53] Figure 8.7 shows the distinction between parallel and ingredient co-branding.

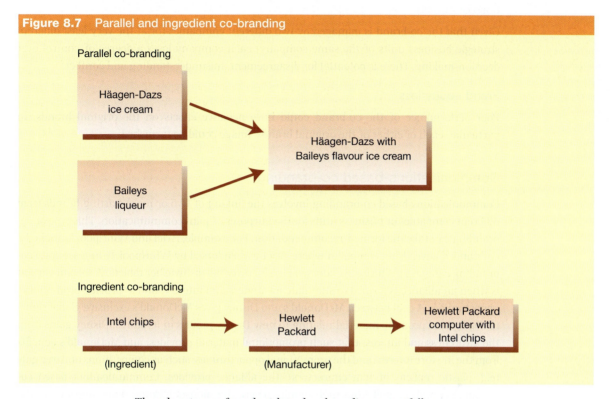

Figure 8.7 Parallel and ingredient co-branding

The advantages of product-based co-branding are as follows.

Added value and differentiation

The co-branding alliance of two or more brands can capture multiple sources of brand equity, and therefore add value and provide a point of differentiation. For example, the aforementioned combination of Häagen-Dazs ice cream with Baileys liqueur flavour creates a brand that adds value through the distinctive flavouring and differentiates the brand from competitive offerings. Another example is the alliance between Nike and Lego's 'Bionicle' action heroes to form 'Bionicle by Nike' trainers. The Bionicle brand adds value and differentiates the co-brand from other trainers.[54] The impact of product-based co-branding has been researched by Kodak, which showed that for a fictional entertainment product 20 per cent of respondents said they would buy under the Kodak name and 20 per cent would buy under the Sony name. However, 80 per cent claimed they would buy if the product carried both names. Clearly the co-brand carried brand equity that was greater than the sum of its parts.[55]

Positioning

A co-brand can position a product for a particular target market. This was the reason Ford formed an alliance with *Elle* magazine to create the Ford Focus Elle, targeting women. The *Elle*-branded Focus has features such as heated leather seats, metallic livery and special wheels in order to appeal to women who choose cars on the basis of look and style. A five-page advertorial appeared in *Elle*, where the brand was positioned as a stylish fashion accessory.[56]

Reduction of cost of product introduction

Co-branding can reduce the cost of product introduction since two well-known brands are combined, accelerating awareness, acceptance and adoption.[57]

There are also risks involved in product-based co-branding, as described below.

Loss of control

Given that the co-brand is managed by two different companies (or at the very least different strategic business units of the same company) each company loses a degree of control over decision-making. There is potential for disagreement, misunderstanding and conflict.

Brand equity loss

Poor performance of the co-brand could have negative effects on the original brands. In particular, each or either of the original brands' image could be tarnished.

Communications-based co-branding

Communications-based co-branding involves the linking of two or more existing brands from different companies or business units for the purposes of joint communication. This type of co-branding can take the form of recommendation. For example, Ariel and Whirlpool launched a co-branded advertising campaign where Ariel was endorsed by Whirlpool.[58] In a separate co-branding campaign Whirlpool endorsed Finish Powerball dishwasher tablets. A second variant is when an alliance is formed to stimulate awareness and interest, and to provide promotional opportunities. A deal between McDonald's and Disney gives McDonald's exclusive global rights to display and promote material relating to new Disney movies in its stores. Disney gains from the awareness and interest that such promotional material provides, and McDonald's benefits from the in-store interest and the promotional opportunities, such as competitions and free gifts (e.g. plastic replicas of film characters), the alliance provides. Communications-based co-branding can also result from sponsorship, where the sponsor's brand name appears on the product being sponsored. An example is Shell's sponsorship of the Ferrari Formula 1 motor racing team. As part of the deal the Shell brand name appears on Ferrari cars.

The advantages of communications-based co-branding are as follows.

Endorsement opportunities

As we have seen, Whirlpool and Ariel engaged in mutual endorsement in their advertising campaign. Endorsement may also be one-way: Shell gains by being associated with the highly successful international motor racing brand, Ferrari.

Cost benefits

One of the parties in the co-brand may provide resources to the other. Shell's deal with Ferrari demands that Shell pays huge sums of money, which helps Ferrari support the costs of motor racing. Also, joint advertising alliances mean that costs can be shared.

Awareness and interest gains

The McDonald's/Disney alliance means that new Disney movies are promoted in McDonald's outlets, enhancing awareness and interest.

Promotional opportunities

As we have discussed, McDonald's gains by the in-store promotional opportunities afforded by its co-branding alliance with Disney.

The risks involved in communications-based co-branding are similar to those of product-based co-branding.

Loss of control

Each party to the co-branding activity loses some of its control to the partner. For example, in joint advertising there could be conflicts arising from differences of opinion regarding creative content and the emphasis given to each brand in the advertising.

Brand equity loss

No one wants to be associated with failure. The poor performance of one brand could tarnish the image of the other. For example, an unsuccessful Disney movie prominently promoted in McDonald's outlets could rebound on the latter. Conversely, bad publicity for McDonald's might harm the Disney brand by association.

Some examples of product and communications-based co-brands are given in Table 8.6.

Table 8.6 Co-branding examples
Parallel co-brands
Häagen-Dazs and Baileys Cream Liqueur form Häagen-Dazs with Baileys flavour ice cream
Ford Focus and *Elle* women's magazine form Ford Focus Elle car
Nike and Lego Bionicle form 'Bionicle by Nike' trainers
NatWest Bank and MasterCard form NatWest MasterCard credit card
Ingredient co-brands
Intel as component in Hewlett Packard computers
Nutrasweet as ingredient in Diet Coke
Scotchgard as stain protector in fabrics
Communications-based co-brands
Ariel and Whirlpool: joint advertising campaign
McDonald's and Disney: joint in-store promotions
Shell and Ferrari: sponsorship

Global and pan-European branding

Global branding is the achievement of brand penetration worldwide. Levitt is a champion of global branding, arguing that intensified competition and technological developments will force companies to operate globally, ignoring superficial national differences.[59] A *global village* is emerging, where consumers seek reliable, quality products at a low price and the marketing task is to offer the same products and services in the same way, thereby achieving enormous global economies of scale. Levitt's position is that the new commercial reality is the emergence of global markets for standardized products and services on a previously unimagined scale. The engine behind this trend is the twin forces of customer convergence of tastes and needs, and the prospect of global efficiencies in production, procurement, marketing, and research and development. Japanese companies have been successful in achieving these kinds of economies to produce high-quality, competitively priced global brands (e.g. Toyota, Sony, Nikon and Fuji).

The creation of global brands also speeds up a brand's time to market by reducing time-consuming local modifications. The perception that a brand is global has also been found to affect positively consumers' belief that the brand is prestigious and of high quality.[60]

In Europe, the promise of pan-European branding has caused leading manufacturers to seek to extend their market coverage and to build their portfolio of brands. Nestlé has widened its brand portfolio by the acquisition of such companies as Rowntree (confectionery) and Buitoni-Perugina (pasta and chocolate), and has formed a joint venture (Cereal Partners) with the US giant General Mills to challenge Kellogg's in the European breakfast cereal market. Mars has replaced its Treets and Bonitos brands with M&Ms, and changed the name of its third largest UK brand, Marathon, to the Snickers name used in the rest of Europe.

The counter-argument to global branding is that it is the exception rather than the rule. It has undoubtedly occurred with high-tech, rapid roll-out products such as audio equipment, cameras, video recorders and camcorders. Furthermore, some global successes, such as Coca-Cola, BMW, Gucci and McDonald's, can be noted, but national varieties in taste and consumption patterns will ensure that such achievements in the future will be limited. For example, the fact that the French eat four times more yoghurt than the British, and the British buy eight times more chocolate than the Italians reflects the kinds of national differences that will affect the marketing strategies of manufacturers.[61] Indeed, many so-called global brands are not standardized, claim the 'local' marketers. For example, Coca-Cola in Scandinavia tastes different from that in Greece.

The last example gives a clue to answering the dilemma facing companies that are considering building global brands. The question is not whether brands can be built on a global scale (clearly they can) but which parts of the brand can be standardized and which must be varied across countries. A useful way of looking at this decision is to separate out the elements that comprise the brand, as shown in Fig. 8.8. Can brand name and image, advertising, service, guarantees, packaging, quality and design, and delivery be standardized or not?

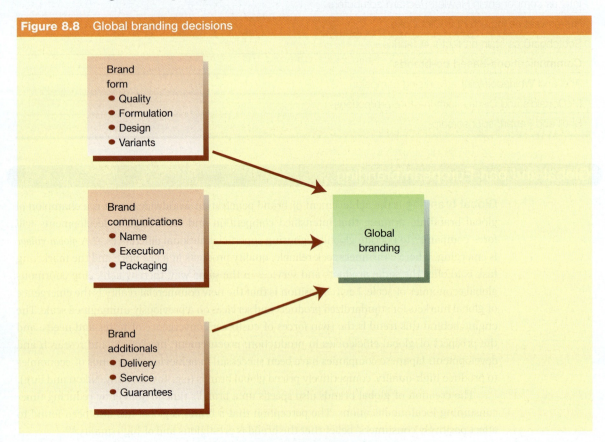

Figure 8.8 Global branding decisions

Gillette's global success with its Sensor razor was based on a highly standardized approach: the product, brand name, the message 'The Best a Man Can Get', advertising visuals and packaging were standardized; only the voice-overs in the advertisement were changed to cater for 26 languages across Europe, the USA and Japan.

Lever Brothers found that, for detergent products, brand image and packaging could be standardized but the brand name, communications execution and brand formulation needed to vary across countries.[62] For example, its fabric conditioner used a cuddly teddy bear across countries but was named differently in Germany (Kuschelweich), France (Cajoline), Italy (Coccolini), Spain (Mimosin), the USA (Snuggle) and Japan (Fa-Fa). Brand image and packaging were the same but the name and formulation (fragrance, phosphate levels and additives) differed between countries.

In other circumstances, the brand form and additions may remain the same (or very similar) across countries but the brand communications may need to be modified. For example, a BMW car may be positioned as having an exclusive image but what Dutch and Italian car buyers consider are the qualities that amount to exclusiveness are very different.[63] Consequently, differing advertising appeals would be needed to communicate the concept of exclusiveness in these countries.

Much activity has taken place over recent years to achieve global and pan-European brand positions. There are three major ways of doing this, as outlined below.[64]

1. *Geographic extension*: taking present brands into the geographic markets.
2. *Brand acquisition*: purchasing brands.
3. *Brand alliance*: joint venture or partnerships to market brands in national or cross-national markets.

Managers need to evaluate the strengths and weaknesses of each option, and Fig. 8.9 summarizes these using as criteria speed of market penetration, control of operations and the level of investment required. Brand acquisition gives the fastest method of developing global brands. For example, Unilever's acquisition of Fabergé, Elizabeth Arden and Calvin Klein immediately made it a major player in fragrances, cosmetics and skincare. Brand alliance usually gives moderate speed. For example, the use of the Nestlé name for the Cereal Partners (General Mills and Nestlé) alliance's breakfast cereal in Europe should help retailer and consumer acceptance. Geographic extension is likely to be the slowest unless the company is already a major global player with massive resources, as brand building from scratch is a time-consuming process.

Figure 8.9 Developing global and pan-European brands

Source: Barwise, P. and T. Robertson (1992) Brand Portfolios, *European Management Journal* 10(3), 279. Copyright © 1992 with kind permission from Elsevier Science Ltd, The Boulevard, Langford Lane, Kidlington OX5 1GB, UK.

Strategy		Criteria for evaluation		
		Speed	Control	Investment
	Geographic expansion	Slow	High	Medium
	Brand acquisition	Fast	Medium	High
	Brand alliance	Moderate	Low	Low

However, geographic extension provides a high degree of control since companies can choose which brands to globalize, and plan their global extensions. Brand acquisition gives a moderate degree of control although many may prove hard to integrate with in-house brands. Brand alliance fosters the lowest degree of control, as strategy and resource allocation will need to be negotiated with the partner.

Finally, brand acquisitions are likely to incur the highest level of investment. For example, Nestlé paid £2.5 billion (€3.6 billion) for Rowntree, a figure that was over five times net asset value. Geographic extension is likely to be more expensive than brand alliance since, in the latter case, costs are shared, and one partner may benefit from the expertise and distribution capabilities of the other. For example, in the Cereal Partners' alliance, General Mills gained access to Nestlé's expertise and distribution system in Europe. Although the specifics of each situation need to be carefully analysed, Fig. 8.9 provides a framework for assessing the strategic alternatives when developing global and pan-European brands.

Corporate identity management

Managers also need to be aware of the importance of the corporate brand as represented by its corporate identity. Corporate identity represents the ethos, aims and values of an organization, presenting a sense of its individuality, which helps to differentiate it from its competitors. A key ingredient is visual cohesion, which is necessary to ensure that all corporate communications are consistent with each other and result in a corporate image in line with the organization's defining values and character. The objective is to establish a favourable reputation with an organization's stakeholders, which it is hoped will be translated into a greater likelihood of purchasing the organization's goods and services, and working for and investing in the organization.[65]

Corporate identity management has emerged as a key activity of senior marketing and corporate management because of the following developments.[66]

- Mergers, acquisitions and alliances have led to many new or significantly changed companies that require new identities (e.g. Diageo).
- Some existing companies have undertaken 're-imaging' by changing the reality of their activities and/or via their communications to make their activities/image more technology orientated (e.g. mmO$_2$).
- The emergence of dotcom and new media companies created many new company identities (e.g. Lastminute.com).

Corporate identity management is concerned with the conception, development and communication of an organization's ethos, aims (mission) and values. Its orientation is strategic and is based on a company's culture and behaviour. It differs from traditional brand marketing directed towards consumers or organizational purchases since it is concerned with all of an organization's stakeholders and the wide-ranging way in which an organization communicates. If managed well it can affect organizational performance by attracting and retaining customers, increasing the likelihood of creating beneficial strategic alliances, recruiting high-quality staff, being well positioned in financial markets, maintaining strong media relations and strengthening staff identification with the company.[67]

An example of the successful use of corporate identity management is Arcadis, an infrastructural engineering company with its headquarters in the Netherlands but with operations all over the world. A strong corporate identity was particularly important to give a sense of unity to a company that had grown largely through acquisition. The company believes that its identity, which brings with it a set of specific values, has produced benefits both with internal staff and external customers.[68]

Not all corporate identity activities are successful, however. An example is the repainting of British Airways' tail fins. Originally, all BA tail fins were the colour of the Union Jack, symbolizing its British heritage. In an attempt at global repositioning, most of them were repainted using the colours of the national emblems of many overseas countries. The move allegedly backfired as passengers, especially businesspeople, disliked the excessive variety in tail-fin design.[69] A second failure in corporate identity management was the ill-fated change in name from the Post Office to Consignia, discussed earlier in this chapter. The new name was designed to reflect a wider range of services (mail delivery, retail outlets and the delivery of packages) than the original name, the Post Office, suggested, and to facilitate entry into global markets under an international identity that could work well across national borders. However, implementation of the corporate identity change was not well managed, with consumers (and the media) believing that the name was to be used on Post Office retail outlets across the country. Furthermore, research showed that the brand values associated with one part of the Post Office, the Royal Mail, were very high. With the appointment of a new chairman, Allan Leighton and widespread derision of the Consignia name among the public, staff and media, the decision was taken to rename the company, the Royal Mail Group.[70]

Dimensions of corporate identity

A corporate identity can be broken down into five dimensions or identity types, namely actual identity, communicated identity, conceived identity, ideal identity and desired identity. This framework is called the AC²ID test and is shown in Fig. 8.10. By analysing each dimension a company can test the effectiveness of its corporate identity.[71]

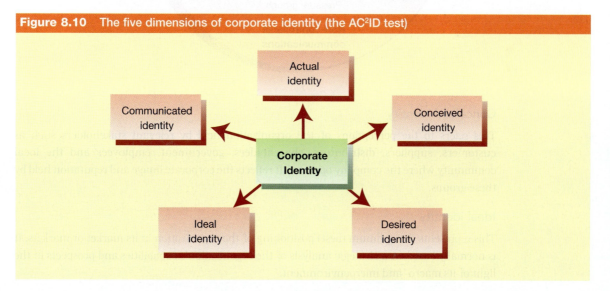

Figure 8.10 The five dimensions of corporate identity (the AC²ID test)

Each of these five dimensions will now be explained.

Actual identity

This represents the reality of the organization and describes what the organization is. It includes the type and quality of the products offered by the organization, the values and behaviour of staff, and the performance of the company. It is influenced by the nature of the corporate ownership, the leadership style of management, organization structure and management policies, and the structure of the industry.

Communicated identity

This is the identity the organization reveals through its 'controllable' corporate communication programme. Typically, communicational tools such as advertising, public relations, sponsorship and visual symbols (corporate names, logos, signs, letterheads, use of colour and design, and word font) are used to present an identity to stakeholders. In addition, communicated identity may derive from 'non-controllable' communications such as word of mouth, media coverage and pressure groups such a Greenpeace. Figure 8.11 illustrates the elements of communicated identity.

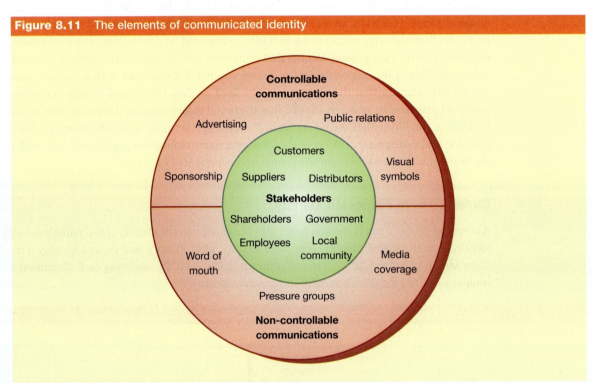

Figure 8.11 The elements of communicated identity

Conceived identity

This refers to the perceptions of the organization held by relevant stakeholders such as customers, suppliers, distributors, shareholders, government, employees and the local community where the company operates. It reflects the corporate image and reputation held by these groups.

Ideal identity

This represents the optimum (best) positioning of the organization in its market or markets. It is normally based on a strategic analysis of the organization's capabilities and prospects in the light of its macro- and microenvironment.

Desired identity

This lives in the hearts and minds of corporate leaders. It is their vision for the organization. This can differ from the ideal identity, which is based on research and analysis. Desired identity is likely to be based on a chief executive's vision, which is influenced more by personality and ego than rational assessment of the organization's strategic position in the marketplace.

Companies, therefore, have multiple identities, and a lack of fit between any two or more of the identities can cause problems that may weaken the company. For example, corporate communications (communicated identity) may be at odds with reality (actual identity); corporate performance and behaviour (actual identity) may fall short of the expectations of key stakeholders (conceived identity); and what is communicated to stakeholders (communicated identity) may differ from what stakeholders perceive (conceived identity). Marketing in Action 8.5 examines a communicated–conceived identity gap at Hilton hotels.

8.5 marketing in action

Corporate Identity Misalignment at Hilton Hotels

An example of a gap between communicated and conceived identities is related to the Hilton hotel chain. In the face of financial difficulties, the US-based company sold off most of its non-American operations including the rights to the Hilton brand name internationally. The non-American operations and rights were acquired by the UK entertainment group Ladbrokes, resulting in the Hilton brand name being used by both the US-based Hilton and Ladbrokes. The two companies increasingly employed different communications strategies to support the Hilton brand in their markets.

This caused confusion among consumers and businesspeople who stayed at Hilton hotels in both markets. In corporate identity terms there was a gap between the widely held perception of Hilton as a single entity (conceived identity) and the two communicated identities. Eventually the two companies realized that this misalignment was weakening both corporate brands, and entered into a formal marketing and brand alliance, including visual identity, marketing programmes, technology and reservation systems.

Based on: Balmer and Greyser (2003)[72]

The AC²ID test, then, is a useful framework for assisting companies in researching, analysing and managing corporate identities. The next section explains how it can be used to do this.

Managing corporate identity programmes

Using the AC²ID test to conduct a corporate identity audit has five stages, known as the REDS² AC²ID Test Process.[73] This results in the identification of a strategy to resolve any gaps between the five identity dimensions. The stages are as described below.

Reveal the five identities

Each of the five identity types are audited. Actual identity is audited by measuring such elements as internal staff values, performance of products and services, and management style. Communicated identity is examined by researching such factors as the communications sent out from the organization and media commentary. Conceived identity is measured by such elements as the corporate image and reputation as perceived by the various stakeholder groups. Ideal identity is audited by measuring such factors as the optimum product features and performance, the optimum set of internal staff values and the optimum management style. Finally, desired identity is examined by researching the vision held by senior management, especially the chief executive.

Examine the ten identity interfaces

Each identity dimension is then compared to the others so that any gaps (misalignments) can be identified. The ten identity interfaces can be used as a checklist of potential problem areas.

To illustrate this stage, Fig. 8.12 shows five interfaces and the kinds of questions that should be asked.

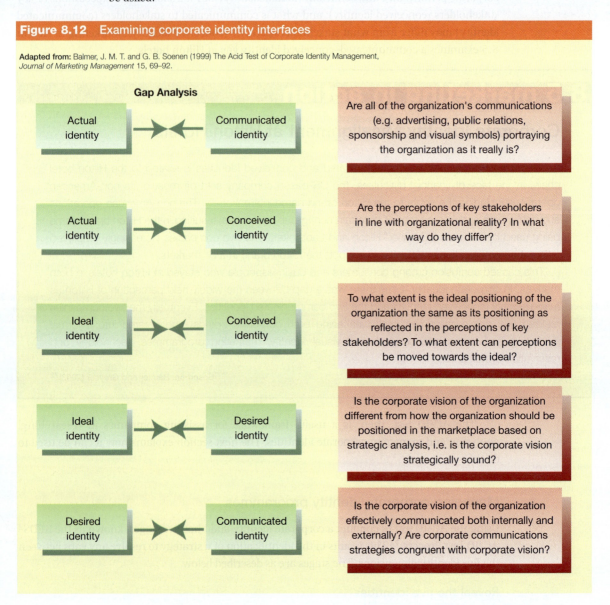

Figure 8.12 Examining corporate identity interfaces

Adapted from: Balmer, J. M. T. and G. B. Soenen (1999) The Acid Test of Corporate Identity Management, *Journal of Marketing Management* 15, 69–92.

Diagnose the situation

The questions posed at the previous stage form the foundation for diagnosing the situation. This involves providing answers to the following questions.

- What are the problems?
- What are their nature?
- What are the implications?

Select the interfaces for attention

Which interfaces should be brought into alignment? Account should be taken of the priorities and the feasibility of the required action.

Strategic choice

What kind of strategies are required to create the corporate identity change needed to bring the interfaces into alignment. Options include reality change (including culture change), modifications to communications strategies, strategic repositioning (including moving into new technologies) and changes in corporation vision and mission.

The REDS^2 AC^{2}ID Test Process, then, encourages management to address the following five questions.[74]

1. What is our current corporate identity?
2. What image is communicated by formal and informal communications?
3. What would be the ideal identity for the organization to acquire in the light of the organization's capabilities and in the light of its micro- and macroenvironment?
4. What corporate identity would senior managers wish their organization to have?
5. How can this required corporate identity be achieved?

As such it provides a practical framework for corporate identity management. It is simple, memorable, logical and operational and, therefore, is a useful tool for managers responsible for corporate branding, corporate communications and corporate identity.[75]

Ethical issues concerning products

There are three major issues regarding ethical issues with products: product safety, planned obsolescence and deceptive packaging.

Product safety

A major concern about product safety has been the issue of the safety of genetically modified products. Vociferous pressure groups such as Greenpeace have spoken out about the dangers of genetic modification. This process allows scientists to manipulate the genetic code of plants to create new characteristics never seen in nature. They are able to isolate any one gene in an organism and insert it into a completely unrelated species. For example, scientists can inject a gene from a bacterium into a grape to make it resistant to viruses; they can engineer maize to make it drought resistant or create potato strains that resist pests. People are sharply divided as to whether this can be safe. Although plant breeders have for thousands of years been tampering with the genes of plants through traditional cross-pollination of plants of the same species, genetic modification goes one step further as it allows scientists to cross the species barrier. This, its critics claim, is fundamentally unnatural. Furthermore, they state, no scientist can be sure that all of this genetic manipulation can be safe. Such concerns, and the attendant publicity have led to one of the pioneers of genetic modification, Monsanto, to back away from further development of genetically modified foods and supermarket chains to ban such produce from their shelves. Supporters state that many new products are introduced with a certain degree of risk being acceptable. For example, a new pharmaceutical product may harm a tiny percentage of users but the utilitarianist principle of 'the greatest good for the greatest number' would support its launch.

It is the reality of modern-day business that new products, such as cars, pharmaceuticals and foods, undergo extensive safety testing before launch. Anything less would violate the consumer's 'right to safety'.

Planned obsolescence

Many products are not designed to last a long time. From the producer's point of view this is sensible as it creates a repeat purchase situation. Hence, cars rust, clothes wear out and fashion items are replaced by the latest styles. Consumers accept that nothing lasts forever, but the issue concerns what is an acceptable length of time before replacement is necessary. One driving force is competition. To quell the Japanese invasion, car manufacturers such as Ford and Volkswagen have made the body shells of their cars much more rust-resistant than before. Furthermore, it has to be recognized that many consumers welcome the chance to buy new clothes, new appliances with the latest features and the latest model of car. Critics argue that planned obsolescence reduces consumers' 'right to choose' since some consumers may be quite content to drive an old car so long as its body shell is free from rust and the car functions well. As we have noted, the forces of competition may act to deter the excesses of planned obsolescence.

Deceptive packaging

This can occur when a product appears in an oversized package to create the impression that the consumer is buying more than is the case. This is known as 'slack' packaging[76] and has the potential to deceive when the packaging is opaque. Products such as soap powders and breakfast cereals have the potential to suffer from 'slack' packaging. A second area where packaging may be deceptive is through misleading labelling. This may take the form of the sin of omission—for example, the failure of a package to state that the product contains genetically modified soya beans. This relates to the consumer's 'right to be informed', and can include the stating of ingredients (including flavouring and colourants), nutritional contents and country of origin on labels. Nevertheless, labelling can be misleading. For example, in the UK, country of origin is only the last country where the product was 'significantly changed'. So oil pressed from Greek olives in France can be labelled 'French' and foreign imports that are packed in the UK can be labelled 'produce of the UK'. Consumers should be wary of loose terminology. For example, smoked bacon may well have received its 'smoked flavour' from a synthetic liquid solution, 'farm fresh eggs' are likely to be un-datemarked eggs of indeterminate age laid by battery hens, and 'farmhouse cheese' may not come from farmhouses but from industrial factories.[77]

The use of loose language and meaningless terms in the UK food and drink industry has been criticized by the Food Standards Agency (FSA). A list of offending words has been drawn up, which includes fresh, natural, pure, traditional and original. Recommendations regarding when it is reasonable to use certain words have been drawn up. For example, 'authentic' should only be used to emphasize the geographic origin of a product and 'home-made' should be restricted to the preparation of the recipe on the premises and must involve 'some degree of fundamental culinary preparation'. The FSA has also expressed concern about the use of meaningless phrases such as 'natural goodness' and 'country-style' and recommended that they should not be used.[78]

Branding and developing economies

Critics of branding accuse the practice of concentrating power and wealth in the hands of companies and economies that are already rich and powerful, whereas poor countries have to compete on price. Supporters of branding claim that it is not branding's fault that poor countries suffer from low wages and that by sourcing from those countries their economies benefit. Ethical Marketing in Action 8.1 discusses some of the issues involved.

8.1 ethical marketing in action

What's in a Name: are Brands Divisive?

Naomi Klein poses the question 'What does Nike make? Trainers? Sportswear? Fashion goods?' The answer is that Nike doesn't make anything—it manages a brand. Others, in countries with cheap labour forces—that is, poor countries—do the making. A pair of Nike ID trainers retails for an average of £100, but the manufacturers see very little of this. In 2001, 31 per cent of Nike's shoes were made in Indonesia; as of July 2001 entry-level full-time wages in Nike contract factories in West Java were equal to or slightly about the legal minimum of 17,000 Rupiahs (£1.22/€1.75) per day.

Nike is not alone: branding 'adds value' to many product offerings. A pair of denim trousers becomes a fashion statement with a Levi's label on it; an addictive and carcinogenic drug becomes a mark of independence, rebellion and midwestern cool when it is branded by Marlboro. Ethical dilemmas arise, not just in the case of specific products but also in a more general way. Branding concentrates power and wealth in a few hands—hands that are already rich and powerful. As in the case of Nike, the world's most successful brands are owned and controlled by its richest countries.

On a global level, this means that the disproportionate power and profits associated with branding continue to accumulate in the wealthy West, whereas poor countries have to compete simply on price. So, while the West concentrates on lucrative image creation, the rest of the world is turned into a collection of low-margin factories. One solution is for the poorer countries to start developing their own brands. To do this they need to develop marketing skills and attract marketing talent. The marketing knowledge you are acquiring now could help redress this balance.

Based on: Klein (2000);[79] www.nike.com/Europe;[80] Oxfam[81]

Ethical dilemma

A company launches a new brand of extra-safe condoms. The packaging and promotion for this product utilize a cartoon theme. Is the approach taken in managing this product ethical?

Review

1 **The concept of a product, brand, product line and product mix**
- A product is anything that is capable of satisfying customer needs.
- A brand is a distinctive product offering created by the use of a name, symbol, design, packaging, or some combination of these intended to differentiate it from its competitors.
- A product line is a group of brands that are closely related in terms of the functions and benefits they provide.
- A product mix is the total set of products marketed by a company.

2 **The difference between manufacturer and own-label brands**
- Manufacturer brands are created by producers and bear their chosen brand name, whereas own-label brands are created and owned by distributors (e.g. supermarkets).

3 **The difference between a core and an augmented product (the brand)**
- A core product is anything that provides the central benefits required by customers (e.g. toothpaste cleans teeth). The augmented product is produced by adding extra functional and/or emotional values to the core product, and combining them in a unique way to form a brand.

4 **Why strong brands are important**

Strong brands are important because they:
- enhance company value
- positively affect consumer perceptions and preferences
- act as a barrier to competition because of their impact on consumer perceptions and preferences
- produce high profits through premium prices and high market share
- provide the foundation for brand extensions
- act as a form of quality certification, which aids the consumer decision-making process
- build trust among consumers.

5 **How to build strong brands**

Strong brands can be built by:
- building quality into the core product
- creating a unique position in the marketplace based on an analysis of brand domain, brand heritage, brand values, brand assets, brand personality and brand reflection
- repositioning to take advantage of new opportunities
- using well-blended communications to create a clear position in the minds of the target audience
- being first into the market with a unique marketing proposition
- taking a long-term perspective
- using internal marketing to train staff in essential skills and to communicate brand strategies so that they understand the company ethos on which the company brand is built.

6 **The differences between family, individual and combined brand names, and the characteristics of an effective brand name**
- A family brand name is one that is used for all products in a range (e.g. Nescafé); an individual brand name does not identify a brand with a particular company

▶
- (e.g. Proctor & Gamble does not appear with Daz); a combination brand name combines family and individual brand names (e.g. Microsoft Windows).
- The characteristics of an effective brand name are that it should evoke positive associations, be easy to pronounce and remember, suggest product benefits, be distinctive, use numerics or alphanumerics when emphasizing technology, be transferable and not infringe on existing registered brand names.

7 Why companies rebrand, and how to manage the process
- Companies rebrand to create a new identity after merger or acquisition, to create a new image/position in the marketplace, following the sale or acquisition of parts of a business where the old name is no longer appropriate, following corporate strategy changes where the old name is considered too limiting, to reflect the fact that a major product brand is more familiar to consumers than the old corporate brand, for international marketing reasons (e.g. name harmonization across national borders), consolidation of brands within a national boundary, and in response to legal problems (e.g. restrictions on its use).
- Managing the rebranding process involves choosing the new brand name and implementing the name change.
- Choosing the new brand name has six stages: setting rebranding objectives, generation of new names, screening to remove any with obvious flaws, information search to identify any infringements of existing brand names, consumer research, and choice of new brand name.
- Implementing the name change requires attention to five key issues: co-ordination among departments and groups; communication to consumers, employees and distributors; discovering what consumers identify with the brand so that communications can incorporate all relevant aspects of the brand; provision of assistance to distributors/retailers so that the change takes place smoothly; and care over the speed of changeover.

8 The concepts of brand extension and stretching, their uses and limitations
- A brand extension is the use of an established brand name on a new brand within the same broad market or product category; brand stretching occurs when an established brand is used for brands in unrelated markets or product categories.
- Their advantages are that they reduce perceived risk of purchase on the part of distributors and consumers, the use of the established brand name raises consumers' willingness to try the new brand, the positive associations of the core brand should rub off on to the brand extension, the awareness of the core brand lowers advertising and other marketing costs, and the introduction of the extension can raise sales of the core brand due to the enhancement of consumers' perception of brand values and image through increased communication.
- The limitations are that poor performance of the brand extension could rebound on the core brand, the brand may lose credibility if stretched too far, sales of the extension may cannibalize sales of the core brand and the use of a brand extension strategy may encourage a focus on minor brand modifications rather than true innovation.

9 The two major forms of co-branding, and their advantages and risks
- The two major forms are product-based (parallel and ingredient) co-branding and communications-based co-branding.

▶

- The advantages of product-based co-branding are added value and differentiation, the enhanced ability to position a brand for a particular target market, and the reduction of the cost of product introduction.
- The risks of product-based co-branding are loss of control and potential brand equity loss if poor performance of the co-brand rebounds on the original brands.
- The advantages of communications-based co-branding are endorsement opportunities, cost benefits, awareness and interest gains, and promotional opportunities.
- The risks of communications-based co-branding are loss of control, and potential brand equity loss.

10 The arguments for and against global and pan-European branding, and the strategic options for building such brands

- The arguments 'for' are that intensified global competition and technological developments, customer convergence of tastes and needs, and the prospect of global efficiencies of scale will encourage companies to create global brands.
- The arguments 'against' are that national varieties in taste and consumption patterns will limit the development of global brands.
- The strategic options are geographic extension, brand acquisition and brand alliances.

11 The dimensions of corporate identity

There are five dimensions (the AC^2ID test):
- actual identity represents the reality of the organization and describes what the organization is
- communicated identity is what is revealed through the organization's 'controllable' corporate communications programme and through 'non-controllable' communication such as word of mouth
- conceived identity refers to the perceptions of the organization held by relevant stakeholders
- ideal identity represents the organization's best positioning in its market(s)
- desired identity is what lives in the hearts and minds of corporate leaders, in particular the chief executive's vision.

12 The management of corporate identity programmes

This involves conducting an audit based on the $REDS^2$ AC^2ID Test Process to:
- reveal the five identities
- examine the ten identity interfaces
- diagnose the situation
- select the interfaces for attention
- address strategic choice.

13 Ethical issues concerning products

- These are product safety, planned obsolescence, deceptive packaging, and branding and developing economies.

Chapter eight Managing Products: Brand and Corporate Identity Management

Key terms

augmented product the core product plus extra functional and/or emotional values combined in a unique way to form a brand

brand a distinctive product offering created by the use of a name, symbol, design, packaging, or some combination of these intended to differentiate it from its competitors

brand assets the distinctive features of a brand

brand domain the brand's target market

brand equity the goodwill associated with a brand name, which adds tangible value to a company through the resulting higher sales and profits

brand extension the use of an established brand name on a new brand within the same broad market or product category

brand heritage the background to the brand and its culture

brand personality the character of a brand described in terms of other entities such as people, animals and objects

brand reflection the relationship of the brand to self-identity

brand stretching the use of an established brand name for brands in unrelated markets or product categories

brand values the core values and characteristics of a brand

co-branding (communications) the linking of two or more existing brands from different companies or business units for the purposes of joint communication

co-branding (product) the linking of two or more existing brands from different companies or business units to form a product in which the brand names are visible to consumers

combination brand name a combination of family and individual brand names

core product anything that provides the central benefits required by customers

corporate identity the ethos, aims and values of an organization, presenting a sense of its individuality, which helps to differentiate it from its competitors

family brand name a brand name used for all products in a range

fighter brands low-cost manufacturers' brands introduced to combat own-label brands

global branding achievement of brand penetration worldwide

individual brand name a brand name that does not identify a brand with a particular company

ingredient co-branding the explicit positioning of a supplier's brand as an ingredient of a product

internal marketing training, motivating and communicating with staff to cause them to work effectively in providing customer satisfaction; more recently the term has been expanded to include marketing to all staff with the aim of achieving the acceptance of marketing ideas and plans

manufacturer brands brands that are created by producers and bear their chosen brand name

own-label brands brands created and owned by distributors or retailers

parallel co-branding the joining of two or more independent brands to produce a combined brand

product line a group of brands that are closely related in terms of the functions and benefits they provide

product mix the total set of products marketed by a company

rebranding the changing of a brand or corporate name

Internet exercise

The Superbrands website is dedicated to highlighting the development of some of the world's most successful brands. Visit and explore the 'Consumer Superbrands' section.

Visit: www.superbrands.org

Questions

(a) What are the characteristics of successful brands?
(b) Discuss the importance of brand values.
(c) Select one of the Superbrands brand case studies and discuss the selected brand's equity.
(d) How can marketing communications influence brand equity?
(e) Using the Superbrands website, discuss the factors that should be considered when selecting a brand name, giving examples.
(f) Explain how a corporate brand differs from a product brand.

Visit the Online Learning Centre at www.mcgraw-hill.co.uk/textbooks/jobber for more Internet exercises.

Study questions

1. Why do companies develop core products into brands?

2. Suppose you were the marketing director of a medium-sized bank. How would you tackle the job of building the company brand?

3. Think of five brand names. To what extent do they meet the criteria of good brand naming as laid out in Table 8.2? Do any of the names legitimately break these guidelines?

4. Do you think that there will be a large increase in the number of pan-European brands over the next ten years or not? Justify your answer.

5. What are the strategic options for pan-European brand building? What are the advantages and disadvantages of each option?

6. Why do companies rebrand product and corporate names? What is necessary for successful implementation of the rebranding process?

7. What are the two main forms of co-branding? What are their advantages and risks?

8. Describe the five dimensions of corporate identity. How can an analysis of these dimensions and their interfaces aid the management of corporate identity?

9. Discuss the major ethical concerns relating to products.

When you have read this chapter log on to the Online Learning Centre at www.mcgraw-hill.co.uk/textbooks/jobber to explore chapter-by-chapter test questions, links and further online study tools for marketing.

case fifteen

Levi's Jeans: Re-engaging the Youth Market

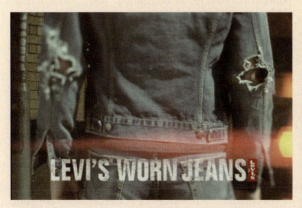

Launched in 2002, Worn Jeans were Levi's attempt to differentiate its product from other jeans brands.

In a conference room at the global headquarters of Levi Strauss & Company in San Francisco, Robert Holloway, the new vice-president of marketing, addressed Levi's new brand management team. 'What kids want is to be acceptable to their peers. They're looking to make an impact with potential partners as well and therefore they want to look right. Part of looking right is wearing what's cool.'

The problem facing Levi Strauss was that jeans were increasingly regarded as 'uncool'. In 1996, the company reported record one-year sales of $7.1 billion and a profit of more than $1 billion. By the end of 1999, sales had fallen to $5.1 billion and the company barely broke even on profits despite closing 30 of its 51 factories and laying off about 15,000 people (40 per cent of its workers).

The root causes go back as far as 1992 when rap music emerged as a cultural phenomenon and baggy trousers were its generational signature. Unfortunately, Levi's failed to connect with young customers. While competitors such as Gap, Diesel, Wrangler and Pepe stole market share, Levi's market share shrank from 31 to 14 per cent. The problem was complacency; for years Levi's had been cool—the kind of cool that seems as if it will never end.

Levi Strauss, a Jewish immigrant from Bavaria, began selling waist overalls from his San Francisco store in 1873 as a utilitarian tool of daily life for farmers, ranchers, miners and factory workers. In the 1950s and 1960s, however, they became associated with teenage rebellion and counter-culture. Marlon Brando, Elvis

The advertising for Type One jeans, launched in 2003, was in typical Levi's avant-garde style.

Presley and Bob Dylan were all photographed wearing Levi's. Based on the proposition 'genuine, original, authentic, real' sales grew tenfold during the late 1960s and early 1970s but it was not until the mid-1980s that the company aggressively used television advertising to launch its 501 Blues campaign. Sales and profits began a continuous 12-year rise. The engine room for this growth was one product: its 501 five-pocket jeans brand, which represented social acceptance and yet a kind of individuality and rebelliousness among its wearers.

But nothing lasts forever. One survey reported that the proportion of US teenage males who considered Levi's to be a 'cool' brand plummeted from 21 per cent to 7 per cent between 1994 and 1998. This was reflected in the comment made by a 16-year-old male when he said that his peers preferred loose brands with non-tapered legs, like the ultra-baggy JNCO jeans: 'But JNCO is more last year. Now it's more Polo, Hilfiger and Boss.' When asked about Levi's he replied, 'If I buy Levi's, it's like I bought Wranglers and people think I'm cheap, but it's still expensive!' Another 15-year-old female stated that her friends will not wear anything from Levi's: 'It doesn't make styles we want. Levi's styles are too tight and for the older generation, like middle-aged people.' She prefers baggy pants from JNCO and Kikwear.

While Levi's remained impervious to the cultural changes in the jeans market, other newer brands have emerged. One major competitor, Gap, began in 1969 ironically as a retail chain selling Levi's exclusively. By staying responsive to consumer changes, the company saw a rapid rise in sales. Two others, Diesel and Pepe, have stolen Levi's rebellious attitude, making Levi's jeans less distinctive in the minds of consumers.

By 2000, traditional styles of jeans (Levi's heartland) had fallen to only 20 per cent of sales, down from more than 50 per cent in 1996. To make matters worse, demographic changes meant that the number of 15–25 year olds in the population was forecast to fall dramatically in future years.

New strategies for the new millennium

The continued segmentation and fragmentation of the UK jeans market has led Levi's to organize its marketing around three customer groups: urban opinion-formers; extreme sports; and regular girls and guys. Each will handle its own new product development, have its own brand managers and marketing team. The core market will remain the 15–25 age group.

In a major attempt to turn around this grim situation, Levi Strauss has developed new marketing strategies. A new range of non-denim jeans, branded Sta-Prest, was launched in 1999 backed up by a major TV advertising campaign starring a toy furry animal called Flat Eric. This campaign was well received by its youth audience.

In 2000, Levi's launched Engineered Jeans, an aggressive modern range billed as a 'reinvention' of the five-pocket style to replace the old 501 brand. Described as the 'twisted original' the new jeans featured side seams that follow the line of the leg, and a curved bottom hem that is slightly shorter at the back to keep it from dragging on the ground. The jeans also have a larger watch pocket to hold items like a pager. Under its youth-orientated Silver Tab brand, Levi's introduced the Mobile Zip-Off Pant, with legs that unzip to create shorts, and the loose Ripcord Pant, which rolls up. Levi's also extended its successful Docker brand to a business-casual line called Dockers Recode using stretch fabrics that appeal to older consumers who passed through their teens wearing Levi's blue jeans.

In 2003, the S-Fit trousers, part of the Dockers range, were launched with anti-radiation pockets for mobile phones in response to consumers' fears about mobile handset radiation. They are premium-priced at over £100 (€144).

Levi Strauss have also innovated on the retail front. In 1999 the company opened its first unbranded store, Cinch!, in London with plans to open other stores with the same format but different names around European capitals. Cinch! will target customers it calls 'cultural connoisseurs': fashionable less mainstream customers. It stocks the new Levi's upmarket Red collection, and the Vintage Clothing and Collectable ranges rather than the mainstream Red Tab or Sta-Prest products. There is no Levi's branding on the store fascia and garments are hung on the walls. Non-Levi's products including Casio watches, and Japanese magazines and art books are also stocked. There is a 'chill-out' television room. Cultural connoisseurs like to 'discover' brands for themselves and appreciate an intimate retail experience.

Levi Strauss has also altered its approach to massified promotion. It believes that a 'massified' image is a hindrance to acceptance among young consumers. It studied how rave promoters publicized their parties using flyers, 'wild posting' on construction sites and lamp-posts, pavement markings and e-mail. It is exploring how such 'viral communications' could be used to infiltrate youth culture. The idea is to introduce the Levi's brand name into the target consumers' clubs, concert venues, websites and fanzines in order for the kids to discover the company's tag for themselves. Levi's is spending massive sums sponsoring and supporting musicians, bands and gigs in order to communicate with today's youth, who are now so smart about media campaigns that the best strategy—as with the Flat Eric campaign—is to try to prod them gently towards the idea that Levi's is again the 'cool' brand. As the president of Levi's advertising agency says, 'If you go into their environment where they are hanging out, and you speak to them in a way that's appropriate, then the buzz created from that is spread, and that's an incredibly powerful way to impact the marketplace.'

In 2002, Levi's Worn Jeans were launched. Worn denim was Levi's attempt to differentiate its product from other jeans brands. Injecting the fabric with two-tone sprays and moulding it to give it a 3D appearance created the worn effect. The launch was supported by commercials showing male and female models slowly rubbing themselves against roads, street furniture and each other in an attempt to create the worn effect on denim. Aimed at 15–25 year olds across Europe, the advertisements ended with the tag-line 'Rub yourself.' A website offered competitions and editorial set within a denim-themed landscape called Worn Jeans World. Visitors could navigate the site using on-screen characters in search of hot spots. The characters had to 'rub' with various tools to access content.

Type One Jeans, made of dark denim with bright stitching, oversized rivets and large pockets, were launched in 2003. Like Worn Jeans, the brand targeted both young men and women. The accompanying campaign more than matched the company's reputation for avant-garde advertising. It featured a group of hybrid mouse-humans, conceived to personify the ad's creative theme of a 'bold new breed' of denim. Before the advertising agency, Bartle Bogle Hegarty, shot the ad, focus groups discussed the plot, where mouse-humans kidnap a cat and blackmail its owner. The research concluded that Levi's should tone down the aggression and superiority, and balance the female and male roles more equally from a script that was skewed towards the females. To create even more interest in the brand, Levi's used a guerrilla marketing technique known as 'self-discovery'. It left documents purporting to be leaked top-secret memos about the launch in bus shelters, bars and pubs. A website was also established in support of the brand.

During this period of innovation, Levi's was faced with the threat of imported cut-price 501 jeans by Tesco, the supermarket chain, and Costco the discount warehouse group. Tesco was selling Levi's 501 jeans, purchased inexpensively in the USA, for £27.99 (€40) compared to £50 (€72) in Levi's-authorized shops. Levi's successfully appealed to the European Court of Justice for this to be prevented.

In the USA, Levi's seemed to be moving in a different direction by creating a cut-price jeans brand to be sold through the discounter Wal-Mart. The new brand, Signature, was Levi's third main brand alongside Levi's and Dockers, and was launched in 2003. Levi's had previously refused to allow its jeans to be sold to discount retailers and supermarkets. The price was set at £15 (€22), just above the £14 (€20) average for jeans in the USA. The range targets men, women and children, and has less detailed finishes than other Levi's lines. For example, the jeans do not have the company's trademark red tab or stitching on the pocket. The move brings Levi's directly into competition with Wrangler and Lee.

Questions

1. Using the anatomy of brand positioning framework, analyse the Levi's brand in 1996 and 1999. Why has the positioning of the brand changed?

2. Do you believe that the Levi's brand positioning is retrievable? Should Levi's relaunch using a different brand name?

3. Assess the steps taken by Levi Strauss to restore Levi's as a successful brand.

4. Explain the apparent contradiction between Levi's concern for cut-priced Levi's appearing in Europe and its decision to launch a discount brand in the USA.

This case was prepared by David Jobber, Professor of Marketing, University of Bradford, based on: Buckley, N. (2002) Levi Strides into Mall's Discount Heart, *Financial Times*, 31 October, 23; Day, J. (1999) Levi's Plans New Stores, *Marketing Week*, 2 September, 7; Espan, H. (1999) Coming Apart at the Seams, *Observer*, Review, 28 March, 1–2; Jardine, A. (2003) Trendsetter, *Marketing*, 27 February, 18; Lee, J. (1999) Can Levi's Ever Be Cool Again?, *Marketing*, 15 April, 28–9; Lee, L. (2000) Can Levi's Ever Be Cool Again?, *Business Week*, 13 March, 144–8; McElhatton, N. (2003) Pre-testing Helps Ad Effectiveness, *Marketing*, 8 May, 27–8; *Marketing*, 10 October, 21.

case sixteen

Reinventing Burberry

It is called 'doing a Gucci' after Domenico De Sole and Tom Ford's stunning success at turning nearly bankrupt Gucci Group into a £7 billion (€10 billion) (market capitalization) fashion powerhouse. Since 1997 when she took over, Rose Marie Bravo's makeover of the 148-year-old Burberry brand looks like following the same path.

The Burberry story began in 1856 when Thomas Burberry opened his first gentlemen's outfitters. By the First World War, business was booming as Burberry won the contract to supply trench coats to the British army. Its reputation grew when it proved its contribution to the national cause. The Burberry check was introduced in the 1920s and became fashionable among the British middle to upper classes. Later, appearances on Humphrey Bogart in *Casablanca* and Audrey Hepburn in *Breakfast at Tiffany's* gave the Burberry trench coat widespread appeal.

Bought by Great Universal Stores in 1955, the brand's huge popularity from the 1940s to the 1970s had waned by the 1980s. A less deferential society no longer yearned to dress like the upper classes and the Burberry brand's cachet fell in the UK. This was partially offset by a surge in sales to the newly rich Japanese and other Asians after they discovered its famous (and trademarked) tan, black, red and white check pattern. By the mid-1990s, the Far East accounted for an unbalanced 75 per cent of Burberry sales. British and American consumers began to regard it as an Asian brand and rather staid. Furthermore, distribution was focused on small shops with few big fashion chains and upmarket stores like Harrods stocking the brand. In the USA, stores like Barney's, Neiman Marcus and Saks only sold Burberry raincoats, not the higher profit margin accessories (e.g. handbags, belts, scarves and wraps).

Change of strategy

These problems resulted in profit falls in the 1990s culminating in a £37 million (€53 million) drop in profits to £25 million (€36 million) in 1997. This prompted some serious managerial rethinking and the recruitment of American Rose Marie Bravo as the new chief executive. Responsible for the turnaround of the US store chain Saks Fifth Avenue, she had the necessary experience to make the radical changes required at Burberry.

One of her first moves was to appoint young designer Roberto Menichetti to overhaul the clothes range. His challenge was to redesign Burberry's raincoats and other traditional products to keep them fresh and attractive to new generations of younger consumers. Furthermore, he sought to extend the Burberry image to a new range of products. The Burberry brand name began to appear on such products as children's clothes, personal products, watches, blue jeans, bikinis, homewares and shoes in order to attract new customers and broaden the company's sales base. Commenting on Menichetti, Bravo said, 'Coming in, I had studied Hermes and Gucci and other great brands, and it struck me that even during the periods when they had dipped a bit, they never lost the essence of whatever made those brands sing. And I thought, "This man will retain what's good and move us forward."'

A second element of her strategy was to bring in advertising agency Baron & Baron and celebrity photographer Mario Testino to shoot ads featuring models Kate Moss and Stella Tennant. Other celebrities, such as the Beckhams, Callum Best, Elizabeth Jagger, Nicole Appleton and Jarvis Cocker, have also featured in Burberry advertising. The focus was to emphasize the new credentials of the Burberry brand without casting off its classic roots. Getting key celebrities to don the Burberry check in its advertising was highly important in achieving this.

A third strand in Bravo's strategy was to sort out distribution. Unprofitable shops were closed and an emphasis placed on flagship stores in cosmopolitan cities. Prestige UK retailers including Harvey Nichols have been selected to stock exclusive ranges. Bravo commented, 'We were selling in 20 small shops in Knightsbridge alone, but we weren't in Harrods.' Also, stores that were selling only raincoats were persuaded to stock high-margin accessories as well. Burberry accessories have increased from 20 per cent to 25 per cent of turnover. This is part of a wider focus on gifts—the more affordable side of luxury that can drive heavy footfall through the stores. As Bravo says, 'Burberry has to be thought of as a gift store. Customers have to feel they can go into Burberry and buy gifts at various price points.'

International expansion is also high on Bravo's priority list; 11 new stores were opened in 2002, including flagship stores in London, New York and Barcelona. The New York store on 57th Street was the

Chapter eight Managing Products: Brand and Corporate Identity Management

realization of a personal dream for Bravo, whose vision was to replace the store it had been running in Manhattan for almost 25 years with one that was bigger, better and far more profitable. It is the biggest Burberry store worldwide and has a number of Burberry 'firsts': a lavish gift department, a large area for accessories, private shopping and an in-store Mad Hatters tea room. It also offers a service called Art of the Trench where customers can get made-to-measure trench coats customized by allowing them to pick their own lining, collar, checks and tartan. The Barcelona store was regarded as vital in helping to reposition the Burberry brand in Spain. Prior to its opening the brand was slightly less fashionable and sold at slightly lower prices than in the UK. The opening of the Barcelona store saw the London product being displayed for the first time as Burberry move towards one global offering. Besides the USA and Spain, Burberry's third priority country is Japan since it is an enormous market for the company already. Future expansion will see another 30 stores opening, bringing the chain up to 100 stores worldwide.

The results of this activity have been astonishing. Profits have been on an upward slope, rising to £110 million (€158 million) in 2002–3 from £85 million (€122 million) a year earlier, a 29 per cent increase. Sales rose 19 per cent to £594 million (€855 million) from £499 million (€719 million). In July 2002, Great Universal Stores floated part of Burberry, its subsidiary, on the stock market, raising £275 million (€396 million).

Burberry does face problems, however. One is the weeding out of grey-market goods, which are offered cheaply in Asia only to be diverted back to western markets at discounts. Not only are sales affected but brand image can be tarnished. Like Dior before it, Burberry is willing to spend the necessary money to try to eliminate this activity. Another problem is that of copycats, which infringe its trademark. Burberry claims to spend about £2 million (€2.88 million) a year fighting counterfeits, running advertisements in trade publications and sending letters to trade groups, textile manufacturers and retailers reminding them about its trademark rights. It uses an Internet-monitoring service to help pick up online discussion about counterfeits. It also works with Customs officials and local police forces to seize fakes and sue infringers.

Models and celebrities are used to advertise the Burberry brand.

Questions

1. How were the clothes bearing the Burberry name augmented to create a brand before the 1980s?

2. What elements of the brand-building factors discussed in this chapter have been used by Rose Marie Bravo since 1997 to rebuild the Burberry brand?

3. What problems might arise in trying to build Burberry into a global brand?

4. What are the dangers inherent in Burberry's strategy since 1997?

This case was prepared by David Jobber, Professor of Marketing, University of Bradford, based on: Anonymous (2002) Burberry, *Marketing*, 1 August, 17; Anonymous (2003) Retail Brief—Burberry Group plc, *Wall Street Journal*, 23 May, 6; Heller, R. (2000) A British Gucci, *Forbes*, 3 April, 84–6; Voyle, S. (2002) Looking beyond the Traditional Trench Coat, *Financial Times*, 12 November, 12; White, E. (2003) Protecting the Real Plaid from a Sea of Fakes, *Wall Street Journal*, 7 May, 1.

chapter nine

Managing products: product life cycle, portfolio planning and product growth strategies

"Nothing lasts forever." — ANONYMOUS

Learning Objectives

This chapter explains:

1. The concept of the product life cycle

2. The uses and limitations of the product life cycle

3. The concept of product portfolio planning

4. The Boston Consulting Group Growth-Share Matrix, its uses and associated criticisms

5. The General Electric Market Attractiveness–Competitive Position model, its uses and associated criticisms

6. The contribution of product portfolio planning

7. Product strategies for growth

This chapter examines the application of a number of tools that can be used in the area of strategic product planning. Product lines and brands need to be managed over time. The product life cycle will be discussed as a tool for helping managers with this task. Its uses and limitations will be explored.

Marketing managers also need to manage brand and product line portfolios. Many companies are multi-product, serving multiple markets and segments. Managers need to address the question of where to place investment for product growth and where to withdraw resources. These and other questions will be dealt with in the second part of this chapter, which examines portfolio planning. The uses and criticisms of the Boston Consulting Group Growth-Share Matrix and the General Electric Market Attractiveness–Competitive Position Model will be explored.

Finally, this chapter discusses the Ansoff Matrix as a tool for analysing product strategies for growth. Whereas product portfolio planning focuses on existing sets of products, the Ansoff Matrix also considers new products and new markets as a means to achieve future growth.

Managing product lines and brands over time: the product life cycle

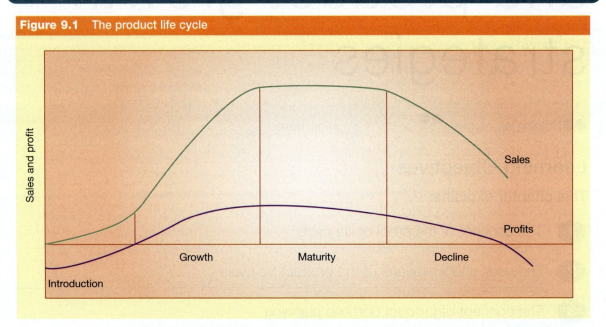

Figure 9.1 The product life cycle

No matter how wide the product mix, both product lines and individual brands need to be managed over time. A useful tool for conceptualizing the changes that may take place during the time that a product is on the market is called the **product life cycle**. It is quite flexible and can be applied to both brands and product lines.[1] For simplicity, in the rest of this chapter, brands and product lines will be referred to as products. We shall now look at the product life cycle, before discussing its uses and limitations.

The classic product life cycle has four stages (see Fig. 9.1): introduction, growth, maturity and decline.

Introduction

When first introduced on to the market a product's sales growth is typically low, and losses are incurred because of heavy development and promotional costs. Companies will be monitoring the speed of product adoption and, if this is disappointing, may terminate the product at this stage. Samsung is one company that invests in new product development to create products that confer new features and benefits for consumers, as the illustration on the next page shows.

Growth

This stage is characterized by a period of faster sales and profit growth. Sales growth is fuelled by rapid market acceptance and, for many products, repeat purchasing. Profits may begin to decline towards the latter stages of growth as new rivals enter the market, attracted by the twin magnets of fast sales growth and high profit potential. The personal computer market was an example of this during the 1980s when sales growth was mirrored by a vast increase in competitors. The end of the growth period is often associated with *competitive shakeout* whereby weaker suppliers cease production. How to survive a shakeout is discussed in Marketing in Action 9.1.

9.1 marketing in action
Surviving a Shakeout

The change from booming growth to a static mature industry can prove traumatic for many companies. The growth phase may have been associated with entrepreneurial drive backed by a strong vision, such as that of Michael Dell who founded Dell Computers Corporation in 1984. With maturity comes the need to put a premium on operational efficiency, a greater sensitivity to customer needs and increased responsiveness to competitor threats For strong, well-positioned companies the looming shakeout provides an opportunity to stabilize the industry and gain market power. For such *adaptive survivors*, there is a need to face three key issues.

1. *Leadership and management style*: survival necessitates the recruitment of talented managers who have experience in large organizations and understand the systematic approach needed to manage a large company. Such a move by Dell Computers changed the orientation from 'growth, growth, growth' to 'liquidity, profitability and growth'.
2. *Resources*: much energy is required to critically evaluate options so that resources are allocated to the most attractive opportunities, and resources withdrawn from past mistakes. For example, Dell Computers invested to increase global sales while withdrawing from retail stores and dropping its failing line of notebook computers.
3. *Controls*: information systems need to be installed to identify such problems as excessive costs, bulging inventories and failure to meet promises to customers.

Smaller, also-ran companies are particularly vulnerable during a shake-out. They need to choose a buffer strategy to provide some protection during the crisis.

- *Market niching*: niches can serve as buffer zones when competitive pressures are not too strong and growth is possible. Managers need to accept a shrinking of aspirations and pruning of operations. Segments where the major companies are underperforming (perhaps because small segment size does not warrant heavy investment) are prime targets.
- *Strategic alliances*: small companies can buffer themselves by forming alliances to pool resources, access expensive assets and increase negotiating power.

If neither of these strategies is viable, then the also-ran company will need to face the decision to sell the company. An early sale may make sense if a buyer can be found who still has an optimistic view of the future. However, patience can be a virtue if the company can survive until prospective buyers have weathered the storm and have gained confidence in their new strategies.

Based on: Day (1997)[2]

Samsung invests in innovation to bring new, exciting products to the marketplace.

Maturity

Eventually sales peak and flatten as saturation occurs, hastening competitive shakeout. The survivors battle for market share by product improvements, advertising and sales promotional offers, dealer discount and price cutting; the result is strain on profit margins particularly for follower brands. The need for effective brand building is acutely recognized during maturity as brand leaders are in the strongest position to resist the pressure on profit margins.[3]

Decline

Sales and profits fall during the decline stages as new technology or changes in consumer tastes work to reduce demand for the product. Suppliers may decide to cease production completely or reduce product depth. Promotional and product development budgets may be slashed and marginal distributors dropped as suppliers seek to maintain (or increase) profit margins.

Uses of the product life cycle

The product life cycle (PLC) concept is useful for product management in several ways, as described below.

Product termination

First, the PLC emphasizes the fact that nothing lasts forever. There is a danger that management may fall in love with certain products. Maybe a company was founded on the success of a particular product; perhaps the product champion of a past success is now the chief executive. Under such circumstances there can be emotional ties with the product that can transcend normal commercial considerations. The PLC underlines the fact that companies have to face the fact that products need to be terminated and new products developed to replace

Table 9.1 Marketing objectives and strategies over the product life cycle

	Introduction	Growth	Maturity	Decline
Strategic marketing objective	Build	Build	Hold	Harvest/manage for cash/divest
Strategic focus	Expand market	Penetration	Protect share/innovation	Productivity
Brand objective	Product awareness/trial	Brand preference	Brand loyalty	Brand exploitation
Products	Basic	Differentiated	Differentiated	Rationalized
Promotion	Creating awareness/trial	Creating awareness/trial/repeat purchase	Maintaining awareness/repeat purchase	Cut/eliminated
Price	High	Lower	Lowest	Rising
Distribution	Patchy	Wider	Intensive	Selective

them. Without this sequence a company may find itself with a group of products all in the decline stage of their PLC.

Growth projections

The second use of the PLC concept is to warn against the dangers of assuming that growth will continue forever. Swept along by growing order books, management can fall into the trap of believing that the heady days of rising sales and profits will continue forever. The PLC reminds managers that growth will end, and suggests a need for caution when planning investment in new production facilities.

Marketing objectives and strategies over the PLC

The PLC emphasizes the need to review marketing objectives and strategies as products pass through the various stages. Changes in market and competitive conditions between the PLC stages suggests that marketing strategies should be adapted to meet them. Table 9.1 shows a set of stylized marketing responses to each stage. Note that these are broad generalizations rather than exact prescriptions but they do serve to emphasize the need to review marketing objectives and strategies in the light of environmental change.

Introduction

The strategic marketing objective is to build sales by expanding the market for the product. The brand objective will be to create product (as well as brand) awareness so that customers will become familiar with generic product benefits.

The marketing task facing pioneer video recorder producers was to gain awareness of the general benefits of the video recorder (e.g. convenient viewing through time-switching, viewing programmes that are broadcast when out of the house) so that the market for video recorders in general would expand. The product is likely to be fairly basic, with an emphasis on reliability and functionality rather than special features to appeal to different customer groups. Promotion will support the brand objectives by gaining awareness for the brand and product type, and stimulating trial. Advertising has been found to be more effective in the beginning of the life of a product than in later stages.[4] Typically price will be high because of the heavy development costs and the low level of competition. Distribution will be patchy as some dealers are wary of stocking the new product until it has proved to be successful in the marketplace.

Growth

The strategic marketing objective during the growth phase is to build sales and market share. The strategic focus will be to penetrate the market by building brand preference. To accomplish this task the product will be redesigned to create differentiation, and promotion will stress the functional and/or psychological benefits that accrue from the differentiation. Awareness and trial are still important but promotion will begin to focus on repeat purchasers. As development costs are defrayed and competition increases, prices will fall. Rising consumer demand and increased salesforce effort will widen distribution.

Maturity

As sales peak and stabilize the strategic marketing objective will be to hold on to profits and sales by protecting market share rather than embark on costly competitive challenges. Since sales gains can only be at the expense of competition, strong challenges are likely to be resisted and lead to costly promotional or price wars. Brand objectives now focus on maintaining brand

9.2 marketing in action

Mobile Marketing Strategies in a Mature Market

The mobile phone market in western Europe has reached saturation. For example, eight out of ten people in the UK aged between 12 and 74 now own a mobile phone. This means that mobile phone companies now operate in a mature market. No longer can profits be fuelled by explosive growth; instead attention has turned to competing for a relatively fixed market of consumers. This has meant a move from customer acquisition to retention, attempts to increase usage rates and lower repeat purchase periods, and heavy investments in innovation. It has also resulted in a period of rationalization as weaker players like Ericsson have significantly reduced costs in an effort to survive. Even the market leader, Nokia, has admitted that it has reached that stage in the product life cycle where a degree of retrenchment and consolidation is needed.

Increased usage of mobile phones has been stimulated by SMS (short message service). This allows consumers to send short text messages at relatively low cost. T-mobile, for example, has encouraged increased usage of its handsets by advertising campaigns using the strapline 'Get more text'.

Nokia is the leader in reducing repeat purchase periods by making mobile phones a fashion accessory. By introducing new, modified, models with desirable design and colour features, the company has encouraged owners to repeat buy on average every 19 months in the UK.

The aim of technological innovation has been to stimulate upgrading. Unfortunately, the first major innovation, Wireless Access Protocol (WAP), which was intended to allow Internet access from mobiles, proved irritatingly cumbersome and failed to attract customers. Multimedia messaging service (MMS) was the next innovation, which by offering consumers the ability to customize text messages with colour pictures and sound has proved more effective in encouraging upgrading.

The big investment has been in 3G technology, for which UK telecommunications companies have invested £22 billion (€32 billion) in licences alone. Technical problems caused delays to the launch but the potential of such features as high-speed data communications, full multimedia messaging with sound and colour, live video streaming and videoconference calls, and a faster, 'always on', wireless Internet service provide a powerful incentive to upgrade.

The maturity stage of the product life cycle may suggest a period of tranquillity for incumbent companies, but competitive and economic forces mean that they face a demanding and volatile marketplace.

Based on: Chandiramani (2002);[5] Cotton and Singh (2003);[6] Keegan (2003);[7] Malkani (2002)[8]

Chapter nine Managing Products: Life Cycle, Portfolio Planning, Growth Strategies

Cathay Pacific promotes the brand values of comfort and provision of high-level facilities for its business-class customers.

loyalty, and promotion will defend the brand stimulating repeat purchase by maintaining brand awareness and values. The illustration for Cathay Pacific shows how the airline promotes its brand values in a mature market. For all but the brand leader, competition may erode prices and profit margins, while distribution will peak in line with sales.

A key focus will be innovation to extend the maturity stage or, preferably, inject growth. This may take the form of innovative promotional campaigns, product improvements, and extensions and technological innovation. Ways of increasing usage and reducing repeat purchase periods of the product will also be sought. Marketing in Action 9.2 shows how mobile phone manufacturers and operators are seeking to revitalize sales in a mature market.

Decline

Falling sales may tempt some companies to raise prices and slash marketing expenditures in an effort to bolster profit margins. The strategic focus, therefore, will be on improving marketing productivity rather than holding or building sales. The brand loyalty that has built up over the years will in effect be exploited to create profits that can be channelled elsewhere in the company (e.g. new products). Product development will cease, the product line depth will be reduced to the bare minimum of brands and the promotional expenditure cut, possibly to zero. Distribution costs will be analysed with a view to selecting only the most profitable outlets. Product elimination is likely as non-viable sales levels are encountered. Many product elimination decisions are based on intuition and judgement rather than formalized analysis.[9]

It is worth noting that the Internet has the capacity to extend the life cycle of many products. Since it is a low-cost global sales channel it can be used to extend the life of products that are in decline, as e-Marketing 9.1 explains.

Product planning

The PLC emphasizes the need for *product planning*. We have already discussed the need to replace old products with new. The PLC also stresses the need to analyse the balance of products that a company markets from the point of view of the PLC stages. A company with all of its products in the mature stage may be generating profits today, but as it enters the decline stage, profits may fall and the company become unprofitable. A nicely balanced product array would see the company marketing some products in the mature stage of the PLC, a number in the growth stage, with the prospect of new product launches in the near future. The growth products would replace the mature products as the latter enter decline, and the new product successes would eventually become the growth products of the future. The PLC is, then, a stimulus to thinking about products as an interrelated set of profit-bearing assets that need to

9.1 e-marketing

The Internet Extends the Product Life Cycle Curve

The Internet has the ability to prolong the life cycle of a company's products. Virtually every product is still available online. For example, a search on Google for a Betamax video (a video technology that is now more than 20 years old), will reveal several sites that still sell or maintain them.

The Internet is a cost-effective channel for companies phasing out 'old' products, and can allow companies to sustain main and spare part production, many years into the future.

The Internet provides companies with a worldwide sales channel, allowing ordering and fulfilment to be focused through a global website rather than using more costly individual country agents and dealerships. The rising costs of order and fulfilment, in the latter stages of the product life cycle, may force companies to cease production. Consider that OKI uses its regional websites (http://europe.oki.com) to extend the product life cycle of its dot matrix printer range.

E-marketplaces can also be used as a mechanism to sell old products and components. Sites like eBay (www.ebay.com) and Dabs.com (www.dabs.com) are online resources allowing companies, and private individuals, to sell 'older' products and parts.

Finally, the Internet is an ideal means of building a *community of interest*; websites arise based around 'product communities'. Many are independent of the manufacturer. They provide, among other things, information on part sourcing and self-maintenance techniques. Sites like Palsite (http://www.palsite.com/home.html) (for old video technologies) provide an example of this phenomenon.

be managed as a group. We shall return to this theme when discussing product portfolio analysis later in this chapter.

The dangers of overpowering

The PLC concept highlights the dangers of overpowering. A company that introduces a new-to-the-world product may find itself in a very powerful position early in its product life cycle. Assuming that the new product confers unique benefits to customers there is an opportunity to charge a very high price during this period of monopoly supply. However, unless the product is patent-protected this strategy can turn sour when competition enters during the growth phase (as predicted by the PLC concept). This situation arose for the small components manufacturer that was the first to solve the technical problems associated with developing a seal in an exhaust recirculation valve used to reduce pollution in car emissions. The company took advantage of its monopoly supply position to charge very high prices to Ford. The strategy rebounded when competition entered and Ford discovered it had been overcharged.[10] Had the small manufacturer been aware of the predictions of the PLC concept it may have anticipated competitive entry during the growth phase, and charged a lower price during introduction and early growth. This would have enabled it to begin a relationship-building exercise with Ford, possibly leading to greater returns in the long run.

Limitations of the product life cycle

The product life cycle is an aid to thinking about marketing decisions, but it needs to be handled with care. Management needs to be aware of the limitations of the PLC so that it is not misled by its prescriptions.

Fads and classics

Not all products follow the classic S-shaped curve. The sales of some products 'rise like a rocket then fall like a stick'. This is normal for *fad* products such as skateboards, which saw phenomenal sales growth followed by a rapid sales collapse as the youth market moved on to another craze.

Other products (and brands) appear to defy entering the decline stage. For example, classic confectionery products and brands such as Mars bars, Cadbury's Milk Tray and Toblerone have survived for decades in the mature stage of the PLC. Nevertheless, research has shown that the classic S-shaped curve does apply to a wide range of products, including grocery food products, pharmaceuticals and cigarettes.[11]

Marketing effects

The PLC is the *result* of marketing activities not the cause. One school of thought argues that the PLC is not simply a fact of life—unlike living organisms—but is simply a pattern of sales that reflects marketing activity.[12] Clearly, sales of a product may flatten or fall simply because it has not received enough marketing attention, or has had insufficient product redesign or promotional support. Using the PLC, argue the critics, may lead to inappropriate action (e.g. harvesting or dropping the product) when the correct response should be increased marketing support (e.g. product replacement, positioning reinforcement or repositioning).

Unpredictability

The duration of the PLC stages is unpredictable. The PLC outlines the four stages that a product passes through without defining their duration. Clearly this limits its use as a forecasting tool since it is not possible to predict when maturity or decline will begin. The exception to this problem is when it is possible to identify a comparator product that serves as a template for predicting the length of each stage. Two sources of comparator products exist: first, countries where the same product has already been on the market for some time; second, where similar products are in the mature or decline stages of their life cycle but are thought to resemble the new product in terms of consumer acceptance. In practice, the use of comparator products is fraught with problems. For example, the economic and social conditions of countries may be so different that simplistic exploitation of the PLC from one country to another may be invalid; the use of similar products may offer inaccurate predictions in the face of ever-shortening product life cycles.

Misleading objective and strategy prescriptions

The stylized marketing objectives and strategy prescriptions may be misleading. Even if a product could accurately be classified as being in a PLC stage, and sales are not simply a result of marketing activities, the critics argue that the stylized marketing objectives and strategy prescriptions can be misleading. For example, there can be circumstances where the appropriate marketing objective in the growth stage is to harvest (e.g. in the face of intense competition), in the mature stage to build (e.g. when a distinct, defensive differential advantage can be developed), and in the decline stage to build (e.g. when there is an opportunity to dominate).

An example of the last strategy is the UK cinema market. Cinemas were clearly in the decline stage of their product life cycle with attendances falling over a period of many years as other evening leisure pursuits gained ground (e.g. restaurants, sports halls, television). The

9.3 marketing in action

Turnaround Strategies in the Decline Stage

The usual prescription for products in the decline stage is to harvest or divest. Nevertheless there can be circumstances where building can be successful. The first example is Skoda, which was in decline until Volkswagen acquired the company. Its build strategy focused on revamping the design and quality of the cars. The negative image of Skoda in the UK meant that a communications campaign that simply highlighted the quality and better features of the car failed. Only when a self-deprecating, humorous campaign targeting those people who rejected Skoda as a credible brand was introduced did Skoda engage consumers' emotions and win the right to be re-evaluated by them.

Seeboard Energy is another example of building in the face of decline. Deregulation of the utilities market created new competitors for the company, which had previously held a monopoly in the distribution of electricity in the south-east of England. Research discovered that one of the problems was that consumers perceived the company as just another big, slow, utility company. The reality, though, was that it was a quite innovative company staffed with young forward-looking people. The build strategy focused on the company's money-saving initiatives underpinned by an advertising campaign that employed the strapline 'relentlessly finding new ways to save you money'. Seeboard Energy delivered on this promise by introducing money-saving methods for consumers and holding its prices at a time when most other energy companies were raising theirs. This was backed up by a major internal training programme to sell the strategy to staff.

Both of these examples (and the earlier example of the revitalization of cinema) show that building in decline is possible so long as the product on offer is appealing to consumers. In the case of Skoda (and cinema), massive investment was needed to put the product right. With Seeboard Energy communication was used to correct misconceptions. What is needed is to understand the fundamental truth about a company or brand. In Skoda's case it was based on a product that exceeded consumer expectations; in Seeboard Energy's case it was based on the fact that they were innovators in the energy market. The Skoda case, also, shows that communicating rational facts may be insufficient: what is needed is to engage with consumers emotionally.

Campaigns that provide an emotional response such as laughter, happiness, joy or tears are often far more powerful than the simple presentation of facts.

Based on: Thatcher (2002)[13]

response of cinema owners was to rationalize (close cinemas) and reduce investment in those that survived to a minimum: a classic harvesting approach. However, one company saw this scenario as a marketing opportunity. Showcase Cinemas were launched during the 1980s offering a choice of around 12 films in modern purpose-built cinemas (with their own car park) near large conurbations. The result was an upturn in cinema attendance (and profits) as customers valued the experience of visiting the convenient upgraded facilities and wide choice of films much more than the old cinema concept. Thus the classic PLC prescription of harvesting in the decline stage was rejected by a company that was willing to invest in order to reposition cinemas as an attractive means of offering evening entertainment. Marketing in Action 9.3 describes two other examples of how decline was arrested.

A summary of the usefulness of the product life cycle concept

Like many marketing tools, the product life cycle should not be viewed as a panacea to marketing thinking and decision-making but as an aid to managerial judgement. By emphasizing the changes that are likely to occur as a product is marketed over time, the concept is a valuable stimulus to strategic thinking. Yet as a prescriptive tool it is blunt. Marketing management must monitor the real-life changes that are happening in the marketplace before setting precise objectives and strategies.

Managing brand and product line portfolios

So far in this chapter we have treated the management of products as separate, distinct and independent entities. However, many companies are multi-product, serving multiple markets and segments. Some of these products will be strong, others weak. Some will require investment to finance their growth, others will generate more cash than they need. Somehow companies must decide how to distribute their limited resources among the competing needs of products so as to achieve the best performance for the company as a whole. Specifically within a product line, management needs to decide which brands to invest in or hold, or from which to withdraw support. Similarly within the product mix, decisions regarding which product lines to build or hold, or from which to withdraw support need to be taken. Managers that focus on individual products often miss the bigger picture that helps ensure the company's entire portfolio of products fits together coherently rather than being a loose confederation of offerings that has emerged out of a series of uncoordinated historical decisions.[14]

Clearly, these are strategic decisions since they shape where and with what brands/product lines a company competes and how its resources should be deployed. Furthermore these decisions are complex because many factors (e.g. current and future sales and profit potential,

9.4 marketing in action

Portfolio Planning to the Core

The composition of a campaign's product portfolio is a vital issue for marketers. Few companies have the luxury of starting with a clean sheet and creating a well-balanced set of products. An assessment of the strengths and weaknesses of the current portfolio is therefore necessary before taking the strategic decisions of which ones to build, hold, harvest or divest.

Major multinationals like Nestlé, Diageo, Procter & Gamble and Unilever constantly review their product portfolios to achieve their strategic objectives. The trend has been to focus on core brands and product categories, and to divest minor, peripheral brands.

Nestlé, for example, has put up for sale some of its best-known British brands as it focuses on key product categories where it can establish and maintain leadership. The brands for sale are Crosse & Blackwell, which includes Branston Pickle and Waistline salad dressing, Gale's honey, Sarson's vinegar, Rowntree's Jelly and Sun-Pat peanut butter. The focus is on the core categories of beverages, confectionery, chilled dairy, milks and nutrition. In line with this strategy, Nestlé has bought the Ski and Munch Bunch dairy brands from Northern Foods. This will give Nestlé a UK business unit with sales of £125 million (€180 million) and a 13 per cent share of the chilled dairy market, propelling it into the number-two position behind Müller.

One advantage of this strategy is to enable maximum firepower to be put behind the core brands. This is the reason Carlsberg-Tetley is dropping minor brands to concentrate its marketing budget on Carlsberg, Carlsberg Export and Tetley beer. Diageo has also consolidated its product portfolio with the sale of Cinzano to Campari. All of these moves are designed to create a product portfolio that can be taken forward to create maximum shareholder value.

Based on: Benady (2002);[15] Mason (2002);[16] Shah (2002);[17] Singh (2002)[18]

cash flow) can affect the outcome. The process of managing groups of brands and product lines is called portfolio planning.

Key decisions regarding portfolio planning involve decisions regarding the choice of which brands/product lines to build, hold, harvest or divest. Marketing in Action 9.4 discusses several companies' approaches to portfolio planning.

In order to get to grips with the complexities of decision-making, two methods have received wide publicity. These are the Boston Consulting Group Growth-Share Matrix and the General Electric Market Attractiveness–Competitive Position portfolio evaluation models. Like the product life cycle these are very flexible tools and can be used at both the brand and product line levels. Indeed, corporate planners can also use them when making resource allocation decisions at the strategic business unit level.

The Boston Consulting Group Growth-Share Matrix

A leading management consultancy, the Boston Consulting Group (BCG), developed the well-known BCG Growth-Share Matrix (see Fig. 9.2). The matrix allows portfolios of products to be depicted in a 2 × 2 box, the axes of which are based on market growth rate and relative market share. The following discussion will be based on an analysis at the product line level.

Market growth rate forms the vertical axis and indicates the annual growth rate of the market in which each product line operates. In Fig. 9.2 it is shown as 0–15 per cent although a different range could be used, depending on economic conditions, for example. In this example the dividing line between high and low growth rates is considered to be 7 per cent. Market growth rate is used as a proxy for market attractiveness.

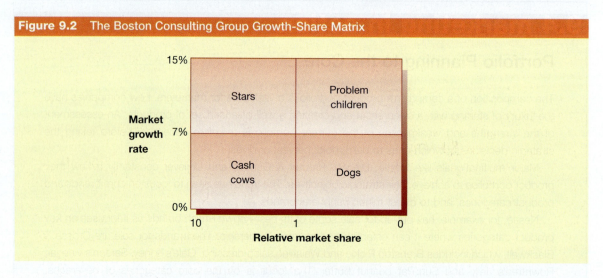

Figure 9.2 The Boston Consulting Group Growth-Share Matrix

Relative market share is shown on the horizontal axis and refers to the market share of each product relative to its largest competitor. It acts as a proxy for competitive strength. The division between high and low market share is 1. Above this figure a product line has a market share greater than its largest competitor. For example, if our product had a market share of 40 per cent and our largest competitor's share was 30 per cent this would be indicated as 1.33 on the horizontal axis. Below 1 we have a share less than the largest competitor. For example, if our share was 20 per cent and the largest competitor had a share of 40 per cent our score would be 0.5.

The Boston Consulting Group argued that cash flow is dependent on the box in which a product falls. Note that cash flow is not the same as profitability. Profits add to cash flow but heavy investment in such assets as plant, equipment and marketing capital can mean that a company can make profits and yet have a negative cash flow.

Stars are likely to be profitable because they are market leaders but require substantial investment to finance growth (e.g. new production facilities) and to meet competitive challenges. Overall cash flow is therefore likely to be roughly in balance. *Problem children* are products in high-growth markets, which cause a drain on cash flow, but these are low-share products; consequently they are unlikely to be profitable. Overall, then, they are big cash users. *Cash cows* are market leaders in mature (low-growth) markets. High market share leads to high profitability and low market growth means that investment in new production facilities is minimal. This leads to a large positive cash flow. *Dogs* also operate in low-growth markets but have low market share. Except for some products near the dividing line between cash cows and dogs (sometimes called *cash dogs*) most dogs produce low or negative cash flows. Relating to their position in the product life cycle, they are the also-rans in mature or declining markets.

What are the strategic implications of the BCG analysis? It can be used for setting strategic objectives and for maintaining a balanced product portfolio.

Guidelines for setting strategic objectives

Having plotted the position of each product on the matrix, a company can begin to think about setting the appropriate strategic objective for each line. As you may recall from Chapter 2, there are four possible strategic objectives: build, hold, harvest and divest. Figure 9.3 shows how each relates to the star, problem children, cash cow and dog categories. However, it should be emphasized that the BCG matrix provides guidelines for strategic thinking and should not be seen as a replacement for managerial judgement.

Figure 9.3 Strategic objectives and the 'Boston box'

Stars	Problem children
Build sales and/or market share	*Build* selectively
Invest to maintain/increase leadership position	Focus on defendable niche where dominance can be achieved
Repel competitive challenges	*Harvest* or *divest* the rest

Cash cows	Dogs
Hold sales and/or market share	*Harvest* or
Defend position	*Divest* or
Use excess cash to support stars, selected problem children and new product development	Focus on defendable niche

- *Stars*: these are the market leaders in high-growth markets. They are already successful and the prospects for further growth are good. As we have seen when discussing brand building, market leaders tend to have the highest profitability so the appropriate strategic objective is to build sales and/or market share. Resources should be invested to maintain/increase the leadership position. Competitive challenges should be repelled. These are the cash cows of the future and need to be protected.

- *Problem children*: as we have seen these are cash drains because they have low profitability and need investment to keep up with market growth. They are called problem children because management has to consider whether it is sensible to continue the required investment. The company faces a fundamental choice: to increase investment (*build*) to attempt to turn the problem child into a star, or to withdraw support by either *harvesting* (raising price while lowering marketing expenditure) or *divesting* (dropping or selling it). In a few cases, a third option may be viable: to find a small market segment (*niche*) where dominance can be achieved. Unilever, for example, identified its speciality chemicals business as a problem child. It realized that it had to invest heavily or exit. Its decision was to sell and invest the billions raised in predicted future winners such as personal care, dental products and fragrances.[19]

- *Cash cows*: the high profitability and low investment associated with high market share in low-growth markets mean that cash cows should be defended. Consequently the appropriate strategic objective is to *hold* sales and market share. The excess cash that is generated should be used to fund stars, problem children that are being built, and research and development for new products.

- *Dogs*: dogs are weak products that compete in low-growth markets. They are the also-rans that have failed to achieve market dominance during the growth phase and are floundering in maturity. For those products that achieve second or third position in the marketplace (*cash dogs*) a small positive cash flow may result, and for a few others it may be possible to reposition the product into a defendable *niche* (as Rover has attempted since the late 1980s). But for the bulk of dogs the appropriate strategic objective is to *harvest* to generate a positive cash flow for a time, or to *divest*, which allows resources and managerial time to be focused elsewhere.

Maintaining a balanced product portfolio

Once all of the company's products have been plotted, it is easy to see how many stars, problem children, cash cows and dogs are in the portfolio. Figure 9.4 shows a product portfolio that is unbalanced. The company possesses only one star and the small circle indicates that sales revenue generated from the star is small. Similarly the two cash cows are also low revenue earners. In contrast the company owns four dogs and four problem children. The portfolio is unbalanced because there are too many problem children and dogs, and not enough stars and

Figure 9.4 The case of an unbalanced product portfolio

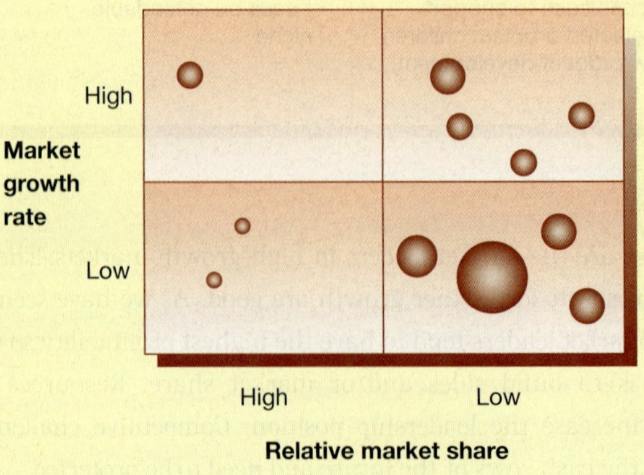

cash cows. What many companies in this situation do is to spread what little surplus cash is available equally between the products in the growth markets.[20] To do so would leave each with barely enough money to maintain market share, leading to a vicious circle of decline.

The BCG remedy would be to conduct a detailed competitive assessment of the four problem children and select one or two for investment. The rest should be harvested (and the cash channelled to those that are being built) or divested. The aim is to build the existing star (which will be the cash cow of the future) and to build the market share of the chosen problem children so that they attain star status.

The dogs also need to be analysed. One of them (the large circle) is a large revenue earner, which despite low profits may be making a substantial contribution to overheads. Another product (on the left) appears to be in the cash dog situation. But for the other two, the most sensible strategic objective may be to harvest or divest.

Criticisms of the BCG Growth-Share Matrix

The simplicity, ease of use and importance of the issues tackled by the BCG Matrix saw its adoption by a host of North American and European companies that wanted to get a handle on the complexities of strategic resource allocation. But the tool has also attracted a litany of criticism.[21] The following list draws together many of the points raised by its critics.

1. The assumption that cash flow will be determined by a product's position in the matrix is weak. For example, some stars will show a healthy positive cash flow (e.g. IBM PCs during the growth phase of the PC market) as will some dogs in markets where competitive activity is low.

2. The preoccupation of focusing on market share and market growth rates distracts managerial attention from the fundamental principle in marketing: attaining a sustainable competitive advantage.

3. Treating the market growth rate as a proxy for market attractiveness, and market share as an indicator of competitive strength is oversimplistic. There are many other factors that have to be taken into account when measuring market attractiveness (e.g. market size, strengths and weaknesses of competitors) and competitive strengths (e.g. exploitable marketing assets, potential cost advantages), besides market growth rates and market share.

4. Since the position of a product in the matrix depends on market share, this can lead to an unhealthy preoccupation with market share gain. In some circumstances this objective makes sense (for example, brand building) but when competitive retaliation is likely the costs of share building may outweigh the gains.

5. The matrix ignores interdependencies between products. For example, a dog may need to be marketed because it complements a star or a cash cow. For example, the dog may be a spare part for a star or a cash cow. Alternatively, customers and distributors may value dealing with a company that supplies a full product line. For these reasons, dropping products because they fall into a particular box may be naive.

6. The classic BCG Matrix prescription is to build stars because they will become the cash cows of the future. However, some products have a very short product life cycle, in which case the appropriate strategy should be to maximize profits and cash flow while in the star category (e.g. fashion goods).

7. Marketing objectives and strategy are heavily dependent on an assessment of what competitors are likely to do. How will they react if we lower or raise prices when

implementing a build or harvest strategy, for example? This is not considered in the matrix.

8. The matrix assumes that products are self-funding. For example, selected problem children are built using cash generated by cash cows. But this ignores capital markets, which may mean that a wider range of projects can be undertaken so long as they have positive net present values of their future cash flows.

9. The matrix is vague regarding the definition of 'market'. Should we take the whole market (e.g. for confectionery) or just the market segment that we operate in (e.g. expensive boxed chocolates)? The matrix is also vague when defining the dividing line between high- and low-growth markets. A chemical company that tends to generate in lower-growth markets might use 3 per cent, whereas a leisure goods company whose markets on average experience much higher rates of growth might use 10 per cent. Also, over what period do we define market growth? These issues question the theoretical soundness of the underlying concepts, and allow managers to manipulate the figures so that their products fall in the right boxes.

10. The matrix was based on cash flow but perhaps profitability (e.g. return on investment) is a better criterion for allocating resources.

11. The matrix lacks precision in identifying which problem children to build, harvest or drop.

General Electric Market Attractiveness–Competitive Position model

As we have already noted, the BCG Matrix enjoyed tremendous success as management grappled with the complex issue of strategic resource allocation. Stimulated by this success and some of the weaknesses of the model (particularly the criticism of its oversimplicity) McKinsey & Co developed a more wide-ranging Market Attractiveness–Competitive Position (MA–CP) model in conjunction with General Electric (GE) in the USA.

Market attractiveness criteria

Instead of market growth alone, a range of market attractiveness criteria were used, such as:

- market size
- market growth rate
- strength of competition
- profit potential
- social, political and legal factors.

Competitive strength criteria

Similarly, instead of using only market share as a measure of competitive strength, a number of factors were used, such as:

- market share
- potential to develop a differential advantage
- opportunities to develop cost advantages
- reputation
- distribution capabilities.

Weighting the criteria

Management was allowed to decide which criteria were applicable for their products. This gave the MA–CP model flexibility. Having decided the criteria, management would then agree upon a weighting system for each set of criteria, with those factors that were more important having a higher weighting. For example, management might decide upon the weights shown in Table 9.2 (which sum to 1.0).

Table 9.2 An example of a weighting system

Market attractiveness

Market size	0.15
Market growth rate	0.20
Strength of competition	0.30
Profit potential	0.30
Social, political and legal factors	0.05
	1.00

Competitive strengths

Market share	0.20
Differential advantage	0.40
Cost advantages	0.05
Reputation	0.10
Distribution capabilities	0.25
	1.00

Each market attractiveness factor is then scored out of 10 (on a scale where 1 denotes 'unattractive' and 10 denotes 'very attractive') to reflect how each product rates on that factor. Similarly, each competitive strength factor is scored out of 10 (on a scale where 1 denotes 'very weak' and 10 denotes 'very strong'). Each score is multiplied by the factor weight and summed to obtain overall market attractiveness and competitive strength scores for each product. These can then be plotted on the MA–CP matrix.

Setting strategic objectives

The model is shown in Fig. 9.5. Like the BCG Matrix the recommendations for setting strategic objectives are dependent on the product's position on the grid. Five zones are shown in Fig. 9.5. The strategic objectives associated with each zone are as follows.[22]

- *Zone 1*: build—manage for sales and market share growth as the market is attractive and competitive strengths are high (equivalent to star products).

- *Zone 2*: hold—manage for profits consistent with maintaining market share as the market is not particularly attractive but competitive strengths are high (equivalent to cash cows).

Figure 9.5 The General Electric Market Attractiveness–Competitive Position model

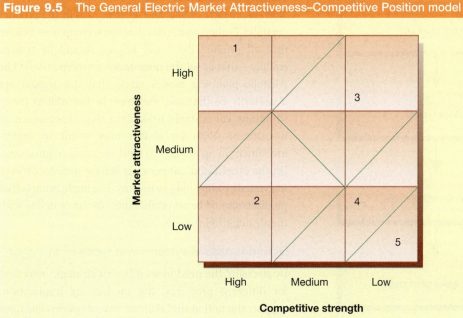

- *Zone 3*: build/hold/harvest—this is the question-mark zone. Where competitors are weak or passive, a build strategy will be used. In the face of strong competitors a hold strategy may be appropriate, or harvesting where commitment to the product/market is lower. (Similar to problem children.)
- *Zone 4*: harvest—manage for cash as both market attractiveness and competitive strengths are fairly low.
- *Zone 5*: divest—improve short-term cash yield by dropping or selling the product (equivalent to dog products).

Criticisms of the GE portfolio model

The proponents of the GE portfolio model argue that the analysis is much richer than BCG analysis—due to more factors being taken into account—and flexible. Critics argue, however, that it is harder to use than the BCG Matrix since it requires managerial agreement on which factors to use, their weightings and scoring. Furthermore, its flexibility provides a lot of opportunity for managerial bias to enter the analysis whereby product managers argue for factors and weightings that show their products in a good light (zone 1). This last point suggests that the analysis should be conducted at a managerial level higher than that being assessed. For example, decisions on which product lines to be built, held, and so on, should be taken at the strategic business unit level, and allocations of resources to brands should be decided at the group product manager level.

The contribution of product portfolio planning

Despite the limitations of the BCG and the GE portfolio evaluation models, both have made a contribution to the practice of portfolio planning. We shall now discuss this contribution and suggest how the models can usefully be incorporated into product strategy.

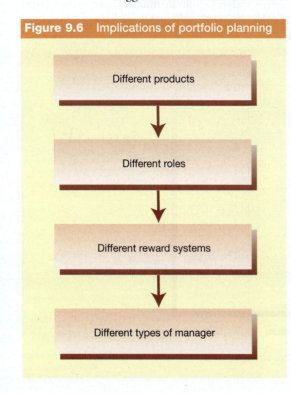

Figure 9.6 Implications of portfolio planning

Different products and different roles

The models emphasize the important strategic point that *different products should have different roles* in the product portfolio. Hedley points out that some companies believe that all product lines and brands should be treated equally—that is, set the same profit requirements.[23] The portfolio planning models stress that this should not necessarily be the case, and may be harmful in many situations. For example, to ask for a 20 per cent return on investment (ROI) for a star may result in under-investment in an attempt to meet the profit requirement. On the other hand, 20 per cent ROI for a cash cow or a harvested product may be too low. The implication is that products should be set profitability objectives in line with the strategic objective decisions.

Different reward systems and types of manager

By stressing the need to set different strategic objectives for different products, the models, by implication, support the notion that *different reward systems and types of manager* should be linked to them. For example, managers of products being built should be marketing led, and rewarded for improving sales and market share. Conversely, managers of harvested (and to some extent cash cow) products should be more cost orientated, and rewarded by profit and cash flow achievement (see Fig. 9.6).

Aid to managerial judgement

Managers may find it useful to plot their products on both the BCG and GE portfolio grids as an initial step in pulling together the complex issues involved in product portfolio planning. This can help them get a handle on the situation and issues to be resolved. The models can then act as an *aid to managerial judgement* without in any way supplanting that judgement. Managers should feel free to bring into the discussion any other factors they feel are not adequately covered by the models. The models can therefore be seen as an aid to strategic thinking in multi-product, multi-market companies.

Product strategies for growth

The emphasis in product portfolio analysis is on managing an *existing* set of products in such a way as to maximize their strengths, but companies also need to look to new products and markets for future growth. The Dyson DC08 (see illustration) is an example of a new product that is an addition to an existing line.

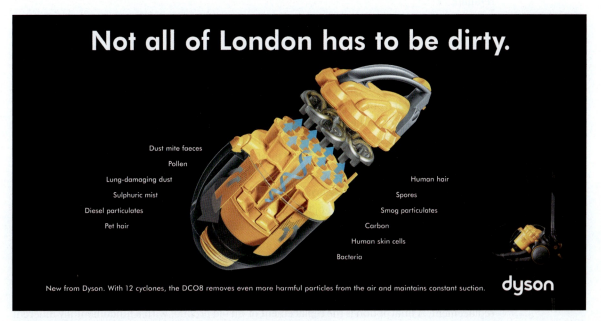

An innovative addition to the Dyson vacuum cleaner product line.

A useful way of looking at growth opportunities is the Ansoff Matrix, as shown in Fig. 9.7.[24] By combining present and new products, and present and new markets into a 2×2 matrix, four product strategies for growth are revealed. Although the Ansoff Matrix does not prescribe when each strategy should be employed, it is a useful framework for thinking about the ways in which growth can be achieved through product strategy.

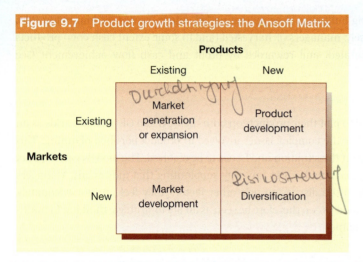

Figure 9.7 Product growth strategies: the Ansoff Matrix

Figure 9.8 shows how the Ansoff Matrix can be used to implement a growth strategy.

The most basic method of gaining **market penetration** in existing markets with current products is by *winning competitors' customers*. This may be achieved by more effective use of promotion or distribution, or by cutting prices. Increasing promotional expenditure is another method of winning competitors' customers, as Cadbury Schweppes did by increasing expenditure by 87 per cent over a four-year period.25 Another way of gaining market penetration is to *buy competitors*. This achieves an immediate increase in market share and sales volume. To protect the penetration already gained in a market, a business may consider methods of *discouraging competitive entry*. *Barriers* can be created by cost advantages (lower labour costs, access to raw materials, economies of scale), highly differentiated products, high switching costs (the costs of changing from existing supplier to a new supplier, for example), and displaying aggressive tendencies to retaliate.

A company may attempt **market expansion** in a market that it already serves by converting *non-users to users* of its product. This can be an attractive option in new markets when non-users form a sizeable segment and may be willing to try the product given suitable inducements. Thus when Carnation entered the powdered coffee whitening market with Coffeemate, a key success factor was its ability to persuade hitherto non-users of powdered whiteners to switch from milk. Lapsed users can also be targeted. Kellogg's has targeted lapsed breakfast cereal users (fathers) who rediscover the pleasure of eating cornflakes when feeding their children. Market expansion can also be achieved by *increasing usage rate*. Colman's attempted to increase the use of mustard by showing new combinations of mustard and food. Kellogg's has also tried to increase the usage (eating) rate of its cornflakes by promoting eating in the evening as well as at breakfast.

The **product development** option involves the development of new products for existing markets.26 One variant is to *extend existing product lines* to give current customers greater choice. When new features are added (with an accompanying price rise) trading up may occur, with customers buying the enhanced-value product on repurchase. *Product replacement* activities involve the replacement of old brands/models with new ones. This is common in the car market and often involves an upgrading of the old model with a new (more expensive) replacement. A final option is the replacement of an old product with a fundamentally different one, often based on technology change. The business thus replaces an old product with an *innovation* (although both may be marketed side by side for a time). The development of the compact disc (CD) is an example.

Market development entails the promotion of *new uses of existing products to new customers*, or the marketing of *existing products (and their current uses) to new market segments*. The promotion of new uses accounted for the growth in sales of nylon, which was first marketed as a replacement for silk in parachutes but expanded into shirts, carpets, tyres, etc. Market development through entering new segments could involve the search for overseas opportunities. Andy Thornton Ltd, an interior design business, successfully increased sales by

Figure 9.8 Strategic options for increasing sales volume

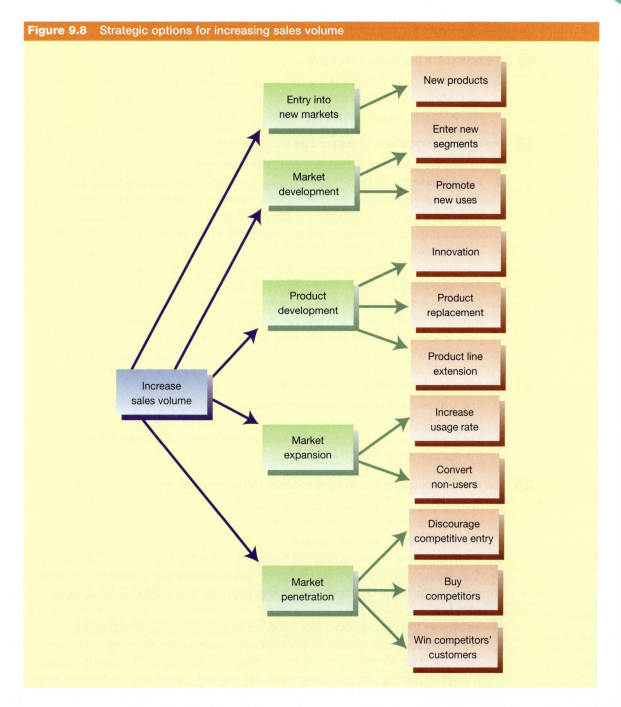

entering Scandinavia and Germany, two geographic segments that provided new expansion opportunities for its services.

The entry into new markets (diversification) option concerns the development of *new products for new markets*. This is the most risky option, especially when the entry strategy is not based on the *core competences* of the business. However, it can also be the most rewarding, as exemplified by Honda's move from motorcycles to cars (based on its core competences in engines) and Sony's move into 8 mm camcorders (based on its core competences in miniaturization and video technology).[27]

Review

1 **The concept of the product life cycle**
- A four-stage cycle in the life of a product illustrated as sales and profit curves; the four stages being introduction, growth, maturity and decline. It is quite flexible and can be applied to both brands and product lines.

2 **The uses and limitations of the product life cycle**
- Its uses are that it emphasizes the need to terminate old and develop new products, warns against the danger of assuming growth will last forever, stresses the need to review marketing objectives and strategies as products pass through the four stages, emphasizes the need to maintain a balanced set of products across the four stages, and warns against the damages of overpowering (setting too high prices early in the cycle when competition is low).
- The limitations are that it is wrong to assume that all products follow the classic S-shaped curve and it is misleading to believe that the product life cycle sales curve is a fact of life; it depends on marketing activity. The duration of the stages are unpredictable, limiting its use as a forecasting tool, and the stylized marketing objectives and strategy prescriptions associated with each stage may be misleading in particular cases.
- Overall it is a valuable stimulus to strategic thinking but as a prescriptive tool it is blunt.

3 **The concept of product portfolio planning**
- This is the process of managing products as groups (portfolios) rather than separate, distinct and independent entities.
- The emphasis is on deciding which products to build, hold, harvest and divest (i.e. resource allocation).

4 **The Boston Consulting Group Growth-Share Matrix, its uses and associated criticisms**
- The matrix allows portfolios of products to be depicted in a 2 x 2 box, the axes of which are based on market growth rate (proxy for market attractiveness) and relative market share (proxy for competitive strength).
- Cash flow from a product is assumed to depend on the box in which a product falls.
- Stars are likely to have cash flow balance; problem children cause a drain on cash flow; cash cows generate large positive cash flow; and dogs usually produce low or negative cash flow.
- Its uses are that the matrix provides guidelines for setting strategic objectives (for example, stars should be built; problem children built selectively, harvested or divested; cash cows held; and dogs harvested or divested), and emphasizes the need to maintain a balanced portfolio with the cash generated by the cash cows being used to fund those being built.
- The criticisms are: the assumption that cash flow is determined by a product's position in the matrix is weak; it distracts management from focusing on sustainable competitive advantage; treating market growth rate and market share as proxies for market attractiveness and competitive strength is oversimplistic; it can lead to an unhealthy preoccupation with market share; it ignores interdependencies between products; building stars may be inappropriate; competitor reactions are ignored; the assumption that products are self-funding ignores capital markets; the theoretical soundness of some of the underlying concepts (e.g. market definition) is questionable; cash flow may not be the best criteria for allocating resources; and the matrix lacks precision in identifying which problem children to build, harvest or divest.

Chapter nine Managing Products: Life Cycle, Portfolio Planning, Growth Strategies

5 **The General Electric Market Attractiveness–Competitive Position model, its uses and associated criticisms**

- The model is based on market attractiveness (e.g. market size, market growth rate, strength of competition) and competitive strength (e.g. market share, potential to develop a differential advantage, cost advantages). By weighting the criteria and scoring products, these can be positioned on a matrix.
- Its advantages over the 'Boston Box' are that more criteria than just market growth rate and market share are used to determine the position of products in the matrix, and it is more flexible.
- Its uses are that the matrix provides guidelines for setting strategic objectives based upon a product's position in the matrix, and that the analysis is much richer than that of the Boston Box because more factors are being taken into account, leading to better resource allocation decisions.
- The criticisms are that it is harder to use than the Boston Box, and its flexibility can provide an opportunity for managerial bias.

6 **The contribution of portfolio planning**

- The models emphasize the important strategic point that different products should have different roles in a product portfolio, and different reward systems and managers should be linked to them.
- The models can be useful as an aid to managerial judgement and strategic thinking, but should not supplant that judgement and thinking.

7 **Product strategies for growth**

- A useful way of looking at growth opportunities is offered by the Ansoff Matrix as it is a practical framework for thinking about how growth can be achieved through product strategy.
- It comprises four general approaches to sales growth: market penetration/expansion, product development, market development and diversification.
- Market penetration and expansion are strategies relating to growing existing products in existing markets. Market penetration depends on winning competitors' customers or buying competitors (thereby increasing market share). Defence of increased penetration may be through discouraging competitive entry. Market expansion may be through converting non-users to users or increasing usage rate. Although market share may not increase, sales growth is achieved through increasing market size.
- Product development is a strategy for developing new products for existing markets. It has three variants: extending existing product lines (brand extensions) to give current customers greater choice; product replacement (updates of old products); and innovation (developing fundamentally different products).
- Market development is a strategy for taking existing products and marketing them in new markets. This may be through the promotion of new uses of existing products to new customers, or the marketing of existing products to new market segments (e.g. overseas markets).
- Diversification (entry into new markets) is a strategy for developing new products for new markets. It is the most risky of the four growth strategies but also potentially the most rewarding.

Key terms

entry into new markets (diversification) the entry into new markets by new products

market development to take current products and market them in new markets

market expansion the attempt to increase the size of a market by converting non-users to users of the product and by increasing usage rates

market penetration to continue to grow sales by marketing an existing product in an existing market

portfolio planning managing groups of brands and product lines

product development increasing sales by improving present products or developing new products for current markets

product life cycle a four-stage cycle in the life of a product illustrated as sales and profits curves, the four stages being introduction, growth, maturity and decline

Internet exercise

Shoe producers spend millions on building their brands. Explore the following shoe websites.

Visit: www.adidas.co.uk
www.drmartens.co.uk
www.puma.co.uk
www.sketchers.com
www.dubarry.ie

Questions

(a) Using the anatomy of brand positioning discussed in this chapter, compare and contrast the shoe brands outlined above.
(b) Why are brand positioning frameworks useful?

Visit the Online Learning Centre at www.mcgraw-hill.co.uk/textbooks/jobber for more Internet exercises.

Study questions

1. The product life cycle is more likely to mislead marketing management than provide useful insights. Discuss.
2. Evaluate the usefulness of the BCG Matrix. Do you believe that it has a role to play in portfolio planning?
3. What is the difference between product and market development in the Ansoff Matrix? Give examples of each form of product growth strategy.
4. How does the GE Matrix differ from the BCG Matrix? What are the strengths and weaknesses of the GE Matrix?
5. Evaluate the contribution of product portfolio planning models to product strategy.

When you have read this chapter log on to the Online Learning Centre at www.mcgraw-hill.co.uk/textbooks/jobber to explore chapter-by-chapter test questions, links and further online study tools for marketing.

case seventeen

Microsoft Xbox Live!: Who will Win the Online Gaming Battle in the Latest Games Console Wars?

The Microsoft Xbox attacked the UK market, exhorting games addicts to 'play more'.

Microsoft launched its much-vaunted games console, the Xbox, in the UK in 2002, to much fanfare and with the catchphrase 'Play More'. The Xbox is the most powerful games console ever, built to the highest of technological specifications. With it, Microsoft is taking on the might of Nintendo and Sony with a $500 million global marketing campaign to muscle in on this industry. It wants a slice of the video games pie, worth an estimated $26.5 billion according to Goldman Sachs, which is comparable to worldwide cinema box office earnings and music sales. Console and hardware sales alone accounted for nearly 33 per cent ($8.7 billion) of the market in 2002. In addition, blockbuster games like *Tomb Raider* can bring in sales of $200–300 million, showing the industry's lucrativeness. For example, the Xbox *Halo* game sold in excess of 2,000,000 units.

Games have been transformed over the past two decades; visuals have come a long way from Atari's Pong and Pac-Man. Now games possesses photo-realism, astonishing 3D graphics, accompanied by Dolby Digital bombastic surround sound. The gaming industry is characterized by five-year cycles, where a games console has roughly a five-year life cycle before being replaced with new, improved technological hardware. Many industry giants have come and gone in this very competitive area. The pioneering Atari had enormous financial difficulties in the mid-1980s and went out of business. Sega, with its all-conquering *Sonic the Hedgehog* and Sega Megadrive, has retrenched from the games console market, concentrating on being only a games developer. In 1999, it launched the Sega Dreamcast console—which flopped dramatically, even though it was the most powerful console of its time, with an online capability—spending a huge marketing budget and even sponsoring the UK's Arsenal football team. However, Sega failed to displace the marketing dominance of Sony, as games addicts held off on hardware purchases until the launch of Sony's PlayStation 2 (PS2). So why has Microsoft entered an arena in which so many others have failed?

As mentioned above, the industry is characterized by a five-year cycle, where hardware is developed and then surpassed by another technological development five years later, making the original hardware obsolete.

Table C17.1	A brief history of popular games consoles		
Launched	Game console	Launched	Game console
1977	Atari Video Computer System (VCS)	1995	Sega Saturn
1982	Sinclair Spectrum	1996	Nintendo 64
1984	Commodore 64	1999	Sega Dreamcast
1985	Nintendo Entertainment System (NES)	2000	Sony PlayStation 2 (PS2)
1986	Commodore Amiga	2002	Nintendo GameCube
1989	Nintendo GameBoy	2002	Microsoft Xbox
1989	Sega Megadrive	2005	Sony PlayStation 3 (PS3)
1995	Sony PlayStation	2006	Microsoft Xbox 2 (Xbox Next)

Hardware is usually launched with a handful of games titles, as it takes games developers roughly between one and two years to launch titles; this means that a glut of games is usually launched after that period. When this five-year cycle ends, the next generation of consoles is launched, with more advanced technological features, and usually with faster processing speeds or larger memory, in many ways mirroring the situation in the PC industry. Table C17.1 illustrates past (and future) video games consoles and their product life cycles.

Traditionally, the games industry has been seen as focused towards children. However, many games are targeted at adults. The best-selling video games are typically those targeted at adults rather than children. Games developers are even launching titles with 18 certificates, banning under-age children and teenagers from buying them. For example, the infamous 18-certificate *Grand Theft Auto* series requires players to take the role of a violent criminal, and they are then rewarded for robbing, shooting and killing people—it was one of the top sellers ever for the PlayStation 2 platform. Game developers are increasingly using movie licensing deals to bolster sales, with movies tie-ins such as the James Bond and Harry Potter films, and the *Lord of the Rings* trilogy. Further licensing deals include those with sports organizations such as the NFL, NBA and FIFA, and third parties such as author Tom Clancy.

Microsoft dominates in its core markets of operating systems and desktop application software, with near monopoly status and power. Its revenues and profits have been healthy and steady. However, sales of PC software will not grow continually, as they have over the past decade. Microsoft now has to look for new avenues of future growth. It has decided that the video-gaming industry is one avenue for future growth, and the company has poured millions into the development of its Xbox. It is a games console, the most sophisticated ever released, that can also play DVDs and—the pièce de resistance—possesses broadband gaming capability. Broadband is a high-speed network connection that allows for real-time Internet gaming and the ultra-quick downloading of software, games and films through the connection. This is the real reason why Microsoft has entered the games console industry. It hopes to use the Xbox and its future reincarnations as a platform through which other Microsoft products can be distributed, and to gain subscription fees from subscribers to the broadband gaming network. The company sells its game console at a loss, hoping to build a large customer base of future potential subscribers and make money from licensing arrangements with games developers. The manufacturer really makes its money through the number of games sold, not the hardware. For every Xbox game developed, Microsoft receives a licensing fee from the games developer.

However, Microsoft is facing one of its toughest challenges ever: strong competitors in the shape of two hardened veterans of past game console wars, Sony with its PS2 and Nintendo with its GameCube. See Table C17.2 for a comparison of the key players in this market.

Table C17.2	Comparison of the key players		
	Microsoft Xbox	**Sony PlayStation 2**	**Nintendo GameCube**
Specification	An Intel 733 MHz processor, the most powerful CPU of any console	128-bit console with Emotion Engine processor 295 MHz processor	485 MHz custom CPU with 162 MHz custom graphics processor
DVD playback	Yes (playback kit required)	Yes	No
Broadband capability	Yes	Yes with network adaptor	Capacity for future modem/broadband connection
Key features	An internal hard drive, for massive storage of game information	Backwards-compatible with PlayStation 1 games	Compatibility with Game Boy Advance
Key games titles	*Halo*, *Splinter Cell*, *Unreal Championship*, *Mech Assault*	*Metal Solid Gear 2*, *Medal of Honour*, *Grand Theft Auto*, *Tomb Raider*	*Star Wars Rogue Leader*, *Sonic Adventure DX*, *Super Smash Brothers*, *Zelda*
Available since	March 2002	November 2000	May 2002
Price	£129	£169	£129

Launching its Xbox in March 2002, Microsoft has been faced with sluggish sales and extra competition thanks to the launch of Nintendo's GameCube. During the latter's launch, Microsoft slashed prices of its Xbox in order to boost sales. Sony launched its PS2 in November 2000 in Europe, getting a good head-start on its competitors' next generation of consoles. Although Sony launched its console with a relatively poor suite of opening games, the console's backward-compatibility (i.e. its ability to play old PlayStation 1 games) proved a major draw. Microsoft launched its Xbox console, with a small selection of blockbuster games, such as *Halo*. Having learned from the past successes of Nintendo, Microsoft firmly believes that developing exclusive games for its platform is key to attracting users to the Xbox console. Microsoft has bought games developers in order to develop games exclusively for the Xbox platform.

However, less than three months after launch, Microsoft was embroiled in a bitter price war, with industry stalwart Sony reducing the price of its consoles, controllers, memory cards and some of its games titles. This price cut showed the Japanese company's clear intention of fighting ferociously for the market dominance it had achieved. This is due to the fact that 60 per cent of Sony's total profits are dependent on its PlayStation business. It repeated the same tactic when launching its first PlayStation in 1995, when it competed against Nintendo and Sega. Furthermore, Nintendo cut the price of its machine from £170 (€245) to £129 (€186) before it was even launched in the UK, five days after Microsoft announced that the Xbox was being reduced from £299 (€430) to £199 (€286). Price slashing has continued unabated, with both Xbox and GameCube now sharing price points at £129, while PlayStation 2 retails at £169 (€243). This was the third price cut in just over a year as Microsoft tried to keep up sales volume.

Microsoft has a very tough fight on its hands if it wants to achieve critical mass. Many industry commentators believe that Microsoft botched its pricing strategy at launch, antagonizing customers who purchased the games console at the high initial launch price and then saw the console available dramatically cheaper within a matter of weeks. In addition, although the Xbox was technologically superior, people were still willing to pay a price premium for the Sony PlayStation brand.

Nintendo is facing enormous pressure with its GameCube offering. Poor sales have led to some high-street retailers, such as Dixons in the UK, threatening not to stock the GameCube or its games because of the lack of volume in that market. The GameCube has failed to replicate the success achieved in its Japanese market, in Europe or the USA. Furthermore, Sony has announced that it is entering the portable game console device market with the launch of PlayStation Portable (PSP), which will compete head to head with Nintendo's GameBoy (the GameBoy has sold over 150 million units since its release in 1989). Sony plans to release its handheld console by the end of 2004. This announcement knocked 10 per cent off Nintendo's share price. Another significant player in the portable gaming market is Finnish mobile phone giant Nokia.

Microsoft Xbox has captured the number-two position in the market, but it is way behind Sony. The PS2 has already sold more than 50 million units; Nintendo GameCube has sold around 9 million, with Microsoft's Xbox selling 10 million. In addition, Microsoft is said to be performing very badly in the key Japanese market. Sony's dominance is attributed to it superior games portfolio and its strong brand image. Sony has upped the pressure on Microsoft by recently announcing a strategic alliance with AOL, the Internet service provider. The companies are jointly trying to exploit the PS2's interactive features, enabling gamers to browse the net, play games online and e-mail through their games consoles. Microsoft has similarly set up alliances with other companies, such as telecoms companies and even that veteran of past games wars, Sega. Sega dropped production of its ailing Dreamcast console in 2001 and now plans to publish titles for Xbox and other platforms. Microsoft claims that it will have launched nearly 300 Xbox games in the USA by the end of 2003 and more than 50 Xbox Live!-enabled titles will be out by Christmas 2003.

All of these games consoles are sold at a loss. Manufacturers hope to make profits from licensing and royalties from games software titles in the future. Microsoft is pinning its hopes largely on Xbox Live!, for which it intends to invest $2 billion dollars into online gaming. Microsoft believes this capability will provide the killer application, which will entice customers to purchase its Xbox. Users of Xbox Live! will be able to go online and play games against people from around the world. Microsoft has publicized the fact that its machine is broadband-ready and that gamers can link online, play against one another and compete in online tournaments. However, analysts have questioned this rationale, as the majority of European households are not yet broadband-ready, with only 4 per cent equipped and with broadband penetration due to rise only slowly over the next five years. Cynics have questioned the viability of this initiative, and wondered why Microsoft has placed so many of its resources in this area. They argue that there is lack of broadband infrastructure and that there are question marks over future revenue streams. Are gamers willing to pay for such a service?

The system will allow all gamers to talk, banter, chat, taunt and trade insults with each other while competing online. Games can sometimes involve up 16 players, all playing online at once. Users obtain a unique login and a password, and then gain access to Xbox Live! When launched in the UK, an Xbox Live! starter kit cost £36 (€52). (A starter kit includes an Xbox communicator headset, an Xbox Live! starter disc, 12 months' subscription to Xbox Live! and Live-enabled demo games.) Subscribers to the service can find friends online, get more games, and download additional levels, weapons and characters. The price covers a year's subscription and an Xbox communicator that allows gamers to interact with other gamers. The platform even allows for 'voice masking'. The communicator has had two main benefits: that of improved gameplay experience, and also that of a powerful word-of-mouth marketing device. Players are interacting with one another, recommending which games to play. At the launch of Xbox Live! in March 2003, Microsoft also launched 12 online games. Subscribers need to be over 18 years of age, with a valid credit card. Subscribers must be over 14 years of age, and with a willing guardian consenting to pay for the subscription. Once the first year's subscription has elapsed, it is automatically renewed and the credit card charged. Parents, or any account owner, can disable voice and/or downloadable content at any time. The IT colossus views this as a long-term investment in the future, as it tries to build a subscriber base for the next generation of consoles.

Sony has responded to Xbox Live! by launching its own online gaming service. PS2 users need a broadband Internet connection (with a paid monthly subscription), a broadband modem, network cables, a £25 (€36) network adaptor (Ethernet) for the PS2, and a PS2 network game: for example, *SOCOM: US Navy SEALs*. Online PS2 gaming is different from Xbox Live! in that there is no central server involved. Gamers simply place their network game in their console and go directly to the game publisher's website. Players can play against opponents of similar skill levels. Furthermore gamers can join friends to compete as teams or, in gamerspeak, 'clans'. Gamers can interact with one another via supplied headset communicators. Sony plans to develop games with both offline and online capability, so that gamers can have a choice of whether to use their standard console as it is or play network gaming. Both the Xbox Live! and the online PS2 require broadband access.

When Bill Gates approved the Xbox in the autumn of 1999, he was told that the console could lose between $900 million to $3.3 billion depending on whether Sony decided to undertake a price war. To any other company, this investment would seem lunacy; however, Microsoft has deep pockets, with an estimated $42 billion in cash reserves and making $3.5 billion profits annually from its operating system. Microsoft does not expect to make a profit in the area until 2005. Currently, it is estimated to be losing at least $150 on every box, which is probably more when shipping, advertising, development overhead costs are factored in.

Much in the same way that razors are sold below cost and their costs are hopefully recouped in the future purchase of replacement blades, the console industry sells its product at below-cost prices, hoping to gain money back on the sale of games, which typically sell for around £40 (€58). For every game sold the console makers make roughly £8 (€11.5) in the form of licensing fees. Microsoft is trying to reduce costs aggressively, moving production and assembly of its Xbox from low-cost Hungary to even-lower-cost China and negotiating with suppliers to reduce costs for component parts. Microsoft is learning about the harsh realities of hardware production, the video games industry and the costs associated with it. It is primarily a software company after all ...

Questions

1. What stage of the product life cycle do you think that Microsoft's Xbox is currently experiencing, in comparison to other products in the games console market? Give reasons for your answer.

2. Using the Ansoff Matrix, discuss how Microsoft is trying to implement a growth strategy in the games console arena.

3. Discuss what you believe to be the key success factors of launching the Microsoft Xbox Live! platform, using the marketing mix 4-Ps framework.

4. Identify what you believe to be the key weaknesses of the Microsoft Xbox Live! business model, if any.

This case was written by Conor Carroll, Lecturer in Marketing, University of Limerick. Copyright © Conor Carroll (2003). The material in the case has been drawn from various published sources.

case eighteen

Unilever Culls for Growth

In February 2000, when Niall FitzGerald, chairman of Unilever, rose in front of his shareholders to reveal his plans for the most comprehensive restructuring and strategy review to hit the company in over 100 years, there was a sharp intake of breath. His four-year 'Path to Growth' strategy was to see 1200 of its 1600 consumer brands axed to concentrate marketing muscle behind 400 high-growth brands. All brands that were not among the top-two sellers in their market segment would be dropped either immediately or over a period of time.

Buyers would be sought for those that were to be divested immediately, the rest would be harvested (milked) and the cash generated ploughed into support for the 400 big brands. This would mean £450 million (€648 million) of extra marketing expenditure put behind such global brands as Magnum ice cream, Dove soap, Knorr soup and Lipton's tea. Local successes, such as Persil washing powder and Colman's mustard in the UK, would also be supported heavily. The promise was to increase profit margins from 11 to 16 per cent and to achieve target annual growth rates of between 4.5 and 5 per cent from its 400 top brands. Brands scheduled to be harvested or divested included Timotei shampoo, Brut deodorant, Radion washing powder, Harmony hairspray, Pear's soap and Jif lemon.

The analysis that Unilever had carried out revealed that only a quarter of Unilever's brands provided 90 per cent of its turnover and that disposing of the other three-quarters would lead to a more efficient supply chain and reduced costs of £1 billion (€1.44 billion) over three years. As FitzGerald explained, 'We were doing too many things. We had too many brands in too many places. Many were just not big enough to move the needle so we had to focus and simplify. That simplification would allow us to take cost out of the business.'

Not everyone was convinced. There were £3.5 billion (€5 billion) of restructuring costs (bigger than most companies' market capitalizations) and the prospect of 25,000 jobs being lost. The exercise would require a highly effective internal communications programme to obtain buy-in from Unilever staff.

By the end of 2002, FitzGerald could claim considerable achievements. Cost savings of over £450 million (€648 million) had already been banked and margins had moved from 11 to 15 per cent. The top 400 leading brands accounted for 88 per cent of sales and achieved an average growth rate of 4.5 per cent. Three businesses had also been bought. Bestfoods, the US foods giant, brought the Hellman's mayonnaise, Knorr soups and Skippy peanut butter brands into the Unilever portfolio; the acquisition of Ben & Jerry's gave the company one of two major brands in the premium ice cream sector; and Slimfast provided major penetration of the diet food market.

Unilever was also busy dropping or selling off Elizabeth Arden, Bachelor's soups, Oxo, Knight's Castille soap, Frish toilet cleaner and Stergene handwashing liquid. The selling off of its upmarket fragrance business, Unilever Cosmetics International, which includes the Calvin Klein range, in August 2002 meant that Unilever no longer competed with L'Oréal and Estée Lauder in cosmetics and fragrances. Some of Unilever's unwanted brands have been bought by small companies. For example, Buck UK bought Unilever's Sqezy – the washing up liquid formerly marketed as 'easy, peasy, lemon Sqezy'. Also, Unilever sold its Harmony hairspray and Stergene fabric conditioner brands to Lornamead. Others, such as Oxo and Bachelor's, have been sold off to larger companies, in this case Campbell Grocery Products.

A number of brand extensions were also planned in 2002, most notably in the Bertolli olive oil, Dove soap, Knorr soup, Lynx (Axe) male grooming and Slimfast diet food brands. The Lynx (Axe) men's deodorant was launched in the USA, three new flavours of Hellman's mayonnaise and an Asian side-dishes range were introduced. In support of its new product development programme, in 2002 Unilever set up its new Unilever Ventures division with £25 million (€36 million) committed over the next three years to invest in new or fledgling business ideas. About 60 per cent of these ideas are to come from within Unilever and 40 per cent from outside. Ventures will spend up to £1.9 million (€2.7 million) on each project and make its vast marketing, research and development, and supply chain 'expertise' available to entrepreneurs it supports.

The result of all this activity was that Unilever posted a 16 per cent increase in 2002 profits, that is £1.5 billion compared to £1.3 billion (€2.1 billion compared to €1.9 billion) in 2001. Sales of its top 400 brands grew 5.4 per cent, above the company's target of between 4.5 and 5 per cent. The company invested £5.1 billion (€7.3 billion) in advertising and promotion, up 8.5 per cent on the 2001 level.

During 2003, Unilever earmarked an additional 20 per cent of marketing investment in its global ice cream portfolio over the next three years. The business is now worth £3.5 billion (€5 billion), about 10 per cent of Unilever's total sales revenue. The ice cream group has a remarkable global brand portfolio. For example, in the UK, Unilever owns Walls; in France, it bought Miko; in Portugal it owns Ola; and in Sweden it owns GB Glace. Over Europe as a whole, Unilever owns and operates more than 12 different ice cream brands, each with its own strong heritage and relationships with customers. Unilever has retained the names of its national brands while replacing original brand symbols with a single heart-shaped logo.

Some of Unilever's brand porfolio

Questions

1. What are the advantages to Unilever of reducing the size of its brand portfolio?

2. To what extent does it appear that Unilever has followed (i) the BCG Growth-Share Matrix, and (ii) the General Electric Market Attractiveness–Competitive Position Model approaches to portfolio planning?

3. What are the attractions to small companies of buying marginal Unilever brands? What are the dangers of doing so?

4. Comment on Unilever's approach to the global marketing of its ice cream brands.

This case was prepared by David Jobber, Professor of Marketing, University of Bradford, based on: Arnold, M. (2002) Unilever Names Brands for Growth, *Marketing*, 21 February 17; Hall, A. (2002) Unilever's Brand Guardian, *Campaign*, 22 November, 5–6; Mason, T. (2002) Unilever Puts its Cash into Ideas, *Marketing*, 10 October, 17; Ritson, M. (2003) Unilever Goes with its 'Heart' to Make Global Brand of Local Ices, *Marketing*, 1 May, 18; Rogers, D. (2002) Unilever Sells Off Fragrance Brands, *Marketing*, 15 August, 4; Singh, S. (2002) Old Brands, New Hands, *Marketing Week*, 11 July, 24–7; Stechler Haes, N. and D. Ball (2003) Unilever's Net Profit Rises 16% on Reorganization Successes, *Wall Street Journal*, 14 February, 5.

chapter ten

Developing new products

> I met R&D people who never left the lab ... and who were so snobbish about the salesforce that they wouldn't know a customer if they tripped over one. I saw financial controllers whose projections sounded exciting but who didn't have a clue about how to make a company grow with new products.
>
> DON FREY, *Learning the Ropes: My Life as a Product Champion*

> Just like flamingos look the same,
> So me and you, just we two
> Got to search for something new.
>
> ROXY MUSIC ('Virginia Plain')

Learning Objectives

This chapter explains:

1. The different types of new products that can be launched
2. How to create and nurture an innovation culture
3. The organizational options applying to new product development
4. Methods of reducing time to market
5. How marketing and R&D staff can work together effectively
6. The stages in the new product development process
7. How to stimulate the corporate imagination
8. The six key principles of managing product teams
9. The diffusion of innovation categories and their marketing implications
10. The key ingredients in commercializing technology quickly and effectively

The life-blood of corporate success is bringing new products to the marketplace. Changing customer tastes, technological advances and competitive pressures mean that companies cannot afford to rely on past product success. Instead they have to work on new product development programmes and nurture an innovation climate to lay the foundations for new product success. The 3M company, for example, places a heavy reliance on new product introduction. Each of its divisions is expected to achieve a quarter of its revenue from products that have been on the market for under six years.

The reality of new product development is that it is a risky activity: most new products fail. But, as we shall see, new product development should not be judged in terms of the percentage of failures. To do so could stifle the spirit of innovation. The acid test is the number of successes. Failure has to be tolerated; it is endemic in the whole process of developing new products.

To fully understand new product development, we need to distinguish between invention and innovation. **Invention is the discovery of new ideas and methods. Innovation occurs when an invention is commercialized by bringing it to market.** Not all countries that are good at invention have the capability to innovate successfully. For example, the UK has an excellent record of invention; among major UK inventions and discoveries are the steam engine, the steamboat, the locomotive, the steam turbine, the electric heater, the hydraulic press, cement, the telegraph, the stethoscope, rubber tyres, the bicycle, television, the computer, the radio valve, radar, celluloid, the hovercraft and the jet engine. In terms of innovation, however, the British fall far short of the Japanese, who have the ability to successfully market products by constantly seeking to improve and develop—a process called Kaizen (sometimes Kaisan).[1] The classic example is the Sony Walkman, which was not an invention in the sense that it was fundamentally new; rather its success (over 75 million have been sold worldwide) was based on the innovation marketing of existing technologies.

Scandinavian countries have many businesses built on a local invention. For example, Tetra Pak was founded by a person who conceived of 'pouring milk into a paper bag'. Lego bricks have revolutionized toys and Gambro invented a machine that can take the place of kidneys. In all these cases, the key was not just the invention but the capability to innovate by bringing the product successfully to market.[2]

A key point to remember is that the focus of innovation should be on providing new solutions that better meet customer needs. Innovative solutions often do not require major breakthroughs in technology. For example, Marks & Spencer leapfrogged the competition in men's suits by being first to sell jackets and trousers separately so that customers could get a better fit. Direct Line became the leader in car insurance by removing the need for brokers through its telemarketing operation. The Body Shop's success was based on the modern woman's concern for the environment, and Dell became the most profitable computer company by becoming the first to market computers directly to its customers.[3] Because many innovations fail, it is important to understand the key success factors in innovation. Marketing in Action 10.1 describes some key findings.

In this chapter we shall ask the question 'What is a new product?' and examine three key issues in new product development, namely organization, developing an innovation culture and the new product development process. Then we shall examine the strategies involved in product replacement, the most common form of new product development. Finally, we shall look at the consumer adoption process, which is how people learn about new products, try them, and adopt or reject them. Throughout this chapter reference will be made to research that highlights the success factors in new product development.

10.1 marketing in action

Keys to Innovation Success

A study of 60 innovations launched by 34 companies and the PIMS database to determine the key success factors in innovation, conducted by Kamran Kashani of IMD and Tony Clayton of PIMS Associates, revealed the following major findings.

- *Innovation success is related to the creation and delivery of added consumer value.* Innovations that produce large improvements in consumer value perform much better than those that fail to show any change in consumer value. Unsurprisingly, radical innovation has greater potential for enhancing performance than small, incremental innovations. Incremental innovations, though, can be very successful provided they meet the first test: the creation and delivery of added consumer value.
- *Speed to market counts.* The most successful new products tend to be those that are launched within one year of the conception of the new idea. There are two reasons for this. First, delay increases the risk of others getting to market first; second, consumer priorities may change.
- *A product's inferior perceived value cannot be compensated for with high communications spending.* High expenditures on advertising and promotion only have a significant effect on performance where the product is already perceived to have high consumer value. High expenditures for inferior products actually worsen the performance: advertising makes bad products fail quicker.

Based on: Murphy (2000)[4]

What is a new product?

Some new products are so fundamentally different from products that already exist that they reshape markets and competition. For example, the pocket calculator created a new market and made the slide rule obsolete. At the other extreme, a shampoo that is different from existing products only by means of its brand name, fragrance, packaging and colour is also a new product. In fact, four brand categories of new product exist.[5]

1. *Product replacements*: these account for about 45 per cent of all new product launches, and include revisions and improvements to existing products (e.g. the Ford Mondeo replacing the Sierra), repositioning (existing products such as Lucozade being targeted at new market segments) and cost reductions (existing products being reformulated or redesigned to cost less to produce).

2. *Additions to existing lines*: these account for about 25 per cent of new product launches and take the form of new products that add to a company's existing product lines. This produces greater product depth. An example is the launch by Weetabix of a brand extension, Fruitibix, to compete with the numerous nut/fruit/cereal product combinations that have been gaining market share. In the Netherlands, Mona introduced a breakfast drink called Goedemorgan (Good Morning) to defend its marketing position against the successful introduction of Honig's Wake Up! Additions can have more strategic objectives, as was the case when Mentadent added a mouthwash to its toothpaste line, which moved the brand into a new product category to expand overall sales of the brand.[6]

3. *New product lines*: these total around 20 per cent of new product launches, and represent a move into a new market. For example, in Europe, Mars has launched a number of ice cream brands, which is a new product line for this company. This strategy widens a company's product mix.

4. *New-to-the-world products*: these total around 10 per cent of new product launches, and create entirely new markets. For example, the video games console, the video recorder and camcorder have created new markets because of the highly valued customer benefits they provide.

Clearly the degree of risk and reward varies according to the new product category. New-to-the-world products normally carry the highest risk since it is often very difficult to predict consumer reaction. Often, market research will be unreliable in predicting demand as people do not really understand the full benefits of the product until it is on the market and they get the chance to experience them. Furthermore, it may take time for the products to be accepted. For example, the Sony Walkman was initially rejected by marketing research since the concept of being seen in a public place wearing earphones was alien to most people. After launch, however, this behaviour was gradually accepted by younger age groups, who valued the benefit of listening to music when on a train or bus, walking down the street, and so on. At the other extreme, adding a brand variation to an existing product line lacks significant risk but is also unlikely to proffer significant returns.

Effective new product development is based on creating and nurturing an innovative culture, organizing effectively for new product development and managing the new product development process. We shall now examine these three issues.

Creating and nurturing an innovative culture

The foundation for successful new product development is the creation of a corporate culture that promotes and rewards innovation. Unfortunately many marketing managers regard their company's corporate culture as a key constraint to innovation.[7] Managers, therefore, need to pay more attention to creating a culture that encourages innovation. Figure 10.1 shows the kinds of attitudes and actions that can foster an innovation culture. People in organizations observe those actions that are likely to lead to success or punishment. The surest way to kill innovative spirit is to conspicuously punish those people who are prepared to create and champion new product ideas through to communication when things go wrong, and to reward those people who are content to manage the status quo. Such actions will breed the attitude 'Why should I take the risk of failing when by carrying on as before I will probably be rewarded?' Research has shown that those companies that have supportive attitudes to rewards and risk, and a tolerant attitude towards failure, are more likely to innovate successfully.[8] This was recognized as early as 1941 in 3M when the former president William McKnight said 'Management that is destructively critical when mistakes are made kills initiative, and it is essential that we have people with initiative if we continue to grow'.[9]

An innovation culture can also be nurtured by senior management visibly supporting new product development in general, and high-profile projects in particular.[10] British Rail's attempt to develop the ill-fated Advanced Passenger Train (APT), which involved new technology, was hampered by the lack of this kind of support. Consequently, individual managers took a subjective view on whether they were for or against the project. Beside sending clear messages about the role and importance of new product development, senior management should reinforce their words by allowing time off from their usual duties to people who wish to develop their own ideas, make available funds and resources for projects, and make themselves accessible when difficult decisions need to be taken.[11]

One company that displays its commitment to innovation is 3M. It invests around 7 per cent of its global sales of around £10 billion (€14.4 billion) in research and development and places a high value on staff input. This is formalized by allowing staff to spend 15 per cent of their work time on their own projects. By motivating staff to dedicate time to new product development, 3M generates 30 per cent of sales from products that are less than four years old.[12]

Finally, management at all levels should resist the temptation of automatic 'nay-saying'. Whenever a new idea is suggested the tendency of the listener is to think of the negatives. For example, suppose you were listening to the first-ever proposal that someone at Marks & Spencer made concerning a move into food retailing. Your response might have been: 'We know nothing about that business', 'The supermarkets have got the economies of scale', 'If we succeed they will undercut us with price' and 'Our customers associate us with clothing; it could undermine our core business.' All of these perfectly natural responses serve only to demotivate the proposer. The correct response is to resist expressing such doubts. Instead, the proposer should be encouraged to take the idea further, to research and develop it. There will come a time to scrutinize the proposal but only after the proposer has received an initial encouraging response. Stifling new ideas at conception serves only to demotivate the proposer from trying again.

Figure 10.1 Creating and nurturing an innovative culture

Marketing in Action 10.2 (overleaf) describes how creative leadership can help to foster an innovative culture.

Organizing effectively for new product development

The second building block of successful innovation is an appropriate organization structure. Most companies use one or a combination of the following methods: project teams, product and brand managers, new product departments and new product committees.

10.2 marketing in action

Creative Leadership and Innovation

The creation and nurturing of an innovative culture relies heavily on the kind of leadership than can release passions, imaginations and energy in a company. This type of creative leader has the following qualities.

- *They design cultures that support innovation*: people are encouraged to adapt continuously to constantly changing circumstances, reject the status quo and operate in a productive discomfort zone.
- *They inspire people*: they know how to electrify relationships between themselves and other people, and produce engagement that stimulates personal growth. They have a clear vision for the future and can motivate people to achieve the corporate mission.
- *They provide insights, not solutions*: they avoid simplistic answers to complex questions but provide support for exploration. In a complex environment, they recognize that there is a need to give form to what is unfolding by asking important questions.
- *They maintain focus, not control*: many organizations are tight on strategy but loose on vision. Creative leaders release the energy and potential of an organization by being tight on vision but looser on strategy. Rather than tight control, they encourage a healthy disequilibrium, and show in their actions how to tolerate uncertainty and live with paradox.

Based on: Francis (2000)[13]

Project teams

Project teams involve the bringing together of staff from such areas as R&D, engineering, manufacturing, finance and marketing to work on a new product development project. Specialized skills are combined to form an effective team to develop the new product concept. This organization form is in line with Kanter's belief that to compete in today's global marketplace, companies must move from rigid functional organizational structures to highly integrated ones.[14] People are assigned to the venture team as a major undertaking and the team is linked directly to top management to avoid having to communicate and get approval from several layers of management before progressing a course of action. This form of organization was used by IBM to successfully develop its first personal computer.

Such teams are sometimes called 'skunkworks' when they are put together in a location physically separate from other employees to work on a project free from bureaucratic intrusion. The team is headed by a product champion (perhaps the person who first conceived the idea) who co-ordinates activities and communicates with senior management. Members of the venture team may continue to manage the product after commercialization. This form of organization is often used in high-technology companies such as Sony, Honda and 3M. Unilever has also moved to establishing a venture unit that focuses on developing new business in targeted areas not currently addressed by existing brands.[15] Its advantages include the fostering of a group identity and common purpose, fast decision-making, and the lowering of bureaucratic barriers.

The Internet is enabling better communication and co-ordination between members of project teams. E-Marketing 10.1 describes how project information can be accessed by team members anywhere in the world so long as they have access to the Internet.

10.1 e-marketing

The Internet as a Tool for New Product Development

The Internet is an increasingly important tool in new product development (NPD). Regardless of whether a new product is a piece of software or a fridge freezer, key co-ordination and data transfer tasks are now facilitated online. The advantage of the Internet over more traditional NPD techniques is its ability to operate in 'real time' between geographically and functionally disparate project teams.

E-mail is the 'killer application on the net' and is used by NPD teams to co-ordinate meetings, provide the latest status, and communicate and discuss project issues. That said, e-mail becomes less useful as the project team grows.

Dedicated software applications become far more useful for tracking project progress (often highlighting, graphically, resources and critical paths), co-ordinating team communications (like videoconferences or chat rooms), storing revised project documentation (like product drawings and specifications) and co-ordinating member actions.

The Internet allows many of these applications to be hosted remotely by a software provider (also known as an ASP or application service provider). Key project information is accessed by team members anywhere in the world, regardless of whether they have the application loaded on their machine; all that is required is access to the Internet.

There is a growing list of online tools used by NPD teams. Examples include applications such as Onproject (www.onproject.com), Projectplace (www.projectplace.com, for project management) and Placeware (http://main.placeware.com, for videoconferencing). Can you think of other online resources these teams are likely to use?

One organizational change that has reduced the product development cycle time is the bringing together of design and manufacturing engineers to work as a team. Traditionally, design engineers would work on product design and then the blueprint would be passed on to production engineers. By working together each group can understand the problems of the other and effectively reduce the time it takes to develop a new product. The process—*simultaneous engineering*—was pioneered in Japan but is being adopted by European companies. For example, Ford of Europe brings together design and production engineers, purchasing engineers, finance and quality control specialists, and support staff to work as teams to develop future Ford cars in long-term collaboration with component suppliers.[16] Fast-moving consumer goods (fmcg) companies also recognize the need to cut time to market. Procter & Gamble has announced that it is reducing new product development times from four years to 18 months. Once more, the old linear path of development is rejected in favour of project teams consisting of brand and marketing managers, external design, advertising and research agency staff, to develop simultaneously the brand and launch strategies.[17] The use of computer-aided technology is also helping this process, as e-Marketing 10.2 demonstrates.

Product and brand managers

Product and brand management entails the assignment of product managers to product lines (or groups of brands within a product line) and/or brand managers to individual brands. These managers are then responsible for their success and have the task of co-ordinating functional areas (e.g. production, sales, advertising and marketing research). They are also often responsible for new product development, including the creation of new product ideas,

10.2 e-marketing

Online Product Development

The modern computer has had an immeasurable impact on accelerating time to market. Designers can now use computer aided design (CAD) systems to develop and evaluate virtual reality prototypes. By linking these systems to computer aided manufacturing (CAM) systems, engineers can often assess the feasibility of manufacturing a new product idea prior to the construction of a new product line. Furthermore, if the manufacturer is willing to overcome reservations about project confidentiality, the firm can provide suppliers with real-time data links, thereby permitting these latter organizations to remain totally informed about all the new product projects as they progress from idea through to manufacture or early prototypes.

Boeing Corporation, for example, adopted a philosophy of linking customers and suppliers into its internal data systems to optimize the development of its next generation of wide-body jet: the 777. The company used a three-dimensional CAD system to design the aircraft, and shared the output from the system with its subcontractors. Customers such as British Airways and United Airlines also participated in the online design process by being permitted to engaged in debates over the implications of alternative cabin layouts suited to their specific operating needs. During prototype construction, subcontractors located anywhere in the world could gain access to the Boeing CAM system to obtain project progress updates and/or gain immediate real-time approval for specification changes when experience of actual manufacturing processes revealed a need to alter component specifications.

The result was that the 777 had fewer geometric errors than its predecessor the 747 after 25 years of production. It was the first aeroplane to fly after no physical mock-up had been made. Now every new aeroplane is made using CAD.

Based on: Chaston (1999);[18] Daniel (2001)[19]

improving existing products and brand extensions. They may be supported by a team of assistant brand managers and a dedicated marketing researcher. In some companies a new product development manager may help product and brand managers in the task of generating and testing new product concepts. This form of organization is common in the grocery, toiletries and drinks industries.

New product departments and committees

The review of new product projects is normally in the hands of high-ranking functional managers, who listen to progress reports and decide whether further funds should be assigned to a project. They may also be charged with deciding new product strategies and priorities. No matter whether the underlying structure is venture team, product and brand management or new product department, a new products committee often oversees the process and services to give projects a high corporate profile through the stature of its membership.

The importance of teamwork

Whichever method (or combination of methods) is used, effective cross-functional teamwork is crucial for success.[20] In particular, as the quotation by Frey at the beginning of this chapter implies, there has to be effective communication and teamwork between R&D and marketing.[21]

Although all functional relationships are important during new product development, the cultural differences between R&D and marketing are potentially the most harmful and difficult to resolve. The challenge is to prevent technical people developing only things that interest them professionally, and to get them to understand the realities of the marketplace.

The role of marketing directors

A study by Gupta and Wileman asked marketing directors of technology-based companies what they believed they could do to improve their relationship with R&D and achieve greater integration of effort.[22] Six major suggestions were made by the marketing directors.

1. *Encourage teamwork*: marketing should work with R&D to establish clear, mutually agreed project priorities to reduce the incidence of pet projects. Marketing, R&D and senior management should hold regular joint project review meetings.

2. *Improve the provision of marketing information to R&D*: one of the major causes of R&D rejecting input from marketing was the lack of quality and timely information. Many marketing directors admitted that they could do a better job of providing such information to R&D. They also believed that the use of information would be enhanced if R&D personnel were made part of the marketing research team so that the questions on their minds could be incorporated into studies. They also felt that such a move would improve the credibility and trust between marketing and R&D.

3. *Take R&D people out of the lab*: marketing should encourage R&D staff to be more customer aware by inviting them to attend trade shows, take part in customer visits and prepare customer materials.

4. *Develop informal relationships with R&D*: they noted that there were often important personality and value differences between the two groups, which could cause conflict as well as being a stimulus to creativity. More effort could be made to break down these barriers by greater socializing, going to lunch together, and sitting with each other at seminars and presentations.

5. *Learn about technology*: the marketing directors believed that improving their 'technological savvy' would help them communicate more effectively with R&D people, understand various product design trade-offs, and comprehend the capabilities and limits of technology to create competitive advantages and provide solutions to customer problems.

6. *Formalize the product development process*: they noted that marketing people were often preoccupied with present products to the neglect of new products, and that the new product development process was far too unstructured. They advocated a more formal process, including formal new project initiation, status reports and review procedures, and a formal requirement that involvement in the process was an important part of marketing personnel's jobs.

The role of senior management

The study also focused on marketing directors' opinions of what senior management could do to help improve the marketing/R&D relationship. We have already noted, when discussing how to create an innovative culture, the crucial role that senior management staff play in creating the conditions for a thriving new product programme. Marketing directors mentioned six major ways in which senior management could play a part in fostering better relations.

1. *Make organizational design changes*: senior management should locate marketing and R&D near to each other to encourage communication and the development of informal relationships. They should clarify the roles of marketing and R&D in developing new products and reduce the number of approvals required for small changes in a project, which would give both R&D and marketing greater authority and responsibility.

2. *Show a personal interest in new product development*: organizational design changes should be backed up by more overt commitment and interest in innovation through early involvement in the product development process, attending product planning and review meetings, and helping to co-ordinate product development plans.

3. *Provide strategic direction*: many marketing directors felt that senior management could provide more strategic vision regarding new product/market priorities. They also needed to be more long term with their strategic thinking.

4. *Encourage teamwork*: senior management should encourage, or even demand, teamwork between marketing and R&D. Specifically, they should require joint R&D/marketing discussions, joint planning and budgeting, joint marketing research and joint reporting to them.

5. *Increase resources*: some marketing directors pointed to the need to increase resources to foster product development activities. The alternative was to reduce the number of projects. Resources should also be provided for seminars, workshops and training programmes for R&D and marketing people. The objective of these programmes would be to develop a better understanding of the roles, constraints and pressures of each group.

6. *Understand marketing's importance*: marketing directors complained of senior management's lack of understanding of marketing's role in new product development and the value of marketing in general. They felt that senior management should insist that marketing becomes involved with R&D in product development much earlier in the process so that the needs of customers are more prominent.

This research has provided valuable insights into how companies should manage the marketing/R&D relationship. It is important that companies organize themselves effectively since cross-functional teamwork and communication has proved to be a significant predictor of successful innovation in a number of studies.[23]

Managing the new product development process

There are three inescapable facts about new product development: it is expensive, risky, and time-consuming. For example, Gillette spent an excess of £100 million over more than ten years developing its Sensor razor brand. The new product concept was to develop a non-disposable shaver that would use new technology to produce a shaver that would follow the contours of a man's face, giving an excellent shave (through two spring-mounted platinum-hardened chromium blades) with fewer cuts. This made commercial sense since shaving systems are more profitable than disposable razors and allow more opportunity for creating a differential advantage. Had the brand failed, Gillette's position in the shaving market could have been damaged irreparably.

Managing the process of new product development is an important factor in reducing cost, time and risk. Studies have shown that having a formal process with review points, clear new product goals and a strong marketing orientation underlying the process leads to greater success whether the product is a physical good or a service.[24]

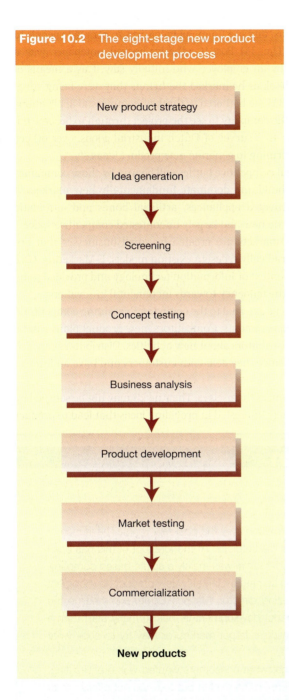

Figure 10.2 The eight-stage new product development process

An eight-step new product development process to provide these characteristics is shown in Fig. 10.2 and consists of setting new product strategy, idea generation, screening, concept testing, business analysis, product development, market testing and commercialization. Although the reality of new product development may resemble organizational chaos, the discipline imposed by the activities carried out at each stage leads to a greater likelihood of developing a product that not only works, but also confers customer benefits. We should note, however, that new products pass through each stage at varying speeds: some may dwell at a stage for a long period while others may pass through very quickly.25

New product strategy

As we have already seen, marketing directors value strategic guidance from senior management about their vision and priorities for new product development. By providing clear guidelines about which products/markets the company is interested in serving, senior management staff can provide a focus for the areas in which idea generation should take place. Also by outlining their objectives (e.g. market share gain, profitability, technological leadership) for new products they can provide indicators for the screening criteria that should be used to evaluate those ideas. An example of a company with a clearly developed new product strategy is Mars, which developed ice cream products that capitalized on the brand equity of its confectionery brand names, such as Twix, Mars and Milky Way.

Idea generation

One of the benefits of developing an innovative corporate culture is that it sparks the imagination. The objective is to motivate the search for ideas so that salespeople, engineers, top management, marketers and other employees are all alert to new opportunities. Interestingly, questioning Nobel Prize winners about the time and circumstances when they had the important germ of an idea that led them to great scientific discovery revealed that it can occur at the most unexpected time: just before going to sleep, on waking up in the morning and at church were some of the occasions mentioned. The common factor seems to be a period of quite contemplation, uninterrupted by the bustle of everyday life and work.

Successful new product ideas are not necessarily based on technological innovation. Often, they are based on novel applications of existing technology (e.g. velcro poppers on disposable nappies) or new visions of markets (e.g. Levi Strauss's vision of repositioning jeans, which were originally used as working clothes, as a fashion statement through its 501 brand).

The sources of new product ideas can be internal to the company: scientists, engineers, marketers, salespeople and designers, for example. Some companies use brainstorming as a technique to stimulate the creation of ideas, and use financial incentives to persuade people to put forward the ideas they have had. The 3M Post-It adhesive-backed notepaper was a successful product that was thought of by an employee who initially saw it as a means of preventing paper falling from his hymn book as he marked the hymns that were being sung. Because of the innovative culture within 3M, he bothered to think of commercial applications and acted as a product champion within the company to see the project through to become the commercial and global success it is today. In a survey of Dutch industrial goods, over 60 per cent of companies claimed to use brainstorming to generate new product ideas.[26]

Hamel and Prahalad argue that global competitive battles will be won by those companies that have the corporate imagination to build and dominate fundamentally new markets.[27] Introducing such products as speech-activated appliances, artificial bones and automatic language translators would effectively create new and largely uncontested competitive space.

Often, fundamentally new products/markets are created by small businesses that are willing to invent new business models or radically redesign existing models. E-Marketing 10.2 (above) discussed these issues within the context of information technology and provided some ways for large companies to break out of the tendency towards incremental innovations.

Sources of new product ideas can also be external to the company. Examining competitors' products may provide clues to product improvements. Competitors' new product plans can be gleaned by training the salesforce to ask distributors about new activities. Distributors can also be a source of new product ideas directly since they deal with customers and have an interest in selling improved products.

A major source of good ideas is consumers themselves. Their needs may not be satisfied by existing products and they may be genuinely interested in providing ideas that lead to product

10.3 marketing in action

Launching the Latin Spirit

The alcoholic drinks market has experienced a transformation over the past few years. The launch of premium bottled spirits has fundamentally changed the marketplace. At the forefront of this has been the launch of Bacardi Breezer. In the mid-1990s, Bacardi-Martini was mainly a spirits-based company. The problem was that both main brands were operating in mature markets. New product development was needed to revitalize sales. The company's marketing director, Maurice Doyle, summed up the dilemma like this: 'The problem with a lot of new product development is that so many start from a brand perspective. They try to make a brand fit a particular target market, or they try to copy what others are doing in order to stay in the market.'

The key was marketing research, which revealed that what consumers wanted was great-tasting, portable alcoholic drinks. Premium packaged beers were on the market but they did not offer ease of taste and traditional spirits did not possess the portability factor.

At the time the drinks market was divided into beer, wine and spirits categories, but Bacardi-Martini realized that the boundaries were about to be blurred by the introduction of fruit-blended spirits in small bottles. Success did not come quickly as pubs and clubs initially resisted putting Bacardi Breezer in behind-bar fridges—traditionally the stronghold of bottled beers such as Budweiser. Initially, it sold only in supermarkets. The breakthrough came through heavy investment in advertising and promotion. Advertising the 'Latin spirit' effect of the brand created demand pull, which saw sales in pubs and clubs soar (see illustration). It is now a £450 million (€648 million) brand in the UK.

Based on: Bower (2000)[28]

Chapter ten Developing New Products

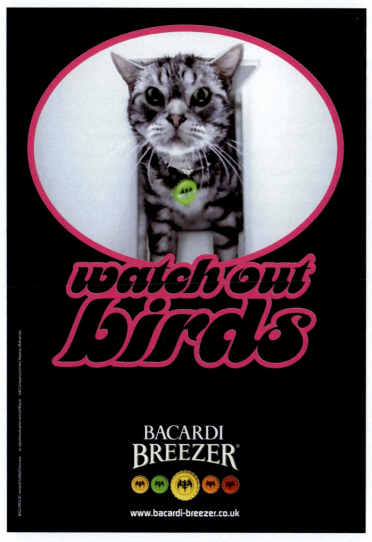

Advertisements for Bacardi Breezer like this one have helped to build a £450 million brand.

improvement. Marketing in Action 10.3 describes how marketing research played a major role in the development of Bacardi Breezer.

In organizational markets, keeping in close contact with customers who are innovators and market leaders in their own marketplaces is likely to be a fruitful source of new product ideas.[29] These *lead customers* are likely to recognize required improvements ahead of other customers as they have advanced needs and are likely to face problems before other product users. Marketing research can play a role in providing feedback when the product line is familiar to customers. For example, the original idea for Hewlett Packard's successful launch of its Desk-Jet printer came from marketing research, which revealed that personal computer users would value a relatively slow-speed printer that approached the quality of a laser printer but sold at less than half the price.[30] Marketing research also uncovered a need for a flexible ceiling covering that prevented cracks in the ceiling reappearing after they had been painted. This new product idea was developed into Polycell's Evenceil, which was a rapid success. However, for radically new products customers may be unable to articulate their requirements and so conventional marketing research may be ineffective as a source of ideas. In this situation, as can be seen in e-Marketing 10.3, companies need to be proactive in their search for new markets rather than relying on customer suggestions.[31]

New product development agencies have been set up to help companies source and test new product ideas. For example, McVitie's, the biscuit manufacturer, approached a UK agency, Redwood Associates, with the brief of identifying a new product concept that, when commercialized, would use an idle production line, which dictated biscuit size, shape and ingredients. Redwood suggested a caramel-flavoured coating for the biscuit and after test marketing the new brand—Gold—was launched successfully in 1988.[36]

Screening

Having developed new product ideas, they need to be screened to evaluate their commercial worth. Some companies use formal checklists to help them judge whether the product idea should be rejected or accepted for further evaluation. This ensures that no important criterion is overlooked. Criteria may be used that measure the attractiveness of the market for the

10.3 e-marketing

Creating Radical Innovation

One of the powerhouses of new ideas in the world's e-commerce industry is the huge number of new firms based in Silicon Valley, California. These 'minnows of business' are frequently challenging the long-established giants in market sectors as diverse as retailing, insurance, book selling and the broadcast media. The reason for their success is that, unlike large corporations, which tend to focus on incremental ideas built upon an existing branch franchise (e.g. Diet Coke from Coca-Cola; Persil detergent tablets from Unilever), these small upstarts in Silicon Valley are often prepared to invent completely new business models (e.g. downloading music from the Internet instead of visiting a retail store) or radically redesign existing models (e.g. Dell selling customized computers via a website).

Silicon Valley's success is due to the fact that large, established corporations usually adopt a disciplined, top-down approach to approving ideas and realizing funds to support R&D. This approach clearly ensures that top management never loses control over its employees; but, at the same time, this attitude communicates a corporate desire for incremental business performance improvement, not a willingness to risk moving the organization into a totally new, radically different range of business activities. Over time, however, even Silicon Valley entrepreneurs can develop conservative habits that lean towards building upon existing expertise and avoiding major risks.

One example is Sun Microsystems, which founded the workstation sector of the computer industry. Having achieved market leadership offering workstations that sold for up to $40,000, one of the company's founders, Andy Bechtolschiem, suggested using a radical new approach to build a $10,000 product. Sun was not willing to fund the idea because it did not follow its favoured strategy of incremental improvements to existing products. Andy left the company and used his own money to fund the prototype. When Sun saw the elegance of his solution, they invited him back to the firm and, together, they launched the extremely successful SPARC workstation.

Avoiding an incremental approach to new product development involves a sharpening of the corporate imagination to become more alive to new market opportunities. Five factors can aid this development.

1. *Escaping the tyranny of served markets*: looking outside markets that are currently served can be assisted by defining core competences and looking at products/markets that lie between existing business units. For example, Motorola's core competences in wireless technology led it to look beyond current products/markets (e.g. mobile phones) and towards global positioning satellite receivers. Looking for white space between business units led Kodak to envisage a market for storing and viewing photographs.

2. *Searching for innovative product concepts*: this can be aided by viewing markets as a set of customer needs and product functionalities. This has led to adding an important function to an existing product (e.g. Yamaha's electronic piano), creating a new way to deliver an existing function (e.g. electronic notepads), or creating a new functionality (e.g. fax machines).

3. *Weakening traditional price–performance assumptions*: traditional price–performance assumptions should be questioned. For example, it was Sony and JVC that questioned the price tag of £25,000 on early video recorders. They gave their engineers the freedom and the technology to design a video recorder that cost less than £500 (€720).

4. *Leading customers*: a problem with developing truly innovative products is that customers rarely ask for them. Successful innovating companies lead customers by imagining unarticulated needs rather than simply following them. They gain insights into incipient needs by talking in-depth to and observing closely a market's most sophisticated and demanding customers. For example, Yamaha set up a facility in London where Europe's most talented

> musicians could experiment with state-of-the-art musical hardware. The objective was not only to understand the customer but also to convey to the customer what might be possible technologically.
>
> (5) *Building a radical innovation hub*: a hub is a group of people who encourage and oversee innovation. It includes idea hunters, idea gatherers, internal venture capitalists, members of project evaluation committees, members of overseeing boards and experienced entrepreneurs. The hub's prime function is to nurture hunters and gatherers from all over the company to foster a stream of innovative ideas. At the centre of each project is a product champion who takes risks, breaks the rules, energizes and rescues, and re-energizes the project.
>
> Based on: Hamel (1999);[32] Hamel and Prahaled (1991);[33] Hunt (2002);[34] Leifer, O'Connor and Rice (2001)[35]

proposed product, the fit between the product and company objectives, and the capability of the company to produce and market the product. Texas Instruments focused on financial and market-based criteria when screening new semiconductor products. To pass its screen, a new product idea had to have the potential to sustain a 15 per cent compound sales growth rate, give 25 per cent return on assets, and be of a unique design that lowered costs or gave a performance advantage. Other companies may use a less systematic approach, preferring more flexible open discussion among members of the new product development committee to gauge likely success.

Concept testing

Once the product idea has been accepted as worthy of further investigation, it can be framed into a specific concept for testing with potential customers. In many instances the basic product idea will be expanded into several product concepts, each of which can be compared by testing with target customers. For example, a study into the acceptability of a new service—a proposed audit of software development procedures that would lead to the award of a quality assurance certificate—was expressed in eight service concepts depending on which parts of the development procedure would be audited (e.g. understanding customer needs, documentation, benchmarking, and so on). Each concept was evaluated by potential buyers of the software to gauge which were the most important aspects of software development that should be audited.[37] Concept testing thus allows the views of customers to enter the new product development process at an early stage.

Group discussion can also be used to develop and test product concepts. For example, a major financial services company decided it should launch an interest-bearing transaction account (product idea) because its major competition had done so.[38] Group discussions were carried out to develop the product idea into a specific product concept (a chequebook feature was rejected in favour of a cash card) with a defined target market (the under-25s). This concept was then developed further using group discussions to refine the product features (a telephone banking service was added) and to select the lifestyle image that should be used to position the new product.

The concept may be described verbally or pictorially so that the major features are understood. Potential customers can then state whether they perceive any benefits accruing from the features. A questionnaire is used to ascertain the extent of liking/disliking what is liked/disliked, the kind of person/organization that might buy the product, how/where/when/how often the product would be used, its price acceptability, and how likely they would be to buy the product.

Considerable ingenuity is needed to research new concepts. For example, research into a new tea shop/tea bar concept avoided the mistake of asking people about it 'cold' (unprepared). This would have resulted in consumers saying negative things like 'only grannies like tea shops' or 'tea isn't fashionable like coffee is'. Instead, in order to establish the tea bar concept as contemporary in feel, a cuttings file of 'articles' about it in fashionable areas such as Soho and Brighton was produced and shown to participants before the market research session took place. Because they felt that the tea bar chain was already up and running and that it was contemporary, the participants became very enthusiastic about it. The research had successfully conveyed the correct concept to the participants and, therefore, their responses were more valid than if they had been asked about their reaction to the concept without the associated image.[39]

Often the last question (buying intentions) is a key factor in judging whether any of the concepts are worth pursuing further. In the grocery and toiletries industries, for example, companies (and their marketing research agencies) often use *action standards* (e.g. more than 70 per cent of respondents must say they intend to buy) based on past experience to judge new product concepts. Concept testing allows a relatively inexpensive judgement to be made by customers before embarking on a costly product development programme. Although not foolproof, obvious non-starters can be eliminated early on in the process.

Business analysis

Based on the results of the concept test and considerable managerial judgement, estimates of sales, costs and profits will be made. This is the **business analysis** stage. In order to produce sensible figures a marketing analysis will need to be undertaken. This will identify the target market, its size and projected product acceptance over a number of years. Consideration will be given to various prices and the implications for sales revenue (and profits) discussed. By setting a tentative price this analysis will provide sales revenue estimates.

Costs will also need to be estimated. If the new product is similar to existing products (e.g. a brand extension) it should be fairly easy to produce accurate cost estimates. For radical product concepts, costings may be nothing more than informal 'guesstimates'.

Break-even analysis, where the quantity needed to be sold to cover costs is calculated, may be used to establish whether the project is financially feasible. *Sensitivity analysis*, in which variations from given assumptions about price, cost and customer acceptance, for example, are checked to see how they impact on sales revenue and profits, can also prove useful at this stage. Optimistic, most likely and pessimistic scenarios can be drawn up to estimate the degree of risk attached to the project.

If the product concept appears commercially feasible, this process will result in marketing and product development budgets being established based on what appears to be necessary to gain customer awareness and trial, and the work required to turn the concept into a marketable product.

Product development

At this stage the new product concept is developed into a physical product. As we have seen, the trend is to move from a situation where this is the sole responsibility of the R&D and/or engineering department. Multi-disciplinary project teams are established with the task of bringing the product to the marketplace. A study by Wheelwright and Clark lays out six key principles for the effective management of such teams.[40]

(1) *Mission*: senior management must agree to a clear mission through a project charter that lays out broad objectives.

(2) *Organization*: the appointment of a heavyweight project leader and a core team consisting of one member from each primary function in the company. Core members should not occupy a similar position on another team.

(3) *Project plan*: creation by the project leader and core team of a contract book, which includes a work plan, resource requirements and objectives against which it is willing to be evaluated.

(4) *Project leadership*: heavyweight leaders not only lead, manage and evaluate other members of the core team, they also act as product champions. They spend time talking to project contributors inside and outside the company, as well as customers and distributors, so that the team keeps in touch with the market.

(5) *Responsibilities*: all core members share responsibility for the overall success of the project as well as their own functional responsibilities.

(6) *Executive sponsorship*: an executive sponsor in senior management is required to act as a channel for communication with top management and to act as coach and mentor for the project and its leader.

The aim is to integrate the skills of designers, engineers, production, finance and marketing specialists so that product development is quicker, less costly and results in a high-quality product that delights customers. For example, the practice of simultaneous engineering means that designers and production engineers work together rather than passing the project from one stage of development to another once the first department's work is finished. Costs are controlled by a method called *target costing*. Target costs are worked out on the basis of target prices in the marketplace, and given as engineering/design and production targets.

Cutting time to market by reducing the length of the product development stage is a key marketing factor in many industries. Allied to simultaneous engineering, companies are using computer-aided design and manufacturing equipment and software (CAD-CAM) to cut time and improve quality. In particular, the use of 3D solid modelling, which completely defines an object in three dimensions on a computer screen and has the ability to compute masses, is very effective in shortening the product development stage.[41]

There are two reasons why product development is being accelerated. First, markets such as personal computers, video cameras and cars change so fast that to be slow means running the risk of being out of date before the product is launched. Second, cutting time to market can lead to competitive advantage. This may be short-lived but is still valuable while it lasts. For example, Rolls-Royce gained an 18-month window of opportunity by cutting lead times on its successful Trent 800 aero-engine.[42]

Marketing has an important role to play in the product development stage. R&D and engineering may focus on the functional aspects of the product, whereas seemingly trivial factors may have an important bearing on customer choice. For example, the foam that appears when washing up liquid is added to water has no functional value: a washing-up liquid could be produced that cleans just as effectively but does not produce bubbles. However, the customer sees the foam as a visual cue that indicates the power of the washing-up liquid. Therefore, to market a brand that did not produce bubbles would be suicidal. Marketing needs to keep the project team aware of such psychological factors when developing the new product. Marketing staff need to make sure that the project team members understand and communicate the important attributes that customers are looking for in the product.

In the grocery market, marketing will usually brief R&D staff on the product concept, and the latter will be charged with the job of turning the concept into reality. For example, Yoplait, the French market leader in fruit yoghurts, found through marketing research that a yoghurt concept based on the following attributes could be a winner:

- top-of-the-range dessert
- position on a health–leisure scale at the far end of the pleasure range—the ultimate taste sensation
- a fruit yoghurt that is extremely thick and creamy.

This was the brief given to the Yoplait research and development team that had the task of coming up with recipes for the new yoghurt and the best way of manufacturing it. Its job was to experiment with different cream/fruit combinations to produce the right product—one that matched the product concept—and to do it quickly. Time to market was crucial in this fast-moving industry. To help them, Yoplait employed a panel of expert tasters to try out the new recipes and evaluate them in terms of texture, sweetness, acidity, colour, smell, consistency and size of the fruit.

Product testing focuses on the functional aspects of the product and on consumer acceptance. Functional tests are carried out in the laboratory and out in the field to check such aspects as safety, performance and shelf life. For example, a car's braking system must be efficient, a jet engine must be capable of generating a certain level of thrust and a food package must be capable of keeping its contents fresh. Product testing of software products by users is crucially important in removing any 'bugs' that have not been picked up by internal testers. E-Marketing 10.4 discusses how Microsoft and Linux product test their operating systems.

Besides conforming to these basic functional standards, products need to be tested with consumers to check acceptability in use. For consumer goods this often takes the form of

10.4 e-marketing

Linux: the Ultimate in Product Development

The market for PC operating systems has been 'monopolized' by Bill Gates and his company Microsoft since the early 1980s. Developing a new Windows operating system (OS) involves substantial testing by Microsoft's in-house team of software engineers before being released to the general public. The first released versions of the new OS often contain 'bugs' that have been missed by Microsoft's engineers and testers. Microsoft's system of development and testing often relies on the general public to fault find and improve the product.

Linus Torvalds, while at the University of Helsinki in 1988, developed a new PC operating system called Linux, which could be improved and amended by anyone (with the skills and talent involved). The latest version can be downloaded to your PC for no, or very little, cost.

Torvalds and a loose-knit group of volunteers in touch via the web, believe that a software development process with little commercial interest and wide ownership is intrinsically more efficient. It is in every Linux user's interest to find faults in old versions and to improve the latest product. Essentially, Linux has created a huge Internet-connected software development team that can, in theory, compete with the might of Microsoft.

Microsoft Windows is still the industry standard. However, Linux presents the first real competitive threat for many years and has forced Microsoft to open elements of its source code to 'selected' external developers—an unprecedented move.

in-house product placement. *Paired companion tests* are used when a new product is used alongside a rival, so that respondents have a benchmark against which to judge the new offering. Alternatively two (or more) new product variants may be tested alongside one another. A questionnaire is administered at the end of the test, which gathers overall preference information as well as comparisons on specific attributes. For example, two soups might be compared on taste, colour, smell and richness. In *monadic placement tests* only the new product is given to users for trial. Although no specific rival is used in the test, in practice users may make comparisons with previously bought products, market leaders or competitive products that are quickly making an impact on the market. For example, Qualcast placed its Concorde electric cylinder lawnmower in a monadic test with potential buyers, and asked questions about its cutting ability, ease of use, reliability and the user's intention to buy. Users indicated that the lawnmower performed efficiently but the intention to buy question revealed that few would buy the machine. When asked why, most said that they preferred the more trendy Flymo hover-mower. This marketing research information led Qualcast to promote the Concorde with the hard-hitting 'It's a Lot Less Bovver than a Hover' advertising campaign. Clearly product placement tests can have communication implications too.

Another way of providing customer input into development is through *product clinics*. For example, prototype cars and trucks are regularly researched by inviting prospective drivers to such clinics where they can sit in the vehicle, and comment on its design, comfort and proposed features. For example, an idea to provide a hook for a woman's handbag in the Ford Mondeo was firmly rejected when researched in this way, and the feature discarded.

Experts can also be used when product testing. For example, the former world champion racing driver Jackie Stewart was used in the development work that led to the launch of the Ford Mondeo. Although there is a danger that expert views may be unrepresentative of the target market, it was found with the Mondeo that Stewart's opinion carried the necessary political clout to force changes in the design of the car that may not have been made without his input.

Information technology is assisting the product development process by allowing various combinations of product features to be displayed on a laptop so that customer preferences can be identified. For example, for a new mobile phone various combinations of size, colour, screen display, keyboard layout and special facilities can be shown to consumers via a laptop, which enables them to construct their ideal product.

In organizational markets, products may be placed with customers free of charge or at below cost to check out the performance characteristics. Parkinson contrasted the attitudes of West German machine tool manufacturers with their less successful British competitors towards product development.[43] The West German companies sought partnerships with customers, and developed and tested prototypes jointly with them. British attitudes were vastly different: marketing research was seen as a way of delaying product development, and customers were rarely involved for fear that they would stop buying existing products.

Market testing

So far in the development process, potential customers have been asked if they intend to buy the product but have never been placed in the position of having to pay for it. **Market testing** takes measurement of customer acceptance one crucial step further than product testing by forcing consumers to 'put their money where their mouth is'. The basic idea is to launch the new product in a limited way so that consumer response in the marketplace can be assessed. Two major methods are used: the simulated market test and test marketing.

The *simulated market test* can take a number of forms, but the principle is to set up a realistic market situation in which a sample of consumers chooses to buy goods from a range provided by the organizing company, usually a marketing research company. For example, a sample of consumers may be recruited to buy their groceries from a mobile supermarket that visits them once a week. They are provided with a magazine in which advertisements and sales promotions for the new product can appear. This method allows measurement of key success indicators such as *penetration* (the proportion of consumers that buy the new product at least once) and *repeat purchase* (the rate at which purchasers buy again) to be made. If penetration is high but repeat purchase low, buyers can be asked why they rejected the product after trial. Simulated market tests are therefore useful as a preliminary to test marketing by spotting problems, such as in packaging and product formulation, that can be rectified before test market launch. They can also be useful in eliminating new products that perform so badly compared to competition in the marketplace that test marketing is not justified.

Test marketing involves the launch of the new product in one or a few geographical areas chosen to be representative of its intended market. Towns or television areas are chosen in which the new product is sold into distribution outlets so that performance can be gauged face to face with rival products. Test marketing is the acid test of new product development since the product is being promoted as it would during a national launch, and consumers are being asked to choose it against competitor products as they would if the new product went national. It is a more realistic test than the simulated market test and therefore gives more accurate sales penetration and repeat purchasing estimates. By projecting test marketing results to the full market, an assessment of the new product's likely success can be made.

Test marketing does have a number of potential problems. Test towns and areas may not be representative of the national market, and thus sales projections may be inaccurate. Competitors may invalidate the test market by giving distributors incentives to stock their product, thereby denying the new product shelf space. Also, test marketing needs to run over a long enough period to measure the repeat purchase rate for the product, since this is a crucial indicator of success for many products (e.g. groceries and toiletries). This can mean a delay in national launch stretching to many months or even years. In the meantime, more aggressive competitors can launch a rival product nationally and therefore gain market pioneer advantages. A final practical problem is gaining the co-operation of distributors. In some instances, supermarket chains refuse to take part in test marketing activities or charge a hefty fee for the service.

The advantages of test marketing are that the information it provides facilitates the 'go/no go' national launch decision, and the effectiveness of the marketing mix elements—price, product formulation/packaging, promotion and distribution—can be checked for effectiveness. Sometimes a number of test areas are used with different marketing mix combinations to predict the most successful launch strategy. Its purpose therefore is to reduce the risk of a costly and embarrassing national launch mistake.

Although commonly associated with fast-moving consumer goods, service companies use test marketing to check new service offerings. Indeed, when they control the supply chain, as is the case with banks and restaurants, they are in an ideal situation to do so. Companies selling to organizations can also benefit from test marketing when their products have short repeat purchase periods (e.g. adhesives and abrasives). For very expensive equipment, however, test marketing is usually impractical, although as we have seen product development with lead users is to be recommended.

On a global scale, many international companies roll out products (e.g. cars and consumer electronics) from one country to another. In so doing they are gaining some of the benefits of test marketing in that lessons learned early on can be applied to later launches.

Commercialization

In this section we shall examine four issues: a general approach to developing a commercialization strategy for a new product, specific options for product replacement strategies, success factors when commercializing technology, and reacting to competitors' new product introductions.

Developing a commercialization strategy for a new product

An effective commercialization strategy relies upon marketing management making clear choices regarding the target market (where it wishes to compete), and the development of a marketing strategy that provides a differential advantage (how it wishes to compete). These two factors define the new product positioning strategy, as discussed in Chapter 7.

A useful starting point for choosing a target market is an understanding of the **diffusion of innovation process**.[44] This explains how a new product spreads throughout a market over time. Particularly important is the notion that not all people or organizations who make up the market will be in the same state of readiness to buy the new product when it is launched. In other words, different actors in the market will have varying degrees of innovativeness—that is, their willingness to try something new. Figure 10.3 shows the diffusion *of innovation* curve which categorizes people or organizations according to how soon they are willing to adopt the innovation.

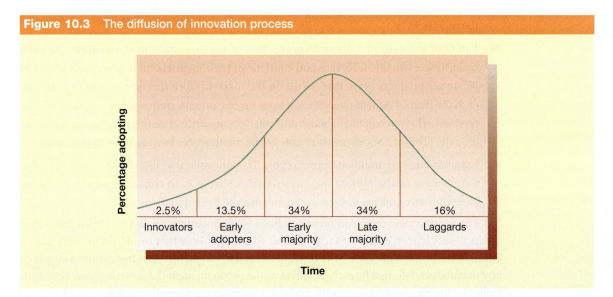

Figure 10.3 The diffusion of innovation process

The curve shows that those actors (*innovators* and *early adopters*) who were willing to buy the new product soon after launch are likely to form a minor part of the total number of actors who will eventually be willing to buy it. As the new product is accepted and approved by these customers, and the decision to buy the new product therefore becomes less risky, so the people that make up the bulk of the market, comprising the *early and late majority*, begin to try the product themselves. Finally, after the product has gained full market acceptance, a group suitably described as the *laggards* adopt the product. By the time the laggards have begun buying the product, the innovators and early adopters have probably moved on to something new.

These diffusion of innovation categories have a crucial role to play in the choice of target market. The key is to understand the characteristics of the innovator and early adopter categories and target them at launch. Simply thinking about the kinds of people or organizations that are more likely to buy a new product early after launch may suffice. If not, marketing research can help. To stimulate the thinking process, Rogers suggests the following broad characteristics for each category.[45]

- *Innovators*: these are often venturesome and like to be different; they are willing to take a chance with an untried product. In consumer markets they tend to be younger, better educated, more confident and more financially affluent, and consequently can afford to take a chance on buying something new. In organizational markets, they tend to be larger and more profitable companies if the innovation is costly, and have more progressive, better-educated management. They may themselves have a good track record in bringing out new products and may have been the first to adopt innovations in the past. As such they may be easy to identify.

- *Early adopters*: these are not quite so venturesome; they need the comfort of knowing someone else has taken the early risk. But they soon follow their lead. They still tend to have similar characteristics to the innovator group, since they need affluence and self-confidence to buy a product that has not yet gained market acceptance. They, together with the innovators, can be seen as opinion leaders who strongly influence other people's views on the product. As such, they have a major bearing on the success of the product. One way of looking at the early adopters is that they filter the products accepted by the innovator group and popularize them, leading to acceptance by the majority of buyers in the market.[46]

- *Early and late majorities*: these form the bulk of the customers in the market. The early majority are usually deliberate and cautious in their approach to buying products. They like to see products prove themselves on the market before they are willing to part with cash for them. The late majority are even more cautious, and possibly sceptical of new products. They are willing to adopt only after the majority of people or organizations have tried the products. Social pressure may be the driving force moving them to purchase.

- *Laggards*: these are tradition-bound people. The innovation needs to be perceived almost as a traditional product before they will consider buying it. In consumer markets they are often the older and less well-educated members of the population.

These categories, then, can provide a basis for segmenting the market for an innovative product (see Chapter 7) and for target market selection.[47] Note that the diffusion curve can be linked to the product life cycle, which was discussed in Chapter 9. At introduction, innovators buy the product, followed by early adopters as the product enters the growth phase. Growth is fuelled by the early and late majority, and stable sales during the maturity phase may be due to repurchasing by these groups. Laggards may enter the market during late maturity or even decline. Thus promotion designed to stimulate trial may need to be modified as the nature of new buyers changes over time.

The second key decision for commercialization is the choice of marketing strategy to establish a differential advantage. Understanding the requirements of customers (in particular, the innovator and early adopter groups) is crucial to this process and should have taken place earlier in the new product development process. The design of the marketing mix will depend on this understanding and the rate of adoption will be affected by such decisions. For example, advertising, promotion and sales efforts can generate awareness and reduce the customer's search costs, sales promotional incentives can encourage trial, and educating users in product benefits and applications has been found to speed the adoption process.[48]

As we have seen, the characteristics of customers affect the rate of adoption of an innovation, and marketing's job is to identify and target those with a high willingness to adopt upon launch. The characteristics of the product being launched also affect the diffusion rate and have marketing strategy implications (see Fig. 10.4).

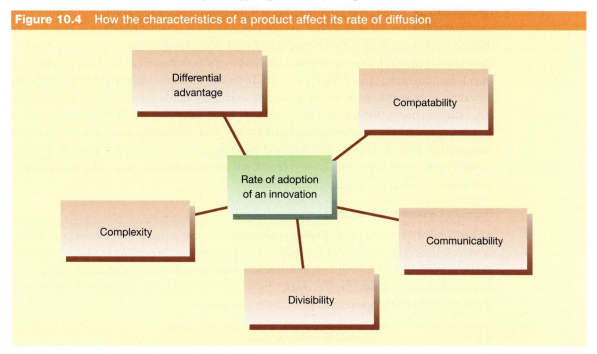

Figure 10.4 How the characteristics of a product affect its rate of diffusion

First, its differential advantage compared to existing products affects the speed of adoption. The more added customer benefits a product gives to a customer the more customers will be willing to buy. The high differential advantage of a fax machine over sending telegrams (e.g. convenience) or letters (e.g. speed) meant fast adoption. In turn, the convenience of e-mail over fax has meant rapid adoption. The differential advantage can be psychological, as when the handheld electronic personal organizer ousted the leather Filofax as a status symbol for the business elite.[49] Note that benefits may be offset by costs. For example, the diffusion of Europe's first high-definition TV (HDTV) set was hampered by its price of £3500 (€5040).

Second, there is the innovation's *compatibility* with people's values, experiences, lifestyles and behaviours. The congruence between personal computers and the lifestyle of many middle-class people helped their diffusion. Conversely, the initial incongruence between the values and experiences of young people and walking in the street wearing earphones was a major hurdle that Sony had to face when marketing its Walkman. Promotion showing opinion leaders using the Walkman was important here. Also the fact that compact disc players could not play vinyl records slowed their adoption initially as people were reluctant to replace their record players with equipment that would make their existing stock of records unplayable.

A third factor affecting diffusion rate is the innovation's *complexity*. Products that are difficult to understand or use may take longer to be adopted. For example, Apple launched its Macintosh computer backed by the proposition that existing computers were too complex to gain widespread adoption. By making its model more user friendly, it hoped to gain fast adoption among the large segment of the population that was repelled by the complexity of using computers.

Fourth, an innovation's *divisibility* also affects its speed of diffusion. Divisibility refers to the degree to which the product can be tried on a limited basis. Inexpensive products can be tried without risk of heavy financial loss. One of the tasks of marketing is to devise launch strategies that allow low cost, risk-free trial of more expensive innovations. For example, Apple devised the 'Test Drive a Mac' scheme, whereby people could try out a Macintosh at a dealer before purchase.

The final product characteristic that affects the rate of diffusion of an innovation is its *communicability*. Adoption is likely to be faster if the benefits and applications of the innovation can be readily observed or described to target customers. If product benefits are long term or difficult to quantify, then diffusion may take longer. For example, Rover's attempt to produce more reliable cars took time to communicate, as buyers' acceptance of this claim depended on their long-term experience of driving the cars. In service industries, marketing innovations like providing more staff to improve the quality of service are hard to quantify in financial terms (i.e. extra revenue generated) and therefore have a low adoption rate by the management of some companies. The marketing implications are that marketing management must not assume that what is obvious to them will be clear to customers. They need to devise a communications strategy that allows potential customers to become aware of the innovation, and understand and be convinced of its benefits.

Product replacement strategies

As we found at the start of this chapter, product replacement is the most common form of new product introduction. A study of the marketing strategies used to position *product replacements* in the marketplace found eight approaches based on a combination of product change and other marketing modifications (i.e. marketing mix and target market changes).[50] Figure 10.5 shows the eight replacement strategies used by companies.

Figure 10.5 Product replacement strategies

Source: Saunders, J. and D. Jobber (1994) Strategies for Product Launch and Deletion, in Saunders, J. (ed.) *The Marketing Initiative*, Hemel Hempstead: Prentice-Hall, 227.

		Product		
		No change	Modified	Technology change
Marketing	No change	No change	Facelift	Inconspicuous technological substitution
	Remix	Remerchandising	Relaunch	Conspicuous technological substitution
	New/market segment	Intangible repositioning	Tangible repositioning	Neo-innovation

(1) *Facelift*: minor product change with little or no change to the rest of the marketing mix or target market. Cars are often given facelifts midway through their life cycle by undergoing minor styling alterations, for example. Japanese companies constantly facelift current electronic products such as video recorders and camcorders by changing product features, a process known as **product churning**.

(2) *Inconspicuous technological substitution*: a major technological change with little or no alteration of the other elements of the marketing mix. The technological change is not brought to the consumer's attention. For example, brand loyalty to instant mashed

potatoes was retained through major technological process and product changes (powder to granules to flakes) with little attempt to highlight these changes through advertising.

(3) *Remerchandising*: a modification of name, promotion, price, packaging and/or distribution, while maintaining the basic product. For example, an unsuccessful deodorant for men was successfully remerchandised with repackaging, heavier advertising, a higher price and new brand name: Brut.

(4) *Relaunch*: both the product and other marketing mix elements are changed. Relaunches are common in the car industry where, every four to five years, a model is replaced with an upgraded version. The replacement of the Ford Sierra with the Mondeo is one example.

(5) *Conspicuous technological substitution*: a major technological change is accompanied by heavy promotional (and other mix changes) to stimulate awareness and trial. An example is the replacement of the Rover Mini with the BMW Mini, which, despite remaining faithful to the character of the original, is technologically a fundamentally different car.

(6) *Intangible repositioning*: the basic product is retained but other mix elements and target customers change. Lucozade is an example of a product that kept its original formulation but was targeted at different customer segments over time.

(7) *Tangible repositioning*: both the product and target market change. In the UK, Kendalls—a downmarket women's accessories chain—was repositioned as Next, a more upmarket women's clothing store.

(8) *Neo-innovation*: a fundamental technology change accompanied by target market and mix changes. For example, Compaq became a market leader in computers for a time by replacing its downmarket, inexpensive IBM PC compatible machines with upmarket, premium-priced computers based on the 286 chip.

Companies, therefore, face an array of replacement options with varying degrees of risk. Figure 10.5 categorizes these options and provides an aid to strategic thinking when considering how to replace products in the marketplace.

Commercializing technology

Superior commercialization of technology has been, and will continue to be, a key success factor in many industries. Some companies, such as Canon, Sony, and Philips, already have the capability to bring sophisticated high-tech products to market faster than other companies that treat the commercialization process in a less disciplined manner. For example, Canon spends heavily on R&D (8 per cent of sales revenues) to maintain its leadership in the laser printer market by fast introduction of innovations such as colour improvements (see illustration overleaf). Consistently beating the competition has been found to rest on four capabilities: being faster to market, supplying a wider range of markets, executing a larger number of product launches, and using a wider breadth of technologies.[51]

Many major market innovations appear in practice to be technologically driven: a technology seeking a market application rather than a market opportunity seeking a technology.[52] Marketing's input in such situations is to provide the insight as to how the technology may provide customer benefits within a prescribed target market. For example, an X-ray brain scanner was developed from a system used to X-ray metal. It was marketing insight that led to its application in medical diagnosis. As we have already discussed, traditional marketing research techniques have only a limited role to play when using technology to create new markets: people find it difficult to articulate their views on subjects that are unfamiliar, and acceptance may come only over time (the diffusion of innovation). Indeed, the price the customer will be asked to pay is usually unclear during the early stage of technological development. A combination of these factors may have been responsible for the first-ever forecast for computers, which predicted worldwide sales of 10 units.

The marketing of technological innovations, therefore, calls for a blend of technology and marketing. The basic marketing question, 'What potential benefits over existing products is this

Innovation at Canon enables the company to preserve its competitive advantage.

product likely to provide?', needs to be asked constantly during product development. This key idea of providing added benefits over the competition can offset price challenges, as Marketing in Action 10.4 explains.

10.4 marketing in action

Innovation at the Speed of Light

Philips, a market leader in the lighting market, faced a strong competitive challenge in the form of cheap, low-energy 'stick' bulbs from China. Its reaction was to commission marketing research, which revealed that consumers wanted both high quality of light and attractive bulb design. The Chinese bulbs scored low on both criteria; in fact, no manufacturer had, at the time, managed to combine energy efficiency and attractive lighting.

The normal cycle in lighting innovation was two years from idea to launch. Philips organized its 'innovation to market' team to bring ideas to market much faster, and focused on high-potential winners.

The result was the launch of the Ambiance low-energy bulb with Softone lighting quality. The product was an immediate success across Europe and effectively repelled the Chinese bulb threat.

By understanding consumers and creating added benefits Philips had created a competitive advantage that offset a major low price threat.

Based on: Murphy (2000)[53]

Furthermore the following lessons from the diffusion of innovation curve need to be remembered.

- The innovator/early adopter segments need to be identified and targeted initially.
- Initial sales are likely to be low: these groups are relatively small.
- Patience is required as the diffusion of an innovation takes time as people/organizations originally resistant to it learn of its benefits and begin to adopt it.
- The target group and message will need to be modified over time as new categories of customer enter the market.

Competitive reaction to new product introductions

New product launches may be in response to new product entries by competitors. Research suggests that when confronted with a new product entry by a competitor, incumbent firms should respond quickly with a limited set of marketing mix elements. Managers should rapidly decide which ones (product, promotion, price and place) are likely to have the most impact, and concentrate their efforts on them.[54]

Competitors' reaction times to the introduction of a new product have been found to depend on four factors.[55] First, response is faster in high-growth markets. Given the importance of such markets, competitors will feel the need to take action speedily in response to a new entrant. Second, response is dependent on the market shares held by the introducing firm and its competitors. Response time is slower when the introducing firm has higher market share and faster for those competitors who have higher market share. Third, response time is faster in markets characterized by frequent product changes. Finally, it is not surprising to find that response time is related to the time needed to develop the new product.

Review

1 **The different types of new products that can be launched**
- There are four types of new product that can be launched: product replacements, additions to existing lines, new product lines and new-to-the-world products.

2 **How to create and nurture an innovative culture**
- Creating and nurturing an innovative culture can be achieved by rewarding success heavily, tolerating a certain degree of failure, senior management sending clear messages about the role and importance of innovation, their words being supported by allowing staff time off to develop their own ideas, making available resources and being accessible when difficult decisions need to be taken, and resisting automatic nay-saying.

3 **The organizational options applying to new product development**
- The options are project teams, product and brand managers, and new product departments and committees. Whichever method is used, effective cross-functional teamwork is essential for success.

4 **Methods of reducing time to market**
- A key method of reducing time to market is the process of simultaneous engineering. Design and production engineers, together with other staff, work together as a team rather than sequentially.
- Consumer goods companies are bringing together teams of brand and marketing managers, external design, advertising and research agency staff to develop simultaneously the brand and launch strategies.

5 **How marketing and R&D staff can work together effectively**
- A study by Gupta and Wileman suggests that marketing and R&D can better work together when teamwork is encouraged, there is an improvement in the provision of marketing information to R&D, R&D people are encouraged to be more customer aware, informal relationships between marketing and R&D are developed, marketing is encouraged to learn about technology, and a formal process of product development is implemented. Senior management staff have an important role to play by locating marketing and R&D close to each other, showing a personal interest in new product development, providing strategic direction, encouraging teamwork, increasing the resources devoted to new product development and enhancing their understanding of the importance of marketing in new product development.

6 **The stages in the new product development process**
- A formal process with review points, clear new product goals and a strong marketing orientation underlying the process leads to greater success.
- The stages are new product strategy (senior management should set objectives and priorities), idea generation (sources include customers, competitors, distributors, salespeople, engineers and marketers), screening (to evaluate their commercial worth), concept testing (to allow the views of target customers to enter the process early), product development (where the concept is developed into a physical product for testing), market testing (where the new product is tested in the marketplace) and commercialization (where the new product is launched).

▶ ⑦ **How to stimulate the corporate imagination**
   - Four ways of stimulating the corporate imagination are: to encourage management to escape the tyranny of served markets by exploring how core competences can be exploited in new markets; to search for innovative product concepts—for example, by creating a new way to deliver an existing function (e.g. the electronic notepad); questioning traditional price–performance assumptions and giving engineers the resources to develop cheaper new products; and gaining insights by observing closely the market's most sophisticated and demanding customers.

⑧ **The six key principles of managing product teams**
   - These are the agreement of the mission, effective organization, development of a project plan, strong leadership, shared responsibilities, and the establishment of an executive sponsor in senior management.

⑨ **The diffusion of innovation categories and their marketing implications**
   - The categories are innovators, early adopters, early and late majorities, and laggards.
   - The marketing implications are that the categories can be used as a basis for segmentation and targeting (initially the innovator/early adopters should be targeted). As the product is bought by different categories, so the marketing mix may need to change.
   - The speed of adoption can be affected by marketing activities—for example, advertising to create awareness, sales promotion to stimulate trial, and educating users in product benefits and applications.
   - The nature of the innovation itself can also affect adoption—that is, the strength of its differential advantage, its compatibility with people's values, experiences, lifestyles and behaviours, its complexity, its divisibility and its communicability.

⑩ **The key ingredients in commercializing technology quickly and effectively**
   - The key ingredients are the ability of technologists and marketing people to work together effectively, simultaneous engineering, constantly asking the question 'What benefits over existing products is this new product likely to provide?', and remembering lessons from the diffusion of innovation curve (i.e. target the innovator/early adopter segments first).

Key terms

brainstorming the technique where a group of people generate ideas without initial evaluation; only when the list of ideas is complete is each idea then evaluated

business analysis a review of the projected sales, costs and profits for a new product to establish whether these factors satisfy company objectives

concept testing testing new product ideas with potential customers

diffusion of innovation process the process by which a new product spreads throughout a market over time

innovation the commercialization of an invention by bringing it to market

invention the discovery of new methods and ideas

market testing the limited launch of a new product to test sales potential

product churning a continuous spiral of new product introductions

project teams the bringing together of staff from such areas as R&D, engineering, manufacturing, finance, and marketing to work on a project such as new product development

simultaneous engineering the involvement of manufacturing and product development engineers in the same development team in an effort to reduce development time

test marketing the launch of a new product in one or a few geographic areas chosen to be representative of the intended market

Internet exercise

Segway launched the Human Transporter to much fanfare in 2001. The Segway HT is a two-wheel transport vehicle that seemingly defies gravity, while its passenger stands vertically on the device. The Segway was seen to be the ideal transport vehicle for urban environments and within industrial complexes. The US Postal Service was seen as the most likely buyer. The Segway even made an appearance on the hit comedy show *Frasier*.

Visit: www.segway.com

Questions

(a) Outline some of the possible problems faced by the inventors of Segway in the commercialization of the technology.
(b) Outline some of the criteria you would have used in deciding to go ahead with a full-scale commercialization of the technology.
(c) Why do you believe that Segway is selling the Human Transporter exclusively on Amazon.com?

Visit the Online Learning Centre at www.mcgraw-hill.co.uk/textbooks/jobber for more Internet exercises.

Study questions

1. Try to think of an unsatisfied need that you feel could be solved by the introduction of a new product. How would you set about testing your idea to examine its commercial potential?

2. The Sinclair C5 was soon withdrawn from market in the UK. The three-wheeled vehicle was designed to provide electric-powered transport over short distances. If you can remember the vehicle, try to think of reasons why the product was a failure. On the other hand, video recorders and fax machines have been huge successes. Why?

3. Why is it difficult for a service company such as a bank to develop new products that have lasting success?

4. You are the marketing manager for a fast-food restaurant chain. A colleague returns from France with an idea for a new dish that she thinks will be a winner.
How would you go about evaluating the idea?

5. What are the advantages and disadvantages of test marketing? In what circumstances should you be reluctant to use test marketing?

6. Your company has developed a new range of spicy-flavoured soups. They are intended to compete against the market leader in curry-flavoured soups. How would you conduct product tests for your new line?

7. What are the particular problems associated with commercializing technology? What are the key factors for success?

8. Discuss how marketing and R&D can form effective teams to develop new products.

When you have read this chapter log on to the Online Learning Centre at www.mcgraw-hill.co.uk/textbooks/jobber to explore chapter-by-chapter test questions, links and further online study tools for marketing.

case nineteen

The Development of a Motoring Icon: The Launch of the New Mini

Small car, big plans: the new Mini is steering a course to international sales success.

Launched in 1959, the original Mini proved to be one of the most enduring fashion and motoring icons of the twentieth century, with production of the car finally coming to a halt in 1998. The announcement in 2000 by BMW, owner of the Mini brand, that it was to invest £200 million (€288 million) in the development and launch of the new Mini was, therefore, received with enormous enthusiasm both by the press and the public.

The small car market

The European car market is intensively competitive, with one of the most crowded parts of this being the so-called 'supermini' segment. With the sector being dominated by some of the mass-market players, such as Renault, Volkswagen, Nissan, Peugeot, Citroën, Ford and Toyota, but also featuring some of the luxury brands such as the Mercedes A-Class and the Audi A2, competition for the Mini was expected to be particularly tough from the outset. However, the attraction of the sector stems from the way in which demand for small city cars is forecast to grow faster than the overall market and far faster than any other sector of the car market.

The target set for the Mini was to capture 4.6 per cent of this sector. In order to do this, a brand strategy was devised that set out 'to distance Mini from what was viewed as comparatively bland competition and capture the car's unique personality in a modern context. References to the past were deliberately avoided'.[1]

The target market

Although a company spokesman said initially that they did not know exactly what kind of customer would be attracted to the new car, the expectation was that customers would probably fall within two main groups. A younger group, aged about 25–35, was expected to buy the Mini as their primary car and was expected to choose the car in preference to a similarly priced Toyota, Volkswagen, Renault or Smart car.

Older buyers, in their forties, with grown-up children and with an urge for some youthful motoring fun were expected to buy it as their second or third car.

The marketing strategy

BMW has described the Mini as central to its strategy of developing premium cars for every size segment of the car market. From the outset, therefore, the marketing team realized that the key to the Mini's success would be how the car was positioned in the market and how it could be differentiated from the competition. They therefore set out to develop an innovative and high-profile strategy. A key element of this in the UK was a £14.4 million (€20.7 million) television and cinema advertising campaign,[2] designed to reflect the product's quirky looks and image, showing 'Mini adventures'. These adventures, which included finding lost cities and helping to save the world from a Martian invasion, led to the Mini achieving the highest awareness per £million spent and, in the case of the cinema, the highest levels of awareness ever recorded by Carlton Cinema. The ad campaign was supported, in turn, by an innovative Internet campaign that made use of Eyeblaster technology, which made it appear as if the site's home pages were being attacked by Martians and disgruntled Zombies. The Mini, of course, then appeared and saved the day.

In the USA, the company ignored television and cinema advertising, and opted instead for a guerrilla marketing campaign that included mounting Minis on top of a fleet of Ford Excursions, one of the world's largest sports utility vehicles. The company also played to the growing backlash against the fuel-hungry SUV (sports utility vehicle) sector. With these vehicles accounting for a quarter of total US vehicle sales, the Mini ads featured the line 'Let's not use the size of our vehicle to compensate for other shortcomings.'

Distribution for the car was based initially on the parent company's BMW dealer network, with all 148 main BMW dealers in the UK (70 Mini-exclusive showrooms in the USA) selling the car either from a separate area in the showroom or from a separate building. Although the same mechanics service both BMW and Mini cars, sales of the Mini are made by dedicated sales teams, each of which were given an initial sales target of 149 cars.

Although the marketing team believed in the product's distinctiveness, they also recognized that one of the most important keys to success within their sector was price. The decisions about the pricing strategy would therefore be a pivotal part of the car's success. Although the original plan was to sell the Mini for about £14,000 (€20,000), the company made a point of learning from the mistakes that Volkswagen had made when it adopted a premium pricing strategy for its new Beetle in 1998, and was then forced to cut prices.

BMW opted for a far more aggressive strategy, with the basic car—the Mini One—costing just over £10,000 (€14,400), rising to £11,600 (€16,704) for the Mini Cooper. However, profit margins for the car were then increased substantially through the series of options that included the roof of the car being painted as a flag, and leather-bound steering wheels, which have added 20 per cent on average to the car's price.

Sales targets and performance

The sales target for the first year was set at around 100,000 units. In the event, global sales proved to be far higher, with 144,000 of the cars reaching the roads in 2002.

In the United States, the Mini's largest market outside Britain, the response to the car was so strong that 25,000 Minis were sold in the first 12 months (the target was 18,000 cars) and waiting lists reached six months or more. The picture in the UK was broadly similar, with dealers not being able to meet demand.

The critics

Although the car has undoubtedly captured the hearts and minds of the motoring public, much of the pre-launch press coverage gave emphasis to the negative aspects of the German acquisition of a British icon. Subsequently, car industry analysts have expressed a number of reservations. Prominent among these have been that whereas most companies update their models every two to three years, BMW has said that it does not intend to freshen the Mini for at least seven. Other critics have said that, as it is, in effect, a fashion item, customers will quickly get bored. Others have pointed to the relatively low levels of productivity (25 cars per employee compared with Nissan's 94 cars per employee), the low selling price of the car and the UK currency base, all of which, it is suggested, will leave BMW struggling to make money from the car.

And so to the future …

The launch of the Mini has proved to be one of the most successful launches ever of a car and has captured the hearts, minds and, most importantly, wallets of an increasingly cynical and demanding car-buying public. The initial launch featured the basic car—the Mini One—and the Mini Cooper, and these were quickly followed by the high-performance Mini Cooper S. The company's plans for the future cover both product and market development, with talk of the possibilities of a diesel-engined version and possibly a 4x4 version. At the same time, the company is moving into a variety of other geographic markets, including China, all of which look as if they too will fall in love with the Mini.

[1] *marketingbusiness*, January 2003, 11.
[2] The advertising spend of £14.4 million (€20.7 million) compares with £19.5 million (€28 million) for Ford's Fiesta, £18.6 million (€27 million) for the Renault Clio and £11 million (€15.8 million) for the Volkswagen Polo.

Questions

1. Assume that you are part of the marketing team for Mini. Using the concept of the diffusion of innovation developed by Rogers, show how your marketing strategy might need to change as you move from the innovators and early adopters that currently make up the market, to other buyer categories.

2. Several commentators have suggested that the Mini is essentially a fashion statement. What are the short- and the long-term marketing implications of this?

3. Referring back to the chapter on branding (Chapter 8), what lessons on brand strategy emerge from the Mini experience?

This case was prepared by Colin Gilligan, Professor of Marketing, Sheffield Hallam University.

case twenty

The UK National Lottery

In 1993 the UK government introduced the National Lottery Act. The UK lagged behind other countries, such as the USA, Spain, South Africa and Australia, which already operated televised lottery draws. In May 1994, the first seven-year licence was awarded to Camelot plc. The first draw took place on 19 November 1994 and, within an hour, an estimated 22 million people had watched the first live Lottery draw on BBC Television. The UK National Lottery quickly became the most successful lottery in the world. However, since its launch in 1994 the UK National Lottery has undergone many changes and Camelot plc now faces the challenge of managing a mature product with declining sales.

The first seven years: 1994–2001

Market research data in the UK, combined with data from overseas lottery markets, identified important product characteristics that the UK National Lottery should have. First, the game had to be easy to play and, second, a large jackpot was required because most people participated for financial gain and the excitement of winning a life-changing sum of money. Camelot plc's marketing strategy recognized the motivating characteristic of excitement and the lure of the jackpot. To encourage people to participate, the Lottery product needed to be simple to play, consumers had to be able to purchase the product easily and the product also had to be affordable. A £1-per-game price was set, a price that would encourage impulse purchase behaviour; although the playing slips contained five to seven 'boards' to encourage multiple plays and hence greater expenditure. In November 1994, 10,000 retailers were selling tickets and by March 1995 this had grown to 14,000. Constant support was readily available from a retailer hotline staffed by 100 people, which on average handled 19,000 calls a week.[1] The siting of Lottery terminals in retail outlets such as supermarkets, newsagents and the like enabled the barrier, or taboo, of entering traditional gambling venues to be overcome. Moreover, the simple nature of handing a completed slip to the retailer also meant it was a relatively fast purchase.

Mass participation was essential as this affected the size of jackpot that could be made available, as well as influencing the amount of funding the five 'good causes' that received 28 per cent of each Lottery pound was allocated. In the National Lottery's first year of operation

The 'Crossed Fingers' logo is a registered trademark of the National Lottery Commission and is reproduced with the kind permission of Camelot Group plc who are the exclusive licensee.

In a Lottery revamp, Camelot is losing its monopoly of the National Lottery with different licences being awarded to run the various lottery games.

weekly jackpots averaged about £8 million (€11.5 million) with the largest ever individual Lottery win being £22,590,829 (€32,530,793).

Consultants employed by Camelot plc recommended that the highest proportion of Lottery outlets should be sited in those areas where there was a greater likelihood of playing, and simple explanatory promotional support was required to educate potential players in the rules of the Lottery. Importantly, the Lottery was to be perceived by the public as a harmless, fun activity. Camelot's communication strategy positioned the UK National Lottery as a fun, exciting game for everyone to play throughout the UK.[2]

The aim of the promotion was to create the largest consumer brand ever launched in the UK.[3] £39 million (€56 million) was spent on an extensive promotional campaign that included TV and radio coverage, posters on 3000 sites, public relations, branding initiatives, external signage, furniture and point-of-sale displays. The National Lottery's logo of crossed fingers and a smile was applied to every piece of promotional material in order to reinforce the message and brand the product with a core identity.[4] As a Camelot executive stated at the time, 'The advertising will emphasize the key motivators for consumers, which are to enjoy a playful moment and also win.'[5] The advertisements had the strapline 'It could be you', fixating on the jackpot prizes available. Many of the initial adverts also informed consumers about how and where to play the game, and the link with the good causes formed another promotional message. One of the key features of Camelot's promotional campaign was the televised Lottery draw. UK television legislation, in regard to public broadcast channels, dictated that the draw had to be part of a 'show' not less than 20 minutes long.

At the launch phase and through the Lottery's first seven years of existence, Camelot plc used branding, an integrated marketing mix and product developments to maintain interest in its core product, the Lottery. Camelot plc recognized that it could not be complacent however, and on 5 February 1997 it introduced a second weekly draw. The introduction of the Wednesday draw offered customers another opportunity to purchase a Lottery ticket. This was followed by the development of the Thunderball draw, launched on the 7 June 1999, a special Millennium draw and Lotto Extra, a jackpot-only game launched in November 2000. There was also a revamp of the televised Lottery draw. All these initiatives were designed to 'push' the market and stimulate demand. However, despite these developments, in 1999 Camelot recorded its first fall in profits since the launch of the game in 1994. Player fatigue, customer realization that the odds of winning the jackpot were 14 million to one and competitor activity, were all seen as contributing to the sales decline.

The next seven years: 2002–2009

In December 2000, Camelot plc was awarded the second UK National Lottery licence, after a bidding process between Camelot plc and the People's Lottery (a consortium led by Richard Branson). The licence began on 27 January 2002. Both Camelot and the People's Lottery bids included games based on new technology (e.g. the Internet). The second seven years of the UK National Lottery sees the UK lottery market move into a maturity phase, which will have marketing implications not only for Camelot plc but also for other gambling organizations. Participation data for the UK National Lottery game is becoming static in terms of demographic profiles as it enters its maturity phase. Experience in foreign markets has also revealed stable participation profiles for mature lotteries. Indeed, research on North American lotteries suggests that the characteristic of mass participation across all social groups declines as lotteries mature.

As the UK National Lottery is now in the mature phase of its life cycle, Camelot plc's strategy has to focus on halting the decline in sales by retaining its core base of customers and stimulating others to play by the introduction of new games. In terms of retention, the influence of entrapment and repetitive purchase behaviour are common issues for many mature brands, but it is an influence that is enhanced with gambling products because of issues of lucky numbers, superstitions, etc. Those Lottery customers who always use the same set of numbers, for instance, continue to play because they are fearful that if they miss a draw that may be the week their numbers 'come up.'

The support for new games (i.e. brand extensions), the maintenance of jackpot prizes and the use of the Internet appear to be the strategies that Camelot is adopting. Camelot is also ensuring that its existing strengths are not neglected. For example, the brand name of 'Camelot' is a recognized brand that will remain for the seven years of the licence. In addition, Camelot's marketing continues to stress the importance of distribution. According to Camelot, by 2001 over 96 per cent of UK households were within two miles of a Lottery outlet and 92 per cent were within one mile. CTN and convenience store outlets remain the largest sectors for Lottery terminals and in total approximately 25,000 retailers operate terminals. On average, independent retailers earn £8,187 (€11,790) in commission from Lottery sales. At the end of January 2002 Camelot launched its retail optimization programme, which is designed to help retailers who are not achieving a minimum weekly sales target to improve their sales over a 24-week period; 155 business executives are employed to support the retail network, giving POS advice, suggesting new sales techniques and solving any operational problems. A telephone hotline offers further retail support.

Further support to the mature Lottery brand can be seen in Camelot's attempts to extend its brand through the introduction of new games such as HotPicks, launched in July 2002. HotPicks is a Lottery game that still involves choosing numbers, but which is designed so that players have a greater chance of winning smaller prizes. The launch of HotPicks was supported by a specific television commercial designed to appeal to young women, and retail outlets were visited by promotional teams handing out leaflets to explain the game. However, in January 2003 Camelot was served with a High Court writ alleging that the HotPicks game infringed another company's brand. No company, particularly one so much in the public spotlight relishes being involved in a legal challenge that may have ramifications for its marketing strategy and brand image. It was also 2002 that saw the introduction of an extra Thunderball draw on Wednesdays. Again, this product development was supported by specific television and print advertisements. In addition, there is the possibility of a daily Lottery draw being introduced.

It is also Camelot's intention to promote a European lottery game, a new product development based on the existing product's strength, namely the size of the jackpot. In December 2002 Camelot signed a letter of intent with La Francaise de Jeux, the French lottery operator and Loterias y Apues-tas del Estado, the Spanish lottery operator to start a Eurolottery. It is forecast that the tickets will cost €2 (£1.40) with a jackpot of €45 million (around £31 million). If new players are attracted by the larger European jackpot offered, larger jackpots, based as they are on participation numbers, will continue to exist. These brand extensions, while stimulating existing purchasers to buy further products, also have the added potential of attracting new players.

All Camelot's brand extensions have been supported by a new marketing communications strategy, introduced by Camelot plc in 2002. As with the launch, Camelot's mix decisions were integrated; perhaps most striking was the renaming of the core game as Lotto, a familiar name in other international lottery markets and thus supporting Camelot's intention to move into Europe. The crossed-fingers logo was modified, and television, print and billboard advertisements were built around the comedian Billy Connolly with the logo 'Live a little, live a Lotto'. The playing slips and POS displays were also redesigned to accommodate the name change. Television commercials featured the impact of Lotto's contribution to good causes by highlighting community schemes that had been funded by Lottery money. The weekly television broadcasts were also redesigned.

However, the Connolly campaign has not been an unqualified success. In a survey by *Marketing* magazine, the Connolly Lotto advertisements were voted the most irritating of 2002, although the ads were also the best recalled commercials of that year. Although the advertisements were remembered by the public, ticket sales were not boosted to a great extent. Camelot, therefore, decided to replace the Connolly campaign three months before it was due to end. The new campaign began in January 2003 and featured real recipients of Lottery grants. The aim of the new campaign was to publicize the Lotto's link with good causes and provide information on the range of different games that are available for the public to play. To support the campaign's link with good causes, Camelot is also keen for all Lotto-funded projects to carry Camelot's crossed-fingers logo to reinforce the brand image.

Other future product developments are focused around the use of the Internet. Camelot's development of its Internet presence was signalled in its licence bid and its aim is to launch an Internet Lottery buying opportunity in summer 2003. Camelot's first Internet game is to be a scratchcard-type game with other Lotto games to follow. This product development offers another opportunity from two potential groups of customers. First, there may be new players who can be categorized initially as 'Internet enthusiasts', who are encouraged to buy Lottery products from their personal computer and, second, there are the existing Lottery purchasers who, via the Internet, are exposed to another channel for their buying behaviour. This second group of players may, for reasons of 'entrapment' or familiarity with the brand name, further increase their spend on Lottery products by buying online in addition to their existing purchase behaviour. At the end of 2002 Camelot also signed an agreement with Sky television to offer interactive games to Sky subscribers, which supports the government's desire for the Lottery to make full use of digital channels. The use of interactive television is also about widening access and, Camelot hopes, increasing sales.

Conclusions

However, despite these product developments and the brand support, Camelot's chief executive's remarks, made at a marketing conference in 2002, some feel damaged the brand and focused attention on the weaknesses of the product: the monopoly of Camelot and, in particular, the poor chance of winning. One thing is certain, the gambling market in the UK is now rather different from that of 1994 when the UK National Lottery game was introduced. The use of a network of Lottery terminals in retail outlets offered a fundamental change in the marketing of gambling. It also caused a significant change in consumer behaviour. The market segments traditionally targeted by gambling providers are not the sole source of Lottery purchases, as demonstrated by the wide participation rates and the proportion of new gamblers prepared to try the UK National Lottery game.

In 1994, Camelot's marketing strategy was innovatory in that it facilitated accessibility and overcame the usual barriers to entry of purchasing a gambling product (e.g. membership rules, the need to enter a specific venue) and focused on the simple rules of play, through the Lottery slip completion and immediacy of purchase. However, the relaxation in legislation, the introduction of me-too products by rival companies and the advances of the Internet are all factors that Camelot has to deal with if it is to improve sales and retain its licence for a third term. Competition from other gambling opportunities is likely to increase due to environmental changes such as new gambling legislation, and Camelot must respond to these competitive pressures. The continued decline in sales figures remains a significant concern for Camelot and one that will be monitored by the government, which is committed to ensuring that the UK National Lottery provides sufficient funds to the five 'good causes' (the Community Fund, the New Opportunities Fund, the Heritage Lottery Fund, the Sports Councils and the Arts Councils).

Postscript

On 3 July 2003, the Department of Culture, Media and Sport published its Lottery Decision Document. The UK government remains committed to the idea of a national lottery but the document outlined a number of measures for revitalizing the Lottery to ensure that good causes continue to receive funding. These measures include greater involvement of the public in grant decision-making, easier grant application processes and opportunities for different companies to run different games.

[1] Brindley, C. S. and R. Hudson-Davies (1996) The Marketing Mix and the National Lottery, *Business Studies Magazine* 8(4) April, 2–5.
[2] Kent-Smith, E. and S. Thomas (1995) Luck had Nothing to do with it. Launching the UK's Largest Consumer Brand, *Journal of the Market Research Society* 37(2), 127–41.
[3] Kent-Smith, E. and S. Thomas (1995) op. cit.
[4] Brindley, C. S. and R. Hudson-Davies (1996) op. cit.
[5] Bowker, I. (1998) cited in *Marketing*, 1 August, 15.

Questions

1. Why does the successful launch of a new product depend on the development of an appropriate mix?
2. Will the Internet halt the decline in Lottery sales?
3. What future product developments are open to Camelot?
4. Is the promotion of the National Lottery ethical?

This case was prepared by Dr Clare Brindley, Department of Business and Management Studies, Crewe and Alsager Faculty, Manchester Metropolitan University.

Pricing strategy

chapter eleven

“Everything is worth what its purchasers will pay for it.”

SYRUS

“There are two fools in every market.
One charges too little; the other charges too much.”

RUSSIAN PROVERB

Learning Objectives

This chapter explains:

1. The economist's approach to price determination

2. The differences between full cost and direct cost pricing

3. An understanding of going-rate pricing and competitive bidding

4. The advantages of marketing-orientated pricing over cost-orientated and competitor-orientated pricing methods

5. The factors that affect price setting when using a marketing-orientated approach

6. When and how to initiate price increases and cuts

7. When and when not to follow competitor-initiated price increases and cuts; when to follow quickly and when to follow slowly

8. Ethical issues in pricing

Price is the odd-one-out of the marketing mix, because it is the revenue earner. The price of a product is what the company gets back in return for all the effort that is put into manufacturing and marketing the product. The other three elements of the marketing mix—product, promotion and place—are costs. Therefore, no matter how good the product, how creative the promotion or how efficient the distribution, unless price covers costs the company will make a loss. It is therefore essential that managers understand how to set prices, because both undercharging (lost margin) and overcharging (lost sales) can have dramatic effects on profitability.

One of the key factors that marketing managers need to remember is that price is just one element of the marketing mix. Price should not be set in isolation; it should be blended with product, promotion and place to form a coherent mix that provides superior customer value. The sales of many products, particularly those that are a form of self-expression—such as drinks, cars, perfume and clothing—could suffer from prices that are too low. As we shall see, price is an important part of positioning strategy since it often sends quality cues to customers.

Understanding how to set prices is an important aspect of marketing decision-making, not least because of changes in the competitive arena that many believe will act to drive down prices in many countries. Since price is a major determinant of profitability, developing a coherent pricing strategy assumes major significance. Marketing in Action 11.1 discusses the major forces that are predicted to drive down prices.

Many people's introduction to the issue of pricing is a course in economics. We will now consider, very briefly, some of the ideas discussed by economists when considering price.

Economists' approach to pricing

Although a full discussion of the approach taken by economists to pricing is beyond the scope of this chapter, the following gives a flavour of some of the important concepts relating to price. The discussion will focus on demand since this is of fundamental importance in pricing. Economists talk of the *demand curve* to conceptualize the relationship between the quantity demanded and different price levels. Figure 11.1 shows a typical demand curve. At a price of P_1, demand is Q_1. As price drops so demand rises. Thus at P_2 demand increases to Q_2. For some

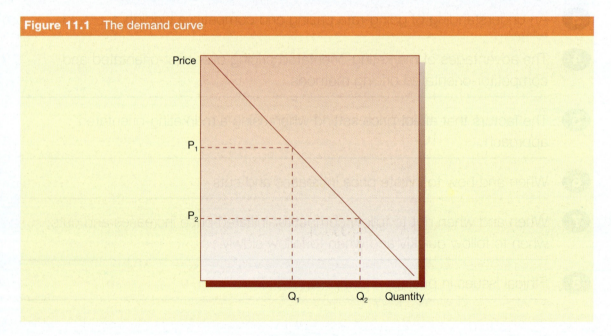

Figure 11.1 The demand curve

11.1 marketing in action

Price Drivers in the Twenty-first Century

Many commentators believe that changes in technology, competitive pressures and consumers' attitudes mean that prices are likely to fall relative to earnings. One item of information supports this view: for the first time in its 16-year history, the Confederation of British Industry (CBI) recorded no increase in retail prices during a three-month period in 1999. So what are the drivers that check the upward movement in prices?

First, technology is having a major impact on prices. This takes two forms: the emergence of the Internet and technological advances that drive down the cost of manufacture. The Internet means that price-discounting new entrants can gain access to global markets at low cost. It also means that the cost of bargain hunting falls. Before the Internet, bargain hunters often needed to spend time and money searching retail outlets for the best offers. Now, with the Internet, search activity is quick and convenient. The other force is technology-driven price reductions. For example, the prices of video recorders, camcorders and mobile phones have fallen dramatically over recent years as advancing technology and economies of scale have driven down costs.

The second force impacting prices is internationalization. As companies globalize so competition intensifies, driving down prices. No longer can local producers rely on a protected home market to maintain high prices. The lowering of trade barriers, for example, through the creation of the single European market, is speeding this process. Consumers are becoming more international in their outlook and are prepared to cross borders to seek bargains such as cheaper alcoholic drinks and cars. Companies are becoming more international in their sourcing policies. For example, Marks & Spencer, which once boasted that the majority of its clothing was sourced in the UK, is increasingly looking abroad for suppliers. Parallel importing is also practised where a retailer sources goods in one country (where prices are low) and sells them in their own country (where prices are higher) at a low price, thus undercutting prices at the manufacturer's traditional outlets.

The third pressure is supply-side induced. The growth in price discounters such as easyJet and Ryanair (airlines), Matalan (clothing), Aldi, Netto and Lidl (grocery) and the emergence of Wal-Mart (grocers and do-it-yourself products) in Europe is transforming the competitive landscape. The concept of everyday low prices is based on companies committed to driving down costs within their supply chain and passing some of the savings back to the consumer. The companies' reward is higher market share and greater economies of scale.

Finally, prices are being checked by the increasing price sensitivity of consumers. The rise in popularity of own-label products is evidence of this fact. Perhaps driven by some of the factors discussed previously, such as the ease of making price comparisons via the Internet and the emergence of price discounters, many consumers are questioning the wisdom of paying top prices for products.

As Marketing in Action 10.4 showed, Philips could resist the emergence of low-priced light bulbs through innovation. The pressure on prices means that innovation and brand building is even more important to differentiate from low-priced competitors. The second implication stems from the fact that price pressure will not hit all markets uniformly. A task of marketing strategists is to predict where its impact will be greatest and to look for markets where downward pressure is relatively weak. It is the latter markets that hold the greatest attraction and they may well be found in services, where the impact of global competition is often less than that for manufactured goods.

Based on: Cook (1999);[1] Mitchell (1999a);[2] Mitchell (1999b);[3] Rodgers (1999);[4] Murphy (2000)[5] products, a given fall in price leads to a large increase in demand. The demand for such products is said to be *price elastic*. For other products, a given fall in price leads to only a small increase in demand. The demand for these products is described as *price inelastic*. Clearly it is useful to know the price elasticity of demand. When faced with elastic demand, marketers know that a price drop may stimulate much greater demand for their products. Conversely, when faced with inelastic demand, marketers know that a price drop will not increase demand appreciably.

An obvious practical problem facing marketers who wish to use demand curve analysis is plotting demand curves accurately. There is no one demand curve that relates price to demand in real life. Each demand curve is based on a set of assumptions regarding other factors such as advertising expenditure, salesforce effectiveness, distribution intensity and the price of competing products, which also affect demand. For the purposes of Fig. 11.1, these have been held constant at a particular level so that one unique curve can be plotted. A second problem regarding the demand curve relates to the estimation of the position of the curve even when other influences are held constant. Some companies conduct experiments to estimate likely demand at various price levels. However, it is not always feasible to do so since they may rely on the co-operation of retailers who may refuse or demand unrealistically high fees. Second, it is very difficult to implement a fully controlled field experiment. Where different regions of the country are involved, differences in income levels, variations in local tastes and preferences, and differences in the level of competitor activities may confound the results. The reality is that while the demand curve is a useful conceptual tool for thinking about pricing issues, in practice its application is limited. In truth, traditional economic theory was not developed as a management tool but as an explanation of market behaviour. Managers therefore turn to other methods of setting prices and it is these methods we shall discuss in this chapter.

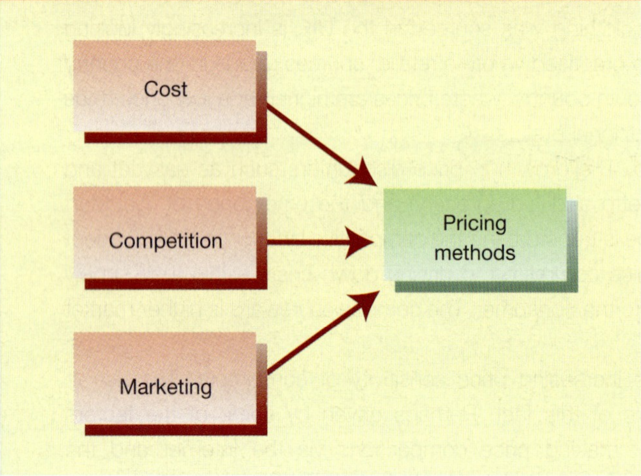

Shapiro and Jackson identified three methods used by managers to set prices (see Fig. 11.2).[6] The first reflects a strong internal orientation and is based on costs. The second is to use competitor-orientated pricing where the major emphasis is on competitor activities. The final approach is called marketing-orientated pricing as it focuses on the value that customers place on a product in the marketplace and its marketing strategy. In this chapter we shall examine each of these approaches and draw out their strengths and limitations. We shall also discuss how to initiate and respond to price changes.

Figure 11.2 Pricing methods

Cost-orientated pricing

Companies often use cost-orientated methods when setting prices.[7] Two methods are normally used: full cost pricing and direct (or marginal) cost pricing.

Full cost pricing

Full cost pricing can best be explained by using a simple example (see Table 11.1). Imagine that you are given the task of pricing a new product (a widget) and the cost figures given in

Table 11.1 Full cost pricing

Year 1

Direct costs (per unit)	= £2
Fixed costs	= £200,000
Expected sales	= 100,000
Cost per unit	
Direct costs	= £2
Fixed costs (200,000 ÷ 100,000)	= £2
Full costs	= £4
Mark-up (10%)	= £0.40p
Price (cost plus mark-up)	= £4.40p

Year 2

Expected sales	= 50,000
Cost per unit	
Direct costs	= £2
Fixed costs (200,000 ÷ 50,000)	= £4
Full costs	= £6
Mark-up (10%)	= £0.60p
Price (cost plus mark-up)	= £6.60p

Table 11.1 apply. Direct costs such as labour and materials work out at £2 per unit. As output increases, more people and materials will be needed and so total costs increase. Fixed costs (or overheads) per year are calculated at £200,000. These costs (such as office and manufacturing facilities) do not change as output increases. They have to be paid whether one or 200,000 widgets are produced.

Having calculated the relevant costs, the next step is to estimate how many widgets we are likely to sell. We believe that we produce a good-quality widget and therefore sales should be 100,000 in the first year. Therefore total (full) cost per unit is £4 and using the company's traditional 10 per cent mark-up, a price of £4.40 is set.

In order to appreciate the problem of using full cost pricing, let us assume that the sales estimate of 100,000 is not reached by the end of the year. Because of poor economic conditions or as a result of setting the price too high, only 50,000 units are sold. The company believes that this level of sales is likely to be achieved next year.

What happens to price? Table 11.1 gives the answer: it is raised because cost per unit goes up. This is because fixed costs (£200,000) are divided by a small expected sales volume (50,000). The result is a price rise in response to poor sales figures. This is clearly nonsense and yet can happen if full cost pricing is followed blindly. A major UK engineering company priced one of its main product lines in this way, and suffered a downward spiral of sales as prices were raised each year with disastrous consequences.

The first problem with full cost pricing, then, is that it leads to an increase in price as sales fall. Second, the procedure is illogical because a sales estimate is made *before* a price is set. Third, it focuses on internal costs rather than customers' willingness to pay. Finally, there may be a technical problem in allocating overheads in multi-product firms.[8]

However, inasmuch as the method forces managers to calculate costs, it does give an indication of the minimum price necessary to make a profit. Once direct and fixed costs have been measured *break-even analysis* can be used to estimate the sales volume needed to balance revenue and costs at different price levels. Therefore the procedure of calculating full costs is useful when other pricing methods are used since full costs may act as a constraint. If they cannot be covered then it may not be worthwhile launching the product.

Direct cost pricing

In certain circumstances, companies may use **direct cost pricing** (sometimes called marginal cost pricing). This involves the calculation of only those costs that are likely to rise as output increases. In the example shown in Table 11.1 direct cost per unit is £2. As output increases, so total costs will increase by £2 per unit. Like full cost pricing, direct cost pricing includes a mark-up (in this case 10 per cent) giving a price of £2.20.

The obvious problem is that this price does not cover full costs and so the company would be making a loss selling a product at this low price. However, there are situations where selling at a price above direct costs but below full cost makes sense. Suppose a company is operating at below capacity and the sales director receives a call from a buyer who is willing to place an order for 50,000 widgets but will pay only £2.20 per unit. If, in management's judgement, to refuse the order will mean machinery lying idle, a strong case for accepting the order can be made since the 0.20p per unit (£10,000) over direct costs is making a contribution to fixed costs that would not be made if the order was turned down. The decision is not without risk, however. The danger is that customers who are paying a higher price become aware of the £2.20 price and demand a similar deal.

Direct cost pricing is useful for services marketing—for example, where seats in aircraft or rooms in hotels cannot be stored; if they are unused at any time the revenue is lost. In such situations, pricing to cover direct costs plus a contribution to overheads is sensible. As with the previous example, the risk is that customers who have paid the higher price find out and complain.

Direct costs, then, indicate the lowest price at which it is sensible to take business if the alternative is to let machinery (or seats or rooms) lie idle. Also, direct cost pricing does not suffer from the 'price up as demand down' problem that was found with full cost pricing, as it does not take account of fixed costs in the price calculation. Finally, it avoids the problem of allocating overhead charges found with full cost pricing for the same reason. However, when business is buoyant it gives no indication of the correct price because it does not take into account customers' willingness to pay. Nor can it be used in the long term as, at some point, fixed costs must be covered to make a profit. Nevertheless, as a short-term expedient or tactical device, direct cost pricing does have a role to play in reducing the impact of excess capacity.

Competitor-orientated pricing

A second approach to pricing is to focus on competitors rather than costs when setting prices. This can take two forms: going-rate pricing and competitive bidding.

Going-rate pricing

In situations where there is no product differentiation—for example, a certain grade of coffee bean—a producer may have to take the going rate for the product. This accords most directly to the economist's notion of perfect competition. To the marketing manager it is anathema. A fundamental marketing principle is the creation of a differential advantage, which enables companies to build monopoly positions around their products. This allows a degree of price discretion dependent upon how much customers value the differential advantage. Even for what appear to be commodity markets, creative thinking can lead to the formation of a differential advantage on which a premium price can be built. A case in point was Austin-Trumans, a steel stockholder, which stocked the same kind of basic steels held by many other stockholders. Faced with a commodity product, Austin-Trumans attempted to differentiate on delivery. It guaranteed that it would deliver on time or pay back 10 per cent of the price to the buyer. So important was delivery to buyers (and so unreliable were many of Austin-Trumans' rivals) that buyers were willing to pay a 5 per cent price premium for this guarantee. The result was that Austin-Trumans were consistently the most profitable company in its sector for a number of years. This example shows how companies can use the creation of a differential advantage to move away from going-rate pricing.

Competitive bidding (Zuschlagsverfahren)

Many contracts are won or lost on the basis of competitive bidding. The most usual process is the drawing up of detailed specifications for a product and putting the contract out to tender. Potential suppliers quote a price that is confidential to themselves and the buyer (sealed bids). All other things being equal, the buyer will select the supplier that quotes the lowest price. A major focus for suppliers, therefore, is the likely bid prices of competitors.

Statistical models have been developed by management scientists to add a little science to the art of competitive bidding.[9] Most use the concept of *expected profit* where:

Expected profit = Profit × Probability of winning

It is clearly a notional figure based on actual profit (bid price − costs) and the probability of the bid price being successful. Table 11.2 gives a simple example of how such a competitive bidding model might be used. Based on past experience the bidder believes that the successful bid will fall in the range of £2000–£2500. As price is increased so profits will rise (full costs = £2000) and the probability of winning will fall. The bidder uses past experience to estimate the probability of each price level being successful. In this example the probability ranges from 0.10 to 0.99. By multiplying profit and probability an expected profit figure can be calculated for each bid price. Expected profit peaks at £160, which corresponds to a bid price of £2200. Consequently this is the price at which the bid will be made.

Table 11.2 Competitive bidding using the expected profit criterion

Bid price (£)	Profit	Probability	Expected
2000	0	0.99	0
2100	100	0.90	90
2200	200	0.80	160*
2300	300	0.40	120
2400	400	0.20	80
2500	500	0.10	50

*Based on the expected profit criterion, recommended bid price is £2200

Unfortunately this simple model suffers from a number of limitations. First, it may be difficult, if not impossible, for managers to express their views on the likelihood of a price being successful in precise statistical probability terms. Note that if the probability of the £2200 bid was recorded as 0.70 rather than 0.80, and likewise the £2300 bid was recorded as 0.50 rather than 0.40, the recommended bid price would move from £2200 (expected profit £140) to £2300 (expected profit £150). Clearly the outcome of the analysis can be dependent on small changes in the probability figures. Second, use of the expected profit criterion is limited to situations where the bidder can play the percentage game over the medium to long term. In circumstances where companies are desperate to win an order, they may decide to trade off profit for an improved chance of winning. In the extreme case of a company fighting for survival, a more sensible bid strategy might be to price at below full cost (£2000) and simply make a contribution to fixed costs, as we discussed above under direct cost pricing.

Clearly the use of competitive bidding models is restricted in practice. However, successful bidding depends on having an efficient competitor information system. One Scandinavian ball-bearing manufacturer, which relied heavily on effective bid pricing, installed a system that was dependent on salespeople feeding into its computer-based information system details of past successful and unsuccessful bids. The salespeople were trained to elicit successful bid prices from buyers, and then to enter them into a customer database that recorded order specifications, quantities and the successful bid price.

Because not all buyers were reliable when giving their salespeople information (sometimes it was in their interest to quote a lower successful bid price than actually occurred), competitors' successful bid prices were graded as category A (totally reliable—the salesperson had seen documentation supporting the bid price or it came from a totally trustworthy source), category B (probably reliable—no documentary evidence but the source was normally reliable) or category C (slightly dubious—the source may be reporting a lower than actual price to persuade us to bid very low next time). Although not as scientific as the competitive bidding model, this system, built up over time, provides a very effective database that salespeople can use as a starting point when they are next asked to bid by a customer.

Marketing-orientated pricing

Marketing-orientated pricing is more difficult than cost-orientated or competitor-orientated pricing because it takes a much wider range of factors into account. In all, ten factors need to be considered when adopting a marketing-orientated approach—these are shown in Fig. 11.3.

Figure 11.3 Marketing-orientated pricing

Marketing strategy

The price of a product should be set in line with *marketing strategy*. The danger is that price is viewed in isolation (as with full cost pricing) with no reference to other marketing decisions such as positioning, strategic objectives, promotion, distribution and product benefits. The result is an inconsistent mess that makes no sense in the marketplace and causes customer confusion.

The way around this problem is to recognize that the pricing decision is dependent on other earlier decisions in the marketing planning process (see Chapter 2). For new products, price will depend on positioning strategy, and for existing products price will be affected by strategic objectives. First, we shall examine the setting of prices for new products. Second, we shall consider the pricing of existing products.

Pricing new products

In this section we shall explore the way in which positioning strategy affects price, launch strategies based upon skimming and penetration pricing, and the factors that affect the decision to charge a high or low price.

Positioning strategy: a key decision that marketing management faces when launching new products is **positioning strategy**. This in turn will have a major influence on price. As discussed in Chapter 7, product positioning involves the choice of target market and the creation of a differential advantage. Each of these factors can have an enormous impact on price.

When strategy is being set for a new product, marketing management is often faced with an array of potential target markets. In each, the product's differential advantage (value) may differ. For example, when calculators were commercially developed for the first time, three distinct segments existed: S1 (engineers and scientists who placed a high value on calculators because their jobs involved a lot of complex calculations); S2 (accountants and bankers who also placed a high value on a calculator because of the nature of their jobs, although not as high as S1); and S3 (the general public, who made up the largest segment but placed a much lower value on the benefits of calculators).[10]

Clearly the choice of target market had a massive impact on the price that could be charged. If engineers/scientists were targeted, a high price could be set, reflecting the large differential advantage of the calculator to them. For accountants/bankers the price would have to be slightly lower, and for the general public a much lower price would be needed. In the event, the S1 segment was chosen and the price set high (around £250/€360). Over time, price was reduced to draw into the market segments S2 and S3 (and a further segment, S4, when exam regulations were changed to allow schoolchildren to use calculators). The development of the market for calculators, based upon targeting increasingly price sensitive market segments, is shown in Fig. 11.4.

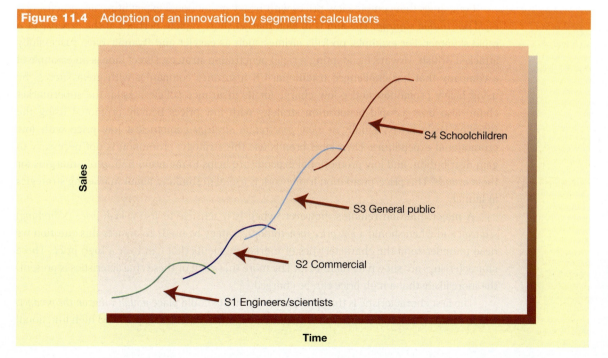

Figure 11.4 Adoption of an innovation by segments: calculators

Two implications follow from this discussion. First, for new products, marketing management must decide on a target market and on the value that people in that segment place on the product (the extent of its differential advantage): only then can a market-based price be set which reflects that value. Second, where multiple segments appear attractive, modified versions of the product should be designed and priced differently, not according to differences in costs, but in line with the respective values that each target market places on the product.

Launch strategies: price should also be blended with other elements of the marketing mix. Figure 11.5 shows four marketing strategies based on combinations of price and promotion. Similar matrices could also be developed for product and distribution, but for illustrative purposes promotion will be used here.

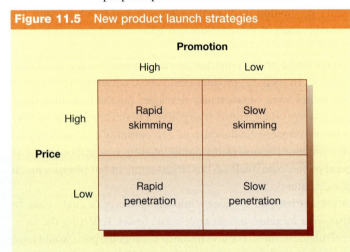

Figure 11.5 New product launch strategies

A combination of high price and high promotion expenditure is called a *rapid skimming strategy*. The high price provides high margin returns on investment and the heavy promotion creates high levels of product awareness and knowledge. Nike usually employs a rapid skimming strategy when it launches new ranges of trainers. A *slow skimming strategy* combines high price with low levels of promotional expenditure. High prices mean big profit margins, but high levels of promotion are believed to be unnecessary, perhaps because word of mouth is more important and the product is already well known (e.g. Rolls-Royce) or because heavy promotion is thought to be incompatible with product image, as with cult products. A company that uses a skimming pricing policy effectively is Bosch, the German car components supplier; it has applied an extremely profitable skimming strategy, supported by patents, to its launch of fuel injection and anti-lock braking systems.[11]

Companies that combine low prices with heavy promotional expenditure are practising a *rapid penetration strategy*. The aim is to gain market share rapidly, perhaps at the expense of a rapid skimmer. For example, no-frills airlines such as easyJet and Ryanair have successfully attacked British Airways by adopting a rapid penetration strategy. Direct Line is an example of a company that has challenged traditional UK insurance companies with great success by using heavy promotion and a low charge for its insurance policies. Asda, the supermarket chain, also uses a rapid penetration strategy with low prices heavily promoted using the strapline 'Asda price'. Finally, a *slow penetration strategy* combines a low price with low promotional expenditure. Own-label brands use this strategy: promotion is not necessary to gain distribution, and low promotional expenditure helps to maintain high profit margins for these brands. This price/promotion framework is useful in thinking about marketing strategies at launch.

A major question remains, however: when is it sensible to use a *high price (skimming) strategy* and when should a *low price (penetration)* strategy be used? To answer this question we need to understand the characteristics of market segments that can bear a high price. These characteristics are shown in Table 11.3. The more that each of these characteristics is present, the more likely that a high price can be charged.[12]

The first characteristic is that the market segment should place a *high value on the product*, which means that its differential advantage is substantial. Calculators provided high functional

Table 11.3	Characteristics of high-price market segments
1	Product provides high value
2	Customers have high ability to pay
3	Consumer and bill payer are different
4	Lack of competition
5	Excess demand
6	High pressure to buy

value to engineers and scientists, other products (for example, perfumes and clothing) may rely more on *psychological value* where brand image is crucial (for example, Chanel perfume or Gucci shoes). Second, high prices are more likely to be viable where *customers have a high ability to pay. Cash rich segments* in organizational markets often correlate with profitability. For example, the financial services sector and the textile industry in Europe may place similar values on marketing consultancy skills but in general the former has more ability to pay.

In certain markets the *consumer of the product is different from the bill payer*. This distinction may form the basis of a high-price market segment. Airlines, for example, charge more for a given flight when the journey is for less than seven days and does not include a Saturday night. This is because that type of air traveller is more likely to be a businessperson, whereas the more price-sensitive leisure travellers who pay for themselves and tend to stay at least a week can travel at a lower fare. Rail travel is often segmented by price sensitivity too. Early-morning long-distance trips are more expensive than midday journeys since the former are usually made by businesspeople.

The fourth characteristic of high-price segments is *lack of competition* among supplying companies. The extreme case is a monopoly where customers have only one supplier from which to buy. When customers have no, or very little, choice of supply, the power to determine price is largely in the hands of suppliers. This means that high prices can be charged if suppliers so wish.

The fifth characteristic of high price segments is *excess demand*. When demand exceeds supply there is the potential to charge high prices. For example, when the demand for diamonds exceeds supply the price of diamonds usually rises.

The final situation where customers are likely to be less price sensitive is where there is *high pressure to buy*. For example, in an emergency situation where a vital part is required to repair a machine that is needed to fulfil a major order, the customer may be willing to pay a high price if a supplier can guarantee quick delivery. The task of the marketing manager is to evaluate the chosen target market for a new product using the checklist provided in Table 11.3. It is unlikely that all five conditions will apply and so judgement is still required. But the more these characteristics are found in the target market, the greater the chances that a high price can be charged.

Table 11.4 lists the conditions when a *low price (penetration) strategy* should be used. The first situation is when an analysis of the market segment using the previous checklist reveals that a low price is the *only feasible alternative*. For example, a product that has no differential advantage launched on to a market where customers are not cash rich, pay for themselves, have little pressure to buy and have many suppliers to choose from has no basis for charging a price premium. At best it could take the going-rate price but, more likely, would be launched using a penetration (low-price) strategy, otherwise there would be no incentive for consumers to switch from their usual brand. The power of consumers to force down prices is nowhere greater than on the Internet. E-Marketing 11.1 discusses the tools available on the Internet to enable consumers to find low prices.

Table 11.4	Conditions for charging low prices
1	Only feasible alternative
2	Market presence *or* domination
3	Experience curve effect/low costs
4	Make money later
5	Make money elsewhere
6	Barrier to entry
7	Predation

11.1 e-marketing

The Internet: where Customers set the Price

The Internet has changed the way companies price products; in fact, nowhere else do consumers have more influence in pricing policy than online. Consider the powerful 'tools' the Internet places at the disposal of online consumers in their quest to find the lowest price—these include search engines and directories, comparison websites and auction sites.

Search engines and directories, like Google and Yahoo!, guide the consumer to thousands of websites where the lowest prices can be found. In theory, these online search tools exert downward pressure on prices; in reality, consumers seldom search for the very lowest price, preferring to access one or two well-known sites. However, new websites are making it even easier to compare prices across the web. Sites like Kelkoo (www.kelkoo.com) and Froogle, developed by Google (www.froogle.com), match the product searched and display only the lowest-priced results. These sites, perhaps, increase pressure on suppliers to update prices more frequently, giving a better deal for consumers and making the implementation of an online pricing policy more complex to control.

Dynamic pricing websites are perhaps the answer, sites like eBay (www.ebay.com) and lastminute.com (www.lastminute.com) find the market value for a product or service by letting customers set the price. Using online auctions, customers bid for desired products or services with the highest bid within a time period affecting the purchase. These sites are among the most successful on the Internet.

There are, however, more positive reasons for using a low price strategy. A company may wish to gain *market presence* or *domination* by pricing its products aggressively. This requires a market containing at least one segment of price-sensitive consumers. As we have already discussed, Direct Line priced its insurance policies aggressively to challenge traditional insurance companies and is now market leader for home and motor insurance in the UK. Penetration pricing for market presence is sometimes followed by price increase once market share has reached a satisfactory level. Mercedes followed this strategy in the US car market by pricing close to the market average in 1967, but had moved to over double the market average price by 1982.[13] The Lexus, Toyota's new luxury model, appears to be following a similar strategy. Ratners, a jewellery chain (now renamed Signet), achieved market domination using price as its major competitive weapon although indiscreet comments by its chairman regarding the quality of its merchandise dampened sales.

Low prices may also be charged to increase output and so bring down costs through the *experience curve effect*. Research has shown that, for many products, costs decline by around 20 per cent when production doubles.[14] Cost economies are achieved by learning how to produce the product more effectively through better production processes and improvements in skill levels. Economies of scale through, for example, the use of more cost-effective machines at higher output levels also act to lower costs as production rises. Marketing costs per unit of output may also fall as production rises. For example, an advertising expenditure of £1 million (€1.44 million) represents 1 per cent of revenue when sales are £100 million (€144 million), but rises to 10 per cent of revenue when sales are only £10 million (€14.4 million). Therefore a company may choose to price aggressively to become the largest producer and therefore, if the experience curve holds, the lowest-cost supplier. Texas Instruments used a penetration pricing strategy for its semiconductors for this reason. By becoming the lowest-cost supplier it had the option of driving out competition by pricing at cost (to match its price, the competition would have to price at below their costs) or pricing above costs and gaining the largest profit margin in the industry. Indeed, ruthless cost cutting may be necessary to achieve profits using low price strategies.

A low price strategy can also make sense when the objective is to *make money later*. Two circumstances can provoke this action. First, the sale of the basic product may be followed by profitable after-sales service and/or spare parts. For example, the sale of an aero-engine at cost may be worthwhile if substantial profits can be made on the later sale of spare parts. Second, the price sensitivity of customers may change over time: initially customers may be price sensitive, implying the need for a low price, but as circumstances change they may become much less sensitive to price. For example, a publisher of management journals based its pricing strategy on this change. A key customer group was librarians who, faced by budget constraints, were price sensitive to new journals. Consequently these were priced low to encourage adoption. Once established in the library their use by students and staff meant that there would be considerable resistance to them being delisted. The strategy, therefore, was to keep price low until target penetration was achieved. Then price was raised consistently above inflation in response to the fall in price sensitivity.

Marketers also charge low prices to *make money elsewhere*. For example, retailers often use loss leaders, which are advertised in an attempt to attract customers into their stores and to create a low-cost image. Supermarkets, much to the annoyance of traditional petrol retailers, use petrol as a loss leader to attract motorists to their stores.[15] Manufacturers selling a range of products to organizations may accept low prices on some goods in order to be perceived by customers as a full-range supplier. In both cases, sales of other higher-priced and more profitable products benefit.

Low prices can also act as a *barrier to entry*. A company may weigh the longer-term benefits of deterring competition by accepting low margins to be greater than the short-term advantages of a high-price, high-margin strategy, which may attract rivals into its market.

Finally, low prices may be charged in an attempt to put other companies out of business. British Airways and TWA were accused of *predatory pricing* against Laker Airlines on its Atlantic routes.

As the Bosch illustration shows, even companies normally associated with premium prices have to take care that their products are not perceived as being out of reach of consumers.

Pricing existing products

The pricing of existing products should also be set within the context of strategy. Specifically, the *strategic objective* for each product will have a major bearing on pricing strategy. As with new products, price should not be set in isolation, but should be

Bosch pays attention to the importance of affordable prices.

consistent with strategic objectives. Four strategic objectives are relevant to pricing: build, hold, harvest and reposition.

- *Build objective*: for price-sensitive markets, a build objective for a product implies a *price lower than the competition*. If the competition raises its prices we would be slow to match it. For price-insensitive markets, the best pricing strategy becomes less clear-cut. Price in these circumstances will be dependent on the overall positioning strategy thought appropriate for the product.

- *Hold objective*: where the strategic objective is to hold sales and/or market share, the appropriate pricing strategy is to *maintain or match price* relative to the competition. This has implications for price changes: if competition reduces prices then our prices would match this price fall.

- *Harvest objective*: a harvest objective implies the maintenance or raising of profit margins even though sales and/or market share are falling. The implication for pricing strategy would be to set *premium prices*. For products that are being harvested, there would be much greater reluctance to match price cuts than for products that were being built or held. On the other hand, price increases would swiftly be matched.

- *Reposition objective*: changing market circumstances and product fortunes may necessitate the repositioning of an existing product. This may involve a *price change*, the direction and magnitude of which will be dependent on the new positioning strategy for the production. As discussed under product replacement strategies (Chapter 10), Brut's repositioning involved new packaging and an increase in price.

The above examples show how developing clear strategic objectives helps the setting of price and clarifies appropriate reaction to competitive price changes. Price setting, then, is much more sophisticated than simply asking 'How much can I get for this product?' The process starts by asking more fundamental questions like 'How is this product going to be positioned in the marketplace?' and 'What is the appropriate strategic objective for this product?' Only after these questions have been answered can price sensibly be determined.

Value to the customer

A second marketing consideration when setting prices is estimating a product's value to the customer. Already when discussing marketing strategy its importance has been outlined: price should be accurately keyed to the value to the customer. In brief, the more value a product gives compared to that of the competition, the higher the price that can be charged. In this section we shall explore a number of ways of estimating value to the customer. This is critical because of the close relationship between value and price. Four methods of estimating value will now be discussed: the buy-response method, trade-off analysis, experimentation and economic value to the customer analysis.

The buy-response method

The **buy-response method** estimates directly the value that customers place on a product by asking them if they would be willing to buy it at varying price levels.[16] The proportion of people who would be willing to buy the product is plotted against price to produce a buy-response curve (see Fig. 11.6). As the figure shows, the curve is usually bell-shaped indicating prices that are too high or too low (indicating poor quality).

Figure 11.6 The buy-response curve

Source: Gabor, A. (1977) *Price as a Quality Indicator in Pricing: Principles and Practices,* London: Heinemann.

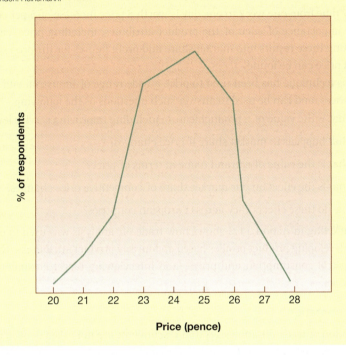

The methodology is as follows.

1. Up to 10 prices are chosen within the range usual for the product field.

2. Respondents are shown the product and asked 'Would you buy X at …?' The price first quoted will be near the average for the product field and the other prices stated at random.

3. The percentage of respondents indicating that they would buy is calculated for each price and plotted to form the buy-response curve.

The curve shows the prices at which willingness to buy drops sharply and thus gives an indication of the acceptable price range for the product (in Fig. 11.6 this would be between 23p and 25p).

Although simple to administer and analyse, the buy-response method suffers from one severe drawback: the methodology focuses the respondent's attention on price, which may induce an unrealistically high price-consciousness.[17] In reality, customers weigh price against product features and the benefits they give. The next technique—trade-off analysis—overcomes this problem.

Trade-off analysis

Trade-off analysis (otherwise known as conjoint analysis) measures the trade-off between price and other product features so that their effects on product preference can be established.[18] Respondents are not asked direct questions about price, instead product profiles consisting of product features and price are described and respondents are asked to name their preferred profile. From their answers, the effect of price and other product features can be measured using a computer model. The following is a brief description of the procedure.

The first step is to identify the most important product features (attributes) and benefits that are expected to be gained as a result of buying the product. Product profiles are then built using these attributes (including price) and respondents are asked to choose which product they would buy from pairs of product profiles. Statistical analysis allows the computation of *preference contributions* that permit the preference for attributes to be compared. For example, if the analysis was for an industrial product, trade-off analysis might show that increasing delivery time from one week to one day is worth a price increase of 5 per cent. In addition, the relative importance of each of the product attributes, including price, can be calculated. By translating these results into market share and profit figures for the proposed new product the optimal price can be found.

This technique has been used to price a wide range of industrial and consumer products and services, and can be used to answer such questions as the following.[19]

(1) What is the value of a product feature including improving service levels in price terms?

(2) What happens to market share if price changes?

(3) What is the value of a brand name in terms of price?

(4) What is the effect on our market share of competitive price changes?

(5) How do these effects vary across European countries?

Marketing in Action 11.2 shows how trade-off analysis was used to price a new German car. By developing product profiles based on four key product attributes—the brand, maximum speed, petrol consumption and price—and interviewing target customers, an optimal price could be set.

Experimentation

A limitation of trade-off analysis is that respondents are not asked to back up their preferences with cash expenditure. Consequently there can be some doubt as to whether what they say they prefer may not be reflected in actual purchase when they are asked to part with their money. *Experimental pricing research* attempts to overcome this drawback by placing a product on sale at different locations with varying prices.

The major alternatives are to use a controlled store experiment or test marketing. In a *controlled store experiment* a number of stores are paid to vary the price levels of the product under test. Suppose 100 supermarkets are being used to test two price levels of a brand of coffee; 50 stores would be chosen at random (perhaps after controlling for region and size) and allocated the lower price, the rest would use the higher price. By comparing sales levels and profit contributions between the two groups of stores the most profitable price would be established. A variant of this procedure would test price differences between the test brand and major rival brands. For example, in half the stores a price differential of 2p may be compared with 4p. In practice, considerable sums need to be paid to supermarkets to obtain approval to run such tests, and the implementation of the price levels needs to be monitored carefully to ensure that the stores do sell at the specified prices.

Test marketing can be used to compare the effectiveness of varying prices so long as more than one area is chosen. For example, the same product could be sold in two areas using an identical promotional campaign but with different prices between areas. A more sophisticated design could measure the four combinations of high/low price and high/low promotional expenditure if four areas were chosen. Obviously, the areas would need to be matched (or differences allowed for) in terms of target customer profile so that the result would be comparable. The test needs to be long enough so that trial and repeat purchase at each price can be measured. This is likely to be between 6 and 12 months for products whose purchase cycle lasts more than a few weeks.

A potential problem of using test marketing to measure price effects is competitor activity designed to invalidate the test results. For example, competitors could run special promotions

11.2 marketing in action

Pricing a German Car using Trade-off Analysis

A German car company used conjoint measurement to set the price for its new Tiger model (name disguised). The managers involved in the decision raised questions like the following: What is the 'price value' of our brand? How much is the customer willing to pay for a higher maximum speed? (There is no speed limit in Germany.) How does petrol consumption relate to price acceptance?

The managers proceeded through the following steps. First, they determined that the most relevant product attributes were brand, maximum speed, petrol consumption and price.

Second, they chose characteristics for each attribute. They would test three brands: one German, one Japanese and their own; three maximum speeds: 200, 220 and 240 kilometres per hour; three levels of petrol consumption: 12, 14 and 16 litres per 100 kilometres; and three prices: €25,000, €30,000 and €35,000.

Third, they designed a questionnaire and collected data. The attributes and characteristics yielded 81 possible product profiles, but the company needed only nine profiles to answer its questions. Researchers developed the nine profiles and presented them to target group respondents in pairs, as shown below. Respondents, interviewed by computer, indicated whether they would buy A or B; 32 such comparisons were presented.

Attribute	Profile A	Profile B
Brand	Tiger	Japanese
Maximum speed	200	240
Petrol consumption	12	16
Price	€30,000	€35,000

From the data, the company calculated preference contributions, numerical values that allow the preference for attributes to be compared. Preference contributions allow you to discover that, say, increasing car speed by 20 kilometres per hour generates the same increase in preference for the car as would decreasing the price by €5,000. Adding up the preference contributions results in an overall preference index.

The greater the difference between the lowest and the highest preference contribution within one attribute (that is, the greater the disparity between preference for, say, the most popular brand and the least popular brand), the more important is this attribute. These differences can be translated into percentage importance weights that add up to 100 per cent. In this case:

Brand	35%
Maximum speed	30%
Price	20%
Petrol consumption	15%

Thus customers in this target group were very interested in brand and maximum speed but less sensitive to price and petrol consumption.

Taking the known attribute levels for the Tiger model, the managers could calculate market share and profits for alternative prices. They found that the optimal price was at the upper end of the price range; they set it slightly below €35,000.

Based on: Simon (1992)[20]

---

in the test areas to make sales levels atypical if they discovered the purpose and location of the test marketing activities. Alternatively, they may decide not to react at all. If they know that a pricing experiment is taking place and that syndicated consumer panel data are being used to measure the results they may simply monitor the results since competitors will be receiving the same data as the testing company.[21] By estimating how successful each price has been, they are in a good position to know how to react when a price is set nationally.

Economic value to the customer analysis

Experimentation is more usual when pricing consumer products. However, industrial markets have a powerful tool at their disposal when setting the price of their products: **economic value to the customer (EVC)** analysis. Many organizational purchases are motivated by economic value considerations since reducing costs and increasing revenue are prime objectives of many companies. If a company can produce an offering that has a high EVC, it can set a high price and yet still offer superior value compared to the competition. A high EVC may be because the product generates more revenue for the buyer than competition or because its operating costs (such as maintenance, operation or start-up costs) are lower over its lifetime. EVC analysis is usually particularly revealing when applied to products whose purchase price represents a small proportion of the lifetime costs to the customer.[22]

Figure 11.7 illustrates the calculation of EVC and how it can be used in price setting. A reference product is chosen (often the market leader) with which to compare costs. In the example, the market leader is selling a machine tool for £50,000. However this is only part of a customer's life-cycle costs. In addition, £30,000 start-up costs (installation, lost production and operator training) and £120,000 post-purchase costs (operator, power and maintenance) are incurred. The total life-cycle costs are, therefore, £200,000.

Our new machine tool (product X) has a different customer cost profile. Technological advances have reduced start-up costs to £20,000 and post-purchase costs to £100,000. Therefore total costs are reduced by £30,000 and the EVC our new product offers is £80,000 (£200,000 – £120,000). Thus the EVC figure is the amount a customer would have to pay to make the total life-cycle costs of the new and reference products the same. If the new machine tool was priced at £80,000 this would be the case. Below this price there would be an economic incentive for customers to buy the new machine tool.

EVC analysis is clearly a powerful tool for price setting since it establishes the upper economic limit for price. Management then has to use judgement regarding how much incentive to give the customer to buy the new product and how much of a price premium to charge. A price of £60,000 would give customers a £20,000 lifetime cost saving incentive while establishing a £10,000 price premium over the reference product. In general, the more entrenched the market leader, the more loyal its customer base and the less well known the newcomer, the higher the cost saving incentive needs to be.

In the second example shown in Fig. 11.7 the new machine tool (product Y) does not affect costs but raises the customer's revenues. For example, faster operation may result in more output, or greater precision may enhance product quality leading to higher prices. This product is estimated to give £40,000 extra profit contribution over the reference product because of higher revenues. Its EVC is, therefore, £90,000 indicating the highest price the customer should be willing to pay. Once more, marketing management has to decide how much incentive to give to customers and how much of a price premium to charge.

EVC analysis can be useful in target market selection since different customers may have varying EVC levels. A decision may be made to target the market segment that has the highest EVC figure since for these customers the product has the greatest differential advantage. The implementation of EVC-based pricing strategy relies on a well-trained salesforce, which is capable of explaining sophisticated economic value calculations to customers, and field-based evidence that the estimates of cost savings and revenue increases will occur in practice.

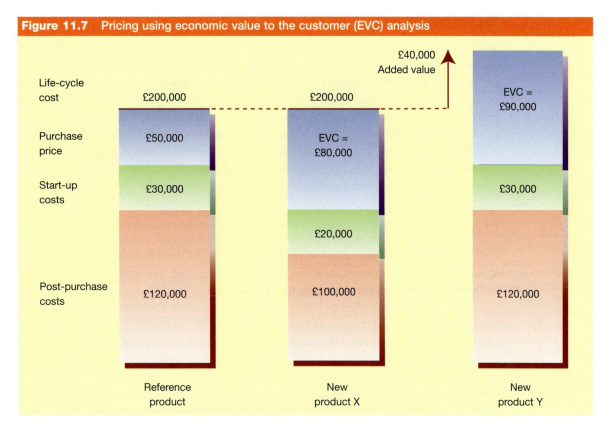

Figure 11.7 Pricing using economic value to the customer (EVC) analysis

Price–quality relationships

A third consideration when adopting a marketing-orientated approach to pricing is the relationship between price and perceived quality. Many people use price as an indicator of quality. This is particularly the case for products where objective measurement of quality is not possible, such as drinks and perfume. But the effect is also to be found with consumer durables and industrial products. A study of price and quality perceptions of cars, for example, found that higher-priced cars were perceived to possess (unjustified) high quality.[23] Also sales of a branded agricultural fertilizer rose after the price was raised above that of its generic competitors despite the fact that it was the same compound. Interviews with farmers revealed that they believed the fertilizer to improve crop yield compared with rival products. Clearly price had influenced quality perceptions.

Product line pricing

Marketing-orientated companies also need to take account of where the price of a new product fits into its existing product line. For example, when Ford developed the Fusion it had to carefully price-position the model range within its existing product line of Ka, Fiesta, Focus and Mondeo.

Some companies prefer to extend their product lines rather than reduce the price of existing brands in the face of price competition. They launch cut-price fighter brands to compete with the low-price rivals. This has the advantage of maintaining the image and profit margins of existing brands.

By producing a range of brands at different price points, companies can cover the varying price sensitivities of customers and encourage them to trade up to the more expensive, higher-margin brands.

Explicability

The capability of salespeople to explain a high price to customers may constrain price flexibility. In markets where customers demand economic justification of prices, the inability to produce cost and/or revenue arguments may mean that high prices cannot be set. In other circumstances the customer may reject a price that does not seem to reflect the cost of producing the product. For example, sales of an industrial chemical compound that repaired grooves in drive-shafts suffered because many customers believed that the price of £500 did not reflect the cost of producing the compound. Only when the salesforce explained that the premium price was needed to cover high research and development expenditure did customers accept that the price was not exploitative.

Competition

Competition factors are important determinants of price. At the very least, competitive prices should be taken into account; yet it is a fact of commercial life that many companies do not know what the competition is charging for its products.

Care has to be taken when defining competition. When asked to name competitors, many marketing managers list companies that supply technically similar products. For example, a paint manufacturer will name other paint manufacturers. However, as Fig. 11.8 illustrates, this is only one layer of competition. A second layer consists of dissimilar products solving the same problem in a similar way. Polyurethane varnish manufacturers would fall into this category. A third level of competition would come from products solving the problem (or eliminating it) in a dissimilar way. Since window frames are often painted, PVC double glazing manufacturers would form competition at this level.

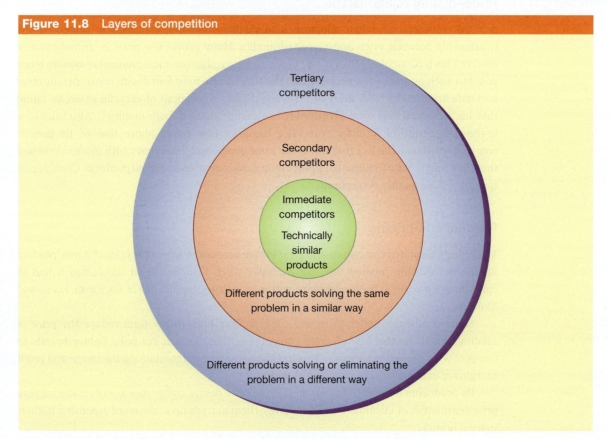

Figure 11.8 Layers of competition

This analysis is not simply academic, as the effects of price changes can be misleading if these three layers of competition are not taken into consideration. For example, if all paint manufacturers raised their prices simultaneously they might believe that overall sales would not be dramatically affected if they mistakenly defined competition as technically similar products. The reality is, however, that such price collusion would make polyurethane varnish and, over a longer period, PVC double glazing more attractive to customers. The implication is that companies must take into account all three levels of competition when setting and changing prices.

In Europe a potential competitive threat is the development of parallel importing, which is the practice of importing goods from low-priced markets into high-priced ones by distributors. This produces the novel effect of a brand competing with itself (on price). The impact of parallel importing on prices is analysed in Marketing in Action 11.3.

11.3 marketing in action

Parallel Importing and Pricing

Parallel importing involves distributors such as retailers buying products in one country (where prices are low) and selling them in another (where prices are higher) at a low price. For example, a pharmaceutical company might sell its drugs in a developing country at a low price only to discover that these discounted drugs are exported to another country where they are in direct competition with the same product sold for higher prices by the same firm.

Not surprisingly, manufacturers have a lot to lose by this activity. First, it lowers average selling prices and therefore reduces profit margins. Second, manufacturers lose control over where and to whom their products are sold. This can damage brand image (compounded by the price drop) as the product range is sold in retail outlets that are incompatible with the brand's position in the marketplace. Finally, the relationship between manufacturers and their traditional distributors can be damaged as the latter see their sales decline in favour of their price-cutting rivals.

An important ruling on parallel importing by the European Court of Justice found in favour of Silhouette, an upmarket Austrian sunglasses manufacturer, which sold 21,000 pairs of an older model to a Bulgarian company on the understanding that they would be sold only in Bulgaria or the former Soviet Union. However, the sunglasses were soon back in Austria being sold at the discount chain Hartlaver at a low price. The court ruled that Silhouette should have the right to choose its distributor.

In another ruling, the European Court of Justice sided with Levi Strauss in its dispute with Tesco, the UK supermarket chain over the distribution of cut-price Levi's 501 jeans. Tesco had been selling the 501s, purchased inexpensively in the USA, for £27.99 (€40) compared to £50 (€72) in Levi's authorized shops.

Levi Strauss argued that its premium brand reputation was in danger of being damaged if any supermarket could sell its products at 'bargain-basement prices'. It also claimed that the staff selling its jeans required special training. Tesco argued that it was in the consumers' interest to be able to buy inexpensive jeans.

The ruling prevents Tesco from importing Levi's products from outside the European Economic Area—the EU, plus Norway, Iceland and Liechtenstein—and selling them at greatly reduced prices. However, the ruling does not prevent Tesco from importing Levi's or other goods such as cheap designer clothes, perfumes and cosmetics from the 'grey market' within Europe.

Based on: Anonymous (1998);[24] Cateora et al. (2000);[25] Mercado et al (2000);[26] Anonymous (2002);[27] Osborn (2001)[28]

Negotiating margins

In some markets, customers expect a price reduction. Price paid is therefore very different from list price. In the car market, for example, customers expect to pay less than the asking price in return for a cash sale. For organizational customers, Marn and Rosiello describe the difference between list price and realized or transaction price as the price waterfall.[29] The difference can be accounted for by order-size discounts, competitive discounts (a discretionary discount negotiated before the order is taken), a fast payment discount, an annual volume bonus and promotional allowances.

Managing this price waterfall is a key element in achieving a satisfactory transaction price. Marketing-orientated companies recognize that such discounting may be a fact of commercial life and build in *negotiating margins* that allow prices to fall from list price levels but still permit profitable transaction prices to be achieved.

Effect on distributors/retailers

When products are sold through intermediaries such as distributors or retailers, the list price to the customer must reflect the margins required by them. When Müller yoghurt was first launched in the UK, a major factor in gaining distribution in a mature market was the fact that its high price allowed attractive profit margins for the supermarket chains. Conversely, the implementation of a penetration pricing strategy may be hampered if distributors refuse to stock the product because the profit per unit sold is less than that for competitive products.

The implication is that pricing strategy is dependent on understanding not only the ultimate customer but also the needs of the distributors and retailers who form the link between them and the manufacturer. If their needs cannot be accommodated, product launch may not be viable or a different distribution system (for example, direct selling) may be required.

Political factors

High prices can be a contentious public issue, which may invoke government intervention. In recent years, public opprobrium has focused on the price of compact discs and children's computer games. Where price is out of line with manufacturing costs, political pressure may act to force down prices. The European Commission and national bodies such as the Competition Commission have been active in discouraging anti-competitive practices such as price-fixing. Indeed, the establishment of the single European market was a result of the desire to raise competitive pressures and thereby reduce prices throughout the European Union.

Companies need to take great care that their pricing strategies are not seen to be against the public interest. Exploitation of a monopoly position may bring short-term profits but incur the backlash of a public inquiry into pricing practices.

Costs

The final consideration that should be borne in mind when setting prices is costs. This may seem in contradiction to the outward-looking marketing-orientated approach but, in reality, costs do enter the pricing equation. The secret is to consider costs alongside all of the other considerations discussed under marketing-orientated price setting rather than in isolation. In this way costs act as a constraint: if the market will not bear the full cost of producing and marketing the product it should not be launched.

What should be avoided is the blind reference to costs when setting prices. Simply because one product costs less to make than another does not imply that its price should be less. Two examples from the car industry illustrate this point. Because the Fiat Tipo is manufactured in a more modern plant than the Fiat Uno it costs less to produce; it is priced higher than the Uno, however, because it is a larger car conferring more customer benefits. Similarly the Rover 400 costs less to manufacture than the Rover 200. Marketing research has shown, however, that because the Rover 400 is a bigger car with a larger boot customers expect to pay more for that model. Rover prices the two models in line with customer expectations, not costs.

Marketers are increasingly using technology to help price products. Marketing in Action 11.4 gives some examples.

11.4 marketing in action

Information Technology Aids Price Setting

Although marketers recognize that, for most pricing decisions, the process is one of taking into account the key factors discussed in this chapter, in some instances prices can be set directly using information technology.

One example of this is the launch of Electronic Shelf Labels by NCR in the USA. Prices are displayed in the supermarkets on small LCD panels. As goods are scanned, computers at head office make a calculation based on the remaining supply of products and the predicted demand, and alter the price in each store. Another is Coca-Cola, which is testing a prototype vending machine that changes the price of each can as the temperature changes.

Roche, a Swiss pharmaceutical company, has also introduced technology to help the salesforce set prices more efficiently. Formerly, price setting was in the hands of salespeople who had wide latitude to set prices deal by deal. Software for every salesperson's laptop computer was introduced to provide accurate—and profitable—price quotes in the field.

Based on: Anonymous (2002);[30] Ritson (2002)[31]

Initiating price changes

Our discussion of pricing strategy so far has looked at the factors that affect it. By taking into account the 10 marketing-orientated factors, managers can judge the correct level at which to set prices. But in a highly competitive world, pricing is dynamic: managers need to know when and how to raise or lower prices, and whether or not to react to competitors' price moves. First, we shall discuss initiating price changes, before analysing how to react to competitors' price changes.

Three key issues associated with initiating price changes are the *circumstances* that may lead a company to raise or lower prices, the *tactics* that can be used, and *estimating competitor reaction*. Table 11.5 (overleaf) illustrates the major points relevant to each of these considerations.

Circumstances

A price increase may be justified as a result of marketing research (for example, trade-off analysis or experimentation) which reveals that customers place a higher *value* on the product than is reflected in its price. *Rising costs*, and hence reduced profit margins, may also stimulate price rises. Another factor that leads to price increases is *excess demand*. A company that cannot

Table 11.5	Initiating price changes	
	Increases	Cuts
Circumstances	Value greater than price Rising costs Excess demand Harvest objective	Value less than price Excess supply Build objective Price war unlikely Pre-empt competitive entry
Tactics	Price jump Staged price increases Escalator clauses Price unbundling Lower discounts	Price fall Staged price reductions Fighter brands Price bundling Higher discounts
Estimating competitor reaction	Strategic objectives Self-interest Competitive situation Past experience	

supply the demand created by its customers may choose to raise prices in an effort to balance demand and supply. This can be an attractive option as profit margins are automatically widened. The final circumstance when companies may decide to raise prices is when embarking on a *harvest objective*. Prices are raised to increase margins even though sales may fall.

Correspondingly, price cuts may be provoked by the discovery that price is high compared to the *value* that customers place on the product, *falling costs* (and the desire to bring down costs further through the experience curve effect), and where there is *excess supply* leading to excess capacity. A further circumstance that may lead to price falls is the adoption of a *build objective*. When customers are thought to be price sensitive, price cutting may be used to build sales and market share. A damper on this tactic would be when a *price war* might be provoked, as happened when Reemtsma Cigarettenfabriken cut the price of its West brand from DM3.80 to DM3.30 in West Germany.[32] This was the first price-cutting move of this severity since the 1940s and led to competitor retaliation that saw the collapse of cigarette prices and margins.

The final circumstance that might lead to price cuts is the desire to *pre-empt competitive entry* into a market. Proactive price cuts—before the new competitor enters—are painful to implement because they incur short-term profit sacrifices but immediately reduce the attractiveness of the market to the potential entrant and reduce the risk of customer annoyance if prices are reduced only after competitive entry.[33] This was the tactic used in 1984 by Cummins Engines, which slashed the prices of its small diesels by 30 per cent to prevent the entry of Japanese companies in its market.[34]

Tactics

Price increases and cuts can be implemented in many ways. The most direct is the *price jump or fall*, which increases or decreases the price by the full amount at one go. A price jump avoids prolonging the pain of a price increase over a long period but may raise the visibility of the price increase to customers. Using *staged price increases* might make the price rise more palatable but runs the risk of a company being charged with 'always raising its prices'. A *one-stage price fall* can have a high-impact dramatic effect that can be heavily promoted, but also has an immediate impact on profit margins. *Staged price reductions* have a less dramatic effect but may be used when a price cut is believed to be necessary but the amount necessary to stimulate sales is unclear. Small cuts may be initiated as a learning process that proceeds until the desired effect on sales has been achieved.

Price can also be raised by using *escalator clauses*. The contracts for some organizational purchases are drawn up before the product has been made. Constructing the product—for example, a new defence system or motorway—may take a number of years. An escalator clause in the contract allows the supplier to stipulate price increases in line with a specified index—for example, increases in industry wage rates or the cost of living.

Price unbundling is another tactic that effectively raises prices. Many product offerings actually consist of a set of products for which an overall price is set (for example, computer hardware and software). Price unbundling allows each element in the offering to be priced separately in such a way that the total price is raised. A variant on this process is charging for services that were previously included in the product's price. For example, manufacturers of mainframe computers have the option of unbundling installation and training services, and charging for them separately.

A final tactic is to maintain the list price but *lower discounts* to customers. In periods of heavy demand for new cars, dealers lower the cash discount given to customers, for example. Quantity discounts can also be manipulated to raise the transaction price to customers. The percentage discount per quantity can be lowered, or the quantity that qualifies for a particular percentage discount can be raised.

Companies that are contemplating a price cut have three options besides a direct price fall. A company defending a premium-priced brand that is under attack from a cut-price competitor may choose to maintain its price while introducing a *fighter brand*. The established brand keeps its premium-price position while the fighter brand competes with the rival for price-sensitive customers. Where a number of products and services that tend to be bought together are priced separately, *price bundling* can be used to effectively lower price. For example, televisions can be offered with 'free three-year repair warranties' or cars offered with 'free labour at first service'. Finally, *discount terms* can be made more attractive by increasing the percentage or lowering the qualifying levels.

Estimating competitor reaction

A key factor in the price change decision is the extent of competitor reaction. A price rise that no competitor follows may turn customers away, while a price cut that is met by the competition may reduce industry profitability. Four factors affect the extent of competitor reaction: their strategic objectives, what is in their self-interest, the competitive situation at the time of the price change, and past experience.

Companies should try to gauge their *competitors' strategic objectives* for their products. By observing pricing and promotional behaviour, talking to distributors and even hiring their personnel, estimates of whether competitor products are being built, held or harvested can be made. This is crucial information: the competitors' response to our price increase or cut will depend upon it. They are more likely to follow our price increase if their strategic objective is to hold or harvest. If they are intent on building market share, they are more likely to resist following our price increase. Conversely, they are more likely to follow our price cuts if they are building or holding, and more likely to ignore our price cuts if they are harvesting.

Self-interest is also important when estimating competitor reactions. Managers initiating price changes should try to place themselves in the position of their competitors. What reaction is in their best interests? This may depend on the circumstances of the price change. For example, if price is raised in response to a general rise in cost inflation, the competition is more likely to follow than if price is raised because of the implementation of a harvest objective.

Price may also depend upon the *competitive situation*. For example, if the competition has excess capacity, a price cut is more likely to be matched than if this is not the case. Similarly, a price rise is more likely to be followed if the competition is faced with excess demand.

Competitor reaction can also be judged by looking at their reactions to previous price changes. While *past experience* is not always a reliable guide, it may provide insights into the way in which competitors view price changes and the likely responses they might make. There is no doubt that the entry of new competitors into a mature market can radically alter price structures.

Reacting to competitors' price changes

When competitors initiate price changes, companies need to analyse their appropriate reactions. Three issues are relevant here: when to follow, what to ignore, and the tactics required if the price change is to be followed. Table 11.6 summarizes the main considerations.

Table 11.6 Reacting to competitors' price changes

	Increases	Cuts
When to follow	Rising costs Excess demand Price-insensitive customers Price rise compatible with brand image Harvest or hold objective	Falling costs Excess supply Price-sensitive customers Price fall compatible with brand image Build or hold objective
When to ignore	Stable or falling costs Excess supply Price-sensitive customers Price rise incompatible with brand image Build objective	Rising costs Excess demand Price-insensitive customers Price fall incompatible with brand image Harvest objective
Tactics: – quick response – slow response	Margin improvement urgent Gains to be made by being customer's friend	Offset competitive threat High customer loyalty

When to follow

Competitive price increases are more likely to be followed when they are due to general *rising cost* levels, or industry-wide *excess demand*. In these circumstances the initial pressure to raise prices is the same on all parties. Following a price rise is also more likely when customers are relatively *price insensitive*, which means that the follower will not gain much advantage by resisting the price increase. Where *brand image is consistent* with high prices, a company is more likely to follow a competitor's price rise as to do so would be consistent with the brand's positioning strategy. Finally, a price rise is more likely to be followed when a company is pursuing a *harvest or hold objective* because, in both cases, the emphasis is more on profit margin than sales/market share gain.

Price cuts are likely to be followed when they are stimulated by general *falling costs* or *excess supply*. Falling costs allow all companies to cut prices while maintaining margins, and excess supply means that a company is unlikely to allow a rival to make sales gains at its expense. Price cuts will also be followed in *price-sensitive markets* since allowing one company to cut price without retaliation would mean large sales gains for the price cutter. The image of the company can also affect reaction to price cuts. Some companies position themselves as low-price manufacturers or retail outlets. In such circumstances they would be less likely to allow a price reduction by a competitor to go unchallenged for to do so would be *incompatible with their brand image*. Finally, price cuts are likely to be followed when the company has a *build* or *hold strategic objective*. In such circumstances an aggressive price move by a competitor would be followed to prevent sales/market share loss. In the case of a build objective, response may be more dramatic with a price fall exceeding the initial competitive move.

When to ignore

The circumstances associated with companies not reacting to a competitive price move are in most cases simply the opposite of the above. Price increases are likely to be ignored when *costs are stable or falling*, which means that there are no cost pressures forcing a general price rise. In the situation of *excess supply* companies may view a price rise as making the initiator less competitive, and therefore allow the price to take place unchallenged, particularly when customers are *price sensitive*. Companies occupying low-price positions may regard a price rise in response to a price increase from a rival to be *incompatible with their brand image*. Finally, companies pursuing a *build objective* may allow a competitor's price rise to go unmatched in order to gain sales and market share.

Price cuts are likely to be ignored in conditions of *rising costs, excess demand* and when servicing *price-insensitive customers*. Premium price positioners may be reluctant to follow competitors' price cuts for to do so would be *incompatible with brand image*. Lastly, price cuts may be resisted by companies using a *harvest objective*.

Tactics

When a company decides to follow a price change it can do so quickly or slowly. A *quick price reaction* is likely when there is an urgent need to *improve profit margins*. Here the competitor's price increase will be welcomed as an opportunity to achieve this objective.

Conversely, a *slow reaction* may be desirable when an *image of being the customer's friend* is being sought. The first company to announce a price increase is often seen as the high-price supplier. Some companies have mastered the art of playing the low-cost supplier by never initiating price increases and following competitors' increases slowly.[35] The key to this tactic is timing the response: too quickly and customers do not notice; too slowly and profit is foregone. The optimum period can be found only by experience but, during it, salespeople should be told to stress to customers that the company is doing everything it can to hold prices for as long as possible.

A *quick response* to a competitor's price fall will happen to ward off a *competitive threat*. In the face of undesirable sales/market share erosion, fast action is needed to nullify potential competitor gains. However, reaction will be slow when a company has a *loyal customer base* willing to accept higher prices for a period so long as they can rely on price parity over the longer term.

Ethical issues in pricing

Key issues regarding ethical issues in pricing are price fixing, predatory pricing, deceptive pricing, price discrimination, penetration pricing and obesity and product dumping.

Price fixing

One of the driving forces towards lower prices is competition. Therefore, it can be in the interests of producers to agree among themselves not to compete on price. This is an act of collusion and is banned in many countries and regions, including the EU. Article 83 of the Treaty of Rome is designed to ban practices preventing, restricting or distorting competition, except where these contribute to efficiency without inhibiting consumers' fair share of the benefit. Groups of companies that collude are said to be acting as a cartel and these are by no means easy to uncover. One of the European Commission's most famous success stories is the uncovering of the illicit cartel among 23 of Europe's top chemical companies from the UK, France, Germany, Belgium, Italy, Spain, the Netherlands, Finland, Norway and Austria. Through collusion, they were able to sustain levels of profitability for low-density polyethylene and PVC in the face of severe overcapacity. Quotas were set to limit companies' attempts to gain market share through price competition and prices were fixed to harmonize the differences between countries to discourage customers from shopping around for the cheapest deals.[36] In the UK, the Office of Fair Trading imposed record fines on retail giants Argos and Littlewoods for the price fixing of toys and games.[37]

Opponents of price fixing claim that it is unethical because it restrains the consumer's freedom of choice and interferes with each firm's interest in offering high-quality products at the best price. Proponents argue that under harsh economic conditions price fixing is necessary to ensure a fair profit for the industry and to avoid price wars that might lead to bankruptcies and unemployment.

Predatory pricing

This refers to the situation where a firm cuts its prices with the aim of driving out the competition. The firm is content to incur losses with the intent that high profits will be generated through higher prices once the competition is eliminated. As we have seen, British Airways and TWA were accused of this practice in trying to eliminate Laker Airlines from their Atlantic routes. More recently easyJet has accused British Airways of predatory pricing through its no-frills subsidiary Go; easyJet claims that the low prices charged by Go are being subsidized by the profits made by British Airways' other operations.

Deceptive pricing

This occurs when consumers are misled by the price deals offered by companies. Two examples are misleading price comparisons and 'bait and switch'. Misleading price comparisons occur when a store sets artificially high prices for a short time so that much lower 'sale' prices can be claimed later. The purpose is to deceive the customer into believing they are being offered bargains. Some countries, such as the UK and Germany, have laws that state the minimum period over which the regular price should be charged before it can be used as a reference price in a sale. Bait and switch is the practice of advertising a very low price on a product (the bait) to attract customers to a retail outlet. Once in the store the salesperson persuades the customer to buy a higher-priced product (the switch). The customer may be told that the lower-priced product is no longer in stock or that it is of inferior quality.

Penetration pricing and obesity

A controversial issue is the question of the ethics of charging low prices for fatty food targeting young people. Critics claim that, by doing so, fast-food companies encourage obesity. Others claim that such companies cannot be blamed when consumers are made well aware by the media of the consequences of eating fatty foods. Ethical Marketing in Action 11.1 discusses the issues involved.

11.1 ethical marketing in action

Penetration Pricing: Should Fast-food Companies take the Blame for Youth Obesity?

Pricing can encourage inappropriate consumption. We know, for example, that reducing the price of alcohol increases the amount of drinking that goes on in a particular society. Given that the World Health Organization estimates that, in the European region, as many as one in four deaths among those under 30 years old is caused by alcohol, this has clear ramifications. By contrast, high prices, such as for designer clothes or even more mundane items like fresh fruit, can limit access by children from low-income families to fashionable trainers or a healthy diet.

This last area—diet—provides an interesting case in point. Fast-food companies have recently come in for trenchant criticism because of their pricing strategy. An article in *The Washington Monthly* highlights the problem. A 'Value Meal', including a coke and fries, delivers 1190 calories—more than half the daily requirement for a teenage girl—for just $3.99. This can be 'King-sized' for a few cents more, raising the calorie count to a massive 1,570. These calories come principally in the form of unhealthy fat and sugar.

Many argue that this type of marketing is contributing to the US epidemic of obesity, an epidemic that is rapidly crossing the Atlantic. In the USA, the Centers for Disease Control and Prevention (CDC) say that, in 2000, the prevalence of obesity among US adults was 19.8 per cent. The figures are increasing for young people: in 2000 there were nearly twice as many overweight children and almost three times as many overweight adolescents as there were in 1980.

In the UK, the proportion of the population that is obese or overweight has been rising in recent years. The prevalence of obesity has now reached 21 per cent in both males and females in England and has almost trebled since 1980. In the UK, around one in four children is overweight and one in ten is obese. In 1995, fast-food market leader McDonald's had 577 outlets in the UK; by 2001, it had 1200. Burger King, the second most popular fast-food chain in the UK, had 685 outlets in 2001. The penetration of 15–19 year olds eating in fast-food restaurants is 74 per cent; for 20–24 year olds it is 68 per cent.

Certainly the two New York teenagers who began legal proceedings against McDonald's in November 2002 felt the company had a case to answer. Their suit alleged that 'McDonald's violated New York State's consumer fraud statutes by deliberately misleading consumers into thinking their cheeseburgers and other products were healthy and nutritious.' It said that the company did not adequately provide information on the health risks associated with fast food, and the children developed health problems from eating its products. However, in January 2003, US District Judge Robert Sweet rejected the lawsuit:

> ❝This opinion is guided by the principle that legal consequences should not attach to the consumption of hamburgers and other fast-food fare unless consumers are unaware of the dangers of each such food. … If consumers know the potential ill-health effect of eating at McDonald's, they cannot blame McDonald's if they, nonetheless, choose to satiate their appetite with a surfeit of supersized McDonald's products.❞

This is an example of just one of the obesity lawsuits against a fast-food franchise. Parallels can be drawn with the 'Big Tobacco' litigation cases in the USA, although, unlike tobacco, fast food is not addictive. However, in November 2002, a report from the investment bank UBS Warburg drew the conclusion that in the longer term, anti-obesity action will hold back producers of fast foods, soft drinks, sugar- and fat-based foods from increasing their revenues. McDonald's is one of a list of companies, ▶

▶ including Tate & Lyle, Hershey's, Cadbury Schweppes, Pepsi and Coca-Cola, which in stock market terms are no longer considered such 'safe' investments as they once were.

Based on: Anonymous (2001);[40] BBC News Online (2002);[41] Godfrey (1989);[42] Key Note (2002);[43] Young and Nestle (2002);[44] www.nysd.uscourts.gov[45]

Price discrimination

This occurs when a supplier offers a better price for the same product to one buyer and not to another, resulting in an unfair competitive advantage. Price discrimination can be justified when the costs of supplying different customers varies, where the price differences reflect differences in the level of competition and where different volumes are purchased. Price discrimination can take place at a regional level. For example, according to the European Commission, UK car prices were 35 per cent higher than elsewhere in Europe before tax.[38] This led to some buyers travelling to mainland Europe to buy new cars and to some dealers planning to import cars for private buyers.[39]

Product dumping

This involves the export of products at much lower prices than charged in the domestic market, sometimes below the cost of production. Products are 'dumped' for a variety of reasons. First, unsold stocks may be exported at a low price rather than risk lowering prices in the home market. Second, products may be manufactured for sale overseas at low prices to fill otherwise unused production capacity. Finally, products that are regarded as unsafe at home may be dumped in countries that do not have such stringent safety rules. For example, the US Consumer Product Safety Commission ruled that three-wheel cycles were dangerous. Many companies responded by selling their inventories at low prices in other countries.[46]

Ethical dilemma

Coffee is a valuable traded commodity with a total value of $50 billion per year. However, there is a vast oversupply and export coffee prices have fallen by more than 70 per cent in the last five years. This fall in world prices to their lowest level ever in real terms has had a dramatic impact on the 85 million people worldwide who depend on coffee for their livelihood. For many coffee farmers, the price obtained for their crop barely provides a living income. For multinational coffee brands this provides a source of supply where prices are low, which they can then sell in western countries where prices are higher. Is this pricing strategy ethical? To find out more you may wish to visit the following websites: Fairtrade Foundation (http://www.fairtrade.org.uk); International Coffee Organization (http://www.ico.org).

Review

1 **The economist's approach to price determination**
- The economist's approach to pricing was developed as an explanation of market behaviour and focuses on demand and supply. There are limitations in applying this approach in practice, which means that marketers turn to other methods in business.

2 **The differences between full cost and direct cost pricing**
- Full cost pricing takes into account both fixed and direct costs. Direct cost pricing takes into account only direct costs such as labour and materials.
- Both methods suffer from the problem that they are internally orientated methods. Direct cost pricing can be useful when the corporate objective is survival and there is a desperate need to fill capacity.

3 **An understanding of going-rate pricing and competitive bidding**
- Going-rate pricing is setting price levels at the rate generally applicable in the market, focusing on competitors' offerings and prices rather than on company costs. Marketers try to avoid going-rate pricing by creating a differential advantage.
- Competitive bidding involves the drawing up of detailed specifications for a product and putting the contract out to tender. Potential suppliers bid for the order with price an important choice criterion. Competitive bidding models have been developed to help the bidding process but they have severe limitations.

4 **The advantages of marketing-orientated pricing over cost-orientated and competitor-orientated pricing methods**
- Marketing-orientated pricing takes into account a much wider range of factors that are relevant to the setting of prices. Although costs and competition are still taken into account, marketers will take a much more customer-orientated view of pricing, including customers' willingness to pay as reflected in the perceived value of the product. Marketers will also evaluate the target market of the product to establish the price sensitivity of customers. This will be affected by such factors as the degree of competition, the degree of excess demand, and the ability of target customers to pay a high price. A full list of factors that marketers take into account is given in point 5 below.

5 **The factors that affect price setting when using a marketing-orientated approach**
- A marketing-orientated approach involves the analysis of marketing strategy, value to the customer, price–quality relationships, explicability, product line pricing, competition, negotiating margins, effect on distributors/retailers, political factors and costs.

6 **When and how to initiate price increases and cuts**
- Initiating price increases is likely to be carried out when value is greater than price, in the face of rising costs, when there is excess demand and where a harvest objective is being followed.
- Tactics are a price jump, staged price increases, escalator clauses, price unbundling and lower discounts.
- Initiating price cuts is likely to be carried out when value is less than price, when there is excess supply, where a build objective is being followed, where a price war is unlikely and when there is a desire to pre-empt competitive entry.
- Tactics are a price fall, staged price reductions, the use of fighter brands, price bundling and higher discounts.

▶ **7** **When and when not to follow competitor-initiated price increases and cuts; when to follow quickly and when to follow slowly**
- Competitor-initiated price increases should be followed when there are rising costs, excess demand, price-insensitive customers, where the price rise is compatible with brand image and where a harvest or hold objective is being followed.
- Competitor-initiated price increases should not be followed when costs are stable or falling, with excess supply, with price-sensitive customers, where the price rise is incompatible with brand image and where a build objective is being followed.
- The price increase should be followed quickly when the need for margin improvement is urgent, and slowly when there are gains to be made by being seen to be the customer's friend.
- Competitor-initiated price cuts should be followed when there are falling costs, excess supply, price-sensitive customers, where the price cut is compatible with brand image, and where a build or hold objective is being followed.
- Competitor-initiated price cuts should not be followed when there are rising costs, excess demand, price-insensitive customers, where the price fall is incompatible with brand image and where a harvest objective is being followed.
- The price cut should be followed quickly when there is a need to offset a competitive threat, and slowly where there is high customer loyalty.

8 **Ethical issues in pricing**
- There are potential problems relating to price fixing, predatory pricing, deceptive pricing, price discrimination and product dumping.

Key terms

buy-response method a study of the value customers place on a product by asking them if they would be willing to buy it at varying price levels

competitive bidding drawing up detailed specifications for a product and putting the contract out to tender

direct cost pricing the calculation of only those costs that are likely to rise as output increases

economic value to the customer (EVC) the amount a customer would have to pay to make the total life-cycle costs of a new and a reference product the same

full cost pricing pricing so as to include all costs and based on certain sales volume assumptions

going-rate pricing pricing at the rate generally applicable in the market, focusing on competitors' offerings rather than on company costs

marketing-oriented pricing an approach to pricing that takes a range of marketing factors into account when setting prices

parallel importing when importers buy products from distributors in one country and sell them in another to distributors who are not part of the manufacturer's normal distribution; caused by big price differences for the same product between different countries

positioning strategy the choice of target market (*where* the company wishes to compete) and differential advantage (*how* the company wishes to compete)

price unbundling pricing each element in the offering so that the price of the total product package is raised

price waterfall the difference between list price and realized or transaction price

trade-off analysis a measure of the trade-off customers make between price and other product features so that their effects on product preference can be established

Internet exercise

Seiko produces a wide range of watches, catering for numerous different markets. Furthermore it markets these watches under a variety of brand names such as Lorus, Pulsar, Spoon, Yema Paris, Dolce & Gabbana, Disney, Nike and the Seiko brand name itself. Explore the company's website, noting the prices of the varied brands on offer.

Visit: www.seiko.co.uk

Questions

(a) Are customers who buy watches price sensitive?
(b) Describe Seiko's general pricing strategy for the brands it markets.
(c) What does the company's positioning strategy have to do with its pricing strategy?
(d) How can Seiko justify the price differences between the various brands it manages?

Visit the Online Learning Centre at www.mcgraw-hill.co.uk/textbooks/jobber for more Internet exercises.

Study questions

1. Accountants are always interested in profit margins; sales managers want low prices to help push sales; and marketing managers are interested in high prices to establish premium positions in the marketplace. To what extent do you agree with this statement in relation to the setting of prices?

2. You are the marketing manager of a company that is about to launch the first voice-activated language translator. The owner talks into the device, the machine electronically translates into the relevant language and speaks to the listener. What factors should you take into consideration when pricing this product?

3. Why is value to the customer a more logical approach to setting prices than cost of production? What role can costs play in the setting of prices?

4. Discuss the advantages and disadvantages of experimentation in assessing customers' willingness to pay.

5. What is economic value to the customer analysis? Under what conditions can it play an important role in price setting?

6. Under intense cost-inflationary pressure you are considering a price increase. What other considerations would you take into account before initiating the price rise?

7. You are the marketing manager of a premium-priced industrial chemical. A competitor has launched a cut-price alternative that possesses 90 per cent of the effectiveness of your product. If you do not react, you estimate that you will lose 30 per cent of sales. What are your strategic pricing options? What would you do?

8. The only reason that companies set low prices is that their products are undifferentiated. Discuss.

9. By far the most criticized ethical issue in marketing is the practice of price fixing. Discuss.

When you have read this chapter log on to the Online Learning Centre at www.mcgraw-hill.co.uk/textbooks/jobber to explore chapter-by-chapter test questions, links and further online study tools for marketing.

case twenty-one

easyJet and Ryanair: Flying High with Low Prices

The story behind the success of Europe's no-frills airlines began in the USA. Southwest Airlines, a Texas-based carrier, was the first to exploit successfully the deregulation of American skies in 1978. Since then, the airline has operated a no-frills, low-fare business model involving no free meals or coffee, only peanuts. The attraction is fares set at about one-fifth of those of the mainstream airlines. Its fleet is made up entirely of one type of aircraft, the Boeing 737, to keep costs down by reducing pilot training and maintenance costs. It flies between secondary airports, which are sometimes over an hour's drive from city centres.

An essential component in the Southwest Airlines approach is fast turnaround times from uncongested airports, which can be as short as 20 minutes with no seat allocation for passengers and with cabin crews doing the cleaning. This means that aircraft can be used for 15 hours per day. In comparison, conventional airlines that run a 'hub and spoke' network fly aircraft for only half that length of time, as aircraft must wait to connect with incoming flights. Southwest Airlines has embraced Internet transactions to cut paperwork and administrative costs, and has rejected corporate acquisitions in favour of organic growth. The result has been a continual stream of profits (unlike other American airlines) and a business that attracts nearly 65 million passengers a year.

In Europe, Southwest Airlines' approach and success has been mirrored by easyJet and Ryanair, who have pioneered low-fare, no-frills flying. Growth has been spectacular, with 26 per cent of consumers travelling with a low-cost airline in 2002 compared with just 13 per cent in 1998. What's more, research has shown that three-quarters of those that have done so think that the no-frills airlines are 'great'. Competition has also intensified, with a number of start-ups such as MyTravel Lite, Jet2 and Flyglobespan in the UK, and Hapag-Lloyd Express, Goodjet and Hellas Jet elsewhere in western Europe.

The growth in the low-cost sector has been fuelled by the burgeoning market for short-haul city breaks, the desire of more adventurous holidaymakers to arrange their own vacation packages, and their wish to own holiday homes in warm, sunny climates. These factors, together with the drive by business to trim back on travel costs, have meant growth rates of 30 per cent per year in passenger numbers in recent times.

The founder of easyJet, Stelios, gets ready for the launch of his new venture, easyCinema. The company says interest has been encouraging with 2,400 seats sold for the opening of the 10-screen box-office-free cinema in Milton Keynes, where tickets are on offer in advance with prices starting at 20p.

Marketing strategy at easyJet

A key element in the success of easyJet has been its approach to pricing. The conventional method of selling airline seats was to start selling at a certain price and then lower it if sales were too low. What Stelios Haji-Ioannou, owner of easyJet, pioneered was the opposite: the start was a low headline price that grabbed attention, then it was raised according to demand. Customers are never told how soon or by how much the price will be changed. This system, called yield management, is designed to allow airline seats to be priced according to supply and demand, and achieve high seat occupancy. This reflects the fact that a particular seat on a specific flight cannot be stored for resale: if it is empty, the revenue is lost.

For the customer the result has been fares much lower than those offered by conventional airlines such as BA and Lufthansa. And so, to be profitable, easyJet has needed to control costs strictly. Following the example of Southwest Airlines, it has achieved this through simplicity (using one aircraft type), productivity (fast turnaround times to achieve high aircraft use) and direct distribution (using the Internet for upfront payment and low administrative charges). Also, onboard costs are reduced by not providing free drinks or meals to passengers.

Although easyJet operates out of secondary airports such as Luton in the UK, it is increasingly using mainstream airports such as Gatwick in a direct attempt to take passengers from more conventional rivals such as BA. Its approach is to fly to relatively few destinations but with a higher frequency on each route. This provides a barrier to entry, and the higher frequency attracts high-volume business travellers that prize schedule over price and are, therefore, willing to pay a little more for the service (the average easyJet seat price [£50, €72] is reported to be higher than that of Ryanair [£34, €49]).

In 2002, easyJet bought rival Go airlines for £374 million (€540 million), a price lower than expected by many analysts. For easyJet, the deal is about creating a route network that stretches across Europe. With the exception of domestic routes, the two airlines had few destinations in common. EasyJet's top routes include Amsterdam, Geneva and Paris, while Go took holidaymakers to Faro, Bologna and Bilbao. There was overlap on only a handful of destinations, both flying to Barcelona, Nice, Majorca and Malaga. Furthermore, the UK bases of the two airlines were complementary, with easyJet operating from Luton, Gatwick and Liverpool, while Go operated from Stansted, Bristol and East Midlands airports. The take-over alone gave easyJet scale and increased buying power, a factor that was important when it decided to abandon its policy of using only Boeing 737s by buying a fleet of aircraft from Airbus in 2002 at a knockdown price. The combined companies were about the same size as Ryanair in terms of passenger numbers.

Under its entrepreneurial leader, Stelios, the easyJet group has moved into other areas, such as car hire and Internet cafés, using the same low-price model. A recent venture is the setting up of easyCinema to challenge the established cinema chains. The motivation was the half-empty cinema auditoriums Stelios saw when visiting conventional cinemas. He could not understand why the price was not varied according to demand (by day and by film). Although some cinemas do reduce prices for midweek screenings, their pricing policies were not considered flexible enough compared to pricing using yield management. Also, Stelios argued, why pay the same to see a blockbuster as to see a flop? And why is the price of the blockbuster the same on the opening night as it is six weeks later? What he proposed was an infinite number of prices depending on supply and demand, following the pattern of his successful airline business.

The easyCinema formula will work as follows. The pricing structure will begin at 20 pence (less than €0.30). People will log on to easyCinema.com, where they will find three options. First, they can select the movie they most want to see, the dates when they can see it and at what prices; second, they can select the day on which they want to visit the cinema, what films are showing and at what prices; and third they can come to the site with a budget of, say, £1 (€1.44) and find all the films that can be seen for £1 or less. Bookings can be made up to two weeks in advance. As with aircraft seats, the likelihood is that the earlier the booking is made, the cheaper the seat will be. Also, after examining costs, Stelios decided not to install food and drink stands saying, 'If ya want popcorn, go to a popcorn vendor. For movies come to easyCinema.' Staff costs are also reduced since there are no tickets. Booking is done through the website and a membership card is printed out that admits visitors to the cinema via a turnstile. Finally, no advertising for unrelated products (e.g. the local curry house) prior to the movie showing will be allowed.

Ryanair's Chief Executive Michael O'Leary celebrated St Patrick's Day by making an announcement at a press conference in London that it was relaunching the operations of the rival no-frills carrier Buzz that it has taken over.

Marketing strategy at Ryanair

Like easyJet, Ryanair has followed the Southwest Airlines business model but, if anything, has been more ruthless at cost-cutting. It provides cheap point-to-point flying from secondary airports, rather than shadowing and undercutting the major carriers as easyJet increasingly does. Sometimes, the airports can be 60 miles from the real destination: for Frankfurt read Hahn, for Hamburg read Lübeck, for Stockholm read Vesteraas or Skavsta, and for Brussels read Charleroi. Ryanair has kept to its single-aircraft policy, the Boeing 737, which it bought second-hand and cheaply, reducing maintenance, spares and crew training. Its new fleet of 737-800s were purchased at record low prices at the bottom of the market. They offer 45 per cent more seats at lower operating costs and the same number of crew.

Turnaround times at airports are fast to keep more aircraft in the air, and online booking, which now accounts for over 90 per cent of bookings, has slashed sales and distribution costs. Ryanair.com has become the largest travel website in Europe, selling more than 800,000 seats per month. Ryanair's focus on cost reduction has resulted in profit margins about double those of easyJet despite the latter's higher prices. Some of the cost savings are passed on to the customers in the form of lower fares (the plan is an average fall in fare levels of 5 per cent per year) to make Ryanair even more attractive to its target market: the leisure customer. In contrast, easyJet is increasingly targeting business passengers. Ryanair is the only European airline to record profits for each of the last 13 years.

Ryanair has also been on the acquisition trail by buying Buzz, the budget division of KLM Royal Dutch Airlines, for £15.8 million (€23 million). Loss-making Buzz was immediately given the Ryanair cost-cutting treatment, including the loss of 440 jobs and new contracts for pilots, which will raise pay but mean longer flying hours. Half of Buzz's routes were axed but Ryanair still intended to increase passenger load from 2 million to 3 million through lower prices (£31.50 [€45] versus £56 [€81] previously) and more frequent flying along the retained routes.

Customer service

The need to trim costs to the bone has meant that some customers have been dissatisfied with the service provided by both airlines. For example, the need for fast turnaround times at airports has meant that customers who check in late are usually refused entry. Where lateness is the fault of another travel provider, such as a rail company, customers have been known to complain bitterly about entry refusal. Fast turnaround times also mean that there is little slack should a flight be delayed, with a knock-on effect on other flights.

Another problem is the reluctance of the no-frills airlines to pay compensation. For example, when easyJet cancelled a flight after it admitted it had no crew to fly the aircraft, it offered a refund of the ticket price but no compensation for the other costs, such as the lost hotel deposit and car parking fees incurred by one of its customers. Ryanair, similarly, was reported to have said, 'We never offer compensation, food or hotel vouchers.' Ryanair also experienced teething problems with lost and delayed luggage after switching baggage contractors, and in the past has appeared reluctant to pay compensation in the case of lost luggage.

Questions

1. How do easyJet and Ryanair achieve success using low-price strategies?

2. What are the advantages and risks associated with low-price strategies?

3. To what extent do the conditions for charging low prices discussed in this chapter hold for easyJet and Ryanair?

4. How successful do you believe easyCinema is likely to be?

This case was prepared by David Jobber, Professor of Marketing at the University of Bradford, and is based on a large number of published sources.

case twenty-two

Hansen Bathrooms (a)

Hansen Bathrooms is a producer of baths, washbasins, toilets and bidets. The company has been in the bathroom market for over 50 years and while sales have never been spectacular, the company has managed to withstand the impact of several economic recessions by prudent cash flow management. Experts in the industry describe Hansen as a traditional, reliable producer that tends to follow market trends rather than lead.

As a response to changing times, Hansen recruited a 30-year-old marketing director, Rob Vincent, and a 25-year-old assistant, Susan Clements. Rob's responsibilities include making suggestions for new bathroom designs, advertising and promotion, and formulating pricing strategies, although the final decisions (except for day-to-day issues) are taken by the board of directors, which is headed by Karl Hansen, the son of the founder of the company.

Rob Vincent and Susan Clements have been in post for nearly two years and, at times, have found the work frustrating because of the board's tendency towards conservatism. However, an exciting development rekindled their enthusiasm. A technologist at the company had developed a special coating that could be applied to all bathroom items (baths, toilets, washbasins and tiles). The coating contained an agent that dispersed the usual grime and grease that accumulated in baths and washbasins, etc. Susan Clements commissioned a market research study which showed that people cleaned their bathroom fittings on average once every two weeks and it was one of the most unpopular household chores. The new coating made this unnecessary. Product trials with a prototype bathroom incorporating the new coating showed that cleaning could easily be extended to once every three months. Respondents in the test were delighted with the reduction in workload. Hansen sought and obtained a patent for the new coating.

Rob felt sure that the board would approve the launch of a new bathroom range using the new coating and was pondering what price to charge. As a starting point Rob set about using Hansen's tried and tested pricing formula. This produced the calculations shown in Table C22.1.

Table C22.1 Rob Vincent's calculations	
Per bathroom (washbasin, toilet and bath)	£
Direct materials	40
Direct labour	40
Total direct cost	80
Fixed cost (150% of direct labour)	60
Total cost	140
Profit mark-up (20% of total cost)	28
Basic price to retailers (BPR)	168
Allowance for promotional costs (10% of BPR)	17
Allowance for retailer discounts (20% of BPR)	34
List price to retailers (LPR)	219
Retailer profit mark-up (100% of LPR)	219
Recommended price to consumers	438

Rob felt very pleased. The price to consumers of £438 was very competitive with the prices charged by other bathroom suppliers (for example, the main two competitors charged £450 and £465). After the usual 25 per cent consumer discount, this would mean the Hansen bathroom would sell for £328 compared to £337 and £348 for its main rivals. 'I wish all my marketing decisions were this easy,' thought Rob. However, before making a final decision he thought he ought to consult Susan.

Questions

1. If you were Susan, would you agree or disagree with Rob Vincent's proposal?
2. What other factors should be taken into account?
3. What alternative strategies exist, if any?

This case was prepared by David Jobber, Professor of Marketing, University of Bradford.

chapter twelve

Advertising

> The codfish lays ten thousand eggs,
> The homely hen lays one,
> The codfish never cackles
> To tell you what she's done.
> And so we scorn the codfish,
> While the humble hen we prize,
> Which only goes to show you
> That it pays to advertise.
>
> ANONYMOUS

Learning Objectives

This chapter explains:

1. The role of advertising in the promotional mix
2. The factors that affect the choice of the promotional mix
3. The key characteristics of the major promotional tools
4. The communication process
5. The nature of integrated marketing communications
6. The differences between the strong and weak theories of how advertising works
7. How to develop advertising strategy: target audience analysis, objective setting, budgeting, message and media decisions, execution and advertising evaluation
8. How campaigns are organized, including advertising agency selection and payment systems
9. Ethical issues in advertising

To many people advertising epitomizes marketing: it is what they believe marketing to be. Readers of this book will recognize the fallacy in this: marketing concerns much broader issues than simply how to advertise. Nevertheless, advertising is an important element in the *promotional mix*. Six major components of the promotional mix are advertising, personal selling, direct marketing, Internet and online marketing, sales promotion and publicity.

1. **Advertising**: any paid form of non-personal communication of ideas or products in the prime media, i.e. television, the press, posters, cinema and radio.
2. **Personal selling**: oral communication with prospective purchasers with the intention of making a sale.
3. **Direct marketing**: the distribution of products, information and promotional benefits to target consumers through interactive communication in a way that allows response to be measured.
4. **Internet and online marketing**: the distribution of products, information and promotional benefits to consumers and businesses through electronic media.
5. **Sales promotion**: incentives to consumers or the trade that are designed to stimulate purchase.
6. **Publicity**: the communication of a product or business by placing information about it in the media without paying for the time or space directly.

In addition to these key promotional tools, the marketer can use exhibitions and sponsorship to communicate with target audiences. These, together with sales promotion and publicity, will be discussed in Chapter 16.

A key marketing decision is the choice of promotional blend needed to communicate to the target audience. Each of the five major promotional tools has its own strengths and limitations and these are summarized in Table 12.1. Marketers will carefully weigh these factors against promotional objectives to decide the amount of resources to channel into each tool. Usually, five considerations will have a major impact on the choice of the promotional mix.

1. *Resource availability and the cost of promotional tools*: to conduct a national advertising campaign may require several million pounds. If resources are not available, cheaper tools such as sales promotion or publicity may have to be used.
2. *Market size and concentration*: if a market is small and concentrated then personal selling may be feasible, but for mass markets that are geographically dispersed, selling to the ultimate customer would not be cost effective. In such circumstances advertising or direct marketing may be the correct choice.
3. *Customer information needs*: if a complex technical argument is required, personal selling may be preferred. If all that is required is the appropriate brand image, advertising may be more sensible.
4. *Product characteristics*: because of the above arguments, industrial goods companies tend to spend more on personal selling than advertising, whereas consumer goods companies tend to do the reverse.
5. *Push versus pull strategies*: a push strategy involves an attempt to sell into channel intermediaries (e.g. retailers) and is dependent on personal selling and trade promotions. A pull strategy bypasses intermediaries to communicate to consumers directly. The resultant consumer demand persuades intermediaries to stock the product. Advertising and consumer promotions are more likely to be used.

Table 12.1 Key characteristics of the six key promotional mix tools

Advertising
- Good for awareness building because it can reach a wide audience quickly
- Repetition means that a brand positioning concept can be communicated effectively; TV is particularly strong
- Can be used to aid the sales effort, to legitimize a company and its products
- Impersonal, lacks flexibility and questions cannot be answered
- Limited capability to close the sale

Personal selling
- Interactive: questions can be answered and objectives overcome
- Adaptable: presentations can be changed depending on customer needs
- Complex arguments can be developed
- Relationships can be built because of its personal nature
- Provides the opportunity to close the sale
- Sales calls are costly

Direct marketing
- Individual targeting of consumers most likely to respond to an appeal
- Communication can be personalized
- Short-term effectiveness can easily be measured
- A continuous relationship through periodic contact can be built
- Activities are less visible to competitors
- Response rates are often low
- Poorly targeted direct marketing activities cause consumer annoyance

Internet and online marketing
- Global reach at relatively low cost
- The number of site visits can be measured
- A dialogue between companies and their customers and suppliers can be established
- Catalogues and prices can be changed quickly and cheaply
- Direct sales possible
- Impersonal and requires consumers to visit a website
- Convenient form of searching for and buying products
- Avoids the necessity of negotiating and arguing with salespeople

Sales promotion
- Incentives provide a quick boost to sales
- Effects may be only short term
- Excessive use of some incentives (e.g. money off) may damage brand image

Publicity
- Highly credible as message comes from a third party
- Higher readership than advertisements in trade and technical publications
- Loss of control: a press release may or may not be used, and its content may be distorted

Two points need to be stressed. First, marketing communications is not the exclusive province of the promotional mix. All of the marketing mix communicates to target customers. The product itself communicates quality; price may be used by consumers as an indicator of quality, and the choice of distribution channel will affect customer exposure to the product. Second, effective communication is not a one-way producer-to-consumer flow. Producers need to understand the needs and motivation of their target audience before they can talk to them in a meaningful way. For example, marketing research may be used to understand large consumer segments before designing an advertising campaign, and salespeople may ask questions of buyers to unfold their particular circumstances, problems and needs before making a sales presentation.

Advertising decisions should not be taken in isolation. Marketers need to consider the complete communication package, with advertising forming one element of the whole. There is a need to blend the components of the promotional mix so that a clear and consistent message is received by target audiences. This has led to the development of integrated marketing communications, which will now be examined.

Integrated marketing communications

An organizational problem many companies face is that the various components of the promotional mix are the responsibility of different departments or agencies. Advertising is controlled by the advertising department in conjunction with an advertising agency. Personal selling strategies are decided by sales management. Publicity is the province of the publicity department and its agency. Other functions are in the charge of direct marketing, Internet and online promotion, and sales promotion. The danger is that the messages sent to consumers become blurred at best and conflicting at worst. For example, advertising messages that convey prestige may be discredited by heavy discounting by the sales team, or frequent use of money-off sales promotions. The logos and typefaces used in advertising may differ from those used in direct mail campaigns.

As the array of communications media expands there is a greater need to co-ordinate the messages and their execution. This has led to the adoption of *integrated marketing communications* by an increasing number of companies. Integrated marketing communications is the concept that companies co-ordinate their marketing communications tools to deliver a clear, consistent, credible and competitive message about the organization and its products. The objective is to position products and organizations clearly and distinctively in the marketplace. As we discussed in Chapter 7, successful positioning is associated with products possessing favourable connotations in the minds of consumers. Integrated marketing communications facilitates the process by which this is achieved by sending out consistent messages through all of the components of the promotional mix so that they reinforce one another. For example, it means that website visuals are consistent with the images portrayed in advertising and that the messages conveyed in a direct marketing campaign are in line with those developed by the public relations department.

Achieving this consistency can be difficult because of office politics. Some advertising creatives are unwilling to be shackled by an overall branding theme that is inconsistent with their latest 'big idea' for a television commercial. Others may feel threatened when an integrated marketing communications campaign calls for a shift in expenditure from advertising to direct or Internet marketing. However, to be successful, these impediments need to be overcome by the appointment of a high-ranking communications officer to oversee the company's communications activities. Perhaps using the title 'marketing communications director', this person is responsible for deciding the extent to which each of the components of the promotional mix will be used based on communication objectives and the role that each can play in their achievement. The person needs to be a visionary and someone with passion, who has the communication ability to persuade everyone of the benefits of an integrated approach to marketing communications.[1]

Integrated marketing communications can lead to improved consistency and clearer positioning of companies and their brands in the minds of consumers. One company that benefited from this approach was American Express, which found that the messages, images and styles of presentation between its advertising and direct marketing vehicles were inconsistent. Using an integrated marketing communications approach, the team worked to produce the consistency required to achieve a clear position among its target audience.

A framework for applying an integrated marketing communications approach is given in Fig. 12.1 The starting point is an understanding of the overall marketing strategy for a product. In particular, the product's target market and differential advantage need to be defined. This leads to the creation of a positioning statement. The communications decisions will then depend on this statement. For example, target market definition will lead to an understanding of the target audience that needs to be reached by communications, and the differential advantage will affect message decisions. Once these issues have been decided, communication objectives will be set and promotional options (e.g. advertising, direct marketing and personal selling) will be evaluated to assess their ability to fulfil objectives and reach the desired audience. Care must be taken to achieve consistency across promotional types in the messages communicated.

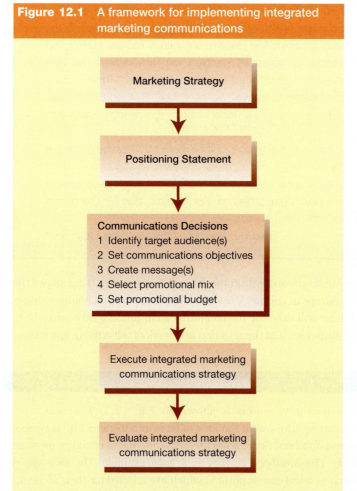

Figure 12.1 A framework for implementing integrated marketing communications

An aggregation of the resources needed to achieve the communication objectives and reach will lead to an estimation of the size of the promotional budget. This will be evaluated for affordability and political acceptability before approval. The chosen integrated communication strategy will be executed and subsequently evaluated in the light of the set objectives.

The move towards integrated marketing communications has led to the rise of *media-neutral planning*. This is the process of solving communication problems through an unbiased evaluation of all media. The focus is on solving communication problems rather than advertising, direct marketing, public relations problems, and so on. Marketing in Action 12.1 discusses some of the opportunities and challenges of media-neutral planning.

12.1 marketing in action

The Opportunities and Challenges of Media-neutral Planning

Media-neutral planning means that, having set communication objectives, all possible media are considered fairly and objectively. The term is sometimes used to back a 'let's do something other than television' or a multimedia approach. However, the process does not necessarily lead to that. It is quite conceivable that the process leads to a television-only campaign, but what it really means is that all media are evaluated rather than rushing into one of the traditional communications media without a full analysis of the options.

This approach has led to some interesting approaches to campaigns. Nike, for example, ran its Scorpion Football campaign not only on television, cinema and posters, but also as a series of events to involve people and give the campaign life beyond the paid-for media. Its competitor, Reebok, staged its Sofa Games in Manchester, Glasgow and Brighton. Featuring skateboarding, BMX and five-a-side football, the events were promoted using radio, e-mail and fly-posting as well as by placing sofas on the street.

Successful media-neutral planning depends on setting media planners free to explore a wide range of options. This can be a problem when media agencies are organized into specialist areas such as the press or television, and clients are organized into separate functions such as advertising or direct marketing. Some companies are reorganizing in recognition of these issues. For example, Vauxhall, the UK arm of General Motors, has restructured its marketing department with customer relationship management (which oversaw direct marketing, for example) merging with advertising. The new department, under one head, is responsible for Vauxhall's advertising, direct mail, online communications, literature and point-of-sale material, as well as all dealer, fleet and after-sales communications. Communication plans will be developed by understanding the benefits, costs and synergies of all media opportunities.

Other problems relate to rewards. Media agencies make most of their money through buying in the traditional media, i.e. television, press, cinema, radio and posters. Media-neutral planning might suggest an events-based strategy for which there is no clear-cut remuneration. Creative people might also have a vested interest in traditional media-planning approaches. For example, they may be biased towards television because they want to win high-profile awards.

Based on: Mills (2002);[2] Kleinman (2002);[3] Ray (2002)[4]

Having placed advertising in its context within the promotional mix, Fig. 12.2 shows the advertising expenditure of 16 European countries to show the context in which advertising is practised. The rest of this chapter will examine the communication process, how advertising works, developing advertising strategies, and the selection and work of advertising agencies.

The communication process

A simple model of the *communication process* is shown in Fig. 12.3. The *source* (or communicator) *encodes* a message by translating the idea to be communicated into a symbol consisting of words, pictures and numbers. Some advertisements attempt to encode a message using the minimum of words. The Marlboro cowboy is a good example. The message is *transmitted* through media such as television or posters, which are selected for their ability to reach the desired target audience in the desired way. Communication requirements may affect

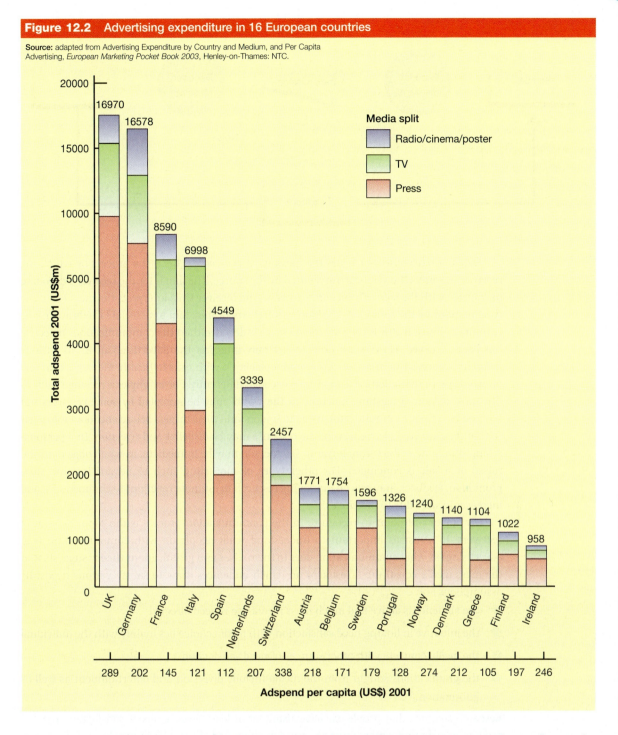

Figure 12.2 Advertising expenditure in 16 European countries

Source: adapted from Advertising Expenditure by Country and Medium, and Per Capita Advertising, *European Marketing Pocket Book 2003*, Henley-on-Thames: NTC.

the choice of media. For example, if the encoded message requires the product to be demonstrated, television and cinema may be preferred to posters and the press. *Noise*—distractions and distortions during the communication process—may prevent transmission to some of the target audience. A television advertisement may not reach a member of the household because of conversation or the telephone ringing. Similarly a press advertisement may not be noticed because of editorial competing for attention.

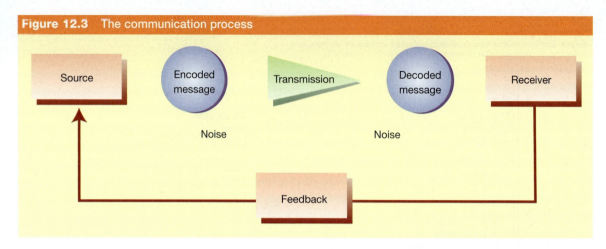

Figure 12.3 The communication process

When a *receiver* sees or hears the message, it is *decoded*. This is the process by which the receiver interprets the symbols transmitted by the source. The aim is for the receiver's decoding to coincide with the source's encoding process. The receiver thus interprets the message in the way intended by the source. A Marlboro advertisement may aim to associate the brand name with masculinity. If this is the way the message is decoded then the communications objective has been achieved. However, a non-smoker may interpret the advertisement in an entirely different way, rejecting the association and replacing it with risks to health. Messages that rely on words more than pictures can also be decoded differently. For example, a message such as 'the most advanced washing machine in the world' may be accepted by some receivers but rejected by others. Communicators need to understand their targets before encoding messages so that they are credible. Otherwise the response may be disbelief and rejection. In a personal selling situation, *feedback* from buyer to salesperson may be immediate, as when objections are raised or a sale is concluded. For other types of marketing such as advertising and sales promotion, feedback may rely on marketing research to estimate reactions to commercials, and increases in sales due to incentives.

An important point to recognize in the communication process is the sophistication of receivers. It is just as important to understand what people do with communication (e.g. advertising) as what communication does to them. Uses and gratifications theory suggests that the mass media constitute a resource on which audiences draw to satisfy various needs. Its assumptions are:

- the audience is active and much mass media use is need directed
- the initiative in linking need satisfaction with media choice lies mainly with the individual
- the media compete with other sources of need satisfaction
- the gratifications sought from the media include diversion and entertainment as well as information.[5]

Research suggests that people use advertising for at least seven kinds of satisfaction, namely product information, entertainment, risk reduction, added value, past purchase reassurance, vicarious experience and involvement.[6] Vicarious experience is the opportunity to experience situations or lifestyles to which an individual would not otherwise have access. Involvement refers to the pleasure of participation in the puzzles or jokes contained in some advertisements. Research among a group of young adults aged 18–24 added other uses of advertising including escapism, ego enhancement (demonstrating their intelligence by understanding the advertisement) and checking out the opposite sex.[7]

Strong and weak theories of how advertising works

For many years there has been considerable debate about how advertising works. The consensus is that there can be no single all-embracing theory that explains how all advertising works because it has varied tasks.[8] For example, advertising that attempts to make an instant sale by incorporating a return coupon that can be used to order a product is very different from corporate image advertising that is designed to reinforce attitudes.

The competing views on how advertising works have been termed the **strong theory of advertising** and the **weak theory of advertising**.[9] The strong theory has its base in the USA and is shown on the left-hand side of Fig. 12.4. A person passes through the stages of awareness, interest, desire and action (AIDA). According to this theory, advertising is strong enough to increase people's knowledge and change people's attitudes, and as a consequence is capable of persuading people who had not previously bought a brand to buy it. It is therefore a conversion theory of advertising: non-buyers are converted to become buyers. Advertising is assumed to be a powerful influence on consumers.

This model has been criticized on two grounds.[10] First, for many types of product there is little evidence that consumers experience a strong desire before action (buying the brand). For example, in inexpensive product fields a brand may be bought on a trial basis without any strong conviction that it is superior to competing brands. Second, the model is criticized because it is limited to the conversion of a non-buyer to a buyer. It ignores what happens after action (i.e. first purchase). Yet in most mature markets advertising is designed to affect people who have already bought the brand at least once.

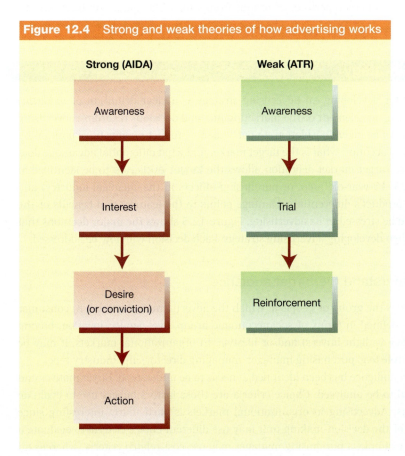

Figure 12.4 Strong and weak theories of how advertising works

The major alternative to the strong advertising theory is shown on the right-hand side of Fig. 12.4. The steps in this model are awareness, trial and reinforcement (ATR). The ATR model, which has received support in Europe, suggests that advertising is a much less powerful influence than the strong theory would suggest. As Ehrenberg explains, 'advertising can first arouse awareness and interest, nudge some customers towards a doubting first trial purchase (with the emphasis on trial, as in "maybe I'll try it") and then provide some reassurance and reinforcement after that first purchase. I see no need for any strong AIDA-like Desire or Conviction before the first purchase is made.'[11] His work in fast-moving consumer goods (fmcg) markets has shown that loyalty to one brand is rare. Most consumers purchase a repertoire of brands. The proportions of total purchases represented by the different brands show little variation over time, and new brands join the repertoire only in exceptional circumstances. A major objective of advertising in such circumstances is to defend brands. It does not work to increase sales by bringing new buyers to the brand advertised. Its main function is to retain existing buyers, and sometimes to increase the frequency with which they buy the brand.[12] Therefore, the target is existing buyers who presumably are fairly well disposed to the brand (otherwise they would not buy it), and advertising is designed to reinforce these favourable perceptions so they continue to buy it.[13]

As we saw when discussing consumer behaviour, level of involvement has an important role in determining how people make purchasing decisions. Jones suggests that involvement may also explain when the strong and weak theories apply.[14] For high-involvement decisions such as the purchase of expensive consumer durables, mail order or financial services, the decision-making process is studied with many alternatives considered and an extensive information search undertaken. Advertising, therefore, is more likely to follow the strong theory either by creating a strong desire to purchase (as with mail order) or by convincing people that they should find out more about the brand (for example, by visiting a showroom). Since the purchase is expensive it is likely that a strong desire (or conviction) is required before purchase takes place.

However, for low-involvement purchase decisions (such as low-cost packaged goods) people are less likely to consider a wide range of brands thoroughly before purchase and it is here that the weak theory of advertising almost certainly applies. Advertising is mainly intended to keep consumers doing what they already do by providing reassurance and reinforcement. Advertising repetition will be important in maintaining awareness and keeping the brand on the consumer's repertoire of brands from which individual purchases will be chosen.

Developing an advertising strategy

The starting point for developing an advertising strategy is a clear definition of *marketing strategy*. Advertising is one element of the marketing mix and decisions regarding advertising expenditure should not be taken in isolation. In particular, a product's competitive positioning needs to be taken into account: what is the target market and what differential advantage does the product possess? Target market definition allows the target audience to be identified in broad terms (e.g. 25–45-year-old men, or purchasing officers in the chemical industry) and recognition of the product's differential advantage points to the features and benefits of the product that should be stressed in its advertising. Figure 12.5 shows the major decisions that need to be taken when developing advertising strategy. Each decision will now be addressed.

Identify and understand the target audience

The target audience is the group of people at which the advertisement is aimed. In consumer markets, it may be defined in terms of socio-economic group, age, gender, location, buying frequency (e.g. heavy vs light buyers) and/or lifestyle. In organizational markets, it may be defined in terms of role (e.g. purchasing manager, managing director) and industry type.

Once the target audience has been identified, it needs to be understood. Buyer motives and choice criteria need to be analysed. Choice criteria are those factors buyers use to evaluate competing products. Advertising in organizational markets is particularly interesting since different members of the decision-making unit may use different choice criteria to evaluate a given product. For example, a purchasing manager may use cost-related criteria, whereas an engineer may place more emphasis on technical criteria. This understanding is vital: it has

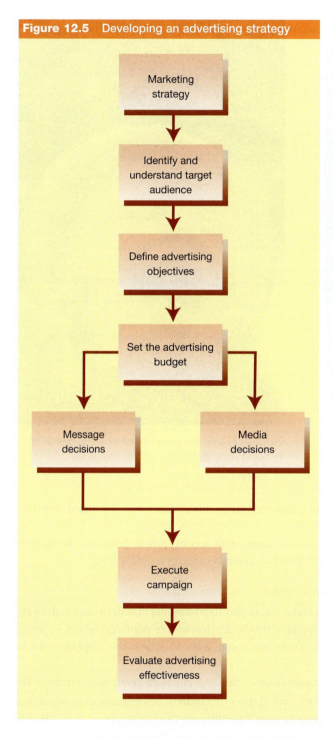

Figure 12.5 Developing an advertising strategy

fundamental implications for message and media decisions. Where costs allow, two different advertisements may be needed with one stressing cost benefits using media read by purchasing managers and another focusing on technical issues in media read by engineers.

Define advertising objectives

Ultimately, advertising is used to stimulate sales and increase profits, but of more operational value is a clear understanding of its *communication objectives*. Advertising can create awareness, stimulate trial, position products in consumers' minds, correct misconceptions, remind and reinforce, and provide support for the salesforce. Each objective will now be discussed.

Create awareness

Advertising can create awareness of a company, a brand, an event, or a solution to a problem. Creating company awareness helps to legitimize a company, its products and representatives to its customers. Instead of customers saying 'I've never heard of them', their response might be 'They are quite well known, aren't they?' In this way advertising may improve the acceptance of products and salespeople. Brand awareness is an obvious precondition of purchase and can be achieved through advertising. For example, when Amstrad launched its first portable computer it ran press advertisements to create awareness of the brand, its price and features.

Advertising can also be used to create awareness of an event: for example, Comet, the UK electrical retailer, ran an ad with copy that read 'Comet Sale Now On'. Finally, advertising can be used to make the target audience aware of a solution to a problem. For example, Hewlett Packard used the following headline in a press advertisement: 'Why can't somebody make a computer that'll get our orders in and out the same day?' 'Somebody does.' The advertisement then explained how Hewlett Packard did this and contained a coupon that could be used to request further information. In this form of advertising, the problem is described, and this description is followed by an explanation of how a solution may be provided.

Stimulate trial

The sale of some products suffers because of lack of trial. Perhaps marketing research has shown that, once consumers try the product, acceptance is high but for some reason only a

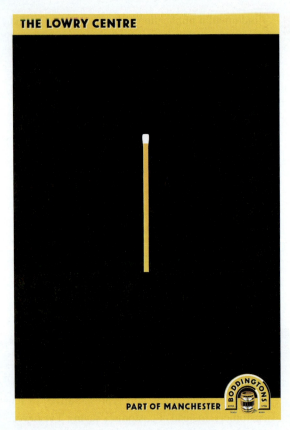
The famous creamy head of Boddingtons beer is visible in this creative execution, which reminds consumers of its northern heritage.

Emirates claims the number-one position based on its being awarded 'Airline of the Year 2002'.

small proportion of the target group has tried it. In such circumstances, advertising that focuses on trial may be sensible. For example, the Irish whiskey brand Jameson ran advertisements that claimed 'You'll never know until you've tried it. Jameson, the spirit of Ireland'. Saab encouraged a trial (test drive) of its diesel range in a similar way.

Position products in consumers' minds

Advertising copy and visuals have a major role to play in positioning brands in the minds of the target audience.[15] Creative positioning involves the development or reinforcement of an image or set of associations for a brand. There are seven ways in which this objective can be achieved.[16]

1. *Product characteristics and customer benefits*: this is a common positioning strategy. For example, BMW uses performance with respect to handling and engineering competence as attributes summed up in the statement 'The Ultimate Driving Machine'. Remy Martin advertisements imbue the brandy with status connections. Other examples are Murphy's Irish Stout ('Like the Murphy's, I'm not bitter'), Stella Artois ('Reassuringly expensive'), Volkswagen ('If only everything in life was as reliable as a Volkswagen'), Galaxy ('Why have cotton when you can have silk?') and Kellogg's All Bran ('The great fibre provider'). The illustration shows one of a series of Boddingtons advertisements, which remind consumers about the beer's creamy head (attribute) while stressing its northern heritage.

A powerful attribute for positioning purposes is being number one. This is because people tend to remember objects that are number one but may easily forget number-two positions. For example, the names of Olympic champions are remembered much better than runners-up, and the name of the highest mountain in a country is remembered much better than the second highest. The advertisement for Emirates (see illustration) is an example of claiming the number-one position. Occasionally two attributes are used, as with Aquafresh toothpaste ('Cavity fighting and fresh breath') and Matey ('Cleans your kids and the bath as well').

(2) *Price quality*: this positioning approach is based on the notion of giving value through quality products sold at low prices. Sainsbury's, the leading UK supermarket chain, has adopted this market position through its tag-line 'Good food costs less at Sainsbury's'. An industrial goods company that adopted a similar positioning strategy was Honeywell, which advertised its control valves as 'Pound for pound the best—all round'.

(3) *Product use*: another positioning method is to associate the product with a use. An example is 'Lemsip is for flu attacks'. The basic idea is that when people think of flu, they automatically remember the brand. A second example is Cadbury's Roses chocolates ('The chocolates to say "thank you"'). The Tio Pepe illustration (below) shows how it positions itself by product use (the perfect aperitif) while depositioning the competition.

(4) *Product user*: another way of positioning is to associate a product with a user or user type. Personalities may be used, such as Andre Agassi (Nike), Linford Christie (Lucozade) and Tim Henman (Adidas). Positioning against user type has been successfully achieved by Audi (upwardly mobile socially) and Guinness (intelligent, individualist).

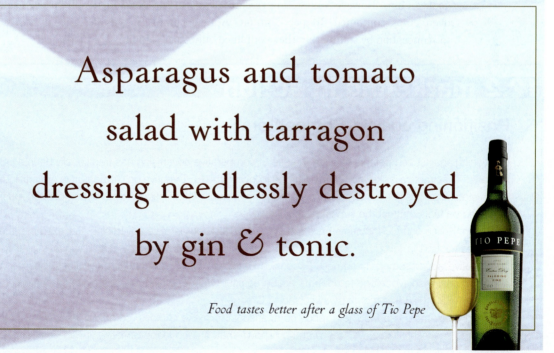

Tio Pepe positions itself as the ideal aperitif.

(5) *Product class*: some products can benefit by positioning themselves within a product class. For example, Red Mountain coffee positioned itself within the ground coffee class with the tag-line 'Ground coffee taste without the grind' and a margarine called 'I Can't Believe It's Not Butter' was positioned within the butter class by virtue of its name and advertising.

(6) *Symbols*: the use of symbols to position brands in the marketplace has been achieved by Michelin (Michelin Man), McDonald's (golden arches) and Apple (a multicoloured apple logo). The use of symbols is particularly effective when the symbol reflects a quality desired in the brand, as with the Andrex puppy (softness).

(7) *Competition*: positioning against well-entrenched competitors can be effective since their image in the marketplace can be used as a reference point. For example, Subaru positioned against Volvo by claiming 'Volvo has built a reputation for surviving accidents. Subaru has built a reputation for avoiding them', based on ABS for better braking and four-wheel drive for better traction. The airline Delta positioned against British Airways' tag-line 'The world's favourite airline' by running the counter-campaign 'We don't want to be the world's favourite airline—we just want to be yours.'

Positioning against competitors can be effective when consumers base their purchase decision on facts. Hence, a well-justified statement claiming a factual advantage against a key competitor can be highly successful. Marketing in Action 12.2 discusses some of the issues involved.

Correct misconceptions

A fourth objective of advertising can be to correct misconceptions that consumers hold against brands. For example, McCain's, the market leader in the UK for oven chips, ran a successful advertising campaign claiming that oven chips contained 40 per cent less fat than home-cooked chips. However, marketing research showed that consumers still believed that their oven chips contained 30 per cent fat. A new campaign was designed to correct this misconception by stating that they contained only 5 per cent fat.

12.2 marketing in action

Positioning against Competitors

Positioning against competitors through the use of comparative advertising has traditionally been a US preserve. The practice is likely to grow in Europe following the EC Directive on Comparative Advertising, which states that it is in the interests of competition and public information. Points of comparison must be based on facts that can be substantiated, however.

Recent British court judgements have broadly supported comparative advertising. For example, the High Court found in favour of Ryanair when it was unsuccessfully sued by British Airways over its comparative advertisement headlined 'Expensive Ba****ds', which compared the airlines' prices on certain routes. Also, Vodafone failed in its action against Orange, which ran ads claiming customers could save £20 (€28.8) a month by switching to Orange.

When consumers use facts (e.g. price comparisons) to make choices, comparative advertising is likely to be successful. However, research has shown that, if used inappropriately, it can demean the brand that is using the technique.

Based on: Grey (2002)[17]

Remind and reinforce

Once a clear position in the minds of the target audience has been established, the objective of advertising may be to remind consumers of the brand's existence, and to reinforce its image. For many leading brands in mature markets, such as Coca-Cola and Mars bars, the objective of their advertising is to maintain top-of-mind awareness and favourable associations. Given their strong market position, a major advertising task is to defend against competitive inroads, thus maintaining high sales, market share and profits.

Provide support for the salesforce

Advertising can provide invaluable support for the salesforce by identifying warm prospects and communicating with otherwise unreachable members of a decision-making unit. Some industrial advertising contains return coupons that potential customers can send to the advertiser indicating a degree of interest in the product. The identification of such warm prospects can enable the salesforce to use its time more efficiently by attempting to call upon them rather than spend time cold calling potential customers who may or may not have an interest in the product.

Given the size and complexity of many organizational decision-making units a salesperson cannot be expected to call on every member. One estimate is that out of 10 decision-making unit members, salespeople manage to talk to three or four on average. Advertising can be used to reach some of the others—for example, the numerous (secretaries) or the inaccessible (managing directors).

Set the advertising budget

The achievement of communication objectives will depend upon how much is spent on advertising. Four methods of *setting budgets* are the percentage of sales, affordability, matching competition, and the objective and task methods.

Percentage of sales

This method bases advertising expenditure on a specified percentage of current or expected sales revenue. The percentage may be based on company or industry tradition. The method is easy to apply and may discourage costly advertising wars if all competitors keep to their traditional percentage. However, the method encourages a decline in advertising expenditure when sales decline, a move that may encourage a further downward spiral of sales. Furthermore, it ignores market opportunities, which may suggest the need to spend more (or less) on advertising. For example, an opportunity to build market share may suggest raising advertising expenditure and, conversely, a decision to harvest a product would suggest reducing expenditure. Finally, the method fails to provide a means of determining the correct percentage to use.

Affordability

This method bases advertising expenditure on what executive judgement regards as an amount that can be afforded. While affordability needs to be taken into account when considering any corporate expenditure, its use as the sole criterion for budget setting neglects the communication objectives that are relevant for a company's products and the market opportunities that may exist to grow sales and profits.

Matching competition

Some companies set their advertising budgets based upon matching expenditure, or using a similar percentage of sales figure as their major competitor. Matching expenditure assumes that the competition has arrived at the correct level of expenditure, and ignores market opportunities and communication objectives. Using a similar percentage of sales ratio similarly lacks strategic vision and can be justified only if it can be shown to prevent costly advertising wars.

Objective and task

This method has the virtue of being logical since the advertising budget depends on communication objectives and the costs of the tasks required to achieve them. It is a popular method in Europe. If the objective is to increase awareness of a brand name from 30 per cent to 40 per cent, the cost of developing the necessary campaign, and using appropriate media (e.g. television, posters) will be calculated. The total cost would represent the advertising budget. In practice, however, the level of effort required to achieve the specified awareness increase may be difficult to estimate. Nevertheless, this method does encourage management to think about objectives, media exposure levels and the resulting costs.

In practice, the advertising budgeting decision is a highly political process.[18] Finance may argue for monetary caution, whereas marketing personnel, who view advertising as a method of long-term brand building, are more likely to support higher advertising spend. The outcome of the debate may depend as much on the political realities within the company as on adherence to any particular budgetary method.

Some companies, notably in food, toiletries and the car industry, spend huge amounts on advertising. For example, in one year alone Procter & Gamble spent over £8 million encouraging consumers to switch from squash to Sunny Delight, the orange drink that became the most successful grocery product launch of the 1990s.[19] A list of the top five advertisers in ten European countries is given in Table 12.2. Procter & Gamble appear in six of the ten countries featured.

Message decisions

Before a message can be decided, a clear understanding of the advertising platform should be acquired. The advertising platform is the foundation on which advertising messages are built. It is the basic selling proposition used in the advertisement (e.g. reliability or convenience). The platform should:

- be important to the target audience
- communicate competitive advantages.

This is why an understanding of the motives and choice criteria of the target audience is essential for effective advertising. Without this knowledge a campaign could be built upon an advertising platform that is irrelevant to its audience.

An advertising message translates the platform into words, symbols and illustrations that are attractive and meaningful to the target audience. In the 1980s IBM realized that many customers bought its computers because of the reassurance they felt when dealing with a well-known supplier. It used this knowledge to develop an advertising campaign based on the advertising platform of reassurance/low risk. This platform was translated into the advertising message 'No one ever got the sack for buying IBM.'

Table 12.2	Top five advertisers in ten European countries
Belgium	**Denmark**
Procter & Gamble	TDC
Belgacom	Sonofon
Unilever	Aller Press
Etat Belge	Orange
Danône Group	CMC Records
Finland	**France**
Sonera	Vivendi Universal
Nokia	France Telecom
Valio	L'Oréal
L'Oréal	PSA Peugeot Citroën
Volvo	Nestlé
Germany	**The Netherlands**
Ferrero	Lever Fabergé
Media Markt & Saturn Verw	Unilever Bestfoods
Procter & Gamble	Procter & Gamble
Haarkosmetik & Parfümer	Iglo Mora Groep
Springer Verlag	Ministerie Van Financien
Norway	**Spain**
Lilleborg Dagligvare	Procter & Gamble
Norsk Tipping As	Danône
Møller Harald As	El Corte Inglés
Telenor Plus	Telefónica Servicios Moviles
Dressmann	Volkswagen-Audi
Sweden	**UK**
Kooperativa Förbundet	COI Communications
ICA	Procter & Gamble
Telia	British Telecom
Volvo	Ford
Svenska Spel	Nestlé

Source: *European Marketing Pocket Book 2003*, Henley-on-Thames: NTC Publications.

Using the right message is important. John Caples, a top direct response copywriter, once wrote:[20]

> I have seen one ad actually sell not twice as much, not three times as much but 19 times as much as another. Both ads occupied the same space. Both were run in the same publication. Both had photographic illustrations. Both had carefully written copy. The difference was that one used the *right* appeal and the other used the *wrong* appeal.

David Ogilvy, an extremely successful advertising practitioner, suggested that press advertisements should follow a number of guidelines.[21]

(1) The message appeal (benefit) should be important to the target audience.

② The appeal should be specific; evidence to support it should be provided.

③ The message should be couched in the customers' language, not the language of the advertiser.

④ The advertisement should have a headline that might:

   (a) promise a benefit

   (b) deliver news

   (c) offer a service

   (d) tell a significant story

   (e) identify a problem

   (f) quote a satisfied customer.

⑤ If body copy (additional copy supporting and flowing from the headline) is to be used:

   (a) long copy is acceptable if it is relevant to the need of the target audience

   (b) long paragraphs and sentences should be avoided

   (c) the copy should be broken up using plenty of white space to avoid it looking heavy to read

   (d) if the advertiser is after enquiries, use a coupon *and* put the company address and telephone number at the end of the body copy. This is particularly important for industrial advertisements when more than one member of the decision-making unit (perhaps from different departments) may wish to send off for further details. With the address and telephone number appearing outside of the coupon, the second enquirer has the relevant information with which to contact the advertiser even if the coupon has already been used.

Most people who read a press advertisement read the headline but not the body copy. Because of this some advertisers suggest that the company or brand name should appear in the headline, otherwise the reader may not know the source of the advertisement. For example, the headlines 'Good food costs less at Sainsbury's' and 'United Colours of Benetton' score highly because in one sentence they link a customer benefit or attribute with the name of the company. Even if no more copy is read the advertiser has got one message across by means of a strong headline. The prominence of visuals also makes them important in conveying the message. The advertisement for Drambuie illustrates how a powerful visual can reinforce the message.

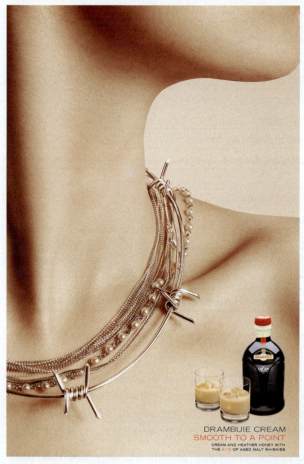

Drambuie: 'the smooth drink with a sting in its tail' is communicated by means of a powerful visual.

Television messages also need to be built on a strong advertising platform. Because television commercials are usually 30 seconds or less in duration, most communicate only one major selling appeal—sometimes called the *single-minded proposition*—which is the single most motivating and differentiating thing that can be said about the brand.[22]

Television advertising often uses one of three creative approaches.[23] First, the *benefits* approach, where the advertisement suggests a reason for the customer to buy (customer benefit). An example is the Red Mountain advertisement 'Ground coffee taste without the grind'. The second approach is more subtle: no overt benefit is mentioned. Instead the intention is to *involve* the viewer. An example of involvement advertising is the commercial for Heinz Spaghetti in which a young couple's son tells them that the tomato on his plate is the sun, the triangles of toast are the mountains, and the Heinz Spaghetti is the sea. When the father enters into the game and asks 'So that's the boat then', the boy responds witheringly 'No, it's a sausage'. The third type of creative approach attempts to register the brand as significant in the market, and is called *salience advertising*. The assumption is that advertising that stands out as being different will cause the brand to stand out as different. An example is the Toshiba 'Tosh' campaign. In that case the significance of Toshiba as a brand was supported by more conventional benefit advertising (e.g. 'Stronger components to last longer').

Television advertising is often used to build a brand personality. The *brand personality* is the message that the advertisement seeks to convey.

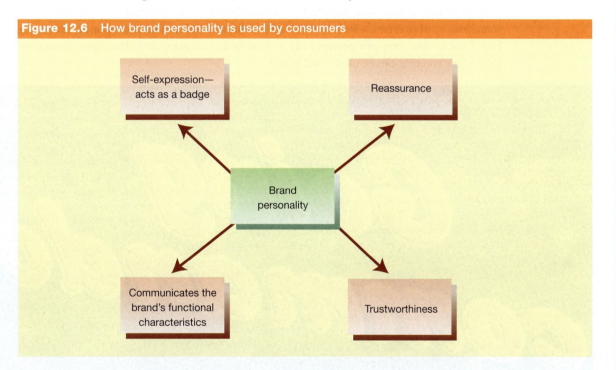

Figure 12.6 How brand personality is used by consumers

Lannon suggests that people use brand personalities in different ways.[24] Figure 12.6 shows that brand personality acts as a form of self-expression, reassurance, a communicator of the brand's function and an indicator of trustworthiness. The value of the brand personality to consumers will differ by product category and this will depend on what they use brand imagery for. In *self-expressive* product categories such as perfumes, cigarettes, alcoholic drinks and clothing, brands act as *badges* for making public an aspect of personality ('I choose this brand [e.g. Holsten Pils bottled lager] to say this about myself').

Brand personality can also act as *reassurance*. For example, the personality of After Eight Mints is sophistication and 'upper-classness', which does not necessarily correspond to the type of people who buy this mass-market brand. What the imagery is doing is providing reassurance that the brand is socially acceptable. Martini advertising also provides this kind of reassurance.

A third use of brand personality is to *communicate the functional characteristics* of the brand. Timotei shampoo advertising is an emotional representation of its functional characteristics: natural, herbal, gentle, pure. Finally, personalities of brands such as Persil and Andrex act to signal *trustworthiness*, a benefit valued by many consumers in their product categories.

Advertisers neglect at their peril the role of *emotion* in consumer decision-making. When choice depends on symbolic meaning helping to define a person's self-concept and sense of identity, and communicate it to other people, decision-making may be largely emotion-driven. Consumers consult their feelings about the decision. For example, a car buyer may ask 'How do I feel about being seen in that car?' If the answer is positive, information search may be confined to providing an objective justification of the choice (for example, the car's reliability, fuel economy, etc.). Television advertising is often used to convey the desired emotional response and the print media to supply objective information. Brands such as Nike with its 'Just do it' attitude, Virgin for its 'us against them' approach and Benetton with its controversial advertising campaigns, including a black stallion mounting a white mare and portraits of American prisoners on death row, have all tried to plug into consumers' emotions.[25] In low-involvement situations, such as with the choice of drinks and convenience foods, humour is sometimes used to create a feeling of warmth about a brand and even regular exposure to a brand name over time can generate the desired feeling of warmth.[26] The Mars illustration shows how emotion can be used to sell brands.

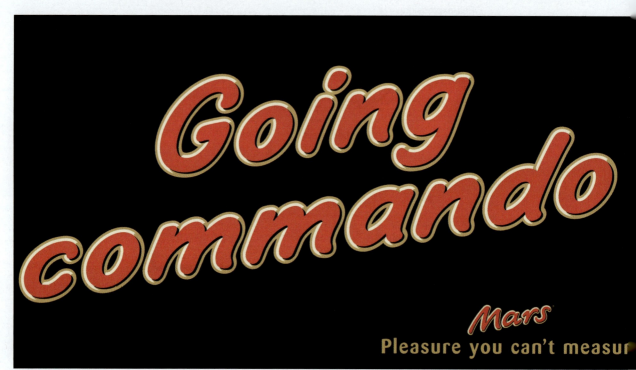

Emotions like pleasure can sell brands, as this humorous poster for Mars bars illustrates.

Media decisions

There used to be a joke among media people that the client's attitude to their part in advertising was 'Ten minutes to go before lunch. Just enough time to discuss media.'[27] As media costs have risen and brands become more sharply targeted, this attitude has disappeared. Two key media decisions are:

① the **media class decision** (for example, television versus the press), and

② the **media vehicle decision** (e.g. a particular newspaper or magazine).

Both decisions will now be examined.

The media class decision

Table 12.3 lists the major media class options (the media mix). The media planner faces the choice of using television, the press, cinema, posters, radio, the Internet or some combination of media classes. Five considerations will be taken into account. First, *creative factors* may have a major bearing on the decision. The key question that needs to be addressed is 'Does the medium allow the communication objectives to be realized?' For example, if the objective is to position the brand as having a high-status aspirational personality, television would be better than posters. However, if the communication objective is to remind the target audience of a brand's existence, a poster campaign may suffice. Each medium possesses its own set of creative qualities and limitations, as described below.

Table 12.3	Media class options
1	Television
2	Press
	National newspapers
	Regional newspapers
	Trade and technical
	Magazines
3	Posters
4	Cinema
5	Radio
6	The Internet

Television: advertisers can demonstrate the product in action. For example, a lawnmower can be shown to cut grass efficiently, or the ease of application of a paint can be demonstrated. The capability of television to combine colour, movement and sound (unlike the press, posters and radio) means that it is often used when brand image building is required. It is easier to create an atmosphere using television than other media that lack its versatility. Advertisements can be repeated over a short time period but it is a transitory medium (unless the commercial is video recorded) so that consumers cannot refer back to the advertisement once it has been broadcast (unlike the press).

Digital television technology means that signals can be compressed, allowing more to be sent to the viewer. The result is the escalation of the number of channels that can be received. The extra 'bandwidth' created by digital technology is likely to reduce costs, enabling small players to broadcast to small target audiences such as small geographical areas and special interest groups (e.g. shoppers). Also, digital technology allows the development of interactive services, promoting the potential for home shopping.[28] During an advertisement, viewers are able to click on the red button on the remote control handset, leading them to an interactive shopping area, the equivalent to an Internet site.[29] This new form of advertising is called interactive TV (iTV) and is discussed in e-Marketing 12.1. The illustration featuring Pampers (overleaf) is an example of promotion featuring interactive television.

12.1 e-marketing

Interactive Television Advertising

Interactive television (iTV) advertising invites viewers to press the red button on the remote control handset to see more information about an advertised product. Viewers may then be asked to request a free sample or brochure, or buy a product, for example. Although in its infancy, iTV is growing, with Sky claiming that around 25 per cent of last-in-break spots on its wholly owned channels carry iTV ads. Sky has also signed a deal with the UK's largest commercial broadcasters, Carlton and Granada, which will add both interactive programming and advertising to ITV.

One of the key drivers of this growth is iTV's ability to provide measurable results for clients, a characteristic that is shared with direct mail. Advertisers can assess campaign performance by measuring response and, for the first time, attribute a financial value to different channels, times of day and even individual slots. It also allows the targeting of niche audiences through the use of specialist television channels that focus on leisure activities such as sport, music and motoring. A third benefit is the ability to provide more in-depth information than a single television or press ad. For example, a car manufacturer could provide a video of a new model and display its features before asking the viewer to request a brochure, thereby generating a lead.

Interactive television advertising can generate direct sales and encourage home shopping. It also has the benefit of not requiring a call centre, with responses being dealt with electronically rather than requiring the hiring of call centre staff to deal with calls, which is a feature of traditional direct response advertising. It is also more convenient for the viewer, who does not have to rush off to the telephone or computer. Also the red button can be more effective than a telephone call, with one advertiser recording a response rate nine times greater via iTV than via a phone number. Longer commercials are more likely to encourage people to respond, with 40-second and 60-second spots generating up to 25 per cent more response than the standard 30-second ad.

The most active sectors are cars, travel and financial services, where the ability to pass on more information to viewers is most highly valued. Grocery brands have been more reluctant to get involved since they tend to be low-involvement purchases.

Based on: Davies (2002);[30] Ray (2003)[31]

Press: factual information can be presented in a press advertisement (e.g. specific features of a compact disc system) and the readers are in control of how long they take to absorb the information. Allied to this advantage is the possibility of re-examination of the advertisement at a later date. But it lacks movement and sound, and advertisements in newspapers and magazines compete with editorial for the reader's attention.

Posters: simplicity is required in the creative work associated with posters because many people (for example, car drivers) will have the opportunity only to glance at a poster. Like the press it is visual only, and is often used as a support medium (backing a television or press campaign) because of its creative limitations. It is believed to be effective for reminder advertising. Carlsberg has used posters effectively using the headline 'Carlsberg—Probably the best lager in the world', showing the necessity for simplicity. Often, poster advertising sites are sold as a package targeting specific audiences. For example, targeting supermarket shoppers can be realized by buying a retail package where advertisers can buy space on panels in supermarket stores; if businesspeople are the target it is possible to buy a package of sites at

Procter & Gamble uses interactive television to promote its Pampers brand.

major airports.[32] The award-winning poster advertisement from Guinness (overleaf), shows the advantages of simplicity, and Marketing in Action 12.3 discusses some of the developments in poster advertising.

12.3 marketing in action

Developments in Poster Advertising

The traditional format of a poster campaign is of a nationally based roadside series of advertisements. The demands of Pan-European marketing, though, are leading to clients requiring access to cross-border outdoor campaigns. For example, the French telecoms company Alcatel requested a poster campaign across France, the Netherlands, Spain, Germany, Italy and Poland. Zenith Media in Paris provided a Europe-wide outdoor campaign running on 40,000 billboards. The launch of Levi's Engineered Jeans was also supported by a pan-European poster campaign. The process has been helped by the consolidation of the European outdoor market into only three suppliers. They offer flexible posting cycles and bespoke packages that reach specific target markets.

Posters are a common sight at football matches. Carlsberg, for example, uses outdoor media there to reach its key target market: males aged 18–44. Other poster locations have gained ground, such as point-of-sale posters in supermarkets, bus shelters, washrooms and university campuses. Like other media, posters present creative opportunities, as when Asda Wal-Mart wrapped a gasometer near the Commonwealth Games Stadium in Manchester with a 35,000 square metre banner. This was seen by millions of viewers in the UK and worldwide, as well as the spectators at the Games.

Whichever location is used, the important message is simplicity. An ad has, on average, just six seconds to get a message across, which has led to the golden rule: 'No more than seven words on a billboard'.

Based on: Beattie (2002);[33] Hanrahan (2002);[34] Hayward (2003);[35] Thurner (2002)[36]

An award-winning advertisement from Guinness, showing how a simple but striking visual can convey the right poster message.

Cinema: advertisements can benefit from colour, movement and sound, and exposure is high due to the captive nature of the audience. Repetition may be difficult to achieve given the fact that people visit cinemas intermittently, but the nature of the audience is predictable, usually between 15 and 25 years of age. However, the popularity of the cinema is growing and companies have been using it to reach audiences besides the traditional youth market, as Marketing in Action 12.4 explains.

12.4 marketing in action

Cinema Renaissance

With people flocking back to the cinema, advertisers are returning to this medium, which has traditionally been the preserve of the young. The rise of the multiplex with its clean, modern image, and first-class sound and picture quality has seen cinema audiences in the UK rise by a third in the last five years. Such factors persuaded BMW to run its UK launch campaign for the new Mini in cinemas months before using television in order to target young, 'early adopters'.

Just as significantly, multiplexes have attracted a new audience that is older and more upmarket. The increase in the number of screens per site means a wide range of films, some of which find an audience with 25–44 year olds, such as *Bridget Jones's Diary* or *Chicago*. This means that the cinema offers new opportunities to reach this important target market.

Based on: Benady (2002);[37] Higham (2002)[38]

Radio: this is creatively limited to sound and thus may be better suited to communicating factual information (for example, a special price reduction) than attempting to create a brand image. The nature of the audience changes during the day (for example, motorists during rush hours) and so a measure of targeting is possible. Production costs are relatively low. The arrival of digital radio is likely to begin in cars as car manufacturers install digital radios into new models on the production line. Radio listening may rise with the growth of the Internet as people listen to the radio while surfing and because radio listening through web browsers is fast becoming a reality.[39]

The Internet: this medium allows global reach to be achieved at relatively low cost. The number of website visits, clicks on advertisements and products purchased can be measured. Interactivity between supplier and consumer is possible either by website-based communication or e-mail. Direct sales are possible, which is driving the growth of e-business in such areas as hotels, travel and information technology. Advertising content can be changed quickly and easily. In the business-to-business area catalogues and price lists can be amended rapidly, and a dialogue between companies and their customers and suppliers can be established.

The disadvantages of Internet advertising are that it is impersonal and requires consumers to visit a website. This may require high expenditure in traditional media, or the placing of expensive banner advertisements on search engines. Although websites themselves can contain high levels of information content, the creative potential of Internet advertisements is limited by size. Finally, Internet ads (particularly 'pop-ups') can be considered intrusive and an irritant.

Some recent developments in Internet advertising are discussed in e-Marketing 12.2.

12.2 e-marketing

New Models in Internet Advertising

At one time, the majority of online revenue was from advertising on websites. These adverts were generally in the form of 'banner ads' (a graphic, a line of copy and a website link). The advertiser would be charged based on the number of online visitors that viewed the ad, calculated on CPM (cost per thousand views; £20 [€28.8] CPM equates to £20 per thousand that arrive on a page where the 'banner ad' is positioned).

Companies soon realized that banner ads were not cost-effective; using website statistics they could tell how many people viewed an ad, how many clicked a link and how many took action (e.g. bought a product). They found that less than 1 per cent of those that viewed a banner clicked on it and less than 1 per cent that arrived at a website bought a product or made an enquiry—often, 10,000 views were required to make one sale; at £20 CPM this equated to £200 (€288) per customer.

Online advertising companies, fearing huge revenue losses, began to innovate. Many offered CPC (cost per click) models; this meant advertisers only paid for traffic that arrived on their site; sites like Google (www.google.co.uk) developed technologies linking banner ads to search results, increasing relevance and (it was hoped) click-through rates; and Overture (www.uk.overture.com) developed a search engine that allowed companies to bid for their position on a search return. New advertising models are being developed all the time; next time you visit a website, consider the advertising models in use.

The second consideration when making the media class decision is the *size of the advertising budget*. Some media are naturally more expensive than others. For example, £250,000 (€360,000) may be sufficient for a national poster campaign but woefully inadequate for television. Advertisers with less than £1 million (€1.44 million) to spend on a national campaign may decide that television advertising is not feasible.

Third, the relative *cost per opportunity to see* is also relevant to the decision: the target audience may be reached much more cheaply using one medium rather than another.

However, the calculation of opportunity to see differs according to media class, making comparisons difficult. For example, in the UK, an opportunity to see for the press is defined as 'read or looked at any issue of the publication for at least two minutes', whereas for posters it is 'traffic past site'.

A fourth consideration is *competitive activity*. Two conflicting philosophies are to compete in the same medium and to dominate an alternative medium. The decision to compete in the same medium may be taken because of a belief that the medium chosen by the major competition is the most effective, and that to ignore it would be to hand the competition a massive communication advantage. Domination of an alternative medium may be sensible for third or fourth players in a product market who cannot match the advertising budgets of the big two competitors. Supposing the major players were using television, the third or fourth competitor might choose press or posters, where it could dominate, achieving higher impact than if it followed the competition into television.

Finally, for many consumer-good producers, *the views of the retail trade* (for example, supermarket buyers) may influence the choice of media class. Advertising expenditure is often used by salespeople to convince the retail trade to increase shelf space for existing brands and to stock new brands. Since distribution is a key success factor in these markets, the views of retailers will be important. For example, if it is known that supermarkets favour television advertising in a certain product market, the selling impact on the trade of £1 million spent on television may be viewed as greater than the equivalent spend of 50:50 between television and the press.

Sometimes a combination of media classes is used in an advertising campaign to take advantage of their relative strengths and weaknesses. For example, a new car launch might use television to gain awareness and project the desired image, with the press being used to supply more technical information. Later, posters may be used as a support medium to remind and reinforce earlier messages.

The media vehicle decision

The media vehicle decision concerns the choice of the particular newspaper, magazine, television spot, poster site, etc. Although creative considerations still play a part, *cost per thousand calculations* are more dominant. This requires readership and viewership figures. In the UK, readership figures are produced by the National Readership Survey, based on 28,000 interviews per year. Viewership is measured by the Broadcasters' Audience Research Board (BARB), which produces weekly reports based on a panel of 4500 households equipped with metered television sets. Traffic past poster sites is measured by Outdoor Site Classification and Audience Research (OSCAR), which classifies 130,000 sites according to visibility, competition (one or more posters per site), angle of vision, height above ground, illumination and weekly traffic past site. Cinema audiences are monitored by Cinema and Video Industry Audience Research (CAVIAR) and radio audiences are measured by Radio Joint Audience Research (RAJAR). Table 12.4 shows how a viewer or reader is measured in terms of opportunity to see.

Table 12.4	Definition of an opportunity to see (OTS)
Television	Presence in room with set switched on at turn of clock minute to relevant channel, provided that presence in room with set on is for at least 15 consecutive seconds
Press	Read or looked at any issue (for at least two minutes) within the publication period (for example, for weeklies, within the last seven days)
Posters	Traffic past site (including pedestrians)
Cinema	Actual cinema admissions

Media buying is a specialized skill and many thousands of pounds can be saved off rate card prices by powerful media buyers. Media buying is accomplished through one of three methods: full service agencies, media specialists or media buying clubs. Full service agencies provide a full range of advertising services for their clients, including media buying. Independent media specialists grew in the early 1990s as clients favoured their focused expertise and negotiating muscle. Media buying clubs were formed by full service agencies joining forces to pool buying power. However, the current trend is back to full service agencies, but with one major difference: today the buying is done by separate profit-making subsidiaries. With very few exceptions, all the world's top media buying operations are now owned by global advertising companies such as Omnicom, WPP, Saatchi & Saatchi and Cordiant.[40]

Today there is more pressure than ever to create critical mass in media buying. With media owners consolidating and advertisers rationalizing, buyers have followed suit to retain buying power. For example, Cordiant and Publicis have established a new venture combining their Zenith and Optimedia media-buying networks.

Buying power enables agencies to acquire and retain clients because advertisers believe that the media houses with the biggest budgets buy cheapest. This means that media buyers need to be of a sufficient size to attract global clients.[41]

Execute campaign

Once the advertisements have been produced and the media selected, they are sent to the relevant media for publication or transmission. A key organizational issue is to ensure that the right advertisements reach the right media at the right time. Each media vehicle has its own deadlines after which publication or transmission may not be possible.

Evaluate advertising effectiveness

Three key questions in *advertising research* are what, when and how to evaluate. What should be measured depends on whatever the advertising is trying to achieve. As we have already seen, advertising objectives include gaining awareness, trial, positioning, correcting misconceptions, reminding and providing support for the salesforce (for example, by identifying warm prospects). By setting targets for each objective, advertising research can assess whether objectives have been achieved. For example, a campaign might have the objective of increasing awareness from 10 to 20 per cent, or of raising beliefs that the product is the 'best value brand on the market' from 15 to 25 per cent of the target consumers.

If advertising objectives are couched in sales or market share terms, advertising research would monitor the sales or market share effects of advertising. Finally, if trade objectives are important, distribution and stock levels of wholesalers and/or retailers, and perhaps their awareness and attitudes, should be measured.

Measurement can take place before, during and after campaign execution. *Pre-testing* takes place before the campaign is run and is part of the creative process. In television advertising, *rough* advertisements are created and tested with target consumers. This is usually done with a *focus group*, which is shown perhaps three alternative commercials and asked to discuss its likes, dislikes and understanding of each one.[42] Stills from the proposed commercial are shown on a television screen with a voice-over. This provides an inexpensive but realistic portrayal of what the commercial will be like if it is shot. The results provide important input from target consumers themselves rather than solely relying on advertising agency views. Voice-overs that are disliked, misunderstanding and lack of credibility of messages are examples of problems that can be identified at the pre-testing stage and, therefore, rectified before the cost of shooting a commercial is incurred. Such research is not without its critics, however. They suggest that the impact of a commercial that is repeated many times cannot be captured in a two-hour group discussion. They point to the highly successful Heineken campaign ('Refreshes the parts that other beers cannot reach'), which was rejected by target consumers in pre-testing.[43]

Press advertisements can be pre-tested using the *folder techniques*.[44] Suppose that two advertisements are being compared, two folders are prepared containing a number of advertisements with which the test advertisements will have to compete for attention. The test advertisements are placed in the same position in each folder. Two matched samples of around 50–100 target consumers are each given one of the folders and asked to go through it. Respondents are then asked to state which advertisements they have noticed (*unaided recall*). They are then shown a list of the advertised brands and asked questions such as which one was most liked, which was least liked, and which they intend to buy. Attention is gradually focused on the test advertisement and respondents are asked to recall its content.

Once the campaign has run, *post-testing* can be used to assess its effectiveness. Sometimes formal post-testing is ignored through laziness, fear or lack of funds. However, checking how well an advertising campaign has performed can provide the information necessary to plan future campaigns. In the UK, image/attitude, statistical analysis of sales data and usage surveys (usage rates, changes in usage) were the most popular TV post-testing techniques.[45] The top three measures used in post-test television advertising research mirror the most popular techniques: image/attitude change, actual sales and usage. Image/attitude change was believed to be a sensitive measure that was a good predictor of behavioural change. Some of those agencies favouring the actual sales measure argued that, despite difficulties in establishing cause and effect, sales change was the ultimate objective of advertising and therefore was the only meaningful measure. Recall was also popular (63 per cent used it regularly). Despite the evidence suggesting that recall may not be a valid measure of advertising effectiveness, those favouring recall gave reasons varying from the sweeping 'It usually means good advertising if good recall is present' to the pragmatic 'Because it shows the advertisement is seen and remembered, it is very reassuring to the client'.

Many of the measures used to evaluate television advertising can also be used for press advertisements. For example, spontaneous recall of a brand name could be measured before and after a press campaign. In addition, readers of a periodical in which the advertisement appeared could be asked to recall which advertisements they saw and, if the test advertisement is recalled, its content. In addition, press advertisements that incorporate coupons to promote enquiries or actual sales can be evaluated by totalling the number of enquirers or the value of sales generated.

The key to evaluating advertising is to consult with the target audience, not rely on industry awards as a measure of effectiveness. These can give very different results. For example, a Norwegian charity won an award for an advertising campaign on which it spent NKr3 million (£300,000/€432,000) only to find that it attracted only NKr1.7 million (£170,000/€245,000) in donations.

Organizing for campaign development

An advertiser has four options when organizing for campaign development. First, small companies may develop the advertising *in co-operation* with people from the media. For example, advertising copy may be written by someone from the company but the artwork and final layout of the advertisement may be done by the newspaper or magazine. Alternatively, commercial radio stations provide facilities for commercials to be produced. Second, the advertising function may be conducted in-house by creating an *advertising department* staffed with copy-writers, media buyers and production personnel. This form of organization locates total control of the advertising function within the company, but since media buying is on behalf of only one company, buying power is low.

Figure 12.7 The structure of a large advertising agency

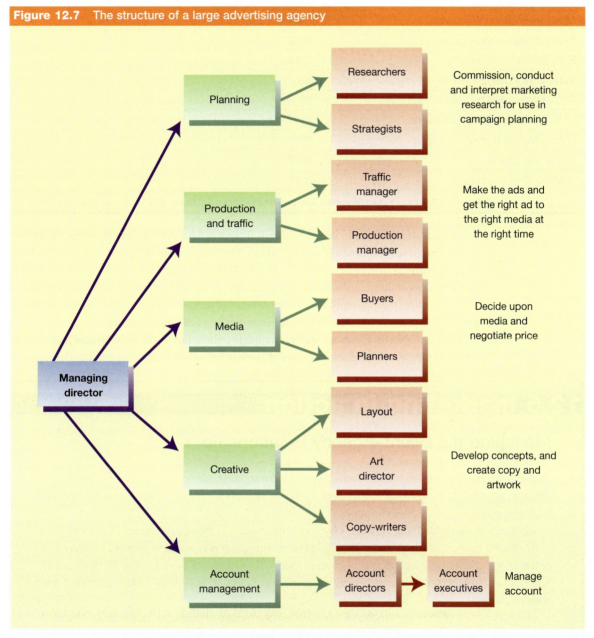

Third, because of the specialist skills that are required for developing an advertising campaign, many advertisers opt to work with an **advertising agency**. Larger agencies offer a full service, comprising creative, media planning and buying, planning and strategy development, market research and production. Figure 12.7 shows the typical structure of a large advertising agency. Key figures in the development of a campaign are account directors and executives, who liaise with client companies and co-ordinate the work of the other departments on behalf of their clients. Because agencies work for many clients they have a wide range of experience, and can provide an objective outsider's view of what is required, and how problems can be solved. Table 12.5 lists the top ten European agencies (by income) in 1998.

Table 12.5 The top ten European advertising agency networks

Agency	Billings ($m)
Y&R Advertising	13358
McCann-Erickson Worldwide	7587
Ogilvy & Mather Worldwide	6182
Euro RSCG	5316
Publicis Worldwide	5267
BBDO Worldwide	4975
DDB Worldwide Communications	4191
D'Arcy Masius Benton & Bowles	3836
TBWA Worldwide	3676
J Walter Thompson Co.	3645

Source: Top European Agency Networks, European Marketing Pocket Book 2003, Henley-on-Thames: NTC.

A fourth alternative is to use in-house staff (or a full service agency) for some advertising functions but to use *specialist agencies* for others. Their attraction, in part, stems from the large volume of business that each specialist controls. This means that they have enormous buying power when negotiating media prices. Alternatively, an advertiser could employ the services of a *creative hot shop* to supplement their own or their full service agency's skills. Saatchi & Saatchi began life as a creative hot shop before developing into a full service agency.

When an advertiser uses an agency, managing the relationship is of critical importance. Marketing in Action 12.5 discusses some of the key issues involved.

12.5 marketing in action

Managing the Client–Agency Relationship

Strong relationships between clients (advertisers) and their agencies can provide the platform for effective advertising. A survey of clients and agencies focused on those issues that were causing problems in achieving this desired state.

Many clients demanded that agencies become more involved in their business, with comments like 'they need to spend more time understanding our challenges and goals' and 'they need to take more notice of the client's view with regard to creative work'. Clearly, clients were looking for agencies to spend more time and attention on understanding their business objectives before beginning the creative process.

The importance of the early stages of the advertising development process was also emphasized by agencies. Some complained about having to deal with junior people at the briefing stage, who had not been trained to write a clear brief. This was critical because unless clients get the briefing stage right things will inevitably go wrong further down the line. This problem was connected to the lack of accessibility of senior marketing staff because they have too much other work to do. This means that briefing is left in the hands of junior staff, who have the power to say 'no' but not 'yes'. This can be very frustrating for agencies. One agency complained about not enough 'ear time' with a senior member of his client's marketing team: 'he is too busy and there is too big an experience gap between him and his team'. Two further consequences of this were insufficient access to business objectives and strategy, and an inability to provide constructive feedback on their proposals.

Based on: Curtis (2002);[46] Curtis (2002)[47]

Agency selection

As with buying any product, agency selection begins by defining requirements clearly. For example, a do-it-yourself or furniture chain may place most emphasis on media selection and buying capabilities so that the lowest cost per thousand can be achieved for its relatively straightforward black and white product information advertisements.[48] On the other hand, a company marketing drinks or perfume may give greater priority to the creative talents of prospective agencies. White describes the selection procedure as follows:[49]

1. define requirements
2. develop a pool list of agencies
3. credentials (e.g. examples of current and previous work, team members, profiles) pitch by agencies
4. issue brief to shortlisted agencies
5. full agency presentation
6. analysis of pitch
7. select winner
8. agree contract details
9. announce winner.

When briefing agencies, the following checklist may be used.

1. *Product history*: e.g. sales, market share, trends, price, past campaigns, competition.
2. *Product features and benefits*: the product's competitive advantages and disadvantages.
3. *Objectives*: the product's marketing and communication objectives.
4. *Target audience*: who they are, their motives and choice criteria.
5. *Timetable*: when the agency presentation is required, when the campaign is planned to commence.
6. *Budget*: how much money is available, which may affect choice of media.

Analysis of the agency presentation will depend on the following six key questions.

1. How good is its creative/media/research work?
2. Does the agency have people you think you can work with?
3. Does your account appear to be important to them?
4. What is their background: who are their clients, how long have they worked with them, is their client list growing or contracting, have they worked in your field before and, if so, why did they lose the account?
5. Are they a full service agency or do they contract out some functions (e.g. media, research)?
6. What do they charge? Do they charge fees as well as commission?

Agency payment systems

The traditional system of agency payment was by *commission* from the media owners. This was because advertising agencies were originally set up on behalf of media owners that wished to provide advertising services to enhance the likelihood of selling advertising space. Hence, it was natural that payment should be from them. Under the commission system, media owners traditionally gave a 15 per cent discount off the rate card (list) price to agencies. For example, a £1 million (€1.44 million) television advertising campaign would result in a charge to the agency of £1 million minus 15 per cent (£850,000/€1,224,000). The agency invoiced the client at the full rate card price (£1 million). The agency commission therefore totalled £150,000 (€216,000).

Large advertisers have the power to demand some of the 15 per cent in the form of a rebate. For example, Unilever announced that it was allowing its advertising agencies 13 per cent commission.[50] Given its worldwide advertising expenditure of £1.5 billion (€1.95 billion) it could probably have demanded a lower figure (possibly 11 per cent) but the company chose not to exercise all of its muscle since it believed that low commission rates ultimately mean poor-quality advertising.

The second method of paying agencies is by *fee*. For smaller clients, commission alone may not be sufficient to cover agency costs. Also, some larger clients are advocating fees rather than commission on the basis that this removes a possible source of agency bias towards media that pay commission rather than a medium like direct mail for which no commission is payable.

The third method of remuneration is through payment by results. This involves measuring the effectiveness of the advertising campaign using marketing research, and basing payment on how well communication objectives have been achieved. For example, payment might be based on how awareness levels have increased, brand image improved or intentions to buy risen. Some agencies are paid by how many sales have been achieved. For example, Holsten Pils pays its agency, TBWA London, by the volume of lager sold; no other payment for its day-to-day work on the client's business is made.[51] Another area where payment by results has been used is media buying. For example, if the normal cost per thousand to reach men in the age range 30–40 is £4.50 (€6.50), and the agency achieves a 10 per cent saving, this might be split 8 per cent to the client and 2 per cent to the agency.[52] Procter & Gamble uses payment by results as the method by which it pays its advertising agencies, which include Saatchi & Saatchi, Leo Burnett, Grey Advertising and D'Arcy Masius Benton & Bowles. Remuneration is tied to global brand sales, so aligning their income more closely with the success (or otherwise) of their advertising.[53]

Ethical issues in advertising

Because it is so visible most people have a view on the value of advertising. Certainly advertising has its critics (and its supporters). Their views will be discussed within the following areas: misleading advertising, advertising's influence on society's values and advertising to children.

Misleading advertising

This can take the form of exaggerated claims and concealed facts. For example, it would be unethical to claim that a car achieved 50 miles to the gallon when in reality it was only 30 miles. Nevertheless, most countries accept a certain amount of puffery, recognizing that consumers are intelligent and interpret the claims in such a way that they are not deceptive. In the UK, the advertising slogan 'Carlsberg—Probably the best lager in the world' is acceptable because of this. However, in Europe, advertisers should be aware that a European directive on misleading advertising states that the burden of proof lies with the advertiser should the claims be challenged. Advertising can also deceive by omitting important facts from the message. Such concealed facts may give a misleading impression to the audience. For example, an advertisement that promotes a food product as 'healthy' because it contains added vitamins might be considered misleading if it failed to point out its high sugar and fat content. Many industrialized countries have their own codes of practice that protect the consumer from deceptive advertising. For example, in the UK the Advertising Standards Authority (ASA) administers the British Code of Advertising Practice. It insists that advertising should be 'legal, decent, honest and truthful'. Ethical Marketing in Action 12.1 gives some examples of how misleading advertising is controlled.

12.1 ethical marketing in action

Controlling Misleading Advertising

Advertising is controlled at both national and European levels to minimize the threat of it misleading consumers. In the UK, the Advertising Standards Authority's code states that an ad 'should not mislead by inaccuracy, ambiguity, exaggeration, omission or otherwise'. One way in which advertising (and branding) can mislead is by unjustifiably linking a brand name to a strong national identity. It was for this reason that the ASA ruled that the umlaut over the 'o' in Möben Kitchens (now Moben Kitchens), a Manchester-based company, should be removed in its advertising. It took the view that the umlaut nurtured the belief that the company was German and that it was trying to gain from that country's reputation for craftsmanship.

Advertisers also have to be careful about the claims they make in their advertising. For example, Procter & Gamble was forced to drop its claim 'Pantene Pro-V is the world's best haircare system', after Lever Fabergé complained to the ASA, which ruled in Lever Fabergé's favour.

Based on: Singh (2002);[54] Thurtle (2001)[55]

Advertising's influence on society's values

Critics argue that advertising images have a profound effect on society. They claim that advertising promotes materialism and takes advantage of human frailties. Advertising is accused of stressing the importance of material possessions, such as the ownership of an expensive car or the latest in consumer electronics. Critics argue that this promotes the wrong values in society. A related criticism is that advertising takes advantage of human frailties such as the need to belong and the desire for status. It promotes the idea that people should be judged on what they possess rather than who they are. For example, advertisements for some cars use status symbol appeals rather than their functional characteristics. Supporters of advertising counter by arguing that these are not human frailties but basic psychological characteristics. They point out that the acquisition of status symbols occurs in societies that are not exposed to advertising messages, such as some African tribes where status is derived from the number of cows a person owns.

Advertising to children

Advertising to children is a controversial issue. Critics argue that children are especially susceptible to persuasion and that they therefore need special protection from advertising. Others counter by claiming that the children of today are remarkably streetwise and can look after themselves. They are also protected by parents who can counteract advertising influence to some extent. Many European countries have regulations that control advertising to children. For example, in Germany advertising specific types of toys is banned and in the UK alcohol advertising is controlled.[56] In Sweden, advertising to under-12s on terrestrial television stations is banned, and in Belgium and Australia advertising within children's programmes is limited.

Countries like the UK have a code of practice to control advertisements aimed at children. The code is designed to avoid the misleading presentation of products and may require advertisers to disclose product information. For example, when advertising toys, accurate information about their size, price and operation should be included.[57] An example of self-regulation at work was the dropping of an advertisement for a soft drink, which featured a gang of ginger-haired middle-aged men taunting a fat youth. The advertisement was withdrawn after numerous complaints were received contending that it encouraged bullying in schools.[58]

Most of the advertising to children is for food (cereals, snacks, sweets and food from fast food outlets), toys, clothes and entertainment products. The emphasis on convenience foods has been criticized for its potential effect on unhealthy eating. This has been countered partially by advertisements that advocate balanced diets and present nutritional information. Nevertheless, the question of whether children understand such information remains unresolved.[59]

Advertisements featuring toys, clothes and entertainment products have been criticized for promoting an acquisitive lifestyle and encouraging 'pester-power', whereby children request their parents to buy them such products, leading to family conflict. However, others point out that advertising may only be one factor in such conflict because some children's products sell well without advertising.[60]

Ethical dilemma

As funding to schools has reduced, pressure is increasing to accept industry-led sponsorship and marketing. Teachers may, therefore, accept materials developed by commercial organizations that wish to involve themselves in helping education. Many individuals are critical of this approach, and urge schools and teachers to exercise careful judgement in their review of such resources. In 2001 a newspaper article reported that more than 140,000 glossy brochures sponsored by US corporate genetic modification giants including Monsanto were being provided to Scottish schools with backing from Scottish Enterprise and schools watchdog HM Inspectorate of Education. Could these brochures be considered a form of advertising to children?

Review

1 The role of advertising in the promotional mix
- Advertising is any paid form of non-personal communication of ideas or products in the prime media, i.e. television, the press, posters, cinema, and radio.
- It possesses strengths and limitations, and should be combined with other promotional tools to form an integrated marketing communications campaign.

2 The factors that affect the choice of the promotional mix
- These are resource availability and the cost of promotional tools, market size and concentration, customer information needs, product characteristics and push versus pull strategies.

3 The key characteristics of the major promotional tools
- Advertising: strong for awareness building, brand positioning, company and brand legitimization, but it is impersonal and inflexible, and has only a limited ability to close a sale.

- Personal selling: strong for interactivity, adaptability, the delivery of complex arguments, relationship building and the closing of the sale, but is costly.
- Direct marketing: strong for individual targeting, personalization, measurement, relationship building through periodic contact, low visibility to competitors, but response rates are often low and can cause annoyance.
- Online marketing: strong for global reach, measurement, establishing a dialogue, quick changes to catalogues and prices, convenience and avoids arguments with salespeople, but impersonal and requires consumers to visit website.
- Sales promotion: strong on providing immediate incentive to buy but effects may be short term and can damage brand image.
- Publicity: strong on credibility, high readership but loss of control.

4 The communications process

- The communication process begins with the source encoding a message that is transmitted through media to the receiver who decodes. Noise (e.g. distractions) may prevent the message reaching the receiver. Feedback may be direct when talking to a salesperson or through marketing research.

5 The value of integrated marketing communications

- Integrated marketing communications is the concept by which companies co-ordinate their marketing communications tools to deliver a clear, consistent, credible and competitive message about the organization and its products.
- Its achievement can be hampered by office politics, and a high-ranking communications officer may be needed to see through its successful implementation.
- Its philosophy has led to the rise in media-neutral planning, which is the process of solving communications problems through an unbiased evaluation of all media.

6 The differences between strong and weak theories of how advertising works

- The strong theory of advertising considers advertising to be a powerful influence on consumers, increasing knowledge, changing attitudes, and creating desire and conviction, and as a consequence persuading people to buy brands.
- The weak theory of advertising considers advertising to be a much less powerful influence on consumers. It suggests that advertising may arouse awareness and interest, nudge some consumers towards trial, and then provide some reassurance and reinforcement after the trial.

7 How to develop advertising strategy: target audience analysis, objective setting, budgeting, message and media decisions, execution, and advertising evaluation

- Advertising decisions should not be taken in isolation but should be based on a clear understanding of marketing strategy, in particular positioning. Then the steps are as follows.
- Identify and understand the target audience: the audience needs to be defined and understood in terms of its motives and choice criteria.
- Define advertising objectives: communicational objectives are to create awareness, stimulate trial, position products in consumer's minds, correct misconceptions, remind and reinforce, and provide support for the salesforce.
- Set the advertising budget: options are the percentage of sales, affordability, matching competition, and objective and task methods.
- Message decisions: messages should be important to the target audience and communicate competitive advantages.

- Media decisions: two key decisions are the choice of media (e.g. television versus the press) and media vehicle (a particular newspaper or magazine).
- Execution: care should be taken to meet publication deadlines.
- Evaluation of advertising: three key questions are what, when and how to evaluate.

8. **How campaigns are organized, including advertising agency selection and payment systems**
    - An advertiser has four organizational options:
        1. advertising can be developed directly in co-operation with the media
        2. an in-house advertising department can be created
        3. a full service advertising agency can be used
        4. a combination of in-house staff (or the full service agency) can be used for some functions and a specialist agency (media or creative) for others.
    - Agency selection should begin with a clear definition of requirements. A shortlist of agencies should be drawn up and each briefed on the product and campaign. Selection will take place after each has made a presentation to the client.
    - Agency payment can be by commission, fee or payment by results.

9. **Ethical issues in advertising.**
    - There are potential problems relating to misleading advertising, advertising's influence on society's values and advertising to children.

Key terms

advertising any paid form of non-personal communication of ideas or products in the prime media, i.e. television, the press, posters, cinema and radio, the Internet and direct marketing

advertising agency an organization that specializes in providing services such as media selection, creative work, production and campaign planning to clients

advertising message the use of words, symbols and illustrations to communicate to a target audience using prime media

advertising platform the aspect of the seller's product that is most persuasive and relevant to the target consumer

direct marketing (1) acquiring and retaining customers without the use of an intermediary; (2) the distribution of products, information and promotional benefits to target consumers through interactive communication in a way that allows response to be measured

integrated marketing communications the concept that companies co-ordinate their marketing communications tools to deliver a clear, consistent, credible and competitive message about the organization and its products

Internet and online marketing the distribution of products, information and promotional benefits to consumers through electronic media

media class decision the choice of prime media, i.e. the press, cinema, television, posters, radio, or some combination of these

media vehicle decision the choice of the particular newspaper, magazine, television spot, poster site, etc.

personal selling oral communication with prospective purchasers with the intention of making a sale

publicity the communication of a product or business by placing information about it in the media without paying for time or space directly

sales promotion incentives to customers or the trade that are designed to stimulate purchase

▶ **strong theory of advertising** the notion that advertising can change people's attitudes sufficiently to persuade people who have not previously bought a brand to buy it; desire and conviction precede purchase

target audience the group of people at which an advertisement or message is aimed

weak theory of advertising the notion that advertising can first arouse awareness and interest, nudge some consumers towards a doubting first trial purchase and then provide some reassurance and reinforcement; desire and conviction do not precede purchase

Internet exercise

Adwatch.tv is a UK television advertising archive, highlighting some of television's latest advertising campaigns. Browse its archive of adverts.
Visit: www.adwatch.tv

Questions

(a) What are the possible objectives of an advertising campaign for a firm?
(b) Discuss what you believe to be essential characteristics of effective advertising, giving examples from the website archive.

Visit the Online Learning Centre at www.mcgraw-hill.co.uk/textbooks/jobber for more Internet exercises.

Study questions

1. Compare the situations where advertising and personal selling are more likely to feature strongly in the promotional mix.

2. Describe the strong and weak theories of how advertising works. Which theory is more likely to apply to the purchase of a car, and the purchase of a soap powder?

3. Within an advertising context, what is 'positioning in the mind of the consumer'? Using examples, discuss the alternative positioning options available to an advertiser.

4. Advertising has no place in the industrial marketing communications mix. Discuss.

5. Media class decisions should always be based on creative considerations, while media vehicle decisions should be determined solely by cost per thousand calculations. Do you agree?

6. Discuss the contention that advertising should be based on the skills of the creative team, not the statistics of the research department.

7. Describe the structure of a large advertising agency. Why should an advertiser prefer to use an agency rather than set up a full-service internal advertising department?

8. Discuss the advantages and limitations of developing pan-European advertising campaigns.

9. As a highly visible communication tool, advertising has its share of critics. What are their key concerns? How far do you agree or disagree with their arguments?

When you have read this chapter log on to the Online Learning Centre at www.mcgraw-hill.co.uk/textbooks/jobber to explore chapter-by-chapter test questions, links and further online study tools for marketing.

case twenty-three

The Repositioning of White Horse Whisky

Market background

United Distillers & Vintners (UDV), the brand owner of Bell's and White Horse, is seeking to recruit a new generation of young drinkers to the whisky market. It has taken the view that this can be achieved by repositioning its White Horse brand so that it shakes free of the old-fashioned imagery currently associated with Scotch whisky. This will involve developing a marketing strategy and advertising campaign that will change the way White Horse is perceived by young people. UDV then intends to promote Bell's in a way that continues to appeal to mainstream, older, established whisky drinkers by continuing to reflect more traditional values.

The Scotch whisky market has been in decline for over 15 years. Drinking patterns generally have moved away from traditional dark spirits (such as rum and whisky) in favour of white spirits (vodka), wine and lagers. Each generation of new drinkers has been attracted to the marketing and promotion of chilled, long, lighter drinks. Brands from exotic countries that combine genuine authenticity with exciting contemporary images have enjoyed persistent growth.

Over time, the profile of whisky drinkers has gradually become older, within a base that is in itself declining (see Tables C23.1 and C23.2). The number of adults drinking whisky at least once a month has declined by around 900,000, and over half the remaining 3.9 million consumers are over 50 years old. The rate of recruitment of people in their twenties and thirties has declined over recent years.

Whisky has always been acknowledged as an 'acquired taste' that was unlikely to appeal to novice drinkers, but rather reflected a more mature palate.

However, people are no longer making the transition to traditional dark spirits in anything like the numbers they did historically. Consumers no longer seem motivated to rise to the challenge of drinking traditional dark spirits (although they are still interested in trying new dark spirits as the growth in malt whisky and bourbon has demonstrated).

Table C23.1 Blended whisky market (000 litre cases)

Year	Cases
1996	10980
1997	10090
1998	9428
1999	9659
2000	9540
2001	8595
2002	8210

Table C23.2 Profile of whisky drinkers

Age	Dec. 1980 %	Dec. 1990 %	Dec. 2002 %
18–24	11	10	9
25–34	19	15	15
35–49	27	24	24
50+	44	50	52
Base 000	4906	4626	3997

The leading brand has consistently remained Bell's (see Table C23.3), but the total share of all the brands is consistently being eroded by less expensive and less famous alternatives. So, in addition to operating in a market that is in overall decline, brands are losing their share of that market.

White Horse whisky is available in some off-licences and in supermarkets like Waitrose and Sainsbury's, where it is among a broad competitive set.

The current image of whisky

UDV commissioned qualitative research in the UK among 18–25 years olds (typically still experimenting) and 25–30 year olds (usually becoming established in their repertoire) to try and understand what the barriers to drinking whisky are and therefore how it might go about challenging these beliefs through its presentation of White Horse.

This research found that there were both product and image barriers to whisky drinking. It is believed to be a strong and overpowering spirit, with a potent bitter smell and 'rough' or 'fiery' taste that will linger unpleasantly after drinking. It is also universally described as a spirit that is very difficult to mix. Repertoires are usually restricted to 'ordinary' mixes such as ice, water, ginger and lemonade. This makes it more difficult to make whisky accessible in a more dilute form, which is typically how young people learn to acquire a taste for spirits; it is rare to be able to take them neat from the beginning.

Table C23.3 Brand share

	1999 %	2000 %	2001 %	2002 %
Bell's	18.9	17.7	17.7	17.0
Teachers	7.4	7.5	6.9	6.2
Famous Grouse	13.4	12.8	12.4	12.9
White Horse	3.1	2.7	2.9	2.3
Grant's	5.3	5.3	5.1	4.8
Whyte & Mackay	4.4	4.6	4.7	4.1
Own-label	18.3	18.9	19.0	18.9
Cheapest on display	8.7	9.1	10.8	12.8

For some, these product barriers can be seen as an initiation test, with the reward being the acknowledgement of being a 'real man'.

Current whisky imagery is seen as outdated and largely irrelevant. For the younger people surveyed, it elicits tired, safe old images of tartan, hills, heather and glens, lochs, bagpipers, open fires, old men drinking on their own, and so on—which are all considered to have once been targeted at their parents or grandparents. These images are not felt to reflect the more authentic, real-life images of Scotland and its rich heritage. Films such as *Braveheart* and recent political moves to give Scotland greater independence are all areas of much greater interest, and offer more compelling images of the dignity and depth of Scotland's rich history.

The consumer

This research project also investigated the values of young people generally, not just with respect to whisky. The findings were as follows.

- Today's young people view balance as a necessity to successful life. They are motivated by success in their desired careers, but the focus for them must also be on enjoyment and escapism in their spare time. They are materialistic, but in a less aggressive way than the young people of the Thatcherite 1980s. To some extent, an environmental awareness and the need to treat and respect the world we live in have softened this.
- The 1990s also brought a shift towards honesty and authenticity—a move away from the contrived, lifestyle-orientated 1980s. Being true to oneself has been identified as being important. Optimism was also in evidence, as it is with many young people who have not been hardened by the reality of life.
- They appreciate quality, sincerity and unpretentiousness. This reflects a going-back-to-basics mentality. They also consider originality, intelligence and a degree of irreverence (or not taking oneself too seriously) to be particularly important. In sum, 'less is more'.
- Humour is seen to be an important vehicle for facing up to the realities of life. Humour that is self-deprecating, subtle and self-referential is particularly liked. Honesty and insight is also appreciated because it credits the viewer with some intelligence.
- The values associated with young people today are also tinged with a degree of vulnerability. The recession of the 1990s has made people recognize that jobs are not for life and that they might underachieve in their lives.

White Horse

White Horse whisky was created in 1890 by Peter Mackie, one of the best-known whisky blenders and distillers of his day. He named it after one of Edinburgh's most famous coaching inns: The White Horse Cellar. Indeed, the brand logo reflects the pub sign design. In its distinctive, modernized, squat bottle, the brand sells for £14.99 (€21.6) per litre, a price below that of Bell's (£16.49/€23.7) and Teachers (£15.79/€23), but above own-label (e.g. Waitrose at £12.99/€18.7).

Yorkshire farmers have always been particularly attached to the brand and created the very smooth and drinkable 'whisky milk'. This consists of a tumbler made up of half cold milk and half White Horse whisky. A favourite way to wind down at the end of a hard day. Alternatively, the brand mixes very well with ginger ale or orange juice.

It is many years since the brand had any advertising support, with most of UDV's effort being behind Bell's. However, it is recognized that the successful targeting of a new generation of young consumers is vital to the future of the whisky market. The recent relaxation of the voluntary code, whereby whisky brands may now be advertised on TV, represents a particular opportunity.

Animal magnetism: UDV aims to make White Horse the thoroughbred choice for young drinkers.

Marketing objective

UDV intends to relaunch White Horse whisky in January 2004. Its aim is to achieve a brand share of 6 per cent in three years. It is expected that 60 per cent of the brand's consumers should be under 50 years of age by that time.

The task

Each syndicate must come up with an advertising strategy based on a budget level of £3 million (€4.3 million) in the first year of advertising. For the purpose of the exercise, in terms of media, they are asked to consider only what their strategy will be (i.e. which target audience should be reached, using which type of media and when), which is the role fulfilled by a media planner, often in conjunction with the creative agency team. They will not be asked to cost out the plan, and will not be given costings for the various media. A simple ratio is included below.

The advertising strategy must answer the following questions.

1. What are the advertising objectives?
2. Who exactly are the people the advertising must affect/reach?
3. What is the main message the advertising must put across and what evidence can be used to support that message?
4. What do we want people to think/feel after seeing the advertising?
5. What should the style of advertising be?
6. Where should the advertising appear (i.e. TV, newspapers, magazines, posters, radio, etc.)? Which would be the primary vehicle and which the secondary support? What percentage of the £3 million (€4.3 million) would be allocated to which media and why?

Issues to consider when developing your media strategy

Today, most creative agencies use a media agency to plan and buy media. The media agency specializes both in understanding how consumers 'consume' media (and therefore which media are most effective in reaching particular audiences) and in being able to negotiate the best-value schedule from the ever-expanding selection of media opportunities. The average person in Britain today is exposed to around 2500 advertising messages a week, so optimum targeting of the media chosen and cut-through of the message displayed are essential.

Consider what target audience can achieve the advertising objectives you have decided upon; then consider what media that target might 'consume' and when might be the most propitious moment to 'approach' them in that medium. Consider both time of day as well as seasonality, and what their activities might be while viewing the medium as this will impact on their frame of mind when seeing the advertising message. You might feel that one medium is not sufficient and that you need to convey your message using a multi-layered effect (e.g. television with direct response, posters with radio, Internet banners with sales promotion, etc.). Consider where and when they can buy the brand, and how this might affect the media chosen. Most types of media are segmented (e.g. different press titles or TV programmes can reach different audiences), so consider a typical example to clarify your answer.

Think about what sort of message you wish to promote. Do you need to explain your positioning and be able to use a lot of words, or is a simple visual able to convey your message? This will dictate whether press or posters, for example, would be most appropriate.

Allow a notional 10 per cent cost for creative production for each medium that you choose.

Use your own consumption of different media to guide you in your media choice, and then consider whether someone in a different consumer age group would react differently and why.

Note

All figures in the tables in this case are indicative.

The author of the book is grateful to Ann Murray Chatterton, Director of Training and Development at the Institute of Practitioners in Advertising (IPA), for permission to publish this case.
Copyright © IPA www.ipa.co.uk

case twenty-four

NFO MarketMind: Brand Tracking and the 'Lettuseat' Advertising Campaign

Introduction

Several marketing research agencies offer different types of tracking study to monitor the effectiveness of advertising a brand and the brand's performance over a specified period of time. NFO WorldGroup is a large market research agency; its MarketMind Brand Tracking System is innovative and unique in the field. This case study is an example taken from a real NFO MarketMind study, although the brand name and product category have been changed for commercial reasons.

The first part of this case study will set the groundwork for the Lettuseat advertising campaign by establishing the contributions from brand tracking studies and the literature, a model of advertising effects upon consumer equity and sales, and the relationship of advertising tasks to the NFO MarketMind measures. This is followed by the tracking study in the Lettuseat advertising campaign.

Contribution of brand tracking studies

Sales may not tell the whole story, or even in some cases may prove to be misleading, so managers are often interested in how their marketing activity influences or changes the mind of the consumer. A consumer's awareness and impressions of, and disposition towards a brand may change and become early indicators of a potential change in behaviour (brand switching, increased usage, change of behaviour, and so on). Some marketers may carry out a study on a sample of their target market of consumers prior to a campaign then repeat this exercise on a fresh sample after the campaign. Measures might include awareness of brands (spontaneous and prompted), brands currently bought, brand preferences, image of brands and recall of advertising or other marketing activities. Changes on any of these measures may be attributed to marketing activity. The problem with only conducting two such 'dipstick' surveys is that two measures in time might not just reflect the effect of a specific marketing activity but also underlying trend(s). This is why continuous tracking (dipsticks at frequent intervals—for instance, weekly or monthly) is preferred. Continuous tracking permits the analyst the opportunity to isolate the effects of marketing activity from trend as well as to understand better how a campaign builds up and then possibly wears out.

Some tracking services are syndicated so anyone can buy them. For instance, the data from a tracking study on hot beverages could potentially be available to all manufacturers in this field for a price.

Over the past few years, brand tracking research has been a significant growth sector of the market research industry, much of it stimulated by the introduction of new approaches, improved methodologies and application to a wider variety of market sectors.

As mentioned above, the example given in this case study is that of a major tracking study called MarketMind by the NFO WorldGroup. The MarketMind view is that all marketing activity, including advertising, has the same fundamental objective—namely to make a contribution to a product's 'consumer equity'.

The value of this case study is to show how a tracking study is used in practice by a research agency for a client company.

Contribution from the literature

If a service or brand is more 'desired' or 'wanted' than those offered by competitors, consumers will be more predisposed towards buying such a service or brand. Assuming that marketplace factors (such as availability, price, and so on) are not a barrier, this should convert into actual sales. A simple model can be formulated, as illustrated in Fig. C24.1, with advertising influencing consumer equity and leading to sales.

An example of one tracking study that was carried out showed demonstrable benefits in terms of public recognition of a new brand that was advertised, leading to the creation of brand equity and increased sales.[1] The television advertisements showed a 'red telephone' with human characteristics because of its activities (moving, jumping into the air and bugle call) for the Direct Line insurance company. The tracking study gave quantifiable evidence of the success of the advertising campaign on television.

Figure C24.1 Advertising's role in influencing equity and sales

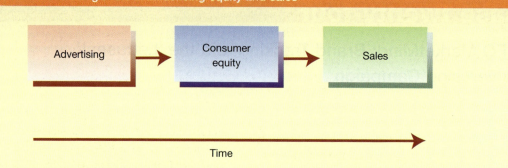

It should be noted that brand equity can be defined in a number of ways.[2] One may talk in terms of the value of a brand should it be sold to another organization. The value of a brand might reflect both its potential and its current status. Current status would take into account its relative 'strength' against competitors in the mind of consumers. Marketers might assess the relative strength of a brand on the basis of one or more performance measures. These might include brand awareness, brand preference and propensity to buy. In addition, the equity of a brand may rest on what consumers associate it with or the set of impressions consumers have of the brand.

Modelling: relevance and significance

It follows that, in order to measure marketing 'effectiveness', we need to monitor this process. But first we need to develop the model because advertising is not usually the only influence on consumer equity and, moreover, consumer equity is not the only influence on sales. Figure C24.2 shows some of the other influences—marketplace factors influencing sales, and marketing factors (both controlled and uncontrolled)—that affect consumer equity. In addition, the advertising executions are placed in a media environment, which acts as both a carrier of and barrier to the advertising's communication.

Figure C24.2 External factors influencing equity and sales

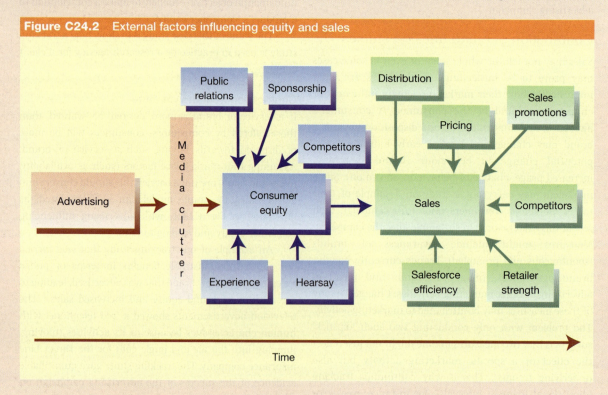

Any brand and advertising tracking system must, therefore, be set up to monitor all the aspects of this model that are relevant and significant to any specific marketing environment. Sensitive and valid measures are required of both the *stimuli* (i.e. the advertising and any other significant marketing activity) and the overall *outcome* (i.e. consumer equity) if we are to have any chance of assessing the contribution of the various stimuli to the outcome.

Advertising awareness and MarketMind measures

In order to maximize our understanding of the efficiency of the advertising, it is clearly useful to be able to disentangle the various elements of reach, impact, communication and branding. Interestingly, many tracking systems are unable to do this, simply because they ask the questions the wrong way.

As an example, if we ask consumers if they have seen any advertising recently for brand X we will *not* get a true measure of the awareness of brand X because …

- some of those who say 'Yes' may simply *think* they've seen advertising, because brand X is familiar to them
- others who say 'Yes' may be thinking about the advertising for something else that they believe, wrongly, is for brand X
- some of those who say 'No' may actually have seen the advertising but don't know that it is for brand X.

The basic problem is that this traditional question format inextricably links the product or *brand name* awareness with the *advertising* awareness.

A way of overcoming this is by initially accessing advertising involvement at the executional level. For instance, with MarketMind the awareness of advertising for the product is obtained by asking consumers *to describe, in their own words, the advertisements they have seen* within a particular product sector. Their descriptions are later validated against the actual advertising to establish a measure called *cut-through*. This represents the proportion of the target audience that recalls the advertising to the extent that *we know* they have seen it—in other words, *true advertising awareness that is unadulterated by product awareness.*

Respondents are also asked to say, unprompted, what the advertising they have just described is trying to tell them. A number of open-ended questions elicit different aspects of the advertising's communication.

The responses to these questions help determine whether or not the advertising message take-out is on-strategy and, along with the descriptions of the advertising itself, will provide a comprehensive picture of the way the advertising communication is contributing to consumers' knowledge of Brand X. In addition, the way respondents describe the advertising will provide insights into the appeal of the advertising on a more emotional level.

This information will be derived from spontaneous advertising descriptions, therefore, providing a 'hard' measure of awareness, indicating where the audience has had some level of *real involvement* with the communication to which it has been exposed. We can be sure, then, that this communication has not only reached but has also gained the attention of the target audience.

Beyond those consumers with strong involvement in the advertising, there will be some consumers who are reached but not involved by the communication. In order to measure the total reach, respondents are shown stimulus materials, such as de-branded stills boards of TV commercials, or played tapes of radio ads and asked if they have seen/heard that particular execution (*recognition*), and which brand or product it was for (*branded recognition*).

This question regime produces a much more accurate, comprehensive, and diagnostic picture of *how* the advertising is working compared with that provided by the traditional methodologies.

The measures themselves relate to the communication tasks in the way described in Table C24.1.

Table C24.1 How the MarketMind measures relate to the communication tasks	
Advertising task	Relevant MarketMind measures
'Reach the target audience'	Recognition
'Penetrate the attention of those reached'	Cut-through
'Communicate the intended messages to those who are attentive'	Message communication (general/people/benefit) and elements recalled, among respondents with cut-through
'Ensure these messages are branded correctly'	Branding levels at cut-through and spontaneous mention of 'brand x' when describing executional details and messages

The Lettuseat advertising campaign

This tracking study shows how Lettuseat salad dressings were advertised on television over a two-year period using several different advertising treatments. The case shows what effect the campaign had overall and what was learned about how the individual treatments worked within the life of the campaign. The campaign is followed from spring 1999 to autumn 2000, encompassing two seasons for the product category.

In 1999, the communication objective of the campaign was to support the sub-brand, Lettuseat Pourable, with the message that Lettuseat pours more easily. This objective was changed in 2000 to communicate having a more subtle flavour that does not overpower food, with the focus back on the parent brand.

Figure C24.3 shows the number of TVRs per week used over the two years (TVRs are television ratings). If 25 per cent of the target market was exposed to a commercial in a commercial break this counts as 25 TVRs. TVRs are simply added up across commercial breaks over a period of time or campaign as one indicator of the weight of a campaign. Other indicators include *opportunities to see* (OTS) and *coverage*. (An OTS of 3.1 means the average opportunities to see a commercial by the target market was 3.1 times. Coverage simply means the penetration of the campaign or the percentage that had any opportunity to see.)

In the first year, the Lettuseat campaign ran from the beginning of the year, with a heavy weight in the spring, shortly before seasonal sales start to pick up, using the advertising execution known as 1999a. This media strategy was designed to remind consumers of the brand as they come into a new season, and to re-establish Lettuseat in its position of brand leader as well as communicating the 'pourable' message for the sub-brand. The campaign then resumed in June, using execution 1999b in order to keep the brand at the forefront of people's minds when they consider salad dressings. Again this was in addition to communicating the message about the sub-brand. Following a change in strategy (see 'Conclusion') a different media plan was used in 2000 with the campaign running only in June and July, with two new executions known as 2000a and 2000b.

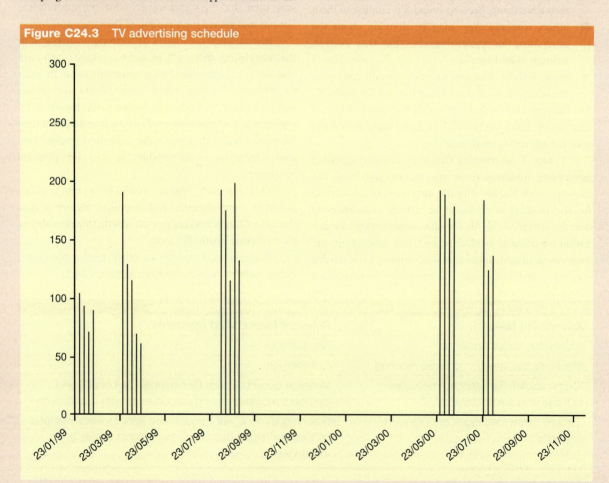

Figure C24.3 TV advertising schedule

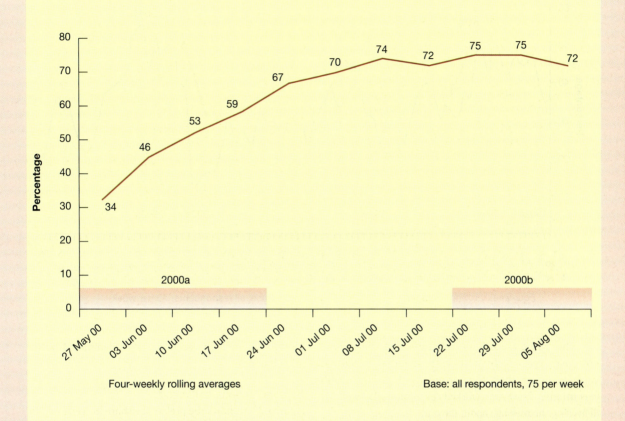

Figure C24.4 Prompted recognition (execution 2000a)

Reaching the target audience

Figure C24.4 shows the recognition of ad 2000a from a de-branded photographic storyboard. Recognition climbed steeply when the ad first came on air, and reached nearly three-quarters of the target audience. It was still remembered some weeks after the first burst, and the second burst maintained that awareness, which otherwise would have been expected to decay. This execution reached the audience well.

Penetrating viewers' attention

Television cut-through is the main measurement of penetration (see Fig. C24.5). This is a hard measure and experience shows that any score over 20 per cent is considered good, and over 40 per cent exceptional, although this must be put into the context of the amount spent. All of the Lettuseat executions achieved exceptional scores. Execution 1999a peaked at 51 per cent with the heavy Easter burst. This was followed by a period of decay down to about 20 per cent before Execution 1999b was aired in June and July. This also performed very well but not as strongly as 1999a, peaking at 40 per cent.

With a long period off-air (i.e. without television advertising) between August 1999 and June 2000, cut-through decayed to around 10 per cent before the next execution, 2000a, was aired. This execution had a very strong impact, taking cut-through back up to 51 per cent with execution 2000b building on this to 54 per cent.

Communicating the messages

Message recall (see Table C24.2) shows how well the different communication objectives have been achieved.

Table C24.2	Message communication			
	Execution			
	1999a	1999b	2000a	2000b
Pours easily	45%	29%	12%	14%
Flavour messages	16%	14%	81%	92%

Base: all who recall relevant execution

Figure C24.5 TV Cut-through 1999–2000

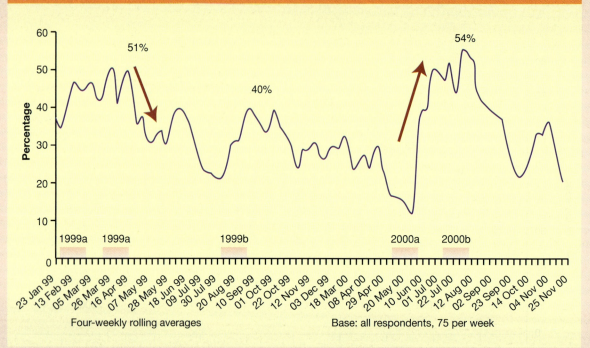

The 1999 executions communicated the desired objectives reasonably well, with the first execution working better than the second. Both of the 2000 executions, however, worked exceptionally well in delivering the message about flavour.

Brand awareness and knowledge

Lettuseat has a strong branding device used in all of its advertising. A high level of correct identification of the brand with the advertising is therefore to be expected. Table C24.3 shows that, for all executions, there is little confusion with competitors. However, neither of the 1999 executions makes a strong association with Lettuseat Pourable. Execution 1999b is better than 1999a, but in both executions it is dominated by the main brand.

Believed image positioning

Figure C24.6 shows the preference share for Lettuseat for having a subtle flavour. This is based on the question 'Which of these brands *would you prefer* to buy if you were looking for a salad dressing with a subtle flavour?'

Although the preference share is always strong because of the brand's dominance in the market, the 2000 executions demonstrate a clear increase in this measure when on-air. This follows a period when a competitor had taken advantage of Lettuseat being off-air to begin to increase its share on this dimension.

Table C24.3 Brand identification

	Execution			
	1999a	1999b	2000a	2000b
Any Lettuseat	86%	89%	87%	84%
Lettuseat only	82%	78%	84%	81%
Lettuseat Pourable	2%	9%	1%	0%
Competitor	5%	5%	4%	6%
Don't know	6%	7%	8%	10%

Base: all who recall relevant execution

Figure C24.6 Brand preference shares (Has subtle flavour)

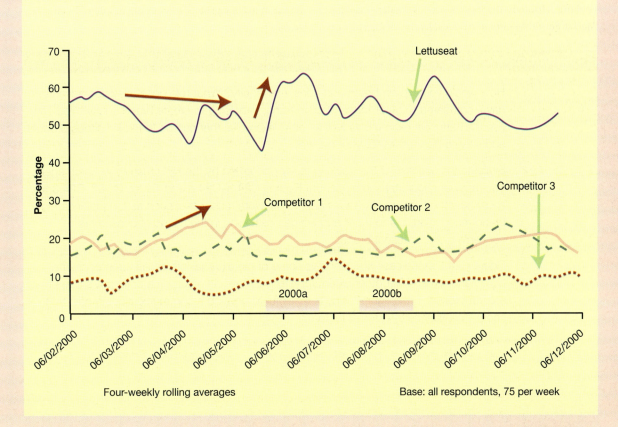

Conclusion

The tracking study clearly showed that the first execution of the 1999 campaign had created cut-through up to the usually high levels for the brand, but that the message delivery and the desired association with the sub-brand were below expectation. The second execution of 1999 had not created the same level of cut-through, nor had it communicated the message as strongly. Although the sub-brand was more strongly communicated than with the other 1999 execution, it was still a long way below satisfactory levels. The failure of the advertising to achieve the desired integrated communication of message and sub-brand was a main factor in the decision to return to advertising the parent brand in 2000 and reinforce one of its key image strengths.

Subsequently the brand was off-air at the beginning of the 2000 season, and a competitor began to mount a challenge on this key image strength. However, the two executions produced for 2000 worked well on all key measures, and saw off this challenge before it significantly damaged Lettuseat's position. Consequently, a decision was made to continue the strategy of reinforcing the parent brand, and to reinforce existing brand strengths. In 2001 the two 2000 executions were used again alongside two new executions that were designed to emphasize other existing band strengths. Thus the company was able to make further use of the two executions produced for 2000.

The tracking study helped the management in the client company to continue to monitor the performance of the brand and its advertising. Therefore, its management was able to make key decisions for the Lettuseat product and its future.

[1] Ashman, S. and K. Clarke, (2000) Optimising Advertising Effectiveness for Direct Line: Quantifying the Major Cost Benefits of Painstaking Television Pre-tests, in Wright, L.T. and M. Crimp (2000) *The Marketing Research Process*, FT Prentice Hall (5th edn), 360–72.

[2] Feldwick, P. (1996) Do we Really Need Brand Equity? Changing Business Dynamics. The Challenge to Marketing Research, *Proceedings of 49th ESOMAR Congress*, Istanbul, Turkey, 3–29. See also Feldwick, P. (1996) What is Brand Equity Anyway, and How do you Measure it?', *Journal of the Market Research Society* 38(2), 85–104.

Further reading about brand literature

Grace, D. and A. O'Cass (2002) Brand Associations: Looking Through the Eye of the Beholder, *Qualitative Market Research—An International Journal* 5(2), 96–111.

Note

NFO WorldGroup is one of the world's largest marketing research agency groups specializing in tailored marketing research.

Questions

1. How would you explain brand and consumer equity? What role does television advertising have, compared to other forms of advertising, in helping to create brand equity? You can use the Lettuseat example as well as other examples that can be found in various product and service businesses for your answer.

2. Evaluate the success of the tracking study performed by the NFO market research agency. Your answer should take into account Figures C24.3–C24.6 and Tables C24.2–C24.3 to show how the tracking study was able to measure responses, such as for audience reach, brand recognition, brand recall and image positioning in the minds of consumers concerning the Lettuseat brand.

3. Figure C24.2 in the case study shows some of the external influences upon consumer equity and sales. What other external influences have an effect on a company's sales that are not present in the figure? Why is it helpful to develop a communications model that will show the influence of external factors?

This case study was prepared by Clive Nancarrow, Professor of Marketing Research at the University of the West of England, Bristol; Len Tiu Wright, Professor of Marketing at De Montfort University, Leicester; and Ian Brace, a director of NFO WorldGroup.

chapter thirteen
Personal selling and sales management

"Everyone lives by selling something." — ROBERT LOUIS STEVENSON

Learning Objectives

This chapter explains:

1. Environmental and managerial forces affecting sales
2. The different types of selling job
3. Sales responsibilities
4. How to prepare for selling
5. The stages in the selling process
6. The tasks of sales management
7. How to design a salesforce
8. How to manage a salesforce
9. Key account management
10. Ethical issues in personal selling and sales management

Personal selling is the marketing task that involves face-to-face contact with a customer. Unlike advertising, promotion, sponsorship and other forms of non-personal communication, personal selling permits a direct interaction between buyer and seller. This two-way communication means that the seller can identify the specific needs and problems of the buyer and tailor the sales presentation in the light of this knowledge. The particular concerns of the buyer can also be dealt with on a one-to-one basis.

This flexibility comes only at a cost. The cost of a car, travel expenses and sales office overheads can mean that the total annual bill for a field salesperson is often twice the level of their salary. In industrial marketing, over 70 per cent of the marketing budget is usually spent on the salesforce. This is because of the technical nature of the products being sold, and the need to maintain close personal relationships between the selling and buying organizations.

However, the nature of the personal selling function is changing. Organizations are reducing the size of their salesforces in the face of greater buyer concentration, moves towards centralized buying, and recognition of the high costs of maintaining a field sales team. The concentration of buying power into fewer hands has also fuelled the move towards relationship management, often through key account selling. This involves the use of dedicated sales teams that service the accounts of major buyers. As the commercial director of HP Foods said:

> Twenty years ago we had between 70 and 100 salespeople. The change in the retail environment from small retailers to central warehouses and supermarkets has meant a big change in the way we communicate with our customers. Instead of sending salespeople out on the road, we now collect a large proportion of our sales by telephone or computer. We have replaced the traditional salesforce with 12 business development executives, who each have a small number of accounts dealing with customers at both national and regional levels.[1]

Selling and sales management are experiencing a period of rapid change. The next section explores the major forces at work.

Environmental and managerial forces affecting sales

A number of major behavioural, technological and managerial forces are influencing how selling and sales management is and will be carried out.[2] These are listed in Table 13.1.

Behavioural forces

Just as customers adapt to their changing environment, so the sales function has to adapt to these forces, which are (i) rising customer expectations, (ii) customer avoidance of buyer–seller negotiations, (iii) the expanding power of major buyers, (iv) globalization of markets and (v) fragmentation of markets.

Rising customer expectations

As consumers experience higher standards of product quality and service so their expectations are fuelled to expect even higher levels in the future. This process may be accelerated by experiences abroad, and new entrants to industries (possibly from abroad) that set new standards of excellence. As the executive of the customer satisfaction research firm J. D. Power explained: 'What makes customer satisfaction so difficult to achieve is that you constantly raise the bar and extend the finish line. You never stop. As your customers get better treatment, they demand better treatment.' The implication for salespeople is that they must accept that both

Table 13.1 Forces influencing selling and sales management practices

Behavioural forces

Rising customer expectations

Customer avoidance of buyer–seller negotiations

Expanding power of major buyers

Globalization of markets

Fragmentation of markets

Technological forces

Salesforce automation
- Laptop computers and software
- Electronic data interchange
- Desktop videoconferencing

Virtual sales offices

Electronic sales channels
- Internet
- Television home shopping

Managerial forces

Direct marketing
- Direct mail
- Telemarketing
- Computer salespeople

Blending of sales and marketing
- Intranets

Qualifications for salespeople and sales managers

Adapted from: Anderson, R. (1996) Personal Selling and Sales Management in the New Millennium, *Journal of Personal Selling and Sales Management* 16(4), 17–32.

consumer and organizational buyer expectations for product quality, customer service and value will continue to rise, and that they must respond to this challenge by advocating and implementing continuous improvements in quality standards.

Customer avoidance of buyer–seller negotiations

Studies have shown that the purchase of a car is the most anxiety-provoking and least satisfying experience in retail buying.[3] Some car salespeople are trained in the art of negotiation, supported by high-pressure sales tactics. Consequently, customers have taken to viewing the purchase as an ordeal to be tolerated rather than a pleasurable occasion to be savoured. In response, some car companies have moved to a 'fixed price, no pressure and full book value for the trade-in' approach. This was used for the successful launch of the Saturn by General Motors in the USA and is the philosophy behind the marketing of Daewoo cars in the UK.

Expanding power of major buyers

The growing dominance of major players in many sectors (notably retailing) is having a profound influence on selling and sales management. Their enormous purchasing power means that they are able to demand and get special services, including special customer status (key account management), just-in-time inventory control, category management and joint funding of promotions. Future success for salespeople will be dependent on their capabilities to respond to the increasing demands of major customers.

Globalization of markets

As domestic markets saturate, companies are expanding abroad to achieve sales and profit growth. Large companies such as Coca-Cola, Colgate-Palmolive and Avon Products now earn the largest proportion of their revenues in foreign markets. The challenges include the correct balance between expatriate and host country sales personnel, adapting to different cultures, lifestyles and languages, competing against world-class brands, and building global relationships with huge customers based in many countries. For example, 3M has a variety of global strategic accounts from industrial high-tech (Motorola, Hewlett Packard, IBM, Texas Instruments) to original equipment manufacturers in electronics, appliances, automotive, electrical, aerospace, furniture, consumer products and healthcare.[4] A major challenge for such a transnational corporation is the co-ordination of global sales teams, which sell to the Nortels, Samsungs, Siemens, or P&Gs of this world, where the customer may be located in over 20 countries and requires special terms of sale, technical support, pricing and customization of products. This complexity means that strategic account managers require both enhanced teamwork and co-ordination skills to ensure that customers receive top-quality service.

Fragmentation of markets

Driven by differences in income levels, lifestyles, personalities, experiences and race, markets are fragmenting to form market segments. This means that markets are likely to become smaller, with an increasing range of brands marketed to cater for the diverse requirements (both functional and psychological) of customers. Marketing and sales managers need to be adept at identifying changes in consumer tastes, and developing strategies that satisfy an increasingly varied and multicultural society.

Technological forces

Three major forces are at play: (i) salesforce automation, (ii) virtual sales offices and (iii) electronic sales channels.

Salesforce automation

Salesforce automation includes laptop and palmtop computers, mobile phones, fax machines, e-mail and sophisticated sales-orientated software, which aid such tasks as journey and account planning, recruitment and selection, and evaluation of sales personnel. In addition, electronic data interchange (EDI) and the Internet provide computer links between manufacturers and resellers (retailers, wholesalers and distributors) allowing the exchange of information. For example, purchase orders, invoices, price quotes, delivery dates, reports and promotional information can be exchanged. Technological innovations have also made possible desktop videoconferencing, enabling sales meetings, training and customer interaction to take place without the need for people to leave their offices.

Virtual sales office

Improved technology has also encouraged the creation of virtual offices, allowing sales personnel to keep in contact with head office, customers and co-workers. The virtual office may be the home or even a car. This can mean large cost and time savings, and enhanced job satisfaction for sales personnel, who are spared some of the many traffic jams that are part of the life of a field salesperson.

Electronic sales channels

The fastest-growing electronic sales channel is undoubtedly the Internet. E-Marketing 13.1 discusses some of the likely effects of the Internet on selling and sales management.

13.1 e-marketing

The Impact of the Internet on Personal Selling and Sales Management

The Internet is predicted to affect selling and sales management in the following ways.

- *Reduction in salesforce size*: the benefits of the Internet, such as low cost and customized transactions, are expected to reduce the size of salesforces. The formation of e-marketplaces has led to business-to-business purchases, which previously would have been the province of the salesforce, being moved online. For example, the US defence contractor United Technologies bought $450 million worth of metals, motors and other products from an e-marketplace in one year and got prices around 15 per cent lower than previously. Furthermore, companies are moving to the Internet to communicate and sell to smaller accounts.

- *Key account management*: by using the Internet to service small customers and deal with some of the details of key account activities, it can free key account managers to focus on long-term relationship building. For example, the Dell Computer salesforce benefits greatly from the customized information provided to its key account customers through the Premier Page website. By using its customized online Premier Page, Dell's biggest customers can configure PCs, pay for them, track their delivery status, and get access to immediate technical support.

- *Sales processes*: the Internet is smoothing communications between sellers and buyers through the use of e-mail and well-designed company websites. In this way, customers can be made aware of shipping dates, inventory status, and other information traditionally delivered in-person by the salesforce. The Internet is also an invaluable tool for the salesperson to use to find information that can be used to support sales presentations.

- *Remote working*: Sales staff can now access their company's internal network through the Internet, using a technology called a Virtual Private Network (VPN). The VPN links remote home computers and laptops into a wider 'virtual' network, using the Internet. This information cannot be viewed by others as the VPN encrypts all data. Field staff have access to real-time information and can update company files and documents instantaneously (e.g. viewing the latest customer details prior to a sales visit).

ASPs (or application service providers) are services that allow every company worker (with appropriate rights) access to the 'same' application and related information, regardless of where they are in the world. All that is needed is Internet access. Providers like Salesforce.com (www.salesforce.com) rent the use of their application to companies. Company sales staff can update customer records as they make client calls and everyone in the company can then view and use the same central information (stored in salesforce.com databanks in the USA).

VPN and ASPs are gaining wide acceptance in allowing companies to integrate the 'remote worker' more fully into the organization. Mobile technologies, like 3G (third generation mobile phones, first launched in the UK by Hutchison 3G), have yet to gain acceptance but promise even greater benefits through connecting field staff 'on the move'.

Based on: Mandel and Hof (2001);[5] Rich (2002);[6] Sharma and Tzokas (2002)[7]

However, another emerging channel is worthy of mention as it will reduce the need for field salesforces. This is television home shopping, where viewers watch cable television presenters promote anything from jewellery to consumer electronics and order by telephone. In effect, the presenter is the salesperson.

Managerial forces

Managers are responding to changes in the environment by developing new strategies to enhance effectiveness. These include: (i) employing direct marketing techniques, (ii) improving the blend between sales and marketing, and (iii) encouraging salespeople to gain professional qualifications.

Direct marketing techniques

The increasing role of direct marketing is reflected in the growth of direct mail and telemarketing activities. However, a third emerging change is the use of computer stations in US retail outlets to replace traditional salespeople. Although in Europe the use of computer-assisted sales in car showrooms has begun with the employment of kiosks where customers can gather product and price information, the process has moved a stage further in the USA, where several Ford dealerships have installed computer stations that fully replace salespeople. Customers can compare features of competitive models, calculate running costs, compute monthly payments, and use the computer to write up the order and telephone it to the factory—all without the intervention of a salesperson.

Blending sales and marketing

Although the development of effective relationships between sales and marketing personnel is recognized by all, often, in practice, blending the two functions into an effective whole is hampered by, among other things, poor communication. The establishment of intranets, which are similar to the Internet except that they are proprietary company networks that link employees, suppliers and customers through their PCs, can improve links and information exchange. Intranets are used for such diverse functions as e-mail, team projects and desktop publishing. Clearly, their use can enhance the effectiveness of a field salesforce that requires fast access to rapidly changing information such as product specifications, competitor news and price updates, and allows the sharing of information between sales and marketing.

Professional qualifications

Finally, sales management is responding to the new challenges by recognizing the importance of professional qualifications. In the UK, this has led to the formation of a new professional body: the Institute of Professional Sales. This body is charged with enhancing the profile of the sales function, promoting best practice, and developing education and training programmes to improve salespeople's and sales managers' professionalism, skills and competences.

Next, we shall examine the different types of seller, the major responsibilities of salespeople, and the process and techniques of personal selling. We shall then explore the tasks of the sales manager including the setting of objectives and strategy, determining salesforce size and organization, and how to recruit, train, motivate and evaluate salespeople.

Types of seller

The diverse nature of the buying situation inevitably means that there are many types of selling job: selling varies according to the nature of the selling task. Figure 13.1 shows that a fundamental distinction is between order-takers, order-creators and order-getters. Order-takers respond to already committed customers; order-creators do not directly receive orders as they talk to specifiers rather than buyers; order-getters attempt to persuade customers to place an order directly.

There are three types of order-taker: inside order-takers, delivery salespeople and outside order-takers. Order-creators are termed 'missionary salespeople'. Order-getters are either frontline salespeople consisting of new business, organizational or consumer salespeople, or sales support salespeople who can be either technical support salespeople or merchandisers.[8] Both types of order-getter are in situations where a direct sale can be made. Each type of selling job will now be discussed.

Order-takers

Inside order-takers

The typical inside order-taker is the retail sales assistant. The customer has full freedom to choose products without the presence of a salesperson. The sales assistant's task is purely transactional: receiving payment and passing over the goods. Another form of inside order-

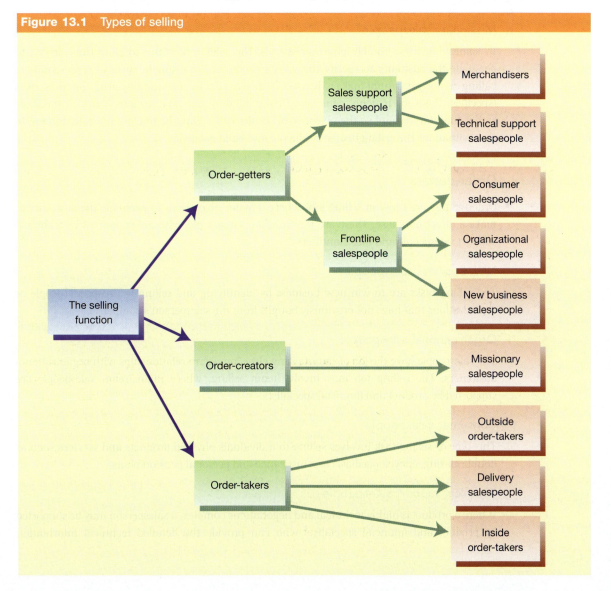

Figure 13.1 Types of selling

taker is the telemarketing sales team, which supports field sales by taking customers' orders over the telephone.

Delivery salespeople

The salesperson's task is primarily concerned with delivering the product. In the UK, milk, newspapers and magazines are delivered to the door. There is little attempt to persuade the household to increase the milk order or number of newspapers taken—changes in order size are customer-driven. Winning and losing orders will be heavily dependent on the reliability of delivery.

Outside order-takers

Unlike inside order-takers, these salespeople visit the customer but also primarily respond to customer requests rather than actively seek to persuade. Unlike delivery salespeople, outside order-takers do not deliver. Outside order-takers are a dying breed, and are being replaced by the more cost-efficient telemarketing teams.

Order-creators

Missionary salespeople

In some industries, notably pharmaceuticals, the sales task is not to close the sale but to persuade the customer to specify the seller's products. For example, medical representatives calling on doctors cannot make a direct sale since the doctor does not buy drugs but prescribes (specifies) them for patients. Similarly, in the building industry, architects act as specifiers rather than buyers and so the objective of a sales call cannot be to close the sale. Instead in these situations the selling task is to educate and build goodwill.

Order-getters

Order-getters are those in selling jobs where a major objective is to persuade the customer to make a direct purchase. These are the frontline salespeople, who are supported by technical support salespeople and merchandisers.

New business salespeople

The selling tasks are to win new business by identifying and selling to prospects (people or organizations that have not previously bought from the salesperson's company).

Organizational salespeople

The salespeople have the job of maintaining close long-term relationships with organizational customers. The selling job may involve team selling, where mainstream salespeople are supported by product and financial specialists.

Consumer salespeople

This type of selling task involves selling to individuals physical products and services such as double glazing, encyclopaedias, cars, insurance and personal pension plans.

Technical support salespeople

Where a product is highly technical and negotiations complex, a salesperson may be supported by product and financial specialists who can provide the detailed technical information required by customers. This may be ongoing as part of a key account team or on a temporary basis, with the specialists being called in to the selling situation when required.

Merchandisers

These provide sales support in retail and wholesale selling. Orders may be negotiated nationally at head office but sales to individual outlets are supported by merchandisers, who give advice on display, implement sales promotions, check stock levels and maintain contact with store managers.

Sales responsibilities

The *primary* responsibility of a salesperson is to increase sales. For order-getters this will usually involve the identification of customer needs, presentation and demonstration, handling objections and closing the sale. These skills will be discussed later in this chapter. However, in order to generate sales successfully, *six enabling functions* are also carried out by many salespeople. These are vital for continuing sales success (see Fig. 13.2):

1. prospecting
2. maintaining customer records and information feedback
3. providing service
4. handling complaints *Beschwerdebehandlung*
5. self-management
6. relationship management.

Figure 13.2 Sales responsibilities

- Prospecting
- Maintaining customer records and information feedback
- Providing service
- Handling complaints
- Self-management
- Relationship management

Profitable sales

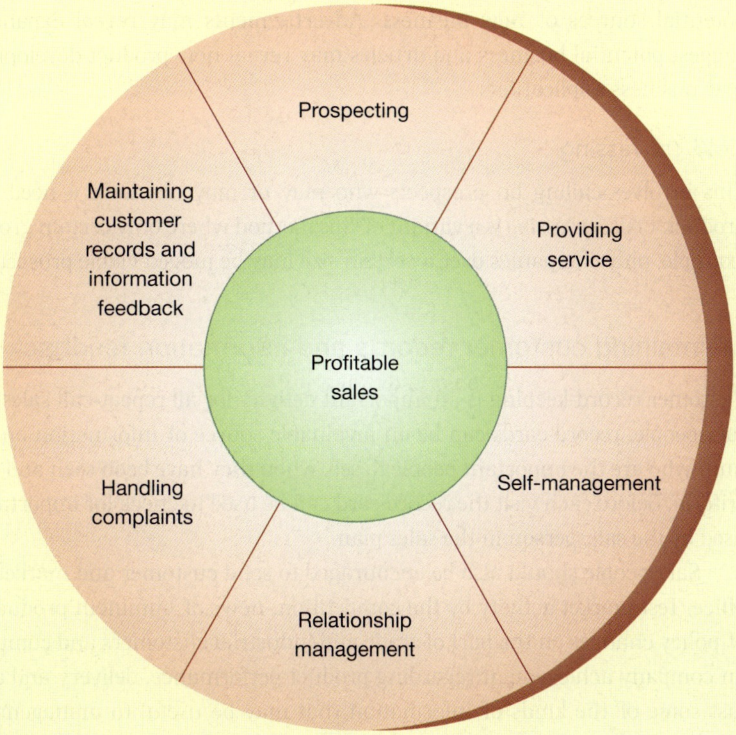

Prospecting

Prospecting is searching for and calling on potential customers. A problem sometimes associated with salespeople who have worked for the same company for many years is that they rely on established customers rather than actively seeking new business. They work in their *comfort zone*, calling on old contacts rather than searching out and selling to new customers. Prospects can be identified from several sources.

Existing customers

Satisfied customers should be asked if they know of anyone who may be interested in the lines of products being sold. This is common practice in insurance and industrial selling, but can be used in other industries too. Having obtained the name of a prospect the salesperson should then ask if the customer's name can be used as an example of a satisfied customer. This is called *reference selling*.

Trade directories

Trade directories such as *Kompass* or *Dun & Bradstreet's Key British Enterprises* can be used to provide the names of prospects. These directories give details such as name, address, telephone number, size of firm and types of product made or distributed. Electronic versions of such directories are normally available.

Enquiries

Enquiries can be stimulated by advertising, direct mail or exhibitions. The enquiry should be dealt with promptly and checked to establish its seriousness and worth. This process of checking leads to establish their potential is called *qualifying*.

The press

It is worthwhile checking the press for advertisements and articles that can give clues to potential sources of new business. Advertisements may reveal expansion plans that may suggest potential business and articles may reveal new product developments that may have new business implications.

Cold canvassing

This involves calling on prospects who may or may not have a need for the salesperson's product. *Cool canvassing* is a variant of this method where only certain groups are called on. For example, only companies over a certain size may be judged viable prospects.

Maintaining customer records and information feedback

Customer record-keeping is an important activity for all repeat-call salespeople. For industrial salespeople, record cards can be an invaluable source of information on the decision-making unit: who are the important people to see, when they have been seen and what are their choice criteria. Before each visit the record card can be used to check for important details that can be used by the salesperson in the sales plan.

Salespeople should also be encouraged to send customer and market information to head office. Test market activity by the competition, news of imminent product launches, rumours of policy changes on the part of trade and industrial customers and competitors, and feedback on company achievement regarding product performance, delivery and after-sales service are just some of the kinds of information that may be useful to management.[9] One method of encouraging feedback of information from salespeople is to reward them not only on the basis of sales but also according to the amount of relevant information they feed back to the company.[10]

Providing service

Salespeople can build goodwill by providing service to their customers. Since they meet many customers each year, they become familiar with solutions to common problems. For example, advice on improving productivity or cutting costs may provide tangible customer benefits.

Salespeople may also be called upon to provide after-sales service to customers. Sales engineers may be required to give advice on the operation of a newly acquired machine or provide assistance in the event of a breakdown. Sometimes they may be able to solve the problem themselves, while in other cases they will call in technical specialists to deal with it.

Handling complaints

Dissatisfied customers tell on average six other people about their cause for complaint. Dealing with complaints quickly and efficiently is therefore a key aspect of selling. The ability of the salesperson to empathize with the customer and react sympathetically can create considerable goodwill. Instead of telling six people of their dissatisfaction, the complainants will then say how well they have been treated.

Self-management

One area that may be delegated to the salesperson is *journey routing*. Many salespeople believe that the most efficient routing plan involves driving out to the furthest customer and then zigzagging back to home base. However, adopting a round-trip approach will usually result in lower mileage.

Call frequencies may also be the responsibility of the salesperson. If so, it is sensible to grade customers according to potential. For example, a grade A customer may be called upon every two weeks, a grade B customer every four weeks, and grade C customers once every two months. One problem with allowing the salesperson discretion over call planning is that they may overcall on established, friendly customers even though they do not have much growth potential.

Relationship management

Many selling situations are not one-off situation-specific encounters but long term. This is particularly true in organizational markets where supplier and trade, governmental or industrial customers work together to create, develop and maintain a network within which both parties thrive.[11] It is within such relationships that the core of marketing activity is found. The management of the relationships with key customers is a major responsibility of salespeople, reflected in the fact that although the number of salespeople overall is falling, the number of key account managers is growing.[12]

Relationship management has already been discussed in Chapter 4. The objective is to build goodwill that is reciprocated by placing orders. To recap, this can be achieved by providing exceptional customer service through:

- technical support
- expertise
- resource support
- improving service levels
- lowering perceived risk.

Videoconferencing is among the newly developed technologies that have changed the way salespeople operate.

In addition, salespeople should develop *trust* through high frequency of contact, ensuring that promises are kept, and reacting quickly and effectively to problems.

Clearly the tasks of salespeople are onerous. Developments in information and telecommunications technology have eased some of the burdens but have created new pressures. Technology has affected the salesperson's job in the areas of organizing (e.g. managing accounts and scheduling calls), presenting (e.g. laptop computers that allow presentations on the road), reporting (e.g. the electronic sending of standardized forms to head office), informing (e.g. carrying CD catalogues of product information), supporting and processing transactions (e.g. checking the progress of customers' orders) and communicating (e.g. e-mail and mobile phones).[13] Some of these issues are discussed in e-Marketing 13.2.

Personal selling skills

Many people's perception of a salesperson is of a slick, fast-talking confidence trickster devoted to forcing unwanted products on innocent customers. Personal experience will tell the reader that this is unrealistic in a world of educated consumers and professional buyers. Success in selling comes from implementing the marketing concept when face to face with customers, not denying it at the very point when the seller and buyer come into contact. The sales interview offers an unparalleled opportunity to identify individual customer needs and match behaviour to the specific customer that is encountered.[16] Indeed, research has shown that such customer-orientated selling is associated with higher levels of salesforce performance.[17]

Research has shown that, far from using high-pressure selling tactics, success is associated with:[18]

- asking questions
- providing product information, making comparisons and offering evidence to support claims
- acknowledging the viewpoint of the customer
- agreeing with the customer's perceptions
- supporting the customer
- releasing tension.

All of these findings are in accord with the marketing concept.

In order to develop personal selling skills it is useful to distinguish six phases of the selling process (see Fig. 13.3). Each of these will now be discussed.

13.2 e-marketing

Technology and the Salesperson's Job

Technological developments in information and telecommunications technology have revolutionized the way salespeople operate. Advances include the following.

- Remote access through portable PCs/laptops/palmtops to branch office or headquarters' computer systems for up-to-the-minute information on order status, price, availability and competitive data. Sales orders and queries can be sent to the sales office and catalogues held on the computer.
- Electronic mail and faxes to speed communications, facilitate links with hard-to-reach people and hold messages sent by other people.
- Word processing, spreadsheet and presentation software for customizing sales letters, automating call reports, preparing quotations and proposals, generating sales forecasts, and preparing text and graphics for presentations.
- Time-management software for journey planning and the automatic updating of call reports.
- Contact management systems that hold information on prospects, customers, sales and competitors to facilitate call planning and execution.
- Mobile phones to ease communication to and from salespeople, and to reduce wasted travelling time.
- Telemarketing software to improve inbound and outbound call productivity.
- Personal digital assistants, which are starting to provide an easy form of data transportation, allowing salesforces to access information on consumer populations and local territories.
- Presentation graphics software such as PowerPoint for text and graphical presentations. Presentations can be stored on disk and projected on to a screen using a special projector with an LCD panel.
- Customer relationship management (CRM) software which, by means of a common database that all customer-facing personnel can access, permits a unified message and image to be presented to customers. A specific application of CRM software is in account management, where information such as contact names, telephone, fax and e-mail numbers, type of business, purpose and dates of meetings/telephone calls, status of customer and details of previous orders is stored, permitting easy access by a range of people including field salespeople and call centre staff.
- The Internet, which allows the promotion and sales of products direct to the customer and improves communication through e-mail, intranets (websites that operate inside an organization) and extranets (websites where access is restricted to approved users, e.g. customers and suppliers). A major growth area is procurement by businesses in e-marketplaces.
- Sales-management software for territory planning, recruitment and selection, training, sales forecasting, evaluation and control.
- Videoconferencing using monitors, screens or mobile phones.

The resulting improvements in productivity do not mean that the job of the salesperson is easier, however. The time savings mean that there is more time for other duties, and greater access to and from the salesperson means that customers and sales management staff expect faster response times.

Based on: Reed (1999);[14] Jobber and Lancaster (2003)[15]

Figure 13.3 The selling process

Preparation

Preparation before a sales visit can reap dividends by enhancing confidence and performance when face to face with the customer. Some situations cannot be prepared for—the unexpected question or unusual objection, for example—but many customers face similar situations, and certain questions and objections will be raised repeatedly. Preparation can help the salesperson respond to these recurring situations.

Salespeople will benefit from gaining knowledge of their own products, competitors' products, sales presentation planning, setting call objectives and understanding buyer behaviour.

Product knowledge

Product knowledge means understanding both product features and the customer benefits that they confer. Understanding product features alone is not enough to convince customers to buy because they buy products for the benefits that the features provide, not the features in themselves. Salespeople need to ask themselves what are the benefits a certain feature provides for customers. For example, a computer mouse (product feature) provides a more convenient way of issuing commands (customer benefit) than using the keyboard. The way to turn features into benefits is to view products from the customer's angle. A by-product of this is the realization that some features may provide no customer benefit whatsoever.

Competitors' products

Knowledge of competitors' products allows their strengths to be offset against their weaknesses. For example, if a buyer claims that a competitor's product has a cost advantage, this may be offset against the superior productivity advantage of the salesperson's product. Similarly, inaccuracies in a buyer's claims can be countered. Finally, competitive knowledge allows salespeople to stress the differential advantage of their products compared to those of the competition.

Sales presentation planning

Preparation here builds confidence, raises the chances that important benefits are not forgotten, allows visual aids and demonstrations to be built into the presentation, and permits the anticipation of objections and the preparation of convincing counter-arguments. Although preparation is vital there should be room left for flexibility in approach since customers have different needs. The salesperson has to be aware that the features and benefits that should be stressed with one customer may have much less emphasis placed on them for another.

Setting call objectives

The key to setting call objectives is to phrase them in terms of what the salesperson wants the customer to do rather than what the salesperson should do. For example:

- for the customer to define what his or her needs are
- for the customer to visit a showroom

- for the customer to try the product, e.g. drive a car
- for the customer to be convinced of the cost saving of 'our' product compared to that of the competition.

This is because the success of the sales interview is customer-dependent. The end is to convince the customer; what the salesperson does is simply a means to that end.

Understanding buyer behaviour

Thought should also be given to understanding *buyer behaviour*. Questions should be asked, such as 'Who are the likely key people to talk to?' 'What are their probable choice criteria?' 'Are there any gatekeepers preventing access to some people, who need to be circumvented?' 'What are the likely opportunities and threats that may arise in the selling situation?' All of the answers to these questions need to be verified when in the actual selling situation but prior consideration can help salespeople to be clear in their own minds about the important issues.

The opening

Initial impressions often affect later perceptions, and so it is important for salespeople to consider how to create a favourable initial response from customers. The following factors can positively shape first impressions.

- Be businesslike in appearance and behaviour.
- Be friendly but not overfamiliar.
- Be attentive to detail, such as holding a briefcase in the hand that is not used for handshaking.
- Observe common courtesies like waiting to be asked to sit down.
- Ask if it is convenient for the customer to see you. This signals an appreciation of their needs (they may be too busy to be seen). It automatically creates a favourable impression from which to develop the sales call, but also a long-term relationship because the salesperson has earned the right to proceed to the next stage in selling: need and problem identification.
- Do not take the sales interview for granted: thank the customer for spending time with you and stress that you believe it will be worthwhile for them.

Need and problem identification

People buy products because they have problems that give rise to needs. For example, machine unreliability (problem) causes the need to replace it with a new one (purchase). Therefore the first task is to identify the needs and problems of each customer. Only by doing so can the salesperson connect with each customer's situation. Having done so, the salesperson can select the product that best fits the customer's need and sell the appropriate benefits. It is benefits that link customer needs to product features as in:

Customer need → Benefit ← Product feature

In the previous example, it would be essential to convince the customer that the salesperson's machine possessed features that guaranteed machine reliability. Knowledge of competitors' products would allow salespeople to show how their machine possessed features that gave added reliability. In this way, salespeople are in an ideal situation to convince customers of a product's differential advantage. Whenever possible, factual evidence of product superiority should be shown to customers. This is much more convincing than mere claims by the salesperson.

Effective needs and problem identification requires the development of questioning and listening skills. The problem is that people are more used to making statements than asking questions. Therefore the art of asking sensible questions that produce a clear understanding of the customer's situation requires training and considerable experience. The hallmark of inexperienced salespeople is that they do all the talking; successful salespeople know how to get the customer to do most of the talking. In this way they gain the information necessary to make a sale.

David Crossland, the entrepreneur who built Airtours (now MyTravel) into one of the UK's biggest travel companies, based his success at selling holidays on his technique of 'just listening' to customers. By asking questions and listening, he picked up clues about what holidays they would prefer from what they said they liked and hated about previous trips.[19]

Presentation and demonstration

The presentation and demonstration provides the opportunity for the salesperson to convince the customer that his or her company can supply the solution to the customer's problem. It should focus on **customer benefits** rather than **product features**. These can be linked using the following phrases:

- which means that
- which results in
- which enables you to.

For example, the machine salesperson might say that the machine possesses proven technology (product feature), *which means that* the reliability of the machine (customer benefit) is guaranteed. Evidence should then be supplied to support this sales argument. Perhaps scientific tests have proved the reliability of the machine (these should be shown to the customer), satisfied customers' testimonials could be produced or a visit to a satisfied customer could be arranged.

In business-to-business markets, some salespeople are guilty of presenting features and failing to communicate the benefit to the business customer. For example, in telecommunications it is not enough to say how fast the line speed is. The benefit derives from the impact that the extra speed has on the customer. It could be that faster speed means reduced call costs, reduced number of lines or increased customer satisfaction.[20]

The salesperson should continue asking questions during the presentation to ensure that the customer has understood what the salesperson has said and to check that what the salesperson has mentioned really is of importance to the customer. This can be achieved by asking, say, 'Is that the kind of thing you are looking for?'

Demonstrations allow the customer to see the product in operation. As such, some of the claims made for the product by the salesperson can be verified. Demonstrations allow the customer to be involved in the selling process through participation. They can, therefore, be instrumental in reducing the *perceived risk* of a purchase and moving the customer towards purchase.

Dealing with objections

It is unusual for salespeople to close a sale without the need to overcome objections. Although objections can cause problems, they should not be regarded negatively since they highlight the issues that are important to the buyer.

The secret of *dealing with objections* is to handle both the substantive and emotional aspects. The substantive part is to do with the objection itself. If the customer objects to the product's price, the salesperson needs to use convincing arguments to show that the price is not too high. But it is a fact of human personality that the argument that is supported by the greater weight of evidence does not always win, since people resent being proved wrong. Therefore, salespeople need to recognize the emotional aspects of objection handling. Under no circumstances should the buyer lose face or be antagonized during this process. Two ways of minimizing this risk are to listen to the objection without interruption, and to employ the agree-and-counter technique.

Listen and do not interrupt

Experienced salespeople know that the impression given to buyers by salespeople that interrupt buyers when they are raising an objection is that the salesperson believes that:

- the objection is obviously wrong
- the objection is trivial
- it is not worth the salesperson's time to let the buyer finish.

Interruption denies buyers the kind of respect they are entitled to receive and may lead to a misunderstanding of the real substance behind the objection.

The correct approach is to listen carefully, attentively and respectfully. The buyer will appreciate the fact that the salesperson is taking the problem seriously, and the salesperson will gain through having a clear and full understanding of what the problem really is.

Agree and counter

The salesperson agrees with the buyer's viewpoint before putting forward an alternative point of view. The objective is to create a climate of agreement rather than conflict, and shows that the salesperson respects the buyer's opinion, thus avoiding loss of face. For example:

> *Buyer*: The problem with your bulldozer is that it costs more than the competition.

> *Salesperson*: You are right, the initial cost is a little higher, but I should like to show you how the full lifetime costs of the bulldozer are much lower than the competition.

Closing the sale

Inexperienced salespeople sometimes think that an effective presentation followed by convincing objection handling should mean that the buyer will ask for the product without the seller needing to close the sale. This does occasionally happen, but more often it is necessary for the salesperson to take the initiative. This is because many buyers still have doubts in their minds that may cause them to wish to delay the decision to purchase.

If the customer puts off buying, the decision may be made when a competitor's salesperson is present, resulting in a lost sale.

Buying signals

The key to closing a sale is to look for **buying signals**. These are statements by buyers that indicate they are interested in buying. For example:

- 'That looks fine.'
- 'I like that one.'
- 'When could the product be delivered?'
- 'I think that product meets my requirements.'

These all indicate a very positive intention to buy without actually asking for the order. They provide excellent opportunities for the salesperson to ask the buyer to make a decision without appearing pushy.

Closing techniques

A variety of closing techniques can be used.

- *Simply ask for the order*: a direct question, such as 'Would you like that one?', may be all that is needed.

- *Summarize and then ask for the order*: with this approach, the salesperson reminds the buyer of the main points of the sales discussion in a manner which implies that the time for decision-making has arrived and that buying is the natural next step: 'Well, Ms Jones, we have agreed that the ZX4 model best meets your requirements of low noise and high productivity at an economical price. Would you like to place an order for this machine?'

- *Concession close*: by keeping a concession back to use in the close, a salesperson may convince an indecisive buyer to place an order: 'I am in a position to offer an extra 10 per cent discount on price if you are willing to place an order now.'

- *Action agreement*: in some situations it is inappropriate to try to close the sale. To do so would annoy the buyer because the sale is not in the hands of one person but a decision-making unit. Many organizational purchasing decisions are of this kind, and the decision may be made in committee without any salesperson being present. Alternatively, the salesperson may be talking to a specifier (such as a doctor or architect) who does not buy directly. In such circumstances, the close may be substituted by an action agreement: instead of closing the sale the salesperson attempts to achieve an action agreement with the customer. For example, in the selling of prescription drugs, either the salesperson or the doctor agree to do something before the next meeting. The salesperson might agree to bring details of a new drug or attempt to get agreement from the doctor to read a leaflet on a drug before the next meeting. This technique has the effect of maintaining the relationship between the parties and can be used as the starting point of the discussion when they next meet.

The follow-up

Once the order is placed there could be a temptation for the salesperson to move on to other customers, neglecting the follow-up visit. However, this can be a great mistake since most companies rely on repeat business. If problems arise, customers have every right to believe that the salesperson was interested only in the order and not their complete satisfaction. By checking that there are no problems with delivery, installation, product use and training (where applicable), the follow-up can show that the salesperson really cares about the customer.

The follow-up can also be used to provide reassurance that the purchase was the right thing to do. As we discussed when analysing consumer behaviour, people often feel tense after deciding to buy an expensive product. Doubts can materialize about the wisdom of spending so much money, or whether the product best meets their needs. This anxiety, known as *cognitive dissonance*, can be minimized by the salesperson reassuring the customer about the purchase during the follow-up phase.

Salespeople operating in overseas markets need to be aware of the cultural nuances that shape business relationships. For example, in the West, a deadline is acceptable whereas in many Middle Eastern cultures, it would be taken as an insult. Marketing in Action 13.1 discusses some of the cultural issues that affect business dealings with Chinese people. Of particular importance are personalized and close business relationships, known as *Guanxi*. *Guanxi* can lead to preferential treatment in the form of easy access to limited resources, increased accessibility to information and preferential credit terms.[26]

13.1 marketing in action

Personal Selling and the Chinese Culture

Cultural factors mean that salespeople need to understand and respect the values of overseas customers and alter their approach accordingly. Visiting salespeople are often invited to long banquets when selling to Chinese people. They usually begin in late morning or early evening. Some Chinese hosts regard visitors as having enjoyed themselves if they become a little intoxicated.

In China, negotiations often last longer than in many western countries. Arriving late for a business appointment is regarded as acceptable behaviour in most western cultures. In Hong Kong, however, this would result in the visitor 'losing face', an extremely serious issue in Chinese culture. Visiting salespeople should avoid creating a situation where a Chinese person might 'lose face' by finding themselves in an embarrassing situation (e.g. by displaying lack of knowledge or understanding). Chinese people like to gather as much information as possible before revealing their thoughts, to avoid losing face or displaying ignorance. Business relations should be built on the basis of harmony and friendship.

Displaying arrogance and the showing of extreme confidence are not admired. Instead, salespeople should make modest, reasoned, down-to-earth points. They should avoid trying to win arguments with customers, who may suffer 'loss of face' and react negatively.

Western salespeople also need to understand the importance of *Guanxi* networks, which provide access to influencers who can make things happen. *Guanxi* is a set of personal relationships/connections on which an individual can draw to secure resources or advantage when doing business. For foreigners, this means having as part of their *Guanxi* network an influential person in an organization or government position. Developing such a network may involve performing favours and the giving of gifts. For example, a businessperson may participate in a public ceremonial function or a profession could send books to a Chinese university. Favours are 'banked' and there is a reciprocal obligation to return a favour. The 'giving of face' is also important. This is done by giving respect, courtesy and praise to other people. The status and reputation of Chinese negotiators should always be recognized, and aggressive behaviour avoided.

Many salespeople make the mistake of using 'self-reference' criteria when selling abroad. They assume that the values and behavioural norms that apply in their own country are equally applicable abroad. To avoid this failing, they need training in the special skills required to sell to people of different cultures.

Based on: Jeannet and Hennessey (2002);[21] Buttery and Leung (1998);[22] Arias (1998);[23] Cateora et al. (2002);[24] Smith (2000)[25]

Sales management

In many respects, the functions of the sales manager are similar to those of other managers. Sales managers, like their production, marketing and finance counterparts, need to recruit, train, motivate and evaluate their staff. However, there are several peculiarities of the job that make effective sales management difficult and the job considerably demanding.

Problems of sales management

Geographic separation

The geographic separation between sales managers and their field salesforce creates problems of motivation, communication and control.

Repeated rejections

Salespeople may suffer repeated rejections when trying to close sales. This may cause attrition of their enthusiasm, attitudes and skills. A major role for sales managers is to provide support and renew motivation in such adverse circumstances.

The salesperson's personality vs the realities of the job

Most people who go into sales are outgoing and gregarious. These are desirable characteristics for people who are selling to customers. However, the reality of the job is that, typically, only 30 per cent of a salesperson's time is spent face to face with customers, with travelling (50 per cent) and administration (20 per cent) contributing the rest.[27] This means that over half of the salesperson's time is spent alone, which can cause frustration in people who enjoy the company of others.

Oversimplification of the task

Some sales managers cope with the difficulties of management by oversimplifying the task. They take the attitude that they are interested only in results. It is their job to reward those who meet sales targets and severely punish those who fail. Such an attitude ignores the contribution that sales management can make to the successful achievement of objectives. Figure 13.4 shows the functions of a sales manager and the relationship between marketing strategy and the personal selling function.

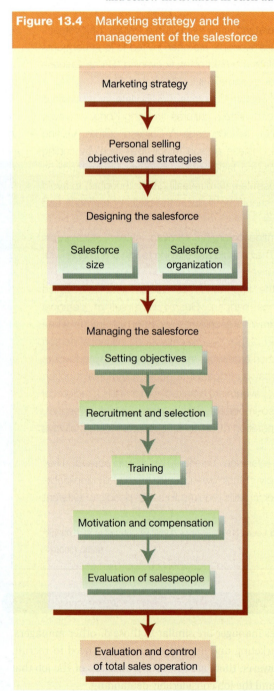

Figure 13.4 Marketing strategy and the management of the salesforce

Marketing strategy

As with all parts of the marketing mix, the personal selling function is not a stand-alone element, but one that must be considered in the light of overall marketing strategy. At the product level, two major marketing considerations are choice of target market and the creation of a differential advantage. Both of these decisions affect personal selling.

Target market choice

The definition of the target market has clear implications for sales management because of its relationship to target accounts. Once the target market has been defined (e.g. organizations in a particular industry over a certain size), sales management can translate that specification into individual accounts to target. Salesforce resources can, therefore, be deployed to maximum effect.

Differential advantage

The creation of a differential advantage is the starting point of successful marketing strategy, but this needs to be communicated to the salesforce and embedded in a sales plan which ensures that the salesforce is able to articulate it convincingly to customers.

Two common dangers

First, the salesforce undermines the differential advantage by repeatedly giving in to customer demands for price concessions. Second, the features that underlie the differential advantage are communicated but the customer benefits are neglected. Customer benefits need to be communicated in terms that are meaningful to customers. This means, for example, that advantages such as higher productivity may require translation into cash savings or higher revenue for financially minded customers.

Four strategic objectives

Marketing strategy also affects the personal selling function through strategic objectives. Each objective—build, hold, harvest and divest—has implications for *sales objectives* and strategy; these are outlined in Table 13.2. Linking business or product area strategic objectives with functional area strategies is essential for the efficient allocation of resources, and effective implementation in the marketplace.[28]

Table 13.2 Marketing strategy and sales management

Strategic marketing objecive	Sales objective	Sales strategy
Build	Build sales volume increase distribution Provide high service levels	High call rates on existing accounts High focus during call Call on new accounts (prospecting)
Hold	Maintain sales volume Maintain distribution Maintain service levels	Continue present call rates on current accounts Medium focus during call Call on new outlets when they appear
Harvest	Reduce selling costs Target profitable accounts Reduce service costs and inventories	Call only on profitable accounts Consider telemarketing or dropping the rest No prospecting
Divest	Clear inventory quickly	Quantity discounts to targeted accounts

Source: Adapted from Strahle, W. and R. L. Spiro (1986) Linking Market Share Strategies to Salesforce Objectives, Activities and Compensation Policies, *Journal of Personal Selling and Sales Management*, August, 11–18.

Personal selling objectives and strategies

As we have seen, selling objectives and strategies are derived from marketing strategy decisions, and should be consistent with other elements of the marketing mix. Indeed, marketing strategy will determine if there is a need for a salesforce at all, or whether the selling role can be accomplished better by using some other medium, such as direct mail. Objectives define what the selling function is expected to achieve. Objectives are typically defined in terms of:

- sales volume (e.g. 5 per cent growth in sales volume)
- market share (e.g. 1 per cent increase in market share)

- profitability (e.g. maintenance of gross profit margin)
- service levels (e.g. 20 per cent increase in number of customers regarding salesperson assistance as 'good or better' in annual customer survey)
- salesforce costs (e.g. 5 per cent reduction in expenses).

Salesforce strategy defines how those objectives will be achieved. The following may be considered:

- call rates
- percentage of calls on existing vs potential accounts
- discount policy (the extent to which reductions from list prices allowed)
- percentage of resources
    - targeted at new vs existing products
    - targeted at selling vs providing after-sales service
    - targeted at field selling vs telemarketing
    - targeted at different types of customers (e.g. high vs low potential)
- improving customer and market feedback from the salesforce
- improving customer relationships.

Once sales managers have a clear idea of what they hope to achieve, and how best to set about accomplishing these objectives, they can make sensible decisions regarding salesforce design.

Designing the salesforce

Two critical design decisions are determining salesforce size and salesforce organization.

Salesforce size

The most practical method for deciding the number of salespeople is called the *workload approach*. It is based on the calculation of the total annual calls required per year divided by the average calls per year that can be expected from one salesperson.[29] The procedure follows seven steps, as outlined below.

1. Customers are grouped into categories according to the value of goods bought and their potential for the future.
2. The call frequency (number of calls per year to an account) is assessed for each category of customer.
3. The total required workload per year is calculated by multiplying the call frequency by the number of customers in each category and then summing for all categories.
4. The average number of calls that can be expected per salesperson per week is estimated.
5. The number of working weeks per year is calculated.
6. The average number of calls a salesperson can make per year is calculated by multiplying (4) and (5).
7. The number of salespeople required is determined by dividing the total annual calls required by the average number of calls one salesperson can make per year.

The formula is:

Number of salespeople = number of customers
× call frequency ÷ average weekly call rate
× number of working weeks per year

An example of how the workload approach can be used will now be given. Steps 1, 2 and 3 may be summarized as shown in Table 13.3.

Table 13.3 The workload approach: an example

Customer group	No of accounts	Call frequency	
A (Over £500,000 per year)	20	x 12	= 240
B (£250,000–£500,000 per year)	100	x 9	= 900
C (£100,000–£249,000 per year)	300	x 6	= 1800
D (Less than £100,000 per year)	500	x 3	= 1500
Total annual workload			= 4440

Step 4 gives:
  Average number of calls per week
  per salesperson = 20

Step 5 gives: Number of weeks = 52
Less: Holidays   4
       Illness   1
       Conferences/meetings 3
       Training   1   = 9
Number of working weeks   = 43

Step 6 gives: Average number of calls
per salesperson per year = 43 x 20
                         = 860

Step 7 gives:

Salesforce size = 4440 / 860 = 6 salespeople

When prospecting forms an important part of the selling job, a separate category (or categories) can be formed with their own call rates to give an estimation of the workload required to cover prospecting. This is then added to the workload estimate based on current accounts to give a total workload figure.

Salesforce organization

There are three basic forms of *salesforce organization*: geographic, product and customer-based structures. The strengths and weakness of each are as follows.

Geographic: the sales area is broken down into territories based on workload and potential, and a salesperson is assigned to each one to sell all of the product range. This provides a simple, unambiguous, definition of each salesperson's sales territory, and proximity to customers encourages the development of personal relationships. It is also a more cost-efficient method of organization than product or customer-based systems. However, when products are technically different and sell in a number of diverse markets, it may be unreasonable to expect a salesperson to be knowledgeable about all products and their applications. Under such circumstances a company is likely to move to a product or customer-based structure.

Product: product specialization is effective where a company has a diverse product range selling to different customers (or at least different people within a given organization). However, if the products sell essentially to the same customers, problems of route duplication (and, consequently, higher travel costs) and multiple calls on the same customer can arise. When applicable, product specialization allows each salesperson to be well informed about a product line, its applications and customer benefits.

Customer-based: salesforces can be organized along market segment, account size, or new versus existing accounts lines. First, computer firms have traditionally organized their salesforce on the basis of industry served (e.g. banking, retailing and manufacturing) in recognition of their varying needs, problems and potential applications. Specialization by these *market segments* allows salespeople to gain in-depth knowledge of customers and to be able to monitor trends in the industry that may affect demand for their products. In some industries, the applications knowledge of market-based salespeople has led them to be known as *fraternity brothers* by their customers.[30] Second, an increasing trend in many industries is towards **key account management**, which reflects the increasing concentration of buying power into fewer but larger customers. These are serviced by a key account salesforce comprising senior salespeople who develop close personal relationships with customers, can handle sophisticated sales arguments and are skilled in the art of negotiation. A number of advantages are claimed for a key account structure.

1. *Close working relationships with the customer*: the salesperson knows who makes what decisions and who influences the various players involved in the decision. Technical specialists from the selling organization can call on technical people (e.g. engineers) in the buying organization, and salespeople can call on administrators, buyers and financial people armed with the commercial arguments for buying.

2. *Improved communication and co-ordination*: the customer knows that a dedicated salesperson or sales team exists so that it is clear who to contact when a problem arises.

3. *Better follow-up on sales and service*: the extra resources devoted to the key account mean that there is more time to follow up and provide service after a major sale has been made.

4. *More in-depth penetration of the DMU*: there is more time to cultivate relationships within the key account. Salespeople can *pull* the buying decision through the organization from the users, deciders and influencers to the buyer, rather than the more difficult task of pushing it through the buyer into the organization, as is done with more traditional sales approaches.

5. *Higher sales*: most companies who have adopted key account selling claim that sales have risen as a result.

6. *The provision of an opportunity for advancement for career salespeople*: a tiered salesforce system with key (or national) account selling at the top provides promotional opportunities for salespeople who wish to advance within the salesforce rather than enter a traditional sales-management position.

The development and management of a key account can be understood as a process that takes place over time between buyers and sellers. The key account management (KAM) relational development model plots the typical progression of a buyer–seller relationship based on the nature of the customer relationship (transactional–collaborative) and the level of involvement with customers (simple–complex).[31] Figure 13.5 shows five stages: Pre-KAM, Early-KAM, Mid-KAM, Partnership-KAM and Synergistic-KAM. A sixth stage (Uncoupling-KAM) represents the breakdown of the relationship, which can happen at any point during the process.

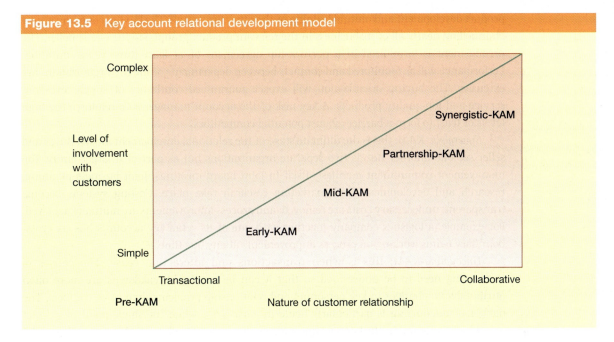

Figure 13.5 Key account relational development model

Pre-KAM: this describes preparation for KAM, or 'prospecting'. The task is to identify those with the potential for moving towards key account status and to avoid wasting investment on those accounts that lack potential. Pre-KAM selling strategies involve making products available while attempting to gather information about customers so that their key account potential can be assessed. Where an account is thought to have potential but breaking into the account is proving difficult, patience and persistence are required. A breakthrough may result from the 'in' supplier doing something wrong—for example, refusing to quote for a low-profit order or failing to repair equipment promptly.

Early-KAM: this involves the exploration of opportunities for closer collaboration by identifying the motives, culture and concerns of the customer. The selling company needs to convince the customer of the benefits of being a 'preferred supplier'. It will seek to understand the customer's decision-making unit and processes, and the problems and opportunities that relate to the value-adding activities. Product adaptations may be made to fit customer needs better. An objective of the sales effort will be to build trust based on consistent performance and open communications. Most communication is channelled through one salesperson (key account manager) and a single contact at the buying organization. This makes for a fragile relationship, particularly as it is likely that the seller is one of many supplying the account. The customer will be monitoring the supplier's performance to assess competence and to identify any problems that might arise. The account manager will be seeking to create a more attractive offering, establish credibility and deepen personal relationships.

Mid-KAM: by now trust has been established and the supplier is one of a small number of preferred sources of the product. The number and range of contacts increase. These may include social events, which help to deepen relationships across the two organizations. The account review process carried out at the selling organization will tend to move upwards to involve senior management because of the importance of the customer and the level of resource allocation. Since the account is not yet exclusive, the activities of competitors will require constant monitoring.

Partnership-KAM: at this stage the buying organization regards the supplier as an important strategic resource. The level of trust will be sufficient for both parties to be willing to share sensitive information. The focus of activities moves to joint problem solving, collaborative product development and mutual training of the other firm's staff. The buying company is now channelling nearly all of its business in the relevant product group(s) to the one supplier. The arrangement is formalized in a partnership agreement of at least three years' duration. Performance will be monitored and contacts between departments of the two organizations are extensive. The buying organization will expect guaranteed continuity of supply, excellent service and top-quality products. A key task of the account manager is to reinforce the high levels of trust to form a barrier against potential competitors.

Synergistic-KAM: this is the ultimate stage of the relational development model. Buyer and seller see one another not as two separate organizations but as part of a larger entity. Top management commitment manifests itself in joint board meetings. Joint business planning, research and development, and marketing research take place. Costing systems become transparent, unnecessary costs are removed, and process improvements are mutually achieved. For example, a logistics company together with one of its retail key accounts has six cross-boundary teams working on process improvements at any one time.[32]

Uncoupling-KAM: this is when transactions and interaction cease. The causes of uncoupling need to be understood so that it can be avoided. Breakdowns are more often attributable to changes in key personnel and relationship problems than price conflicts. The danger of uncoupling is particularly acute in early-KAM when the single point of contact prevails. If, for example, the key account manager leaves to be replaced by someone who, in the buyer's eyes, is less skilled, or there is a personality clash, the relationship may end. A second cause of uncoupling is breach of trust. For example, the breaking of a promise over a delivery deadline, product improvement or equipment repair can weaken or kill a business relationship. The key to handling such problems is to reduce the impact of surprise. The supplier should let the buying organization know immediately a problem becomes apparent. It should also show humility when discussing the problem with a customer. Companies, also, uncouple through neglect. Long-term relationships can foster complacency and customers can perceive themselves as being taken for granted. Cultural mismatches can occur—for example, when the customer stresses price whereas the supplier focuses on life-cycle costs. Difficulties can also occur between bureaucratic and entrepreneurial styles of management. Product or service quality problems can also provoke uncoupling. Any kind of performance problem, or the perception that rivals now offer superior performance can trigger a breakdown in relations. 'In' suppliers must build entry barriers by ensuring that product quality is constantly improved and any problems dealt with speedily and professionally. Not all uncoupling is instigated by the buying company. A key account may be de-rated or terminated because of loss of market share or the onset of financial problems that impair the attractiveness of the account.

Some companies adopt a *three-tier system*, with senior salespeople handling key accounts, sales representatives selling to medium-sized accounts and a telemarketing team dealing with small accounts. Telemarketing is a systematic programme placing outbound sales calls to customers and prospects, and receiving orders and enquiries from them. It is discussed in some detail in Chapter 14.

The importance of key account management on a worldwide scale is reflected in the employment of global account managers by many multinational organizations. *Global account management* (GAM) is the process of co-ordinating and developing mutually beneficial long-term relationships with a select group of strategically important customers (accounts) operating in globalized industries.[33] Global account managers perform two key roles: (i) managing the internal interface between global and national account management, which is often embedded in a headquarters/subsidiary relationship; (ii) managing the external interface between the supplier and the dispersed activities of its global accounts.[34]

Multinational customers are increasingly buying on a centralized or co-ordinated basis and seek suppliers who are able to provide consistent and seamless service across countries.[35] Consequently, suppliers are developing and implementing GAM and are creating global account managers to manage the interface between seller and buyer on a global basis.

A third way of organizing along customer lines is by *new versus existing accounts*. One sales team focuses on the skills of prospecting while another services existing customers. This recognizes the differing skills involved, and the possible neglect of opening new accounts by salespeople who may view their time as being more profitably spent with existing customers.

In practice, a combination of structures may be used to gain the economies of the geographic form with the specialization inherent in the product or customer-based systems. For example, a company using a two-product-line structure may divide into geographically based territories with two salespeople operating in each one.

Managing the salesforce

Besides deciding personal selling objectives and strategies, and designing the salesforce, the company has to manage the salesforce. This requires setting specific salesperson objectives, recruitment and selection, training, motivation and compensation, and evaluation of salespeople. These activities have been shown to improve salesperson performance, indicating the key role sales managers play as facilitators helping salespeople to perform better.[36]

Setting objectives

In order to achieve aggregate sales objectives, individual salespeople need to have their own sales targets to achieve. Usually, targets are set in sales terms (sales quotas) but, increasingly, profit targets are being used, reflecting the need to guard against sales being bought cheaply by excessive discounting. To gain commitment to targets, consultation with individual salespeople is recommended but in the final analysis it is the sales manager's responsibility to set targets. Payment may be linked to their achievement.

Sales management may also wish to set input objectives such as the proportion of time spent developing new accounts, and the time spent introducing new products. They may also specify the number of calls expected per day, and the precise customers who should be called upon.

Recruitment and selection

The importance of recruiting high-calibre salespeople cannot be overestimated. A study into salesforce practice asked sales managers the following question: 'If you were to put your most successful salesperson into the territory of one of your average salespeople, and made no other changes, what increase in sales would you expect after, say, two years?'[37] The most commonly stated increase was 16–20 per cent, and one-fifth of all sales managers said they would expect an increase of over 30 per cent. Clearly the quality of salespeople that sales managers recruit has a substantial effect on performance.

When recruiting salespeople, a commonly held assumption is that money is the most valued attraction. This has been challenged in a study by Galbraith, Kiely and Watkins, which examined the features of the job that were of more interest and value to salespeople.[38] Their findings showed that working methods and independence were more important than earnings as the key attraction to a selling career and that independence was also the most highly valued aspect of doing the selling job. The implication of this study is that sales managers need to discover the reasons why people want to become salespeople in their industry so that they can develop recruitment strategies that reflect those desires.

The recruitment and selection process follows five stages:

1. preparation of the job description and personnel specification
2. identification of sources of recruitment and methods of communication
3. design of the application form and preparation of a shortlist
4. the interview
5. use of supplementary selection aids.

We will now look at each of these in more detail.

Preparation of the job description and personnel specification: a job description will normally include details of job title, duties and responsibilities, and to whom the salesperson will report, the technical requirements (e.g. product knowledge), geographic area to be covered, and the degree of autonomy given to the salesperson.

This job description acts as a blueprint for the personnel specification, which details the type of person the company is seeking. For example, the technical aspects of the job may require a salesperson with an engineering degree or to have worked in a particular industry. The personnel specification will also determine the qualities sought in the recruit. Modern practice is to distinguish between essential and desirable criteria for selection. The criteria will be based on the qualities needed to perform the job and will be used when drawing up the shortlist and deciding on the successful applicant.

Based on extensive research, Mayer and Greenberg reduced the number of qualities believed to be important for effective selling to empathy and ego drive.[39] **Empathy** is the ability to feel as the buyer feels: to be able to understand customer problems and needs. **Ego drive** is the need to make a sale in a personal way, not merely for money. These qualities can be measured using a psychological test, such as the Minnesota Multiphasic Personality Inventory.

Identification of sources of recruitment and methods of communication: sources of recruitment include company personnel, recruitment agencies, education, competitors, other industries, and unemployed people. Advertising is the most common method of communication, with national and local press the most often used media. Recruiters should not attempt to squeeze copy into the smallest possible space since size of advertisement is correlated with impact. The advertisement should contain a headline that attracts the attention of possible applicants.

Design of the application form and preparation of a shortlist: the design of the application form should allow the sales manager to check if the applicant is qualified in the light of the personnel specification. It thus provides a common basis for drawing up a shortlist of candidates, provides a foundation for the interview and is a reference point at the post-interview decision-making stage. Shortlisted candidates must meet all the essential criteria for selection.

The interview: most companies employ a screening interview and a selection interview. The overall objective of the interview is to form a clear and valid impression of the strengths and weaknesses of each candidate in terms of the personnel specification. The following criteria may be used:

- physical requirements (e.g. speech, appearance)
- attainments (e.g. educational attainment, previous sales success)
- qualities (e.g. drive, ability to communicate)
- disposition (e.g. maturity, sense of responsibility)
- interests (e.g. any interests that may have a positive impact on building customer relationships).

The interview should start with a few easy-to-answer questions that allow the candidate to talk freely and relax. Interviewers should be courteous and appear interested in what the candidate says. Open questions (e.g. 'Can you tell me about your experiences selling cosmetics?') should be used during the interview to encourage candidates to express themselves. Probes can be used to prompt further discussion or explanation. For example, the candidate might say 'The one-week introductory sales training course was a waste of my time', to which the interviewer might respond 'That's interesting; why was that?' At the end of the interview the candidate should be told when the decision will be made and how it will be communicated.

Use of supplementary selection aids: some companies use psychological tests as an aid to candidate selection, although their use has been criticized on the grounds that many measure personality traits or interests that do not predict sales success. Consequently, before the use of such tests, validation is necessary to show that test scores are likely to correlate with sales success. A test that may be useful in selecting car salespeople may be useless when filling a vacancy for an aero-engine sales job.

Another selection aid is the use of role-playing in order to gauge the potential of applicants. Obviously, previous sales experience has to be allowed for, and the limitations of the exercise need to be recognized. At best, role-playing may be useful in estimating potential in making short-term sales, but is unlikely to provide a reliable guide when the emphasis is on building long-term relationships with customers.

Training

Many sales managers believe that their salespeople can best train themselves by doing the job. This approach ignores the benefits of a training programme that provides a frame of reference in which learning can take place. The importance of training is supported by research, which has found a positive link between training and sales performance.[40] Training should include not only product knowledge but also skills development. Success at selling comes when the skills are performed automatically, without consciously thinking about them, just as a tennis player or footballer succeeds.

A training programme should include knowledge about the company (its objectives, strategies and organization), its products (features and benefits), its competitors and their products, selling procedures and techniques, work organization (including report preparation), and relationship management. Salespeople need to be trained in the management of long-term customer relationships as well as context-specific selling skills.[41]

Lectures, films, role-playing and case studies can be used in a classroom situation to give knowledge and understanding and to develop competences. These should be followed up with in-the-field training, where skills can be practised face to face with customers. Sales managers and trainers should provide feedback to encourage on-the-job learning. In particular the sales manager needs to:

- analyse each salesperson's performance
- identify strengths and weaknesses
- communicate strengths
- gain agreement that a weakness exists
- train the salesperson in how to overcome the weakness
- monitor progress.

Sales managers themselves need training in the considerable range of skills that they require, including analytical, teaching, motivational and communicational skills, and the ability to organize and plan. Some of the skills are not essential to be able to sell (e.g. teaching and motivating others), hence the adage that the best salespeople do not always make the best sales managers.

Motivation and compensation

Effective motivation is based on a deep understanding of salespeople as individuals, their personalities and value systems. In one sense, sales managers do not motivate salespeople—they provide the enabling conditions in which salespeople motivate themselves. Motivation can be understood through the relationship between needs, drives and goals. Luthans stated that, 'the basic process involves needs (deprivations) which set drives in motion (deprivations with direction) to accomplish goals (anything which alleviates a need and reduces a drive)'.[42] For example, the need for more money may result in a drive to work harder in order to receive increased pay.

Motivation has been the subject of much research over many years. Maslow, Herzberg, Vroom, Adams and Likert, among others, have produced theories that have implications for the motivation of salespeople.[43] Some of their important findings are summarized in the list below.

- Once a need is satisfied it no longer motivates.
- Different people have different needs and values.
- Increasing the level of responsibility/job enrichment, giving recognition of achievement and providing monetary incentives work to increase motivation for some people.
- People tend to be motivated if they believe that effort will bring results, results will be rewarded and the rewards are valued.
- Elimination of disincentives (such as injustices or unfair treatment) raises motivational levels.
- There is a relationship between the performance goals of sales managers and those of the salespeople they lead.

The implication of these findings are that sales managers should:

- get to know what each salesperson values and what each one is striving for (unrealized needs)

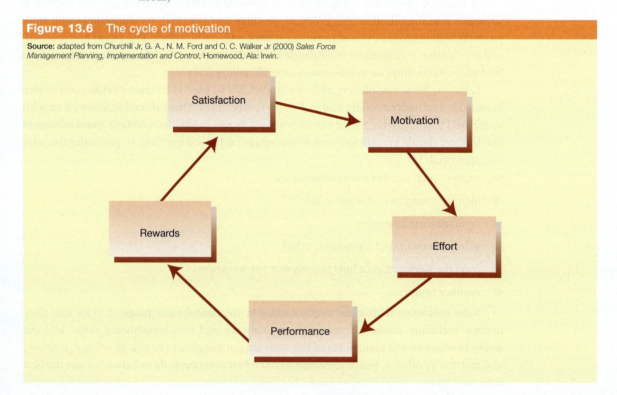

Figure 13.6 The cycle of motivation

Source: adapted from Churchill Jr, G. A., N. M. Ford and O. C. Walker Jr (2000) *Sales Force Management Planning, Implementation and Control*, Homewood, Ala: Irwin.

- be willing to increase the responsibility given to salespeople in mundane jobs
- realize that training can improve motivation as well as capabilities by strengthening the link between effort and performance
- provide targets that are believed to be attainable yet provide a challenge to salespeople
- link rewards to the performance they want improved
- recognize that rewards can be both financial and non-financial (e.g. praise).

Churchill, Ford and Walker developed a **salesforce motivation** model that integrated the work of the motivational theorists (in particular Vroom and Herzberg).[44] This model is shown in Fig. 13.6, and suggests that there is a cycle of motivation. The higher the salesperson's motivation, the greater the effort, resulting in higher performance. Better performance leads to greater rewards and job satisfaction. The cycle is completed through higher satisfaction causing still more motivation.

The implications for sales managers are that they should:

- convince salespeople that they will sell more by working harder or by being trained to work smarter (e.g. more efficient call planning, developing selling skills)
- convince salespeople that the rewards for better performance are worth the extra effort; this implies that the sales manager should give rewards that are valued, and attempt to sell the worth of those rewards to the salesforce (for example, a sales manager might build up the worth of a holiday prize by stating what a good time he or she had personally when there).

Motivation can be affected by the type of compensation plan used by a company. However, as revealed by the research of the motivational theorists, not all people are equally motivated by money. Darmon revealed that there are five types of salespeople, defined by their goal structure.[45]

1. *Creatures of habit*: these salespeople try to maintain their standard of living by earning a predetermined amount of money.
2. *Satisfiers*: these salespeople perform at a level just sufficient to keep their jobs.
3. *Trade-offers*: these salespeople allocate their time based upon a personally determined ratio between work and leisure that is not influenced by the prospect of higher earnings.
4. *Goal-orientated*: these salespeople prefer recognition as achievers by their peers and superiors, and tend to be sales-quota orientated with money mainly serving as recognition of achievement.
5. *Money-orientated*: these salespeople aim to maximize their earnings. Family relationships, leisure and even health may be sacrificed in the pursuit of money.

Consequently, sales managers must categorize their salespeople before deciding their motivational and compensation plan. For example, if a salesforce consists of creatures of habit, satisfiers and trade-offers, increasing commission opportunities is unlikely to be successful. However, where most of the salesforce are goal-orientated or money-orientated, improving commission opportunities is likely to be effective in raising motivation and performance.

Compensation plans are not only determined by motivational considerations. The nature of the selling task, which may determine if the payment of commission is feasible, is another major factor. We shall now examine three types of compensation: fixed salary, commission only and salary plus commission/bonus.

- *Fixed salary*: because payment is not directly tied to sales, salespeople paid by fixed salary are more willing to carry out tasks that do not result in short-term sales, such as providing technical back-up, completing information feedback reports and prospecting, than those paid by commission only. A fixed salary also provides the income security that many salespeople value, although the direct incentive to earn more money by increasing sales is lost. Also the system may lead to perceived injustices if higher-performing salespeople are not being paid more than their lower-achieving colleagues.

- *Commission only*: the lack of a fixed element to income provides a strong incentive to sell, perhaps too strong at times, leading to overbearing salespeople desperate to close sales. Other disadvantages are an unwillingness to take time off from direct selling tasks to attend training courses or fill in reports, and a tendency for there to be high turnover of staff in jobs where commission only is the norm—for example, in insurance selling.

- *Salary plus commission/bonus*: this hybrid system provides some incentive to sell, with an element of security. Usually salary makes up about 70 per cent of income. This system is attractive to ambitious salespeople who wish to combine a base level of income with the opportunity to earn more by greater effort and ability. For these reasons it is the most commonly used method of payment.[46] Bonuses are usually paid on the achievement of some task, such as achieving a sales target or opening a certain number of new accounts.

For many companies their market is the world, which means that they are faced with motivating international salesforces. Marketing in Action 13.2 discusses some of the problems involved and their solutions.

13.2 marketing in action

Motivating an International Salesforce

Sales managers should not assume that a motivation and compensation system that works well in their home country will work in overseas markets: the values and expectations of their foreign-based salespeople need to be understood. For example, in Europe financial incentives are often used to motivate salespeople but in Japan and the Middle East commission is rarely used. Instead, non-financial factors such as increased responsibility or greater job security are more common. An understanding of local customs is essential. In Japan, for example, salary increases are based on seniority. Political factors can also determine the level of fringe benefits provided for employees.

Care needs to be taken over salaries paid to an overseas salesforce when it consists of a mixture of expatriates and local salespeople. Because a salary increase often accompanies an expatriate's overseas move, they may be paid more than local recruits. If this becomes common knowledge, the motivation of locally recruited salespeople may decline.

A common complaint among international salespeople is that their head office does not understand them. They often feel alone or deserted. Their motivation can be boosted through the setting of realistic sales targets, giving them full support and improving communication.

Based on: Cundif and Hilger (1988);[47] Hill *et al*. (1991);[48] Cateora *et al*. (2002)[49]

Evaluation of salespeople

Salesforce evaluation provides the information necessary to check if targets are being achieved, and provides the raw information to guide training and motivation. By identifying the strengths and weakness of individual salespeople, training can be focused on the areas in need of development, and incentives can be aimed at weak spots such as poor prospecting performance.

Often, performance will be compared to standards of performance such as sales or profit quotas, although other comparisons such as salesperson-to-salesperson or current-to-past sales are also used. Two types of performance measures are used, based on quantitative and qualitative criteria.

Quantitative measures of performance: salespeople can be assessed on input, output and hybrid criteria. Output criteria include:

- sales revenue
- profits generated
- gross profit margin
- sales per active account
- number of new accounts opened.

Input criteria include:

- number of calls
- calls per active account
- calls on new accounts (prospects)
- number of prospects visited.

Hybrid criteria are formed by combining output and input criteria, for example:

- sales revenue per call
- profit per call
- prospecting success ratio = number of new accounts opened ÷ number of prospects visited.

These quantitative measures can be compared against target figures to identify strengths and weaknesses. Many of the measures are diagnostic, pointing to reasons why a target is not being reached. For example, a poor call rate might be a cause of low sales achievement. Some results will merit further investigation. For example, a low prospecting success ratio should prompt an examination of why new accounts are not being opened despite the high number of prospects visited.

Qualitative measures of performance: whereas quantitative criteria will be measured with hard figures, qualitative measures rely on soft data. They are intrinsically more subjective and include assessment of:

- sales skills, e.g. questioning, making presentations
- customer relationships, e.g. how much confidence do customers have in the salesperson, and whether rapport is good
- product knowledge, e.g. how well informed is the salesperson regarding company and competitor products
- self-management, e.g. how well are calls prepared, routes organized
- co-operation and attitudes, e.g. to what extent does the salesperson show initiative, follow instructions?

The use of quantitative and qualitative measures is interrelated. For example, a poor sales per call ratio will mean a close qualitative assessment of sales skills, customer relationships and product knowledge.

A final form of qualitative assessment does not focus on the salesperson directly but the likelihood of *winning or losing an order*. Particularly for major sales, a sales manager needs to be able to assess the chances of an order being concluded successfully in time to rectify the situation if things seem to be going astray. Unfortunately, asking salespeople directly will rarely result in an accurate answer. This is not because they are trying to deceive but because they may be deluding themselves. The answer is to ask a series of who, when, where, why and how questions to probe deeper into the situation. It also means working out acceptable and unacceptable responses. Table 13.4 provides an illustration of how such questions could be employed in connection with a major computer sale.

Table 13.4 Winning and losing major orders

Question	Poor (losing answer)	Good (winning answer)
Who will authorize the purchase	The director of MIS.	The director of MIS, but it requires an executive director's authorization, and we've talked it over with this person
When will they buy?	Right away. They love the new model.	Before the peak processing load at the year end.
Where will they be when the decision is made: in the office alone, in their boss's office, in a meeting?	What different does that make? I think they have already decided.	At a board meeting. But don't worry, the in-supplier has no one on its board and we have two good customers on it.
Why will they buy from us? Why not their usual supplier?	They and I go way back. They love our new model.	The next upgrade from the in-supplier is a big price increase, and ours fits right between its models. They are quite unhappy with the in-supplier about that.
How will the purchase be funded?	They've lots of money, haven't they?	The payback period on reduced costs will be about 14 months and we've a leasing company willing to take part of the deal.

The losing answers are thin and unconvincing. The salesperson may be convinced that the sale will be achieved but the answers show that this is unlikely. The winning answers are much more assured and credible. The sales manager can be confident that there is no need to take action.

However, with the losing answer the sales manager will need to act and the response will depend on how important the sale and the salesperson are to the company. If they both have high potential, the sales manager should work with the salesperson. He or she should be counselled so that they know why they are being helped and what they will learn from the experience. The aim is to conclude the sale and convince the salesperson that their personal development will be enhanced by the experience.

If the salesperson has high potential but not the sale, only a counselling session is needed. Care should be taken not to offend the salesperson's ego. When only the sale has high potential, the alternatives are not so pleasant. Perhaps the salesperson could be moved to a more suitable post. When neither the salesperson nor the sale has potential, the only question to ask is whether the salesperson is redeployed before or after the sale is lost.

Evaluation and control of the total sales operation

Evaluation of the total personal selling function is necessary to assess its overall contribution to marketing strategy. The results of this assessment may lead to more cost-efficient means of servicing accounts being introduced (e.g. direct mail or telemarketing), the realization that the selling function is under-resourced, or the conclusion that the traditional form of sales organization is in need of reform. One company that suspected its salesforce had become complacent moved every salesperson to a different territory. Despite having to forge new customer relationships, sales increased by a quarter in the following year.

Evaluation of the personal selling function should also include assessing the quality of its relationship with marketing and other organizational units. Salespeople that manage the external relationship with distributors (e.g. retailers) must collaborate internally with their colleagues in marketing to agree joint business objectives and to develop marketing programmes (for example, new products and promotions) that meet the needs of distributors, as well as consumers, so that they are readily adopted by them. This means that close collaboration and good working relations are essential.[50]

Ethical issues in personal selling and sales management

Four ethical issues that salespeople may have to face are deception, the hard sell, bribery and reciprocal buying.

Deception

A dilemma that, sooner or later, faces most salespeople is the choice of telling the customer the whole truth and risk losing the sale, or misleading the customer to clinch it. The deception may take the form of exaggeration, lying or withholding important information that significantly reduces the appeal of the product. Such actions should be avoided by influencing salespersons' behaviour by training, by sales management encouraging ethical behaviour by their own actions and words, and by establishing codes of conduct for their salespeople. Nevertheless, from time to time evidence of malpractice in selling reaches the media. For example, in the UK it was alleged that some financial services salespeople mis-sold pensions by exaggerating the expected returns. The scandal cost the companies involved millions of pounds in compensation.[51]

Ethical Marketing in Action 13.1 discovers some of the issues surrounding the selling of dried milk for babies in developing countries.

The hard sell

Personal selling is also criticized for employing high-pressure sales tactics to close a sale. Some car dealerships have been deemed unethical by using hard-sell tactics to pressure customers into making a quick decision on a complicated purchase that may involve expensive credit facilities. Such tactics encouraged Daewoo to approach the task of selling cars in a fundamentally different way.

Bribery

This is the act of giving payment, gifts or other inducements to secure a sale. Bribes are considered unethical because they violate the principle of fairness in commercial negotiations. A major problem is that in some countries bribes are an accepted part of business life: to compete, bribes are necessary. When an organization succumbs, it is usually castigated in its home country if the bribe becomes public knowledge. Yet without the bribe it may have been operating at a major commercial disadvantage. Companies need to decide whether they are going to market in countries where bribery is commonplace. Taking an ethical stance may cause difficulties in the short term but in the long run the positive publicity that can follow may be of greater benefit.

13.1 ethical marketing in action

Nurse Knows Best:
the Inappropriate Selling of Infant Formula

Nestlé and its marketing of infant formula (dried milk used to bottle-feed babies) provide one of the most evocative examples of unethical selling. In the 1970s and 1980s Nestlé sold its formula products in the developing world using saleswomen dressed to look like nurses. This created the impression, among a vulnerable target group, that the product was endorsed by the medical profession and represented a healthy and desirable alternative to breastfeeding. In reality, its use can be problematic. It required the mother to have money and ongoing access to both the product (once breastfeeding has been stopped it can seldom be restarted) and a reliable, clean water supply. There are also difficulties associated with reading or following mixing instructions. On top of this, medical opinion consistently advises that 'breast is best'; the World Health Organization advocates breastfeeding exclusively for the first four to six months where possible. According to UNICEF, 'if every baby were exclusively breastfed from birth, an estimated 1.5 million lives would be saved each year'.

Aid agencies, Non-Governmental Organizations (NGOs) concerned with child health and church groups all protested loudly about Nestlé's marketing. A major boycott of its products was organized. This culminated in a World Health Organization-sponsored International Code of Marketing Breastmilk Substitutes (see Table 13.5 for the code's key tenets), which Nestlé agreed to honour. But the row rumbles on. Some groups feel it is virtually impossible for a commercial company to market infant formula ethically; the commercial imperative will always win out. Indeed, Nestlé itself complained that its profile has forced it to behave ethically, but that its less well-known competitors are continuing to market formula in unethical ways and are gaining competitive advantage as a result.

Table 13.5   Key tenets of the 1991 International Code of Marketing of Breastmilk Substitutes

- No advertising of any of these products to the public.
- No free samples to mothers.
- No promotion of products in healthcare facilities, including distribution of free or low-cost supplies.
- No company sales representatives to advise mothers.
- No gifts or personal samples to health workers.
- No words or pictures idealizing artificial feeding, or pictures of infants on labels on infant milk containers.
- Information to health workers should be scientific and factual.
- All information on artificial infant feeding, including that on labels, should explain the benefits of breastfeeding, and the costs and hazards associated with artificial feeding.
- Unsuitable products, such as sweetened condensed milk, should not be promoted for babies.
- Manufacturers and distributors should comply with the code's provisions even if countries have not adopted laws or other measures.

Certainly, NGOs and non-profit organizations working in the field list numerous transgressions of the code, such as direct advertising to the consumer in Armenia, and lobbying the government of Pakistan to dilute the code and allow the provision of free supplies to large hospitals in Bangkok.

This last issue led the UNICEF nutrition project officer for Thailand to confirm: 'UNICEF's position is that all free supplies to hospitals and health facilities must be stopped to protect breastfeeding.' In addition to anecdotal evidence, academic studies have found that manufacturers of breast milk substitutes have used national healthcare systems in West Africa, Bangladesh, Poland, South Africa and Thailand to promote their products and to distribute free samples to mothers.

More powerfully, Jim Lindenberger, ex-director of Best Start Social Marketing, a leading US non-profit organization, states:

❝Most infant formula companies violate the code at some level, marketing and selling a product which health organizations around the world have [linked] to severely harmful effects on infants in developing countries.❞

For the marketing student the key lesson is that the way products are sold raises its own ethical dilemmas that need to be carefully addressed, and that the moral and financial bottom lines can often conflict—at least in the short term. Note that the product itself is actually not the problem. Infant formula may not be as good as breast milk, but it provides a real and valuable alternative for mothers who cannot breastfeed, either for physical or lifestyle reasons. The ethical dilemmas arise in the way it is marketed, and, especially, sold—hence the code.

Based on: INFACT (www.infactcanada.ca/obstinat/htm) 2003;[52] www.babymilkaction.org/pages/campaign 2003;[53] Aguayo, Ross, Kanon and Ouedraogo (2003);[54] www.ibfan.org;[55] Lindenberger (2003);[56] Taylor (1998)[57]

Reciprocal buying

Gegengeschäfte

Another practice that might be considered unethical is reciprocal buying. This is where a customer only agrees to buy from a supplier if that supplier agrees to purchase something from the buying organization. This may be considered unfair to other competing suppliers, who may not agree to such an arrangement or may not be in a position to buy from the customer. Supporters of reciprocal buying argue that it is reasonable for a customer to extract the best terms of agreement from a supplier; if this means reaching agreement to sell to the supplier then so be it. Indeed, counter-trade, where goods may be included as part of the payment for supplies has been a feature of international selling for many years and can benefit poorer countries and companies that cannot afford to pay in cash.

Ethical dilemma

Pyramid selling is a scheme where the primary purpose is to earn money through recruiting other individuals. Individuals are encouraged to join through the promise that they will receive payments for introducing further participants. The Department of Trade and Industry in the UK refers to such schemes as illegitimate and illegal if, 'while purporting to offer business opportunities, the sole purpose of the scheme is to make money by recruiting other participants, rather than trading in goods or services'. Other countries similarly consider this a 'bogus' form of selling. The main problem with pyramid selling is that it requires an infinite supply of new participants if everyone is to make money; supply will always be finite, thus saturation point is generally reached quickly and later recruits have little chance of recovering their money. Do you think that pyramid schemes encourage deceptive selling? You may wish to visit the relevant page of the DTI's website at http://www.dti.gov.uk/ccp/topics1/facts/pyramid.htm.

Review

1 **Environmental and managerial forces affecting sales**
- The environmental forces are behavioural (rising customer expectations, customer avoidance of buyer–seller negotiations, the expanding power of major buyers, globalization of markets and fragmentation of markets) and technological (salesforce automation, the virtual sales office and electronic channels).
- The managerial forces are the growth in direct marketing techniques, the development of effective relationships between sales and marketing, and recognition of the importance of professional qualifications.

2 **The different types of selling job**
- Selling jobs fall into three categories: (i) order-takers (inside order-takers, delivery salespeople and outside order-takers), (ii) order-creators (missionary salespeople) and (iii) order-getters (frontline salespeople such as new business salespeople, organizational salespeople and sales support salespeople like technical support salespeople and merchandisers).

3 **Sales responsibilities**
- The primary responsibility of salespeople is to increase sales, but six enabling functions are prospecting, maintaining customer records and information feedback, providing service, handling complaints, self-management, and customer relationship management.

4 **How to prepare for selling**
- Salespeople should prepare for selling by gaining knowledge of their own and competitors' products, planning sales presentations, setting call objectives and seeking to understand buyer behaviour.

5 **The stages in the selling process**
- The stages are preparation, the opening, need and problem identification, presentation and demonstration, dealing with objections, closing the sale and follow-up.

6 **The tasks of sales management**
- The tasks of a sales manager are to understand marketing strategy, set personal selling objectives and strategies, design the salesforce (salesforce size and organization), manage the salesforce (set salesperson objectives, recruitment and selection, training, motivation and compensation, and evaluation of salespeople), and evaluation and control of the total sales operation.

7 **How to design a salesforce**
- Designing a salesforce requires determining salesforce size and deciding salesforce organization.
- A useful method of determining salesforce size is the workload method.
- Salesforces can be organized by geographic, product and customer (market segment, account size or new vs existing accounts) structures.

8 How to manage a salesforce

- Managing a salesforce requires setting specific salesperson objectives, recruitment and selection, training, motivation and compensation, and evaluation of salespeople.
- Setting objectives: targets should be set in consultation with salespeople.
- Recruitment and selection: the stages are preparation of the job description and personnel specification, identification of sources of recruitment and methods of communication, design of the application form and preparation of a shortlist, the interview, and the use of supplementary selection aids.
- Training: sales managers need to analyse each salesperson's performance, identify strengths and weaknesses, communicate strengths, gain agreement that a weakness exists, provide training to overcome any weaknesses, and monitor progress.
- Motivation and compensation: sales managers should understand what each salesperson values, be willing to give extra responsibilities and training, provide challenging yet attainable targets, link rewards to performance, and recognize that rewards can be both financial and non-financial (e.g. praise) to improve motivation. Compensation plans can be fixed salary, commission only or salary plus commission/bonus.
- Evaluation of salespeople: sales managers should use an array of measures, which can be quantitative (input and output) and qualitative (e.g. sales skills and ability to manage customer relationships).

9 Key account management

- Key account management is an approach to selling that focuses resources on major customers and uses a team selling approach.
- Its advantages are close working relationships with customers, improved communication and co-ordination, better follow-up on sales and service, more in-depth penetration of the decision-making unit, higher sales and the provision of an opportunity for the advancement of career salespeople.
- The stages in the key account management relational development model are Pre-KAM, Early-KAM, Partnership-KAM, Synergistic-KAM and Uncoupling-KAM.

10 Ethical issues in personal selling and sales management

- There are potential problems relating to deception, the hard sell, bribery and reciprocal buying.

Key terms

buying signals statements by a buyer that indicate s/he is interested in buying

customer benefits those things that a customer values in a product; customer benefits derive from product features

ego drive the need to make a sale in a personal way, not merely for money

empathy to be able to feel as the buyer feels, to be able to understand customer problems and needs

key account management an approach to selling that focuses resources on major customers and uses a team selling approach

product features the characteristics of a product that may or may not convey a customer benefit

prospecting searching for and calling on potential customers

salesforce evaluation the measurement of salesperson performance so that strengths and weaknesses can be identified

salesforce motivation the motivation of salespeople by a process that involves needs, which set encouraging drives in motion to accomplish goals

target accounts organizations or individuals whose custom the company wishes to obtain

Internet exercise

A number of firms pursue direct selling to consumers, door to door. Firms like Tupperware and Ann Summers have become synonymous with home-based parties, where their sales agents sell products to interested parties at organized events. Explore some of the following websites.

Visit: www.avon.uk.com
www.tupperware.co.uk
www.kleeneze.co.uk
www.betterware.co.uk

Questions

(a) Discuss the reasons why these firms adopt the direct selling approach.
(b) As a sales manager, how would you try and motivate your sales agents?
(c) Identify and discuss the numerous criteria that are used to assess an individual's sales performance, highlighting what you believe to be the most effective.
(d) Direct sales agents are recruited from all walks of life. However many people contend that 'salespeople are born not made'. Do you agree or disagree with this statement? Give reasons for your answer, discussing what you believe to be the essential characteristics needed to have a successful career in sales.

Visit the Online Learning Centre at www.mcgraw-hill.co.uk/textbooks/jobber for more Internet exercises.

Study questions

1. Select a car with which you are familiar. Identify its features and translate them into customer benefits.

2. Imagine you are face to face with a customer for that car. Write down five objections to purchase and prepare convincing responses to them.

3. You are the new sales manager of a company selling abrasives to the motor trade. Your salesforce is paid by fixed salary, and you believe it to be suffering from motivational problems. Discuss how you would handle this.

4. Because of its inherent efficiency the only sensible method of organizing a salesforce is by geographically defined territories. Discuss.

5. Quantitative methods of salesforce organization are superior to qualitative methods because they rely on hard numbers. Evaluate this statement.

6. A company wishes to strengthen its relationships with key customers. How might it approach this task?

7. The key to sales success lies in closing the sale. Discuss.

8. How practical is the workload approach to deciding salesforce size?

9. What are the key stages in the key account relational development model? What implications do they have for marketing to organizational customers?

10. From your own personal experience, do you consider salespeople to be unethical? Can you remember any sales encounters when you have been subject to unethical behaviour?

When you have read this chapter log on to the Online Learning Centre at www.mcgraw-hill.co.uk/textbooks/jobber to explore chapter-by-chapter test questions, links and further online study tools for marketing.

case twenty-five

Glaztex

Glaztex plc was a UK-based supplier of bottling plant used in production lines to transport and fill bottles. Two years ago it opened an overseas sales office targeting Scandinavia, Germany, France and the Benelux countries. It estimated that there were over 1000 organizations in those countries that had bottling facilities, and that a major sales push in northern Europe was therefore warranted. Sales so far had been disappointing with only three units having been sold. Expectations had been much higher than this, given the advantages of its product over that produced by its competitors.

Technological breakthroughs at Glaztex meant that its bottling lines had a 10 per cent speed advantage over the nearest competition with equal filling accuracy. A major problem with competitor products was unreliability. Downtime due to a line breakdown was extremely costly to bottlers. Tests by Glaztex engineers at its research and development establishment in the UK had shown its system to be the most reliable on the market. Glaztex's marketing strategy was based around high-quality, high-price competitive positioning. It believed that the superior performance of its product justified a 10 per cent price premium over its major competitors, which were all priced at around £1 million (€1.44 million) for a standard production line. Salespeople were told to stress the higher speed and enhanced reliability when talking to customers. The sales organization in northern Europe consisted of a sales manager with four salespeople assigned to Scandinavia, Germany, France and the Benelux countries respectively. A technical specialist was also available when required. When a sales call required specialist technical assistance, a salesperson would contact the sales office to arrange for the technical specialist to visit the prospect, usually together with the salesperson.

Typically, four groups of people inside buying organizations were involved in the purchase of bottling equipment—namely the production manager, the production engineer, the purchasing officer and, where large sums of money were involved (over £1.5 million/€2.2 million), the technical director. Production managers were mainly interested in smooth production flows and cost savings. Production engineers were charged with drawing up specifications for new equipment, and in large firms, they were usually asked to draw up state-of-the-art specifications. The purchasing officers, who were often quite powerful, were interested in the financial aspects of any purchase, and technical directors, while interested in technical issues, also appreciated the prestige associated with having state-of-the-art technology.

John Goodman was the sales executive covering France. While in the sales office in Paris, he received a call from Dr Leblanc, the technical director of Commercial SA, a large Marseille-based bottling company, which bottled under licence a number of major soft drink brands. It had a reputation for technical excellence and innovation. Goodman made an appointment to see Dr Leblanc on 7 March. He was looking forward to making his first visit to this company. The following extracts are taken from his record of his sales calls.

7 March

Called on Dr Leblanc who told me that Commercial SA had decided to purchase a new bottling line as a result of expansion, and asked for details of what we could provide. I described our system and gave him our sales literature. He told me that three of our competitors had already discussed their systems with him. As I was leaving, he suggested that I might like to talk to M. Artois, their production engineer to check specifications.

8 March

Visited M. Artois who showed me the specifications he had drawn up. I was delighted to see that our specifications easily exceeded them, but was concerned that his specifications seemed to match those of one of our competitors, Hofstead Gm, almost exactly. I showed M. Artois some of our technical manuals. He did not seem impressed.

11 March

Visited Dr Leblanc who appeared very pleased to see me. He asked me to give him three reasons why they should buy from us. I told him that our system was more technologically advanced than the competition's, was more reliable and had a faster bottling speed. He asked me if I was sure it was the most technologically advanced. I said that there was no doubt about it. He suggested I contact M. Bernard the purchasing manager. I made an appointment to see him in two days' time.

13 March

Called on M. Bernard. I discussed the technical features of the system with him. He asked me about price. I told him I would get back to him on that.

15 March

Visited Dr Leblanc who said a decision was being made within a month. I repeated our operational advantages and he asked me about price. I told him I would give him a quote as soon as possible.

20 March

Saw M. Bernard. I told him our price was £1.1 million. He replied that a major competitor had quoted less than £1 million. I replied that the greater reliability and bottling speed meant that our higher price was more than justified. He remained unimpressed.

21 March

Had a meeting with Mike Bull, my sales manager, to discuss tactics. I told him that there were problems. He suggested that all purchasing managers liked to believe they were saving their company money. He told me to reduce my price by £50,000 to satisfy M. Bernard's ego.

25 March

Told M. Bernard of our new quotation. He said he still did not understand why we could not match the competition on price. I repeated our technical advantages over the competition and told him that our 10 per cent faster speed and higher reliability had been proven by our research and development engineers.

30 March

Visited Dr Leblanc who said a meeting had been arranged for 13 April to make the final decision but that our price of £1.05 million was too high for the likes of M. Bernard.

4 April

Hastily arranged a meeting with Mike Bull to discuss the situation. Told him about Dr Leblanc's concern that M. Bernard thought our price was too high. He said that £1 million was as low as we could go.

5 April

Took our final offer to M. Bernard. He said he would let me know as soon as a decision was made. He stressed that the decision was not his alone; several other people were involved.

16 April

Received a letter from M. Bernard stating that the order had been placed with Hofstead Gm. He thanked me for the work I had put into the bid made by Glaztex.

Questions

1. Analyse the reasons for the failure to win the order and discuss the lessons to be learnt for key account management.

This case was prepared by Professor David Jobber, Professor of Marketing, University of Bradford.

case twenty-six

Selling Exercise

You are the salesperson in the electrical department of a small store. For the past few minutes a man has been looking at the range of torches you have for sale. He comes up to you and says, 'I'm looking for a good torch.'

Take the interview from this point. You have a display of six torches (A–F) with features as described in Table C26.1.

Table C26.1 Six torches

Torch	Cost (excl. batteries)	Batteries	Light rays	Duration of light on new batteries	Construction material	Size/weight (incl. batteries)
A	£12	2 × 6V £1.50 each	Beam/spread by focus	10 hrs	Metal/plastic	20 cm 1.5 kg
B	£4	2 × 1.5V 70p each	Beam	2.5 hrs	Plastic	16 cm 1 kg
C	£2	2 × 1.5V 70p each	Beam	2 hrs	Plastic	12 cm 0.75 kg
D	£2.50	2 × 1.5V 70p each	Spread	2 hrs	Plastic	10 cm 0.5 kg
E	£2.00	2 × pencil 35p each	Weak spread	2 hrs	Plastic	12 cm 0.25 kg
F	£1.70	2 × pencil 35p each	Weak beam	1.25 hrs	Plastic	8 cm 0.20 kg

Torch	Colours	Brightness	Other features
A	Various	8w 0.5w red bulb	Supplied with a 10-foot lead to plug into car cigarette lighter. Has a red bulb in opposite end to use as car light in emergencies. Made in UK.
B	Red/white	3w	Complete with hanging hook and push button flasher. Made in Far East.
C	Red/white	2w	Complete with bicycle bracket and turn switch. Made in France.
D	Various	1.5w	Neat and convenient shape. Hand held. Made in Far East.
E	Yellow/red	1.5w	Neat and small. Made in Hong Kong.
F	Red	0.5w	Made in Far East.

This case was prepared by Robert Edwards, Zeneca.

Direct marketing

chapter fourteen

14

❝There is nothing more exciting than getting a favourable response by mail.❞ ROBERT STONE

Learning Objectives

This chapter explains:

1. The meaning of direct marketing
2. The reasons for the growth in direct marketing activity
3. The nature and uses of database marketing
4. The nature of customer relationship management
5. How to manage a direct marketing campaign
6. The media used in direct marketing
7. Ethical issues in direct marketing

In recent years, direct marketing has established itself as a major component of the promotional mix. Whereas mass advertising reaches a wide spectrum of people, some of whom may not be in the target audience and may only buy at some later unspecified date, direct marketing uses media that can more precisely target consumers and request an immediate direct response. Although the origins of direct marketing lie in direct mail and mail-order catalogues, today's direct marketers use a wide range of media, including telemarketing, direct response advertising, the Internet and online computer shopping to interact with people. No longer is direct marketing synonymous with 'junk mail'—it has grown to be an integral part of the relationship marketing concept, where companies attempt to establish ongoing direct and profitable relationships with customers. Expenditure on direct marketing in Europe has grown in recent years. Expenditure by country is given in Fig. 14.1.

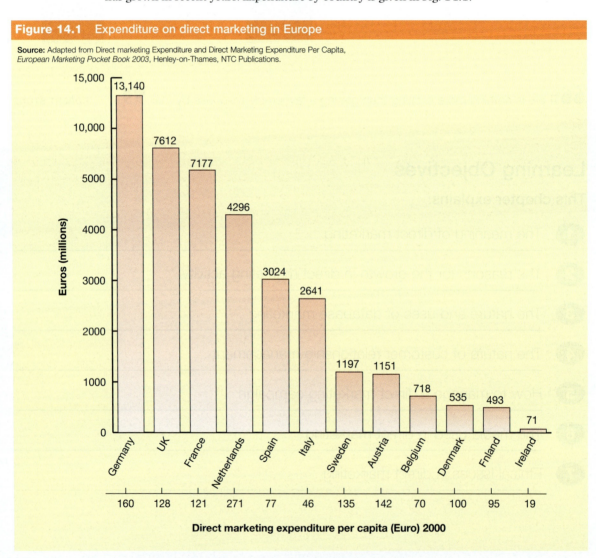

Figure 14.1 Expenditure on direct marketing in Europe

Source: Adapted from Direct marketing Expenditure and Direct Marketing Expenditure Per Capita, *European Marketing Pocket Book 2003*, Henley-on-Thames, NTC Publications.

In this chapter, we will examine the types of media, including the potential of the new interactive electronic communications systems, that direct marketers use to reach their targets. We will explore the issues relating to database management and customer relationship management. The management of a direct marketing campaign will be analysed, including the need for integrated communications, setting objectives, targeting, achieving customer retention and creating action plans. Finally, a number of ethical issues will be discussed.

First, however, we begin by describing what direct marketing is and the reasons for its growing popularity among marketers.

Defining direct marketing

Direct marketing attempts to acquire and retain customers by contacting them without the use of an intermediary. Unlike many other forms of communication, it usually requires an immediate response, which means that the effectiveness of most direct marketing campaigns can be assessed quantitatively.

A definition of direct marketing is:

> The distribution of products, information and promotional benefits to target consumers through interactive communication in a way that allows response to be measured.

Direct marketing campaigns are not necessarily short-term, response-driven activities. More and more companies are using direct marketing to develop ongoing direct relationships with customers. Some marketers believe that the cost of attracting a new customer is five times that of retaining existing customers. Direct marketing activity can be one tool in the armoury of marketers in their attempt to keep current customers satisfied and spending money. Once a customer has been acquired, there is the opportunity to sell that customer other products marketed by the company. Direct Line, a UK insurance company, became market leader in motor insurance by bypassing the insurance broker to reach the consumer directly through direct response television advertisements using a freefone number and financial appeals to encourage car drivers to get in touch. As well as selling motor insurance, their trained telesales people offer substantial discounts on other insurance products, including buildings and contents insurance. In this way, Direct Line has built a major business through using a combination of direct marketing methods.

Direct marketing covers a wide array of methods including:

- direct mail
- telemarketing (both inbound and outbound)
- mobile marketing
- direct response advertising (coupon response or 'phone now')
- catalogue marketing
- electronic media (Internet, e-mail, interactive TV)
- inserts (leaflets in magazines)
- door-to-door leafleting.

The first four of these direct marketing channels will be analysed later in the chapter when discussing media selection for a campaign. Electronic media will be discussed in Chapter 15. A survey of large consumer goods companies across Europe by the International Direct Marketing Network measured the use of these techniques (excluding catalogue marketing and online channels).[1] It was found that 84 per cent of companies used some form of direct marketing, but there was wide variation between countries. For example, 40 per cent used outbound telemarketing in Germany whereas none did in France. Overall, direct mail was the most commonly used technique (52 per cent) followed by coupon advertisements in the press (41 per cent). Telemarketing was not widely employed, although its use is more often associated with business-to-business marketing.

Another European study of consumer and business-to-business direct marketing, by Ogilvy & Mather Direct, found that the split was 65:35 of all activity across Europe.[2] However, there were national differences. For example, in the Netherlands business-to-business direct marketing accounted for 60 per cent of marketing. In all countries, targeted direct mail to a custom-built database was seen as highly effective in business-to-business marketing, as was outbound telemarketing (usually in conjunction with direct mail). Inbound telemarketing (examined in detail on page 526) was considered essential for business customers. Advertising in the national press was rated highly in the UK, Denmark and Germany. Business magazines and inserts scored highest in the Netherlands and Sweden.

Much of this activity is carried out within national boundaries. The number of consumer direct marketers who run large-scale pan-European campaigns are few. These include American Express, Yves Rocher, Polaroid and Mattel. Business-to-business direct marketing activity is more international, with companies such as Rank Xerox, IBM and Hewlett Packard treating Europe as a single market for many years.

Direct marketing activity, including direct mail, telemarketing and telephone banking, is regulated by a European Commission Directive that came into force at the end of 1994. Its main provisions are that:

- suppliers cannot insist upon pre-payments
- consumers must be told the identity of the supplier, the price, quality of the product and any transport changes, the payment and delivery methods, and the period over which the solicitation remains valid
- orders must be met within 30 days unless otherwise indicated
- a cooling-off period of 30 days is mandatory and cold calling by telephone, fax or electronic mail is restricted unless the receiver has given prior consent.

As with all marketing communications, direct marketing campaigns should be integrated both within themselves and with other communication tools such as advertising, publicity and personal selling. Unco-ordinated communication leads to blurred brand images, low impact and customer confusion.

Growth in direct marketing activity

Like other communication areas, such as sales promotion, direct marketing activities have grown over the last 10 years. Smith outlines five factors that have fuelled this rise.[3]

1 Market and media fragmentation

The trend towards market fragmentation has limited the capability of mass-marketing techniques to reach market segments with highly individualized needs. As markets segment, the importance of direct marketing media to target distinct consumer groups with personalized appeals will grow. One growing segment is women in paid employment who have less time to shop. Direct marketing can satisfy their need for speed and convenience through shopping by telephone or mail using a credit card as a mechanism for payment. Also, specialist interest groups (e.g. bird watchers or personal computer enthusiasts) can be reached directly and efficiently by direct mail and by inserts in direct response advertising in specialist magazines.

The growth of specialist media (media fragmentation) has meant that direct response advertising is more effective since market niches can be tightly targeted. The range of specialist magazines in bookshops these days and the emergence of specialist TV channels such as MTV mean that it is easier to reach a closely defined target segment.

2 Developments in technology

The rise in accessibility of computer technology and the increasing sophistication of software, allowing the generation of personalized letters and telephone scripts, has eased the task of direct marketers. Large databases holding detailed information on individuals can be stored, updated and analysed to enhance targeting. Automated telephone systems make it possible to handle dozens of calls simultaneously, reducing the risk of losing potential customers. Furthermore, developments in technology in telephone, cable and satellite television and the Internet have triggered the rise in home-based electronic shopping.

3 The list explosion

The increased supply of lists and their diversity (e.g. 25,000 Rolls-Royce owners, 20,000 women executives, 100,000 house improvers or 800 brand managers in fmcg and service companies) has provided the raw data for direct marketing activities. List brokers act as an intermediary in the supply of lists of names and addresses from list owners (often either companies who have built lists through transactions with their customers, or organizations that have compiled lists specifically for the purpose of renting them). List brokers thus aid the process of finding a suitable list for targeting purposes. Lists are rented usually on a one-time-use basis. To protect the supplier against multiple use by the client, 'seeds' are planted on the list. These are usually employees of the list broking firm who will receive the mailing so that any multiple mailings from a once-only list will easily be identified.

4 Sophisticated analytical techniques

By using geodemographic analysis, households can be classified into a neighbourhood type—for example, 'modern private housing, young families' or 'private flats, single people'. These, in turn, can be cross-referenced with product usage, media usage and lifestyle statements to create market segments that can be targeted by direct mail (geodemographic information contains the postcode for households).

5 Co-ordinated marketing systems

The high costs of personal selling have led an increasing number of companies to take advantage of direct marketing techniques such as direct response advertising and telemarketing to make salesforces more cost-effective. For example, a coupon response advertisement or direct mail may generate leads that can be screened by outbound telemarketing. Alternatively, inbound telemarketing can provide the mechanism for accommodating enquiries stimulated by other direct marketing activities.

Database marketing

At the heart of much direct marketing activity is the marketing database, since direct marketing depends on customer information for its effectiveness. A marketing database is an electronic filing cabinet containing a list of names, addresses, telephone numbers, lifestyle and transactional data. Information such as the types of purchase, frequency of purchase, purchase value and responsiveness to promotional offers may be held.

Database marketing is defined as follows.⁴

> An interactive approach to marketing that uses individually addressable marketing media and channels (such as mail, telephone and the salesforce) to:
> - provide information to a target audience
> - stimulate demand
> - stay close to customers by recording and storing an electronic database memory of customers, prospects and all communication and transactional data.

Some key characteristics of database marketing are that, first, it allows direct communication with customers through a variety of media, including direct mail, telemarketing and direct response advertising. Second, it usually requires the customer to respond in a way that allows the company to take action (such as contact by telephone, sending out literature or arranging sales visits). Third, it must be possible to trace the response back to the original communication.⁵

The computer provides the capability of storing and analysing large quantities of data from diverse sources and presenting information in a convenient, accessible and useful format.⁶ The creation of a database relies on the collection of information on customers, which can be sourced from:

- company records
- responses to sales promotions
- warranty and guarantee cards
- offering samples that require the consumer to give name, address, telephone number, etc.
- enquiries
- exchanging data with other companies
- salesforce records
- application forms (e.g. to join a credit or loyalty scheme)
- complaints
- responses to previous direct marketing activities
- organized events (e.g. wine tastings).

Collecting information is easiest for companies that have direct contact with their customers such as those in financial services or retailing. However, even for those where the sales contact is indirect, building a database is often possible. For example, Seagram, the drinks company, built up a European database through telephone and written enquiries from consumers, sales promotional returns, tastings in store, visits to company premises, exhibitions, and promotions that encouraged consumers to name like-minded friends or colleagues.⁷

Typical information stored on a database

Figure 14.2 shows typical information that is recorded on a database. This is described in more detail below.⁸

Customer and prospect information

This provides the basic data required to access customers and prospects (e.g. name, address, telephone number) and contains their general behavioural characteristics (e.g. psychographic

Figure 14.2 A marketing database

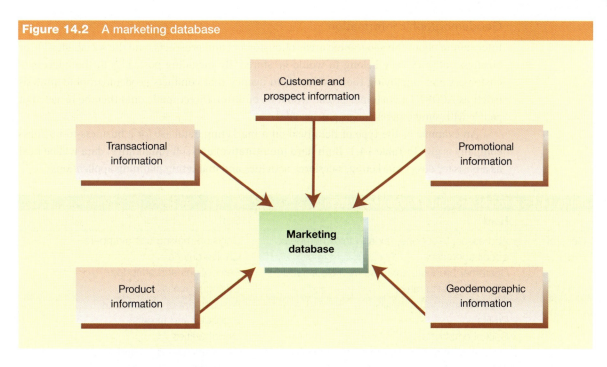

and behavioural data). For organizational markets, information on key decision-makers and influencers, and the choice criteria they use would also be stored.

Transactional information

Past transactions are a key indicator of likely future transactions. Transactional data must be sufficiently detailed to allow FRAC (frequency, recency, amount and category) information to be extracted for each customer. *Frequency* refers to how often a customer buys. Both the average frequency and the trend (is the customer tending to buy more or less frequently?) is of use to the direct marketer. *Recency* measures when the customer last bought. If customers are waiting longer before they rebuy (i.e. recency is increasing) the reasons for this (e.g. less attractive offers or service problems) need to be explored. *Amount* measures how much a customer has bought and is usually recorded in value terms. Analysis of this data may reveal that 20 per cent of customers are accounting for 80 per cent of the value of transactions. Finally, *category* defines the type of product being bought. Cross-analysing category data with type of customer (e.g. geodemographics or lifestyle data) can reveal the customer profile most likely to buy a particular product. Also, promotions can be targeted at those individuals known to be interested in buying from a particular product category.

Promotional information

This covers information on what promotional campaigns have been run, who has responded to them and what the overall results were in terms of contacts, sales and profits. The database will contain information on which customers were targeted, and the media and contact strategy employed.

Product information

This information would include which products have been promoted, who responded, when and from where.

Geodemographic information

Information about the geographic areas of customers and prospects, and the social, lifestyle or business category they belong to would be stored. By including postcodes in the address of customers and employing the services of an agency that conducts geodemographic analysis (such as ACORN) a customer profile would be built up. Direct mail could then be targeted at people with similar geodemographic profiles.

An example of the type of data held on a marketing database for a business-to-business company is give in Table 14.1. Both hard (quantitative) and soft (qualitative) data will be held as a basis for direct marketing, salesforce activities and marketing planning applications.

Table 14.1   A major account information system

	Hard	Soft
General	Addresses, telephone, fax and telex numbers, e-mail addresses Customer products sold and markets served (size and growth rates) Sales volume and revenue Profits Capital employed Operating ratios (e.g. return on capital employed, profit margin)	Decision-making unit members Choice criteria Perceptions and attitudes Buying process Assessment of relationships Problems and threats Opportunities Suppliers' strengths and weaknesses Competitors' strengths and weaknesses Environmental changes affecting account now and in the future
Specific	Suppliers' sales to account by product Suppliers' price levels and profitability by product Details of discounts and allowances Competitors' products, price levels and sales Contract expiry dates	

How might a marketing database be used?

One application is to target those people who are more likely to respond to a direct marketing campaign. For example, a special offer on garden tools from a mail-order company could be targeted at those people who have purchased gardening products in the past. Another example would be a car dealer which, by holding a database of customers' names and addresses and dates of car purchase, could use direct mail to promote service offers and new model launches. Telemarketing campaigns can be targeted in a similar way.

A marketing database can also be used to strengthen relationships with customers. For example, Highland Distillers switched all of its promotional budget for its Macallan whisky brand from advertising to direct marketing. It built a database of 100,000 of its more frequent drinkers (those who consume at least five bottles a year), mailing them every few months with interesting facts about the brand, whisky memorabilia and offers.[9]

Database marketing can be used strategically to improve customer retention with long-term programmes established to maximize customer lifetime value. This issue will be discussed further when we examine customer retention strategies. Many retailers have created loyalty schemes where customers apply for a card that entitles them to discounts but also enables the retailer to record and store transactional data (e.g. which products are bought, their frequency, value, etc.) on an individual basis. Marketing in Action 14.1 shows how a database could be used by a retailer.

14.1 marketing in action

Using a Marketing Database in Retailing

The potential for using marketing databases is enormous, allowing integrated planning of marketing communications. Suppose a retailer wanted to increase sales and profits using a database. How might this happen? First, the retailer analyses its database to find distinct groups of customers for whom the retailer has the potential to offer superior value. The identification of these target market segments allows tailored products, services and communications to be aimed at them.

The purchasing patterns of individuals are established by means of a loyalty card programme. The scheme's main objective is to improve customer loyalty by rewarding varying shopping behaviours differently. The scheme allows customers to be tracked by frequency of visit, expenditure per visit and expenditure per product category. Retailers can gain an understanding of the types of products that are purchased together. For example, Boots, the UK retailer, uses its Advantage card loyalty scheme to conduct these kinds of analyses. One useful finding is that there is a link between buying films and photoframes and the purchase of new baby products. Because its products are organized along category lines it never occurred to the retailer to create a special offer linked to picture frames for the baby products buyer, yet these are the kinds of products new parents are likely to want.

Integrated marketing communications is possible using the marketing database, as the system tracks what marketing communications (e.g. direct mail, promotions) customers are exposed to, and measures the cost-effectiveness of each activity via electronic point of sale data and loyalty cards.

The retailer's customers are classified into market segments based on their potential, their degree of loyalty and whether they are predominantly price- or promotion-sensitive. A different marketing strategy is devised for each group. For example, to trade up high-potential, promotionally sensitive, low-loyalty shoppers who do their main shopping elsewhere, high-value manufacturers' coupons for main shopping products are mailed every two months until the consumer is traded up to a different group. Also, high-loyalty customers can be targeted for special treatment such as receiving a customer magazine.

The Tesco Clubcard also gathers a rich stream of information. It is used to define segments—for example, discount-driven 'price sensitives', 'foodies', 'heavy category users', and 'brand loyalists', testing consumer response to promotions, and testing the effects of different prices. Different regional media selection strategies can be tested by monitoring in-store responses. It is also used to communicate more effectively with consumers. Promotions can be targeted more precisely: for example, targeting dog food offers to dog owners, direct mail can be sent out to targeted segments such as 'healthy living' types, and tailored e-mail campaigns developed. Product assortments in stores can also be fine-tuned according to the buying habits of customers.

The success of the Boots Advantage card and the Tesco Clubcard has prompted the launch of the Nectar loyalty card (see the illustration on page 514). A key difference is that it is a joint initiative, with the founders (Sainsbury's, BP, Barclaycard and Debenhams) quickly being joined by Vodafone, First Quench (which owns Threshers and Bottoms Up off-licences) and Adams (the children's clothes retailer). Within the first six months, 11 million cardholders had been signed up by the original four members. The opportunity to offer attractive rewards to customers, and thereby increase loyalty, as well as the data-gathering opportunities make Nectar an exciting proposition.

Based on: Wilson (1999);[10] James (2003);[11] Mitchell (2002);[12] O'Hara (2003)[13]

Copyright and all intellectual property rights owned by Loyalty Management UK Limited. Advert developed by WCRS/Solid State Industries Limited.
The Nectar loyalty scheme is a joint initiative among several companies.

The main applications of database marketing are as follows.

- *Direct mail*: a database can be used to select customers for mailings.
- *Telemarketing*: a database can store telephone numbers so that customers and prospects can be contacted. Also when customers contact the company by telephone, relevant information can be stored, including when the next contact should be made.
- *Distributor management systems*: a database can be the foundation on which information is provided to distributors and their performance monitored.
- *Loyalty marketing*: highly loyal customers can be selected from the database for special treatment as a reward for their loyalty.
- *Target marketing*: other groups of individuals or businesses can be targeted as a result of analysing the database. For example, buyer behaviour information stored by supermarkets can be used to target special promotions to those individuals likely to be receptive to them. For example, a consumer promotion for wine could be sent to wine drinkers exclusively.
- *Campaign planning*: using the database as a foundation for sending consistent and co-ordinated campaigns and messages to individuals and market segments.
- *Marketing evaluation*: by recording responses to marketing mix inputs (e.g. price promotions, advertising messages and product offers) it is possible to assess how effective different approaches are to varying individuals and market segments.

The development of database marketing has taken a step further with the growth of customer relationship management systems that use databases as the foundation for managing customer relationships. The next section discusses these systems.

Customer relationship management

Customer relationship management (CRM) is a term for the methodologies, technologies and e-commerce capabilities used by firms to manage customer relationships.[14] In particular, CRM software packages aid the interaction between the customer and the company, enabling the company to co-ordinate all of the communication effort so that the customer is presented with a unified message and image. CRM companies offer a range of information technology-based services such as call centres, data analysis and website management. The basic principle behind CRM is that company staff have a single-customer point of view of each client.[15] As customers are now using multiple channels more frequently, they may buy one product from a salesperson and another from a website. A website may provide product information, which is used to buy the product from a distributor. Interactions between a customer and a company may take place through the salesforce, call centres, websites, e-mail, fax services or distributors (see Fig. 14.3).

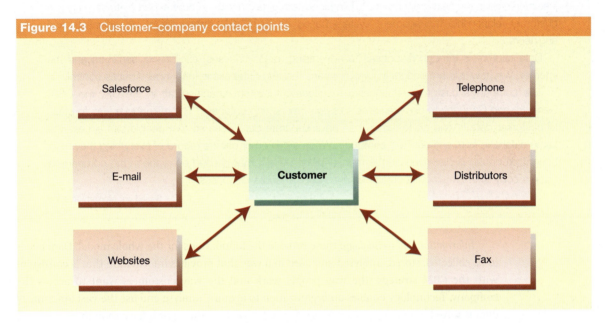

Figure 14.3 Customer–company contact points

Therefore it is crucial that no matter how a customer contacts a company, frontline staff have instant access to the same data about the customer, such as his/her details and past purchases. This usually means the consolidation of the many databases held by individual departments in a company into one centralized database that can be accessed by all relevant staff on a computer screen. E-Marketing 14.1 describes how a CRM system has brought benefits in a business-to-business situation.

Customer relationship management is much more than simply the technology, however. A thorough examination of the CRM process is provided by the QCi customer management model (see Fig. 14.4). This model can be used by companies to understand how well they are managing their customers.[17] Each of the elements of the model will now be discussed.

Analysis and planning: effective CRM begins by understanding the value, attitudes and behaviour of various customers and prospects. Once this has been achieved customers and prospects should be segmented so that planning activity can be as effective as possible. The planning will focus on such areas as the cost-effective retention and acquisition of customers.

Proposition: once segments of customers are identified and understood, the proposition to each segment needs to be defined, and appropriate value-based offers planned. The proposition will be defined in terms of such issues as price, brand and service, and should drive the experience the customer can expect when dealing with the organization, its product and its distributors. The proposition must then be communicated to both customers and the people responsible for delivering it.

14.1 e-marketing

Customer Relationship Management in Business-to-Business Markets

Adept Scientific markets products and services for scientific, technical, mathematical and industrial engineering applications on desktop computers. Its success is based on relationship building: it is not just interested in the next order but in building long-term relationships. A central part of its strategy is a customer relationship management system based on a 300,000-strong list of UK scientists and engineers.

Data capture is through responses to advertising, press releases, exhibitions, seminars and the Internet. Very few lists are bought in, which means that the database is fully under Adept's control.

The company's customer relationship management system enables staff in the UK, the USA, Denmark and Germany to use the same sales and marketing database. The main focus was to place all customer data in one place rather than have separate databases so that people can access the same database from any desktop computer. When a customer calls, a record of everything they have bought previously is displayed on the monitor. When direct mail is used everyone in the company is given a copy of the mailing, its objectives and how to handle responses.

Based on: Morgan (2001)[16]

Information and technology: these provide the foundations for the whole model. Data needs to be collected, stored, analysed and used in a way that provides information that is consistent with the CRM strategy, the way people work and the way customers want to access the company. Technology enables an organization to acquire, analyse and use the vast amounts of data involved in managing customers. It needs to deliver the right information to the relevant people at the right time so that they can achieve their role in managing customers.

People and organization: an organization's frontline staff need to be recruited, trained, developed and motivated to deliver high standards of customer relations. Key elements are an organizational structure that supports effective customer management, role identification, training requirements and resources, and employee satisfaction. It is these 'soft' elements that are so crucial to CRM success, as e-Marketing 14.2 (overleaf) explains.

Process management: in an environment where customer contact can take place at several different points, processes can be difficult to implement and manage. Nevertheless, clear and consistent processes for managing customer relations need to be developed and reviewed in the light of changing customer requirements.

Customer management activity: this concerns the implementation of the plans and processes to deliver the proposition(s) to target segment(s). This involves:

- targeting customer and prospect groups with clearly defined propositions
- enquiry management—this starts as soon as an individual expresses an interest and continues through qualification, lead handling and outcome reporting
- welcoming—this covers new customers and those upgrading their relationship; it covers simple 'thank you' messages to sophisticated contact strategies
- getting to know—customers need to be persuaded to give information about themselves; this information needs to be stored, updated and used; useful information includes attitude and satisfaction information and relationship 'healthchecks'

Figure 14.4 The QCi customer management model

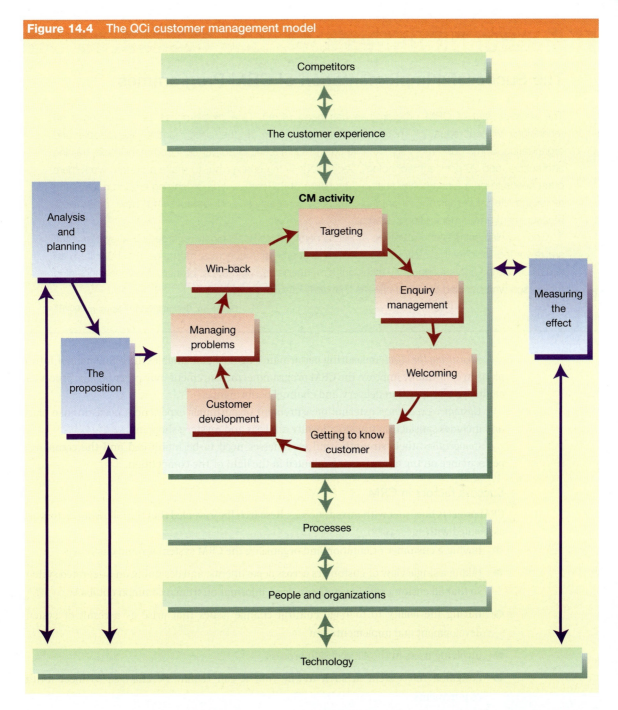

- customer development—decisions need to be made regarding which customers to develop through higher levels of relationship management activity, and which to maintain or drop
- managing problems—this involves early problem identification, complaint handling and 'root cause' analysis to spot general issues that have the potential to cause problems for many customers
- win-back—activities include understanding reasons for loss, deciding which customers to try to win back, and developing win-back programmes that offer lost customers the chance to come back and good reason to do so.

14.2 e-marketing

The Successful Implementation of CRM Programmes

The success rate of CRM programmes has been mixed. One problem has been the focus on technology without equal or more attention being given to the softer factors like people and organization. Some observers estimate that success is a result of 80 per cent communication, training and culture, and 20 per cent technology. Technology is the enabler but to make a system work there often needs to be a fundamental shift in the culture of the company; reorganizing around customers, reviewing decision-making, changing business processes and establishing new objectives, measurement and remuneration systems.

One key element is staff motivation. At HSBC bank, which has a highly regarded CRM system, staff are rewarded for effective customer contact. If a customer requests a mortgage brochure from an HSBC call centre and subsequently takes out a mortgage at a high-street branch, everyone—including the person who handled the initial call—is financially rewarded.

Based on: Gofton (2002);[18] Newing (2002)[19]

Measuring the effect: measuring performance against plan enables the refinement of future plans to continually improve the CRM programme; measurement may cover people, processes, campaigns, proposition delivery and channel performance.

Customer experience: external measurement of customer experiences needs to take place and includes satisfaction tracking, loyalty analysis and mystery shopping.

Competitors: their strengths and weaknesses need to be monitored and the company's performance on the above issues evaluated in the light of the competition.

Success factors in CRM

CRM projects have met with mixed success. Research has revealed that the following factors are associated with success:[20]

- having a customer orientation and organizing the CRM system around customers
- taking a single view of customers across departments, and designing an integrated system so that all customer-facing staff can draw information from a common database
- having the ability to manage cultural change issues that arise as a result of system development and implementation
- involving users in the CRM design process
- designing the system in such a way that it can readily be changed to meet future requirements
- having a board-level champion of the CRM project, and commitment within each of the affected departments to the benefits of taking a single view of the customer and the need for common strategies—for example, prioritizing resources on profitable customers
- creating 'quick wins' to provide positive feedback on the project programmes
- ensuring face-to-face contact (rather than by paper or e-mail) between marketing and IT staff
- piloting the new system before full launch.

Managing a direct marketing campaign

As we shall see, the marketing database is an essential element in creating and managing a direct marketing campaign. However, it is not the starting point for campaign development. As with all promotional campaigns, direct marketing should be fully integrated with all marketing mix elements to provide a coherent *marketing strategy*. Direct marketers need to understand how the product is being *positioned* in the marketplace, which means that its target market and differential advantage must be recognized.

It is crucial that messages sent out as part of a direct marketing campaign do not conflict with those communicated by other channels such as advertising or the salesforce. The integrating mechanism is a clear definition of marketing strategy. Figure 14.5 shows the steps in the management of a direct marketing campaign. Each will now be discussed.

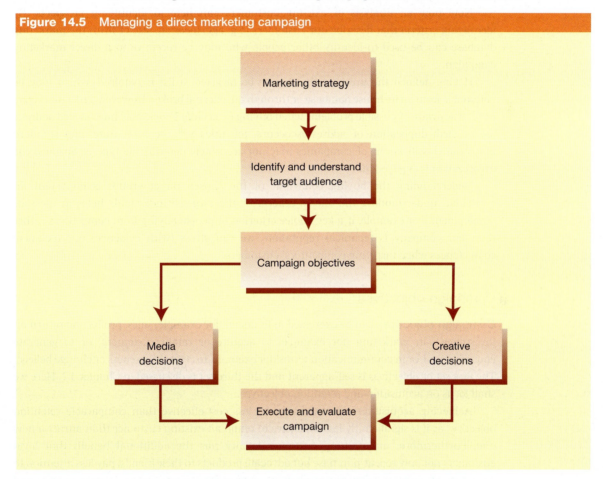

Figure 14.5 Managing a direct marketing campaign

Identify and understand target audience

David Ogilvy, the famous advertising guru, once wrote: 'Never sell to a stranger.' The needs and purchasing behaviour of the target audience must be understood from the start.

The target audience is the group of people at which the direct marketing campaign is aimed. The usual ways of segmenting consumer and organizational markets described in Chapter 7 can be applied.

Companies like Experian provide segmentation breakdowns, such as by lifestyle, that can be used for targeting. However, a particularly useful method of segmentation for direct marketing purposes is as follows.

- *Competitors' customers*: all people who buy the types of product our company produces but from our competitors.
- *Prospects*: people who have not bought from our company before but qualify as potential purchasers (e.g. our customers are large companies, therefore other large companies should be targeted).
- *Enquirers*: people who have contacted the organization and shown interest in one or more products but, as yet, have not bought.
- *Lapsed customers*: people who have purchased in the past but appear to have ceased buying.
- *Referrals*: people who have been recommended to the organization as potential customers.
- *Existing customers*: people who are continuing to buy.

Note how an analysis of existing customers can help in identifying prospects. By identifying criteria that describe our customers (e.g. age, location, size of firm) the marketing database can be used to identify other people who may be receptive to a direct marketing campaign.

Having defined the group(s) that are to be targeted, a list is required, which may be obtainable from an in-house database or through an external broker. However, direct marketers need to be aware of possible problems when buying externally. People may have moved address, job or died; duplication of addresses occurs, job titles may be inaccurate, and standard industrial classifications of companies may not accurately describe the type of business the organization is engaged in.

Understanding the buying behaviour of the chosen target groups is important. In particular, understanding the choice criteria of the targeted individuals helps in message development. For example, if a key choice criterion of people buying from competitors rather than our company is technical reputation, we can stress (with evidence) our technical competences when targeting competitors' customers.

Campaign objectives

Campaign objectives can be expressed in financial (for example, sales, profits and return on investment), in marketing (for example, to acquire or retain customers, or to generate enquiries) and/or in communication terms (for example, to create awareness or change beliefs). The first set of objectives is self-apparent and the third set is discussed in Chapter 12. Here we shall focus on acquisition and retention objectives.

Achieving acquisition objectives may be less cost-effective than comparable retention objectives as it is significantly less expensive to retain an existing customer than attract a new one. Furthermore, maintaining customer loyalty has the additional benefit that loyal customers not only repeat-purchase but advocate products to their friends, pay less attention to competitive brands and often buy product line extensions.[21] Nevertheless, in order to grow and offset lost customers, direct marketing campaigns aimed at attracting new customers are inevitable. When measuring the attractiveness of a potential customer, the concept of *lifetime value* is important. This measures the profits that can be expected from customers over their expected life with a company. Banks know, for example, that gaining student accounts has very high lifetime value since switching between banks is unusual. This means that the allowable marketing cost per acquisition (or how much a company can afford to spend to acquire a new customer) can be quite high. If the calculation was based on potential profits while a student, the figure would be much lower. The establishment of a marketing database can, over time, provide valuable information on buying patterns, which aids the calculation of lifetime value.

Where a marketing database does not hold information on prospects and where external lists are either unavailable or unreliable, another option is 'member-get-member' programmes. Existing members (e.g. of motoring organizations) or customers (e.g. of an insurance company) are incentivized to recruit new people to join or buy from the organization. For example, the Royal Society for the Protection of Birds (RSPB) launched a 'Recruit a Friend and Help Yourself to a Free Pocket Organiser' campaign targeted at young ornithologists. New members were offered free gifts as an incentive to join.

Once acquired, the objective is to retain the business of the customer. This is because keeping customers has a direct impact on profitability. A study conducted by Pricewaterhouse showed that a 2 per cent increase in customer retention has the same profit impact as a 10 per cent reduction in overhead costs.[22] Customer loyalty programmes have blossomed as a result, with direct marketing playing a key role. Retention programmes are aimed at maximizing a customer's lifetime value to the company. Maintaining a long-term relationship with a customer provides the opportunity to up-sell, cross-sell and renew business. Up-selling involves the promotion of higher-value products—for example, a more expensive car. Cross-selling entails the switching of customers to other product categories, as when a music club promotes a book collection. Renewal involves the timing of communication to existing customers when they are about to repurchase. For example, car dealers often send direct mail promotional material two years after the purchase of a car, since many people change cars after that period.

Launched in 1995, Tesco's Clubcard scheme has opened a world of promotional offers to its customers, which has served to enhance repeat buying and customer loyalty.

Often, the achievement of retention objectives depends on the identification of a company's best customers defined in terms of current and potential profitability. FRAC data (discussed earlier in this chapter), which measure purchasing behaviour in terms of frequency (how often), recency (how recent), amount (of what volume and value) and category (what product type) forms the basis of this analysis. The identity and profile of high-value customers are then drawn up. Profiling enables the identification of similar types of individuals or organizations for the achievement of acquisition programmes. Major international airlines have developed frequent-flyer schemes along these lines. Their best customers (often business travellers) are identified by analysis of their database and rewarded for their loyalty. By collecting and analysing data the airlines identify and profile their frequent flyers, learn how best to develop a relationship with them, and attempt to acquire new customers with similar profiles. Databases can therefore be used to segment customers so that the most attractive groups can be targeted with a tailored direct marketing campaign.

The importance of customer retention has prompted many supermarkets to develop store loyalty cards, which are swiped through a machine at the checkout. The loyalty card contains customer information such as the name and address of the individual, so that purchasing data, such as expenditure per visit, the range of products purchased, the brands purchased, when and how often the customer shops and which branch was used can be linked to individuals. This means that supermarkets such as Tesco and Sainsbury's in the UK know what sort of products and services to offer in different stores and to different customers. One proponent of loyalty schemes claimed, 'Profiling based on spend, frequency and product gives more information about a customer than knowing where someone lives or what their salary is. We won't need demographic information any more.'[23]

Direct mail can be used to send targeted promotional offers to people who are known to purchase from a particular product category. For example, a special offer for an Australian red wine could be sent to people who are known to drink red wine. Tesco's Clubcard scheme began in 1995 and has been widely regarded as successful. Customers accumulate points that are electronically added to the card when it is swiped at the checkout. Effectively, points mean money off future purchases at the checkout (plus other promotional offers). Thus the more money a customer spends the greater the points and the higher the discounts on future purchases. This process, it is claimed, generates higher rates of repeat buying and loyalty benefiting the store, as well as providing in-depth purchasing data.

Despite their growth in such industries as petrol retailing, airlines (see the illustration), supermarkets and hotels, loyalty schemes have attracted their critics. Loyalty schemes may simply raise the cost of doing business and, if competitors respond with 'me-toos', the final outcome may be no more than minor tactical advantages.[24] The costs are usually very high when technology, software, staff training, administration, communications and the costs of the rewards are taken into account. Shell, for example, is reported to have spent £20 million (€28.8 million) on hardware and software alone to support its Smart card, which allows drivers to collect points when purchasing petrol.[25] The danger is that loyalty schemes cost too much when price has become more important in the competitive arena.[26] A second criticism is that the proliferation of loyalty schemes is teaching consumers promiscuity. Evidence from a MORI poll found that 25 per cent of loyalty card holders are ready to switch to a rival scheme if it has better benefits.[27] Far from seeing a loyalty scheme as a reason to stay with a retailer, consumers may be using such schemes as criteria for switching. Third, the basis of loyalty schemes, rewarding loyal customers, is questioned. A company that has a band of loyal customers is presumably already doing something right. Rather than giving them discounts, why not do more of that (e.g. wide product range, better service)? Even if loyal customers spend a little more, do the extra revenues justify the extra costs? Nevertheless, loyalty schemes are seen by many companies as an essential element in doing business. What needs to be questioned by marketing managers is whether exceptional loyalty can be expected from such schemes, what are the true costs and whether focusing on a select group of customers (as with frequent-flyer schemes) leads to the neglect of others.

Loyalty programmes are popular with airlines such as KLM.

Media decisions

Direct marketers have a large number of media which they can use to reach customers and prospects. Each of the major media will now be examined.

Direct mail

Direct mail is material sent through the postal service to the recipient's home or business address with the purpose of promoting a product and/or maintaining an ongoing relationship. Direct mail at its best allows close targeting of individuals in a way not possible using mass advertising media. For example, Heinz employs direct mail to target its customers and prospects. Since it markets 360 products, above-the-line advertising for all of them is impossible. By creating a database based on responses to promotions, lifestyle questionnaires and rented lists, Heinz has built a file of 4.6 million households. Each one now receives the four-times-a-year 'At Home' mailpack, which has been further segmented to reflect loyalty and frequency of purchase. Product and nutritional information is combined with coupons to achieve product trials.[28] Skoda has also used direct mail successfully. Cold prospects were sent a Skoda badge (see the illustration) inviting them to 'live with it for a while' and were encouraged to take the rest of the car for a test drive when they were comfortable with the badge. Research showed that negative feeling towards the brand dropped from 42 per cent to 34 per cent of car buyers, partly as a result of this direct mail campaign.

An award-winning direct mail campaign featuring a Skoda badge.

A major advantage of direct mail is its cost. For example, in business-to-business marketing, it might cost £50 (€72) to visit potential customers, £5 (€7.2) to telephone them but less than £1 (€1.44) to send out a mailing.[29]

A key factor in the effectiveness of a direct mail campaign is the quality of the mailing list. Mailing lists are variable in quality. For example, in one year in the UK, 100 million items were sent back marked 'return to sender'.[30] List houses supply lists on a rental or purchase basis. Since lists go out of date quickly, it is usually preferable to rent. *Consumer lists* may be compiled from subscriptions to magazines, catalogues, membership of organizations, etc. Alternatively, consumer lifestyle lists are compiled from questionnaires. The electoral roll can also be useful when combined with geodemographic analysis. For example, if a company wished to target households living in modern private housing with young families, the electoral roll can be used to provide the names and addresses of people living in such areas.

One problem with consumer lists is people moving house and dying. Specialized data-suppression services, such as the 'gone away suppression file' offered by the REaD Group, can reduce this difficulty. It claims to identify over 94 per cent of all home movements and over 80 per cent of deceased people.[31] *Business-to-business lists* may be bought from directory producers such as the *Kompass* or *Key British Enterprises* directories, from trade magazine subscription lists (e.g. *Chemicals* or *Purchasing Managers' Gazette*) or from exhibition lists (e.g. Which Computer Show). Perhaps the most productive mailing list is that of a company's own customers: the *house list*. This is because of the existing relationship that a company enjoys with its own customers. Also of use would be the names of past buyers who have become inactive, enquirers, and those who have been referred or recommended by present customers of the company. It is not uncommon for a house list to be far more productive than an outside-compiled list.[32] Customer behaviour such as products purchased, recency, frequency and expenditure can also be stored on the database.

The management of direct mail involves asking the following five questions.[33]

1. *Who?* Who is the target market? Who are we trying to influence? The illustration featuring Saab is an example of a closely targeted campaign.

2. *What?* What response is required? A sale, an enquiry?

③ *Why?* Why should they buy or make an enquiry? Is it because our product is faster, cheaper, or whatever?

④ *Where?* Where can they be reached? Can we obtain their home or work address?

⑤ *When?* When is the best time to reach them? Often this is weekends for consumers, and Tuesday, Wednesday or Thursday for businesspeople (Monday can be dominated by planning meetings and on Friday they may be busy clearing their desks for the weekend).

This award-winning direct mail campaign for Saab closely targeted fortysomething professionals. They were sent a map of Europe accompanied by a pin and informed that, wherever they were driving to—whether it be the supermarket or the south of France—the Saab 9–5 would provide the most rewarding driving experience.

Other management issues include the organization required for addressing and filling the envelopes; *mailing houses* provide these services, and for large mailings the postal service needs to be notified so that the mailing can be scheduled.

Direct mail allows *specific targeting to named individuals*. For example, by hiring lists of subscribers to gardening catalogues a manufacturer of gardening equipment could target a specific group of people that would be more likely to be interested in a promotional offer than the public in general. *Elaborate personalization* is possible and the results directly measurable. Since the objective of direct mail is immediate—usually a sale or an enquiry—success can easily be measured. Some organizations, such as Reader's Digest, spend money researching alternative creative approaches before embarking on a large-scale mailing. Such factors as type of promotional offer, headlines, visuals and copy can be varied in a systematic manner, and by using code numbers on reply coupons response can be tied to the associated creative approach.

The effectiveness of direct mail relies heavily on the quality of the list. Poor lists raise costs and can contribute to the criticism of *junk mail* since recipients are not interested in the contents of the mailing. *Initial costs* can be much higher than advertising in terms of cost per thousand people reached, and response can be low (an average response rate of 2 per cent is often quoted). Added to these costs is the expense of setting up a database. In these terms direct mail should be viewed as a medium- to long-term tool for generating repeat business from a carefully targeted customer group. An important concept is the *lifetime value of a customer*, which is the profit made on a customer's purchase over the customer's lifetime.

Some enlightened companies are taking steps to improve the effectiveness of their direct mail by more focused targeting. Marketing in Action 14.2 describes how Toyota is changing its direct mail strategy.

14.2 marketing in action

Toyota Targets the Responsive Car Buyer

Anyone who has suffered the unfocused direct mail campaigns from the financial services industry trying to sell credit cards and loans will be delighted to hear that Toyota is employing a different strategy. Its previous strategy was to send 'cold' mailings to millions of people who had never made contact with the company.

The problem was that only 10 per cent of people are looking for a car at any one time. Also research has shown that, even for popular brands like Volkswagen, only 20 per cent of these potential buyers would consider purchasing that brand of car. The result was that cold direct mail in the automotive sector was likely to catch the wrong people at the wrong time. Toyota was concerned that not only were such mass mailings costly but they might damage the company's brand image.

The new approach is to support above-the-line advertising with carefully targeted direct mail to 'brand considerers': people who have contacted Toyota in the past through media such as its website, showrooms or by telephone. David Miller, a partner in Toyota's direct marketing agency comments, 'Our role will be to maximize conversion. What we are not doing is sending out cold direct mail to people who may not be in the market or be interested in the Toyota brand. It's just a waste of money.'

This enlightened approach will not only save Toyota money, it will remove the danger of its direct mailings tarnishing its brand image. With direct mail response rates running at around 3 per cent, brand owners must always ask the question 'What damage am I doing to my brand among the other 97 per cent?'

Based on: Benady (2002);[34] Charles (2002)[35]

The UK direct mail industry is regarded as one of the most professional, with a reputation for adopting new mailing techniques quickly. Figure 14.6 (overleaf) shows the volume of direct mail in 12 European countries.

In central and eastern Europe, consumer and business reaction to direct mail is almost always positive. It is seen as something new, interesting and important. Practical, factual appeals work best. For example, the benefit may refer to a family's health or a company's access to capital. The major problem of direct mail in this region is the poor quality of the mailing lists.[36]

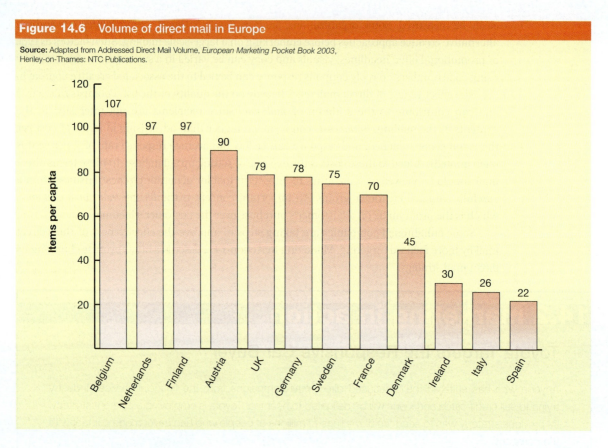

Figure 14.6 Volume of direct mail in Europe

Source: Adapted from Addressed Direct Mail Volume, *European Marketing Pocket Book 2003*, Henley-on-Thames: NTC Publications.

Telemarketing

Telemarketing is a marketing communication system where trained specialists use telecommunications and information technologies to conduct marketing and sales activities.

Inbound telemarketing occurs when a prospect contacts the company by telephone, whereas outbound telemarketing involves the company calling the prospect. Developments in IT have affected both forms. For example, Quick Address is a package that enables telemarketing people handling inbound calls to quickly identify the address and account details of the caller with the minimum amount of typing time, and also ensure it is accurate. The caller is asked for their name and postcode (either for the household or company). From this, the correct address will appear on the computer screen. If the caller wishes to purchase (using a credit card, for example) over the telephone, the tedium of giving (and spelling) their address to allow postage is removed. This has gained penetration in such areas as selling football or theatre tickets. Even more sophisticated developments in telecommunications technology allow the caller to be identified even before the agent has answered the call. The caller's telephone number is relayed into the customer database and outlet details appear on the agent's screen before the call is picked up. This service (called *integrated telephony*) has gained penetration in the customer service area.

An integrated telemarketing package would, in response to an incoming call, bring up the customer's file on the computer screen, record the order, check stocks, and provide field salespeople with updated inventory information and estimated delivery times.

A more controversial technological development is the use of interactive voice response (IVR), where the caller talks to a machine rather than a person. IVR is beneficial when the nature of calls is specific such as a brochure request. It can also be used to cover busy periods including the period following a direct response television advertisement. When the majority of callers want the same basic information, IVR permits this to be provided quickly and accurately. It is sometimes used in conjunction with a personalized service when a caller requires it. The main disadvantage of the approach is some callers may dislike dealing with a machine and prefer to talk to a person. Also some queries may not be covered by the automated service.[37]

Computerization can also enhance productivity in outbound telemarketing. Large databases can store information that can easily be accessed by telemarketing agents. Call lists can be allocated to agents automatically. Scripts can be created and stored on the computer so that operators have ready and convenient access to them on-screen. Orders can be processed automatically and follow-up actions (such as call-back in one month or send literature) can be recorded and stored. In addition, productivity can be raised by auto-diallers.

A major technological advance is predictive dialling, which makes multiple outbound calls from a call centre. Calls are only delivered to agents when the customer answers, therefore cutting out wasted calls to answer machines, engaged signals, fax machines and unanswered calls. It is claimed to dramatically improve call centre efficiency by providing agents with a constant flow of calls. However, agents get no time to psych themselves up for the call (they are alerted by a bleep and the relevant details appear on a screen). Call centre staff have to work extremely intensively.[38]

Telemarketing automation also allows simple keystroke retrieval of critical information such as customer history, product information or schedules. If the prospect or customer is busy, automated systems can reschedule a callback and allow the operator to recall the contact on screen at a later date simply by pressing a single key.

The versatility of telemarketing

Telemarketing can be used in a number of roles, and it is this versatility that has seen telemarketing activities grow in recent years. Its major roles are those described below.

Direct selling: when the sales potential of a customer does not justify a face-to-face call from a salesperson, telemarketing can be used to service the account. The telephone call may simply take the form of an enquiry about a re-ordering possibility, and as such does not require complex sales arguments that need face-to-face interaction. Alternatively, an inbound telephone call may be the means of placing an order in response to a direct mail or television advertising campaign. For example, freefone facilities are often used for order placing in conjunction with the advertising of record collections on television.

Supporting the salesforce: customers may find contacting the field salesforce difficult given the nature of their job. A telemarketing operation can provide a communications link to the salesforce, and an enquiry- or order-handling function. In this way customers know that there is someone at the supplier company who they can contact easily if they have a problem, enquiry or wish to place an order.

Generating and screening leads: an outbound telemarketing team can be used to establish contact with prospective customers and attempt to arrange a salesforce visit. Alternatively, it can be used to screen leads that have been generated by direct mail or coupon response to advertising. People who have requested further information can be contacted by telephone to ascertain their potential (qualifying a lead) and, if qualified, to try to arrange a salesforce visit.

Marketing database building and updating: a secondary source of information, such as a directory, can provide a list of companies that partially qualify them for inclusion in a marketing database. However, the telephone may be required to check that they fulfil other conditions. For example, one criterion may be that they are textile companies. A directory such as *Kompass* may be used to identify them; however, a telephone call may be necessary to check that they have a marketing department, which may be a second condition for entry on to the database. The updating (*cleaning*) of lists may require a telephone call, for example, to check that the name of the marketing director on the database is accurate.

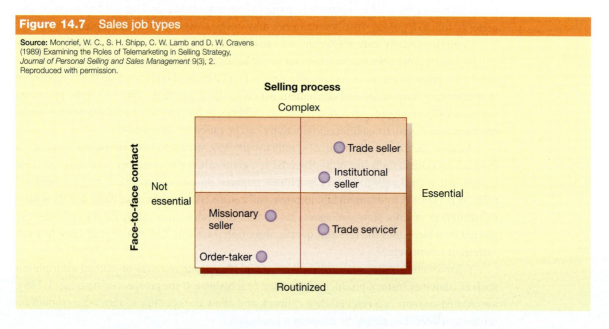

Figure 14.7 Sales job types

Source: Moncrief, W. C., S. H. Shipp, C. W. Lamb and D. W. Cravens (1989) Examining the Roles of Telemarketing in Selling Strategy, *Journal of Personal Selling and Sales Management* 9(3), 2. Reproduced with permission.

Applications of telemarketing

When used professionally, telemarketing can be a most cost-efficient, flexible and accountable medium.[39] The telephone permits two-way dialogue that is instantaneous, personal and flexible, albeit not face to face.

As we have seen, telemarketing is often linked to field selling activities. The link between telemarketing and five field job types was developed by Moncrief.[40] The job types were described in terms of the amount of face-to-face contact required and the complexity of the selling process. The face-to-face contact (horizontal dimension) of Fig. 14.7 is particularly useful to illustrate the possible roles of telemarketing in selling strategy.

The missionary seller (making new initial customer contact) and the order-taker job types offer potential opportunities of using telemarketers as the organization's primary salesforce. The role of telemarketing in the institutional seller, trade servicer and trade seller job categories is to supplement field selling efforts. The more routinized the selling process (the vertical dimension of Fig. 14.7), the more likely telemarketing is to make an important supplemental contribution to face-to-face selling. An assessment of the need for face-to-face contact indicates whether telemarketing is appropriate in a supporting and/or a primary role in an organization's selling strategy. In some selling situations, both primary and supporting telemarketing strategies may be appropriate.

Telemarketing as a supporting role: the need for this role occurs when face-to-face contact is required, but selected buyer–seller activities can be accomplished by telemarketing personnel. These activities may include taking orders and handling re-orders. Successful implementation of a telemarketing support effort requires close co-ordination of field and telemarketing salespeople. Moncrief *et al.* point out that research suggests that the supporting role creates a major organizational design task, and resistance from field personnel will be likely to occur.[41] A carefully formulated plan is essential to assure co-operation of telemarketing and the field salesforce. When face-to-face interaction is needed, telemarketing plays a secondary role in selling strategy.

Primary role: telemarketing can provide a complete sales and customer support effort for selling situations in which face-to-face contact is not required. Conditions that suggest using telemarketing in a primary role include a routinized selling process, low cash value of purchases, a large and widely dispersed customer base, and non-technical products. Regardless of other considerations, a significant factor in deciding not to use face-to-face contact lies in the cost of field sales calls and the margins available to cover these costs.

Combination role: some companies have adopted selling strategies that utilize telemarketing in both supporting and primary roles. Organizations that may benefit from this strategy are those with large and widely dispersed customer bases, whose purchasers range from very small accounts to very large accounts. The accounts signed to the primary telemarketing functions are those that cannot economically be served on a face-to-face basis. Telemarketers often have primary responsibility for smaller customers and provide backup services for other customers when face-to-face salespeople are not available.

No role: importantly, certain selling situations are not appropriate for any type of telemarketing support. Conditions that may require face-to-face customer contact by a field salesperson greatly reduce or eliminate telemarketing's value—for example, where the selling process complexity, contact requirements and importance of the purchase demand face-to-face contact.

Guidelines for telemarketing

An eight-step guide to telephone selling has been published by the Bell Telephone System of America. It runs as follows.[42]

1. Identify yourself and your company.
2. Establish rapport: this should come naturally since you have already researched your potential clients and their business.
3. Make an interesting comment (e.g. to do with cost savings or a special offer).
4. Deliver your sales message: emphasize benefits over features (e.g. your production people will like it because it helps to overcome downtime through waiting for the material to set).
5. Overcome objections: be skilled at objection-handling techniques.
6. Close the sale: when appropriate do not be afraid to ask for the order (e.g. 'Would you like to place an order now?') or fulfil another sales objective (e.g. 'Can I send you a sample?').
7. Action agreement: arrange for a sales call or the next telephone call.
8. Express your thanks.

The advantages of telemarketing

There are a number of reasons why telemarketing has grown in recent years. First, it has lower costs per contact than a face-to-face salesperson visit. Second, it is less time consuming than personal visits. Third, the growth in telephone ownership has increased access to households, and the use of toll-free lines (800 or 0800 numbers) has reduced the cost of responding by telephone. Next, the increasing sophistication of new telecommunications technology has encouraged companies to employ telemarketing techniques. For example, digital networks allow the seamless transfer of calls between organizations. The software company Microsoft and its telemarketing agency can smoothly transfer calls between their respective offices. If the caller then asks for complex technical information it can be transferred back to the relevant Microsoft department.[43] Finally, despite the reduced costs (compared to a personal visit) the telephone retains the advantage of two-way communication.

The disadvantages of telemarketing

Telemarketing is not a panacea since it suffers from a number of disadvantages. First, it lacks the visual impact of a personal visit and it is not possible to assess the mood or reactions of the buyer through observing body language, especially facial expressions. It is easier for a customer to react negatively over the telephone and the number of rejections can be high. Telephone selling can be considered intrusive and some people may object to receiving unsolicited telephone calls. Finally, although cost per contact is cheaper than a personal sales call, it is more expensive than direct mail or media advertising. Labour costs can be high, although computerized answering can cut the cost of receiving incoming calls.

A threat to the continuing growth of telemarketing is the growth of the Internet. E-Marketing 14.3 discusses some of the issues involved.

14.3 e-marketing

Telemarketing Versus the Web

One of the key driving forces behind the growth of telemarketing has been the reduction in costs, allowing expensive salespeople and retail outlets to be replaced with cheaper telephone-based services. Huge call centres where perhaps a hundred people operate telephones, making and receiving calls, have emerged. Now the same logic is being applied to the replacement of call centres with websites. Customers communicating with companies via e-mail can drastically cut the volume of telephone traffic, and companies are eager to encourage such a change. One industry observer estimates that at the moment it costs about 65p (€0.93) per transaction in an outlet, 32p (€0.46) per telephone transaction and 2.5p (€0.36) per Internet transaction.

Many companies are encouraging Internet bookings. For example, airlines such as easyJet and Ryanair, and financial services companies such as Egg and First Direct, have set up systems to enable transactions to be carried out on the Internet.

These trends have been closely monitored by telemarketing bureaux. Their response has been to develop call centres into contact centres. These offer a full package of telephone, e-mail, fax, web chat, web self-service and web enquiries. Web self-service uses a section of the client's website to give out automatic responses to standard questions, which frees up the operator's time to deal with more complex enquiries. This means that contact centres like those for Cisco could handle a situation where a customer rings to ask about an e-mail he/she sent regarding an order placed on Cisco's website.

Based on: Booth (1999);[44] Moran (2002);[45] Murphy (2002);[46] Reed (1999)[47]

Mobile marketing

Mobile marketing (the sending of short text messages direct to mobile phones) is extremely successful. Every month in the UK over a billion chargeable text messages are sent. Marketers have been quick to spot the opportunities of this medium to communicate, particularly to a youth audience. Marketers now send out messages to potential customers via their mobile phones to promote such products as fast food, movies, banks, alcoholic drinks, magazines and books. A new acronym, SMS (short messaging service) has appeared to describe this new medium, which is available on all mobile phones that use the global system for mobile communications (GMS), which dominates the second generation (2G) standard.[48] The advantages of this approach for marketers are as follows.[49]

- *Cost effective*: the cost per message is between 15p (€0.22) and 25p (€0.36) compared with 50p (€0.72) to 75p (€1.1) per direct mail shot, including print production and postage.

- *Personalized*: like direct mail each message is sent to individuals, in contrast to traditional advertising.

- *Targeting*: given that SMS use among 15–25 year olds is 86 per cent, and 87 per cent among 25–34 year olds in the UK, mobile marketing has high potential as a youth targeting tool.[50]

- *Interactive*: the receiver can respond to the text message, setting up the opportunity for two-way dialogue.

- *Customer relationship building*: by establishing an ongoing dialogue with consumers it can aid the relationship-building process.

- *Time flexible*: unlike direct mail, mobile marketing can be sent at various times of the day, giving greater flexibility when trying to reach the recipient.

- *Immediate and measurable*: the results of the mobile campaign can be immediate (for example, the number of people taking up an offer) and the results measurable.

- *Database building*: creative use of mobile marketing allows marketers to gather consumer information, which can be stored on a database.

To illustrate some of these advantages, Marketing in Action 14.3 describes how Cadbury and Kiss 100, a radio station, use mobile marketing.

14.3 marketing in action

Mobile Marketing at Cadbury and Kiss

Mobile marketing can be used for short-term promotional purposes and for long-term relationship building. An example of the former is the promotional campaign run by Cadbury. A total of 65 million Cadbury chocolate bars (brands included Crunchie, Caramel, Time Out and Dairy Milk) carried a promotion inviting consumers to 'text and win'. The prizes were worth £1 million (€1.44 million) and included 100 chances to win £5000 (€7200) in cash, widescreen televisions, PlayStations, DVD players, Palm Pilots and CDs. Almost 5 million text responses were received. Each wrapper contained a code, which the person texted in, and a winner or loser message was flashed back.

Although this highly successful campaign was primarily designed to boost sales, Cadbury received a further bonus. It was possible to tell which of the brands the response was linked to. Also the time of consumption could be measured, assuming the response came straight after the chocolate bar was consumed. This meant that consumption could be correlated with external factors such as the weather.

Kiss 100 is a London-based radio station that targets the youth market. It uses mobile marketing to build long-term relationships with listeners and to add a 'fun' element to that relationship. At the heart of the process is the HeySexy database. In order to join the database, listeners either text in their details, call the phone line or subscribe via the Kiss website. Information on gender and date of birth is gathered, and all channels have prompts for members to 'unsubscribe' if they so wish.

The main purpose of the database is to encourage listening and loyalty. 'Listen-to-win' methods encourage members to tune in, and prizes include SMS games, offers and competitions. For example, a 'Text to win' competition invited Kiss listeners to text in when a particular record was played. Other relationship-building initiatives were a highly popular text greeting from a Kiss DJ on each member's birthday, and an anonymous Valentine's Day service. Listeners texted in the mobile number of their loved one with a message, to be forwarded by Kiss. This resulted in almost 4000 messages being sent, including several marriage proposals and one acceptance!

Based on: Cowlett (2002);[51] Reid (2002)[52]

Mobile marketing does have certain limitations though.[53] These are as follows.

- *Short text messages*: the number of words in a text message is limited to 160 characters. Future technological advances may remove this limitation.
- *Visually unexciting*: 2G systems do not permit picture messaging. Although multimedia messaging services and 3G technology allow picture messaging, the extra cost may deter its widespread use.
- *Wear-off*: while mobile marketing is still novel, response rates are good, but sceptics argue that once the novelty has worn off and consumers receive more and more advertising/promotion-related messages the effectiveness of the medium will wane.
- *Poor targeting*: as with poorly targeted direct mail, 'junk' text messages cause customer annoyance and lead to poor response rates.

An important consideration as mobile marketing develops is gaining consumer acceptance. A number of key rules should be followed, as outlined below.[54]

- *Permission*: mobile communications are very personal and any unwelcome intrusion runs the risk of consumer rejection. Therefore, permission-based mobile marketing is essential when using mobile phones as communication channels. In the UK, the Mobile Marketing Association (MMA) was set up to ensure that consumers were protected from spamming. Three sets of regulations govern mobile marketing: the Data Protection Act, the MMA code of conduct and the New Electronic Communications Directive. The Data Protection Act requires companies to indicate how often they will be communicating to people and also what types of message will be sent. All consumers must have a clear and easy way of opting out (e.g. using SMS or the web). The MMA code of conduct states that mobile marketing must be an opt-in system with a clear and free opt-out route. The New Electronic Communications Directive states that mobile marketing must be an opt-in system with a clear and free opt-out route.
- *Targeting*: since mobile phones are extremely personal devices with the brand, fascia colour, size and ringtone reflecting, often, the owner's personality, messages sent to consumers via the phone must be highly relevant and targeted. This can be achieved through direct communication, or by using Mosaic or Prizm lifestyle segmentation data.
- *Value added*: the communication should be of value to the recipient. This can take the form of entertainment or special access to products and information.
- *Interactive*: mobile marketing should engage consumers in a two-way dialogue. Today's youth love to talk back, and often demand the right to talk back to the message sender. Rather than developing one-way 'push' campaigns, companies should explore the possibilities of integrating voice and text-based games, images and sounds to take full advantages of this developing medium.

At the moment, mobile marketing is not just acceptable, it is actually popular. Research by the Mobile Marketing Association showed that 68 per cent of consumers would be likely to recommend the service to their friends, and 43 per cent said they would respond to messages positively, perhaps by visiting a website or viewing an advertisement.[55]

Direct response advertising

Direct response advertising appears in the prime media, such as television, newspapers and magazines, but differs from standard advertising as it is designed to elicit a direct response such as an order, enquiry or request for a visit. Often a freefone telephone number is included in the advertisement or for the print media a response coupon is used. This mechanism combines the ability of broadcast media to reach large sections of the population with direct marketing techniques that allow a swift response on behalf of both prospect and company.

Most telephone numbers are just tacked on to the end of an advertisement. There are a few examples, though, where the telephone number or call for action has been incorporated into the creative treatment. The most notable are the creative use of numbers such as 40 40 40 by the leisure group Forte and 2-8 2-8 2-0 (mimicking the sound of an owl) by the insurance company Guardian Royal Exchange, which has an owl as its emblem.

Direct response television (or interactive television as it is sometimes called) has experienced fast growth. It is an industry worth £3 billion (€4.3 billion) globally and comes in many formats. The most basic is the standard advertisement with telephone number; 60-, 90- or 120-second advertisements are sometimes used to provide the necessary information to persuade viewers to use the freefone number for ordering. Other variants are 25-minute product demonstrations (generally referred to as infomercials) and live home shopping programmes broadcast by companies such as QVC.

Not all direct response television is focused on immediate sales. As was discussed in Chapter 12, on advertising, the format may be a standard advertisement on a digital channel, which requires the viewer to press the red button on the remote control handset to access further information and/or request a brochure or free sample. Another form is the interactive television advertisement that allows access to the Internet. This relies on digital technology and connection to a telephone line. The advantage is that marketers can get direct response to a mass-market advertisement, but whether viewers will interrupt their programme viewing to surf the web is questionable.[56]

A popular misconception regarding direct response television (DRTV) is that it is suitable only for products such as music compilations and cut-price jewellery. In Europe, a wide range of products is marketed (such as leisure and fitness products, motoring and household goods, books and beauty care products) through pan-European satellite channels such as Eurosport, Super Channel and NBC. Quantum International, the European market leader in this field, has adopted a strategy of marketing products not yet available through other outlets. As with other media, DRTV has to adapt to local cultural variations. For example, in the UK, the credit card is an accepted method of payment, while in Germany there is a reluctance to use this method. This means that Quantum's UK operation is based on payments by credit card, while cash is used in its German counterpart.[57]

Four circumstances increase the likelihood of DRTV application and success.

1. Goods that benefit from demonstration or a service that needs to be explained.
2. A product that has mass consumer appeal (although specialist products could be placed on a single-interest channel).
3. A good DRTV promotion must make good television to attract and maintain the interest of the audience.
4. DRTV should be supported by an efficient telemarketing operation to handle the response generated by the advertisement.

Catalogue marketing

Catalogue marketing is the sale of products through catalogues distributed to agents and customers, usually by mail or at stores if the catalogue marketer is a store owner. Catalogue marketing is popular in Europe, with such organizations as Otto Versand and Quelle Schikedanz (Germany), GUS and Next Directory (UK) and Trois Suisse and La Redoute (France). Many of them operate in a number of countries: La Redoute, for instance, has operations in

France, Belgium, Norway, Spain and Portugal, and Trois Suisse operates in France, the Netherlands, Belgium, Austria, Germany, Italy, Spain, Portugal and the UK. Catalogue marketing is popular in Austria because legislation restricts retail opening hours.[58]

A common form of catalogue marketing is mail order, where catalogues are distributed and, traditionally, orders received by mail. This form of marketing suffered from an old-fashioned downmarket image and was based on an agency system where agents passed around the catalogue among friends and relatives, collecting and sending orders to the mail-order company in return for commission. Delivery was slow (up to 28 days) and the range of merchandise usually targeted at lower-status social groups who valued the credit facility of weekly payment. Some enterprising companies, notably Next and Trois Suisse, saw catalogue marketing as an opportunity to reach a new target market: busy, affluent, middle-class people, who valued the convenience of choosing products at home.

Marketing in Action 14.4 describes how Next and other upmarket niche retailers have successfully moved into catalogue marketing.

14.4 marketing in action

Niche Marketing with Catalogues

Short on time, bothered about standards and more concerned with quality than price, today's consumer is driving the growth of upmarket niche catalogue marketing. The clothing retailer Next was the first to exploit this new marketing opportunity and others have followed in its path.

One such company is Boden, which is now a £40 million a year business with a database of around 200,000 active shoppers. It was founded in 1991 using catalogues to market menswear and has now expanded, with separate catalogues for women, children and babies. Its target market is affluent families with children and two working parents. The convenience of home shopping is highly valued by them.

Other companies that have been successful in targeting affluent, aspirational consumers using catalogue marketing are Ocean (home furnishings), and the White Company (linen). Target consumers are those who are prepared to pay a little more for high-quality, stylish products. All of those mentioned above are direct catalogue retailers, rejecting the use of agents in favour of supplying catalogues directly to consumers.

Based on: Voyle (2001)[59]

The Next Directory story is an example of how store retailers can use catalogue marketing to reach a wider range of customers. Laura Ashley, Habitat and Marks & Spencer are other examples, some of which charge for their catalogues. Some retailers, notably Argos in the UK, base their entire operation on a catalogue; a wide range of products, including household goods, cameras, jewellery, toys, mobile phones, furniture and gardening equipment, is sold through the Argos catalogue. A customer can select at home, visit a catalogue shop where only a restricted selection of goods is on display and purchase products instantly. Argos's success is based on low prices and an efficient service and inventory system that controls costs and ensures a low out-of-stock situation.

When used effectively, catalogue marketing to consumers provides a convenient way of selecting products at home that allows discussion between family members in a relaxed atmosphere away from crowded shops and streets. Often, credit facilities are available. For remote rural locations it provides a valuable service, obviating the necessity to travel long distances to town shopping centres. For catalogue marketers, the expense of high-street locations is removed and there is the opportunity to display a wider range of products than could feasibly be achieved in a shop. Distribution can be centralized, lowering costs. Nevertheless, catalogues are expensive to produce (hence the need for some retailers to charge for them) and they require regular updating, particularly when selling fashion items. They do not allow goods to be tried (e.g. a vacuum cleaner) or tried on (e.g. clothing) before purchase. Although products can be seen in the catalogue, variations in colour printing can mean that the curtains or suite that are delivered do not have exactly the same colour tones as those that appear on the printed page.

Catalogue marketers have taken full advantage of the potential of database marketing to segment their customers, record purchasing behaviour (types of products bought, when, sizes, etc.) and monitor creditworthiness. Some develop 'scoring systems' to enable them to predict the chances of payment defaults, high merchandise return ratios and low ordering rates, based on an individual's location and personal characteristics.[60]

Catalogues are also important in business-to-business markets. They provide an invaluable aid to the salesperson when calling on customers and, when in their hands, are a perpetual sales aid, acting as a reference book and allowing them to select and order at their convenience (often by telephone). Many companies place their catalogue on their website so that it is readily available to customers.

Business-to-business catalogues often contain an enormous amount of information, such as product specifications and prices. Once in the hands of customers and prospects, direct mail and telemarketing campaigns can be used to persuade them to consult their catalogues. It is hardly surprising, then, that for any supplier of a wide range of products, such as component and office supply companies, the catalogue remains a key marketing tool, whether supplied by hard copy or electronically.

Integrated media campaigns

In Chapter 12, on advertising, the need for *integrated marketing communications* was stressed. Communications strategy must be consistent with, and reinforce, other elements of the marketing mix (product, place and price). Within the promotional mix (advertising, personal selling, direct marketing, sales promotion and publicity) the same consistency and reinforcement should apply. Following this logic, messages sent out using various direct marketing media should also form a coherent whole. For example, information disseminated through the Internet should be consistent with that sent out via a direct mail campaign.

In practice, direct marketing does not always use multiple contacts or multiple media. A marketer wishing to attract delegates to a conference might use a single-medium, single-stage campaign—that is, one direct mailing to the target audience. A campaign designed to retain customers (e.g. subscribers to a charity or magazine) might use a single-medium, multiple-stage campaign. Three direct mail letters might be sent to encourage renewal. However, direct marketers have the opportunity to use a combination of media in sequence to achieve their objectives. This is termed a multiple-medium, multiple-stage campaign.

A business-to-business company marketing a new adhesive might place a direct response advertisement in trade magazines to stimulate trial and orders. A response coupon, freefone telephone number and e-mail address would be provided, and prospects invited to choose their most convenient method of contact. An inbound telemarketing team would be trained to receive calls and take either orders or requests for samples for trial. Another team would deal with mail and e-mail correspondence. An outbound telemarketing team would follow up prospects judged to be of small and medium potential and the salesforce targeted at large potential customers and prospects. The sequence would be as shown in Fig. 14.8 (overleaf).

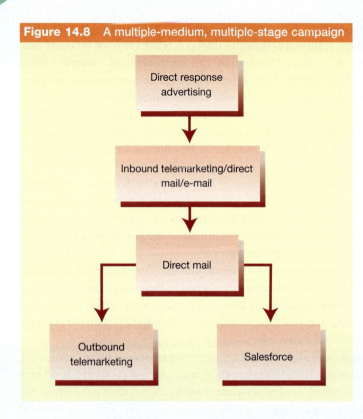

Figure 14.8 A multiple-medium, multiple-stage campaign

In this way, the company has identified prospects, generated an initial sales response, created interest in the new product, begun a dialogue with customers and prospects and, where necessary, arranged demonstrations. Each medium has been used to its best advantage, and salesforce time and effort targeted at prospects and customers who have both the interest and potential to justify a sales call.

Creative decisions

Most direct marketing campaigns have different objectives from those of advertising. Whereas advertising usually attempts to create awareness and position the image of a brand in prospects' minds, the aim of most direct marketing is to make a sale. It is more orientated to immediate action than advertising. Recipients of direct marketing messages (particularly through direct mail) need to see a clear benefit in responding. For example, Direct Line's success in the motor insurance business was built on a clear customer benefit—substantial cost savings from insuring with that company rather than the traditional insurance company—using direct response advertising and a highly efficient telemarketing team. Positioning Direct Line as a telemarketing-based motor insurer was achieved through advertising featuring a red telephone supported on wheels. Its *creative strategy* was consistent with the objectives and message of the campaign.

A *creative brief* will include the following elements (see Fig. 14.9).

- *Communication objectives*: what is the campaign hoping to achieve? Common objectives for direct marketing are sales volume and value, number of orders or enquiries, and cost-effectiveness. These will be outlined in more detail when discussing campaign evaluation.

- *Product benefits (and weaknesses)*: the product features will be identified as well as their associated customer benefits. Features can be linked to benefits by the phrases 'which results in' or 'which means that'. Key sources of competitive advantage will be spotlighted, which means that a thorough analysis of competitor products' strengths and weaknesses will have to be made.

- *Target market analysis*: target customers and prospects will be profiled and/or identified individually, and their needs and purchasing behaviour analysed. It is essential that creative people understand the types of people they are communicating with, since messages, to be effective, must be important to the target audience, not simply the 'pet' ideas of the creatives.

- *Development of the offer*: the offer should be valued by the target audience (pre-testing offers through group discussions and/or small-scale tests can measure the attractiveness of alternative offers). Some offers are price related. For example, an offer for a Capital One Visa credit card announced 'Lowest Rate in the UK for Credit Card Purchases 7.9 per cent APR Variable and No Annual Fee'. This message was emblazoned on the envelope and letter, and was supported by financial data showing cost savings compared to the competition. Other offers may take the form of free gifts. Monthly magazines often offer three free copies for a year's subscription. Another example is Legal & General Direct, a financial services company, which offered a free pen to all those who asked for a home insurance quote and a free telephone/radio alarm clock to those who took up insurance with them.

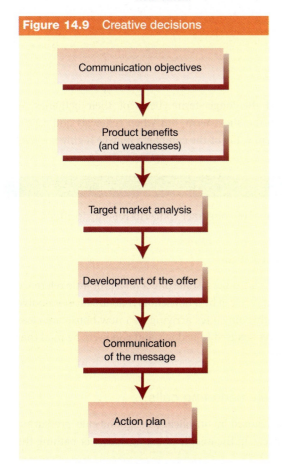

Figure 14.9 Creative decisions

- *Communication of the message*: as seen in the previous example, the offer or key message can be communicated on the envelope as well as the internal contents. Supporting evidence should be provided wherever possible. Several enclosures in a direct mail shot can be included, each with a different objective, but each should have one clear single-minded purpose. Recipients must be told clearly how to respond. Research has shown that including a freefone number as well as the usual freepost envelope can increase response by 50–125 per cent.[61] Today's direct marketers also have the option of including e-mail addresses. Letters should be personalized and the tone of the communication carefully thought out. Should a razzmatazz high-pressure sell or a gentler more subtle approach be used? Pre-testing various approaches can give invaluable information on this issue. Scripts are often used in telemarketing to communicate messages. When combined with powerful software and information technology (as discussed earlier, when we looked at telemarketing) they can provide an efficient way of communicating with customers and prospects. Mobile phone text messaging is another option for communicating the message. This is a growing medium, particularly for targeting youth audiences.

- *Action plan*: decisions regarding when the campaign should be run, how often, and suggestions regarding the most appropriate media to use to communicate the message and achieve the campaign's objectives must be made. For telemarketing campaigns, estimates of the number of operators required and when need to be produced.

Execute and evaluate the campaign

Execution of the campaign may be in-house or through the use of a specialist agency. Direct marketing activity usually has clearly defined short-term objectives against which performance can be measured. Some of the most frequently used measurements are:

- response rate (the proportion of contacts responding)
- total sales (volume and value)
- number of contacts purchasing
- sales rate (percentage of contacts purchasing)

- number of enquiries
- enquiry rate
- cost per contact
- cost per enquiry
- cost per sale
- conversion rate from enquiry to sale
- average order value
- renewal rate
- repeat purchase rate.

Direct marketers should bear in mind the longer-term effects of their activities. A campaign may seemingly be unprofitable in the short term, but when renewals and repeat purchases are taken into account the long-term value of the campaign may be highly positive.

Ethical issues in direct marketing

The use of direct marketing has raised a number of consumer concerns relating to ethics.

The quantity of poorly targeted direct mail

Although designed to foster close targeting of consumers, some direct mail is of little reference to the recipient. The double-glazing promotion received by a household that already has double glazing or the direct mail shot promoting bathroom suites arriving at a new house are clear sources of irritation. Much worse is the distress caused to widows and widowers by mail that continues to arrive for their deceased partner.

The timing and intrusive nature of telemarketing calls

Consumers also complain of the annoyance caused by unsolicited telephone calls pressuring them to buy products at inconvenient times (e.g. in the middle of eating dinner or bathing the baby).

The content of direct mail envelopes

Most direct mail enclosures are harmless, but attempts to be novel and different have led some direct marketers to include devices that have been considered offensive or dangerous. One campaign targeted at marketing managers enclosed a bullet as an attention-getting measure. The response of some recipients was that someone somewhere had them in their sights! The complaints poured in, resulting in a severe reprimand for the culprit. Bullets, scissors and devices that make ticking sounds are all evidence that some direct marketers have paid insufficient attention to the potentially annoying and harmful effects of their actions.

Invasion of privacy

Many consumers fear that every time they subscribe to a club, society or magazine, apply for a credit card, or buy anything by telephone or direct mail, their names, addresses and other information will be entered on to a database that will guarantee a flood of mail from the supplier. Furthermore, where country legislation does not restrict it, their names will be sold, without their knowledge, to other direct marketing organizations, which are free to send further unsolicited mail.

The direct marketing industry and governments are responding to the public concerns noted above. Ethical Marketing in Action 14.1 discusses some developments.

14.1 ethical marketing in action

Consumer Protection in Direct Marketing

Consumer protection in direct marketing is a combination of national laws, Europe-wide directives, the use of suppression files and company actions. National laws, such as the Data Protection Act in the UK, set out principles for the collection and use of personal data. These include the need for transparency where a person should be informed, before his or her personal data are collected, of the purposes for which it will be used, and given the opportunity not to supply the data. Personal data should also be kept secure, which means that staff dealing with personal data need to be trained in how to deal with requests to disclose such data.

In 2003 the European Commission's data protection directive was intended to guarantee people a right to privacy and to create a level playing field for European commerce. However, the result was that the member states' national laws were left largely unaffected meaning that pan-European direct marketing campaigns still need to comply with individual national laws, which can differ substantially in their coverage. One of the toughest is regulated by the Spanish Data Protection Authority, which has fined Reader's Digest and Microsoft €1 million (£675,000) each for holding data longer than they should.

Another method of protection is to provide the opportunity for people who do not wish to receive direct mail or unsolicited telephone calls to enter their details on to a suppression file. This is a list of names, addresses and telephone numbers that direct marketers should check against their own lists and then remove any names appearing on it. In the UK, two suppression lists exist: the Mailing Preference Service and the Telephone Preference Service, with over 300,000 and 75,000 people registered respectively.

A major factor in getting these instruments accepted by the direct marketing industry has been the threat of EC directives. If the industry did not regulate itself, the fear was that Europe would impose restrictive legislation on it.

Finally, companies have a responsibility for addressing public concerns. Some companies, like Barclays, a UK bank, are doing so. Barclays has moved into direct marketing for personal loans. A few years ago all current account customers would have received a direct mail shot. Now an in-house team prepares a target list using software that analyses its customer database. Less than 10 per cent of current account customers are chosen as suitable recipients based on analysis of an array of characteristics.

Based on: Coad (2003);[62] Fell (2002)[63]

Ethical dilemma

A socially responsible company supplying locally produced organic food products has been offered a supply of packaging from overseas at a rate significantly cheaper than that offered by its current local supplier. This offer is, however, contrary to the company's values on local supply and the reduction of environmental impact. The positive impact is that this saving would enable the company to invest in some direct marketing for its products that have only recently entered the market. Should the company change to the cheaper supplier?

Review

1 **The meaning of direct marketing**
- Direct marketing is the distribution of products, information and promotional benefits to target customers through interactive communication in a way that allows response to be measured.
- It includes such methods as direct mail, telemarketing, direct response advertising, catalogue marketing, electronic media, inserts, and door-to-door leafleting.

2 **The reasons for the growth of direct marketing activity**
- Direct marketing activity has grown because of market and media fragmentation, developments in technology, the list explosion, sophisticated analytical techniques, and co-ordinated marketing systems.

3 **The nature and uses of database marketing**
- Database marketing is an interactive approach to marketing that uses individually addressable marketing media and channels to provide information to a target audience, stimulate demand and stay close to customers.
- It is used in direct mail to provide a database for mailings, in telemarketing to provide a database for telephone contact, in distributor management systems to provide a database for supplying information and monitoring distributors, in loyalty marketing for the selection of highly loyal customers to be given special treatment, in target marketing to target groups of consumers based on their behaviour, in campaign planning to use a database as a foundation to send consistent messages, and in marketing evaluation by using a database to hold responses to marketing mix variables (e.g. price promotions).

4 **The nature of customer relationship management**
- Customer relationship management (CRM) is the term that describes the methodologies, technologies and e-commerce capabilities used by firms to manage customer relationships.
- The basic principle behind CRM is that company staff have a single-customer point of view of each client.
- Companies can assess how well they are managing their customer relationships by examining the following areas: analysis and planning, the proposition made to each customer segment, how well information and technology are being used, how well people are being managed and supported by an effective organizational structure, the efficiency of customer-impinging processes, the effectiveness of the implementation of the customer management activity, the quality of measuring performance against plan and against competitors, and the quality of the customer experience.
- Success in CRM projects is associated with having a customer orientation, taking a single view of customers across departments, having the ability to manage cultural change, involving users in the design process, having a project champion on the board and a commitment to the benefits of CRM across affected departments, creating 'quick wins', ensuring face-to-face contact between marketing and information technology staff, and piloting the new system before launch.

5 How to manage a direct marketing campaign
- A direct marketing campaign should not be designed in isolation but based on a clear understanding of marketing strategy in particular positioning. Then the steps are as follows.
- Identify and understand the target audience: never sell to a stranger. Who is to be reached, their motives and choice criteria need to be understood.
- Campaign objectives: these can be expressed in financial (e.g. sales), in marketing (e.g. acquire or retain customers) or communication (e.g. change beliefs) terms.
- Media decisions: major media options are direct mail, telemarketing, mobile marketing, direct response advertising, catalogue marketing and the Internet (which is discussed in the next chapter).
- Creative decisions: a creative brief will include a statement of communication objectives, product benefits (and weaknesses), target market analysis, development of the offer, communication of the message, and an action plan.
- Execute and evaluate the campaign: execution of the campaign may be in-house or through the use of a specialist agency. Evaluation should be taken against defined objectives such as total sales, number of enquiries, cost per sale and repeat purchase rate.

6 The media used in direct marketing
- The major media are direct mail, telemarketing, direct response advertising, catalogue marketing and the Internet (which is discussed in the next chapter).
- Direct mail: advantages are that it allows specific targeting to named individuals, elaborate personalization, and measurement; disadvantages are that poor lists give rise to intrusive junk mail, initial costs can be higher than advertising and response can be low.
- Telemarketing: advantages are that it is less costly and time consuming than a face-to-face salesperson visit, the growth of telephone ownership means it has wide reach, toll-free lines have reduced the cost of responding, sophisticated software has increased the efficiency of using telemarketing and, compared to advertising and other non-personal promotional methods, it has the advantage of two-way communication; disadvantages are that it lacks visual impact of a personal visit, body language cannot be judged, rejections can be high, unwanted unsolicited telephone calls can cause consumer annoyance, and costs per contact are higher than for direct mail and advertising.
- Mobile marketing: advantages are that it can be cost effective, personalized, it allows targeting of specific groups, is interactive, allows customer relationship building, is time flexible, is immediate and measurable, allows database building; disadvantages are that messages must be short, it is visually unexciting, may suffer from wear-off and there is the potential of poor targeting, causing consumer annoyance.
- Direct response advertising: advantages are that the combination of advertising and direct marketing techniques (e.g. telemarketing) allows a swift response, a wide audience can be reached and, when direct response television is used, goods can be demonstrated, services explained, more in-depth information provided, and samples and brochures requested and sent; disadvantages are that not all products are suited to direct response advertising and, for infomercials and home shopping programmes, reach can be low.

▶
- Catalogue marketing: advantages are that product selection can be in the convenience of the home, for people in remote rural locations it removes the need to travel long distances, costs can be reduced by avoiding expensive high-street locations and centralizing distribution, and a wider range of goods can be displayed in a catalogue compared to a shop; disadvantages are that catalogues are expensive to produce and require regular updating, goods cannot be tried or tried on before the order is placed, and colour tones in the catalogue may not match those of the delivered product.

7 Ethical issues in direct marketing
- There are potential problems relating to the quantity of poorly targeted direct mail, the timing and intrusive nature of telemarketing calls, the content of direct mail envelopes and invasion of privacy.

Key terms

campaign objectives goals set by an organization in terms of, for example, sales, profits, customers won or retained, or awareness creation

catalogue marketing the sale of products through catalogues distributed to agents and customers, usually by mail or at stores

customer relationship management the methodologies, technologies and e-commerce capabilities used by firms to manage customer relationships

database marketing an interactive approach to marketing that uses individually addressable marketing media and channels to provide information to a target audience, stimulate demand and stay close to customers

direct mail material sent through the postal service to the recipient's house or business address promoting a product and/or maintaining an ongoing relationship

direct response advertising the use of the prime advertising media such as television, newspapers and magazines to elicit an order, enquiry or request for a visit

mobile marketing the sending of text messages to mobile phones to promote products and build relationships with consumers

telemarketing a marketing communications system whereby trained specialists use telecommunications and information technologies to conduct marketing and sales activities

Internet exercise

With mobile penetration rates much higher than those for the Internet, many firms view mobile marketing as a more effective way of interacting with their core audiences. Flytext is a firm that specializes in the creation of SMS and mobile marketing campaigns. Visit its site and look at its mobile marketing campaigns.

Visit: www.flytext.com

Questions

(a) List the strengths and weaknesses associated with mobile marketing campaigns.
(b) What do you believe to be key factors in launching a successful mobile marketing campaign?
(c) Do you believe that mobile marketing campaigns will lose their effectiveness once there is saturation of the medium as a marketing communications platform? Explain your reasoning.

Visit the Online Learning Centre at www.mcgraw-hill.co.uk/textbooks/jobber for more Internet exercises.

Study questions

1. Compare the strengths and weaknesses of direct mail and telemarketing.
2. What are the key differences between direct marketing and media advertising?
3. Define direct marketing. What are the seven forms of direct marketing? Give an example of how at least three of them can be integrated into a marketing communications campaign.
4. What is database marketing? Explain the types of information that are recorded on a database.
5. What are the stages of managing a direct marketing campaign? Why is the concept of lifetime value of a customer important when designing a campaign?
6. What are the advantages and disadvantages of loyalty schemes? Why are many companies employing such schemes?
7. What benefits does catalogue marketing provide to consumers and companies? Compare the traditional catalogue marketing approach with its modern equivalent.
8. Discuss the major concerns relating to ethics in direct marketing.

When you have read this chapter log on to the Online Learning Centre at www.mcgraw-hill.co.uk/textbooks/jobber to explore chapter-by-chapter test questions, links and further online study tools for marketing.

case twenty-seven

The Launch of Nectar: Will the Nectar Loyalty Scheme Reap Rewards?

The Nectar (www.nectar.com) loyalty programme was launched in September 2002 to much fanfare. The scheme was backed by £50 million (€72 million) worth of TV, radio, press advertising and direct marketing to support the launch. Just over two months after its launch, Nectar claimed that it was the UK's biggest loyalty scheme, surpassing Tesco's Clubcard and Boots' Advantage schemes. A number of organizations have joined forces to launch the loyalty programme. Sainsbury's, Barclaycard, Debenhams and BP amalgamated their existing loyalty schemes under one umbrella brand called Nectar. All of the partners' existing rewards programmes, such as Sainsbury's Reward card, Barclaycard's Profiles card and BP's Premier scheme, were to be phased out within a year of the launch of Nectar and their members have been encouraged to transfer to the Nectar scheme. It is Debenhams first foray into the field of loyalty programmes.

Consumers who use their Nectar cards at reward partners, will collect points, which can be then redeemed for free flights, meals, vouchers etc. An independent company called Loyalty Management UK (LMUK) co-ordinates the Nectar scheme. The programme's management is outsourced to LMUK, allowing the consortium's partners to concentrate on their own businesses. The scheme proposes to be the biggest loyalty scheme in the UK, overtaking (as mentioned above) Tesco's Clubcard, and Air Miles, and aiming to capture 50 per cent of the UK's 25 million households. Ironically, LMUK's chairman, Keith Mills was the founder of Nectar's chief rival Air Miles.

Loyalty programmes are nothing new in the UK, people can still remember collecting Green Shield Stamps. The Nectar scheme is different from traditional loyalty schemes in that merchants are pooling their resources, which helps spread the costs associated with setting up the infrastructure and the running of such an initiative. Furthermore, card subscribers can pool their points from a variety of firms rather than a single merchant, greatly enhancing their points-earning potential and making rewards more attainable. Interested users simply pick up a Nectar registration leaflet and card from a Sainsbury's store, a Barclays Bank, a Debenhams department store, a participating BP service station, a participating Thresher Group store, Vodafone outlets, Adams or participating Ford dealers. Card subscribers return the completed registration form by post, or they can register online.

Shoppers can view how many points they have collected by viewing them online in My Nectar or by phoning the Nectar call centre. Nectar points are exchanged for Nectar vouchers (500 points = 1 Nectar voucher). These vouchers are collected at the card subscriber's home Sainsbury's (the store where they first used their card) or again via the Nectar call centre, from where the vouchers are sent out in the post. Some rewards (such as flights) can only be redeemed through the call centre.

Table C27.1   Nectar reward programme participants

Nectar points are collected by:
- shopping at Sainsbury's—2 Nectar points for £1
- using Barclaycard—2 Nectar points for £1
- filling up at participating BP filling stations—1 Nectar point for 1 litre of fuel
- shopping at Debenhams department stores—2 Nectar points for £1
- shopping at Adams, children's clothes retailer—2 Nectar points for £1
- shopping at Thresher group, off-licences—2 Nectar points for £1
- using Vodafone—2 Nectar points for every £1 spent on calls, text messages, ringtones etc.
- using Ford dealers—2 Nectar points for £1 on servicing, repairs and MOTs of Ford cars.

Table C27.2 Some of the Nectar rewards programme participants

Holidays, flights and travel	Eating out	Excursions
Lunn Poly	McDonald's	Legoland
British Midland BMI	Garfunkels	Alton Towers
Virgin Atlantic	Brewsters	Madame Tussauds
KLM	Brewers Fayre	Tower of London
Singapore Airlines	TGI Fridays	Driving Experiences
Eurotunnel	Planet Hollywood	Health & Spa Getaways
Stena	Café Uno	Adventure Excursions
DFDS Seaways	Est Est Est	*(sailing, scuba diving,*
Best Western Hotels	Medieval Banquet	*white-water rafting, jet skiing etc.)*
Heathrow Express		
Groceries and wine	**Good causes**	**Entertainment**
Argos	NSPCC	Odeon
Sainsbury's	Red Cross	Blockbuster
Laithwaithes	Free Kick	
Adams	Tommy's	
Kodak Express	Future Forest	

A major coup for Nectar is the signing up of Vodafone as an issuing partner. It dropped Nectar's rival Air Miles in 2000 because it claimed that customers preferred cheaper charges at the time. One core differential advantage that Nectar has over Air Miles is that it can attract shoppers who want 'aspirational' rewards such as a flight to Australia, as well as those shoppers who simply want basic rewards such as free video rental. The Nectar scheme differentiates the market, attracting both high and low spenders. Loyalty schemes try to entice new shoppers and reward existing customers. Nectar is trying to mimic the success of a similar scheme in Germany called Payback. The Payback scheme is not reliant on a single supermarket retailer, however it joined up several big brands in different sectors to create a broad appeal. Payback combined brands such as a leading grocery brand, a department store, a pharmacy chain, an Internet service provider and a credit card company.

Nectar believes that it has several key advantages over other loyalty schemes. First, the costs of operating such a scheme are greatly reduced due to the shared costs of having multiple partners involved. Second, partners in the scheme can avail themselves of a much richer data bank on their customers, analysing their purchases across a cross-section of different products, purchased in many different outlets. Finally, by leveraging several big brands rather than one single supermarket, the loyalty scheme has a much broader appeal. Hopefully, customers perceive the rewards as more attainable due to the number of different participating partners available. Barclays hopes to entice new customers to avail themselves of its Barclaycard product, by offering 500 Nectar bonus points to new customers.

Trouble arose for Nectar during its first week of operation. Subscribers were encouraged to register for the scheme via the Nectar website; for doing so, members would be rewarded an additional 100 bonus points. However, the website collapsed under the strain of demand, when it experienced 100,000 hits per minute. The website was allegedly forced to close when customers could view the personal data of other shoppers. The collapse of the website forced LMUK to direct customers towards the Nectar call centre. LMUK was forced to pull press and TV advertising, which featured Sainsbury's successful celebrity endorser Jamie Oliver, just a week after launch because it could not cope with the tide of registrations. Nectar came under fire from industry rivals as a result, by highlighting that a significant number had not been registered (i.e. had not given their personal

Table C27.3 Typical rewards

Meal at McDonald's	500 points
Movie rental at Blockbuster	500 points
Cinema ticket for West End Odeon	2000 points
£10 off shopping at Sainsbury's	2000 points
Single Heathrow Express ticket	2000 points
Ticket for Madame Tussauds	2500 points
London to Paris flight ticket	6000 points
London to New York flight ticket	36,500 points
London to Tokyo flight ticket	163,500 points

details), which negated the usefulness of the purchase information gathered. Subscribers don't have to register until they want to claim their rewards.

At the launch of the Nectar loyalty programme, Sainsbury's came under fire from the media, which lambasted the scheme as offering poor value to customers. Shoppers would now have to spend more than under Sainsbury's old Reward card scheme to avail themselves of free deals with Nectar. To earn a free flight to Amsterdam, for example, a shopper would have to spend £3000 (€4320) under the Nectar scheme, yet under the old scheme only £2500 (€4680). Newspapers such as the *Guardian* highlighted stories of weary points collectors having to collect thousands more points due to changes in the reward structure. One exasperated elderly woman was shown to have collected 12,927 points on her Barclaycard (the equivalent of having spent £129,270 [€186,150]) and was just 73 points short of obtaining her dream holiday of a return flight to Australia on the old scheme. As a result of the changes, the 70-year-old lady needed another 74,500 Nectar points. More problems arose when the Independent Television Commission ordered Nectar to amend its television ads due to them being misleading. Some 71 BP filling stations were not participating in the Nectar scheme, as they share sites with Safeway supermarkets. In future, Nectar had to make clear this restriction.

Tesco launched its Clubcard loyalty programme back in 1995. It was primarily used to make improvements to supply chain management, but this has evolved into improving relationships with customers. Tesco has also introduced a limited number of partners to its Clubcard loyalty scheme, and shoppers can now also earn points by shopping in retailers such as H. Samuel and Allders department store. However, Tesco still controls the branding of the loyalty scheme and manages its operation. Tesco also rewards customers who spend over £60 (€86) a week with additional points.

Air Miles (www.airmiles.co.uk), a British Airways subsidiary, ran a £20 million (€29 million) promotional campaign to minimize Nectar's impact on its business. This was a pre-emptive strike, just before the launch of Nectar. The Great Air Miles Giveaway reduced the number of points needed for over 500,000 flights. In addition, Air Miles has added the House of Fraser and BT as partners. Furthermore, Tesco renewed its Clubcard loyalty scheme programme by offering its cards at its checkouts for the first time, launching an offers magazine called *FreeTime* and emphasizing its tie-up with Air Miles in its marketing communications. Another competitor in the loyalty programme arena is the independent BuyandFly! points scheme. Partners within the BuyandFly! scheme include Odeon, *OK!* magazine, Domino's Pizza and Jet petrol stations.

LMUK feels that the core strength of the Nectar scheme is the variety of firms participating in it, making it hard for other schemes to replicate and giving it a unique selling point to interested subscribers. In November 2002, LMUK announced that Nectar had overtaken Tesco's Clubcard as the UK's most popular scheme, attracting 11.1 million active users. Tesco had previously stated in its press releases that it had 10 million users. Tesco hit back by claiming that its Clubcard scheme has 13.14 million users who have used their card in the past 12 months. This was an effort to reassert its claim that Tesco's Clubcard was the UK's 'most popular loyalty scheme'. Boots then entered the race to see who was the biggest by announcing that it had 14 million holders of its Advantage card; however, only 10.5 million of these had used their card in the past three months.

Air Miles has 6.5 million registered users. When Sainsbury's terminated its contract with Air Miles in 2001, it estimated that it accounted for a fall of 1 per cent sales revenue in one quarter. Commentators suggest that some shoppers switched to shops that participated in the Air Miles scheme having accumulated substantial points in the past and wanting to cash in their points.

Selling flights to loyalty programmes represents a highly lucrative revenue stream for airlines. A surprisingly high proportion of airline income derives from sales of frequent-flyer tickets to retailers, credit card companies and hotels for their loyalty programmes. In the USA, the top five airlines earned close on $2 billion (£1.37 billion/€1.97 billion) from sales of frequent-flyer points. For airlines, loyalty programmes are profit earners, whereas for other merchants, they represent significant costs. Airlines simply fill seats, which would otherwise not be filled; yet other merchants are rewarding customers with gifts that cost money (e.g. £10 [€14.4] shopping vouchers). Advocates of loyalty programmes argue that the information obtained from loyalty schemes helps organizations better understand their customers and their needs, helping readjust their product and service offering as a result. This information can be data-mined using customer relationship management software programs, analysing a firm's customers over time, their preferred brands, their buying patterns, their response to price promotions, and so on. This information in turn helps stores with the development of new products, and the future design and layout of stores. They view this data as essential feedback from customers, which is even more important than the loyalty itself.

Many retailers, such as Asda and Safeway, have abandoned loyalty programmes in favour of EDLP (everyday low pricing) strategies or BOGOF (buy one get one free) offers. They feel that customers are attracted into their stores by offering good value-for-money deals, not through complicated reward schemes. Many retailers believe that the costs simply outweigh any benefits of running a loyalty programme (the costs of offering a loyalty programme can be quite substantial). Not only does the organization have to consider the cost of the rewards, such as a free flight, but also the operating costs of running the initiative. In 2000, it is estimated that the top 16 retailers in Europe spent over $1 billion (£685 million/€986 million) on consumer loyalty programmes. Costs include the issuing of cards, operating a call centre, mailing costs, staffing costs, the design and operation of the customer database, and so on. When Safeway pulled the plug on its loyalty scheme, it was costing the firm £60 million (€86 million) a year to run. Asda cancelled trials of its points card in 1999 after testing in 19 of its stores. Opponents of loyalty programmes argue that the level of outlay required would be better allocated to improving customer service levels within stores or offering customers better deals, which they find both tangible and valuable.

Research has shown that customers really value things like good customer service, low prices, availability of toilets and in-store coffee shops rather than loyalty programmes. Safeway experienced a growth in its sales figures after its programme was axed due to better promotions offered by the store as a result. Customer loyalty improvements are very elusive for retailers and other merchants; many commentators feel that loyalty cards simply repay loyal customers rather than increasing their loyalty to the brand. Independent research has shown that some retailers (such as Asda, Waitrose and Morrisons), which have no loyalty schemes in place, in fact have higher scores for loyal shoppers. Recently, some US academics have found a weak correlation between profitability and customer longevity, which goes against popular marketing notions that regular customers are cheaper to serve, less price sensitive and create positive word of mouth for the firm. People often stay loyal to a brand simply because of inertia and the whole inconvenience of changing.

Many consumers are apathetic towards loyalty programmes, as they feel the rewards are minuscule in comparison to the expenditure needed to obtain them and that it takes too long to save up for the reward to justify the effort. For instance, the standard rebate for a loyalty scheme is 1 per cent on the amount of money spent. In other words, a supermarket shopper would have to spend over £1000 (€1440) in a supermarket to receive £10 (€14.40) off their shopping bill, which to many shoppers is very uninspiring. In addition, loyalty schemes have been criticized for their messy and lengthy redemption procedures. Furthermore, there is a proliferation of competing loyalty cards available. Wallets are being weighed down with tonnes of plastic. Shoppers may possess a wide array of cards on the off-chance that they may purchase an item from Homebase, Boots, Game, WHSmith or other merchants, and avail themselves of any incentive or discount on offer.

So will Nectar's loyalty programme be rewarding for both Nectar's partners and, more importantly, their cardholders? Only time will tell.

Questions

1. Discuss the advantages and disadvantages associated with retailer loyalty programmes such as Nectar's from both a customer and retailer perspective.

2. Discuss the main applications for the information gathered on customers who use their Nectar loyalty cards.

3. What do you believe are the key factors in launching a successful loyalty reward programme?

4. Outline the strategic options available to Air Miles, in response to the growing threat from Nectar, recommending what you believe to be the best option available and giving reasons for your answer.

This case was written by Conor Carroll, Lecturer in Marketing, University of Limerick. Copyright © Conor Carroll (2003). The material in the case has been drawn from a variety of published sources.

case twenty-eight

Customer Relationship Management and Value Creation

Organizations exist to provide value to their customers and other stakeholders (shareholders, for example). By providing this value to their customers, organizations' sales and profits are normally enhanced, and this in turn leads to higher dividends and share prices.

Organizations need to understand how value can be created and destroyed so that they can take appropriate action. One tool managers can use is the customer management model (developed by QCi) discussed in this chapter. The model can be used to analyse the contribution that customer management can make to providing value for an organization.

This exercise is designed to stimulate thought about how value is created and destroyed by managers through their activities when managing customers. To recap, the main elements of the QCi customer relationship management model are as follows.

- *Analysis and planning*: creating value through understanding the value, attitudes and behaviour of customers, and effective planning.
- *Proposition*: creating value through developing a proposition that is effective in keeping and developing those customers the organization wishes to manage.
- *Information and technology*: creating value by the efficient use and dissemination of information.
- *People and organization*: creating value through effective people and organization.
- *Process management*: creating value by using customer-centric processes.
- *Customer management activity*: creating value by effective acquisition, retention, development and recovery activities.
- *Measuring the effect*: creating value by measuring performance.
- *Customer experience*: creating value by understanding the customer experience.
- *Competitors*: creating value by understanding competitors.

Question

1 For each of the above elements, list two ways of (i) creating value and (ii) destroying value. To start you off, this is what an answer to the first element (analysis and planning) would look like.

Analysis and planning

(i) Value is created by:

- understanding which customers you want to manage
- retaining those that are worth keeping.

(ii) Value is destroyed by:

- a lack of customer knowledge
- servicing high-cost/low-revenue customers.

This case was written by Tracy Harwood, Senior Lecturer in Marketing, De Montfort University, and Michael Starkey, Senior Lecturer in Marketing, De Montfort University.

chapter fifteen

Internet marketing

> ❝The minute you start to do business on the web, you ... have to think about your competition as global, your readers as global, your suppliers as global, and your partners as global.❞
>
> THOMAS FRIEDMAN, *Killing Goliath.com*

Learning Objectives

This chapter explains:

1. The concept of Internet marketing
2. The range of activities that comprise e-commerce, and the forms of e-commerce market exchanges
3. Factors affecting the adoption of Internet marketing
4. Benefits and limitations the Internet offers to consumers and companies
5. Organizational competences for online success
6. How to achieve competitive advantage online
7. The key components of an e-commerce marketing mix

In 1989 the first commercial transactions occurred across the computer networks that form the Internet. Over the next few years the number of computers connected to the Internet increased exponentially, giving connected companies and their customers the opportunity to explore the value of this digital trading environment. It should be noted that the Internet is not the first digital trading environment to be used by consumers. In 1981, the French government launched the Télétel project, which although originally implemented as a means of improving telephone services soon began to offer its users the chance to buy goods and services online (see e-Marketing 15.1).

In 1991, the invention of the World Wide Web (WWW) by Tim Berners-Lee, based on the http (hyper text transfer protocol), provided millions of technically unqualified users with the opportunity to access the vast online resource of text, graphics and multimedia content. Shortly afterwards, web browsers were developed, e.g. Microsoft's Internet Explorer and Netscape Navigator to help guide users around the Internet and the web. Globally, tens of thousands of companies (both established and new market entrants) sought to establish ways to exploit this new commercial medium. This early period of the Internet's commercial development was likened to the Californian gold rush era of 1849; companies seeking to benefit from using the Internet for trading rapidly became involved in activities such as registering domain names and creating websites, then waiting for a return on their investment. For many, the financial return did not materialize and the dotcom boom period turned into dotcom bust. The overinflated paper value of Internet companies dwindled overnight and more traditional companies retrenched their online activities. While companies such as eBay, Lastminute.com, Yahoo!, Priceline and Amazon have survived, others such as Napster, Clickmango, Boxman and Ready2shop have collapsed.

However, despite its somewhat turbulent beginnings, the Internet is having a widespread impact on companies in the USA and Europe. Research by e-Business W@tch,[3] an initiative established to ensure widespread provision of relevant e-business information, has revealed that nearly 70 per cent of European companies have created websites. However, there is considerable variation in uptake across industrial sectors. Tourism and financial services are very proactive adopters, whereas the chemical and electronics industries are disappointed by the outcomes of belonging to the e-economy. The proactive stance of companies operating in consumer industries is perhaps in view of the fact that Europeans, on average, spent €430 (£300) online between August and October 2002. Additionally, future predictions suggest that European online consumers will buy more products online than American consumers.[4] This research highlights two significant issues likely to affect online success: (i) the types of products and services a company sells; (ii) the markets served (business-to-business, business-to-consumer, business-to-government).

Table 15.1 (page 552) lists the common Internet and e-commerce terms that are currently in use.

The remainder of this chapter explores the context of Internet marketing, the range of online marketing activities, the forms of e-commerce, the benefits and limitations to consumers and businesses of becoming involved with e-commerce activities, how to assess the competences needed for online success, the competitive advantages of online marketing and the design of an e-commerce marketing mix.

More than just a website

Although the media tend to focus on organizations and their web-based activities, it is important to recognize that exploiting Internet technologies is much more than just putting a brochure online.

15.1 e-marketing

Early Entry into E-commerce

i-minitel is a service of France Télécom
The home page of Minitel's new web-based services (www.i-minitel.com).

Minitel France Telecom videotext system

There now are 7 million 'Minitels' in France. The Minitel was originally a telephone-like terminal with a screen that could decode and display text-based information. These terminals provide access to one in every five French households, Post Office patrons and French office workers. There are over 26,000 online services, including banking and shopping. Originally the government-owned France Telecom freely distributed the terminals, connected to a telephone line. However, new hardware has been developed that increases methods and speed of access. Additionally, freely available terminal emulation software has also been distributed globally, greatly increasing access to Minitel services. Furthermore, at the end of 2000, France Telecom launched i-Minitel (see illustration), with new high-speed, easy-to-use software that enables Minitel's services to be accessed from PCs and Apple Macs. A few months later it unveiled 'Et hop Minitel', which enables companies to publish their web content on the system.

Based on: Kessler (1995);[1] McGrath (2001)[2]

The **Internet** and the **World Wide Web** have revolutionized commercial trading around the globe. Increasingly, organizations have begun to find ways to incorporate these new technologies into their promotional campaigns and channel strategies, offering customers different ways to communicate, receive information and buy goods. The Internet phenomenon has sparked a period of rapid new product development, partly driven by enhanced technological knowledge and partly driven by demand. The nature of communication between not only businesses and consumers but also the technologies employed are changing, as is illustrated by the example of Bluetooth Technology.

Table 15.1 A glossary of common Internet and e-commerce terms
Browser: computer software such as Netscape Navigator or Internet Explorer that can guide the user around the Internet
Chatroom: a site that allows visitors to communicate with each other about a topic of common interest to them
Click-through: the number of times a site visitor 'clicks' on to an Internet page
Domain name: this is the address most Internet sites have, which performs the role of being the 'telephone number' for individuals wishing to reach them
Dotcom: term referring to a business that uses Internet technologies to trade; the term came into popular usage around 1997
E-commerce: electronic (or 'e-') commerce is the description applied to a wide range of technologies used to streamline business interactions; examples of these technologies include the Internet, electronic data interchange (EDI), e-mail, electronic payment systems, advanced telephone systems, hand-held digital appliances, interactive televisions, self-service kiosks and smart cards
EDI (electronic data interchange): this is a pre-Internet technology, which was developed to permit organizations to use linked computers for the rapid exchange of information
E-marketing: the achievement of marketing objectives through the utilization of electronic communication technologies, including mobile devices
Extranet: a website where access is restricted to approved users
Firewall: computer software that protects the customer's online purchase transaction from being accessed by others
Hit: a single request from a browser to an Internet server
Home page: a website's welcome page providing details of site contents and guidance about using the site
Hyper text transfer protocol (http): the language protocol that underpins the web and enables the linking of documents to parts of other documents, subsequently allowing users to navigate their way around the Internet
Internet marketing: the achievement of marketing objectives through the utilization of Internet and web-based technologies
Internet service provider (ISP): companies such as Dixons Freeserve and AOL, which offer users access to the Internet; ISP software can be obtained over the Internet, from computer discs or on CD-Roms supplied by the ISP
Intranet: a website that operates inside an organization and does not offer access to any users external to the organization
Portal: a website that serves as an 'entry point' to the World Wide Web; portals usually offer guidance on using the Internet and 'search engines' that permit keyword searches
TCP/IP: the language protocol that enables different machines using differing operating languages to communicate with each other
Website: a www file that contains text, pictures and/or sound

Bluetooth's mission (see illlustration) is to facilitate 'interoperability' through the use of wireless technologies. This means that all kinds of peripherals, from commercial printers and computers to domestic fridges and microwaves, can interconnect and exchange data. In the commercial setting this provides increased opportunities for mobile networking and flexible working solutions. In the home, online shopping can become an automated process.

Essentially what is happening on a global basis is that technologies such as telecommunications, satellite broadcasting, digital television and IT are on a convergence path through which the world is being offered a more flexible, faster and extremely low-cost way of exchanging information. Hence when discussing this new technology, it is safer not to restrict

©2003 Bluetooth SIG. Inc.
The official Bluetooth wireless information site (www.bluetooth.com).

any assessment of opportunity to the role of the Internet. Instead the debate should be expanded to cover all aspects of information interchange. This is increasingly being recognized by organizations, which are moving to exploit the huge diversity of opportunities now offered by online marketing. It should also be recognized that before the advent of the World Wide Web, organizations had been conducting business electronically for decades.

For example, many large firms have been using a technology known as electronic data interchange (EDI) to manage their relationships with both suppliers and customers. EDI, often described as 'paperless trading', is the placing of orders with suppliers and carrying out financial transactions via dedicated network connections. EDI messages look similar to e-mail messages but are fundamentally different due to the internal structure, which facilitates the automatic processing of orders and financial transactions. Previously, EDI exchanges used agreed message standards and proprietary software, thus tying users into expensive systems. However, Internet-based EDI overcomes the need for such software and in doing so lowers the barriers to adoption, providing opportunities for small and medium-sized businesses to trade online. Internet-based systems, or extranets, set up between specific trading partners also provide a less costly option.

Internet marketing and e-commerce

In 1996, Hoffman and Novak[5] stated that, 'Because the web presents a fundamentally different environment for marketing activities than traditional media, conventional marketing activities are being transformed.' One of the unique properties of this evolving digital marketing environment to be highlighted was its capacity for many-to-many communications. As a result of the advent of this new communication model, it was suggested that the role of the consumer and the importance of interactive technologies would increase significantly. Notwithstanding these (and other) unique properties facilitated by the widespread uptake of Internet technologies, over a decade of commercial global trading online has revealed that the 'the fundamentals of businesses have not changed.'[6] In other words, the traditional marketing concept provides a set of guiding principles for companies wishing to integrate a wide range of Internet and digital technologies into their business activities.

There has been some debate as to how to refer to such activities. 'Internet marketing' is a term originally used and generally considered to mean 'the achievement of corporate goals through meeting and exceeding customer needs better than the competition' through the utilization of digital Internet technologies. More recently the term e-marketing has been coined, referring to the utilizations of a wider range of network communication technologies, including mobile phones and digital television, in the pursuit of marketing objectives. An additional term, 'online marketing', is also sometimes used to refer to marketing firms when they become members of marketing logistics networks where there are flows of information, goods, services and experiences, as well as payment and credit.[7]

The widening application of digital technologies suggests that marketers should extend their thinking beyond the Internet to encompass all of the platforms that permit a firm to do business electronically.[8] E-commerce involves applying a wide range of digital technologies to streamline business interactions, including Internet, EDI, e-mail, electronic payment systems, advanced telephone systems, hand-held digital appliances, interactive television, self-service kiosks and smart cards. E-Marketing 15.2 discusses how Wal-Mart has used e-commerce and Internet technologies to gain competitive advantage.

15.2 e-marketing

Technology-driven Success at Wal-Mart

In 1980 Wal-Mart was a small niche retailer based in the southern states of the USA, yet within 10 years the company became the largest and most profitable retailer in the world. The fundamental competence driving this success was its early entry into exploiting information technology to develop its 'cross-docking' technique of inventory management. This is a computer-based just-in-time system, which keeps inventory on the move through the value chain. Goods are continuously delivered to its warehouses, almost instantaneously picked for reshipment, repacked and forwarded to stores. The result is that Wal-Mart can run 85 per cent of goods through its own warehouse system and purchase truckloads from suppliers to the extent that it achieves a 3 per cent handling cost advantage that supports the funding of everyday low prices.

The system took years to evolve and is based around investing in the latest available technology. For example, the company developed a satellite-based EDI system using a private satcom system that sends daily point-of-sale data to 4000 suppliers. Wal-Mart continues to adopt new technology and has recently requested that all suppliers should use the latest EDI technology for all exchange transactions.

The company also worked with Procter & Gamble to develop its 'Efficient Customer Response', an integrated, computer-based system that provides the benchmark against the company's entire supply chain operations. Additionally, in order to ensure that employees have access to critical information, store and aisle managers are provided with detailed information on customer buying patterns and a video link to permit stores to share success stories.

Wal-Mart has not only benefited from technology-driven efficiency gains in business-to-business markets but also in consumer markets. Wal-Mart.com is, according to *USA Today*, currently one of the top five Internet shopping websites in terms of visitors.

15.3 e-marketing

Successful E-procurement Systems

The home page of Coors Brewers Ltd (formerly known as Bass Brewers plc).

Some large manufacturing companies in traditional industries have reportedly been slow to respond to the opportunities presented by the Internet. However, this is not so in the case of Coors Brewers Ltd. The organization's proactive approach towards the use of Internet technologies (see illustration) has produced many benefits for the company and its employees. Moreover, these activities have received recognition from leading purchasing practitioners in the form of a Kelly's Award, which is given for demonstrating benefits through innovation that bring commercial success in the field of purchasing. Indeed, one judge commented that the company's use of Internet technologies was:

> A good example of a company reassessing its purchasing strategy and taking gradual steps to get staff ready for e-procurement ... and shows some demonstrable benefits over the last three years—for example, purchasing card, website and supplier rationalization.

The purchasing group at Coors Brewers Ltd achieved this success through commitment to finding new ways of making improvements to existing methods of procurement. Early in the project the development team decided that solutions would involve Internet-based technologies. One of the key questions they had to solve was which company could provide appropriate solutions. After a global search, the team found a suitable company that could offer acceptable and reliable technological solutions, and provide access to a global trading network.

In the meantime, part of the development team focused on the practicalities of how to provide buyers with access to the goods needed to fulfil the company's purchasing requirements. The solution was to create catalogues of suppliers' goods that are relevant to buying requirements—in essence, a specially tailored online catalogue. This approach enables buyers to have instant access to the range of goods their particular department needs to purchase, while eliminating superfluous items (e.g.

> buyers in manufacturing do not want to purchase business gifts and, conversely, marketers are not interested in purchasing aluminium cans). This streamlined approach helps to avoid system overload. The system also provides mechanisms for negotiating terms of service, price and delivery.
>
> Part of the success of Coors Brewers' e-procurement system is due to the development team's approach towards its implementation. It was decided at the outset that it was important for the new e-procurement system to be readily accepted by existing procurement personnel. In order to encourage its usage the development team created an identity for the system, an important part of which was its ability to lighten workloads. Additionally, they named the system ERIC. This focus on the human side of the implementation, in conjunction with technological expertise and support, helped to ensure the success of ERIC.
>
> Source: http://www.purchasingawards.com/last-winners.html[9]

Once a company decides to embrace e-commerce as a path via which to exploit new entrepreneurial opportunities, then an immediate outcome is that the organization's knowledge platform becomes much more closely linked with other knowledge sources elsewhere within the market system, such as suppliers and customers. The reason why this occurs is that once buyers and sellers become electronically linked, the volumes of data interchange dramatically increase as trading activities begin to occur in real time. The outcome is the emergence of very dynamic, rapid responses by both customer and supplier to changing circumstances within their market system. E-Marketing 15.3 (see preceding page) examines how Coors Brewers Ltd has proactively responded to new opportunities created by digital technologies.

E-commerce market exchanges

The extent of e-commerce is borne out by the fact that all possible combinations of exchange between consumers and business organizations take place (see Fig. 15.1). *Business-to-business* exchanges take place through the use of EDI interchanges, and companies such as Cisco have transferred nearly all of their purchases to the Internet. This is probably the largest form of e-commerce at present.

Figure 15.1 Forms of e-commerce

	From business	From consumer
To business	B2B Cisco	C2B Priceline
To consumer	B2C Amazon	C2C eBay

The most apparent form of e-commerce is from *business-to-consumer*, with established retailers such as Tesco setting up online shopping facilities and in doing so creating additional channels to market via the Internet. Amazon.com has built a global book-selling operation by using Internet technologies. Consumers are becoming accustomed to trading electronically and this form of e-commerce is forecast to escalate.

E-commerce from *consumer-to-business* is less common but demonstrates the versatility of the Internet. An example is the approach adopted by Priceline.com, whereby would-be passengers 'name their own price' for services such as hotel accommodation and airline tickets. The service providers then decide

These materials have been reproduced with the permission of eBay Inc. Copyright © EBAY INC. ALL RIGHTS RESERVED
eBay offers consumers the opportunity to buy a wide range of products at the right price.

whether or not to accept offers based on current availability. Priceline is currently still profiting from this innovative business model.

The Internet also permits consumers to trade with other consumers via auctions (*consumer-to-consumer*). Would-be sellers can offer products through such sites as eBay or QXL to potential customers. The advertisement for eBay provides insight into the depth of the assortment of goods available for trading between sellers and buyers.

Factors affecting the adoption of Internet marketing

When managers are first confronted by the Internet, it is not unusual for them to be overwhelmed by both the apparent complexity of the technology and the diversity of the alternative pathways via which a firm can engage in Internet marketing and e-commerce. Van Slyke and Bélanger[10] suggest several key considerations likely to impact on a business involved with Internet technologies; operational efficiency, channel conflict, new markets and competition, financial investment and market changes.

Moreover, the extent to which an organization proceeds through such levels of Internet adoption is contingent on a number of factors.[11] This research focused on levels of Internet adoption among UK retailers and highlighted three dominant and interacting themes likely to influence the extent to which the Internet is used as a transactional sales channel.

1. *Internal factors*: those resulting from or belonging to a process, activity or member of personnel over which the company has complete control, e.g. does the organization have a clear strategic vision and is the product range suitable for online trading?

2. *Environmental factors*: those resulting from or belonging to a process, activity or member of personnel over which the company does not have complete control, e.g. the extent to which competitors are using the Internet and the likelihood of the target market wanting to use the Internet to shop or gather information.

③ *The Internet's comparative advantage*: circumstances where the Internet offers a comparative advantage compared to using traditional retailing methods, e.g. technological capabilities—speed and interactivity, remote access to new markets around the globe.

This proposition has been encapsulated in a model of the factors affecting the future development of the Internet, as illustrated graphically in Fig. 15.2.

Figure 15.2 Factors affecting the likely uptake and application of the Internet as a channel for direct sales

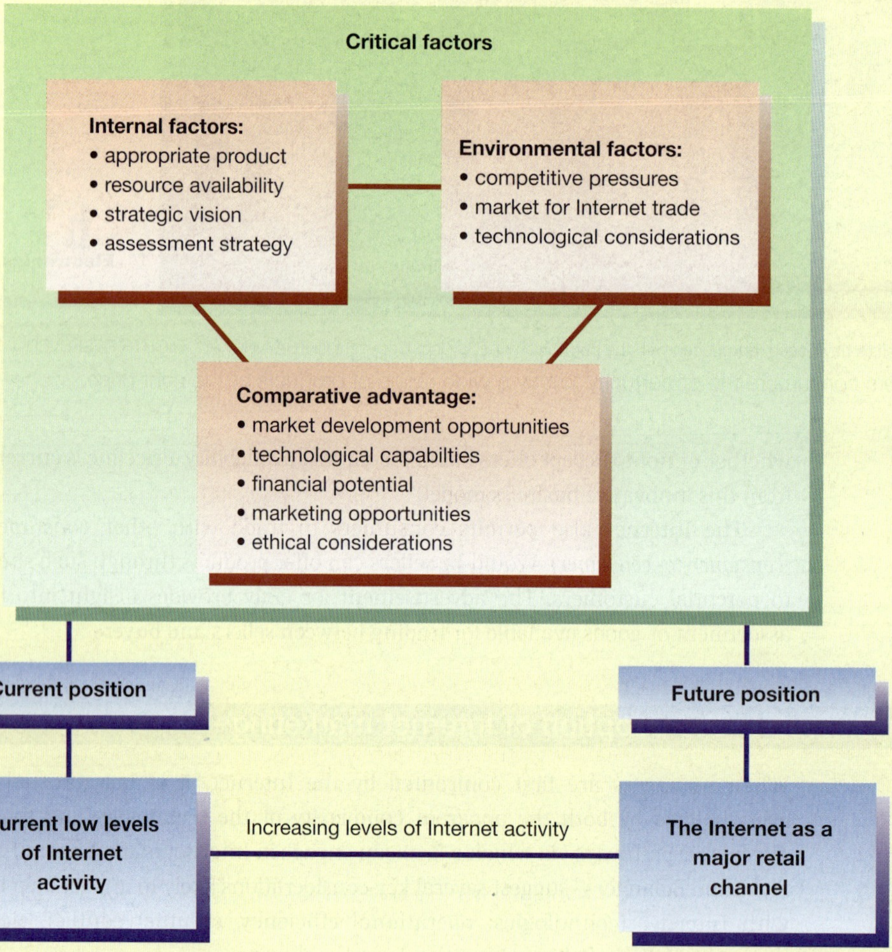

Critical factors

Internal factors:
- appropriate product
- resource availability
- strategic vision
- assessment strategy

Environmental factors:
- competitive pressures
- market for Internet trade
- technological considerations

Comparative advantage:
- market development opportunities
- technological capabilties
- financial potential
- marketing opportunities
- ethical considerations

Current position → **Current low levels of Internet activity** — Increasing levels of Internet activity → **Future position** → **The Internet as a major retail channel**

The benefits and limitations of the Internet and e-commerce

In order to maximize opportunities to meet and exceed customer expectations, an organization should assess the benefits and limitations of Internet technologies. By posing questions such as 'Does the Internet change the target or scope of the market?', 'Does the Internet help satisfy customer needs?' and 'Will customers use the Internet over the long term?' an organization can begin to identify how to differentiate its e-commerce offer from that of the competition (see Table 15.2).

Table 15.2 Potential benefits and limitations of Internet technologies to consumers	
Benefits	**Limitations**
Convenience in terms of being able to provide access 24 hours a day, 365 days a year. Furthermore, the customer can permit avoidance of driving to a store, searching for products or queuing at the checkout.	*Delivery times* are not quite so flexible. The logistical complexities of getting physical goods the last mile to the customer's home can mean that the customer must stay in and wait until the goods arrive.
As an *information resource*, the Internet enables the end user to acquire detailed information about products, pricing and availability without leaving their home or the office.	*Information overload*: the amount of information that can be accessed via the Internet by an end user can be overwhelming.
Multimedia: through exploitation of the latest technology, customers can gain a better understanding of their needs by, for example, examining 3D displays of car interiors or hotel accommodation.	*Access to technology*: the greater the capacity to incorporate multimedia content into e-commerce operations, the higher the required specifications of the computer to download such content. Many consumers in and around the globe do not have access to even the most basic means of accessing the Internet (see e-Marketing 15.4, page 560).
New products and services can be purchased in areas such as online financial services, and there is the ability to mix together audio, music and visual materials to customize the entertainment goods being purchased.	*Security*: many consumers are concerned about using credit and/or debit cards to purchase goods online for fear that their details will be captured by 'crackers'.
Lower prices: it is possible to search for the lowest price available for brands. Specific sites (e.g. Kelkoo and Froogle) allows consumers to surf the Internet to find the best available price.	*Cost implications:* the consumer has to make an initial investment in suitable computer equipment, pay for consumables like printer ink and fund the cost of downloading company information.

The impact of the geography of the Internet is not the only consideration for an organization planning an online operation. E-commerce and Internet technologies also offer the benefits and limitations listed in Table 15.3 (page 561) to commercial organizations.

Thus, having reviewed the potential benefits and limitations, the organization is then at the stage where it can begin to determine an entry point into e-commerce. Most organizations will soon realize that the Internet is a technological tool, the use of which will evolve and change as the organization gains experience of trading in cyberspace. Hart et al.[15] discovered that UK retailers had different approaches towards Internet adoption. Initially, Internet technologies were found to be used to provide a range of information about a company on a website. The next stage was to incorporate various forms of interactive marketing into the website—for example, surveys and e-mail questionnaires to encourage direct, two-way communication with customers. The final stage involved permitting customers to use an online marketing platform to place orders and make payments via the Internet.

As Internet technologies continue to evolve so too do the opportunities to trade in new and exciting markets. While UK retailers have begun to migrate to the web, providing opportunities to trade with their customers online, many of their customers have become involved in developing online links with one another in online communities. E-Marketing 15.5 (page 562) discusses this evolutionary stage of Internet marketing.

15.4 e-marketing

Internet Geography

An Internet map of the world and (inset) of Asia.

The size of the Internet and the current geographic dispersion of Internet users is important if an organization is to gain a better understanding of the potential of online markets. Three aspects to consider are as follows.

1. *Internet traffic*: the large map in the illustration shows the Internet's global infrastructure mapped against a map of the real world, and provides details of the technological infrastructure and the density of hosts in particular geographical regions. The map provides a clear indication of where the major routes for data traffic exist around the globe. It is important to note, however, that the infrastructure connecting all of these networks is only part of the Internet universe. A great deal of data traffic is local.

2. *Number of hosts*: the Internet Software Consortium has been measuring the size of the Internet since 1993 by counting the number of hosts. The first survey recorded just 1,313,000 hosts. The survey in January 2003 recorded, 171,638,297 hosts, giving an indication of the extent to which the Internet has grown in a single decade.

3. *User distribution*: North America continues to have the largest number of Internet users but, interestingly, the USA does not have the highest density of users per head of population. In Iceland nearly 78 per cent of the population are connected to the Internet whereas in the USA the figure is around 60 per cent. The size and density of user populations vary considerably from country to country but the density of user populations tends to follow the Internet infrastructure as shown on the global Internet map in the illustration. Highly developed countries tend to have significantly larger numbers of Internet users than less economically developed countries. In Asia (see the illustration, insert), very highly populated countries like India (7 million Internet users) and China (48.5 million Internet users) have a very low density of Internet users as a percentage of their populations. However, it is important to note that the user population in China is growing rapidly (approximately 2146.67 per cent since 1999).

▶ Although assessing the size of the Internet in terms of the number of users and the size of the technological infrastructure is a difficult task, it is important for organizations to consider the technological constraints in conjunction with the target market in order to assess the viability of some of the new markets that can now be accessed via the Internet.

Based on: Internet Software Consortium;[12] Chaffey et al. (2003);[13] Cyberatalas[14]

Table 15.3 Potential benefits and limitations of Internet technologies to organizations

Benefits	Limitations
Investment reduction through actions such as replacing retail outlets with an online shopping mall or saving on paper by converting a sales catalogue into an electronic form.	*Operational costs:* organizations are likely to incur increased logistical costs and, in the case of retailers, the cost of selecting goods for the consumer prior to delivery (a particularly high cost in the case of the grocery retailer).
Reduced order costs: e-procurement systems can significantly reduce the costs associated with handling a purchase order by streamlining order entry systems and reducing administration costs.	*Set-up costs:* moving from a paper-based system to a fully integrated e-procurement system can have high cost implications: investment in networked systems to enable e-procurement systems to interface with back-office systems, cost of human resources skills, etc.
Improved distribution because once information-based products such as magazines or software are made available online the company can achieve global distribution without having to invest in obtaining placements in traditional outlets.	*Short-termism*: companies should adopt a strategic focus towards the adoption of e-commerce and look for opportunities to create long-term economic value rather than the short-term gain achieved through technologically facilitated cost reductions.
Reduced personal selling costs because the role of the salesperson as a provider of one-to-one information can be replaced with an interactive website.	*High-cost content*: end users have high expectations of the up-to-dateness of website content. Not only does content have to be regularly updated but also there are high cost implications for content creation.
Relationship building because, via a website, a firm can acquire data on customers' purchase behaviour that can be used to develop higher levels of customer service.	*Connective to transactional relationships*: the focus on price reductions by online suppliers as a mechanism to attract customers can undermine the very nature of a relationship. It can become difficult to build a relationship based on anything but price.
Customized promotion because, unlike traditional media such as television or print advertising, the firm can develop communications materials on the website designed to meet the needs of small, specific groups of customers.	*Over-specialization* while it is technically possible to target a segment of one using Internet technologies, an organization should always question the profitability of adopting such a strategy.
New market opportunities because e-commerce permits firms, whether they are large or small, to offer their products or services to any market in the world.	*Technological deserts*: parts of the world are poorly served by telecommunications and network access providers; as a result some parts of the world do not have access to the Internet.
Marketing research opportunities because e-mail and website-based surveys provide a low-cost method of questioning large samples, although the representativeness of the sample needs to be considered as does the acquisition of e-mail lists and the potential resentment that unsolicited e-mail questionnaires can cause. The Internet also provides a rich source of secondary information through websites.	*Authenticity*: not all Internet users respond to Internet surveys by providing factual data. Potentially, false or deliberately incorrect responses can bias research findings and give misleading results.

15.5 e-marketing

Network Communities

According to Cova and Cova,[16] citizens of the world are interested in finding social links and associated identities. They refer to the forces that are shaping postmodern societies as being 'tribal', so called because there is no central power to maintain social order, and groups form around 'non-rational and anarchic elements—locality, kinship, emotion and passion'. Tribes are difficult to quantify in terms of traditional segmentation variables: while there are common threads that bind a tribe together, identifying the nature of this common passion is a highly complex task due to a general lack of logic and coherence.

Internet tribes are growing rapidly through the use of e-mail, web-based discussion forums and Internet chat (*chatrooms*). For an organization to interact with tribal groups they should establish ways of using a website to build a long-term relationship through the provision of value-added services that provide effective support but do not exploit membership of the tribe. Car manufacturers such as Citroën and Volkswagen support many enthusiasts' sites, the immediate value of which for the organization is to reinforce the emotional bonds between the product and the consumer via the web. With the creation of such 'virtual community centres', organizations can begin to gain benefits from network communities of consumers. Friends Reunited has taken this model a step further by charging a small entrance fee to those wishing to become an active member of the tribe (see the illustration).

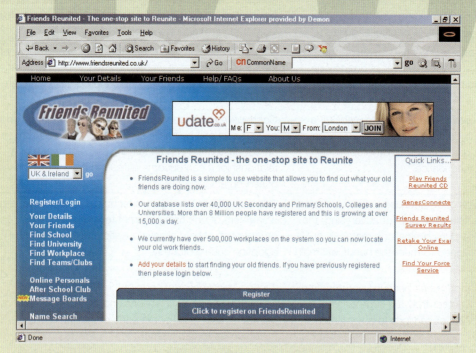

Friends Reunited.com has created a virtual community and a financial success.

Based on: Cova and Cova (2002);[16] Rauch and Thunquist;[17] www.citroen.mb.ca/citroenet;[18] www.vwvortex.com;[19] http://friends_reunited.com[20]

Assessing online competence

For the marketer, Internet marketing primarily offers both a new promotional medium and an alternative channel to market. In view of this situation, it seems reasonable to propose that success in online markets will be influenced by the degree to which a firm can develop unique capabilities in the area of exploiting superior technical knowledge and internal organizational routines as the basis for supporting competitive advantage. Moreover, companies with particular skills and capabilities might be able to out-perform their rivals, creating sustainable competitive advantage and superior performance.

This perspective leads to the conclusion that Internet marketing provides an important example of how the 'resource-based' view of the firm will provide the basis for determining whether a firm will achieve market success.[21] By drawing on a resource-based view of the firm, it seems reasonable to propose that successful implementation of an online marketing plan will be critically dependent on the firm having appropriate competences for managing strategy, finance management and operations. These are shown in Fig. 15.3.

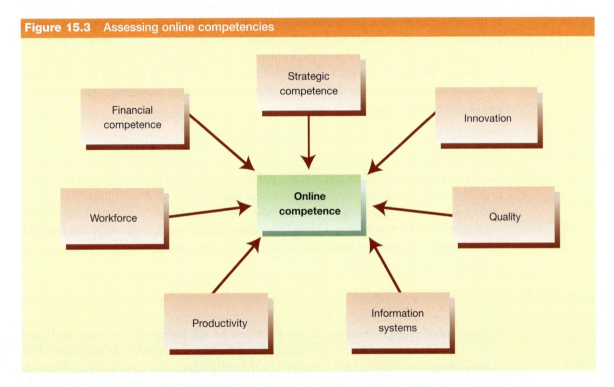

Figure 15.3 Assessing online competencies

Strategic competence

The long-term survival of all organizations is critically dependent upon their ability to identify new market trends, and to determine how the internal capabilities of the organization can be used to exploit emerging opportunities. In the case of online marketing, Ghosh has proposed that the following four distinct strategic marketing opportunities exist:[22]

1. establishing a direct link with customers (or others with whom the firm has an important relationship) to complete transactions or exchange trade information more easily (e.g. Staples, the office superstore chain, selling supplies online to large corporate customers)

2. utilizing the technology to bypass others within a value chain (e.g. online retailers such as the bookstore Amazon.com)

③ developing and delivering new products and services (e.g. the online share trading system developed by Charles Schwab in the USA)

④ becoming a dominant player in the electronic channel of a specific industry by creating and setting new business rules (e.g. Dell Computer's dominance in the electronic direct selling of computers to large corporate customers).

Financial competence

To be successful, it is crucial that the organization has the financial resources required to fund the level of investment needed to support any new marketing strategy. To those lacking in Internet trading experience, initial examination would tend to indicate that creation of a website is an extremely low-cost proposition. All that seems to be needed is to register a domain name and to then use low-cost software (e.g. Microsoft's FrontPage) to construct the organization's web pages. Porter[23] suggests that organizations should proceed with caution and seek to ensure that use of the Internet will create long-term *economic value* not just a short-term increase in *revenues*. He continues, saying that distorted revenues, interim cost savings and rising share prices should not be used to justify investment in the new economy. As a result, organizations need to evaluate their competitive positions carefully and then develop coherent e-commerce business strategies. In other words, the ease with which a website can apparently be created needs to be evaluated against the expertise of creating, managing and maintaining an effective and efficient online business.

Innovation

Rapid development of Internet technologies has created many business opportunities. In order to prosper in the e-commerce trading environment organizations need to continually engage in finding new ways of improving their products and process technologies. Unfortunately for the e-marketer, at the 'click of a button' the competition can rapidly gain an in-depth understanding of your operation, which adds a new dimension to competitor analysis and planning competitive strategies.

Workforce

In most online markets, because all firms understand the nature of customer needs and internal operations utilize very similar computer technologies, it is often extremely difficult to achieve a long-term sustainable advantage over the competition. Two variables that are clearly critical influencers of customer satisfaction are (i) the speed and accuracy of service delivery, and (ii) sustaining the technical reliability of all online systems. The importance of these variables does mean that the e-marketer will need to ensure that the human resource management (HRM) practices within their organization are focused on continually investing in upgrading employee skills in order that all staff are capable of fulfilling their job roles to a standard that exceeds that which is achieved by the competition. Furthermore, the e-marketer should seek to understand what causes certain employees to consistently achieve high performance standards within the organization and then determine how effective management of these factors can contribute to sustaining a market lead over the competition.

Appropriate HRM practices for achieving optimal workforce performance of back-office staff will usually be based around the same principles that are to be found in any type of organization. At the moment, the greatest HRM problem facing the e-commerce industry is the recruitment, retention and ongoing skills development of the technical staff responsible for the development and operation of e-commerce systems.

Quality

Correction-based quality is founded on what is now considered to be an outmoded concept—namely waiting until something goes wrong and then initiating remedial work to correct the fault. By moving to prevention quality, the organization develops processes that minimize the occurrence of the mistakes that have been causing the defects to occur. One outcome of the efforts by the large multinational firms to improve service quality is that customers now have much higher expectations of their suppliers and, furthermore, are willing to proactively seek out alternative suppliers.

In relation to the management of quality, online marketing can be treated as a service business. As with any service business, customer loyalty is critically dependent upon the actions of the supplier being able to totally fulfil the expectations of the customer. The critical variables influencing whether the customer perceives that expectations are being met include reliability, tangibles, responsiveness, assurance and empathy.[24]

In many service encounters, the customer is forced to accept some degree of supplier failing and continue to patronize the same service source because the supplier is the most conveniently placed (e.g. the businessperson who frequents a somewhat poor hotel because it is located next to a customer's office; the consumer who uses a local store because the nearest supermarket is some miles away). It is important, however, for the online marketer to recognize that the 'loyalty due to convenience' scenario will rarely apply to customers purchasing in cyberspace. For example, if the website visited fails to fulfil expectations, then at the click of a button the potential customer can instantaneously travel to a new location offering a higher level of service quality.[25] Amazon is a good example of how service quality can be achieved online, as e-Marketing 15.6 discusses.

Productivity

Productivity is usually measured in terms of the level of value-added activities per employee and/or per number of hours worked. By increasing productivity in terms of value-added/employee or per hours of labour input, a firm can expect to enjoy an increase in

15.6 e-marketing

Online Service at Amazon

Possibly one of the most effective examples of what can be achieved in terms of service quality is provided by Amazon, the world's largest online bookstore (although it sells much more besides books). Jeff Bezos founder of Amazon.com set out to create the world's most customer-centric company and has succeeded in building a firm that currently serves customers in over 200 countries around the globe. Jeff's original aim was to develop an online business that would enable customers to find anything they might want to buy online at a discounted price.

The company is in constant pursuit of this aim, and has recently begun to expand its product portfolio to include new product categories such as apparel in the USA, and kitchen and home ranges in parts of Europe. Amazon.com offers customers rapid access to its site and, once there, the user is presented with search engines, book reviews, a 'shopping trolley' and a wide variety of delivery alternatives. Once an order has been placed, Amazon.com automatically confirms the order by e-mail, and then enables the customer to track the delivery status of their order online. Post-purchase, the customer is offered personalized recommendations based on prior purchases.

profitability. Given the major influence of productivity on organizational performance, it is clear that this is an area of internal competence that will have a significant influence on any marketing plan. In relation to online marketing, possibly the two most important elements of the productivity equation are customer interface productivity and logistics productivity. In the case of customer interface productivity, this can usually be improved by ensuring that, through investment in the latest computer technologies, virtually all aspects of customer needs, from product enquiry through to ordering, can occur without any human intervention by supplier employees. Additionally, however, where human support *is* needed, this must be delivered by highly trained support staff, aided by the latest online customer assistance tools in order to sustain the productivity of the interface. Then, once an order is placed, the employee productivity of the back-office staff involved in order processing, order assembly and product delivery must be of the highest level. E-Marketing 15.7 shows how high levels of productivity are achieved by the Dell Corporation.

15.7 e-marketing

E-commerce Productivity

An excellent example of e-commerce productivity is provided by Dell Corporation, the world's largest computer direct marketing operation. Customers visiting the Dell website are provided not just with an effective ordering system but, in addition, a multitude of tools for answering technical questions and for configuring their own personalized compuer design. If customers hit a problem, by the click of a button they will be put in telephone contact with a highly trained Dell service employee who can offer an appropriate solution. Once an order is placed, the Dell automated procurement, manufacturing and distribution system ensures that logistics productivity is at a standard that is the envy of the competition.

Information systems

For those firms that decide the Internet can provide the primary channel through which to attract new customers and retain the loyalty of existing customers, poorly integrated information systems are not an acceptable option. Success can only occur if all data flows are integrated, and to stay ahead of the competition continuous investment must be made in further upgrading and enhancing the company information systems. Hence, information management competence is clearly critical if a firm is seeking to base its brand differentiation on the Internet around offering online services superior to those delivered by the competition. The secret of the success of most e-commerce operations is that they have exploited one or more of these characteristics as a strategy through which to deliver a purchase proposition superior to that available from their offline competitors.

Competitive online advantage and strategy

Marketers have long accepted that success demands identification of some form of *competitive advantage* capable of distinguishing an organization from other firms operating in the same market sector. The unique properties of the Internet offer some opportunities to establish new forms of competitive advantage. These include highly tailored product assortments and customized products, instant response, uninterrupted trading hours and more informed customer services. The secret of the success of most e-commerce operations is that they have exploited such advantages, created by Internet technologies, in order to deliver a purchase proposition that is superior to that of their offline competitors.

Lower costs and prices

Lower prices

The Internet permits suppliers to make contact with customers without using an intermediary. The savings generated by the removal of the intermediary from the transaction can be passed on to the customer in the form of lower prices. An example of this form of competitive advantage is provided by the UK airline easyJet. This firm, established some years ago, is now the country's leading 'no-frills', low-price airline. Similar to operators in the USA, the company uses smaller regional airports and limits the scale of ground and in-flight services offered to customers. The advent of the Internet has permitted the company to create an automated, online flight enquiry, booking service and ticket assurance system, which has replaced all other forms of ticket booking.

Lower costs

Large manufacturing companies in traditional industries have reportedly been slow to respond to the opportunities presented by the Internet. However, a key driver for the adoption of such technologies has been the opportunities for cost reduction, especially within the purchasing function.

Improved service quality

In most service markets it is almost impossible to offer a product proposition that is very different from that of the competition. As a result, one of the few ways of gaining a competitive advantage is through being able to deliver a superior level of customer service. A key influencer of service quality is the speed of information interchange between the supplier and the customer. The information interchange capability of the Internet offers some interesting opportunities to create competitive advantage. For many years, Federal Express has been a global leader in the application of IT to provide a superior level of customized delivery services to major corporate customers. The firm has enhanced its original customer-service software system, COSMOS, by providing major clients with terminals and software that use the Internet to take them into the Federal logistics management system. In effect, Federal Express now offers customers the ability to create a state-of-the-art distribution system without having to make any investment in self-development of shipping expertise inside their own firms (www.fedex.com).

Greater product variety

The average high-street retail shop is physically restricted in terms of the amount of space that is available to display goods. Hence its customers, who may have already faced the inconvenience of having to travel to the retailer's location, may encounter the frustration of finding that the shop does not carry the item they wish to purchase. Online retailers (pureplays, 'clicks and bricks') can avoid the space restrictions of their 'bricks and mortar' competitors. As a result, they can use their website to offer a much greater variety of goods to potential customers.

Product customization

Over the past 20 years, many manufacturers have come to realize that adoption of just-in-time (JIT) production can offer the potential to customize products to meet the needs of individual customers. For example, computer giant Dell exploited JIT to assist it to build a product to meet the specific needs of each customer. One obstacle to the implementation of a product customization strategy is the volume of information interchange required between the customer and supplier during the design, selection and pricing phases of the purchase transaction. Internet technologies can remove this obstacle. By creating a website, the supplier can offer the buyer a vast amount of information. Dell's utilization of direct marketing techniques permitted it to be a 'first mover' in exploiting Internet technologies as part of its strategy to offer customized products. Customers who visit the Dell website are offered assistance in selecting the type of technology most suited to their needs. These data provide the inputs to an online help system, which guides the customer through the process of evolving the most appropriate specification from a range of choices. Once a final selection is made, the customer receives an instant quote on both the price of their purchase and the date upon which it will be delivered.

A key factor influencing the ability of firms to exploit the Internet as part of a product customization strategy has been the increasing availability of lower-cost computer hardware and very affordable, powerful software tools. This has had the effect of rapidly driving down the cost of analysing the huge amounts of data that are generated by customers visiting websites. This trend has sparked off a new concept in market research, which is known as **data warehousing (or data mining)**. Baker and Baker[26] have proposed that this new approach should be based on exploiting information provided by customers to:

- classify customers into distinct groups based on their purchase behaviour
- model relationships between possible variables such as age, income and location, to determine which of these influence purchase decisions
- cluster data into finite clusters that define specific customer types
- use this knowledge to tailor products and other aspects of the marketing mix, such as promotional message or price, to meet the specific needs of individual customers.

Customers' use of the Internet in both business-to-business and consumer goods markets means that e-commerce firms can use data warehousing to gain in-depth insights into the behaviour of their customers. As a result, mass customization has become a practical reality for firms that in the past were positioned as mass marketers. The reason for this situation is that when customers start surfing the net they are asked to provide detailed information to potential suppliers. One can link together information on pages visited, responses to questions asked as customers register with a site, personal addresses (e-mail) and payment card details to build highly detailed customer profiles. Jeff Bezos (founder of Amazon.com), has used the analogy that the e-commerce retailer can behave like the small-town shopkeeper of yesteryear because of this deep understanding of the customers that visit the online store. Armed with such in-depth knowledge, like the shopkeeper in a village store, the large retailer can personalize service to suit the specific needs of every individual customer across a widely dispersed geographic domain.

As with the mass-customization opportunities available to large firms, the Internet also permits small firms to become involved in the practice of one-to-one marketing. The outcome is that niche marketers now find it feasible to operate as 'micro-nichers', customizing products to meet individual customer needs. Acumin, for example, is a web-based vitamin company that blends vitamins, herbs and minerals according to the specific instruction of the customer. New York's CDucTIVE offers customers the facility of designing their own CDs online to contain their favourite mix of music tracks.

Selecting an e-commerce marketing mix

Selecting an **e-commerce marketing mix** can be guided by applying established marketing management principles as the basis for defining how Internet technologies are to be integrated into a firm's existing operations. In many organizations, e-commerce marketing mix proposals will be based around enhancing existing offline activities by utilizing the Internet and the web to provide new sources of information, customer–supplier interaction and/or alternative purchase transaction channels.

In view of this situation, it seems logical to propose that the selection of an e-commerce marketing mix will involve processes similar to those utilized in conventional, offline marketing planning activities. Notwithstanding these similarities, Internet technologies have facilitated new facets to some of the traditional marketing management concepts and these are now discussed. The areas that need to be examined are illustrated in Fig. 15.4 (overleaf).

Marketing audit and SWOT analysis

Within the marketing audit there should be coverage of the strategic situation facing the organization. This will be based on a description of e-market size, e-market growth trends, e-customer benefit requirements, utilization of the marketing mix to satisfy e-customer needs, e-commerce activity of key competitors and the potential influence of changes in any of the variables that constitute the core and macro-environmental elements of the e-market system. This review should include analysis of whether the firm is merely going to service end user market needs or will concurrently seek to integrate e-commerce systems with those of key suppliers.

The internal e-capabilities of the organization are reviewed within the context of whether they represent strengths or weaknesses that might influence future performance. One of the key issues will be that of whether staff have appropriate e-commerce operational skills, whether new staff will need to be recruited or aspects of the project outsourced to specialist e-commerce service providers. Another issue is the degree to which existing databases can be integrated into a new e-commerce system on either a real-time or batch-processing basis.

E-market circumstances are assessed in relation to whether these represent opportunities or threats. Consideration will need to be given to whether the move is proactive or a reactive response to initiatives already implemented by the competition.

Other issues to be examined include: (i) the degree to which existing markets will be served through e-commerce, and (ii) whether e-commerce will be used to support entry into new markets. Combining the external and internal market analysis will permit execution of the SWOT analysis. The SWOT analysis, when linked with the situation review, will provide the basis for defining which key issues will need to be managed in order to develop an effective e-commerce plan for the future.

Marketing objectives and strategy

The degree to which e-commerce marketing objectives will be defined can vary tremendously. Some organizations will merely restrict aims to increasing the effectiveness of their promotional activities. Others may specify overall forecasted e-sales and desired e-market share targets. Some organizations may extend this statement by breaking the market into specific e-market target segments, detailed aims for e-sales, e-expenditure and e-profits for each product and/or e-market sector. The e-marketing core strategy will define how, by positioning the company in a specific way, stated marketing objectives will be achieved.

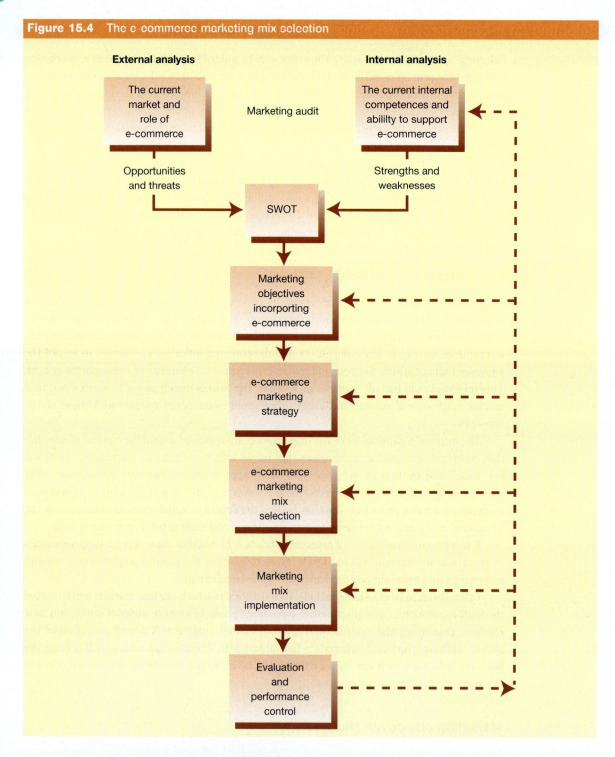

Figure 15.4 The e-commerce marketing mix selection

E-commerce marketing mix

The Internet's unique properties have the potential to have an impact across the whole of the marketing mix (see Fig. 15.5). Marketing mix considerations will need to be extended to cover how each element within the e-commerce mix (product, price, promotion and distribution/place) will be utilized to support the specified strategy. Internet technologies bring new unique properties to each element in the marketing mix, which need careful consideration if strategic goals are to be met.

Figure 15.5 Internal marketing and the marketing mix

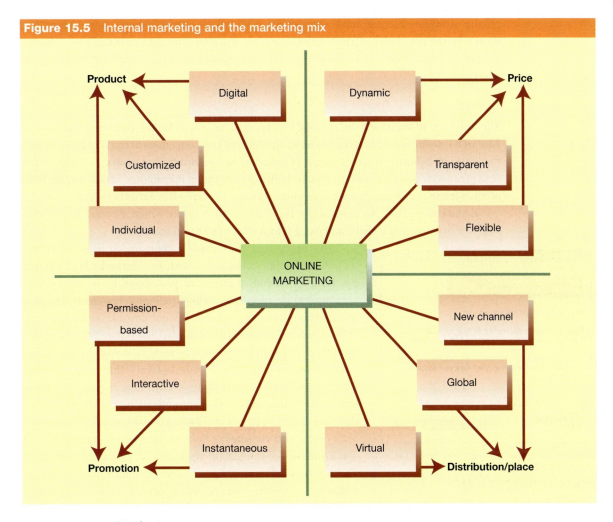

Product

There are several ways that the Internet offers an opportunity for product enhancement:

- *individual*—personal specifications can lead to highly individual products being created
- *customized*—Tesco's online shopping website captures details of shoppers' regular purchase choices and then provides a customized list of favourites; the main benefit for the customer is speedier online shopping
- *digital*—emergence of the Internet has facilitated the growth and distribution of bit-based products; bit-based products are digital goods and services that can be delivered via the Internet straight to an online customer's desktop—for example, information, software upgrades, computer games, flight bookings and hotel reservations; once the customer makes the payment they can download the product regardless of the physical location of the supplier or the buyer; information in the form of market analysts' and consultants' reports is another form of bit-based product and the market for such goods has grown significantly since the commercialization of the Internet.

Price

A major impact of Internet technologies on economics is that they potentially reduce the search costs that buyers incur when looking for information about new products and services. The net effect is a reduction in suppliers' power to control and therefore charge higher prices as pricing strategies become more *transparent*. Additionally, prices become more *dynamic*, as shown by the popularity of the auction site eBay. Priceline.com demonstrates how collective buying can change the price paid by the consumer, creating an opportunity for *flexible* pricing strategies.

Promotion

The Internet is becoming increasingly important as a marketing communications tool. Research has discovered that the web is used extensively by consumers in the USA as a research tool.[27] When using the Internet as part of a marketing communication strategy a company can send *permission-based* e-mailings, regular bulletins containing information about, say, the latest product features and any promotional offers that the customer has agreed to accept.

E-Marketing 15.8 discusses some basic issues to consider when viewing e-mail as a potential promotional vehicle, and using it as a viral marketing tool.

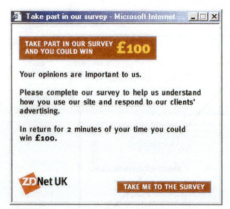

Used with permission from CNET Networks US Ltd. Copyright 2003. All rights reserved.

Pop-up produced by ZDNet.

This agreement can enable a company to begin to build a longer-term online relationship with the customer. Furthermore, the Internet enables a customer to respond by *interacting* with communication messages, unlike traditional broadcast and print media where a two-way dialogue is not possible on a large scale. *Interactive* features can be incorporated into online promotions in a number of different forms, such as surveys, competitions, banner advertisements and interstitials (adverts that pop up when Internet users visits particular websites and/or pages). Another innovative characteristic of communications via the Internet is that they can be *instantaneous*, as data is transmitted through fibre-optic cables and via satellite links at the speed of light, providing opportunities for immediate responses to enquiring customers. The Internet offers a range of new communication tools and techniques, which can be incorporated into a company's integrated marketing communications strategy, e.g. viral marketing (the spreading of messages via e-mail lists and between individuals—in other words, electronic word of mouth), interstitials (pop-ups and pop-under ads), banner advertisements (static, animated or interactive). The illustration on this page displays an example of a pop-up ad; viral marketing is discussed in e-Marketing 15.8.

Companies will need to establish an integrated communications strategy for online media in just the same manner as they would for more traditional media. However, when using the Internet, the scale of an e-commerce promotional plan will be strongly influenced by the degree to which a company already has a strong offline market presence. Thus, for example, when Tesco, the largest UK supermarket chain, began to offer an online grocery-purchasing service, the launch promotional campaign was quite simple. As the company already has strong brand recognition in the market, the main aim of its promotional activity was to register awareness for its website address. This was achieved by using traditional channels such as some television advertising, mail shots to Tesco loyalty card holders and in-store merchandising displays.

Promotional planning for an e-commerce start-up is more difficult because the company has the dual task of (i) communicating the benefits of using the firm's online facilities, and (ii) registering awareness for its website address. Although there appears to be little solid data on the scale of the promotional spending required for a successful e-commerce launch, the Boston Consulting Group has estimated that in the consumer goods markets, the expenditure will have to at least double that required to build website awareness for a company that already has a well-established offline operation. Evidence is now growing that it is this need for massive promotional expenditure that represents the largest aspect of risk in the launch of a new e-commerce business. An early example of the scale of risk is the attempt by the UK firm

15.8 e-marketing

E-mail Marketing

E-mail marketing is available to everyone with an Internet connection, an e-mail account and basic applications (e.g. Windows 98).

Most e-mail packages (e.g. Microsoft Outlook) will allow simple messages to be sent to a distribution list; this is simply the name given to a group of e-mail addresses (for example, 'sales prospects', 'friends' or 'weekend vacationers'). Through defining the customer base in this way, a few messages can be sent to hundreds of customers.

As a company learns more about its customer base over time (e.g. purchase history, business sector, position) then messages can be made more personal. Microsoft Word's 'mail merge' functionality allows users to compose a standard message and, through integrating basic spreadsheet information like first name and location, personalize it, as the following example shows.

> Dear <Field1>
> As a past customer of our <Field2> branch we are happy to announce …

Personalizing messages can increase their effectiveness but does not mean they can be sent to anyone. Spam (unsolicited mail) costs companies billions every year and e-mail marketers *must* adhere to the Data Protection Act 1998 and may even be required to register with the data protection registrar (www.dpr.gov.uk).

E-mail messages should only be sent to those that give permission, and personal data should never be used or stored in ways the provider is unaware of. A 2003 EU Directive requires companies to ask consumers to opt in to receiving e-mails and to indicate when they are using 'cookies', which are placed in a user's computer to track visits to websites, and will then have the opportunity to reject them.

E-mail is used to implement what is known as viral marketing. Many companies are using viral marketing techniques to promote their products to a wider online audience. Viral marketing is not a new concept by any means; it is the electronic version of word of mouth. Viral messages are spread every day, e.g. when a joke is received via e-mail and then sent on to friends.

Companies attempt to harness this viral effect by building messages that are suitably engaging and promote an aspect of their company with content that customers want to read and send on. This requires some creativity and a strong understanding of the customer base.

Humour is one way of creating a strong viral (or pass-along) effect. Pepsi (www.pepsi.com) famously e-mailed a series of streaming video adverts prior to the 2002 World Cup, stealing a march on its largest competitor.

'Giving something for nothing' is another effective means of increasing the viral effect. Hotmail (www.hotmail.com) became the number-one web-based e-mail supplier, with over 14 million users worldwide, most from a message sent to a handful of paid 'e-mail' users. The prospect of free e-mail was hard to resist and it was impossible not to tell others. Companies like 5pm.co.uk (www.5pm.co.uk) now sends e-mails promoting specific off-peak restaurant deals, only redeemable through unique links noted on the e-mail, with the intention that these will be passed on to 'new' customers. Almost everything has viral marketing potential—even you. If you don't have an e-mail signature file you are missing a viral marketing opportunity.

Based on: Anonymous (2003)[28]

boo.com to launch a global online sports clothing business. The company invested over £75 million (€108 million) in the creation and launch of the new business. Unfortunately, revenue inflows from sales were much lower than expected and the outcome was that, in May 2000, boo.com went into receivership and was taken over by fashion-mall.com.

A key consideration for companies is getting their websites identified by search engines. This requires marketing their websites to the search engines so that they can easily be found by web users. A second consideration is trying to improve the placing of a website on search engine page rankings. The higher the placing, the more likely a web user will visit the website.

Distribution (place)

The Internet has created opportunities for companies to utilize a *new channel* to market. This channel provides a conduit through which communication messages can be distributed but, additionally, it provides a channel where transactions can take place. Moreover, the Internet has distinct advantages over traditional channels in reducing barriers to entry. The location issue, considered to be the key determinant of retail patronage[29] in the physical sense, is reduced, along with the enormous capital investment in stores. Trading exchanges take place in a virtual market space, created by computer networks and layers of application software. As previously discussed, these networks spread around the globe.

It has been suggested that by removing the physical protection to the goods on offer (e.g. the retail store) the Internet may also provide the opportunity for increased competition. New market entrants in the guise of 'virtual merchants' can easily combine commerce software with scheduling and distribution in order to bypass traditional distributors. The Internet could therefore present a threat by fundamentally changing the distribution channels for consumer products.[30]

The potential increase in competition brought about by the advent of e-commerce is causing many firms to reassess their approach to utilizing distribution systems to acquire and sustain competitive advantage. One approach to determining an optimal mix decision when selecting an e-commerce distribution channel is to assume that there are two critical dimensions influencing the decision: whether to retain control or delegate responsibility for transaction management and logistics management.

Possibly the most frequently encountered e-commerce distribution model is that of retaining control over transactions and the delegation of distribution. This is the standard model that is in use among most online tangible goods retailers. These organizations, having successfully sold a product to a website visitor, will use the global distribution capabilities of organizations such as FedEx or UPS to manage all aspects of distribution logistics.

In the majority of offline consumer goods markets, the commonest distribution model is to delegate both transaction and logistics processes (e.g. major brands such as Coca-Cola being marketed via supermarket chains). This can be contrasted with the online world where absolute delegation of all processes is a somewhat rarer event. The reason for this situation is that many firms, having decided that e-commerce offers an opportunity for revising distribution management practices, perceive cyberspace as a way to regain control over transactions by cutting out intermediaries and selling direct to their end-user customers. This process, in which traditional intermediaries may be squeezed out of channels, is usually referred to as *disintermediation*. Hence, for those firms engaged in assessing the e-commerce distribution aspects of their marketing mix, there is the need to recognize that the technology has the following implications.

1. Distance ceases to be a cost influencer because online delivery of information is substantially the same no matter what the destination of the delivery.
2. Business location becomes an irrelevance because the e-commerce corporation can be based anywhere in the world.
3. The technology permits continuous trading, 24 hours a day, 365 days a year.

A characteristic of offline distribution channels is the difficulty that smaller firms face in persuading intermediaries (e.g. supermarket chains) to stock their goods. This scenario is less applicable in the world of e-commerce. Firms of any size face a relatively easy task in establishing an online presence. Market coverage can then be extended by developing trading alliances based upon offering to pay commission to other online traders who attract new customers to the company's website. This ease of entry variable will reduce the occurrence of firms' marketing effort being frustrated because they are unable to gain the support of intermediaries in traditional distribution channels. Eventually, e-commerce may lead to a major increase in the total number of firms offering goods and services across world markets. As this occurs, markets will become more efficient and many products will be perceived as commodities, with the consequent outcome that average prices will decline.

Marketing mix implementation

Once all the issues associated with e-commerce marketing mix selection have been resolved, these variables will provide the basis for specifying the technological infrastructure that will be needed to support the planned e-commerce operation. In some cases the firm will decide to manage all of these matters in-house, but in others the firm may outsource a major proportion of its e-commerce operations to specialist subcontractors. An example of an e-commerce market where the supplier tends to manage all aspects of the distribution management function is the financial services sector. Online banks usually wish to retain absolute control over both the transaction and delivery processes. The alternative of the e-commerce transaction being delegated, but delivery responsibility retained, can be found in the airline industry. Many of the airlines use online service providers such as www.cheapflights.co.uk to act as retailers of their unsold seat capacity. Regardless of the actual arrangement of the infrastructure solutions, the key concepts to be aware of are integration and interoperability. The greater the extent to which components of the e-commerce operation are linked across the full range of business activities, the greater the opportunities.

An action plan is needed in order that all employees can be provided with detailed descriptions of all actions to be taken to manage the e-marketing mix. This plan will include timings and definitions of which specific individual(s)/department(s) are responsible for managing the marketing mix. Financial forecasts provide a detailed breakdown of e-revenue, cost of e-goods, all e-expenditures and resultant e-profits.

Evaluation and performance control

Evaluation and control systems need to be created that permit management to rapidly identify variance of actual performance versus forecast for all aspects of the marketing mix. Management also requires mechanisms that generate diagnostic guidance on the cause of any variance. To achieve this aim, control systems should focus on the measurement of key variables within the plan such as targeted e-market share, e-customer attitudes, awareness objectives for e-promotion, e-market distribution targets by product and expected versus actual behaviour of the competition. In addition, measurement of the effectiveness of e-marketing activities should be carried out on several levels: monitoring data traffic flows, and assessing the timeliness and suitability of online content.[31]

Ethical issues in Internet marketing

The growth of marketing through the use of Internet technologies has had many beneficial effects, such as increasing customer choice and convenience, and enabling smaller companies to compete in global markets. In addition to such potential commercial benefits, the Internet phenomenon has had an impact at the ethical level.

The digital divide

The historical timeline of the development of Internet technologies reveals that in the early days it served highly specialized purposes and was used by expert technologists. Expansion and changes in the development of the World Wide Web have made Internet technology more accessible to a greater number of people, but there remains a virtual divide between the technology's 'haves' and 'have nots'. Hoffman and Novak[32] examined the impact of race on Internet adoption and concluded that educational attainment is crucial if the digital divide is to be closed.

Public and private organizations around the globe need to find create solutions to improve Internet access for all citizens regardless of their demographic background, as they should not be deprived of Internet access due to financial restrictions, a poor education and/or a lack of computer skills. From a commercial perspective, it is also important to acknowledge that while the networks forming the Internet reach around the globe, access is far from equal and equitable.

Social exclusion

Another ethical consideration is the fear that the Internet excludes the poorest members of society from partaking of the benefits of online shopping since they cannot afford a computer and the associated charges.[33] For example, Prudential, the financial services company, has faced strong criticism for the way Egg, its high-interest savings bank, cut itself off from mainstream customers by offering Internet-only access, thereby creating a system that ensures it attracts only the wealthiest customers. Some utility companies, too, may be discriminating against low-income groups by offering cut-price energy only over the Internet.[34] Conversely, many other public- and private-sector organizations throughout the European Union are committed to finding ways to support sectors of the community that are currently excluded from the growing knowledge economy. The Abbey National, working in conjunction with the charity Age Concern, has invested in free computer and Internet taster sessions for the over-50s as part of the UK's initiative to encourage use of the Internet.

Intrusions on privacy

Some Internet users are very wary of online shopping because of the information provided about them by cookies. These are tiny computer files that a marketer can download on to the computer of online shoppers that visit the marketer's website, to record their visits. Cookies serve many useful functions. They remember users' passwords so that they do not have to log on each time they revisit a site; they remember users' preferences so they can be provided with the right pages or data; and they remember the contents of consumers' shopping baskets from one visit to the next. However, because they can provide a record of users' movements around the web, cookies can give a very detailed picture of people's interests and circumstances.[35] For example, cookies contain information provided by visitors, such as product preferences, personal data and financial information, including credit card numbers.[36] From a marketer's point of view, cookies allow customized and personalized content for online shoppers. However, most Internet users probably do not know that this information is being collected and stored, and would object if they knew. (Incidentally, online users can check if their drive contains cookies by opening any file named 'cookies'.) Some people fear that companies will use this information to build psychographic profiles that enable them to influence a customer's behaviour. Others simply object that information about them is being held without their express permission. Although users are identified by a code number rather than a name and address (and this, therefore, does not violate the EU data protection directive), the fear is that direct marketing databases will be combined with information on online shopping behaviour to create a vast new way of peering into people's private lives.

Another form of invasion of privacy is the sending of unsolicited e-mails (spam). Recipients find spam intrusive and annoying. One remedy is for Internet service providers to install protection against spam on behalf of their customers. The EU's Electronic Data

15.1 ethical marketing in action

Marketing to 'Cybertots': Online or Out of Line?

The number of children using the Internet is growing rapidly. In the UK alone, an estimated 8.6 million youngsters have regular access to the Internet and spend an average of six hours every month online. This trend has been met with a corresponding increase in the amount of online marketing activity that targets children.

The dynamic and interactive characteristics of this new medium greatly enhance its potential appeal to children. The Internet encourages both exploration and interaction, and marketers have sought to create online environments that are both exciting and accessible to them. Bright and diverse colours, bold graphics, animation and sound, enable advertisers to create interactive fun-filled environments capable of inducing in children a psychological 'flow state' and engaging them for extended periods of time. Commercial messages can be skilfully woven into these environments, making it difficult for children to distinguish between editorial and advertising, and therefore to recognize they are being targeted with a sales pitch.

These sites are also extremely valuable to marketers who wish to collect demographic and personal use information about their young markets to inform their future efforts. They may either ask for the information directly, or get it more covertly by simply monitoring each child's online activities electronically. Technology capable of tracking 'mouse clicks' is now available, and the resulting data can be used to monitor how individual children interact with different forms of advertising.

The direct solicitation of information becomes part of the fun of the website. For example, on the Kellogg's Coco Pops site, children are encouraged to 'join the gang' in order to receive 'jungle e-mails from Coco' and 'other goodies'. To do this, they need to provide their full name, date of birth and e-mail address (those under 14 years are asked to provide a parent's name and e-mail address). Similarly, to participate fully in some of the interactive games (e.g. to enable their high scores to be recorded) children are required to register with the site. Shortly after they register, children are sent an e-mail encouraging them to revisit the site to help Coco the Monkey find Crafty Croc!

In the case of Coco Pops, children receive immediate and unsolicited e-mails 'from' the product 'spokescharacter' encouraging them to return to the site. In this way, contact information and product spokescharacters are used to create and foster ongoing and loyal relationships between youngsters and the brand.

Where marketers obtain more detailed information from children, such as their individual interests, tastes and preferences, they become capable of even more powerful target marketing. With this kind of information, they can communicate directly with each child, proposing products, brands or online content that they know will directly match their individual interests.

Advertising to children online poses several ethical considerations for marketers. Are they deliberately tricking children by merging advertising with other website content? Are children capable of recognizing the difference? Are children aware that the personal information that is being solicited from them will be used for future marketing purposes? Do they realize that their every mouse click is being monitored? Do the parental consent checks really work? What do you think?

Based on: Datamonitor (2002);[38] Montgomery (1996);[39] Montgomery and Pasnik (1996);[40] www.cocopops.co.uk[41]

Protection Directive states that marketers must not send e-mails to consumers who have not expressly stated their wish to receive them.

A disturbing trend is the growth in unsolicited e-mails from companies to consumers, with over half of UK consumers (57 per cent) reporting a growth according to a survey of 400 consumers conducted by anti-spam technology company Brightnoil. Worryingly, over two-thirds of respondents defined spam as 'marketing or promotional e-mails from unknown companies or individuals', and over half of the sample found spam annoying or extremely annoying. Brightnoil's global vice-president of marketing, François Lavaste, comments:

> E-mail is an excellent medium, but it is a mistake to use it without prior consent. It is better suited to the later stages of developing a relationship. We believe the best solution is for Internet service providers to install the protection on behalf of their customers, who shouldn't have to worry about it.[37]

The EU's Electronic Data Protection Directive stipulates that marketers must not send e-mails to consumers that have not expressly stated their wish to receive them. By October 2002 seven countries had signed up, with a deadline of October 2003.

Marketing to children

Another potential ethical issue is that of using the Internet to market to children. The Internet is a very popular medium with youngsters and there are ethical issues that companies need to keep in mind. Ethical Marketing in Action 15.1 (page 577) discusses some of the important issues involved.

Ethical dilemma

Napster software enabled millions of users to share and download music mp3 files from one another's computer hard drives. This infringed copyright laws and Napster was eventually taken to court, where it was subsequently ordered to cease operating. Those contesting the practices of Napster argued that this file sharing was theft and victims included the record companies, musicians, technicians and producers. Supporters of the technology, however, argued that rather than causing loss of revenue, file sharing was a valuable promotional tool. Despite the ruling against Napster, similar companies offer file-sharing facilities to copyright music free of charge. Is the provision of free music over the Internet ethical?

Review

1 **The concept of Internet marketing**

- Internet marketing is the achievement of corporate goals through meeting and exceeding customer needs better than the competition, through the utilization of digital Internet technologies.

2 **The range of activities that comprise e-commerce, and the forms of e-commerce market exchanges**

- E-commerce involves applying a wide range of digital technologies, including Internet, EDI, e-mail, electronic payment systems, advanced telephone systems, handheld digital appliances, interactive television, self-service kiosks and smart cards.

▶
- Forms of e-commerce market exchange are business-to-business (e.g. Cisco), business-to-consumer (e.g. Amazon), consumer-to-business (e.g. Priceline) and consumer-to-consumer (e.g. eBay).

3 **Factors affecting the adoption of Internet marketing**
- Internal factors: appropriate product, resource availability, clear strategic vision and strategy for assessing Internet capabilities.
- Environmental factors: extent to which competitors are using the Internet, the extent to which the target market wants to use the Internet to shop or gather information, and technological considerations.
- Comparative advantage: the extent to which the Internet can offer a potential advantage over traditional competition, such as providing speed and interactivity, and gaining access to global markets.

4 **Benefits and limitations the Internet offers customers and companies**
- The benefits for customers are convenience, information provision, multimedia advantages, the provision of new products and services, and lower prices.
- The limitations for customers are lack of flexibility with delivery times, information overload, the need for access to advanced technology, security concerns, and the need for a substantial upfront investment in computer equipment.
- The benefits for organizations are investment reduction, reduced order costs, improved distribution, reduced personal selling costs, relationship building opportunities, customized promotion, new market opportunities and market research opportunities.
- The limitations for organizations are higher operational costs (e.g. logistical costs), high set-up costs, the danger of short-termism, the need to update content regularly, the danger of creating price-based transactional relationships with customers, over-specialization by targeting unviable small groups of consumers, the creation of technological deserts, and the lack of authenticity of market research results.

5 **Organizational competences for online success**
- Strategic competence: the ability to identify new market trends and to determine how the internal capabilities of the organization can be used to exploit emerging opportunities.
- Financial competence: the required level of resources to fund the necessary investment.
- Innovation: the ability to innovate in order to stay ahead of the competition.
- Workforce: human resource management practices need to be employed to recruit, retain, train, motivate and develop staff with the necessary skills to deliver speedy and accurate service, and to sustain high levels of online technical reliability.
- Quality: using prevention-quality systems to minimize error and fulfil customer expectations.
- Productivity: two key areas are customer interface productivity and logistics productivity. Employing the latest computer technology and highly trained staff helps to achieve high levels of productivity.
- Information systems: data flows need to be integrated, and the upgrading of the company's information system is required to stay ahead of the competition.

6 **How to achieve competitive advantage online**
- The Internet offers some opportunities to establish competitive advantage through lower costs and prices, improved service quality, greater product variety and the potential to customize products.

▶

▶ **7** **The key components of an e-commerce marketing mix**

- The selection of an e-commerce marketing mix will involve similar processes to those used in conventional offline planning: marketing audit and SWOT analysis, marketing objectives and strategy, the design of the marketing mix and implementation, evaluation and control.
- The Internet's unique properties have the potential to affect all elements of the marketing mix, as outlined below.
- Product: individual personal specifications, customized shopping and delivery of bit-based digital goods and services to customers (e.g. hotel reservations).
- Price: reduction in search costs means that pricing strategies become more transparent, auction sites make prices more dynamic, and collective buying creates an opportunity for flexible pricing strategies.
- Promotion: opportunities include permission-based e-mails, banner advertisements and interstitials (pop-ups). Interaction between sender and recipient is possible and communications are instantaneous. Viral marketing can be used to spread messages through consumer groups. An integrated communications strategy needs to be established.
- Distribution: the Internet has provided a new channel to market in which transactions can take place and where the physical presence of a store is not required. The cost of online delivery of information is not dependent on distance; location is irrelevant because the e-commerce corporation can be based anywhere, and trading can be 24 hours a day, 365 days a year. Reach can be global.

Key terms

data warehousing (or data mining) the storage and analysis of customer data, gathered from their visits to websites, for classificatory and modelling purposes so that products, promotions and price can be tailored to the specific needs of individual customers

domain names global system of unique names for addressing web servers; the Domain Name System (DNS) is the method of administering such names; each level in the system is given a name and is called a domain: gTDL refers to global top-level domains (e.g. .com, .edu, .org), ccTDL refers to country code top-level domains of which there are around 250 (e.g. .uk, .fr, .it, .tv); domain names are maintained by the Internet Corporation for Assigned Names (ICANN) (www.icann.org) and are constantly under review; ICANN also deals with cases of cybersquatting; domain name registration is required if a company wants to establish a web presence

e-business a term originally used by IBM to describe technological solutions that enable an organization to optimize its business operations through the adoption of digital technologies

e-commerce the use of technologies such as the Internet, electronic data interchange, e-mail and electronic payment systems to expedite business interactions

e-commerce marketing mix the extension of the traditional marketing mix to include the opportunities afforded by new electronic media such as the Internet

electronic data interchange (EDI) a pre-Internet technology developed to enable organizations' computers to exchange documents (e.g. purchase orders) with one another in a secure environment via a dedicated computer link

▶ **e-marketing** the achievement of marketing objectives through the utilization of electronic communication technologies, including mobile devices

e-procurement the purchasing of goods and services (in business markets) via the Internet

http (hypertext transfer protocol) A standard invented by Tim Berners-Lee in 1991 to enable computers across the Internet to receive and send web content

Internet global web of computer networks, which permits instantaneous communication and transactions between individuals and organizations; the structure of these networks is based on links between special computers called servers and routers, which store and direct data across the networks respectively

Internet marketing the achievement of marketing objectives through the utilization of Internet and web-based technologies

viral marketing electronic word of mouth, where promotional messages are spread using e-mail from person to person

website a collection of various files including text, graphics, video and audio content created by organizations and individuals; website content is transmitted across the Internet using http

World Wide Web a collection of computer files that can be accessed via the Internet, allowing organizations to include documents containing text, images, sound and video

Internet exercise

The strategic role of a website can vary significantly from those designed to serve an organization's *communication objectives* to those that provide an organization with a new or additional channel to market. Sometimes the strategic function of the website can be obscured through overly creative application of multimedia content. Nevertheless, it is important to understand the purpose set for any website to facilitate reflection on performance and to assist with competitor analysis. Some suggested sites to visit, which have various strategic functions, are listed below.

Visit: http://www.accor.com
http://www.accorhotels.com/accorhotels/index.html
http://www.bmw.co.uk (BMW UK)
http://www.bmwgroup.com (BMW)
http://www.uk.thebodyshop.com/web/tbsuk/index.jsp (Body Shop plc)
http://www.wellbeing.com/index.jsp (Boots Company plc)

Questions

(a) Find three company websites that you think are serving different strategic functions.
(b) Analyse the content of each site in order to clarify how the website potentially adds value from the customers' perspective (either business-to-business or business-to-consumer).
(c) Identify any gaps.
(d) Score the websites in terms of their ability to meet the strategic function.

Visit the Online Learning Centre at www.mcgraw-hill.co.uk/textbooks/jobber for more Internet exercises.

Study questions

1. Marketing on the Internet is a growing business. Why is this so? What are the barriers to its more rapid expansion?

2. Discuss the ways that the operations of organizations are likely to change as a result of the development of e-commerce.

3. What are the benefits of the Internet and e-commerce to customers and organizations? Are there any potential disadvantages and pitfalls of marketing on the Internet?

4. Discuss the key competences necessary to implement an online marketing plan successfully.

5. Discuss the unique characteristics the Internet offers that can be used as a basis for competitive advantage.

6. How can the marketing mix be extended and utilized to support an e-marketing strategy?

7. Discuss the key ethical issues relating to the Internet and online marketing.

8. With reference to e-Marketing 15.3, what are the advantages and pitfalls for an organization like Coors Brewers of having access to a global online purchasing system? Explain why you think giving an e-procurement system an identity could help with its implementation.

When you have read this chapter log on to the Online Learning Centre at www.mcgraw-hill.co.uk/textbooks/jobber to explore chapter-by-chapter test questions, links and further online study tools for marketing.

case twenty-nine

Google: a Victim of its Own Success?

> The world's biggest, best-loved search engine owes its success to supreme technology and a simple rule: don't be evil. Now the geek icon is finding that moral compromise is just the cost of doing big business.[1]

During September 1998, Google was launched. This innovative approach to searching the Internet uses the world's biggest index to find useful online information resources.[2] Google, created by graduate students Larry Page and Sergey Brin of the Computer Science Department at Stanford University, USA, has rapidly become a very successful search engine, accounting for around 80 per cent of Internet searches worldwide. In terms of visitor numbers, this currently means that in excess of 28 million visitors spend around 15 million hours a month using Google-driven sites to find online information resources.[3] Google's success can be attributed to several key factors.

Innovative computer technology

Smart algorithms (mathematical instructions that computers can understand) devised by Larry and Sergey helped to resolve the problem faced by many Internet users of how to find relevant information. Google's system is in principle straightforward: by focusing on page rankings rather than just indexing contents, the search engine is able to provide more relevant search results than earlier search tools such as Yahoo!, AltaVista and Excite. Search tools are used to crawl the web, checking the content of pages, but are in fact oblivious to the actual meaning of the content. As a result they are unable to differentiate between relevant and irrelevant web pages when delivering search results.

However, by adopting a rank-ordering system, logging pages according to the number of links from other web pages and the structure of these connections, has enabled Google to become a quasi-intelligent search tool. To assist the ranking process, Google also checks font sizes, whether a word appears in the page title, the position on the page in which a word appears and a range of other page characteristics in order to give an indication of the significance of the search term within a given page. Overall, technological advances made at the product design stage contributed to Google's instant success by

Sergey Brin, President of Google, delivers a keynote speech to the company.

providing a product that was quickly perceived by Internet users as superior to the competition. Accordingly, the Google brand has been able to differentiate itself from the competition mainly by introducing the customer benefit of 'relevance' to online searching.

E-commerce business model

Google's financial success, a rarity among Internet businesses, can be explained by the business model adopted by Larry and Sergey, and their constant focus on building and, perhaps more importantly, maintaining brand values.

Initially, the success was based on licensing the company's search technology to third parties. It currently provides search services for a number of leading search engines (see Fig. C29.1). Indeed, a recent survey by Nielsen/NetRatings[4] showing the audience reach of the

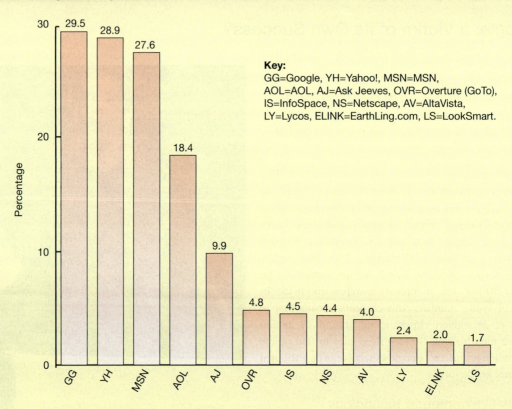

Figure C29.1 US digital media universe audience reach (Home and work users, January 2003)

Source: Nielsen/NetRatings for SearchEngineWatch.com.

Key:
GG=Google, YH=Yahoo!, MSN=MSN,
AOL=AOL, AJ=Ask Jeeves, OVR=Overture (GoTo),
IS=InfoSpace, NS=Netscape, AV=AltaVista,
LY=Lycos, ELINK=EarthLing.com, LS=LookSmart.

top 12 search engines, helps demonstrate the extent of Google's success as the company is the 'search provider' for Yahoo!, AOL, Ask Jeeves, Netscape and Hotbot.[5]

In addition to licensing search technology, Larry and Sergey eventually decided to explore the search engine's capacity to generate advertising revenue. In 1998, the key question puzzling many dotcom entrepreneurs was how to harness Internet and web technologies profitably. Most of Google's direct competitors had already opted for business models that relied on generating advertising revenue. A key problem with this approach was that formerly uncluttered customer interfaces became cluttered with a variety of static and interactive banner advertisements and pop-ups (for example, AltaVista, whose name means literally 'The view from above'). The outcome was that many loyal Internet users (searchers) rapidly became dissatisfied customers. Nevertheless, the Google team decided to use advertising to generate revenue. However, they used a text-based approach to advertise sponsored links, enabling the home page to remain uncluttered. Instantly, Internet searchers were highly satisfied by this approach and, almost overnight, Google became an internationally recognised brand.

In addition to having a successful financial business model, the company also adopted a lean and flexible operations strategy. According to Vogelstein,[6] what lies behind Google's success is its network of data centres based around Santa Clara, USA. Thousands of computer servers provide a search capacity much greater than the company's rivals generating approximately eight times the capacity of competitors. However, these computers are built in-house and run on the free Linux operating system. Consequently, Google benefits, as repairs and upgrades are comparatively low cost. Low operating costs facilitated the company's development during the early days.

The future

Larry and Sergey had a good idea and implemented it in a manner that enabled the company to differentiate itself from the competition, while protecting itself by raising market entry barriers. Currently, Google is a private company and its key responsibility is to ensure that it meets the needs of its customers. However, this is becoming increasingly difficult. The company's phenomenal success and world dominance as a search engine/provider could be about to create major difficulties for its most valuable asset: its brand identity. Sergey Brin has been the defender of Google's conscience 'but in doing so he imposes his worldview on everyone else'[7]— approximately 80 per cent of the world's online populations. Google's idealistic standpoint is being brought into question, its mission to 'Do good by users', remaining 'pure' throughout, is becoming more difficult to maintain. On the one hand, Sergey has sanctioned closing down web pages considered to be making inappropriate comments and has also acquiesced to legal pressures to close down sites offering controversial viewpoints. On the other hand, Google has been shut down by a national government. The Chinese government decided to block access to Google as it was considered to allow access to dissident political viewpoints. Instantly, Sergey engaged in some deft negotiations with the Chinese government in order to work out a compromise. A few days later, access to Google was restored, much to the delight of the 46 million Internet users in China.

It will, inevitably, become increasingly difficult for Google to 'delight' all of its Internet searchers and, therefore, policy decisions will need to be made, but where will such decisions lead? Will Google compromise its 'purity' in order to retain visitor numbers?

[1] McHugh, J. (2003) Google vs Evil, *Wired* 11(1) 130–5.
[2] Naughton, J. (2002) Web Masters, *Observer*, 15 December, 27.
[3] McHugh, J. (2003) op. cit.
[4] http://www.searchenginewatch.com/reports/article.php/2156451.
[5] http://www.searchenginewatch.com/reports/article.php/2156401.
[6] Vogelstein, F. (2002) Looking for a Dot-com Winner? Search no Further, *Fortune* 145(11) 65–8.
[7] McHugh, J. (2003) op. cit.

Questions

1. What are Google's sources of online competence?

2. How does Google differentiate itself from the competition and, in doing so, create competitive advantage?

3. Should Google aim to maintain its competitive advantage using its current approach to online advertising (text-based only) or should the company allow banner and other forms of online advertising, which could provide significant opportunities for income generation?

This case was prepared by Dr Fiona Ellis-Chadwick, Lecturer in Marketing and e-Commerce, Loughborough University.

case thirty

Thin Red Line

Thin Red Line is a shirt retailing company based in West London. It currently has a retail store on Fulham Road, offers a direct mail service and is in the early stages of retailing shirts on the Internet. The firm was born when Hereward Cleghorn-Brown and Tim Haller were offered some unused space in the back room of Cleghorn-Brown's mother's office, conveniently situated on Savile Row, home of some of the best hand-made shirts in the world. A shirt company need only mention that it has an office on this prestigious road and it can add a significant mark-up to the price of its goods.

Haller and Cleghorn-Brown, therefore, decided to capitalize on this and began their own mail-order shirt company from their Savile Row address. Their idea was simple: good-quality shirts for affluent young people at an affordable and competitive price. They created a brochure that was distributed by mail and reinforced through word of mouth. They learned a great deal in the first two years of trading and with their products, premium location and leisure shirts at a good price, their results also improved with experience.

They were soon set to grow the business with a product that was ready for a retail outlet. By this time the partners had specialized, with Cleghorn-Brown having taken over marketing affairs, and Haller handling the financial aspects of the firm. They borrowed sufficient funds to rent a store in London's fashionable neighbourhood of Fulham, which was an ideal location for their products. There was only one other shirt store in the district, which seemed to be doing very well, and the area was well known for its affluent young shoppers. Thin Red Line invested heavily in store layout and directed its efforts toward reinforcing the premium value of its shirts.

By late 1998 the store had an annual turnover of £250,000 (€360,000) and employed two sales assistants. Its product range continues to expand and has been extended to include cufflinks and boxer shorts. Free collar stiffeners are given away with each purchase, and the company also believes in attempting to explain to customers the more technical aspects of choosing and wearing shirts correctly (see the illustration).

'Six Reasons to Shop with Us!'—from the Thin Red Line website.

Target market and current market share

While Thin Red line has not commissioned any formal market research in this area, the partners are enthusiastic 'do-it-yourself' marketing researchers and strategists. They believe that the target market consists of all business shirt wearers. Further segmentation narrows this focus to affluent professional men and women aged 20 to 65. The trendy design of the retail store is more geared towards the younger, 20–40, age group, reflecting the underlying demographic of the population of Fulham. Thin Red Line also believes that younger people are more prepared to switch brands or try new styles. The firm attempts to concentrate on all 'successful' men and women in established industries (e.g. banking, finance, insurance and law), where suits and formal dress codes are still in place.

Currently, Thin Red Line estimates to have captured approximately 25–30 per cent of the Fulham Road shirt market. However, it understands that it only has a negligible share of the UK shirt market, and has not really made any impact at all internationally.

Competition

Thin Red Line's major competitors span the UK, and with the advent of the Internet, a number of these have attempted to trade globally. Currently, Thin Red Line regards its main competitors as shirt manufacturers and retailers in the UK that are either mail-order vendors or located in the Fulham area, and that attempt to serve the young/affluent sector of the market. These include:

- Thomas Pink (www.thomaspink.co.uk)
- Charles Tyrwhitt (www.ctshirts.co.uk)
- Cavenagh (www.cavenagh.co.uk), and
- TM Lewin (www.lewin.co.uk).

Cleghorn-Brown and Haller have discovered that the Charles Tyrwhitt website is very successful and turned over about £2 million (€2.88 million) in 1998. This is thought to be as a direct result of Tyrwhitt's exploitation of its extensive mail-order database and marketing expenditure, which is concentrated on inserts in magazines such as the *Economist* and *Country Life*. All the firm's promotional material features the website and its URL quite prominently. Thomas Pink is thought to be successful for similar reasons, although the firm has recently increased prices to around £55 (€79) per shirt, which moves it further away from the value side of the market.

The birth of Thin Red Line.com

Cleghorn-Brown has always been fascinated by technology, and the Internet has interested him greatly since 1997. In early 1998, he began investigating how Thin Red Line could utilize the Internet to grow and develop its business. Because choices were hampered by a lack of funds to invest in new projects such as this, he taught himself HTML programming and built a website for Thin Red Line on his own.

By the end of 1998, he had created a non-functional web presence for Thin Red Line. However, it was not until February 1999 that he managed to create a site that let customers browse through pages displaying the various products the firm had on offer. He admitted that he had no strategy for the firm's web presence at this time and just wanted to see what happened.

To the surprise of Cleghorn-Brown and Haller, the web page enjoyed quite a large number of hits (an average of 3897 per month) during the first six months of 1999, which resulted in a reasonable average purchase size of £85.62 (€123) per online transaction. Cleghorn-Brown began to hope for even more than this from the Internet, and he started to look at various ways of maximizing the potential of the medium for Thin Red Line.

Suitability of Thin Red Line to e-commerce

In an attempt to align their thinking on the role of e-commerce in their overall strategy, Cleghorn-Brown and Haller spent a morning in July 1999 completing a checklist contained in a report in the *Financial Times*, entitled 'Creating Value through the Internet'. This questionnaire had been devised to help a firm assess its e-commerce capability. The partners were surprised at how consistent their answers were when they compared them—with a few exceptions they had both given the same responses.

According to the report:

- if the total score was between 70 and 100, the company is well positioned to achieve success on the Internet
- between 50 and 70, the firm still has considerable work to do to make the Internet work for it
- if the score is less than 50, e-commerce is unlikely to be successful and a major rethink is required.

Thin Red Line scored 42.

After the exercise however, Cleghorn-Brown was sceptical about the validity of the checklist. 'First,' he argued to Tim Haller, 'this scoring system has been devised by two Arthur Andersen consultants. I think they just want to make small firms like ours feel that they need to seek more consulting advice!

'Second, there are a number of the questions that are not totally applicable to our situation. For example, "Are you using e-commerce to consolidate your suppliers and cut costs?" That's dumb. Thin Red Line only has one supplier, and therefore our score has been affected accordingly.' Tim Haller was less doubtful. 'I think this questionnaire does have some utility. It does highlight our current lack of strategic intent towards e-commerce. It also reflects our need to develop an Internet perspective, increase online sales and extend our overall site strategy. Perhaps we do need a rethink.' The checklist used, and Thin Red Line's scoring on it are shown in Table C30.1.

Table C30.1 The *Financial Times* e-commerce checklist as completed by Cleghorn-Brown and Haller (averaged)

Question	Possible answers	Score
Do you have a strong 'customer proposition'?	We have a unique proposition, which has clear benefits to the customer and has already been successfully test-marketed.	20 points
	Our customer proposition is good, and we believe it will be received positively by customers when it is launched.	10 points
	Ours is essentially a 'me-too' offering—but it seems to work for our competitors.	5 points
	Score out of 20 (insert your score here)	**5**
Is senior management fully committed?	Senior management is committed to fundamental changes and our company has already appointed a senior executive to lead our e-commerce initiatives.	15 points
	Senior management understands e-commerce and appears to be prepared to make changes to make our e-commerce initiatives work.	8 points
	Senior management has an elementary understanding of e-commerce but our e-commerce initiatives are only being driven by one or two middle managers.	4 points
	Score out of 15 (insert your score here)	**8**
Have you adapted your sales and distribution (or procurement) processes for 'cyberspace'?	With the help of our key customers, we have fundamentally redesigned our key processes and have carefully planned the implementation of these changes to ensure that our e-commerce offering will work effectively.	15 points
	We have agreed to make some changes to our key processes such as sales and distribution.	8 points
	Our existing processes are more or less the same as before. Although there may be some teething problems, we're sure we'll be able to work through issues as they arise.	4 points
	Score out of 15 (insert your score here)	**8**
Are you providing valuable content for your customers?	Our Internet site is one of the most innovative in the industry and is updated constantly using a variety of in-house and externally commissioned content material.	10 points
	We regularly update our site with new material although we have never considered going to external providers to improve the range and quality of our content.	5 points
	Our Internet site is well designed and easy to navigate. We provide information on our products and services and we even have a picture of our CEO on the site.	2 points
	Score out of 10 (insert your score here)	**2** ▶

Table C30.1 continued		
Question	Possible answers	Score
Are you using e-commerce to consolidate your suppliers and cut costs?	Since agreeing to introduce e-commerce for procurement, we have planned to halve the number of suppliers we deal with and our procurement costs through obtaining more favourable rates from our remaining suppliers.	10 points
	We will probably reduce the number of suppliers as a result of implementing e-commerce in our company.	5 points
	Our policy is to maintain a wide range of suppliers in order to maintain competition between them.	2 points
	Score out of 10 (insert your score here)	**2**
Do your customers contribute to your e-commerce offering?	We have designed our offering with the help of our customers, who have the flexibility to design and order their own products, while we have been able to reduce costs in our traditional distribution channels.	10 points
	Our customers can provide us with feedback, which we will use as an input to our design process.	5 points
	We have a good traditional website that is generating leads for us.	2 points
	Score out of 10 (insert your score here)	**2**
Have you created links to other sites or alliances with other companies?	We have researched our offering in great detail and have created formal alliances with a number of other organizations. This generates a 'club' atmosphere among our customers and builds loyalty to our Internet site.	10 points
	We have started to create links with a number of organizations to make our e-commerce offering more attractive to customers.	5 points
	Our website should generate a reasonably high volume of traffic.	2 points
	Score out of 10 (insert your score here)	**5**
Are you thinking big, starting small and scaling quickly?	We have an ambitious end game, resources committed to a number of options and will invest heavily in successful ventures.	10 points
	We are ambitious but only investing in one option to achieve our objectives.	5 points
	We are testing the water with an e-commerce venture and will see how it goes.	2 points
	Score out of 10 (insert your score here)	**10**
	Overall score (out of a maximum of 100)	**42**

Both Cleghorn-Brown and Haller are firmly convinced that as products, shirts are imminently suited to online shopping. The product appeals to a wide section of potential customers. Generally, Thin Red Line's shirts are bought by professional men who have little time for, or interest in, buying office attire.

Reorders are received on a regular basis, and customers tend to become very loyal to a brand, if for no other reason than they know what they are getting. Shirts can be displayed and conveyed well visually, as the company realized in the beginning when it compiled its brochure. Buying a shirt does not constitute a complex purchase, and therefore a customer will feel happy reordering a shirt. Shirt sizes are effectively 'graded', and therefore the products within each category are fairly standardized. Almost the only exception is that Thin Red Line offers arm extensions to its shirts at a price of £9 (€13).

Haller believes that brand loyalty is very strong and that purchasers would be unlikely to buy a Thin Red Line shirt unless they had gone to the physical store and had experienced the shirt. The Internet is not able to offer this experience, but does provide an extremely easy and convenient way to reorder a product. Both partners are convinced that, in general, consumers will buy online because of increased convenience and customization.

Thin Red Line's website: www.thinredline.com

The Thin Red Line website offers a full 'brochure' experience that allows Internet surfers to browse through the current range of products. Despite the relatively large number of photographs on the site, the pages open quickly. The website also allows effortless and secure (Secure Server Software, SSL) online purchasing with a shopping basket function similar to that used by online giants such as Amazon.com and Barnes and Noble. Thin Red Line promises 48-hour worldwide dispatch. Any dialogue with Thin Red Line is answered instantly by an automatic response from the firm, and the partners believe that these activities meet the need for immediacy of interaction that Internet users now expect.

The site is fast, clear and easy to navigate. Selecting styles and colours is simple and adding items to the shopping basket is prompted by 'ADD TO ORDER' buttons. The front page of the site is shown in the illustration.

Evaluating the website's effectiveness

Haller and Cleghorn-Brown concur that the end goal of the website is to promote and facilitate online purchasing, to increase sales, reduce costs and improve profitability. However, they talk continually about the fact that this is not possible without visitors to the site. Their interim objective is to attract and retain visitors to the site. Both Cleghorn-Brown and Haller have become enthusiastic, although admittedly amateur, marketing researchers on the site. 'While we confess to all kinds of research sins, such as small samples, rushed jobs and an obvious lack of formal marketing research training, Tim and I are rather proud of some of the approaches and results we have achieved and the data we have gathered,' says Cleghorn-Brown.

'For example,' he continues, 'we have calculated a ratio of visitors to hits on the site, as well as a ratio of purchases to visitors [see Table C30.2]. Our goal is obviously to increase the ratio of purchases to visitors, but we believe that before we can do this, we need to "up" the visits-to-hits ratio. And then before we can do that well, we really need to increase the number of hits, which is of course the 64,000-dollar question facing everyone on the net.'

'Our ultimate goal is that our website sales should exceed our retail store sales,' says Haller. 'I budgeted for revenue in 2000 of £350,000 (€504,000).' His analysis of how many additional active visitors to the website would be required to convert into £150,000 (€216,000) worth of revenue in 2000 is shown in Table C30.3.

Cleghorn-Brown and Haller have gathered other information they believe is pertinent to their online business. For example, they have established that 58 per cent of the visitors type in the domain name directly, 35 per cent find the site through search engines, and 7 per cent through a Thin Red Line link on other websites. Some of their current ideas for promoting the Thin Red Line website are as follows.

A sample page from the Thin Red Line website (www.thinredline.com).

Table C30.2 An analysis of surfer activity on Thin Red Line's website using an average from May through August 1999

$$\text{Contact efficiency} = \frac{\text{Active visitors to the site}}{\text{Hits on the site}} = \frac{1481}{3897} = 38\%$$

(Active visitors are considered to be those who go beyond the first page)

$$\text{Conversion efficiency} = \frac{\text{Purchases}}{\text{Active visitors}} = \frac{12}{1481} = 0.8\%$$

- Printing the web address and e-mail address on all of the company's literature, stationary and display advertising. If the prospects believe that they can receive more information about Thin Red Line's products and services then they will visit the site.
- Giving prospects a reason to visit the site. 'We would like to offer something of value to prospects, whether it's saving money on a "shirt of the month", as Charles Tyrwhitt does, or "What's new in fashion", as [Thomas] Pink does, or simply the opportunity to learn more about Thin Red Line,' says Cleghorn-Brown.
- Promote the site using traditional media. 'Perhaps we should spend more money on print advertising and ensure that the web address and e-mail address are featured prominently,' says Cleghorn-Brown. Haller counters, 'That's great, where will the money come from?'

Other information gathered by the firm is the fact that visitors to the Thin Red Line website currently stay an average of 1.5 minutes, and that the longer they stay on the site the more likely they are to purchase. The partners agree that keeping people engaged on the website for longer periods of time is key to success.

Thin Red Line's target market is a professional between the ages of 25 and 45. The male/female split is 75/25 per cent respectively. In order to investigate these issues in more detail, Cleghorn-Brown sent a survey by e-mail to 25 professionals between the ages of 25 and 45; 10 responses were received, 50 per cent male and 50 per cent female; six respondents were between the ages of 25 and 30, and four were 31 or older.

The respondents were asked to spend 10 minutes surfing the Thin Red Line website as a potential buyer and then rate a series of statements. The items were rated on a Likert-type scale ranging from 1 = strongly disagree, through to 5 = strongly agree. 'In summary, I learned the following,' says Cleghorn-Brown: 'People felt in control when exploring the site and believed that the website allowed them to control the interaction. People also disagreed that they were aware of distractions on the site, although only a few of them felt that they were totally absorbed in what they were doing while exploring the site.

'People also felt that their curiosity was not highly stimulated throughout the interaction, and also that their imagination had not really been aroused by the site. On a more positive note, the site appeared to be interesting to the surfers, but the vote was split on whether the site was fun to explore.' He summarizes: 'My conclusion at present, based on this small survey, is that the Thin Red Line website is good (7 out of 10 respondents said they would visit the site again) but not brilliant. I would like to find ways of improving the customer's curiosity and interest levels, and to give them more opportunity to have fun on the site.'

Table C30.3 Tim Haller's estimates on additional £150,000 revenue from the website in 2000

Revenue goal	£150,000
Average spend per customer	£85.62
No. of annual purchasers required	1752
Current no. of purchasers per month	146
No. of additional active visitors needed per month (at an 8% conversion efficiency)	18,249
No. of additional hits needed per month (at a 38% contact efficiency)	48,024
The current monthly average number of active visitors is 1481 and the current average number of monthly visitors is 3897	

Current and emerging website strategy

'I think we have to admit that we did not have an entry strategy for our website,' Cleghorn-Brown reflects. 'I think our attitude has been, "Let's see what happens." But we both have very high aspirations for the site, and like to think that our strategies are now emerging. First, we intend to accelerate overall profits for the firm by getting sales from the website to exceed sales from the store.

'Second, we want our branding to become synonymous with the Internet, and not our retail store. Ultimately, we want to get back to our roots and be a mail-order company, but based only on the Internet, with no printing and postage costs in our marketing efforts. We think that the potential savings that derive from online versus postal brochure distribution are enormous.'

Haller adds, 'We lose approximately 10 per cent of our mail-order database customers because they move and don't inform us of their new address; e-commerce provides several advantages because we know immediately who is no longer there because of the undelivered e-mail message. This dramatically cuts down on wasted catalogues and postage charges. Furthermore, our competitors are seen as shirt stores or mail-order companies who also have a website, but they are viewed primarily as stores. We want to be perceived primarily as a web-based company with an outlet in Fulham. Perhaps people will want to try on their first Thin Red Line shirt before buying, but after that we want them to reorder the same size shirt online, without having to come back in to the store.'

'We are now thinking about rebranding everything with www.thinredline.com as the major brand signal (boxes, bags, shirt labels, letterhead, etc.),' adds Cleghorn-Brown. 'Coupled with media attention, we want to promote this change of perception. From this relaunch, we are hoping to receive 10,000 new registrations, which can be used to create a more detailed database. We think this would be a bold but potentially sound move.'

Haller reflects, 'Instead of letting things simply keep evolving like this, I think the time has come to sit down for a few days, away from the hustle and bustle of the store. Let's involve our supplier, and even the assistants—after all, they talk to and help customers who buy shirts. My uncle has a huge room in a renovated barn on his farm in Oxfordshire. It would be ideal. We could even have an agenda.'

'Now that would be something!' Cleghorn-Brown counters. 'Maybe we would even stick to it!'

Questions

1. Assess the suitability of Thin Red Line to e-commerce.
2. Of what strategic use might e-commerce be to Thin Red Line?
3. Produce a SWOT analysis of Thin Red Line in relation to e-commerce.
4. Evaluate the effectiveness of Thin Red Line's website. How might it be improved?
5. Summarize your recommendations to Thin Red Line.

Graduate students David Harmston, Jill Schwabl and Rian van der Merwe prepared this case under the supervision of Professor Leyland Pitt as the basis for class discussion rather than to illustrate either effective or ineffective handling of an administrative situation.

Other promotional mix methods

chapter sixteen

> Advertising brings the horse to water, sales promotion makes it drink. — JULIAN CUMMINS

> Don't tell my mother I'm in public relations, she thinks I play piano in a brothel. — JACQUES SEQUELA

Learning Objectives

This chapter explains:

1. The growth in sales promotion
2. The major sales promotion types
3. The objectives and evaluation of sales promotion
4. The objectives and targets of public relations
5. The key tasks and characteristics of publicity
6. The guidelines to use when writing a news release
7. The objectives and methods of sponsorship
8. How to select and evaluate a potential sponsored event or programme
9. The objectives, conduct and evaluation of exhibitions
10. The reasons for the growth in product placement and its risks
11. Ethical issues in sales promotion and public relations

In Chapters 12, 13, 14 and 15 we examined the role and use of advertising, personal selling, direct marketing and Internet marketing in the promotional mix. This chapter provides an analysis of other methods of promoting products: sales promotion, public relations and publicity, sponsorship, exhibitions and product placement. Traditionally, these were regarded as playing a secondary role compared to advertising and personal selling. In recent years, though, one common factor has linked them all: they are all growth areas in the promotional mix, and marketing people need to know how to manage them effectively. Each method needs to be used as part of a consistent communication programme so that all elements of the promotional mix support and reinforce one another. The message needs to be consistent with the product's positioning strategy.

Sales promotion

As we saw in Chapter 12, sales promotions are incentives to consumers or the trade that are designed to stimulate purchase. Examples include money off and free gifts (consumer promotions), discounts and salesforce competitions (trade promotions). Incentives to in-company salespeople are sometimes included within the definition of sales promotion but these have been dealt with in Chapter 13, and consequently will not be discussed in this chapter.

A vast amount of money is spent on sales promotion. Peattie and Peattie explain the growth in sales promotion as follows.[1]

- *Increased impulse purchasing*: the retail response to greater consumer impulse purchasing is to demand more sales promotions from manufacturers.

- *Sales promotions are becoming respectable*: through the use of promotions by market leaders and the increasing professionalism of the sales promotion agencies.

- *The rising cost of advertising and advertising clutter*: these factors erode advertising's cost effectiveness.

- *Shortening time horizons*: the attraction of the fast sales boost of a sales promotion is raised by greater rivalry and shortening product life cycles.

- *Competitor activities*: in some markets, sales promotions are used so often that all competitors are forced to follow suit.[2]

- *Measurability*: measuring the impact of sales promotions is easier than for advertising since their effect is more direct and, usually, short term. The growing use of electronic point-of-sale (EPOS) scanner information makes measurement easier.

The effects of sales promotion

Sales promotion is often used to provide a short, sharp shock to sales. In this sense it may be regarded as a short-term tactical device. Figure 16.1 shows a typical sales pattern. The sales promotion boosts sales during the promotion period because of the incentive effect. This is followed by a small fall in sales to below normal level because some consumers will have stocked up on the product during the promotion. The long-term sales effect of the promotion could be positive, neutral or negative. If the promotion has attracted new buyers, who find that they like the brand, repeat purchases from them may give rise to a positive long-term effect.[3] Alternatively, if the promotion (e.g. money off) has devalued the brand in the eyes of consumers, the effect may be negative.[4] Where the promotion has caused consumers to buy the brand only because of its incentive value, with no effect on underlying preferences, the long-term effect may be neutral.[5] An international study of leading grocery brands has shown that the most likely long-term effect of a price promotion for an existing brand is neutral. Such promotions tend to attract existing buyers of the brand rather than new buyers during the promotional period.[6]

Some sales promotions may have a more strategic focus, however. Smith describes how Pears, the premium-priced transparent soap, is supported by the annual Miss Pears competition.[7] The competition attracts 20,000 entries each year and the photograph of the winning child is featured on the Pears soap cartons. The objective of the promotion is to enhance Pears' caring family image.

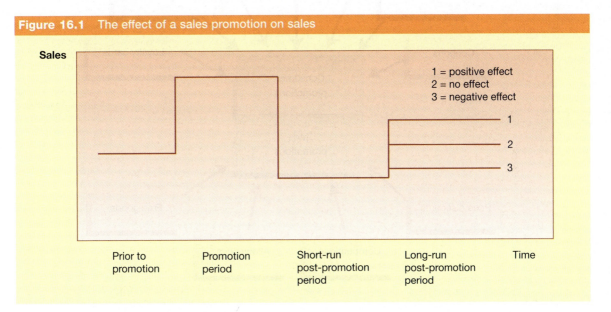

Figure 16.1 The effect of a sales promotion on sales

Major sales promotion types

Sales promotion can be directed at the consumer or the trade (see Fig. 16.2). Major consumer sales promotion types are money off, bonus packs, premiums, free samples, coupons, prize promotions and loyalty cards. A sizeable proportion of sales promotions are directed at the trade, including price discounts, free goods, competitions and allowances.

Money off

Money-off promotions provide a direct value to the customer, and therefore an unambiguous incentive to purchase. They have a proven track record of stimulating short-term sales increases. However, price reductions can easily be matched by the competition and if used frequently can devalue brand image. Consumer response may be 'If the brand is that good why do they need to keep reducing the price?'

Bonus packs

These give *added value* by giving consumers extra quantity at no additional cost. **Bonus packs** are often used in the drinks, confectionery and detergent markets. For example, cans of lager may be sold on the basis of '12.5 per cent extra free!' Because the price is not lowered, this form of promotion runs less risk of devaluing brand image. Extra value is given by raising quantity rather than cutting price. With some product groups, this encourages buyers to consume more. For example, a Mars bar will be eaten or a can of lager drunk whether there is extra quantity or not. The illustrations on page 597 show the use of bonus pack promotions for Lucozade and Sainsbury's Cerveza de España.

Figure 16.2 Consumer and trade promotions

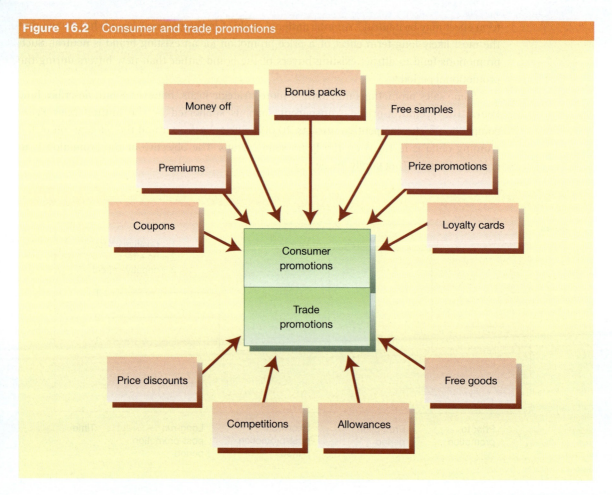

Premiums

Premiums are any merchandise offered free or at low cost as an incentive to purchase a brand. There are three major forms: free in- or on-pack gifts, free-in-the-mail offers, and self-liquidating offers.

Free in- or on-pack gifts: gifts may be given away free with brands. For example, Twiglets, a snack food, was promoted by enclosing a small can of Appletize, a fizzy apple drink, in its pack; PG Tips, a brand of tea, used a plastic dinosaur attached to the outside of its packaging to promote sales. A free in-pack promotion for Nestlé Sporties and an on-pack promotion for Nestlé Frosted Shreddies are shown in the illustrations on page 598. Occasionally the gift is a free sample of one brand that is banded to another brand (*banded pack offer*). The free sample may be a new variety or flavour that benefits by getting trial. In other cases the brands are linked, as when Nestlé promoted its Cappuccino brand by offering a free KitKat to be eaten while drinking the coffee, and Cadbury ran a similar promotion with a packet of Cadbury's Chocolate Chip Cookies attached to its Cadbury's Chocolate Break, a milk chocolate drink.

When two or more items are banded together the promotion is called a multibuy and can involve a number of items of the same brand being offered together. Multibuys are a very popular form of promotion. They are frequently used to protect market share by encouraging consumers to stock up on a particular brand when two or more items of the same brand are packaged together. However, unlike price reductions, they do not encourage trial because consumers do not bulk buy a brand they have not tried before. When multibuys take the form of two different brands, range trial can be generated. For example, a manufacturer of a branded

Lucozade energy drink featuring a bonus offer.

Extra value is provided by this bonus pack of Sainsbury's Cerveza de España.

coffee launching a new brand of tea could band the two brands together, thus leveraging the strength of the coffee brand to gain trial of the new tea brand.[8]

Free-in-the-mail offers: this sort of promotion involves the collection of packet tops or labels, which are sent in the mail as proof of purchase to claim a free gift or money-off voucher; Kellogg's Ricicles has been promoted by such an offer. Gifts can be quite valuable because redemption rates can be low (less than 10 per cent redemption is not unusual). This is because of *slippage*: consumers collect labels with a view to mailing them but never collect the requisite number.

Self-liquidating offers: these are similar to free-in-the-mail offers except that consumers are asked to pay a sum of money to cover the costs of the merchandise plus administration and postage charges. The consumer benefits by getting the goods at below normal cost because the manufacturer passes on the advantage of bulk buying and prices at cost. The manufacturer benefits by the self-funding nature of the promotion, although there is a danger of being left with surplus stocks of the merchandise. A self-liquidating offer used to promote the Weetabix Bananabix brand is shown in the illustration overleaf.

Free samples

Free samples of a brand may be delivered to the home or given out in a store. The idea is that having tried the sample a proportion of consumers will begin to buy it. For new brands or brand extensions (for example, a new shampoo or fabric conditioner) this form of promotion is an effective if expensive way of gaining consumer trial. However, sampling may be ineffective if the brand has nothing extra to offer the consumer. For existing brands that have a low trial but

Nestlé Sporties: a free in-pack gift to appeal to children.

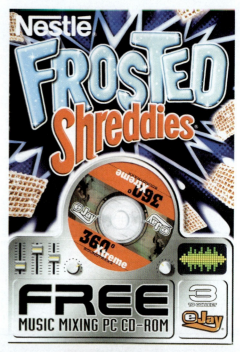

Nestlé Frosted Shreddies uses a free on-pack gift to promote the brand.

A self-liquidating offer used to promote the Weetabix Bananabix brand.

high purchasing rate, sampling may be effective. As it would appear that many of those who try the brand like it and buy it again, raising the trial rate through free samples could have a beneficial long-term effect. Marketing in Action 16.1 shows just how successful sampling can be.

Coupons

There are three ways of couponing. Coupons can be delivered to the home, appear in magazines or newspapers, or appear on packs. *Home couponing*, after home sampling, is the best way to achieve trial for new brands.[11] *Magazine or newspaper couponing* is much cheaper than home delivery and can be used to stimulate trial, but redemption rates are much lower at around 5 per cent on average. The purpose of *on-pack couponing* is to encourage initial and repeat purchasing of the same brand, or trial of a different brand. A brand carries an on-pack coupon redeemable against the consumer's next purchase, usually for the same brand. Redemption rate is high, averaging around 40 per cent.[12] The coupon can offer a higher face value than the equivalent cost of a money-off pack since the effect of the coupon is on both initial and repeat sales. However, it is usually less effective in raising initial sales than money off because there is no immediate saving and its appeal is almost exclusively to existing consumers.[13]

16.1 marketing in action

Sampling for Success

For new food brands nothing beats getting the product into consumers' mouths. Sampling can achieve this, and add fun and interaction to the consumer experience. It can also be remarkably successful.

A sampling campaign for McCain's Home Fries (oven chips), Rosti and Pizza Fingers in Asda, Sainsbury's and Tesco supermarkets rose by over 100 per cent in one week, while the average increase over eight weeks was over 900 per cent. The campaign featured chefs preparing food in stores to encourage free tasting, point-of-purchase competitions and a 40-foot branded trailer parked in the supermarket car park.

Another successful sampling campaign was for the Enjoy! frozen food brand owned by Bird's Eye Walls. This was the biggest ever hot food sampling in the UK and led to a 200 per cent sales increase in participating retailers. Alongside supermarkets, the campaign covered railway stations, high streets, city centres and the Ideal Home Exhibition by means of a mobile trailer where contemporary and innovative products from the Enjoy! range were cooked. Not only were short-term sales higher but loyalty as a response to trial broke records.

Based on: Gannaway (2002);[9] Hemsley (2002)[10]

Prize promotions

There are three main types of *prize promotion*: competitions, draws and games. Unlike other promotions, the cost can be established in advance and does not depend on the number of participants. *Competitions* require participants to exercise a certain degree of skill and judgement. For example, a competition to win free cinema seats might require entrants to name five films based upon stills from each. Entry is usually dependent on at least one purchase. Compared to premiums and money off, competitions offer a less immediate incentive to buy, and one that requires time and effort on the part of entrants. However, they can attract attention and interest in a brand. *Draws* make no demands on skill or judgement: the result depends on chance (see the Little Chef 'Win a Mini' free prize draw illustration, overleaf). For example, a supermarket may run an out-of-the-hat draw, where customers fill in their name and address on an entry card and on a certain day a draw is made. Another example of a draw is when direct mail recipients are asked to return a card on which there is a set of numbers. These are then compared against a set of winning numbers.

An example of a *game promotion* is where a newspaper encloses a series of bingo cards and customers are told that, over a period of time, sets of bingo numbers will be published. If these numbers form a line or full house on a bingo card a prize is won. Such a game encourages repeat purchase of the newspaper.

The national laws governing sales promotions in Europe vary tremendously and local legal advice should be taken before implementing a sales promotion. The UK, Ireland, Spain, Portugal, Greece, Russia and the Czech Republic have fairly relaxed laws about what can be done. Germany, Luxembourg, Austria, Norway, Switzerland and Sweden are much more restrictive. For example, in Sweden free mail-ins, free draws and money-off-next-purchase promotions, and in Norway self-liquidating offers, free draws, money-off vouchers and money-off-next-purchase, are not allowed.

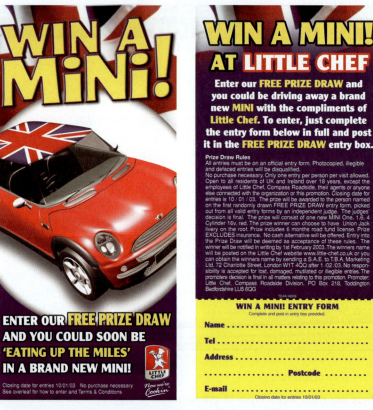

Little Chef: promotion using a free prize draw.

Loyalty cards

A major development in retailing is the offering of *loyalty cards* to customers, who gain points every time they spend money at an outlet. Points can be swapped for money-off vouchers to be used against purchases at the store or for bargain offers on other purchases such as cinema tickets. The intention is to attract customers back to the outlet, but the retailer gains other advantages. The card contains information on the customer including his or her name and address and, when it is swiped through the checkout machine, detailed information on purchases is recorded. This means that the purchasing behaviour of individual customers is known to the retailer, which can then use this information to, among other things, target tailored direct mail promotions at those who are likely to be responsive since it is known that they purchase within a product category (e.g. wine) or buy certain types of product within a category (e.g. herbal tea).

Loyalty cards are very popular, with over 90 per cent of people in the UK holding at least one loyalty card and, of these, 78 per cent carrying more than one loyalty card. Many loyalty card schemes are specific to an individual company, such as the Tesco Clubcard, but the Nectar card is a joint venture between several companies such as Debenhams, Sainsbury's, BP, Barclaycard and Vodafone—it boasts over 11 million customers.[14]

Price discounts

The trade may be offered (or may demand) *discounts* in return for purchase. The concentration of buying into fewer trade outlets has placed increasing power with these organizations. This power is often translated into discounts from manufacturers. The discount may be part of a joint promotion, whereby the retailer agrees to devote extra shelf space, buy larger quantities, engage in a joint competition and/or allow in-store demonstrations.

Free goods

An alternative to a price discount is to offer more merchandise at the same price. For example, the *baker's dozen* technique involves offering 13 items (or cases) for the price of 12.

Competitions

This involves a manufacturer offering financial inducements or prizes to distributors' salesforces in return for achieving sales targets for their products. Alternatively, a prize may be given to the salesforce with the best sales figures.

Allowances

A manufacturer may offer an *allowance* (a sum of money) in return for retailers providing promotional facilities in store (*display allowance*). For example, an allowance would be needed to persuade a supermarket to display cards on its shelves indicating that a brand was being sold at a special low price. An *advertising allowance* would be paid by a manufacturer to a retailer for featuring its brands in the retailer's advertising.

Sales promotion objectives

The most basic objective of any sales promotion is to provide extra value that encourages purchase. When targeted at consumers the intention is to stimulate consumer pull; when the trade is targeted distribution push is the objective. We will now look at specific sales promotion objectives.

Fast sales boost

As we saw when discussing the effects of sales promotion, the usual response is for sales volume to increase. Short-term sales increases may be required for a number of reasons, including the need to reduce inventories or meet budgets prior to the end of the financial year, moving stocks of an old model prior to a replacement, and to increase stockholding by consumers and distributors in advance of the launch of a competitor's product.[15] Promotions that give large immediate benefits, such as money off or bonus packs, have bigger effects on sales volume than more distant promotions such as competitions or self-liquidators. What needs to be realized, however, is that sales promotion should not be used as a means of patching up more fundamental inadequacies such as inferior product performance or poor positioning.

A sales promotion that went seriously wrong was Hoover's attempt to boost sales of its washing machines, vacuum cleaners, refrigerators and tumble driers by offering two free US flight tickets for every Hoover product purchased over £100. The company was the target of much bad publicity as buyers discovered that the offer was wreathed in difficult conditions (found in the promotion's small print) and complained bitterly to Hoover and the media. In an attempt to limit the danger done to its reputation, the company announced that it would honour its offer to its customers, at an estimated cost of £20 million.

Encourage trial

Sales promotions can be highly successful by encouraging trial. If new buyers like the brand, the long-term effect of the promotion may be positive. Home sampling and home couponing are particularly effective methods of inducing trial. Promotions that simply give more product (e.g. bonus packs) are likely to be less successful since consumers will not place much value on the extra quantity until they have decided they like it.

Encourage repeat purchase

Certain promotions, by their nature, encourage repeat purchase of a brand over a period of time. Any offer that requires the collection of packet tops or labels (e.g. free mail-ins and promotions such as bingo games) is attempting to raise repeat purchase during the promotional period. Loyalty cards are designed to offer consumers an incentive to repeat purchase at a store.

Stimulate purchase of larger packs

Promotions that are specifically linked to larger pack sizes may persuade consumers to switch from the less economical smaller packs. For example in the UK, Unilever ran a highly successful promotion linked to its jumbo-sized Persil detergent packs, offering vouchers for free rail travel.

Gain distribution and shelf space

Trade promotions are designed to gain distribution and shelf space. These are major promotional objectives since there is a strong relationship between sales and these two factors. Discounts, free gifts and joint promotions are methods used to encourage distributors to stock brands. Also, consumer promotions that provide sizeable extra value may also persuade distributors to stock or give extra shelf space.

Evaluating sales promotion

There are two types of research that can be used to evaluate sales promotions: *pre-testing research* is used to select, from a number of alternative promotional concepts, the most effective in achieving objectives; *post-testing research* is carried out to assess whether or not promotional objectives have been achieved.

Pre-testing research

Three major pre-testing methods are group discussions, hall tests and experimentation. **Group discussions** may be used with target consumers to test ideas and concepts. They can provide insights into the kinds of promotions that might be valued by them, and allow assessment of several promotional ideas so that some can be tested further and others discounted. Group discussions should be used as a preliminary rather than a conclusive tool.

Hall tests involve bringing a sample of target consumers to a room that has been hired, usually in a town or city location so that alternative promotional ideas can be tested. For example, a bonus pack, a free gift and a free-in-the-mail offer might be tested. The promotions are ranked on the basis of their incentive value. No more than eight alternatives should be tested and the promotions should be of a similar cost to the company.[16] Usually a sample of 100 to 150 is sufficient to separate the winners from the losers.

Experimentation closes the gap between what people say they value and what they actually value by measuring actual purchase behaviour in the marketplace. Usually two panels of stores are used to compare two promotional alternatives, or one promotion against no promotion (control). The two groups of stores must be chosen in such a way that they are comparable (a matched sample) so that the difference in sales is due to the two promotions rather than differences in the stores themselves. Experimentation may be used in a less sophisticated way where one or a small number of stores is used simply as a final check on promotional response before launching a promotion nationally. For service companies, the process may be even easier. Leaflets are produced to communicate the offer and are distributed to a sample of target consumers.[17] Group discussions and hall tests can be used prior to an experiment to narrow the promotional alternatives to a manageable few.

Post-testing research

After the sales promotion has been implemented, the effects must be monitored carefully. Care should be taken to check sales both during *and* after the promotion so that post-promotional sales dips can be taken into account (a *lagged effect*). In certain situations a sales fall can precede a promotion (a *lead effect*). If consumers believe a promotion to be imminent they may hold back purchases until it takes place. Alternatively, if a retail sales promotion of consumer durables (e.g. gas fires, refrigerators, televisions) is accompanied by higher commission rates for salespeople, they may delay sales until the promotional period.[18] If a lead effect is possible, sales prior to the promotion should also be monitored.

Ex-factory sales figures are usually an unreliable guide to consumer uptake at the retail level. Consequently, consumer panels and retail audits (see Chapter 5) are usually employed to measure sales effects. Consumer panel data also reveal the types of people who responded to the sales promotion. For example, they would indicate whether any increase in sales was due to heavy buyers stocking up or new buyers trying the brand for the first time. Retail audit data could be used to establish whether the promotion was associated with retail outlets increasing their stock levels, a rise in the number of outlets handling the brand, as well as measuring sales effects.

An attempt may also be made to assess the long-term impact of a sales promotion. However, in money promotion-prone markets—such as food, drink and toiletries—the pace of promotional activity means that it is impossible to disentangle the long-term effects of one promotion from another.

Public relations and publicity

A company is dependent on many groups if it is to be successful. The marketing concept focuses on customers and distributors, but the needs and interests of other groups are also important, such as employees, shareholders, the local community, the media, government and pressure groups. Public relations is concerned with all of these groups and may be defined as:

> ❝ ... the management of communications and relationships to establish goodwill and mutual understanding between an organization and its public. ❞

Public relations is therefore more wide ranging than marketing, which focuses on markets, distribution channels and customers. By communicating to other groups, public relations creates an environment in which it is easier to conduct marketing.[19] These publics are shown in Fig. 16.3.

Public relations activities include publicity, corporate advertising, seminars, publications, lobbying and charitable donations. It can accomplish many objectives, as outlined below.[20]

1. *Prestige and reputation*: it can foster prestige and reputation, which can help companies to sell products, attract and keep good employees, and promote favourable community and government relations.
2. *Promotion of products*: the desire to buy a product can be helped by the unobtrusive things that people read and see in the press, radio and television. Awareness and interest in products and companies can be generated.
3. *Dealing with issues and opportunities*: the ability to handle social and environmental issues to the mutual benefit of all parties involved.
4. *Goodwill of customers*: ensuring that customers are presented with useful information, are treated well and have their complaints dealt with fairly and speedily.

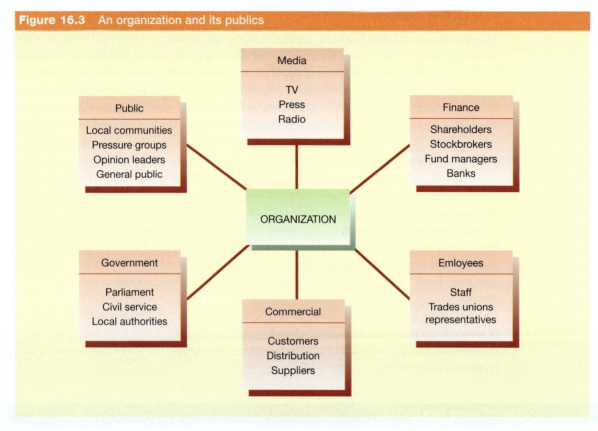

Figure 16.3 An organization and its publics

5. *Goodwill of employees*: promoting the sense of identification and satisfaction of employees with their company. Activities such as internal newsletters, recreation activities, and awards for service and achievement can be used.

6. *Overcoming misconceptions*: managing misconceptions about a company so that unfounded opinions do not damage its operations.

7. *Goodwill of suppliers and distributors*: building a reputation as a good customer (for suppliers) and a reliable supplier (for distributors).

8. *Goodwill of government*: influencing the opinions of public officials and politicians so that they feel the company operates in the public interest.

9. *Dealing with unfavourable publicity*: responding quickly, accurately and effectively to negative publicity such as an oil spill or an air disaster.

10. *Attracting and keeping good employees*: creating and maintaining respectability in the eyes of the public so that the best personnel are attracted to work for the company.

A study by Kitchen and Proctor showed that public relations is a growth area in the UK.[21] The three major reasons for this were recognition by marketing teams of the power and value of public relations, increased advertising costs leading to an exploration of more cost-effective communication routes, and improved understanding of the role of public relations.

Communications associated with public relations can take two forms. Asymmetric communications involve an organization communicating with its publics but never, or rarely, taking any action as a result of feedback. For example, consultation about a new building project may take place, but no satisfactory organizational response may result. In contrast, symmetric communications involves two-way communication between an organization and its publics (e.g. through public meetings) and this consultation informs organizational strategic decision-making. For example, public concern about a building project may result in landscaping and the reduction in the number of houses to be built. The second approach is particularly important when seeking to maintain good community relations.

Public relations activity is aided by technological developments, as described below.

- *Video news releases*: coverage of a public relations event is edited to three to four minutes and sent to television and news departments around the world via cassette, vision circuits or by satellite. No commentary is added and the releases can be edited and voice-overs included as news departments see fit. TV is very choosy about which stories it will use. The brand must play only a supporting role in the story as overtly promotional messages are almost always rejected. Birth control pill manufacturer Schering obtained an audience of nearly six million through a VNR for its sponsorship of an exhibition on fertility control.

- *Videoconferencing*: this is two-way communication of both words and pictures via telephone lines. The process can be used to manage pan-European sales and marketing conferences.

- *Satellite conferencing*: this can be used to transmit a message from one location to many sites around Europe. It is gaining in popularity for pan-European product launches, press conferences and conventions.

- *Video magazines*: this medium can be used for disseminating a corporate message to customers and employees. Compared with print magazines it is more personal and can create a sense of involvement for remote subsidiaries.

Publicity

A major element of public relations is publicity. It can be defined as communication about a product or organization by the placing of news about it in the media without paying for the time or space directly. Three key tasks of a publicity department are:[22]

1. responding to requests from the media—although a passive service function, it requires well-organized information and prompt responses to media requests

2. supplying the media with information on events and occurrences relevant to the organization—this requires general internal communication channels and knowledge of the media

3. stimulating the media to carry the information and viewpoint of the organization—this requires creative development of ideas, developing close relationships with media people and understanding their needs and motivations.

The characteristics of publicity

Information dissemination may be through news releases, news conferences, interviews, feature articles, photocalls and public speaking (at conferences and seminars, for example). No matter which method is used to carry the information, publicity has five important characteristics.

1. *The message has high credibility*: the message has higher credibility than advertising because it appears to the reader to have been written independently (by a media person) rather than by an advertiser. Because of this high credibility, it can be argued that it is more persuasive than a similar message used in an advertisement.

2. *No direct media costs*: since space or time in the media is not bought there is no direct media cost. However, this is not to say that it is cost-free. Someone has to write the news release,

take part in the interview or organize the news conference. This may be organized internally, by a press officer or publicity department, or externally, by a public relations agency.

3) *Lose control of publication*: unlike advertising, there is no guarantee that the news item will be published. This decision is taken out of the control of the organization and into the hands of an editor. A key factor in this decision is whether the item is judged to be newsworthy. The item must be *distinctive* in the sense of having *news value*. For example, the organization that is first to launch a voice-activated personal computer will receive massive publicity; the second company to do so will barely get any. The topic of the news item must also be judged to be of *interest* to a publication's readers. Table 16.1 lists a number of potentially newsworthy topics.

4) *Lose control of content*: there is no way of ensuring that the viewpoint expressed by the news supplier is reflected in the published article. For example, a news release might point to an increase in capital expenditure to deal with pollution, but this might be used negatively (for example, saying the increase is inadequate).

5) *Lose control of timing*: an advertising campaign can be co-ordinated to achieve maximum impact. The timing of the publication of news items, however, cannot be controlled. For example, a news item publicizing a forthcoming conference to encourage attendance could appear in a publication after the event has taken place or, at least, too late to have any practical effect on attendance.

Writing news releases

Perhaps the most popular method of disseminating information to the media is through the news release. By following a few simple guidelines (as outlined below), the writer can produce news releases that please editors and therefore stand a greater chance of being used.[23]

- *The headline*: make the headline factual and avoid the use of flamboyant, flowery language that might irritate editors. The headline should briefly introduce the story, e.g. 'A New Alliance to be Formed between Virgin and Delta Airlines'.

- *Opening paragraph*: this should be a brief summary of the whole release. If this is the only part of the news release that is published the writer will have succeeded in getting across the essential message.

- *Organizing the copy*: the less important ideas should be placed towards the end of the news release. The further down the paragraph, the more chance of its being cut by an editor.

Table 16.1 Potentially newsworthy topics

Being or doing something first

Marketing issues
- New products
- Research breakthroughs: future new products
- Large orders/contracts
- Sponsorships
- Price changes
- Service changes
- New logos
- Export success

Production issues
- Productivity achievements
- Employment changes
- Capital investments

Financial issues
- Financial statements
- Acquisitions
- Sales/profit achievements

Personal issues
- Training awards
- Winners of company contests
- Promotions/new appointments
- Success stories
- Visits by famous people
- Reports of interviews

General issues
- Conferences/seminars/exhibitions
- Anniversaries of significant events

- *Copy content*: like headlines, copy should be factual not fanciful. An example of bad copy would be 'We are proud to announce that Virgin Airlines, the world's most innovative airline, will fly an exciting new route to Singapore'. Instead, this should read 'A new route to Singapore will be flown by Virgin Airlines'. Whenever possible, statements should be backed up by facts. For example, a statement claiming 'fuel economy' for a car should be supported by figures.

- *Length*: news releases should be as short as possible. Most are written on one page, some are merely one paragraph. The viewpoint that long releases should be sent to editors so that they can cut out the parts they do not want is a fallacy. Editors' self-interest is that their job should be made as easy as possible; the less work they have to do amending copy the greater the chances of its publication.

- *Layout*: the release should contain short paragraphs with plenty of *white space* to make it appear easy to read. There should be good-sized margins on both sides, and the copy should be double-spaced so that amendments and printing instructions can be inserted by the editor. When a story runs to a second or third page, 'more' should be typed in the bottom right-hand corner and succeeding pages numbered with the headline repeated in the top left-hand corner.

Publicity can be a powerful tool for creating awareness and strengthening the reputation of organizations. For example, it was the inherent newsworthiness of Anita Roddick's Body Shop business with its emphasis on environmental and animal-friendly products that provided media coverage, not advertisements. The trick is to motivate everyone in an organization to look for newsworthy stories and events, not simply to rely on the publicity department to initiate them.

Public relations and publicity should be part of an integrated communications strategy so that they reinforce the messages consumers receive from other communication vehicles. Marketing in Action 16.2 discusses some important issues.

Sponsorship

Sponsorship has been defined by Sleight as:[28]

> ... a business relationship between a provider of funds, resources or services and an individual, event or organization which offers in return some rights and association that may be used for commercial advantage.

Potential sponsors have a wide range of entities and activities from which to choose, including sports, arts, community activities, teams, tournaments, individual personalities or events, competitions, fairs and shows. Sports sponsorship is by far the most popular sponsorship medium as it offers high visibility through extensive television press coverage, the ability to attract a broad cross-section of the community and to service specific niches, and the capacity to break down cultural barriers.[29]

Vodafone is very active in sports sponsorship, with a portfolio that includes Manchester United, the Australian rugby team and Ferrari. These links help to build the image of Vodafone as being a global force. For example, when Manchester United tours Asia with its stars, Vodafone laps up coverage both in the Far East and Asia, and the Ferrari sponsorship gives it television exposure in over 200 countries. It has formed a sponsorship strategy team in Germany, which interacts with local teams in key markets. The aim is to ensure that all of its markets are exploiting sponsorship opportunities to the maximum extent.[30]

16.2 marketing in action

Integrated Public Relations

The development of integrated communications agencies all too often meant offering advertising, direct marketing and sales promotion. Public relations was not usually included, being seen as little more than the sending out of press releases. Yet there have been examples of public relations playing a strategic role in an integrated communications campaign. For example, Unilever faced restrictions on the health claims it could use when advertising Flora margarine. The solution was to lead with a public relations campaign reporting medical research, which found that polyunsaturated fats were relatively good for health. This was supported by an advertising campaign that focused on the message that Flora was 'rich in polyunsaturates'.

There are three methods of establishing integrated communications. The first is for clients to bring all their specialist agencies around a table and insist on an integrated approach. Another is to use a large international agency that can offer a complete package, such as the Young & Rubicam group, which owns the PR agency Burson-Marsteller. Finally, clients can choose a single integrated agency that includes public relations in its offering. One practical problem is that no matter which option is chosen, the different agencies or sections within agencies may fight for a bigger share of the communications budget. Even using one agency does not prevent this, since each section may operate as a separate profit centre. A problem from the client side is that this may give the strategic thinking role to those representing advertising. The other communication areas are then asked to fall in line, even if it is very difficult to translate the advertising message into public relations, sales promotion or a direct marketing campaign.

The demand for integrated communications campaigns has seen a sharp rise in the number of single integrated agencies, often formed by the purchase of public relations agencies by organizations traditionally focusing on advertising. This recognizes the importance of public relations in the service offering to those clients that demand a one-stop-shop experience. For example, the advertising agency Ogilvy & Mather worked with Ogilvy PR on the launch of the Ford Ka.

The role of the client in achieving integrated public relations is vital. Unless the client provides strong leadership, clear objectives and develops a co-operative culture, the various parties will fight each other for credit, resources and importance.

Based on: Gofton (1996);[24] Flack (1999);[25] Jones (2002);[26] Leyland (2002)[27]

Companies should be clear about their reasons for spending money on sponsorship. The five principal objectives of sponsorship are to gain publicity, create entertainment opportunities, foster favourable brand and company associations, improve community relations and create promotional opportunities.

Gaining publicity

Sponsorship provides ample opportunities to create publicity in the news media. Worldwide events such as major golf, football and tennis tournaments supply the platform for global media coverage. Sponsorship of such events can provide brand exposure to millions of people. Some events, such as athletics championships, have mass audience appeal, while others such as golf have a more upmarket profile. Dunhill's sponsorship of major golf tournaments allows the brand name to be exposed to its more upmarket customer segment.

The publicity opportunities of sponsorship can produce major *awareness* shifts. For example, Canon's sponsorship of football in the UK raised awareness of the brand name from 40 per cent to 85 per cent among males; awareness of the name of an insurance company sponsoring a national cricket competition increased from 2 to 16 per cent; and Texaco's prompted recall improved from 18 to 60 per cent because of motor racing sponsorship.[31]

Sponsorship can also be used to position brands in the marketplace. For example, Procter & Gamble spent the entire marketing budget for its shampoo Wash & Go, totalling £6 million (€8.4 million), on sponsoring the English Premier League. The intention is to position it as a sports brand, with the strapline 'A simply great supporter of football', among its target market of young, active males.[32]

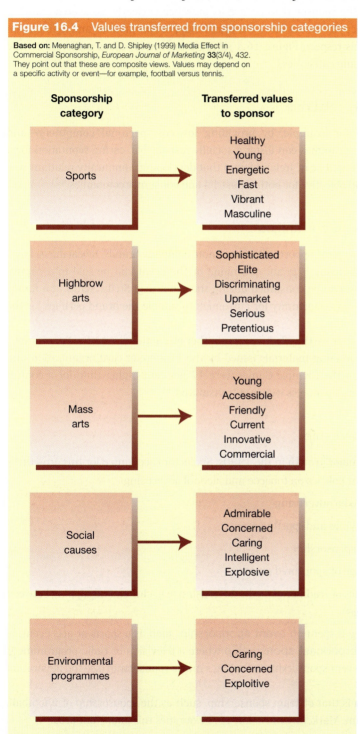

Figure 16.4 Values transferred from sponsorship categories

Based on: Meenaghan, T. and D. Shipley (1999) Media Effect in Commercial Sponsorship, *European Journal of Marketing* **33**(3/4), 432. They point out that these are composite views. Values may depend on a specific activity or event—for example, football versus tennis.

Creating entertainment opportunities

A major objective of much sponsorship is to create entertainment opportunities for customers and the trade. Sponsorship of music, the performing arts and sports events can be particularly effective. For example, BMW supported classical concerts in stately homes in the UK to provide dealers with customer entertainment opportunities.[33] The Tetley Bitter sponsorship deal with the England Cricket Team provided not only wide publicity but also important opportunities to invite key customers to watch test matches. Often, sports personalities are invited to join the sponsors' guests. Attendance at sponsored events can also be used to reward successful employees.

Fostering favourable brand and company associations

The third objective of sponsorship is to create favourable associations for a brand and company. For example, sponsorship of athletics by SmithKline Beecham for its Lucozade Sport brand reinforces its market position and its energy associations. Dunhill's golf sponsorship is consistent with its upmarket positioning, and Stella Artois' tennis sponsorship had a major impact in establishing the brand in the premium lager market segment. Marlboro's motor racing sponsorship and Budweiser's sponsorship of the television programme showing American football reinforce their masculine images.

Both the sponsor and the sponsored activity become involved in a relationship with a transfer of values from activity to sponsor. The audience, finding the sponsor's name, logo and other symbols threaded through the event, learns to associate sponsor and activity with one another. The task facing the sponsor is to ensure its presence is clearly associated with the activity and transfer the activity values on to the brand. Support promotions and mainstream advertising can help in this respect. Figure 16.4 shows some broad values conferred on the sponsor from five sponsorship categories.

Improving community relations

Sponsorship of schools—for example, by providing low-cost personal computers—and supporting community programmes can foster a socially responsible, caring reputation for a company. A survey in the Republic of Ireland found that developing community relations was the most usual sponsorship objective for both industrial and consumer companies.[34]

Creating promotional opportunities

Sponsored events provide an ideal opportunity to promote company brands. Sweatshirts, bags, pens, etc., carrying the company logo and the name of the event can be sold to a captive audience. Where the brand can be consumed during the event (e.g. Stella Artois at a tennis tournament) this provides an opportunity for customers to sample the brand perhaps for the first time.

Sponsorship can also improve the effectiveness of other promotional vehicles. For example, responses to the direct marketing materials issued by the Visa credit card organization and featuring its sponsorship of the Olympic Games were 17 per cent higher than for a control group to whom the sponsorship images were not transmitted.[35]

Expenditure on sponsorship

Sponsorship experienced major growth in the 1990s. Six factors accounted for this growth:[36]

1. restrictive government policies on tobacco and alcohol advertising
2. escalating costs of media advertising
3. increased leisure activities and sporting events
4. the proven record of sponsorship
5. greater media coverage of sponsored events
6. the reduced efficiencies of traditional media advertising (e.g. clutter, and zapping between television programmes).

Although most money is spent on **event sponsorship**, such as a sports or arts event, of increasing importance is **broadcast sponsorship** where a television or radio programme is the focus. An example of event sponsorship is Carling's music sponsorship (see the illustration opposite).

Another growth area is that of team sponsorship, such as the sponsorship of a football, rugby or motor racing team. Marketing in Action 16.3 examines this important area.

Carling moved out of football to sponsor top music events featuring major artists who were taken back to their roots by playing in venues where they first started. This Jamiroquai gig for 300 people became a Channel 4 television programme seen by almost 750,000 viewers. Other sponsored music events include the Leeds and Reading Festivals.

16.3 marketing in action

Sports Sponsorship

Sports sponsorship includes the money spent by companies to associate themselves with events and teams (including football clubs) across a range of sports from show-jumping to golf. It includes the millions of pounds that Vodafone, the mobile phone group, spends each year to have its name on Manchester United shirts and the body of Michael Schumacher's Formula 1 Ferrari. It also covers the £26 million the 15 official partners of the World Cup (including Coca-Cola, MasterCard, Yahoo! and Gillette) paid for the privilege of advertising in the stadiums and using the World Cup logo. Sports sponsorship also includes the monies paid to sports organizations such as the FA Premier League in the UK (see the illustration overleaf).

Companies pay this kind of money to associate their brands with international glamour (e.g. motor racing), success (e.g. Manchester United) and for their brands to be seen at high-profile events (e.g. the World Cup) that attract hundreds of millions of viewers worldwide.

Sponsorship presents successful teams with unprecedented opportunities. For example, besides the Vodafone deal, Manchester United has negotiated multi-million-pound global sponsorship and licensing deals with Budweiser, Nike and Wilkinson Sword. Such partnerships have led to co-branding opportunities such as the Manchester United Protector 3D Diamond razor from Wilkinson Sword.

Based on: Anonymous (2002);[37] Gibson (2002);[38] Jones (2002)[39]

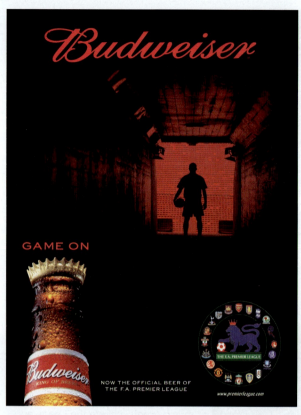

Budweiser sponsors the FA Premier League in the UK.

Broadcast sponsorship of programmes can extend into the sharing of production costs. This is attractive to broadcasters, who face increasing costs of programming; and sponsors, who gain a greater degree of influence in negotiations with broadcasters, an opportunity to benefit from cheaper advertising, and the rights to exploit the programme, its characters and actors for promotional purposes. In Europe, composite programmes like Unilever's game show *Wheel of Fortune*, which can be customized for each market, already achieves some success.[40]

Accompanying the growth of event sponsorship has been the phenomenon of **ambush marketing**. Originally this term referred to the activities of companies that tried to associate themselves with an event (e.g. the Olympics) without paying any fee to the event owner. The activity is legal so long as no attempt is made to use an event symbol, logo or mascot. More recently the term has been broadened to include a range of activities such as sponsoring the television coverage of a major event, sponsoring national teams and the support of individual sportspeople.

Selection and evaluation of an event or programme to sponsor

Selection

Selection of an event or programme to sponsor should be undertaken by answering a series of questions.

- *Communications objectives*: What are we trying to achieve? Are we looking for awareness or image, improvement in community relations or entertainment opportunities? Does the personality of the event match the desired brand image?

- *Target market*: Who are we trying to reach? Is it the trade or final customers? How does the profile of our customer base match the likely audience of the sponsored event or programme?

- *Risk*: What are the associated risks? What are the chances that the event or programme might attract adverse publicity (e.g. football hooliganism tainting the image of the sport and, by implication, the sponsor)? To what extent would termination of the sponsorship contract attract bad publicity (e.g. mean the closing of a theatre)?

- *Promotional opportunities*: What are the potential sales promotion and publicity opportunities?

- *Past record*: If the event or programme has been sponsored before, what were the results? Why did the previous sponsor withdraw?

- *Cost*: Does the sponsorship opportunity represent value for money?

Evaluation

This process should lead to a clear idea of why an event or programme is being sponsored. Understanding *sponsorship objectives* is the first step in evaluating sponsorship's success. As we have seen, Canon used football sponsorship to improve awareness levels and market research was carried out as a monitor. Sponsorship of a school by providing personal computers would be monitored by measuring coverage in local newspapers, and on radio stations and possibly television.

For major sponsorship deals, evaluation is likely to be more formal and involve the measurement of *media coverage and name mentions/sightings* using a specialist monitoring agency. For example, Volvo's £2 million (€2.8 million) sponsorship of tennis resulted in 1.4 billion impressions (number of mentions or sightings, audience size) which it calculated was worth £12 million (€16.8 million) in media advertising.[41]

Meenaghan[42] recommends the following evaluation procedure designed to measure the effects of the exposure.

1. Determination of the company's brand's present position in terms of pre-sponsorship awareness and image with the target audience, and the setting of objectives.

2. Tracking to detect movements in customer awareness and attitudes towards the company/brand.

3. Post-sponsorship comparison of performance levels against initial objectives.

However, a survey into the evaluation of football sponsorship found that while two-thirds of companies evaluated their sponsorship activities few went beyond the basic measurement of media coverage.[43]

Exhibitions

Exhibitions are unique in that of all the promotional tools available they are the only one that brings buyers, sellers and the competitors together in a commercial setting. In Europe, the Cologne trade exhibitions bring together 28,000 exhibitors from 100 countries with 1.8 million buyers from 150 countries.[44] Overall, the number of exhibitions, exhibitors and visitors is growing. Nevertheless, the perceived value of exhibitions is debatable. The following comments illustrate the wide variation of opinion.

> While all elements within the communication program are vital, perhaps only the exhibition will involve all disciplines, and will present the greatest opportunity to present Gould as a total company.[45]

> Exhibitions are usually a form of mass hysteria. It is a foregone conclusion that they are very expensive. Even though there may be thousands of visitors, there are also thousands of exhibits.

> The retention factor is very debatable ... every time we exhibit at a trade show, our conclusion is 'never again'.[46]

Despite these differing views, exhibitions appear to be an important part of the industrial promotion mix. One study into the relative importance of promotional media placed exhibitions as a source of information in the industrial buying process second only to personal selling, and ahead of direct mail and print advertising.[47]

Their importance is mirrored in the expansion of the number of exhibitions taking place in Europe despite the fact that the difficulty in evaluating their success means that they are often the first to suffer when a marketing budget needs to be cut.[48] Besides the usual major industry exhibitions, such as motor shows, more specialized lifestyle exhibitions are emerging, targeting niche markets. For example, the Cosmo Show, featuring cosmetics, targets young women and attracts over 55,000 visitors. The 1999 event was the launch pad for Olay Colour (formerly Oil of Ulay) to reveal its new identity and for the launch of Cussons new moisturizer Aqua Source.[49]

Exhibitors sometimes create the unusual to impress visitors. For example, Orange took two stands at the GSM exhibition in Cannes. One was dedicated to products while the other was a relaxation and massage area. This stand had no salespeople, just a team of masseurs offering head and neck massages, comfy chairs and coffee. Many visitors remarked that it was their favourite area of the show.[50]

Exhibition objectives

Exhibitions can achieve a number of objectives, including:
- an opportunity to reach an audience with a distinct interest in the market and the products on display
- create awareness and develop relationships with new prospects
- strengthen existing customer relationships
- provide product demonstrations
- determine and stimulate needs of customers
- gather competitive intelligence
- introduce a new product
- recruit dealers or distributors
- maintain/improve company image
- deal with service and other customer problems
- generate a mailing list
- make a sale.

Bonoma has organized many of these objectives into a matrix depending on whether the objective concerns current or potential customers, and selling versus non-selling objectives (Fig. 16.5).[51] Research into why companies exhibit at trade shows found that the major reasons were:[52]
- to generate leads/enquiries
- to introduce a new product or service
- because competitors are exhibiting
- to recruit dealers or distributors.

Whatever objectives are set, they should be clear and measurable. This enables the exhibitor to identify the real opportunities presented by the event and allows the degree of success of the exhibition to be evaluated.[53]

In no other medium will advertising, publicity, sales promotion, product demonstration, sales staff, key management, present customers and prospects join together in a live event that offers the opportunity to impress key audience perceptions of the company, its operations and products.[54]

Figure 16.5 Exhibition objectives

Source: adapted from Bonoma, T. V. (1985) Get More out of your Trade Shows, in Gumpbert, D. E. (ed.), *The Marketing Renaissance*, New York: Wiley. Copyright © 1985 John Wiley & Sons Inc. Reprinted by permission.

	Selling objectives	Non-selling objectives
Current customers	Maintain relationships Transmist benefits Remedy serve problmes Stimulate extra sales	Maintain image Demonstrate products Gather competitive intelligence Widen exposure
Potential customers (prospects)	Contact prospects Determine needs Transmit benefits Commit to follow-up or sale	Contact prospects Foster image building Demonstrate products Gather competitive intelligence

Planning for an exhibition

Success at an exhibition involves considerable pre-event planning. Clear objectives should be set, selection criteria for evaluating exhibition attendance determined, and design and promotional strategies decided. Pre-show promotions to attract visitors to the stand include direct mail, telephoning, a personal sales call before the event and an advertisement in the trade or technical press. New media can also be used to good effect, as e-Marketing 16.1 explains.

16.1 e-marketing

Exhibition Promotion through Viral Marketing

Marsh-McBirney, Inc., a flowmeter manufacturer based in Maryland, USA, makes innovative use of viral marketing to draw interest to its stand every year at a major US industry trade fair. Marsh-McBirney realized that it had little chance of receiving any attention at the WEFTEC 2002 trade event: not only were there thousands of other companies attending (its booth number was 4547), it was also up against much larger competitors with larger promotional budgets.

It decided to drive traffic to its stand by sending an e-mail to its customer base prior to the event. The message offered to measure customers' baseball pitch speed using the same technology that operates in the company's flowmeters. The fastest pitch would receive an autographed baseball, but there were other prizes too: a baseball card was given to anyone bringing along the printed e-mail and everyone that came along was given the chance to win a bat signed by the famous Sammy Sosa. With an offer like this it was intended that the initial e-mail should be passed on to a much wider audience than the initial customer base (viral marketed).

Marsh-McBirney operated one of the most popular stands at the event. It also succeeded in building brand awareness and driving potential customers to its stand (who would otherwise have ignored it). It did all this while demonstrating its product in action. Through a little creative thinking, tying the product to an area of heightened interest such as baseball, and using e-business technology to disseminate its message to a much wider audience, this company has managed to turn a potential strike-out into a home run.

A high degree of professionalism is required by the staff who attend the exhibition stand. The characteristics of a good exhibitor have been found to be:[55]

- exhibiting a wider range of products, particularly large items that cannot be demonstrated on a sales call
- staff always in attendance at the stand—visitors should never hear that 'the person who covers that product is not here right now'
- well-informed staff
- informative literature available
- seating area or office provided on the stand
- refreshments provided.

Evaluating an exhibition

Post-show evaluation will examine performance against objectives. This is a learning exercise that will help to judge whether the objectives were realistic, how valuable the exhibition appears to have been and how well the company was represented.

Quantitative measures include:

- the number of visitors to the stand
- the number of key influencers/decision-makers who visited the stand
- how many leads/enquiries were generated
- the cost per lead/enquiry
- the number and value of orders
- the cost per order
- the number of new distributorships opened/likely to be opened.

Other more subjective, qualitative criteria include:

- the worth of competitive intelligence
- interest generated in the new products
- the cultivation of new/existing relationships
- the value of customer query and complaint handling
- the promotion of brand values.

Sales and marketing may not always agree on the key evaluation criteria to use. For example, sales may judge the exhibition on the number of leads while marketing may prefer to judge the show on the longer-term issue of the promotion of brand values.[56]

Finally, since a major objective of many exhibitors is to stimulate leads and enquiries, mechanisms must be in place to ensure that these are followed up promptly. Furthermore, the leads generated at an exhibition can be used to build a marketing database for future direct mail campaigns.

Product placement

Product placement is the deliberate placing of products and/or their logos in movies and television, usually in return for money. The appearance of brands in these media is unlikely to be by accident: usually vast sums of money are paid by brand owners to secure exposure. For example, Steven Spielberg's sci-fi film *Minority Report* featured more than 15 major brands, including Gap, Nokia, Pepsi, Guinness, Lexus and Amex, with their logos appearing on video billboards throughout the film. These product placements earned DreamWorks and 20th Century Fox $25 million, which went some way towards reducing the $102 million production costs for the film.[57] As is related in Case 32 at the end of this chapter, product placement was prominent in the Bond movie *Die Another Day*, with 007 wearing an Omega watch, driving an Aston Martin, making calls on a Philips mobile phone, flying BA with Samsonite luggage and listening to a Sony stereo.[58]

The growth in product placement

Product placement is growing for the following reasons.

- *Mass-market reach*: as media fragments (for example, due to the growth of digital television channels), it becomes increasingly hard to reach mass markets. Films can reach hundreds of millions of consumers worldwide, creating rapid brand awareness.
- *Positive associations*: brands can benefit from the positive images in a film or television programme. For example, for James Bond to be seen driving an Aston Martin or Jaguar imparts the Bond association of sophistication, masculinity and coolness to the car.
- *Credibility*: many consumers do not realize that brands have been product-placed. The brands are seen being used rather than appearing in a paid-for advertisement. This can add to the credibility of the associations sought.
- *Message repetition*: movies are often repeated on television and bought on video or DVD, creating opportunities for brand message repetition.
- *Avoidance of advertising bans*: with bans on advertising certain products, such as cigarettes, in particular media, product placement is an opportunity to reach large audiences.
- *Targeting*: by choosing an appropriate movie or television programme, specific market segments can be reached. For example, product placement in 'teen' movies can reach younger age groups.
- *Branding opportunities*: new brands can be launched linked to the film. For example, Philips launched a range of James Bond-branded shaving products to coincide with the launch of *Die Another Day*.[59]
- *Promotional opportunities*: placements in movies can provide promotional opportunities by creating related websites. For example, the *Die Another Day* website provided streamed video clips of Bond using a range of placed products in scenes from the film. Also, a section of the website was devoted to '007 partners' where a gallery of logos was visible and links to the brand partner website provided.[60]
- *Measurement*: market research companies, such as CinemaScore in the USA, conduct viewer exit surveys to measure which brands were noticed during the showing of a movie.[61]

Risks associated with product placement

Although product placement, as we have seen, has many strong points, there are also certain risks involved.

- *Movie/programme failure*: just as brands can benefit from movie or television successes, failures can tarnish brand image by association.
- *Lack of prominence*: the brand may be overshadowed by action in the film and not be noticed.
- *Audience annoyance*: blatant product placement may cause audience annoyance, tarnishing any brand association.
- *Loss of control*: although brand owners who pay large fees for having their products placed in films and television will be able to exercise some control over how these are portrayed, other people, such as directors and editors, reduce their degree of control compared to standard advertisements.

Ethical issues in sales promotion and public relations

Ethical concerns regarding sales promotion and public relations include the use of trade inducements, malredemption of coupons, the use of third-party endorsements and the promotion of anti-social behaviour.

Use of trade inducements

Retailers sometimes accept inducements from manufacturers to encourage their salespeople to push the manufacturers' products. This often takes the form of bonus payments to salespeople. The result is that there is an incentive for salespeople to pay special attention to those product lines that are linked to such bonuses when talking to customers. Customers may, therefore, be subjected to pressure to buy products that do not best meet their needs.

Malredemption of coupons

This ethical issue concerns the behaviour of customers in supermarkets who attempt to redeem reduced-price coupons without buying the associated product. When faced with a large shopping trolley of goods it is easy for supermarket checkout attendants to accept coupons without verification. The key to stopping this practice is thorough training of supermarket employees so that they always check coupons against goods purchased.

Third-party endorsements

Another ethical question is related to the use of third-party endorsements to publicize a product, where a person gives a written, verbal and/or visual recommendation of the product. A well-known, well-respected person is usually chosen but given that payment often accompanies the endorsement the question arises as to its credibility. Supporters of endorsements argue that consumers know that endorsers are usually paid and are capable of making their own judgements regarding their credence.

Promoting anti-social behaviour

The promotion of events that can lead to anti-social behaviour also raises ethical issues. For example, a 'promotion night' in pubs and clubs can lead to excessive drinking. Drunkenness, crime and violence may follow. These issues are discussed in Ethical Marketing in Action 16.1.

16.1 ethical marketing in action

Happy Hours: Sad Results?

Pubs and clubs often have to fight hard for custom. One competitive strategy is the 'promotion night', where special deals are used to attract drinkers. These have their origins in the 'happy hour', when drinks are sold cheaply to encourage custom at traditionally quiet times. An ulterior motive may be to keep drinkers beyond the designated time and profit from perhaps greater spending once the special prices are finished.

Happy hours have, however, raised concerns. The criminal justice pressure group Nacro, for example, recently released research showing that such promotions are associated with violence and drunkenness, and can exacerbate existing drinking and anti-social behaviour problems; 41 per cent of victims of 'contact crime' judged the offender to be under alcoholic influence. One of the main recommendations of Nacro's report is to '[discourage] rapid drinking by restricting happy hours and other promotions that encourage rapid consumption of drinks'. Alcohol Concern highlights research in Cardiff and Bristol hospitals' Accident and Emergency departments, which provides 'clear evidence of the increased vulnerability of binge drinkers (the practice of drinking large quantities at one sitting) particularly to assault'.

In recent years, happy hours have become more elaborate, especially in the fiercely competitive and very lucrative youth sector: 35 per cent of the male 16–24 age group drink over 21 alcohol units per week and 22 per cent of the female 16–24 age group drink over 14 units a week.* A typical promotion might include a stream of specials throughout the evening such as 'the never ending vodka glass' for an hour at the beginning and end of the evening, and a special offer on vodka/Red Bull to 'recharge your batteries'. It is easy to see how this could create problems like drunkenness and accidents. Arguably, such practices may also be linked to the recent increase in 'binge drinking', a field in which young Britons lead Europe. This is not just a matter of headaches and red faces 'the morning after'; real health consequences result. The World Health Organization (WHO) estimates that, in Europe, one in four male deaths among the under-30s is directly attributable to alcohol.

The information presented in this vignette demonstrates that ethical issues are present in sales promotion decisions as in other forms of marketing. Marketers need to think through the implications of their practices and recognize that competitive advantage and higher sales may come at a more than monetary price. What do you think?

* The recommended weekly maximum intake of alcohol is 21 units for men and 14 units for women. One unit is the equivalent of half a pint of beer, or one glass of wine.

Based on: Alcohol Concern (1998);[62] Roberts et al (2001);[63] Shepherd and Brickley (1996);[64] British Crime Survey (1996);[65] WHO Global Burden of Disease 2000 Study (2001)[66]

Ethical dilemma

Fair trade products are those that provide producers with a living wage and improved working conditions. The fair trade mark in the UK is awarded and regulated by the Fairtrade Foundation. The Fairtrade Foundation was set up by CAFOD, Christian Aid, New Consumer, Oxfam, Traidcraft and the World Development Movement. The mark is given to products that meet internationally recognized standards of fair trade. To receive the fair trade mark products must contain a minimum of 20 per cent dry weight ingredients that are fairly traded. Thus for a product to be labelled and promoted as fair trade all the product ingredients need not actually be fairly traded. Is this promotion of fair trade ethical?

Review

1 **The growth in sales promotion**
- The reasons for growth are increased impulse purchasing, the growing respectability of sales promotions, the rising costs of advertising and advertising clutter, shortening time horizons for goal achievement, competitor activities and the fact that their sales impact is easier to measure than that of advertising.

2 **The major sales promotion types**
- Major consumer promotions are money off, bonus packs, premiums (free in- or on-pack gifts, free-in-the-mail offers and self-liquidating offers), free samples, coupons, prize promotions (competitions, draws and games), and loyalty cards; major trade promotions are price discounts, free goods, competitions and allowances.

3 **The objectives and evaluation of sales promotion**
- The objectives of sales promotion are to provide a fast sales boost, encourage trial, encourage repeat purchase, stimulate purchase of larger packs, and gain distribution and shelf space.
- Sales promotion can be evaluated using pre-testing research (group discussions, hall tests and experimentation) and post-testing research (consumer panel and retail audit data).

4 **The objectives and targets of public relations**
- The objectives of public relations are to foster prestige and reputation, promote products, deal with issues and opportunities, enhance the goodwill of customers and employees, correct misconceptions, improve the goodwill of suppliers, distributors and government, deal with unfavourable publicity, and attract and keep good employees.
- The targets of public relations are the general public, the media, the financial community, government, commerce (including customers) and employees.

5 **The key tasks and characteristics of publicity**
- Three key tasks are: responding to requests from the media; supplying the media with information on events relevant to the organization; stimulating the media to carry the information and the viewpoint of the organization.
- The characteristics of publicity are that the message has higher credibility than advertising, there are no direct media costs and no control over what is published (content), whether the item will be published or when it will be published.

6 **The guidelines to use when writing a news release**
- The guidelines are: make the headline factual and briefly introduce the story; the opening paragraph should be a summary of the whole release; the copy should be organized by placing the less important messages towards the end; copy should be factual and backed up by evidence; the release should be short; the layout should contain short paragraphs with plenty of white space.

7. The objectives and methods of sponsorship
- The objectives of sponsorship are to gain publicity, create entertainment opportunities, foster favourable brand and company associations, improve community relations and create promotional opportunities.
- The two key methods of sponsorship are event sponsorship (such as a sports or arts event) and broadcast sponsorship (where a television or radio programme is sponsored).

8. How to select and evaluate a potential sponsored event or programme
- Selection should be based on asking what we are trying to achieve (communication objectives), who we are trying to reach (target market), what are the associated risks (e.g. adverse publicity), what are the potential promotional opportunities, what is the past record of sponsorship of the event or programme, and what are the costs.
- Evaluation should be based on measuring results in terms of sponsorship objectives (e.g. changes in awareness and attitudes). Formal evaluation involves measurement of media coverage and name mentions/sightings using a specialist monitoring agency.

9. The objectives, conduct and evaluation of exhibitions
- Objectives of exhibitions can be classified as selling objectives to current customers (e.g. stimulate extra sales), selling objectives to potential customers (e.g. determine needs and transmit benefits), non-selling objectives to current customers (e.g. maintain image and gather competitive intelligence) and non-selling objectives to potential customers (e.g. foster image building and gather competitive intelligence).
- Staff conduct at an exhibition should ensure that there is always someone in attendance to talk to visitors, staff should be well-informed, provide informative literature, and a seating area/office and refreshments should be provided.
- Evaluation of an exhibition includes number of visitors/key influencers/decision-makers who visit the stand, number of leads/enquiries/orders/new dealerships generated and cost per lead/enquiry/order. Qualitative evaluation includes the worth of competitive intelligence, and interest generated in new products.

10. The reasons for the growth in product placement and its risks
- Product placement activity is growing because of its mass-market reach, ability to confer positive associations to brands, high credibility, message repetition, its ability to avoid advertising bans, its targeting capabilities, the opportunities it provides for new linked brands and promotions, and the ability to measure its impact on audiences.
- Its risks are that the movie or television programme may fail, tarnishing brand image; there is the possibility that the placement may not get noticed or cause annoyance; and there is also the reduction in control, compared to advertisements, concerning how the brand will be portrayed in the movie or television programme.

11. Ethical issues in sales promotion and public relations
- There are potential problems relating to the use of trade inducements, malredemption of coupons, the use of third-party endorsements to publicize a product, and the promotion of anti-social behaviour.

Key terms

ambush marketing originally referred to the activities of companies that try to associate themselves with an event (e.g. the Olympics) without paying any fee to the event owner; now means the sponsoring of the television coverage of a major event, national teams and the support of individual sportspeople

bonus pack giving a customer extra quantity at no additional cost

broadcast sponsorship a form of sponsorship where a television or radio programme is the focus

consumer panel data a type of continuous research where information is provided by household consumers on their purchases over time

consumer pull the targeting of consumers with communications (e.g. promotions) designed to create demand that will pull the product into the distribution chain

distribution push the targeting of channel intermediaries with communications (e.g. promotions) to push the product into the distribution chain

event sponsorship sponsorship of a sporting or other event

exhibition an event that brings buyers and sellers together in a commercial setting

experimentation the application of stimuli (e.g. two price levels) to different matched groups under controlled conditions for the purpose of measuring their effect on a variable (e.g. sales)

group discussion a group, usually of six to eight consumers, brought together for a discussion focusing on an aspect of a company's marketing

hall tests bringing a sample of target consumers to a room that has been hired so that alternative marketing ideas (e.g. promotions) can be tested

money-off promotions sales promotions that discount the normal price

premiums any merchandise offered free or at low cost as an incentive to purchase

product placement the deliberate placing of products and/or their logos in movies and television, usually in return for money

public relations the management of communications and relationships to establish goodwill and mutual understanding between an organization and its public

retail audit data a type of continuous research tracking the sales of products through retail outlets

sponsorship a business relationship between a provider of funds, resources or services and an individual, event or organization that offers in return some rights and association that may be used for commercial advantage

Internet exercise

Due to audience and media fragmentation, advertisers are seeking different ways to capture the attention of their targeted audience and to stand out from the rest of the clutter. Cunningstunts is a promotions agency that tries to maximize publicity by gaining editorial coverage from the media on its promotional stunts. It famously projected a nude picture of Gail Porter (now Hipgrave) in a pose for *FHM* magazine, on to the House of Commons, which gained huge publicity coverage. Take a look at some of its past exploits.

Visit: www.cunningstunts.net

Questions

(a) Discuss the reasons why other promotional methods, like the ones used by Cunningstunts, are increasing in their importance.
(b) Comment on the effectiveness of the types of campaign conducted by Cunningstunts.
(c) How can the effectiveness of these publicity stunts be measured?
(d) Are all forms of publicity good for a firm? Discuss.

Visit the Online Learning Centre at www.mcgraw-hill.co.uk/textbooks/jobber for more Internet exercises.

Study questions

1. When you next visit a supermarket, examine three sales promotions. What types of promotion are they? What are their likely objectives?

2. Why would it be wrong to measure the sales effect of a promotion only during the promotional period? What are the likely long-term effects of a promotion?

3. Distinguish between public relations and publicity. Is it true that publicity can be regarded as free advertising?

4. There is no such thing as bad publicity. Discuss.

5. The major reason for event sponsorship is to indulge senior management in their favourite pastime. Discuss.

6. Exhibitions are less effective than personal selling and more costly than direct mail, so why use them?

When you have read this chapter log on to the Online Learning Centre at www.mcgraw-hill.co.uk/textbooks/jobber to explore chapter-by-chapter test questions, links and further online study tools for marketing.

case thirty-one

Community Relations: Building Masts for 3G Phones

Third-generation (3G) mobile phones went on sale to the public in March 2003. Supported by generous advertising and a significant PR campaign, the handsets represented the first opportunity to retrieve some of the massive licence fees, amounting to some £22 billion (€32 billion), demanded by the UK government. As a new niche commodity, the 3G phones were something of a challenge. Initial pricing had the NEC e606 and the Motorola A830 at £400 (€576), with other versions available at higher prices. But, by May 2003, major retail outlets were discounting by 60 per cent or more.

Hutchison 3g is a mobile multimedia company, one of five organisations awarded licences by the UK government to run third-generation wireless services. It is the only company focusing solely on 3G, and is co-owned by Hutchison Whampoa (previously owner of Orange), KPN Mobile from the Netherlands and NTT DoCoMo, Japan's largest mobile phone company. The company's competitors include the four other UK mobile phone operators to have won 3G licences: Orange, mmO$_2$, T-mobile and Vodafone. Of these, the UK quoted companies have come under strong institutional pressure to write down the value of their 3G licences, with mmO$_2$ reducing its by £6 billion (€8.6 billion) in May 2003 and Vodafone putting up strong arguments to shareholders for not following suit. Hutchison 3g itself had to call on a £1 billion (€1.44 billion) loan facility from its three main shareholders in the first quarter of 2003 (according to the *Financial Times* of 10 March 2003).

Launched in May 2002 as 3, Hutchison 3g's goal was to be the first provider in the UK. In order to achieve its aim, 3 had to build a series of new base stations, because most of the existing ones served 2G operators and had limited capacity.

3's handsets were launched in March 2003, a calculated risk given that the handsets themselves were not actually in the shops until May that year. Prior to the launch date (set appropriately at 3 March 2003), 3 began demonstrating its handsets to industry and media analysts in January (*PR Week*, 4 April 2003).

Mobile handsets work by converting users' voices or data into radio waves that are transmitted to other handsets via a national network of base stations. Each base station covers a specific area and forms part of a patchwork of overlapping cells nationwide. But individual stations can only handle a certain number of users at any one time, so in order to provide efficient service and coverage, it was important that 3 had the network in place to meet demand. Base stations have antennae that can be attached to existing structures, buildings, towers or masts.

The siting of mobile phone base stations, particularly those attached to masts, has aroused considerable controversy in some parts of the country. In Sheffield, 200 residents signed a petition and raised strong objections at a public meeting, following the erection of four masts in the same street (*Sheffield Star*, 1 April 2002). The visual effect of masts is not the only consideration: concerns have also been expressed about the emissions of radio frequency radiation, the loss of value to properties, noise and vibration, the way in which planning applications are dealt with, and the inconsistencies in public consultation. For example, in some cases, Hutchison 3g and other providers have 'permitted rights' under the current regulations, thereby relaxing the requirement to seek full planning permission for every new base station.

In 1999, the UK government had asked the Independent Expert Group on Mobile Phones (IEGMP), chaired by Sir William Stewart, to investigate the possible health effects of mobile phone technology, including base stations. Published in 2000, IEGMP's report indicated no general risk to the health of people living near base stations, on the basis that exposure to non-ionizing radio waves was expected to be a small fraction of the limits set in international guidelines. Nevertheless, it advocated a 'precautionary approach' in respect of masts, including further study of base stations sited near schools. Subsequent research into emissions from masts to schools showed that they ranged from 'thousands to hundreds of thousands below exposure guidelines set by the International Commission on non-ionising radiological protection' (*Manchester Evening News*, April 2002).

The logic of the 'precautionary approach' is based on the action of power control, whereby radio frequency exposure levels are reduced the closer one is to the base station itself. In other words, according to one review, 'base stations should be placed as close as possible to schools, etc., exactly the opposite of the objectors' demands (Manchester City Council Telecom Masts Inquiry, March 2001). The Stewart Report stressed that if there was any question of a risk to health, this was posed by the mobile phones themselves, rather than the masts. Yet at five public meetings held by the Stewart Inquiry, it was the fear of masts rather than phones that was raised. In addition, experts in electromagnetic frequencies at the World Health Organization have spoken of gaps in knowledge that 'have been identified for further research to better assess health risks'.

Hutchison 3g has always maintained its commitment 'to open consultation with local communities and stakeholders'. Where considered necessary, the company's initial phase of community consultation has included:

- letters and information leaflets to the immediate neighbours or those further afield, depending on site specifics
- letter and information leaflets to the community council, together with request for meeting
- letter and information leaflet to local council member, together with request for meeting
- key stakeholder briefing session through a structured round table meeting
- one day drop-in centres, appropriately advertised, serviced by Hutchison 3g staff involved in acquisitions, planning and community affairs.

An inquiry conducted by Manchester City Council's physical environment and scrutiny committee in March 2001 concluded that 'the operators were very open about their plans and [that they had] presented detailed numbers to the inquiry'. But the commitment has been treated with some scepticism. As one radio interviewer put it to the vice chair of the IEGMP, local communities will not necessarily understand the science needed to make the appropriate decisions.

Questions

1) There is a view that public relations should aspire to genuinely symmetrical communication. Define the terms 'symmetric' and 'asymmetric', and give your views on how far the mobile phone operators, as exemplified in this case study, have met this recommendation.

2) Discuss the term, 'community relations', identifying the relevant stakeholders and publics in this case study.

3) Devise an outline community relations campaign plan based on this case study. Set objectives and strategy, showing how the results may be measured.

The information on which this case study is based was supplied by the Community Affairs Department of Hutchison 3g. The case was prepared by Alan Rawel, Head of Education and Training, Institute of Public Relations, London.

The positioning of mobile phone masts raises aesthetic, environmental and health concerns.

case thirty-two

Movie Marketing: How Studios Make and Spend Fortunes, Creating Hype for their Blockbusters

Movies are a fickle business. Studios can invest millions into the marketing of a movie but still come out with a box office flop. The movie *Titanic* broke all box office records, with a worldwide take of $1,835,300,000, and a budget of $200 million. However, this type of performance is very much the exception rather than the rule. In 2001, the average studio movie cost $47.7 million to make and an additional $31 million to market. Blockbuster movies such as *Godzilla* spent in excess of $50 million simply marketing the movie. Box office revenue is not the only revenue studios make. There are very lucrative markets for companion books, soundtracks, posters, rental DVDs, collector DVDs and, of course, the multitude of merchandising opportunities available. For example, *Monsters Inc* was estimated to have earned in excess of $110 million on the first day of its release on DVD.

Pictures have an extremely short life span when released at the cinema. The typical life span of a movie at the box office is six weeks. They need to make an impact in their first three weeks of release. In some cases, studios need to achieve large opening weekends to recoup the costs of a picture. If there is negative word of mouth about a picture, primarily from critics and the media, this can be devastating to a movie's chance of success (e.g. as was the case with *The Avengers*). Timing is crucial, especially in such a competitive marketplace, where new products are introduced every week. Studios have to time their release dates so as to reach the market at the most opportune time and avoid competition, which is likely to poach suitable demographic audiences from their movie.

The typical launch strategy for films is to pre-market the movie before the release date, building up audience interest and launching the movie on a large-scale basis, simultaneously launching the movie in thousands of cinemas. The movie industry is very much a seasonal business, with two prime seasons: winter and summer. Furthermore, some films are launched at peak times when their audience is more likely to go to the cinema (e.g. launching children's films during the school holidays).

Release calendars are constantly reshuffled so films can maximize their chances of success. Big-budget movies try to open on bank holidays, trying to gain large opening weekends, thus gaining further publicity. Other movies try to find ideal release dates so as not to clash with other films of a similar genre or those that are a competitive threat. Table C32.1 illustrates the importance of timing a film's release because of the competitive threats of similar movies.

Table C32.1	Battle of the 'event movies'			
Year and battle	1992 'Columbus'	1997 'Volcanoes'	1998 'Asteroids'	2000 'Mars'
Movies	1492—Conquest of Paradise vs Christopher Columbus: The Discovery	Dante's Peak vs Volcano	Deep Impact vs Armageddon	Mission to Mars vs Red Planet
Verdict	Both total flops: 1492 cost $47m to make, but only grossed just over $7m in the USA	Dante's Peak was relatively successful, while Volcano didn't explode at the box office	Both commercial successes, with Armageddon raking in over $500 million	Both $90 million budgeted turkeys were commercial flops

Some of the crucial factors in determining the likelihood of success for a movie are the type of movie theme, the film's promotional strategy, its distribution strategy and, of course, the quality of the movie, as listed below:

- movie theme (genre of movie)
- promotion strategy (creative strategy, media budget, choice of media vehicles, media schedule, media interest, publicity and word of mouth generated)
- distribution strategy (release pattern and distribution intensity)
- movie quality (production values, direction, acting, cinematography, script)
- cast (movie stars themselves can be viewed as brands, adding extra pulling power to a film).

Movies can be classified into several categories, as outlined in Table C32.2. These categories highlight a film's genre and the demographic appeal of a movie.

Table C32.2 Movie categories

'High concept'	'Franchise movies'	'Oscar hype'
These movies are built around single-concept ideas, with a large focus on scale and effects. They are frequently called 'event movies'.	Movies created in the hope of developing sequels to the original films. Huge cash cows for studios in terms of merchandising and spin-off opportunities	Material well respected by critics and the general public alike. Favourites at award ceremonies. Awards generate additional box office revenue due to the extra kudos.
Examples include: ● Titanic ● Pearl Harbor ● Apollo 13.	Examples include: ● Harry Potter ● Lord of the Rings ● Tomb Raider.	Examples include:* ● American Beauty ● A Beautiful Mind ● Life is Beautiful.
'Chick flicks'	'Bullets not Broadway'	'Sleeper hits'
Movies that appeal primarily to a female audience, including the genres of drama, romance, comedy or suspense.	Movies that appeal primarily to a male audience, including the genres of action, sci-fi, comedy or suspense.	Low-budget movies that gain popularity through positive word of mouth and slowly build up screen coverage.
Examples include: ● Pretty Woman ● Dirty Dancing ● Sleepless in Seattle.	Examples include: ● Con Air ● XXX ● Face Off.	Examples include: ● The Blair Witch Project ● The Full Monty ● My Big Fat Greek Wedding.
'Magic kingdom'	'Star power movies'	'Turkeys and straight to video'
Primarily focused on children, but also appealing to the accompanying adult audiences. Typically animation feature films. Huge earners.	Movies that use the pulling power of their leading actor(s) or actress(es) to gain extra box office revenue.	Movies that vanish without a trace despite large budgets, and appear quickly on video/DVD format, in some cases bypassing cinemas altogether.
Examples include: ● The Lion King ● Shrek ● A Bug's Life.	Examples include: ● Ocean's Eleven ● Vanilla Sky ● Heat.	Examples include: ● Pluto Nash ● Meet Joe Black ● The Postman ● D-Toxx.

* Please note: this category does not only include those films that have the words 'beauty' or 'beautiful' in their titles!

Opening weekends are crucial in the determination of a film's success. If a film has a successful opening weekend, studios breathe a sigh of relief in that they may recoup some of their costs, even if the film opens to negative reviews. The biggest-ever opening weekend was that for *Spider-Man*, which collected $114 million dollars. However, every year sees a surprise sleeper hit doing very well at the box office; examples include *The Blair Witch Project*, *My Big Fat Greek Wedding* and *The Full Monty*. Such films that are launched on limited release, with minuscule promotional budgets; however, due to positive word of mouth from audiences, more people attend the movies based on recommendations. This extra demand is spotted by cinema chains, which then show the movies in extra screens, further increasing sales and building up positive word of mouth. This is what is called gaining 'sales momentum'. As a result of this extra revenue, a studio can launch national advertising campaigns to prolong this sales momentum, with promotional tag-lines such as 'Surprise Hit of The Year!' and positive audience testimonials. Figure C32.1 shows the difference in box office takings between a sleeper hit (*My Big Fat Greek Wedding*) and a typical revenue pattern (*Panic Room*).

So what marketing tools are used to create the hype behind a movie? Table C32.3 has the answer.

Trailers can cost huge amounts of money. Studios can typically spend $600,000 on the production of a movie trailer. There are three typical movie trailers that will accompany a movie: the full two-and-a-half-minute theatrical trailer; a variety of 30-second TV spot trailers; and teaser trailers. A teaser trailer, for example, may not show any footage of the movie except the logo of the film and when it is due for release, such as *Terminator 3*, where the teaser was launched a year before the movie was due for release. (See www.apple.com/trailers for examples of the latest film trailers.) These are used to build up audience interest and anticipation for a movie, generating word of mouth. For Superbowl 2002, the major film studios bought 30-second teaser trailers for their upcoming summer movies, such as *XXX*, *Signs*, *Austin Powers 3*, *Harts War*, *Bad Company* and *Collateral Damage*. Each 30-second clip is a mere snip, costing only $2 million dollars. Spending that type of money does not necessarily guarantee success, as half of those movies promoted were commercial flops (for example, *Bad Company*, starring Anthony Hopkins and Chris Rock, cost Touchstone Pictures $80 million, but only made $30 million at the US box office).

Publicity is a huge weapon in the arsenal of a studio's marketing strategy. The core aim of publicity is getting as much (positive) media exposure as possible. Newspapers, magazines and television programmes continually vie for insights into celebrity lifestyles. Good publicists aim to get their movie stars on the cover of a magazine, arrange interviews on talk shows, arrange press conferences, and so on. Their role is to get the media talking about a particular movie star and their latest film. This process takes place before and during a film's release, helping to

Figure C32.1 Comparison of box office takings

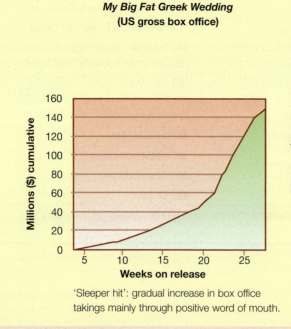

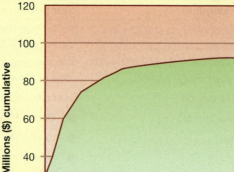

'Sleeper hit': gradual increase in box office takings mainly through positive word of mouth.

'Traditional': strong opening weekend, with diminishing returns as the weeks progress.

Table C32.3 How to promote a blockbuster

- Television advertising (30-second spot adverts)
- Cinema advertising (full trailer advertising)
- Teaser trailer advert (year before film launch)
- 'Making of' documentaries
- Featurettes
- Movie festivals
- Awards (Oscars, Baftas, Cannes, Venice, Sundance, etc.)
- Internet sites and promotion
- Merchandising — Movie tie-ins with fast-food outlets, food and drink companies, etc.
  - Toys
  - Video games
- News stories (celebrity gossip, box office records)
- Press junkets
- News conferences (TV/radio interviews)
- Gala premieres
- Celebrity parties
- Reviewer quotes (e.g. *Total Film* magazine—'a rollercoaster of a movie')
- Magazine content (reviews, profiles, interviews)

build awareness of the film. Movie studios strive for publicity, as they do not have to pay for this type of exposure. For example, the movie *Vanilla Sky*, starring Tom Cruise, garnered huge publicity before it was even released due to the star's relationship with his leading lady Penelope Cruz. The couple's photos were ubiquitous in the media, and their 'celebrity newsworthiness' generated substantial word of mouth about the film, as well as audience interest. Many studios throw press junkets, where they invite the press to a private screening, provide 10-minute interviews with the talent and, of course, wine and dine the ever fickle press, giving them freebies, providing accommodation, all in order to get good editorial coverage.

According to academic research, seven out of ten pictures lose money, two break even, and only one stands a reasonable chance of being a huge success. Studios try to build up the expectations of consumers by packaging a movie with popular actors, respected directors, expensive budgets, exotic locations and easily recognized script material such as a best-selling book, TV spin-off, comic book or video game adaptation. By adding these elements, studios improve the overall awareness of a film, building up audience interest. The studio's aim is to gain sales and momentum as quickly as possible. Film critics play an important role in helping consumers decide their choice of films, as their opinions decrease audience uncertainty

Star vehicle: BMW used the James Bond movie *Goldeneye* (starring Pierce Brosnan, pictured) to launch its Z3 roadster.

about the quality of a film. Since movies are intangible and unique, film-goers find it hard to judge the quality of a movie prior to seeing it. Columbia Pictures (owned by Sony) went a step too far in trying to get a recommendation for its films by concocting its own critic, the fictitious David Manning. Its marketing department created fabricated quotes about films such as *The Animal*, *A Knight's Tale* and *Vertical Limit*, and used them in promotional campaigns for the films. Furthermore, it went further still by using its own employees in (apparently unbiased) screen testimonials promoting Columbia's very own film, Mel Gibson's *The Patriot*.

One of the best ways of generating word of mouth, and to gain free editorial and media coverage, is film award ceremonies and festivals such as the Oscars. *Variety*, the movie trade magazine, stated that Oscar-related

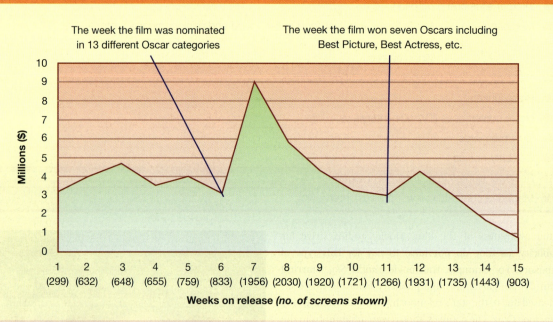

Figure C32.2 *Shakespeare in Love* weekend, US gross box office

Table C32.4	A comparison of the movie marketing techniques		
	Pearl Harbor 'High concept'	*Shakespeare in Love* 'Oscar hype'	*My Big Fat Greek Wedding* 'Sleeper hit'
Year	2001	1998	2002
Background	Big action blockbuster, laden with special effects, 'next big thing', labelled actors.	Oscar-winning romantic comedy with well-known actors in lead roles.	Low-budget comedy with no well-known actors except for one well-known TV personality.
Budget	$152 million	$25 million	$5 million
Hype machine	$5 million extravaganza on board an aircraft carrier in Hawaii with 2500 specially invited guests, for press interviews, concert, fireworks and world premiere; gained massive worldwide media coverage.	Aimed to win Oscars and did. Promoted heavily for nominations and spent $7 million to do so. Gamble paid off earning the film extra publicity and revenue.	Started publicity by generating buzz in the American Greek community. Aided by this initial success, the studio invested $19 million in media advertising support to keep the momentum.
Worldwide box office	$450 million	$289 million	$160 million

advertising in its paper and on its website exceeded $10 million in 2002, a 20 per cent increase on the previous year (though not up on the *Saving Private Ryan* vs *Shakespeare in Love* year of 1998). The studio behind *Shakespeare in Love* spent $7 million in a marketing campaign designed to snatch an Oscar, which amounts to more than $1700 spent per Oscar Academy voter. The studio released the film in a limited number of cinema theatres before the 31 December deadline in 1997 so that it could be eligible for Oscar contention. The movie, which grabbed the Best Picture award, gained, on average, 27 per cent of its box office gross after the awards were announced (see Figure C32.2). The effect of achieving 13 Oscar nominations and winning seven awards was twofold in that it increased the longevity of the film at cinemas as well as the number of screens the film was shown in.

The promotional techniques used by movies vary depending on the monetary resources available to generate publicity, the targeted audience and the overall genre of the movie. Table C32.4 illustrates that different techniques are used to generate publicity for a film. Crucially, promoting movies is primarily aimed at building audience awareness and generating positive word of mouth about a movie.

Furthermore, studios garner money from product placement in their movies. Recent examples include *Minority Report*, which was set in 2054, but included brand names such as Lexus, Nokia, American Express, Gap, Reebok and Pepsi. In some cases brands are integrated into the very storyline of the film, as was the case in Tom Hanks' *Castaway*, where his character plays a FedEx manager sent around the world to make sure packages arrive on time—a FedEx plane even crashes into the sea! Product placement is where companies pay movie studios fees for having their product used or to have it shown directly in the film. Companies use product placement for a variety of reasons, namely cost effectiveness, to increase global reach and to create brand associations with a film. For example, BMW launched its innovative and popular Z3 roadster in the James Bond movie *Goldeneye*. The car achieved huge publicity and instant coolness as the new 'Bond car'. In Bond's most recent escapade, the movie earned $70 million before it was even shown, through marketing tie-in deals with 20 different advertisers (see Table C32.5). Not every product got screen time, but advertisers could use the Bond endorsement in their own adverts.

To sum up, the main motto of movie marketing is that 'you have to spend money to make money'.

Table C32.5 Product placement and marketing tie-ins featured in 'Bond 20', *Die Another Day*		
Jaguar (*owned by Ford*)	Finlandia vodka	Norelco shavers
Aston Martin (*owned by Ford*)	7-Up	Revlon
Thunderbird (*owned by Ford*)	Bollinger champagne	Ty Nant (spring water)
Samsonite	Brioni suits	Visa
Plantronics (*phone headsets*)	Sony Ericsson	Philips
Bombardier (*skidoos*)	Omega	Mattel 'Bond Girl Barbie'
Heineken	Swatch	British Airways
Club Med	Kodak	Energizer batteries

Questions

1) What do you believe are the key factors in launching a movie successfully?

2) Evaluate the different promotional vehicles available to movie studios in launching their blockbuster movies, commenting on their efficiency and cost effectiveness.

3) Discuss the role of critics in movie marketing.

4) Discuss why you believe marketers are investing vast sums of money in movie product placement.

5) Outline and discuss the risks associated with movie product placement.

This case was written by Conor Carroll, Lecturer in Marketing, University of Limerick. Copyright © Conor Carroll (2002). The material in the case has been drawn from a variety of published sources.

chapter seventeen

Distribution

> *Uphill slow, downhill fast*
> *Cargo first, safety last.*
>
> US TRUCKING MOTTO, CIRCA 1950

Learning Objectives

This chapter explains:

1. The functions and types of channels of distribution

2. How to determine channel strategy

3. The three components of channel strategy: channel selection, intensity and integration

4. The five key channel management issues: member selection, motivation, training, evaluation and conflict management

5. The cost–customer service trade-off in physical distribution

6. The components of a physical distribution system: customer service, order processing, inventory control, warehousing, transportation and materials handling

7. How to improve customer service standards in physical distribution

8. Ethical issues in distribution

Producing products that customers want, pricing them correctly and developing well-designed promotional plans are necessary but not sufficient conditions for customer satisfaction. The final part of the jigsaw is distribution: the *place* element of the marketing mix. Products need to be available in adequate quantities, in convenient locations and at times when customers want to buy them. In this chapter we shall examine the functions and types of distribution channels, the key decisions that determine channel strategy, how to manage channels and issues relating to the physical flow of goods through distribution channels (physical distribution management).

Producers need to consider not only the needs of their ultimate customer but also the requirement of channel intermediaries, those organizations that facilitate the distribution of products to customers. For example, success for Müller yoghurt in the UK was dependent on convincing a powerful retailer group (Tesco) to stock the brand. The high margins the brand supported were a key influence in Tesco's decision. Without retailer support Müller would have found it uneconomic to supply consumers with its brand. Clearly, establishing a supply chain that is efficient and meets customers' needs is vital to marketing success. This supply chain is termed a channel of distribution, and is the means by which products are moved from producer to the ultimate customer. Gaining distribution outlets does not come easily. Advertising to channel intermediaries is sometimes used to explain the benefits of the brand to encourage stocking, as the Dyson trade ad illustrates.

Gaining distribution outlets does not come easily. Advertising to channel intermediaries is sometimes used to promote the benefits of stocking a brand.

The choice of the most effective channel of distribution is an important aspect of marketing strategy. The development of supermarkets effectively shortened the distribution channel between producer and consumer by eliminating the wholesaler. Prior to their introduction the typical distribution channel for products like food, drink, tobacco and toiletries was producer to wholesaler to retailer. The wholesaler would buy in bulk from the producer and sell smaller quantities to the retailer (typically a small grocery shop). By building up buying power, supermarkets could shorten this chain by buying direct from producers. This meant lower costs to the supermarket chain and lower prices to the consumer. The competitive effect was to drastically reduce the numbers of small grocers and wholesalers in this market. By being more efficient and better meeting customers' needs, supermarkets had created a competitive advantage for themselves.

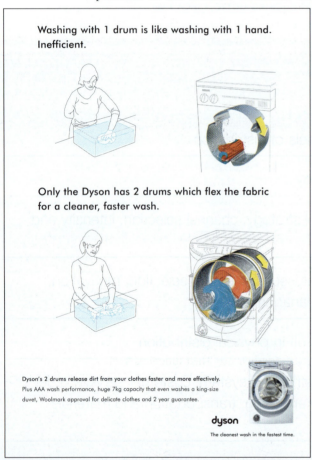

This trade advertisement for the Dyson washing machine appeared in electrical retail magazines.

More recently the Internet has been playing a key role in distribution. One area where the Internet is having a major impact is by providing customer support and service in the express delivery market, as e-Marketing 17.1 explains.

17.1 e-marketing

Express Delivery Companies: Leaders in Online Support and Service

The courier and express delivery marketplace is worth around £1.6 billion (€2.3 billion). E-business technology has revolutionized this market and the activities of its three largest players (DHL, FedEx and United Parcel Force)—over half of their business-to-business transactions now take place over the Internet. Competition within this marketplace is fierce and is driving the use of technology in customer support and service.

DHL began business in 1969 and is majority owned by Deutsche Post World Net. It retains around 40 per cent of the express delivery marketplace worldwide and boasts a network of hubs and logistic centres covering 227 countries. The DHL website (www.dhl.com) is the main source of customer support and service. It provides increasing levels of relevant and 'real-time' information.

Among its service features, DHL provides customers with delivery quotes and allows them to organize collection and delivery details in real time, online. It also provides an online tracking service that provides up-to-the-minute status on packages and parcels.

Technology provides new levels of customer support and service for DHL, but also begs the question 'Where will new sources of service advantage come from?' DHL is well aware of this problem and looks at every area for potential advantage. By allowing its online tracking tool to be integrated within customer websites, DHL provides a valuable service for its immediate customers—tying them to one supplier in a market where switching costs are low—and further promotes the DHL brand.

Based on: Key Notes (2001)[1]

Next, we shall explore the functions of channel intermediaries and then examine the different types of channels that manufacturers can use to supply their products to customers.

Functions of channel intermediaries

The most basic question to ask when deciding channel strategy is whether to sell directly to the ultimate customer or to use channel intermediaries such as retailers and/or wholesalers. To answer this question we need to understand the functions of channel intermediaries—that is, what benefits might producers derive from their use. Their functions are to reconcile the needs of producers and customers, to improve efficiency by reducing the number of transactions or creating bulk, to improve accessibility by lowering location and time gaps between producers and consumers, and to provide specialist services to customers. Each of these functions is now examined in more detail.

Reconciling the needs of producers and consumers

Manufacturers typically produce a large quantity of a limited range of goods, whereas consumers usually want only a limited quantity of a wide range of goods.[2] The role of channel intermediaries is to reconcile these conflicting situations. For example, a manufacturer of tables sells to retailers that each buy from a range of manufacturers of furniture and furnishings. The manufacturer can gain economies of scale by producing large quantities of tables, and each retailer provides a wide assortment of products offering its customers considerable choice under one roof.

A related function of channel intermediaries is *breaking bulk*. A wholesaler may buy large quantities from a manufacturer (perhaps a container load) and then sell smaller quantities (such as by the case) to retailers. Alternatively, large retailers such as supermarkets buy large quantities from producers, and break bulk by splitting the order between outlets. In this way, producers can produce large quantities while consumers are offered limited quantities at the point of purchase.

Improving efficiency

Channel intermediaries can improve distribution efficiency by *reducing the number of transactions* and *creating bulk for transportation*. Figure 17.1 shows how the number of transactions between three producers and three customers is reduced by using one intermediary. Direct distribution to customers results in nine transactions, whereas the use of an intermediary cuts the number of transactions to six. Distribution (and selling) costs and effort, therefore, are reduced.

Small producers can benefit by selling to intermediaries, which then combine a large number of small purchases into bulk for transportation. Without the intermediary it may prove too costly for each small producer to meet transportation costs to the consumer. Agricultural products such as coffee, vegetables and fruit, which are grown by small producers, sometimes benefit from this arrangement.

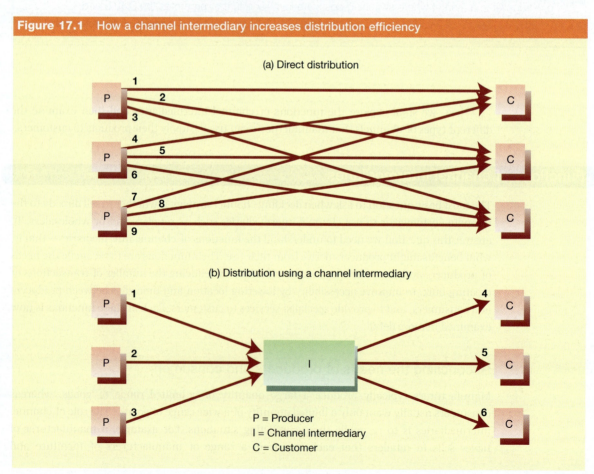

Figure 17.1 How a channel intermediary increases distribution efficiency

Improving accessibility

Two major divides that need to be bridged between producers and consumers are the location and time gaps. The *location gap* derives from the geographic separation of producers from the customers they serve. Many of the cars produced in the UK by Nissan and Toyota are exported to Europe. Car dealers in Europe provide customer access to these cars in the form of display and test drive facilities, and the opportunity to purchase locally rather than deal direct with the producer thousands of miles away.

The *time gap* results from discrepancies between when a manufacturer wants to produce goods and when consumers wish to buy. For example, manufacturers of spare parts for cars may wish to produce Monday to Friday but consumers may wish to purchase throughout the week and especially on Saturday and Sunday. By opening at the weekend, car accessory outlets bridge the time gap between production and consumption.

Providing specialist services

Channel intermediaries can perform specialist customer services that manufacturers may feel ill-equipped to provide themselves. Distributors may have long-standing expertise in such areas as selling, servicing and installation to customers. Producers may feel that these functions are better handled by channel intermediaries so that they can specialize in other aspects of manufacturing and marketing activity.

Types of distribution channel

All products whether they be consumer goods, industrial goods or services require a channel of distribution. Industrial channels tend to be shorter than consumer channels because of the small number of ultimate customers, the greater geographic concentration of industrial customers, and the greater complexity of the products that require close producer–customer liaison. Service channels also tend to be short because of the intangibility of services and the need for personal contact between the service provider and consumer.

Consumer channels

Figure 17.2 (overleaf) shows four alternative consumer channels. Each one is described briefly below.

Producer direct to consumer

Cutting out distributor profit margin may make this option attractive to producers. Direct selling between producer and consumer has been a feature of the marketing of Avon Cosmetics and Tupperware plastic containers. As discussed in Chapter 14, direct marketing is of growing importance in Europe and includes the use of direct mail, telephone selling and direct response advertising.

The Internet is creating new opportunities to supply consumers direct rather than through retailers. E-Marketing 17.2 discusses the developments in the music industry whereby downloadable music is being offered to consumers via their PCs.

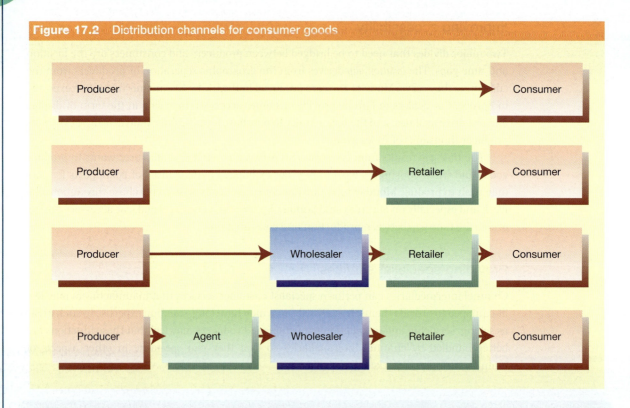

Figure 17.2 Distribution channels for consumer goods

17.2 e-marketing

The Internet: Making the Music Industry Rethink Distribution

The music industry has been affected more than most by Internet technology. Napster (www.napster.com) revolutionized music distribution a number of years ago, through a technology called peer-to-peer (P2P). This allowed users to swap files (in this case music files) and access, literally, millions of songs free of charge. This process has been challenged in the law courts by the major record companies and this has forced Napster to cease trading as a P2P provider and introduce a new pay model.

P2P and file sharing has been no more than a 'wake-up call' for the music industry. It missed the Internet as an opportunity to download music and sell physical product (e.g. CDs), it failed to recognize the public antipathy towards CD over-pricing and it missed a key trend in people using PCs to download, store and play music.

These trends are forcing record companies and music resellers to adapt. EMI and others now offer music by their artists straight to the consumer in downloadable format. Virgin now sells music in downloadable format through its Virgin JamCast service. In addition, it also sells CDs and other related materials through its online store (www.virgin.com/megastores/uk). The question some are asking is 'If record companies can sell artist material from a website straight to the consumer, can artists also produce their material for direct consumption?' Furthermore, do record companies 'really' need the music resellers to get their product out there? As always, the Internet promises big changes—in this case it may just deliver.

Producer to retailer to consumer

The growth in retailer size has meant that it becomes economic for producers to supply retailers directly rather than through wholesalers. Consumers then have the convenience of viewing and/or testing the product at the retail outlet. Supermarket chains exercise considerable power over manufacturers because of their enormous buying capabilities.

Producer to wholesaler to retailer to consumer

For small retailers (e.g. small grocery or furniture shops) with limited order quantities, the use of wholesalers makes economic sense. Wholesalers can buy in bulk from producers, and sell smaller quantities to numerous retailers. The danger is that large retailers in the same market have the power to buy directly from producers and thus cut out the wholesaler. In certain cases, the buying power of large retailers has meant that they can sell products to their customers cheaper than a small retailer can buy from the wholesaler. Longer channels like this tend to occur where retail oligopolies do not dominate the distribution system. In Europe, long channels involving wholesalers are common in France and Italy. In France, for example, the distribution of vehicle spare parts is dominated by small independent wholesalers.[3]

Producer to agent to wholesaler to retailer to consumer

This long channel is sometimes used by companies entering foreign markets. They may delegate the task of selling the product to an agent (who does not take title to the goods). The agent contacts wholesalers (or retailers) and receives commission on sales. Overseas sales of books are sometimes generated in this way.

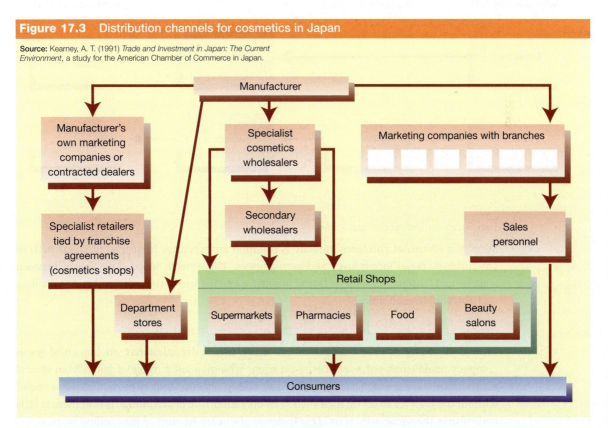

Figure 17.3 Distribution channels for cosmetics in Japan

Source: Kearney, A. T. (1991) *Trade and Investment in Japan: The Current Environment*, a study for the American Chamber of Commerce in Japan.

Some companies use multiple channels to distribute their products. Grocery products, for example, use both producer to wholesaler to retailer (small grocers), and producer to retailer (supermarkets). In Japan, distribution channels to consumers tend to be long and complex, with close relationships between channel members, a fact that has acted as a barrier to entry for foreign companies. An example of the complexity of Japanese distribution channels for cosmetics is given in Fig. 17.3 (see preceding page).[4]

Industrial channels

Common industrial (business to business) distribution channels are illustrated in Fig. 17.4. Usually a maximum of one channel intermediary is used.

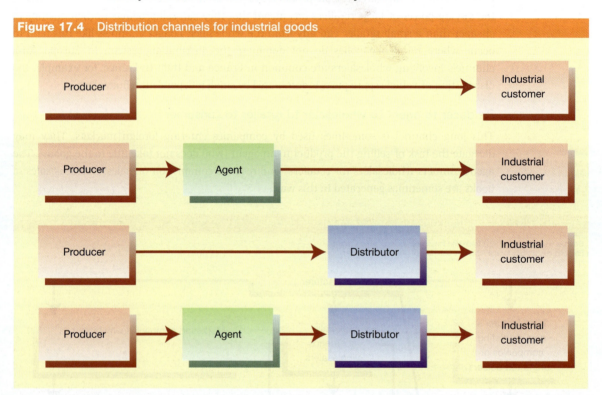

Figure 17.4 Distribution channels for industrial goods

Producer to industrial customer

Supplying industrial customers directly is common for expensive industrial products such as gas turbines, diesel locomotives and aero-engines. There needs to be close liaison between supplier and customer to solve technical problems, and the size of the order makes direct selling and distribution economic.

Producer to agent to industrial customer

Instead of selling to industrial customers using their own salesforce, an industrial goods company could employ the services of an agent who may sell a range of goods from several suppliers (on a commission basis). This spreads selling costs and may be attractive to companies without the reserves to set up their own sales operation. The disadvantage is that there is little control over the agent, who is unlikely to devote the same amount of time selling on products compared with a dedicated sales team.

Producer to distributor to industrial customer

For less expensive, more frequently bought industrial products, distributors are used. These may have both internal and field sales staff.[5] Internal staff deal with customer-generated enquiries and order placing, order follow-up (often using the telephone) and checking inventory levels. Outside sales staff are more proactive: their practical responsibilities are to find new customers, get products specified, distribute catalogues and gather market information. The advantage to customers of using distributors is that they can buy small quantities locally.

Producer to agent to distributor to industrial customer

Where industrial customers prefer to call upon distributors, the agent's job will require selling into these intermediaries. The reason why a producer may employ an agent rather than a dedicated salesforce is usually cost based (as previously discussed).

Services channels

Distribution channels for services are usually short: either direct or using an agent. Since stocks are not held, the role of the wholesaler, retailer or industrial distributor does not apply. Figure 17.5 shows the two alternatives whether they be to consumer or industrial customers.

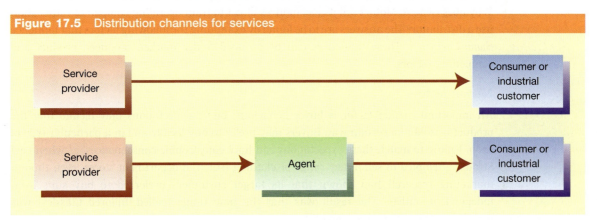

Figure 17.5 Distribution channels for services

Service provider to consumer or industrial customer

The close personal relationships between service providers and customers often mean that service supply is direct. Examples include healthcare, office cleaning, accountancy, marketing research and law.

Service provider to agent to consumer or industrial customer

A channel intermediary for a service company usually takes the form of an agent. Agents are used when the service provider is geographically distant from customers, and where it is not economical for the provider to establish its own local sales team. Examples include insurance, travel, secretarial and theatrical agents.

Channel strategy

Channel strategy decisions involve the selection of the most effective distribution channel, the most appropriate level of distribution intensity and the degree of channel integration (see Fig. 17.6). Each of these decisions will now be discussed.

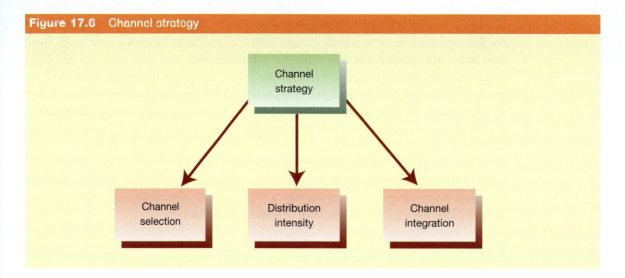

Figure 17.6 Channel strategy

Channel selection

Why does Procter & Gamble sell its brands through supermarkets rather than selling direct? Why does General Motors sell its locomotives direct to train operating companies rather than use a distributor? The answers are to be found by examining the following factors that influence *channel selection*. These influences can be grouped under market, producer, product and competitive factors.

Market factors

An important market factor is buyer behaviour: buyer expectations may dictate that the product be sold in a certain way. Buyers may prefer to buy locally and in a particular type of shop. Failure to match these expectations can have catastrophic consequences, as when Levi Strauss attempted to sell a new range of clothing (suits) in department stores, even though marketing research had shown that its target customers preferred to buy suits from independent outlets. The result was that the new range (called Tailored Classics) was withdrawn from the marketplace.

Buyer needs regarding product information, installation and technical assistance also have to be considered. A judgement needs to be made about whether the producer or channel intermediary can best meet these needs in terms of expertise, commitment and cost. For example, products that require facilities for local servicing, such as cars, often use intermediaries to carry out the task. Where the service requirement does not involve large capital investment the producer may carry out the service. For example, suppliers of burglar alarms employ their staff to conduct annual inspection and servicing.

The willingness of channel intermediaries to market a product is also a market-based factor that influences channel decisions. Direct distribution may be the only option if distributors refuse to handle the product. For industrial products, this may mean the recruitment of salespeople, and for consumer products direct mail may be employed to communicate to and supply customers. The profit margins demanded by wholesalers and retailers, and the commission rates expected by sales agents also affect their attractiveness as channel intermediaries. These costs need to be assessed in comparison with those of a salesforce.

The location and geographical concentration of customers also affects channel selection. The more local and clustered the customer base, the more likely direct distribution is feasible. Direct distribution is also more prevalent when buyers are few in number and buy large quantities. A large number of small customers may mean that using channel intermediaries is the only economical way of reaching them (hence supermarkets).

Producer factors

A constraint on the channel decision is when the producer lacks adequate resources to perform the functions of the channel. Producers may lack the financial and managerial resources to take on channel operations. Lack of financial resources may mean that a salesforce cannot be recruited, and sales agents and/or distributors are used instead. Producers may feel that they do not possess the customer-based skills to distribute their products and prefer to rely on intermediaries.

The product mix offered by a producer may also affect channel strategy. A wide mix of products may make direct distribution (and selling) cost effective. Narrow or single product companies, on the other hand, may find the cost of direct distribution prohibitive unless the product is extremely expensive.

The final product influence is the desired degree of control of channel operations. The use of independent channel intermediaries reduces producer control. For example, by distributing their products through supermarkets, manufacturers lose total control of the price charged to consumers. Furthermore, there is no guarantee that new products will be stocked. Direct distribution gives producers control over such issues.

Product factors

Large complex products are often supplied direct to customers. The need for close personal contact between producer and customer, and the high prices charged, mean that direct distribution and selling is both necessary and feasible. Perishable products such as frozen food, meat and bread require relatively short channels to supply the customer with fresh stock. Finally, bulky or difficult to handle products may require direct distribution because distributors may refuse to carry them if storage or display problems arise.[6]

Competitive factors

If the competition controls traditional channels of distribution—for example, through franchise or exclusive dealing arrangements—an innovative approach to distribution may be required. Two alternatives are to recruit a salesforce to sell direct or to set up a producer-owned distribution network (see the section on vertical marketing systems, under 'Conventional marketing channels', below). Producers should not accept that the channels of distribution used by competitors are the only ways to reach target customers. Direct marketing provides opportunities to supply products in new ways. Increasingly, traditional channels of distribution for personal computers through high-street retailers are being circumvented by direct marketers, who use direct response advertising to reach buyers. The emergence of the more computer-aware and experienced buyer, and the higher reliability of these products as the market reaches maturity has meant that a local source of supply (and advice) is less important.

Distribution intensity

The second channel strategy decision is the choice of *distribution intensity*. The three broad options are intensive, selective and exclusive distribution.

Intensive distribution

Intensive distribution aims to achieve saturation coverage of the market by using all available outlets. With many mass-market products, such as cigarettes, foods, toiletries, beer and newspapers, sales are a direct function of the number of outlets penetrated. This is because consumers have a range of acceptable brands from which they can choose. If a brand is not available in an outlet, an alternative is bought. The convenience aspect of purchase is paramount. New outlets may be sought that hitherto had not stocked the products, such as the sale of confectionery and grocery items at petrol stations.

Selective distribution

Market coverage may also be achieved through **selective distribution**, in which a producer uses a limited number of outlets in a geographical area to sell its products. The advantages to the producer are the opportunity to select only the best outlets to focus its efforts to build close working relationships and to train distributor staff on fewer outlets than with intensive distribution, and, if selling and distribution is direct, to reduce costs. Upmarket aspirational brands are often sold in carefully selected outlets. Retail outlets and industrial distributors like this arrangement since it reduces competition. Selective distribution is more likely to be used when buyers are willing to shop around when choosing products. This means that it is not necessary for a company to have its products available in all outlets. Products such as audio and video equipment, cameras, personal computers and cosmetics may be sold in this way.

Problems can arise when a retailer demands distribution rights but is refused by producers. This happened in the case of Superdrug, a UK discount store chain, which requested the right to sell expensive perfume but was denied by manufacturers who claimed that the store did not have the right ambience for the sale of luxury products. Superdrug maintained that its application was refused because the chain wanted to sell perfumes for less than their recommended prices. A Monopolies and Mergers Commission investigation supported current practice. European rules allow perfume companies to confine distribution to retailers who measure up in terms of décor and staff training. Manufacturers are not permitted to refuse distribution rights on the grounds that the retailer will sell for less than the list price.[7]

Exclusive distribution

This is an extreme form of selective distribution in which only one wholesaler, retailer or industrial distributor is used in a geographic area. Cars are often sold on this basis with only one dealer operating in each town or city. This reduces a purchaser's power to negotiate prices for the same model between dealers since to buy in a neighbouring town may be inconvenient when servicing or repairs are required. It also allows very close co-operation between producer and retailer over servicing, pricing and promotion. The right to **exclusive distribution** may be demanded by distributors as a condition for stocking a manufacturer's product line. Similarly, producers may wish for exclusive dealing where the distributor agrees not to stock competing lines.

Exclusive dealing can reduce competition in ways that may be considered contrary to consumers' interests. The European Court of Justice rejected an appeal by Unilever over the issue of exclusive outlets in Germany. By supplying freezer cabinets Unilever maintained exclusivity by refusing to allow other competing ice creams into them. The court's ruling may affect ice cream distribution in other European countries including the UK.[8] Also, Coca-Cola, Schweppes Beverages and Britvic's exclusive ties with the leisure trade (such as sports clubs) were broken by the Office of Fair Trading, making competitive entry easier.[9]

However, the European Court rejected an appeal by the French Leclerc supermarket group over the issue of the selective distribution system used by Yves St Laurent perfumes. The judges found that the use of selective distribution for luxury cosmetic products increased competition and that it was in the consumer's and manufacturer's interest to preserve the image of such luxury products.

Channel integration

Channel integration can range from conventional marketing channels, comprising an independent producer and channel intermediaries, through a franchise operation, to channel ownership by a producer. Producers need to consider the strengths and weaknesses of each system when setting channel strategies.

Conventional marketing channels

The independence of channel intermediaries means that the producer has little or no control over them. Arrangements such as exclusive dealing may provide a degree of control, but separation of ownership means that each party will look after their own interests. Conventional marketing channels are characterized by hard bargaining and, occasionally, conflict. For example, a retailer may believe that cutting the price of a brand is necessary to move stock, even though the producer objects because of brand image considerations.

However, separation of ownership means that each party can specialize in the function in which it has strengths: manufacturers produce, intermediaries distribute. Care needs to be taken by manufacturers to stay in touch with customers and not abdicate this responsibility to retailers.

A manufacturer that dominates a market through its size and strong brands may exercise considerable power over intermediaries even though they are independent. This power may result in an **administered vertical marketing system** where the manufacturer can command considerable co-operation from wholesalers and retailers. Major brand builders such as Procter & Gamble and Lever Brothers had traditionally held great leverage over distribution but, recently, power has moved towards the large dominant supermarket chains through their purchasing and market power. Marks & Spencer is a clear example of a retailer controlling an administered vertical marketing system. Through its dominant market position it is capable of exerting considerable authority over its suppliers.

Franchising

A **franchise** is a legal contract in which a producer and channel intermediaries agree each member's rights and obligations. Usually, the intermediary receives marketing, managerial, technical and financial services in return for a fee. Franchise organizations such as McDonald's, Benetton, Hertz, the Body Shop and Avis combine the strengths of a large sophisticated marketing-orientated organization with the energy and motivation of a locally owned outlet. Franchising is also commonplace in the car industry, where dealers agree exclusive deals with manufacturers in return for marketing and financial backing. Although a franchise operation gives a degree of producer control there are still areas of potential conflict. For example, the producer may be dissatisfied with the standards of service provided by the outlet, or the franchisee may believe that the franchising organization provides inadequate promotional support. Goal conflict can also arise. For example, some McDonald's franchisees are displeased with the company's rapid expansion programme, which has meant that new restaurants have opened within a mile of existing outlets. This has led to complaints about lower profits and falling franchise resale values.[10] A franchise agreement provides a **contractual vertical marketing system** through the formal co-ordination and integration of marketing and distribution activities. Some franchises exert a considerable degree of control over marketing operations. A case in point is Benetton, which is discussed in Marketing in Action 17.1.

17.1 marketing in action

International Franchising: the Case of Benetton

Benetton operates out of 5000 stores in 120 countries. The company has traditionally run a franchise operation. Each Benetton franchisee pays a one-off lump sum—so-called 'key money'—with no ongoing fee payments. In return, the franchisee benefits from Benetton's brand name, which is synonymous with fashion and colour, and exclusive rights to distribution within a given geographic area.

Benetton exercises considerable control over the franchise operation, choosing the location of outlets, determining retail prices, store layout and the colour blocking of the clothes. Some control is also taken over stocking: some product ranges have to be bought by the franchisee; once purchased, they cannot be returned to Benetton. Instead, twice-yearly sales periods in January and August provide opportunities to offload surplus stock. Sales periods are important to a Benetton franchisee, with up to 40 per cent of revenue being generated then.

Franchising gives Benetton considerable flexibility: if things go wrong Benetton is sheltered from some of the financial implications. For example, in the USA, 300 shops closed but the company was protected as it did not own any of them.

Benetton's manufacturer-and-design-only model is changing, however, with a move into directly owned and operated stores. These are mainly megastores carrying complete casual womenswear, menswear, childrenswear and underwear collections, as well as a wide selection of accessories.

The key driver into directly owned megastores is the consumer's desire to shop in big, bright, friendly retail outlets. A key benefit is to bring Benetton closer to the consumer. As a manufacturer, Benetton had no effective way of monitoring consumer trends and evaluating how its product lines were performing. In contrast, the fast-growing Zara outlets are directly owned by Inditex, which has been successful in quickly transferring catwalk styles to the high street. A retail presence allows Benetton to design its products to more closely align with consumer tastes. The company has also established closer contact with its franchisees by linking them to the company intranet.

This dual distribution strategy is not without its risks—not least the potential alienation of franchise holders and the need to develop a new managerial skill set.

Based on: www.Benetton.com;[11] Ivey (2002);[12] Vignalli, Schmidt and Davies (1993)[13]

Three economic explanations of why a producer might choose franchising as a means of distribution have been proposed. Franchising may be a means of overcoming resource constraints, as an efficient system to overcome producer–distributor management problems and as a way of gaining knowledge of new markets.[14] Franchising allows the producer to overcome internal resource constraints by providing access to the franchisee's resources. For example, if the producer has limited financial resources, access to additional finances may come from the franchisee. The second explanation of franchising relates to the problems of managing geographically dispersed operations. In such situations, producers may value the notion of the owner-manager who has a vested interest in the success of the business. Although some control may still be necessary, the franchisee benefits directly from increases in sales and profits and so has a financial incentive to manage the business well. Finally, franchising may be a way for a producer to access the local knowledge of the franchisee. Franchising may therefore be attractive when a producer is expanding into new markets and where potential franchisees have access to information that is important in penetrating such markets.

Franchising can occur at four levels of the distribution chain.

1. *Manufacturer and retailer*: the car industry is dominated by this arrangement. The manufacturer gains retail outlets for its cars and repair facilities without the capital outlay required by ownership.
2. *Manufacturer and wholesaler*: this is commonly used in the soft drinks industry. Manufacturers such as Schweppes, Coca-Cola and Pepsi grant wholesalers the right to make up and bottle their concentrate in line with their instructions, and to distribute the products within a defined geographic area.
3. *Wholesaler and retailer*: this is not as common as other franchising arrangements but is found with car products and hardware stores. It allows wholesalers to secure distribution of their product to consumers.
4. *Retailer and retailer*: an often used method that frequently has its roots in a successful retailing operation seeking to expand geographically by means of a franchise operation, often with great success. Examples include McDonald's, Benetton, Pizza Hut and KFC.

Channel ownership

Total control over distributor activities comes with channel ownership. This establishes a **corporate vertical marketing system**. By purchasing retail outlets, producers control their purchasing, production and marketing activities. In particular, control over purchasing means a captive outlet for the manufacturer's products. For example, the purchase of Pizza Hut and KFC by Pepsi has tied these outlets to the company's soft drinks brands.

The advantages of control have to be weighed against the high price of acquisition and the danger that the move into retailing will spread managerial activities too widely. Nevertheless corporate vertical marketing systems have operated successfully for many years in the oil industry where companies such as Shell, Texaco and BP own not only considerable numbers of petrol stations but also the means of production.

Channel management

Once the key channel strategy decisions have been made, effective implementation is required. Specifically, a number of channel management issues must be addressed (see Fig. 17.7). These are the selection, motivation, training and evaluation of channel members, and managing conflict between producers and channel members.

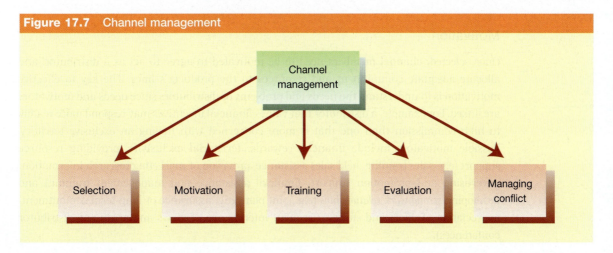

Figure 17.7 Channel management

Selection

For some producers (notably small companies) the distribution problem is not so much channel selection as channel acceptance. Their task is to convince key channel intermediaries (especially retailers) to stock their products. However, let us assume that we have a certain amount of discretion in choosing specific channel members to distribute our product. Selection then involves identifying candidates and developing *selection criteria*.

Identifying sources

Sources for identifying candidates include trade sources, reseller enquiries, customers of distributors and the field salesforce.[15] *Trade sources* include trade associations, exhibitions and trade publications. Talking to trade associations can lead to the supply of names of prospective distributors. Other trade publications may be published commercially and the names of possible distributors may be compiled. Exhibitions provide a useful means of meeting and talking to possible distributors. Sometimes channel members may be proactive in contacting a producer to express an interest in handling their products. Such *reseller enquiries* show that the possible distributor is enthusiastic about the possibility of a link. *Customers of distributors* are a useful source since they can comment on their merits and limitations. Finally, if a producer already has a *field salesforce* calling on intermediaries, salespeople are in a good position to seek out possible new distributors in their own territory.

The use of target country-based distributors is a common method of foreign market entry in Europe. A study of the sources of identifying overseas distribution found that the five most common methods were personal visits to search the market, the national trade board, customer and colleagues' recommendations, and trade fairs.[16]

Developing selection criteria

Common selection criteria include market, product and customer knowledge, market coverage, quality and size of the salesforce (if applicable), reputation among customers, financial standing, the extent to which competitive and complementary products are carried, managerial competence and hunger for success, and the degree of enthusiasm for handling the producer's lines. In practice, selection may be complex because large, well-established distributors may carry many competing lines and lack enthusiasm for more. Smaller distributors, on the other hand, may be less financially secure and have a smaller salesforce but be more enthusiastic and hungry for success. The top selection criteria of overseas distributors are market knowledge, enthusiasm for the contract, hunger for success, customer knowledge, and the fact that the distributor does not carry competitors' products.

Motivation

Once selected, channel members need to be motivated to agree to act as a distributor, and allocate adequate commitment and resources to the producer's lines. The key to effective motivation is to understand the needs and problems of distributors since needs and motivators are linked. For example, a distributor that values financial incentives may respond more readily to high commission than one that is more concerned with having an exclusive territory. Possible motivators include financial rewards, territorial exclusivity, providing resource support (e.g. sales training, field sales assistance, provision of marketing research information, advertising and promotion support, financial assistance and management training) and developing *strong work relationships* (e.g. joint planning, assurance of long-term commitment, appreciation of effort and success, frequent interchange of views and arranging distributor conferences).

In short, management of independent distributors is best conducted in the context of informal *partnerships*.[17] Producers should seek to develop strong relationships with their distributors based on a recognition of their performance and integrated planning and operations. For example, jointly determined sales targets could be used to motivate and evaluate salespeople, who might receive a bonus on achievement. A key element in fostering a spirit of partnership is to provide assurances of a long-term business relationship with the distributor (given satisfactory performance). This is particularly important in managing overseas distributors as many fear that they will be replaced by the producer's own salesforce once the market has been developed. The effort to develop partnerships appears to be worthwhile: a study of Canadian exporters and their British distributors found that success was related to partnership factors like joint decision-making, and close and frequent contact with distributors.[18]

The most popular methods cited by export managers and directors to motivate their overseas distributors were territorial exclusivity, provision of up-to-date product and company information, regular personal contact, appreciation of effort and understanding of the distributors' problems, attractive financial incentives, and provision of salespeople to support the distributors' salesforce.[19] Given overseas distributors' fears that they may be replaced, it was disappointing to note that only 40 per cent of these exporters provided assurances of a long-term business commitment to their distributors as a major motivator.

Mutual commitment between channel members is central to successful relationship marketing. Two types of commitment are affective commitment that expresses the extent to which channel members like to maintain their relationship with their partners, and calculative commitment where channel members need to maintain a relationship. Commitment is highly dependent on interdependence and trust between the parties.[20]

Training

The need to train channel members obviously depends on their internal competences. Large-market supermarket chains, for example, may regard an invitation by a manufacturer to provide marketing training as an insult. However, many smaller distributors have been found to be weak on sales management, marketing, financial management, stock control and personnel management, and may welcome producer initiatives on training.[21] From the producer's perspective, training can provide the necessary technical knowledge about a supplier company and its products, and help to build a spirit of partnership and commitment.

However, the training of overseas distributors by British exporters appears to be the exception rather than the rule.[22] When training is provided, it usually takes the form of product and company knowledge. Nevertheless when such knowledge is given it can help to build strong personal relationships and give distributors the confidence to sell those products.

Evaluation

The evaluation of channel members has an important bearing on distributor retention, training and motivation decisions. Evaluation provides the information necessary to decide which channel members to retain and which to drop. Shortfalls in distributor skills and competences may be identified through evaluation, and appropriate training programmes organized by producers. Where a lack of motivation is recognized as a problem, producers can implement plans designed to deal with the root causes of demotivation (e.g. financial incentives and/or fostering a partnership approach to business).[23]

It needs to be understood, however, that the scope and frequency of evaluation may be limited where power lies with the channel member. If producers have relatively little power because they are more dependent on channel members for distribution than channel members are on individual producers for supply, in-depth evaluation and remedial action will be restricted. Channel members may be reluctant to spend time providing the producers with comprehensive information on which to base evaluation. Remedial action may be limited to tentative suggestions when producers suspect there is room for improvement.

Where manufacturer power is high, through having strong brands and many distributors from which to choose, evaluation may be more frequent and wider in scope. Channel members are more likely to comply with the manufacturer's demands for performance information and agree for their sales and marketing efforts to be monitored by the manufacturer.

Evaluation criteria include sales volume and value, profitability, level of stocks, quality and position of display, new accounts opened, selling and marketing capabilities, quality of service provided to customers, market information feedback, ability and willingness to meet commitments, attitudes and personal capability.

Although the evaluation of overseas distributors and agents is more difficult than that for their domestic counterparts, two studies have shown that over 90 per cent of producers do carry out evaluation, usually at least once a year.[24] For distributors, sales-related criteria were most widely applied, with sales volume, sales value and creating new business three of the top four most commonly applied measures. Channel inputs were also widely used, with provision of market feedback, customer services, selling/marketing inputs and keeping commitments cited frequently. Given the importance of distributors in marketing to Europe, it is important that such evaluation takes place. However, a somewhat disappointing finding was that, with the exception of value of sales, less than half of the exporters used mutually *agreed objectives* to evaluate performance. Such a method is consistent with the partnership approach to channel management, and provides clarity and commitment to objectives since both parties have contributed to setting them. The most common method was to *compare against past performance*, which requires great care to ensure that account is taken of changes in the competitive environment over time.

Managing conflict

When producers and channel members are independent, conflict inevitably occurs from time to time. The intensity of conflict can range from occasional, minor disagreements that are quickly forgotten, to major disputes that fuel continuous bitter relationships.[25]

Sources of channel conflict

The major sources of *channel conflict* are differences in goals, differences in views on the desired product lines carried by channel members, multiple distribution channels, and inadequacies in performance.

- *Differences in goals*: most resellers attempt to maximize their own profit. This can be accomplished by improving profit margin, reducing inventory levels, increasing sales, lowering expenses and receiving greater allowances from suppliers. In contrast, producers might benefit from lower margins, greater channel inventories, higher promotional expenses and fewer allowances given to channel members. These inherent conflicts of interest mean that there are many potential areas of disagreement between producers and their channel members.

- *Differences in desired product line*: resellers that grow by adding product lines may be regarded as disloyal by their original suppliers. For example, WHSmith a UK retailer, originally specialized in books, magazines and newspapers but has grown by adding new product lines such as computer disks, videotape and software supplies. This can cause resentment among its primary suppliers, who perceive the reseller as devoting too much effort to selling secondary lines. Alternatively, retailers may decide to specialize by reducing their product range. For example, in Europe there has been a growth in the number of speciality shops selling, for example, athletics footwear. A sports outlet that decides to narrow its product range will wish to increase the assortment of the specialized items that make it distinct. This can cause conflict with its original suppliers of these product lines since the addition of competitors' brands makes the retailer appear disloyal.[26]

- *Multiple distribution channels*: in trying to achieve market coverage, a producer may use multiple distribution channels. For example, a producer may decide to sell directly to key accounts because their size warrants a key account salesforce, and use channel intermediaries to give wide market coverage. Conflict can arise when a channel member is denied access to a lucrative order from a key account because it is being serviced directly by the producer. Disagreements can also occur when the producer owns retail outlets that compete with independent retailers that also sell the producer's brands. For example, Clarks, a footwear manufacturer, owns a chain of outlets that compete with other shoe outlets that sell Clarks' shoes.[27]

- *Inadequacies in performance*: an obvious source of conflict is when parties in the supply chain do not perform to expectations. For example, a channel member may underperform in terms of sales, level of inventory carried, customer service, standards of display and salesperson effectiveness. Producers may give poor delivery, inadequate promotional support, low profit margins, poor-quality goods and incomplete shipments. These can all be potential areas of conflict.

Avoiding and resolving conflict

How can producers and channel members avoid and resolve conflict? There are several ways of managing conflict.

- *Developing a partnership approach*: this calls for frequent interaction between producer and resellers to develop a spirit of mutual understanding and co-operation. Producers can help channel members with training, financial help and promotional support. Distributors, in turn, may agree to mutually agreed sales targets and provide extra sales resources. The objective is to build confidence in the manufacturer's products and relationships based on trust. When conflicts arise there is more chance they will be resolved in a spirit of co-operation. Organizing staff exchange programmes can be useful in allowing each party to understand the problems and tensions of the other to avoid giving rise to animosity.

- *Training in conflict handling*: staff who handle disputes need to be trained in negotiation and communication skills. They need to be able to handle high-pressure conflict situations without resorting to emotion and *blaming behaviour*. Instead, they should be able to handle such situations calmly and be able to handle concession analysis, in particular the identification of *win-win situations*. These are situations where both the producer and reseller benefit from an agreement.

- *Market partitioning*: to reduce or eliminate conflict from multiple distribution channels, producers can try to partition markets on some logical basis, such as customer size or type. This can work if channel members accept the basis for the partitioning. Alternatively, different channels can be supplied with different product lines. For example, Hallmark sells its premium greetings cards under its Hallmark brand name to upmarket department stores, and its standard cards under the Ambassador name to discount retailers.[28]

- *Improving performance*: many conflicts occur for genuine reasons. For example, poor delivery by manufacturers or inadequate sales effort by distributors can provoke frustration and anger. Rather than attempt to placate the aggrieved partner, the most effective solution is to improve performance so that the source of conflict disappears. This is the most effective way of dealing with such problems.

- *Channel ownership*: an effective but expensive way of resolving conflicting goals is to buy the other party. Since producer and channel member are under common ownership, the common objective is to maximize joint profits. Conflicts can still occur but the dominant partner is in a position to resolve them quickly. Some producers in Europe have integrated with channel intermediaries successfully. For example, over 40 per cent of household furniture is sold through producer-owned retail outlets in Italy.[29]

- *Coercion*: In some situations, conflict resolution may be dependent on coercion, where one party forces compliance through the use of force. For example, producers can threaten to withdraw supply, deliver late or withdraw financial support; channel members, on the other hand, can threaten to delist the manufacturer's products, promote competitive products and develop own-label brands. In Europe, the increasing concentration of retailing into groups of very large organizations has meant that the balance of power has moved away from the manufacturers. The development of own-label brands has further strengthened the retailers' position, while giving them the double advantage of a high profit margin (because their purchase price is low) and a low price to the customer. Manufacturers' power in the supply chain is increased when they are large with high market share. By having a large and loyal customer base, manufacturers' brands become essential for distributors to stock. This increases manufacturers' negotiating power. Also by dominating a product category (e.g. Unilever and Proctor & Gamble in detergents) manufacturers gain power over distributors. By using multiple channels of distribution (e.g. direct as well as through distributors) and using a wide selection of distributors, the power of any one distributor is reduced. Control over distributors can also be gained by franchising and channel ownership (where manufacturers own retail outlets).

Physical distribution

In the first part of this chapter we examined channel strategy and management decisions, which concern the choice of the correct outlets to provide product availability to customers in a cost-effective manner. Physical distribution decisions focus on the efficient movement of goods from producer to intermediaries and the consumer. Clearly, channel and physical distribution decisions are interrelated, although channel decisions tend to be made earlier.

Physical distribution is defined as a 'set of activities concerned with the physical flows of materials, components and finished goods from producer to channel intermediaries and consumers'.

The aim is to provide intermediaries and customers with the right products, in the right quantities, in the right locations, at the right time. Physical distribution activities have been the subject of managerial attention for some time because of the potential for cost savings and improving customer service levels. Cost savings can be achieved by reducing inventory levels, using cheaper forms of transport and shipping in bulk rather than small quantities. Customer service levels can be improved by fast and reliable delivery, including just-in-time delivery, holding high inventory levels so that customers have a wide choice and the chances of stockouts are reduced, fast order processing, and ensuring products arrive in the right quantities and quality.

In the clothing industry, fast-changing fashion demands mean that companies such as H&M and Zara use extremely short lead times to create a competitive advantage over their slower, more cumbersome, rivals. The methods used by H&M were discussed in Case 1 (at the end of Chapter 1) and the Zara distribution operation is discussed in Marketing in Action 17.2.

Physical distribution management concerns the balance between cost reduction and meeting customer service requirements. Trade-offs are often necessary. For example, low inventory and slow, cheaper transportation methods reduce costs but lower customer service levels and satisfaction. Determining this balance is a key marketing decision as physical distribution can

17.2 marketing in action

Managing the Supply Chain the Zara Way

Zara, the Spanish clothing company, has revolutionized the fashion industry. Its key competitive advantage lies in its ability to match fashion trends that change quickly. This relies on an extremely fast and responsive supply chain.

Zara uses its stores to find out what consumers want, what styles are selling, what colours are in demand, and which items are hot sellers and which failures. The data is fed back to Zara headquarters through a sophisticated marketing information system. At the end of each day, Zara sales assistants report to the store manager using wireless headsets to communicate inventory levels. The store managers then inform the Zara design and distribution departments at headquarters about what consumers are buying, asking for and avoiding. Top-selling items are requested and low-selling items are withdrawn from shops within a week.

Garments are made in small production runs to avoid over exposure, and no item stays in the shops for more than four weeks, which encourages Zara shoppers to make repeat visits. Whereas the average high-street store in Spain expects shoppers to visit on average three times a year, Zara shoppers visit up to 17 times.

The company's designers use the feedback from the stores when preparing new designs. The fabrics are cut and dyed at Zara's own highly automated manufacturing facilities, which gives it control over this part of the supply chain. Seamstresses in 350 independently owned workshops in Spain and Portugal stitch about half of the pre-cut pieces into garments; the other half are stitched in-house.

The finished garments are sent back to Zara's headquarters with its state-of-the-art logistics centre where they are electronically tagged, quality checked and sorted into distribution lots for shipping to their destinations.

So efficient are Zara's production and distribution systems that the average turnaround time from design to delivery is 10 to 15 days, with around 12,000 garments being marketed each year. In this way, Zara stays on top of fashion trends rather than being outpaced by the market.

Based on: Anonymous (2002);[30] Jobber and Fahy (2003);[31] Mitchell (2003);[32] Roux (2002)[33]

be a source of competitive advantage. A useful approach is to analyse the market in terms of customer service needs and price sensitivity. The result may be the discovery of two segments:

- segment 1—low service needs, high price sensitivity
- segment 2—high service needs, low price sensitivity.

Unipart was first to exploit segment 2 in the do-it-yourself car repair and servicing market. It gave excellent customer service ('The answer's yes. Now what's the question?') but charged a high price. This analysis, therefore, defined the market segment to target and the appropriate marketing mix. Alternatively, both segments could be targeted with different marketing mixes. In industrial markets, large companies may possess their own service facilities while smaller firms require producer or distributor service as part of the product offering and are willing to pay a higher price. For example, Norsk Kjem, a Norwegian chemical company, discovered that the market for one of its product lines—wetting agents used in many processes to promote the retention and even distribution of liquids—was segmented in this way.[34] Small firms had less technical expertise and lower price sensitivity, and they ordered smaller quantities than larger companies. This meant that Norsk Kjem required different physical distribution (including service levels) and price structures for the two market segments.

Not only are there trade-offs between physical distribution costs and customer service levels, but there are also possible conflicts between elements of the physical distribution system itself. For example, an inventory manager may favour low stocks to reduce costs, but if this leads to stock-outs this may raise costs elsewhere: the freight manager may have to accept higher costs resulting from fast freight deliveries. Low-cost containers may lower packaging costs but raise the cost of goods damaged in transit. This fact, and the need to co-ordinate order processing, inventory and transportation decisions, mean that physical distribution needs to be managed as a system with a manager overseeing the whole process. A key role that the physical

17.3 marketing in action

The Human Element in Distribution

Unipart has transformed itself from a car parts manufacturer into one of the UK's biggest distribution companies. Today, only 10 per cent of Unipart's sales come from its original business of parts manufacturing. The rest come from distribution contracts covering a vast range of products with companies like Vodafone, Hewlett Packard, Virgin Trains and Jaguar.

The objective is to be as quick and accurate as possible in translating orders into deliveries. The company's success is partly based on taking principles from lean manufacturing to distribution services. Unipart's staff are organized along the lines of production cells in car factories. They are grouped into small teams that meet daily to talk about problems and opportunities for improvement.

The work by an employee in picking up specific items from a warehouse rack might be analysed. The result could be a new and more efficient warehouse layout or to use a different system to feed orders from customers more quickly.

Unipart, in addition, organizes 'improvement circles' of about five people, mainly from Unipart but sometimes including customers, suppliers and transport groups. They usually meet once a week for about an hour and focus on how their experiences can be used to solve problems. Other people who might benefit from their work can find the information on the company's internal website. For example, if someone types 'windscreen glass' into the website's search engine all the previous work on how to make or distribute this product more efficiently is provided.

Based on: Marsh (2002)[35]

distribution manager would perform would be to reconcile the conflicts inherent in the system so that total costs are minimized subject to required customer service levels.

In an age when the Internet and information technology is driving advances in distribution systems, it is easy to forget how important the human element is in supply chain management. Marketing in Action 17.3 examines how Unipart, one of the UK's biggest distribution businesses is getting the most out of its staff.

The physical distribution system

A system is a set of connected parts managed in such a way that overall objectives are achieved. The physical distribution system contains the following parts (see Fig. 17.8).

- *Customer service*: What level of customer service should be provided?
- *Order processing*: How should the orders be handled?
- *Inventory control*: How much inventory should be held?
- *Warehousing*: Where should the inventory be located? How many warehouses should be used?
- *Transportation*: How will the products be transported?

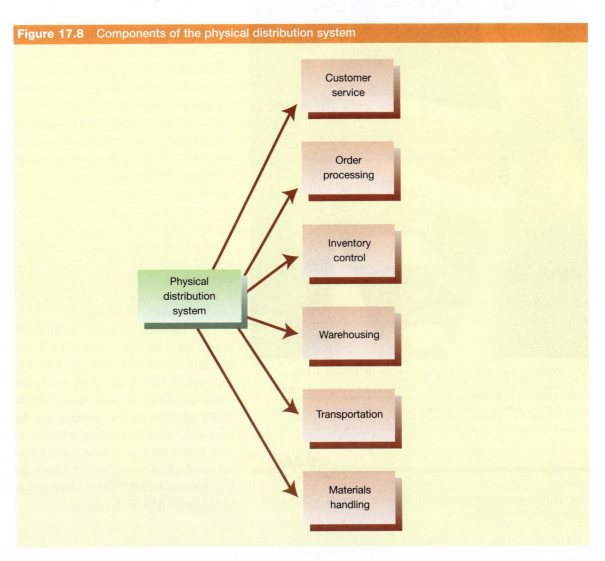

Figure 17.8 Components of the physical distribution system

- *Materials handling*: How will the products be handled during transportation?

Companies like DHL provide specialist expertise in these areas, as the illustration below shows. Each of the above questions will now be explored.

Customer service

Customer service standards need to be set. For example, a customer service standard might be that 90 per cent of orders are delivered within 48 hours of receipt and 100 per cent are delivered within 72 hours.

Higher customer service standards normally mean higher costs as inventory levels need to be higher. Since inventory ties up working capital, the higher the inventory level the higher the working capital charge. The physical distribution manager needs to be aware of the costs of fulfilling various customer service standards (e.g. 80, 90 and 100 per cent of orders delivered within 48 hours) and the extra customer satisfaction that results from raising standards.

In some cases customers value consistency in delivery time rather than speed. For example, a customer service standard of guaranteed delivery within five working days may be valued more than 60 per cent within two, 80 per cent within five and 100 per cent within seven days. Since the latter standard requires delivery at 60 per cent within two days it may require higher inventory levels than the former. Therefore, by understanding customer requirements, it may be possible to increase satisfaction while lowering costs.

Customer service standards should be given considerable attention because they may be the differentiating factor between suppliers: they may be used as a key customer choice criterion. Methods of improving customer service standards in physical distribution are listed in Table 17.1. By examining ways of improving product availability and order cycle time, and raising information levels and flexibility, considerable goodwill and customer loyalty can be created.

The Internet is providing the means of improving customer service for some distribution companies. For example, if a customer of Federal Express wants to track a package over the Internet, it simply types 'FedEx' and the package number. On the computer screen will appear where it is, who signed for it and what time it was delivered. Also, since the customer no longer needs to call Federal Express, it is saving FedEx $10 million a year.[36]

DHL provides specialist physical distribution services, in this case on an international basis.

Table 17.1 Methods of improving customer service standards in physical distribution

Improve product availability

Raise in-stock levels

Improve accuracy, speed and reliability of deliveries

Improve order cycle time

Shorten time between order and delivery

Improve consistency between order and delivery time

Raise information levels

Improve salesperson information on inventory

Raise information levels on order status

Be proactive in notifying customer of delays

Raise flexibility

Develop contingency plans for urgent orders

Ensure fast reaction time to unforeseen problems (e.g. stolen goods, damage in transit)

Technological developments are enabling distribution companies to offer customers the ability to integrate their delivery operations with other business functions. They can provide technology to cover the whole order cycle from the moment the goods are ordered through to electronic invoicing using the Internet.[37] Companies like PeopleSoft (see illustration) are providing specialist technological help to companies that wish to improve their ability to satisfy customers through better supply chain management.

PeopleSoft Supply Chain Management uses technology to improve efficiency and customer service.

Order processing

Reducing time between a customer placing an order and receiving the goods may be achieved through careful analysis of the components that contribute to the order-processing time. A computer link between salesperson and order department may be effective. Electronic data interchange can also speed order-processing time by checking the customer's credit rating, and whether the goods are in stock, issuing an order to the warehouse, invoicing the customer and updating the inventory records. Marketing in Action 17.2, on Zara, discusses some European developments.

Many *order-processing systems* are inefficient because of unnecessary delays. Basic questions can spot areas for improvement, such as what happens when a sales representative receives an order? What happens when it is received in the order department? How long does it take to check inventory? What are the methods for checking inventory? Many companies are moving to computer-based systems to bring efficiency to this area.

Inventory control

Inventory levels can be a source of conflict between finance and marketing management. Since inventory represents costs, financial managers seek stock minimization; marketing management, acutely aware of the customer problems caused by stock-outs, want large inventories. In reality a balance has to be found, particularly as inventory cost rises at an increasing rate as customer service standards near 100 per cent. This means that to always have in stock every conceivable item that a customer might order would normally be prohibitively expensive for companies marketing many items. One solution to this problem is to separate items into those that are in demand and those that are slower-moving. This is sometimes called the 80:20 rule since for many companies 80 per cent of sales are achieved by 20 per cent of products. A high customer service standard is then set for the high-demand 20 per cent (e.g. in stock 95 per cent of the time) but a much lower standard used for those items less in demand (e.g. in stock 70 per cent of the time).

Two related *inventory decisions* are knowing when and how much to order so that stocks are replenished. As inventory for an item falls, a point is reached when new stock is required. Unless a stock-out is tolerated the *order point* will be before inventory reaches zero. This is because there will be a *lead time* between ordering and receiving inventory. The *just-in-time inventory system* (discussed in Chapter 4) is designed to reduce lead times so that the order point (the stock level at which reordering takes place), and overall inventory levels for production items, are low. The key to the just-in-time system is the maintenance of a fast and reliable lead time so that deliveries of supplies arrive shortly before they are needed.

The order point depends on three factors: the viability of the order lead time, fluctuation in customer demand, and the customer service standard. The more variable the lead time between ordering and receiving stock, and the greater the fluctuation in customer demand, the higher the order point. This is because of the uncertainty caused by the variability, leading to the need for safety (buffer) stocks in case lead times are unpredictably long or customer demand unusually high. The higher the customer service standard, the higher the need for safety stocks, and hence the higher the order point. A simple inventory control system is shown in Fig. 17.9.

How much to order depends on the cost of holding stock and order-processing costs. Orders can be small and frequent or large and infrequent. Small, frequent orders raise order-processing costs but reduce inventory-carrying costs; large, infrequent orders raise inventory costs but lower order-processing expenditure. Therefore a trade-off between the two costs is required to achieve an economic order quantity (EOQ), the point at which total costs are lowest. Its calculation is shown diagrammatically in Fig. 17.10. Numerically it can be calculated as follows:

$$EOQ = \sqrt{\frac{2DO}{IC}}$$

where

D = annual demand in units
O = cost of placing an order
I = annual inventory cost as percentage of the cost of one unit
C = cost of one unit of the product

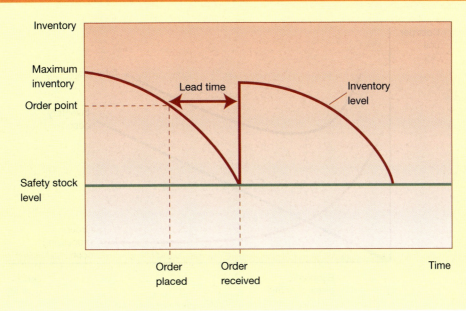

Figure 17.9 Inventory control

As an example let us assume that:

Annual demand = 4000 units
Cost of placing an order = £4
Per unit annual inventory cost = 20p or 10 per cent of the unit cost (£2)
Cost of one unit = £2

$$EOQ = \sqrt{\frac{2 \times 4000 \times 4}{0.10 \times 2}} = \sqrt{\frac{32\,000}{0.20}}$$

$$= \sqrt{160\,000} = 400 \text{ units per order}$$

Therefore the most economic order size, taking into account inventory and order-processing costs, is 400 units.

Suppliers can build strong relationships with their customers through automated inventory restocking systems, as Marketing in Action 17.2, on Zara, describes.

Warehousing

Warehousing involves all the activities required in the storing of goods between the time they are produced and the time they are transported to the customer. These activities include breaking bulk, making up product assortments for delivery to customers, storage and loading. *Storage warehouses* hold goods for moderate or long time periods whereas *distribution centres* operate as central locations for the fast movement of goods. Retailing organizations use regional distribution centres where suppliers bring products in bulk. These shipments are broken down into loads, which are then quickly transported to retail outlets. Distribution centres are usually highly automated with computer-controlled machinery facilitating the movement of goods. A computer reads orders and controls forklift trucks that gather goods and move them to loading bays.

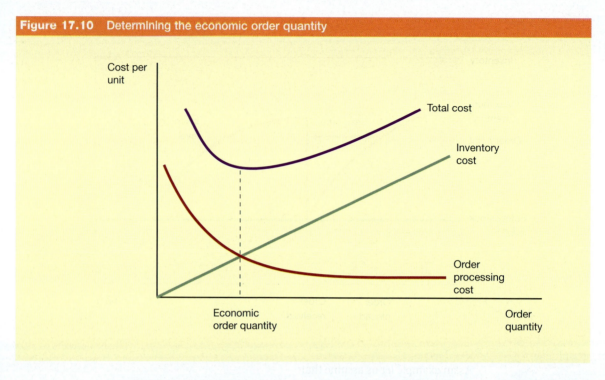

Figure 17.10 Determining the economic order quantity

Warehousing strategy involves the determination of the location and the number of warehouses to be used. At one extreme is one large central warehouse to serve the entire market; at the other is a number of smaller warehouses that are based near to local markets. In Europe, the removal of trade barriers between countries of the EU has reduced transportation time and costs. This change, together with distribution focus being on regional rather than national markets, has fuelled the trend towards fewer, larger warehouses where economies of scale can reduce costs. As with most physical distribution decisions, the optimum number and location of warehouses is a balance between customer service and cost considerations. Usually the more locally based warehouses a company uses, the better the customer service but the higher the cost.

The need for greater efficiency in the supply chain has led to a new generation of warehouse management systems. Marketing in Action 17.4 discusses how Lever Fabergé is applying such systems to improve warehouse efficiency.

Transportation

Customer service ultimately depends on the ability of the physical distribution system to transport products on time and without damage. Timely delivery is even more important with the group use of the just-in-time system. Therefore the choice of *transportation mode* is vital to the successful implementation of marketing strategy. The five major transport methods are rail, road, air, water and pipelines. Each has its strengths and limitations.

Rail

Railways are efficient at transporting large, bulky freight on land over large distances. Rail is often used to transport coal, chemicals, oil, aggregates and nuclear flasks. A problem, though, is lack of flexibility. For many companies the use of rail would mean transport by lorry to and from a rail depot. Furthermore for small quantities the use of rail may prove uneconomic. In the UK British Rail withdrew its Speedlink service in which container loads of various goods

17.4 marketing in action

Smart Warehouses at Lever Fabergé

In traditional warehouse systems, goods are logged in manually and time is wasted chasing paperwork and correcting errors, while stock gets mislaid and pallets mixed up. A new generation of warehouse management systems (WMS) uses IT to organize, optimize and, ultimately, replace the labour-intensive tasks of receiving goods and selecting items for orders.

One application is at Lever Fabergé, the UK trading arm of Anglo-Dutch consumer products giant Unilever. A distribution centre at Doncaster, Yorkshire, has been built to store and distribute all of its personal care products. The new warehouse will virtually eliminate errors, with features such as paperless picking via radio data terminals, advanced shipping notification and real-time order status checking.

Its WMS is designed to let its customers and partners do their own order progress chasing if they wish and to receive pre-delivery advice via the Internet. They can be told which goods are arriving, their origin, weight and even expiry date.

As such technology-based systems become more widespread, the old image of the warehouse being the dim and dusty world of pallets and brown coats will begin to fade.

Based on: Nairn (2002)[38]

from different producers were combined into one rail load. However, the building of the Channel Tunnel between Britain and mainland Europe has given a boost to rail transport. British Rail and French railway company SNCF have built freight terminals to encourage rail transport across the Channel.

Rail is more environmentally friendly than road and is ideally suited to freight when it moves 400 kilometres or more in large regular quantities from supplier's siding to customer's siding. Where there is no siding, the journey is usually costlier than road, and more likely to incur theft or damage to goods in transit. Furthermore, distributors of foodstuffs and perishables are obliged by health authorities to transport their products at controlled temperatures. They may be reluctant to rely on freight as it may be difficult to access if delayed.

Road

Motorized transport by road has the advantage of flexibility because of direct access to companies and warehouses. This means that lorries can transport goods from supplier to receiver without unloading en route. Furthermore, speed is likely to increase and costs fall in Europe as a result of the advent of the single European market. With cross-border restrictions removed—drivers spent an average of 30 per cent of their time waiting or filling in forms at border crossings prior to 1993—road transport in Europe is likely to grow.[39] However, the growth of road transport in Europe, and particularly the UK, has received considerable criticism because of increased traffic congestion and the damage done to roads by heavy juggernauts.

Air

The key advantages of air freight are its speed and long-distance capabilities. Its speed means that it is often used to transport perishable goods and emergency deliveries. Furthermore, in a period when companies are seeking to reduce inventories, air freight can be used to supply inventories under just-in-time systems. With the growth in international trade, air freight is predicted to be a growth activity. Its major disadvantages are high cost and the need to transport goods by road to and from air terminals.

In 1996 the European Air Shippers' Council published a set of recommendations to air carriers regarding guaranteed delivery and lead times. Although freight can account for up to 20 per cent of an airline's revenues, it is often treated unfairly in terms of investment. The report recommends that carriers focus their attention on providing better service to supply chain managers.

Water

Water transportation is slow but inexpensive. Inland transportation is usually associated with bulky, low-value, non-perishable goods such as coal, ore, grain, steel and petroleum. Ocean-going ships carry a wider range of products. When the cost benefits of international sea transportation outweigh the speed advantage of air freight, water shipments may be chosen. A large proportion of long-haul deliveries between Europe and the Pacific Rim is by sea transport. As with air freight, water transport normally needs road transportation of goods to and from docks.

Pipeline

Pipelines are a dependable and low-maintenance form of transportation for liquids and gases. However, their construction is expensive and time consuming. They are usually associated with natural gas, water and crude petroleum. Ownership is in the hands of the companies that use them.

Materials handling

Materials handling involves the activities related to the moving of products in the producer's plant, warehouses and transportation depots. Modern storage facilities tend to be of one storey, allowing a high level of automation. In some cases, robots are used to conduct materials-handling tasks. Lowering the human element in locating inventory and assembling orders has reduced error and increased the speed of these operations.

Two key developments in materials handling are unit handling and containerization. *Unit handling* achieves efficiency by combining multiple packages on to pallets that can be moved by forklift trucks. *Containerization* involves the combining of many quantities of goods (e.g. car components) into a single large container. Once sealed they can easily be transferred from one form of transport to another. For example, a container could be loaded on to a lorry and taken to a rail freight terminal to form part of a train load of containers destined for the docks. There the container can easily be transferred to a ship for transportation to a destination thousands of miles away. Since individual items are not handled, damage in transit is reduced.

An important element in materials handling is the quality of packaging. It is necessary to evaluate not only the appearance and cost of packaging, but also the ability to repackage into larger quantities for transportation. Packages must be sturdy enough to withstand the rigours of physical distribution, such as harsh handling and stacking.

Ethical issues in distribution

Five key ethical issues in distribution are the use of slotting allowances, grey markets, exclusive dealing, restrictions on supply, and fair trading.

Slotting allowances

The power shift from manufacturers to retailers in the packaged consumer goods industry has meant that slotting allowances are often demanded to take products. A slotting allowance is a fee paid to a retailer in exchange for an agreement to place a product on the retailer's shelves. Critics argue that they represent an abuse of power and work against small manufacturers who cannot afford to pay the fee. Retailers argue that they are simply charging rent for a valuable, scarce commodity: shelf space.[40]

Grey markets

These occur when a product is sold through an unauthorized distribution channel. When this occurs in international marketing the practice is called parallel importing. Usually a distributor buys goods in one country (where prices are low) and sells them in another (where prices are high) at below the going market price. This causes anger among members of the authorized distribution channel, who see their prices being undercut. Furthermore, the products may well be sold in downmarket outlets that discredit the image of the product, which has been built up by high advertising expenditures. Nevertheless, supporters of grey markets argue that they encourage price competition, increase consumer choice and promote the lowering of price differentials between countries.

Exclusive dealing

This is a restrictive arrangement whereby a manufacturer prohibits distributors that market its products from selling the products of competing suppliers. The act may restrict competition and restrict the entry of new competitors and products into a market. It may be found where a large supplier can exercise power over weaker distributors. The supplier may be genuinely concerned that anything less than an exclusive agreement will mean that insufficient effort will be made to sell its products by a distributor and that unless such an agreement is reached it may be uneconomic to supply the distributor.

Restrictions in supply

A concern of small suppliers is that the power of large manufacturers and retailers will mean that they are squeezed out of the supply chain. In the UK, farmers and small grocery suppliers have joined forces to demand better treatment from large supermarket chains, which are forging exclusive deals with major manufacturers. They claim the problem is made worse by the growth of category management where retailers appoint 'category captains' from their suppliers, who act to improve the standing of the whole product category such as breakfast cereals or confectionery. The small suppliers believe this forces them out of the category altogether as category captains look after their own interests. They would like to see a system similar to that in France where about 10 per cent of shelf space is by law given to small suppliers.[41]

Fair trading

One problem of free market forces is that when small commodity producers are faced with large powerful buyers the result can be very low prices. This can bring severe economic hardship to the producers, who may be situated in countries of the developing world. In the face of a collapse in world coffee prices, a fair trading brand, Cafédirect, was launched. The company was founded on three principles: to influence positively producers' income security, to act as an example and catalyst for change, and to improve consumer understanding of fair trade values. It pays suppliers a minimum price for coffee beans, pegged above market fluctuations and provides tailor-made business support and development programmes. There are now more than 50 fair trade products on sale in the UK, including Ridgways tea and Divine chocolate, and sales are rising.[42] The growth in fair trade products is discussed in Ethical Marketing in Action 17.1.

17.1 ethical marketing in action

Fair Trade Expansion

The concern that small suppliers of commodity products like coffee beans or tea receive inadequate prices has fuelled the growth in the fair trade movement. Products like Cafédirect and companies such as the Body Shop have pioneered the move towards fair prices for suppliers in developing countries.

Many supermarkets, in turn, have provided shelf room for fairly traded products. The leader in this field is the Co-op, a UK supermarket and convenience store chain. Founded in the nineteenth century to give low-wage workers a better deal, it has returned to its roots by trying to carve out a niche as the ethical choice among supermarkets. For example, all of its own-label chocolate is fair trade labelled, in a move that is expected to double sales of fair trade chocolate in the UK.

Fair trade coffee is also a growing sector. Coffee bar chains such as Costa Coffee and Pret A Manger offer a fair trade variety. In fact, all Pret A Manger filter coffee is fair trade. The Co-op has also introduced own-label fair trade coffee.

These moves will go a little way to helping the 25 million people who depend on coffee production for their livelihoods and are facing poverty because of falling prices. The price of coffee beans reached a 30-year low in 2002, resulting in farmers selling it for much lower than production costs. Ultimately, the success of fair trade ventures depends on consumers being willing to try and repeat-buy fair trade products.

Based on: Benady (2002);[43] Charles (2002)[44]

Ethical dilemma

A vital element in distribution success is a customer's decision on 'place' of purchase. For consumers concerned about ethical issues this can involve some dilemma. Take the example of the fair trade coffee Cafédirect. This product was founded on the basis of providing producers with income security and is popular among ethically concerned consumers. This product may be purchased in supermarkets, some charity shops (including Oxfam) and alternative outlets (including wholefood outlets and One World fair trade outlets). Which distribution outlet would provide the most ethical option?

Review

1) The functions and types of channels of distribution

- The functions are to reconcile the needs of producers and consumers, improving efficiency, improving accessibility and providing specialist services.
- Four types of consumer channel are producer direct to consumer, producer to retailer to consumer, producer to wholesaler to retailer to consumer, and producer to agent to wholesaler to retailer to consumer.
- Four types of industrial channels are producer to industrial customer, producer to agent to industrial customer, producer to distributor to industrial customer, and producer to agent to distributor to industrial customer.
- Two types of service channel are service provider to consumer or industrial customer, and service provider to agent to consumer or industrial customer.

2) How to determine channel strategy

- Channel strategy should be determined by making decisions concerning the selection of the most effective distribution channel, the most appropriate level of distribution intensity and the correct degree of channel integration.

3) The three components of channel strategy: channel selection, intensity and integration

- Channel selection is influenced by market factors (buyer behaviour, ability to meet buyer needs, the willingness of channel intermediaries to market a product, the profit margins required by distributors and agents compared with the costs of direct distribution, and the location and geographic concentration of customers), producer factors (lack of resources, the width and depth of the product mix offered by a producer, and the desired level of control of channel operations), product factors (complexity, perishability, extent of bulkiness and difficulty of handling), and competitive factors (need to choose innovative channels because traditional channels are controlled by the competition or because a competitive advantage is likely to result).
- Channel intensity options are intensive distribution to achieve saturated coverage of the market by using all available outlets, selective distribution, where a limited number of outlets in a geographical area are used, and exclusive distribution, which is an extreme form of selective distribution where only one wholesaler, retailer or industrial distributor is used in a geographic area.
- Channel integration can range from conventional marketing channels (where there is separation of ownership between producer and distributor, although the manufacturer power of channel intermediaries may result in an administered vertical marketing system), franchising (where a legal contract between producers and channel intermediaries defines each party's rights and obligations, leading to a contractual marketing system) and channel ownership (where the manufacturer takes control over distributor activities through ownership, leading to a corporate vertical marketing system).

4) The five key channel management issues: member selection, motivation, training, evaluation and conflict management

- Selection of members involves identifying sources (the trade, reseller enquiries, customers of distributors and the field salesforce) and establishing selection criteria (market coverage, quality and size of the salesforce, reputation, financial standing, extent of competitive and complementary products, managerial competence, hunger for success, and enthusiasm).

- Motivation of distributors involves understanding the needs and problems of distributors, and methods include financial rewards, territorial exclusivity, providing resource support, the development of strong work relationships (possibly in the context of informal partnerships).
- Training may be provided where appropriate. It can provide the necessary technical knowledge about a supplier company and its products, and help to build a spirit of partnership and commitment.
- Evaluation criteria include sales volume and value, profitability, level of stocks, quality and position of display, new accounts opened, selling and marketing capabilities, quality of service, market information feedback, willingness and ability to meet commitments, attitudes and personal capability. Evaluation should be based on mutually agreed objectives.
- Conflict management sources are differences in goals, differences in desired product lines, the use of multiple distribution channels by producers, and inadequacies in performance. Conflict-handling approaches are developing a partnership approach, training in conflict handling, market partitioning, improving performance, channel ownership and coercion.

5 The cost–customer service trade-off in physical distribution

- Physical distribution management concerns the balance between cost reduction and meeting customer service requirements. An example of a trade-off is incompatibility between low inventory and slow, cheaper transportation methods that reduce costs, and the lower customer service levels and satisfaction that results.

6 The components of a physical distribution system: customer service, order processing, inventory control, warehousing, transportation and materials handling

- The system should be managed so that its components combine to achieve overall objectives. Management needs to answer a series of questions related to each component: customer service (What levels of service should be provided?); order processing (How should orders be handled?); inventory control (How much inventory should be held?); warehousing (Where should the inventory be located and how many warehouses should be used?); transportation (How will the products be transported?); materials handling (How will the products be handled during transportation?).

7 How to improve customer service standards in physical distribution

- Customer service standards can be raised by improving product availability (e.g. by increasing inventory levels), improving order cycle time (e.g. faster order processing), raising information levels (e.g. information on order status) and raising flexibility (e.g. fast reaction time to problems).

8 Ethical issues in distribution

- There are potential problems relating to slotting allowances, grey markets, exclusive dealing, restrictions on supply, and fair trading.

Key terms

administered vertical marketing system a channel situation where a manufacturer that dominates a market through its size and strong brands may exercise considerable power over intermediaries even though they are independent

channel integration the way in which the players in the channel are linked

channel intermediaries organizations that facilitate the distribution of products to customers

channel of distribution the means by which products are moved from the producer to the ultimate consumer

channel strategy the selection of the most effective distribution channel, the most appropriate level of distribution intensity and the degree of channel integration

contractual vertical marketing system a franchise arrangement (e.g. a franchise) that ties together producers and resellers

corporate vertical marketing system a channel situation where an organization gains control of distribution through ownership

economic order quantity the quantity of stock to be ordered where total costs are at the lowest

exclusive distribution an extreme form of selective distribution where only one wholesaler, retailer or industrial distributor is used in a geographical area to sell the products of a supplier

franchise a legal contract in which a producer and channel intermediaries agree each other's rights and obligations; usually the intermediary receives marketing, managerial, technical and financial services in return for a fee

intensive distribution the aim of this is to provide saturation coverage of the market by using all available outlets

safety (buffer) stocks stocks or inventory held to cover against uncertainty about resupply lead times

selective distribution the use of a limited number of outlets in a geographical area to sell the products of a supplier

Internet exercise

Australian Homemade is an ice cream/chocolate restaurant franchise operation. The group is rapidly expanding in Europe, but has yet to set up an operation in the UK. Visit its website and browse the section on franchising opportunities.

Visit: www.australianhomemade.com

Questions

(a) How does the Australian Homemade franchise concept work?
(b) What are the benefits for Australian Homemade in adopting a franchise format in order to launch successfully in the UK market?
(c) What are the weaknesses associated with franchising for the franchisor and the franchisee?

Visit the Online Learning Centre at www.mcgraw-hill.co.uk/textbooks/jobber for more Internet exercises.

Study questions

1. What is the difference between channel decisions and physical distribution management? In what ways are they linked?
2. Of what value are channels of distribution? What functions do they perform?
3. The best way of distributing an industrial product is direct from manufacturer to customer. Discuss.
4. Why is channel selection an important decision? What factors influence choice?
5. What is meant by the partnership approach to managing distributors? What can manufacturers do to help build partnerships?
6. Describe situations that can lead to conflict between channel members. What can be done to avoid and resolve conflict?
7. Why is there usually a trade-off between customer service and physical distribution costs? What can be done to improve customer service standards in physical distribution?
8. A distributor wishes to estimate the economic order quantity for a spare part. Annual demand is 5000 units, the cost of placing an order is £5, and the cost of one spare part is £4. The per-unit annual inventory cost is 50p. Calculate the economic order quantity.
9. Unlike advertising, the area of distribution is free from ethical concerns. Discuss.

When you have read this chapter log on to the Online Learning Centre at www.mcgraw-hill.co.uk/textbooks/jobber to explore chapter-by-chapter test questions, links and further online study tools for marketing.

case thirty-three

The Trouble with TopUps: Vodafone Causes a Stir by Lowering the Margins of Retailers

Vodafone (www.vodafone.ie) has incurred the wrath of Irish retailers, sparking a feud between the two parties. The company has reduced retailer margins for pre-paid mobile call credit, a product called TopUps. Vodafone, the world's biggest mobile phone operator, bought Eircell, an Irish mobile phone operator in 2000. The company is now the largest mobile phone operator in the country with an estimated customer base of over 1.7 million. Ready to Go is the brand name of its pre-paid mobile phone service.

Customers can buy a mobile phone (which is heavily subsidized) and do not need to sign any contracts; in addition, they receive no monthly bills with rental fees or connection charges. Customers are simply billed on their usage per second and their account is debited. Once their account is fully used, customers have to top it up with call credit. Customers can view their credit by dialling a freefone number, which is free to call 24 hours a day.

Call charges for Ready to Go options are typically higher than monthly contract options. Ireland's mobile phone industry is extremely lucrative. At present, Irish mobile phone penetration rate is static at 77 per cent, the seventh highest penetration rate in Europe. There are approximately 2.97 million mobile phone subscribers in Ireland. Three mobile phone operators have a presence in the Irish market: Vodafone, O_2 (formerly BT mobile phone operations) and Meteor, which have a 57 per cent, 40 per cent and 3 per cent market share respectively. The marketplace can effectively be described as a duopoly.

Customers have traditionally used retail outlets to purchase their call credit. In order to issue TopUp codes nationwide, Vodafone uses two main wholesalers. One wholesaler is responsible for distribution of the physical cards and the other for electronic distribution of TopUp codes using a network of electronic terminals. Retailers order TopUp cards via a free fax number or by establishing a standing order with the TopUp wholesaler. Over the past three years, Vodafone has encouraged retailers to invest in electronic terminals to issue the majority of TopUp codes. An Irish company called Alphyra manages the operation of these terminals. It currently has about 5000 terminals placed in Irish retailer premises. These terminals also cater for Vodafone's competitors, O_2 and Meteor, by issuing top-up codes to the pre-paid mobile market. Alphyra's terminals are found in nearly all grocery outlets, ranging from large supermarkets to newsagents, service stations to mobile phone outlets. In excess of 95 per cent of retailers use these terminals for the issuing of e-TopUps to mobile phone customers. Vodafone needs to utilize an intensive distribution system for its pre-paid services to facilitate future growth and satisfy the convenience needs of customers. This intensive distribution system allows Vodafone's customers to gain access to call credit in thousands of different locations.

At the launch of its pre-paid mobile services, Vodafone relied solely on its retailer distribution network to supply call credit. However, the company has now developed multiple channels of distribution for its customers to gain access to call credit, due to advances in technology and creating strategic alliances with key partners such as banks. Table C33.1 (overleaf) illustrates the variety of channels available to customers. To create an intensive distribution strategy, margins on the supply of call credit were quite high in comparison to other product lines carried by retailers. Since the company's critical mass has been achieved, the company is now trying to wean retailers off these relatively high margins.

Table C33.1 Vodafone TopUp channels

TopUp channels available

- Retail chains: e.g. Tesco
- Independent retailers: corner stores, newsagents, etc.
- Online: at www.vodafone.ie
- Bank ATMs: customers can top up at a variety of bank ATMs
- Text top-ups: customers have to register online at Vodafone's website and use their credit or laser cards to top up, by simply texting their desired amount of credit and providing a personal identification number (PIN)
- Credit card: by simply dialling Vodafone's call centre and paying by credit card over the phone; call credit can be purchased in a range of denominations
- TopUp vending machines: stand-alone TopUp dispensers placed in retail outlets
- E-TopUps: using one of Alphyra's 5000 electronic terminals at retail outlets
- Go cards: by buying Ready to Go cards at any one of 6000 retail outlets; cards can be purchased in a range of denominations
- Any of Vodafone's stores: Vodafone has adopted a forward integration strategy (i.e. it is getting involved in retailing) by opening over 41 Vodafone-branded outlets throughout the country

Obviously, due to the size of the market and the pervasiveness of the mobile phone in modern society, this is a very valuable revenue earner for the retail trade. The margins on call credit were a great source of revenue for retailers. Previously, in order to build a distribution base, the margin for call credit was 12 per cent, which enticed retailers to stock call credit for mobile phones and invest in electronic terminals. Now, mobile call credit is for many retailers a 'must have' item to stock, similar to everyday items such as bread and milk, because of huge consumer demand. Table C33.2 illustrates the margin structure for Vodafone TopUps up until 9 September 2002. The margin rates for all of other mobile companies were similar.

Table C33.2 Previous margin structure for Vodafone TopUps

RRP (recommended retail price)	Current retailer margin	Gross	Net	VAT
€40	10%	€36.00	€29.75	€6.25
€25	10%	€22.50	€18.60	€3.90
€20	10%	€18.00	€14.88	€3.12
€15	10%	€13.50	€11.16	€2.34
€10	10%	€9.00	€7.44	€1.56

In late August 2002, Vodafone issued a communication regarding the changes to retailer margins. The memo stated a number of reasons for the decrease in margins. It noted that the pre-paid mobile phone market had grown by 80 per cent and 60 per cent respectively over the past two years and that it was an important revenue earner for retailers. Furthermore, it explained new marketing initiatives such as the extension of expiry dates for call credit, and stated that in order to facilitate this 'investment in the consumer it was necessary for Vodafone to rebalance the margins' (see Table C33.3). A spokesperson for Vodafone asserted the claim that 'customers will actually benefit because we will be redirecting our investment towards more customer friendly services'. Only smaller denominations of TopUps, of €10 and €15, were affected by the change in margins. This followed a similar cut in margins from 12 per cent to 10 per cent on the sales of top-up cards in the previous year, resulting in the loss of 5.5 per cent margin in the course of a year for many independent retailers.

Table C33.3 New margin structure for Vodafone TopUps as of 9 September 2002

RRP (recommended retail price)*	Current retailer margin	Gross	Net	VAT
€15	6.5%	€14.02	€11.59	€2.43
€10	6.5%	€9.35	€7.73	€1.62

* Other denominations are unaffected by the change

As a result of this reduction in margins, retailers were irate, particularly small independent retailers. This anger was embodied in the reaction of two national retailer representative groups: the Irish Retail Newsagents Association (IRNA) and the Retail Grocery, Dairy, and Allied Trades Association (RGDATA). The conflict took a dramatic turn when the IRNA issued notices to all its members on the Vodafone margin issue in early September. The IRNA is one of Ireland's largest trade organizations, representing independent news retailers in Ireland, with nearly 1300 members, who own more than 1500 outlets in Ireland. The notice read that 'because of action by Vodafone we regret that a handling charge of 40c on €10 and 60c on €15 TopUps will apply'. This notice was placed in the majority of small newsagents around the country, and numerous retailers started charging these surcharges to Vodafone customers. According to RGDATA director general Ailish Forde, 'This is a clear example of a large and powerful company cutting their costs at the expense of small retailers who rely strongly on the sale of these smaller-denomination electronic top-ups. For many of our members, the sale of these smaller units represents 95 per cent of their total card sales with card sales making up about 20 per cent of their annual turnover'. Forde continued, 'We believe that retailers will now have no choice but to look at offers from other operators in the market. Retailers are not in a position to endure such excessive price cuts.'

In some cases, retailers stopped selling Vodafone TopUp credits, while in other cases, some retailers intended to impose a surcharge on consumers to cover the costs of providing the service. There have also been reports of some retailers removing all Vodafone notices and marketing material from their stores. In a number of cases, some retailers have threatened to change their own mobile networks and switch to one of Vodafone's competitors. Other retailers have used the conflict for opportunistic promotion. Tesco launched national print and broadcast advertising designed to highlight to customers that mobile phone top-ups were available from its outlets, with 'no handling fees charged'. These retailer surcharges were bound to alienate customers and increase the churn rate (i.e. level of switching) of customers to other mobile networks. Vodafone now had a serious marketing dilemma to face. What was the most appropriate response?

The first retaliatory blow by Vodafone was launched on 14 October when it placed full-page adverts in the national newspapers, highlighting where customers could find recommended retail outlets that did not charge a surcharge for its TopUps. This was followed by smaller-scale adverts, including the same message, over the following days. These ads highlighted other channels customers could use to get their Vodafone TopUps. The other mobile phone operators are now adopting a wait-and-see approach before altering their margin structures. This conflict between retailers and Vodafone may offer them a strategic opportunity. On 1 October Vodafone issued a letter from its chief executive, Paul Donovan, to three national retail trade associations, which restated its position that margins will remain, and accused some retailers of 'profiteering' by charging handling fees in excess of the margin reduction. Furthermore, Donovan stated that 'Vodafone Ireland shall not implement any further reductions on e-TopUp wholesale margins until at least 2004.' Another Vodafone spokesperson stated that Vodafone now offers the same margins as the National Lottery to retailers, which is exactly the same type of electronic transaction. Some national retail chains and petrol forecourt chains are not asking customers for a surcharge. In addition, the spokesperson stated that its pre-paid mobile products deliver between 800,000 and 900,000 customers to retailers' stores, many on a weekly basis, and that these customers buy more than just TopUps.

Vodafone's advertising counter-offensive is still ongoing, with heavy media spend promoting other suitable channels for TopUps and listing recommended retailers that are not charging a surcharge. An example of the type of advertising copy can be seen in Fig. C33.1.

Figure C33.1 Ad copy for Vodafone

Source: copy of Vodafone advert taken from *Sunday Independent*, 20 October 2002, S1.

The row escalated further when RGDATA lodged a complaint to the Competition Authority, Ireland's competition watchdog. The complaint specified that certain retailers were getting preferential treatment. The trade association claimed that high-street retail chains were obtaining commissions as high as 13 per cent on normal €10 and €15 TopUps. RGDATA complained to the watchdog that Vodafone was abusing its power, placing smaller retailers at a disadvantage, due to the mobile company's dominant position. Other trade associations reaffirmed their positions by issuing notices to say that retailers can legally charge handling fees, and that they may be set at whatever levels they wish. Vodafone further upped the ante by offering customers 10 per cent extra call credit for those who topped up via ATMs, using text TopUps or online.

This issue has unleashed a multitude of problems for Vodafone, leaving it with difficult decisions to face. Stark choices have to be made by Vodafone managers. How can they avoid further escalation of this conflict and diffuse the situation?

Questions

1. How can a manufacturer achieve dominance of a supply chain?

2. In your opinion, who controls the balance of power in this case? Justify your answer.

3. Discuss the possible implications of these margin cuts for Vodafone's relationship with retailers.

4. What are the strategic options available to both Vodafone and the affected retailers? Furthermore, recommend a course of action for Vodafone, giving reasons for your answer.

This case was written by Conor Carroll, Lecturer in Marketing, University of Limerick. Copyright © Conor Carroll (2002). The material in the case has been drawn from a variety of published sources.

case thirty-four

Avon and L'Oréal: Keep Young and Beautiful!

When book salesman David McConnell began giving away small vials of perfume as sweeteners for his customers, little did he know what a huge empire he was laying the foundations for. He soon realized that people were more interested in the perfumes than they were in the books, so he started the California Perfume Company in 1886, selling perfumes door to door. In 1939 the company became Avon.

In 1958 the first 'Avon ladies' appeared in Britain, immaculately dressed and made-up, and began knocking on the doors of suburban homes, selling cosmetics to housewives who were unable to get out to the shops, or whose villages and towns lacked shops with a reasonable selection of cosmetics. These Avon ladies sold cosmetics and also recruited new salespeople, so the company grew with all the power of a chain letter. Currently Avon sells over 7500 products in 25 languages, throughout 143 countries. In 2002 the company turned over $6 billion (£2.3 billion/€3.3 billion) worldwide and made $534.6 million (£205.6 million/€296 million) in profits. The UK market share is second only to Boots, making the company a profit of £326 million (€469 million) in 2002. This is approaching the same level as competitor L'Oréal's entire UK turnover (£443 million/€638 million in 2001).

The success of Avon is not based on the cosmetics themselves: they are good, but nothing special, and the packaging ranges from the dowdy to the garish. The corporate image is not exactly upmarket either: firms such as L'Oréal and Olay regard Avon as something of a joke, perhaps because of its direct-selling approach, which puts it in the same class as double glazing and door-to-door brush salesmen in some people's eyes. However, Avon products end up in some surprising handbags: fashion writers and film stars use the products, just a few of the one in three women in Britain who use Avon. Avon has no presence on the high street: the products are only sold through its 160,000 Avon ladies, who still travel round selling to customers in their own homes. For this is the real strength of Avon: it distributes its products directly to people's homes, which caters for the housebound, the housewives with small children, those who live too far from the shops and those who have too little time to go and shop. It is the distribution method that overcomes all the other drawbacks.

The Avon way of selling cosmetics.

In Iceland, Avon ladies traverse glaciers with the products in backpacks; in South America they kayak up the Amazon and barter the cosmetics for gold nuggets, food or wood (two dozen eggs buys a Bart Simpson deodorant). In Turkey, one woman who had lost everything in an earthquake rebuilt her family's wealth single-handed by selling Avon from tent to tent in the refugee camp. In Milton Keynes, Avon's top saleslady delivers the cosmetics from a specially adapted bicycle.

Avon also runs a website for transsexuals and transvestites. For obvious reasons, these individuals have a desperate need for make-up experts who can advise them in their own homes. Alice, a transvestite who has become an Avon lady, says 'Avon's services are priceless to those who are still too shy to buy make-up on the high street. Men just beginning to wear make-up have less idea of what to use than a young girl who might be just starting to use cosmetics.'

The sales cycle for Avon is three weeks. At the beginning of the period, a new brochure is issued and delivered by hand to each customer. The sales lady collects the orders, then posts or e-mails them to Avon. One week later the products are delivered to the representative, who then delivers the products, collects the money and sends Avon its cut. Top Avon sales ladies are rumoured to earn around £30,000 (€43,000) a year, but most earn less—frequently they are themselves limited in their career possibilities by location, by children, or by their husbands' working patterns. Avon offers them the flexibility to work around their other commitments. Having said that, Avon is regularly included in 'top 100 companies to work for' lists, and has many employees with 40 years' service or more. Perhaps the greatest success story in the company is Sandy Mountford, who joined the company as a sales rep at age 34 and was UK president of the company 16 years later.

Avon's competitor, L'Oréal, is another global company. Its main UK brands are Maybelline, L'Oréal of Paris and Garnier. L'Oréal competes in the same market as Avon, but follows a more traditional distribution route. It has a main distribution centre for the UK in Manchester, from which 3200 different products are shipped: in 2002, 38,000 tonnes of products were shipped from this one depot. The company also distributes direct from its factory near Llantrisant in South Wales; half the production output of this factory is exported. The difference between L'Oréal and Avon could not be greater, however. L'Oréal distributes through retailers, mainly supermarkets and chemists, and distributes its professional haircare range through hairdressing salons.

Worldwide, L'Oréal is the larger of the two companies, with sales of €14 million (£10 million) earning profits of €1.4 million (£1 million). L'Oréal is only present in 130 countries, however. The company's distribution method requires strong advertising support: TV advertising is the mainstay of the company's UK marketing communications, largely because of its appeal to retailers.

L'Oréal's professional hairdressing products are distributed in two ways: direct to salons via a national network of sales representatives and through specialist hairdressing cash-and-carry outlets such as Aston and Fincher. These cash-and-carries are strictly for professional hairdressers: the public are not permitted to buy L'Oréal professional haircare products because the strength of the chemicals used is much greater than that of home-haircare products. Even more exclusive is the Kerastase brand, which is only distributed to salons that meet exacting technical standards and whose staff have been specially trained in the use of the products. In return, L'Oréal guarantees that only a limited number of Kerastase salons will operate in a given area.

L'Oréal supports its professional hairdressers by providing training courses both in-salon and at its own training school in London, and also by providing advice over the Internet. Colorweb is a software system that enables hairdressers to enter the colour of the client's hair, the amount of grey hair, the amount of previous colouring remaining in the hair, and several other dimensions in order to be told exactly which mix of L'Oréal products to use. This has been a highly successful approach to deskilling the previously esoteric art of hair colouring, which relied heavily on the experience, judgement and training of the stylist.

Unlike Avon, L'Oréal has maintained an upmarket brand image, which has been expensive to keep up. Its Garnier and Maybelline brands are frequently to be seen on TV, as is its 'Because you're worth it!' tag-line. Support for its distributor network is clearly a major expense: Avon's annual prizes of holidays for top salespeople cost peanuts by comparison. Yet Avon has achieved a much higher profit level, turnover level and even brand recognition in the UK. Perhaps distribution is more than just a way of getting goods to customers—perhaps there are strategic implications too.

L'Oréal requires strong advertising support for its distribution methods.

Questions

1. How would you categorize Avon's distribution strategy?
2. Which company do you think has the most control over its distribution? Why?
3. Why does L'Oréal have so many more distribution channels than Avon?
4. If Avon is so successful, why doesn't L'Oréal have its own door-to-door salesforce?
5. How would you categorize the Kerastase brand in terms of distribution?
6. What are the main advantages of Avon's distribution system over L'Oréal's?
7. What are the main advantages of L'Oréal's distribution system over Avon's?

This case study was prepared by Jim Blythe, Reader in Marketing, Glamorgan University.

part three

Competition and Marketing

18 Analysing competitors and creating a competitive advantage

19 Competitive marketing strategy

chapter eighteen

Analysing competitors and creating a competitive advantage

"The race is not always to the swift, nor the battle to the strong, but that is the way to bet."

DAMON RUNYON

Learning Objectives

This chapter explains:

1. The determinants of industry attractiveness
2. How to analyse competitors
3. The difference between differentiation and cost leadership strategies
4. The sources of competitive advantage
5. The value chain
6. How to create and maintain a differential advantage
7. How to create and maintain a cost leadership position

Satisfying customers is a central tenet of the marketing concept, but it is not enough to guarantee success. The real question is whether a firm can satisfy customers better than the competition. For example, many car manufacturers market cars that give customer satisfaction in terms of appearance, reliability and performance. They meet the basic requirements necessary to compete. Customer choice, however, will depend on creating a little more value than the competition. This extra value is brought about by establishing a competitive advantage—a topic that will be examined later in this chapter.

Since corporate performance depends on both customer satisfaction and being able to create greater value than the competition, firms need to understand their competitors as well as their customers. By understanding its competitors, a firm can better predict their reaction to any marketing initiative that the firm might make, and exploit any weaknesses they might possess. Competitor analysis is thus crucial to the successful implementation of marketing strategy. The discussion will begin by examining competitive industry structure: rivalry between firms does not take place within a vacuum. For example, the threat of new competitors and the bargaining power of buyers can greatly influence the attractiveness of an industry and the profitability of each competitor.

Analysing competitive industry structure

An *industry* is a group of firms that market products that are close substitutes for each other. In common parlance we refer to the car, oil or computer industry, indicating that the definition of an industry is normally product-based. It is a fact of life that some industries are more profitable than others. For example, the car, steel, coal and textile industries have had poor profitability records for many years, whereas the book publishing, television broadcasting, pharmaceuticals and soft drinks industries have enjoyed high long-run profits. Not all of this difference can be explained by the fact that one industry provides better customer satisfaction than another. There are other determinants of industry attractiveness and long-run profitability that shape the rules of competition. These are the threat of entry of new competitors, the threat of substitutes, the bargaining power of buyers and of suppliers, and the rivalry between the existing competitors.[1] Where these forces are intense, below-average industry performance can be expected; where these forces are mild, superior performance is common. Their influence is shown diagrammatically in Fig. 18.1, which is known as the Porter model of competitive industry structure. Each of the 'five forces' in turn comprises a number of elements that, together, combine to determine the strength of each force and its effect on the degree of competition. Each force is discussed below.

The threat of new entrants

New entrants can raise the level of competition in an industry, thereby reducing its attractiveness. For example, in Denmark, new foreign entrants such as Sweden's SE-Banken have hit the largest banks, Den Danske Bank and Unibank, and Norway's Finax.[2] The threat of new entrants depends on the barriers to entry. High entry barriers exist in some industries (e.g. pharmaceuticals), whereas other industries are much easier to enter (e.g. restaurants). Key *entry barriers* include:

- economies of scale
- capital requirements
- switching costs
- access to distribution
- expected retaliation.

Figure 18.1 The Porter model of competitive industry structure

Source: adapted from Porter; M. E. (1998) *Competitive Strategy*, New York; Free Press, 4.
Reprinted with permission of the Free Press, an imprint of Simon and Schuster. Copyright © 1980 by Free Press.

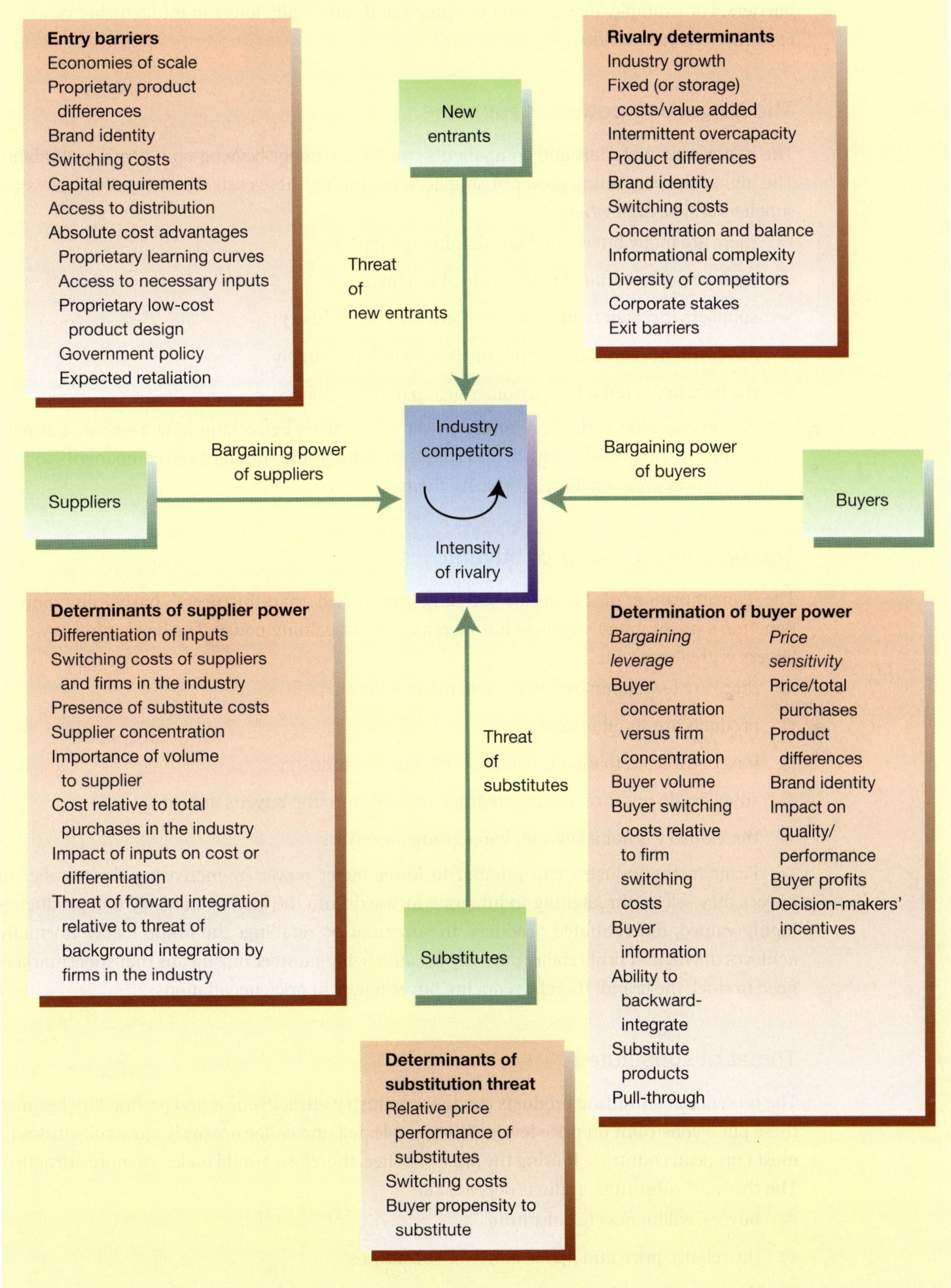

Entry barriers
Economies of scale
Proprietary product differences
Brand identity
Switching costs
Capital requirements
Access to distribution
Absolute cost advantages
  Proprietary learning curves
  Access to necessary inputs
  Proprietary low-cost product design
Government policy
Expected retaliation

Rivalry determinants
Industry growth
Fixed (or storage) costs/value added
Intermittent overcapacity
Product differences
Brand identity
Switching costs
Concentration and balance
Informational complexity
Diversity of competitors
Corporate stakes
Exit barriers

New entrants
Threat of new entrants

Suppliers — Bargaining power of suppliers → Industry competitors (Intensity of rivalry) ← Bargaining power of buyers — Buyers

Determinants of supplier power
Differentiation of inputs
Switching costs of suppliers and firms in the industry
Presence of substitute costs
Supplier concentration
Importance of volume to supplier
Cost relative to total purchases in the industry
Impact of inputs on cost or differentiation
Threat of forward integration relative to threat of background integration by firms in the industry

Determination of buyer power

Bargaining leverage	Price sensitivity
Buyer concentration versus firm concentration	Price/total purchases
Buyer volume	Product differences
Buyer switching costs relative to firm switching costs	Brand identity
Buyer information	Impact on quality/performance
Ability to backward-integrate	Buyer profits
Substitute products	Decision-makers' incentives
Pull-through	

Threat of substitutes

Substitutes

Determinants of substitution threat
Relative price performance of substitutes
Switching costs
Buyer propensity to substitute

For present competitors, industry attractiveness can be increased by raising entry barriers. High promotional and R&D expenditures, and clearly communicated retaliatory actions to entry are some methods of raising barriers. Some managerial actions can unwittingly lower barriers. For example, new product designs that dramatically lower manufacturing costs can ease entry for newcomers.

The bargaining power of suppliers

The cost of raw materials and components can have a major bearing on a firm's profitability. The higher the bargaining power of suppliers, the higher these costs. The bargaining power of suppliers will be high when:

- there are many buyers and few dominant suppliers
- there are differentiated highly valued products
- suppliers threaten to integrate forward into the industry
- buyers do not threaten to integrate backward into supply
- the industry is not a key customer group to the suppliers.

A firm can reduce the bargaining power of suppliers by seeking new sources of supply, threatening to integrate backward into supply, and designing standardized components so that many suppliers are capable of producing them.

The bargaining power of buyers

The concentration of European retailing has raised manufacturers' bargaining power. Benetton's use of many suppliers has increased its bargaining power. The bargaining power of buyers is greater when:

- there are few dominant buyers and many sellers
- products are standardized
- buyers threaten to integrate backwards into the industry
- suppliers do not threaten to integrate forwards into the buyer's industry.
- the industry is not a key supplying group for buyers.

Firms in the industry can attempt to lower buyer power by increasing the number of buyers they sell to, threatening to integrate forwards into the buyer's industry and producing highly valued, differentiated products. In supermarket retailing, the brand leader normally achieves the highest profitability partially because being number one means that supermarkets need to stock the brand, thereby reducing buyer power in price negotiations.

Threat of substitutes

The presence of substitute products can lower industry attractiveness and profitability because these put a constraint on price levels. For example, tea and coffee are fairly close substitutes in most European countries. Raising the price of coffee, therefore, would make tea more attractive. The threat of substitute products depends on:

- buyers' willingness to substitute
- the relative price and performance of substitutes
- the costs of switching to substitutes.

The threat of substitute products can be lowered by building up switching costs, which may be psychological—for example, by creating strong distinctive brand personalities—and maintaining a price differential commensurate with perceived customer values.

Industry competitors

The intensity of rivalry between competitors in an industry will depend on the following factors.

- *Structure of the competition*: there is more intense rivalry when there are a large number of small competitors or a few equally balanced competitors, and less rivalry when a clear leader (at least 50 per cent larger than the second) exists with a large cost advantage.
- *Structure of costs*: high fixed costs encourage price-cutting to fill capacity.
- *Degree of differentiation*: commodity products encourage rivalry, while highly differentiated products that are hard to copy are associated with less intense rivalry.
- *Switching costs*: rivalry is reduced when switching costs are high because the product is specialized, the customer has invested a lot of resources in learning how to use the product or has made tailor-made investments that are worthless with other products and suppliers.
- *Strategic objectives*: when competitors are pursuing build strategies, competition is likely to be more intense than when playing hold or harvesting strategies.
- *Exit barriers*: when barriers to leaving an industry are high due to such factors as lack of opportunities elsewhere, high vertical integration, emotional barriers or the high cost of closing down plant, rivalry will be more intense than when exit barriers are low.

Firms need to be careful not to spoil a situation of competitive stability. They need to balance their own position against the well-being of the industry as a whole. For example, an intense price or promotional war may gain a few percentage points in market share but lead to an overall fall in long-run industry profitability as competitors respond to these moves. It is sometimes better to protect industry structure than follow short-term self-interest.

A major threat to favourable industry structure is the use of a no-frills, low-price strategy by a minor player seeking positional advantage. For example, the launch of generic products in the pharmaceutical and cigarette industries has lowered overall profitability.

Despite meeting customers' needs with high-quality, good-value products, firms can 'compete away' the rewards. An intensive competitive environment means that the value created by firms in satisfying customer needs is given away to buyers through lower prices, dissipated through costly marketing battles (e.g. advertising wars) or passed on to powerful suppliers through higher prices for raw materials and components.

In Europe the competitive structure of industries was fundamentally changed with the advent of the single European market. The lifting of barriers to trade between countries has radically altered industry structure by affecting its underlying determinants. For example, the threat of new entrants and the growth in buyer/supplier power through acquisition or merger are fundamentally changing the competitive climate of many industries.

Competitor analysis

The analysis of how industry structure affects long-run profitability has shown the need to understand and monitor competitors. Their actions can spoil an otherwise attractive industry, their weaknesses can be a target for exploitation, and their response to a firm's marketing initiatives can have a major impact on their success. Indeed, firms that focus on competitors' actions have been found to achieve better business performance than those who pay less attention to their competitors.[3] Competitive information can be obtained from marketing research surveys, recruiting competitors' employees (sometimes interviewing them is sufficient), secondary sources (e.g. trade magazines, newspaper articles), distributors, stripping down competitors' products and gathering competitors' sales literature.

Competitor analysis seeks to answer five key questions.

1. Who are our competitors?
2. What are their strengths and weaknesses?
3. What are their strategic objectives and thrust?
4. What are their strategies?
5. What are their response patterns?

These issues are summarized in Fig. 18.2. Each question will now be examined.

Figure 18.2 Competitor analysis

Who are our competitors?

The danger when identifying competitors is that competitive myopia prevails. This malady is reflected in a narrow definition of competition resulting in too restricted a view of which companies are in competition. Only those companies that are producing technically similar products are considered to be the competition (e.g. paint companies). This ignores companies purchasing substitute products that perform a similar function (e.g. polyurethane varnish firms) and those that solve a problem or eliminate it in a dissimilar way (e.g. PVC double-glazing companies). The actions of all of these types of competitors can affect the performance of our firm and therefore need to be monitored. Their responses also need to be assessed as they will determine the outcome of any competitive move that our firm may wish to make. For example, we need to ask how likely it would be that polyurethane varnish companies would follow any price move we might wish to make.

Beyond these current competitors the environment needs to be scanned for potential entrants into the industry. These can take two forms: entrants with technically similar products and those invading the market with substitute products. Companies with similar core competences to the present incumbents may pose the threat of entering with technically similar products. For example, Xerox's skills in office automation provided the springboard for it to enter (unsuccessfully) the computer market. The source of companies entering with substitute products may be more difficult to locate, however. A technological breakthrough may transform an industry by rendering the old product obsolete as when the calculator replaced the slide rule, or when the car replaced the horse-drawn buggy. In such instances it is difficult to locate the source of the substitute product well in advance. Figure 18.3 illustrates this competitive arena.

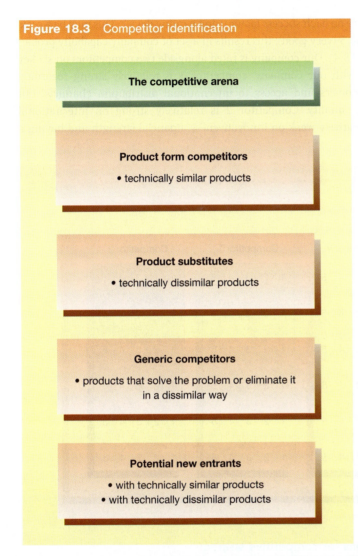

Figure 18.3 Competitor identification

What are their strengths and weaknesses?

Having identified our competitors the next stage is to complete a competitor audit in order to assess their relative strengths and weaknesses. A precise understanding of competitor strengths and weaknesses is an important prerequisite of developing competitor strategy. In particular, it locates areas of competitive vulnerability. Military strategy suggests that success is most often achieved when strength is concentrated against the enemy's greatest weakness.[4] This analogy holds true for business, as the success of Japanese companies in the car and motorcycle industries demonstrates.

The process of assessing competitors' strengths and weaknesses may take place as part of a marketing audit (see Chapter 2). As much internal, market and customer information should be gathered as is practicable. For example, financial data concerning profitability, profit margins, sales and investment levels, market data relating to price levels, market share and distribution channels used, and customer data concerning awareness of brand names, and perceptions of brand and company image, product and service quality, and selling ability may be relevant.

Not all of this information will be accessible, and some may not be relevant. Management needs to decide the extent to which each element of information is worth pursuing. For example, a decision is required regarding how much expenditure is to be allocated to measuring customer awareness and perceptions through marketing research.

This process of data gathering needs to be managed so that information is available to compare our company with its chief competitors on the *key factors for success* in the industry. A three-stage process can then be used, as follows.

1 Identify key factors for success in the industry

These should be restricted to about six to eight factors otherwise the analysis becomes too diffuse.[5] Their identification is a matter of managerial judgement. Their source may be functional (such as financial strength or flexible production) or generic (for example, the ability to respond quickly to customer needs, innovativeness, or the capability to provide other sales services). Since these factors are critical for success they should be used to compare our company with its competitors.

2 Rate our company and competitors on each key success factor using a rating scale

Each company is given a score on each success factor using a rating device. This may be a scale ranging from 1 (very poor) to 5 (very good); this results in a set of company capability profiles (an example is given in Fig. 18.4). Our company is rated alongside two competitors on six key success factors. Compared with our company, competitor 1 is relatively strong regarding technical assistance to customers and access to international distribution channels, but relatively weak on product quality. Competitor 2 is relatively strong on international distribution channels but relatively weak on innovativeness, financial strength and having a well-qualified workforce.

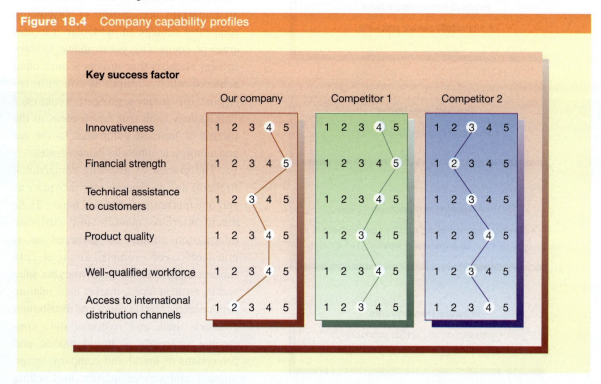

Figure 18.4 Company capability profiles

3 Consider the implications for competitive strategy

The competitive profile analysis is then used to identify possible competitive strategies. This analysis would suggest that our company should consider taking steps to improve technical assistance to customers to match or exceed competitor 1's capability on this factor. At the moment, our company enjoys a differential advantage over competitor 1 on product quality. Our strength in innovativeness should be used to maintain this differential advantage and competitor 1's moves to improve product quality should be monitored carefully.

Competitor 2 is weaker overall than competitor 1 and our company. However, it has considerable strengths in having access to international distribution channels. Given our company's weakness in this area, a strategic alliance with or take-over of competitor 2 might be sensible if our company's objective is to expand internationally. Our company's financial strength and competitor 2's financial weakness suggests that a take-over might be feasible.

What are their strategic objectives and thrust?

The third part of competitor analysis is to infer their *strategic objectives*. Companies may decide to build, hold or harvest products and strategic business units (SBUs). To briefly recap, a build objective is concerned with increasing sales and/or market share, a hold objective suggests maintaining sales and/or market share, and a harvest objective is followed when the emphasis is on maximizing short-term cash flow through slashing expenditure and raising prices whenever possible. It is useful to know what strategic objectives are being pursued by competitors because their response pattern may depend upon objectives. Looking at this topic from a product perspective, if we are considering building market share of our product by cutting price, a competitor who is also building is almost certain to follow; one who is content to hold sales and market share is also likely to respond, but a company following a harvest objective for its product is much less likely to reduce price because it is more concerned with profit margin than unit sales.

Conversely, if we are considering a price rise, a competitor pursuing a build strategy is not likely to follow; the price of a product subject to a hold objective is now likely to rise in line with our increase; and a company using a harvest objective will almost certainly take the opportunity to raise its product's price, maybe by more than our increase.

Knowing competitors' strategic objectives is also useful in predicting their likely strategies. For example, a build objective is likely to be accompanied by aggressive price and promotional moves, a hold objective with competitive stability, and a harvest objective with cost- rather than marketing-orientated strategies.

Strategic thrust refers to the future areas of expansion a company might contemplate. Broadly, a company can expand by penetrating existing markets more effectively with current products, launching new products in existing markets or by growing in new markets with existing or new products. Knowing the strategic thrust of competitors can help our strategic decision-making. For example, knowing that our competitors are considering expansion in North America but not Europe will make expansion into Europe a more attractive strategic option for our company.

What are their strategies?

At the product level, competitor analysis will attempt to deduce positioning strategy. This involves assessing a competitor product's target market and differential advantage. The marketing mix strategies (e.g. price levels, media used for promotion, and distribution channels) may indicate target market, and marketing research into customer perceptions can be used to assess relative differential advantages.

Companies and products need to be monitored continuously for changes in positioning strategy. For example, Volvo's traditional positioning strategy, based on safety, has been modified to give more emphasis to performance and style.

Strategies can also be defined in terms of competitive scope. For example, are competitors attempting to service the whole market or a few segments of a particular niche? If a niche player, is it likely that they will be content to stay in that segment or will they use it as a beachhead to move into other segments in the future? Japanese companies are renowned for their use of small niche markets as springboards for market segment expansion (e.g. the small car segments in the USA and Europe).

Competitors may be playing the cost-leadership game, focusing on cost-reducing measures rather than expensive product development and promotional strategies. (Cost leadership will be discussed in more detail later in this chapter.) If competitors are following this strategy it is more likely that they will be focusing research and development expenditure on process rather than product development in a bid to reduce manufacturing costs.

What are their response patterns?

A key consideration in making a strategic or tactical move is the likely response of competitors. As we have discussed, understanding competitor objectives and strategies is helpful in predicting competitor reactions. Indeed, a major objective of competitor analysis is to be able to predict competitor response to market and competitive changes. Competitors' past behaviour is also a guide to what they might do. Market leaders often try to control competitor response by retaliatory action. These are called *retaliatory* competitors because they can be relied on to respond aggressively to competitive challenges. Len Hardy, ex-chairman of Lever Brothers, explained the role of a retaliation as follows:

> ❝A leader must enforce market discipline, must be ruthless in dealing with any competitive challenge. If you make a price move and a competitor undercuts it, then he should be shown that this action has been noticed and will be punished. If he is not punished he will repeat the move—and soon your leadership will be eroded.[6]❞

Thus by punishing competitor moves, market leaders can condition competitors to behave in predicted ways—for example, by not taking advantage of a price rise by the leader.

It is not only market leaders that retaliate aggressively. Where management is known to be assertive, and our move is likely to have a major impact on their performance, a strong response is usual.

The history, traditions and managerial personalities of competitors also have an influence on competitive response. Some markets are characterized by years of competitive stability with little serious strategic challenge to any of the incumbents. This can breed complacency, with predictably slow reaction times to new challenges. For example, innovation that offers superior customer value may be dismissed as a fad and unworthy of serious attention.

Another situation where competitors are unlikely to respond is where their previous strategies have restricted their scope for retaliation. An example of such a *hemmed-in competitor* was a major manufacturer of car number plates that were sold to car dealerships. A new company was started by an ex-employee who focused on one geographical area, supplying the same quality product but with extra discount. The national supplier could not respond since to give discount in that particular region would have meant granting the discount nationwide.

A fourth type of competitor may respond selectively. Because of tradition or beliefs about the relative effectiveness of marketing instruments a competitor may respond to some competitive moves but not others. For example, extra sales promotion expenditures may be matched but advertising increases (within certain boundaries) may be ignored. Another reason for selective response is the varying degree of visibility of marketing actions. For example, giving extra price discounts may be highly visible, but providing distributors with extra support (e.g. training, sales literature, loans) may be less discernible.

A final type of competitor is totally *unpredictable* in its response pattern. Sometimes there is a response and, at other times, there is no response. Some moves are countered aggressively; with others reaction is weak. No factors explain these differences adequately; they appear to be at the whim of management.

Some companies use role-play to assess competitor reactions: their most knowledgeable managers act out the roles of key competitors to aid prediction of their response to a proposed marketing initiative.[7] Interestingly, research has shown that managers tend to over-react more frequently than they under-react to competitors' marketing activities.[8]

Competitive advantage

The key to superior performance is to gain and hold a competitive advantage. Firms can gain a competitive advantage through *differentiation* of their product offering, which provides superior customer value, or by managing for *lowest delivered cost*. Evidence for this proposition was provided by Hall, who examined the competitive strategies pursued by the two leading firms (in terms of return on investment) in eight mature industries characterized by slow growth and intense competition.[9] In each industry the two leading firms offered either high product differentiation or the lowest delivered cost. In most cases, an industry's return on investment leader opted for one of the strategies, while the second-placed firm pursued the other.

Competitive strategies

These two means of competitive advantage, when combined with the competitive scope of activities (broad vs narrow), result in four generic strategies: differentiation, cost leadership, differentiation focus, and cost focus. The differentiation and cost leadership strategies seek competitive advantage in a broad range of market or industry segments, whereas differentiation focus and cost focus strategies are confined to a narrow segment.[10]

Differentiation

Differentiation strategy involves the selection of one or more choice criteria that are used by many buyers in an industry. The firm then uniquely positions itself to meet these criteria. Differentiation strategies are usually associated with a premium price, and higher than average costs for the industry as the extra value to customers (e.g. higher performance) often raises costs. The aim is to differentiate in a way that leads to a price premium in excess of the cost of differentiating. Differentiation gives customers a reason to prefer one product over another and thus is central to strategic marketing thinking. Key to the success of Dyson, the vacuum cleaner and washing machine manufacturer, is differentiation, as Marketing in Action 18.1 explains.

18.1 marketing in action

Differentiation at Dyson

Successful differentiation relies on creating something different from the competition on attributes that customers value. James Dyson did just that with his bagless vacuum cleaner, which out-performed its rivals by providing greater suction and greater convenience through eliminating the need to buy and install bags into which traditional vacuum cleaners deposited dirt and dust. The vacuum cleaners looked different too, using yellow as a distinctive colour. Within two years the Dyson Dual Cyclone became the fastest-selling vacuum cleaner in the UK, and is now available in 22 countries.

Success does not come easily though, as Dyson was almost bankrupted by the legal costs of establishing and protecting his patent. Further innovations were required to create more differentiation, including the Root 8 Cyclone, which sucks up more dust by using eight cyclones instead of two.

Continuing to exploit better performance as a differentiator, Dyson launched the Contrarotator washing machine, which has two drums spinning in opposite directions. This produces the customer benefits of allowing greater loads while cleaning more effectively. It became the best-selling machine in the £500-plus sector within 18 months of its launch.

Based on: Anonymous (2002);[11] Anonymous (2002)[12]

Cost leadership

This strategy involves the achievement of the lowest cost position in an industry. Many segments in the industry are served and great importance is attached to minimizing costs on all fronts. So long as the price achievable for its products is around the industry average, cost leadership should result in superior performance. Thus cost leaders often market standard products that are believed to be acceptable to customers. Heinz and United Biscuits are believed to be cost leaders in their industries. They market acceptable products at reasonable prices, which means that their low costs result in above-average profits. Some cost leaders need to discount prices in order to achieve high sales levels. The aim here is to achieve superior performance by ensuring that the cost advantage over the competition is not offset by the price discount. No-frills supermarket discounters like Costco, KwikSave, Aldi and Netto fall into this category.

Differentiation focus

With this strategy, a firm aims to differentiate within one or a small number of target market segments. The special needs of the segment mean that there is an opportunity to differentiate the product offering from the competition's, which may be targeting a broader group of customers. For example, some small speciality chemical companies thrive on taking orders that are too small or specialized to be of interest to their larger competitors. Differentiation focusers must be clear that the needs of their target group differ from the broader market (otherwise there will be no basis for differentiation) and that existing competitors are underperforming.

Cost focus

With this strategy a firm seeks a cost advantage with one or a small number of target market segments. By dedicating itself to the segment, the cost focuser can seek economies that may be ignored or missed by broadly targeted competitors. In some instances, the competition, by trying to achieve wide market acceptance, may be over-performing (for example, by providing unwanted services) to one segment of customers. By providing a basic product offering, a cost advantage will be gained that may exceed the price discount necessary to sell it.

Choosing a competitive strategy

The essence of corporate success, then, is to choose a generic strategy and pursue it with gusto. Below-average performance is associated with the failure to achieve any of these generic strategies. The result is no competitive advantage: a *stuck-in-the-middle position* that results in lower performance than that of the cost leaders, differentiators or focusers in any market segment. An example of a company that made the mistake of moving to a stuck-in-the-middle position was General Motors with its Oldsmobile car. The original car (the Oldsmobile Rocket V8) was highly differentiated, with a 6-litre V8 engine, which was virtually indestructible, very fast and highly reliable. In order to cut costs, this engine was replaced by the same engine that went into the 5-litre Chevrolet V8. This had less power and was less reliable. The result was catastrophic: sales plummeted.

Firms need to understand the generic basis for their success and resist the temptation to blur strategy by making inconsistent moves. For example, a no-frills cost leader or focuser should beware of the pitfalls of moving to a higher cost base (perhaps by adding expensive services). A focus strategy involves limiting sales volume. Once domination of the target segment has been achieved there may be a temptation to move into other segments in order to achieve growth with the same competitive advantage. This can be a mistake if the new segments do not value the firm's competitive advantage in the same way.

In most situations differentiation and cost leadership strategies are incompatible: differentiation is achieved through higher costs. However, there are circumstances when both can be achieved simultaneously. For example, a differentiation strategy may lead to market share domination, which lowers costs through economies of scale and learning effects; or a highly differentiated firm may pioneer a major process innovation that significantly reduces manufacturing costs leading to a cost-leadership position. When differentiation and cost leadership coincide, performance is exceptional since a premium price can be charged for a low-cost product.

Sources of competitive advantage

In order to create a differentiated or lowest cost position, a firm needs to understand the nature and location of the potential *sources of competitive advantage*. The nature of these sources are the superior skills and resources of a firm. Management benefits by analysing the superior skills and resources that are contributing, or could contribute, to competitive advantage (i.e. differentiation or lowest cost position). Their location can be aided by value chain analysis. A **value chain** is the discrete activities a firm carries out in order to perform its business.

Superior skills

Superior skills are the distinctive capabilities of key personnel that set them apart from the personnel of competing firms.[13] The benefit of superior skills is the resulting ability to perform functions more effectively than other firms. For example, superior selling skills may result in closer relationships with customers than competing firms achieve. Compaq Computers built strong relationships with corporate retailers by offering attractive margins and exclusive franchises.[14] Superior quality assurance skills can result in higher and more consistent product quality.

Superior resources

Superior resources are the tangible requirements for advantage that enable a firm to exercise its skills. Superior resources include:

- the number of sales people in a market
- expenditure on advertising and sales promotion
- distribution coverage (the number of retailers who stock the product)
- expenditure on R&D
- scale of and type of production facilities
- financial resources
- brand equity
- knowledge.

Core competences

The distinctive nature of these skills and resources make up a company's **core competences**. For example, a core competence of Sony is miniaturization. Building on this capability, Sony launched the first minidisc digital Walkman in Europe in 1993. Minidisc technology allows recording from conventional compact discs in high-quality digital stereo on to a disc one-third of the size of standard CDs. These can then be played in the Walkman in the same way as compact cassettes. By creating superior sound quality in a convenient format, Sony has used its core competence to create a competitive advantage.

Value chain

A useful method for locating superior skills and resources is the value chain.[15] All firms consist of a set of activities that are conducted to design, manufacture, market, distribute and service its products. The value chain categorizes these into primary and support activities (see Fig. 18.5). This enables the sources of costs and differentiation to be understood and located.

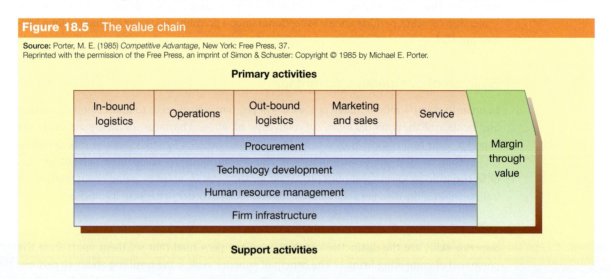

Figure 18.5 The value chain

Source: Porter, M. E. (1985) *Competitive Advantage*, New York: Free Press, 37.
Reprinted with the permission of the Free Press, an imprint of Simon & Schuster: Copyright © 1985 by Michael E. Porter.

Primary activities include in-bound physical distribution (e.g. materials handling, warehousing, inventory control), operations (e.g. manufacturing, packaging), out-bound physical distribution (e.g. delivery, order processing), marketing (e.g. advertising, selling, channel management) and service (e.g. installation, repair, customer training).

Support activities are found within all of these primary activities, and consist of purchased inputs, technology, human resource management and the firm's infrastructure. These are not defined within a given primary activity because they can be found in all of them. Purchasing can take place within each primary activity, not just in the purchasing department; technology is relevant to all primary activities, as is human resource management; and the firm's infrastructure, which consists of general management, planning, finance, accounting and quality management, supports the entire value chain.

By examining each value-creating activity, management can look for the skills and resources that may form the basis for low cost or differentiated positions. For example, an analysis of the effectiveness of a company's website activities should reveal its competitive advantages and disadvantages compared to the competition, as e-Marketing 18.1 explains.

To the extent that skills and resources exceed (or could be developed to exceed) those of the competition, they form the key sources of competitive advantage. Not only should the skills and resources within value-creating activities be examined, the *linkages* between them should be examined too. For example, greater co-ordination between operations and in-bound physical distribution may give rise to reduced costs through lower inventory levels.

Value chain analysis can extend to the value chains of suppliers and customers. For example, just-in-time supply could lower inventory costs; providing salesforce support to distributors could foster closer relations. Thus, by looking at the linkages between a firm's value chain and those of suppliers and customers, improvements in performance can result that can lower costs or contribute to the creation of a differentiated position.

Overall, the contribution of the value chain is in providing a framework for understanding the nature and location of the skills and resources that provide the basis for competitive

18.1 e-marketing

Measuring Competitiveness: the Purpose of a Website Audit

A website audit measures the relative effectiveness of a company's website activities. It looks at three aspects of online competitiveness: technology, usability and marketing.

The technology used to build a website can put companies at a significant disadvantage vis-à-vis their competitors. For example, websites that are built using 'frame-based' technologies (e.g. www.grangemanor.co.uk) or 'flash-based' technologies (e.g. www.happell.co.uk) are seldom found on search engines (search engines are unable to capture and store much information from these types of site).

The usability of a site affects its relative competitiveness and involves assessing more 'subjective' aspects of the website. It looks at the effectiveness of the site content, design, navigation and functionality for a typical user. For example, does the content site tell the user succinctly what it is about? Does the design reflect the type of company it is and the industry it is involved in? Can the user navigate to a piece of information and return to the home page? Does the site allow the user an appropriate level of interaction—for example, through online contact forms?

How well the site is marketed online is assessed by looking at where it ranks on the major search engines and directories. Rather than testing the site across numerous search engines, sites like EchoEcho (www.echoecho.com) provide a tool to do this automatically.

The result of the website audit is an assessment of the relative competitiveness of a website. Companies serious in this area will carry out audits with different customer groups and compare against their competitors.

advantage. Furthermore, the value chain provides the framework for cost analysis. Assigning operating costs and assets to value activities is the starting point of cost analysis so that improvement can be made, and cost advantages defended. For example, if a firm discovers that its cost advantage is based on superior production facilities, it should be vigilant in upgrading those facilities to maintain its position against competitors. Similarly, by understanding the sources of differentiation, a company can build on these sources and defend against competitive attack. For example, if differentiation is based on skills in product design, then management knows that sufficient investment in maintaining design superiority is required to maintain the firm's differentiated position. Also, the identification of specific sources of advantage can lead to their exploitation in new markets where customers place a similar high value on the resultant outcome. For example, Marks & Spencer's skills in clothing retailing were successfully extended to provide differentiation in food retailing.

Creating a differential advantage

Although skills and resources are the sources of competitive advantage, they are translated into a differential advantage only when the customer perceives that the firm is providing value above that of the competition.[16] The creation of a differential advantage, then, comes with the marrying of skills and resources with the key attributes (choice criteria) that customers are looking for in a product offering. However, it should be recognized that the distinguishing competing attributes in a market are not always the most important ones. For example, if customers were asked to rank safety, punctuality and onboard service in order of importance

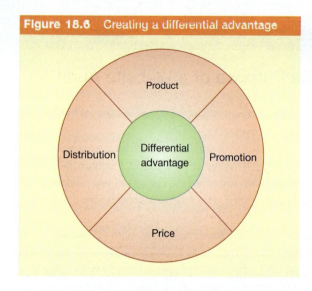

Figure 18.6 Creating a differential advantage

when flying, safety would undoubtedly be ranked at the top. Nevertheless, when choosing an airline, safety would rank low because most airlines are assumed to be safe. This is why airlines look to less important ways of differentiating their offerings (e.g. by giving superior onboard service).

A differential advantage can be created with any aspect of the marketing mix. Product, distribution, promotion and price are all capable of creating added customer value (see Fig. 18.6). The key to whether improving an aspect of marketing is worthwhile is to know whether the potential benefit provides value to the customer. Table 18.1 lists ways of creating differential advantages and their potential impact on customer value.

Table 18.1 Creating a differential advantage using the marketing mix

Marketing mix	Differential advantage	Value to the customer
Product	Performance	Lower costs; higher revenue; safety; pleasure; status
	Durability	Longer life; lower costs
	Reliability	Lower maintenance and production costs; higher revenue; fewer problems
	Style	Good looks; status
	Upgradability	Lower costs; prestige
	Technical assistance	Better-quality products; closer supplier–buyer relationships
	Installation	Fewer problems
Distribution	Location	Convenience; lower costs
	Quick/reliable delivery	Lower costs; fewer problems
	Distributor support	More effective selling/marketing; close buyer–seller relationships
	Delivery guarantees	Peace of mind
	Computerized reordering	Less work; lower costs
Promotion	Creative/more advertising	Superior brand personality
	Creative/more sales promotion	Direct added value
	Co-operative promotions	Lower costs
	Well-trained salesforce	Superior problem-solving
	Dual selling	Sales assistance; higher sales
	Fast, accurate quotes	Lower costs; fewer problems
	Free demonstrations	Lower risk of purchase
	Free or low-cost trial	Lower risk of purchase
	Fast complaint handling	Fewer problems; lower costs
Price	Lower price	Lower cost of purchase
	Credit facilities	Lower costs; better cash flow
	Low-interest loans	Lower costs; better cash flow
	Higher price	Price–quality match

Product

Product performance can be enhanced by such devices as raising speed, comfort and safety levels, capacity and ease of use, or improving taste or smell. For example, raising the speed of operation of a scanner can lower the cost of treating hospital patients. Improving comfort levels (e.g. of a car), taste (e.g. of food), or smell (e.g. of cosmetics) can give added pleasure to consumption. Raising productivity levels of earth-moving equipment can bring higher revenue if more jobs can be done in a given period of time. The illustration for Virgin Atlantic shows how it is trying to offer better performance through superior service.

The *durability* of a product has a bearing on costs since greater durability means a longer operating life. The Panasonic Toughbook advertisement (see illustration on page 695) promotes the durability of the brand as a key differential advantage. Improving product *reliability* (i.e. lowering malfunctions or defects) can lower maintenance and production costs, raise revenues through lower downtime and reduce the hassle of using the product. Product *styling* can also give customer value through the improved looks that good style brings. This can confer status to the buyer and allow the supplier to charge premium prices, as with Bang & Olufsen hi-fi equipment. Marketing in Action 18.2 discusses how style can be used as a differentiator.

The capacity to *upgrade* a product (to take advantage of technological advances) or to meet changing needs (e.g. extra storage space in a computer) can lower costs, and confer prestige by maintaining state-of-the-art features. The illustration featuring the Apple iMac computer shows how style can be used to create a differential advantage.

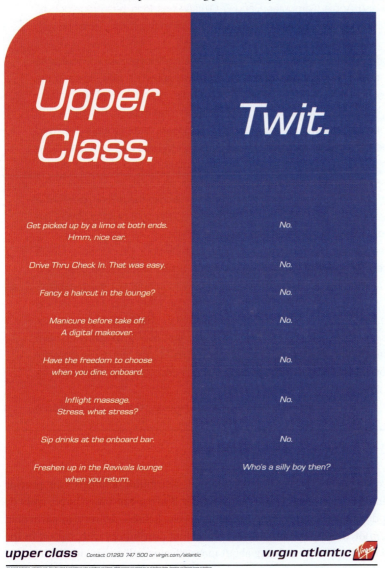

Virgin differentiates by offering superior service.

Products can be augmented by the provision of *guarantees* that give customers peace of mind and lower costs should the product need repair, as well as giving *technical assistance* to customers, so that they are provided with better-quality products. Both parties benefit from closer relationships and from the provision of product *installation*, which means that customers do not incur problems in properly installing a complex piece of equipment.

18.2 marketing in action

Using Style to Differentiate Products

Two companies that have successfully used style to differentiate their products from those of the competition are Bang & Olufsen and Apple Computer. Bang & Olufsen has long been regarded as the style leader in audio and television equipment, and Apple created a stir in the computer world with the launch of its iMac.

Bang & Olufsen has built a worldwide reputation for quality and a fanatically loyal customer base. Its sleek, tastefully discrete designs and high standards of production have earned it elite status in the market. For decades, these factors have formed the basis of its advertising and marketing strategy. The company recognizes that style needs to be displayed distinctively in retail outlets. This has led to the creation of 'concept shops' where subtle images are projected on to walls and products displayed in free-standing areas constructed from translucent walls. The company's view is that you cannot sell Bang & Olufsen equipment when it is sandwiched between a washing machine and a shelf of videos. The concept shop gives the right look to make the most of the products.

Although not the market leader overall, Apple's iMac leads the competition in the design, publishing and education segments. It also sells well in the consumer market: over 30 per cent of iMac buyers are first-time home computer owners. A key point of differentiation is its looks. As Steve Jobs, chief executive at Apple, explains, 'If you look at it, our industry has done a pretty poor job of listening to its customers in the consumer market. The industry sold big, ugly beige ... boxes that took up desks and everything else. The customers were saying "My God, I don't know how to connect all these cables", "My God, this thing is too noisy", "My God, this doesn't fit on my desk", and "My God, I have to hide it when visitors come over".' The result was the colourful, curvaceous all-in-one iMac. No consumer could mistake the distinctive design of the new model. The result was that over 2 million units have been sold and Apple's market share in the USA has risen to a respectable 11 per cent. So successful has Apple been in creating a strong brand identity with its iMac that the company has withstood the challenge of a flood of iMac lookalikes.

Based on: McIntosh (1999);[17] Pickford (1999);[18] Whiteling (2002)[19]

Distribution

Wide distribution coverage and/or careful selection of distributor *locations* can provide convenient purchasing for customers. *Quick and/or reliable delivery* can lower buyer costs by reducing production downtime and lowering inventory levels. Reliable delivery, in particular, reduces the frustration of waiting for late delivery. Providing distributors with *support* in the form of training and financial help can bring about more effective selling and marketing, and offers both parties the advantage of closer relationships. Working with organizational customers to introduce *computerized reordering* systems can lower their costs, reduce their workload and increase the cost for them of switching to other suppliers.

Promotion

A differential advantage can be created by the *creative use of advertising*. For example, Heineken was differentiated by the use of humour and the tag-line 'Heineken refreshes the parts other beers cannot reach' at a time when many other lagers were promoted by showing groups of men in public houses enjoying a drink together. *Spending more on advertising* can also aid

Panasonic stresses the durability (and style) of its Toughbook PC as a key differentiator.

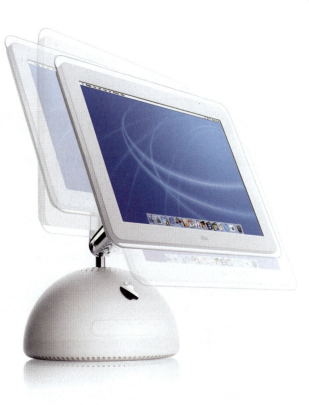

Apple uses style to create a differential advantage for its iMac computer.

differentiation by creating a stronger brand personality than competitive brands. Similarly, using *more creative sales promotional methods* or simply *spending more on sales incentives* can give direct added value to customers. By engaging in *co-operative promotions* with distributors, producers can lower their costs and build goodwill.

The salesforce can also offer a means of creating a differential advantage. Particularly when products are similar, a *well-trained salesforce* can provide superior problem-solving skills for their customers. Part of the success of IBM in penetrating the mainframe computer market in the early 1980s was due to its well-trained salesforce, which acted as problem solver and information consultant for its customers. *Dual selling*, whereby a producer provides salesforce assistance to distributors, can lower the latter's costs and increase sales. For example, a chemical company might supply product specialists who support a distributor's salesforce by providing technical expertise when required. Sales responsiveness in the form of *fast, accurate quotes* can lower customer costs by making transactions more efficient, and reduce the hassle associated with ordering supplies. Furthermore, *free demonstrations* and *free (or low cost) trial* arrangements can reduce the risk of purchase for customers. Finally, *superior complaint handling* procedures can lower customer costs by speeding up the process, and reduce the inconvenience that can accompany it.

Price

Using low price as a means of gaining differential advantage can fail unless the firm enjoys a cost advantage and has the resources to fight a price war. For example, Laker Airways challenged British Airways in transatlantic flights on the basis of lower price, but lost the battle when British Airways cut its prices to compete. Without a cost advantage and with fewer resources, Laker Airways could not survive BA's retaliation. Budget airlines such as Ryanair and easyJet have challenged more traditional airlines by charging low prices based on low costs, as e-Marketing 18.2 discusses.

18.2 e-marketing

Low-cost Airlines: Using the Internet to Build Competitive Advantage

The model for budget, or 'no-frills', airlines was first developed in the USA by Southwest Airlines in the 1970s. The premise of this budget airline was to get passengers to their destination for less, with an 'adequate' level of service. This model, highly successful for Southwest, has since been copied by Ryanair, easyJet, Go, Buzz and others.

The competitive advantage of budget airlines is in maintaining low operating costs while increasing revenue, and the Internet has helped them do both.

The majority of budget carriers use the Internet as the main distribution channel, while traditional airlines still rely on intermediaries. In fact, the sole order method of Ryanair (www.ryanair.co.uk) is online, where it takes 600,000 bookings per week. In addition, the Internet enables e-ticketing and reduces other material costs as customers receive all information online.

The largest area of competitive advantage is in maximizing seat revenue, and all carriers have sophisticated yield management systems. Maximizing seat revenue involves charging just enough to fill the flight but not so little that margins are cut. It is impossible to optimize revenues when sales are achieved through the airline and a network of travel agencies—the flow of information is too slow. However, through sole use of the Internet, budget carriers can update prices instantaneously, maximizing flight profitability.

Technology provides huge advantages for these companies but (as Ryanair and others have proved) it is also easy to copy their advances. These companies need to be aware of new ways of retaining their competitive advantage

Based on: Key Note (2002)[20]

A less obvious means of lowering the effective price to the customer is to offer *credit facilities* or *low-interest loans*. Both serve to lower the cost of purchase and improve cash flow for customers. Finally, a *high price* can be used as part of a premium positioning strategy to support brand image. Where a brand has distinct product, promotional or distributional advantages, a premium price provides consistency within the marketing mix.

This analysis of how the marketing mix can be used to develop a differential advantage has focused on how each action can be translated into value to the customer. It must be remembered, however, that for a differential advantage to be realized, a firm needs to provide not only customer value but also value that is superior to that offered by the competition. If all firms provide distributor support in equal measure, for example, distributors may gain value, but no differential advantage will have been achieved.

Fast reaction times

In addition to using the marketing mix to create a differential advantage, many companies are recognizing the need to create *fast reaction times* to changes in marketing trends. For example, Benetton has installed state-of-the-art communications, manufacturing and distribution technology to give it flexibility and a fast reaction time. Using advanced telecommunications, the company receives sales information from around the world 24 hours a day, every day of the year. It boasts that if everyone decided to wear nothing but hats tomorrow, it would be ready to produce 50 million hats within a week.[21]

Sustaining a differential advantage

When searching for ways to achieve a differential advantage, management should pay close attention to factors that cannot easily be copied by the competition. The aim is to achieve a *sustainable differential advantage*. Competing on low price can often be copied by the competition, meaning that any advantage is short-lived. Means of achieving a longer-term advantage include:

- patent-protected products
- strong brand personality
- close relationships with customers
- high service levels achieved by well-trained personnel
- innovative product upgrading
- creating high entry barriers (e.g. R&D or promotional expenditures)
- strong and distinctive internal processes that deliver the above and are difficult to copy.[22]

Eroding a differential advantage

However, many advantages are contestable. For example, IBM's stronghold on personal computers was undermined by cheaper clones. Three mechanisms are at work that can erode a differential advantage:[23]

1. technological and environment changes that create opportunities for competitors by eroding the protective barriers (e.g. long-standing television companies are being challenged by satellite television)
2. competitors learn how to imitate the sources of the differential advantage (e.g. competitors engage in a training programme to improve service capabilities)
3. complacency leads to lack of protection of the differential advantage.

Creating cost leadership

Creating a cost-leadership position requires an understanding of the factors that affect costs. Porter has identified 10 major *cost drivers* that determine the behaviour of costs in the value chain (see Fig. 18.7).[24]

Economies of scale

Scale economies can arise from the use of more efficient methods of production at higher volumes. For example, United Biscuits benefits from more efficient machinery that can produce biscuits more cheaply than that used by Fox's Biscuits, which operates at much lower volume. Scale economies also arise from the less-than-proportional increase in overheads as production volume increases. For example, a factory with twice the floor area of another factory is less than twice the price to build. A third scale economy results from the capacity to spread the cost

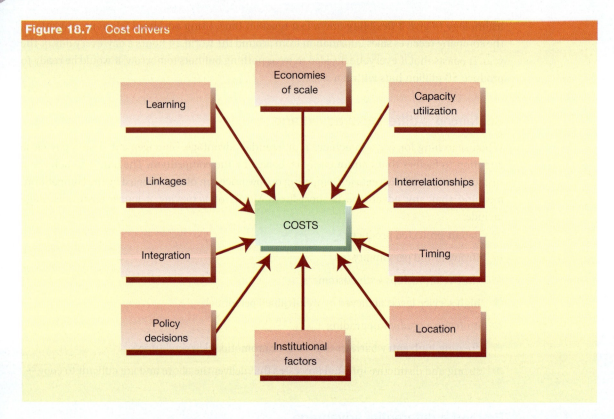

Figure 18.7 Cost drivers

of R&D and promotion over a greater sales volume. However, economies of scale do not proceed indefinitely. At some point, diseconomies of scale are likely to arise as size gives rise to overcomplexity and, possibly, personnel difficulties.

Learning

Costs can also fall as a result of the effects of learning. For example, people learn how to assemble more quickly, pack more efficiently, design products that are easier to manufacture, lay out warehouses more effectively, cut driving time and reduce inventories. The effect of learning on costs was seen in the manufacture of fighter planes for the Second World War. The time to produce each plane fell over time as learning took place. The combined effect of economies of scale and learning as cumulative output increases has been termed the experience curve. The Boston Consulting Group has estimated that costs are reduced by approximately 15–20 per cent on average each time cumulative output doubles. This suggests that firms with greater market share will have a cost advantage through the experience curve effect, assuming all companies are operating on the same curve. However, a move towards a new manufacturing technology can lower the experience curve for adopting companies, allowing them to leap-frog more traditional firms and thereby gain a cost advantage even though cumulative output may be lower.

Capacity utilization

Since fixed costs must be paid whether a plant is manufacturing at full or zero capacity, under-utilization incurs costs. The effect is to push up the cost per unit for production. The impact of capacity utilization on profitability was established by the PIMS (profit impact of marketing strategy) studies, which have shown a positive association between utilization and return on investment.[25] Changes in capacity utilization can also raise costs (e.g. through the extra costs of hiring and laying off workers). Careful production planning is required for seasonal products such as ice cream and fireworks, in order to smooth output.

Linkages

These describe how the costs of activities are affected by how other activities are performed. For example, improving quality-assurance activities can reduce after-sales service costs. In the car industry, the reduction in the number of faults on a new car reduces warranty costs. The activities of suppliers and distributors also link to affect the costs of a firm.

For example, the introduction of a just-in-time delivery system by a supplier reduces the inventory costs of a firm. Distributors can influence a firm's physical distribution costs through their warehouse location decision. To exploit such linkages, though, the firm may need considerable bargaining power. In some instances it can pay a firm to increase distributor margins or pay a fee in order to exploit linkages. For example, Seiko paid its US jewellers a fee for accepting its watches for repair and sending them to Seiko; this meant that Seiko did not need local services facilities and its overall costs fell.[26]

Interrelationships

Sharing costs with other business units is another potential cost driver. Sharing the costs of R&D, transportation, marketing and purchasing lower costs. Know-how can also be shared to reduce costs by improving the efficiency of an activity.

Integration

Both integration and de-integration can affect costs. For example, owning the means of physical distribution rather than using outside contractors could lower costs. Ownership may allow a producer to avoid suppliers or customers with sizeable bargaining power. De-integration can lower costs and raise flexibility. For example, by using many small clothing suppliers, Benetton is in a powerful position to keep costs low while maintaining a high degree of production flexibility.

Timing

Both first movers and late entrants have potential opportunities for lowering costs. First movers in a market can gain cost advantages: it is usually cheaper to establish a brand name in the minds of customers if there is no competition. Also, they have prime access to cheap or high-quality raw materials and locations. However, late entrants to a market have the opportunity to buy the latest technology and avoid high market development costs.

Policy decisions

Firms have a wide range of discretionary policy decisions that affect costs. Product width, level of service, channel decisions (e.g. small number of large dealers vs large number of small dealers), salesforce decisions (e.g. in-company salesforce vs sales agents) and wage levels are some of the decision areas that have a direct impact on costs. Southwest Airlines, for example, cuts costs by refusing to waste time assigning seats and does not wait for late arrivals. The overriding concern is to get the aeroplane in and out of the gate quickly so that it is in the air earning money. Southwest flies only one kind of aircraft, which also keeps costs down.[27] Care must be taken not to reduce costs on activities that have a major bearing on customer value.

For example, moving from a company-employed salesforce to sales agents may not only cut costs but also destroy supplier–customer relationships.

Location

The location of plant and warehouses affects costs through different wage, physical distribution and energy costs. Dyson, for example, manufactures its vacuum cleaners in Malaysia to take advantage of low wage costs.[28] Locating near customers can lower out-bound distributional costs, while locating near suppliers reduces in-bound distributional costs.

Institutional factors

These include government regulations, tariffs and local content rules. For example, regulations regarding the maximum size of lorries affect distribution costs.

Firms employing a cost leadership strategy will be vigilant in pruning costs. This analysis of cost drivers provides a framework for searching out new avenues for cost reduction. In European retailing, the entry of cost leaders in the form of no-frills, bulk purchase warehouse clubs is predicted to have a major impact on food and consumer durable purchasing. Furthermore, by converting their cost advantage (and lower margins) into low prices they are creating a differential advantage over their more expensive rivals.

Review

1 The determinants of industry attractiveness
- Industry attractiveness is determined by the degree of rivalry between competitors, the threat of new entrants, the bargaining power of suppliers and buyers, and the threat of substitute products.

2 How to analyse competitors
- Competitor analysis should identify competitors (product from competitors, product substitutes, generic competitors and potential new entrants); audit their capabilities; analyse their objectives, strategic thrust and strategies; and estimate competitor response patterns.

3 The difference between differentiation and cost leadership strategies
- Differentiation strategy involves the selection of one or more choice criteria used by buyers to select suppliers/brands and uniquely positioning the supplier/brand to meet those criteria better than the competition.
- Cost leadership involves the achievement of the lowest cost position in an industry.

4 The sources of competitive advantage
- Competitive advantage can be achieved by creating a differential advantage or achieving the lowest cost position.
- Its sources are superior skills, superior resources, and core competences. A useful method of locating superior skills and resources is value chain analysis.

5 The value chain
- The value chain categorizes the value-creating activities of a firm. The value chain divides these into primary and support activities. Primary activities are in-bound physical distribution, operations, out-bound physical distribution, marketing and service. Support ▶

activities are found within all of these primary activities, and consist of purchased inputs, technology, human resource management and the firm's infrastructure.
- By examining each value-creating activity, management can search for the skills and resources (and linkages) that may form the basis for low cost or differentiated positions.

6 How to create and maintain a differential advantage

- A differential advantage is created when the customer perceives that the firm is providing value above that of the competition.
- A differential advantage can be created using any element in the marketing mix: superior product, more effective distribution, better promotion and better value for money by lower prices. A differential advantage can also be created by developing fast reaction times to changes in marketing trends.
- A differential advantage can be maintained (sustained) through the use of patent protection, strong brand personality, close relationships with customers, high service levels based on well-trained staff, innovative product upgrading, the creation of high entry barriers (e.g. R&D or promotional expenditures), and strong and distinctive internal processes that deliver the earlier points and are difficult to copy.

7 How to create and maintain a cost leadership position

- Cost leadership can be created and maintained by managing cost drivers, which are economies of scale, learning effects, capacity utilization, linkages (e.g. improvements in quality assurance can reduce after-sales service costs), interrelationships (e.g. sharing costs), integration (e.g. owning the means of distribution), timing (both first movers and late entrants can have low costs), policy decisions (e.g. controlling labour costs), location, and institutional factors (e.g. government regulations).

Key terms

competitive advantage the attempt to achieve superior performance through differentiation to provide superior customer value or by managing to achieve lowest delivered cost

competitive scope the breadth of a company's competitive challenge, e.g. broad or narrow

competitor audit a precise analysis of competitor strengths and weaknesses, objectives and strategies

core competences the principal distinctive capabilities possessed by a company—what it is really good at

differential advantage a clear performance differential over the competition on factors that are important to target customers

differentiation strategy the selection of one or more customer choice criteria and positioning the offering accordingly to achieve superior customer value

entry barriers barriers that act to prevent new firms from entering a market, e.g. the high level of investment required

experience curve the combined effect of economies of scale and learning as cumulative output increases

industry a group of companies that market products that are close substitutes for each other

value chain the set of a firm's activities that are conducted to design, manufacture, market, distribute, and service its products

Internet exercise

The airline industry is in a state of turmoil for a number of reasons, such as the events of 11 September 2001, the success of low-cost airlines, increasing deregulation and many well-established airlines facing bankruptcy. In the UK, competition is getting fiercer. Budget airlines have exploded on to the scene offering flights for as little as £1.99 (€2.9) each way. Analyse the state of the airline industry.

Visit: www.britishairways.co.uk
www.ryanair.com
www.easyjet.com
www.flybmi.com
www.bmibaby.com

Questions

(a) Using the skills you have learnt in this chapter, conduct an external analysis of the airline industry, using Porter's 'five forces' model.
(b) BMI and BMIBABY are owned by the same company. Discuss the strategic implications associated with having two very different strategies.
(c) What are the dangers associated with having two different generic strategies for the airline?

Visit the Online Learning Centre at www.mcgraw-hill.co.uk/textbooks/jobber for more Internet exercises.

Study questions

1. Using Porter's 'five forces' framework, discuss why profitability in the European textile industry is lower than in book publishing.
2. For any product of your choice identify the competition using the four-layer approach discussed in this chapter.
3. Why is competitor analysis essential in today's turbulent environment? How far is it possible to predict competitor response to marketing actions?
4. Distinguish between differentiation and cost-leadership strategies. Is it possible to achieve both positions simultaneously?
5. Discuss, with examples, ways of achieving a differential advantage.
6. How can value chain analysis lead to superior corporate performance?
7. Using examples, discuss the impact of the advent of the single European market on competitive structure.
8. What are cost drivers? Should marketing management be concerned with them, or is their significance solely the prerogative of the accountant?

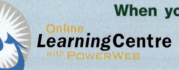

When you have read this chapter log on to the Online Learning Centre at www.mcgraw-hill.co.uk/textbooks/jobber to explore chapter-by-chapter test questions, links and further online study tools for marketing.

case thirty-five

Wal-Mart Grows Asda

The ASDA Wal-Mart store at Patchway, on the M5, near Bristol. The American retailer signalled the beginning of its assault on the British supermarket industry with the unveiling of its first UK supercentre. The store officially opened to the public in 2000.

In the spring of 1999, the shareholders of Kingfisher, the UK retail group, were smiling. They had just seen their share price rocket from around £5 (€7.2) to over £9 (€13) in less than a year with the news that Kingfisher was to take over Asda, the UK supermarket chain. Geoffrey Mulcahy, who headed Kingfisher, saw the move as another step towards his ambition of being a 'world-class retailer', where the efficiencies of buying merchandise in massive quantities, managing large stores, and achieving lower prices and higher sales turnover would reap further benefits for shareholders, employees and customers alike.

Mulcahy, the normally taciturn former Harvard MBA (he even calls his 40-foot boat *No Comment*), had turned around the ailing Woolworth's chain by selling off its city sites to release cash that could be used for investment. He discovered that Woolworth's owned a small do-it-yourself chain called B&Q. By building large retail 'sheds' backed up by service provided by ex-plumbers, electricians and the like, an advertising campaign based on the tag-line 'You can do it when you B&Q it!', and low prices, the chain became a success story of the 1990s, beating off me-too rivals such as Do It All, Sainsbury's Homebase and US invaders such as Texas. By adding the electrical goods retailer Comet and the health and beauty products chain Superdrug, Kingfisher was on the road to fulfilling Mulcahy's dream—taking over Asda was the next step. Sadly, his vision was to be shattered by Wal-Mart, the US predator that wanted to expand its European presence, which had already begun by the acquisition of the German warehouse chain Wertkauf.

Mulcahy was well aware that Wal-Mart was lurking in the wings, but all the talk was that the US retailer was cool about entering the UK market where retail competition was intense and planning restrictions made the likelihood of opening the kind of vast 'supercentres' it operates in the USA unlikely. All that changed one June Monday morning when he received a 7 am telephone call from Archie Norman, Asda's chief executive, to say that he had 'a bit of a problem'. The 'problem' was that Asda had agreed a deal with Wal-Mart.

Wal-Mart USA

Enter any Wal-Mart store in the USA and consumers are struck by the sheer scale of the operation. These are stores of over 200,000 square feet in which seven UK superstores could be accommodated. Next come the 'greeters', who welcome customers into the stores, give them their card in case they need help and put a smiley sticker on them. Then come the prices where, for example, a cotton T-shirt that would sell for the equivalent of around $15 (£9.40/€13.5) in a UK department store sells for $1 (£0.60/€0.90) in Wal-Mart. The choice of products is wide ranging, from clothes via groceries and pharmaceuticals to electrical goods. Stores are well organized with the right goods always available, kept neat and clean in appearance and with goods helpfully displayed.

At the heart of the Wal-Mart operation are its systems and information technology: 1000 information technologists run a 24-terabyte database; its information collection, which comprises up to 65 million transactions (by item, time, price and store), drives most aspects of its business. Within 90 minutes of an item being sold, Wal-Mart's distribution centres are organizing its replacement. Distribution is facilitated by state-of-the-art delivery tracking systems. So effective is the system that when a flu epidemic hit the USA, Wal-Mart followed its spread by monitoring flu remedy sales in its stores. It then predicted its movement from east to west so that Wal-Mart stores were adequately stocked in time for the rise in demand in their local areas.

Wal-Mart also uses real-time information systems to let consumers decide what appears in its stores. The Internet is used to inform suppliers what was sold the day before. In this way, it only buys what sells.

Its relationship with its suppliers is unusual in that they are only paid when an item is sold in its stores. Not only does this help cash flow, it also ensures that the interests of manufacturer and Wal-Mart coincide. Instead of the traditional system where once the retailer had purchased stock it was essentially the retailer's problem to sell it, if the product does not sell it hurts the manufacturer's cash flow more than Wal-Mart's. Consequently, at a stroke, the supplier's and retailer's interests are focused on the same measures and rewards. There is no incentive for the supplier to try to sell Wal-Mart its under-performing brands since they will suffer in the same way as the retailer if they fail to sell in the store.

Its success is reflected in its ability to outperform its rivals (sales are four times greater than its nearest competitor, KMart). Recent plans include returning to the high street with smaller stores to compete with so-called 'mom and pop' local grocers. It is not without its critics, though, who claim that Wal-Mart's success has driven high-street stores out of business, leaving derelict, boarded-up downtown streets. Christened 'Sprawl-Mart' by its critics, it has been accused of being anti-union, and for causing the demise of the aforementioned mom and pop stores.

Wal-Mart staff are called 'associates' and are encouraged to tell top management what they believe is wrong with their stores. They are offered share options and encouraged to put the customer first.

Wal-Mart's overseas operations

Since 1992 Wal-Mart has moved internationally and, with the exception of Germany, has trounced the competition. In Canada and Mexico it is already market leader in discount retailing. In Canada it bought Woolco in 1994, quickly added outlets, and by 1997 became market leader with 45 per cent of the discount store market—a remarkable achievement. In countries such as China and Argentina it has been surprisingly successful and, in 2002, achieved international sales of over $35 billion (£22 billion/€31.7 billion).

In 1998 it entered Europe with the buying of Germany's Wertkauf warehouse chain, quickly followed by the acquisition of 74 Interspar hypermarkets. It immediately closed stores, then reopened them with price cuts on 1100 items, making them 10 per cent below competitors' prices. The German eye for a bargain has meant that it has rapidly gained market share.

Wal-Mart's entry into the UK was the next step in its move into the European market. Asda was a natural target since it shared Wal-Mart's 'everyday low prices' culture. It was mainly a grocery supermarket but also sold clothing. Its information technology systems lagged badly behind those of its UK supermarket competitors, but it has acted as 'consumer champion' by selling cosmetics and over-the-counter pharmaceuticals for cheaper prices than those charged by traditional outlets. It has also bought branded products such as jeans from abroad to sell at low prices in its stores. Wal-Mart decided to keep the Asda store name rather than rebranding it as Wal-Mart. However, in 2002 the Wal-Mart name was incorporated on carrier bags, till receipts and lorries for the first time. The phrase 'part of the Wal-Mart Family' appeared under the Asda name, with 'Wal-Mart' in the strong blue colour associated with the supermarket's US owner. Asda also changed its tag-line, 'Permanently low prices', to Wal-Mart's 'Always low prices'. Although supermarket fascias continue to carry the Asda logo only, the largest store format was renamed Asda Wal-Mart Supercentre. (Most of Asda's stores are located in the north of the UK.)

The early signs are that the acquisition is a success with sales and profits rising. A major move was to create a speciality division that operates pharmacy, optical, jewellery, photography and shoe departments. The aim was to make store space work harder (i.e. improve sales revenue and profits per square metre). Asda has also benefited from the introduction of thousands of new non-food items across a wide range of home and leisure categories. Space has been made for these extra products in existing food-dominated supermarkets by decreasing the amount of facing devoted to food and reducing pack sizes.

The George line of clothing has been a huge success and was expanded to include a lower-priced version of the brand called Essentially George. In 2003, two stand-alone 10,000-square-foot clothing stores were opened, branded George, in Leeds and Croydon city centres. The stores carry the complete line of George-brand men's, women's and children's clothing at prices the same as those offered in the George departments in Asda supermarkets.

Besides expanding its product lines, Asda has also focused on cutting prices, aided by its inclusion in the Wal-Mart stable, which brings it enormous buying power. For example, since the take-over, it has made 60 per cent savings on fabrics and 15 per cent on buttons. This has meant price reductions on such clothing items as jeans, ladies tailored trousers, skirts, silk ties and baby pyjamas. In four years, the price of George jeans has fallen from £15 (€21.6) to £6 (€8.6).

Asda has also embarked on an ambitious expansion plan with the number of stores increasing from 229 to over 260. Also, floor space has been increased in many existing supermarkets with the addition of mezzanine floors to avoid increasingly restrictive planning laws. In 2003, Wal-Mart/Asda entered the battle to take over Safeway, which would, if successful, give it a much greater presence in the south of England.

Questions

1. What are Wal-Mart's sources of competitive advantage? How do these sources manifest themselves in creating competitive advantage for Wal-Mart customers?

2. Does Wal-Mart's acquisition of Asda make competitive sense?

3. What impact is Wal-Mart's entry into the UK likely to have on the retail sector and consumers?

This case was prepared by David Jobber, Professor of Marketing, University of Bradford, based on the following sources: Alexander, G. (1999) Wal-Mart Weighs Up Plan to Invade UK, *Sunday Times*, 7 February, 7; Bummer, A. (1999) Uncle Sam Invades, *Guardian*, G2, 15 June, 2–3; Farrelly, P. (1999) The Wonder of Woolies Takes on the World, *Observer*, 25 April, 7; Hamilton, K. (1999) Wal-Smart, *Sunday Times*, 20 June, 5; Laurance, B. (1999) How America Shoplifted Asda, *Observer*, 20 June, 5; Merrilees, B. and D. Miller (1999) Defensive Segmentation Against a Market Spoiler Rival, *Proceedings of the Academy of Marketing Conference*, Stirling, July, 1–10; Mitchell, A. (1999) Wal-Mart Arrival Heralds Change for UK Marketers, *Marketing Week*, 24 June, 42–3; Voyle, S. (2000) Wal-Mart Expands Asda in Drive for Market Share, *Financial Times*, 10 January, 21; Anonymous (2002) Asda Reaps Reward for International Division, *DSN Retailing Today*, 25 February, 1; Bowers, S. (2003) Hunter to Raise the Stakes, *Guardian*, 6 January, 17; Teather, D. (2003) Asda's £360m Plan Will Create 3,900 Jobs, *Guardian*, 19 February, 23; Troy, M. (2003) 'Buy' George! Wal-Mart's Asda Takes Fashion to UK's High Street, *DSN Retailing Today*, 23 June, 1.

case thirty-six

StoraEnso: Using an Ethics Code to Create a Competitive Advantage

Ethics scandals among businesses are reported on a weekly basis in newspapers, television or other media. Sometimes the scandals could have been avoided, other times not. Many firms nevertheless adopt ethics codes as a strategy in trying to avoid such scandals and bad publicity.

Different surveys report various results of how usual ethics codes are in business firms. According to a study in the United Kingdom[1] about half of the firms have written codes of practice. Another survey reports that 95 per cent of *Fortune* 500 companies have ethics codes.[2] However, the use of ethics codes differs among countries. The Americans seem to be the ones who use ethics codes the most, with almost every firm using one. In Europe, however, it is not as common to use ethics codes. In France, Germany and the UK, for instance, about half of firms have such codes.[3]

This case study gives an example of a firm that recently decided to adopt an ethics code. This was done partly because it was seen as a way to create a competitive advantage, partly as a way to ensure that the whole firm had a common frame of ethical conduct and partly as a way of marketing the firm to stakeholders.

StoraEnso: a Nordic firm on the global market

StoraEnso is one of the leading integrated forestry companies—one that has a worldwide approach to its business. It is the world's second largest producer of paper and board as of the first quarter of 2002, being only narrowly superseded by International Paper. Its total paper and board capacity is 15 million tonnes per year. UPM-Kymmene is its closest competitor, with roughly 12 million tonnes per year. The five core areas of production at StoraEnso are magazine paper, newsprint, fine paper, packaging boards and timber products.

The company is listed on the Helsinki, Stockholm and New York stock exchanges. A key organizational asset of the firm is its global marketing network, which has enabled StoraEnso to achieve annual sales of approximately €13.5 billion. The year 2000 brought a big leap forward in sales and profit, and the figures stabilized in 2001. Sales continue to grow in absolute terms, though the operating profit as a percentage of sales has diminished from 18 per cent to 11 per cent.

Leader of the StoraEnso Group in January 2002 was CEO Jukka Härmälä, with the position of deputy CEO being held by Björn Hägglund. The senior management team heads some 43,000 employees in over 40 countries, so the company is clearly a global corporation with worldwide influence. However, its main regions for activity are Finland, Sweden, Germany and North America. The company is owned largely by Finnish and Swedish institutions, together with private shareholders from both of these countries. Other groups not defined here hold a 36 per cent minority of shares. It is remarkable that these other shareholders only have voting power amounting to 13 per cent.[4]

StoraEnso aims to position itself as a local company, in parallel with its image as a global firm. Its customers are primarily publishers, printing houses and merchants on one hand, and packaging, joinery and construction industries on the other. Thus, StoraEnso works mainly in the business-to-business environment.

Ethical profiling as strategic planning

In 1999 the company took a first step towards ethical profiling of the group in launching the programme 'Mission, Vision and Values'. In a few brief lines, the strategy of StoraEnso was formulated in statements of its goal (mission), its aim (vision) and its priorities (values).[5] Through this programme the firm focused on its environmental and economical sustainability. However, in order to incorporate factors of social responsibility in its ethical profiling, StoraEnso worked out a more thorough set of principles to guide its actions and behaviour. This document—Principles for Corporate Social Responsibility—was officially embraced and adopted on 12 December 2001.

The background of the company's ethical document, or code, derives from the UN declaration of Human Rights, the UN Global Compact and the core International Labor Organization (ILO) conventions. However, the document was designed and formulated by the top management levels of StoraEnso itself. Referring to the adopted principles, CEO Jukka Härmälä said:

> Historically, many communities developed around sawmills or paper mills, and responsibility was typically a local concept, but today one must also consider responsibility at the global level. At a time of intensifying consolidation, responsibility in all operations is the way to prepare for a truly global presence ...[6]

StoraEnso has gained a good position in rankings of sustainability-related issues by external organizations. The company is included in the FTSE4Good global index series for socially responsible investors. The initiator behind this index series is FTSE—the leading expert in creating and managing equity indexes, which is jointly owned by the London Stock Exchange and the *Financial Times*. To be included in the index series, a company is evaluated in terms of its approach to environmental sustainability, its relationship with stakeholders and its support of human rights.[7] StoraEnso has also been included in the Dow Jones Sustainability Index since its establishment in 1999.[8]

Top-driven code

The initiation of the ethical principles programme has come from the very top tier of management—the director of corporate social responsibility is the officer that formulated the principles. As a result, the initiative can be said to be top-driven, aiming to affect the whole corporation in time. This is expected to take a few years.[9] In a letter to shareholders, CEO Jukka Härmälä and chairman Claes Dahlbäck wrote with reference to the adopted ethical code:

> In 2001 StoraEnso formulated its Principles for Corporate Social Responsibility. This marked an important milestone in our commitment to the value-creation process. In a time of intensified globalization, growth must go hand in hand with responsible business conduct. ... Expanding the business to countries outside the traditional home area is demanding in terms of integrating local and corporate cultures. We intend to be responsible wherever we operate.[10]

In looking more closely at this excerpt, it is first remarkable to see how the principles are addressed as being a value-creation process and not seen as a bottleneck making business activities unnecessarily complicated. The message is therefore that the adopted document is positively related to the process of adding value to the company. StoraEnso sees the ethics code as a source of competitive advantage. Second, the CEO and chairman say that growth *must go hand in hand* with responsible business conduct. The necessity of responsibility as a part of the company's growth is stated as non-negotiable. StoraEnso thereby defines itself as a mature corporation according to criteria established by research on moral maturity in business organizations.[11] After this bold and straight talk, at the end of the quotation humility can be discerned as the letter continues, 'We intend to be responsible wherever we operate.' In choosing this formulation, the managers indicate their awareness of the problems of cultural relativity and economic development, factors also addressed by stating their commitment to integrating local and corporate cultures. Cultural relativity and economic development are issues that make an ethnocentric definition of ethical principles complex, as the values can indeed vary from culture to culture and region to region.[12]

Principles for corporate social responsibility: a critical analysis

As indicated, the code follows principles stated by the United Nations and the International Labor Organization. The code is clearly intended for promoting long-term profitability and is seen as a way of adding and creating value. It addresses three purposes of sustainable development: (i) social, (ii) environmental, and (iii) economic. A significant feature of the statement is that StoraEnso makes it very clear that it expects the same level of commitment to ethical issues and business excellence from its stakeholders.[13] This expectation is not, however, systematically controlled as yet and it is reasonable to ask whether the firm's stakeholders know of this demanding expectation. One might get the impression that this wording sounds better than the situation it describes. As a result, the intention is possibly more impressive than the realization, as director of corporate social responsibility Mikael Hannus hints.[14]

The code consists of seven parts: business practice, communication, community involvement, reduction in workforce, human rights, integration of the principles and, finally, a section defining the firm's stakeholders. As for business practice and communication, equity among stakeholders and openness towards them is emphasized. Employees must avoid conflicts of a private nature in conducting business interests, and they are also encouraged to engage in local community activities.[15]

Consequently, it can be seen that in these statements StoraEnso also wishes to exert an influence on the private lives of its employees. At the same time, the firm shows that these private lives are important to the image of the firm as well, in that it draws no clear line between business and private life. Hence, one may perceive the corporation as an individual actor, with employees that make up the personality of the firm itself. As a result, the firm *is* what the stakeholders *are*. In a sense, StoraEnso has a soul, an image and a personality that is not based on business transactions and activities alone—but also takes its form from activities outside the business itself. This is quite remarkable and shows that the aims of the corporation really go beyond 'just' conducting business.

The section of the code that defines principles linked to human rights is influenced by the views of the United Nations. Only in a few paragraphs have specific lines of thought been put out as prohibitions. These address issues such as child labour, legal hours for working and the payment of wages.[16]

In the section covering the integration of the principles into the organization, StoraEnso gives itself a realistic time frame to implement the ideas expressed in the document in the corporation as a whole. The seriousness of embracing the principles is demonstrated in its didactic tone, commanding its stakeholders and employees to integrate these principles in their everyday activities. However, no threat is posed as a possible consequence of breaking the principles. According to Hannus, however, some stakeholders realize that they are not in a long-term relationship with StoraEnso unless they conform to the standard it sets.[17]

The last paragraph in this section is very interesting, stating that 'we respect cultural differences ... but we will not compromise on our Principles of Corporate Social Responsibility'.[18] Having adopted the ethical principles as non-negotiable makes the principles part of the core values of the corporation. Researchers define core values as explicitly non-negotiable.[19] But in addition to this, core values need to be values that already exist in an organization as the core functions around which the business activities are set. Thus, core values should not need to be enforced as they are already present within the working culture. First, the ethical principles are seen as non-negotiable, which makes them by definition core values.

Second, StoraEnso indicates that time will be given for spreading and implementing the principles throughout the organization. This indicates that the principles are not pre-existing but need to be implemented. The principles are then, by definition, peripheral values but not core values. However, peripheral values are seen as adjustable to local culture and custom, whereas core values are not. As a result, one gets the feeling that StoraEnso is in a way mixing up the ideas of core values with peripheral values and that its ethical principles are not yet the core values they are said to be. This may imply difficulties for the organization should a scandal or a negative incident occur that contradicts its ethical code. The code can become part of the core values but, to date, this researcher argues that it is not.[20]

Finally, in the principles of social responsibility, the key stakeholders are defined at the very end: customers, employers, investors, partners, the civil society and other societal and governmental bodies. Surprisingly even over-state institutions such as the United Nations are seen as stakeholders.[21]

Conclusion

A few trends show the growing seriousness of using codes of conduct in business firms. Globalization has pressured firms like StoraEnso to develop public statements of their core values and principles that are used in all locations. By publishing their principles in a global forum, the firms are, in a way, communicating with their stakeholders worldwide. The codes are also usually the result of top management initiatives and pro-action. Thus, the codes are part of top management strategy planning and implementation. Also, one can assume that the ethical consciousness of these managers has increased as result of the codification of ethical values in the business.[22] This is probably the situation with StoraEnso. All of the above-mentioned trends show how ethics codes have become, and still are becoming, of importance to international business firms.

As for this case study, one can in conclusion say that StoraEnso has made a big effort in bringing ethical issues to the forefront of the competition in its industry. The process of the code's implementation has not finished and one might consider it probable that some changes to the code may come into being as the process of implementation of its strategy evolves.

More information on the StoraEnso ethics code can be found at www.storaenso.com.

Chapter eighteen Analysing Competitors and Creating a Competitive Advantage

[1] Pearson, G. (1995) *Integrity in Organizations. An Alternative Business Ethic,* London: McGraw-Hill International.
[2] Steiner, G. A. and J. F. Steiner (1997) *Business, Government, and Society. A Managerial Perspective*, text and cases, Singapore: McGraw-Hill. See also Treviño, L. and K. Nelson (1999) *Managing Business Ethics. Straight Talk About How To Do It Right*, New York: John Wiley & Son, 216.
[3] Gasparski, W. W. (2000) *Codes of Ethics, Their Design, Introduction and Implementation: A Polish Case*, paper presented at the Second World Congress of Business, Economics and Ethics, 19–23 July 2000, São Paulo.
[4] *Global Local Responsible. Key Facts. Full Year 2001.* StoraEnso web publication at www.storaenso.com, consulted on 3 April 2002.
[5] StoraEnso (2001) Annual Report, 4.
[6] Press release, 12 December 2001 at 15:00 GMT.
[7] Press release, 11 July 2001 at 11:45 GMT.
[8] StoraEnso (2001), 8.
[9] Mikael Hannus, Director of Corporate Social Responsibility, in personal interview, 5 April 2002.
[10] StoraEnso (2001), 8.
[11] See e.g. Reidenbach, R. E. and D. Robin (1991) A Conceptual Model of Corporate Moral Development, *Journal of Business Ethics*, April.
[12] See e.g. Chonko, Lawrence B. (1995) *Ethical Decision-Making in Marketing*, New York: Sage Publications, 44; Laczniak, E. R. and P. E. Murphy (1993) *Ethical Marketing Decisions: The Higher Road*, Needham Heights: Allyn & Bacon, 211.
[13] StoraEnso Endorses Principles for Corporate Social Responsibility, press release, 12 December 2001, at www.storaenso.com, consulted on 3 April 2002.
[14] In interview on April 5, 2002.
[15] The StoraEnso Principles for Corporate Social Responsibility (2001), 2.
[16] The StoraEnso Principles for Corporate Social Responsibility (2001), 2–3.
[17] In interview on 5 April 2002.
[18] The StoraEnso Principles for Corporate Social Responsibility (2001), 3.
[19] Fuller, D. A. (1999) *Sustainable Marketing. Managerial–Ecological Issues*, Thousand Oaks, London, New Delhi: Sage Publications; also Laczniak and Murphy (1993) op. cit., 218.
[20] Director Hannus was also somewhat unclear on this point as to whether the code is representing the core values or not.
[21] The StoraEnso Principles for Corporate Social Responsibility (2001), 4.
[22] Berenbeim (2000) Global Ethics, *Executive Excellence* 17(5), 7ff.

StoraEnso Included in Index of Social Responsibility, press release, 11 July 2001, at www.storaenso.com, consulted on 3 April 2002.

Questions

(1) How would you assess StoraEnso's ethical code as a marketing planning function?

(2) What slogan was primarily used by StoraEnso to cover its business mission? What do you think of it?

(3) In what way does the ethics code help StoraEnso achieve a stronger position in the market? Use Porter's 'five forces' model, if you like.

(4) Do you think StoraEnso succeeds in making the ethics code part of its core strategy? Is the code a competitive advantage?

This case was prepared by Lise-Lotte Lindfelt MBA, Doctoral Researcher, Department of Business Administration, Åbo Akademi University, Finland.

Competitive marketing strategy

chapter nineteen

> **"**The easiest victories are in those places where there is no enemy.**"** ANONYMOUS ARMY GENERAL

Learning Objectives

This chapter explains:

1 The nature of competitive behaviour

2 How military analogies can be applied to competitive marketing strategy

3 The attractive conditions and strategic focus necessary to achieve the following objectives: build, hold, niche, harvest, divest

4 The nature of frontal, flanking, encirclement, bypass and guerrilla attacks

5 The nature of position, flanking, pre-emptive, counter-offensive and mobile defences, and strategic withdrawal

In many markets, competition is the driving force of change. Without competition companies satisfice: they provide satisfactory levels of service but fail to excel. Where there is a conflict between improving customer satisfaction and costs, the latter often take priority since customers have little choice and cost-cutting produces tangible results. Competition, then, is good for the customer as it means that companies have to try harder or lose their customer base. A case in point is the impact of Eurotunnel on cross-Channel ferry operators. As Barratt commented:[1]

> One thing is certain: Eurotunnel's plans have galvanized the ferry operators and the Dover Harbour Board into making long-overdue changes to their operating procedures. P&O European Ferries announced this month that from next spring [1993] it will operate a cross-Channel service every 45 minutes. Check-in time will also be cut from 30 minutes to 20 minutes.
>
> Dover Harbour Board has met the challenge by drastically streamlining the loading and unloading process. Last month, for the first time, I drove off the ferry at Dover and went straight out of the terminal without stopping—just the briefest pause to wave the passports at the immigration officer.

When developing marketing strategy, companies need to be aware of their own strengths and weaknesses, customer needs, and the competition. This three-pronged approach to strategy development has been termed the 'strategic triangle' and is shown in Fig. 19.1. This framework recognizes that to be successful it is no longer sufficient to be good at satisfying customers' needs: companies need to be better than the competition. In Chapter 18 we discussed various ways of creating and sustaining a competitive advantage. In this chapter we shall explore the development of marketing strategies in the face of competitive activity and challenges. First, we shall look at alternative modes of competitive behaviour and then, drawing on military analogy, examine when and how to achieve strategic marketing objectives.

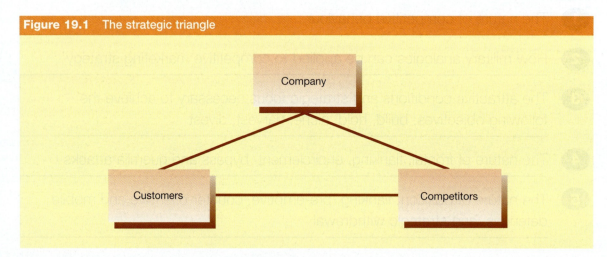

Figure 19.1 The strategic triangle

Competitive behaviour

Rivalry between firms does not always lead to conflict and aggressive marketing battles. Competitive behaviour can take five forms: conflict, competition, co-existence, co-operation and collusion.[2]

Conflict

Conflict is characterized by aggressive competition, where the objective is to drive competitors out of the marketplace. British Airways and TWA's successful battle with Laker is an example of competitive conflict where the financial muscle of the established airlines brought down their price-cutting competitor. More recently British Airways' unsuccessful attempt to discredit Virgin Atlantic with its so-called 'dirty tricks' campaign is another manifestation of conflict.

Competition

The objective of competition is not to eliminate competitors from the marketplace but to perform better than them. This may take the form of trying to achieve faster sales and/or profit growth, larger size or higher market share. Competitive behaviour recognizes the limits of aggression. Competitor reaction will be an important consideration when setting strategy. Players will avoid spoiling the underlying industry structure, which is an important influence on overall profitability. For example, price wars will be avoided if competitors believe that their long-term effect will be to reduce industry profitability.

Co-existence

Three types of co-existence can occur. First, co-existence may arise because firms do not recognize their competitors owing to difficulties in defining market boundaries. For example, a manufacturer of fountain pens may ignore competition from jewellery companies since its definition may be product-based rather than market-centred (i.e. the gift market). Second, firms may not recognize other companies they believe are operating in a separate market segment. For example, Waterman is likely to ignore the actions of Bic pens as they are operating in different market segments. Third, firms may choose to acknowledge the territories of their competitors (for example, geography, brand personality, market segment or product technology) in order to avoid harmful head-to-head competition.

Co-operation

This involves the pooling of the skills and resources of two or more firms to overcome problems and take advantage of new opportunities. A growing trend is towards **strategic alliances** where firms join together through a joint venture, licensing agreement, or joint research and development contract to build a long-term competitive advantage. In today's global marketplace, where size is a key source of advantage, co-operation is a major type of competitive behaviour.

Collusion

The final form of competitive behaviour is collusion, whereby firms come to some arrangement that inhibits competition in a market. For example, vitamin manufacturers from France, Germany, Japan and Switzerland, including Aventis, BASF and Roche, were found guilty of collusion in the areas of price fixing and setting sales quotas by the European Commission.[3] Collusion is more likely where there are a small number of suppliers in each national market, the price of the product is a small proportion of buyer costs, where cross-national trade is restricted by tariff barriers or prohibitive transportation costs, and where buyers are able to pass on high prices to their customers.

Developing competitive marketing strategies

The work of such writers as Ries and Trout, and Kotler and Singh has drawn attention to the relationship between military and marketing 'warfare'.[4,5] Their work has stressed the need to develop strategies that are more than customer based. They placed the emphasis on attacking and defending against the competition, and used military analogies to guide strategic thinking. They saw competition as the enemy and thus recognized the relevance of the principles of military warfare as put forward by such writers as Sun Tzu and von Clausewitz to business.[6,7] As von Clausewitz wrote:

> ❝Military warfare is a clash between major interests that is resolved by bloodshed—that is the only way in which it differs from other conflicts. Rather than comparing it to an art we could more accurately compare it to commerce, which is also a conflict of human interests and activities.❞

Indeed, military terms have been used in business and marketing for many years. Terms such as *launching a campaign, achieving a breakthrough, company division* and *strategic business unit* are common in business language. Frequently, sales and service personnel are referred to as *field forces*.[8]

The context in which we shall explore the development of competitive marketing strategy is the achievement of *strategic marketing objectives*. Four of these objectives have already been discussed (to *build, hold, harvest* and *divest*), to which a fifth objective—to *niche*—may be added. The discussion of each objective will focus on the *attractive conditions* that favour its adoption, and the **strategic focus**, which comprises the strategies that can be employed to achieve the objective.*

Build objectives

Attractive conditions

A *build objective* is suitable in *growth markets*. Because overall market sales are growing, all players can achieve higher sales even if the market share of one competitor is falling. This is in marked contrast to mature (no growth) markets where an increase in the sales of one player has to be at the expense of the competition (zero sum game).

Some writers point out that if competitors' expectations are high in a growth market (for example, because they know that the market is growing) they may retaliate if those expectations are not met.[9] While this is true, their reaction is not likely to be as strong or protracted as in a no-growth situation. For example, if expectations have led to an expansion of plant capacity that is not fully utilized because of competitor activity, the situation is not as serious as when over-capacity exists in a no-growth market. In the former case, market growth will help fill capacity without recourse to aggressive retaliatory action, whereas, in the latter, capacity utilization will improve only at the expense of the competition.

A build objective also makes sense in growth markets because new users are being attracted to the product. Since these new users do not have established brand or supplier loyalty it is logical to invest resources into attracting them to our product offering. Provided the

---

* The format of this part of Chapter 19 is similar to that of 'Offensive and Defensive Marketing Strategies' in *Competitive Positioning* by John Saunders and Graham Hooley (London: Prentice-Hall). This is because the approach was developed by the author of the current text and Graham Hooley when they worked together at the University of Bradford School of Management.

product meets their expectations, trial during the growth phase can lead to the building of goodwill and loyalty as the market matures. One company that has pursued a build objective in growth markets is Cisco Systems, as e-Marketing 19.1 explains.

19.1 e-marketing

Building in Growth Markets: the Case of Cisco

A company that successfully pursued a build objective in a growth market was Cisco Systems. For 15 years the firm doubled its size every year on the back of the Internet boom, resulting in a company that, by 2000, had 29,000 employees, revenue of $12 billion (£7.5 billion/€10.7 billion) and profits of $3 billion (£1.9 billion/€2.7 billion) a year.

Cisco makes vital equipment for global communications. The backbone of its product line are 'routers', which are high-powered computers that direct traffic around the Internet and corporate intranets. On them, data such as e-mail or web pages are sent around in small packages with an 'address label'. Routers inspect the label and work out the best path for a package to take, and pass it to the next router. Cisco's expertise in this market is such that it supplies 80 per cent of Internet routers.

Cisco also built sales and profits through diversification and acquisition. This has led to moves into other networking hardware, such as premium-priced switches for telephone networks. Cisco's customers not only include large multinationals but also telephone network operators such as Telia in Sweden.

As with most markets, the growth years have been followed by a slowdown. While growth has stagnated in the early years of the new millennium, Cisco is still a powerful cash generator, with a cash pile topped only by Microsoft. Its cash reserves of $21 billion (£13.2 billion/€18.7 billion) has been made possible by gross profit margins of 68 per cent—a figure that makes the mouths of other technology companies water.

In classic portfolio-planning style, Cisco is using its healthy cash flow and reserves to finance a move into new markets that may help it replace some of the growth it can no longer count on from its core products. This has produced a stream of promising products, including storage and security systems, and technology to transmit voice calls over IP networks.

Based on: Anonymous (2000);[10] Taylor (2000);[11] Morrison and Waters (2002)[12]

A build objective is also attractive in mature (no growth) markets where there are *exploitable competitive weaknesses*. For example, Japanese car producers exploited US and European car manufacturers' weaknesses in reliability and build quality; Travelworld, a UK travel agency, exploited its competitors' weakness in providing customer service to would-be holidaymakers; Rowntree Macintosh exploited a weakness in Cadbury's Dairy Milk chocolate bar that had been reduced in thickness to maintain its price as the cost of sugar rose. Group discussion research discovered that chocolate bar buyers were dissatisfied with the new 'thinness' of the Cadbury product. Rowntree Macintosh responded with the successful launch of Yorkie, a thicker product positioned on a 'chunkiness' platform. Exploitable competitive weaknesses allow the creation of a differential advantage.

A third attractive condition for building sales and market share is when the company has *exploitable corporate strengths*. For example, Casio built on its core competence in microelectronics to move from calculators to watches. Marks & Spencer exploited its strength as a reliable, trustworthy retailer to launch a low-risk, medium-return range of unit trusts. As one financial analyst commented, 'M&S unit trusts will never be in the top ten, but they will never be in the bottom ten either!'

When taking on a market leader, an attractive, indeed a necessary, condition is *adequate corporate resources*. The financial muscle that usually accompanies market leadership and the importance of the situation mean that forceful retaliation can be expected. We have already given the example of Laker failing to have the financial capability to win a price war against British Airways and TWA.

Finally, a build objective is attractive when *experience curve effects* are believed to be strong. Some experience curve effects (the combined impact on costs of economies of scale and learning) are related to cumulative output: by building sales faster than the competition, a company can achieve the position of cost leader as United Biscuits has done in the UK.

Strategic focus

A build objective can be achieved in four ways: through market expansion, winning market share from the competition, by merger or acquisition, and by forming strategic alliances.

Market expansion

This is brought about by creating new users or uses, or by increasing frequency of purchase. *New users* may be found by expanding internationally, as Tesco has done, or by moving to larger target markets, as with Lucozade, which was initially targeted at ill children but now has mass-market appeal. *New uses* can be promoted, as when Johnson's Baby Lotion was found to be used by women as a facial cleanser. The technique of brand extension can be used in new use situations. The umbrella based Flash has been extended from a bath cleaner to floors and cookers in this way. *Increasing frequency of use* may rely on persuasive communications—for example, by persuading people to clean their teeth twice a day rather than only once. Kellogg's attempted to increase the frequency of consumption of its Corn Flakes brand by suggesting that it can be eaten as a snack during the day and at night rather than solely at breakfast time, a move that ran the risk of blurring its distinct brand image.

Winning market share

If a market cannot be expanded, a build strategy implies gaining marketing success at the expense of the competition. In these circumstances the principles of offensive warfare sometimes apply. These are to consider the strength of the leader's position, to find a weakness in the leader's strength and attack at that point. A classic example of these principles being applied in a political context was the 1988 US presidential election. In July 1988 the challenger Michael Dukakis was 17 percentage points ahead of George Bush Snr in the opinion polls. By October 1988 when the election was held, Bush won by 17 percentage points. How did Bush do it? The answer was that Bush identified a weakness in Dukakis's position and attacked remorselessly at that point:

> ❝The post-mortem has already begun. The consensus is that Dukakis allowed Bush to 'define' him, to paint him as a dangerous un-American left-winger before he could present himself to the voters on his own terms.[13]❞

Clearly in politics the concepts of positioning and competitive strategy apply just as forcefully as in product marketing.

In business, companies seek to win market share through product, distribution, promotional innovation and penetration pricing. Kotler and Singh have identified five competitor confrontation strategies (see Fig. 19.2) designed to win sales and market share.[14]

Frontal attack involves the challenger taking on the defender head on. If the defender is a market leader, the success of a head-on challenge is likely to depend on four factors.[15] First, the

Figure 19.2 Attack strategies

Source: Kotler, P. and R. Singh (1981) Marketing Warfare in the 1980s, *Journal of Business Strategy*, Winter, 30–41. Reprinted with permission of Faulkner and Gray.

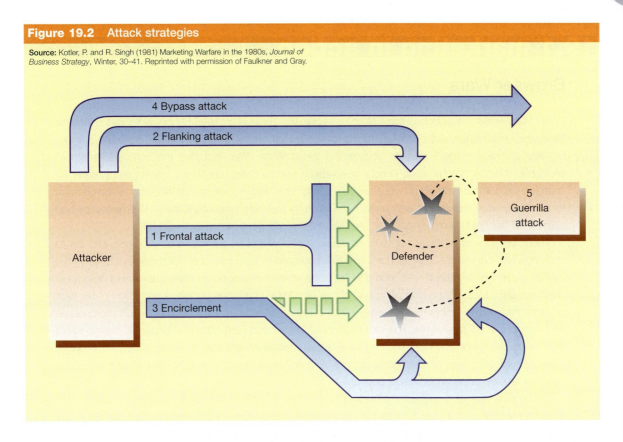

challenger should have a clear and sustainable *competitive advantage*. If the advantage is based on cost leadership this will support a low price strategy to fight the market leader. A distinct differential advantage provides the basis for superior customer value. Sustainability is necessary to delay the leader's capability to respond.

Second, the challenger should achieve proximity *in other activities*. In the earth-moving market, John Deere took on Caterpillar with a machine that gave buyers productivity gains; it failed, however, due to its inability to match Caterpillar in after-sales service.

Third, success is more likely if there is some *restriction on the leader's ability to retaliate*. Restrictions include patent protection, pride, technological lead times and the costs of retaliation. Where a differential advantage or cost leadership position is supported by *patent protection*, imitation by the market leader will be very difficult. *Pride* may hamper retaliation; the market leader refused to imitate because to do so would admit that the challenger had outsmarted the leader. Where the challenge is based on a technological innovation it may take the leader *time to put in place the new technology*. John Deere's challenge to Caterpillar was based on a hydrostatic drive that would take Caterpillar two to three years to install in its own machines. Furthermore, retaliation may be difficult for the market leader because of the *costs* involved. Earlier in the book, we discussed the difficulty of a car number plate market leader offering the discounts given by a regional competitor as, to do so, would mean giving discounts nationally. The risk of damaging brand image and lowering profit margins may also deter market leaders from responding to price challenges.

Finally, the challenger needs *adequate resources* to withstand the battle that will take place should the leader retaliate. After studying 30 such battles, General von Clausewitz observed that only two had been won by a side with inferior manpower. Napoleon supported the principle of superior force when he said, 'God is on the side of the big battalions.'[16]

19.1 marketing in action

Browser Wars

When Marc Anderson launched the first commercial web browser in 1995 his newly floated company, Netscape, was valued at $2.7 billion. Its value was based on the potential that its pioneer Navigator browser software made it easy to access the World Wide Web. Not that the software itself was profitable; it could not be since it was given away free to computer users. Profits were made by charging the companies that run websites for its Netscape 'server' software. (The server is the platform for providing online services to web users.) The strategy was so successful that by 1996 Netscape had claimed 85 per cent market share, and the value of the company had risen to $6 billion.

The future looked anything but rosy, however. A strong rival by the name of Microsoft was set to challenge Netscape's dominance. The company marketed its own package but this was inferior to the market leader and Microsoft was regarded as being at least a year behind Netscape's technology. To catch up, Bill Gates, the boss at Microsoft, threw hundreds of millions of dollars and 2000 of his best programmers at the problem. The result was the launch of Internet Explorer 3.0, which matched its rival's performance. Meanwhile, financial economics meant that Netscape had begun to charge users $49 for its Navigator software. Microsoft's financial muscle meant that it would supply its browser software free of charge and its domination of PC software meant that Internet Explorer would be supplied as part of the Windows 95 package to 46 million users in 1997.

By the time Internet Explorer 4.0 (IE4) was launched in late 1997, Microsoft held 36 per cent market share in the USA and 47 per cent of the UK browser market. One of the main features of IE4 is the introduction of 'push technology', which enables users to receive several streams of automatically updated information on their screens. This has major appeal to media owners such a Pearson (which owns the *Financial Times*) since it means that live news can flow on to users' screens automatically, rather than having websites that have to be visited.

A major twist in the 'browser wars' story took place when Microsoft faced an anti-trust lawsuit brought by the US government. Microsoft was accused of exploiting its monopoly power in order to reduce competition. Part of the action threatened the practice of integrating its Internet Explorer software with its Windows operating system, which resulted in the shutting out of its main competitors. However, the US Department of Justice abandoned its claim that this was illegal and the latest version continues to be bundled with Windows XP.

Today, Microsoft's Internet Explorer holds over 65 per cent of the browser market and Netscape, unable to survive alone, has been sold to America Online (AOL). Microsoft's superior resources and market power had proved too much for the market pioneer.

Based on: Barksdale (1996);[17] Garrett (1997);[18] Alexander (1999);[19] Alexander (1999);[20] Marsh(1998);[21] Anonymous (2000);[22] Anonymous (2001);[23] Spiegel and Abrahams (2001)[24]

In emerging markets, the resources of early challengers can play a vital role in attacking the market pioneer. Marketing in Action 19.1 discusses how Microsoft attacked Netscape in the early market development of the Internet web browser market.

An example of a challenge to a market leader that succeeded because most of these conditions were met was IBM's attack on Apple, the market leader in the personal computer market.[25] Initially slow into the segment, IBM developed a computer that possessed a competitive advantage over Apple based on a 16-bit processor that was faster and more powerful than Apple's 8-bit machine. IBM also persuaded software houses to develop a wide range of software that would run only on its machines. Buyers would therefore have a wider choice of software from which to choose if they bought an IBM rather than an Apple computer (a major differential advantage). IBM also managed to achieve proximity to Apple in other activities, particularly in terms of reliability and after-sales service.

Apple refused to follow IBM's route regarding software, preferring to remain distinctive (perhaps pride was a factor here). Instead it retaliated by launching the Macintosh based on an *ease of use* differential advantage. IBM, therefore, still held the software edge.

IBM's massive resources, based on its mainframe computer cash cows, enabled it to launch a powerful promotional campaign aimed at the business market. IBM's ability to create a differential advantage, its ability, initially, to match Apple on other activities, Apple's inability to generate as wide a range of software as IBM, and IBM's superior resources made up the platform that led to IBM overtaking Apple as market leader. However, IBM's inability to sustain its differential advantage with software as IBM clones entered the market with cheaper prices has been a major factor in its recent downturn in sales and profits.[26]

As Table 19.1 illustrates, many markets are characterized by head-to-head competition between the major protagonists. It is not only companies that compete head to head: countries do so too. For example, Malaysia and Singapore are rivals since both countries want to be the region's financial centre, both want to be its air and sea transport hub, and each is competing to attract direct investment from leaders in information technology.[27]

Table 19.1 Major marketing head to heads

Companies	Competitive area
Nike vs Reebok	Footwear
Sega vs Sony	Computer games
Ever Ready vs Duracell	Batteries
Coca-Cola vs Pepsi	Soft drinks
McDonald's vs Burger King	Fast-food restaurants
GEC-Alsthom vs Asea Brown Boveri	Power engineering
Unilever vs Procter & Gamble	Fast-moving consumer goods
Unilever vs Mars	Ice cream
Motorola vs Nokia	Mobile telephones
IBM vs Fujitsu	Computers
Microsoft vs Netscape	Internet web browsers

A **flanking attack** involves attacking unguarded or weakly guarded ground. In marketing terms it means attacking geographical areas or market segments where the defender is poorly represented. For example, in the USA as major supermarket chains moved out of town, the 7-11 chain prospered by opening stores that provided the convenience of local availability and longer opening hours.

The attack by Japanese companies on the European and US car markets was a flanking attack—on the small car segment—from which they have expanded into other segments including sports cars. The success of Next, the retail clothing chain, was based on spotting an underserved, emerging market segment: working women aged 25–40 who were finding it difficult to buy stylish clothes at reasonable prices.

Another example of a flanking attack was when Mars attacked Unilever's Walls ice cream subsidiary in Europe by launching a range of premium brands such as its ice cream Mars bar and a series of ice cream versions of its chocolate brands, such as Snickers, Galaxy and Bounty. This flanking attack was regarded by Unilever as a major threat to its ice cream business. Its response was to launch a range of premium brands, including Magnum and Gino Ginelli, and to defend vigorously its *shop exclusivity deals*, which prevent competitors from selling its products in shops that sell Walls ice cream, and *freezer exclusivity*, which prohibits competitors from placing their ice cream in Unilever-supplied freezer cabinets.

The advantage of a flanking attack is that it does not provoke the same kind of response as a head-on confrontation. Since the defender is not challenged in its main market segments, there is more chance that it will ignore the challenger's initial successes. If the defender dallies too long, the flank segment can be used as a beachhead from which to attack the defender in its major markets, as Japanese companies have repeatedly done.

An encirclement attack involves attacking the defender from all sides. Every market segment is hit with every combination of product features to completely encircle the defender. An example is Seiko, which produces over 2000 different watch designs for the worldwide market. These cover everything the customer might want in terms of fashion and features. One of its watches, which targets young men, is illustrated below. A variant on the encirclement-attack approach is to cut off supplies to the defender. This could be achieved by the acquisition of major supply companies.

A bypass attack circumvents the defender's position, as the German army did in 1940 when it bypassed the Maginot Line, built by the French to protect themselves from invasion.

In business, a bypass attack changes the rules of the game, usually through technological leap-frogging as Casio did when bypassing Swiss analogue watches with digital technology. A bypass attack can also be accomplished through diversification. An attacker can bypass a defender by seeking growth in new markets with new products, as Marks & Spencer has done with its move into financial services.

A guerrilla attack hurts the defender with pin-pricks rather than blows. Just as the French Resistance used guerrilla tactics against the German forces in the Second World War, not to defeat the enemy but to weaken it, so in business the underdog can make life uncomfortable for its stronger rivals. Unpredictable price discounts, sales promotions or heavy advertising in a few television regions are some of the tactics attackers can use to cause problems for defenders.

Guerrilla tactics may be the only feasible option for a small company facing a larger competitor. Such tactics allow the small company to make its presence felt without the dangers

Seiko produces hundreds of different watches to cater for diverse customer tastes; here, a technologically advanced watch—the Seiko Perpetual Calendar—has been designed to appeal to young men.

of a full-frontal attack. By being unpredictable, guerrilla activity is difficult to defend against. Nevertheless, such tactics run the risk of incurring the wrath of the defender, who may choose to retaliate with a full-frontal attack if sufficiently provoked.

The role of guerrilla marketing in enabling small companies to compete again larger rivals through the use of the Internet is discussed in e-Marketing 19.2.

19.2 e-marketing

Guerrilla Marketing: an Online Concept

The marketing techniques that allow small companies to compete effectively against their much larger competitors can collectively be termed *guerrilla* marketing techniques. The metaphor derives from guerrilla warfare, where large armies are often defeated by their smaller adversaries, through their expert knowledge of the terrain and through developing strategies that play to their advantages of speed and flexibility over size and might.

In an online context, *guerrilla* marketing encompasses marketing techniques such as e-mail and viral marketing, discussion forums and newsgroups, search engine optimization and website linking. (All of these techniques have been described in more detail in previous e-marketing vignettes.) The techniques described do not involve a large financial investment but they do involve knowledge of the subject area and the desire to change. Companies like Buccleuch Scotch Beef in search engine optimization and 5pm.co.uk in e-mail and viral marketing are examples of *guerrilla* marketers: they are punching above their weight through use of their online marketing techniques.

There is also the case of Talking Newspapers (www.tnuk.co.uk), an online service providing audio versions of selected newspapers and magazines to the visually impaired. This service competes with much larger charitable organizations for the online user. However, through website linking it is now driving serious traffic to its site. The owner of Talking Newspapers spends an hour or two every week surfing the web to find sites to link to. There are now over 250 sites where he has a presence, including the *Radio Times* section of the BBC's website. Can you think of any *guerrilla* marketers?

Merger or acquisition

A third approach to achieving a build objective is to merge with or acquire competitors. By joining forces, costly marketing battles are avoided, and purchasing, production, financial, marketing and R&D synergies may be gained. Further, a merger can give the scale of operation that may be required to operate as an international force in the marketplace. Mergers are not without their risks, though, not least when they involve parties from different countries. Differences in culture, language, business practices, and the problems associated with restructuring may cause terminal strains. For example, the problems faced by AOL and Time Warner following their merger are partly attributable to the culture strains of welding a nifty e-culture to a sedate media business.[28] Two European examples of merger failure are Dunlop and Pirelli (rubber) and Hoechst and Hoogovens (steel). Indeed, a study by McKinsey & Co. management consultants into the success or failure of 319 mergers and acquisitions claimed that about half had been successful in terms of post-acquisition return on equity and assets, and whether or not they exceeded the acquirer's cost of capital.[29]

In marketing terms, mergers and acquisitions give an immediate sales boost and, when the players operate in the same market, an increase in market share. However, companies considering merger have to be very careful that the benefits exceed the costs, as Marketing in Action 19.2 illustrates.

19.2 marketing in action

Counting the Cost of Mergers and Acquisitions

Mergers and acquisitions remain a popular tool for growing businesses. Lured by the potential benefits of complementary businesses that allow the merger partners to increase sales revenues, and the cost savings that can be made, a large number of companies are following this route to strategic development, including:

- Ford—Volvo
- Vodafone Airtouch—Mannesmann
- Renault—Nissan
- Glaxo Wellcome—SmithKline Beecham
- Wal-Mart—Asda
- America On Line—Time Warner
- Carrefour—Promodès
- Hewlett Packard—Compaq.

But studies have shown that 65 per cent of mergers fail to benefit shareholders. There are several reasons for this. One is poor implementation. A key issue is the blending of two different corporate cultures. It is not so much a problem of open warfare but a situation where the cultures of the two partners do not meld quickly enough to take advantage of new opportunities; meanwhile the marketplace has moved on. A second issue is that, often, too little time is spent before a merger thinking about whether the two organizations really are compatible and what the possible negative consequences might be. A classic case is PepsiCo's acquisition of major fast-food operators KFC, Pizza Hut and Taco Bell.

The marriage of a soft drinks manufacturer and fast-food companies seemed highly sensible. The offers were complementary: cola and fast food is like bees and honey. Pepsi was guaranteed distribution in a high-growth market in a way that automatically excluded Coca-Cola from key outlets. There were also numerous opportunities for joint promotional initiatives. What was underestimated were the problems. Becoming partners with KFC meant that rival fast-food outlets, such as McDonald's, rejected Pepsi in favour of Coca-Cola. So what appeared to be a route to expansion actually tethered Pepsi, leaving Coke a free rein.

The Pepsi link also constrained its fast-food outlets, particularly in countries where Pepsi was a poor also-ran to Coca-Cola. In these markets, their fast-food outlets wanted to give the customers what they wanted (Coca-Cola) but could not do so because of their ownership. The result was conflict rather than synergy.

A third issue with mergers is deciding who is in charge. Mergers of equals can be dangerous because it is not always clear who is the boss. This can lead to indecision while more nimble competitors move ahead.

A fourth problem is staff related. Top managers and salespeople become recruitment targets for competitors and redundancies damage morale.

Two key questions that companies need to ask themselves are: (i) 'What advantages will the merger or acquisition bring that competitors will find difficult to match?' and (ii) 'Would the premium that is usually paid to the shareholders of the acquired company be better spent elsewhere—for example, on improved customer service?'

Based on: Mitchell (2000);[30] Shapinker (2000);[31] London (2002)[32]

Forming strategic alliances

A final option for companies seeking to build is the strategic alliance. The aim is to create a long-term competitive advantage for the partners, often on a global scale. The partners typically collaborate by means of a joint venture (a jointly owned company), licensing agreements, long-term purchasing and supply arrangements, or joint R&D programmes. Strategic alliances maintain a degree of flexibility not apparent with a merger or acquisition.

A major motivation for strategic alliances is the sharing of product development costs and risks. For example, the cost of developing and creating manufacturing facilities for a new car targeted at world markets exceeds £2 billion (€2.9 billion), and developing a new drug can cost over £25 million (€36 million). Sharing these costs may be the only serviceable economic option for a medium-sized manufacturer in either of these industries.

Marketing benefits can accrue too. For example, access to new markets and distribution channels can be achieved, time to market reduced, product gaps filled and product lines widened.[33] It was to take advantage of marketing opportunities in financial services that Tesco partnered a bank. Furthermore, a strategic alliance can be the initial stage to a merger or acquisition, allowing each party to assess their abilities to work together effectively. Marketing in Action 19.3 describes how three strategic alliances have been used successfully to build sales, market share and profits.

A third reason for alliances is because mergers and acquisitions are sometimes not possible because of legal restrictions or national sensitivities. Many airline alliances, such as the multi-airline Star Alliance, led by United Airlines of the USA and Lufthansa of Germany, are formed for this reason.[38]

Table 19.2 Some key European and US strategic alliances

Companies	Competitive area
Electrolux—AEG	Household appliances
Maersk—P&O	Shipping services to the Middle East
Rolls-Royce—Pratt & Whitney	Aero-engines
GEC—Alsthom	Power engineering
Hoechst—Mitsubishi	Disperse dyes
Lufthansa—United Airlines	Air travel
Nestlé—Baxter Healthcare	Clinical nutrition
Nestlé—General Mills	Ready-to-eat breakfast cereals
Nestlé—Coca-Cola	Ready-to-drink tea and coffee
Unilever—PepsiCo	Develop and distribute tea-based products in the USA
Unilever—BSN	Develop and market products combining ice cream and yoghurt
Glaxo—Roche	Pharmaceuticals
Ford—GM	Cars
Seagram—Bertelsmann	Sell discs online
Microsoft—BT	Internet and corporate data communications services
Psion—Ericsson—Nokia—Motorola	Computer and telecommunications products
Pilkington—Saint Gobain	Glass

19.3 marketing in action

Building through Strategic Alliances

Europe has encountered a wave of strategic alliances, creating a borderless world where firms adapt to a changing environment by constantly changing shape. Instead of going it alone, they form partnerships with their rivals for mutual benefit. Nowhere was the joining of arch-rivals for dual gain more striking than the alliance between Glaxo, the UK pharmaceutical company, and Hoffman-La Roche of Switzerland to market Zantac, a drug for treating stomach ulcers. Rather than building a large sales and distribution network to cover all US hospitals, Glaxo gave Hoffman-La Roche the rights to all US sales through its established distribution network. Similar deals were struck with Sankyo (Japan), Merck (Germany) and Fournier (France). The result was that Zantac became the most successful pharmaceutical product of all time.

A second spectacular success for the strategic alliance was JVC's attempt to establish VHS as the global standard for video recording. Faced with a powerful rival—Sony's Betamax format which possessed superior picture quality—JVC formed a myriad of alliances with consumer electronics firms around the world. VHS was licensed to Japanese video recorder manufacturers, joint ventures were formed with Thorn-EMI-Ferguson (UK) and Telefunken (Germany), and JVC supplied RCA-branded video recorders to the US market.

A third success story was the alliance between German, French, UK, Belgian and Spanish aircraft manufacturers to compete with the US market leaders Boeing and McDonnell Douglas for civil transportation aircraft. The objectives of the European alliance were to gain the development and production expertise for civil aircraft for the twenty-first century, and to share the enormous R&D costs of a new aircraft. The result was that Airbus Industrie developed and built a full range of civil aircraft, pushing McDonnell Douglas into third place in the industry.

These three examples show how the strategic alliance can be used to build sales, market share and profits. This is not to say that it is a panacea for growth. Cultural problems and differing managerial styles can cause the demise of an alliance. For example, the ill-fated alliance between the Metal Box Company (UK) and Carnaud (France) in packaging was plagued with these kinds of problems. Eurotunnel, too, suffered from the differences between the British and French way of doing business. For example, while British managers attended meetings to make decisions, the French went to find out what the boss had decided to do.

Nevertheless, the advantages of strategic alliances as a basis for growth are leading to a flurry of activity within the mobile computing sector. The big prize is leadership in the market for Internet access through mobile phones. These devices enable users to retrieve and answer their e-mail, surf the net or buy goods and services anywhere rather than being limited to PC access. This requires the combining of handheld cellular and Internet technologies, leading to an alliance between Microsoft and BT, the formation of the Symbian alliance between Psion, the UK computer company, and Ericsson, Nokia and Motorola, the world's top-three mobile phone manufacturers, and an alliance between Siemens and Yahoo!.

A trend in high-technology markets is for large businesses to form alliances with smaller innovative companies. For example, Intel, the microchip manufacturer, has long experience of forming alliances with smaller firms. One benefit is to help its understanding of specific emerging technologies concerning microchip production. Other industrial giants that do likewise are DuPont (chemicals), Nokia (mobile phones), General Electric (diverse range of areas, including software and fuel cells) and Rolls-Royce (aero-engines).

Based on: Ohmae (1989);[34] Alexander (1999);[35] Cane (2000);[36] Marsh (2003)[37]

Table 19.3 Build objectives
Attractive conditions
Growth markets
Exploitable competitive weaknesses
Exploitable corporate strengths
Adequate corporate resources
Strategic focus
Market expansion
● new users
● new uses
● increasing frequency of use
Winning market share
● product innovation
● distribution innovation
● promotional innovation
● penetration pricing
● competitor confrontation
Merger or acquisition
Forming strategic alliances

A key factor in benefiting from strategic alliances is the desire and ability to learn from the alliance partner. Japanese companies have excelled at this, while European and US companies have traditionally lagged. The risk is that the alliance leaks technological and core capabilities to the partner, thereby giving away important competitive information. This one-way transfer of skills should be avoided by building barriers to capability seepage: core competences should be protected at all costs. This is easier when a company has few alliances, when only a limited part of the organization is involved, and when the relationships built up in the alliance are stable.[39]

The number of strategic alliances in Europe has grown since 1984, particularly in the electronics, car, aerospace and food industries.[40] For example, Philips has formed alliances with SGS Thomson (semiconductors), Grundig (video equipment, cordless telephones), Motorola (semiconductors), Kodak (photo-CDs) and Matsushita (intelligent audio-visual products).[41] Table 19.2 lists some of the other major alliances involving European and US firms.

A summary of the key attractive conditions and strategic focuses for build objectives is given in Table 19.3.

Hold objectives

Hold objectives involve defending a company's current position against would-be attackers. The principles of defensive warfare are, therefore, relevant. Perhaps the principle that has the most relevance in business is the recognition that strong competitive moves should always be blocked. Earlier, when discussing attack strategies, we saw how George Bush Snr successfully applied a principle of offensive warfare by identifying a weakness in his opponent and concentrating a major attack at that point.

It was Dukakis's failure to implement this principle of defensive warfare that compounded his problems. He recognized that Bush's attack should have been countered immediately:

> ❝There was a poignant moment last week when a young boy told him [Dukakis] he would be playing his part in a school mock election. What advice did he have? 'Respond to the attacks immediately,' said Dukakis, grinning.[42]❞

The lesson was not lost on Bill Clinton during his successful challenge to George Bush Snr in the 1992 presidential election. His strategists established a 24-hour-response capability to any Bush attack. As predicted, Bush attempted to position Clinton as a man of high taxes. Clinton was accused in a television advertisement of increasing taxes if elected. The advertisement featured the kinds of people who would suffer as a result of the extra tax they would have to pay. Within 24 hours Clinton ran his own advertisement quoting the *Washington Post* as stating that the Republican ad was misleading. This fast response capability was believed by the Democrats to be a major factor in Clinton's ability to maintain his opinion poll lead and emerge the victor in the election. In the UK, the Labour Party studied the electoral tactics of the Clinton administration and many, such as the fast-response capability, were implemented in its successful challenge to the Conservative government in 1997.

We shall now analyse the conditions that make a hold objective attractive, and the strategic focus necessary to achieve the objective.

Attractive conditions

The classic situation where a hold objective makes strategic sense is a *market leader in a mature or declining market*. This is the standard cash cow position discussed as part of the Boston Consulting Group market share/market growth rate analysis. By holding on to market leadership, a product should generate positive cash flows that can be used elsewhere in the company to build other products and invest in new product development. Holding on to market leadership per se makes sense because brand leaders enjoy the marketing benefits of bargaining power with distribution outlets, and brand image (the number one position), as well as enjoying experience curve effects that reduce costs. Furthermore, in a declining market, maintaining market leadership may result in becoming a virtual monopolist as weaker competitors withdraw.

A second situation where holding is suitable is in *growth markets when the costs of attempting to build sales and market share outweigh the benefits*. This may be the case in the face of aggressive rivals, who will respond strongly if attacked. In such circumstances it may be prudent to be content with the status quo, and avoid actions that are likely to provoke the competition.

Strategic focus

A hold objective may be achieved by monitoring the competition or by confronting the competition.

Monitoring the competition

In a market that is characterized by competitive stability, the required focus is simply to *monitor the competition*. Perhaps everyone is playing the 'good competitor' game, content with what they have, and no one is willing to destabilize industry structure. Monitoring is necessary to check that there are no significant changes in competitor behaviour but, beyond that, no change in strategy is required.

Confronting the competition

In circumstances where rivalry is more pronounced, strategic action may be required to defend sales and market share from aggressive challenges. The principles of defensive warfare provide a framework for identifying strategic alternatives that can be used in this situation. Figure 19.3 illustrates six methods of defence derived from military strategy.[43]

Position defence involves building a fortification around one's existing territory as the French did with their Maginot Line. Unfortunately, this static defence strategy was unsuccessful because the Germans simply went around it. In marketing, the analogy is to build a fortification around existing products. This reflects the philosophy that the company has good products, and all that is needed is to price them competitively and promote them effectively. This is more likely to work if the products have differential advantages that are not easily copied—for example, through patent protection. Also marketing assets like brand names and reputation may provide a strong defence against aggressors, although it can be a dangerous strategy. For example, Ever Ready's refusal to develop an alkaline battery in the face of an aggressive challenge to its market leadership by Duracell was an example of position defence. Instead it stuck with its zinc-carbon product, which had a shorter life than its alkaline rival, and invested

Figure 19.3 Defence strategies

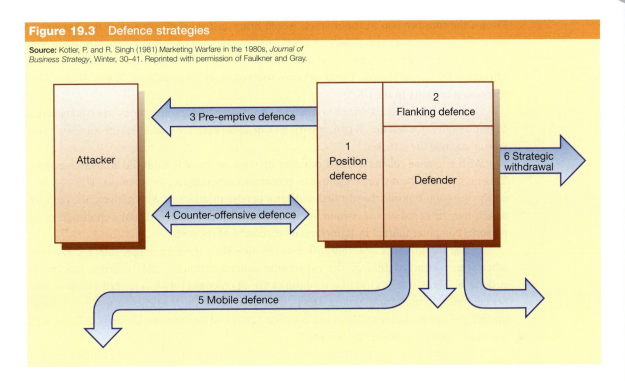

Source: Kotler, P. and R. Singh (1981) Marketing Warfare in the 1980s, *Journal of Business Strategy*, Winter, 30–41. Reprinted with permission of Faulkner and Gray.

£2 million (€2.6 million) in promotion. Only after Hanson acquired the company did Ever Ready develop its own alkaline battery.[44]

Land Rover and Range Rover provide another instance of an unsuccessful position defence. Based on a belief in their invincibility, they conducted little new product development. This created the opportunity for Subaru to introduce its cheaper, 'fun' four-wheel-drive vehicles. Only belatedly did Land Rover respond by developing the successful Discovery model.

Flanking defence is characterized by the defence of a hitherto unprotected market segment. The danger is that if the segment is left unprotected, it will provide a beachhead for new entrants to gain experience in the market and attack the main market later. This means that if it helps to avoid or slow down competitive inroads, it can make sense for a defender to compete in a segment that, in pure short-term profitability terms, looks unattractive. A further problem is that the defence of the segment may be half-hearted as it is not central to the main business. An example is General Motors and Ford's weak attempts to build a small car to compete with Volkswagen and the Japanese companies. The products—the Vega and Pinto—suffered from poor build quality and unreliability, and proved ineffective in defending the exposed flank.

Failure to defend an emerging market segment can have catastrophic consequences. For example, Distillers, which was dominant in the market for blended Scotch whisky with its Johnny Walker, Dewars and White Horse brands, ignored the growing malt whisky and white spirit segments. This preoccupation with the declining blended whisky segment resulted in disappointing performance and a successful take-over by Guinness.

Pre-emptive defence follows the philosophy that the best form of defence is to attack first. This may involve continuous innovation and new product development, a situation characteristic of the camcorder market. Japanese manufacturers are caught up in a continuous spiral of product introductions (known as product *churning*). Failure to maintain this rate of change would soon lead to product obsolescence and market share collapse.

A pre-emptive defence may also be used to dissuade a would-be attacker. For example, ICI, the market leader in the UK chemical fertilizer market, feared that Norsk Hydro's purchase of

Fisons, the number two in the market, would bring a strong offensive from the Norwegian company. ICI's strategy was to launch a pre-emptive defence by severely cutting the price of its fertilizer brands, thereby reducing profitability, which made future plant expansion less attractive to Norsk Hydro. These actions succeeded in discouraging Norsk Hydro from increasing capacity in the UK.[45]

Counter-offensive defence: a defender can choose from three options when considering a counter-offensive defence. It can embark on a head-on counter-attack, hit the attacker's cash cow or encircle the attacker.

With a *head-on counter-attack* a defender matches or exceeds what the attacker has done. This may involve heavy price cutting or promotion expenditure, for example. This can be a costly operation but may be justified to deter a persistent attacker. Alternatively, the counter-attack may be based on innovation, as when Apple counter-attacked IBM's challenge in the personal computer market by launching its successful Macintosh.

Hitting the attacker's cash cow strikes at the attacker's resource supply line. For example, when Xerox attacked IBM in the mainframe computer market, IBM counter-attacked by striking at Xerox's cash cow (the medium-range photocopier) with a limited range of low-priced copiers plus leasing arrangements that were particularly attractive to Xerox's target market (smaller businesses). The result was that Xerox sold its computer business to Honeywell, and concentrated on defending copiers.[46]

The third strategic option is to *encircle the attacker*. This strategy was successfully employed by Heublein when its Smirnoff vodka brand was attacked by the cheaper Wolfsmidt brand in the USA. Its response was to maintain the price of Smirnoff while launching two new brands, one at the same price as Wolfsmidt and one at a lower price. This manoeuvre successfully defended Heublein's position as market leader in the vodka market.

When a company's major market is under threat a mobile defence may make strategic sense. The two options are diversification and market broadening. A classic example of a company using *diversification* as a form of mobile defence is Imperial Tobacco, which responded to the health threat to its cigarette business by diversifying into food and leisure markets. *Market broadening* involves broadening the business definition, as film companies like Warner Brothers did in the face of declining cinema audiences. By defining its business as entertainment provider rather than film maker, it successfully moved into television, gambling and theme parks.

A strategic withdrawal, or contraction defence, requires a company to define its strengths and weaknesses, and then to hold on to its strengths while divesting its weaknesses. This results in the company concentrating on its core business. An example is Diageo, which withdrew from the fast-food business by selling Burger King, and from food by selling Pillsbury to concentrate on premium drinks.[47] Nokia also practised strategic withdrawal, moving initially from a paper, rubber goods and cables group into computers, consumer electronics and telecoms, and then, very successfully, concentrating on mobile telecoms (mainly mobile telephones and telecoms infrastructure). Along with Motorola and Ericsson, Nokia dominates the mobile handset market. At the product level, Woolworth rationalized its product lines to specialize on strong areas such as do-it-yourself products, gardening items and confectionery, and ceased selling food and white goods (e.g. refrigerators) in its stores.

A strategic withdrawal allows a company to focus on its core competences and is often required when diversification has resulted in too wide a

Table 19.4 Hold objectives

Attractive conditions
Market leader in a mature or declining market
Costs exceed benefits of building

Strategic focus
Monitoring the competition
Confronting the competition

spread of activities away from what it does really well. Peters and Waterman termed this focus on core skills and competences *sticking to your knitting*.[48]

Table 19.4 summarizes the key points for hold objectives.

Niche objectives

A company may decide to pursue a market niche objective by pursuing a small market segment or even a segment within a segment. In doing so, it may avoid competition with companies that are serving the major market segments. However, niche-orientated companies, if successful, run the risk that larger competitors are attracted into the segment. For example, the initial success of Sock Shop, a niche provider of stylish men's socks, stimulated large department stores such as Marks & Spencer to launch their own competitive ranges.

Attractive conditions

Nicheing may be the only feasible objective for companies with a small budget and where strong competitors are dominating the main segments. As such, it may be an attractive option for small companies that lack the resources to compete directly against the major players. But there need to be pockets within the market that provide the opportunity for profitable operations, and in which a competitive advantage can be created. Typical circumstances where these conditions apply are when the major players are under-serving a particular group of customers as they attempt to meet the needs of the majority of customers, and where the market niche is too small to be of interest to them.

Strategic focus

A key strategic tool for a niche-orientated company is *market segmentation*. Management should be vigilant in its search for underserved segments that may provide profitable opportunities. The choice will depend upon the attractiveness of the niche and the capability of the company to serve it. Once selected, effort—particularly research and development expenditure—will be focused on serving customer needs. *Focused R&D expenditure* gives a small company a chance to make effective use of its limited resources.[49] The emphasis should be on creating and sustaining a *differential advantage* through intimately understanding the needs of the customer group, and focusing attention on satisfying those needs better than the competition. Finally, niche operators should be wary of pursuing growth strategies by broadening their customer base. Often this will lead to a blurring of the differential advantage upon which their success has been built. Indeed, since some niche companies trade on *exclusivity*, to broaden their market base would by definition run the risk of diluting their differential advantage. TVR, which specializes in distinctive, high-performance sports cars, is a company that consistently pursues a niche objective. TVR consciously *thinks small*, eschewing unsustainable growth in favour of profitability. The emphasis is on high margin not high volume. Table 19.5 summarizes this brief discussion of niche objectives.

Table 19.5 Niche objectives
Attractive conditions
Small budget
Strong competitors dominating major segments
Pockets existing for profitable operations
Creating a competitive advantage
Strategic focus
Market segmentation
Focused R&D
Differentiation
Thinking small

Harvest objectives

A company embarking upon a **harvest objective** attempts to improve unit profit margins even if the result is falling sales. Although sales are falling, the aim is to make the company or product extremely profitable in the short term, generating large positive cash flows that can be used elsewhere in the business (for example, to build stars and selected problem children, or to fund new product development).

Attractive conditions

Also-ran products or companies in *mature or declining markets* (dogs) may be candidates for harvesting, since they are often losing money, and taking up valuable management time and effort.[50] Harvesting actions can move them to a profitable stance, and reduce management attention to a minimum. In *growth markets* harvesting can also make sense where the *costs of building or holding exceed the benefits*. These are problem children companies or products that have little long-term potential. Harvesting is particularly attractive if a *core of loyal customers* exists, which means that sales decline to a stable level. For example, a SmithKline Beecham hair product, Brylcreem, was harvested but sales decline was not terminal as a group of men who used the product in their adolescence continued to buy it in later life. This core of loyal customers meant it was still profitable to market Brylcreem, although R&D and marketing expenditure was minimal. More recently, Brylcreem has been repositioned as a hair gel targeting young men. A final attractive condition is where future breadwinners exist in the company or product portfolio to provide future sales and profit growth potential. Obviously harvesting a one-product company is likely to lead to its demise.

Strategic focus

Implementing a harvest objective begins with *eliminating research and development expenditure*. The only product change that will be contemplated is *reformulations* that reduce raw material and/or manufacturing costs. *Rationalization of the product line* to one or a few top sellers cuts costs by eliminating expensive product variants. *Marketing support is reduced* by slashing advertising and promotional budgets, while every opportunity is taken to *increase price*.

Table 19.6 summarizes the attractive conditions and strategic focus for achieving harvest objectives.

Table 19.6   Harvest objectives
Attractive conditions
Market is mature or declining (dog products)
In growth markets where the costs of building or holding exceed the benefits (selected problem children)
Core of loyal customers
Future breadwinners exist
Strategic focus
Eliminate R&D expenditure
Product reformulation
Rationalize product line
Cut marketing support
Consider increasing price

Divest objectives

A company may decide to divest itself of a strategic business unit or product. In doing so it may stem the flow of cash to a poorly performing area of its business.

Attractive conditions

Divestment is often associated with *loss-making products or businesses* that are a drain on both financial and managerial resources. *Low-share products or businesses in declining markets* (dogs) are prime candidates for divestment. Other areas may be considered for divestment when it is judged that the *costs of turnaround exceed the benefits*. As such, also-rans in growth markets may be divested, sometimes after harvesting has run its full course. However, care must be taken to examine interrelationships within the corporate portfolio. For example, if a product is making a loss it would still be worthwhile supporting it if its removal would *adversely affect sales of other products*. In some industrial markets, customers expect a supplier to provide a full range of products. Consequently, even though some may not be profitable, sales of the whole range may be affected if the loss makers are dropped.

Strategic focus

Because of the drain on profits and cash flow, once a decision to divest has been made, the focus should be to *get out quickly so as to minimize costs*. If a buyer can be found then some return may be realized; if not, the product will be withdrawn or the business terminated.

Table 19.7 summarizes the attractive conditions and strategic focus relating to divestment.

Table 19.7 Divest objectives
Attractive conditions
Loss-making products or businesses: drain on resources
Often low share in declining markets
Costs of turnaround exceed benefits
Removal will not significantly affect sales of other products
Strategic focus
Get out quickly; minimize the costs

Review

1 **The nature of competitive behaviour**
- Competitive behaviour can take five forms: conflict, competition, co-existence, co-operation and collusion.

2 **How military analogies can be applied to competitive marketing strategy**
- Military analogies are used to guide strategic thinking because of the need to attack and defend against competition.
- Attack strategies are the frontal attack, the flanking attack, encirclement, the bypass attack and the guerrilla attack.
- Defence strategies are the position defence, the flanking defence, the pre-emptive defence, the counter-offensive defence, the mobile defence, and strategic withdrawal.

3 **The attractive conditions and strategic focus necessary to achieve the following objectives: build, hold, niche, harvest and divest**

- Build objectives: attractive conditions are growth markets, exploitable competitive weaknesses, exploitable corporate strengths and adequate corporate resources; strategic focus is market expansion, winning market share, merger or acquisition, and forming strategic alliances.
- Hold objectives: attractive conditions are market leader in a mature or declining market, and costs exceed benefits of building; strategic focus is monitoring the competition, and confronting the competition.
- Niche objectives: attractive conditions are small budget, strong competitors dominating major segments, pockets exist for profitable operations, and opportunity to create a competitive advantage; strategic focus is market segmentation, focused R&D, differentiation and thinking small.
- Harvest objectives: attractive conditions are market is mature or declining, growth markets where the cost of building or holding exceeds the benefits, a core of loyal customers and future breadwinners exists; strategic focus is eliminate R&D expenditure, reformulate product, rationalize the product line, cut marketing expenditure and consider increasing price.

4 **The nature of frontal, flanking, encirclement, bypass and guerrilla attacks**

- Frontal attack: the challenger takes on the defender head on.
- Flanking attack: this involves attacking unguarded or weakly guarded ground (e.g. geographical areas or market segments).
- Encirclement attack: the defender is attacked from all sides (every market segment is hit with every combination of product features).
- Bypass attack: the defender's position is circumvented by, for example, technological leap-frogging or diversification.
- Guerrilla attack: the defender's life is made uncomfortable through, for example, unpredictable price discounts, sales promotions or heavy advertising in a few selected regions.

5 **The nature of position, flanking, pre-emptive, counter-offensive and mobile defences, and strategic withdrawal**

- Position defence: building a defence around existing products, usually through keen pricing and improved promotion.
- Flanking defence: defending a hitherto unprotected market segment.
- Pre-emptive defence: usually involves continuous innovation and new product development, recognizing that the best form of defence is attack.
- Counter-offensive defence: a counter-attack that takes the form of a head-on counter-attack, an attack on the attacker's cash cow or an encirclement of the attacker.
- Mobile defence: moving position by diversification or broadening the market by redefining the business.
- Strategic withdrawal: holding on to the company's strengths while divesting its weaknesses (e.g. weak strategic business units or product lines), resulting in the company focusing on its core business.

Key terms

bypass attack circumventing the defender's position, usually through technological leap-frogging or diversification

competitive behaviour the activities of rival companies with respect to each other; this can take five forms—conflict, competition, co-existence, co-operation and collusion

counter-offensive defence a counter-attack that takes the form of a head-on counter-attack, an attack on the attacker's cash cow or an encirclement of the attacker

divest to improve short-term cash yield by dropping or selling off a product

encirclement attack attacking the defender from all sides, i.e. every market segment is hit with every combination of product features

flanking attack attacking geographical areas or market segments where the defender is poorly represented

flanking defence the defence of a hitherto unprotected market segment

frontal attack a competitive strategy where the challenger takes on the defender head on

guerrilla attack making life uncomfortable for stronger rivals through, for example, unpredictable price discounts, sales promotions or heavy advertising in a few selected regions

harvest objective the improvement of profit margins to improve cash flow even if the longer-term result is falling sales

hold objective a strategy of defending a product in order to maintain market share

mobile defence involves diversification or broadening the market by redefining the business

niche objective the strategy of targeting a small market segment

position defence building a fortification around existing products, usually through keen pricing and improved promotion

pre-emptive defence usually involves continuous innovation and new product development, recognizing that attack is the best form of defence

strategic alliance collaboration between two or more organizations through, for example, joint ventures, licensing agreements, long-term purchasing and supply arrangement

strategic focus the strategies that can be employed to achieve an objective

strategic withdrawal holding on to the company's strengths while getting rid of its weaknesses

Internet exercise

The digital camera industry is very competitive with a multitude of firms vying for consumers. Digital cameras are reshaping the photographic industry. Visit the following related websites.

Visit: www.pentax.co.uk
www.nikon.co.uk
www.olympus.co.uk
www.polaroid.co.uk
www.konica.co.uk
www.fuji.co.uk

Questions

(a) Discuss the competitive marketing strategies employed by these competitors.
(b) What strategies would you recommend to Pentax in the face of such intense competition?

Visit the Online Learning Centre at www.mcgraw-hill.co.uk/textbooks/jobber for more Internet exercises.

Study questions

1. Why do many monopolies provide poor service to their customers?
2. Discuss the likely impact of the single European market on competitive behaviour.
3. Compare and contrast the conditions conducive to building and holding sales/market share.
4. Why is a position defence risky?
5. Why are strategic alliances popular in Europe? How do they differ from mergers?
6. A company should always attempt to harvest a product before considering divestment. Discuss.
7. In defence it is always wise to respond to serious attacks immediately. Do you agree? Explain your answer.

When you have read this chapter log on to the Online Learning Centre at www.mcgraw-hill.co.uk/textbooks/jobber to explore chapter-by-chapter test questions, links and further online study tools for marketing.

case thirty-seven

The Battle over Safeway and the Fight for UK Retailer Dominance

On 9 January 2003, Morrisons (www.morrisons.plc.uk) the UK's fifth-largest supermarket retailer made an audacious bid for Safeway, the UK's fourth-largest supermarket retailer. The move would radically reshape the UK's £100 billion (€144 billion) grocery market. A full-scale bidding war between the key retail players erupted, when the markets learnt that the board of Safeway had accepted a £2.9 billion (€4.12 billion) all-share take-over bid from Morrisons. The move shook the market as Morrisons had been regarded as solely focused in the north of the country and had grown entirely organically, shunning mergers or acquisitions. The bid has started a supermarket sweep for Safeway, with the pages of business papers speculating on the future owners and the implications. Numerous potential suitors were linked to the supermarket chain, such as Tesco, Sainsbury's, Asda, Marks & Spencer, BHS owner Philip Green, French giant Carrefour, and even the infamous buyout specialist KKR Kohlberg Kravis Roberts. They all want a piece of Safeway because of the chain's valuable retail sites. Strict UK planning regulations have curtailed the development of large retail sites, restricting retail chains' prospects for future UK development of their large supermarket formats.

Safeway (www.safeway.co.uk) was originally owned by California-based Safeway Food Stores Ltd. Its first UK store was opened in Bedford in 1962. In 1987, the Argyll Group subsequently bought out the supermarket chain: it bought the UK arm of Safeway for £681 million (€980 million) from the American company. Eventually the Argyll Group changed its name to Safeway plc, and is now the fourth-biggest food retailer in the UK (see Table C37.1).

Table C37.1 Safeway at a glance

- Founded in 1962
- £9 billion sales
- 8 million shoppers every week
- 90,000 employees
- 477 stores in the UK
- Possesses a store portfolio of convenience stores, supermarkets, superstores and hypermarkets; the average size of its superstores is around 31,000 square feet of sales area, and typically one store would employ around 250 staff and sell a range of up to 22,000 products
- Classified as a 'high–low' operator (i.e. more of an upmarket operator, however competes strongly with rivals on price on selected 'must have' grocery items)
- 170 stores have on-site petrol stations; the firm has a strategic alliance with BP
- Launched financial products in conjunction with Abbey National

Safeway has several types of outlet: hyperstores, superstores, supermarkets, convenience stores, and petrol forecourt retailing stores (in conjunction with BP). Some of Safeway's hyperstores carry over 22,000 different product lines, with in excess of 40 per cent of that range being Safeway own-brand. The company has four own-brand options: 'The Best' premium range, 'The Safeway' standard range, an economy line called 'Safeway Savers' and a variety of sub-brands. In 1999, Safeway's boss Carlos Criado-Perez was headhunted from US retail colossus Wal-Mart in order to revitalize the Safeway brand. Under his leadership, Safeway realized that it couldn't compete on price with larger rivals, so the firm went upmarket, creating retail theatres, pizza ovens, bakeries, etc.

However, Safeway still competes on price for 'must have' shopping item categories. The main focus of the revitalization was based on creating a more upmarket image for the retail brand, refitting Safeway supermarkets and focusing on fresh produce. This strategy focused on offering customers four main propositions: offering great-value products, being the best at offering consistently high-quality fresh products, being the best in terms of availability of products through efficient supply chain systems and, finally, aiming to be best at customer service in the retail sector. Extensive store refits were undertaken, concentrating on improved layouts, offering a wider assortment to customers and focusing on using the latest visual merchandising techniques. Over 180 stores underwent these face-lifts. Initially, the strategy seemed to be working, but it was not creating the desired levels of growth for the company.

The audacious bid by Morrisons for its larger rival (Safeway is four times bigger—see Table C37.2) took both the industry and the stock market by surprise. Morrisons was always regarded as a very successful regional operator, or as a possible take-over target, but not as a major-league player. So why has Morrisons placed a £2.9 billion bet on the Safeway chain?

The UK grocery retailing industry is very dynamic and subject to numerous drivers of change. The industry is experiencing a number of changes, such as changing consumer tastes, consumers demanding higher levels of service and convenience and changing consumer shopping practices; it is also faced with lower growth levels, leading to intense competition between retailers. These changes have led to several key implications for retailers.

Retailers are developing new store formats in new areas (e.g. convenience stores, petrol forecourt retailing etc.), increasing their focus on sales of high margin, non-food items (e.g. CDs and DVDs), developing new markets abroad (e.g. Tesco recently entered the Japanese market). Indeed, Tesco (the market leader) has gone from strength to strength due to its internationalization strategy and its move into the convenience store sector. Retailers must continue to develop new and improved customer service offerings. Many are extending and developing their own-label ranges (e.g. many retailers have different classes of own-label goods, ranging from premium to economy). Finally, improving their supply chain management operational efficiencies is seen as essential.

Retailers are placing a greater focus on the building of store brand image through effective positioning and differentiation. In this increasingly competitive environment, achieving growth through merger and acquisition activity is seen as a viable strategic direction. Many UK retail giants are lining up to get a piece of Safeway's valuable property portfolio (see Table C37.3).

Table C37.2 Morrisons versus Safeway: how they compare

	Safeway	Morrisons
Stores	477	113
Sales (ex-VAT)	£8.6 billion	£3.9 billion
Market share growth (1997—2002)	0.5%	1.4%
Sales area (sq ft)	10,296	4,039
Operating profit	£416.5 million	£229.8 million
Operating profit margin	4.9%	5.9%
Operating profit per sq ft	£40.70	£57.80

Source: Verdict Research

Table C37.3 The suitors

Morrisons	ASDA Wal-Mart	Tesco
Market share = 5.9%	Market share = 15.9%	Market share = 25.8%
UK stores = 119	UK stores = 258	UK stores = 730
Employees = 43,000	Employees = 117,000	Employees = 265,000
Pre-tax profit = £229.8 million	Pre-tax profit =(£7.6 billion: Wal-Mart)	Pre-tax profit = £1.2 billion
The Competition Commission's (CoCom) preferred bidder. It will transform Morrisons into a major retail player. If it fails, it may buy the offloaded stores from the successful bidder, but will struggle to gain the same type of market share as the three market leaders.	Seen as the favourite in the take-over battle, with deep pockets for any drawn-out take-over battle. If Asda wins it becomes number two overnight. Severe setback if Sainsbury's wins as it increases the gap behind the two market leaders.	Unlikely to get approval from CoCom, however it may pick up off-loaded stores from the successful bidder. Tesco would prefer, if it is excluded from bidding, that Morrisons would win rather than Asda, as its leadership position may otherwise be under threat.
Sainsbury's	**Philip Green**	
Market share = 17.4%	Owner of the Arcadia group (Top Shop, Wallis, Evans, Burton, Miss Selfridge, etc.) and BHS stores.	
UK stores = 463		
Employees = 174,000		
Pre-tax profit = £571 million		
If it wins it consolidates its position as number two. Would have to sell approximately 90 stores. If it loses, it is under threat of losing its status as the UK's number-two retail operator, which would be regarded as a disaster for the company.	No grocery interests. As a result he is exempt from any CoCom merger inquiry. Has said he is interested in Safeway. Trades unions have been openly opposed to a possible take-over by Green.	

The highly regarded Sir Ken Morrison runs the Morrisons chain. The Yorkshire septuagenarian emerged as the unlikely driving force behind creating the UK's fourth largest retailing group. Sir Ken Morrison took over the family business over 45 years ago, and has since transformed a few shops and market stalls into a billion-pound retail chain. Ken Morrison is regarded as the doyen of UK grocery retailing, with boundless energy and enthusiasm for the business. He has reported growth every single year since he floated the chain in 1967. Furthermore, the chain boasts extraordinary levels of consumer loyalty. The Bradford-based company is well defended from unwanted suitors by the fact that 30 per cent of the company is owned by the Morrison family, worth around £1 billion (€1.44 billion). From the humble beginnings of the first Morrisons supermarket in Bradford, the company has enjoyed unprecedented success, which has primarily been derived from organic growth, and has not been reliant on mergers or acquisitions, unlike other UK supermarket giants. The last time Morrisons acquired another company was back in 1978.

The chain believes in offering customers a 'no-frills', great-value-for-money proposition. It believes that customers value low prices and promotions such as BOGOFs (buy one get one free) rather than sophisticated loyalty reward programmes or Internet shopping. If the Morrisons bid succeeds it will have 16.1 per cent of the market, placing it neck and neck with third-placed rival Asda/Wal-Wart. Morrisons has long desired to move south; however, with increasingly difficult planning restrictions in place over retail site developments in the UK, acquisition seems the only viable alternative. Morrisons is highly vertically integrated, with its own abattoir and its own factories that manufacture food; it also packs its own fresh produce, and the company even makes its own plastic bags. One of its factories packs in the region of 400,000 packs of cheese, and produces and packs over 350,000 sausages per week. Close on 55 per cent of its sales are derived from its own-brand range. It believes the advantages of a vertically integrated system are that Morrisons has a tighter control over quality, it minimizes wastage and eliminates costly intermediaries in the supply chain, the firm has greater market understanding, and that it offers flexibility in adapting to changes in demand.

The deal gathered momentum after Safeway's chairman met Sir Ken Morrison at a trade event in October 2002. Morrisons was always seen by the trade and media as very much a northern company. In order to woo Safeway investors, Morrisons hired investment bankers for the first time and courted financial public relations advisers to help seal the deal. The main focus of this campaign was on transferring Morrisons' highly successful retail formula to Safeway's stores. This formula relies on a focus on selling high-quality products at low prices—its 'the very best for less' proposition, offering 1000 specials at any one time, including approximately 150 BOGOF promotions. The firm believes in price transparency offering the same prices in all of its stores in the UK. It has a strong fresh-food proposition, including the in-store Market Street (a collection of specialist fresh-food counters, which tries to replicate the experience of buying fresh produce from market traders). Morrisons wants to apply its sales performance levels to Safeway stores. Furthermore, the Safeway brand will be retained for use in the convenience store format within the new retailing group.

Morrisons firmly believes that having a 'big four' rather than a 'big three' (including just Tesco, Sainsbury's and Asda) would be much better for competition in the retail sector. However, some industry commentators believe that the Morrisons formula may be stretched to the limit in terms of its resources, due to its high reliance on vertically integrated systems. New distribution networks would be required, with new suppliers and more support for existing Safeway suppliers needed. If the Morrisons deal is successful, it envisages five key tasks in integrating Safeway into the Morrisons framework. First, to integrate all of Safeway's regional distribution centres (one of a network of large warehouses operated for a single retailer where merchandise is consolidated prior to delivery to its local stores) in order to handle the Morrisons product range. Second, converting and refurbishing 358 of Safeway's stores (those over 15,000 square feet) into the Morrisons format. It is estimated that the cost of this conversion will total £360 million (€518 million) over three years. Third, investment in central packing and production facilities for the newly enlarged group. In the proposal £450 million (€648 million) is allocated towards an additional abattoir, new packing and production facilities for the enlarged retail group. Fourth, centralizing core functions at the Bradford headquarters, such as buying and IT. Finally, creating a cultural change at Safeway, by adopting Morrisons' philosophy of least cost/best value, through intensive training and employee-rotation programmes.

Many analysts feel that Morrisons would find it difficult to subsume an organization nearly four times bigger than itself in size, whereas other bidders would have better resources to facilitate a seamless take-over. The longer a drawn-out bidding war ensues, the greater the danger of losing the key Safeway staff that will be needed to make the integration work. Many at Safeway's headquarters in Middlesex fear for their jobs, so they are distracted by the take-over battle, and their motivation and morale is low.

In its submission to Safeway investors, Morrisons used case studies to illustrate its experience and past successes when converting other stores to the Morrisons format. They highlighted a former Co-op store Morrisons acquired in 1998, and after a quick conversion (in 10 days) and, later, a major refurbishment at a cost of £5 million (€7.2 million), sales per week at the store rose by 59 per cent and customer spend increased by 22 per cent in two years. The submission stated that the creation of a 'fourth force' in UK retailing would benefit competition, as well as customers and suppliers alike.

Sainsbury's declared its intention to table a counter-offer for Safeway, valuing the supermarket chain at £3.15 billion (€4.5 billion), and offering Safeway shareholders a cash and share offer. Sainsbury's was the market leader until 1995, when it fell behind Tesco due to falling sales. Under new leadership, the company has updated its image, introduced new product ranges and store formats, and dramatically improved its supply chain management. Even if Sainsbury's loses the battle, it may pick up much sought-after extra retail sites from the successful bidder because of geographical overlaps and/or Competition Commission (CoCom) recommendations. If the Sainsbury's bid fails it will concentrate on its recovery plan, buying stores and opening new stores. Sir Peter Davis, CEO of Sainsbury's, in the company's submission to CoCom, has argued that a successful Sainsbury's bid would benefit customers, with further price reductions due to scale efficiencies and greater food choice. A successful Sainsbury's bid would be a counter-balance to the increasingly used discount retailing of Asda and Morrisons. If Sainsbury's is successful in its bid, it envisions that costs savings of £300 million (€432 billion) could be achieved, 1700 job cuts, and the disposal of 90 stores to satisfy CoCom. Previously, in 2002, Asda and Sainsbury's considered a joint bid for Safeway, only to fall out over how the spoils would be split between the two companies.

If Asda wins there will be huge overlaps in Scotland, which would force it to sell particular outlets to avoid the wrath of competition watchdogs. Asda has very deep pockets thanks to its behemoth US owner Wal-Mart, which employs nearly a million people and has sales over £150 billion (€216 billion). The chain wants to dominate UK grocery retailing, like it does in the USA. Some of the 'big three' may consider joint bids to cherry-pick particular Safeway stores and also in order to circumvent competition watchdog concerns. The Transport and General Workers Union backs Sainsbury's in the battle for Safeway, as it is concerned about the power of rival bidders such as Asda, Tesco and Philip Green. Sainsbury's has won union approval for the deal over its long-standing relationships with British suppliers, whereas other bidders have practised 'ruthless bargaining' with suppliers.

Consumers, suppliers and regulatory authorities alike are concerned over the ever-increasing power of retailers due to their sheer size and concentration. Any successful bid would have to clear two regulatory authorities: the Office of Fair Trading (OFT) and the Competition Commission (CoCom). These regulatory authorities can get involved in the process when an actual or proposed merger will create or intensify a market share of 25 per cent of the supply of particular goods and services in the UK, or involve the take-over of assets exceeding £70 million (€101 million). These government regulators examine bidders' market share over many years, as well as their geographic dispersion (there is a 15-minute driving time rule), shopper choice in a neighbourhood, impact on other supermarkets post-merger and, importantly, the balance of power between suppliers and retailers. Authorities view having competitive rivalry within the sector as benefiting customers. They would view the Morrisons bid as having the fewest obstacles due to its smaller size and the geographic fit of the proposed merged entity with very few overlaps. However, the Morrisons bid was referred to the merger inquiry due to local, as opposed to national, competition concerns that other rival bids may face.

CoCom would baulk if Tesco, Sainsbury's or Asda/Wal-Mart gained control over Safeway, as this would be viewed as bad for customer choice. Morrisons believes that a deal with Safeway would generate annual savings of £250 million (€360 million); this would mainly arise from trading benefits and buying synergies, and from 1200 job losses through the elimination of duplicate functions. CoCom is examining bid proposals from Tesco, the biggest UK-based supermarket company, Sainsbury's, Morrisons and Wal-Mart-owned Asda. All of the retail chains had to make detailed submissions to the CoCom merger inquiry. Retail mogul Philip Green, owner of high-street fashion names BHS and Arcadia, escaped investigation as he has no grocery business interests. At this stage of the take-over battle, Morrisons is the only one to have made a formal bid, valuing Safeway at around £2.9 billion (€4.18 billion). If the Morrisons bid fails, it will receive a £30 million (€43 million) 'break fee', for getting the ball rolling over the take-over battle. It is likely that Morrisons may have to sweeten the deal with an extra cash offer (a £1-a-share offer) to beat rivals.

If Morrisons wins, this would be seen as levelling the playing field. However, financial analysts believe that its bid is not high enough and has a major disadvantage in that it is an all-share offer, whereas the Sainsbury's offer would be half cash and Asda's is likely to be an all-cash offer. Unless the competition authorities intervene, these bigger rivals have the financial clout to up the price for this prized retail asset. Safeway is seen as the last acquisition opportunity in the UK's competitive supermarket sector. The stakes are high, and everyone wants a piece of the action.

Questions

1. What motivates retailers to pursue a merger and acquisition strategy?
2. What are the risks associated with pursuing a merger and acquisition strategy?
3. Critically analyse the competitive marketing strategy adopted by Morrisons in its bid for the larger Safeway retail chain.

This case was written by Conor Carroll, Lecturer in Marketing, University of Limerick. Copyright © Conor Carroll (2003). The material in the case has been drawn from a variety of published sources.

case thirty-eight

Mitsubishi Ireland: Building the Black Diamond Brand

Mitsubishi Ireland operates in the consumer electronics industry, which has been characterized by some major changes in recent years. Increased globalization and the ongoing growth in power of retailers had led Mitsubishi Electric—its parent company—to cease production of colour televisions (CTVs) and video cassette recorders (VCRs) at its two plants in the UK. Country subsidiaries throughout Europe were told to exit the CTV and VCR businesses in favour of more profitable products in growth markets, such as mobile phones and air conditioners. However, this move presented real problems for the Irish subsidiary.

Mitsubishi Ireland had long been a market leader in CTVs and VCRs and these products were the mainstay of its operations. Furthermore, the Irish market was very small relative to other European countries, affording only limited opportunities for other products in the Mitsubishi range. However, its response to the crisis was innovative and dramatically successful. The company launched a new brand of CTVs and VCRs called Black Diamond; these are made by Vestel, one of Europe's largest original equipment manufacturers (OEMs). Extensive marketing to an initially sceptical dealer base and to the general public resulted in rapid acceptance of the new brand. In one year, the company managed to replace all its Mitsubishi-made CTVs and VCRs with this new range, and this transition was accompanied not with a loss in market share but an actual increase.

As he looked to the future, Fergus Madigan, Mitsubishi Ireland's managing director, pondered the strategic implications of the success of Black Diamond. Technological change was becoming a feature of the industry, with implications for the nature of the Black Diamond range and for positioning the Black Diamond brand in the marketplace. It was clear that some very important decisions lay ahead.

Mitsubishi Ireland

Mitsubishi Electric has a presence in 39 countries around the world. Most of its key R&D and production activities continue to be in Japan, although the company has significant operations in China, Taiwan and the USA. Mitsubishi Electric Europe's registered office is in the Netherlands, with its main corporate office located in London. It has significant operations in the UK, France and Germany, as well as offices in Belgium, the Czech Republic, Ireland, Italy, Portugal, the Russian Federation, Spain and Sweden. Mitsubishi's Irish subsidiary (MEU-IR) was established in 1981 as a branch office of Mitsubishi UK. With an initial staff of eight, the company generated over IR£1 million (€1.27 million) in sales in the first year. Since then, its growth rate has been very impressive, peaking at sales levels of IR£70 million (€88.84 million) in 2000, by which time employment levels had risen to 49 people.

CTVs and VCRs have been the mainstay of MEU-IR's operations over the years. Mitsubishi has a long tradition in television manufacturing, having launched its first television in 1953 and its first colour television in 1960. Though its market share in many European countries was very low, Mitsubishi has been a leading player in the Irish market and its brand is well known and associated with high-quality, technologically advanced products. When its sales of CTVs and VCRs peaked at over IR£14 million (€17.77 million) in 1990, these products represented almost three-quarters of the company's turnover for that year. Since then, its dependence on this sector has reduced as the company has expanded the range of products it offers on the Irish market and, by 1997, CTVs and VCRs accounted for one-third of its turnover.

Mitsubishi Ireland currently has 45 employees and it is essentially an integrated sales and marketing company (see Fig. C38.1). The majority of its staff are attached to one of its five support groups—namely, marketing, customer support, logistics and purchasing, distribution, and finance. The personnel and capabilities of these groups are then shared across its six major product divisions. Consumer goods—that is, CTVs and VCRs—is still its biggest division but is closely followed by its air-conditioner business, which accounts for about 30 per cent of turnover. Equally important are the display products division, which mainly involves the sale of monitors to personal computer companies such as Gateway; and the cellular mobile telecommunications division, which primarily markets the Mitsubishi mobile phone brand, Trium. The company also supplies digital security systems such as monitors and time-lapse VCRs, and some factory automation equipment, including programmable logic components, drives and circuit breakers.

Figure C38.1 Mitsubishi Electric Irl. Ltd: company structure

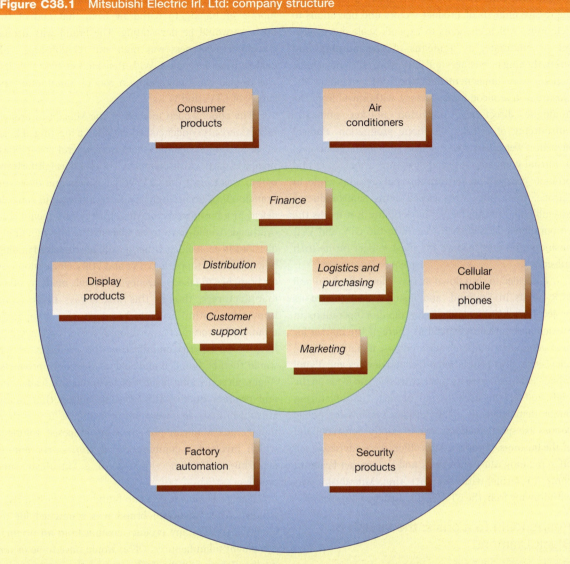

Therefore, the company has a diverse customer base, ranging from manufacturers that need production line equipment, to mobile phone network providers, to individuals looking for a new television. However, there are also commonalties across these businesses. For example, Mitsubishi's reputation for audio-visual products enhances its competitiveness in display products and security systems, as well as in its consumer division. And while some of its businesses involve working directly with industrial customers, its two main divisions—consumer products and air conditioning—require capabilities in managing a dealer network.

1998: a shock for Mitsubishi Ireland

After almost three-quarters of a century of continuous profitability, Mitsubishi Corporation reported heavy losses for the year ending 31 March 1998, in common with a number of other major Japanese corporations. Profits had been rising steadily throughout the 1990s, though the fiscal year 1997 had seen an 86 per cent profit fall to ¥8.5 billion. However, for the first time in its history, Mitsubishi posted a loss in 1998 and it was substantial at ¥105.9 billion (about US$800 million). The fall was attributed to several factors. In terms of products, the bottom had fallen out of the semiconductor market, with the average price of a 16M DRAM dropping to a third of what it had been 12 months earlier, and competition continued to be severe in the audio-visual market. Geographically, the stagnation of the Japanese economy and the economic turmoil that gripped the South-East Asian economies of Thailand, South Korea and Indonesia had also adversely affected performance.

To deal with these losses, Mitsubishi undertook an aggressive analysis of product sectors and operations to determine which elements to expand, scale down, spin off or eliminate, as a means of streamlining and strengthening its business and improving efficiency. Quick actions were implemented in the USA, including the closure of a semiconductor factory, withdrawal from the analogue direct-view television market and the outsourcing of cellular telephone production. Radical measures were also taken in Japan, such as the creation of a 'virtual company' internal structure to cut costs and promote competition between internal divisions while, in Europe, some lines were closed at its semiconductor assembly and testing facility in Germany. But it was the corporation's decision with regard to the CTV and VCR business that was to have the most impact on its Irish subsidiary.

It decided to shut down its two colour television and VCR plants in Scotland, and instead strengthened its projection television and display monitor operations in Mexico and moved to expand its share of the market for next-generation audio-visual products, including digital televisions, next-generation projection devices and digital broadcasting services. Its strategy was now to focus on the high end of the audio-visual market, manufacturing major items such as colour display systems for public venues like sports stadiums, and to exit the consumer end of the business. European sales offices were advised to sell off remaining Mitsubishi stock and the market began to come to terms with the fact that Mitsubishi was withdrawing from the CTV/VCR industry in Europe.

Responding to a crisis: the launch of Black Diamond

The decision to close the two Scottish plants came as a hammer blow to Mitsubishi Ireland. Of all Mitsubishi's European offices, Ireland more than most depended on the sales of CTVs and VCRs. Mitsubishi CTVs and VCRs had achieved strong brand recognition and the Irish branch had a market share in this sector that was the envy of its European counterparts. But now it looked as though all the good work of the previous 20 years was going to be wasted. Fergus Madigan decided that immediate action was necessary. He called together his management team of Denis Boyd (head of sales), Colm Mulcahy (marketing manager) and John Fitzgerald (field sales manager) on several occasions during February 1998 to consider the options. Immediately, it became clear that making a graceful exit from the business was not going to be one of them. Too much effort had been put in for that to be considered. More critically, consumer products were the heart and soul of the Irish branch and the effect on staff morale of having to withdraw from that end of the business would be devastating. The brand was strong, consumer awareness was high and relationships with dealers were very good. With that kind of base, all that was needed was to figure out a way of maintaining the supply of CTVs and VCRs.

The options open to each of the Mitsubishi branch offices were also under consideration at a meeting at head office in London. Though there were several possibilities, none was particularly palatable. The most straightforward option was to exit the CTV/VCR business and downsize branch offices accordingly. Aside from having to concede defeat in a business sector, this strategy also meant that overheads would have to be allocated to the remaining divisions in each office. Other possibilities involved finding new sources of supply for CTVs and VCRs. One option was for branches to take an agency for brands made by other manufacturers, though this was always likely to be unpopular within Mitsubishi given the company's reputation for product innovation. A second option was to have a third party manufacture the products, which would then be branded and sold as Mitsubishi products. Again, given its long history of technological leadership and product quality, this was an option that many Mitsubishi managers were not in favour of. It was then that Fergus Madigan presented his proposed solution, which involved a combination of third-party manufacturing and the development of a Mitsubishi sub-brand.

The development of a sub-brand was clearly a risky strategy. The Mitsubishi brand was renowned for its quality, therefore any product coming from an original equipment manufacturer (OEM) would have to be of top quality. Convincing the dealer base of the merits of this proposal would be critical to its success. Dealers were likely to be very sceptical about the idea, given the number of strong brands already on the market. Then there was the tricky issue of what brand name to use on any new products as, obviously, they were not being manufactured by Mitsubishi. Despite these challenges, MEU-IR decided to progress with the idea. It first set about finding an OEM. During the spring of 1998, a number of alternatives were considered, including a French company, an Italian company and two Korean companies. Then Mitsubishi began talks with a Turkish company, Vestel. Initial discussions looked positive. Vestel was a well-established firm that had a lot of experience in manufacturing consumer electronics products and had spare capacity in a large production facility at Ismir. It was also one of the largest OEM manufacturers in Europe, and Turkey was starting to establish a reputation for itself as a producer of consumer products and white goods.

As the discussions progressed, Michael Clancy, Mitsubishi's main technical specialist, spent two months in Turkey, where he worked with Vestel's production people to ensure that its product quality matched Mitsubishi's exacting standards. Relations between the two parties during this period were sometimes strained as Vestel struggled to match the strict criteria set by Mitsubishi. At one stage, Michael Clancy brought the complete production line at the Turkish plant to a halt because he was not happy with the quality of the product. However, both sides persisted and, by June 1998, Vestel was manufacturing two colour televisions for Mitsubishi: a 21-inch text and a 21-inch Nicam. The next step was to ensure that these products presented no problems when in actual use. In terms of television signals, Ireland is a fringe area and the technology required to achieve quality reception is much greater than that necessary in mainland European areas. Michael Clancy spent a further two months taking the televisions around the country to ensure that they worked well whether they were used in areas served by aerial or cable, as reception qualities tended to vary significantly. No problems were detected and Mitsubishi was confident that it had products that matched its quality requirements.

The Black Diamond brand

At the same time as it worked on solving the difficult problem of finding a suitable supplier, the management of Mitsubishi also faced the additional challenge of how to brand the new range given that it was not a Mitsubishi-manufactured product. The selection of a brand name was a difficult one, involving hours of discussions. The management team had a number of names to choose from, including Blue Diamond, Black Diamond, Diamond Vision and Diva. Blue Diamond had been a Mitsubishi sub-brand during the period 1979 to 1985. In those days the picture tube took a short period to warm up when the television was turned on, and to cool down again when it was turned off, and during that time the screen had a slightly blue tint—hence the name Blue Diamond. As the technology advanced, this warm-up/cool-down period was virtually eliminated and, in 1990, Mitsubishi had used the name Black Diamond for its television range as a way of conveying the quality of its products and to describe the sharp visual picture provided by its televisions.

The Black Diamond brand name was a registered name of Mitsubishi Ireland but had not been used since 1995 because it was felt then that the use of the sub-brand was confusing customers. Diamond Vision was an attractive proposition as it was the name used on Mitsubishi's range of large outdoor screens, and would confer an image of technological advancement on the new range. Diva was a very successful Mitsubishi brand in countries like Singapore, Australia and New Zealand.

The company also considered a two-brand strategy. There was the possibility of having products made by a Japanese OEM, which could be branded Diva and positioned as top of the range, while Black Diamond could be used for its mid-market products. But it was felt that as Diva had no brand recognition in Ireland, it would be a very hard sell there. The company finally decided to go with Black Diamond, primarily because it had recognition among employees as well as dealers and customers in the marketplace. In addition, research had shown that it was a name that stood on its own.

But there were also important risks. When it was last on the market, Black Diamond had a product association—namely the Black Diamond tube. This time it would have to stand on its own as a brand. Then there was the issue of whether Black Diamond would be too closely associated with CTVs. Discussions led to the consideration of White Diamond for white goods and Red Diamond for audio. At one stage, Fergus Madigan became totally exasperated at a management meeting. They had not even launched the brand and already it seemed that it was being stretched all over the place. A deep breath was taken and a decision was made to go with Black Diamond as the brand name. However, it was necessary to make some changes to the logo in order to accommodate the OEM product (see the illustration overleaf). The name Mitsubishi was taken off the top bar, which was now left blank though the words 'TV & Video' were subsequently added to the top bar in 1999. Subsequently, when the new brand proved successful in the marketplace, it was decided to drop the words 'TV & Video' as well as the strong black lines from the logo to allow it to be more versatile and suitable for use on other products such as audio and white goods.

Motivation of staff was also a critical issue at this time, as they too needed to be assured that the company had a strategy to cope with the closure of the two CTV/VCR plants. In January 1999, Fergus Madigan brought all his staff to Paris for the company's annual conference. It was at this conference that management was to present its reviews of the past year, as well as an outline of budgets and targets for the forthcoming year. It was essential to show at this stage that the company was in a position of strength while all the uncertainty was going on. This Paris event was repeated in 2000.

Evolution of the Black Diamond logo.

In a very short space of time the management of Mitsubishi Ireland was well on its way to turning around a potentially disastrous situation. The closure of the Scottish plants had been announced in February 1998, yet by June of that year, the company had convinced its corporate office that it still had a future in CTVs and VCRs. It had established a relationship with a third party and was confident that this partner could deliver top-quality products. It also had a brand name that captured the functional and symbolic attributes of the new range. But the strategy was not without significant risks. If Black Diamond failed, reputations would be severely dented, and the confidence and morale of employees would take a serious blow. MEU-IR's management knew their credibility was on the line, both in terms of the Irish marketplace and within the Mitsubishi corporation. It was now time to take their new strategy to the marketplace, and this was likely to be the most difficult hurdle of all.

The launch of Black Diamond

The new Black Diamond range was always going to face a difficult birth. The closure of the CTV and VCR plants in the UK had created a great deal of uncertainty among the dealer base, which was concerned as to whether there would be adequate service and support available for the existing Mitsubishi stock they held. At the same time, Mitsubishi's competitors in the Irish market sought to make as much capital as possible out of the unprecedented development. They targeted dealers aggressively, questioning Mitsubishi's commitment to the business and seeking to make the most out of the unexpected opportunity created by the potential withdrawal of one of the dominant firms in the market. So when Mitsubishi launched its new range of Black Diamond televisions at its annual August trade show, it faced a sceptical and worried dealer base.

Members of the Consumer Electronics Distributors Association (CEDA), which includes all the leading brands on the Irish market, each hold an annual trade show, usually in August, to showcase new products and marketing initiatives. These shows were a particularly important part of the calendar when the dealer base was made up of mostly small, independent brown goods specialists as they created the opportunity to build relationships with a disparate dealer network. Though less important as the dealer base consolidated, the 1998 show was a critical one for Mitsubishi. As usual, the show was held at Mitsubishi's premises in Dublin. No effort was spared in convincing dealers of both the quality of the new range of televisions and of Mitsubishi's commitment to the CTV and VCR business. Customers were walked through a display of the entire Mitsubishi consumer product range, including CTVs, VCRs, dehumidifiers, monitors, batteries, tapes, and so on, to demonstrate that Mitsubishi Ireland, far from withdrawing from the consumer market was more committed to it than ever before. The new Black Diamond range was presented at the end of the tour and customers were given a technical demonstration of the product, comparing it with other brands to convince them of its quality. They were also invited to have their own engineers take sets away to examine and assess them.

The show was a tremendous success and dealers agreed to stock the two new televisions. As the pre-Christmas period is the most important buying time during the year, Mitsubishi brought out a third Black Diamond CTV—a silver 21-inch Nicam model—which was also adopted by dealers and well received by the market. The initial positioning of Black Diamond was a central factor in these early successes. Black Diamond was positioned as a Mitsubishi sub-brand. Sub-branding is very popular in the consumer electronics area with brands like Sony's PlayStation being particularly well known. In its other divisions, Mitsubishi Ireland had some strong sub-brands such as Mr Slim and City Multi in air conditioners, and Trium in mobile phones. It pursued a deliberate strategy of keeping a very close association between its new products and the highly credible Mitsubishi name by marketing them as 'Black Diamond distributed by Mitsubishi'. This approach greatly assisted with the acceptance of the new range in the marketplace. Another difficult hurdle—the dealers—had been surmounted and the way was now clear for a full-scale launch of the Black Diamond range in 1999.

Black Diamond in 1999

It was 1999 that saw the full transition to the Black Diamond range as the remaining Mitsubishi stock was sold off. By the end of that year the Black Diamond CTV range had been expanded to include 28-inch and 32-inch televisions as well as a top-of-the-range 42-inch plasma television. In addition, two new Black Diamond VCRs were added to the four Mitsubishi-made VCR brands offered. Across each of the different product categories, the Black Diamond range was positioned as a top-quality, competitively priced product. Prices for each of the different models were in the mid range, which effectively placed Black Diamond in direct competition with other leading brands like Philips.

Promotion of the new range was critical in 1999. The major emphasis continued to be on securing dealer loyalty and pushing the product through the channel. In February of that year, Mitsubishi took representatives of 24 of its leading dealers to Paris for a two-day product preview. The main purpose of this event was to unveil the full 1999 Black Diamond range and to demonstrate again the company's commitment to the CTV/VCR business by showing the promotional support that would be used to drive the brand. It also served as a useful forum for getting dealer feedback on their initial experiences with Black Diamond. These trade efforts proved to be very successful and all the major dealers in Ireland, such as Power City, DID Electrical, ESB Retail, the DSG Group and Shop Electric, agreed to stock the new range.

Key to building the Black Diamond brand were the advertising concepts used on point-of-sale material and in advertisements targeted at the end user. Two tag-lines were used in all the promotional literature, namely 'quality makes all the difference' and 'see the difference'. The former was used to reinforce the quality image of the products and to convey that Black Diamond was a brand the consumer could trust. 'See the difference' suggested that the only way televisions can be evaluated is to look at them, and this tag-line showed the company's confidence in its new brand. The main visual used in the advertising was eye-catching and provocative. Rather than showing a television, it showed the body of a woman with a diamond superimposed on it. The message of the visual was simply a reinforcement of the brand name but the concept did a very effective job of creating awareness in the marketplace (see the illustration below).

Televisions were shown in some product-specific advertising. For example, its silver 21-inch Nicam television, which was launched for the Christmas 1998 market, showed a Christmas scene on the TV screen, while a sumo wrestler featured on the screen of its 28-inch television to convey the image of size. Some silver 21-inch Nicam CTV sets were offered as prizes on the popular Irish

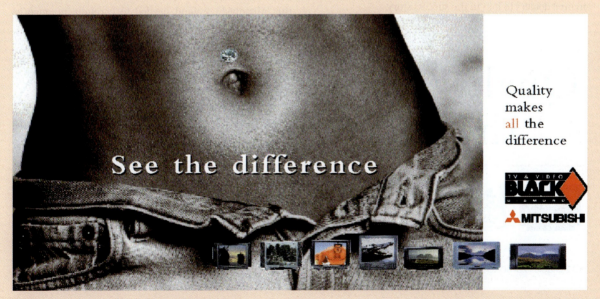

Print advertising for Black Diamond television.

TV programme *The Late Late Show*. Being the first sets of their kind on the Irish market, they help to associate the name Black Diamond with innovation. The full Black Diamond range of colour televisions was combined to form a banner line that was included in much of its advertising and point of sale material (see the illustration below). The main advertising media used during the year were press and point of sale; a schedule for the IR£2 million (€2.53 million) promotional budget for the year is shown in Table C38.1.

The performance of Black Diamond

The success of Black Diamond took everyone in the industry by surprise. From a situation of having to consider exiting the business just under two years previously, Mitsubishi Ireland had managed to develop a new line of products and had successfully launched them on to the market. But what is perhaps more remarkable is that the transition from Mitsubishi-made products to the Vestel-manufactered range resulted not only in the company maintaining its share of the market, but actually increasing it (see Table C38.2 on page 748). Market share figures for 1999 show that MEU-IR had significantly strengthened its position as the dominant player in the large-screen CTV market, but it also assumed dominance of the VCR sector and made significant inroads into Philips' leadership of the portable TV sector. By the end of 1999, this success was reflected in the company's dealer-based promotional material, which carried the tag-line 'from Brand New ... to Brand Leader'. The advertising talked about the success of Black Diamond as well as MEU-IR's support for the brand, and invited dealers to join in the success story.

New challenges for Black Diamond

Although the launch of Black Diamond had been dramatically successful, Mitsubishi Ireland could not afford to become complacent. Many new challenges lay ahead, with perhaps the most significant being the increased penetration of new technologies. 'Home cinema' was a term that had been circulating in the industry for many years, but its promise finally appeared to be fulfilled during the early years of the twenty-first century. Widescreen televisions (i.e. from 24 to 36 inches) were the star performers in the industry, accounting for 45 per cent of the total television sector in 2001. This represented a growth of over 35 per cent on the previous year, and is driven by advances in the Pure Flat and 100 Hz digital picture technologies. It was anticipated that demand for widescreen and plasma televisions would remain strong throughout 2002, helped by the World Cup taking place in Japan and South Korea. To capitalize on this potential opportunity, Mitsubishi Ireland engaged the services of Mick McCarthy, the Republic of Ireland's team manager, to front its advertising for 2002. At the same time, demand for portable CTVs has continued to decline and major price pressure is being felt in this sector.

Significant shake-up is also taking place in the VCR/DVD sector. DVDs are the industry success story, cited by the *Guinness Book of World Records* as the fastest-growing paid-for consumer entertainment product in history. In Ireland, DVD sales were increasing at a rate of 100 per cent during the years 2000 and 2001. Not surprisingly the VCR market is contracting, falling from €32 million in 2000 to €27 million in 2001. Overall, the trend towards large home entertainment systems meant that Mitsubishi Ireland needed to carefully manage its

The Black Diamond banner line.

Table C38.1 Mitsubishi advertising and promotion plan, 1999

Media/percentage budget allocation	Jan	Feb	Mar	Apr	May	Jun	Jul	Aug	Sep	Oct	Nov	Dec
Corp. advertising												
Newspapers		X	X	X	X	X	X	X	X	X	X	X
Trade magazines			X	X	X		X	X	X	X	X	
Production		X	X	X	X	X	X	X	X		X	X
Dealer advertising/incentives												
Dealer support			X					X				X
Golf day									X			
Dealer trip		X										
Roadshow (May)					X							
Roadshow (Sept)									X			
User promotions												
Administration		X		X		X		X		X		X
Handouts				X		X		X		X		
Trade promotions												
Trade show (April)				X								
Trade show (Sept)									X			
Paris launch		X										
Sponsorship												
Special		X		X		X		X		X		X
Point-of-sale												
April		X	X	X								
September							X	X	X			
Brochures			X		X		X		X		X	
Exhibitions												
Dealer shows		X									X	
Public relations												
CEDA		X				X				X		
PR			X		X		X		X		X	
Research		X				X				X		
Sundry A&P												
Freight		X		X		X		X		X		X
Photography			X		X		X		X		X	
Printing		X		X		X		X		X		X

product range. On the plus side, the move to high-value products had driven the value of the Irish CTV market to €196 million in 2001, an increase of 26 per cent on 2000. While the company had largely held the share gains made in 1999 through 2000 and 2001, it needed a clear competitive marketing strategy for the years ahead given the uncertainty created by technological and market changes.

Table C38.2 Market share (percentage)

	Portable CTV	Large-screen CTV	Total CTV	VCR
Mitsubishi	27	40	32	32
Philips	36	18	30	29
Panasonic	12	12	12	12
Sanyo	12	10	9	11
Sony	5	9	8	7
Grundig	4	4	3	1
Others	4	7	6	8

Questions

1. Evaluate the launch of the Black Diamond brand. Why was it so successful?

2. Develop a competitive marketing strategy for the Black Diamond brand.

This case was written by John Fahy, Professor of Marketing, University of Limerick, Ireland. Copyright © John Fahy, 2003. This case is intended to serve as a basis for class discussion rather than to show either effective or ineffective management. The author gratefully acknowledges the support and assistance of the management staff of Mitsubishi Electric Irl. Ltd in the development of this case.

part four

Marketing Implementation and Application

- **20** Managing marketing implementation, organization and control
- **21** Marketing services
- **22** International marketing

chapter twenty

Managing marketing implementation, organization and control

❝God grant me the serenity to accept things I cannot change, courage to change things I can, and the wisdom to know the difference.❞
REINHOLD NIEBUHR

❝There is nothing more difficult than to take the lead in the introduction of a new order of things.❞
MACHIAVELLI

Learning Objectives

This chapter explains:

1. The relationship between marketing strategy, implementation and performance
2. The stages that people pass through when they experience disruptive change
3. The objectives of marketing implementation and change
4. The barriers to the implementation of the marketing concept
5. The forms of resistance to marketing implementation and change
6. How to develop effective implementation strategies
7. The elements of an internal marketing programme
8. The skills and tactics that can be used to overcome resistance to the implementation of the marketing concept and plan
9. Marketing organizational structures
10. The nature of a marketing control system

Designing marketing strategies and positioning plans that meet today's and tomorrow's market requirements is a necessary but not a sufficient condition for corporate success. They need to be translated into action through effective implementation. This is the system that makes marketing happen in companies: it is the face of marketing that customers see in the real world. As we shall see, how implementation is managed has a crucial bearing on business outcomes, and its accompanying process—the management of change—must be accomplished with skill and determination if strategies and plans are to become marketing practice.

This chapter examines the relationship between strategy, implementation and performance, how people react to change, and the objectives of implementation. It then explores the kinds of resistance that can surface when implementing the marketing concept and strategic marketing decisions. Finally, a framework for gaining commitment is laid out before looking at the skills and tactics that marketing managers can use to bring about marketing implementation and change. A key factor in implementing a change programme is top management support. Without its clear, visible and consistent backing a major change programme is likely to falter under the inertia created by vested interests.[1]

As new technologies emerge, companies need more than ever to embrace change and take the steps necessary to adapt to changing circumstances. In this way, they can turn potential threats into opportunities, as e-Marketing 20.1 describes.

This chapter also examines how companies organize their marketing activities and establish control procedures to check that objectives have been achieved.

20.1 e-marketing

The Internet as a Change Agent: the Case of Reuters

Few companies have recognized the power of the Internet to improve their operations, fewer still have made the decision to put the Internet at the very heart of their operations; those that have include Cisco, Dell, Sun and Reuters.

Reuters, unlike the others, is an 'old economy' organization; it began in 1850 when Paul Julius Reuters used carrier pigeons to send stock market news across a gap in the telegraph line between Berlin and Paris. Reuters was also the world's first online company, exchanging information as early as the 1970s through its own (and the world's largest) private communications network.

However, the Internet was destined to put Reuters out of business. Who could possibly need a proprietary network when information could be transferred over an open, public network?

Rather than wait for the inevitable, Reuters decided to turn a threat into an opportunity by being first to move. It set up the Reuters Greenhouse Fund, the aim of which was to invest in the technologies that could put Reuters out of business. It was among the first to invest in Yahoo! and Verisign.

These were more than just investments, Reuters was learning and changing. For example, it provided content to Yahoo! and a further 900 web portals. It also used Verisign's online security protocol to transfer confidential information to its clients.

Through treating the Internet as an area of innovation and learning, Reuters has been able to turn risk into opportunity and has put the Internet at the heart of its operations.

Based on: Kanter (2001)[2]

Marketing strategy, implementation and performance

Marketing strategy concerns the issues of *what* should happen and *why* it should happen. Implementation focuses on actions: *who* is responsible for various activities, *how* the strategy should be carried out, *where* things will happen and *when* action will take place.

Managers devise marketing strategies to meet new opportunities, counter environmental threats and match core competences. The framework for strategy development was discussed in Chapter 2, which dealt with marketing planning. Although implementation is a consequence of strategy, it also affects strategy and should form part of the strategy development process. The proposition is straightforward: strategy, no matter how well conceived from a customer perspective, will fail if people are incapable of carrying out the necessary tasks to make the strategy work in the marketplace. Implementation capability, then, is an integral part of strategy formulation. The link between strategy and implementation is shown in Fig. 20.1. Implementation affects marketing strategy choice. For example, a company that traditionally has been a low-cost, low-price operator may have a culture that finds it difficult to implement a value-added, high-price strategy. Strategy also determines implementation requirements: for example, a value-added, high-price strategy may require the salesforce to refrain from price discounting.

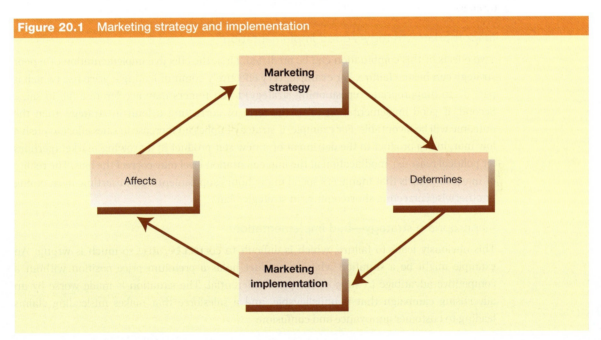

Figure 20.1 Marketing strategy and implementation

Combining strategies and implementation

Bonoma has argued that combinations of appropriate/inappropriate strategy and good/poor implementation will lead to various business outcomes.[3] Figure 20.2 shows the four-cell matrix, with predicted performances.

Appropriate strategy—good implementation

This is the combination most likely to lead to success. No guarantee of success can be made, however, because of the vagaries of the marketplace, including competitor actions and reactions, new technological breakthroughs and plain bad luck; but with strong implementation backing sound strategy, marketing management has done all it can to build success.

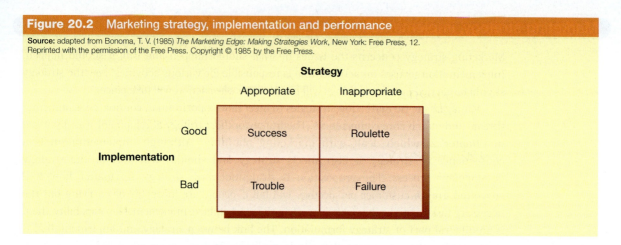

Figure 20.2 Marketing strategy, implementation and performance

Source: adapted from Bonoma, T. V. (1985) *The Marketing Edge: Making Strategies Work*, New York: Free Press, 12. Reprinted with the permission of the Free Press. Copyright © 1985 by the Free Press.

Appropriate strategy—bad implementation

This combination is likely to lead to trouble if sub-standard performance is attributed to poor strategy. Management's tendency to look for strategy change in response to poor results will result in a less appropriate strategy being grafted on to an already wayward implementation system.

Inappropriate strategy—good implementation

Two effects of this combination can be predicted. First, the effective implementation of a poor strategy can hasten failure. For example, very effectively communicating a price rise (which is part of an inappropriate repositioning strategy) to customers may accelerate a fall in sales. Second, if good implementation takes the form of correcting a fault in strategy, then the outcome will be favourable. For example, if strategy implies an increase in sales effort to push a low margin *dog* product to the detriment of a new *star* product in a growing market (perhaps for political reasons), modification at the implementation level may correct the bias. The reality of marketing life is that managers spend many hours supplementing, subverting, overcoming or otherwise correcting shortcomings in strategic plans.

Inappropriate strategy—bad implementation

This obviously leads to failure, which is difficult to correct because so much is wrong. An example might be a situation where a product holds a premium price position without a competitive advantage to support the price differential. The situation is made worse by an advertising campaign that is unbelievable, and a salesforce that makes misleading claims leading to customer annoyance and confusion.

Implications

So what should managers do when faced with poor performance? First, strategic issues should be separated from implementation activities and the problem diagnosed. Second, when in doubt about whether the problem is rooted in strategy or implementation, implementation problems should be addressed first so that strategic adequacy can be assessed more easily.

Implementation and the management of change

The implementation of a new strategy may have profound effects on people in organizations. Brand managers that discover their product is to receive fewer resources (harvested) may feel bitter and demoralized; a salesperson that loses as a result of a change in the payment system

Change can be assisted by the presence of a charismatic leader like Richard Branson.

may feel equally aggrieved. The implementation of a strategy move is usually associated with the need for people to adapt to *change*. The cultivation of change, therefore, is an essential ingredient in effective implementation. Some companies have charismatic leaders, like Virgin and Richard Branson, which can help the cultivation of change (see illustration).

A key ingredient in the management of change is getting the speed of change right. Proctor & Gamble suffered by trying to change too quickly. The new chief executive Durk Jaeger's vision was to transform P&G into a global brand powerhouse with Organization 2005, a six-year plan to improve sales and become truly global. But the upheaval left too many loyal managers alienated; costs were slashed but the required growth did not materialize. As Chris Lapuente explains:

> ❝What we tried to do was change the whole organization back to front, with a promise of record earnings. Virtually everybody changed jobs. And we were excited and inspired by the new vision and direction. It was very intoxicating.
>
> This is a winning culture and everybody signed up for it. The problem was that we didn't get the balance right between speed, stretch, innovation and commitments. We were far, far too impatient.[4]❞

It is helpful to understand the emotional stages that people pass through when confronted with an adverse change. These stages are known as the **transition curve** and are shown in Fig. 20.3.[5]

Figure 20.3 The transition curve

Source: Wilson, G. (1993) *Making Change Happen*, London: Pitman, 7. Reproduced with kind permission of Pitman Publishing.

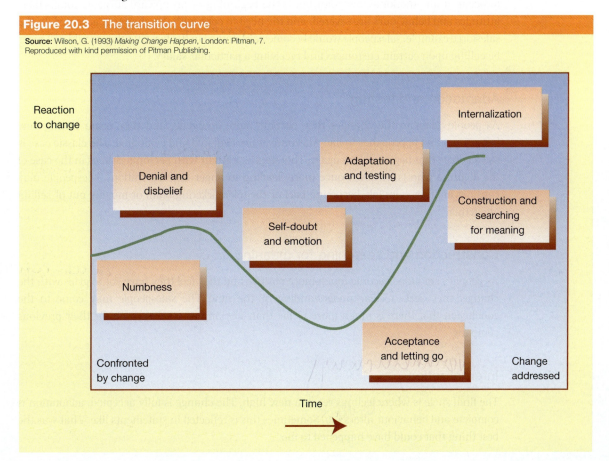

Numbness

The first reaction is usually shock. The enormity of the consequences leads to feelings of being overwhelmed, despair and numbness. The outward symptoms include silence and lack of overt response. The news that a field salesforce is to be replaced by a telemarketing team is likely to provoke numbness in the field salespeople.

Denial and disbelief

Denial and disbelief may follow numbness, leading to trivializing the news, denying it or joking about it. The aim is to minimize the psychological impact of the change. News of the abandonment of the field salesforce may be met by utter disbelief, and sentiments such as 'They would never do that to us.'

Self-doubt and emotion

As the certainty of the change dawns, so personal feelings of uncertainty may arise. The feeling is one of powerlessness, of being out of control: the situation has taken over the individual. The likely reaction is one of anger: both as individuals and as a group, salesforce staff are likely to vent their anger and frustration on management.

Acceptance and letting go

Acceptance is characterized by tolerating the new reality and letting go of the past. This is likely to occur at an emotional low point but is the beginning of an upward surge as comfortable attitudes and behaviours are severed, and the need to cope with the change is accepted. In the salesforce example, salespeople would become accustomed to the fact that they would no longer be calling upon certain customers and receiving a particular salary.

Adaptation and testing

As people adapt to the changes they become more energetic, and they begin testing new behaviours and approaches to life. Alternatives are explored and evaluated. The classic case is the divorcee that begins dating again. This stage is fraught with personal risk, as in the case of the divorcee who is let down once more, leading to anger and frustration. Salespeople may consider another sales job, becoming part of the telemarketing team or moving out of selling altogether.

Construction and searching for meaning

As people's emotions become much more positive and they feel they have got to grips with the change, they seek a clear understanding of the new. The salespeople may come to the conclusion that there is much more to life than working as a salesperson for their previous company.

Internalization

The final stage is where feelings reach a new high. The change is fully accepted, adaptation is complete and behaviour alters too. Sometimes this is reflected in statements like 'That was the best thing that could have happened to me.'

Implications

Most people pass through all the above stages, although the movement from one stage to the next is rarely smooth. The implication for managing marketing implementation is that the acceptance of fundamental change such as the reprioritizing of products, jobs or strategic business units will take time for people to accept and come to terms with. The venting of anger and frustration is an accompanying behaviour to this transition from the old to the new, and should be accepted as such. Some people will leave as part of the fifth stage—the testing of new behaviours—but others will see meaning in and internalize the changes that have resulted from strategic redirection.

Objectives of marketing implementation and change

The overriding objective of marketing implementation and change from a strategic standpoint is the successful execution of the marketing plan. This may include:

- gaining the support of key decision-makers in the company for the proposed plan (and overcoming the opposition of others)
- gaining the required resources (e.g. people and money) to be able to implement the plan
- gaining the commitment of individuals and departments in the company who are involved in frontline implementation (e.g. marketing, sales, service and distribution staff)
- gaining the co-operation of other departments needed to implement the plan (e.g. production and R&D).

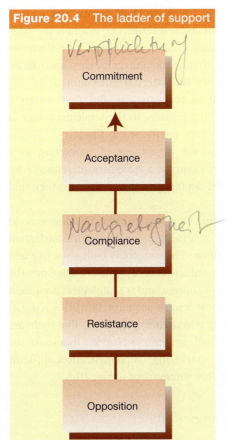

Figure 20.4 The ladder of support

For some people, the objectives and execution of the plan are consonant with their objectives, interests and viewpoints; gaining support from them is easy. But there are likely to be others who are involved with implementation from whom support is not so readily gained. They are the losers and neutrals. Loss may be in the form of lower status, a harder life or a reduction in salary. Neutrals may be left untouched overall with gains being balanced by losses. For some losers, support will never be forthcoming, for others they may be responsive to persuasion, whereas neutrals may be more willing to support change.

The ladder of support

What does support mean? Figure 20.4 illustrates the degree of support that may be achieved; this can range from outright opposition to full commitment.

Opposition

The stance of direct opposition is taken by those with much to lose from the implementation of the marketing strategy, and who believe they have the political strength to stop the proposed change. Opposition is overt, direct and forceful.

Resistance

With resistance, opposition is less overt and may take a more passive form such as delaying tactics. Perhaps because of the lack of a strong power base, people are not willing to display open hostility but, nevertheless, their intention is to hamper the implementation process.

Compliance

Compliance means that people act in accordance with the plan but without much enthusiasm or zest. They yield to the need to conform but lack conviction that the plan is the best way to proceed. These reservations limit the lengths to which they are prepared to go to achieve its successful implementation.

Acceptance

A higher level of support is achieved when people accept the worth of the plan and actively seek to realize its goals. Their minds may be won but their hearts are not set on fire, limiting the extent of their motivation.

Commitment

Commitment is the ultimate goal of an effective implementation programme. People not only accept the worth of the plan but also pledge themselves to secure its success. Both hearts and minds are won, leading to strong conviction, enthusiasm and zeal. This can be encouraged by making people feel valued. Halifax, for example, uses members of staff in its television advertising to promote its financial services (see illustrations).

Barriers to the implementation of the marketing concept

Over the following pages we shall discuss the various forms of opposition and resistance, and examine the skills and tactics necessary to deal with them. This reflects the growing realism that marketing managers need to be adept at managing the internal environment of the company as well as the external. But first we shall examine some of the barriers to the implementation of the marketing concept mentioned in Chapter 1. This is necessary because the acceptance of marketing as a philosophy in a company is a necessary prerequisite for the successful development of marketing strategy and implementation.

The marketing concept states that business success will result from creating greater customer satisfaction than the competition. The concept is both seductive and tautological. It is seductive because it encapsulates the essence of business success, and is tautological because it is necessarily true. So why do so many companies score so badly at marketing effectiveness? The fact is that there are inherent *personal and organizational barriers* that make the achievement of marketing implementation difficult in practice. These are summarized in Fig. 20.5.

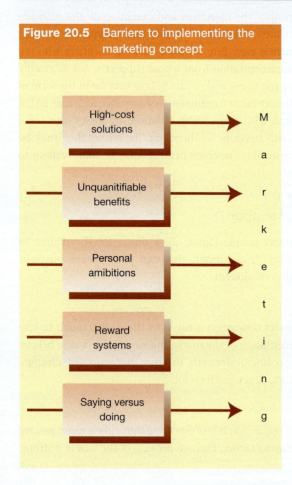

Figure 20.5 Barriers to implementing the marketing concept

High-cost solutions

Often giving what the customer wants involves extra costs. In today's heavily competitive environment most

Staff feel valued when included in key organizational practices/activities. The Halifax use members of staff when advertising their financial services products in both of these advertisements.

companies will meet customers' low-cost solutions. Therefore many marketing recommendations to beat competition will involve higher costs. Travelworld, a travel agency, was founded on giving better service to its customers. The chief executive recognized that the competition often required customers to queue at peak periods when booking a holiday. This he felt was unacceptable when customers were involved in a major transaction: a holiday is one of the highest-expenditure items for families each year. The solution was to hire enough staff at his outlets to ensure that queuing was not a problem. He came from a marketing background and accepted the higher costs involved.

Meeting customer requirements can also conflict with production's desire to gain cost economies of scale, and the finance director's objective of inventory reduction. Customers invariably differ in their requirements—they have different personalities, experiences and lifestyles—and to meet individual requirements is clearly not feasible. A solution to this problem is to group customers into segments that have similar needs and to target one product or service offering to each group. This allows the production manager to reap some economies of scale, and marketing to tailor offerings to the marketplace.

It was the failure of Henry Ford to compromise that almost led to his company's downfall.[6] He continued to make the Model T in the face of competition from General Motors, which was making a range of cars in many colours (including pink) because Americans no longer wanted the drab old Model T and could afford something more glamorous. Ford's predilection with economies of scale lost him number-one position in the ranking of US car companies, a position that Ford has never managed to regain.

To a finance director stocks mean working capital tied up and interest charges to be made. To the marketing director stocks mean higher service levels and thus higher customer satisfaction. In the retailing of paint, for example, an out-of-stock situation is likely to mean a lost customer. Once more the marketing approach of giving customers what they want is a high-cost solution. Clearly, a compromise needs to be reached and target market segmentation can provide its basis. Unipart, a supplier of spare parts for cars, recognized that inventory cost control procedures meant that the competition was holding low stocks. This resulted in customer dissatisfaction when an urgently needed part, say a distributor cap, could not be provided when required. Unipart's strategy was to target those motorists (do-it-yourselfers) that valued instant (or very quick) parts provision and were willing to pay a little more for the service. Its tag-line, 'The answer's yes. Now what's the question?', reflected the company's strategy. It identified a *high-price, high-service* segment and chose to serve those customers. In other situations, a *low-price, low-service* segment may be identified, and low stocks and a low price may be the appropriate response.

Unquantifiable benefits

A problem with marketing recommendations is that they are often unquantifiable in the sense that it is difficult to measure the exact increase in revenue (and profits) that will result from their implementation. A case that illustrates this point is that of a business school faced with a customer problem. The student car park was regularly being raided by thieves who stole radios and cars. One marketing solution was to employ at least one security guard. The extra cost could easily be quantified, not so the economic benefits to the business school, however. On a purely commercial basis, it is impossible to say what the marginal revenue would be. On a similar theme, what is likely to be the reduced revenue from removing one platform attendant from a railway station? The cost saving is immediate and quantifiable; the reduced customer satisfaction through not having someone to answer queries is not.

Personal ambitions

Personal ambitions can also hinder the progress of marketing in an organization. The R&D director may enjoy working on challenging, complex technical problems at the cutting edge of scientific knowledge. Customers may simply want products that work. Staff may want an easy life, which means that the customer is neglected.

Reward systems

It is a basic tenet of motivation theory that behaviour is influenced by reward systems.[7] Unfortunately organizations are prone to reward individuals in ways that conflict with marketing-orientated action. A problem that Sir John Egan had when he took over at Jaguar was that staff in the buying department were rewarded by the savings they made on their purchases. Consequently the emphasis when negotiating with suppliers was price. In order to meet these demands suppliers were compromising quality and the result was unreliable cars. The joke in the USA was that you needed two Jaguars just to make sure that one started in the morning. Egan told his purchasing department to negotiate higher prices in return for better quality. Sales staff who are rewarded by incentives based on sales revenue may be tempted to give heavy discounts, which secure easy sales in the short term but may ruin positioning strategies and profits. Webster argues that the key to developing a market-driven, customer-orientated business lies in how managers are evaluated and rewarded.[8] If managers are evaluated on the basis of short-term profitability and sales, they are likely to pay heed to these criteria and neglect market factors such as customer satisfaction, which ensure the long-term health of an organization.

Saying versus doing

Another force that blocks the implementation of the marketing concept is the gap between what senior managers say and what they do. Webster suggests that senior management must give clear signals and establish clear values and beliefs about serving the customer.[9] However, Argyris found that senior executives' behaviour often conflicted with what they said—for example, they might say 'Be customer orientated' and then cut back on marketing research funds.[10] This resulted in staff not really believing that management was serious about achieving a customer focus.

Implications

The implications are that marketing managers have to face the fact that some people in the organization will have a vested interest in blocking the introduction and growth of marketing in an organization, and will have some ammunition (e.g. the extra costs, unquantifiable benefits) to achieve their aims. Marketing implementation, then, depends on being able to overcome the opposition and resistance that may well surface as a result of developing market-driven plans. The following sections discuss the nature of such resistance, and ways of dealing with it.

Forms of resistance to marketing implementation and change

Opposition to the acceptance of marketing and the implementation of marketing plans is direct, open and conflict driven. Often, arguments such as the lack of tangible benefits and the extra expense of marketing proposals, will be used to cast doubt on their worth. Equally likely, however, is the more passive type of *resistance*. Kanter and Piercy suggest ten forms of resistance:[11,12]

1. criticism of specific details of the plan
2. foot-dragging
3. slow response to requests
4. unavailability
5. suggestions that, despite the merits of the plan, resources should be channelled elsewhere
6. arguments that the proposals are too ambitious
7. hassle and aggravation created to wear the proposer down
8. attempts to delay the decision, hoping the proposer will lose interest
9. attacks on the credibility of the proposer with rumour and innuendo
10. deflation of any excitement surrounding the plan by pointing out the risks.

Market research reports supporting marketing action can also be attacked. Johnson describes the reaction of senior managers to the first marketing research report commissioned by a new marketing director.[13]

> As a diagnostic statement the research was full, powerful, prescriptive. The immediate result of this analysis was that the report was rubbished by senior management and directors. The analysis may have been perceived by its initiator as diagnostic but it was received by its audience as a politically threatening statement.

In general, there are ten ways of blocking a marketing report.[14] These are described in Marketing in Action 20.1 (overleaf).

Ansoff argues that the level of resistance will depend on how much the proposed change is likely to disrupt the culture and power structure of the organization and the speed at which the change is introduced.[16] The latter point is in line with the previous discussion about how people adapt to adverse change, requiring time to come to terms with disruptions. The greatest level of opposition and resistance will come when the proposed change is implemented quickly and is a threat to the culture and politics of the organization; the least opposition and resistance will be found when the change is consonant with the existing culture and political structure, and is introduced over a period of time. Further, Pettigrew states that resistance is likely to be low when a company is faced with a crisis, arguing that a common perception among people that the organization is threatened with extinction also acts to overcome inertia against change.[17]

20.1 marketing in action

Ten Ways of Blocking a Marketing Report

Reports that present critical conclusions or unpopular recommendations to an audience of managers are likely to meet stiff opposition. There are 10 devices used by managers to block an undesired report.

1. *Straight rejection*: the report and its writer/commissioner are dismissed without further discussion. This approach requires political strength and self-confidence
2. *Bottom drawer*: the report is effectively 'bottom drawered' by praising its contents but taking no action on its recommendations. The writer/commissioner, happy to receive praise, does not press the matter further.
3. *Mobilizing political support*: recognizing there is strength in numbers, the opposer gathers support from other managers who are threatened by the report.
4. *Criticizing the details*: a series of minor technical criticisms are raised to discredit the report, such as poor question wording and unrepresentative samples.
5. *But in the future*: the report is recognized as being accurate for today but does not take into account future events and so should not be implemented.
6. *Working on emotions*: make the writer feel bad by asking 'How can you do this to me?'
7. *Invisible man tactic*: the opposer is never available for comment on the report.
8. *Further study is required*: the report is returned for further work.
9. *The scapegoat*: 'I have no problems with this report but I know the boss/head office, etc. will not approve of it.'
10. *Deflection*: an extension of criticizing the details, where attention is directed at areas where the opposer's knowledge is sufficient to contradict some points made by the writer/commissioner and so discredit the whole report.

Based on: Pettigrew (1974)[15]

Developing implementation strategies

Faced with the likelihood of resistance from vested interests, a **change master** needs to develop an implementation strategy that can deliver the required change.[18] The importance of a change master is discussed in Marketing in Action 20.2, which examines change at Xerox.

A change master is a person who is responsible for driving through change within an organization. This necessitates a structure for thinking about the problems to be tackled and the way to deal with them. Figure 20.6 illustrates such a framework. The process starts with a definition of objectives.

Implementation objectives

These are formulated at two levels: what we would like to achieve (*would-like objectives*) and what we must achieve (*must-have objectives*). Framing objectives in this way recognizes that we may not be able to achieve all that we desire. Would-like objectives are our preferred solution: they define the maximum that the implementer can reasonably expect.[20] Must-have objectives define our minimum requirements: if we cannot achieve these then we have lost and the plan or strategy will not succeed. Between the two points there is an area for negotiation, but beyond our must-have objective there is no room for compromise.

20.2 marketing in action

A Master of Change at Xerox

The history of Xerox illustrates the importance of being able to implement strategy. Here was a company with a coherent strategy and excellent products pushed close to bankruptcy by its inability to get things done. Its salvation was the appointment of Anne Mulcahy, a Xerox employee for 25 years, to chief executive officer with a brief to act as a change master.

When she took over, the organization was losing on every front. A failed reorganization of the North American salesforce had alienated customers. A botched consolidation of administrative centres had caused chaos with billing and revenue collection. Added to this, growth markets such as Brazil and Thailand had soured, competition was intensifying and the balance sheet was overloaded with debt.

Ms Mulcahy's first move was a 90-day mission, talking to customers and employees. As she explains, 'There was such confusion and complexity in the company that I could have wasted a lot of time addressing symptoms that were not at the heart of what was wrong.'

Her turnaround plan was simple but brutal: overheads would be cut by $1 billion, unprofitable businesses would close and assets would be sold to repay debt. Central to the successful implementation of this plan was her long-standing and respected position at Xerox. In the eyes of staff at Xerox she had earned the right to change the company. Her position as an insider also meant that she knew the capabilities of other Xerox managers to hand-pick a new team. Her philosophy is that someone must feel that they 'own' each change initiative that takes place.

Also playing a key part in the process was the use of the severity of the crisis to push for change. 'I used it as a vehicle to get things done that wouldn't have been possible in times of business as usual,' she says.

Finally, though many of the operations and strategy committees are the same, the way she runs them has changed. A case in point was an operations committee meeting to discuss customer satisfaction. The functional experts made a good presentational job, and break-out sessions were allowing full participation, but suddenly Ms Mulcahy realized that they were slipping into old Xerox ways of nice presentations, nice process, but never addressing the tough issues. The meeting was refocused to face up to the hard decisions that would really make a difference to customer satisfaction.

Based on: London and Hill (2002)[19]

By clearly defining these objectives at the start, we know what we would like, the scope for bargaining, and the point where we have to be firm and resist further concessions. For example, suppose our marketing plan calls for a move from a salary-only payment system for salespeople to salary plus commission. This is predicted to lead to strong resistance from salespeople and some sales managers, who favour the security element of fixed salary. Our would-like objective might be a 60:40 split between salary and commission. This would define our starting point in

Figure 20.6 Managing implementation

attempting to get this change implemented. But in order to allow room for concessions, our must-have objective would be somewhat lower, perhaps an 80:20 ratio between salary and commission. Beyond this point we refuse to bargain: we either win or lose on the issue. In some situations, however, would-like and must-have objectives coincide: here there is no room for negotiation, and persuasive and political skills are needed to drive through the issue.

Strategy

All worthwhile plans and strategies necessitate substantial human and organizational change inside companies.[21] Marketing managers, therefore, need a practical mechanism for thinking through strategies to drive change. One such framework is known as internal marketing, sometimes called the 'missing half' of the marketing programme.[22]

Originally the idea of internal marketing was developed within the area of services marketing, where it was applied to develop, train, motivate and retain employees at the customer interface in such areas as retailing, catering and financial services.[23] However, the concept can be expanded to include marketing to all employees with the aim of achieving successful marketing implementation. The framework is appealing as it draws an analogy with external marketing structures such as market segmentation, target marketing and the marketing mix. The people inside the organization to whom the plan must be marketed are considered *internal customers*. We need to gain the support, commitment and participation of sufficient of these to achieve acceptance and implementation of the plan. For those people where we fail to do this we need to minimize the effectiveness of their resistance. They become, in effect, our competitors in the internal marketplace.

Internal market segmentation

As with external marketing, analysis of customers begins with market segmentation. One obvious method of grouping internal customers is into three categories.

(1) *Supporters*: those who are likely to gain from the change or are committed to it.

(2) *Neutrals*: those whose gains and losses are in approximate balance.

(3) *Opposers*: those who are likely to lose from the change or are traditional opponents.

These three market segments form distinct *target groups* for which specific *marketing mix* programmes can be developed (see Fig. 20.7).

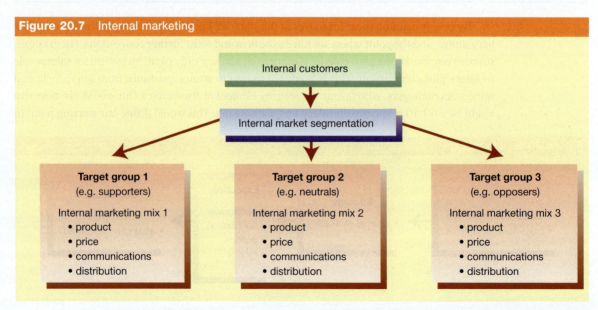

Figure 20.7 Internal marketing

Internal marketing mix programmes

Product is the marketing plan and strategies that are being proposed, together with the values, attitudes and actions that are needed to make the plan successful. Features of the product may include increased marketing budgets, extra staff, different ways of handling customers, different pricing, distribution and advertising, and new product development strategies. The product will reflect our would-like objectives; however, it may have to be modified slightly to gain acceptance from our opponents. Hence the need for must-have objectives.

The *price* element of the marketing mix is what we are asking our internal customers to pay as a result of accepting the marketing plan. The price they pay may be lost resources, lower status, fear of the unknown, harder work and rejection of their pet projects because of lack of funds. Clearly, price sensitivity is a key segmentation variable that differentiates supporters, neutrals and opposers.

Communications is a major element of the internal marketing mix and covers the communications media and messages used to influence the attitudes of key players. A combination of personal (presentations, discussion groups) and non-personal (the full report, executive summaries) can be used to inform and persuade. Communication should be two-way: we should listen as well as inform. We should also be prepared to adapt the product (the plan) if necessary in response to our internal customers' demands. This is analogous to adaptation of a new product in the external marketplace as a result of marketing research. Communication objectives will differ according to the target group, as follows.

- *Supporters*: to reinforce existing positive attitudes and behaviour, mobilize support from key players (e.g. chief executive).
- *Neutrals*: the use of influence strategies to build up perception of rewards and downgrade perceived losses; display key supporters and explain the benefits of joining 'the team'; negotiate to gain commitment.
- *Opposers*: disarm and discredit; anticipate objections and create convincing counter-arguments; position them as 'stuck in their old ways'; bypass by gaining support of opinion and political leaders; negotiate to lower resistance.

Opposition to the proposals may stem from a misunderstanding on the part of staff of the meaning of marketing. Some people may equate marketing with advertising and selling rather than the placing of customer satisfaction as central to corporate success. An objective of communications, therefore, may be to clarify the real meaning of marketing, or to use terms that are more readily acceptable such as 'improving service quality'.[24]

Distribution describes the places where the product and communications are delivered to the internal customers such as meetings, committees, seminars, informal conversations and away-days. Consideration should be given to whether presentations should be direct (proponents to customers) or indirect (using third parties such as consultants). Given the conflicting viewpoints of the three target segments, thought should be given to the advisability of using different distribution channels for each group. For example, a meeting may be arranged with only supporters and neutrals present. If opposers tend to be found in a particular department, judicious selection of which departments to invite may accomplish this aim.

Execution

In order to execute an implementation strategy successfully, certain skills are required, and particular tactics need to be employed. Internal marketing has provided a framework to structure thinking about implementation strategies. Within that framework, the main skills are persuasion, negotiation and politics.

Persuasion

The starting point of persuasion is to try to understand the situation from the internal customer's standpoint. The new plan may have high profit potential, the chance of real sales growth and be popular among external customers, but if it causes grief to certain individuals and departments in the organization, resistance may be expected. As with personal selling, the proponents of the plan must understand the needs, motivations and problems of their customers before they can hope to develop effective messages. For example, appealing to a production manager's sense of customer welfare will fail if that person is interested only in smooth production runs. In such a situation the proponent of the plan needs to show how smooth production will not be affected by the new proposals, or how disruption will be marginal or temporary.

The implementer also needs to understand how the features of the plan (e.g. new payment structure) confer customer benefits (e.g. the opportunity to earn more money). Whenever possible, evidence should be provided to support claims. Objectives should be anticipated and convincing counter-arguments produced. Care should be taken not to bruise egos unnecessarily.

Negotiation

Implementers have to recognize that they may not get all they want during this process. By setting would-like and must-have objectives (see earlier in this chapter) they are clear about what they want and have given themselves negotiating room wherever possible. Two key aspects of negotiation will be considered next: concession analysis and proposal analysis.

The key to **concession analysis** is to value the concessions the implementer might be prepared to make from the viewpoint of the opponent. By doing this it may be possible to identify concessions that cost the implementer very little and yet are highly valued by the opponent. For example, if the must-have objective is to move from a fixed salary to a salary plus commission, a salesperson's compensation plan conceding that the proportions should be 80:20 rather than 70:30 may be trivial to the implementer (an incentive to sell is still there) and yet highly valued by the salesperson as they will gain more income security and value the psychological bonus of winning a concession from management. By trading concessions that are highly valued by the opponent and yet cost the implementer little, painless agreement can be reached.

Proposal analysis: another sensible activity is to try to predict the proposals and demands that opponents are likely to make during the process of implementation. This provides time to prepare a response to them rather than relying on quick decisions during the heat of negotiation. By anticipating the kinds of proposals opponents are likely to make, implementers can plan the types of counter-proposal they are prepared to make.

Politics

Success in managing implementation and change also depends on the understanding and execution of political skills. Understanding the sources of power is the starting point from which an assessment of where power lies and who holds the balance can be made. The five sources are reward, expert, referent, legitimate and coercive power.[25]

Reward power derives from the implementer's ability to provide benefits to members in the organization. The recommendations of the plan may confer natural benefits in the form of increased status or salary for some people. In other cases, the implementer may create rewards for support—for example, promises of reciprocal support when required, or backing for promotion. The implementer needs to assess what each target individual values and whether the natural rewards match those values, or whether created rewards are necessary. A limit on the use of reward power is the danger that people may come to expect rewards in return for support. Created rewards, therefore, should be used sparingly.

Expert power is based on the belief that implementers have special knowledge and expertise that renders their proposals more credible. For example, a plan outlining major change is more likely to be accepted if produced by someone who has a history of success rather than a novice. Implementers should not be reluctant to display their credentials as part of the change process.

Referent power occurs when people identify with and respect the architect of change. That is why charismatic leadership is often thought to be an advantage to those who wish to see change implemented.

Legitimate power is wielded when the implementer insists on an action from a subordinate as a result of their hierarchical relationship and contract. For example, a sales manager may demand compliance with a request for a salesperson to go on a training course or a board of directors may exercise its legitimate right to cut costs.

The strength of **coercive power** lies with the implementer's ability to punish those who resist or oppose the implementation of the plan. Major organizational change is often accompanied by staff losses. This may be a required cost-cutting exercise but it also sends messages to those not directly affected that they may be next if further change is resisted. The problem with using coercive power is that, at best, it results in compliance rather than commitment.

Applications of power

The balance of power will depend on who holds the sources of power and how well they are applied. Implementers should pause to consider any sources of power they hold, and also the sources and degree of power held by supporters, neutrals and opposers. Power held by supporters should be mobilized, those neutrals who wield power should be cultivated, and tactics should be developed to minimize the influence of powerful opposers. The tactics that can be deployed will be discussed shortly, but two applications of power will be discussed first: overt and covert power plays.

Overt power plays are the visible, open kind of power plays that can be used by implementers to push through their proposals. Unconcealed use of the five sources of power is used to influence key players. The use of overt power by localized interests, who battle to secure their own interests in the process of change has been well documented.[26]

Covert power plays are a more disguised form of influence. Their use is more subtle and devious than that of overt power plays. Their application can take many forms including agenda setting, limiting participation in decisions to a few select individuals/departments, and defining what is and what is not open to decision for others in the organization.[27]

Tactics

The discussion of overt and covert power plays has introduced some of the means by which implementers and change agents can gain acceptance of their proposals and overcome opposition. We shall now examine in more detail the array of tactics that can be used to achieve these ends. The discussion so far has described the kinds of resistance and opposition that may arise when trying to implement the marketing concept and, more specifically, marketing plans and strategies. We have also examined the skills that are needed to win implementation battles. We shall now outline the tactics that can be used to apply those skills in the face of some hostile reaction within the organization. These can be grouped into tactics of persuasion, politics, time and negotiation (see Fig. 20.8), and are based on the work of a number of authorities.[28] They provide a wide-ranging checklist of approaches to mobilizing support and overcoming resistance.

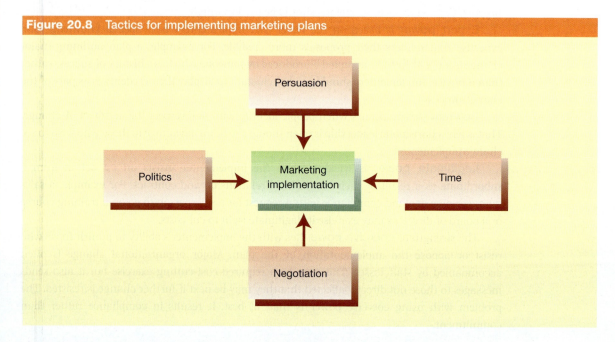

Figure 20.8　Tactics for implementing marketing plans

Persuasion

- *Articulate a shared vision*: the vision—a picture of the destination aspired to and the desired results of the change—needs to be spread to the key players in the organization. For example, if the marketing plan calls for a reduction in staffing levels, the vision that this is required to reposition the company for greater competitiveness needs to be articulated. Without an understanding of the wider picture, people may regard the exercise as 'just another cost drive'.[29] Since most change involves risk and discomfort, a clear vision of its purpose and consequences can make the risk acceptable and the discomfort endurable.

- *Communicate and train*: implementation of the marketing concept or a fundamentally different marketing plan means that many individuals have to reorientate and engage in new activities. To achieve this requires a major commitment to communicating the nature and purpose of the change, as well as to training staff in the new skills to be mastered. Major changes require face-to-face communication at discussion sessions and management education seminars. Formal training programmes are needed to upgrade skills and introduce new procedures.

- *Eliminate misconceptions*: a major part of the communication programme will be designed to eliminate misconceptions about the consequences of the change. Unfounded fears and anxieties should be allayed. Certain individuals will exaggerate the negative consequences of the proposed changes, and their concerns need to be addressed.

- *Sell the benefits*: the needs of key players have to be identified and the benefits of the change sold to them on that basis. The benefits may be economic (e.g. increased salary) or psychological (e.g. increased status, enhanced power). Whereas shared vision provides evidence of a wider general benefit (e.g. increased competitiveness) personal benefits should also be sold. This recognizes the fact that individuals seek to achieve not only organizational goals but also personal ambitions.

- *Gain acceptance by association*: position the plan against some well-accepted organizational doctrine such as *customer service* or *quality management*. Because the doctrine is heavily backed, the chances of the plan being accepted and implemented are enhanced. Another positioning strategy is to associate the plan with a powerful individual (e.g. the chief executive). The objective is to create the viewpoint that if the boss wants the plan, there is no point in opposing it.

- *Leave room for local control over details*: leaving some local options or local control over details of the plan creates a sense of ownership on the part of those responsible for implementation, and encourages adaptation to different situations. Thought should be given to the extent of uniformity in execution, and the areas where local adoption is both practical and advisable.

- *Support words with action*: when implementation involves the establishment or maintenance of a marketing-orientated culture, it is vital to support fine words with corresponding action. As we saw when discussing resistance to the marketing concept, it is easy for managers to contradict their words with inappropriate actions (e.g. stressing the need to understand customers and then cutting the marketing research budget). An illustrative case of how management actions supported the culture they were trying to create is the story of a regional manager of US company United Parcel Service (UPS), who used his initiative to untangle a misdirected shipment of Christmas presents by hiring an entire train and diverting two UPS-owned 727s from their flight plans.[30] Despite the enormous cost (which far exceeded the value of the business), when senior management learned what he had done they praised and rewarded him: their actions supported and reinforced the culture they wanted to foster. As this story became folklore at UPS, its staff knew that senior management meant business when they said that the customer had to come first.

- *Establish two-way communication*: it is important that the people who are responsible for implementation feel that they can put their viewpoints to senior management, otherwise the feeling of top-down control will spread and resistance will build up through the belief that 'no one ever listens to us'. It is usually well worth listening to people lower down the management hierarchy and especially those who come face to face with customers. One way of implementing this approach is through staff suggestion schemes, but these need to be managed so that staff believe it is worth bothering to take part. Marketing in Action 20.3 discusses how Asda's successful scheme works.

Politics

- *Build coalitions*: the process of creating allies for the proposed measures is a crucial step in the implementation process. Two groups have special significance: power sources that control the resources needed for implementation such as information (expertise or data), finance and support (legitimacy, opinion leadership and political backing); and stakeholders, who are those people likely to gain or lose from the change.[33] Discussion with potential losers may reveal ways of sharing some rewards with them ('Invite the

20.3 marketing in action

Good Ideas Mean Successful Implementation

Asda, the UK supermarket chain acquired by Wal-Mart in 1999, has a policy of tapping into the collective wisdom of its 85,000 staff. It runs two schemes aimed at involving staff in the day-to-day running of the company. The first, entitled Colleague Circles, encourages its staff (Asda calls them colleagues) to put forward suggestions for improved customer service. The best ideas are presented at an annual meeting called the National Circle. The objective is to make it as easy as possible for colleagues to pass on ideas based on their experience with customers.

The second scheme, called 'Tell Tony', invites staff to make suggestions direct to Asda's chief executive officer Tony Denunzio. A key ingredient is that if someone writes to the CEO, they get a reply from the CEO. The scheme reflects the belief in Asda that everyone is equally valued and their contribution respected. It promotes a culture in which everyone takes responsibility for improving the business. The most promising are rewarded with 'star points' that can be redeemed against a catalogue of offers including clothes and holidays.

Neither scheme is intended to provide a vehicle for ideas that fundamentally change the strategy of Asda, but to improve Asda's operations in small ways. For example, one suggestion was based on the problem of clearing up litter and trolleys around rose bushes that were used to landscape car parks. The thorns were proving painful and so the roses were replaced with shrubs and trees that made a tiny part of Asda's operations easier and more efficient.

Evidence shows that suggestion schemes only work if people believe their suggestions will be considered and some implemented. Inviting staff to make suggestions can improve motivation and quality of work including the achievement of high standards of customer service. Staff can never complain that 'no one ever listens to us'!

Based on: White (1999);[31] www.asda.co.uk[32]

opposition in'). At the very least, talking to them will reveal their grievances and so allow thought to be given to how these may be handled. Another product of these discussions with both potential allies and foes is that the original proposals may be improved by accepting some of their suggestions.

- *Display support*: having recruited powerful allies these should be asked for a visible demonstration of support. This will confirm any statements that implementers have made about the strength of their backing ('gain acceptance by association'). Allies should be invited to meetings, presentations and seminars so that stakeholders can see the forces behind the change.

- *Invite the opposition in*: thought should be given to creating ways of sharing the rewards of the change with the opposition. This may mean modifying the plan and how it is to be implemented to take account of the needs of key players. So long as the main objectives of the plan remain intact, this may be a necessary step towards removing some opposition.

- *Warn the opposition*: critics of the plan should be left in no doubt as to the adverse consequences of opposition. This has been called *selling the negatives*. However, the tactic should be used with care because statements that are perceived as threats may stiffen rather than dilute resistance, particularly when the source does not have a strong power base.

- *Use of language*: in the political arena the potency of language in endorsing a preferred action and discrediting the opposition has long been apparent. For example, during the Gulf War the following terminology was used:[34]

We (UN) have:	They (Iraq) have:
Army, Navy and Air Force	the war machine
reporting guidelines	censorship
press briefings	propaganda
We:	*They:*
suppress	destroy
eliminate	kill
neutralize	kill
We launch:	*They launch:*
first strikes	sneak missile attacks
pre-emptively	without provocation
Our men are:	*Their men are*
boys, lads	troops, hordes.

Language can be used as a weapon in the implementation battle with critics being labelled 'outdated', 'backward looking' and 'set in their ways'. In meetings, implementers need to avoid the temptation to *overpower* in their use of language. For people without a strong power base (such as young newcomers to a company) using phrases like 'We must take this action' or 'This is the way we have to move' to people in a more senior position (e.g. a board of directors) will provoke psychological resistance even to praiseworthy plans. Phases like 'I suggest' or 'I have a proposal for you to consider' recognize the inevitable desire on the part of more senior management to feel involved in the decision-making rather than being treated like a rubber stamp.

- *Decision control*: this may be achieved by agenda setting (i.e. controlling what is and is not discussed in meetings), limiting participation in decision-making to a small number of allies, controlling which decisions are open for debate in the organization, and timing important meetings when it is known that a key critic is absent (e.g. on holiday, or abroad on business).

- *The either/or alternative*: finally, when an implementation proposal is floundering, a powerful proponent may decide to use the either/or tactic in which the key decision-maker is required to choose between two documents placed on the desk: one asks for approval of the implementation plan, the other tenders the implementer's resignation.

Time

- *Incremental steps*: people need time to adjust to change, therefore consideration should be given to how quickly change is introduced. Where resistance to the full implementation package is likely to be strong, one option is to submit the strategy in incremental steps. A small, less controversial strategy is implemented first. Its success provides the impetus for the next implementation proposals, and so on.

- *Persistence*: this tactic requires the resubmission of the strategy until it is accepted. Modifications to the strategy may be necessary on the way but the objective is to wear down the opposition by resolute and persistent force. The game is a battle of wills, and requires the capability of the implementer to accept rejection without loss of motivation.
- *Leave insufficient time for alternatives*: a different way of using time is to present plans at the last possible minute so that there is insufficient time for anyone to present or implement an alternative. The proposition is basically 'We must move with this plan as there is no alternative'.
- *Wait for the opposition to leave*: for those prepared to play a waiting game, withdrawing proposals until a key opposition member leaves the company or loses power may be feasible. Implementers should be alert to changes in the power structure in these ways as they may present a window of opportunity to resubmit hitherto rejected proposals.

Negotiation

- *Make the opening stance high*: when the implementer suspects that a proposal in the plan is likely to require negotiation, the correct opening stance is to start high but be realistic. There are two strong reasons for this. First, the opponent may accept the proposal without modification; second, it provides room for negotiation. When deciding how high to go, the limiting factor is the need to avoid unnecessary conflict. For example, asking for a move from a fixed salary to a commission-only system with a view to compromising with salary plus commission is likely to be unrealistic and to provoke unnecessary antagonism among the salesforce.
- *Trade concessions*: sometimes it may be possible to grant a concession simply to secure agreement to the basics of the plan. Indeed, if the implementer has created negotiating room, this may be perfectly acceptable. In other circumstances, however, the implementer may be able to trade concession for concession with the opponent. For example, a demand from the salesforce to reduce list price may be met by a counter-proposal to reduce discount levels. A useful way of trading concessions is by means of the *if ... then* technique: '*If* you are prepared to reduce your discount levels from 10 to 5 per cent, I am *then* prepared to reduce list price by 5 per cent.'[35] This is a valuable tool in negotiation because it promotes movement towards agreement and yet ensures that concessions given to the opponent are matched by concessions in return. Whenever possible, an attempt to create *win-win* situations should be made where concessions that cost the giver very little are highly valued by the receiver.

Evaluation

Finally, during and after the implementation process, evaluation should be made to consider what has been achieved and what has been learned. Evaluation may be in terms of the degree of support gained from key players, how well the plan and strategy have been implemented in the marketplace (e.g. by the use of customer surveys), the residual goodwill between opposing factions, and any changes in the balance of power between the implementers and other key parties in the company.

Marketing organization

Marketing organization provides the context in which marketing implementation takes place: companies may have no marketing departments; those that do may have functional, product-based market-centred or matrix organizational structures.

No marketing department

As we have seen this is a common situation. Small companies that cannot afford the luxury of managerial specialism, production or financially driven organizations, and companies that eschew marketing because they believe it to be nothing more than glitz, glamour and promotion are unlikely to have a marketing department. In small companies, the owner-manager may carry out some of the functions of marketing, such as developing customer relationships, providing market feedback and product development. In larger companies, which may use the traditional production, finance, personnel and sales functional division, the same task may be undertaken by those departments, especially sales (e.g. customer feedback, sales forecasting). The classic case of a company that has scorned the popular concept of marketing is Anita Roddick's Body Shop. Despite being based on many of the essentials of marketing (e.g. a clearly differentiated product range, clear, consistent positioning and effective PR) the Body Shop has refused to set up a marketing department. However, the growth of me-too brands led to the need to reappraise the role of marketing through the establishment of a marketing department in 1994.[36]

It should be noted that not all companies that do not have a marketing department are poor at marketing; nor does the existence of a marketing department guarantee marketing orientation. As we have seen, many marketing departments carry out only a selected range of marketing functions and lack the power to influence key customer-impinging decisions or to drive through a marketing-orientated philosophy within the business. Marketing should be seen as a company-wide phenomenon, not something that should be delegated exclusively to the marketing department.

Functional organization

As small companies grow, the most likely emergence of a formal marketing structure is as a section within the sales department. As the importance of marketing is realized and the company grows, the status of marketing may rise with the appointment of a marketing manager on equivalent status with the sales manager who reports to a marketing director (see Fig. 20.9a). If the marketing director title is held by the previous sales director, little may change in terms of company philosophy: marketing may subsume a sales support role. An alternative route is to set up a *functional structure* under a sales director and a marketing director (see Fig. 20.9b). Both have equal status and the priorities of each job may lead to conflict (see Table 20.1). A study of Fazer, a Finnish confectionery firm, showed that these conflicts can be heightened by the different backgrounds of marketing people who had business training and salespeople who trusted more on personal experience and skills.[37] The preferred solution, then, is to appoint a marketing director who understands and has the power to implement marketing strategies that recognize sales as one (usually a key) element of the marketing mix.

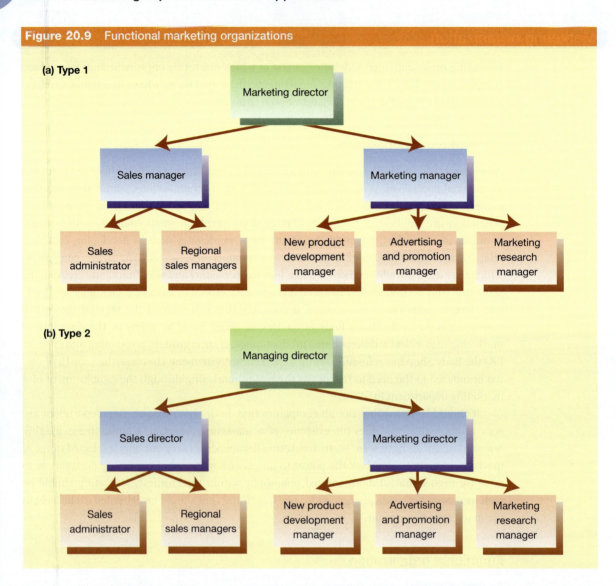

Figure 20.9 Functional marketing organizations

Functionalisms bring the benefit of specialization of task and a clear definition of responsibilities, and is still the most common form of marketing organization.[38] However, as the product range widens and the number of markets served increases, the structure may become unwieldy with insufficient attention being paid to specific products and markets since no one has full responsibility for a particular product or market.

Product-based organization

The need to give sufficient care and attention to individual products has led many companies (particularly in the fast-moving consumer goods field) to move to a product-based structure. For example, Nestlé moved from a functional to a product management system in 1992. A common structure is for a product manager to oversee a group of brands within a product field (e.g. lagers, shampoos) supported by brand managers who manage specific brands (see Fig. 20.10). Their role is to co-ordinate the business management of their brands. This involves dealing with advertising, promotion and marketing research agencies, and function areas within the firm. Their dilemma stems from the fact that they have responsibility for the

Table 20.1 Potential areas of conflict between marketing and sales

Area	Sales	Marketing
Objectives	Short-term sales	Long-term brand/market building
Marketing research	Personal experience with customers/trade	Market research reports
Pricing	Low prices to maximize sales volume. Discount structure in the hands of the salesforce	Price set consistent with positioning strategy. Discount structure built into the marketing implementation plan
Marketing expenditure	Maximize resources channelled to the salesforce	Develop a balanced marketing mix using a variety of communication tools
Promotion	Sales literature, free customer give-aways, samples, business entertainment	Design a well-blended promotional mix including advertising, promotion and public relations

commercial success of their brands without the power to force through their decisions as they have no authority over other functional areas such as sales, production and R&D. They act as ambassadors for their brands, attempting to ensure adequate support from the salesforce, and sufficient marketing funds to communicate to customers and the trade through advertising and promotion.

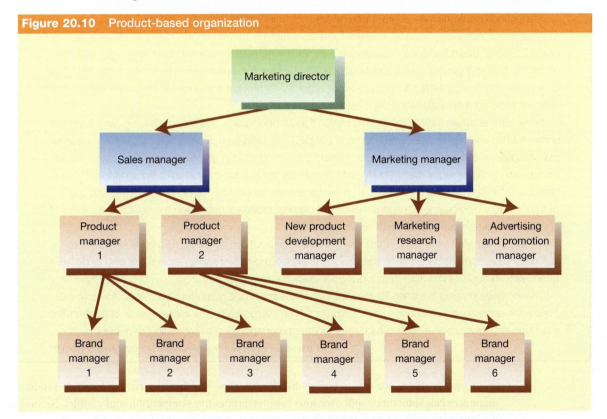

Figure 20.10 Product-based organization

The advantages of a *product-based organization* are that adequate attention is given to developing a co-ordinated marketing mix for each brand, and assigning specific responsibility means that speed of response to market or technological developments is quicker than relying on a committee of functional specialists. A by-product of the system is that it provides excellent training for young businesspeople as they are required to come into contact with a wide range of business activities.

20.4 marketing in action

The Growth of the Category Manager

The criticisms levelled at the brand management system—conflict, cost and inwardly focused—and the demands of the trade have led major marketing organizations to look at category management as an alternative. Instead of separate brand managers, category teams manage several brands, with specialists handling advertising, sales promotion, line extensions and packaging, and customizing each category's product mix, merchandising and promotions on a store-by-store basis. The result is that brands are managed as a portfolio, thus reducing conflict, the number of management layers are reduced, thus lowering costs, and the customer (or at least the trade) is in sharper focus.

Usually, a retailer will appoint a leading supplier as 'category captain', who makes recommendations for the category as a whole. If the merchandising, stocking, pricing and promotional proposal make sense, the retailer accepts the plan. If not, the retailer will consult other suppliers before asking the category captain to present a new plan.

Two additional forces are encouraging the growth of category management. First, retailers are using information technology and databases to manage categories as their unit of analysis. Consequently, they expect their suppliers also to possess a category perspective. Indeed, some multinational retailers are expecting one worldwide contact person for a category to provide the 'big picture' necessary to manage cross-nationally. Second, category management promotes greater clarity in strategy across brands. Brand positions within categories can be more readily defined, and resource allocation decisions involving promotional budgets and product innovations can be made strategically. The goal is to make the brands within a category work together to provide the greatest collective impact and reap the maximum operational efficiencies.

Lever Brothers has moved down this route. It no longer has a marketing director. Two business units—fabrics and homecare—with two core, parallel marketing teams, have been set up. A *consumer marketing team* focuses on the consumer/brand marketing, and a *category marketing team* moulds brand plans to fit the requirements of retailers, especially the supermarket chains. For example, if a new brand or extension is being considered, it would be developed only if it makes sense in the trade's vision of the category. The category management team can help retailers determine the best category mix of brands for a given store or a specific community.

An accompanying change is that the old sales department at Lever Brothers has become a *customer development department*, recognizing the changing role of salespeople as looking to develop business with customers rather than looking for quick sales.

These developments have led to the ideas of three important marketing concepts: the three Cs. These are *consumers*, *categories* and *customers*. The reorganization is more than a change in the management structure; it reflects a fundamental change of approach to marketing and sales.

Based on: Aaker and Joachimsthaler (2000);[40] Ambler (2001)[41]

However, there are a number of drawbacks. First, the healthy rivalry between product managers can sometimes spill over into counter-productive competition and conflict. Second, the system can breed new layers of management, which can be costly. For example, brand managers might be supplemented by assistants and as brands are added so new brand managers need to be recruited. Big strides have been taken to reduce inefficiency. A UK study by Booze, Allen and Hamilton, which is reported in Richards,[39] showed that the percentage of brand managers handling just one brand had dropped from 45 per cent in 1990 to 33 per cent in 1994, and the number of brand managers working on more than three brands had jumped from 30 to 46 per cent. Also, companies such as Procter & Gamble and Unilever are eliminating layers of management in the face of increasing demands from supermarkets to trim prices (and thus increase efficiency). Procter & Gamble, for example, has eliminated the title of assistant brand manager. Third, brand managers are often criticized for spending too much time coordinating in-company activities and too little time talking to customers. In response to these problems some companies are introducing category management to provide a focus on a category of brands. Marketing in Action 20.4 discusses the growth of category management.

Market-centred organization

Where companies sell their products to diverse markets, *market-centred organizations* should be considered. Instead of managers focusing on brands, *market managers* concentrate their energies on understanding and satisfying the needs of particular markets. The salesforce, too, may be similarly focused. For example, Fig. 20.11 shows a market-centred organization for a hypothetical computer manufacturer. The specialist needs and computer applications in manufacturing, education and financial services justify a sales and marketing organization based on these market segments.

Occasionally, hybrid product/market-centred organizations based on distribution channels are appropriate. For example, at Philips, old organizational structures based on brands or products have been downgraded, replacing them with a new focus on distribution channels. Product managers who ensure that product designs fit market requirements still exist. However, under a new combined sales and marketing director the emphasis has moved to markets. Previously, different salespeople would visit retailers selling different products from

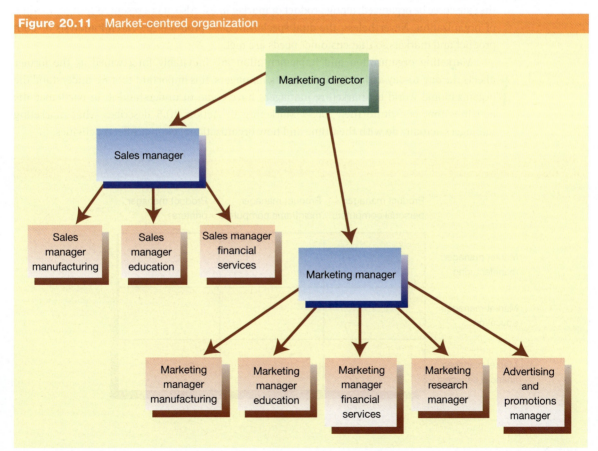

Figure 20.11 Market-centred organization

the Philips range. This has been replaced by dedicated sales teams concentrating on channels such as the multiples, the independents and mail order.[42]

The enormous influence of the trade in many consumer markets has forced other firms, besides Philips, to rethink their marketing organization. This has led to the establishment of *trade marketing* teams, which serve the needs of large retailers.

The advantage of the market-centred approach is the focus it provides on the specific customer requirements of new opportunities, and developing new products that meet their customer needs. By organizing around customers, it embodies the essence of the marketing concept. However, for companies competing in many sectors it can be resource-hungry.

Matrix organization

For companies with a wide product range selling in diverse markets, a *matrix structure* may be necessary. Both product and market managers are employed to give due attention to both facets of marketing activity. The organizational structure resembles a grid, as shown in Fig. 20.12, again using a hypothetical computer company. Product managers are responsible for their group of products' sales and profit performance, and monitor technological developments that impact on their products. Market managers focus on the needs of customers in each market segment.

For the system to work effectively, clear lines of decision-making authority need to be drawn up because of the possible areas of conflict. For example, who decides the price of the product? If a market manager requires an addition to the product line to meet the special needs of some customers, who has the authority to decide if the extra costs are justified? How should the salesforce be organized: along product or market lines? Also, it is a resource-hungry method of organization. Nevertheless, the dual specialism does promote the careful analysis of both product and markets so that customer needs are met.

Marketing organization and implementation are inevitably intertwined as the former affects the day-to-day activities of marketing managers. It is important that we understand the organizational world as marketing managers have come to understand it, in particular the activities that constitute their job.[43] Marketing in Action 20.5 describes what marketing managers actually do with their time and how organizational change affects activities.

Figure 20.12 Matrix organization

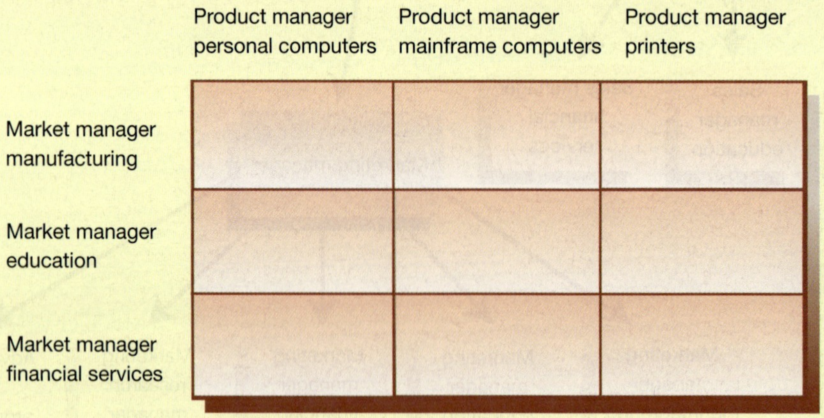

	Product manager personal computers	Product manager mainframe computers	Product manager printers
Market manager manufacturing			
Market manager education			
Market manager financial services			

20.5 marketing in action

What Marketing Managers Really Do

Marketing managers fully recognize their crucial role in planning for the future but the realities of the job often mean that the short-term pressures of dealing with administrative tasks leave little time for strategic planning. One survey of 50 brand and marketing managers found that short-term business accounted for 83 per cent of their day, broken down as follows:

- 29 per cent on marketing operations or 'maintenance'
- 23 per cent working with other functions
- 11 per cent preparing and giving presentations
- 8 per cent on administration
- 6 per cent travelling
- 6 per cent training.

This left only 17 per cent of the day available for 'future marketing'.

Organizational structures can influence how much time is spent on various tasks. Virgin, for example, has flattened structures, which gives individuals more responsibility. As a result there are fewer meetings. One executive reported that he had only three meetings a month: one for manufacturing where all the divisions meet, one for marketing (if needed) and one for sales. Since there were few layers of middle management, work was invigorating because 'you spend your time doing what you are meant to be doing'. This contrasted with his experience in an advertising agency where much wasted effort was spent presenting the same information to different groups of colleagues, clients and their colleagues. When the process of preparing contact reports, monthly updates and three-monthly reviews was added, the time left over for strategic thinking was minimal.

One area of the marketing mix where marketing has less influence than it should is pricing. In a survey of marketing directors only 39 per cent said they had a high influence on price. Since price is the revenue-earning element of the marketing mix it is quite disturbing to find that marketing does not play a more prominent role in many companies.

Based on: Leggett (1996);[44] Murphy (2002)[45]

Marketing control

Marketing control is an essential element of the marketing planning process because it provides a review of how well marketing objectives have been achieved. A framework for controlling marketing activities is given in Fig. 20.13. The process begins by deciding marketing objectives, leading to the setting of performance standards. For example, a marketing objective of 'widening the customer base' might lead to the setting of the performance standard of 'generating 20 new accounts within 12 months'. Similarly the marketing objective of 'improving market share' might translate into a performance standard of 'improving market share from 20 per cent to 25 per cent'. Some companies set quantitative marketing objectives, in which case performance standards are automatically derived.

The next step is to locate responsibility. In some cases responsibility ultimately falls on one person (e.g. the brand manager), in others it is shared (e.g. the sales manager and salesforce). It is important to consider this issue since corrective or supportive action may need to focus on those responsible for the success of marketing activity.

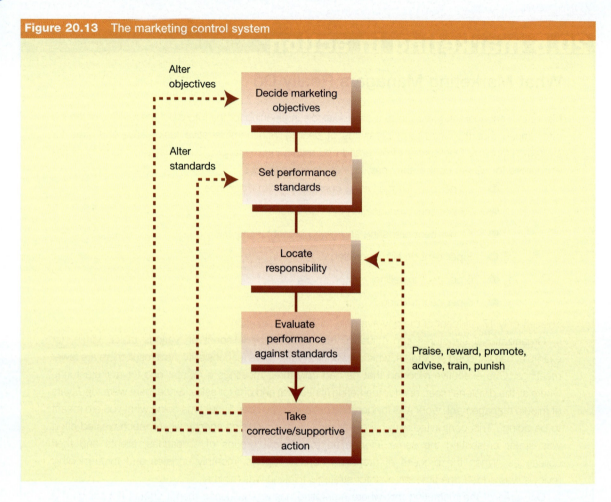

Figure 20.13 The marketing control system

Performance is then evaluated against standards, which relies on an efficient information system, and a judgement has to be made about the degree of success and/or failure achieved, and what corrective or supportive action is to be taken. This can take various forms.

- First, failure that is attributed to poor performance of individuals may result in the giving of advice regarding future attitudes and actions, training and/or punishment (e.g. criticism, lower pay, demotion, termination of employment). Success, on the other hand, should be rewarded through praise, promotion and/or higher pay.

- Second, failure that is attributed to unrealistic marketing objectives and performance standards may cause them to be lowered for the subsequent period. Success that is thought to reflect unambitious objectives and standards may cause them to be raised next period.

- Third, the attainment of marketing objectives and standards may also mean modification next period. For example, if the marketing objective and performance standard of opening 20 new accounts is achieved, this may mean the focus for the next period may change. The next objective may focus on customer retention, for instance.

- Finally, the failure of one achieved objective to bring about another may also require corrective action. For example, if a marketing objective of increasing calls to new accounts does not result in extra sales, the original objective may be dropped in favour of another (e.g. improving product awareness through advertising).

Strategic control

Two types of control system may be used. The first concerns major strategic issues and answers the question 'Are we doing the right thing?' It focuses on company strengths, weaknesses, opportunities and threats, and the process of control is through a marketing audit. This was discussed in depth in Chapter 2 under the heading 'The process of marketing planning' and will not be elaborated upon here.

Operational control

The second control system concerns day-to-day ongoing marketing activities, and is called operational control. Key methods of operational control are *customer satisfaction measurement*, *sales and market share analysis*, and *cost and profitability analysis*. Although focused on operational issues, this information can also usefully be fed into the marketing audit.

Customer satisfaction measurement

An increasingly common barometer of marketing success is customer satisfaction measurement. This is an encouraging sign as customer satisfaction is at the heart of the marketing concept. Although this measure does not appear directly on a company's profit and loss account, it is a fundamental condition for corporate success. The process involves the setting of customer satisfaction criteria, the design of a questionnaire to measure satisfaction on those criteria, the choice of which customers to interview, and the analysis and interpretation of results. The use of a market research agency is advised to take advantage of their skills and unbiased viewpoint. One industrial marketing research agency advocates interviewing three customer groups to give a valid picture of customer satisfaction and marketing effectiveness:

- 10 current customers
- 10 lapsed customers (who bought from us in the past but don't now)
- 10 non-customers (who are in the market for the product but hitherto have not bought from us).

Invaluable information can be gained concerning customer satisfaction, how effective the salesforce is, why customers have switched to other suppliers, and why some potential customers have never done business with our company.

Sales and market share analysis

Sales analysis compares actual with target sales. The starting point is to compare overall sales revenue. Negative variance may be due to lower sales volume, or lower prices. Product, customer and regional analysis will be carried out to discover where the shortfall arose. A change in the product mix could account for a sales fall, with more lower-priced products being sold. The loss of a major customer may also account for a sales decline. Regional analysis may identify a poorly performing area sales manager or salesperson. These findings would point the direction of further investigations to uncover the reasons for such outcomes.

Market share analysis evaluates a company's performance in comparison to that of its competitors. Sales analysis may show a healthy increase in revenues but this may be due to market growth rather than an improved performance over competitors. An accompanying decline in market share would sound warning bells regarding relative performance. Again, these findings would stimulate further investigation to root out the causes.

It should be recognized that a market share decline is not always a symptom of poor performance. This is why outcomes should always be compared to marketing objectives and performance standards. If the marketing objective was to harvest a product, leading to a performance standard of a 5 per cent increase in profits, its achievement may be accompanied by a market share decline (through the effect of a price rise). This would be a perfectly satisfactory outcome given the desired objective.

Cost and profitability analysis

Cost analysis deals with expenses and, when compared to sales revenue, provides the basis for profitability analysis. Profitability analysis provides information on the profit performance of key aspects of marketing such as products, customers or distribution channels. The example given focuses on products. The hypothetical company sells three types of product: paper products, printers and copiers. The first step is to measure marketing inputs to each of these products. These are shown in Table 20.2. Allocation of sales calls to products is facilitated by separate sales teams for each group.

Table 20.2	Allocating functional costs to products		
Products	Salesforce (number of sales calls per year)	Advertising (number of one-page ads placed)	Order processing (number of orders placed)
Paper products	500	20	1000
Printers	400	20	800
Copiers	250	10	200
Total	1150	50	2000
Total cost	£190,000	£130,000	£80,000
Functional cost per unit	£165 per call	£2600 per ad	£40 per order

If the sales teams were organized on purely geographic lines, an estimate of how much time was devoted to each product, on average, at each call would need to be made. Table 20.2 shows how the costs of an average sales call, advertising insertion and order are calculated. This provides vital information to calculate profitability for each product.

Table 20.3 shows how the net profit before tax is calculated. The results show how copiers are losing money. Before deciding to drop this line the company would have to take into account the extent to which customers expect copiers to be sold alongside paper products and printers, the effect on paper sales of dropping copiers, the possible annoyance caused to customers that already own one of their copiers, the extent to which copiers cover overheads that otherwise would need to be paid for from paper products and printer sales, the scope for pruning costs and increasing sales, and the degree to which the arbitrary nature of some of the cost allocations has unfairly treated copier products.

Table 20.3 Profitability statement for products (£)

	Paper products	Printers	Copiers
Sales	1,000,000	700,000	300,000
Cost of goods sold	500,000	250,000	250,000
Gross margin	500,000	450,000	50,000
Marketing costs			
Salesforce (at £165 per call)	82,500	66,000	41,250
Advertising (at £2600 per advertisement)	52,000	52,000	26,000
Order processing (at £40 per order)	40,000	32,000	8,000
Total cost	174,500	150,000	72,250
Net profit (or loss) before tax	325,500	300,000	(25,250)

Review

1. The relationship between marketing strategy, implementation and performance

- Strategy, no matter how well conceived, will fail if people are incapable of carrying out the necessary tasks (implementation) to make the strategy work in the marketplace.
- Appropriate strategy with good implementation will have the best chance of successful outcomes; appropriate strategy with bad implementation will lead to trouble, especially if the substandard implementation leads to strategy change; inappropriate strategy with good implementation may hasten failure or may lead to actions that correct strategy and therefore produce favourable outcomes; and inappropriate strategy with bad implementation will lead to failure.

2. The stages that people pass through when they experience disruptive change

- The stages are numbness, denial and disbelief, self-doubt and emotion, acceptance and letting go, adaptation and testing, construction and meaning, and internalization.

3. The objectives of marketing implementation and change

- The overall objective is the successful execution of the marketing plan.
- This may require gaining the support of key decision-makers, gaining the required resources and gaining the commitment of relevant individuals and departments.

4. The barriers to the implementation of the marketing concept

- The barriers are the fact that new marketing ideas often mean higher costs, the potential benefits are often unquantifiable, personal ambitions (e.g. the desire of R&D staff to work on leading-edge complex problems) may conflict with the customer's desire to have simple but reliable products, reward systems may reward short-term cost savings, sales and profitability rather than long-term customer satisfaction, and there may be a gap between what managers say (e.g. 'be customer-orientated') and what they do (e.g. cut back on marketing research funds).

5. The forms of resistance to marketing implementation and change

- The ten forms of resistance are criticisms of specific details of the plan; foot-dragging; slow response to requests; unavailability; suggestions that, despite the merits of the plan, resources should be channelled elsewhere; arguments that the proposals are too ambitious; hassle and aggravation created to wear the proposers down; attempts to delay the decision; attacks on the credibility of the proposer; and pointing out the risks of the plan.

▶ **6 How to develop effective implementation strategies**
- A change master is needed to drive through change.
- Managing the implementation process requires the setting of objectives ('would like' and 'must have'), strategy (internal marketing), execution (persuasion, negotiation, politics and tactics) and evaluation (who wins, and what can be learned).

7 The elements of an internal marketing programme
- An internal marketing programme mirrors the structures used to market externally such as market segmentation, targeting and the marketing mix.
- The people to whom the plan must be marketed within the organization are known as internal customers. These can be segmented into three groups: supporters, neutrals and opposers. These form distinct target markets that require different internal marketing mixes to be designed to optimize the chances of successful adoption of the plan.

8 The skills and tactics that can be used to overcome resistance to the implementation of the marketing concept and plan
- The skills are persuasion (the needs, motivations and problems of internal customers need to be understood before appealing messages can be developed), negotiation (concession and proposal analysis) and political skills (the understanding of the sources of power, and the use of overt and covert power plays).
- The tactics are persuasion (articulating a shared vision, communicating and training, eliminating misconceptions, selling the benefits, gaining acceptance by association, leaving room for local control over details, supporting words with action, and establishing two-way communication); politics (building coalitions, displaying support, inviting the opposition in to share the rewards, warning the opposition of the consequences of opposition, the use of appropriate language, controlling the decision-making process and the use of the either/or alternative (either accept or I tender my resignation); timing (incremental steps, persistence, leaving insufficient time for alternatives, and waiting for the opposition to leave); and negotiation (starting high and trading concessions).

9 Marketing organizational structures
- The options are no marketing department, functional, product-based, market-centred or matrix organizational structures.

10 The nature of a marketing control system
- There are two types of marketing control: strategic and operational control systems.
- Strategic control systems answer the question 'Are we doing the right things?' and are based on a marketing audit.
- Operational control systems concern day-to-day ongoing marketing activities, and cover customer satisfaction measurement, sales and market share analysis, and cost and profitability analysis.

Key terms

category management the management of brands in a group, portfolio or category, with specific emphasis on the retail trade's requirements

change master a person that develops an implementation strategy to drive through organizational change

coercive power power inherent in the ability to punish

concession analysis the evaluation of things that can be offered to someone in negotiation valued from the viewpoint of the receiver

cost analysis the calculation of direct and fixed costs, and their allocation to products, customers and/or distribution channels

covert power play the use of disguised forms of power tactics

customer satisfaction measurement a process through which customer satisfaction criteria are set, customers are surveyed and the results interpreted in order to establish the level of customer satisfaction with the organization's product

expert power power that derives from an individual's expertise

legitimate power power based on legitimate authority, such as line management

market share analysis a comparison of company sales with total sales of the product, including sales of competitors

marketing control the stage in the marketing planning process or cycle when performance against plan is monitored so that corrective action, if necessary, can be taken

overt power play the use of visible, open kinds of power tactics

profitability analysis the calculation of sales revenues and costs for the purpose of calculating the profit performance of products, customers and/or distribution channels

proposal analysis the prediction and evaluation of proposals and demands likely to be made by someone with whom one is negotiating

referent power power derived by the reference source, e.g. when people identify with and respect the architect of change

reward power power derived from the ability to provide benefits

sales analysis a comparison of actual with target sales

trade marketing marketing to the retail trade

transition curve the emotional stages that people pass through when confronted with an adverse change

Internet exercise

Nestlé is one of the world's largest companies, with operations spanning the globe. It holds a wide-ranging product portfolio including confectionery, bottled water, breakfast cereals, pasta, and so on.

Visit: www.nestle.co.uk
www.nestle.com

Questions

(a) Discuss why this firm may need global marketing controls.
(b) What internal and external factors may influence the organizational structure of Nestlé?
(c) What organizational structure is best suited to Nestlé's needs?

Visit the Online Learning Centre at www.mcgraw-hill.co.uk/textbooks/jobber for more Internet exercises.

Study questions

1. Think of a situation when your life suffered from a dramatic change. Using Fig. 20.3 for guidance, recall your feelings over time. How closely did your experiences match the stages in the figure? How did your feelings at each stage (e.g. denial and disbelief) manifest themselves?

2. Can good implementation substitute for an inappropriate strategy? Give an example of how good implementation might make the situation worse and an example of how it might improve the situation.

3. What might be the objectives of market implementation and change? Distinguish between gaining compliance, acceptance and commitment.

4. Why do some companies fail to implement the marketing concept?

5. Describe the ways in which people may resist the change that is implied in the implementation of a new marketing plan. Why should they wish to do this?

6. What is internal marketing? To what extent does it parallel external marketing strategy?

7. Describe the skills that are necessary to see a marketing plan through to successful implementation.

8. What tactics of persuasion are at the implementer's disposal? What are the advantages and limitations of each one?

9. Without the use of political manoeuvres, most attempts at marketing implementation will fail. Discuss.

10. Discuss the options available for organizing a marketing department. How well is each form likely to serve customers?

11. Discuss the problems involved in setting up and implementing a marketing control system.

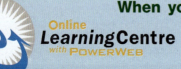

When you have read this chapter log on to the Online Learning Centre at www.mcgraw-hill.co.uk/textbooks/jobber to explore chapter-by-chapter test questions, links and further online study tools for marketing.

case thirty-nine

Jambo Records

The butterflies in Laura Martell's stomach this Sunday evening seemed to be a different species from the ones that had been fluttering there a week ago. Last Sunday she had been looking forward to starting her new job as marketing manager at Jambo Records, one of the UK's leading independent record labels. After two years working as a marketing assistant with one of the five 'major' record companies, she had finally landed her dream job. However, after her first full week at Jambo, the job was beginning to look more like a nightmare, and she was feeling increasingly in limbo and uncertain about how things were likely to develop.

During the week, she had learnt more about the background to her appointment, and it helped to explain why she had got off to a difficult start. The creating of a marketing manager's position at Jambo had been at the bank's insistence as part of a recent refinancing deal. The last 12 months had been a difficult time for Jambo: a protracted court battle with one of the label's leading acts had been resolved in the company's favour, but had left the label facing an unexpectedly large bill for legal costs. The other difficulties surrounded the purchase of a nightclub aimed at building the Jambo brand, and emulating the likes of the Ministry of Sound, Cream and Knitting Factory. This proved to be a disaster, largely blamed on a poor choice of location and a failure to invest enough in promotion after the club opened late and considerably over its refurbishment budget. Eight months later, the club was sold on at a substantial loss in both financial and public relations terms.

Industry analysts forecast that Jambo would be next in a procession of independent labels to be absorbed within one of the majors. However, Chris Rubold, the founder, CEO and largest shareholder of Jambo, had gone to the bank in search of refinancing, armed with the company's first-ever business plan. His proposals had ultimately been accepted, but with certain conditions attached, and Laura's job was one of those conditions.

Her first day had started promisingly. Chris Rubold had made her feel very welcome, and had introduced her to the rest of the management team. He also kept stressing how her arrival marked a new era for Jambo, since 'they were now really going to take marketing seriously'. The company seemed to be structured around three areas, each relating to an area of music, and loosely labelled 'hip-hop', 'house/dance' and 'songs/guitars'. Each area had its own product manager responsible for creating the physical product and getting it into the music retailers, and an A&R (artists and repertoire) manager responsible for finding, signing and generally looking after the recording artists. The finance/purchasing manager and office manager completed the management introductions for the morning. There were two marketing assistants, who handled a myriad of logistical tasks, although one seemed largely concerned with artwork and packaging issues, while the other seemed mostly taken up with organizing concerts and personal appearances. Everybody seemed to report directly to Chris.

After a while, Chris left Laura to her own devices and to settle into her new office, telling her that he hoped that she would be able to pick up the marketing ball for Jambo and run with it, because 'I won't have a lot of time to think about our marketing. I'm going to be much more involved in the technological development of the company. So far we've been slow in picking up the opportunities that the Internet and mp3 provide, but now we're chasing hard to catch up. How we deliver our music to the customer is going to be the key to success in the twenty-first century, and if we can get the technology right, we could be among the winners. But getting it right isn't easy: mp3 has stolen a lead, and you've got over 25 million consumers already swapping mp3 music files for free through the Napster community. Now there's Windows Media offering the same kind of audio capabilities, and the AB Music Player from AT&T—who knows what the standard will be in five years' time, but we've got to be ready for it. Then we've also got to make decisions about how much product we make available digitally online. Do we try to re-author all our tracks for mp3, Liquid Audio and any other popular format? Or just our current stuff, or just our most popular stuff? It isn't just a question of getting the music to the audience, we've got to work out how we're going to charge for it as well. People have got so used to free mp3 files on the net, that getting them to pay for them could be tricky. So, with all that to worry about, for the next few months I'm going to be up to my eyeballs in the technology, and won't have much time to think about the marketing.'

By the second day, things had begun to deteriorate. In a radio interview, Jambo's biggest-selling solo artist complained that he had left one of the 'big five' labels to 'escape from the suits and hairdos but now they've followed me to Jambo'. Later, he went on to intimate that at the end of his current contract, he would be dispensing with record companies altogether, and would distribute his music direct to fans via the Internet. It also came to light that on the website of one of the label's highest-profile guitar bands, the band and its fans had been corresponding on the subject, and postings from members of the band made it clear they were disappointed that Jambo was 'going corporate'.

Most of Tuesday and Wednesday were taken up with more introductions and meetings. Laura met the rest of the staff, a few of the artists, had a tour of the company's recording studio and attended an album launch. Wednesday afternoon was taken up with a sales meeting. The UK market was first on the agenda, and Chris Rubold outlined the situation: 1999 had not been a good year for the UK record industry generally, with album sales down 5.9 per cent from 1998. Overall revenues were only protected by the rise in the trade price of singles of almost 24 per cent. Jambo had under-performed compared to the market with an album decline of almost 7 per cent, and single sales were static compared to 1 per cent overall market growth. More worryingly, none of the new artists broken during the past 12 months had made a significant contribution to overall sales. The major bright spot had been the organization of a new summer festival of Jambo's dance acts in Ayia Napa. This had been a big success and had generated considerable positive media coverage, including some excellent TV coverage. This had fed through into healthy third- and fourth-quarter sales growth for most of the artists involved.

Next came the USA and Gabriella Roche, product manager for hip-hop, who had recently returned from there, was enthusiastic about Jambo's partnership with US distributor/promoter Sparkle Distribution. She said, 'Sparkle really likes our stable of artists, and has made a fantastic effort to push them. It has easily exceeded the targets we set for airplay on the college radio circuit for our guitar bands, and it has really exceeded expectations in terms of getting airplay for some of our hip-hop artists in the big metropolitan areas. I know that might not sound like a big deal, but in the US market, getting radio airplay is a big step towards getting an artist to chart. Of course, if we bring it back to actual sales figures, I have to admit they are disappointing, but it isn't for want of trying. With a music market of over $14 billion (£8.8 billion/€12.7 billion), we only need a tiny slice of it to succeed, and it's growing at over 2 per cent compared to pretty flat sales in most of Europe. But America is tough for indie labels to crack, particularly because so much of the distribution into independent record stores is dominated by two big players: Valley and Orchid.'

Last came Europe. It was confirmed that industry-wide sales for 1999 across Europe had been 'flat', but the first quarter of 2000 had seen promising growth in the Scandinavian trio of Sweden, Norway and Finland. International Federation of Phonographic Industry figures suggested that these had grown by 30 per cent, 11 per cent and 7 per cent respectively (although the Swedish figure reflected a growth in exports as much as domestic consumption). Denmark, by contrast, remained flat, and more worryingly in terms of its size, so did Germany following a drop in sales value during 1999. Peter Allt, product manager for house/dance, said that he was looking into an idea to improve Jambo's position on the continent: 'A couple of other independent labels have established small regional offices in Germany, and we could look to follow suit. We could put together a little project team—perhaps one product manager, one A&R manager—and they could go out for six months or a year and try to promote our current artists, and maybe find some new ones.'

By this stage Laura felt that she had done a lot of listening and learning, but now the time had come to contribute to a meeting. The safest way to do this to begin with, she thought, was to ask a few intelligent questions. 'Why Germany?' she asked. 'Well,' said Peter, 'we know their English is pretty good, which will help, and I've got a few useful contacts out there. It's a big market in which dance is strong, and others have done it, which suggests it's a smart thing to do.' Laura sensed that her question hadn't been entirely welcome, and she lapsed back into silence and listened to the others debating the potential costs and benefits of Peter's idea.

On Thursday morning, Laura decided that it was time to get proactive and make progress on one of several ideas she had brought with her into the job, convinced they could make a positive impact at Jambo. She went to see Phil Stone, A&R manager for songs/guitars to explain her idea. She began, 'I really appreciate the importance of the A&R manager's role; given the pace of change in the industry, the whole business depends on you turning up good new artists. The trouble is, there's a limit to how many bands any one individual can get around to meeting up with and checking out. I know demo tapes are another way of picking people up, but there's a mountain of incoming demo tapes in reception that seems to be getting bigger every day. Why don't we follow the lead of websites like Dealwithepic.com, which the Epic label has put together? It allows bands to upload demos through the website, and they are given a guarantee that they will be given a listen by A&R staff. It's been pretty successful: they had 50 uploads on the first day the system went live.'

Laura waited for a reaction, but it wasn't what she had hoped for. Phil said that if she thought she could replace him with a website, she'd 'got another think coming' and that he didn't have time for any more of 'this nonsense' because he had to go and meet up with some 'real people' at an artist's store visit. Over lunch she suggested to the product managers that they could insert customer feedback cards into their CDs. This could help gather useful information about customers, and would only need a bit of merchandise offered as a draw prize to encourage a response. This idea, like the last, went down like the proverbial lead balloon. 'The music business', one of her new colleagues explained, 'is all about getting the music right. If the music is right, and the radio stations play it, the music markets itself.' Another commented that it was a pity the nightclub had closed down, as that had proved a really good way of finding out about what customers wanted. 'If a new track went down really well at the club, within a couple of weeks you could have it out as a single and moving up the charts.'

Friday, fortunately, was relatively uneventful, and Laura was glad to get to the weekend. Now, she pondered what she should do and say in the week ahead. She was convinced that Jambo's enthusiasm for trying to break artists into the American market was misplaced. The British presence had been eroding rapidly over recent years to the point where in 1999 no UK artists featured in the 80 US biggest-selling albums. Only Fatboy Slim and Charlotte Church had come even close, by selling just over a million units. Nobody in the current Jambo stable looked likely to take America by storm and, if it did happen, they could still capitalize through a licensing agreement with one of the majors.

The 'German project' also looked ill-judged. Jambo's continental business was invaluable, but very fragmented, and Laura could see little reason why it would be easier to develop further from Berlin as opposed to London. A more effective method might be through joining forces with NetBeat, the multilingual music portal, which specializes in partnerships with independent record labels to promote their artists across the continent. NetBeat sells CDs, mp3 downloads and music merchandise, and provides editorial content slanted towards the different continental music markets. It could prove an ideal way to create continental penetration without excessive costs. It would also side-step the distribution strangle-hold held by a handful of channels in countries like Italy.

She dug out some of the market research reports she had salvaged from her last job, and browsed through them. Several of them said the same thing, that western Europe and North America were not going to see much growth in the near future, it was the Latin American and Asia Pacific markets that were up and coming—but could they really form part of Jambo's future plans?

Laura knew that Jambo, like most of the rest of the industry, was at a turning point. It needed to improve sales, it needed to find good new artists and it needed to respond appropriately to the changes being ushered in by new technology. Jambo, like other independent labels, faced some real opportunities. The prospect of online delivery of recordings could allow it to compete more effectively against the majors' giant production and promotion systems. The merger of EMI and Warner, two of the five majors, could also create opportunities. Analysts were forecasting a shake-out of artists following this merger, and a trend towards the majors increasingly shedding artists viewed as incapable of generating sales on an international scale. Again, this could prove beneficial to the independents. Laura was convinced that, as Jambo's marketing manager, she could play a leading role in helping the company grasp these opportunities. First, however, she needed to get her colleagues to take marketing a little more seriously.

Questions

1. Why do you think Laura had such a difficult first week?
2. What can she do to improve things at Jambo?
3. What difficulties might she face in trying to move Jambo towards more formalized marketing?

This case was prepared by Ken Peattie, Professor of Marketing, Cardiff University, and James Roberts, Informed Sources International. This case is a fictionalized account based on actual events.

case forty

Hansen Bathrooms (b)

Rob Vincent had taken Susan Clements' advice (see Case twenty-two). The coating on the Hansen bathroom furniture created extra value for consumers and should be reflected in a higher price. A market research survey had shown beyond doubt that households valued the benefits that the coating produced: cleaning could be extended from once every two weeks to once every three months.

Accordingly, Rob had recommended to the board a consumer price of £470 (€676). This was only £5 (€7.20) and £20 (€29) more than the prices of the two main competitors. After the usual 25 per cent discount, the price differential would be even less. But the board remained unconvinced.

The first meeting to discuss pricing strategy for the new Hansen bathroom range—featuring a new, patent-protected coating which contained an agent that dispersed grime and grease from basins and washbasins, etc.—had taken place three weeks ago. No conclusion had been drawn. Consequently, a second meeting had been arranged to thrash out a coherent strategy.

Rob decided to play it tough. At 30 he was considerably younger than anyone else on the board; the rest of the members were in their fifties. Rob began, 'I recommended a price of £470 three weeks ago and that recommendation still stands! I hope my arguments have sunk in since our last meeting because quite honestly they are watertight. Let's go through them once again:

'One: the new coating provides tangible customer value—cleaning is extended from once every two weeks to once every three months.

'Two: marketing research has shown that the customer is delighted with this change.

'Three: our bathroom design and quality of fittings match those of the competition.

'Four: our main competitors are priced at £450 and £465; our price premium reflects the added value that the coating provides.

'Five: the higher price feeds directly into our bottom-line profit figures.'

'Thank you, Rob,' said Karl Hansen, the chairman of the board, 'We are well aware of the price impact on profit margins, but at £470 we will sell fewer units than if we enter the market at £440, which gives the consumer two incentives to buy: price and value.'

'I totally agree,' opined Jack Sunderland, the sales director. 'The foundation of this company has been built on volume. We need volume to keep our factories working.'

'But you will get volume,' interrupted Rob, 'the market wants this product. What we need to do is to cash in on a major technological improvement.'

'It certainly is that,' agreed Chris Henderson, the technical director, 'the coating has taken five years to develop and is fully protected by patent. But I thought demand fell as price increased. I tend to agree with Karl and Jack.'

'Not necessarily. In this case I feel a price premium is fully justified. The market research proves it,' continued Rob.

'Could we try out two price levels?' said John France, the finance director, 'We have strong ties with Outram Brothers, a major bathroom retailer. I'm sure Bill Outram would agree to a few trials.'

'Absolutely not!' shouted Rob, 'We must act decisively. Every week we wait is lost profit for us.'

'Yes,' said Hansen, 'but your suggestion is too risky, Rob. We need to follow our tried-and-tested approach. I propose that we launch at £440. If the public like it, we can always raise the price later. Do I have agreement?'

Later that day Rob told Susan about the outcome: 'I can't believe those old guys could reach a decision like that. They refuse to accept the facts. All they like to do is eat a hearty lunch in the executive dining room and sleep it off in the afternoon. If they went jogging like me at lunchtime they might realize that work is more than about food and drink. Do you know, Sue, the only time I've been in that dining room is when old man Hansen took me in there for a drink on my appointment.'

Questions

1. What do you think of Rob Vincent as a manager?
2. How well has he marketed his pricing proposals internally?
3. Can you suggest a better internal marketing approach?

This case was prepared by David Jobber, Professor of Marketing, University of Bradford.

chapter twenty-one

Marketing services

21

Closed for lunch.❞   SIGN ON DOOR OF MOSCOW RESTAURANT

Learning Objectives

This chapter explains:

1. The nature and special characteristics of services
2. Managing customer relationships
3. Managing service quality, productivity and staff
4. How to position a service organization and brand
5. The services marketing mix
6. The major store and non-store retailing types
7. The theories of retail evolution
8. Key retail marketing decisions
9. The nature and special characteristics of non-profit marketing

This chapter discusses the special issues concerning the marketing of services. This is not to imply that the principles of marketing covered in earlier chapters of this book do not apply to services; rather it reflects the particular characteristics of services and the importance of service firms to the economy. In most industrialized economies, expenditure on services is growing. For example, in the European Union figures compiled by the European Commission show that the percentage share of gross domestic product attributable to the services sector rose from 38 per cent in 1970 to almost 50 per cent by 1990. There are a number of reasons for this.[1]

(1) Advances in technology have led to more sophisticated products that require more design, production and maintenance services.

(2) Growth per capita income has given rise to a greater percentage being spent on luxuries such as restaurant meals, overseas holidays and weekend hotel breaks, all of which are service intensive. Greater discretionary income also fuels the demand for financial services such as investment trusts and personal pensions.

(3) A trend towards outsourcing means that manufacturers are buying services that are outside the firm's core expertise (such as distribution, warehousing, and catering).

(4) Deregulation has increased the level of competition in certain service industries (e.g. telecommunications, television, airlines), resulting in expansion.

Retailing is an important element of services. Because of this, some of the special marketing considerations relevant to retailing will be covered later in this chapter. Marketing in the non-profit sector will also be discussed, with hospitals, national television companies, employment services, museums, charities, schools and universities all being service-orientated. First, we shall examine the nature of services.

The nature of services

Cowell states that 'what is significant about services is the relative dominance of *intangible attributes* in the make-up of the "service product". Services are a special kind of product. They may require special understanding and special marketing efforts.'[2] Pure services do not result in ownership, although they may be linked to a physical good. For example a machine (physical good) may be sold with a one-year maintenance contract (service).

Many offerings, however, contain a combination of the tangible and intangible. For example, a marketing research study would provide a report (physical good) that represents the outcome of a number of service activities (discussions with client, designing the research strategy, interviewing respondents and analysing the results). This distinction between physical and service offerings can, therefore, best be understood as a matter of degree rather than in absolute terms. Figure 21.1 shows a physical goods–service continuum, with the position of each offering dependent upon its ratio of tangible/intangible elements. At the pure goods end of the scale is clothing, as the purchase of a skirt or socks is not normally accompanied by a service. Carpet purchases may involve an element of service if they require professional laying. Machinery purchase may involve more service elements in the form of installation and maintenance. Software design is positioned on the service side of the continuum since the value of the product is dependent on design expertise rather than the cost of the physical product (disk). Marketing research is similarly services based, as discussed earlier. Finally, psychotherapy may be regarded as a pure service since the client receives nothing tangible from the transaction.

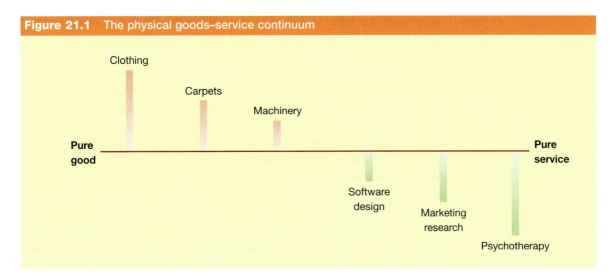

Figure 21.1 The physical goods–service continuum

We have already touched on one characteristic of services that distinguishes them from physical goods: intangibility. There are, in fact, four key distinguishing characteristics: intangibility, inseparability, variability and perishability (see Fig. 21.2).

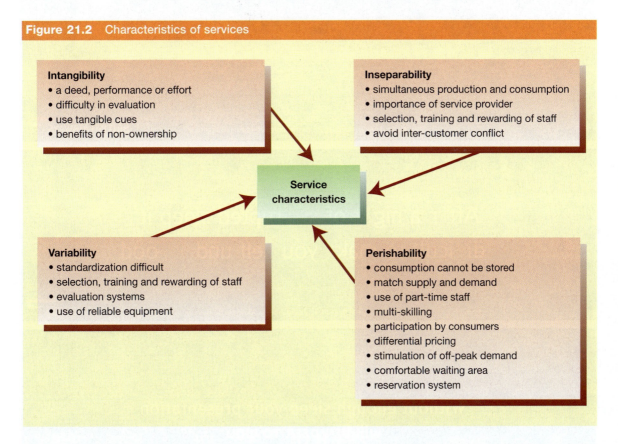

Figure 21.2 Characteristics of services

Intangibility

Pure services cannot be seen, tasted, touched, or smelled before they are bought—that is, they are intangible. Rather a service is *a deed, performance* or *effort*, not an object, device or thing.[3] This may mean that a customer finds difficulty in evaluating a service before purchase. For example, it is virtually impossible to judge how enjoyable a holiday will be before taking it because the holiday cannot be shown to a customer before consumption.

For some services, their intangibility leads to *difficulty in evaluation* after consumption. For example, it is not easy to judge how thorough a car service has been immediately afterwards: there is no way of telling if everything that should have been checked has been checked.

The challenge for the service provider is to *use tangible cues* to service quality. For example, a holiday firm may show pictures of the holiday destination, display testimonials from satisfied holidaymakers and provide details in a brochure of the kinds of entertainment available. A garage may provide a checklist of items that are required to be carried out in a service, and an indication that they have been.

The task is to provide evidence of service quality. McDonald's does this by controlling the physical settings of its restaurants and by using its 'golden arches' as a branding cue. By having a consistent offering, the company has effectively dealt with the difficulties that consumers have in evaluating the quality of a service. Standard menus and ordering procedures have also ensured uniform and easy access for customers, while allowing quality control.[4] Companies try to communicate tangible benefits to consumers, as the illustration for British Airways shows.

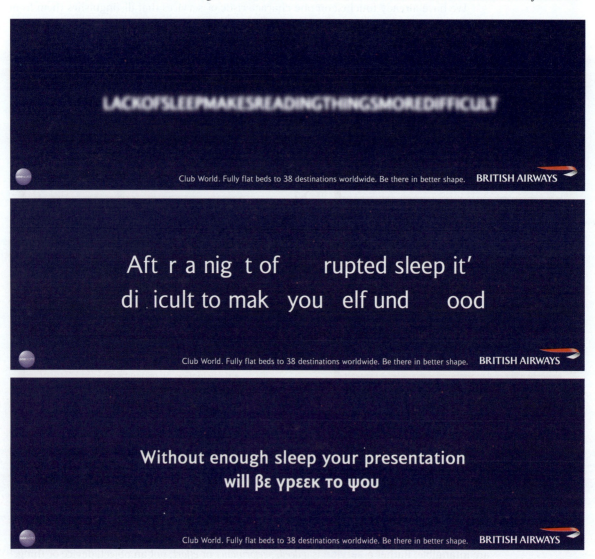

British Airways communicates the intangible benefit of a good night's sleep on its long-haul flights.

Intangibility also means that the customer cannot own a service. Payment is for use or performance. For example, a car may be hired or a medical operation performed. Service organizations sometimes stress the *benefits of non-ownership* such as lower capital costs and the spreading of payment charges.

Inseparability

Unlike physical goods, services have inseparability—that is, they have *simultaneous production and consumption*. For example, a haircut, a medical operation, psychoanalysis, a holiday and a rock concert are produced and consumed at the same time. This contrasts with a physical good, which is produced, stored and distributed through intermediaries before being bought and consumed. This illustrates the *importance of the service provider*, which is an integral part of the satisfaction gained by the consumer. How service providers conduct themselves may have a crucial bearing on repeat business over and above the technical efficiency of the service task. For example, how courteous and friendly the service provider is may play a large part in the customer's perception of the service experience. The service must be provided not only at the right time and in the right place but also in the right way.[5]

Often, in the customer's eyes, the photocopier service engineer or the insurance representative *is* the company. Consequently, the *selection, training and rewarding of staff* who are the frontline service people are of fundamental importance in the achievement of high standards of service quality. This notion of the inseparability of production and consumption gave rise to the idea of relationship marketing in services. In such circumstances, managing buyer–seller interaction is central to effective marketing and can only be fulfilled in a relationship with the customer.[6]

Furthermore, the consumption of the service may take place in the presence of other consumers. This is apparent with restaurant meals, air, rail or coach travel, and many forms of entertainment, for example. Consequently, enjoyment of the service is dependent not only on the service provided, but also on other consumers. Therefore service providers need to identify possible sources of nuisance (e.g. noise, smoke, queue jumping) and make adequate provision to *avoid inter-customer conflict*. For example, a restaurant layout should provide reasonable space between tables and non-smoking areas so that the potential for conflict is minimized.

Marketing managers should not underestimate the role played by customers in aiding other customers in their decision-making. A study into service interactions in IKEA stores found that almost all customer–employee exchanges related to customer concerns about 'place' (e.g. 'Can you direct me to the pick-up point?') and 'function' (e.g. 'How does this chair work?'). However, interactions between customers took the form of opinions on the quality of materials used in products, advice on bed sizes and how to move around the in-store restaurant. Many customers appeared to display a degree of product knowledge or expertise bordering on that of contact personnel.[7]

Variability

Service quality may be subject to considerable variability, which makes standardization difficult. Two restaurants within the same chain may have variable service owing to the capabilities of their respective managers and staff. Two marketing courses at the same university may vary considerably in terms of quality depending on the lecturers. Quality variations among physical products may be subject to tighter controls through centralized production, automation and quality checking before dispatch. Services, however, are often conducted at multiple locations, by people who may vary in their attitudes (and tiredness), and are subject to simultaneous production and consumption. The last characteristic means that a service fault (e.g. rudeness) cannot be quality checked and corrected between production and consumption, unlike a physical product such as misaligned car windscreen wipers.

The potential for variability in service quality emphasizes the need for rigorous selection, training, and rewarding of staff in service organizations. Training should emphasize the standards expected of personnel when dealing with customers. *Evaluation systems* should be developed that allow customers to report on their experiences with staff. Some service organizations, notably the British Airports Authority, tie reward systems to customer satisfaction surveys, which are based, in part, on the service quality provided by their staff.

Service standardization is a related method of tackling the variability problem. For example, a university department could agree to use the same software package when developing overhead transparencies for use in lectures. The *use of reliable equipment* rather than people can also help in standardization—for example, the supply of drinks via vending machines or cash through bank machines. However, great care needs to be taken regarding equipment reliability and efficiency. For example, bank cash machines have been heavily criticized for being unreliable and running out of money at weekends.

Perishability

The fourth characteristic of services is their **perishability** in the sense that *consumption cannot be stored* for the future. A hotel room or an airline seat that is not occupied today represents lost income that cannot be gained tomorrow. If a physical good is not sold, it can be stored for sale later. Therefore it is important to *match supply and demand* for services. For example, if a hotel has high weekday occupancy but is virtually empty at weekends, a key marketing task is to provide incentives for weekend use. This might involve offering weekend discounts, or linking hotel use with leisure activities such as golf, fishing or hiking.

Service providers also have the problem of catering for peak demand when supply may be insufficient. A physical goods provider may build up inventory in slack periods for sale during peak demand. Service providers do not have this option. Consequently, alternative methods need to be considered. For example, supply flexibility can be varied through the *use of part-time staff* during peak periods. *Multi-skilling* means that employees may be trained in many tasks. Supermarket staff can be trained to fill shelves and work at the checkout at peak periods. *Participation by consumers* may be encouraged in production (e.g. self-service breakfasts in hotels). Demand may be smoothed through *differential pricing* to encourage customers to visit during off-peak periods (for example, lower-priced cinema and theatre seats for afternoon performances). *Stimulation of off-peak demand* can be achieved by special events (e.g. golf or history weekends for hotels). If delay is unavoidable then another option is to make it more acceptable—for example, by providing a comfortable waiting area with seating and free refreshments. Finally, a *reservation system*, as commonly used in restaurants, hair salons and theatres, can be used to control peak demand and assist time substitution.

Managing services

Four key aspects of managing services are managing customer relationships, managing service quality, managing service productivity, managing service staff and positioning services.

Managing customer relationships

Relationship marketing in services has attracted much attention in recent years as organizations focus their efforts on retaining existing customers rather than only attracting new ones. It is not a new concept, however, since the idea of a company earning customer loyalty was well known to the earliest merchants, who had the following saying: 'As a merchant, you'd better have a friend in every town.'[8] Relationship marketing involves the shifting from activities concerned with attracting customers to activities focused on current customers and how to retain them. Although the idea can be applied to many industries it is particularly important in services since there is often direct contact between service provider and consumer—for example, doctor and patient, hotel staff and guests. The quality of the relationship that develops will often determine its length. Not all service encounters have the potential for a long-term relationship, however. For example, a passenger at an international airport who needs road transportation will probably never meet the taxi driver again, and the choice of taxi supplier will be dependent on the passenger's position in the queue rather than free choice. In this case the exchange—cash for journey—is a pure transaction: the driver knows that it is unlikely that there will ever be a repeat purchase.[9] Organizations, therefore, need to decide when the practice of relationship marketing is most applicable. The following conditions suggest potential areas for the use of relationship marketing activities:[10]

- where there is an ongoing or periodic desire for the service by the customer, e.g. insurance or theatre service versus funeral service
- where the customer controls the selection of a service provider, e.g. selecting a hotel versus entering the first taxi in an airport waiting line
- where the customer has alternatives from which to choose, e.g. selecting a restaurant versus buying water from the only utility company service in a community.

Having established the applicability of relationship marketing to services, we will now explore the benefits of relationship marketing to organizations and customers, and the customer retention strategies used to build relationships and tie customers closer to service firms.

Benefits for the organization

There are six benefits to service organizations in developing and maintaining strong customer relationships.[11]

(1) *Increased purchases*: a study by Reichheld and Sasser[12] has shown that customers tend to spend more each year with a relationship partner than they did in the preceding period. This is logical as it would be expected that as the relationship develops, trust would develop between the partners, and as the customer becomes more and more satisfied with the quality of services provided by the supplier so it will give a greater proportion of its business to the supplier.

(2) *Lower cost*: the start-up costs associated with attracting new customers are likely to be far higher than the cost of retaining existing customers. Start-up costs will include the time of salespeople making repeat calls in an effort to persuade a prospect to open an account, the advertising and promotional costs associated with making prospects aware of the company and its service offering, the operating costs of setting up accounts and systems, and the time costs of establishing bonds between the supplier and customer in the early stages of the relationship. Furthermore, costs associated with solving early teething problems and queries are likely to fall as the customer becomes accustomed to using the service.

(3) *Lifetime value of a customer*: the lifetime value of a customer is the profit made on a customer's purchases over the lifetime of that customer. If a customer spends

£80 (€115.2) in a supermarket per week, resulting in £8 (€11.5) profit, uses the supermarket 45 times a year over 30 years, the lifetime value of that customer is £10,800 (€15,550). Thus a bad service experience early on in this relationship, which results in the customer defecting to the competition, would be very expensive to the supermarket, especially when the costs of bad word of mouth are added, as this may deter other customers from using the store.

(4) *Sustainable competitive advantage*: the intangible aspects of a relationship are not easily copied by the competition. For example, the friendships and high levels of trust that can develop as the relationship matures can be extremely difficult for competitors to replicate. This means that the extra value to customers that derives from the relationship can be a source of sustainable competitive advantage for suppliers.[13]

(5) *Word of mouth*: word of mouth is very important in services due to their intangible nature, which makes them difficult to evaluate prior to purchase. In these circumstances, potential purchasers often look to others who have experienced the service (e.g. a hotel) for personal recommendation. A firm that has a large number of loyal customers is more likely to benefit from word of mouth than another without such a resource.

(6) *Employee satisfaction and retention*: satisfied, loyal customers benefit employees in providing a set of mutually beneficial relationships and less hassle. This raises employees' job satisfaction and lowers job turnover. Employees can spend time improving existing relationships rather than desperately seeking new customers. This sets up a virtuous circle of satisfied customers, leading to happy employees that raise customer satisfaction even higher.

The net result of these six benefits of developing customer relationships is high profits. A study has shown across a variety of service industries that profits climb steeply when a firm lowers its customer defection rate.[14] Firms could improve profits from 25 to 85 per cent (depending on the industry) by reducing customer defections by just 5 per cent. The reasons are that loyal customers generate more revenue for more years and the costs of maintaining existing customers are lower than the costs of acquiring new customers. An analysis of a credit card company revealed that improving the defection rate from 10 to 20 years increased the lifetime value of this customer from $135 to $300.

Benefits for the customer

Entering into a long-term relationship can also reap the following four benefits for the customer.

(1) *Risk and stress reduction*: since the intangible nature of services makes them difficult to evaluate before purchase, relationship marketing can benefit the customer as well as the firm. This is particularly so for services that are personally important, variable in quality, complex and/or subject to high-involvement buying.[15] Such purchases are potentially high risk in that making the wrong choice has severe negative consequences for the buyer. Banking, insurance, motor servicing and hairstyling are examples of services that exhibit some or all of the characteristics—importance, variability, complexity and high involvement—that would cause many customers to seek an ongoing relationship with a trusted service provider. Such a relationship reduces consumer stress as the relationship becomes predictable, initial problems are solved, special needs are accommodated and the consumer learns what to expect. After a period of time, the consumer begins to trust the service provider, can count on a consistent level of quality service and feels comfortable in the relationship.[16]

(2) *Higher-quality service*: experiencing a long-term relationship with a service provider can also result in higher levels of service. This is because the service provider becomes knowledgeable about the customer's requirements. For example, doctors get to know the medical history of their patients, and hairstylists learn about the preferences of their clients. Knowledge of the customer built up over a series of service encounters facilitates the tailoring or customizing of the service to each customer's special needs.

(3) *Avoidance of switching costs*: maintaining a relationship with a service supplier avoids the costs associated with switching to a new provider. Once a service provider knows a customer's preferences and special needs, and has tailored services to suit them, to change would mean educating a new provider and accepting the possibility of mistakes being made until the new provider has learnt to accommodate them. This results in both time and psychological costs to the customer. Bitner suggests that a major cost of relocating to a new geographic location is the need to establish relationships with unfamiliar service providers such as banks, schools, doctors and hairdressers.[17]

(4) *Social and status benefits*: customers can also reap social and status benefits from a continuing relationship with a supplier. Since many service encounters are also social encounters, repeated contact can assume personal as well as professional dimensions. In such circumstances, service customers may develop relationships resembling personal friendships. For example, hairdressers often serve as personal confidantes, and restaurant managers may get to know some of their customers personally. Such personal relationships can feed one's ego (status) as when a hotel customer commented, 'When employees remember and recognize you as a regular customer you feel really good.'[18]

Developing customer retention strategies

The benefits of developing long-term relationships with customers mean that it is worthwhile for services organizations to consider designing customer retention strategies. This involves the targeting of customers for retention, bonding, internal marketing, promise fulfilment, building of trust and service recovery (see Fig. 21.3), as described below.

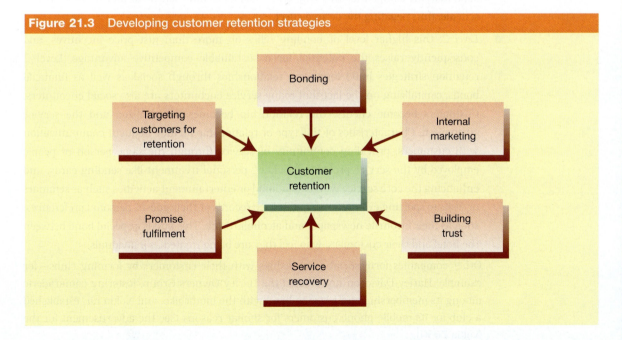

Figure 21.3 Developing customer retention strategies

1. *Targeting customers for retention*: not all customers are worthy of relationship building. Some may be habitual brand switchers, perhaps responding to the lowest deal currently on offer; others may not generate sufficient revenue to justify the expense of acquiring them and maintaining the relationship; and, finally, some customers may be so troublesome, and their attitudes and behaviour cause so much disruption to the service provider, that the costs of servicing them outweigh the benefits. Firms need, therefore, to identify those customers with whom they wish to engage in a long-term relationship, those for whom a transactional marketing approach is better suited, and those with whom they would prefer not to do business. This is the classical market segmentation and targeting approach discussed in Chapter 7. The characteristics of those customers that are candidates for a relationship marketing approach are high-value, frequent-use, loyalty-prone customers for whom the actual and potential service offerings that can be supplied by the firm have high utility.

    Targeting customers for retention involves the analysis of loyalty and defection-prone customers. Service suppliers need to understand why customers stay or leave, what creates value for them, and their profile. Decisions can then be made regarding which types of customer defector they wish to try to save (e.g. price or service defectors) and the nature of the value-adding strategy that meets their needs, while at the same time maintaining bonds with loyalty-prone customers.[19]

2. *Bonding*: retention strategies vary in the degree to which they bond the parties together. One framework that illustrates this idea distinguishes between three levels of retention strategy based on the types of bond used to cement the relationship.[20]

    - *Level 1*: at this level the bond is primarily through financial incentives, for example, higher discounts on prices for larger-volume purchases or frequent-flyer or loyalty points resulting in lower future prices. The problem is that the potential for a sustainable competitive advantage is low because price incentives are easy for competitors to copy even if they take the guise of frequent-flyer or loyalty points. Most airlines and supermarkets compete in this way and consumers have learnt to join more than one scheme, thus negating the desired effect.

    - *Level 2*: this higher level of bonding relies on more than just price incentives, and consequently raises the potential for a sustainable competitive advantage. Level 2 retention strategies build long-term relationships through social as well as financial bonds, capitalizing on the fact that many service encounters are also social encounters. Customers become clients, the relationship becomes personalized and the service customized. Characteristics of this type of relationship include frequent communication with customers, providing community of service through the same person or people employed by the service provider, providing personal treatment like sending cards, and enhancing the core service with educational or entertainment activities such as seminars or visits to sporting events. Some hotels keep records of their guests' personal preferences, such as their favourite newspaper and alcoholic drink. This builds a special bond between the hotel and their customers, who feel they are being treated as individuals.

    Other companies form social relationships with their customers by forming clubs—for example, Harley-Davidson has created the Harley Owners Group, fostering camaraderie among its membership and a strong bond with the motorbike, and Nokia has established a club for its mobile phone customers for similar reasons (see the advertisement for the Nokia 7650).

Nokia has established a club for owners of its mobile phones.

- *Level 3*: this top level of bonding is formed by financial, social and structural bonds. Structural bonds tie service providers to their customers through providing solutions to customers' problems that are designed into the service delivery system. For example, logistics companies often supply their clients with equipment that ties them into their systems. When combined with financial and social bonds, structural bonds can create a formidable barrier against competitor inroads and provide the basis for a sustainable competitive advantage.

(3) *Internal marketing*: a fundamental basis for customer retention is high-quality service delivery. This depends on high-quality performance from employees since the service product is a performance and the performers are employees.[21] Internal marketing concerns training, communicating to and motivating internal staff. Staff need to be trained to be technically competent at their job as well as to be able to handle service encounters with customers. To do this well, they must be motivated and understand what is expected of them. Service staff act as 'part-time marketers' since their actions can directly affect customer satisfaction and retention.[22] They are critical in the 'moments of truth' when they and customers come into contact in a service situation.

A key focus of an internal marketing programme should be employee selection and retention. Service companies that suffer high rates of job turnover are continually employing new, inexperienced staff to handle customer service encounters. Employees that have worked for the company for years know more about the business and have had the opportunity to build relationships with customers. By selecting the right people and managing them in such a way that they stay loyal to the service organization, higher levels of customer retention can be achieved through the build-up of trust and personal knowledge gained through long-term contact with customers.

(4) *Promise fulfilment*: the fulfilment of promises is a cornerstone for maintaining service relationships. This implies three key activities: *making* realistic promises initially, and *keeping* those promises during service delivery by *enabling* staff and service systems to deliver on promises made.[23]

Making promises is done through normal marketing communications channels such as advertising, selling and promotion, as well as the specific service cues that set expectations such as the dress of the service staff, and the design and décor of the establishment. It is important not to over-promise with marketing communications or the result will be disappointment, and consequently customer dissatisfaction and defection. The promise should be credible and realistic. Some companies adhere to the adage 'under-promise and over-deliver'.

A necessary condition for promises to be kept is the enabling of staff and service systems to deliver on the promises made. This means staff must have the skills, competences, tools, systems and enthusiasm to deliver. Some of these issues have been looked at in the earlier discussion of internal marketing, and are dependent on the correct recruitment, training and rewarding of staff, and on providing them with the right equipment and systems to do their jobs.

The final activity associated with promise fulfilment is the keeping of promises. This relies on service staff or technology such as the downloading of software via the Internet. The keeping of promises occurs when the customer and the service provider interact: the 'moment of truth' mentioned earlier. Research has shown that customers judge employees on their ability to deliver the service right the first time, their ability to recover if things go wrong, how well they deal with special requests, and on their spontaneous actions and attitudes.[24] These are clearly key dimensions that must play a part in a training programme and should be borne in mind when selecting and rewarding service staff; not all service encounters are equal in importance, however. Research conducted on behalf of Marriott hotels has shown that events occurring early in a service encounter affect customer loyalty the most. Based on these findings Marriott developed its 'First 10 Minutes' strategy. It is hardly surprising that first impressions are so important since before then the customer has had no direct contact with the service provider and will be uncertain of the outcome.

Finally, we need to recognize that the keeping of promises does not depend solely on service staff and technology. Because service delivery is often in a group setting (e.g. listening to a lecture, watching a film or travelling by air) the quality of the experience can be as dependent on the behaviour of other customers as that of the service provider. Lovelock, Vandermerwe and Lewis label the problem customers 'jaycustomers'.[25] These are people who act in a thoughtless or abusive way, causing problems for the organization, its employees and other customers. One particular kind of jaycustomer is the belligerent person who shouts abuse and threats at service staff because of some service malfunction. Staff need to be trained to develop the self-confidence and assertiveness required to deal with such situations, and do so using role-play exercises. If possible, the jaycustomer should be moved away from other customer contact to minimize the discomfort of the latter. Finally, where the service employee does not have the authority to resolve the problem, more senior staff should be approached to settle a dispute.

(5) *Building trust*: customer retention relies heavily on building trust. This is particularly so for service firms since the intangibility of services means that they are difficult to evaluate before buying and experiencing them (indeed some, such as car servicing, are hard to evaluate after purchasing them). Purchasing a service for the first time can leave the customer with a feeling of uncertainty and vulnerability, particularly when the service is personally important, variable in quality, complex and subject to high-involvement purchasing. It is not surprising that customers who have developed trust in a supplier in these circumstances are unlikely to switch to a new supplier and undergo the uncomfortable feelings of uncertainty and vulnerability all over again.

Companies that wish to build up their trustworthiness should keep in touch with their customers by regular two-way communication to develop feelings of closeness and openness, provide guarantees to symbolize the confidence they feel in their service delivery as well as reducing their customers' perceived risk of purchase, and to operate a policy of fairness and high standards of conduct with their customers.[26]

(6) *Service recovery*: service recovery strategies should be designed to solve the problem and restore the customers' trust in the firm, and to improve the service system so that the problem does not recur in the future.[27] They are crucial because the inability to recover service failures and mistakes loses customers both directly and through their tendency to tell other actual and potential customers about their negative experiences.

The first ingredient in a service recovery strategy is to set up a tracking system to identify system failures. Customers should be encouraged to report service problems since it is those customers that do not complain that are least likely to purchase again. Systems should be established to monitor complaints, follow up on service experiences by telephone calling, and to use suggestion boxes for both service staff and customers.

Second, staff should be trained and empowered to respond to service complaints. This is important because research has shown that the successful resolution of a complaint can cause customers to feel more positive about the firm than before the service failure. If a second problem occurs, though, this effect (called the 'recovery paradox') disappears.[28] The first response from a service provider to a genuine complaint is to apologize. Often this will take the heat out of the situation and lead to a spirit of co-operation rather than recrimination. The next step is to attempt to solve the problem quickly. Marriott hotels facilitates this process by empowering frontline employees to solve customers' problems quickly, even though this may mean expense to the hotel, and without recourse to seeking approval from higher authority. Other key elements in service recovery are to appear pleasant, helpful and attentive, show concern for the customer and be flexible. Regarding problem resolution, service staff should provide information about the problem, take action and should appear to put themselves out to solve the problem.[29] Marketing in Action 21.1 describes complaint handling at Virgin Trains.

21.1 marketing in action

Complaint Handling at Virgin Trains

When customers complain to Chris Green, chief executive, or Richard Branson the owner of Virgin Trains, about service failures their complaint is dealt with by a member of a team of three specially assigned to handle the stream of queries, complaints, criticisms and occasionally compliments that are sent or telephoned in. The first step is to assess the complaint carefully. Most customers are wanting an explanation, information and\or reassurance, and it is important to understand what they are seeking. This is followed by research. For example, if someone complains about a delay, the operational log will be checked to find out why it happened so an explanation can be given. The third step is to find out what action is being taken to improve the situation. This could take the form of increased spending on new trains, and this information will be conveyed to the customer.

As part of their job the team of three get out on the rail network to see the service in action for themselves. It is important for them to experience what people are talking about and meet staff so that they can see what issues need to be dealt with.

Most complaints arrive by letter but occasionally irate customers complain over the telephone. The keys to responding to angry customers are to imagine yourself in their shoes, to be polite and informative. Whether the complaint is by letter or telephone, the response must be fresh. Even though similar complaints occur quite regularly, the temptation to reply with a standard letter needs to be resisted.

Based on: Thorpe (2000)[30]

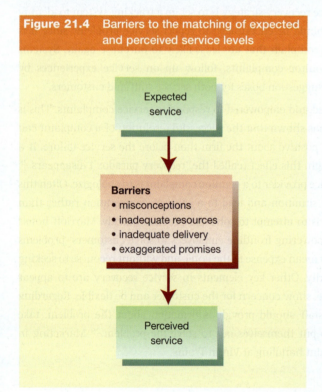

Figure 21.4 Barriers to the matching of expected and perceived service levels

Finally, a service recovery strategy should encourage learning so that service recovery problems are identified and corrected. Service staff should be motivated to report problems and solutions so that recurrent failures are identified and fixed. In this way, an effective service recovery system can lead to improved customer service, satisfaction and higher customer-retention levels.

Managing service quality

Intuitively, it makes sense to suggest that improving service quality will increase customer satisfaction, leading to higher sales and profits. Indeed, it has been shown that companies that are rated higher on service quality perform better in terms of market share growth and profitability.[31] Yet, for many companies, high standards of service quality remain elusive. There are four causes of poor perceived quality (see Fig. 21.4). These are the barriers that separate the perception of service quality from what customers expect.[32]

Barriers to the matching of expected and perceived service levels

The **misconception barrier** arises from management's misunderstanding of what the customer expects. Lack of marketing research may lead managers to misconceive the important service attributes that customers use when evaluating a service, and the way in which customers use attributes in evaluation. For example, a restaurant manager may believe that shortening the gap between courses may improve customer satisfaction, when the customer actually values a pause between eating.

Inadequate resources barrier: managers may understand customer expectations but be unwilling to provide the resources necessary to meet them. This may arise because of a cost reduction or productivity focus, or simply because of the inconvenience it may cause.

Inadequate delivery barrier: managers may understand customer expectations and supply adequate resources but fail to select, train and reward staff adequately, resulting in poor or inconsistent service. This may manifest itself in poor communication skills, inappropriate dress, and unwillingness to solve customer problems.

Exaggerated promises barrier: even when customer understanding, resources and staff management are in place, a gap between customer expectations and perceptions can still arise through exaggerated promises. Advertising and selling messages that build expectations to a pitch that cannot be fulfilled may leave customers disappointed even when receiving good service. For example, a tourist brochure that claims a hotel is 'just a few minutes from the sea' may lead to disappointment if the walk takes 10 minutes.

Service quality can be improved by using the Internet. E-Marketing 21.1 describes how Egg provides value to time-pressured consumers by giving 24-hour, 7-day-a-week access to their finances.

21.1 e-marketing

Online Financial Services

Tremendous opportunities are presented to banks and other financial organizations to service existing and new customers through the Internet. From a standing start more than five years ago, there are now 6 million Internet bank accounts in the UK. Driving this Internet banking and financial service phenomenon are the need for improved services to allow customers 24/7 access to their finances, and to compete with a growing number of financial service providers (including non-financial organizations like Tesco or Virgin) at a time when it has never been easier, as a customer, to switch providers.

The ability for customers to deposit funds, earn interest and transfer monies online without the physical infrastructure normally associated with a full banking service (secure high-street premises, tellers, printed currency, strongboxes, etc.) has considerably reduced average transaction costs (£0.01 per transaction for Internet banking compared with £0.70 per transaction for a full branch service). In addition to most traditional financial service organizations offering Internet services there are now also around 20 banks that exist only on the Internet.

Egg (www.egg.co.uk) was launched in October 1998 and is the UK's leading online financial services company; by 2002 it had amassed almost 2 million customers. Egg is based on the Internet but uses additional channels to communicate with customers, including iTV (interactive television) and telephone. Egg's main target market is young, busy professionals. This is because this segment of consumers value the 24-hour, 7-day-a-week access Egg provides.

Based on: Shearer (2003)[33]

Meeting customer expectations

A key to providing service quality is the understanding and meeting of *customer expectations*. To do so requires a clear picture of the criteria used to form these expectations, recognizing that consumers of services value not only the *outcome* of the service encounter but also the *experience* of taking part in it. For example, an evaluation of a haircut depends not only on the quality of the cut but also the experience of having a haircut. Clearly, a hairdresser needs not only technical skills but also the ability to communicate in an interesting and polite manner. Ten criteria may be used when evaluating the outcome and experience of a service encounter.[34]

1. *Access*: is the service provided at convenient locations and times with little waiting?
2. *Reliability*: is the service consistent and dependable?
3. *Credibility*: can customers trust the service company and its staff?
4. *Security*: can the service be used without risk?
5. *Understanding the customer*: does it appear that the service provider understands customer expectations?
6. *Responsiveness*: how quickly do service staff respond to customer problems, requests and questions?
7. *Courtesy*: do service staff act in a friendly and polite manner?
8. *Competence*: do service staff have the required skills and knowledge?
9. *Communication*: is the service described clearly and accurately?
10. *Tangibles*: how well managed is the tangible evidence of the service (e.g. staff appearance, décor, layout)?

These criteria form a useful checklist for service providers wishing to understand how their customers judge them. A self-analysis may show areas that need improvement, but the most reliable approach is to check that customers use these criteria and to conduct marketing research to compare performance against competition. Where service quality is dependent on a succession of service encounters (for example, a hotel stay may encompass the check-in, the room itself, the restaurant, breakfast and check-out), each should be measured in terms of their impact on total satisfaction so that corrective actions can be taken.[35] Questionnaires have now been developed that allow the measurement of perceived customer satisfaction at distinct stages of the service-delivery process (for example, the stages encountered while visiting a museum).[36]

Measuring service quality

A scale called *SERVQUAL* has been developed to aid the measurement of *service quality*.[37] Based on five criteria—reliability, responsiveness, courtesy, competence and tangibles—it is a multiple-item scale that aims to measure customer perceptions and expectations so that gaps can be identified. The scale is simple to administer with respondents indicating their strength of agreement or disagreement with a series of statements about service quality using a Likert scale.

Managing service productivity

Productivity is a measure of the relationship between an input and an output. For example, if more people can be served (output) using the same number of staff (input), productivity per employee has risen. Clearly there can be conflict between improving service productivity (efficiency) and raising service quality (effectiveness). For example, a doctor who reduces consultation time per patient or a university that increases tutorial group size raise productivity at the risk of lowering service quality. Table 21.1 shows how typical operational goals that seek to minimize costs can cause marketing concerns. Marketers need to understand why operations managers have such goals, and operations managers need to recognize the implications of their actions for customer satisfaction.[38]

Table 21.1 Marketing and operations' views on operational issues		
Operational issues	Typical operations goals	Common marketing concerns
Productivity improvement	Reduce unit cost of production	Strategies may cause decline in service quality
Standardizaton versus customization	Keep costs low and quality consistent: simplify operations tasks; recruit low-cost employees	Consumers may seek variety, prefer customization to match segmented needs
Batch vs unit processing	Seek economies of scale, consistency, efficient use of capacity	Customers may be forced to wait, feel 'one of a crowd', be turned off by other customers
Facilities layout and design	Control costs; improve efficiency by ensuring proximity of operationally related tasks; enhance safety and security	Customers may be confused, shunted around unnecessarily, find facility unattractive and inconvenient
Job design	Minimize error, waste and fraud; make efficient use of technology; simplify task for standardization	Operationally orientated employees with narrow roles may be unresponsive to customer needs
Management of capacity	Keep costs down by avoiding wasteful under-utilization of resources	Service may be unavailable when needed; quality may be compromised during high-demand periods
Management of queues	Optimize use of available capacity by planning for average throughput; maintain customer order, discipline	Customers may be bored and frustrated during wait, see firm as unresponsive

Source: Lovelock, C. (1992) Seeking Synergy in Service Operations: Seven Things Marketers Need to Know about Service Operations, *European Management Journal* 10(1), 22–9. Reprinted with permission from Elsevier Science Ltd, The Boulevard, Langford Lane, Kidlington OX5 1GB, UK.

Clearly a balance must be struck between productivity and service quality. At some point quality gains become so expensive that they are not worthwhile. However, there are ways of improving productivity without compromising quality. Technology, obtaining customer involvement in production of the service, and balancing supply and demand are three methods of achieving this.

Technology

Technology can be used to improve productivity and service quality. For example, airport X-ray surveillance equipment raises the throughput of passengers (productivity) and speeds the process of checking-in (service quality). Automatic cash dispensers in banks increase the number of transactions per period (productivity) while reducing customer waiting time (service quality). Automatic vending machines increase the number of drinks sold per establishment (productivity) while improving accessibility for customers (service quality). Computerization can also raise productivity and service quality. For example, Direct Line, owned by the Royal Bank of Scotland, is based on computer software that produces a motor insurance quote instantaneously. Callers are asked for a few details (such as how old they are, where they live, what car they drive and number of years since their last claim) and this is keyed into the computer, which automatically produces a quotation.[39]

Online reservation systems are now commonplace in the travel and hotel industries. Booking costs are reduced and queuing problems, so often found with telemarketing operations, eliminated. E-Marketing 21.2 describes how Travel Inn has benefited from developing an online reservation system.

21.2 e-marketing

E-business in the Hotel Industry

The hotel industry in the UK comprises several large chains, including Hilton, Jarvis, Moathouse, Travelodge and Travel Inn. Travel Inn is the leading brand in the budget hotel market with 285 hotels and 30 per cent market share. The budget hotel industry in the UK is highly competitive and many such hotel chains have turned to e-business technology to increase bookings and gain competitive advantage.

Travel Inn (www.travelinn.co.uk) is no different, and from the first steps of developing a brochure-ware website (one offering general information) it introduced a new reservation system that provides online access to room availability and allows room bookings to be made via the website.

The success of this online resource is in no small part due to considerable offline advertising. Shortly after 11 September 2001, Travel Inn launched a £3 million marketing campaign aimed at 25–55-year-old businesspeople; the main thrust being to reinforce the brand and to promote the website address. Web traffic grew as a result and online bookings now account for 15 per cent of all reservations.

Can Travel Inn's use of e-business technology maintain its position in the hotel industry? This remains to be seen. Many hotel chains are more heavily involved in using customer data to manage relationships better, e.g. through targeted e-mail marketing, reduced check-in times, increased customer preferences, and so on. In this sense Travel Inn could still do more but so could its nearest competitors.

Based on: Lee (2003)[40]

Retailers have benefited from electronic point of sale (EPOS) and electronic data interchange (EDI). Timely and detailed sales information can aid buying decisions and provide retail buyers with a negotiating advantage over suppliers. Other benefits from this technology include better labour scheduling, and stock and distribution systems.

Customer involvement in production

The inseparability between production and consumption provides an opportunity to raise both productivity and service quality. For example, self-service breakfast bars and petrol stations improve productivity per employee and reduce customer waiting time (service quality). The effectiveness of this tactic relies heavily on customer expectations, and on managing transition periods. It should be used when there is a clear advantage to customers in their involvement in production. In other instances, reducing customer service may reduce satisfaction. For example, a hotel that expected its customers to service their own rooms would need a persuasive communications programme to convince customers that the lack of service was reflected in cheaper rates.

Balancing supply and demand

Because services cannot be stored, balancing supply and demand is a key determinant of productivity. Hotels or aircraft that are less than half full incur low productivity. If in the next period, the hotel or airline is faced with excess demand, the unused space in the previous period cannot be used to meet it. The combined result is low productivity and customer dissatisfaction (low service quality). By smoothing demand or increasing the flexibility of supply, both productivity and service quality can be achieved.

Smoothing demand can be achieved through differential pricing and stimulating off-peak demand (e.g. weekend breaks). Increasing supply flexibility may be increased by using part-time employees, multi-skilling and encouraging customers to service themselves.

Managing service staff

Many services involve a high degree of contact between service staff and customers. This is true for such service industries as healthcare, banking, catering and education. The quality of the service experience is therefore heavily dependent on staff–customer interpersonal relationships. John Carlzon, the head of Scandinavian Airlines System (SAS), called these meetings *moments of truth*. He explained that SAS faced 65,000 moments of truth per day and that the outcomes determined the success of the company.

Research on customer loyalty in the service industry showed that only 14 per cent of customers who stopped patronizing service businesses did so because they were dissatisfied with the quality of what they had bought. More than two-thirds stopped buying because they found service staff indifferent or unhelpful.[41] Clearly, the way in which service personnel treat their customers is fundamental to success in the service industry.

Also, frontline staff are important sources of customer and competitor information and, if properly motivated, can provide crucial inputs in the development of new service products.[42] For example, discussions with customers may generate ideas for new services that customers would value if available on the market.

In order for service employees to be in the frame of mind to treat customers well, they need to feel that their company is treating them well. In companies where staff have a high regard for the human resources policy, customers also have a positive opinion of the service they receive.

The *selection of suitable people* is the starting point of the process. Personality differences mean that it is not everyone who can fill a service role. The nature of the job needs to be defined and the appropriate personality characteristics needed to perform effectively outlined. Once selected, training is required to familiarize recruits to the job requirements and the culture of the organization. Orientation is the process by which a company helps new recruits understand the organization and its culture. Folklore is often used to show how employees have made outstanding contributions to the company.

Socialization allows the recruit to experience the culture and tasks of the organization. Usually, the aim is creative individualism, whereby the recruit accepts all of the key behavioural norms but is encouraged to display initiative and innovation in dealing with problems. Thus standards of behaviour are internalized, but the creative abilities of the individual are not subjugated to the need to conform.

Service quality may also be affected by the degree to which staff are *empowered*, or given the authority to satisfy customers and deal with their problems. For example, each member of staff of Marriott hotels is allowed to spend up to £1000 on their own initiative to solve customer problems. The company uses some of the situations that have arisen where employees have acted decisively to solve a customer problem in their advertising. The advantage is quicker response times since staff do not have to consult with their supervisors before dealing with a problem.[43] However, empowerment programmes need to recognize the increased responsibility thrust on employees. Not everyone will welcome this, and reward systems need to be thought through (e.g. higher pay or status).

Pret A Manger empowers staff in a different way. Following application and interview, prospective job candidates are paid to work for one day in a Pret store. The people working in that store then make the final decision as to whether the candidate is taken on. This empowers staff and ensures that only staff with the right attitude are employed.[44]

Maintaining a motivated workforce in the face of irate customers, faulty support systems and the boredom that accompanies some service jobs is a demanding task. The motivational factors discussed when examining salesforce management are equally relevant here and include recognition of achievement, role clarity, opportunities for advancement, the interest value of the job, monetary rewards, and setting challenging but achievable targets. Some service companies (e.g. Holiday Inn) give employee-of-the-month awards as recognition of outstanding service. A key factor in avoiding demotivation is to monitor support systems so that staff work with efficient equipment and facilities to help them carry out their job.

Service evaluation is also important in managing staff. Customer feedback is essential to maintaining high standards of service quality. McDonald's continually monitors quality, service, cleanliness and value (QSCV), and if a franchisee fails to meet these standards they are dropped. The results of customer research should be fed back to employees so that they can relate their performance standards to customer satisfaction. Enlightened companies tie financial incentives to the results of such surveys.

Positioning services

Positioning is the process of establishing and keeping a distinctive place in the market for a company and its products. Most successful service firms differentiate themselves from the competition on attributes that their target customers value highly. They develop service concepts that are highly valued, and communicate to target customers so that they accurately perceive the position of the service. For example, Credit Suisse Financial Products positions itself as a specialist in risk management products and services.

The positioning task entails two decisions:

1. choice of target market (where to compete)
2. creation of a differential advantage (how to compete).

These decisions are common to both physical products and services. Creating a differential advantage is based on understanding the target customers' requirements better than the competition. Figure 21.5 shows the relationship between *target customer needs* and the *services marketing mix*. On the left of the figure is an array of factors (choice criteria) that customers may use to judge a service. How well a service firm satisfies those criteria depends on its marketing mix (on the right of the figure). Marketing research can be useful in identifying important choice criteria but care needs to be taken in such studies. Asking customers which are the most important factors when buying a service may give misleading results. For example, the most important factor when travelling by air may be safety. However, this does not mean that customers use safety as a choice criterion when deciding which airline to use. If all major airlines are perceived as being similar in terms of safety, other less important factors like the quality of in-flight meals and service may be the crucial attributes used in decision-making.

Target marketing

The basis of target marketing is market segmentation. A market is analysed to identify groups of potential customers with similar needs and price sensitivities. The potential of each of these

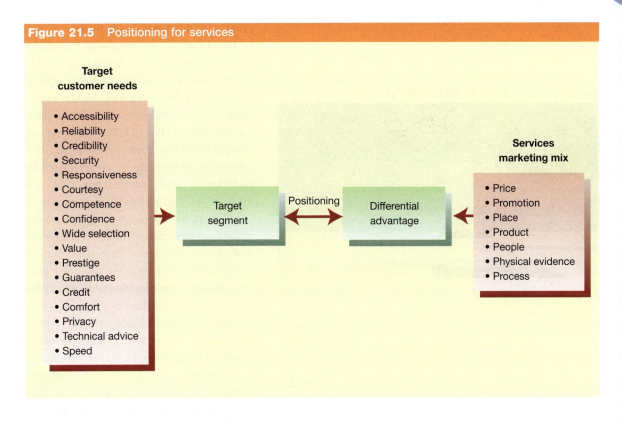

Figure 21.5 Positioning for services

segments is assessed on such factors as size, growth rate, degree of competition, price sensitivity, and the fit between its requirements and the company's capabilities.

Note that the most attractive markets are often not the biggest, however, as these may have been identified earlier and will already have attracted a high level of competition. There may, however, be pockets of customers who are underserved by companies that are compromising their marketing mix by trying to serve too wide a customer base. The identification of such customers is a prime opportunity during segmentation analysis. Target marketing allows service firms to tailor their marketing mix to the specific requirements of groups of customers more effectively than trying to cater for diverse needs.

Marketing managers also need to consider those potential customers that are not directly targeted but may find the service mix attractive. Those customers that are at the periphery of the target market are called halo customers and can make a substantial difference between success and failure (see Fig. 21.6). For example, Top Shop, a UK clothing retailer targeting 16–24 year olds, was very successful in attracting this group to its shops but financial performance was marred by the lack of interest from its halo customers: those who fell outside this age bracket but nevertheless may have found Top Shop's clothing to their taste.

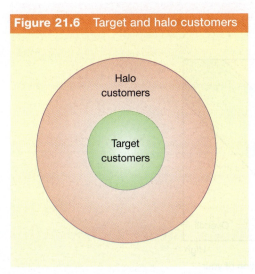

Figure 21.6 Target and halo customers

Differential advantage

Understanding customer needs will be the basis of the design of a new service concept that is different from competitive offerings, is highly valued by target customers, and therefore

This ad for P&O Cruises communicates the company's expertise, giving consumers confidence in its competence at organizing cruises in the Caribbean.

creates a differential advantage. It will be based on the creative use of marketing-mix elements, resulting in such benefits as more reliable or faster delivery, greater convenience, more comfort, higher-quality work, higher prestige or other issues (listed on the left of Fig. 21.5). Some service companies stress their expertise in their advertising to meet the customer's need for confidence and competence, as the illustration featuring P&O Cruises shows.

Research can indicate which choice criteria are more or less valued by customers, and how customers rate the service provider's performance on each.[45] Figure 21.7 shows three possible outcomes: *under-performance* results from performing poorly on highly valued choice criteria; *overkill* arises when the service provider excels at things of little consequence to customers; and the *target area* is where the supplier performs well on criteria that are of high value to customers and less well on less-valued criteria. Differentiation is achieved in those areas that are of most importance, while resources are not wasted improving service quality levels in areas that are unimportant to customers. The result is the achievement of both effectiveness and efficiency in the service operation.

Figure 21.7   Achieving differentiation in service quality

Source: Christopher, M. and R. Yallop (1990) Audit your Customer Service Quality, *Focus*, June/July. Reprinted with kind permission of Martin Christopher.

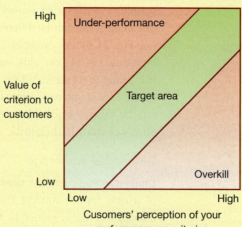

The services marketing mix

The **services marketing mix** is an extension of the 4-Ps framework introduced in Chapter 1. The essential elements of *product*, *promotion*, *price* and *place* remain, but three additional variables—*people*, *physical evidence* and *process*—are included to produce a 7-Ps mix.[46] The need for the extension is due to the high degree of direct contact between the firm and the customer, the highly visible nature of the service assembly process, and the simultaneity of production and consumption. While it is possible to discuss people, physical evidence and process within the original 4-Ps framework (for example, people could be considered part of the product offering) the extension allows a more thorough analysis of the marketing ingredients necessary for successful services marketing. Each element of the marketing mix will now be examined.

Product: physical products can be inspected and tried before buying, but pure services are intangible; you cannot go to a showroom to see a marketing research report or medical operation that you are considering. This means that service customers suffer higher perceived risk in their decision-making and that the three elements of the extended marketing mix—people, physical evidence and process—are crucial in influencing the customer's perception of service quality. These will be discussed later.

The *brand name* of a service can also influence the perception of a service. Four characteristics of successful brand names are as follows.[47]

1. *Distinctiveness*: it immediately identifies the services provider and differentiates it from the competition.
2. *Relevance*: it communicates the nature of the service and the service benefit.
3. *Memorability*: it is easily understood and remembered.
4. *Flexibility*: it not only expresses the service organization's current business but is also broad enough to cover foreseeable new ventures.

Credit cards provide examples of effective brand names: Visa suggests internationality and Access emphasizes easy accessibility to cash and products. Obviously the success of the brand name is heavily dependent on the service organization's ability to deliver on the promise it implies.

Although trial of some services is impossible, for others it can be achieved. For example, some hotels invite key decision-makers of social clubs (for example, social secretaries of pensioner groups) to visit their hotels free of charge to sample the facilities and service. The hotels hope that they will recommend a group visit to their members.

Service providers such as airlines are constantly seeking ways of differentiating themselves from their competitors. For example, the quality of the physical products that accompany a service can be used as a basis for differentiation.

Promotion: the intangible element of a service may be difficult to communicate. For example, it may be difficult to represent courtesy, hard work and customer care in an advertisement. Once again, the answer is to use *tangible cues* that will help customers understand and judge the service. A hotel can show its buildings, swimming pool, friendly staff and happy customers. An investment company can provide tangible evidence of past performance. Testimonials from satisfied customers can also be used to communicate services benefits. Netto, the Danish-based supermarket chain, used testimonials from six customers in its UK advertising to explain the advantages of shopping there.

Advertising can be used to communicate and reinforce the image of a service. For example, store image can enhance customer satisfaction and build store loyalty.[48] The illustration featuring Norway (overleaf) is an example of using advertising to communicate the benefits of a service.

New media can also be used to promote services. For example, some online retailers use targeted e-mail to encourage customers to visit their sites. The travel and leisure retailer Lastminute.com sends more than two million e-mails to customers every week with content tailored to fit the recipient's age and lifestyle.[49]

Personal selling can also be effective in services marketing because of the high perceived risk inherent in many service purchases. For example, a salesperson can explain the details of a personal pension plan or investment opportunity, answer questions and provide reassurance.

Because of the high perceived risk inherent in buying services, salespeople should develop lists of satisfied customers to use in reference selling. Also salespeople need to be trained to ask for referrals. Customers should be asked if they know of other people or organizations that might benefit from the service. The customer can then be used as an entrée and point of reference when approaching and selling to the new prospect.

This advertisement for Norway communicates the benefits of holidaying there.

Word of mouth is critical to success for services because of their experiential nature. For example, talking to people that have visited a resort or hotel is more convincing than reading holiday brochures. Promotion, therefore, must acknowledge the dominant role of personal influence in the choice process and stimulate word of mouth communication. Cowell suggests four approaches, as follows.[50]

① Persuading satisfied customers to inform others of their satisfaction (e.g. American Express rewards customers that introduce others to its service).

② Developing materials that customers can pass on to others.

③ Targeting opinion leaders in advertising campaigns.

④ Encouraging potential customers to talk to current customers (e.g. open days at universities).

Communication should also be targeted at employees because of their importance in creating and maintaining service quality. Internal communications can define management expectations of staff, reinforce the need to delight the customer and explain the rewards that follow from giving excellent service. External communications that depict service quality can also influence internal staff if they include employees and show how they take exceptional care of their customers.

Care should be taken not to exaggerate promises in promotional material since this may build up unachievable expectations. For example, Delta Airlines used the advertising slogan 'Delta is ready when you are.' This caused problems because it built up customers' expectations that the airline would always be ready—an impossible task. This led Delta to change its slogan to the more realistic 'We love to fly and it shows.'[51]

The unethical promotion of service products has caused problems in some sectors. A study of senior managers in UK insurance companies revealed an awareness of a range of ethical problems. The design of commission systems which may encourage bias towards products that provide greater returns to the salesperson, and the promotion of inappropriate products were of particular concern.[52]

Price: price is a key marketing tool for three reasons. First, as it is often difficult to evaluate a service before purchase, price may act as an indicator of perceived quality. For example, in a travel brochure the price charged by hotels may be used to indicate their quality. Some companies expect a management consultant to charge high fees, otherwise they cannot be particularly good. Second, price is an important tool in controlling demand: matching demand and supply is critical in services because they cannot be stored. Creative use of pricing can help to smooth demand. Third, a key segmentation variable with services is price sensitivity. Some customers may be willing to pay a much higher price than others. Time is often used to segment price-sensitive and price-insensitive customers. For example, the price of international air travel is often dependent on length of stay. Travellers from Europe to the USA will pay a lot less if they stay a minimum of six nights (including Saturday). Airlines know that customers who stay for less than that are likely to be businesspeople who are willing and able to pay a higher price.

Many companies do not take full advantage of the opportunities to use price creatively in the marketing of their services. For example, in the industrial services sector, one study found that firms 'generally lack a customer orientation in pricing; emphasize formula-based approaches that are cost-oriented; are very inflexible in their pricing schemes; do not develop price differentials based on elasticity of different market segments; and rarely attempt to measure customer price sensitivity'.[53]

Some services, such as accounting and management consultancy, charge their customers fees. A strategy needs to be thought out concerning fees. How far can fees be flexible to secure or retain particular customers? How will the fee level compare to that of the competition? Will there be an incentive built in to the fee structure for continuity, forward commitment or the use of the full range of services on offer? Five pricing techniques may be used when setting fee levels.

1. *Offset*: low fee for core service but recouping with add-ons.
2. *Inducement*: low fee to attract new customers or to help retain existing customers.
3. *Diversionary*: low basic fees on selected services to develop the image of value for money across the whole range of services.
4. *Guarantee*: full fee payable on achievement of agreed results.
5. *Predatory*: competition's fees undercut to remove them from the market; high fees charged later.

Place: distribution channels for services are usually more direct than for many physical goods. Because services are intangible, the services marketer is less concerned with storage, the production and consumption is often simultaneous, and the personal nature of services means that direct contact with the service provider (or at best its agent) is desirable. Agents are used when the individual service provider cannot offer a sufficiently wide selection for customers. Consequently, agents are often used for the marketing of travel, insurance and entertainment. However, the advent of the Internet means that direct dealings with the service provider are becoming more frequent.

Growth for many service companies means opening new facilities in new locations. Whereas producers of physical goods can expand production at one site to serve the needs of a geographically spread market, the simultaneous production and consumption of hotel, banking, catering, retailing and accounting services, for example, means that expansion often means following a multi-site strategy. The evaluation of store locations is therefore a critical skill for services marketers. Much of the success of top European supermarket chains has been due to their ability to choose profitable new sites for their retailing operations.

People: because of the simultaneity of production and consumption in services, the firm's personnel occupy a key position in influencing customer perceptions of product quality.[54] In fact, service quality is inseparable from the quality of the service provider. Without courteous, efficient and motivated staff, service organizations will lose customers. A survey has shown that one in six consumers have been put off making a purchase because of the way they were treated by staff.[55] An important marketing task, then, is to set standards to improve the quality of service provided by employees and monitor their performance. Without training and control, employees tend to be variable in their performance, leading to variable service quality.

Training is crucial so that employees understand the appropriate forms of behaviour. British Airways trains its staff to identify and categorize different personality types of passengers, and to modify their behaviour accordingly. Staff (e.g. waiters) need to know how much discretion they have to talk informally to customers, and to control their own behaviour so that they are not intrusive, noisy or immature. They also need to be trained to adopt a warm and caring attitude to customers. This has been shown to be linked to customers' perceptions of likeability and service perception, as well as loyalty to the service provider.[56] Finally, they need to adopt a customer-first attitude rather than putting their own convenience and enjoyment before that of their customers. This is not to say that staff should not enjoy their work. As Ross Urquhart, managing director of brand experience consultancy RPM, puts it:

> ❝When people enjoy their work it is clear from their body language and the tone of their voice. They give off positive messages about their employer and will go the extra mile for their clients too. The company brand enjoys a very real boost as a result.[57]❞

Marketing should also examine the role played by customers in the service environment and seek to eliminate harmful interactions. For example, the enjoyment of a restaurant meal or air travel will very much depend on the actions of other customers. At Christmas, restaurants are often in demand by groups of work colleagues for staff parties. These can be rowdy affairs that can detract from the pleasure of regular patrons. This situation needs to be managed, perhaps by segregating the two types of customer in some way.

Physical evidence: this is the environment in which the service is delivered, and any tangible goods that facilitate the performance and communication of the service. Customers look for clues to the likely quality of a service by inspecting the tangible evidence. For example, prospective customers may gaze through a restaurant window to check the appearance of the waiters, the décor and furnishings. The ambience of a retail store is highly dependent on décor, and colour can play an important role in establishing mood because colour has meaning. For example, black signifies strength and power, whereas green suggests mildness. The interior of jet aircraft is pastel-coloured to promote a feeling of calmness, whereas many nightclubs are brightly coloured, with flashing lights to give a sense of excitement.

The layout of a service operation can be a compromise between operations' need for efficiency, and marketing's desire to serve the customer effectively. For example, the temptation to squeeze in an extra table at a restaurant or extra seating in an aircraft may be at the expense of customer comfort.

Process: this is the procedures, mechanisms and flow of activities by which a service is acquired. Process decisions radically affect how a service is delivered to customers. For example, a self-service cafeteria is very different from a restaurant. Marketing managers need to know if self-service is acceptable (or indeed desirable). Queuing may provide an opportunity to create a differential advantage by reduction/elimination, or making the time spent waiting more enjoyable. Certainly waiting for service is a common experience for customers and is a strong determinant of overall satisfaction with the service and customer loyalty. Research has shown that an attractive waiting environment can prevent customers becoming irritated or bored very quickly, even though they may have to wait a long time. Both appraisal of the wait and satisfaction with the service improved when the attractiveness of the waiting environment (measured by atmosphere, cleanliness, spaciousness and climate) was rated higher.[58] Providing a more effective service (shorter queues) may be at odds with operations as the remedy may be to employ more staff.

Reducing delivery time—for example, the time between ordering a meal and receiving it— can also improve service quality. As discussed earlier, this need not necessarily cost more if customers can be persuaded to become involved in the production process, as successfully reflected in the growth of self-service breakfast bars in hotels.

Finally, Berry suggests seven guidelines when implementing a positioning strategy.[59]

(1) Ensure that *marketing* happens at all levels, from the marketing department to where the service is provided.

(2) Consider introducing *flexibility* in providing the service; when feasible, customize the service to the needs of customers.

(3) Recruit *high-quality staff*, treat them well and communicate clearly to them; their attitudes and behaviour are the key to service quality and differentiation.

(4) Attempt to market to *existing customers* to increase their use of the service, or to take up new service products.

(5) Set up a *quick-response facility* to customer problems and complaints.

(6) Employ *new technology* to provide better services at lower cost.

(7) Use *branding* to clearly differentiate service offerings from those of the competition in the minds of target customers.

Retailing

Retailing is an important service industry: it is the activity involved in the sale of products to the ultimate consumer. Retailing is a major employer of the European Union's workforce and its international nature is increasing despite laws such as France's Loi Royer, Belgium's Loi Cadenas and Germany's Baunutzungsverordnung, which restrict retail developments above certain sizes.

The purchasing power of retailers has meant that manufacturers have to maintain high service levels and good relations with them. Many are turning to trade marketing teams to provide dedicated resources to service their needs. Marketing in Action 21.2 describes these developments.

Consumer decision-making involves not only the choice of product and brand, but also the choice of retail outlet. Most retailing is conducted in stores such as supermarkets, catalogue shops and departmental stores, but non-store retailing such as mail order and automatic vending also accounts for a large amount of sales. Retailing provides an important service to customers, making products available when and where customers want to buy them.

Store choice may be dependent on the buying scenario relevant to consumers in a market. For example, two unique choice situations in Germany are relevant for grocery shopping: shopping for daily household needs (*Normaleinkauf*) and grocery shopping for stocking up for weekly or monthly household needs (*Vorratseinkauf*). The stores chosen for the former activity are largely different to those used for the latter.[64]

21.2 marketing in action

Trade Marketing

The growing importance of retailers to the success of brand marketing is being reflected in the formation of trade marketing teams to service their needs. The traditional consumer marketing organization of product managers that controlled brands and a separate salesforce to sell to the trade is gradually being replaced. A combination of the move to key account management on the part of the salesforce, and the brand manager's lack of appreciation of what retailers actually want, has prompted many successful European consumer goods companies to set up a trade marketing organization. Its role is to bridge the gap between brand management and the salesforce.

Trade marketers focus on retailer needs. What kinds of products do they want, in which sizes, with which packaging, at what prices and with what kind of promotion? Supermarkets are demanding more tailored promotions. For example, a large supermarket chain also owned a group of hotels. It demanded from a drinks supplier that the next competition promotion offer holiday breaks in its hotels as prizes (paid for by the manufacturer).

The information on trade requirements is fed back to brand-management staff, which develop appropriate products. The trade marketers then brief the salesforce on how best to communicate the value of these to retailers. In this way, trade marketing is designed to ensure that the retailer's needs are met by the brand marketing mix co-ordinated by consumer marketing personnel.

Eventually, trade marketing might provide the integrating force to link the marketing function with key account management under one organizational unit. So far this has proved difficult to achieve because of the different backgrounds and cultures of sales and brand management. For example, sales may be more inclined to support promotions that boost short-term sales, whereas brand management may be wary of promotions that may endanger the image of the brand. Most large consumer companies have paused part-way by setting up a hybrid, trade marketing unit with a co-ordinating role; others, as we have seen, have moved to category management as a means of forging stronger links with the trade.

The key drivers behind the adoption of trade marketing are: (i) the need for improved communication and co-ordination between sales and brand marketing so that trade requirements are built into brand plans; (ii) new trade marketing-related tasks such as planning trade orientated promotions, developing expertise in the use of computer models (e.g. space planning or direct product profitability software) and providing information to account handlers on customers, consumers and competitors; and (iii) the move to category management by many retailers, which invites a corresponding response from manufacturers in order to improve their trade marketing service and relationships.

Based on: Ohbora et al. (1992);[60] Dewsnap (1997);[61] Nicholas (1999);[62] Dewsnap and Jobber (2000)[63]

Many large retailers exert enormous power in the distribution chain because of the vast quantities of goods they buy from manufacturers.

This power is reflected in their ability to extract 'guarantee of margins' from manufacturers. This is a clause inserted in a contract that ensures a certain profit margin for the retailer irrespective of the retail price being charged to the customer. One manufacturer is played against another and own-label brands are used to extract more profit.[65]

Major store and non-store types

Supermarkets

These are large self-service stores traditionally selling food, drinks and toiletries, but range broadening by some supermarket chains means that such items as non-prescription pharmaceuticals, cosmetics and clothing are also being sold. While one attraction of supermarkets is their lower prices compared with small independent grocery shops, the extent to which price is a key competitive weapon depends on the supermarket's positioning strategy. For example, in the UK Sainsbury's, Waitrose and Tesco rely less on price than KwikSave, Aldi or Netto.

Department stores

So called because related product lines are sold in separate departments, such as men's and women's clothing, jewellery, cosmetics, toys, and home furnishings, in recent years department stores have been under increasing pressure from discount houses, speciality stores and the move to out-of-town shopping. Nevertheless, they are still surviving in this competitive arena.

Speciality shops

These outlets specialize in a narrow product line. For example, many town centres have shops selling confectionery, cigarettes and newspapers in the same outlet. Many speciality outlets sell only one product line, such as Tie Rack and Sock Shop. Specialization allows a deep product line to be sold in restricted shop space. Some speciality shops, such as butchers and greengrocers, focus on quality and personal service.

Discount houses

These sell products at low prices by bulk buying, accepting low margins and selling high volumes. Low prices, sometimes promoted as sale prices, are offered throughout the year. As an executive of Dixons, a UK discounter of electrical goods, commented, 'We only have two sales—each lasting six months.' Many discounters operate from *out-of-town retail warehouses* with the capacity to stock a wide range of merchandise.

Category killers

These are retail outlets with a narrow product focus but, unusually, with a pronounced width and depth to that product range. Category killers emerged in the USA in the early 1980s as a challenge to discount houses. They are distinct from speciality shops in that they are bigger and carry a wider and deeper range of products within their chosen product category, and are distinguished from discount houses in their focus on only one product category. Two examples of the category killer are Toys 'Я' Us and Nevada Bob's Discount Golf Warehouses.[66]

Convenience stores

These stores offer customers the convenience of close location and long opening hours every day of the week. Because they are small they pay higher prices for their merchandise than supermarkets, and therefore have to charge higher prices to their customers. Some of these stores join buying groups such as Spar or Mace to gain some purchasing power and lower prices. But the main customer need they fulfil is for top-up buying—for example, when short of a carton of milk or loaf of bread. Although average purchase value is low, convenience stores prosper because of their higher prices and low staff costs: many are family businesses.

Catalogue stores

These retail outlets promote their products through catalogues that are either posted or are available in the store for customers to take home. Purchase is in city-centre outlets, where customers fill in order forms, pay for the goods and then collect them from a designated place in the store. In the UK, Argos is a successful catalogue retailer selling a wide range of discounted products such as electrical goods, jewellery, gardening tools, furniture, toys, car accessories, sports goods, luggage and cutlery.

Mail order

This non-store form of retailing may also employ catalogues as a promotional vehicle but the purchase transaction is conducted via the mail. Alternatively, outward communication may be by direct mail, television, magazine or newspaper advertising. Increasingly orders are being placed by telephone, a process facilitated by the use of credit cards as a means of payment. Goods are then sent by mail. A growth area is the selling of personal computers by mail order. By eliminating costly intermediaries, products can be offered at low prices. Otto-Versand, the German mail-order company, owns Grattan, a UK mail-order retailer, and has leading positions in Austria, Belgium, Italy, the Netherlands and Spain. Its French rival, La Redoute, has expanded into Belgium, Italy and Portugal. Mail order has the prospect of pan-European catalogues, central warehousing and processing of cross-border orders.

Automatic vending

Vending machines offer such products as drinks, confectionery, soup and newspapers in convenient locations, 24 hours a day. No sales staff are required although restocking, servicing and repair costs can be high. Cash dispensers at banks have improved customer service by permitting round-the-clock access to savings. However, machine breakdowns and out-of-stock situations can annoy customers.

Theories of retail evolution

Three retailing theories explain the changing fortunes of different retailing types, and how one type is replaced by another. These are the **wheel of retailing**, the **retail accordion** and the **retail life cycle**.

The wheel of retailing

This theory suggests that new forms of retailing begin as cut-price, low-cost and narrow-profit-margin operations. Eventually, the retailer trades up by improving display and location, providing credit, delivery and sales services, and by raising advertising expenditures. The retailer thus matures as a high-cost, high-price conservative operator, making it vulnerable to new, lower-price entrants.[67] The theory has been the subject of much debate, but anecdotal evidence concerning department stores, supermarkets and catalogue stores suggests that many began as low-price operators that subsequently raised costs and prices, creating marketing opportunities for new, low-price competitors, developments that are consistent with the theory.

The retail accordion

This theory focuses on the width of product assortment sold by retail outlets and claims a general—specific—general cycle. The cycle begins with retailers selling a wide assortment of goods, followed by a more focused range; this, in turn, is replaced by retailers expanding their range.[68] The theory was developed with regard to the evolution of the entire retail system and is broadly in accord with experience in the USA where the general store of the nineteenth century was superseded by the specialist retailers of the early twentieth. These then gave way to the post-1940s mass merchandisers.

The retail life cycle

The concept of a retail life cycle is based on the well-known product life cycle, which states that new types of retailing pass through the stages of birth, growth, maturity and decline.[69] A retailing innovation enjoying a competitive advantage over existing forms is rewarded by fast sales growth. During the growth stage, imitators are attracted by its success, and by the end of this phase problems arise through over-ambitious expansion. Maturity is characterized by high competition, and is replaced by decline as new retail innovations take over. Evidence suggests that variety stores and counter-service grocery stores evolved in this manner.[70]

Key retail marketing decisions

The three theories of retailing explain the evolution in retailing methods, but there is nothing inevitable about the demise of a given retailer. The key is to anticipate and adapt to changing environmental circumstances. We shall now explore some of the key retailing decisions necessary to prosper in today's competitive climate.

The basic framework for deciding retail marketing strategy is that described earlier in this chapter, when services were discussed. However, there are a number of specific issues that relate to retailing and are worthy of separate discussion. These are retail positioning, store location, product assortment and services, price and store atmosphere. These call for decisions to be taken against a background of rapid change in information technology. E-Marketing 21.3 describes some developments and their impact on retail marketing decisions.

21.3 e-marketing

Information Technology in Retailing

Retailers are no strangers to information technology developments, with electronic point of sale (EPOS) systems allowing the counting of products sold, money taken and faster service at checkouts. More recent innovations, such as loyalty cards, however, have shifted the focus to understanding the customer. By monitoring individual purchasing patterns, direct mail promotions can be targeted at named individuals and adapted to match their known preferences and likely purchases. In-store product assortments can be matched more closely to purchasing patterns. In the USA, retailers are tailoring in-store promotions and discounts to individuals. One supermarket has a scheme where shoppers swipe their loyalty cards through 'readers' as they enter the shop and a list of money-off vouchers, based on their previous spending patterns, is printed.

A key technological development that is changing the way products are bought is the Internet. Online shopping is growing as more people become accustomed to electronic payment and fears over security subside. Already e-commerce has made inroads in books, information technology, travel and groceries. One success story is Tesco.com, the Internet arm of the UK supermarket chain. It now takes revenues of around £1 million (€1.44 million) a day. Shoppers can visit Tesco.com's website to order their groceries, which are delivered for a charge of £5 (€7.20). The company uses its loyalty card scheme to target direct mail at those shoppers likely to value this service. For example, shoppers who appear to be price sensitive and, therefore, unlikely to be willing to pay the delivery charge are excluded from the mailing.

With direct mail being used to generate trial, e-mail is employed to keep the interest ongoing. But the main driver of success is the fact that the system works. Shoppers go to the site, choose the items they want, pay by credit card and at the prescribed time (within a chosen two-hour range) the Tesco delivery people arrive with the produce.

Multimedia kiosks are also changing the face of retailing. In the USA, consumer electronics retailer Best Buy has equipped stores with interactive kiosks offering information on 65,000 CDs, 12,000 videos and 2000 software packages as an alternative to consulting sales assistants.

Information technology is also improving links between manufacturers and retailers. Electronic data interchange (EDI) allows them to exchange purchase orders, invoices, delivery notes and money electronically rather than using paper-based systems.

Based on: Gray (2000);[71] Voyle (2000);[72] Reid (2002)[73]

Retail positioning

As with all marketing decisions, **retail positioning** involves the choice of target market and differential advantage. Targeting allows retailers to tailor their marketing mix, which includes product assortment, service levels, store location, prices and promotion, to the needs of their chosen customer segment. Differentiation provides a reason to shop at one store rather than another. A useful framework for creating a differential advantage has been proposed by Davies, who suggests that innovation in retailing can come only from novelty in the process offered to the shopper, or from novelty in the product or product assortment offered to the shopper.[74] Figure 21.8 shows that differentiation can be achieved through *process innovation* or *product innovation*, or a combination of the two (*total innovation*). UK catalogue retailer Argos has offered innovation in the process of shopping, whereas Next achieved success through product innovation (stylish clothes at affordable prices). Toys 'Я' Us is an example of both product and process innovation through providing the widest range of toys at one location (production innovation) and thereby offering convenient, one-stop shopping (process innovation). By way of contrast, Woolworth by not offering differentiation in either of these dimensions, has lost market share in toys. The customer is offered a limited choice, no price advantage and the risk of having to shop around to be sure of finding a suitable toy.

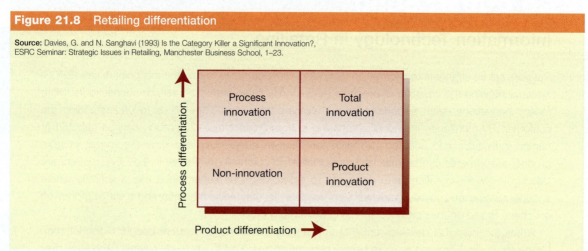

Figure 21.8 Retailing differentiation

Source: Davies, G. and N. Sanghavi (1993) Is the Category Killer a Significant Innovation?, ESRC Seminar: Strategic Issues in Retailing, Manchester Business School, 1–23.

Western retailers have achieved major successes in Asia by creating differential advantages over local competitors, thereby establishing superior retail positioning, as Marketing in Action 21.3 explains.

Store location

Convenience is an important issue for many shoppers, and so store location can have a major bearing on sales performance. Retailers have to decide on regional coverage, the towns and cities to target within regions, and the precise location within a given town or city. Location for Ted Baker, the clothes-to-home-furnishings fashion retailer is absolutely key as the company does not advertise. Ted Baker is at Gatwick and Heathrow airports, Bluewater and Glasgow but also in Miami, Paris and New York's Bloomingdales. Its London store sits opposite Paul Smith, the designer clothes store, in one of the city's trendiest enclaves.[76] Many retailers begin life as regional suppliers, and grow by expanding geographically. In the UK, for example, the Asda supermarket chain expanded from the north of England, while the original base for Sainsbury's was in the south of England.

The choice of town or city will depend on such factors as correspondence with the retailer's chosen target market, the level of disposable income in the catchment area, the

21.3 marketing in action

Retail Positioning in Asia

For centuries, Asian consumers have shopped in 'wet markets' where people jostle among stalls and haggle over the prices of fresh produce being unloaded throughout the day from trolleys. Asian retailing is undergoing a massive transformation, however, due to the influx of western multinationals with the skills, resources, technology and culture to run megastores.

The early movers into Asia include Carrefour, Wal-Mart, Royal Ahold, Tesco, Makro and Casino. They create superior retail positioning against local competitors by creating differential advantages through the use of air conditioning—an advantage to both shopper and produce in such hot climates—and the convenience of one-stop shopping. They support these benefits with superior logistics networks. Unlike local retailers they have centralized purchasing and the resources necessary to set up their own distribution network and to source cheap local produce.

Not all Asian markets have welcomed western retailers with open arms, however. Hong Kong, for example, has proved resistant under the near-duopoly between Jardine Matheson, a trading house, and Li Ka-shing, a Chinese tycoon. There have, also, been mistakes, with Carrefour displaying a tendency to locate some outlets in the wrong place and making its offerings 'too French'. Wal-Mart, too, was once guilty of selling clothes to the Chinese in rather too generous American sizes.

The lesson is that Asian consumers may well be attracted by trendy foreign names, wide aisles, one-stop shopping and air conditioning, but they also demand a local touch.

Based on: Anonymous (2001)[75]

availability of suitable sites and the level of competition. The choice of a particular site may depend on the level of existing traffic (pedestrian and/or vehicular) passing the site, parking provision, access to the outlet for delivery vehicles, the presence of competition, planning restrictions and the opportunity to form new retailing centres with other outlets. For example, an agreement between two or more non-competing retailers (e.g. Marks & Spencer and Tesco) to site outlets together out of town means greater drawing power than could be achieved individually. Having made that decision, the partners will look for suitable sites near their chosen towns or cities.

The location of stores can be greatly aided by geographic information systems (GIS) that profile geographical areas according to such variables as disposable income, family size, age and birth rates. We saw in Chapter 7, on market segmentation and positioning, how such systems can be used to segment markets and allow tailored marketing mixes to be designed. Marketing in Action 21.4 discusses how they can be used in location decisions.

Product assortment and services

Retailers have to decide upon the breadth of their product assortment and its depth. A supermarket, for example, may decide to widen its product assortment from food, drink and toiletries to include clothes and toys; this is called *scrambled merchandising*. Within each product line it can choose to stock a deep or shallow product range. Some retailers, like Tie Rack, Sock Shop and Toys 'Я' Us, stock one deep product line, as mentioned above. Department stores, however, offer a much broader range of products including toys, cosmetics, jewellery, clothes, electrical goods and household accessories. Some retailers begin with one product line and gradually broaden their product assortment to maximize revenue per customer. For example, petrol stations broadened their product range to include motor accessories and, more recently, confectionery, drinks, flowers and newspapers. A by-product of this may be to reduce

21.4 marketing in action

Locating Stores Using Geographic Information Systems

Geographic information systems (GIS) allow marketers to understand the profiles of people living in specific geographic areas. Such information is clearly of interest to retailers when deciding on the location of new outlets. For example, Asda, the UK supermarket chain, uses GIS data as a method of finding new store locations. By understanding the number and profile of consumers living in different geographical areas, it can plan its stores (and product assortment) to be located in the right areas to serve its target market. Asda property systems manager, John Atkinson, commented, 'By using a combination of the number and type of people who live within a 15-minute drive time of a site, we are able to establish the size and type of store needed, and what products should be stocked.'

For organizations planning locations for baby products outlets, schools and hospitals, birth statistics can be invaluable. High-street retailer Mothercare, which has over 200 stores throughout the UK, uses birth data as part of its new store planning process. School and maternity hospital location decisions are also dependent on birth rates, which can differ enormously in different parts of the country.

Some specialist consultancies like SPA Marketing Systems can provide more refined information than simple birth rates in their GIS. Information on the number of children born in a specified area, the father's occupation and the mother's age, both of which reflect the family's affluence, can be supplied. Younger mothers tend to be less affluent than older mums, allowing the targeting of more well-off families to be achieved with a certain degree of precision.

Based on: Hayward (2001);[77] Hayward (2002)[78]

---

customers' price sensitivity since selection of petrol station may be based on the ability to buy other products rather than the lowest price.

The choice of product assortment will be dependent on the positioning strategy of the retailer, customer expectations and, ultimately, on the profitability of each product line. Slow-moving unprofitable lines should be dropped unless they are necessary to conform with the range of products expected by customers. For example, customers expect a full range of food products in a supermarket.

Another product decision concerns own-label branding. Large retailers may decide to sell a range of own-label products to complement national brands. Often the purchasing power of large retail chains means that prices can be lower and yet profit margins higher than for competing national brands. This makes the activity an attractive proposition for many retailers. Consumers also find own-label brands attractive, with many of them in the grocery field being regarded as being at least equal to, if not better then, established manufacturer brands.[79] Supermarkets have moved into this area, as have UK electrical giants such as Dixons, which uses the Chinon brand name for cameras and Saisho for brown goods such as hi-fi and televisions, and Currys, which has adopted the Matsui brand name. In both cases the use of a Japanese-sounding name (even though some of the products were sourced in Europe) was believed to enhance their customer appeal.

Finally, retailers need to consider the nature and degree of *customer service*. Discount stores traditionally provided little service but, as price differentials have narrowed, some have sought differentiation through service. For example, many electrical goods retailers provide a comprehensive after-sales service package for their customers. Superior customer service may make customers more tolerant of higher prices and even where the product is standardized (as in fast-food restaurants) training employees to give individual attention to each customer can increase loyalty to the outlet.[80]

Price

For some market segments price is a key factor in store choice. Consequently, some retailers major on price as their differential advantage. This requires vigilant cost control and massive buying power. A recent trend is towards *everyday low prices* favoured by retailers rather than higher prices supplemented by promotions supported by manufacturers. Retailers such as B&Q, the do-it-yourself discounter, maintain that customers prefer predictable low prices rather than occasional money-off deals, three-for-the-price-of two offers and free gifts. Supermarket chains are also pressurizing suppliers to provide consistently low prices rather than temporary promotions. This action is consistent with the desire to position themselves on a low-price platform.

The importance of price competitiveness is reflected in the alliance of European food retailers called Associated Marketing Services. Retailers such as Argyll (UK), Ahold (the Netherlands), ICA (a federation of Swedish food retailers) and Casino (France) have joined forces to foster co-operation in the areas of purchasing and marketing of brands. Its range of activities includes own branding, joint buying, the development of joint brands and services, and the exchange of information and skills. A key aim is to reduce cost price since this accounts for 75 per cent of the sales price to customers.[81]

Some supermarkets sell *no-frills products*. These are basic commodities, such as bread, sugar and soft drinks, sold in rudimentary packaging at low prices. KwikSave, for example, sells such products in its own-label No Frills range in plain white packaging with black lettering. Such products appeal to the price-conscious shopper who wants standard products at low prices, and help to position KwikSave as a low-price supermarket. This is important given the competitive threats of Aldi and Netto in the UK.

Retailers need to be aware of the negative consequences of setting artificial 'sales' prices. The use of retail 'sales' by outlets to promote their merchandise can lead to increasing scepticism as to their integrity, especially those that 'must end soon' but rarely do, and the 'never to be repeated' bargain offers that invariably are.[82]

Store atmosphere

This is created by the design, colour and layout of a store. Both exterior and interior design affect atmosphere. External factors include architectural design, signs, window display and use of colour, which together create an identity for a retailer and attract customers. Retailers aim to create a welcoming rather than an intimidating mood. The image that is projected should be consonant with the ethos of the shop. The Body Shop, for example, projects its environmentally caring image through the green exterior of its shops, and window displays that feature environmental issues.

Interior design also has a major impact on atmosphere. Store lighting, fixtures and fittings, and layout are important considerations. Supermarkets that have narrow aisles that contribute to congestion can project a negative image, and poorly lit showrooms can feel intimidating. Colour, sound and smell can affect mood. As we have discussed earlier in this chapter, colour has meaning and can be used to create the desired atmosphere in a store. Supermarkets often use music to create a relaxed atmosphere, whereas some boutiques use pop music to attract their target customers. Departmental stores often place perfume counters near the entrance, and supermarkets may use the smell of baking bread to attract their customers.

The success of Stew Leonard's supermarket in Connecticut, USA, in projecting a fun atmosphere for shoppers has attracted the attention of European retailers. The Quinn's supermarket chain in Ireland has emulated its success, and other chains, such as Asda in the UK, provide a face-painting service for children at holiday times to make grocery shopping more fun.

Marketing in non-profit organizations

Non-profit organizations attempt to achieve some other objective than profit. This does not mean they are uninterested in income as they have to generate cash to survive. However, their primary goal is non-economic—for example, to provide cultural enrichment (an orchestra), to protect birds and animals (Royal Society for the Protection of Birds, Royal Society for the Prevention of Cruelty to Animals), to alleviate hunger (Oxfam), to provide education (schools and universities), to foster community activities (community association), and to supply healthcare (hospitals) and public services (local authorities). Their worth and standing is not dependent on the profits they generate. They are discussed in this chapter as most non-profit organizations operate in the services sector. Indeed, non-profit organizations account for over half of all service provision in most European countries.

Marketing is of growing importance to many non-profit organizations because of the need to generate funds in an increasingly competitive arena. Even organizations that rely on government-sponsored grants need to show how their work is of benefit to society: they must meet the needs of their customers. Many non-profit organizations rely on membership fees or donations, which means that communication to individuals and organizations is required, and they must be persuaded to join or make a donation. This requires marketing skills, which are increasingly being applied. Such is the case with political parties, which use marketing techniques to attract members (and the fees their allegiance brings) and votes at elections.[83] Advertising is also used by charities such as The Samaritans to communicate with their target audiences (see the illustration).

Advertising is not the exclusive preserve of profit-orientated organizations; non-profit organizations such as The Samaritans also advertise.

Characteristics of non-profit marketing

There are a number of characteristics of *non-profit marketing* that distinguish it from that conducted by profit-orientated marketing organizations.[84]

Education vs meeting current needs

Some non-profit organizations see their role as not only meeting the current needs of their customers but also educating them in terms of new ideas and issues, cultural development and social awareness. These goals may be in conflict with maximizing revenue or audience figures. For example, a public broadcasting organization like the BBC may trade off audience size for some of these objectives, or an orchestra may decide that more esoteric pieces of classical music should be played rather than the more popular pieces.

Multiple publics

Most non-profit organizations serve several groups, or publics. The two broad groups are *donors*, who may be individuals, trusts, companies or government bodies, and *clients*, who include audiences, patients and beneficiaries.[85] The need is to satisfy both donors and clients, complicating the marketing task. For example, a community association may be part-funded by the local authority and partly by the users (clients) of the association's buildings and facilities. To succeed both groups have to be satisfied. The BBC has to satisfy not only its viewers and listeners, but also the government, which decides the size of the licence fee that funds the BBC's activities.

Non-profit organizations need to adopt marketing as a coherent philosophy for managing multiple public relationships.[86]

Measurement of success and conflicting objectives

For profit-orientated organizations success is measured ultimately in terms of profitability. For non-profit organizations measuring success is not so easy. In universities, for example, is success measured in research terms, number of students taught, the range of qualifications or the quality of teaching? The answer is that it is a combination of these factors, which can lead to conflict: more students and a larger range of courses may reduce the time available for research. Decision-making is therefore complex in non-profit-orientated organizations.

Public scrutiny

While all organizations are subject to public scrutiny, public-sector non-profit organizations are never far from the public's attention. The reason is that they are publicly funded from taxes. This gives them extra newsworthiness as all taxpayers are interested in how their money is being spent. They have to be particularly careful that they do not become involved in controversy, which can result in bad publicity.

Marketing procedures for non-profit organizations

Despite these differences, the marketing procedures relevant to profit-orientated companies can also be applied to non-profit organizations. Target marketing, differentiation and marketing-mix decisions need to be made. We shall now discuss these issues with reference to the special characteristics of non-profit organizations.

Target marketing and differentiation

As we have already discussed, non-profit organizations can usefully segment their target publics into donors and clients (customers). Within each group, sub-segments of individuals and organizations need to be identified. These will be the targets for persuasive communications and the development of services. The needs of each group must be understood. For example, donors may judge which charity to give to on the basis of awareness and reputation, the confidence that funds will not be wasted on excessive administration and the perceived worthiness of the cause. The charity needs, therefore, not only to promote itself but also to gain publicity for its cause. Its level of donor funding will depend on both factors. The brand name of the charity is also important. 'Oxfam' suggests the type of work the organization is mainly concerned with—relief of famine—and so is instantly recognizable. 'Action in Distress' is also suggestive of its type of work.

Market segmentation and targeting are key ingredients in the marketing of political parties. Potential voters are segmented according to their propensity to vote (obtainable from electoral registers) and the likelihood that they will vote for a particular party (obtainable from door-to-door canvassing returns). Resources can then be channelled to the segments most likely to switch votes in the forthcoming election, via direct mail and doorstep visits. Focus groups provide a feedback mechanism for testing the attractiveness of alternative policy options and gauging voters' opinions on key policy areas such as health, education and taxation. By keeping in touch with public opinion, political parties have the information to differentiate themselves from their competitors on issues that are important to voters. While such marketing research is unlikely to affect the underlying beliefs and principles on which a political party is based, it is a necessary basis for the policy adaptations required to keep in touch with a changing electorate.[87]

Developing a marketing mix

Many non-profit organizations are skilled at *event marketing*. Events are organized to raise funds, including dinners, dances, coffee mornings, book sales, sponsored walks and theatrical shows. Not all events are designed to raise funds for the sponsoring organization. For example, the BBC hosts the Comic Relief and Children in Need *telethons* to raise money for worthy causes.

The pricing of services provided by non-profit organizations may not follow the guidelines applicable to profit-orientated pricing. For example, the price of a nursery school place organized by a community association may be held low to encourage poor families to take advantage of the opportunity. Some non-profit organizations exist to provide free access to services—for example, the National Health Service in the UK. In other situations, the price of a service provided by a non-profit organization may come from a membership or licence fee. For example, the Royal Society for the Protection of Birds (RSPB) charges an annual membership fee. In return, members receive a quarterly magazine and free entry to RSPB reserves. The BBC receives income from a licence fee that all television owners have to pay. The level of this fee is set by government, as noted above, making relations with political figures an important marketing consideration.

Like most services, distribution systems for many non-profit organizations are short, with production and consumption simultaneous. This is the case for hospital operations, consultations with medical practitioners, education, nursery provision, cultural entertainment and many more services provided by non-profit organizations. Such organizations have to think carefully about how to deliver their services with the convenience that customers require. For example, although the Hallé Orchestra is based in Manchester, over half of its performances are in other towns or cities.

Many non-profit organizations are adept at using promotion to further their needs. The print media are popular with organizations seeking donations for worthy causes such as famine relief in Africa. Direct mail is also used to raise funds. Mailing lists of past donors are useful here, and some organizations use lifestyle geodemographic analyses to identify the type of person that is more likely to respond to a direct mailing. Non-profit organizations also need to be aware of the publicity opportunities that may arise because of their activities. Many editors are sympathetic to such publicity attempts because of their general interest to the public. Sponsorship is also a vital income source for many non-profit organizations, as Marketing in Action 21.5 explains.

Public relations has an important role to play to generate positive word-of-mouth communications and to establish the identity of the non-profit organization (e.g. a charity). Attractive fund-raising settings (e.g. sponsored lunches) can be organized to ensure that the exchange proves to be satisfactory to donors. A key objective of communications efforts should be to produce a positive assessment of the fundraising transaction and to reduce the perceived risk of the donation so that donors develop trust and confidence in the organization, and become committed to the cause.[89]

21.5 marketing in action

Sponsoring the Arts

Arts sponsorship is an activity that offers companies public relations and promotional opportunities, corporate hospitality possibilities and the chance to put something into the community (the 'warm glow' effect). Traditionally, arts sponsorship was easy: if the company chairperson or spouse liked Bach or Bacon, a cheque was written to pay for a concert or an art show. Today it is not that simple. The emphasis is on reciprocal benefits, where the arts organization contributes to the welfare of the sponsor and the sponsor improves the efficiency of an often poorly managed arts organization. For example, during Allied Domecq's sponsorship of the Royal Shakespeare Company, the RSC lighting engineers advised on creating the right atmosphere in the drinks company's pubs and voice coaches gave speech training to improve presentation skills. In the opposite direction, sponsors are sending accountants, computer specialists and marketing gurus into arts companies as mentors.

In an age when companies are finding differentiation difficult, some companies are ploughing millions into arts sponsorship as a means of distinguishing themselves from the competition. An example is Orange, the UK's largest arts sponsor, which has sponsored the Orange prize for women novelists, filming and film awards, and a Bristol-based project to create museums devoted to science and technology. The latter project includes an Imaginarium, a sphere-shaped structure that traces developments in the digital communications revolution through the display of Orange products. The aim is to associate the brand name with technological innovation and to distinguish itself as a cut above its rivals in the intensely competitive mobile phone market.

There was a time when sponsoring the arts was something done on a whim, but now sponsorships have to fulfil business objectives. Orange, for example, launched a text poetry competition on National Poetry Day, inviting mobile phone users to text in a poem. The business objective was directly linked to the need to boost revenue from texting.

Based on: Murphy (2002)[88]

Review

1 **The nature and special characteristics of services**
- Services are a special kind of product that may require special understanding and special marketing efforts because of their special characteristics.
- The key characteristics of pure services are intangibility (they cannot be touched, tasted or smelled); inseparability (production and consumption takes place at the same time, e.g. a haircut); variability (service quality may vary, making standardization difficult); and perishability (consumption cannot be stored, e.g. a hotel room).

2 **Managing customer relationships**
- Relationship marketing involves shifting from activities concerned with attracting new customers to activities focused on retaining existing customers.
- The benefits to the organization are increased purchases, lower costs, maximizing lifetime value of customers, sustainable competitive advantage, gaining word of mouth, and improved employee satisfaction and retention.
- The benefits to the customer are risk and stress reduction, higher-quality service, avoidance of switching costs, and social and status advantages.
- Customer retention strategies are targeting customers worthy of retention, bonding, internal marketing, promise fulfilment, building of trust, and service recovery.

3 Managing service quality, productivity and staff

- Two key service quality concepts are customer expectations and perceptions. Customers may be disappointed with service quality if their service perceptions fail to meet their expectations. This may result because of four barriers: the misconception barrier (management's misunderstanding of what the customer expects); the inadequate resources barrier (management provides inadequate resources); inadequate delivery barrier (management fails to select, train and adequately reward staff); and the exaggerated promises barrier (management causes expectations to be too high because of exaggerated promises).
- Service quality can be measured using a scale called SERVQUAL, which is based on five criteria: reliability, responsiveness, courtesy, competence and tangibles (e.g. quality of restaurant décor).
- Service productivity can be improved without reducing service quality by using technology (e.g. automatic cash dispensers); customer involvement in production (e.g. self-service petrol stations); and balancing supply and demand (e.g. differential pricing to smooth demand).
- Staff are critical in service operations because they are often in contact with customers. The starting point is the selection of suitable people, socialization allows the recruit to experience the culture and tasks of the organization, empowerment gives them the authority to solve customer problems, they need to be trained and motivated, and evaluation is required so that staff understand how their performance standards relate to customer satisfaction.

4 How to position a service organization or brand

- Positioning involves the choice of target market (where to compete) and the creation of a differential advantage (how to compete). These decisions are common to both physical products and services. However, because of the special characteristics of services, it is useful for the services marketer to consider not only the classical 4-Ps marketing mix but also an additional 3-Ps—people, physical evidence and process—when deciding how to meet customer needs and create a differential advantage.

5 The services marketing mix

- The service marketing mix consists of 7-Ps: product, price, place, promotion, people (important because of the high customer contact characteristic of services), physical evidence (important because customers look for cues to the likely quality of a service by inspecting the physical evidence, e.g. décor), and process (because the process of supplying a service affects perceived service quality).

6 The major store and non-store retailing types

- These are supermarkets, department stores, speciality shops, category killers (narrow product focus but with a pronounced width and depth to their product range), convenience stores, catalogue stores, mail order and automatic vending.

7 Theories of retail evolution

- There are three theories: (i) the wheel of retailing suggests that new forms of retailing begin as cut-price, low-price and narrow-profit-margin operations, but later the retailer trades up by adding on services to become a high-cost, high-price conservative operator; (ii) the retail accordion claims a general, wide assortment, specific/focused, general merchandiser sequence of retail evolution; and (iii) the retailer life cycle states that new types of retailing pass through the stages of birth, growth, maturity and decline.

8 Key retail marketing decisions
- Key retailing decisions are retail positioning, store location, product assortment and services, price and store atmosphere.

9 The nature and special characteristics of non-profit marketing
- Non-profit organizations attempt to achieve some other objective than profit. For example, an orchestra's primary objective may be cultural enrichment. Non-profit organizations are still interested in income as they have to generate cash to survive.
- Their special characteristics are that they may wish to pursue educational objectives as well as meeting the current needs of customers; they often serve multiple publics—for example, donors (e.g. the government) and clients (e.g. audiences); the difficulty of measuring success given multiple, sometimes conflicting objectives; and the close public scrutiny of public-sector organizations because of their funding from taxes.

Key terms

exaggerated promises barrier a barrier to the matching of expected and perceived service levels caused by the unwarranted building up of expectations by exaggerated promises

halo customers customers that are not directly targeted but may find the product attractive

inadequate delivery barrier a barrier to the matching of expected and perceived service levels caused by the failure of the service provider to select, train and reward staff adequately, resulting in poor or inconsistent delivery of service

inadequate resources barrier a barrier to the matching of expected and perceived service levels caused by the unwillingness of service providers to provide the necessary resources

inseparability a characteristic of services, namely that their production cannot be separated from their consumption

intangibility a characteristic of services, namely that they cannot be touched, seen, tasted or smelled

misconception barrier a failure by marketers to understand what customers really value about their service

perishability a characteristic of services, namely that the capacity of a service business, such as a hotel room, cannot be stored—if it is not occupied, this is lost income that cannot be recovered

retail accordion a theory of retail evolution that focuses on the cycle of retailers widening and then contracting product ranges

retail life cycle a theory of retailing evolution that is based on the product life cycle, stating that new types of retailing pass through birth, growth, maturity and decline

retail positioning the choice of target market and differential advantage for a retail outlet

service any deed, performance or effort carried out for the customer

services marketing mix product, place, price, promotion, people, process and physical evidence (the '7-Ps')

variability a characteristic of services, namely that, being delivered by people, the standard of their performance is open to variation

wheel of retailing a theory of retailing development which suggests that new forms of retailing begin as low-cost, cut-price and narrow-margin operations and then trade up until they mature as high-price operators, vulnerable to a new influx of low-cost operators

Internet exercise

easyCar is a car rental company that is an offshoot of easyJet, the successful low-cost airline operator. easyCar is competing against well-established players such as Avis, Hertz and National. Visit the following websites.

Visit: www.easycar.com
www.avis.co.uk
www.hertz.co.uk
www.nationalcar.co.uk

Questions

(a) Discuss how easyCar differentiates itself against its well-established competitors.
(b) How does easyCar try to eliminate the impact of variability in terms of the services it offers?
(c) What brand values does each of these car rental firms encapsulate?

Visit the Online Learning Centre at www.mcgraw-hill.co.uk/textbooks/jobber for more Internet exercises.

Study questions

1. The marketing of services is no different to the marketing of physical goods. Discuss.

2. What are the barriers that can separate expected from perceived service? What must service providers do to eliminate these barriers?

3. Discuss the role of service staff in the creation of a quality service. Can you give examples from your own experiences of good and bad service encounters?

4. Use Fig. 21.7 to evaluate the service quality provided on your college course. First, identify all criteria that might be used to evaluate your course. Second, score each criterion from one to ten, based on its value to you. Third, score each criterion from one to ten based on your perception of how well it is provided. Finally, analyse the results and make recommendations.

5. Of what practical value are the theories of retail evolution?

6. Identify and evaluate how supermarkets can differentiate themselves from their competitors. Choose three supermarkets and evaluate their success at differentiation.

7. Discuss the problems of providing high-quality service in retailing in central and eastern Europe.

8. How does marketing in non-profit organizations differ from that in profit-orientated companies? Choose a non-profit organization and discuss the extent to which marketing principles can be applied.

9. Discuss the benefits to organizations and customers of developing and maintaining strong customer relationships.

When you have read this chapter log on to the Online Learning Centre at www.mcgraw-hill.co.uk/textbooks/jobber to explore chapter-by-chapter test questions, links and further online study tools for marketing.

case forty-one

The Leith Agency

The Leith Agency in Edinburgh (www.leith.co.uk) is a small, dynamic advertising agency. It is very much a service-orientated company, but also produces tangible products in the form of advertisements for television, cinema, print media, billboards and radio, to name a few. It was founded in 1984 and John Denholm is now chairman of the agency. John graduated from St Andrews University with an MA (Hons) degree in Economics. He began his marketing career with Boots, Scottish & Newcastle, and, later, worked with Hall Advertising as account director. After this appointment, John founded The Leith Agency and it has grown substantially over the years into a brand that is well known in Scotland and beyond, particularly for its creativity.

Creativity

With regards to advertising agencies, it is stated that agencies are particularly creative because what they *produce* and *sell* is 'creativity'. With reference to The Leith Agency, the creative ideas produced by individuals within the agency leads to creative strategies in order to communicate a message, reposition a client's brand or contribute to the new product development process. The clients of The Leith Agency are other businesses; making this a business-to-business transaction. Therefore, the agency's main activity is producing creative advertisements for its business clients. It does not offer additional services such as consultancy. Therefore, creativity plays an essential role within the organization and the philosophy of the agency centres around producing creative advertisements and servicing its clients efficiently.

Structure

The Leith Agency has 39 employees and five main departments. These departments consist of account management, account planning, creatives, creative services and TV/production. Within these departments there are directors, managers, deputies, executives and assistants, who all work closely together to provide clients with creative solutions to their problems. In brief, the account planning department receives a brief from a client and is involved with the strategic thinking behind a campaign, before, during and after the launch. The account management department is in contact with the client on a day-to-day basis, converses with them and arranges meetings. This department also works closely with account planning to provide a detailed strategic brief for the creative department, which generates the creative ideas behind a campaign. The ideas go back to account planning and account management, which inform the client of the creative ideas proposed by the agency. If the ideas are accepted, the creative services department is responsible for the production of print media, and organizes the size of the advertisements and where they will be placed. Finally, the TV/production department is responsible for television campaigns.

The Leith Agency: clients

The Leith Agency has many well-known clients, and includes local-based organizations such as the Edinburgh Club and Beat 106, and other Scottish-based organizations such as Irn-Bru, Bank of Scotland, Orangina, Tennents and Standard Life. Other international clients include Honda, Coinstar, Carling and Bass Brewers. Therefore, The Leith Agency's clients not only operate at the local level but on a national level as well. The Leith Agency also works with different strategic partners to offer its clients an integrated service. These strategic partners include OneAgency, Dow Carter and Newtone6 who compliment the services offered by The Leith Agency by providing direct marketing, new media and design support.

Creative output: Tennents lager

It is clear that business clients utilize The Leith Agency for a diverse range of strategies in order to reinforce or reposition their brand. One of the most successful campaigns has been that of Tennents lager. Tennents lager is the most popular beer brand in Scotland, accounting for over one in four pints consumed. Its sheer presence in Scotland made it hard to position it to younger drinkers as a brand 'for them'. The challenge for The Leith Agency was to get 18–25-year-old drinkers to think again about Tennents Lager by challenging their perceptions of the brand, as market research revealed that it was 'their dad's pint'. The Leith Agency decided that it needed to turn the brand's ubiquity—its greatest weakness—into a strength. The opportunity identified by The Leith Agency was that if Tennents lager is 'drunk by everyone' then it must attract some interesting and unusual drinkers as well as the 'boring folk down the local'.

Creative strategy: Tennents lager

The creative strategy focused on the relationship with these unusual drinkers and their highly idiosyncratic relationship with Tennents lager, celebrating comic and anarchic extremes of behaviour in the chase for a pint. This extreme behaviour has been portrayed in advertisements featuring a masochist, showing the extreme behaviour of a man who punishes himself in the pursuit of a pint. Other creative advertisements involved the portrayal of a feminist who enjoyed a pint of lager, obviously to appeal to female drinkers.

The advertising campaign has evolved over 10 years and has been used in other aspects of the communication mix, such as relationship marketing, promotions and sponsorship. The results of this creative output is that brand awareness increased by 50 per cent as a result of the advertising and that 18–24 year olds prefer the Tennents brand over Budweiser and Miller. In addition, in 1999, Tennents lager achieved its highest market share of 65 per cent. It is clear from this example that the creative output was a success for Tennents lager as well as The Leith Agency. The agency has won several awards for this campaign from the Institute of Practitioners in Advertising (IPA) effectiveness awards.

The IPA

The IPA (www.ipa.co.uk) is the industry body and professional institute for the UK's thriving and highly potent advertising business. It is non-profit making and is funded by member subscriptions. To be a member of the IPA is the highest professional recognition that an advertising agency can achieve. Membership is by election and agencies must demonstrate that they are professional companies in the eyes of their peers and the media. Agencies must also be independent companies and be able to mount a national advertising campaign, be financially stable with a gross income of over £250,000 (€360,000), and uphold the legal and ethical standards set down by the industry's regulatory bodies. There are over 200 IPA members in the UK and 23 members of the Scottish IPA, of which The Leith Agency is a member. Collectively, the members of the IPA handle more than 80 per cent of all advertising billings in the UK.

Each year, the Scottish IPA decides which advertising agencies have produced outstanding campaigns, and awards certain agencies either a grand prix award, special award, gold, silver, bronze or commendation for the effectiveness of an advertising campaign. The Leith Agency has won many of these awards through advertising campaigns for the public sector such as HEBS, charities such as the Big Issue and consumer goods advertising for companies such as Warburtons and Glayva. More recently, the agency has won awards for advertisements produced for Standard Life, Honda and Beat 106.

It is clear that the IPA has strict guidelines that must be adhered to for an agency to become a member. In addition, it is a self-regulatory body that recognizes the creative efforts produced by advertising agencies through industry awards. The industry awards are an important communication tool for advertising agencies as they send out positive messages, not only to industry peers but to potential clients that an agency has produced effective and creative output. Through the creative work that The Leith Agency has produced and the recognition from the IPA awards, the agency would appear to be effective, reliable and offer a high-quality product compared to some of its competitors. This is what is defined as a strong brand.

Building the Leith brand: creative output

The Leith Agency recognizes the potential of creative output in building the Leith brand. As the creative work is judged by the company's clients as well as industry peers, word of mouth becomes an important communication tool, in the form of referrals. These referrals not only increase business for the company but also strengthen the corporate brand. Therefore, producing effective, creative output is one of the agency's main goals. This is achieved by providing an internal culture where individuals are supported by 'adequate processes' in order to produce creative advertisements as well as service their clients efficiently. To explore this further, and the agency's marketing strategy in general, it is necessary to consider the 7-Ps of service-based organizations: product, price, place, promotion, people, processes and physical evidence.

Product

The Leith Agency is utilized by its business clients to produce creative advertisements in order to communicate a message to its own market. As a business entity, the agency is positioned and perceived to be 'Scottish, down-to-earth and dependable'. It is one of the most successful agencies in Scotland and it is felt that this is the case because of two points. First, the agency's proposition or positioning statement is clear: 'great ads without the grief'. It is felt that the agency has people who are 'grounded' and 'pragmatic', who understand that creativity is only a means to an end; it is not some higher art form that needs to be protected from business processes (thought to be an unusual view within this industry sector). Therefore, the agency's unique proposition is to be collaborative in terms of servicing its clients, and to be effective and creative when producing the tangible product.

Price

The Leith Agency is paid a set fee, which is negotiated at the beginning of the contract with its business clients. Previously, the advertising industry was based on a commission of 15 per cent and was paid by the media owner (for example, a television company) to the agencies involved in producing the advertisements. However, this has its pluses and minuses. Agencies were paid the 15 per cent commission regardless of the effectiveness of the advertising campaign. Therefore, good agencies received less money than poor agencies, as an ineffective campaign would probably need more money spent on it. So, in theory, chairman John Denholm states that divorcing the income from commission is right, as the set fee is a way of monitoring the industry and is often performance based as well. However, this has meant that advertising agencies in general receive less money, which has affected margins across the industry.

Place

The Leith Agency has been for many years, and until recently, a 'single-location distributor'. However, the agency could no longer rely on one outlet (its Edinburgh office) and now has an office in London. This is not because premises are necessary to deliver the end product, as this can be done electronically. It was thought to be crucial in terms of winning business as the main marketing decision-makers are based in London.

Promotion

The Leith Agency's communication strategy centres on both above-the-line and below-the-line activities. Above-the-line consists mainly of public relations (PR) and corporate brand building through sponsorship and videos. With regard to PR, this is actively pursued through media attention such as *The Drum* (a local Scottish paper) or *Campaign* magazine. Articles written on The Leith Agency in these editions is an appropriate way to receive free publicity. As the agency is a small independent, operating in an unstable Scottish market, marketing budgets are kept to a minimum. Therefore, advertising in the trade press is infrequent. The Leith Agency, albeit infrequently, sponsors local events in Edinburgh. Examples of these include the Edinburgh Science Festival and the agency's recent plans to sponsor the Marketing Society's annual dinner. This is done basically to create and reinforce awareness of and interest in the Leith brand. Below-the-line activities include one-to-one relationship marketing, direct marketing, promotional videos, pitches and presentations, which are used to 'woo' potential clients. This is the main form of communication, as close contact with clients is crucial to building a relationship and developing trust.

People

Within any industry, ensuring employees are rewarded is crucial in maintaining morale. The Leith Agency subscribes to the IPA salary survey and is felt to be as competitive as its competitors. However, because of low inflation, increases in salary have been minimal. The employees within the agency also receive an end-of-year bonus. However, due to the recession within the Scottish advertising industry over the last few years, bonuses within the agency have also been minimal. The wider environment has also affected profit margins and formal training is relatively stagnant. However, The Leith Agency does have a relatively flexible, 'open door' management ethos. As such, mentoring is a crucial part of the training process. In terms of promotion, the agency is extremely top heavy, which is reflective of the advertising industry in general. Therefore, there is a 'glass ceiling' effect in terms of promotional opportunities. Also, there is low staff turnover, which makes it difficult to climb the corporate ladder.

Processes

The processes within The Leith Agency are two-fold: first, servicing the client and, second, producing tangible products. Within this particular agency, servicing the client involves collaboration and building long-term relationships based on trust. However, The Leith Agency does not have a 'written down' service strategy but has addressed this as it was felt that it would be beneficial to the agency. Producing the tangible product involves an avoidance of becoming 'creatively precious' as this can result in clients buying something they do not necessarily believe in. Also, there are processes in place to support the creative process. These include intrinsically motivated employees, a flexible management approach, high levels of autonomy and control over workloads, challenging and interesting work, team-based work groups, sufficient resources, encouragement of risks and a tolerance of failure. However, barriers to the creative process do exist within the agency. These include insincere recognition of ideas (lip-service) and lack of promotional opportunities. There is also a question mark over the extent of extrinsic rewards within the agency as these are restricted to an end-of-year bonus, which has not been paid for the last two years because of the economic downturn in the Scottish market and the opening of The Leith Agency in London. There is also doubt about formal training within the agency because of tighter margins and profitability, which means there is less money to invest in programmes such as formal training.

Physical evidence

Physical evidence is very much related to the employees within the agency. Because of the close one-to-one relationships that the agency has with its clients, employees physically represent the Leith brand. This means a shared perception of daily practices is crucial in dealing with its business clients. Physical evidence also takes the form of the tangible product. The advertisements that The Leith Agency produces are a reflection of the Leith brand. It is therefore extremely important that the agency produces effective and creative advertising campaigns for its customers. The Leith brand itself also physically manifests itself in terms of the name, where it is based and has an emotional perception attached to it. Leith Chairman John Denholm highlights how he thinks the brand is perceived:

> A bit flash, a bit arrogant and a bit pleased with themselves. ... I think when people meet us and think, something odd here: they are quite normal human beings. It is quite an unflash sort of place ... in Scotland creativity in business equals you must be a 'bunch of nutters' who are difficult to deal with. In fact we are Scottish, dependable and down to earth.

Conclusion

This case study on The Leith Agency has provided an insight into how a small independent advertising agency in Scotland operates. This is highlighted through the company history and through the use of the 7-Ps for services marketing. As the agency is predominately a service-based business-to-business operator, the use of the 7-Ps framework has highlighted the significance of people, processes and physical evidence. In addition, as the tangible product is just as important as the service encounter, it was highlighted that supporting the creative process in order to produce the creative output is of extreme importance.

Within The Leith Agency many supports were identified, such as a flexible management style, team-based work groups, high amounts of autonomy and control, challenging and interesting work, to name a few. Supporting the creative process is crucial within this industry sector as creative output is scrutinized by industry peers and recognized through awards such as those presented by the IPA. Therefore, supporting this process is beneficial in the long term as it can, if the response and feedback is favourable, strengthen the Leith brand, through word of mouth, peer recognition and industry referrals.

Questions

1. Discuss the 7-Ps of services marketing. How crucial are the last three elements—people, processes and physical evidence—to The Leith Agency?

2. How important is creative output in terms of strengthening the corporate brand?

3. Why is The Leith Agency's presence in London necessary at this time?

This case study was prepared by Christine Band, Lecturer in Marketing, Napier University.

case forty-two

Hope Community Resources, Inc.

Prior to the 1960s, there were no services within the state of Alaska for people with developmental difficulties. Those in need of services were removed from their families, friends and communities, and were sent to other states within the USA to live in institutions, where they received minimal custodial care. With the establishment of Hope Community Resources, Inc. (Hope) in 1968, Alaskans with developmental problems were brought back to the state of Alaska where care could be provided. Hope is a private, non-profit agency operating in the state of Alaska, USA. All of Hope's activities are guided by a mission statement that clearly identifies its purpose. The mission of Hope is 'to provide services and supports requested and designed by individuals and families who experience disabilities, resulting in choice, control, family preservation and community inclusion'.

Hope has believed from its inception that no one should have to live in an institution. Hope provides support services for the developmentally disabled, based on each individual's and family's needs. Every attempt is made to keep families together and avoid 'out of home' placements.

The services provided by Hope include in-home assistance, foster care, supported employment, supported living and assisted living. Supported living provides various levels of training and supervision to individuals moving into or living in settings that maximize their independence. To this end, Hope has assisted people with developmental difficulties in acquiring and owning their own homes. Assisted living provides 24-hour residential care for adults in one of Hope's group homes. In the group homes, people with developmental difficulties can live together in the community, thus involving them in community activities and relationships. At present, Hope provides its services to over 700 individuals in Alaska.

Hope's funding

In 2000, Hope had a total income of $23 million (£14 million/€20 million), which had increased from almost $14 million (£8.7 million/€12.5 million) in 1994. The majority of this income came from Medicaid. Medicaid is the largest programme providing medical and health-related services to America's poorest people. It covers approximately 36 million individuals, including children, the aged, the blind and the disabled. Hope's other income sources were the State of Alaska, individual fees, capital projects, fundraising and other revenues. A breakdown of Hope's funding sources in 2000 may be seen in Table C42.1. Recently Hope established Hope Industries Inc., a for-profit subsidiary of Hope Community Resources. The sole purpose of Hope Industries is to provide additional revenue to Hope Community Resources. Hope Industries has set up its first venture in an attempt to generate income and is continuing to evaluate new business opportunities that have the

Table C42.1 Hope Community Resources, Inc. funding sources, 2000		
	$	%
Medicaid	$17,777,509	77.0
State of Alaska	$2,542,935	11.0
Individual fees	$1,129,321	4.9
Capital projects	$664,858	2.9
Fundraising	$585,516	2.5
Other revenue	$383,479	1.7
Total	**$23,083,479**	**100.0**

potential to make a contribution to Hope Community Resources.

Even though a small proportion of Hope's total funds came from fundraising (only 2.5 per cent), this still remains an important part of Hope's operations. Hope's PR department has been very active in developing and promoting several fundraising events each year. The best-known fundraising event is the 'Walk and Roll for Hope'. This is a state-wide, pledge-based walking, biking and roller-blading event that is run in many areas of Alaska. The event generated a net income of over $28,000 (£17,500/€25,200) in 2000. However, this compared poorly to the income generated through this event in previous years. For example, in 1997, it generated over $84,000 (£52,700/€75,800). Other fundraising events organized by Hope in 2000 included a Christmas bazaar, an end-of-summer auction, barbecue and a celebrity golf classic. Although these events raised valuable funds for Hope, management was concerned that such events were raising less money than in previous years (see Table C42.2). Although Hope had many donors, few of these were making large contributions. In addition, most donors were individuals rather than large corporations. This may have been due to the fact that there was little promotion of Hope's many giving opportunities. For example, individuals could contribute to an endowment fund, bequests, annuities and trusts. They could also contribute to any of Hope's fundraising events and, in addition to cash gifts, could donate products such as household goods, food, household appliances and specialized medical equipment that could be used in Hope's group homes. Individuals could also volunteer their time, particularly during fundraising events. Apart from individual donors, corporate donors were not made aware of the many sponsorship opportunities within Hope and had not been targeted directly for donations. Hope's local focus may also have limited its ability to engage in fundraising outside the State of Alaska.

The organization's image

As 2000 drew to a close, senior management at Hope became increasingly concerned about Hope's image.

There was a feeling that Hope had lost its connection with the public, and there was a perception among senior management that the general public was unclear about what Hope had to offer the community. Hope had not refined its communication with the public as it grew, and top management feared that Hope had become so big that it had lost its 'charity' or 'mom and pop' image, and was now seen as an impersonal, money-grabbing organization. It was believed that this may have caused the decline in income from its main fundraising events.

There was also a concern that there were few proactive attempts to educate the public and businesses about Hope's services and giving opportunities. Hope had no marketing department and nobody within the organization was given sole responsibility for the marketing function. Any marketing activities that took place were organized by the PR department. Many PR spokespeople were being used to promote the organization, which was leading to inconsistent communication. The organization had no marketing plan, there were no measurable marketing objectives in place and no marketing budget.

In-depth analysis

In December 2000, a marketing consultant was invited to Hope's head office in Anchorage, Alaska, to conduct an in-depth analysis of the organization and to advise on how the use of marketing would assist Hope. A number of

Table C42.2 Net income from main fundraising events		
Event	1997 ($)	2000 ($)
Walk and Roll for Hope (Anchorage)	84,413	28,056
Christmas bazaar	4,381	2,950
End-of-summer auction	12,665	13,146
Barbecue	15,952	19,889
Celebrity golf classic	—	−7,351

meetings took place throughout the month of December in the course of this analysis. Present at these meetings were the marketing consultant, the director, the associate director, Hope's business development director, the administrator of PR and resource development and members of the PR team. Important information about Hope was obtained from these meetings and also from documentation available within Hope and from one-to-one meetings with management and staff.

As part of an investigation of Hope, the marketing consultant deemed it important to engage in a competitor analysis. Hope's competitors were identified as all other non-profit organizations that depend on donations from individuals and corporations. Hope's main competitor in Alaska at that time was established in 1957, and was a multi-faceted organization that served more than 500 children and adults in Anchorage with developmental and other disabilities and mental illnesses. Like Hope, this organization had no dedicated marketing department. However, the associate director of this organization assumed responsibility for the marketing of the organization. Having come from the for-profit sector and having worked in the banking industry, the associate director had a strong belief in the value of marketing. He saw how marketing was used in the for-profit sector to create awareness, provide information, educate the public, change attitudes and influence consumer decision-making, and he believed that marketing could be used successfully in the non-profit sector for the same purposes.

This competitor undertook extensive market research in the late 1990s to identify public perceptions of its organization. The results indicated that the public had a very narrow view of the services it provided. As a result, it engaged in an extensive TV advertising campaign at a cost of $60,000 (£37,600/€54,150), aimed at educating the public about the organization and its activities. This advertising campaign was later supported by the use of bus, radio and print advertisements. This competitor also employed a marketing consultant to develop a marketing plan for the organization. He recommended a marketing budget of $300,000 (£188,260/€270,000) for 2000. The organization did not spend the recommended $300,000 in 2000, but did spend $125,000 (£78,400/€113,000) on marketing that year (1 per cent of turnover). Management of this competitive organization also had something to say about Hope's image. They believed that the public saw Hope as a large, impersonal state-wide organization. A representative of this competing organization stated, 'Hope would say that they are people centred, but the perception is that they are not. Hope have become so big that they have lost that focus on people first.' This statement seemed to confirm everything that top management at Hope had feared.

The role of marketing at Hope

Having completed an in-depth analysis of Hope and its main competitors, the marketing consultant prepared and presented an interim report to Hope's management team. The report outlined the information collected as a result of the analysis, and made some strong recommendations to management. The marketing consultant expressed a need for a change in how Hope interacted with its publics and the use of marketing was seen as crucial in bringing about this change. One important issue raised by the consultant was the need to discover if there was a lack of awareness and understanding of Hope and, if so, to what extent and why. It was believed that market research would provide the answer to this question and would aid in the development of a marketing plan. However, market research can be a lengthy process. To avoid this delay in implementing marketing in Hope, the consultant recommended that a two-pronged approach be used.

It was recommended that a marketing campaign be implemented immediately to raise the visibility of the organization and, in the meantime, market research be conducted to devise a more tailored marketing programme aimed at dealing with perceptions unveiled as a result of marketing research. The marketing approach recommended is summarized in Table C42.3.

Table C42.3 Recommended marketing approach for Hope		
Phase	Purpose	Time frame
I Immediate marketing	Create awareness Communicate the benefits of contributions	Jan.–June 2001
II Future marketing	Use market research to learn more about current perceptions	Jan.–June 2001
	Use the results to design and implement a specific marketing plan	July–Dec. 2001 Jan.–Dec. 2002

Phase I: immediate marketing

It was recommended that marketing be used immediately to create awareness and visibility of the Hope name. It was also agreed that there should be a focus on the benefits to be obtained by making a contribution or donation to Hope. In the past, a lot of Hope's PR efforts had been focused on attracting people to participate in fundraising events without giving them a reason to participate. It was also advised that there was a need to show people how their donations are used to benefit the community. In order to increase visibility, and to get this new advertising message across, the use of newspaper, TV, cinema and vehicle advertising was recommended, along with video presentations and new signage at the organization's head office in Anchorage.

Phase II: future marketing

The marketing consultant strongly advised on the need to develop a marketing plan for Hope that would clearly outline the organization's objectives, the marketing strategies to be used, the budget required and procedures for implementing, controlling and evaluating the marketing effort. The purpose of future marketing strategies for Hope would be to build on existing awareness and to create a deeper understanding of Hope and what it had to offer.

However, before this future marketing could be planned for, it was seen as necessary to conduct marketing research among Hope's various publics to identify their perceptions of the organization. These publics included the general public, employees, the board of directors, clients and guardians, the State of Alaska, and businesses. It was recommended that focus-group interviews be conducted with the various publics identified above.

Hope's management, staff and competitors already had their own views on what public perceptions of the organization were, but formalized market research was deemed necessary to accurately identify public perceptions of Hope vis-à-vis the competition. In addition, it was the consultant's belief that marketing research would help identify new or emerging marketing opportunities and would aid in assessing the effectiveness of previous organizational decisions. It would also provide further information for the development of a marketing plan and would assist in the development of Hope's promotion.

It was recommended that an external marketing research agency be employed to conduct this research, rather than use internal staff. An external agency would help bring objectivity to the exercise and would be more experienced in the use and analysis of market research techniques. It was advised that a marketing budget be created to make implementation of these recommendations possible. Hope management decided to make $50,000 (£31,000/€45,000) available for marketing in 2001 and $100,000 (£62,000/€89,000) in 2002 (approximately 0.4 per cent of turnover).

Market research results

In June 2001, a number of focus-group interviews were conducted by a contracted market research consultancy as recommended. These interviews were held with four of Hope's publics: employees who care for the disabled, team leaders/directors, potential donors, and current donors. Specific details of these four focus groups may be seen in Table C42.4.

Table C42.4	Focus-group participants	
Group 1	Direct care employees	4 women
Group 2	Team leaders/directors	8 women, 2 men
Group 3	Potential donors* (open to the idea of giving, but not currently giving to specific organizations)	5 women, 2 men
Group 4	Donors* (people who currently give regularly to specific organizations)	9 women, 2 men

* Donor group participants each received $50 for their time

The results of the focus-group interviews were grouped under the following headings: advertising, education, fundraising and awareness. In terms of advertising, there was significant interest and support among all groups in seeing Hope communicate its mission via advertising. There was a general consensus that a lot of people were not aware of the good work that Hope was doing and that the organization needed to get its message out to the public.

In terms of education, the focus-group results clearly showed that there was an agreement that Hope should have stronger links with the educational institutions in Alaska. There was discussion about creating an education department to work in tandem with the schools, not only to promote fundraising for Hope, but also to increase children's awareness and acceptance of people's differences.

When it came to discussing Hope's fundraising activities, many recommendations were made by all groups. There seemed to be a significant lack of awareness of the connection between Hope and the Walk and Roll for Hope. Many of the donor focus group participants believed that the walk was for generic 'hope' for all people, and that the funds were to be divided among several charitable organizations. There was a recommendation to rebrand the Walk for Hope and to integrate it more fully into the organization's advertising and PR plans. A legacy strategy was also recommended, i.e. to encourage those parents that currently take part in the walk to encourage their children to do so too. There was agreement among all groups that there was a great need to encourage recurrent giving. It was advised that Hope create a donor newsletter that could inform donors of ongoing initiatives, show personal stories of those who have benefited from donor contributions and could act as a thank you to donors for making a contribution to Hope.

The final issue discussed concerned awareness of Hope and its activities. The results of the focus-group interviews showed a need to create greater awareness of the organization, correct misperceptions and convey the good mission of Hope. The role of PR was emphasized as a means of illustrating Hope's good work. PR was also recommended as a means of creating awareness as it tends to be cheaper than advertising and may carry more credibility as it is not an obvious commercial message.

Marketing activities in Hope

As a result of these focus group findings, a number of changes were made to Hope's marketing activities in 2001 and 2002. In an attempt to increase people's awareness of Hope and its fundraising events, a series of advertisements were used throughout both 2001 and 2002 to educate the public. In order to more fully integrate Hope's advertising and PR plans, a new slogan was developed that was used in almost all advertisements promoting Hope and its fundraising events. This slogan, 'Helping People With Disabilities Achieve Independence', was seen as a means of clearly communicating the organization's core values.

As stated previously, a marketing budget of $100,000 was available for 2002. All marketing activity was organized by the PR department, which also had responsibility for the marketing budget. Hope's PR department also created a marketing/PR calendar for 2002, outlining the timing of the various forms of promotion used. Hope used a number of TV advertisements to promote its work. These TV ads typically showed a developmentally disabled person in Hope's care integrating with the community and retaining a sense of independence. These advertisements were also accompanied by a number of public service announcements (PSAs) to promote specific fundraising events. A number of radio advertisements were also used for promotion purposes, and an example of one such radio advertisement can be seen in Figure C42.1.

Figure C42.1   Hope radio advertisement 2002
Hope Community Resources: 30-second radio spot
Hope Community Resources promotes a quality of life for individuals who experience a disability. Keeping families together is a very important part of Hope's program. We all want to be treated with dignity and respect. Hope is working to make that possible for those Alaskans who experience disabilities. Hope is here, helping the individual and the family to live life with respect and dignity.
Hope Community Resources
Helping people with disabilities achieve independence

Newspaper advertisements were used to promote Hope's main fundraising events, such as the Walk and Roll for Hope and the Hope auction.

Poster advertisements were also used to inform the public of most fundraising events, including the celebrity golf classic. Cinema advertising was used to promote some of the fundraising events and vehicle advertising was also an important promotional vehicle.

In an attempt to make more businesses aware of Hope and the giving opportunities available, the PR department created a brochure illustrating sponsorship opportunities in 2002. This brochure was mailed to businesses throughout Alaska in an attempt to encourage them to make a contribution to Hope, either through a cash donation or sponsorship of an event or advertisement. The brochure explained the many sponsorship options businesses could choose from. For example, a business could sponsor Hope bus signs, newspaper advertisements or cinema advertisements. Alternatively, they could sponsor prizes for the Walk and Roll for Hope or promotional gifts (such as hats, visors or squeezy bottles). Other sponsorship options included making cash contributions, or volunteering on the day of the main fundraising events. Very importantly, this brochure outlining the sponsorship options also clearly indicated the benefits to the companies that availed themselves of these sponsorship options. As 2002 drew to a close, management at Hope was anxious to assess the effectiveness of its new marketing focus and wondered what lay ahead for Hope in 2003.

Questions

1. How is non-profit marketing different from marketing in the for-profit sector? Are there any difficulties associated with non-profit marketing?

2. How should Hope assess the effectiveness of its marketing efforts in 2001 and 2002? Do you think Hope's current communications mix needs to be adapted? If so, in what way?

3. Although some marketing activities have been undertaken by Hope, a marketing plan has yet to be developed. Outline the main components of a marketing plan for Hope.

This case was prepared by Marie O'Dwyer, Lecturer in Marketing at Waterford Institute of Technology, Ireland.

chapter twenty-two

International marketing

> ❝I want to be a good Frenchman in France and a good Italian in Italy. My strategy is to go global when I can and stay local when I must.❞
>
> ERIC JOHANNSON, President of Electrolux

Learning Objectives

This chapter explains:

1. The reasons why companies seek foreign markets
2. The factors that influence which foreign markets to enter
3. The range of foreign market entry strategies
4. The factors influencing foreign market entry strategies
5. The influences on the degree of standardization or adaptation
6. The special considerations involved in designing an international marketing mix
7. How to organize for international marketing operations

Today's managers need international marketing skills to be able to compete in an increasingly global marketplace. They require the capabilities to identify and seize opportunities that arise across the world. Failure to do so brings stagnation and decline, not only to individual companies but also to whole regions.

The importance of international marketing is reflected in the support given by governmental bodies set up to encourage and aid export activities. Such organizations often provide help in gathering information on foreign markets, competitors and their products, and barriers to entry. They disseminate such information through libraries, abstract services and publications. Furthermore, they organize business missions to foreign countries, provide exhibition space at international trade fairs and may give incentives to firms to attend such fairs. Often, they employ trade officers in important foreign markets to help exporters gather marketing research information and find prospective customers for their products.[1] The importance of such government-sponsored activities in assisting the exporting performance of firms was supported by the findings of a study of Greek exporters.[2]

The emergence of the international marketplace known as the World Wide Web has the potential to transform international transactions. Suppliers and customers can communicate electronically across the world through sending e-mail messages and setting up interactive websites. Small companies can gain access to global markets without the need for expensive salesforces or retail outlets. Transactions can be accomplished by giving credit card details and clicking a button. Not all markets will be fundamentally changed by Internet marketing because of delivery considerations and the fact that many customers may prefer to buy such things as clothing and furniture after personal contact and viewing. Nevertheless, established players in mature global markets are analysing the potential of the Internet to provide opportunities and threats to their businesses.

The purpose of this chapter, then, is to explore four issues in developing international marketing strategies. First, the question of whether to go international or stay domestic is addressed; second, the factors that impact upon the selection of countries in which to market are considered; third, foreign market entry strategies are analysed; finally, the options available for developing international marketing strategies are examined.

Deciding whether to go international

Figure 22.1 Going international

Many companies shy away from the prospect of competing internationally. They know their domestic market better, and they would have to come to terms with the customs, language, tariff regulations, transport systems and volatile currencies of foreign countries. On top of that, their products may require significant modifications to meet foreign regulations and different customer preferences. So, why do companies choose to market abroad? There are seven triggers for international expansion (see Fig. 22.1).

Saturated domestic markets

The pressure to raise sales and profits, coupled with few opportunities to expand in current domestic markets, provide one condition for international expansion. This has been a major driving force behind Marks & Spencer's moves into Europe and the USA, and its interest in expanding its activities into Japan and China.[3] Many of the foreign expansion plans of European supermarket chains were fuelled by the desire to take a proven retailing formula out of their saturated domestic market into new overseas markets.

Small domestic markets

In some industries, survival means broadening scope beyond small national markets to the international arena. For example, Philips and Electrolux (electrical goods) could not compete against the strength of global competitors by servicing their small domestic market alone. For them, internationalization was not an option: it was a fundamental condition for survival.

Low-growth domestic markets

Often recession at home provides the spur to seek new marketing opportunities in more buoyant overseas economies. This was the reason for the international moves of Andy Thornton, a small company specializing in the refurbishment of commercial premises. Survival in the severe UK recession of the early 1990s was achieved through winning contracts in countries such as Denmark, Sweden and Germany.

Customer drivers

Customer-driven factors may also affect the decision to go international. In some industries customers may expect their suppliers to have an international presence. This is increasingly common in advertising, with clients requiring their agencies to co-ordinate international campaigns. A second customer-orientated factor is the need to internationalize operations in response to customers expanding abroad.

Competitive forces

There is a substantial body of research which suggests that when several companies in an industry go abroad, others feel obliged to follow suit to maintain their relative size and growth rate.[4] This is particularly true in oligopolistic industries. A second competitive factor may be the desire to attack, in their own home market, an overseas competitor that has entered our domestic market. This may make strategic sense if the competitor is funding its overseas expansion from a relatively attractive home base.

Cost factors

High national labour costs, shortages of skilled workers, and rising energy charges can raise domestic costs to uneconomic levels. These factors may stimulate moves towards foreign direct investment in low-cost areas such as Taiwan, Korea, and central and eastern Europe. Expanding into foreign markets can also reduce costs by gaining economies of scale through an enlarged customer base.

Portfolio balance

Marketing in a variety of regions provides the opportunity to achieve portfolio balance as each region may be experiencing different growth rates. At any one time, the USA, Japan, individual

European and Far Eastern countries will be enjoying varying growth rates. By marketing in a selection of countries, the problems of recession in some countries can be balanced by the opportunities for growth in others.

Deciding which markets to enter

Having made the commitment to internationalize, marketing managers require the analytical skills necessary to pick those countries and regions that are most attractive for overseas operations. Two sets of factors will govern this decision: macroenvironmental issues and microenvironmental issues. These are shown in Fig. 22.2.

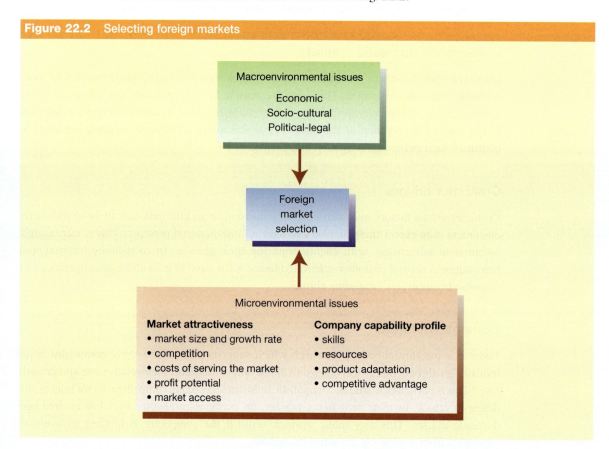

Figure 22.2 Selecting foreign markets

Macroenvironmental issues

These consist of *economic*, *socio-cultural* and *political-legal* influences on market choice.

Economic influences

A country's size, per capita income, stage of economic development, infrastructure, and exchange rate stability and conversion affect its attractiveness for international business expansion. Small markets may not justify setting up a distribution and marketing system to supply goods and services. Low per-capita income will affect the type of product that may sell in that country. The market may be very unattractive for car manufacturers but feasible for bicycle producers. Less developed countries, in the early stages of economic development, may demand inexpensive agricultural tools but not computers.

The economic changes that have taken place in central and eastern Europe have had varying effects on each country's attractiveness. For example, the move from centrally planned to market-based economy of Poland initially caused a rise in unemployment to 400,000 people, and a 40 per cent fall in purchasing power of some households as government subsidies and price controls were abolished.[5] However, these shocks were followed by greater investment on the part of western countries and a fall in inflation from as high as 250 per cent to 3.4 per cent.[6]

Another economic consideration is a nation's infrastructure. This comprises the transportation structures (roads, railways, airports), communication systems (telephone, television, the press, radio) and energy supplies (electricity, gas, nuclear). A poor infrastructure may limit the ability to manufacture, advertise and distribute goods, and provide adequate service back-up. Some central and eastern European countries suffer because of this. In other areas of Europe infrastructure improvements are enhancing communications—for example, the ambitious, if costly, Eurotunnel that links the UK with mainland Europe, and the bridge and tunnel that connect the two main parts of Denmark.

Finally, exchange rate stability and conversion may affect market choice. A country that has an unstable exchange rate or one that is difficult to convert to hard currencies such as the dollar or mark may be considered too risky to enter.

Socio-cultural influences

Differences in socio-cultural factors between countries are often termed *psychic distance*. These are the barriers created by cultural disparities between the home country and the host country, and the problems of communication resulting from differences in social perspectives, attitudes and language.[7] This can have an important effect on selection. International marketers sometimes choose countries that are psychically similar to begin their overseas operations. This has a rationale in that barriers of language, customs and values are lower. It also means that less time and effort is required to develop successful business relationships.[8] Johanson and Vahlne, on the basis of four Swedish manufacturing firms, showed that firms often begin by entering new markets that are psychically close (culturally and geographically), gaining experience in these countries before expanding operations abroad into more distant markets.[9] Erramilli states that this is also true of service firms that move from culturally similar foreign markets into less familiar markets as their experience grows.[10] Language, in particular, has caused many well-documented problems for marketing communications in international markets. Marketing in Action 22.1 describes some of the classic mistakes that have been made.

Political–legal influences

Factors that potential international marketers will consider are: the general attitudes of foreign governments to imports and foreign direct investment; political stability; and trade barriers. Negative attitudes towards foreign firms may also discourage imports and investment because of the threat of protectionism and expropriation of assets. Positive governmental attitudes can be reflected in the willingness to grant subsidies to overseas firms to invest in a country and a willingness to cut through bureaucratic procedures to assist foreign firms and their imports. The willingness of the UK government to grant investment incentives to Japanese firms was a factor in Nissan, Honda and Toyota setting up production facilities there.

Eagerness to promote imports has not always been a feature of Japanese attitudes, however. Until recently, imports of electrical goods were hampered by the fact that each one had to be inspected by government officials. Also their patent laws rule that patents are made public after 18 months but are not granted for four to six years. In many western countries

22.1 marketing in action

Classic Communication Faux Pas

Language differences have caused innumerable problems for international marketers, and can provide a barrier to foreign market entry. The problem is particularly acute in countries like Britain, where one-third of its small and medium-sized companies admit to having communication difficulties abroad. This contrasts with Belgium, where 92 per cent of companies employ foreign language specialists, closely followed by the Netherlands and Luxembourg. It is no excuse to claim that English is a world business language and consequently there is no need to develop foreign language skills. As the former German Chancellor Willy Brandt once exclaimed, 'If I am selling to you I will speak English, but if you are selling to me dann müssen Sie Deutsch sprechen!'

Here are some classic examples of translations that have gone wrong.

- A Thai dry cleaners: 'Drop your trousers here for best results'.
- A sign in Hong Kong tailor: 'Ladies may have a fit upstairs'.
- A Moscow guide to a Russian Orthodox monastery: 'You are welcome to visit the cemetery where famous Russian and Soviet composers, artists, and writers are buried daily, except Thursdays'.
- A Portuguese restaurant that offers 'butchers' mess from the oven'.
- A Spanish sports shop called 'The Athlete's Foot'.
- A French dress shop advertising 'Dresses for street walking'.

The world of advertising is not without its humorous errors in translation:

- Come alive with Pepsi: Rise from the grave with Pepsi (German)
- Avoid embarrassment—use Parker pens: Avoid pregnancy—use Parker pens (Spanish).
- Cleans the really dirty parts of your wash—Cleans your private parts (French)
- Body by Fisher: Corpse by Fisher (Flemish)
- Chrysler for power: Chrysler is an aphrodisiac (Spanish)
- Tropicana orange juice: Tropicana Chinese juice (Cuba)
- Tomato paste: Tomato glue (Arabic).

Based on: Halsal (1994);[11] Egand and McKiernan (1994);[12] Cateora et al. (2002)[13]

patents remain secret until they are granted. The Japanese system discourages high-technology and other firms that wish to protect their patents from entering Japan.

Countries with a history of political instability may be avoided because of the inevitable uncertainty regarding their future. Countries such as Iraq and Lebanon have undoubtedly suffered because of the political situation.

Finally, a major consideration when deciding which countries to enter will be the level of tariff barriers. Undoubtedly the threat of tariff barriers to imports to the countries of the EU has encouraged US and Japanese foreign direct investment into Europe. Within the single market the removal of trade barriers is making international trade in Europe more attractive, as not only tariffs fall but, in addition, the need to modify products to cater for national regulations and restrictions is reduced.

Microenvironmental issues

While the macroenvironmental analysis provides indications of how attractive each country is to an international marketer, microenvironmental analysis focuses on the attractiveness of the particular market being considered, and the company capability profile.

Market attractiveness

Market attractiveness can be assessed by determining market size and growth rate, competition, costs of serving the market, profit potential and market access.

- *Market size and growth rate*: large, growing markets (other things being equal) provide attractive conditions for market entry. Research supports the notion that market growth is a more important consideration than market size.[14] It is expectations about future demand rather than existing demand that are important, particularly for foreign direct investment.

- *Competition*: markets that are already served by strong, well-entrenched competitors may dampen enthusiasm for foreign market entry. Volatility of competition also appears to reduce the attractiveness of overseas markets. Highly volatile markets, with many competitors entering and leaving the market and where market concentration is high, are particularly unattractive.[15]

- *Costs of serving the market*: two major costs of servicing foreign markets are distribution and control. As geographic distance increases, so these two costs rise. Many countries' major export markets are in neighbouring countries—such as the USA, whose largest market is Canada. Costs are also dependent on the form of market entry. Obviously, foreign direct investment is initially more expensive than using distributors. Some countries may not possess suitable low-cost entry options, making entry less attractive and more risky. Long internal distribution channels (e.g. as in Japan) can also raise costs as middlemen demand their profit margins. If direct investment is being contemplated, labour costs and the supply of skilled labour will also be a consideration. Finally, some markets may prove unattractive because of the high marketing expenditures necessary to compete in them.

- *Profit potential*: some markets may be unattractive because industry structure leaves them with poor profit potential. For example, the existence of powerful buying groups may reduce profit potential through their ability to negotiate low prices.

- *Market access*: some foreign markets may prove difficult to penetrate because of informal ties between existing suppliers and distributors. Without the capability of setting up a new distribution chain, this would mean that market access would effectively be barred. Links between suppliers and customers in organizational markets would also form a barrier. In some countries and markets, national suppliers are given preferential treatment. The German machine tool industry is a case in point, as is defence procurement in many western European countries.

Company capability profile

Company capability to serve a foreign market also needs to be assessed: this depends on skills, resources, product adaptation and competitive advantage.

- *Skills*: does the company have the necessary skills to market abroad? If not, can sales agents or distributors compensate for any shortfalls? Does the company have the necessary skills to understand the requirements of each market?

- *Resources*: different countries may have varying market servicing costs. Does the company have the necessary financial resources to compete effectively in them? Human resources also need to be considered as some markets may demand domestically supplied personnel.
- *Product adaptation*: for some foreign markets, local preferences and regulations may require the product to be modified. Does the company have the motivation and capability to redesign the product?
- *Competitive advantage*: a key consideration in any market is the ability to create a competitive advantage. Each foreign market needs to be studied in the light of the company's current and future ability to create and sustain a competitive advantage.

Deciding how to enter a foreign market

Once a firm has decided to enter a foreign market, it must choose a mode of entry—that is, select an institutional arrangement for organizing and conducting international marketing activities.

The choice of foreign market entry strategy is likely to have a major impact on a company's performance overseas.16 Each mode of entry has its own associated levels of commitment, risks, control and profit potential. The major options are indirect exporting, direct exporting, licensing, joint ventures, and direct investment either in new facilities or through acquisition (see Fig. 22.3).

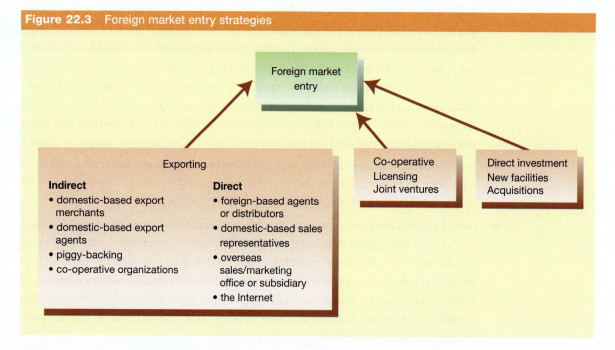

Figure 22.3 Foreign market entry strategies

Indirect exporting

Indirect exporting involves the use of independent organizations within the exporter's domestic market; these include the following.

1. *Domestic-based export merchants* who take title to the products and sell them abroad.
2. *Domestic-based export agents* who sell on behalf of the exporter but do not take title to the products; agents are usually paid by commission.

(3) *Piggy-backing*, whereby the exporter uses the overseas distribution facilities of another producer.

(4) *Co-operative organizations*, which act on behalf of a number of producers and are partly controlled by them; many producers of primary products such as fruit and nuts export through co-operative organizations.

Indirect exporting has three advantages. First, the exporting organization is domestically based, thus communication is easier than using foreign intermediaries. Second, investment and risk are lower than setting up one's own sales and marketing facility. Third, use can be made of the exporting organization's knowledge of selling abroad.

Direct exporting

As exporters grow more confident, they may decide to undertake their own exporting task. This will involve building up overseas contracts, undertaking marketing research, handling documentation and transportation, and designing marketing-mix strategies. Direct exporting modes include export through foreign-based agents or distributors (independent middlemen), a domestic-based salesforce, an overseas sales/marketing office or subsidiary, and via the Internet.

Foreign-based agents or distributors

Most companies use agents or distributors in some or all of their exporting abroad. Over 60 per cent of US companies use them for some or all of their export activity, and for European firms the figure rises to over 70 per cent.[17] Agents may be *exclusive*, where the agreement is between the exporter and the agent alone; *semi-exclusive*, where the agent handles the exporter's goods along with other non-competing goods from other companies; or *non-exclusive*, where the agent handles a variety of goods, including some that may compete with the exporter's products.

Distributors, unlike agents, take title to the goods, and are paid according to the difference between the buying and selling prices rather than commission. Distributors are often appointed when after-sales service is required as they are more likely to possess the necessary resources than agents.

The advantages of both agents and distributors are that they are familiar with the local market, customs and conventions, have existing business contracts and employ foreign nationals. They have a direct incentive to sell through either commission or profit margin, but since their remuneration is tied to sales they may be reluctant to devote much time and effort to developing a market for a new product. Also, the amount of market feedback may be limited as the agent or distributor may see themselves as a purchasing agent for their customers rather than a selling agent for the exporter.

Overall, exporting through independent middlemen is a low-investment method of market entry although significant expenditure in marketing may be necessary. Also it can be difficult and costly to terminate an agreement with them, suggesting that this option should be viewed with care and not seen as an easy method of market entry.

Domestic-based sales representatives

As the sales representative is a company employee, greater control of activities compared to that when using independent middlemen can be expected. Whereas a company has no control over the attention an agent or distributor gives to its products or the amount of market feedback provided, it can insist that various activities be performed by its sales representatives.

Also the use of company employees shows a commitment to the customer that the use of agents or distributors may lack. Consequently they are often used in industrial markets, where there are only a few large customers that require close contact with suppliers, and where the size of orders justifies the expense of foreign travel. This method of market servicing is also found when selling to government buyers and retail chains, for similar reasons.

Overseas sales/marketing office or subsidiary

This option displays even greater customer commitment than using domestic-based sales representatives, although the establishment of a local office requires a greater investment. However, the exporter may be perceived as an indigenous supplier, improving its chances of market success. In some markets, where access to distribution channels is limited, selling direct through an overseas sales office may be the only feasible way of breaking into a new market. The sales office or subsidiary acts as a centre for foreign-based sales representatives, handles sales distribution and promotion, and can act as a customer service centre.

For the company contemplating exporting for the first time, there are many potential pitfalls.[18]

The Internet

The global reach of the Internet means that companies can now engage in exporting activities direct to customers. By creating a website overseas, customers can be made aware of a company's products and ordering can be direct. Products can be supplied straight to the customer without the need for an intermediary. E-Marketing 22.1 discusses how a service company used the Internet to build its export business.

22.1 e-marketing

Considerations in Using the Internet to Export

The Internet provides a low-cost route to international markets. By building a website and displaying it live on the Internet a company can make its products and services available to the online population (655 million people in over 190 countries). The use of electronic communications, and web-based customer support and service can provide an exporter with a means of building strong relationships with quality customers. In addition, exporting activities can be supported by a number of online marketing techniques that are international in scope, including search engine optimization and website linking.

Due in part to the benefits of Internet exporting, Gael Software decided to sell one of its products, MindGenius (www.ygnius.com), exclusively over the Internet. Before making this decision, Gael had to consider the potential risks of doing this. Would it receive payment, would the software be copied illegally, could it allow users to try the software without giving it away? It found technical solutions for these problems and has now made over 100,000 sales to 104 countries worldwide. In addition, it is able to use e-mail marketing software to track prospects from the trial-download stage and intervene to increase sales conversions.

The Internet is not only a channel to market but also a rich research tool. Sites like International Growth (www.internationalgrowth.org) offer skills and resources for specific industries, in this case for UK software and computer services companies. It provides (free) market research reports, a skills area, and information on the main international marketing issues to consider.

Licensing

Licensing refers to contracts in which a foreign licensor provides a local licensee with access to one or a set of technologies or know-how in exchange for financial compensation.[19] The licensee will normally have exclusive rights to produce and market the product within an agreed area for a specific period of time in return for a *royalty* based on sales volume. A licence may relate to the use of a patent for either a product or process, copyright, trademarks and trade secrets (e.g. designs and software), and know-how (e.g. product and process specifications).

Licensing agreements allow the exporter to enter markets that otherwise may be closed for exports or other forms of market entry, without the need to make substantial capital investments in the host country. However, control of production is lost and the reputation of the licensor is dependent on the performance of the licensee. A grave danger of licensing is the loss of product and process know-how to third parties, which may become competitors once the agreement is at an end.

The need to exploit new technology simultaneously in many markets has stimulated the growth in licensing by small high-tech companies that lack the resources to set up their own sales and market offices, engage in joint ventures or conduct direct investment abroad. Licensing is also popular in R&D-intensive industries such as pharmaceuticals, chemicals and synthetic fibres, where rising research and development costs have encouraged licensing as a form of reciprocal technology exchange.

Sometimes the licensed product has to be adapted to suit local culture. For example, packaging that uses red and yellow, the colours of the Spanish flag, is seen as an offence to Spanish patriotism; in Greece purple should be avoided as it has funereal associations; and the licensing of a movie, TV show or book whose star is a cute little pig will have no prospect of success in Muslim countries, where the pig is considered an unclean animal.[20]

In Europe, licensing is encouraged by the European Union (EU), which sees the mechanism as a way of offering access to new technologies to companies lacking the resources to innovate; this provides a means of technology sharing on a pan-European scale. Licensing activities have been given exemption in EU competition law (which means that companies engaged in licensing cannot be accused of anti-competitive practices), and *tied purchase* agreements whereby licensees must buy components from the licensor have not been ruled anti-competitive since they allow the innovating firm protection from loss of know-how to other component suppliers.

Franchising

Franchising is a form of licensing where a package of services is offered by the franchisor to the franchisee in return for payment. The two types of franchising are *product* and *trade name franchising*, the classic case of which is Coca-Cola selling its syrup together with the right to use its trademark and name to independent bottlers, and *business format franchising* where marketing approaches, operating procedures and quality control are included in the franchise package as well as the product and trade name. Business-format franchising is mainly used in service industries such as restaurants, hotels and retailing, where the franchisor exerts a high level of control in the overseas market since quality-control procedures can be established as part of the agreement. For example, McDonald's specifies precisely who should supply the ingredients for its fast-food products wherever they are sold to ensure consistency of quality in its franchise outlets.

The benefits to the franchisor are that franchising may be a way of overcoming resource constraints, as an efficient system to overcome producer–distributor management problems and as a way of gaining knowledge of new markets.[21] Franchising provides access to the franchisee's resources. For example, if the franchisor has limited financial resources, access to additional finance may be supplied by the franchisee.

Franchising may overcome producer–distributor management problems in managing geographically dispersed operations through the advantages of having owner-managers that have vested interests in the success of the business. Gaining knowledge of new markets by tapping into the franchisee's local knowledge is especially important in international markets where local culture may differ considerably between regions.

There are risks, however. Although the franchisor will attempt to gain some control of operations, the existence of multiple, geographically dispersed owner-managers makes control difficult. Service delivery may be inconsistent because of this. Conflicts can arise through dissatisfaction with the standard of service, lack of promotional support and the opening of new franchises close to existing ones, for example. This can lead to a breakdown of relationships and deteriorating performance. Also, initial financial outlays can be considerable because of expenditures on training, development, promotional and support activities.

The franchisee benefits by gaining access to the resources of the franchisor, its expertise (sometimes global) and buying power. The risks are that it may face conflicts (as discussed above) that render the relationship unviable.

Franchising is also exempt from EC competition law as it is seen as a means of achieving increased competition and efficient distribution without the need for major investment. It promotes standardization, which reaps scale economies with the possibility of some adaptation to local tastes. For example, McDonald's includes salad in its product range in Germany and France, and Benetton allows a degree of freedom to its franchisees to stock products suitable to their particular customers.[22]

Joint ventures

Two types of joint venture are *contractual* and *equity* joint ventures. In contractual joint ventures no joint enterprise with a separate personality is formed. Two or more companies form a partnership to share the cost of an investment, the risks and long-term profits. The partnership may be to complete a particular project or for a longer term co-operative effort.[23] They are found in the oil exploration, aerospace and car industries, and in co-publishing agreements.[24] An equity joint venture involves the creation of a new company in which foreign and local investors share ownership and control.

Joint ventures are sometimes set up in response to government conditions for market entry or because the foreign firm lacks the resources to set up production facilities alone. Also the danger of expropriation is less when a company has a national partner than when the foreign firm is the sole owner.[25] Finding a national partner may be the only way to invest in some markets that are too competitive and saturated to leave room for a completely new operation. Many of the Japanese/US joint ventures in the USA were set up for this reason. The foreign investor benefits from the local management talent, and knowledge of local markets and regulations. Also, joint ventures allow partners to specialize in their particular areas of technological expertise in a given project. Finally, the host firm benefits by acquiring resources from its foreign partners. For example, in Hungary host firms have gained through the rapid acquisition of marketing resources, which has enabled them to create positions of competitive advantage.[26]

There are potential problems, however. The national partner's interests relate to the local operation, while the foreign firm's concerns relate to the totality of its international operations. Particular areas of conflict can be the use made of profits (pay out vs plough back), product line and market coverage of the joint venture, and transfer pricing.

In Europe, incentives for joint research projects are provided through the European Strategic Programme for Research and Development in Information Technology (ESPRIT) so long as the project involves companies from at least two member states. Equity joint ventures are common between companies from western European and eastern European countries. Western European firms gain from low-cost production and raw materials, while former eastern bloc companies acquire western technology and know-how. Eastern European governments are keen to promote joint ventures rather than wholly owned foreign direct investment in an attempt to prevent the exploitation of low-cost labour by western firms.

Direct investment

This method of market entry involves investment in foreign-based assembly or manufacturing facilities. It carries the greatest commitment of capital and managerial effort. Wholly owned direct investment can be through the acquisition of a foreign producer (or by buying out a joint venture partner) or by building *new facilities*. Acquisition offers a quicker way into the market and usually means gaining access to a qualified labour force, national management, local knowledge, and contacts with the local market and government. In saturated markets, acquisition may be the only feasible way of establishing a production presence in the host country.[27] However, co-ordination and styles of management between the foreign investor and the local management team may cause problems. Whirlpool, the US white goods (washing machines, refrigerators, etc.) manufacturer, is an example of a company that has successfully entered new international markets using acquisition. The company has successfully entered European markets through its acquisition of Philips' white goods business and its ability to develop new products that serve cross-national Euro-segments. European companies have also gained access to North American markets through acquisition. For example, ABN-Amro has built up market presence in the USA through a series of acquisitions to become the largest foreign bank in that country.[28]

Wholly owned direct investment offers a greater degree of control than licensing or joint ventures, and maintains the internalization of proprietary information. It accomplishes the circumvention of tariff and non-tariff barriers, and lowers distribution costs compared with domestic production. A local presence means that sensitivity to customers' tastes and preferences is enhanced, and links with distributors and the host nation's government can be forged. Foreign direct investments can act as a powerful catalyst for economic change in the transition from a centrally planned economy. Foreign companies bring technology, management know-how and access to foreign markets.[29] Direct investment is an expensive option, though, and the consequent risks are greater. If the venture fails, more money is lost and there is always the risk of expropriation. Furthermore, closure of plant may mean substantial redundancy payments.

The creation of the single European market allows free movement of capital across the EU, removing restrictions on direct investment using greenfield sites. Foreign direct investment through acquisition, however, may be subject to investigation under EC competition policy. American firms, in particular, sought to acquire European firms prior to 1992 in an attempt to secure a strong position in the face of the threat of 'Fortress Europe'.

The selection of international market entry mode is dependent on the trade-offs between the levels of control, resources and risk of losing proprietary information and technology. Figure 22.4 summarizes the levels associated with exporting using middlemen, exporting using company staff, licensing, joint ventures and direct investment.

Considerable research has gone into trying to understand the factors that have been shown to have an impact on selection of market entry method. Both external (country

Figure 22.4 Selecting a foreign market entry mode: control, resources and risk

Level	Risk of losing proprietary information	Resources	Control
High		Direct investment	Direct investment Exporting (own staff)
Medium	Licensing Joint venture	Joint venture Exporting (own staff)	Joint venture Licensing
Low	Exporting (own staff) Exporting (middlemen) Direct investment	Licensing Exporting (middlemen)	Exporting (middlemen)

environment and buyer behaviour) and internal (company issues) factors have been shown to influence choice. A summary of these research findings is given in Table 22.1.

Developing international marketing strategy

Standardization or adaptation

A fundamental decision that managers have to make regarding their international marketing strategy is the degree to which they standardize or adapt their marketing mix around the world (these are referred to, respectively, as the adapted marketing mix and the standardized marketing mix). Many writers on the subject discuss standardization and adaptation as two distinct options. Pure standardization means that a company keeps the same marketing mix in all countries to which it markets. The commercial reality, however, is that few mixes are totally standardized. The brands that are most often quoted as being standardized are Coca-Cola, McDonald's and Levi Strauss. It is true that many elements of their marketing mixes are identical in a wide range of countries but even here adaptation is found.

First, in Coca-Cola, the sweetness and carbonization vary between countries. For example, sweetness is lowered in Greece and carbonation lowered in eastern Europe. Diet Coke's artificial sweetener and packaging differ between countries.[44] Second, Levi Strauss uses different domestic and international advertising strategies.[45] As Dan Chow Len, Levi's US advertising manager, commented:

> The markets are different. In the US, Levi's is both highly functional and fashionable. But in the UK, its strength is as a fashion garment. We've tested UK ads in American markets. Our primary target market at home is 16–20 year olds, and they hate these ads, won't tolerate them, they're too sexy. Believe it or not, American 16–20 year olds don't want to be sexy. ... When you ask people about Levi's here, it's quality, comfort, style affordability. In Japan, it's the romance of America.[46]

Third, in McDonald's, menus are changed to account for different customer preferences. For example, in France and Germany salads are added to the menu, as mentioned above. The proportion of meat in the hamburgers also varies between countries.

Table 22.1 Factors affecting choice of market entry method

External variables

Country environment

- Large market size and market growth encourage direct investment
- Barriers to imports encourage direct investment[30]
- The more the country's characteristics are rated favourable, the greater the propensity for direct investment[31]
- The higher the country's level of economic development, the greater the use of direct investment
- Government incentives encourage direct investment
- The higher the receiving company's technical capabilities, the greater the use of licensing
- Government intervention in foreign trade encourages licensing[32]
- Geocultural distance encourages independent modes, e.g. agents, distributors[33]
- Psychical distance does not favour integrated modes, e.g. own salesforce, overseas sales/marketing offices[34]
- Low market potential does not necessarily preclude direct investment for larger firms[35]

Buyer behaviour

- Piecemeal buying favours independent modes
- Project and protectionist buying encourages co-operative entry, e.g. licensing and joint ventures[36]

Internal variables

Company issues

- Lack of market information, uncertainty and perception of high investment risk lead to the use of agents and distributors[37]
- Large firm size or resources encourage higher level of commitment[38]
- Perception of high investment risk encourages joint ventures[39]
- Small firm size or resources encourage reactive exporting[40]
- Limited experience favours integrated entry modes[41]
- Service firms with little or no experience of foreign markets tend to prefer full control modes, e.g. own staff, overseas sales/marketing offices
- Service firms that expand abroad by following their clients' expansion plans tend to favour integrated modes[42]
- When investment rather than exporting is preferred, lack of market information leads to a preference for co-operative rather than integrated modes[43]

Source: Whitelock, J. and D. Jobber (1994) The Impact of Competitor Environment on Initial Market Entry in a New, Non-Domestic Market, *Proceedings of the Marketing Educaton Group Conference*, Coleraine, July, 1008–17.

Most global brands adapt to meet local requirements. Even high-tech electronic products have to conform to national technical standards and may be positioned differently in various countries. As Unilever chairman Michael Perry has warned, most brands will remain national:

> Global brands are simply local brands reproduced many times. Although it may be true that increasingly we address even larger numbers of consumers we do well to remember that we continue to do that one-to-one.[47]

How, then, do marketers tackle the standardization–adaptation issue? A useful rule of thumb was cited at the start of this chapter: go global (standardize) when you can, stay local (adapt) when you must. Figure 22.5 provides a grid for thinking about the areas where standardization may be possible, and where adaptation may be necessary. For a car like the

Mercedes' style and technology cross national borders.

Mercedes C-Class, featured in the illustration, the product elements may be standardized to a high degree, although the positioning of the car may differ between countries. Standardization is an attractive option because it can create massive economies of scale.

For example, lower manufacturing, advertising and packaging costs can be realized. Also the logistical benefit of being able to move stock from one country to another to meet low-stock situations should not be underestimated. This has led to the call to focus on similarities rather than differences between consumers across Europe, and the rest of the world. Proctor & Gamble, for example, standardizes most of its products across Europe, so Pampers nappies and Pringles crisps are the same in all western European countries, although P&G's detergent Daz does differ.[48] However, there are a number of barriers to developing standardized global brands. These are discussed in Marketing in Action 22.2.

Developing global and regional brands requires commitment from management to a coherent marketing programme. The sensitivities of national managers need to be accounted for as

Figure 22.5 A grid to aid thinking about standardization and adaptation of the marketing mix

	Full adaptation	Full standardization
Product positioning		
Product formulation		
Product design		
Service offering		
Brand name		
Pack design		
Advertising proposition		
Creating presentation		
Sales promotion		
Personal selling style		
Price		
Discount structure		
Credit terms		
Distribution channels		

they may perceive a loss of status associated with greater centralized control. One approach is to have mechanisms that ensure the involvement of national managers in planning, and that

22.2 marketing in action

Barriers to Developing Standardized Global Brands

The cost of the logistical advantages of developing standardized global marketing approaches has meant that many companies have looked carefully at standardizing their approach to the European market. Mars, for example, changed the name of its chocolate bar Marathon in the UK to conform to its European brand name Snickers. Full standardization of the marketing mix is difficult, however, because of five problems.

1. *Culture and consumption patterns*: different cultures demand different types of product (e.g. beer and cheese). Some countries use butter to cook with rather than to spread on bread; people in different countries wash clothes at different temperatures; UK consumers like their chocolate to be sweeter than people in mainland Europe; and in South America hot chocolate is a revitalizing drink to have at breakfast, whereas in the UK it is a comfort drink to have just before going to bed. The failure of KFC in India is believed to be due to its standardized offering of plain fried chicken while McDonald's has succeeded by adapting its offering—for example, the Maharajeh Mac made from chicken and local spices—to the Indian palate. Consumer electrical products are less affected, though.

2. *Language*: brand names and advertising may have to change because of language differences. For example, the popular French drink PSCHITT would probably require an alteration of its brand name if launched in the UK.

3. *Regulations*: while national regulations are being harmonized in the single market, differences still exist—for example, with colourings and added vitamins in food.

4. *Media availability and promotional preferences*: varying media practices also affect standardization. For example, wine cannot be advertised on television in Denmark, but in the Netherlands this is allowed. Beer cannot be advertised on television in France, but this is allowed in most other European countries. In Italy, levels of nudity in advertising that would be banned in some other countries are accepted. Sales promotions may have to change because of local preferences. For example, French shoppers prefer coupons and twin packs, whereas their British counterparts favour X per cent extra free.

5. *Organizational structure and culture*: the changes necessary for a standardized approach may be difficult to implement where subsidiaries have, historically, enjoyed considerable power. Also where growth had been achieved through acquisition, strong cultural differences may lead to differing views about pan-European brand strategy.

The reality is that full standardization is rarely possible. Even brands that are regarded as global, such as Sony, Nike, Visa, IBM, Disney, Heineken, McDonald's and Pringles, are not as identical globally as they may first appear. For example, Visa uses different logos in some countries, Heineken is positioned as a mainstream beer in some countries but as a premium beer in others, Pringles uses different flavours and advertising executions in different countries, and although McDonald's core food items are consistent across countries some products are customized to local tastes. Setting the objective as being to develop a standardized global brand should not be the priority; instead, global brand leadership—strong brands in all markets backed by effective global brand management—should be the goal.

Based on: De Chernatony (1993);[49] Aaker and Joachimsthaler (2002);[50] Benady (2003);[51] Kirby (2000);[52] Luce (2002)[53] encourage them to make recommendations. The key is to balance this local involvement with the need to look for similarities rather than differences across markets. It is the essential differences in consumer preferences and buyer behaviour that need to be recognized in marketing mix adaptation, rather than the minor nuances. Managers must also be prepared to invest heavily and over a long time period to achieve brand penetration. Success in international markets does not come cheaply or quickly. Market research should be used to identify the required positioning in each global market segment.[54]

This discussion has outlined the difficulties in achieving a totally standardized marketing mix package. Rather the tried-and-tested approach of market segmentation based on understanding consumer behaviour and identifying international target markets, which allows the benefits of standardization to be combined with the advantages of customization, is recommended. The two contrasting approaches are summarized in Fig. 22.6.

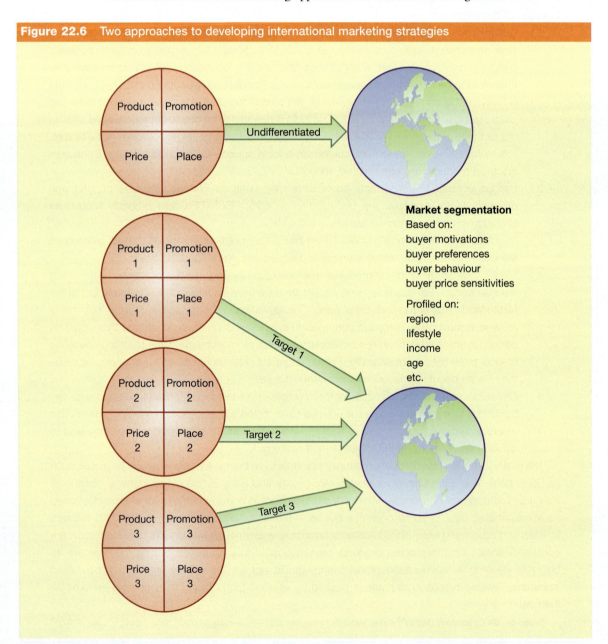

Figure 22.6　Two approaches to developing international marketing strategies

International marketing mix decisions

When developing an international marketing mix, marketers need to avoid falling into the trap of applying national stereotypes to country targets. As with domestic markets, overseas countries contain market segments that need to be understood before a tailored marketing mix can be designed. Marketing in Action 22.3 discusses some of the complexities of the Chinese market.

22.3 marketing in action

Marketing to China

Since joining the World Trade Organization, China has been widely regarded as the world's greatest marketing opportunity. But marketers must remember that of its 1.3 billion population less than 10 per cent of Chinese people have incomes sufficient to afford western products.

The Chinese market is a grouping of regional markets differentiated by local cultures that originate from the country's ancient substructure of provinces. In economic terms, the provinces along China's eastern coast, where many of its major cities lie, are more open to outside influence and more developed than those of the interior. There are also important differences between the traditions and diet of people from the northern provinces and those from the rice-cultivating lands in the south.

The implication is that marketing advantage can be gained by developing products, most notably food and drink, that reflect local variations in taste. The US sports drink company Gatorade is an example of a company that has applied this approach successfully. Different flavours were offered in different cities to appeal to local tastes. It identified that in the northern city of Beijing people like sweet tastes, while the Cantonese prefer sour flavours, such as lemon and lime.

Marketers also need to recognize differences in circumstances between home and overseas markets that can fundamentally affect the success of international operations. For example, in China, B&Q the do-it-yourself retailer, failed to appreciate that newly bought flats tend to be empty shells without wiring, plumbing, kitchens, bathrooms or even dividing walls. Although B&Q's store in Shanghai was advertised as a 'one-stop-shop for home improvement' it did not offer designers, a decoration service or furniture, leaving customers disappointed. The answer was to redesign B&Q stores in China to overcome the problems: floor space was doubled by adding a top floor with furniture and soft furnishings, and decorating and building services were offered.

Based on: Benady (2003);[55] Clegg (2002)[56]

Once a thorough understanding of the target market has been achieved, marketing managers can then tailor a marketing mix to fit those requirements. We will now explore some of the special considerations associated with developing an effective *international marketing mix*.

Product

Some companies rely on global markets to provide the potential necessary to justify their huge research and development costs. For example, in the pharmaceutical industry, Glaxo SmithKline's Zantac and Zovirax could not have been developed (R&D costs exceeded £30 million in both cases) without a worldwide market. Canon's huge research and development budget is also justified by the potential of global markets. For example, the bubble-jet and laser-beam computer printers it invented formed the basis upon which it has built world market shares of 30 and 65 per cent, respectively.[57] Once developed, the company can offer a standardized product to generate huge positive cash flow as the benefits that these products provide span national boundaries.

A second situation that supports a standardized product is where the brand concept is based on *authentic national heritage* across the globe: Scotch whisky, Belgian chocolate and French wine are relevant examples. Clearly, there are sound marketing reasons for a standard product. A third basis for standardization is where a global market segment of like-minded people can be exploited. This is the basis for the success of such products as Swatch and Rolex watches, Gucci fashion accessories and Chanel perfume. Where brands make statements about people, the *international properties* of the brand add significantly to its appeal.

In other cases, however, products need to be modified. Product adaptations come in two forms: permanent and temporary.[58] A company may make a fairly standard product worldwide, but make adaptations for particular markets. For example, the Barbie doll is a standardized product for most countries but in Japan, based on market research, it had to be redesigned by making it smaller, darkening hair colour and giving it smaller breasts. This was a *permanent adaptation*. However, the change may be only a *temporary adaptation* if the local consumer needs time to adjust gradually to a new product. This often occurs with food products. For example, when McDonald's entered Japan it had to alter the red meat content of its hamburgers because Japanese consumers preferred fat to be mixed with beef. Over time, the red meat content has been increased making it almost as high as it is in the USA. Also when Mister Donut was introduced in Japan the cinnamon content was reduced as market research had shown that the Japanese customers did not like the taste. Over time, the cinnamon content was increased to US levels.[59]

Many products that appear to be the same are modified to suit differing tastes. For example, the ubiquitous Mars bar has different formulations in northern and southern Europe, with northern Europeans favouring a sweeter taste. Also, the movement of large multinational companies to seek global brand winners can provide opportunities for smaller companies to exploit emerging market segments. For example, in the Netherlands, a small company took the initiative to sell environmentally friendly products, and captured one-quarter of the household cleaning market.[60]

Brand names may require modification because of linguistic idiosyncrasies. Many companies are alive to this type of problem now. Mars, for example, changed the name of its Magnum ice cream in Greece to Magic. However, in France McVitie's is having problems trying to convince consumers that the word 'digestive' has nothing to do with stomach disorders. Brand name changes also occur in the UK with Brooke Bond PG Tips being called Scottish Blend in Scotland and coming in distinctive Scottish packaging.[61]

Promotion

A survey of agency practitioners found that the use of standardized advertising campaigns is set to increase in the future.[62] Standard campaigns can realize cost economies and a cohesive positioning statement in a world of increasing international travel. Standardization allows the multinational corporation to maintain a consistent image identity throughout the world, and minimizes confusion among consumers who travel frequently.[63] As with all standardization–adaptation debates, the real issue is one of degree. Rarely can a campaign be transferred from one country to another without any modifications because of language difference. The clever use of pop music (an international language) in Levi's advertising is one exception, however. Coca-Cola is also close to the full standardization position with its one-sound, one-sight, one-appeal philosophy. Benetton also succeeded in running a global advertising campaign based on the 'United Colours of Benetton' theme. Yet research has found that full standardization of advertising is rare.[64]

Other companies find it necessary to adopt different positions in various countries, resulting in the need for advertising adaptation. In Mexico, Nestlé managed to position the drinking of instant coffee as an upmarket activity. It is actually smarter to offer guests a cup of instant coffee than ground coffee. This affects the content of its advertising. When brands are used differently in various countries, the advertising may need to be changed accordingly. For example, Schweppes tonic water is very much a mixer (e.g. drunk with gin) in the UK and Ireland, but is drunk on its own in Spain and France. Marketing in Action 22.4 gives examples of regulations on advertising in various countries.

22.4 marketing in action

Global Advertising Taboos

Standardized advertising campaigns are hampered by the rules and regulations in various countries around the world. These prevent certain types of advertising from appearing. Here are some examples.

France	ban on alcohol advertising
Easter Europe	alcohol advertising banned or heavily restricted; for example, in the Czech Republic drink cannot be poured, and ads cannot show people enjoying it; in Bulgaria no bottles, glasses, or any actors drinking can be shown
Sweden	no TV advertising of toys to children under 12
Nordic countries	strict regulations on tobacco advertising
Finland	children may not sing or speak the name of a product
UK	TV tobacco ads banned
Austria	children not allowed to appear in an ad unless accompanied by a parent or comparable adult figure
Lithuania	petfood ads banned before 11 pm
Malaysia	cannot wear baseball caps worn back to front (claimed to be indicative of gang influences and the undesirable side of western society); blue jeans cannot appear in ads (other colours are acceptable)
Asia	men with long hair banned from ads
Muslim countries	women can appear only if suitably attired; certain parts of the body (e.g. armpits) are not allowed to be shown for religious reasons
Korea	all models, actors and actresses in ads have to be Korean
Belgium, Luxembourg and Germany	ban on comparative advertising
Kuwait	ban on advertising cigarettes, lighters, pharmaceuticals, alcohol, airlines and chocolates

Based on: Richmond (1994);[65] Cateora et al. (2002)[66]

An analysis of the extent of advertising adaptation that is necessary can be assisted by separating the advertising proposition from the creative presentation of that proposition. The advertising platform is the aspect of the seller's product that is most persuasive and relevant to the potential customer: it is the fundamental proposition that is being communicated. The *creative presentation* is the way in which that proposition is translated into visual and verbal statements.[67] Table 22.2 gives some examples. Advertising platforms, being broad statements of appeal, are more likely to be transferable than creative presentations. If this is the case, the solution is to keep the platform across markets but change the creative presentation to suit local

Table 22.2 Adapting advertising for global markets		
Product category	Advertising platform	Creative presentation
Four-wheel-drive vehicles	Off-the-road technology	Jeep's 'We wrote the book on 4-wheel drive'
Toothpaste	Cosmetic benefits	Colgate's 'ring of confidence'
Airline travel	In-flight service quality	British Airways' 'It's the way we make you feel that makes you fly British Airways. The World's Favourite airline'
Washing detergent	Heavy-duty cleaning	Procter & Gamble's 'Tide gets out the dirt kids get into'

demands. In other cases both platform and presentation can be used globally, as was the case with the British Airways campaign mentioned in Table 22.2.

Advertising can be used to position brands using one of three strategies, as outlined below.[68]

1. **Global consumer positioning**: this strategy defines the brand as a symbol of a given global culture. For example, a jeans brand could be positioned as one worn by adult, upper-middle-class men who are globally cosmopolitan. The objective would be to have consumers identify the brand as a sign of membership in a globally cosmopolitan segment. Real-world examples include Sony ('My First Sony'), which positioned one of its brands as appropriate for young people around the world; Philips ('Let's Make Things Better'), whose advertisements featured people from different countries; and Benetton ('The United Colours of Benetton') whose slogan emphasizes the unity of humankind and promotes the idea that people all over the world consume the brand.

2. **Foreign consumer culture positioning**: with this strategy the brand is associated with a specific foreign culture. It becomes symbolic of that culture so that the brand's personality, use occasion and/or user group are associated with a foreign culture. For example, Gucci in the USA is positioned as a prestigious and fashionable Italian product and Singapore Airlines' use of the 'Singapore Girl' in its global advertising campaign and the positioning of Louis Jadot wine as a 'taste' of France are two further examples.

3. **Local consumer culture positioning**: this involves the association of the brand with local consumer culture. The brand is associated with local cultural meanings, reflects the local culture's norms and identities, is portrayed as consumed by local people in the national culture and/or depicted as locally produced for local people. For example, Dr Pepper soft drink is positioned in the USA as part of the 'American' way of life. In international advertising, it could be used when a good is produced or a service supplied locally.

Selling styles may also require adaptation because of cultural imperatives. Various cultures have different *time values*: In Latin American cultures, salespeople are often kept waiting a long time for a business appointment and in Spain delay in answering correspondence does not mean the matter has low priority but may reflect the fact that close family relatives take absolute priority and, no matter how important other business is, all other people are kept waiting. In the West, deadlines are common in business but in many Middle Eastern countries a deadline is taken as an insult and may well lose the overseas salesperson business.

The concept of space has different meanings in different cultures too. In the West the size of an executive's office is often taken to indicate status. In the Arab world this is not the case: a managing director may share the same office with clerks. In western cultures business is often conducted at a distance, say six feet or more. In the Middle East and Latin America, business discussions are often carried out in close proximity, involving physical contact to which the western salesperson needs to get accustomed.

The unwritten rules of doing business are often at variance too. In the West business may be discussed over lunch or at dinner in the businessperson's home. In India, this would violate hospitality rules. Western business relies on the law of contract for sales agreements but in Muslim culture a person's word is just as binding. In fact, a written contract may be seen as a challenge to his or her honour.[69] Salespeople need to adapt their behaviour to accommodate the expectations of customers abroad. For example, in Japan, sales presentations should be low key with the use of a moderate, deliberate style reflecting their preferred manner of doing business. Salespeople should not push for a close of sale; instead they should plan to cultivate relationships through sales calls, courtesy visits, the occasional lunch and other social events.

A study by Campbell, Graham, Jolibert and Meissner suggests that sales negotiation outcomes may depend on country factors in the West.[70] In Germany the *hard sell* approach was positively related to negotiation success; in France similarity (in terms of background and personality) was important; in the UK the role of the negotiator had a significant bearing on outcomes with buyers outperforming sellers; and in the USA adopting a problem-solving approach was related to negotiation success.

The Internet is creating opportunities for companies to advertise globally by setting up a website. Using electronic media as a promotional tool may be hampered by the need to set price lists, however. Where prices are currently very different across national borders some companies may decide that the risks of establishing a global Internet presence outweigh the advantages.

Country images may have a role to play in the selection of goods in overseas markets. For example, a negative image of a country may influence a consumer's attitudes towards products originating from that country. Country of origin is sometimes used to promote products abroad when associations are believed to be favourable and the extent to which the national image is considered suitable for the specific type of product being marketed. For example, the product categories most often promoted by means of the Danish image are foodstuffs and dairy produce, design goods and products related to agriculture.[71]

A clear instance of the power of country images is the case of the Toyota Corolla, which is built on the same assembly line as the near-identical GM Prism in the USA. However, because of the added value of Japanese origin, the Corolla commands a 10 per cent price premium.[72]

Price

Price setting is a key marketing decision because price is the revenue-generating element of the marketing mix. Poor pricing decisions can undermine years of toil on fashioning strategy and pruning costs. As Leszinski states:

> ❝As Europe moves towards a single market, lack of attention to pricing is a serious problem. The stakes are unusually high. ... On average, a 1 per cent increase results in a 12 per cent improvement in a company's operating margin. This is four times as powerful as a 1 per cent increase in its volume. But the sword cuts both ways. A price decrease of 5 to 10 per cent will eliminate most companies' profits. As the single market develops, decreases of this magnitude can easily happen: the existing price differentials across Europe for some products are in the region of 20 to 40 per cent.[73]❞

In the face of more intense global competition, international marketers need to consider six issues when considering cross-national pricing decisions:

① calculating extra costs and making price quotations

② understanding the competition and customers

③ using pricing tactics to undermine competitor actions

④ parallel importing

⑤ transfer pricing

⑥ counter-trade.

Each of these special considerations will now be explored.

Calculating extra costs and making price quotations: the extra costs of doing business in a foreign market must be taken into account if a profit is to be made. *Middlemen and transportation costs* need to be estimated. Distributors may demand different mark-ups and agents may require varying commission levels in different countries. The length of the distribution channel also needs to be understood, as do the margins required at each level before a price to the consumer can be set. These can sometimes almost double the price in an overseas market compared to at home. Overseas transportation may incur the additional costs of insurance, packaging and shipping. *Taxes and tariffs* also vary from country to country. Although there are moves to standardize the level of value added tax in the single market there are still wide variations. Denmark, in particular, is a high-tax economy. A tariff is a fee charged when goods are brought into a country from another country. Although tariff barriers have fallen among the member states of Europe, they can still be formidable between other countries. Companies active in international business need to protect themselves against the costs of *exchange rate fluctuations*. Nestlé, for example, lost $1 million in six months due to adverse exchange rate moves.[74] Companies are increasingly asking that transactions be written in terms of the vendor company's national currency, and *forward hedging* (which effectively allows future payments to be settled at around the exchange rate in question when the deal was made) is commonly practised.

Care should be taken when *quoting a price* to an overseas customer. The contract may include such items as credit, who is responsible for the goods during transit, and who pays insurance and transportation charges (and from what point). As we have seen, the currency in which payment is made can have a dramatic effect on profitability. This must be spelled out. Finally, the quantity and quality of the goods must be defined. For example, the contract should specify whether a 'ton' is a metric 'tonne' or an imperial 'ton'. Quality standards to be used when evaluating shipments should be agreed so that future arguments regarding returned-as-defective products may be minimized. The price charged, then, in a quotation can vary considerably depending on these factors.

Understanding the competition and customers: as with any pricing decision these factors play a major role. The difference is that information is often more difficult to acquire for exporters because of the distances involved. When making pricing moves, companies need to be aware of the present *competitors' strategic degrees of freedom*, how much room they have to react, and the possibility of the price being used as a weapon by companies entering the market from a different industry. Where prices are high and barriers to entry low, incumbent firms are especially vulnerable.

Companies also need to be wary of using self-reference criteria when evaluating overseas customer's perceptions. This occurs when an exporter assumes that the choice criteria that are important to his overseas customers are the same as those used by his domestic customers. The viewpoints of domestic and foreign consumers to the same product can be very different. For example, a small Renault car is viewed as a luxury model in Spain but utilitarian in Germany. This can affect the price position vis-à-vis competitors in overseas markets.

Using pricing tactics to undermine competitor actions: four tactics can be used in the face of competitor activity.[75]

1. *Disguise price reductions*: rather than reduce advertised list price, which is visible to competitors and may lead to a downward price spiral, cuts should be communicated directly to customers via the salesforce or direct mail by such methods as changes in the terms of sale (training included), reduced service charges or revised discount structures.

2. *Abolish printed lists*: quote price directly on a customer-by-customer basis. This creates uncertainty in the market as competitors are less confident of knowing what to quote against.

3. *Build barriers to price switching*: try to build up switching costs. For example, in the mobile phone market, the problems involved for users in changing numbers and acquiring a new handset limit switching between providers and raise their price flexibility.

4. *Respond to competitor attacks decisively*: for example, an electrical components supplier that held market leadership was successfully attacked by a competitor on price. The situation was not helped by the leader's policy of strictly following a printed price list along with predictable discounts for large accounts. A major plank of the leader's response was to target the aggressor's largest account with massive discounts. Although the customers stayed loyal, the aggressor understood the message and refrained from continuing its price attack.

International marketers need to understand how to use such pricing tactics in the face of increasingly fierce global competition.

Parallel importing: a major consideration in international markets is the threat of parallel imports. These occur when importers buy products from distributors in one country and sell them in another to distributors who are not part of the manufacturer's normal distribution system. The motivation for this practice occurs when there are large price differences between countries, and the free movement of goods between member states means that it is likely to grow. Companies protect themselves by:

- lowering price differentials
- offering non-transferable service/product packages
- changing the packaging—for example, a beer producer by offering differently shaped bottles in various countries ensured that the required recyclability of the product was guaranteed only in the intended country of sale.[76]

Another means of parallel importing (or 'grey market' trading as it is sometimes called) is by supermarkets buying products from abroad to sell in their stores at reduced prices. A landmark legal battle was won by Levi Strauss to prevent Tesco, the UK supermarket chain, from selling Levi's jeans imported cheaply from outside Europe. Marketing in Action 22.5 discusses the issues surrounding the case.

22.5 marketing in action

Levi's versus Tesco: the Case of 'Grey' Jeans

In a historic legal case, the European Court of Justice sided with Levi Strauss in its dispute with Tesco, the UK supermarket chain, over the distribution of cut-price Levi's 501 jeans. The court ruled that Levi Strauss could prevent Tesco from importing its products from outside the European Economic Area—at the time of the judgment this covered the EU plus Norway, Iceland and Liechtenstein—and selling them at greatly discounted prices. Before the ruling Tesco was selling Levi's 501 jeans, bought cheaply in the USA, for £27.99 compared to £50 in Levi's authorized shops.

Levi Strauss argued that its premium brand reputation was in danger of being damaged if any supermarket could sell its products at 'bargain-basement prices'. It also claimed that the staff selling its jeans needed special training. Levi Strauss said its victory would help other brand owners 'who invest heavily in research and development'. These sentiments were supported by the British Brands Group, which applauded the 'vote of confidence in the integrity of brand manufacturers'. Nevertheless, the European consumer lobby, BEUC, claimed the ruling was a bad day for consumers: 'transnational corporations use trademark law to restrict competition and charge higher prices in Europe'.

While admitting to 'disappointment', Tesco recognized that the ruling did not prevent it from importing Levi's or other goods such as cheap designer clothes, perfumes and cosmetics from the grey market within Europe. This is because the EU's 1989 Trademark Directive states that brand owners cannot dictate distribution of their products once they have been sold within the EEA. Tesco lost its case because the jeans were imported outside of the EEA. The directive states that in such circumstances, the brand owner must give permission for them to be sold.

Based on: Anonymous (2001);[77] Benady (2003);[78] Finch (2002);[79] Osborn (2001)[80]

Transfer pricing: this is the price charged between profit centres (e.g. manufacturing company to foreign subsidiary) of a single company. Transfer prices are sometimes set to take advantage of lower taxation in some countries than others. For example, a low price is charged to a subsidiary in a low-tax country and a high price in one where taxes are high. Similarly, low transfer prices may be set for high-tariff countries. Transfer prices should not be based solely on taxation and tariff considerations, however. For example, transfer pricing rules can cause subsidiaries to sell products at higher prices than the competition even though their true costs of manufacture are no different.

Counter-trade: not all transactions are concluded in cash; goods may be included as part of the asking price. Four major forms of counter-trade are as follows.

1. *Barter*: payment for goods with other goods, with no direct use of money; the vendor then has the problem of selling the goods that have been exchanged.

2. *Compensation deals*: payment using goods and cash. For example, General Motors sold $12 million worth of locomotives and diesel engines to former Yugoslavia and received $8 million in cash plus $4 million worth of cutting tools.[81]

3. *Counter-purchase*: the seller agrees to sell a product to a buyer and receives cash. The deal is dependent on the original seller buying goods from the original buyer for all or part of the original amount.

4. *Buy-backs*: these occur when the initial sale involves production plant, equipment or technology. Part or all of the initial sale is financed by selling back some of the final product. For example, Levi Strauss set up a jeans factory in Hungary that was financed by the supply of jeans back to the company.

A key issue in setting the counter-trade 'price' is valuing the products received in exchange for the original goods, and estimating the cost of selling on the bartered goods. However, according to Shipley and Neale, this forms 20–30 per cent of world trade with yearly value exceeding $100 billion.[82]

Place

A key international market decision is whether to use importers/distributors or the company's own personnel to distribute a product in a foreign market. Initial costs are often lower with the former method, so it is often used as an early method of market entry. For example, Sony and Panasonic entered the US market by using importers. As sales increased they entered into exclusive agreements with distributors, before handling their own distribution arrangements by selling directly to retailers.[83]

International marketers must not assume that overseas distribution systems resemble their own. As we have mentioned, Japan is renowned for its long, complex distribution channels; in Africa, distribution bears little resemblance to that in more developed countries. An important consideration when evaluating a distribution channel is the power of its members. Selling directly to large powerful distributors such as supermarkets may seem attractive logistically but their ability to negotiate low prices needs to be taken into account.

Customer expectations are another factor that has a bearing on the channel decision. For many years, in Spain, yoghurt was sold through pharmacies (as a health product). As customers expected to buy yoghurt in pharmacies, suppliers had to use them as an outlet. Regulations also affect the choice of distribution channel. For example, over-the-counter (OTC) pharmaceuticals are sold only in pharmacies in Belgium, France, Spain and Italy, whereas in Denmark, the UK and Germany, other channels (notably grocery outlets) also sell them.

As with domestic marketing, the marketing mix in a foreign market needs to be blended into a consistent package that provides a clear position for the product in the marketplace. Furthermore, managers need to display high levels of commitment to their overseas activities as this has been shown to be a strong determinant of performance.[84]

Organizing for international operations

The starting point for organizing for international marketing operations is, for many companies, the establishment of an export department. As sales, the number of international markets and the complexity of activities increase, so the export department may be replaced by a more complex structure. Bartlett and Ghoshal describe four types of structure for managing a worldwide business enterprise: international, global, multinational and transnational organization.[85]

International organization

The philosophy of management is that overseas operations are appendages to a central domestic operation. Subsidiaries form a co-ordinated federation with many assets, resources, responsibilities and decisions decentralized, but overall control is in the hands of headquarters. Formal management planning and control systems permit fairly tight headquarters–subsidiary links.

Global organization

The management philosophy is that overseas operations should be viewed as 'delivery pipelines' to a unified global market. The key organizational unit is the centralized hub that controls most strategic assets, resources, responsibilities and decisions. The centre enforces tight operational control of decisions, resources and information.

Multinational organization

A multinational mentality is characterized by a regard for overseas operations as a portfolio of independent businesses. Many key assets, responsibilities and decisions are decentralized. Control is through informal headquarters–subsidiary relationships supported by simple financial controls.

Transnational organization

This organizational form may be described as a complex process of co-ordination and co-operation in an environment of shared decision-making. Organizational units are integrated with large flows of components, products, resources, people and information among interdependent units. The transnational organization attempts to respond to an environment that is characterized by strong simultaneous forces for both global integration and national responsiveness.[86]

Centralization vs decentralization

A key determinant of the way international operations are organized is the degree to which the environment calls for global integration (centralization) versus regional responsiveness (decentralization). Centralization reaps economies of scale and provides an integrated marketing profile to channel intermediaries that, themselves, may be international, and customers that are increasingly geographically mobile. Confusion over product formulations, advertising approaches, packaging design and labelling, and pricing is eliminated by a co-ordinated approach. (However, too much centralization can lead to the *not invented here syndrome*, where managers in one country are slow to introduce products that have been successful in others, or fail to fully support advertising campaigns that have been conceived elsewhere.)

Decentralization maximizes customization of products to regional tastes and preferences. Since decentralized decision-making is closer to customers, speed of response to new opportunities is quicker than with a centralized organizational structure. Relationships with the trade and government are facilitated by local decision-making.

Many companies feel the pressure of both sets of forces, hence the development of the transnational corporation. European integration has led many companies to review their overseas operations with the objective of realizing global economies wherever possible. European centralized marketing teams carry the responsibility for looking at the longer-term strategic picture alongside national marketing staff who deal less with advertising theme development and brand positioning, and more with handling retailer relationships.[87] The result is loss of responsibility and power for national marketing managers. This is a sensitive issue, and many companies are experimenting with the right blend of centralization and national power.[88] Desire to preserve national identity and resentment of centralized European interference can run deep. One British company, owned by a German parent for more than a decade, still battled to preserve its national identity by holding its own formal board meetings and publishing its own separate annual report.[89] When Pampers was launched across Europe by Procter & Gamble, an employee found that 'as soon as it was known that I was from the European Technical Centre ... my local support dried up'.[90] Marketing in Action 22.6 describes how some European companies have approached the task of moving towards a more global approach to their marketing operations.

22.6 marketing in action

Managing the Process of Globalization

The fact that national marketing managers often lose responsibility and power in moves to a more centralized marketing approach means that simply preaching the virtues of globalization will not gain their commitment. Neither is compelling business logic likely to remove their opposition.

One approach to developing support is through the creation of *taskforces*. A business area is selected where the urgency of need is most clear; and where positive early results can begin a 'ripple effect', creating champions for change within the company. Procter & Gamble, for example, created a taskforce of national product managers to decide upon common brand requirements. A freight company, under intense pressure from international buying groups, set up a pricing taskforce to thrash out a co-ordinated European pricing strategy. One by-product of the taskforce approach is that it provides top management with a forum for identifying potential Euro-managers.

For some intransigent national managers, removing them from office may be the only effective solution. But there are less blatant methods. One approach is to put responsibility for planning prospective changes in the hands of the individual managers most threatened by them. For example, the roles of national marketing managers could be expanded to include responsibility for developing brands across Europe. Another way forward is to establish an accountability and compensation system for national marketing managers that reflects their new situation. When a centralized approach is needed, they are more willing to give up power in return for what makes them succeed.

Companies such as Coca-Cola, McDonald's, Shell and HSBC employ a global marketing director to co-ordinate worldwide operations. Such a role is not for the faint-hearted: much of their time is spent travelling and they have to combine an ability to digest reams of consumer research with the talent to persuade, through powerful argument, local marketing executives to adopt a strategy. HSBC's global marketing chief managed to achieve the right balance between the need to create a global positioning statement for its advertising and local demands for a bank by the use of the tag-line 'HSBC—the world's local bank' (see the illustration overleaf).

To minimize conflict, some companies are trying to build tiered systems where the marketing decisions that are centrally determined and those that are subject to local control are clearly defined. For example, the brand positioning and advertising theme issues may be determined centrally but the creative interpretation of them is decided locally.

Whichever approach is used, a system that shares insights, methods and best practice should be established. The system should provide a global mechanism to identify first-hand observations of best practice, communicate them to those who would benefit from them, and allow access to a store of best-practice information when required. To do this, companies need to nurture a culture where these ideas are communicated. This can be helped by rewarding the people who contribute. Tracking employees who post insights and examples of best practice, and rewarding them during annual performance reviews is one method. Regular meetings can also aid communication, especially when they include workshops that engage the participants in action-orientated learning. Sometimes the sharing of information at these meetings is less important than the establishment of personal relationships that foster subsequent communications and interactions. Technological developments can also make communication easier and quicker, such as the formation of intranets that allow global communication of best practice news, competitor actions and technological change. Of more lasting use, however, is the sending of teams to see best practice at first hand to facilitate the depth of understanding not usually achieved by descriptive accounts.

Based on: Mazur (1993);[91] Aaker and Joachimsthaler (2000);[92] Anonymous (2002);[93] Benady (2003)[94]

Part four Marketing Implementation and Application

*TEXTPHONE 08000 283 516. Calls may be monitored and/or recorded for quality purposes. Lines are open 8.00am to 10.00pm every day (except Christmas Day, Boxing Day and New Year's Day).

You'll find a local business banker in every branch of HSBC.

Unless they're out.

© John Offenbach

At HSBC Bank, we believe that every branch should have a local business banker. Someone who's accessible, who you can talk to about your business face to face. Whether it be at a local branch or, if it's easier, we can come to you. As a global bank we understand the importance of local business. It's what makes us the world's local bank. **For more information or to receive a 'Moving to HSBC' brochure or a business 'Start-up pack' call 08000 321 322* or visit www.ukbusiness.hsbc.com**

HSBC
The world's local bank

Issued by HSBC Bank plc

TO RECEIVE YOUR FREE BUSINESS START-UP PACK ☐ OR YOUR MOVING TO HSBC BROCHURE ☐
SEND THIS COUPON TO HSBC BANK PLC, FREEPOST NWW 1502, MANCHESTER M45 9AZ

TITLE .... SURNAME .... FIRST NAME .... ADDRESS ....
.... POSTCODE ☐☐☐☐ ☐☐☐☐
DAYTIME TEL NO. (INC STD) .... EVENING TEL NO. (INC STD) .... EMAIL ....
DO YOU HOLD OTHER HSBC ACCOUNTS? ☐ YES ☐ NO (PLEASE TICK). IF SO PLEASE COULD YOU FILL IN YOUR SORT CODE ☐4☐ ☐0☐ ☐☐☐☐
ACCOUNT NO ☐☐☐☐☐☐☐☐ MAY WE SEND YOU INFORMATION ABOUT OUR PRODUCTS AND SERVICES IN FUTURE? ☐

HSBC's global positioning statement: 'HSBC The world's local bank'.

Review

1 **The reasons why companies seek foreign markets**
- The reasons are to find opportunities beyond saturated domestic markets, to seek expansion beyond small, low-growth domestic markets, to meet customer expectations, competitive forces (e.g. the desire to attack an overseas competitor), cost factors (e.g. to gain economies of scale), and the achievement of a portfolio balance where problems of economic recession in some countries can be balanced by growth in others.

2 **The factors that influence which foreign markets to enter**
- The factors are macroenvironmental issues (economic, socio-cultural and political-legal) and microenvironmental issues (market attractiveness, which can be assessed by analysing market size and growth rate, degree of competition, the costs of serving the market, profit potential and market accessibility) and company capability profile (skills, resources, product adaptability and the ability to create a competitive advantage).

3 **The range of foreign market entry strategies**
- Foreign market entry strategies are indirect exporting (using, for example, domestic-based export agents), direct exporting (using, for example, foreign-based distributors); licensing (using, for example, a local licensee with access to a set of technologies or know-how); joint venture (where, for example, two or more companies form a partnership to share the risks, costs and profits) and direct investment (where, for example, a foreign producer is bought or new facilities built).

4 **The factors influencing foreign market entry strategies**
- The factors are the risk of losing proprietary information (for example, direct investment may be used to avoid this risk), resources (for example, when resources are low, exporting using agents or distributors may be favoured) and the desired level of control (for example, when high control is desired direct investment or exporting using the company's staff may be preferred).

5 **The influences on the degree of standardization or adaptation**
- A useful rule of thumb is to go global (standardize) when you can and stay local (adapt) when you must.
- The key influences are cost; the need to meet local regulations, language and needs; the sensitivities of local managers, who may perceive a loss of status associated with greater centralized control; media availability and promotional preferences; and organizational structure and culture (for example, where subsidiaries hold considerable power).

6 **The special considerations involved in designing an international marketing mix**
- The special considerations are huge research and development costs, where a brand concept is based on an authentic national heritage that transcends global boundaries, where a global segment of like-minded people can be exploited, and where a cohesive positioning statement makes sense because of increasing global travel. All of these considerations favour a standardized marketing mix. Where there are strong local differences an adapted marketing mix is required.

▸ **7 How to organize for international marketing operations**
- Many companies begin with an export department but this may be replaced later by more complex structures.
- Four types of structure for managing a worldwide business enterprise are: international (where overseas operations are appendages to a central domestic operation); global (where overseas operations are delivery pipelines to a unified global market); multinational (where overseas operations are managed as a portfolio of independent businesses); and transnational organizations (which are characterized by a complex process of co-ordination and co-operation in an environment of shared decision-making).

Key terms

adapted marketing mix an international marketing strategy for changing the marketing mix for each international target market

centralization in international marketing it is the global integration of international operations

contractual joint venture two or more companies form a partnership but no joint enterprise with a separate identity is formed

counter-trade a method of exchange where not all transactions are concluded in cash; goods may be included as part of the asking price

decentralization in international marketing it is the delegation of international operations to individual countries or regions

direct exporting the handling of exporting activities by the exporting organization rather than by a domestically based independent organization

direct investment market entry that involves investment in foreign-based assembly or manufacturing facilities

equity joint venture where two or more companies form a partnership that involves the creation of a new company

foreign consumer culture positioning positioning a brand as associated with a specific foreign culture (e.g. Italian fashion)

franchising a form of licensing where a package of services is offered by the franchisor to the franchisee in return for payment

global consumer culture positioning positioning a brand as a symbol of a given global culture (e.g. young cosmopolitan men)

indirect exporting the use of independent organizations within the exporter's domestic market to facilitate export

licensing a contractual arrangement in which a licensor provides a licensee with certain rights, e.g. to technology access or production rights

local consumer culture positioning positioning a brand as associated with a local culture (e.g. local production and consumption of a good)

self-reference criteria the use of one's own perceptions and choice criteria to judge what is important to consumers. In international markets, the perceptions and choice criteria of domestic consumers may be used to judge what is important to foreign consumers

standardized marketing mix an international marketing strategy for using essentially the same product, promotion, distribution, and pricing in all the company's international markets

transfer pricing the price charged between the profit centres of the same company, sometimes used to take advantage of lower taxes in another country

Internet exercise

L'Oréal, the global cosmetics and beauty company, has links to numerous country-specific websites. However, the content—such as text and visuals—alters depending on the country. Starting out from the main website below, visit some of the different country-specific websites for L'Oréal to explore any differences between them.

Visit: www.loreal.com

Questions

(a) Discuss how L'Oréal is adopting a global marketing strategy.
(b) Why should L'Oréal have an understanding of the different cultural nuances for its different international markets?
(c) Is it possible for L'Oréal to standardize its marketing mixes? Explain your reasoning.
(d) What types of product are easily globalized, and why?

Visit the Online Learning Centre at www.mcgraw-hill.co.uk/textbooks/jobber for more Internet exercises.

Study questions

1. What are the factors that drive companies to enter international markets?

2. Joint ventures are a popular method of entering markets in Europe. Choose an example (many are given in this book) and research its background (and outcomes if any).

3. For a company of your choice, research its reasons for expanding into new foreign markets, and describe the moves that have been made.

4. Using information in this chapter and from Chapter 17, on distribution, describe how you would go about selecting and motivating overseas distributors.

5. Why are so many companies trying to standardize their global marketing mixes? With examples, show the limitations to this approach.

6. What are the factors that influence the choice of market entry strategy?

7. Select a familiar advertising campaign in your country and examine the extent to which it is likely to need adaptation for another country of your choice.

8. Describe the problems of pricing in overseas markets and the skills required to price effectively in the global marketplace.

When you have read this chapter log on to the Online Learning Centre at www.mcgraw-hill.co.uk/textbooks/jobber to explore chapter-by-chapter test questions, links and further online study tools for marketing.

case forty-three

Going International: the Case of McDonald's

Who are McDonald's?

Mention the name McDonald's and you will find that nearly everyone has a reaction. This ground-breaking quick-service restaurant brand is seen by many as 'the epitome of US cultural imperialism', a runaway marketing success, but is reviled by some because of its popularity amid accusations of selling fatty food.[1] Acclaimed as one of the premier global brands[2] (Interbrand[3] lists it as the world's eighth most valuable) McDonald's is the world's largest food-service company, proudly boasting over 30,000 restaurants in 121 countries worldwide, serving a whopping 46 million customers daily.[4]

Founded in the 1950s by a milkshake salesperson, McDonald's has taken the American burger and fries meal concept to the masses. In the late 1970s in south-east England consumers had to drive some distance to find a McDonald's; now they are ubiquitous. Big Macs follow wherever hungry people go: into football stadiums, motorway rest areas, aeroplanes, trains and even ski resorts. Put simply, McDonald's is a counter service, family restaurant phenomenon that has taken the world by storm.

Why has the global brand of McDonald's been so successful?

The McDonald's recipe for success at first glance seems obvious: fast service enabled by a limited menu, a focus on cleanliness, family-friendly facilities and good value for money. The emergence of a cash-rich, time-poor lifestyle, shopping mall meccas and societal acceptance of a more casual approach to eating on the run (aptly named grazing) helped underscore the emergence of McDonald's and, effectively, the birth of the fast-food industry as we know it today. Economic growth fuelled the purses and wallets of eager consumers, keen to feast on the American dream food.

Innovations in food-preparation technology and service delivery provided a fast-service format that customers appreciated and a cost base that competitors found hard to match. Snappy counter service surrounded with repugnant bright yellow self-seating areas helped McDonald's grab market share of both the traditional fish'n'chip shop take-away and the diner/table service markets, with waiter labour cost savings passed on to consumers through lower prices. McDonald's was also in the leading group of companies to introduce franchising in the global marketplace, augmenting organic restaurant growth by harnessing the management, cultural and entrepreneurial capabilities and capital of local businesspeople around the world.

McDonald's conquers the world!

Consumers may see a Big Mac as a cheap way to fuel up, a quick fix to suppress their offspring's relentless nagging, fast and easy food, a good place to stop to use a clean toilet or a safe place to eat on their own. Whatever the reason for visiting McDonald's, buying a McBurger, fries and drink will not give you much change from a fiver in England. But what if you were lining up to place your order in Moscow, Beijing or Mumbai? The *Economist*,[5] recognizing the pervasiveness of the McDonald's brand, has created a Big Mac Index using the concept of purchasing price parity to help derive an alternative exchange rate calculation based on the real cost of like-for-like goods in different currencies. The burger is used as a pseudo-'basket of goods' and can highlight if a currency holds 'fair' market value. It is claimed to be a good exchange rate tracker over the longer term, having seen both burger prices tumble and currency values shift. Generally speaking, the cheapest burgers can be purchased in the emerging economies, where currencies tend to be undervalued, but even at around $1.20 (approximately half the price of a Euro zone or US Big Mac) how different might buyer behaviour be if a McDonald's experience equates to 5 per cent of your monthly income?

McDonald's launched its first international operation in 1967, moving boldly into Canada, the only market that has been allowed to modify the brand image (a maple leaf appears above the golden arches). Next Europe beckoned, followed by Asia and South America. In the 1990s eastern Europe succumbed, surprisingly even some Arabic states opened their doors to the McDonald's 'global realization' strategy.[6] Global conquest did not happen quickly or easily, however. The Canadian organization set up the first McDonald's in the communist Soviet Union in 1990 after 14 years of negotiations. To ensure high-quality, fresh ingredients, farms were set up to supply the restaurants, and the city of Moscow struck innovative barter deals that saw the burger company manage large real-estate developments. Prepared to queue for hours in the bitter cold, many young Russians still remember the excitement of experiencing their first taste of America.

Eric Schlosser,[7] in *Fast Food Nation*, says 'Fast food chains have become totems of Western economic development.' Schlosser also explains that Ronald McDonald has lead from the front, opening up new markets for foreign franchisors, supported by US foreign policy, which runs programmes at its embassies to help American franchisors find overseas partners.

The McDonald's corporation claims expertise in franchising, marketing and training, and a 'proven ability'[8] to operate in a variety of economic business and cultural conditions. It is intriguing, then, that McDonald's itself has not been able to diversify successfully into the global restaurant business beyond its flagship brand. The burger giant has resorted to purchasing a number of established branded restaurant formats, including a coffee bar (Aroma Café, now sold), Chipotle Mexican, Donatos Pizzeria and Boston Market, with little international success thus far. In January 2001 McDonald's purchased a minority share (33 per cent) of the fast-growing UK sandwich take-away chain Pret A Manger, a move that seemed to signal its intention to take a second brand to the global marketplace. Pret, a chain of some 130 outlets,[9] prides itself on selling fresh food with no additives, made on site, with excess stock being given away to charitable causes at the end of each day. The Pret A Manger management team has used McDonald's expertise, local business partners and funds to open wholly owned stores in New York, Hong Kong and Tokyo, but in spring 2003 it is claimed that Pret had no plans to introduce franchising nor to launch more international locations.[10] Although the McDonald's know-how and capital helped fuel Pret's expansion (40 new stores) it is claimed that the Oak Brook, Illinois, management team is not involved in the operation of Pret A Manger.

Truly global?

'You know what to expect when you eat at McDonald's; there will be no surprises' is a refrain that resonates. Whether or not you love the gherkin that is found nestling on a dollop of tomato sauce in a standard hamburger, you know when you peel back the plastic wrapper that there is going to be a gherkin waiting for you. Most of us have been conditioned to believe that McDonald's is a no-surprises eating experience—it is the same everywhere. Not true! Cross any border and visit the nearest McDonald's and you will find a host of variations, from price to product, even in the presentation. In the Netherlands, beer is on the menu. The Germans regularly enjoy a Chinese week, with five guest menu items including fried shrimp and egg rolls. The Canadians tuck into a McPizza and Thailand boasts the pork Samurai burger. In India you will not find pork or beef but goat and lamb burgers, and over half the menu card is devoted to tasty vegetarian options. In Japan the menu is heavily tailored, with ingredients such as cabbage and teriyaki sauce.

Although many believe that McDonald's is the same everywhere, clearly this is a misconception. McDonald's country teams have considerable autonomy to develop and market new product lines. Its UK division has experimented with curry and Italian variants and, in the USA, in response to stagnating sales, barbecue bacon burgers, sausage breakfast burritos, mozzarella sticks and grilled chicken flatbreads have been introduced to freshen up what some claim is a tired customer proposition. Critics[11] have accused McDonald's of being slow off the mark in responding to changing customer tastes, but there is a solid record for product innovation inside the global arches. Plastic salad boxes have long been on the menu, but McDonald's is said[12] to be testing several low-fat products in its UK outlets (perhaps based on the Canadian Lighter Choices menu, which boasts a soya bean McVeggie burger, salad with fat-free dressing and a granola-topped fruit and yoghurt parfait).[13] In addition to introducing lower-fat menu options, McDonald's will be providing on-packaging calorie and fat content information for the first time as it tries to counter the obesity lobby.[14]

Being a leading global cultural icon has not made life easy for the all-American McDonald's corporation. Not only has it lost high-profile court cases (Stella Liebeck won over $2.8 million (£1.76 million/€2.5 million) in 1992 after scalding herself with boiling coffee),[15] it is also targeted by environmentalists, terrorists and, most recently, by obesity lobbyists. McDonald's has long paid the price of celebrity: one lobby abates to be replaced by another, and the latest speculative lawsuit is from a group of obese New York teenagers who blame McDonald's (and others) for their size and health problems including diabetes, heart problems and high blood pressure.[16] In 2002 insensitive remarks from an American diplomat stoked up a riot at the Riyadh McDonald's in Saudi Arabia.

One burger too far?

McDonald's has demonstrated impressive growth by expanding into markets across the globe, increasing restaurant penetration in existing markets and stretching its product range to include exciting breakfasts, coffee and the McFlurry ice cream option. The pugnacious corporate communications[17] do not worry themselves with the threat of over-penetration causing cannibalization or, having seen below expectation performance since quarter four, 1999,[18] that the McDonald's brand might be coming towards the end of its extended growth phase. Given a growing world population and assuming that everyone eats three meals a day, McDonald's believes it enjoys less than 1 per cent[19] of all meal occasions, a share position that allows plenty of upside growth. Competition is, however, aggressively snapping at the base of the golden arches. A new genre of restaurants seems to have emerged, dubbed 'fast casual'. These outlets offer consumers fresher, healthier, more varied food in a more inviting ambience.[20] A McDonald's spokesperson, despite corporate fighting talk, has even been quoted as saying that 'one brand can't be all things to all people'.[21] One highly successful franchise format, Subway, the made-to-order-sandwich chain, now has more outlets in the USA than McDonald's, which is closing 1000 restaurants.[22] Is fast casual the new food retail business model that will displace the kings of the quick service? Having already held back the tide of many challengers, is it perhaps in the emergence of this group of new competitors, the fast casuals, that McDonald's will find its ultimate contest?

[1] Murray, I. (2002) Ronald McDonald Feels the Pricks of his Conscience, *Marketing Week*, 12 September, 106.
[2] Aaker, D. (1991) *Managing Brand Equity*, New York: Free Press, 68.
[3] Anonymous (2002) Can Mac Fight Back?, *Marketing*, 17 October, 23.
[4] www.mcdonalds.com (2002) investor fact sheet.
[5] Anonymous (2000) Big MacCurrencies, 29 April, www.economist.com.
[6] Schlosser, E. (2002) *Fast Food Nation*, England: Penguin, 229.
[7] Schlosser (2002) op. cit.
[8] www.mcdonalds.com (2002) investor fact sheet, 2.
[9] www.pret.com, visited March 2003.
[10] www.pret.com, visited 7 March 2003.
[11] Warren, M. (2002) Has the Balloon Burst for McDonald's?, *Daily Telegraph*, 7 December, 21.
[12] Kleinman, M. (2002) UNICEF Forgoes Kids Link to McDonalds, *Marketing*, 22 August, 1.
[13] Dobson, S. (2002) The Golden Arches Lightens Up: McDonald's Restaurants of Canada, *Marketing Magazine* 107(50), 14.
[14] Kleinman, M. (2003) McDonald's to Put Fat Level on Packs, *Marketing*, 6 February, 1.
[15] Bourne, D. (2002) McDonald's Misled Customers Over Use of Beef Extract, *FHM*, March, 104.
[16] Warren (2002) op. cit.
[17] www.mcdonalds.com (2002) investor fact sheet.
[18] Zuber, A. (2002) McD Sales Still Sliding; Leaner Profits Expected, *Nation's Restaurant News* 36(39), 6, 14ff.
[19] www.mcdonalds.com (2002) investor fact sheet.
[20] Anonymous (2002) Fast Food in America, Not so Fast, *Economist*, 7 December, 89.
[21] Hayes, J. (2002) Fast-food Giants Awaken Amid Flurry of Competition, *Nation's Restaurant News* 36(41), 58.
[22] Warren (2002) op. cit.

Questions

1. McDonald's allows its global brand offering to be tailored to better meet different consumer needs and wants. What are the advantages and disadvantages of this strategy? Are there examples of truly global brands that are never customized?

2. What have been the key factors that have led to McDonald's global success?

3. McDonald's has fuelled its impressive growth performance by operating a franchise system (in addition to wholly owned restaurants). What are the risks and potential benefits of choosing the franchising option?

4. The McDonald's franchise has enabled many entrepreneurs around the world to build their own successful businesses. Would you think about setting up a McDonald's franchise? What are the key issues you would consider?

5. In 2001 McDonald's purchased a share of the fast-growing UK-originating sandwich bar company Pret A Manger, looking for a franchise vehicle that had perhaps a healthier customer perception. What strategy would you adopt to ensure a greater exposure for McDonald's to a growing trend towards healthier eating?

This case was prepared by Justin O'Brien, Manager Global Selling, British Airways, and Eleanor Hamilton, Director of the Entrepreneurship Unit, Lancaster University Management School.

case forty-four

British Airways World Cargo

British Airways is the world's largest international airline, carrying more passengers from one country to another than any of its competitors. In 1999–2000, more than 41 million people chose to fly on the 538,000 flights it operated. Some 30 million of those passengers flew internationally, representing around 1 in every 15 people flying from one country to another worldwide.

British Airways operates 321 aircraft, covering a worldwide route network of 233 destinations in 96 countries. The group employs more than 60,000 people in over 100 countries worldwide. London's Heathrow Airport (the world's largest international airport) and Gatwick Airport are its main operating bases. The company's spectacular, purpose-built headquarters are at Waterside, near Heathrow Airport.

British Airways' stated corporate mission is 'to be the undisputed leader in world travel'.

British Airways World Cargo

British Airways World Cargo (BAWC) is the fifth-largest international cargo airline. In 1999–2000, the airline carried 897,000 tonnes of freight, mail and courier shipments across a global network spanning more than 160 destinations in over 80 countries, generating revenues of £556 million (€800 million).

Cargo is a core business activity for British Airways: 90 per cent of all cargo is carried in the holds of passenger aircraft, supplemented with additional outsourced freighter capacity on key routes in Asia, the Americas, Africa and the Indian sub-continent. The airline transports a wide variety of products, including fresh fruit, flowers and vegetables, pharmaceuticals, a vast range of high-tech products, spare parts for cars and ships, textiles and fashion goods, and even family pets relocating overseas with their owners. BAWC was also the largest carrier of Beaujolais Nouveau to markets all over the world in November 1999. The airline's freighter and passenger services carried more than 1800 tonnes of 1999 'Beaujo' to destinations in the USA, Japan and Australia.

Customers include freight forwarders such as BAX Global, Danzas AEI and Expeditors; integrators such as FedEx and DHL; and niche forwarders such as Jag Freight.

British Airways World Cargo's services aim to combine speed and flexibility with value for money. The organization has undertaken a five-year, £250 million (€360 million)-plus global change programme, which is nearing completion. The programme has included investments in facilities, new technology and training. The aim is to make BAWC the first-choice cargo airline for customers transporting goods anywhere in the world.

British Airways introduce a corporate service style

British Airways takes great pride in seeking to deliver the highest levels of innovative customer service. In January 2000, it unveiled £600 million (€864 million) worth of new customer services and products, to be introduced over the next two years. This is the biggest investment of its kind in airline history. It includes flat beds in the Club World long-haul business cabin, and a fourth cabin, World Traveller Plus, for full-fare economy passengers on long-haul flights.

In further efforts to improve the quality of its service delivery, British Airways recently introduced a 'corporate service style'. Employees across the airline, both those in customer-facing roles and those in support functions, were encouraged to adopt this service style when interacting with customers and with their colleagues.

The development of the service style included qualitative research with BA passengers and staff in the UK and in key overseas markets. The research identified customer needs, which BA's brand management team translated into 'service style standards' or attributes of the service style. Service style behaviours, or behaviour intended to support those service style attributes, were also defined.

Service style for British Airways World Cargo

In spring 2000, a project was instigated to consider whether British Airways service style could be adapted for British Airways World Cargo. BAWC operates as an autonomous contribution centre within BA. All central functions are located at the World Cargo Centre in Heathrow and not at the airline's Waterside headquarters. The BAWC commercial and operational offices throughout the world are, on the whole, separate from British Airways' passenger operations.

Some important branding issues were raised. The British Airways' brand lends a significant amount of brand value to the BAWC brand. As a result, the BAWC brand character has traditionally mirrored that of British Airways. On an operational level, BAWC is dependent on BA aircraft and flight crew to facilitate the delivery of its products and services.

On the other hand BAWC operates in a predominantly business-to-business market, and currently occupies a different position in that marketplace (a follower not a leader). The passenger side of British Airways is pursuing a strategy of product leadership, whereas BAWC is pursuing a strategy of operational excellence.

The project was to focus on formulating a service style for BAWC. It was identified that the service style needed to strike a balance between being appropriate to national cultures around the world and maintaining consistency across those cultures. The air cargo market in which BAWC operates is becoming increasingly global, and building a 'global brand' and ensuring that its customers experience similar service regardless of where they are was viewed as vital to the organization.

The process of developing a service style for British Airways World Cargo

The initial question was whether BAWC should seek to adapt the existing British Airways service style or create a completely new service style for BAWC. There was some debate. One argument was that an adaptation of the existing British Airways service style might be inappropriate, because the research for it was conducted in a passenger, rather than a cargo, context. Others argued that as the BAWC brand derives significant brand equity from the BA brand, it could be important that the BAWC service style mirrors that of BA. This approach, it was argued, would encourage consistency of experience when customers interact with BA and BAWC. It was also pointed out that a number of key decision-makers within BAWC's customers are known to be frequent flyers with the airline. In the meantime, British Airways had taken the decision that the whole of its organization would be embracing the new service style across all its operations and all the countries where it operates. On balance, it was concluded that BAWC should now develop a service style by adapting the existing British Airways service style to reflect the differences between the passenger and cargo operations.

Questions were raised about the development of a specified service style. Three approaches were considered:

1. a global set of service style standards and behaviours, developed centrally and consistently implemented across the world
2. a global set of service style standards and behaviours, centrally developed and adapted to different national cultures
3. a global set of service style standards and behaviours, centrally developed and locally adapted to different national cultures.

Table C44.1   Service style attributes revealed by the BAWC research exercise
Recognition
What does the customer experience?
I feel that BAWC people recognize me as an individual.
Customer focus
What does the customer experience?
When I am with BAWC people, I feel as though I am their number-one priority.
Effective action
What does the customer experience?
BAWC people take accountability and deliver.
Being proactive
What does the customer experience?
BAWC people focus on what they can do, not what they can't.
Delivering on our promises
What does the customer experience?
BAWC people understand my requirements and deliver a solution of standard processes and services.
Teamwork
What does the customer experience?
I see BAWC people across the world work as a team to deliver for me.

To explore these issues an extensive research exercise was carried out within British Airways and BAWC. A draft BA service style for BAWC was produced, and feedback obtained from overseas managers and BAWC service delivery teams. Proposals were evaluated in the light of a number of models taken from the management literature on culture and cultural differences.

The service style attributes, which emerged from the research, were as listed in Table C44.1.

The recommended approach was the third option: to articulate the BA service style for BAWC through the eyes of the customer and provide the local BAWC offices with a menu of behaviours intended to create that customer experience. The local offices could define how they would create that customer experience by selecting the behaviours appropriate to the national culture and agreeing 'their' service style with the BAWC brand management team in London. The objective was to maintain a consistency of brand throughout the world, while delivering a customer experience appropriate to the national culture.

An example of a 'BA service style for BAWC menu' is shown in Table C44.2.

Table C44.2   Example of a 'BA service style for BAWC menu'

Recognition

What does the customer experience?

I feel that BAWC people recognize me as an individual.

How can you do it?

- Approach customers who may require assistance.
- Give immediate attention to approaching customers.
- Acknowledge and greet each customer. Be welcoming.
- Introduce yourself by name.
- Use the customer's name.
- Smile.
- Establish eye contact.
- Maintain open body language.
- Maintain a confident and friendly tone of voice.
- Maintain a smart appearance—exceed the uniform standards.
- Wear your name badge.
- Be calm and in control.
- Acknowledge all customer 'thank yous'.
- End each customer interaction with a pleasant close.
- On farewell, ask if any further assistance is required.

What is it not?

- Displaying low energy levels.
- Not making eye contact.
- Being uncertain about the task or the next steps.
- Being aloof.
- Being indifferent.
- Having a lack of pride.

Customer focus

What does the customer experience?

When I'm with BAWC people, I feel as though I'm their number-one priority.

Table C44.2   continued

How do you do it?
- Show empathy.
- Demonstrate respect.
- Show care and consideration.
- Listen to customers' needs and concerns.
- Treat all customers' concerns and issues as a priority.
- Maintain a presence at all customer-facing points.
- Maintain a welcoming and approachable posture.
- Face the customer.
- Have an optimistic attitude.
- Keep personal items out of sight.
- If still finishing a task from the last customer, do not ignore approaching customers; greet them and explain when you will be available.
- Clarify your understanding of the problem or issue directly with the customer. On no account should a customer be expected to repeat themselves to one of your colleagues. Ask all incoming calls if you can put them on hold until your current transaction is over (unless the call concerns the current transaction).
- Politely ask all interruptions (including other customers) to kindly wait until your current transaction is over.

What is it not?
- Leaving the customer contact point unmanned.
- Having your back to the customer.
- Hiding in the office!
- Having newspapers or magazines on desks or counters.
- Talking to colleagues while customers are present.
- Ignoring customers.
- Dismissing or invalidating customers' questions and concerns.
- 'I hear what you say but ...'
- Justifying your actions.
- Picking an argument.
- Deliberately making the situation worse.
- Interrupting the customer.
- Using inappropriate language.
- Believing that customers are an irritation or inconvenience.

Questions

1. Why would an organization like BAWC consider introducing a corporate service style?
2. What difficulties might be encountered when implementing a common service style across a global organization spanning different cultures?
3. Evaluate the advantages and disadvantages of the approach finally recommended to BAWC.

This case was prepared by Eleanor Hamilton, Director of the Entrepreneurship Unit, Lancaster University Management School, and Sion O'Connor, Brand Manager, British Airways World Cargo.

References

Chapter 1

1. Drucker, P. F. (1999) *The Practice of Management*, London: Heinemann.
2. Rosenberg, L. J. and J. A. Czepeil (1983) A Marketing Approach to Customer Retention, *Journal of Consumer Marketing* 2, 45–51.
3. Grönroos, C. (1989) Defining Marketing: A Market-Oriented Approach, *European Journal of Marketing* 23(1), 52–60.
4. Houston, F. S. (1986) The Marketing Concept: What It Is and What It Is Not, *Journal of Marketing* 50, 81–7.
5. Levitt, T. (1969) *The Marketing Mode*, New York: McGraw-Hill.
6. Parkinson, S. T. (1991) World Class Marketing: From Lost Empires to the Image Man, *Journal of Marketing Management* 7(3), 299–311.
7. Morgan, R. E. and C. A. Strong (1998) Market Orientation and Dimensions of Strategic Orientation, *European Journal of Marketing* 32(11/12), 1051–73.
8. Simms, J. (2002) Building Brand Growth, *Marketing*, 26 September, 26–7.
9. Brown, R. J. (1987) Marketing: A Function and a Philosophy, *Quarterly Review of Marketing* 12(3), 25–30.
10. Jobber, D. and J. Fahy (2003) *Foundations of Marketing*, Maidenhead: McGraw-Hill; and Nichola, J. (2001) Where Did It All Go Wrong?, *Marketing Business*, November, 7.
11. Abell, D. F. (1978) Strategic Windows, *Journal of Marketing*, July, 21–6.
12. Anonymous (1989) Fortress Europe, *Target Marketing* 12(8), 12–14.
13. Brownlie, D. and M. Saren (1992) The Four Ps of the Marketing Concept: Prescriptive, Polemical, Permanent and Problematical, *European Journal of Marketing* 26(4), 34–47.
14. Wensley, R. (1990) The Voice of the Consumer? Speculations on the Limits to the Marketing Analogy, *European Journal of Marketing* 24(7), 49–60.
15. Bloom, P. N. and S. A. Greyser (1981) The Maturity of Consumerism, *Harvard Business Review*, Nov–Dec, 130–9.
16. Tauber, E. M. (1974) How Marketing Research Discourages Major Innovation, *Business Horizons*, 17 (June), 22–6.
17. Brownlie and Saren (1992) op. cit.
18. McGee, L. W. and R. L. Spiro (1988) The Marketing Concept in Perspective, *Business Horizons*, May–June, 40–5.
19. Rothwell, R. (1974) SAPPHO Updated: Project SAPPHO Phase II, *Research Policy*, 3.
20. Brown, S. (2001) Torment Your Customers (They'll Love It), *Harvard Business Review*, October 83–8.
21. White, D. (1999) Delighting in a Superior Service, *Financial Times*, 25 November, 17.
22. Jones, T. O. and W. E. Sasser Jr (1995) Why Satisfied Customers Defect, *Harvard Business Review*, Nov–Dec, 88–99.
23. Morgan, A. (1996) Relationship Marketing, *Admap*, October, 29–33.
24. White D. (1999) Delighting in a Superior Service, *Financial Times*, 25 November, 17.
25. Roythorne, P. (2003) Under Surveillance, *Marketing Week*, 13 March, 31–2.
26. Ryle, S. (2003) Every Little Helps Leahy Tick, *Observer*, 13 April, 18.
27. Samuel, J. (1992) Marketing Air Waves, *Guardian Weekend*, 3 October, 39.
28. Freeman, L. and L. Wentz (1990) P&G's First Soviet TV Spot, *Advertising Age*, 12 March, 56–7.
29. Anonymous (2001) Young Hopefuls, *Marketing Week*, 11 January, 21.
30. Singh, S. (2002) Glitz and Glamour, *Marketing Week*, 22 August, 36–7.
31. Anonymous (2002) Glamour, *Campaign*, 11 January, 27.
32. Booms, B. H. and M. J. Bitner (1981) Marketing Strategies and Organisation Structures for Service Firms, in Donnelly, J. H. and W. R. George (eds) *Marketing of Services*, Chicago: American Marketing Association, 47–52.
33. Rafiq, M. and P. K. Ahmed (1992) The Marketing Mix Reconsidered, *Proceedings of the Marketing Education Group Conference*, Salford, 439–51.
34. Ford, D., H. Håkansson and J. Johanson (1986) How Do Companies Interact? *Industrial Marketing and Purchasing* 1(1), 26–41.
35. Buttle, F. (1989) Marketing Services, in Jones, P. (ed.) *Management in Service Industries*, London: Pitman, 235–59.
36. Hooley, G. and J. Lynch (1985) Marketing Lessons from UK's High-Flying Companies, *Journal of Marketing Management* 1(1), 65–74.
37. Narver, J. C. and S. F. Slater (1990) The Effect of a Market Orientation on Business Profitability, *Journal of Marketing* 54 (October), 20–35.
38. Pelham, A. M. (2000) Market Orientation and Other Potential Influences on Performance in Small and Medium-Sized Manufacturing Firms, *Journal of Small Business Management* 38(1), 48–67.
39. Narver, J. C., R. L. Jacobson and S. F. Slater (1999) Market Orientation and Business Performance: An Analysis of Panel Data, in R. Deshpande (ed.) *Developing a Market Orientation*, Thousand Oaks, CA: Sage Publications, 195–216.
40. Slater, S. F. and J. C. Narver (1994) Does Competitive Environment Moderate the Market Orientation Performance Relationship, *Journal of Marketing* 58, January, 46–55.
41. Pelham, A. M. and D. T. Wilson (1996) A Longitudinal Study of the Impact of Market Structure, Firm Structure, and Market Orientation Culture of Dimensions of Small Firm Performances, *Journal of the Academy of Marketing Science* 24(1), 27–43.
42. Pulendran, S., R. Speed and R. E. Wilding II (2003) Marketing Planning, Market Orientation and Business Performance, *European Journal of Marketing* 37(3/4), 476–97.
43. Hooley, G., J. Lynch and J. Shepherd (1990) The Marketing Concept: Putting the Theory into Practice, *European Journal of Marketing* 24(9), 7–23.
44. Hooley, Lynch and Shepherd (1990) op. cit.
45. Narver and Slater (1990) op. cit.

Chapter 2

1. Day, G. S. (1984) *Strategic Marketing Planning: The Pursuit of Competitive Advantage*, St Paul, MN: West, 41.
2. Weitz, B. A. and R. Wensley (1988) *Readings in Strategic Marketing*, New York: Dryden, 4.
3. Piercy, N. (2002) *Market-led Strategic Change: Transforming the Process of Going to Market*, Oxford: Butterworth-Heinemann.
4. Day (1984) op. cit., 48.
5. Ackoff, R. I. (1987). Mission Statements, *Planning Review* 15(4), 30–2.
6. Hooley, G. J., A. J. Cox and A. Adams (1992) Our Five Year Mission: To Boldly Go Where No Man Has Been Before …, *Journal of Marketing Management* 8(1), 35–48.
7. Abell, D. (1980) *Defining the Business: The Starting Point of Strategic Planning*, Englewood Cliffs, NJ: Prentice-Hall, Ch. 3.
8. Levitt, T. (1960) Marketing Myopia, *Harvard Business Review*, July-August, 45–6.
9. Wilson, I. (1992) Realizing the Power of Strategic Vision, *Long Range Planning* 25(5), 18–28.
10. Day, G. S. (1999) *Market Driven Strategy: Processes for Creating Value*, New York: Free Press, 16–17.

11. Davidson, H. (2002) *The Committed Enterprise*, Oxford: Heinemann.
12. Maitland, A. (2003) How to Profit from Recession, *Financial Times*, 7 February, 11.
13. Mitchell, A. (2002) Can Brands Claim to Have Passion with No Vision, *Marketing Week*, 13 June, 34–5.
14. Anonymous (2002) Hard to Copy, *Economist*, 2 November, 79.
15. Desmond, E. W. (1998) Can Canon Keep Clicking?, *Fortune*, 2 February, 58–64.
16. Piercy (1997) op. cit., 259.
17. Jackson, T. (1999) How to Teach Old Dogs Valuable New Tricks, *Financial Times*, 26 May, 15.
18. Barker, T. (2000) Freeserve Taken Over for £1.6 bn, *Financial Times*, 7 December, 27.
19. McDonald, M. H. B. (2002) *Marketing Plans*, London: Butterworth-Heinemann, 2nd edn.
20. Day (1999) op. cit., 9.
21. Porter, M. E. (1980) *Competitive Strategy: Techniques for Analysing Industries and Competitors*, New York: Free Press, Ch. 2.
22. Phillips, L. W., D. R. Chang and R. D. Buzzell (1983) Product Quality, Cost Position and Business Performance: A Test of Some Key Hypotheses, *Journal of Marketing* 47(Spring), 26–43.
23. Drucker, P. F. (1993) *Management Tasks, Responsibilities, Practices*, New York: Harper and Row, 128.
24. Piercy, N. (1986) The Role and Function of the Chief Marketing Executive and the Marketing Department, *Journal of Marketing Management* 1(3), 265–90.
25. Leppard, J. W. and M. H. B. McDonald (1991) Marketing Planning and Corporate Culture: A Conceptual Framework which Examines Management Attitudes in the Context of Marketing Planning, *Journal of Marketing Management* 7(3), 213–36.
26. Greenley, G. E. (1986) *The Strategic and Operational Planning of Marketing*, Maidenhead: McGraw-Hill, 185–7.
27. Terpstra, V. and R. Sarathy (1991) *International Marketing*, Orlando, FL: Dryden, Ch. 17.
28. Oktemgil, M. and G. Greenley (1997) Consequences of High and Low Adaptive Capability in UK Companies, *European Journal of Marketing* 31(7), 445–66.
29. Raimond, P. and C. Eden (1990) Making Strategy Work, *Long Range Planning* 23(5), 97–105.
30. Driver, J. C. (1990) Marketing Planning in Style, *Quarterly Review of Marketing* 15(4), 16–21.
31. Saker, J. and R. Speed (1992) Corporate Culture: Is It Really a Barrier to Marketing Planning?, *Journal of Marketing Management* 8(2), 177–82. For information on marketing and planning in small and medium-sized firms see Carson, D. (1990) Some Exploratory Models for Assessing Small Firms' Marketing Performance: A Qualitative Approach, *European Journal of Marketing* 24(11) 8–51, and Fuller, P. B. (1994) Assessing Marketing in Small and Medium-Sized Enterprises, *European Journal of Marketing* 28(12), 34–9.
32. O'Shaughnessy, J. (1995) *Competitive Marketing*, Boston, Mass: Allen & Unwin.
33. Greenley, G. (1987) An Exposition into Empirical Research into Marketing Planning, *Journal of Marketing Management* 3(1), 83–102.
34. Armstrong, J. S. (1982) The Value of Formal Planning for Strategic Decisions: Review of Empirical Research, *Strategic Management Journal* 3(3), 197–213.
35. McDonald, M. H. B. (1984) The Theory and Practice of Marketing Planning for Industrial Goods in International Markets, Cranfield Institute of Technology, PhD thesis. A more recent study has also confirmed that marketing planning is linked to commercial success: Pulendran, S., R. Speed and R. E. Wildin II (2003) Marketing Planning, Marketing Orientation and Business Performance, *European Journal of Marketing* 37(3/4), 476–97.
36. Mintzberg, H. (1975) The Manager's Job: Folklore and Fact, *Harvard Business Review*, July–August, 49–61.
37. McDonald, M. H. B. (1989) The Barriers to Marketing Planning, *Journal of Marketing Management* 5(1), 1–18.
38. McDonald (2002) op. cit.
39. Abell, D. F. and J. S. Hammond (1979) *Strategic Market Planning*, Englewood Cliffs, NJ: Prentice-Hall.

Chapter 3

1. Leeflang, P. S. H. and W. F. van Raaij (1995) The Changing Consumer in the European Union: A Meta-Analysis, *International Journal of Research in Marketing* 12, 373–87.
2. Blackwell R. D., P. W. Miniard and J. F. Engel (2001) *Consumer Behavior*, Orlando, FL: Dryden, 174.
3. Woodside, A. G. and W. H. Mote (1979) Perceptions of Marital Roles in Consumer Processes for Six Products, in Beckwith et al. (eds) *American Marketing Association Educator Proceedings*, Chicago: American Marketing Association, 214–19.
4. Donation, S. (1989) Study Boosts Men's Buying Role, *Advertising Age*, 4 December, 48.
5. Anonymous (1990) Business Bulletin, *Wall Street Journal*, 17 May, A1.
6. Weinberg, C. B. and R. S. Winer (1983) Working Wives and Major Family Expenditures: Replication and Extension, *Journal of Consumer Research* 7 (September), 259–63.
7. Bellante, D. and A. C. Foster (1984) Working Wives and Expenditure on Services, *Journal of Consumer Research* 11 (September), 700–7.
8. Swasey, A. (1990) Family Purse Strings Falls into Young Hands, *Wall Street Journal*, 2 February, B1.
9. Blackwell, Miniard and Engel (2001) op. cit., 16–28.
10. Hawkins, D. I., R. J. Best and K. A. Coney (1989) *Consumer Behaviour: Implications for Marketing Strategy*, Boston, Mass: Irwin, 536.
11. O'Shaughnessey, J. (1987) *Why People Buy*, New York: Oxford University Press, 161.
12. Baumgartner, H. and J. Bem Steenkamp (1996) Exploratory Consumer Buying Behaviour: Conceptualisation and Measurement, *International Journal of Research in Marketing* 13, 121–37.
13. Kuusela, H., M. T. Spence and A. J. Kanto (1998) Expertise Effects on Prechoice Decision Processes and Final Outcomes: A Protocol Analysis, *European Journal of Marketing* 32(5/6), 559–76.
14. Creusen, M. E. H. and J. P. L. Schoormans (1997) The Nature of Differences between Similarity and Preference Judgements: A Replication and Extension, *International Journal of Research in Marketing* 14, 81–7.
15. Blackwell, Miniard and Engel (2001) op. cit., 34.
16. Elliott, R. and E. Hamilton (1991) Consumer Choice Tactics and Leisure Activities, *International Journal of Advertising* 10, 325–32.
17. Ajzen, I. and M. Fishbein (1980) *Understanding Attitudes and Predicting Social Behaviour*, Englewood Cliffs, NJ: Prentice-Hall.
18. See e.g. Budd, R. J. and C. P. Spencer (1984) Predicting Undergraduates' Intentions to Drink, *Journal of Studies on Alcohol* 45(2), 179–83; Farley, J., D. Lehman and M. Ryan (1981) Generalizing from 'Imperfect' Replication, *Journal of Business* 54(4), 597–610; Shimp, T. and A. Kavas (1984) The Theory of Reasoned Action Applied to Coupon Usage, *Journal of Consumer Research* 11, 795–809.
19. Ehrenberg, A. S. C. and G. J. Goodhart (1980) *How Advertising Works*, J. Walter Thompson/MRCA.
20. Wright, P. L. (1974) The Choice of a Choice Strategy: Simplifying vs Optimizing, Faculty Working Paper no. 163, Champaign, Ill: Department of Business Administration, University of Illinois.
21. Rothschild, M. L. (1978) Advertising Strategies for High and Low Involvement Situations, *American Marketing Association Educator's Proceedings*, Chicago: 150–62.
22. Rothschild (1978) op. cit.

23. For a discussion of the role of involvement in package labelling see Davies, M. A. P. and L. T. Wright (1994) The Importance of Labelling Examined in Food Marketing, *European Journal of Marketing* 28(2) 57–67.
24. Elliott, R. (1997) Understanding Buyers: Implications for Selling, in D. Jobber (ed.) *The CIM Handbook of Selling and Sales Strategy*, Oxford: Butterworth-Heinemann.
25. See Elliott, R. (1998) A Model of Emotion-Driven Choice, *Journal of Marketing Management* 14, 95–108; Rook, D. (1987) The Buying Impulse, *Journal of Consumer Research* 14(1), 89–99.
26. Hawkins, Best and Coney (1989) op. cit., 664–5.
27. Bedell, G (2003) *The Observer Review*, 19 January, 1–2.
28. See Carrigan, M. and A. Attala (2001) The Myth of the Ethical Consumer—Do Ethics Matter in Purchase Behaviour? *Journal of Consumer Marketing* 18(7) 560–77; and Follows, S.B. and D. Jobber (1999) Environmentally Responsible Behaviour: A Test of a Consumer Model, *European Journal of Marketing* 34(5/6), 723–46.
29. Carrigan and Attala (2001) op. cit.
30. Mowen, J. C. (1988) Beyond Consumer Decision Making, *Journal of Consumer Research* 5(1), 15–25.
31. Elliot and Hamilton (1991) op. cit.
32. Anonymous (2002) Who's Wearing the Trousers?, *Economist*, 8 September, 27–9.
33. Carter, M. (2002) Ruthlessly Shopping for Comfort, *Financial Times*, 20 May, 12.
34. Dwek, R. (2002) Apple Pushes Design to Core of Marketing, *Marketing Week*, 24 January, 20.
35. Hawkins, Best and Coney (1989) op. cit., 30.
36. Blackwell, Miniard and Engel (2001) op. cit., 29.
37. Bettman, J. R. (1982) A Functional Analysis of the Role of Overall Evaluation of Alternatives and Choice Processes, in Mitchell, A. (ed.) *Advances in Consumer Research 8*, Ann Arbor, Mich: Association for Consumer Research, 87–93.
38. Laurent, G. and J. N. Kapferer (1985) Measuring Consumer Involvement Profiles, *Journal of Marketing Research* 12 (February), 41–53.
39. Blackwell, Miniard and Engel (2001) op. cit., 363.
40. Williams, K. C. (1981) *Behavioural Aspects of Marketing*, London: Heinemann.
41. Hawkins, Best and Coney (1989) op. cit., 275.
42. Ratneshwar, S., L. Warlop, D. G. Mick and G. Seegar (1997) Benefit Salience and Consumers' Selective Attention to Product Features, *International Journal of Research in Marketing* 14, 245–9.
43. Levin, L. P. and G. J. Gaeth (1988) Framing of Attribute Information Before and After Consuming the Product, *Journal of Consumer Research* 15 (December), 374–78.
44. Key, A. (2000) The Colour-Coded Secrets of Brands, *Marketing*, 6 January, 21.
45. Jones, H. (1996) Psychological Warfare, *Marketing Week*, 2 February, 32–5.
46. Kemp, G. (2000) Elastic Brands, *Marketing Business*, October, 40–2.
47. Hawkins, Best and Coney (1989) op. cit., 317.
48. Ries, A. and J. Trout (2001) *Positioning: The Battle for Your Mind*, New York: Warner.
49. Luthans, F. (2001) *Organisational Behaviour*, San Francisco: McGraw-Hill.
50. Maslow, A. H. (1954) *Motivation and Personality*, New York: Harper & Row, 80–106.
51. Van Trijp, H. C. M., W. D. Hoyer and J. J. Inman (1996) Why Switch? Product Category-Level Explanations for True Variety-Seeking Behaviour, *Journal of Marketing Research* 33, August, 281–92.
52. Kassarjan, H. H. (1971) Personality and Consumer Behaviour Economics: A Review, *Journal of Marketing Research*, November, 409–18.
53. Ackoff, R. L. and J. R. Emsott (1975) Advertising at Anheuser-Busch, Inc., *Sloan Management Review*, Spring, 1–15.
54. Lunn, T., S. Baldwin and J. Dickens (1982) Monitoring Consumer Lifestyles, *Admap*, November, 18–23.
55. O'Brien, S. and R. Ford (1988) Can we at Last Say Goodbye to Social Class? *Journal of the Market Research Society* 30(3), 289–332.
56. Singh, S. (2001) No Stopping to Eat or Drink, *Marketing Week*, 5 July, 38–9.
57. Carter, M. (2002) Branding Takes a Road Test, *Financial Times*, 17 April, 14.
58. Murphy, D. (2001) Connecting with On-line Teenagers, *Marketing*, 27 September, 31–2.
59. Bamossy, G. and S. Dawson (1991) A Comparison of the Culture of Consumption between Two Western Cultures: A Study of Materialism in the Netherlands and United States, *Proceedings of the European Marketing Academy Conference*, Dublin, May, 147–68.
60. Anonymous (1981) *An Evaluation of Social Grade Validity*, London: Market Research Society.
61. O'Brien and Ford (1988) op. cit., 309.
62. Baker, K., J. Germingham and C. Macdonald (1979) The Utility to Market Research of the Classification of Residential Neighbourhoods, *Market Research Society Conference*, Brighton, March, 206–17.

Chapter 4

1. Corey, E. R. (1991) *Industrial Marketing: Cases and Concepts*, Englewood Cliffs, NJ: Prentice-Hall.
2. Jobber, D. and G. Lancaster (2003) *Selling and Sales Management*, London: Pitman, 27.
3. Bishop, W. S., J. L. Graham and M. H. Jones (1984) Volatility of Derived Demand in Industrial Markets and its Management Implications, *Journal of Marketing*, Fall, 95–103.
4. Webster, F. E. and Y. Wind (1972) *Organizational Buying Behaviour*, Englewood Cliffs, NJ: Prentice-Hall, 78–80. The sixth role of initiator was added by Bonoma, T. V. (1982) Major Sales: Who Really does the Buying, *Harvard Business Review*, May–June, 111–19.
5. Cline, C. E. and B. P. Shapiro (1978) *Cumberland Metal Industries (A): Case Study*, Boston, Mass: Harvard Business School.
6. Benady, D. (2001) If Undelivered, *Marketing Week*, 20 December, 31–3.
7. Reed, A. (2001) Netting Customers, *Marketing Week*, 31 May, 75–6.
8. Thatcher, M. (2001) Hitting New Targets, *Marketing Business*, March, 37–9.
9. Robinson, P. J., C. W. Faris and Y. Wind (1967) *Industrial Buying and Creative Marketing*, Boston, Mass: Allyn & Bacon.
10. Jobber and Lancaster (2003) op. cit., 35.
11. Draper, A. (1994) Organisational Buyers as Workers: The Key to their Behaviour, *European Journal of Marketing* 28(11) 50–62.
12. Parker, D. (1996) The X Files, *Marketing Week*, 8 March, 73–4.
13. For a discussion of the components of risk see Stone, R. N. and K. Gronhaug (1993) Perceived Risk: Further Considerations for the Marketing Discipline, *European Journal of Marketing* 27(3) 39–50.
14. Jobber, D. (1994) What Makes Organisations Buy, in Hart, N. (ed.) *Effective Industrial Marketing*, London: Kogan Page, 100–18.
15. Mazur, L. (2002) Increasing Momentum, *Marketing Business*, June, 16–19.
16. Cardozo, R. N. (1980) Situational Segmentation of Industrial Markets, *European Journal of Marketing* 14(5/6), 264–76.
17. Robinson, Faris and Wind (1967) op. cit.
18. Lee, L. and D. W. Dobler (1977) *Purchasing and Materials Management: Text and Cases*, New York: McGraw-Hill, 265.

19. Forbis, J. L. and N. T. Mehta (1981) Value-Based Strategies for Industrial Products, *Business Horizons*, May–June, 32–42.
20. Hutt, M. D. and T. W. Speh (1997) *Business Marketing Management*, New York: Dryden Press, 3rd edn, 40.
21. Done, K. (1992) 0 to 130,000 in 14 Weeks, *Financial Times*, 23 September, 11.
22. Brierty, E. G., R. W. Eckles and R. R. Reeder (1998) *Business Marketing*, Englewood Cliffs, NJ: Prentice-Hall, 105.
23. Kotler, P. (2003) *Marketing Management*, New Jersey: Pearson.
24. Moffat, S. (2003) The Case of Covisint (Working Paper), University of Strathclyde.
25. Blenkhorn, D. L. and P. M. Banting (1991) How Reverse Marketing Changes Buyer–Seller's Roles, *Industrial Marketing Management* 20, 185–91.
26. Anderson, F. and W. Lazer (1978) Industrial Lease Marketing, *Journal of Marketing* 42 (January), 71–9.
27. Morris, M. H. (1988) *Industrial and Organisation Marketing*, Columbus, OH: Merrill, 323.
28. Gummerson, E. (1996) Relationship Marketing and Imaginary Organisations: A Synthesis, *European Journal of Marketing* 30(2) 33–44.
29. Andreassen, T. W. (1995) Small, High Cost Countries Strategy for Attracting MNC's Global Investments, *International Journal of Public Sector Management* 8(3), 110–18.
30. Ravald, A. and C. Grönroos (1996) The Value Concept and Relationship Marketing, *European Journal of Marketing* 30(2), 19–30.
31. Takala, T. and O. Uusitalo (1996) An Alternative View of Relationship Marketing: A Framework for Ethical Analysis, *European Journal of Marketing* 30(2), 45–60.
32. Geyskens, I., J.-B. E. M. Steenkamp and N. Kumar (1998) Generalizations About Trust in Marketing Channel Relationships Using Meta-Analysis, *International Journal of Research in Marketing* 15, 223–48; and Selnes, F. (1998) Antecedents and Consequences of Trust and Satisfaction in Buyer–Seller Relationships, *European Journal of Marketing* 32(3/4), 305–22.
33. See e.g. Ford, D. (1980) The Development of Buyer–Seller Relationships in Industrial Markets, *European Journal of Marketing* 14(5/6), 339–53; Hakansson, H. (1982) *International Marketing and Purchasing of Industrial Goods: An Interaction Approach*, New York: Wiley; Turnbull, P. W. and M. T. Cunningham (1981) *International Marketing and Purchasing*, London: Macmillan; Turnbull, P. W. and J. P. Valla (1986) *Strategies for Industrial Marketing*, London: Croom-Helm.
34. Thornhill, J. and A. Rawsthorn (1992) Why Sparks are Flying, *Financial Times*, 8 January, 12.
35. Pollack, B. (1999) The State of Internet Marketing, *Direct Marketing*, January, 18–22.
36. Bowen, D. (2002) The Hidden Art of Persuading Your Customers to Click Here, *Financial Times*, 9 July, 16.
37. Ford (1980) op. cit.
38. Thornhill and Rawsthorn (1992) op. cit.
39. See Lovelock, C. H. (1983) Classifying Services to Gain Strategic Marketing Insight, *Journal of Marketing* 47, Summer, 9–20; Wray, B., A. Palmer and D. Bejou (1994) Using Neural Network Analysis to Evaluate Buyer–Seller Relationships, *European Journal of Marketing* 28(10), 32–48.
40. See Shaw, V. (1994) The Marketing Strategies of British and German Companies, *European Journal of Marketing* 28(7), 30–43; Meissner, H. G. (1986) A Structural Comparison of Japanese and German Marketing Strategies, *Irish Marketing Review* 1, Spring, 21–31.
41. Jackson, B. B. (1985) Build Customer Relationships that Last, *Harvard Business Review*, Nov–Dec, 120–5.
42. Bannister, N. (1999) 21,000 Go in Nissan Rescue, *Guardian*, 19 October, 22.
43. Milner, M. and N. Bannister (1999) op. cit.
44. Hayward, D. (2002) Promise of Big Benefits in the B2B Arena, *Financial Times*, 1 May, 5.
45. Zineldin, M. (1998) Towards an Ecological Collaborative Relationship Management: A 'Co-operative Perspective', *European Journal of Marketing* 32(11/12), 1138–64.
46. London, S. (2002) The Next Core Competence is Getting Personal, *Financial Times*, 13 December, 14.
47. Shipley, D. (1991) Key Customer Services, private papers.
48. Jackson (1985) op. cit., 127.

Chapter 5

1. National Statistics (2003) Labour Market Trends, Office for National Statistics: London, S48–S49.
2. Abell, J. N. (1990) Europe 1992: Promises and Prognostications, *Financial Executive* 6(1), 37–41.
3. Mercado S., R. Welford, and K. Prescott (2001) *European Business: An Issue-Based Approach*, Harlow: FT Pearson.
4. Mercado, Welford and Prescott (2001) op. cit.
5. Mercado, Welford and Prescott (2001) op. cit.
6. Johnson, D and C. Turner (2000) *European Business*, London: Routledge.
7. Stone, N. (1989) The Globalization of Europe: An Interview with Wisse Dekker, *Harvard Business Review*, May–June, 90–5.
8. Friberg, E. G. (1989) 1992: Moves Europeans are Making, *Harvard Business Review*, May–June, 85–9.
9. Drucker, P. K. (1988) Strategies for Survival in Europe in 1993, *McKinsey Quarterly*, autumn, 41–5.
10. Lorenz, C. (1992) Transparent Moves to European Unity, *Financial Times*, 24 July, 16.
11. Friberg (1989) op. cit.
12. Guido, G. (1991) Implementing a Pan European Marketing Strategy, *Long Range Planning* 24(5), 23–33.
13. Quelch, J. A. and R. D. Buzzell (1989) Marketing Moves through EU Crossroads, *Sloan Management Review* 31(1), 63–74.
14. Whitelock, J. and E. Kalpaxoglou (1991) Standardized Advertising for the Single European Market? An Exploratory Study, *European Business Review* 91(3), 4–8.
15. Geroski, P. and K. P. Gugler (2001) *Corporate Growth Convergence in Europe*, Centre for Economic Performance, Discussion Paper 2838.
16. Quelch, J. A., E. Joachimsthaler and J. L. Nueno (1991) After the Wall: Marketing Guidelines for Eastern Europe, *Sloan Business Review*, winter, 82–93.
17. Fairlamb, D. and J. Rossant (2002) Mega Europe, *Business Week*, 18 November, 23–30.
18. Brown, P. (1992) Rise of Women Key to Population Curb, *Guardian*, 30 April, 8.
19. Roberto, E. (1975) *Strategic Decision-Making in a Social Program: The Case of Family-Planning Diffusion*, Lexington, Mass: Lexington Books.
20. James, D. (2001) B2-4B Spells Profits, *Marketing News*, 5 November, 13.
21. Haut Conseil de la Population et de la Famille (1989) *Vieillissement et Emploi, Vieillissement et Travail*, Paris: Documentation Française, 31.
22. Johnson, P. (1990) Our Ageing Population: The Implications for Business and Government, *Long Range Planning* 23(2), 55–62.
23. Johnson (1990) op. cit.
24. Mole, J. (1990) *Mind Your Manners*, London: Industrial Society.
25. Wolfe (1991) The 'Eurobuyer'; How European Businesses Buy, *Marketing Intelligence and Planning* 9(5), 9–15.
26. Writers, F. T. (1992) Queuing for Flawed Fantasy, *Financial Times*, 13/14 June, 5.

27. For a discussion of some green marketing issues see Pujari, D. and G. Wright (1999) Integrating Environmental Issues into Product Development: Understanding the Dimensions of Perceived Driving Forces and Stakeholders, *Journal of Euromarketing* 7(4), 43–63; Peattie, K. and A. Ringter (1994) Management and the Environment in the UK and Germany: A Comparison, *European Management Journal* 12(2), 216–25.
28. Buxton, P. (2000) Companies with a Social Conscience, *Marketing*, 27 April, 33–4.
29. Slavin, T. (2000) Canny Companies Come Clean, *Observer*, 27 June, 16.
30. Anonymous (2002) Irresponsibility, *Economist*, 23 November, 80.
31. Crowe, R. (2001) Corporate Gloss Obscures the Hard Facts, *Financial Times*, 11 December, 18.
32. Anderson, P. (1999) Give and Take, *Marketing Week*, 26 August, 39–41.
33. Anderson (1999) op. cit.
34. Berkowitz, E. N., R. A. Kerin, S. W. Hartley and W. Rudelius (2000) *Marketing*, Boston, MA: McGraw-Hill.
35. Reed, C. (2000) Ethics Frozen Out in the Ben & Jerry Ice Cream War, *Observer*, 13 February, 3; Anonymous (2000) Slippery Slopes, *Economist*, 15 April, 85.
36. Business Portrait (1997) Early Riser Reaches the Top, *European*, 17–23 April, 32.
37. Hadjikhani, A. and H. Hakansson (1996) Political Actions in Business Networks: A Swedish Case, *International Journal of Research in Marketing* 13, 431–47.
38. Pass, C. and B. Lowes (1992) Maintaining Competitive Markets: UK and EU Merger Policy, *Management Decisions* 30(4), 44–51.
39. Anonymous (2002) Fixing for a Fight, *Economist*, 20 April, 71–2.
40. Ritson, M. (2002) Companies Walk a Tightrope as EU Free Trade Law Begins to Bite, *Marketing*, 7 November, 16.
41. Mitchell, A. (1992) The Ripening of Green Toiletries, *Marketing*, 13 February, 12.
42. Cookson, C. (1992) It Grows on Trees, *Financial Times*, 12 August, 8.
43. See Schypek, J. (1992) Germany on Trial over Green Packaging, *Marketing*, 2 July, 14–16; and Thornhill, J. (1992) The Hiccs Come Out of the Sticks, *Financial Times*, 5 February, 11.
44. Muhlbacker, H., M. Botschen and W. Beutelmeyer (1997) The Changing Consumer in Austria, *International Journal of Research in Marketing* 14, 309–20.
45. See Wilkstrom, S. R. (1997) The Changing Consumer in Sweden, *International Journal of Research in Marketing* 14, 261–75; Laaksonen, P., M. Laaksonen and K. Moller (1998) The Changing Consumer in Finland, *International Journal of Research in Marketing* 15, 169–80.
46. Schypek (1992) op. cit.
47. Cane, A. (2002) Far From Up and Running, *Financial Times Creative Business*, 18 June, 5.
48. McCartney, N. (2002) The Generation Gap, *Financial Times Wireless Report*, 16 October, 2–5.
49. Nakamoto, N. (2001) A Pioneering But Risky Mobile Call, *Financial Times*, 1 October, 18.
50. Anonymous (1993) Europe's Technology Policy: How Not to Catch Up, *Economist*, 9 January, 21–3.
51. Daniel, C. (2001) Psion Opts to Close its Future in Handheld Organisers, *Financial Times*, 12 July, 18.
52. Littlewood, F. (1999) Driven by Technology, *Marketing*, 11 March, 9.
53. Ansoff, H. I. (1991) *Implementing Strategic Management*, Englewood Cliffs, NJ: Prentice-Hall.
54. Brownlie, D. (2002) Environmental Analysis, in Baker, M. J. (ed.) *The Marketing Book*, Butterworth-Heinemann, Oxford.
55. Brownlie (2002) op. cit.
56. Diffenbach, J. (1983) Corporate Environmental Analysis in Large US Corporations, *Long Range Planning* 16(3), 107–16.

Chapter 6

1. Van Bruggen, A., A. Smidts and B. Wierenga (1996) The Impact of the Quality of a Marketing Decision Support System: An Experimental Study, *International Journal of Research in Marketing* 13, 331–43.
2. Jobber, D. and C. Rainbow (1977) A Study of the Development and Implementation of Marketing Information Systems in British Industry, *Journal of the Marketing Research Society* 19(3), 104–11.
3. Jain, S. C. (1999) *Marketing Planning and Strategy*, South Western Publishing.
4. Moutinho, L. and M. Evans (1992) *Applied Marketing Research*, Colorado Springs, CO: Wokingham: Addison-Wesley, 5.
5. Kotler, P., W. Gregor and W. Rodgers (1977) The Marketing Audit Comes of Age, *Sloan Management Review*, Winter, 25–42.
6. Fletcher, W. (1997) Why Researchers are so Jittery, *Financial Times*, 3 March, 16.
7. ESOMAR Annual Study of the Marketing Research Industry (2001), published by ESOMAR (2000), Amsterdam.
8. Cook, R. (1999) Focus Groups Have to Evolve if they are to Survive, *Campaign*, 9 July, 14.
9. Hemsley, S. (1999) Paid Informers, *Marketing Week*, 19 August, 45–7.
10. Flack, J. (2002) Not So Honest Joe, *Marketing Week*, 26 September, 43.
11. ESOMAR Annual Study of the Marketing Research Industry (2001), published by ESOMAR, Amsterdam.
12. Miles, L. (2002) Making a Research Relationship Work, *Marketing*, 10 October, 29–30.
13. Foss, B. and M. Stone (2001) *Successful Customer Relationship Marketing*, Kogan Page, London.
14. Pritchard, S (2003) Clicking the Habits, *Financial Times IT Review*, 5 February, 4.
15. Crouch, S. and M. Housden (2003) *Marketing Research for Managers*, Oxford: Butterworth-Heinemann, 253.
16. Crouch and Housden (2003) op. cit., 260.
17. Wright, L. T., and M. Crimp (2000) *The Marketing Research Process*, London: Prentice-Hall, 16.
18. Clegg, A. (2001) Policy and Opinion, *Marketing Week*, 27 September, 63–5.
19. Gray, R. (1999) Tracking the Online Audience, *Marketing*, 18 February, 41–3.
20. Goulding, C. (1999) Consumer Research, Interpretive Paradigms and Methodological Ambiguities, *European Journal of Marketing* 33(9/10), 859–73.
21. Peter, J. P., J. C. Olson, and K. G. Grunert (1999) *Consumer Behaviour and Marketing Strategy*, Maidenhead: McGraw-Hill.
22. Cozens, C. (2001) Sharpening the Focus, *Guardian*, 21 May, 58.
23. Earnshaw, D. (2001) Big Brother is Getting on a Bit, *Marketing Week*, 14 June, 36.
24. Gofton, K. (2001) The Search for the Holy Grail, *Campaign*, 15 June, 26–7.
25. James, M. (2002) Big Brother is Watching You, *Marketing Business*, November/December, 26–7.
26. Ritson, M. (2002) The Best Research Comes from Living the Life of Your Customer, *Marketing*, 18 July, 16.
27. Singh, S. (2001) Big Brother Keeps an Eye on Buying Habits, *Marketing Week*, 31 May, 22.
28. Yu, J. and H. Cooper (1983) A Quantitative Review of Research Design Effects on Response Rates to Questionnaires, *Journal of Marketing Research* 20 February, 156–64.
29. Falthzik, A. and S. J. Carroll (1971) Rate of Return for Close v Open-ended Questions in a Mail Survey of Industrial Organisations, *Psychological Reports* 29, 1121–2.
30. O'Dell, W. F. (1962) Personal Interviews or Mail Panels, *Journal of Marketing* 26, 34–9.

31. See Kanuk, L. and C. Beroncon (1975) Mail Surveys and Response Rates: A Literature Review, *Journal of Marketing Research* 12 (November), 440–53; Jobber, D. (1986) Improving Response Rates to Industrial Mail Surveys, *Industrial Marketing Management* 15, 183–95; Jobber, D. and D. O'Reilly (1998) Industrial Mail Surveys: A Methodological Update, *Industrial Marketing Management* 27, 95–107.
32. Murphy (2002) Questions and Answers, *Marketing Business*, April, 37.
33. Anonymous (2002) Audi Shifts Customer Research up a Gear, *Marketing Week*, 21 March, 37.
34. Price, R. (1992) Soccer Diary, *Guardian*, 19 December, 16.
35. See Kotler *et al*. (1977) op. cit.
36. Jobber, D. (1985) Questionnaire Design and Mail Survey Response Rates, *European Research* 13(3), 124–9.
37. Reynolds, N. and A. Diamantopoulos (1998) The Effect of Pretest Method on Error Detection Rates: Experimental Evidence, *European Journal of Marketing* 32(5/6), 480–98.
38. Sigman, A. (2001) The Lie Detectors, *Campaign*, 15 June, 29.
39. Crouch and Housden (2003) op. cit.
40. Jobber, D. and M. Watts (1986) Behavioural Aspects of Marketing Information Systems, *Omega* 14(1), 69–79; Wierenga, B. and P. A. M. Oude Ophis (1997) Marketing Decision Support Systems: Adoption, Use and Satisfaction, *International Journal of Research in Marketing* 14, 275–90.
41. Ackoff, R. L. (1967) Management Misinformation Systems, *Management Science* 14(4) 147–56.
42. Piercy, N. and M. Evans (1983) *Managing Marketing Information*, Beckenham: Croom Helm.
43. See Deshpande, R. and S. Jeffries (1981) Attitude Affecting the Use of Marketing Research in Decision-Making: An Empirical Investigation, in *Educators' Conference Proceedings*, Chicago: American Marketing Association, 1–4; Lee, H., F. Acito and R. L. Day (1987) Evaluation and Use of Marketing Research by Decision Makers: A Behavioural Simulation, *Journal of Marketing Research* 14 (May); 187–96.
44. Schlegelmilch, B. (1998) *Marketing Ethics: An International Perspective*, London: International Thomson Business Press.
45. Benady, D. (2001) Burst Bubbles, *Marketing Week*, 22 November, 25–6.

Chapter 7

1. Steiner, R. (1999) How Mobile Phones Came to the Masses, *Sunday Times*, 31 October, 6.
2. Wind, Y. (1978) Issues and Advances in Segmentation Research, *Journal of Marketing Research*, August, 317–37.
3. Van Raaij, W. F. and T. M. M. Verhallen (1994) Domain-specific Market Segmentation, *European Journal of Marketing* 28(10), 49–66.
4. Sampson, P. (1992) People are People the World Over: The Case for Psychological Market Segmentation, *Marketing and Research Today*, November, 236–44.
5. Hooley, G. J., J. Saunders and N. Piercy (2003) *Marketing Strategy and Competitive Positioning: The Key to Market Success*, Hemel Hempstead: Prentice-Hall, 148.
6. Anonymous (2002) Best Use of Research Award, Campaign Media Awards, 29 November, 25.
7. Cook, V. J. Jr and W. A. Mindak (1984) A Search for Constants: The 'Heavy-User' Revisited!, *Journal of Consumer Marketing* 1(4), 79–81.
8. O'Shaughnessy, J. (1995) *Competitive Marketing: A Strategic Approach*, London: Routledge.
9. Ehrenberg, A. S. C. and G. J. Goodhardt (1978) *Market Segmentation*, New York: J. Walter Thompson.
10. Anonymous (2002) Examples of Excellence, *Marketing*, 2 May, 15.
11. Reed, D. (1995) Knowledge is Power, *Marketing Week*, 9 December, 46–7.
12. Sampson (1992) op. cit.
13. Lord, R. (2002) China's WTO Entry is not a Passport to Profit, *Campaign*, 16 August, 24–5.
14. Oliver, R. (2002) Exploding the Myth, *Campaign*, 16 August, 30.
15. Ackoft, R. L. and J. R. Emsott (1975) Advertising at Anheuser-Busch, Inc., *Sloan Management Review*, Spring, 1–15.
16. Lannon, J. (1991) Developing Brand Strategies across Borders, *Marketing and Research Today*, August, 160–8.
17. Young, S. (1972) The Dynamics of Measuring Unchange, in Haley, R. I. (ed.) *Attitude Research in Transition*, Chicago: American Marketing Association, 61–82.
18. Tynan, A. C. and J. Drayton (1987) Market Segmentation, *Journal of Marketing Management* 2(3), 301–35.
19. Considine, P. (1999) The Young Ones, *Campaign*, 17 September, 31.
20. Green, H. (1999) New Generation, New Media, *Campaign*, 17 September, 34.
21. Willman, J. (1999) Elida Returns to its Youth to Find Secrets of Success, *Financial Times*, 5 November, 16.
22. Bosworth, C. (2002) Playing Hard to Get, *Marketing Business*, Nov./Dec., 24.
23. Ray, A. (2002) Using Outdoor to Target the Young, *Marketing*, 31 January, 25.
24. O'Brien, S. and R. Ford (1988) Can We at Last Say Goodbye to Social Class?, *Journal of the Market Research Society* 30(3), 289–332.
25. Kossoff, J. (1988) Europe: Up for Sale, *New Statesman and Society*, 7 October, 43–4.
26. Garrett, A. (1992) Stats, Lies and Stereotypes, *Observer*, 13 December, 26.
27. Mitchell, V.-W. and P. J. McGoldrick (1994) The Role of Geodemographics in Segmenting and Targeting Consumer Markets: A Delphi Study, *European Journal of Marketing* 28(5), 54–72.
28. Hayward, C. (2002) Who, Where, Win, *Marketing Week*, 12 September, 43.
29. Kossoff (1988) op. cit.
30. See Wind, Y. and R. N. Cardozo (1974) Industrial Market Segmentation, *Industrial Marketing Management*, 3, 153–66; R. E. Plank (1985) A Critical Review of Industrial Market Segmentation, *Industrial Marketing Management* 14, 79–91.
31. Wind and Cardozo (1974) op. cit.
32. Moriarty, R. T. (1983) *Industrial Buying Behaviour*, Lexington, Mass: Lexington Books.
33. Corey, R. (1978) *The Organisational Context of Industrial Buying Behaviour*, Cambridge, Mass: Marketing Science Institute, 6–12.
34. See Abell, D. F. and J. S. Hammond (1979) *Strategic Market Planning: Problems and Analytical Approaches*, Hemel Hempstead: Prentice-Hall; G. S. Day (1986) *Analysis for Strategic Market Decisions*, New York: West; Hooley, Saunders and Piercy (2003) op. cit.
35. Walters, D. and D. Knee (1989) Competitive Strategies in Retailing, *Long Range Planning* 22(6), 74–84.
36. Laurance, B. (1990) It was Niche Work if You Could Get It, *Guardian*, 10 February, 12.
37. Richards, H. (1996) Discord Amid the High Notes, *The European*, 16–22 May, 23.
38. Anonymous (2000) Saga, Dealing in Satisfaction, *Observer*, 19 March, 29.
39. Anonymous (2002) Over 60 and Overlooked, *Economist*, 10 August, 57–8.
40. Anonymous (2002) Shades of Grey, *Campaign*, 29 November, 27.
41. Curtis, J. (2002) Grey Hair, Wrinkles and Money to Burn, *FT Creative Business*, 8 October, 8–10.
42. Zikmund, W. G. and M. D'Amico (1999) *Marketing*, St Paul, MN: West, 249.
43. Anonymous (2001) A Long March, *Economist*, 14 July, 79–82.
44. Benady, D. (2003) King Customer, *Marketing Week*, 8 May, 24–7.
45. Ries, A. and J. Trout (2001) *Positioning: The Battle for your Mind*, New York: Warner.

46. Cullen, M. (2001) Fantasy Ireland, *Campaign*, 14 September, 28.
47. Anonymous (2002) Holsten's £15m for Pils Keeps Those Daddies Coming, *The Grocer*, 23 February, 68.
48. Anonymous (2001) Burbridge Shoots Becks, *Creative Review*, June, 13.
49. Clark, A. (2001) The Thin End of the Dynastic Wedge, *Guardian*, 25 July, 24.
50. Hedburg, A. (2001) An American Storm Brewing in the UK, *Marketing Week*, 6 September, 21.
51. Smith, C. (2002) Lager's Success in the UK Reflects Top Quality Marketing, *Marketing*, 15 August, 15.
52. Brech, P. (2000) MacKenzie Plans Sports Revolution, *Marketing*, 20 January, 9.
53. Platford, R. (1997) Fast Track to Approval, *Financial Times*, 24 April, 27.
54. Anonymous (2002) Changing Perceptions, *Marketing Business*, April, 12.
55. Jobber, D. and J. Fahy (2003) *Foundations of Marketing*, Maidenhead: McGraw-Hill.

Chapter 8

1. DeKimpe, M. C., J.-B. E. M. Steenkamp, M. Mellens and P. Vanden Abeele (1997) Decline and Variability in Brand Loyalty, *International Journal of Research in Marketing* 14, 405–20.
2. Chernatony, L. de (1991) Formulating Brand Strategy, *European Management Journal* 9(2), 194–200.
3. K. L. Keller (2003) *Strategic Brand Management*, New Jersey: Pearson.
4. East, R. (1997) *Consumer Behaviour*, Hemel Hempstead: Prentice-Hall Europe.
5. Benady, D. (2002) Copycat Packaging, *Marketing Week*, 5 December, 31.
6. Charles, G (2003) Crunch Time for Copycats, *Marketing Week*, 13 February, 24–7.
7. Smith, R. (2002) Key to Tapping into a Premium Market, *Marketing*, 4 April, 25.
8. Simms, J. (2001) The Value of Disclosure, *Marketing*, 2 August, 26–7.
9. De Chernatony, L. and M. H. B. McDonald (1998) *Creating Powerful Brands*, Oxford: Butterworth-Heinemann.
10. Doyle, P. (2001) *Marketing Management and Strategy*, Hemel Hempstead: Prentice-Hall.
11. Buzzell, R. and B. Gale (1987) *The PIMS Principles*, London: Collier Macmillan.
12. Reyner, M. (1996) Is Advertising the Answer?, *Admap*, September, 23–6.
13. Ehrenberg, A. S. C., G. J. Goodhardt and T. P. Barwise (1990) Double Jeopardy Revisited, *Journal of Marketing* 54 (July), 82–91.
14. See S. King (1991) Brand Building in the 1990s, *Journal of Marketing Management* 7(1), 3–14; and P. Doyle (1989) Building Successful Brands: The Strategic Options, *Journal of Marketing Management* 5(1), 77–95.
15. Buzzell and Gale (1987) op. cit.
16. Lemmink, J. and H. Kaspar (1994) Competitive Reactions to Product Quality Improvements in Industrial Markets, *European Journal of Marketing* 28(12), 50–68.
17. Brierley, S (2002) Avoiding the Bland Trap During Times of Recession, *Marketing Week*, 24 October, 27.
18. Simms J. (2002) Can Brands Grow Without Ads?, *Marketing*, 2 May, 22–3.
19. King (1991) op. cit.
20. Pieters, R. and L. Warlop (1999) Visual Attention during Brand Choice: The Impact of Time Pressure and Task Motivation, *International Journal of Research in Marketing* 16, 1–16.
21. For example, Urban, G. L., T. Carter, S. Gaskin and Z. Mucha (1986) Market Share Rewards to Pioneering Brands: An Empirical Analysis and Strategic Implications, *Management Science* 32 (June), 645–59, showed that for frequently purchased consumer goods the second firm in the market could expect only 71 per cent of the market share of the pioneer and the third only 58 per cent of the pioneer's share. Also Lambkin, M. (1992) Pioneering New Markets: A Comparison of Market Share Winners and Losers, *International Journal of Research in Marketing* 9(1), 5–22, found that those pioneers that invest heavily from the start in building large production scale, in securing wide distribution and in promoting their products achieve the strongest competitive position and earn the highest long-term returns.
22. Leibernan, M. B. and D. B. Montgomery (1988) First Mover Advantage, *Strategic Management Journal* 9, 41–56.
23. Nayak, P. R. (1991) *Managing Rapid Technological Development*, London: A. D. Little.
24. Oakley, P. (1996) High-tech NPD Success through Faster Overseas Launch, *European Journal of Marketing* 30(8), 75–81.
25. Reinertsen, R. G. (1983) Whodunit? The Search for the New Product Killers, *Electronic Business*, 9 July, 62–6.
26. Tellis, G. and P. Golder (1995) First to Market, First to Fail? Real Causes of Enduring Market Leadership, *Sloan Management Review* 37(2), 65–76.
27. Cadbury, A. (1988) *Annual Report of Cadbury Schweppes*, Bournville.
28. King (1991) op. cit.
29. Wilkinson, A. (1999) Trebor Slims Down for Leaner Branding, *Marketing Week*, 26 August, 20.
30. Miller, R. (1999) Science Joins Art in Brand Naming, *Marketing*, 27 May, 31–2.
31. Anonymous (2002) You Wait All Year Then, *Marketing Week*, 24 October, 63.
32. Benady, D. (2002) The Trouble with Facelifts, *Marketing Week*, 6 June, 21–3.
33. See Keller, K.L. (2003) *Strategic Brand Management*, New Jersey: Pearson Education; Riezebos, R. (2003) *Brand Management*, Harlow: Pearson Education.
34. Thurtle, G. (2002) Papering over the Cracks, *Marketing Week*, 7 March, 25–7.
35. Furness, V. (2002) Lego Revamp to Axe Sub-Brands, *Marketing Week*, 17 October, 9.
36. Rogers, D. (2001) MyTravel Brand Takes on World's Top Operators, *Marketing*, 20 November, 3.
37. Keller (2003) op. cit.
38. Kapferer, J.-N. (1997) *Strategic Brand Management*, London: Kogan Page.
39. Pandya, N. (1999) Soft Selling Soap Brings Hard Profit, *Guardian*, 2 October, 28.
40. Beale, C. (1999) Tommy Hilfiger Kicks Off £8m Media Review, *Campaign*, 15 October, 5.
41. Sullivan, M. W. (1990) Measuring Image Spillovers in Umbrella-branded Products, *Journal of Business*, July, 309–29.
42. Sharp, B. M. (1990) The Marketing Value of Brand Extension, *Marketing Intelligence and Planning* 9(7), 9–13.
43. Aaker, D. A. and K. L. Keller (1990) Consumer Evaluation of Brand Extensions, *Journal of Marketing* 54 (January), 27–41.
44. Aaker, D. A. (1990) Brand Extensions: The Good, the Bad and the Ugly, *Sloan Management Review*, Summer, 47–56.
45. Bottomley, P. A. and J. R. Doyle (1996) The Formation of Attitudes towards Brand Extensions: Testing and Generalising Aaker and Keller's Model, *International Journal of Research in Marketing* 13, 365–77.
46. Roberts, C. J. and G. M. McDonald (1989) Alternative Naming Strategies: Family versus Individual Brand Names, *Management Decision* 27(6), 31–7.

47. Grime, I., A. Diamantopoulos and G. Smith (2002) Consumer Evaluations of Extensions and their Effects on the Core Brand: Key Issues and Research Propositions, *European Journal of Marketing* 36(11/12), 1415–38.
48. Saunders, J. (1990) Brands and Valuations, *International Journal of Advertising* 9, 95–110.
49. Bennett, R. C. and R. G. Cooper (1981) The Misuse of the Marketing Concept: An American Tragedy, *Business Horizons*, Nov.–Dec., 51–61.
50. Sharp (1990) op. cit.
51. Prickett, R. (2003) Listen … Selectively, *Marketing Week*, 23 January, 43.
52. Aaker (1990) op. cit.
53. Riezebos, R. (2003) *Brand Management*, Harlow: Pearson Education.
54. Chandiramani, R. (2002) Lego Strikes Deal with Nike for Kid's 'Bionicle' Trainers, *Marketing*, 7 November, 1.
55. Aaker, D. A. and E. Joachimsthaler (2000) *Brand Leadership*, New York: Free Press.
56. Brech, P. (2002) Ford Focus Targets Women with *Elle* Tie, *Marketing*, 8 August, 7.
57. Keller, K.L. (2003) *Strategic Brand Management*, New Jersey: Pearson.
58. Kapferer, J.-N. (1997) *Strategic Brand Management*, London: Kogan Page.
59. Levitt, T. (1983) The Globalisation of Marketing, *Harvard Business Review*, May–June, 92–102.
60. Steenkamp, J.-B. E. M., R. Batra and D. L. Alden (2003) How Perceived Brand Globalness Creates Brand Value, *Journal of International Business Studies* 34(1), 53–65.
61. Barwise, P. and T. Robertson (1992) Brand Portfolios, *European Management Journal* 10(3), 277–85.
62. Halliburton, C. and R. Hünerberg (1993) Pan-European Marketing-Myth or Reality, *Proceedings of the European Marketing Academy Conference*, Barcelona, May, 490–518.
63. Kern, H., H. Wagner and R. Hassis (1990) European Aspects of a Global Brand: The BMW Case, *Marketing and Research Today*, February, 47–57.
64. Barwise and Robertson (1992) op. cit.
65. Riel, C. B. M. and J. M. T. Balmer (1997) Corporate Identity: The Concept, its Measurement and Management, *European Journal of Marketing* 31(5/6), 340–55.
66. Balmer, J. M. T. and S. A. Greyser (2002) Managing the Multiple Identities of the Corporation, *California Management Review* 44(3), 72–86.
67. Balmer, J. M. T. and S. A. Greyser (2003) *Revealing the Corporation*, London: Routledge.
68. Gander, P. (2000) Image Bank, *Marketing Week*, 16 March, 43–4.
69. Martin, M. and I. Heath (1989) BA Redesign was Global Failure, *Marketing*, 2 December, 21.
70. See Benady, D. (2002) The Trouble with Facelifts, *Marketing Week*, 6 June, 20–3; Cozens, C. (2002) Don't Blame Me for Consignia, *Guardian*, 8 May, 8–9; Thurtle, G. (2002) Papering Over the Cracks, *Marketing Week*, 7 March, 25–7.
71. Balmer and Greyser (2003) op. cit. The term 'AC^{2}ID test' was trademarked by J. M. T. Balmer in 1999.
72. Balmer and Greyser (2003) op. cit.
73. See Balmer, J. M. T. and G. B. Soenen (1999) The ACID Test of Corporate Identity Management, *Journal of Marketing Management* 15, 69–92, Balmer and Greyser (2003) op. cit. The REDS^2 Acid Test Process was trademarked by J. M. T. Balmer in 1999.
74. Balmer and Soenen (1999) op. cit.
75. Davies, G. with R. Chun, R. V. Da Silva and S. Roper (2003) *Corporate Reputation and Competitiveness*, London: Routledge. This study provides empirical evidence of a link between corporate identity/image, customer and employee satisfaction, and financial performance.
76. Smith, N. C. (1995) Marketing Strategies for the Ethics Era, *Sloan Management Review*, Summer, 85–97. See also T. W. Dunfee, N. C. Smith and W. T. Ross Jr (1999) Social Contracts and Marketing Ethics, *Journal of Marketing* 63 (July), 14–32.
77. Young, R. (1999) First Read the Label, Then Add a Pinch of Salt, *The Times*, 30 November, 2–4.
78. Anonymous (2001) An End to the Packet Racket, *Marketing Week*, 2 August, 3; and Benady, D. (2001) Will They Eat Their Words, *Marketing Week*, 2 August, 24–6.
79. Klein, N. (2000). *No Logo. Taking Aim at the Brand Bullies*. London: HarperCollins.
80. www.nike.com/Europe.
81. Oxfam Community Aid Abroad: the Nikewatch Campaign. Website: http://www/caa.org.au/campaigns/nike/index.html.

Chapter 9

1. Polli, R. and V. Cook (1969) Validity of the Product Life Cycle, *Journal of Business*, October, 385–400.
2. Day, G. (1997) Strategies for Surviving a Shakeout, *Harvard Business Review*, March–April, 92–104.
3. Doyle, P. (1989) Building Successful Brands: The Strategic Options, *Journal of Marketing Management* 5(1), 77–95.
4. Vakratsas, D. and T. Ambler (1999) How Advertising Works: What Do We Really Know? *Journal of Marketing* 63, January, 26–43.
5. Chandiramani, R. (2002) Mobile Phone Advertising Enters a New Era, *Marketing*, 25 April, 15.
6. Cotton, D. and S. Singh (2003) Young, Hip and Upwardly Mobile, *Marketing Week*, 9 January, 28.
7. Keegan, V. (2003) Greater Expectations, *Guardian Online*, 20 March, 5.
8. Malkani, G. (2002) Devices and Stratagems to Make Mobile Phones Sexy Again, *Financial Times*, 3 February, 12.
9. See Greenley, G. E. and B. L. Barus (1994) A Corporative Study of Product Launch and Elimination Decisions in UK and US Companies, *European Journal of Marketing* 28(2) 5–29; Hart, S. J. (1989) Product Deletion and Effects of Strategy, *European Journal of Marketing* 23(10), 6–17; Avlonitis, G. J. (1987) Linking Different Types of Product Elimination Decisions to their Performance Outcome, *International Journal of Research in Marketing* 4(1), 43–57.
10. Cline, C. E. and B. P. Shapiro (1979) *Cumberland Metal Industries (A): Case Study*, Cambridge, Mass: Harvard Business School.
11. Polli and Cook (1969) op. cit.
12. Dhalia, N. K. and S. Yuspeh (1976) Forget the Product Life Cycle Concept, *Harvard Business Review*, Jan.–Feb., 102–12.
13. Thatcher, M. (2002) Reviving Brands, *Marketing Business*, February, 29–30.
14. Shah, R. (2002) Managing a Portfolio to Unlock Real Potential, *Financial Times*, 21 August, 13.
15. Benady (2002) Dormant for Long Enough, *Marketing Week*, 29 August, 20–3.
16. Mason, T. (2002) Nestlé Sells Big Brands in Core Category Focus, *Marketing*, 7 February, 5.
17. Shah, R. (2002) Managing a Portfolio to Unlock Real Potential, *Financial Times*, 21 August, 13.
18. Singh, S. (2002) Old Brands, New Brands, *Marketing Week*, 11 July, 24–7.
19. Brierley, D. (1997) Spring-Cleaning a Statistical Wonderland, *European*, 20–26 February, 28.
20. Hedley, B. (1977) Boston Consulting Group Approach to the Business Portfolio, *Long Range Planning*, February, 9–15.
21. See e.g. Day, G. S. and R. Wensley (1983) Marketing Theory with a Strategic Orientation, *Journal of Marketing*, Fall, 79–89; Haspslagh, P. (1982) Portfolio Planning: Uses and Limits, *Harvard Business Review*, Jan.–Feb., 58–73; Wensley, R. (1981) Strategic Marketing: Betas, Boxes and Basics, *Journal of Marketing*, Summer, 173–83.

22. Hofer, C. and D. Schendel (1978) *Strategy Formulation: Analytical Concepts*, St Paul, MN: West.
23. Hedley (1977) op. cit.
24. Ansoff, H. L. (1957) Strategies for Diversification, *Harvard Business Review*, Sept.–Oct., 114.
25. Mitchell, A. (2003) A Plea From the Top for a Marketing Revolution, *Marketing Week*, 20 March, 34–5.
26. Ansoff, I. (1957) Strategies for Diversification, *Harvard Business Review*, Sept.–Oct., 113–24.
27. Prahalad, C. K. and G. Hamel (1990) The Core Competence of the Corporation, *Harvard Business Review*, May–June, 79–91.

Chapter 10

1. Pearson, D. (1993) Invent, Innovate and Improve, *Marketing*, 8 April, 15.
2. Richard, H. (1996) Why Competitiveness is a Dirty Word in Scandinavia, *European*, 6–12 June, 24.
3. Doyle, P. (1997) From the Top, *Guardian*, 2 August, 17.
4. Murphy, D. (2000) Innovate or Die, *Marketing Business*, May, 16–18.
5. Booz, Allen and Hamilton (1982) *New Product Management for the 1980s*, New York: Booz, Allen and Hamilton, Inc.
6. Hultink, E., A. Griffin, H. S. J. Robben and S. Hart (1998) In Search of Generic Launch Strategies for New Products, *International Journal of Research in Marketing* 15, 269–85.
7. Matthews, V. (2002) Caution Versus Creativity, *Financial Times*, 17 June, 12.
8. See Gupta, A. K. and D. Wileman (1990) Improving R&D/Marketing Relations: R&D Perspective, *R&D Management* 20(4), 277–90; Koshler, R. (1991) Produkt—Innovationasmanagement als Erfolgsfaktor, in Mueller-Boehling, D. *et al.* (eds) *Innovations—und Technologiemanagement*, Stuttgart: C. E. Poeschel Verlagi; Shrivastava, P. and W. E. Souder (1987) The Strategic Management of Technological Innovation: A Review and a Model, *Journal of Management Studies* 24(1), 24–41.
9. Aceland, H. (1999) Harnessing Internal Innovation, *Marketing*, 22 July, 27–8.
10. See Booz, Allen and Hamilton (1982) op. cit.; Maidique, M. A. and B. J. Zirger (1984) A Study of Success and Failure in Product Innovation: The Case of the US Electronics Industry, *IEEE Transactions in Engineering Management*, EM-31 (November), 192–203.
11. See Bergen, S. A., R. Miyajima and C. P. McLaughlin (1988) The R&D/Production Interface in Four Developed Countries, *R&D Management* 18(3), 201–16; Hegarty, W. H. and R. C. Hoffman (1990) Product/Market Innovations: A Study of Top Management Involvement among Four Cultures, *Journal of Product Innovation Management* 7, 186–99; Cooper, R. G. (1979) The Dimensions of Industrial New Product Success and Failure, *Journal of Marketing* 43 (Summer), 93–103; Johne, A. and P. Snelson (1988) Auditing Product Innovation Activities in Manufacturing Firms, *R&D Management* 18(3), 227–33.
12. Aceland, H. (1999) op. cit.
13. Francis, T. (2000) Divine Intervention, *Marketing Business*, May, 20–2.
14. Kanter, R. M. (1983) *The Change Masters*, New York: Simon & Schuster.
15. Mitchell, A. (2003) The Tyranny of the Brand, *Marketing Business*, January, 17.
16. Done, K. (1992) From Design Studio to New Car Showroom, *Financial Times*, 11 May, 10.
17. Buxton, P. (2000) Time to Market is NPD's Top Priority, *Marketing*, 30 March, 35–6.
18. Chaston, I. (1999) *New Marketing Strategies*, London: Sage.
19. Daniel, C. (2001) Lifelike Models that Leap off the Screen, *Financial Times*, 24 December, 8.
20. See Hise, R. T., L. O'Neal, A. Parasuraman and J. U. NcNeal (1990) Marketing/R&D Interaction in New Product Development: Implications for New Product Success Rates, *Journal of Product Innovation Management* 7, 142–55; Johne and Snelson (1988) op. cit.; Walsh, W. J. (1990) Get the Whole Organisation Behind New Product Development, *Research in Technological Management*, Nov.–Dec., 32–6.
21. Frey, D. (1991) Learning the Ropes: My Life as a Product Champion, *Harvard Business Review*, Sept.–Oct., 46–56.
22. Gupta, A. K. and D. Wileman (1991) Improving R&D/Marketing Relations in Technology-based Companies: Marketing's Perspective, *Journal of Marketing Management* 7(1), 25–46.
23. See Dwyer, L. M. (1990) Factors Affecting the Proficient Management of Product Innovation, *International Journal of Technological Management* 5(6), 721–30; Gupta and Wileman (1990) op. cit.; Adler, P. S., H. E. Riggs and S. C. Wheelwright (1989) Product Development Know-How, *Sloan Management Review* 4, 7–17.
24. Brentani, U. de (1991) Success Factors in Developing New Business Services, *European Journal of Marketing* 15(2), 33–59; Johne, A. and C. Storey (1998) New Source Development: A Review of the Literature and Annotated Bibliography, *European Journal of Marketing* 32(3/4), 184–251.
25. Cooper, R. G. and E. J. Kleinschmidt (1986) An Investigation into the New Product Process: Steps, Deficiencies and Impact, *Journal of Product Innovation Management*, June, 71–85.
26. Nijssen, E. J. and K. F. M. Lieshout (1995) Awareness, Use and Effectiveness of Models and Methods for New Product Development, *European Journal of Marketing* 29(10), 27–44.
27. Hamel, G. and C. K. Prahalad (1991) Corporate Imagination and Expeditionary Marketing, *Harvard Business Review*, July–August, 81–92.
28. Bower, F. (2000) Latin Spirit, *Marketing Business*, October, 24–5.
29. Parkinson, S. T. (1982) The Role of the User in Successful New Product Development, *R&D Management* 12, 123–31.
30. Nevens, T. M., G. L. Summe, and B. Uttal (1990) Commercializing Technology: What the Best Companies Do, *Harvard Business Review*, May–June, 154–63.
31. Johne, A. (1992) Don't Let your Customers Lead You Astray in Developing New Products, *European Management Journal* 10(1), 80–4.
32. Hamel, G. (1999) Bringing Silicon Valley Inside, *Harvard Business Review*, Sept.–Oct., 71–84.
33. Hamel, G. and C. K. Prahaled (1991) Corporate Imagination and Expeditionary Marketing, *Harvard Business Review*, July–August, 81–92.
34. Hunt, J. W. (2002) Crucibles of Innovation, *Financial Times*, 18 January, 18.
35. Leifer, R. G., C. O'Connor and M. Rice (2001) Implementing Radical Innovation in Mature Firms: The Role of Hubs, *Academy of Management Executives* 15(3) 61–70.
36. Weston, C. (1992) Brand New Ideas to Help Adapt to a Fast-Changing Marketplace, *Guardian*, 2 June, 12.
37. Jobber, D., J. Saunders, G. Hooley, B. Gilding and J. Hatton-Smooker (1989) Assessing the Value of a Quality Assurance Certificate for Software: An Exploratory Investigation, *MIS Quarterly*, March, 19–31.
38. Edgett, S. and S. Jones (1991) New Product Development in the Financial Services Industry: A Case Study, *Journal of Marketing Management* 7(3), 271–84.
39. Matthews, V. (2002) Caution Versus Creativity, *Financial Times*, 17 June, 12.
40. Wheelwright, S. and K. Clark (1992) *Revolutionizing Product Development*, New York: Free Press.
41. Baxter, A. (1992) Shifting to High Gear, *Financial Times*, 14 May, 15.
42. Pullin, J. (1997) Time is Money on the Way to Market, *Guardian*, 5 April, 99.

43. Parkinson (1982) op. cit.
44. Rogers, E. M. (1983) *Diffusion of Innovations*, New York: Free Press.
45. Rogers (1983) op. cit.
46. Zinkmund, W. G. and M. D'Amico (1999) *Marketing*, St Paul, MN: West.
47. Easingwood, C. and C. Beard (1989) High Technology Launch Strategies in the UK, Industrial *Marketing Management* 18, 125–38.
48. See Mahajan, V., E. Muller and R. Kerin (1987) Introduction Strategy for New Product with Positive and Negative Word-of-Mouth, *Management Science* 30, 1389–404; Robertson, T. S. and H. Gatignon (1986) Competitive Effects on Technology Diffusion, *Journal of Marketing* 50 (July), 1–12; Tzokas, N. and M. Saren (1992) Innovation Diffusion: The Emerging Role of Suppliers Versus the Traditional Dominance of Buyers, *Journal of Marketing Management* 8(1), 69–80.
49. Daniel, C. (2001) Psion Quits Handheld Organiser Market, *Financial Times*, 12 July, 1.
50. Saunders, J. and D. Jobber (1994) Product Replacement Strategies: Occurrence and Concurrence, *Journal of Product Innovation Management* (November).
51. Nevens, Summe and Uttal (1990) op. cit.
52. Brown, R. (1991) Managing the 'S' Curves of Innovation, *Journal of Marketing Management* 7(2), 189–202.
53. Murphy, D. (2000) Innovate or Die, *Marketing Business*, May, 16–19.
54. Gatignon, H., T. S. Robertson and A. J. Fein (1997) Incumbent Defence Strategies Against New Product Entry, *International Journal of Research in Marketing* 14, 163–76.
55. Bowman, D. and H. Gatignon (1995) Determinants of Competitor Response Time to a New Product Introduction, *Journal of Marketing Research* 33, February, 42–53.

Chapter 11

1. Cook, R. (1999) Does Price Advertising Kill Brands, *Campaign*, 16 April, 19.
2. Mitchell, A. (1999a) Technology Breaks Chain Linking Price with Value, *Marketing Week*, 11 November, 54–5.
3. Mitchell, A. (1999b) Lure of Discounters Will Raise Price Awareness, *Marketing Week*, 9 December, 9.
4. Rodgers, D. (1999) How Many Brands Can Fly the Budget Skies, *Marketing*, 16 September, 15.
5. Murphy, D. (2000) Innovate or Die, *Marketing Business*, May, 16–9.
6. Shapiro, B. P. and B. B. Jackson (1978) Industrial Pricing to Meet Customer Needs, *Harvard Business Review*, Nov.–Dec., 119–27.
7. See Shipley, D. (1981) Pricing Objectives in British Manufacturing Industry, *Journal of Industrial Economics* 29 (June), 429–43; Jobber, D. and G. J. Hooley (1987) Pricing Behaviour in the UK Manufacturing and Service Industries, *Managerial and Decision Economics* 8, 167–71.
8. Christopher, M. (1982) Value-in-Use Pricing, *European Journal of Marketing* 16(5), 35–46.
9. Edelman, F. (1965) Art and Science of Competitive Bidding, *Harvard Business Review*, July–August, 53–66.
10. Brown, R. (1991) The S-Curves of Innovation, *Journal of Marketing Management* 7(2), 189–202.
11. Simon, H. (1992) Pricing Opportunities—and How to Exploit Them, *Sloan Management Review*, Winter, 55–65.
12. Jobber, D. and D. Shipley (1998) Marketing-Orientated Pricing Strategies, *Journal of General Management* 23(4), 19–34.
13. Simon (1992) op. cit.
14. Abell, D. F. and J. S. Hammond (1979) *Strategic Marketing Planning*, Englewood Cliffs, NJ: Prentice-Hall.
15. Eastham, J. (2002) Prices Down, Numbers Up, *Marketing Week*, 20 June, 22–5.
16. Gabor, A. (1977) *Price as a Quality Indicator in Pricing: Principles and Practices*, London: Heinemann.
17. Simon, H. and E. Kucher (1992) The European Pricing Time Bomb: And How to Cope with it, *European Management Journal* 10(2), 136–45.
18. Kucher, E. and H. Simon (1987) Durchbruch bei der Preisentscheidung: Conjoint-Measurement, eine neue Technik zur Gewinnoptimierung, *Harvard Manager* 3, 36–60.
19. Cattin, P. and D. R. Wittink (1989) Commercial Use of Conjoint Analysis: An Update, *Journal of Marketing*, July, 91–6.
20. Simon, H. (1992) Pricing Opportunities and How to Exploit Them, *Sloan Management Review*, Winter, 62. Copyright © 1992 by the Sloan Management Review Association. Reproduced with permission. All rights reserved.
21. Moutinho, L. and M. Evans (1992) *Applied Marketing Research*, Wokingham: Addison-Wesley, 161.
22. Forbis, J. L. and N. T. Mehta (1979) Economic Value to the Customer, McKinsey Staff Paper, Chicago: McKinsey & Co., Inc., February, 1–10.
23. Erickson, G. M. and J. K. Johansson (1985) The Role of Price in Multi-Attribute Product-Evaluations, *Journal of Consumer Research*, September, 195–9.
24. Anonymous (1998) Grey Market Ruling Delights Brand Owners, *Financial Times*, 17 July, 8.
25. Cateora, P. R., J. L. Graham and P. N. Ghauri (2002) *International Marketing*, London: McGraw-Hill.
26. Mercado, S. Welford, R. and K. Prescott (2000) *European Business: An Issue-Based Approach*, Harlow: FT Prentice-Hall.
27. Anonymous (2002) Consumers Fall for Levi Message, *Guardian*, 21 November, 25.
28. Osborn, A. (2001) Levi's Wins Fight to Halt Tesco Price Cuts, *Guardian*, 21 November, 13.
29. Marn, M. V. and R. L. Rosiello (1992) Managing Price, Gaining Profit, *Harvard Business Review*, Sept.–Oct., 84–94.
30. Anonymous (2002) The Price is Wrong, *Economist*, 25 May, 71–2.
31. Ritson, M. (2002) Who Needs Marketers for Price When Vending Machines Will Do, *Marketing*, 27, June, 16.
32. Simon (1992) op. cit.
33. Simon (1992) op. cit.
34. Schacht, H. (1988) Leading a Company through Change, *Harvard Business School Seminar*, 11 November.
35. Ross, E. B. (1984) Making Money with Proactive Pricing, *Harvard Business Review*, Nov.–Dec., 145–55.
36. Mercado, Welford and Prescott (2000) op. cit.
37. Sherwood, B. (2003) OFT's Action Man Takes on Price Fixing of Toys, *Financial Times*, 20 February, 3.
38. Mitchell, A. (2000) Why Car Trade is Stalling Over New Pricing Policy, *Marketing Week*, 17 February, 40–1.
39. Griffiths, J. (2000) Dealers Draw up Plan to Import Cheap New Cars, *Financial Times*, 19 January, 1.
40. Anonymous (2001) Fixing a Fat Nation: Why Diets and Gyms Won't Save us from the Obesity Epidemic, *Washington Monthly*, December. Available online at http://www.washingtonmonthly.com/features/2001/0112.farley.cohen.html.
41. BBC News Online (2002) McDonald's Targeted in Obesity Lawsuit, 22 November. Available online at http://news.bbc.co.uk.
42. Godfrey, C. (1989) Factors Influencing the Consumption of Alcohol and Tobacco: The Use and Abuse of Economic Models, *British Journal of Addiction* 84, 1123–38.
43. Key Note (2002) Fast Food & Home Delivery Outlets, 2002 Market Report, Hampton: Key Note Ltd.
44. Young, L.R. and M. Nestle (2002) The Contribution of Expanding Portion Sizes to the US Obesity Epidemic, *American Journal of Public Health* 92, 246–9.
45. http://www.nysd.uscourts.gov/courtweb/pdf/DO2NYSC/03-00649.PDF.
46. Schlegelmilch, B. (1998) *Marketing Ethics: An International Perspective*, London: International Thomson Business Press.

Chapter 12

1. Eagle, L. and P. J. Kitchen (2000) IMC, Brand Communications, and Corporate Cultures, *European Journal of Marketing* 34(5/6), 667–86.
2. Mills, D. (2002) Introduction to Media-Neutral Planning, *Campaign* Report, 8 November, 3.
3. Kleinman, M. (2002) Vauxhall Shifts to a Media-Neutral Stance, *Marketing*, 19 December, 9.
4. Ray, A. (2002) How to Adopt a Neutral Stance, *Marketing*, 27 June, 27.
5. Katz, E., M. Gurevitch and H. Haas (1973) On the Use of the Mass Media for Important Things, *American Sociological Review* 38, 164–81.
6. Crosier, K. (1983) Towards a Praxiology of Advertising, *International Journal of Advertising* 2, 215–32.
7. O'Donohoe, S. (1994) Advertising Uses and Gratifications, *European Journal of Marketing* 28(8/9), 52–75.
8. Wright, L. T. and M. Crimp (2000) *The Marketing Research Process*, London: Prentice-Hall, 180.
9. Jones, J. P. (1991) Over-promise and Under-delivery, *Marketing and Research Today*, November, 195–203.
10. Ehrenberg, A. S. C. (1992) Comments on How Advertising Works, *Marketing and Research Today*, August, 167–9.
11. Ehrenberg (1992) op. cit.
12. Jones (1991) op. cit.
13. Dall'Olmo Riley, F., A. S. C. Ehrenberg, S. B. Castleberry, T. P. Barwise and N. R. Barnard (1997) The Variability of Attitudinal Repeat-Rates, *International Journal of Research in Marketing* 14, 437–50.
14. Jones (1991) op. cit.
15. Ries, A. and J. Trout (2001) *Positioning: The Battle for your Mind*, New York: McGraw-Hill.
16. Aaker, D. A., R. Batra and J. G. Myers (1996) *Advertising Management*, New York: Prentice-Hall.
17. Grey, R. (2002) Fighting Talk, *Marketing*, 20 September, 26.
18. Piercy, N. (1987) The Marketing Budgeting Process: Marketing Management Implications, *Journal of Marketing* 51(4), 45–59.
19. Finch, J. (2000) P&G Brings Delight to the Ad Business, *Guardian*, 2 March, 29.
20. In Ogilvy, D. (1983) *Ogilvy on Advertising*, London: Pan, 70–102.
21. Ogilvy (1983) op. cit.
22. Saatchi & Saatchi Compton (1985) *Preparing the Advertising Brief* 9.
23. Hall, M. (1992) Using Advertising Frameworks: Different Research Models for Different Campaigns, *Admap*, March, 17–21.
24. Lannon, J. (1991) Developing Brand Strategies across Borders, *Marketing and Research Today*, August, 160–7.
25. Tomkins, R. (1999) Images with the Power to Shock, *Financial Times*, 18 February, 10.
26. Elliott, R. (1997) Understanding Buyer Behaviour: Implications for Selling, in D. Jobber (ed.) *The CIM Handbook of Selling and Sales Strategy*, Oxford: Butterworth-Heinemann.
27. Syedain, H. (1992) Taking the Expert Approach to Media, *Marketing*, 4 June, 20–1.
28. *Campaign* Report (1997) Global Review of Digital TV, *Campaign*, 30 May, 8–10.
29. See Furber, R. (2000) Early Start, *Marketing Week*, 9 March, 65–6; Reed, D. (2000) Rapid Response, *Marketing Week*, 25 May, 63–5.
30. Davies, O. (2002) Interactive TV is Set to Transform Ads Landscape, *Marketing*, 20 November, 28.
31. Ray, A. (2003) Press the Red Button, *Marketing Business*, April, 28–30.
32. Tomkins, R. (1999) Reaching New Heights of Success, *Financial Times*, 28 May, 16.
33. Beattie, T. (2002) Private Eye, *Campaign*, 1 March, 24.
34. Hanrahan, M. (2002) Increase Poster Power with Moving Image, *Marketing Week*, 2 May, 14.
35. Hayward, C. (2003) Getting into Outdoor, *Marketing Week*, 30 January, 39–41.
36. Thurner, R. (2002) Outdoor Advertising—A Strong Single Currency, *Marketing Week*, 10 January, 14.
37. Benady, D. (2002) Record Audiences Still Cinema Doubts, *Marketing Week*, 21 February, 14.
38. Higham, N. (2002) Blockbusting Ad Revenue Comes to the Silver Screen, *Marketing Week*, 18 October, 19.
39. Croft, M. (1999) Listeners Keep Radio On Air, *Marketing Week*, 8 July, 30–1.
40. See Fletcher, W. (1999) Independents May Have Had Their Day, *Financial Times*, 27 August, 15; Anonymous (2000) Star Turn, *Economist*, 11 March, 91.
41. Tomkins, R. (2001) Media Buyers Get Hitched and Attend Critical Mass, *Financial Times Creative Business*, 24 July, 2.
42. Jobber, D. and A. Kilbride (1986) How Major Agencies Evaluate TV Advertising in Britain, *International Journal of Advertising*, 5, 187–95.
43. Bell, E. (1992) Lies, Damned Lies and Research, *Observer*, 28 June, 46.
44. Wright and Crimp (2000) op. cit.
45. Jobber and Kilbride (1986) op. cit.
46. Curtis, J. (2002) Clients Speak Out on Agencies, *Marketing*, 28 March, 22–3.
47. Curtis, J. (2002) Agencies Speak Out on Clients, *Marketing*, 4 April, 20–1.
48. Smith, P. R. (2001) *Marketing Communications: An Integrated Approach*, London: Kogan Page, 116.
49. Smith (2001) op. cit.
50. Mead, G. (1992) Why the Customer is Always Right, *Financial Times*, 8 October, 17.
51. Dignam, C. (2002) The New Deal, *Financial Times Creative Business*, 13 August, 6.
52. Smith (2001) op. cit.
53. See Tomkins, R. (1999) Getting a Bigger Bang for the Advertising Buck, *Financial Times*, 24 September, 17; Waters, R. (1999) P&G Ties Advertising Agency Fees to Sales, *Marketing Week*, 16 September, 1.
54. Singh, S. (2002) ASA Slams P&G Claims About its Pantene Brand, *Marketing Week*, 31 October, 6.
55. Thurtle, G. (2001) Are National Links Good for a Brand? *Marketing Week*, 20 September, 21–2.
56. Schlegelmilch, B. (1998) *Marketing Ethics: An International Perspective*, London: International Thomson Business Press.
57. Oates, C., M. Blades and B. Gunter (2003) Marketing to Children, *Journal of Marketing Management* 19(4), 401–10.
58. Anonymous (2000) IPA Chief Denies Tango Ad Own Goal, *Marketing Week*, 9 March, 12.
59. Oates, C., M. Blades and B. Gunter (2003) op. cit.
60. Proctor, J. and M. Richards (2002) Word-of-Mouth Marketing: Beyond Pester Power, *International Journal of Advertising and Marketing to Children* 3(3), 3–11.

Chapter 13

1. Rines, S. (1995) Forcing Change, *Marketing Week*, 1 March, 10–13.
2. See Anderson, R. E. (1996) Personal Selling and Sales Management in the New Millennium, *Journal of Personal Selling and Sales Management* 16(4), 17–52; Magrath, A. J. (1997) A Comment on 'Personal Selling and Sales Management in the New Millennium', *Journal of Personal Selling and Sales Management* 17(1), 45–7.
3. Anonymous (1996) Revolution in the Showroom, *Business Week*, 19 February, 70–6.
4. Magrath (1997) op. cit.
5. Mandel, M. J. and R. D. Hof (2001) Rethinking the Internet: Down But Hardly Out, *Business Week*, 26 March, 128.
6. Rich, G. A. (2002) The Internet: Boom or Bust to Sales Organizations, *Journal of Marketing Management* 18(3/4), 287–300.

7. Sharma, A. and N. Tzokas (2002) Personal Selling and Sales Management in the Internet Environment: Lessons Learned, *Journal of Marketing Management* 18(3/4), 249–58.
8. This classification of selling types is supported by the research of McMurry, R. N. (1961) The Mystique 4of Super-Salesmanship, *Harvard Business Review,* 26 (March–April), 114–32; McMurry, R. N. and J. S. Arnold (1968) *How to Build a Dynamic Sales Organisation*, New York: McGraw-Hill; Montcrief, W. C. (1986) Selling Activity and Sales Position Taxonomies for Industrial Salesforces, *Journal of Marketing Research* 23(3), 261–70.
9. Jobber, D. and G. Lancaster (2003) *Selling and Sales Management,* Harlow: Prentice-Hall.
10. Wickstrom, S. (1996) The Customer as Co-producer, *European Journal of Marketing* 30(4), 6–19.
11. Gummesson, E. (1987) The New Marketing: Developing Long Term Interactive Relationships, *Long Range Planning* 20, 10–20.
12. Abberton Associates (1991) *Balancing the Salesforce Equation: The Changing Role of the Sales Organisation in the 1990s*, Thame: CPM Field Marketing Ltd.
13. Widmier, S. M., D. W. Jackson Jr. and D. B. McCabe (2002) Infusing Technology into Personal Selling, *Journal of Personal Selling and Sales Management* 22(3), 189–98.
14. Reed, D. (1999) Field Force, *Marketing Week*, 23 September, 55–7.
15. Jobber and Lancaster (2003) op. cit.
16. Weitz, B. A. (1981) Effectiveness in Sales Interactions: A Contingency Framework, *Journal of Marketing* 45, 85–103.
17. Román, S., S. Ruiz and J. L. Munuera (2002) The Effects of Sales Training on Salesforce Activity, *European Journal of Marketing* 36(11/12), 1344–66.
18. Schuster, C. P. and J. E. Danes (1986) Asking Questions: Some Characteristics of Successful Sales Encounters, *Journal of Personal Selling and Sales Management*, May, 17–27.
19. Walters, J. (2000) Journey's End For the King of the Costas, *Observer*, 19 November, 9.
20. Brooke, K. (2002) B2B and B2C Marketing is not so Different, *Marketing Business*, July/August, 39.
21. Jeannet, J. P. and H. D. Hennessey (2002) *Global Marketing Strategies*, Boston: Houghton-Mifflin.
22. Buttery, E. A. and T. K. P. Leung (1998) The Difference between Chinese and Western Negotiations, *European Journal of Marketing* 32(3/4), 374–89.
23. Arias, J. T. G. (1998) A Relationship Marketing Approach to *Guanxi*, *European Journal of Marketing* 32(1/2), 145–56.
24. Cateora, P. R., J. L. Graham and P. N. Ghauri (2002) *International Marketing*, London: McGraw-Hill.
25. Smith, D. A. (2000) What's the Buzz on *Guanxi*? *Marketing Business*, December/January, 53.
26. Lee, D.-J., J. H. Pae and Y. H. Yong (2001) A Model of Close Business Relationships in China (*Guanxi*), *European Journal of Marketing* 35(1/2), 51–69.
27. McDonald, M. H. B. (2002) *Marketing Plans*, London: Heinemann.
28. Strahle, W. and R. L. Spiro (1986) Linking Market Share Strategies to Salesforce Objectives, Activities and Compensation Policies, *Journal of Personal Selling and Sales Management*, August, 11–18.
29. Talley, W. J. (1961) How to Design Sales Territories, *Journal of Marketing* 25(3), 16–28.
30. Magrath, A. J. (1989) To Specialise or Not to Specialise?, *Sales and Marketing Management* 14(7), 62–8.
31. Millman, T. and K. Wilson (1995) From Key Account Selling to Key Account Management, *Journal of Marketing Practice* 1(1), 9–21.
32. McDonald, M. and B. Rogers (1998) *Key Account Management*, Oxford: Butterworth-Heinemann.
33. Wilson, K., S. Croom, T. Millman and D. Weilbaker (2000) The SRT-SAMA Global Account Management Study, *Journal of Selling and Major Account Management* 2(3), 63–84.
34. Wilson, K. and T. Millman (2003) The Global Account Manager as Political Entrepreneur, *Industrial Marketing Management* 32, 151–8.
35. Montgomery, G. and P. Yip (1999) Statistical Evidence on Global Account Management Programs, *Fachzeitschrift Für Marketing THEXIS* 16(4), 10–13.
36. Piercy, N., D. W. Cravens and N. A. Morgan (1998) Salesforce Performance and Behaviour Based Management Processes in Business-to-Business Sales Organisations, *European Journal of Marketing* 32(1/2), 79–100.
37. P. A. Consultants (1979) *Salesforce Practice Today: A Basis for Improving Performance*, Cookham: Institute of Marketing.
38. Galbraith, A. J., Kiely and T. Watkins (1991) Salesforce Management: Issues for the 1990s, *Proceedings of the Marketing Education Group Conference*, Cardiff, July, 425–45.
39. Mayer, M. and G. Greenberg (1964) What Makes a Good Salesman, *Harvard Business Review* 42 (July–August), 119–25.
40. See DeCormier, R. and D. Jobber (1993) The Counsellor Selling Method: Concepts and Constructs, *Journal of Personal Selling and Sales Management* 13(4), 39–60; Ronán, S., S. Ruiz and J. L. Munuera (2002) The Effects of Sales Training on Salesforce Activity, *European Journal of Marketing* 36(11/12), 1344–66.
41. Wilson, K. (1993) Managing the Industrial Salesforce in the 1990s, *Journal of Marketing Management* 9(2), 123–40.
42. Luthans, F. (1997) *Organizational Behaviour*, New York: McGraw-Hill.
43. See Maslow, A. H. (1954) *Motivation and Personality*, New York: Harper & Row; Herzberg, F. (1966) *Work and the Nature of Man*, Cleveland: W Collins; Vroom, V. H. (1964) *Work and Motivation*, New York: Wiley; Adams, J. S. (1965) Inequity in Social Exchange, in Berkowitz, L. (ed.) *Advances in Experimental Social Psychology 2*, New York: Academic Press; Likert, R. (1961) *New Patterns of Sales Management*, New York: McGraw-Hill.
44. Churchill Jr, G. A., N. M. Ford and O. C. Walker Jr (2000) *Salesforce Management: Planning, Implementation and Control*, Homewood, Ala: Irwin.
45. Darmon, R. Y. (1974) Salesmen's Response to Financial Initiatives: An Empirical Study, *Journal of Marketing Research*, November, 418–26.
46. See Avlonitis, G., C. Manolis and K. Boyle (1985) Sales Management Practices in the UK Manufacturing Industry, *Journal of Sales Management* 2(2), 6–16; Shipley, D. and D. Jobber (1991) Salesforce Motivation, Compensation and Evaluation, *The Services Industries Journal* 11(2), 154–70.
47. Cundiff, E. and M. T. Hilger (1988) *Marketing in the International Environment*, Englewood Cliffs, NJ: Prentice-Hall.
48. Hill, J. S., R. R. Still and U. O. Boya (1991) Managing the International Salesforce, *International Marketing Review* 8(1), 19–31.
49. Cateora, P. R., J. L. Graham and P. H. Ghauri (2002) *International Marketing*, London: McGraw-Hill.
50. Dewsnap, B. and D. Jobber (2002) A Social Psychological Model of Relations Between Marketing and Sales, *European Journal of Marketing* 36(7/8), 874–94.
51. Mackintosh, J. (1999) Pensions Mis-selling Cost May Rise by £1bn, *Financial Times*, 18/19 December, 2.
52. INFACT (www.infactcanada.ca/obstinat/htm) 2003.
53. www.babymilkaction.org/pages/campaign 2003.
54. Aguayo V. M., J. S. Ross, S. Kanon, A. N. Ouedraogo (2003) Monitoring Compliance with the International Code of Marketing of Breastmilk Substitutes in West Africa: Multisite Cross Sectional Survey in Togo and Burkina Faso, *British Medical Journal* 326(7381), 127–32.
55. This summary of the International Code of Marketing Breastmilk Substitutes is from the International Baby Food Action Network's website at http://www/ibfan.org.
56. Lindenberger, J. (2003) Personal communication with G. Hastings, February 2003.
57. Taylor, A. (1998) Violations of the International Code of Marketing of Breastmilk Substitutes: Prevalence in Four Countries, *British Medical Journal* 316(7138), 1117–22.

Chapter 14

1. North, B. (1995) Consumer Companies Take Direct Stance, *Marketing*, 20 May, 24–5.
2. Guide 26 (1993) International Direct Marketing, *Marketing*, 22 April, 23–6.
3. Smith, P. R. (2001) *Marketing Communications: An Integrated Approach*, London: Kogan Page.
4. Stone, M., D. Davies and A. Bond (1995) *Direct Hit: Direct Marketing with a Winning Edge*, London: Pitman.
5. Fletcher, K., C. Wheeler and J. Wright (1990) The Role and Status of UK Database Marketing, *Quarterly Review of Marketing*, Autumn, 7–14.
6. Linton, I. (1995) *Database Marketing: Know What Your Customer Wants*, London: Pitman.
7. Nancarrow, C., L. T. Wright and J. Page (1997) Seagram Europe and Africa: The Development of a Consumer Database Marketing Capability, *Proceedings of the Academy of Marketing*, July, Manchester, 1119–30.
8. Stone, Davies and Bond (1995) op. cit.
9. Murphy, C. (2002) Catching up with its Glitzier Cousin, *Financial Times*, 24 July, 13.
10. Wilson, R. (1999) Discerning Habits, *Marketing Week*, 1 July, 45–8.
11. James, M. (2003) The Quest for Fidelity, *Marketing Business*, January, 20–2.
12. Mitchell, A. (2002) Consumer Power Is on the Cards in Tesco Plan, *Marketing Week*, 2 May, 30–1.
13. O'Hara, M. (2003) Vodafone Joins Loyalty Scheme, *Guardian*, 18 February, 22.
14. Foss, B. and M. Stone (2001) *Successful Customer Relationship Marketing*, London: Kogan Page.
15. Dempsey, J. (2001) An Elusive Goal Leads to Confusion, *Financial Times Information Technology Supplement*, 17 October, 4.
16. Morgan (2001) The Art of the Targeted Mailshot, *Financial Times*, 13 September, 17.
17. See Foss and Stone (2001) op. cit.; Woodcock, N., M. Starkey, J. Stone, P. Weston, and J. Ozimek (2001) *State of the Nation II: 2002, An Ongoing Global Study of how Companies Manage their Customer*, QCi Assessment Ltd, West Byfleet.
18. Gofton, K. (2002) Support for the Frontline, *Financial Times Creative Business*, 12 May, 8.
19. Newing, R. (2002) Customers not Impressed by Wonderful Technology, *Financial Times IT Review*, 6 November, 7.
20. See Ryals, L., S. Knox and S. Maklan (2002) *Customer Relationship Management: Building the Business Case*, London: FT Prentice Hall; H. Wilson, E. Daniel and M. McDonald (2002) Factors for Success in Customer Relationship Management Systems, *Journal of Marketing Management* 18(1/2), 193–200.
21. Stone, Davies and Bond (1995) op. cit.
22. Murphy, J. (1997) The Art of Satisfaction, *Financial Times*, 23 April, 14.
23. A quotation by G. Harrison in Rines, S. (1995) Blind Data, *Marketing*, 17 November, 26–7.
24. Dowling, G. R. and M. Uncles (1997) Do Loyalty Programs Really Work? *Sloan Management Review* 38(4), 71–82.
25. Burnside, A. (1995) A Never Ending Search for the New, *Marketing*, 25 May, 31–5.
26. East, R. and W. Lomax (1999) Loyalty Value, *Marketing Week*, 2 December, 51–5.
27. Murphy, C. (1999) Addressing the Data Issue, *Marketing*, 28 January, 31.
28. Clegg, A. (2000) Hit or Miss, *Marketing Week*, 13 January, 45–9.
29. Benady, D. (2001) If Undelivered, *Marketing Week*, 20 December, 31–3.
30. Michell, A. (1995) Preaching the Loyalty Message, *Marketing Week*, 1 December, 26–7.
31. Reed, D. (1996) Direct Fight, *Marketing Week*, 1 November, 45–7.
32. Baier, M. (1985) *Elements of Direct Marketing*, New York: McGraw-Hill, 184.
33. Bird, D. (2000) *Commonsense Direct Marketing*, London: Kogan Page, 180.
34. Benady, A. (2002) Evolution of the Modern Mail, *Financial Times Creative Business*, 23 April, 2–3.
35. Charles, G. (2002) Time Cold Direct Mail Was Junked?, *Marketing Week*, 10 October, 22.
36. Guide 26 (1993) op. cit.
37. Miller, R. (1999) Phone Apparatus, *Campaign*, 18 June, 35–6.
38. Miller (1999) op. cit.
39. McHatton, N. R. J. (1988) *Total Telemarketing*, New York: Wiley, 269.
40. Moncrief, W. C. (1986) Selling Activity and Sales Position Taxonomies for Industrial Sales Forces, *Journal of Marketing Research* 23(2), 261–70.
41. Moncrief, W. C., S. H. Shipp, C. W. Lamb and D. W. Cravens (1989) Examining the Roles of Telemarketing in Selling Strategy, *Journal of Personal Selling and Sales Management* 9(3), 1–20.
42. Jobber, D. and G. Lancaster (2003) *Selling and Sales Management*, London: Pitman, 192–3.
43. Stevens, M. (1993) A Telephony Revolution, *Marketing*, 16 September, 38.
44. Booth, E. (1999) Will the Web Replace the Phone? *Marketing*, 4 February, 25–6.
45. Moran, N. (2002) Centres Develop New Calling, *Financial Times IT Review*, 18 September, 2.
46. Murphy, D. (2002) High Tech Ways to Help the Customer, *Marketing*, 12 September, 27.
47. Reed, D. (1999) Back-up Call, *Marketing Week*, 18 November, 45–7.
48. McCartney, N. (2003) Getting the Message Across, *Financial Times IT Review*, 15 January, 3.
49. See Anonymous (2002) Can SMS Ever Replace Traditional Direct Mail, *Marketing Week*, 26 September, 37; and McCartney (2003) op. cit.
50. Middleton, T. (2002) Sending out the Winning Message, *Marketing Week*, 16 May, 43–5.
51. Cowlett, M. (2002) Text Messaging to Build Youth Loyalty, *Marketing*, 31 October, 29.
52. Reid, A. (2002) The SMS Work that Increased Cadbury's Cut of a Flat Market, *Campaign*, 1 March, 17.
53. McCartney (2003) op. cit.
54. De Kerckhove, A. (2002) Introduction to Making Mobile Marketing Work, *Campaign*, 22 March, 3.
55. Blythe, J. (2003) in Jobber, D. and G. Lancaster, *Selling and Sales Management*, Harlow: F.T. Pearson.
56. Murphy, D. (2001) Dare to Be Digital, *Marketing Business*, December/January, 3–5.
57. Carman, D. (1996) Audiences Dial 'S' for Shopping, *European*, 4–10 April, 13.
58. Mühlbacher, H., M. Botshen and W. Beutelmeyer (1997) The Changing Consumer in Austria, *International Journal of Research in Marketing* 14, 309–19.
59. Voyle, S. (2001) Bond Street Without the Border, *Financial Times*, 5 October, 16.
60. Stone, Davies and Bond (1995) op. cit.
61. Roman, E. (1995) *The Cutting Edge Strategy for Synchronizing Advertising, Direct Mail, Telemarketing and Field Sales*, Lincolnwood IL: NTC Business Books.
62. Coad, T. (2003) Dog's Breakfast, *Marketing Week*, 27 February, 49–50.
63. Fell, J. (2002) How to Keep it Legal, *FT Creative Business*, 20 May, 12.

Chapter 15

1. Selhofer, H. (2002) European Union e-business Watch (2002) http://www.ebusiness-watch.org/marketwatch/database/overview_tables.htm.
2. Kulla, M. (2003) European Online Consumers Challenging US For E-commerce Leadership, AOL Europe, 3 March, at http://www.media.aol.co.uk/ukpress_view.cfm?release_num=55253050.
3. Kessler, J. (1995) The French Minitel: Is There Digital Life Outside of the 'US ASCII' Internet? A Challenge or Convergence? *D-Lib Magazine*, December, San Francisco, CA, at http://www.dlib.org/dlib/december95/12kessler.html (visited 10 January 2002).
4. McGrath, D. (2001) Minitel: The Old New Thing, *Wired News*, 18 April, at http://www.wired.com/news/technology/0,1282,42943,00.html (visited 18 January 2002).
5. Hoffman, D. and T. Novak (1997) A New Marketing Paradigm for Electronic Commerce, *The Information Society* 13, 43–54.
6. Barwise, P., A. Eleberse and K. Hammond (2002) Marketing and the Internet: A Research Review, in Weitz, B. and R. Wensley (eds), Handbook of Marketing, London: Sage.
7. Adam, S., R. Mulye, R. Deans and D. Palihawadana (2002) E-marketing in Perspective: A Three Country Comparison of Business Use of the Internet, *Marketing Intelligence and Planning* 20(4) 243–51.
8. Seybold, P. B. and R. T. Marshak (1998) *Customer.com: How to Create a Profitable Business Strategy for the Internet and Beyond*, New York: Random House.
9. Kelly's Awards, at http://www.purchasingawards.com/last-winners.html.
10. Van Slyke, C. and F. Bélanger (2003) *E-Business Technologies: Supporting the Net-enhanced Organization*, USA: John Wiley & Sons.
11. Doherty, N. F., F. E. Ellis-Chadwick and C. A. Hart (1999) Cyber Retailing in the UK: The Potential of the Internet as a Retail Channel, *International Journal of Retail and Distribution Management* 27(1), 22–36.
12. Internet Software Consortium, at http://www.isc.org/ds/new-survey.html.
13. Chaffey, D., R. Mayer, K. Johnston and F. Ellis-Chadwick (2003) *Internet Marketing: Strategy, Implementation and Practice*, Prentice Hall London.
14. Cyberatlas, at http://cyberatlas.Internet.com/big_picture/geographics/article/0,,5911_151151,00.html.
15. Hart, C., N. Doherty and F. Ellis-Chadwick (2002) Retailer Adoption of the Internet–Implications for Retail Marketing *European Journal of Marketing* 34(8) 954–74.
16. Cova, B. and V. Cova (2002) Tribal Marketing: The Tribalisation of Society and its Impact on the Conduct of Marketing, *European Journal of Marketing*.
17. Rauch, D. and G. Thunqvist (2000) *Virtual Tribes: Postmodern Consumers in Cyberspace*, unpublished Masters thesis, Stockholm University: The Market Academy.
18. http://www.citroen.mb.ca/citroenet/.
19. http://www.vwvortex.com/.
20. http://friends_reunited.com.
21. Fahy, J. (2000) The Resource-Based View of the Firm: Some Stumbling-Blocks on the Road to Understanding Sustainable Competitive Advantage, *Journal of European Industrial Training* 24(2), 94–104.
22. Ghosh, S. (1998) Making Business sense of the Internet, Harvard Business Review, March–April, 127–35.
23. Porter M. E. (2001) Strategy and the Internet, *Harvard Business Review*, March, 63–78.
24. Parasuraman, A., V.A. Zeithmal and L. L. Berry (1988) A Conceptual Model of Service Quality and its Implications for Future Research, *Journal of Marketing* 48, Fall, 34–45.
25. Shapiro, C. and H. R. Varian (1999) *Information Rules*, Harvard, MA: Harvard Business School Press.
26. Baker, S. and K. Baker (1998) Mine Over Matter, *Journal of Business Strategy* 19(4), 22–7.
27. Morganosky, M. and B. Cude (2002) Consumer Demand for Online Food Retailing: Is it Really a Supply Side Issue? *International Journal of Retail and Distribution Management* 30(10) 451–8.
28. Anonymous (2003) EU Rules Aim to Outlaw Spam, *Marketing Business*, May 2003.
29. Finn, A. and Louviere, J. J. (1990) Shopping-centre Patronage Models: Fashioning a consideration Set Segmentation Solution, *Journal of Business Research* 21, 259–75.
30. Doherty, Ellis-Chadwick and Hart (1999) op. cit.
31. Chaffey, Mayer, Johnston and Ellis-Chadwick (2003) op. cit.
32. Novak, T. P. and D. L. Hoffman (1998) Bridging the Digital Divide: The Impact of Race on Computer Access and Internet Use, 2 February, Project 2000, Vanderbilt University, at http://www2000.ogsm.vanderbilt.edu/papers/race/science.html (visited 19 October 2000).
33. Cowe, R. (2000) Dark Side of the Web, *Guardian*, 24 February, 7.
34. Benady, D. (2000) Class War, *Marketing Week*, 27 January, 28–31.
35. Tomkins, R. (2000) Cookies Leave a Nasty Taste, *Financial Times*, 3 March, 16.
36. Berkowitz, E. N., R. A. Kerin, S. W. Hartley and W. Rudelius (2000) *Marketing*, Boston, MA: Irwin McGraw-Hill.
37. Anonymous (2002) UK Consumers have had Enough of Spam E-mail, *Marketing Week*, 31 October, 39.
38. Datamonitor (2002) Marketing Food and Drinks to the Internet Generation: Effective Youth Targeting and Profit Opportunities, *Reuters Business Insight Consumer Goods Report*.
39. Montgomery, K. C. (1996) Children in the Digital Age, *American Prospect*, 27, July–August.
40. Montgomery, K. C. and S. Pasnik (1996) *Web of Deceit*, Washington: Center for Media Education.
41. http://www.cocopops.co.uk.

Chapter 16

1. Peattie, K. and S. Peattie (1993) Sales Promotion: Playing to Win?, *Journal of Marketing Management* 9, 255–69.
2. Lal, R. (1990) Manufacturer Trade Deals and Retail Price Promotion, *Journal of Marketing Research* 27(6), 428–44.
3. Rothschild, M. L. and W. C. Gaidis (1981) Behavioural Learning Theory: Its Relevance to Marketing and Promotions, *Journal of Marketing* 45, Spring, 70–8.
4. Tuck, R. T. J. and W. G. B. Harvey (1972) Do Promotions Undermine the Brand?, *Admap*, January, 30–3.
5. Brown, R. G. (1974) Sales Response to Promotions and Advertising, *Journal of Advertising Research* 14(4), 33–9.
6. Ehrenberg, A. S. C., K. Hammond and G. J. Goodhardt (1994) The After-Effects of Price-Related Consumer Promotions, *Journal of Advertising Research* 34(4), 1–10.
7. Smith, P. R. (2001) *Marketing Communications: An Integrated Approach*, London: Kogan Page, 240–3.
8. Killigran, L. and R. Cook (1999) Multibuy Push May Backfire, *Marketing Week*, 16 September, 44–5.
9. Gannaway, B. (2002) Brand Building with Sampling, *Marketing*, 25 April, 29.
10. Hemsley, S. (2002) Extra Sensory Perception, *Marketing Week*, 21 November, 41–2.
11. Davidson, J. H. (2003) *Offensive Marketing*, Harmondsworth: Penguin, 249–71.
12. Cummins, J. (2002) *Sales Promotion*, London: Kogan Page, 79.
13. Davidson (2003) op. cit.
14. Dourado, P. (2003) Plastic Population, *Marketing Week*, 24 April, 35–7.

15. Cummins (2002) op. cit.
16. Collins, M. (1986) Research on 'Below the Line' Expenditure, in Worcester, R. and J. Downham (eds) *Consumer Market Research Handbook*, Amsterdam: North Holland, 537–50.
17. Cummins (2002) op. cit.
18. Doyle, P. and J. Saunders (1985) The Lead Effect of Marketing Decisions, *Journal of Marketing Research* 22(1), 54–65.
19. White, J. (1991) *How to Understand and Manage Public Relations*, London: Business Books.
20. Lesly, P. (1991) *The Handbook of Public Relations and Communications*, Maidenhead: McGraw-Hill, 13–19.
21. Kitchen, P. J. and T. Proctor (1991) The Increasing Importance of Public Relations in Fast Moving Consumer Goods Firms, *Journal of Marketing Management* 7(4), 357–70.
22. Lesly (1991) op. cit.
23. Jefkins, F. (1985) Timing and Handling of Material, in Howard, W. (ed.) *The Practice of Public Relations*, Oxford: Heinemann, 86–104.
24. Gofton, K. (1996) Integrating the Delivery, *Marketing*, 31 October (Special Supplement on Choosing and Using Public Relations), 8–10.
25. Flack, J. (1999) Public Speaking, *Marketing Week*, 4 November, 51–2.
26. Jones, H. (2002) At Close Quarters, *Campaign*, 7 February, 25.
27. Leyland, A. (2002) One-Stop-Shopping, *Campaign*, 8 March, 28.
28. Sleight, S. (1989) *Sponsorship: What it is and How to Use it*, Maidenhead: McGraw-Hill, 4.
29. Bennett, R. (1999) Sports Sponsorship, Spectator Recall and False Consensus, *European Journal of Marketing* 33(3/4), 291–313.
30. Fry, A. (2001) How to Profit from Sponsorship Sport, *Marketing*, 16 August, 25.
31. Mintel (1991) *Sponsorship, Special Report*, London: Mintel International Group Ltd.
32. McKelvey, C. (1999) TV Washout, *Marketing Week*, 2 December, 27–9.
33. Meenaghan, T. and D. Shipley (1999), Media Effects in Commercial Sponsorship, *European Journal of Marketing* 33(3/4), 328–47.
34. Haywood, R. (1984) *All About PR*, Maidenhead: McGraw-Hill, 186.
35. Crowley, M. G. (1991) Prioritising the Sponsorship Audience, *European Journal of Marketing* 25(11), 11–21.
36. Miles, L. (1995) Sporting Chancers, *Marketing Director International* 6(2), 50–2.
37. Anonymous (2002) Wilkinson Sword Scores Global Sponsorship Deal with Man U, *Marketing Week*, 25 July, 7.
38. Gibson, N. (2002) Advertisers Bet their Shirts on Sport, *Financial Times*, 20 March, 24.
39. Jones, H. (2002) Fair Play, *Marketing Business*, June, 21–3.
40. Meenaghan, T. (1991) Sponsorship: Legitimising the Medium, *European Journal of Marketing* 25(11), 5–10.
41. Smith (1993) op. cit.
42. Meenaghan, T. (1991) The Role of Sponsorship in the Marketing Communications Mix, *International Journal of Advertising* 10, 35–47.
43. Thwaites, D. (1995) Professional Football Sponsorship–Profitable or Profligate?, *International Journal of Advertising* 14, 149–64.
44. O'Hara, B., F. Palumbo and P. Herbig (1993) Industrial Trade Shows Abroad, *Industrial Marketing Management* 22, 233–7.
45. Couretas, J. (1984) Trade Shows and the Strategic Mainstream, *Business Marketing* 69, 64–70.
46. Anonymous (1979) Trade Shows are Usually a Form of Mass Hysteria, *Industrial Marketing* 64(4), 6–10.
47. Parasuraman, A. (1981) The Relative Importance of Industrial Promotional Tools, *Industrial Marketing Management* 10, 277–81.
48. Zappaterra, Y. (1999) Proving Your Worth, *Marketing*, 25 February, 35–6.
49. McLuhan, R. (1999) Hitting the Target at Lifestyle Events, *Marketing Week*, 20 May, 27–8.
50. Prickett, R. (2002) The Key to the Show, *Marketing Week*, 12 September, 49–51.
51. Bonoma, T. V. (1985) Get More Out of your Trade Shows, in Gumpert, D. E. (ed.) *The Marketing Renaissance*, New York: Wiley.
52. Trade Show Bureau (1983) *The Exhibitor: Their Trade Show Practices*, Research Report No. 19, East Orleans, Mass: Trade Show Bureau.
53. Russell, I. (1999) Driving Force, *Marketing Week*, 7 October, 69–73.
54. Couretas (1984) op. cit.
55. Lancaster, G. and H. Baron (1977) Exhibiting for Profit, *Industrial Management*, November, 24–7.
56. Blaskey, J. (1999) Proving Your Worth, *Marketing*, 25 February, 35–6.
57. Anonymous (2002) The Ten Top Product Placements in Features, *Campaign*, 17 December, 36.
58. Anonymous (2002) op. cit.
59. Kleinman, M. (2002) Philips to Launch 007 Shaving Range, *Marketing*, 4 April, 3.
60. Wheelright, G. (2003) Bond Encourages Surfers to Buy Another Day, *Financial Times IT Review*, 15 January, 2.
61. Keller, K. L. (2003) *Strategic Brand Management*, New Jersey: Pearson.
62. Alcohol Concern (1998) Factsheet 2, available online at http//www.alcoholconcern.org.uk.
63. Roberts, M., C. Fox and J. McManus (2001) *Drink and Disorder. Alcohol, Crime and Anti-Social Behaviour: 'A Nacro Policy Report'*, London: Nacro Publications.
64. Shepherd, J. P. and M. R. Brickley (1996) The Relationship Between Alcohol Intoxication, Stressors and Injury in Urban Violence, *British Journal of Criminology* 36(4): 546–72.
65. The 1996 British Crime Survey. Home Office Statistical Bulletin, 19/96.
66. WHO Global Burden of Disease 2000 Study, WHO European Ministerial Conference on Young People and Alcohol, Stockholm, February 2001.

Chapter 17

1. Key Note Report (2001) Courier and Express Services.
2. Stern, L. W. and El-Ansany (1995) *Marketing Channels*, Englewood Cliffs, NJ: Prentice-Hall, 6.
3. Dudley, J. W. (1990) *1992 Strategies for the Single Market*, London: Kogan Page, 327.
4. Kearney, A. T. (1991) *Trade Investment in Japan: The Current Environment*, a study for the American Chamber of Commerce in Japan, June, 16.
5. Narus, J. A. and J. C. Anderson (1986) Industrial Distributor Selling: The Roles of Outside and Inside Sales, *Industrial Marketing Management* 15, 55–62.
6. Rosenbloom, B. (1987) *Marketing Channels: A Management View*, Hinsdale, Ill: Dryden, 160.
7. Laurance, B. (1993) MMC in Bad Odour Over Superdrug Ruling, *Guardian*, 12 November, 18.
8. Anonymous (1993) EC Rejects Unilever Appeal on Cabinets, *Marketing*, 25 February, 6.
9. Meller, P. (1992) Isostar Enters the Lucozade League, *Marketing*, 2 July, 9.
10. Helmore, E. (1997) Restaurant Kings or Just Silly Burgers, *Observer*, 8 June, 5.
11. See www.Benetton.com.
12. Ivey, J. (2002) Benetton Gambles on Colour of the Future, *Corporate Finance*, June, 13–15.
13. Vignalli, C., R. A. Schmidt and B. J. Davies (1993) The Benetton Experience, *International Journal of Retail and Distribution Management* 21(3), 53–9.

14. Hopkinson, G. C. and S. Hogarth Scott (1999) Franchise Relationship Quality: Microeconomic Explanations, *European Journal of Marketing* 33(9/10), 827–43.
15. Rosenbloom (1987) op. cit.
16. Shipley, D. D., D. Cook and E. Barnett (1989) Recruitment, Motivation, Training and Evaluation of Overseas Distributors, *European Journal of Marketing* 23(2), 79–93.
17. Shipley, Cook and Barnett (1989) op. cit.
18. Rosson, P. and I. Ford (1982) Manufacturer: Overseas Distributor Relations and Export Performance, *Journal of International Business Studies* 13, Fall, 57–72.
19. Shipley, Cook and Barnett (1989) op. cit.
20. Kumar, N., L. K. Scheer and J.-Bem Steenkamp (1995) The Effects of Perceived Interdependence on Dealer Attitudes, *Journal of Marketing Research* 32 (August), 248–56.
21. See Shipley, D. D. and S. Prinja (1988) The Services and Supplier Choice Influences of Industrial Distributors, *Service Industries Journal* 8(2), 176–87; Webster, F. E. (1976) The Role of the Industrial Distributor in Marketing Strategy, *Journal of Marketing* 40, 10–16.
22. Shipley, Cook and Barnett (1989) op. cit.
23. See Pegram, R. (1965) *Selecting and Evaluating Distributors*, New York: National Industrial Conference Board, 109–25; Shipley, Cook and Barnett (1989) op. cit.
24. Philpot, N. (1975) Managing the Export Function: Policies and Practice in Small and Medium Companies, *Management Survey Report No. 16*, British Institute of Management; Shipley, Cook and Barnett (1989) op. cit.
25. Magrath, A. J. and K. G. Hardy (1989) A Strategic Paradigm for Predicting Manufacturer–Reseller Conflict, *European Journal of Marketing* 23(2), 94–108.
26. Magrath and Hardy (1989) op. cit.
27. Magrath and Hardy (1989) op. cit.
28. Hardy, K. G. and A. J. Magrath (1988) Ten Ways for Manufacturers to Improve Distribution Management, *Business Horizons*, Nov.–Dec., 68.
29. Magrath and Hardy (1989) op. cit.
30. Anonymous (2002) Chain Reaction, *Economist*, 2 February, 1–3.
31. Jobber, D. and J. Fahy (2003) *Foundations of Marketing*, Maidenhead: McGraw-Hill.
32. Mitchell, A. (2003) When Push Comes to Shove, It's All About Pull, *Marketing Week*, 9 January, 26–7.
33. Roux, C. (2002) The Reign of Spain, *Guardian*, 28 October, 6–7.
34. Hardy, K. G. (1985) Norsk Kjem A/S case study, University of Western Ontario, Canada
35. Marsh, P. (2002) Insights off the Production Line, *Financial Times*, 21 March, 17.
36. Barksdale, J. (1996) Microsoft Would Like to Squash Me Like a Bug, *Financial Times*, Special Report on IT, 2 October, 2.
37. Hastings, P. (2002) Industry Seek Ways to Get it Together, *Financial Times IT Review*, 2 October, 8.
38. Nairn, G. (2002) More than Just Boxing Clever, *Financial Times IT Review*, 2 October, 7.
39. Samiee, S. (1990) Strategic Considerations of the EC 1992 Plan for Small Exporters, *Business Horizons*, March–April, 48–56.
40. Schlegelmilch, B. (1998) *Marketing Ethics: An International Perspective*, London: International Thomson Business Press.
41. McCawley, I. (2000) Small Suppliers Seek Broader Shelf Access, *Marketing Week*, 17 February, 20.
42. Carter, M. (1999) Commercial Taste for an Ethical Brew, *Financial Times*, 22 October, 17.
43. Benady, D. (2002) Instant Profits at What Costs, *Marketing Week*, 26 September, 24–7.
44. Charles, G. (2002) Costs Versus Consciences, *Marketing Week*, 5 December, 22–5.

Chapter 18

1. Porter, M. E. (1998) *Competitive Strategy: Techniques for Analysing Industries and Competitors*, New York: Free Press.
2. Graham, G. (1997) Competition is Getting Tougher, *Financial Times*, Special Report on Danish Banking, 9 April, 2.
3. Noble, C. H., R. K. Sinha and A. Kumar (2002) Market Orientation and Alternative Strategic Orientations: A Longitudinal Assessment of Performance Implications, *Journal of Marketing* 66, October, 25–39.
4. Von Clausewitz, C. (1908) *On War*, London: Routledge & Kegan Paul.
5. Macdonald, M. (2002) *Marketing Plans*, Oxford: Butterworth-Heinemann.
6. Dudley, J. W. (1990) *1992: Strategies for the Single Market*, London: Kogan Page.
7. Ross, E. B. (1984) Making Money with Proactive Pricing, *Harvard Business Review* 62, Nov.–Dec., 145–55.
8. Leeflang, P. H. S. and D. R. Wittink (1996) Competitive Reaction versus Consumer Response: Do Managers Over-react? *International Journal of Research in Marketing* 13, 103–19.
9. Hall, W. K. (1980) Survival Strategies in a Hostile Environment, *Harvard Business Review* 58, Sept.–Oct., 75–85.
10. Porter (1980) op. cit.
11. Anonymous (2002) Dyson—Great British Brands, *Marketing*, 1 August, 21.
12. Anonymous (2002) Marketing Week/CIM Effectiveness Awards, *Marketing Week*, 16 November, 60.
13. Day, G. S. and R. Wensley (1988) Assessing Advantage: A Framework for Diagnosing Competitive Superiority, *Journal of Marketing* 52, April, 1–20.
14. Day, G. S. (1999) *Market Driven Strategy: Processes for Creating Value*, New York: Free Press.
15. Porter, M. E. (1998) *Competitive Advantage*, New York: Free Press.
16. For methods of calculating value in organizational markets, see Anderson, J. C. and J. A. Narus (1998) Business Marketing: Understand What Customers Value, *Harvard Business Review*, Nov.–Dec., 53–65.
17. McIntosh, N. (1999) No Sleeping on the Jobs, *Guardian*, 23 September, 8–9.
18. Pickford, J. (1999) Sounds Like a Better Vision, *Financial Times*, 1 December, 15.
19. Whiteling, I. (2002) Innovate Don't Imitate, *Marketing Week*, 2 May, 41–2.
20. Key Note Report (2002) *The Airline Industry*.
21. Bruce, L. (1987) The Bright New Worlds of Benetton, *International Management*, Nov., 24–35.
22. De Chernatony, L., F. Harris and F. Dall'Olmo Riley (2000) Added Value: Its Nature, Roles and Sustainability, *European Journal of Marketing* 34(1/2), 39–56.
23. Day (1999) op. cit.
24. Porter (1998) op. cit.
25. Buzzell, R. D. and B. T. Gale (1987) *The PIMS Principles*, New York: Free Press.
26. Porter (1998) op. cit.
27. McNulty, S. (2001) Short on Frills Big on Morale, *Financial Times*, 31 October, 14.
28. Marsh, P. (2002) Dismay at Job Losses as Dyson Shifts Production to Malaysia, *Financial Times*, 6 February, 3.

Chapter 19

1. Barratt, F. (1992) Britain Lets Down the Drawbridge, *Independent*, 19 September, 43.
2. Easton, G. and L. Araujo (1986) Networks, Bonding and Relationships in Industrial Markets, *Industrial Marketing and Purchasing* 1(1), 8–25.
3. Anonymous (2002) Fixing for a Fight, *Economist*, 20 April, 71–2.
4. Ries, A. and J. Trout (1997) *Marketing Warfare*, New York: McGraw-Hill.
5. Kotler, P. and R. Singh (1981) Marketing Warfare in the 1980s, *Journal of Business Strategy*, Winter, 30–41.
6. Sun Tzu (1963) *The Art of War*, London: Oxford University Press.
7. Von Clausewitz, C. (1908) *On War*, London: Routledge & Kegan Paul.
8. Jeannet, J.-P. (1987) *Competitive Marketing Strategies in a European Context*, Lausanne: International Management Development Institute, 101.
9. See Aaker, D. and G. S. Day (1986) The Perils of High-Growth Markets, *Strategic Management Journal* 7, 409–21; Wensley, R. (1982) PIMS and BCG: New Horizons or False Dawn?, *Strategic Management Journal* 3, 147–58.
10. Anonymous (2000) The Dogfood Danger, *Economist*, 8 April, 82–6.
11. Taylor, P. (2000) Reshaping the Global Landscape of IT, *Financial Times*, Information Technology Survey, 2 February, 1.
12. Morrison, S. and R. Waters (2002) Cisco Has the Edge Despite IT Upheaval, *Financial Times*, 6 November, 33.
13. Hoggart, S. (1988) President for Slumberland, *Observer*, 6 November, 15.
14. Kotler and Singh (1981) op. cit.
15. Porter, M. E. (1998) *Competitive Advantage*, New York: Free Press, 514–17.
16. Von Clausewitz (1908) op. cit.
17. Barksdale, J. (1996) Microsoft World Like to Squash Me Just Like a Bug, *Financial Times*, Special Report on IT, 2 October, 2.
18. Garrett, A. (1997) Wrestling for the Soul of the Internet, *Observer*, 5 October, 7.
19. Alexander, G. (1999) Shocked Gates Ready to Sue for Peace, *Sunday Times*, 7 November, 1.
20. Alexander, G. (1999) Humbled Microsoft Ready to Back Down, *Sunday Times*, 28 March, 11.
21. Marsh, H. (1998) Microsoft's Real Trial is Trust, *Marketing*, 3 December, 16–17.
22. Anonymous (2000) After the Verdict, *Economist*, 8 April, 81–2.
23. Anonymous (2001) Not off the Hook, *Economist*, 15 September, 68–9.
24. Spiegel, P. and P. Abrahams (2001) Microsoft Rivals Criticise Legal Deal, *Financial Times*, 2 November, 21.
25. Hooley, G., J. Saunders and N. Piercy (2003) *Marketing Strategy and Competitive Positioning*, London: Prentice-Hall, 224.
26. Fagan, M. (1991) Unhappy Anniversary for IBM, *Financial Times*, 15 October, 16.
27. Kynge, J. (1997) Malaysia: A Technological Transformation, *Financial Times*, Survey, 19 May, 3.
28. Anonymous (2002) When Something Is Rotten, *Economist*, 27 July, 61–2.
29. Mercado, S., R. Welford and K. Prescott (2000) *European Business: An Issue-based Approach*, Harlow: FT Prentice-Hall.
30. Mitchell, A. (2000) Why AOL/Time Warner Union will Prove Barren, *Marketing Week*, 20 January, 38–9.
31. Shapinker, M. (2000) Marrying in Haste, *Financial Times*, 12 April, 22.
32. London, S. (2002) Secrets of a Successful Partnership, *Financial Times*, 6 February, 12.
33. Lorenz, C. (1992) Take your Partner, *Financial Times*, 17 July, 13.
34. Ohmae, K. (1989) The Global Logic of Strategic Alliances, *Harvard Business Review*, March–April, 143–54.
35. Alexander, G. (1999) Alliances Form in Battle to Dominate Mobile Computing, *Sunday Times*, 14 February, 7.
36. Cane, A. (2000) Playing the Mobile Phone Card, *Financial Times*, 10 February, 13.
37. Marsh, P. (2003) A Synchronised Swim in the Pool, *Financial Times*, 24 January, 14.
38. Shapinker, M. (2001) Tips for a Beautiful Relationship, *Financial Times*, 11 July, 14.
39. Lorenz, C. (1992) The Risks of Sleeping with the Enemy, *Financial Times*, 16 July, 11.
40. Bronder, C. and R. Pritzl (1992) Developing Strategic Alliances: A Conceptual Framework for Successful Cooperation, *European Management Journal* 10(4), 412–21.
41. Nakamoto, M. (1992) Plugging into Each Other's Strengths, *Financial Times*, 27 March, 21.
42. Hoggart (1988) op. cit.
43. Kotler and Singh (1981) op. cit.
44. Urry, M. (1992) Takeover put Spark into Battery Maker, *Financial Times*, 14 April, 21.
45. Jeannet (1987) op. cit.
46. James, B. J. (1984) *Business Wargames*, London: Abacus.
47. Eastham, J. (2002) Thin Times Ahead for Burger King, *Marketing Week*, 1 August, 19–20.
48. Peters, T. J. and R. H. Waterman Jr (1995) *In Search of Excellence: Lessons from America's Best-Run Companies*, New York: Harper & Row.
49. Hammermesh, R. G., M. J. Anderson and J. E. Harris (1978) Strategies for Low Market Share Businesses, *Harvard Business Review* 50(3), 95–102.
50. Hedley, B. (1977) Strategy and the Business Portfolio, *Long Range Planning*, February, 9–15.

Chapter 20

1. Johannessen, J.-A., J. Olaisen and A. Havan (1993) The Challenge of Innovation in a Norwegian Shipyard Facing the Russian Market, *European Journal of Marketing* 27(3), 23–38.
2. Kanter, R. M. (2001) *Evolve: Succeeding in the Digital Culture of Tomorrow*, HBS Press.
3. Bonoma, T. V. (1985) *The Marketing Edge: Making Strategies Work*, New York: Free Press.
4. Mazur, L. (2002) No Pain, No Gain, *Marketing Business*, September, 10–13.
5. Wilson, G. (1993) *Making Change Happen*, London: Pitman.
6. Abopdaher, D. (1986) *A Biography of Iacocca*, London: Star.
7. Stanton, W. J., R. H. Buskirk and R. Spiro (2002) *Management of a Sales Force*, Boston, Mass: Irwin.
8. Webster, F. E. Jr (1988) Rediscovering the Marketing Concept, *Business Horizons* 31 (May–June), 29–39.
9. Webster (1988) op. cit.
10. Argyris, C. (1966) Interpersonal Barriers to Decision Making, *Harvard Business Review* 44 (March–April), 84–97.
11. Kanter, R. M. (1988) *The Change Masters*, London: Allen & Unwin.
12. Piercy, N. (2001) *Marketing-Led Strategy Change*, Oxford: Butterworth-Heinemann.
13. Johnson, G. (1987) *Strategic Change and the Management Process*, Oxford: Basil Blackwell.
14. Pettigrew, A. M. (1974) The Influence Process between Specialists and Executives, *Personnel Review* 3(1), 24–30.
15. Pettigrew, A. M. (1974) op. cit.
16. Ansoff, I. and E. McDonnell (1990) *Implanting Strategic Management*, Englewood Cliffs, NJ: Prentice-Hall.
17. Pettigrew, A. M. (1985) *The Awakening Giant: Continuity and Change in ICI*, Oxford: Basil Blackwell.
18. Kanter (1988) op. cit.

19. London, S. and A. Hill (2002) A Recovery Strategy Worth Copying, *Financial Times*, 16 October, 12.
20. Kennedy, G., J. Benson and J. MacMillan (1984) *Managing Negotiations*, London: Business Books.
21. Piercy, N. (1990) Making Marketing Strategies Happen in the Real World, *Marketing Business*, February, 20–1.
22. Piercy, N. and N. Morgan (1991) Internal Marketing: The Missing Half of the Marketing Programme, *Long Range Planning* 24(2), 82–93.
23. See Grönroos, C. (1985) Internal Marketing: Theory and Practice, in Bloch, T. M., G. D. Upah and V. A. Zeithaml (eds) *Services Marketing in a Changing Environment*, Chicago: American Marketing Association; Gummesson, E. (1987) Using Internal Marketing to Develop a New Culture: The Case of Ericsson Quality, *Journal of Business and Industrial Marketing* 2(3), 23–8; Mudie, P. (1987) Internal Marketing: Cause of Concern, *Quarterly Review of Marketing*, Spring–Summer, 21–4.
24. Laing, A. and L. McKee (2001) Willing Volunteers or Unwilling Conscripts? Professionals and Marketing in Service Organizations, *Journal of Marketing Management* 17(5/6), 559–76.
25. French, J. R. P. and B. Raven (1959) The Bases of Social Power, in Cartwright, D. (ed.) *Studies in Social Power*, Ann Arbor, Mich: University of Michigan Press, 150–67.
26. See Hickson, D. J., C. R. Hinings, C. A. Lee, R. E. Schneck and J. M. Pennings (1971) A Strategic Contingencies Theory of Intraorganizational Power, *Administrative Science Quarterly* 16(2), 216–29; Hinings, C. R., D. J. Hickson, J. M. Pennings and R. E. Schneck (1974) Structural Conditions of Intraorganizational Power, *Administrative Science Quarterly* 19(1), 22–44.
27. Wilson, D. C. (1992) *A Strategy of Change: Concepts and Controversies in the Management of Change*, London: Routledge.
28. See Kanter, R. M., B. A. Stein and T. D. Jick (1992) *The Challenge of Organizational Change*, New York: Free Press; Kanter (1988) op. cit.; Piercy (2001) op. cit.; Ansoff and McDonnell (1990) op. cit.
29. Kanter, Stein and Jick (1992) op. cit.
30. Bonoma, T. V. (1984) Making your Marketing Strategy Work, *Harvard Business Review* 62 (March–April), 68–76.
31. White, D. (1999) Good Ideas Come from Little Boxes, *Financial Times*, 15 September, 18.
32. www.asda.co.uk.
33. Kanter, Stein and Jick (1992) op. cit.
34. Wilson (1993) op. cit.
35. Kennedy, Benson and MacMillan (1984) op. cit.
36. Hewitt, M. (1994) Body Shop Opens its Doors to Marketing, *Marketing*, 26 May, 20.
37. Eriksson, P. and K. Räsänen (1998) The Bitter and the Sweet: Evolving Constellations of Product Mix Management in a Confectionery Company, *European Journal of Marketing* 32(3/4), 279–304.
38. Workman J. P. Jr, C. Homburg and K. Gruner (1998) Marketing Organisation: an Integrative Framework of Dimensions and Determinants, *Journal of Marketing* 62, July, 21–41.
39. See Richards, A. (1994) What is Holding Back Today's Brand Managers?, *Marketing* 3 (3, February), 16–17.
40. Aaker, D. and E. Joachimsthaler (2000) *Brand Leadership*, New York: Free Press, 10–11.
41. Ambler, T. (2001) Category Management is Best Deployed for Brand Positioning, *Marketing*, 29 November, 18.
42. Mitchell, A. (1994) Dark Night of Marketing or a New Dawn?, *Marketing*, 17 February, 22–3.
43. Brownlie, D. and M. Saren (1997) Beyond the One-Dimensional Marketing Manager: The Discourse of Theory, Practice and Relevance, *International Journal of Research in Marketing* 14, 147–61.
44. Leggett, D. (1996) Hours Not to Reason Why, *Marketing*, 31 October, 26–7.
45. Murphy, D. (2002) Cause and Effect, *Marketing Business*, October, 22–4.

Chapter 21

1. Gross, A. C., P. M. Banting, L. N. Meredith and I. D. Ford (1993) *Business Marketing*, Boston, Mass: Houghton Mifflin, 378.
2. Cowell, D. (1995) *The Marketing of Services*, London: Heinemann, 35.
3. Berry, L. L. (1980) Services Marketing is Different, *Business Horizons*, May–June, 24–9.
4. Edgett, S. and S. Parkinson (1993) Marketing for Services Industries: A Review, *Service Industries Journal* 13(3), 19–39.
5. Berry (1980) op. cit.
6. Aijo, T. S. (1996) The Theoretical and Philosophical Underpinnings of Relationship Marketing, *European Journal of Marketing* 30(2), 8–18; Grönroos, C. (1990) *Services Management and Marketing: Managing the Moments of Truth in Service Competition*, Lexington, MA: Lexington Books.
7. Baron, S., K. Harris and B. J. Davies (1996) Oral Participation in Retail Service Delivery: A Comparison of the Roles of Contact Personnel and Customers, *European Journal of Marketing* 30(9), 75–90.
8. Grönroos, C. (1994) From Marketing Mix to Relationship Marketing: Towards a Paradigm Shift in Marketing, *Management Decision* 32(2), 4–20.
9. Egan, C. (1997) Relationship Management, in Jobber, D. (ed.) *The CIM Handbook of Selling and Sales Strategy*, Oxford: Butterworth-Heinemann, 55–88.
10. Berry, L. L. (1995) Relationship Marketing, in Payne, A., M. Christopher, M. Clark and H. Peck (eds) *Relationship Marketing for Competitive Advantage*, Oxford: Butterworth-Heinemann, 65–74.
11. Zeithaml, V. A. and M. J. Bitner (2002) *Services Marketing*, New York: McGraw-Hill, 174–8.
12. Reichheld, F. F. and W. E. Sasser Jr (1990) Zero Defections: Quality Comes to Services, *Harvard Business Review*, Sept.–Oct., 105–11.
13. Roberts, K., S. Varki and R. Brodie (2003) Measuring the Quality of Relationships in Consumer Services: An Empirical Study, *European Journal of Marketing* 37(1/2), 169–96.
14. Reichheld and Sasser Jr (1990) op. cit.
15. Berry, L. L. (1995) Relationship Marketing of Services—Growing Interest, Emerging Perspectives, *Journal of the Academy of Marketing Science* 23(4), 236–45.
16. Bitner, M. J. (1995) Building Service Relationships: It's All About Promises, *Journal of the Academy of Marketing Science* 23(4), 246–51.
17. Bitner (1995) op. cit.
18. Parasuraman, A., L. L. Berry and V. A. Zeithaml (1991) Understanding Customer Expectations of Service, *Sloan Management Review*, Spring, 39–48.
19. Berry (1995) op. cit.
20. Berry, L. L. and A. Parasuraman (1991) *Marketing Services*, New York: Free Press, 136–42.
21. Berry (1995) op. cit.
22. Gummesson, E. (1987) The New Marketing–Developing Long-term Interactive Relationships, *Long Range Planning* 20, 10–20.
23. Bitner (1995) op. cit.
24. See Bitner, M. J., B. H. Booms and M. S. Tetreault (1990) The Service Encounter: Diagnosing Favourable and Unfavourable Incidents, *Journal of Marketing* 43, January, 71–84; Bitner, M. J., B. H. Booms and L. A. Mohr (1994) Critical Service Encounters: The Employee's View, *Journal of Marketing* 58, October, 95–106.
25. Lovelock, C. H., S. Vandermerwe and B. Lewis (1999) *Services Marketing–A European Perspective*, New York: Prentice-Hall, 176.
26. Berry (1995) op. cit.
27. Kasper, H., P. van Helsdingen and W. de Vries Jr (1999) *Services Marketing Management*, Chichester: Wiley, 528.
28. Maxham III, J. G. and R. G. Netemeyer (2002) A Longitudinal Study of Complaining Customers' Evaluations of Multiple Service Failures and Recovery Efforts, *Journal of Marketing* 66, October, 57–71.

29. Johnson, R. (1995) Service Failure and Recovery: Impact, Attributes and Process, in Swartz, T. A., D. E. Bowen and S. W. Brown (eds) *Advances in Services Marketing and Management* 4, 52–65.
30. Thorpe, A. (2000) On ... Handling Complaints, *Guardian*, 10 April, 3.
31. Buzzell, R. D. and B. T. Gale (1987) *The PIMS Principles: Linking Strategy to Performance*, New York: Free Press, 103–34.
32. Parasuraman, A., V. A. Zeithaml and L. L. Berry (1985) A Conceptual Model of Service Quality and its Implications for Future Research, *Journal of Marketing*, Fall, 41–50.
33. Shearer, E. (2003) A Strategic E-business review of Egg, Working Paper, University of Strathclyde.
34. Parasuraman, Zeithaml and Berry (1985) op. cit.
35. Danaher, P. J. and J. Mattson (1994) Customer Satisfaction during the Service Delivery Process, *European Journal of Marketing* 28(5), 5–16.
36. De Ruyter, K., M. Wetzels, J. Lemmink and J. Mattsson (1997) The Dynamics of the Service Delivery Process: A Value-Based Approach, *International Journal of Research in Marketing* 14, 231–43.
37. Zeithaml, V. A., A. Parasuraman and L. L. Berry (1988) SERVQUAL: A Multiple Itemscale for Measuring Consumer Perceptions of Service Quality, *Journal of Retailing* 64(1), 13–37.
38. Lovelock, C. (1992) Seeking Synergy in Service Operations: Seven Things Marketers Need to Know about Service Operations, *European Management Journal* 10(1), 22–9.
39. Mudie, P. and A. Cottam (1997) *The Management and Marketing of Services*, Oxford: Butterworth-Heinemann, 211.
40. Lee, B. (2003) The Impact of E-business on the Hotel Sector, Working Paper, University of Strathclyde.
41. Schlesinger, L. A. and J. L. Heskett (1991) The Service-Driven Service Company, *Harvard Business Review*, Sept.–Oct., 71–81.
42. Lievens, A. and R. K. Moenaert (2000) Communication Flows During Financial Service Innovation, *European Journal of Marketing* 34(9/10), 1078–110.
43. Bowen, D. E. and L. L. Lawler (1992) Empowerment: Why, What, How and When, *Sloan Management Review*, Spring, 31–9.
44. Hiscock, J. (2002) The Brand Insiders, *Marketing*, 23 May, 24–5.
45. Christopher, M. and R. Yallop (1990) Audit your Customer Service Quality, *Focus*, June–July, 1–6.
46. Booms, B. H. and M. J. Bitner (1981) Marketing Strategies and Organisation Structures for Service Firms, in Donnelly, J. H. and W. R. George (eds) *Marketing of Services*, Chicago: American Marketing Association, 47–51.
47. Berry, L. L., E. E. Lefkowith and T. Clark (1980) In Services: What's in a Name?, *Harvard Business Review*, Sept.–Oct., 28–30.
48. Bloemer, J. and K. de Ruyter (1998) On the Relationship Between Store Image, Store Satisfaction and Store Loyalty, *European Journal of Marketing* 32(5/6), 499–513.
49. Cole, G. (2003) Window Shopping, *Financial Times IT Review*, 5 February, 4.
50. Cowell (1984) op. cit.
51. Sellers, P. (1988) How to Handle Customers Gripes, *Fortune* 118 (October), 100.
52. Diacon, S. R. and C. T. Ennew (1996) Ethical Issues in Insurance Marketing in the UK, *European Journal of Marketing* 30(5), 67–80.
53. Morris, M. H. and D. Fuller (1989) Pricing an Industrial Service, *Industrial Marketing Management* 18, 139–46.
54. Rafiq, M. and P. K. Ahmed (1992) The Marketing Mix Reconsidered, *Proceedings of the Annual Conference of the Marketing Education Group*, Salford, 439–51.
55. Wilkinson, A. (2002) Employees can get the Message Across, *Marketing Week*, 3 October, 20.
56. Lemmink, J. and J. Mattsson (1998) Warmth During Non-Productive Retail Encounters: The Hidden Side of Productivity, *International Journal of Research in Marketing* 15, 505–17.
57. Sumner-Smith, D. (2001) A Winning Strategy, *Marketing Business*, May, 26–8.
58. Pruyn, A. and A. Smidts (1998) Effects of Waiting on the Satisfaction with the Service: Beyond Objective Times Measures, *International Journal of Research in Marketing* 15, 321–34.
59. Berry, L. L. (1987) Big Ideas in Services Marketing, *Journal of Services Marketing*, Fall, 5–9.
60. Ohbora, T., A. Parsons and H. Riesenbeck (1992) Alternative Routes to Global Marketing, *McKinsey Quarterly* 3, 52–74.
61. Dewsnap, B. (1997) Trade Marketing, in D. Jobber (ed.) *The CIM Handbook of Selling and Sales Strategy*, Oxford: Butterworth-Heinemann, 104–25.
62. Nicholas, R. (1999) Thirsty Work, *Marketing Week*, 11 November, 79–83.
63. Dewsnap, B. and D. Jobber (2000) The Sales–Marketing Interface in Consumer Packaged-Goods Companies: A Conceptual Framework, *Journal of Personal Selling and Sales Management* 20(2), 109–19.
64. Thelen, E. M. and A. G. Woodside (1997) What Evokes the Brand or Store? Consumer Research on Accessibility Theory Applied to Modelling Primary Choice, *International Journal of Research in Marketing* 14, 125–45.
65. Krishnan, T. V. and H. Soni (1997) Guaranteed Profit Margins: A Demonstration of Retailer Power, *International Journal of Research in Marketing* 14, 35–56.
66. Davies, G. and N. Sanghavi (1993) Is the Category Killer a Significant Innovation? *ESRC Seminar: Strategic Issues in Retailing*, Manchester Business School, 1–23.
67. Brown, S. (1990) Innovation and Evolution in UK Retailing: The Retail Warehouse, *European Journal of Marketing* 24(9), 39–54.
68. Hollander, S. C. (1966) Notes on the Retail Accordion, *Journal of Retailing* 42(2), 24.
69. Davidson, W. R., A. D. Bates and S. J. Bass (1976) The Retail Life Cycle, *Harvard Business Review* 54 (Nov.–Dec.), 89–96.
70. Knee, D. and D. Walters (1985) *Strategy in Retailing: Theory and Application*, Oxford: Philip Adam.
71. Gray, R. (2000) E-tail Must Deliver on Web Promises, *Marketing*, 2 March, 37–8.
72. Voyle, S. (2000) Food E-tailers Struggle to Get the Recipe Right, *Financial Times*, 15 February, 17.
73. Reed, A. (2002) Tesco.com Leads the Way with Completely Integrated Thinking, *Campaign*, 19 April. 14.
74. Davies, G. (1992) Innovation in Retailing, *Creativity and Innovation Management* 1(4), 230.
75. Anonymous (2001) A Hyper Market, *Economist*, 7 April, 88–9.
76. Ryle, S. (2002) How to Get Ahead in Advertising at No Cost, *Observer*, 1 December, 8.
77. Hayward, C. (2001) The Child-Catchers, *Marketing Week*, 18 October, 45–6.
78. Hayward, C. (2002) Who, Where, Win, *Marketing Week*, 12 September, 43.
79. Burt, S. (2000) The Strategic Role of Retail Brands in British Grocery Retailing, *European Journal of Marketing* 34(8), 875–90.
80. Bloemer, S., K. de Ruyter and M. Wetzels (1999) Linking Perceived Service Quality and Service Loyalty: A Multi-Dimensional Perspective, *European Journal of Marketing* 33(11/12), 1082–106.
81. Elg, U. and U. Johansson (1996) Networking When National Boundaries Dissolve: The Swedish Food Sector, *European Journal of Marketing* 30(2), 61–74.
82. Betts, E. J. and P. J. McGoldrick (1996) Consumer Behaviour with the Retail 'Sales', *European Journal of Marketing* 30(8), 40–58.
83. See Lock, A. and P. Harris (1996) Political Marketing—Vive La Difference, *European Journal of Marketing* 30(10/11), 21–31; Butler, P. and N. Collins (1996) Strategic Analysis in Political Markets, *European Journal of Marketing* 30(10/11), 32–44.
84. Bennett, P. D. (1988) *Marketing*, New York: McGraw-Hill, 690–2.
85. Shapiro, B. (1992) Marketing for Non-Profit Organisations, *Harvard Business Review*, Sept.–Oct., 123–32.

86. Balabanis, G., R. E. Stables and H. C. Phillips (1997) Market Orientation in the Top 200 British Charity Organisations and its Impact on their Performance, *European Journal of Marketing* 31(8), 583–603.
87. For an in-depth examination of political marketing, see Butler, P. and N. Collins (1994) Political Marketing: Structure and Process, *European Journal of Marketing* 28(1) 19–34.
88. Murphy, C. (2002) Real Value from Reflected Glory, *Financial Times*, 17 September, 15.
89. Hibbert, S. A. (1995) The Market Positioning of British Medical Charities, *European Journal of Marketing* 29(10), 6–26.

Chapter 22

1. Cuyvers, L., P. de Pelsmacker, G. Rayp and I. T. M. Roozen (1995) A Decision Support Model for the Planning and Assessment of Export Promotion Activities by Government Export Promotion Institutions—the Belgian Case, *International Journal of Research in Marketing* 12, 173–86.
2. Katsikeas, C. S., N. F. Piercy and C. Ioannidis (1996) Determinants of Export Performance in a European Context, *European Journal of Marketing* 30(6), 6–35.
3. Laurence, B. (1994) M&S Plans £1 Billion Investment, *Guardian*, 25 May, 14.
4. See Aharoni (1966) *The Foreign Investment Decision Process*, Boston, Mass: Harvard University Press; Aagarwal, S. and S. N. Ramaswami (1992) Choice of Foreign Market Entry Mode: Impact of Ownership, Location and Internalisation Factors, *Journal of International Business Studies*, Spring, 1–27; Knickerbocker, F. T. (1973) *Oligopolistic Reaction and Multinational Enterprise*, Boston, Mass: Harvard University Press.
5. Borrell, J. (1990) Living with Shock Therapy, *Time*, 11 June, 31.
6. Tully, S. (1990) Poland's Gamble Begins to Pay Off, *Fortune*, 27 August, 91–6.
7. Litvak, I. A. and P. M. Banting (1968) A Conceptual Framework for International Business Arrangements, in King, R. L. (ed.) *Marketing and the New Science of Planning*, Chicago: American Marketing Association, 460–7.
8. Conway, T. and J. S. Swift (2000) International Relationship Marketing, *European Journal of Marketing* 34(1/2), 1391–413.
9. Johanson, J. and J.-E. Vahlne (1977) The Internationalisation Process of the Firm: A Model of Knowledge Development and Increasing Foreign Market Commitments, *Journal of International Business Studies* 8(1), 23–32.
10. Erramilli, M. K. (1991) Entry Mode Choice in Service Industries, *International Marketing Review* 7(5), 50–62.
11. Halsall, M. (1994) Nova Means 'Does Not Go' in Spanish: Why British Firms Need to Learn the Language of Customers, *Guardian*, 11 April, 16.
12. Egan, C. and P. McKiernan (1994) *Inside Fortress Europe: Strategies for the Single Market*, Wokingham: Addison-Wesley, 118.
13. Cateora, P. R., J. L. Graham and P. J. Ghauri (2002) *International Marketing*, London: McGraw-Hill, 377.
14. Knickerbocker (1973) op. cit.
15. Whitelock, J. and D. Jobber (1994) The Impact of Competitor Environment on Initial Market Entry in a New, Non-Domestic Market, *Proceedings of the Marketing Education Group Conference*, Coleraine, July, 1008–17.
16. Young, S., J. Hamill, C. Wheeler and J. R. Davies (1989) *International Market Entry and Development*, Englewood Cliffs, NJ: Prentice-Hall.
17. West, A. (1987) *Marketing Overseas*, London: Pitman.
18. For comprehensive coverage of the problem faced by exporters, see Katsikeas, C. S. and R. E. Morgan (1994) Differences in Perceptions of Exporting Problems based on Firm Size and Export Market Experience, *European Journal of Marketing* 28(5), 17–35.
19. Young, Hamill, Wheeler and Davies (1989) op. cit.
20. Bloomgardon, K. (2000) Branching Out, *Marketing Business*, April, 12–3.
21. Hopkinson, G. C. and S. Hogarth-Scott (1999) Franchise Relationship Quality: Microeconomic Explanations, *European Journal of Marketing* 33(9/10), 827–43.
22. Welford, R. and K. Prescott (1996) *European Business*, London: Pitman.
23. Wright, R. W. (1981) Evolving International Business Arrangements, in Dhawan, K. C., H. Etemad and R. W. Wright (eds) *International Business: A Canadian Perspective*, Reading, MA: Addison Wesley.
24. Young, Hamill, Wheeler and Davies (1989) op. cit.
25. Terpstra, V. and R. Sarathy (1999) *International Marketing*, Fort Worth, Texas: Dryden.
26. Hooley, G., T. Cox, D. Shipley, J. Fahy, J. Beracs and K. Kolos (1996) Foreign Direct Investment in Hungary: Resource Acquisition and Domestic Competitive Advantage, *Journal of International Business Studies* 4, 683–709.
27. Terpstra and Sarathy (1999) op. cit.
28. Smit, B. (1996), Dutch Bank Moves Deeper into the Mid West, *European*, 28 Nov.–4 Dece., 25.
29. Ghauri, P. N. and K. Holstius (1996) The Role of Matching in the Foreign Market Entry Process in the Baltic States, *European Journal of Marketing* 30(2), 75–88.
30. Buckley P. J., H. Mirza and J. R. Sparkes (1987) Foreign Direct Investment in Japan as a Means of Market Entry: The Case of European Firms, *Journal of Marketing Management* 2(3), 241–58.
31. Goodnow, J. D. and J. E. Hansz (1972) Environmental Determinants of Overseas Market Entry Strategies, *Journal of International Business Studies* 3(1), 33–50.
32. Contractor, F. J. (1984) Choosing between Direct Investment and Licensing: Theoretical Considerations and Empirical Tests, *Journal of International Business Studies* 15(3), 167–88.
33. Anderson, E. and A. T. Coughlan (1987) International Market Entry and Expansion via Independent or Integrated Channels of Distribution, *Journal of Marketing* 51, January, 71–82.
34. Klein, S. and J. R. Roth (1990) Determinants of Export Channel Structure: The Effects of Experience and Psychic Distance Reconsidered, *International Marketing Review* 7(5), 27–38.
35. See Agarwal and Ramaswami (1992) op. cit.; Knickerbocker (1973) op. cit.
36. Sharma, D. D. (1988) Overseas Market Entry Strategy: The Technical Consultancy Firms, *Journal of Global Marketing* 2(2), 89–110.
37. Johanson and Vahlne (1977) op. cit.
38. Johanson, J. and J.-E. Vahlne (1990) The Mechanisms of Internationalisation, *International Marketing Review* 7(4), 11–24.
39. Buckley, Mirza and Sparkes (1987) op. cit.
40. Sharma (1988) op. cit.
41. Klein and Roth (1990) op. cit.
42. Erramilli (1991) op. cit.
43. Buckley, Mirza and Sparkes (1987) op. cit.
44. Quelch, J. A. and E. J. Hoff (1986) Customizing Global Marketing, *Harvard Business Review*, May–June, 59–68.
45. Banerjee, A. (1994) Transnational Advertising Development and Management: An Account Planning Approach and a Process Framework, *International Journal of Advertising* 13, 95–124.
46. Mayer, M. (1991) *Whatever Happened to Madison Avenue? Advertising in the '90s*, Boston, Mass: Little, Brown, 186–7.
47. Mitchell, A. (1993) Can Branding Take on Global Proportions? *Marketing*, 29 April, 20–1.
48. Mazur, L. (2002) No Pain, No Gain, *Marketing Business*, September, 10–13.
49. Chernatony, L. de (1993) Ten Hints for EC-wide Brands, *Marketing*, 11 February, 16.
50. Aaker, D. A. and E. Joachimsthaler (2000) *Brand Leadership*, New York: Free Press, 303–9.
51. Benady, D. (2003) Uncontrolled Immigration, *Marketing Week*, 20 February, 24–7.

52. Kirby, K. (2000) Globally Led Locally Driven, *Marketing Business*, May, 26–7.
53. Luce, E. (2002) Hard Sell to a Billion Consumers, *Financial Times*, 15 April, 14.
54. Chernatony, L. de (1993) Ten Hints for EC-wide Brands, *Marketing*, 11 February, 16.
55. Benady. D. (2003) Home Truths About Global Marketing, *Marketing Week*, 6 February, 20.
56. Clegg, A. (2002) Crossing Cultures, *Marketing Week*, 28 February, 69–70.
57. Dawkins, W. (1996) Time to Pull Back the Screen, *Financial Times*, 19 November, 14.
58. Dudley, J. W. (1989) *1992: Strategies for the Single Market*, London: Kogan Page.
59. Ohmae, K. (1985) *Triad Power*, New York: Free Press.
60. Mitchell (1993) op. cit.
61. Harris, P. and F. McDonald (1994) *European Business and Marketing: Strategic Issues*, London: Chapman.
62. Duncan, T. and J. Ramaprasad (1993) Ad Agency Views of Standardised Campaigns for Multinational Clients, Conference of the American Academy of Advertising, Chicago, Ill, 17 April.
63. Papavassiliou, N. and V. Stathakopoulos (1997) Standardisation versus Adaptation of International Advertising Strategies: Towards a Framework, *European Journal of Marketing* 31(7), 504–27.
64. Harris, G. and S. Attour (2003) The International Advertising Practices of Multinational Companies: A Content Analysis Study, *European Journal of Marketing* 37(1/2), 154–68.
65. Richmond, S. (1994) Global Taboos, in World Advertising, *Campaign Report*, 13 May, 19–21.
66. Cateora, P. R., J. L. Graham and P. N. Ghauri (2002) op. cit., 376.
67. Killough, J. (1978) Improved Pay-offs from Transnational Advertising, *Harvard Business Review*, July–Aug., 58–70.
68. Alden, D. L., J.-B. E. M. Steenkamp and R. Batra (1998) Brand Positioning Through Advertising in Asia, North America, and Europe: The Role of Global Consumer Culture, *Journal of Marketing* 63, January, 75–87.
69. Jobber, D. and G. Lancaster (2003) *Selling and Sales Management*, London: Pitman.
70. Campbell, N. C. G., J. L. Graham, A. Jolibert and H. G. Meissner (1988) Marketing Negotiations in France, Germany, the United Kingdom and the United States, *Journal of Marketing* 52, April, 49–62.
71. Niss, N. (1996) Country of Origin Marketing Over the Product Life Cycle: A Danish Case Study, *European Journal of Marketing* 30(3), 6–22.
72. See Powell, C. (2000) Why We Really Must Fly the Flag, *Observer*, Business Section, 25 April, 4 and Yip, G. (2003) *Total Global Strategy*, Englewood Cliffs, NJ: Prentice-Hall, 88.
73. Leszinski, R. (1992) Pricing for the Single Market, *McKinsey Quarterly* 3, 86–94.
74. Cateora, P. R. and P. Ghauri (2002) *International Marketing*, Homewood, Ala: Irwin.
75. Garda, R. A. (1992) Tactical Pricing, *McKinsey Quarterly* 3, 75–85.
76. Leszinski (1992) op. cit.
77. Anonymous (2001) Consumers Fall for Levi Message, *Guardian*, 21 November, 25.
78. Benady, D. (2003) Uncontrolled Immigration, *Marketing Week*, 20 February, 24–7.
79. Finch, J. (2002) Tesco Loses Fight to Sell Cheap Levi's, *Guardian*, 1 August, 20.
80. Osborne, A. (2001) Levi's Wins Fight to Halt Tesco Price Cuts, *Guardian*, 21 November, 13.
81. Cateora and Ghauri (2002) op. cit.
82. Shipley, D. and B. Neale (1988) Countertrade: Reactive or Proactive, *Journal of Business Research*, June, 327–35.
83. Darlin, D. (1989) Myth and Marketing in Japan, *Wall Street Journal*, 6 April, B1.
84. Chadee, D. D. and J. Mattsson (1998) Do Service and Merchandise Exporters Behave and Perform Differently? *European Journal of Marketing* 32(9/10), 830–42.
85. Bartlett, C. and S. Ghoshal (1991) *Managing Across Borders: The Transnational Solution*, Cambridge, Mass: Harvard Business School Press.
86. Ghoshal, S. and N. Nohria (1993) Horses for Courses: Organizational Forms of Multinational Corporations, *Sloan Management Review*, Winter, 23–35.
87. Mazur, L. (1993) Brands sans Frontières, *Observer*, 28 November, 8.
88. Ohbora, T., A. Parsons and H. Riesenbeck (1992) Alternative Routes to Global Marketing, *McKinsey Quarterly* 3, 52–74.
89. Blackwell, N., J.-P. Bizet, P. Child and D. Hensley (1992) Creating European Organisations that Work, *McKinsey Quarterly* 2, 31–43.
90. Bartlett, C. (1991) Procter & Gamble Europe, Cambridge, Mass: Harvard Business School Case, No. 9-384-139.
91. Mazur (1993) op. cit.
92. Aaker, D. A. and E. Joachimsthaler (2000) *Brand Leadership*, New York: Free Press, 310–14.
93. Anonymous (2002) Ex-Admen Who Must Act Globally and Think Locally, *Campaign*, 15 March, 18.
94. Benady, D. (2003) The Global Power Struggle, *Marketing Week*, 27 March, 24–7.

Glossary

ad hoc research a research project that focuses on a specific problem, collecting data at one point in time with one sample of respondents

adapted marketing mix an international marketing strategy for changing the marketing mix for each international target market

administered vertical marketing system a channel situation where a manufacturer that dominates a market through its size and strong brands may exercise considerable power over intermediaries even though they are independent

advertising any paid form of non-personal communication of ideas or products in the prime media, i.e. television, the press, posters, cinema and radio, the Internet and direct marketing

advertising agency an organization that specializes in providing services such as media selection, creative work, production and campaign planning to clients

advertising message the use of words, symbols and illustrations to communicate to a target audience using prime media

advertising platform the aspect of the seller's product that is most persuasive and relevant to the target consumer

ambush marketing originally referred to the activities of companies that try to associate themselves with an event (e.g. the Olympics) without paying any fee to the event owner; now means the sponsoring of the television coverage of a major event, national teams and the support of individual sportspeople

attitude the degree to which a customer or prospect likes or dislikes a brand

augmented product the core product plus extra functional and/or emotional values combined in a unique way to form a brand

awareness set the set of brands that the consumer is aware may provide a solution to the problem

beliefs descriptive thoughts that a person holds about something

benefit segmentation the grouping of people based on the different benefits they seek from a product

bonus pack giving a customer extra quantity at no additional cost

brainstorming the technique where a group of people generate ideas without initial evaluation; only when the list of ideas is complete is each idea then evaluated

brand a distinctive product offering created by the use of a name, symbol, design, packaging, or some combination of these intended to differentiate it from its competitors

brand assets the distinctive features of a brand

brand domain the brand's target market

brand equity the goodwill associated with a brand name, which adds tangible value to a company through the resulting higher sales and profits

brand extension the use of an established brand name on a new brand within the same broad market or product category

brand heritage the background to the brand and its culture

brand personality the character of a brand described in terms of other entities such as people, animals and objects

brand reflection the relationship of the brand to self-identity

brand stretching the use of an established brand name for brands in unrelated markets or product categories

brand values the core values and characteristics of a brand

broadcast sponsorship a form of sponsorship where a television or radio programme is the focus

business analysis a review of the projected sales, costs and profits for a new product to establish whether these factors satisfy company objectives

business mission the organization's purpose, usually setting out its competitive domain, which distinguishes the business from others of its type

buy-response method a study of the value customers place on a product by asking them if they would be willing to buy it at varying price levels

buying centre a group that is involved in the buying decision (also known as a decision-making unit)

buying signals statements by a buyer that indicate s/he is interested in buying

bypass attack circumventing the defender's position, usually through technological leap-frogging or diversification

campaign objectives goals set by an organization in terms of, for example, sales, profits, customers won or retained, or awareness creation

catalogue marketing the sale of products through catalogues distributed to agents and customers, usually by mail or at stores

category management the management of brands in a group, portfolio or category, with specific emphasis on the retail trade's requirements

cause-related marketing the commercial activity by which businesses and charities or causes form a partnership with each other to market an image, good or service for mutual benefit

centralization in international marketing it is the global integration of international operations

change master a person that develops an implementation strategy to drive through organizational change

channel integration the way in which the players in the channel are linked

channel intermediaries organizations that facilitate the distribution of products to customers

channel of distribution the means by which products are moved from the producer to the ultimate consumer

channel strategy the selection of the most effective distribution channel, the most appropriate level of distribution intensity and the degree of channel integration

choice criteria the various attributes (and benefits) people use when evaluating products and services

classical conditioning the process of using an established relationship between a stimulus and a response to cause the learning of the same response to a different stimulus

co-branding (communications) the linking of two or more existing brands from different companies or business units for the purposes of joint communication

co-branding (product) the linking of two or more existing brands from different companies or business units to form a product in which the brand names are visible to consumers

coercive power power inherent in the ability to punish

cognitive dissonance post-purchase concerns of a consumer arising from uncertainty as to whether a decision to purchase was the correct one

cognitive learning the learning of knowledge, and development of beliefs and attitudes without direct reinforcement

combination brand name a combination of family and individual brand names

competitive advantage the attempt to achieve superior performance through differentiation to provide superior customer value or by managing to achieve lowest delivered cost

competitive behaviour the activities of rival companies with respect to each other; this can take five forms—conflict, competition, co-existence, co-operation and collusion

competitive bidding drawing up detailed specifications for a product and putting the contract out to tender

competitive scope the breadth of a company's competitive challenge, e.g. broad or narrow

competitor analysis an examination of the nature of actual and potential competitors, and their objectives and strategies

competitor audit a precise analysis of competitor strengths and weaknesses, objectives and strategies

competitor targets the organizations against which a company chooses to compete directly

concept testing testing new product ideas with potential customers

concession analysis the evaluation of things that can be offered to someone in negotiation valued from the viewpoint of the receiver

consumer decision-making process the stages a consumer goes through when buying something—namely, problem awareness, information search, evaluation of alternatives, purchase and post-purchase evaluation

consumer panel household consumers who provide information on their purchases over time

consumer panel data a type of continuous research where information is provided by household consumers on their purchases over time

consumer pull the targeting of consumers with communications (e.g. promotions) designed to create demand that will pull the product into the distribution chain

continuous research repeated interviewing of the same sample of people

contractual joint venture two or more companies form a partnership but no joint enterprise with a separate identity is formed

contractual vertical marketing system a franchise arrangement (e.g. a franchise) that ties together producers and resellers

control the stage in the marketing planning process or cycle when the performance against plan is monitored so that corrective action, if necessary, can be taken

core competences the principal distinctive capabilities possessed by a company—what it is really good at

core product anything that provides the central benefits required by customers

core strategy the means of achieving marketing objectives, including target markets, competitor targets and competitive advantage

corporate identity the ethos, aims and values of an organization, presenting a sense of its individuality, which helps to differentiate it from its competitors

corporate vertical marketing system a channel situation where an organization gains control of distribution through ownership

cost analysis the calculation of direct and fixed costs, and their allocation to products, customers and/or distribution channels

counter-offensive defence a counter-attack that takes the form of a head-on counter-attack, an attack on the attacker's cash cow or an encirclement of the attacker

counter-trade a method of exchange where not all transactions are concluded in cash; goods may be included as part of the asking price

covert power play the use of disguised forms of power tactics

culture the traditions, taboos, values and basic attitudes of the whole society in which an individual lives

customer analysis a survey of who the customers are, what choice criteria they use, how they rate competitive offerings and on what variables they can be segmented

customer benefits those things that a customer values in a product; customer benefits derive from product features

customer relationship management the methodologies, technologies and e-commerce capabilities used by firms to manage customer relationships

customer satisfaction the fulfilment of customers' requirements or needs

customer satisfaction measurement a process through which customer satisfaction criteria are set, customers are surveyed and the results interpreted in order to establish the level of customer satisfaction with the organization's product

customer value perceived benefits minus perceived sacrifice

customized marketing the market coverage strategy where a company decides to target individual customers and develops separate marketing mixes for each

data the most basic form of knowledge, the result of observations

data warehousing (or mining) the storage and analysis of customer data, gathered from their visits to websites, for classificatory and modelling purposes so that products, promotions and price can be tailored to the specific needs of individual customers

database marketing an interactive approach to marketing that uses individually addressable marketing media and channels to provide information to a target audience, stimulate demand and stay close to customers

decentralization in international marketing it is the delegation of international operations to individual countries or regions

decision-making process the stages that organizations and people pass through when purchasing a physical product or service

decision-making unit (DMU) a group of people within an organization who are involved in the buying decision (also known as the buying centre)

depth interviews the interviewing of consumers individually for perhaps one or two hours, with the aim of understanding their attitudes, values, behaviour and/or beliefs

descriptive research research undertaken to describe customers' beliefs, attitudes, preferences and behaviour

differential advantage a clear performance differential over the competition on factors that are important to target customers

differential marketing strategies market coverage strategies where a company decides to target several market segments and develops separate marketing mixes for each

differentiated marketing a market coverage strategy where a company decides to target several market segments and develops separate marketing mixes for each

differentiation strategy the selection of one or more customer choice criteria and positioning the offering accordingly to achieve superior customer value

diffusion of innovation process the process by which a new product spreads throughout a market over time

direct cost pricing the calculation of only those costs that are likely to rise as output increases

direct exporting the handling of exporting activities by the exporting organization rather than by a domestically based independent organization

direct investment market entry that involves investment in foreign-based assembly or manufacturing facilities

direct mail material sent through the postal service to the recipient's house or business address promoting a product and/or maintaining an ongoing relationship

direct marketing (1) acquiring and retaining customers without the use of an intermediary; (2) the distribution of products, information and promotional benefits to target consumers through interactive communication in a way that allows response to be measured

direct response advertising the use of the prime advertising media such as television, newspapers and magazines to elicit an order, enquiry or request for a visit

distribution analysis an examination of movements in power bases, channel attractiveness, physical distribution and distribution behaviour

distribution push the targeting of channel intermediaries with communications (e.g. promotions) to push the product into the distribution chain

divest to improve short-term cash yield by dropping or selling off a product

domain names global system of unique names for addressing web servers; the Domain Name System (DNS) is the method of administering such names; each level in the system is given a name and is called a domain: gTDL refers to global top-level domains (e.g. .com, .edu, .org), ccTDL refers to country code top-level domains of which there are around 250 (e.g. .uk, .fr, .it, .tv); domain names are maintained by the Internet Corporation for Assigned Names (ICANN) (www.icann.org) and are constantly under review; ICANN also deals with cases of cybersquatting; domain name registration is required if a company wants to establish a web presence

e-business a term originally used by IBM to describe technological solutions that enable an organization to optimize its business operations through the adoption of digital technologies

e-commerce the use of technologies such as the Internet, electronic data interchange, e-mail and electronic payment systems to expedite business interactions

e-commerce marketing mix the extension of the traditional marketing mix to include the opportunities afforded by new electronic media such as the Internet

economic order quantity the quantity of stock to be ordered where total costs are at the lowest

economic value to the customer (EVC) the amount a customer would have to pay to make the total life-cycle costs of a new and a reference product the same

effectiveness doing the right thing, making the correct strategic choice

efficiency a way of managing business processes to a high standard, usually concerned with cost reduction; also called 'doing things right'

ego drive the need to make a sale in a personal way, not merely for money

electronic data interchange (EDI) a pre-Internet technology developed to enable organizations' computers to exchange documents (e.g. purchase orders) with one another in a secure environment via a dedicated computer link

e-marketing the achievement of marketing objectives through the utilization of electronic communication technologies, including mobile devices

empathy to be able to feel as the buyer feels, to be able to understand customer problems and needs

encirclement attack attacking the defender from all sides, i.e. every market segment is hit with every combination of product features

entry barriers barriers that act to prevent new firms from entering a market, e.g. the high level of investment required

entry into new markets (diversification) the entry into new markets by new products

environmental scanning the process of monitoring and analysing the marketing environment of a company

e-procurement the purchasing of goods and services (in business markets) via the Internet

equity joint venture where two or more companies form a partnership that involves the creation of a new company

ethics the moral principles and values that govern the actions and decisions of an individual or group

event sponsorship sponsorship of a sporting or other event

evoked set the set of brands that the consumer seriously evaluates before making a purchase

exaggerated promises barrier a barrier to the matching of expected and perceived service levels caused by the unwarranted building up of expectations by exaggerated promises

exchange the act or process of receiving something from someone by giving something in return

exclusive distribution an extreme form of selective distribution where only one wholesaler, retailer or industrial distributor is used in a geographical area to sell the products of a supplier

exhibition an event that brings buyers and sellers together in a commercial setting

experience curve the combined effect of economies of scale and learning as cumulative output increases

experimental research research undertaken in order to establish cause and effect

experimentation the application of stimuli (e.g. two price levels) to different matched groups under controlled conditions for the purpose of measuring their effect on a variable (e.g. sales)

expert power power that derives from an individual's expertise

exploratory research the preliminary exploration of a research area prior to the main data-collection stage

family brand name a brand name used for all products in a range

fighter brands low-cost manufacturers' brands introduced to combat own-label brands

flanking attack attacking geographical areas or market segments where the defender is poorly represented

flanking defence the defence of a hitherto unprotected market segment

focus group a group normally of six to eight consumers brought together for a discussion focusing on an aspect of a company's marketing

focused marketing a market coverage strategy where a company decides to target one market segment with a single marketing mix

foreign consumer culture positioning positioning a brand as associated with a specific foreign culture (e.g. Italian fashion)

franchise a legal contract in which a producer and channel intermediaries agree each other's rights and obligations; usually the intermediary receives marketing, managerial, technical and financial services in return for a fee

franchising a form of licensing where a package of services is offered by the franchisor to the franchisee in return for payment

frontal attack a competitive strategy where the challenger takes on the defender head on

full cost pricing pricing so as to include all costs and based on certain sales volume assumptions

geodemographics the process of grouping households into geographic clusters based on information such as type of accommodation, occupation, number and age of children, and ethnic background

global branding achievement of brand penetration worldwide

global consumer culture positioning positioning a brand as a symbol of a given global culture (e.g. young cosmopolitan men)

going-rate pricing pricing at the rate generally applicable in the market, focusing on competitors' offerings rather than on company costs

group discussion a group, usually of six to eight consumers, brought together for a discussion focusing on an aspect of a company's marketing

guerrilla attack making life uncomfortable for stronger rivals through, for example, unpredictable price discounts, sales promotions or heavy advertising in a few selected regions

hall tests bringing a sample of target consumers to a room that has been hired so that alternative marketing ideas (e.g. promotions) can be tested

halo customers customers that are not directly targeted but may find the product attractive

harvest objective the improvement of profit margins to improve cash flow even if the longer-term result is falling sales

hold objective a strategy of defending a product in order to maintain market share

http (hypertext transfer protocol) a standard invented by Tim Berners-Lee in 1991 to enable computers across the Internet to receive and send web content

inadequate delivery barrier a barrier to the matching of expected and perceived service levels caused by the failure of the service provider to select, train and reward staff adequately, resulting in poor or inconsistent delivery of service

inadequate resources barrier a barrier to the matching of expected and perceived service levels caused by the unwillingness of service providers to provide the necessary resources

indirect exporting the use of independent organizations within the exporter's domestic market to facilitate export

individual brand name a brand name that does not identify a brand with a particular company

industry a group of companies that market products that are close substitutes for each other

information combinations of data that provide decision-relevant knowledge

information framing the way in which information is presented to people

information processing the process by which a stimulus is received, interpreted, stored in memory and later retrieved

information search the identification of alternative ways of problem-solving

ingredient co-branding the explicit positioning of a supplier's brand as an ingredient of a product

innovation the commercialization of an invention by bringing it to market

inseparability a characteristic of services, namely that their production cannot be separated from their consumption

intangibility a characteristic of services, namely that they cannot be touched, seen, tasted or smelled

integrated marketing communications the concept that companies co-ordinate their marketing communications tools to deliver a clear, consistent, credible and competitive message about the organization and its products

intensive distribution the aim of this is to provide saturation coverage of the market by using all available outlets

interaction approach an approach to buyer–seller relations that treats the relationships as taking place between two active parties

internal marketing training, motivating and communicating with staff to cause them to work effectively in providing customer satisfaction; more recently the term has been expanded to include marketing to all staff with the aim of achieving the acceptance of marketing ideas and plans

Internet global web of computer networks, which permits instantaneous communication and transactions between individuals and organizations; the structure of these networks is based on links between special computers called servers and routers, which store and direct data across the networks respectively

Internet and online marketing the distribution of products, information and promotional benefits to consumers through electronic media

Internet marketing the achievement of marketing objectives through the utilization of Internet and web-based technologies

invention the discovery of new methods and ideas

just-in-time (JIT) this concept aims to minimize stocks by organizing a supply system that provides materials and components as they are required

key account management an approach to selling that focuses resources on major customers and uses a team selling approach

legitimate power power based on legitimate authority, such as line management

licensing a contractual arrangement in which a licensor provides a licensee with certain rights, e.g. to technology access or production rights

life-cycle costs all the components of costs associated with buying, owning and using a physical product or service

lifestyle the pattern of living as expressed in a person's activities, interests and opinions

lifestyle segmentation the grouping of people according to their pattern of living as expressed in their activities, interests and opinions

local consumer culture positioning positioning a brand as associated with a local culture (e.g. local production and consumption of a good)

macroenvironment a number of broader forces that affect not only the company but the other actors in the environment, e.g. social, political, technological and economic

macrosegmentation the segmentation of organizational markets by size, industry and location

manufacturer brands brands that are created by producers and bear their chosen brand name

market development to take current products and market them in new markets

market expansion the attempt to increase the size of a market by converting non-users to users of the product and by increasing usage rates

market penetration to grow sales by marketing an existing product in an existing market

market segmentation the process of identifying individuals or organizations with similar characteristics that have significant implications for the determination of marketing strategy

market share analysis a comparison of company sales with total sales of the product, including sales of competitors

market testing the limited launch of a new product to test sales potential

marketing audit a systematic examination of a business's marketing environment, objectives, strategies and activities, with a view to identifying key strategic issues, problem areas and opportunities

marketing concept the achievement of corporate goals through meeting and exceeding customer needs better than the competition

marketing control the stage in the marketing planning process or cycle when performance against plan is monitored so that corrective action, if necessary, can be taken

marketing environment the actors and forces that affect a company's capability to operate effectively in providing products and services to its customers

marketing information system a system in which marketing information is formally gathered, stored, analysed and distributed to managers in accordance with their informational needs on a regular, planned basis

marketing mix a framework for the tactical management of the customer relationship, including product, place, price, promotion (the 4-Ps); in the case of services three other elements to be taken into account are process, people and physical evidence

marketing objectives there are two types of marketing objective: strategic thrust, which dictates which products should be sold in which markets, and strategic objectives, i.e. product-level objectives, such as build, hold, harvest and divest

marketing orientation companies with a marketing orientation focus on customer needs as the primary drivers of organizational performance

marketing planning the process by which businesses analyse the environment and their capabilities, decide upon courses of marketing action and implement those decisions

marketing research the gathering of data and information on the market

marketing structures the marketing frameworks (organization, training and internal communications) upon which marketing activities are based

marketing systems sets of connected parts (information, planning and control) that support the marketing function

marketing-oriented pricing an approach to pricing that takes a range of marketing factors into account when setting prices

media class decision the choice of prime media, i.e. the press, cinema, television, posters, radio, or some combination of these

media vehicle decision the choice of the particular newspaper, magazine, television spot, poster site, etc.

microenvironment the actors in the firm's immediate environment that affect its capability to operate effectively in its chosen markets—namely, suppliers, distributors, customers and competitors

microsegmentation segmentation according to choice criteria, DMU structure, decision-making process, buy class, purchasing structure and organizational innovativeness

misconception barrier a failure by marketers to understand what customers really value about their service

mobile defence involves diversification or broadening the market by redefining the business

mobile marketing the sending of text messages to mobile phones to promote products and build relationships with consumers

modified rebuy where a regular requirement for the type of product exists and the buying alternatives are known but sufficient change (e.g. a delivery problem) has occurred to require some alteration to the normal supply procedure

money-off promotions sales promotions that discount the normal price

motivation the process involving needs that set drives in motion to accomplish goals

new task refers to the first time purchase of a product or input by an organization

niche objective the strategy of targeting a small market segment

omnibus survey a regular survey, usually operated by a marketing research specialist company, which asks questions of respondents for several clients on the same questionnaire

operant conditioning the use of rewards to generate reinforcement of response

overt power play the use of visible, open kinds of power tactics

own-label brands brands created and owned by distributors or retailers

parallel co-branding the joining of two or more independent brands to produce a combined brand

parallel importing when importers buy products from distributors in one country and sell them in another to distributors who are not part of the manufacturer's normal distribution; caused by big price differences for the same product between different countries

perception the process by which people select, organize and interpret sensory stimulation into a meaningful picture of the world

perishability a characteristic of services, namely that the capacity of a service business, such as a hotel room, cannot be stored—if it is not occupied, this is lost income that cannot be recovered

personal selling oral communication with prospective purchasers with the intention of making a sale

personality the inner psychological characteristics of individuals that lead to consistent responses to their environment

place the distribution channels to be used, outlet locations, methods of transportation

portfolio planning managing groups of brands and product lines

position defence building a fortification around existing products, usually through keen pricing and improved promotion

positioning the choice of target market (where the company wishes to compete) and differential advantage (how the company wishes to compete)

positioning strategy the choice of target market (**where** the company wishes to compete) and differential advantage (**how** the company wishes to compete)

pre-emptive defence usually involves continuous innovation and new product development, recognizing that attack is the best form of defence

premiums any merchandise offered free or at low cost as an incentive to purchase

price (1) the amount of money paid for a product; (2) the agreed value placed on the exchange by a buyer and seller

price unbundling pricing each element in the offering so that the price of the total product package is raised

price waterfall the difference between list price and realized or transaction price

product a good or service offered or performed by an organization or individual, which is capable of satisfying customer needs

product churning a continuous spiral of new product introductions

product development increasing sales by improving present products or developing new products for current markets

product features the characteristics of a product that may or may not convey a customer benefit

product life cycle a four-stage cycle in the life of a product illustrated as sales and profits curves, the four stages being introduction, growth, maturity and decline

product line a group of brands that are closely related in terms of the functions and benefits they provide

product mix the total set of products marketed by a company

product placement the deliberate placing of products and/or their logos in movies and television, usually in return for money

product portfolio the total range of products offered by the company

production orientation a business approach that is inwardly focused either on costs or on a definition of a company in terms of its production facilities

profile segmentation the grouping of people in terms of profile variables, such as age and socio-economic group, so that marketers can communicate to them

profitability analysis the calculation of sales revenues and costs for the purpose of calculating the profit performance of products, customers and/or distribution channels

project teams the bringing together of staff from such areas as R&D, engineering, manufacturing, finance, and marketing to work on a project such as new product development

promotional mix advertising, personal selling, sales promotions, public relations, direct marketing, and Internet and online promotion

proposal analysis the prediction and evaluation of proposals and demands likely to be made by someone with whom one is negotiating

prospecting searching for and calling on potential customers

psychographic segmentation the grouping of people according to their lifestyle and personality characteristics

public relations the management of communications and relationships to establish goodwill and mutual understanding between an organization and its public

publicity the communication of a product or business by placing information about it in the media without paying for time or space directly

qualitative research exploratory research that aims to understand consumers' attitudes, values, behaviour and beliefs

reasoning a more complex form of cognitive learning where conclusions are reached by connected thought

rebranding the changing of a brand or corporate name

reference group a group of people that influences an individual's attitude or behaviour

referent power power derived by the reference source, e.g. when people identify with and respect the architect of change

relationship marketing the process of creating, maintaining and enhancing strong relationships with customers and other stakeholders

repositioning changing the target market or differential advantage, or both

research brief a written document stating the client's requirements

research proposal a document defining what the marketing research agency promises to do for its client and how much it will cost

retail accordion a theory of retail evolution that focuses on the cycle of retailers widening and then contracting product ranges

retail audit a type of continuous research tracking the sales of products through retail outlets

retail audit data a type of continuous research tracking the sales of products through retail outlets

retail life cycle a theory of retailing evolution that is based on the product life cycle, stating that new types of retailing pass through birth, growth, maturity and decline

retail positioning the choice of target market and differential advantage for a retail outlet

reverse marketing the process whereby the buyer attempts to persuade the supplier to provide exactly what the organization wants

reward power power derived from the ability to provide benefits

rote learning the learning of two or more concepts without conditioning

safety (buffer) stocks stocks or inventory held to cover against uncertainty about resupply lead times

sales analysis a comparison of actual with target sales

sales promotion incentives to customers or the trade that are designed to stimulate purchase

salesforce evaluation the measurement of salesperson performance so that strengths and weaknesses can be identified

salesforce motivation the motivation of salespeople by a process that involves needs, which set encouraging drives in motion to accomplish goals

sampling process a term used in research to denote the selection of a sub-set of the total population in order to interview them

secondary research data that has already been collected by another researcher for another purpose

selective attention the process by which people screen out those stimuli that are neither meaningful to them nor consistent with their experiences and beliefs

selective distortion the distortion of information received by people according to their existing beliefs and attitudes

selective distribution the use of a limited number of outlets in a geographical area to sell the products of a supplier

selective retention the process by which people only retain a selection of messages in memory

self-reference criteria the use of one's own perceptions and choice criteria to judge what is important to consumers. In international markets, the perceptions and choice criteria of domestic consumers may be used to judge what is important to foreign consumers

service any deed, performance or effort carried out for the customer

services marketing mix product, place, price, promotion, people, process and physical evidence (the '7-Ps')

simultaneous engineering the involvement of manufacturing and product development engineers in the same development team in an effort to reduce development time

social responsibility the ethical principle that a person or organization should be accountable for how its acts might affect the physical environment and general public

sponsorship a business relationship between a provider of funds, resources or services and an individual, event or organization that offers in return some rights and association that may be used for commercial advantage

standardized marketing mix an international marketing strategy for using essentially the same product, promotion, distribution, and pricing in all the company's international markets

straight rebuy refers to a purchase by an organization from a previously approved supplier of a previously purchased item

strategic alliance collaboration between two or more organizations through, for example, joint ventures, licensing agreements, long-term purchasing and supply arrangement

strategic business unit a business or company division serving a distinct group of customers and with a distinct set of competitors, usually strategically autonomous

strategic focus the strategies that can be employed to achieve an objective

strategic issues analysis an examination of the suitability of marketing objectives and segmentation bases in the light of changes in the marketplace

strategic objectives product-level objectives relating to the decision to build, hold, harvest or divest products

strategic thrust the decision concerning which products to sell in which markets

strategic withdrawal holding on to the company's strengths while getting rid of its weaknesses

strong theory of advertising the notion that advertising can change people's attitudes sufficiently to persuade people who have not previously bought a brand to buy it; desire and conviction precede purchase

SWOT analysis a structured approach to evaluating the strategic position of a business by identifying its strengths, weaknesses, opportunities and threats

target accounts organizations or individuals whose custom the company wishes to obtain

target audience the group of people at which a direct marketing campaign is aimed

target market a segment that has been selected as a focus for the company's offering or communications

target marketing selecting a segment as a focus for the company's offering or communications

team selling the use of the combined efforts of salespeople, product specialists, engineers, sales managers and even directors to sell products

telemarketing a marketing communications system whereby trained specialists use telecommunications and information technologies to conduct marketing and sales activities

test marketing the launch of a new product in one or a few geographic areas chosen to be representative of the intended market

total quality management the set of programmes designed to constantly improve the quality of physical products, services and processes

trade marketing marketing to the retail trade

trade-off analysis a measure of the trade-off customers make between price and other product features so that their effects on product preference can be established

transfer pricing the price charged between the profit centres of the same company, sometimes used to take advantage of lower taxes in another country

transition curve the emotional stages that people pass through when confronted with an adverse change

undifferentiated marketing a market coverage strategy where a company decides to ignore market segment differences and develops a single marketing mix for the whole market

value analysis a method of cost reduction in which components are examined to see if they can be made more cheaply

value chain the set of a firm's activities that are conducted to design, manufacture, market, distribute, and service its products

variability a characteristic of services, namely that, being delivered by people, the standard of their performance is open to variation

vicarious learning learning from others without direct experience or reward

viral marketing electronic word of mouth where promotional messages are spread using e-mail from person to person

weak theory of advertising the notion that advertising can first arouse awareness and interest, nudge some consumers towards a doubting first trial purchase and then provide some reassurance and reinforcement; desire and conviction do not precede purchase

website a collection of various files including text, graphics, video and audio content created by organizations and individuals; website content is transmitted across the Internet using http

wheel of retailing a theory of retailing development which suggests that new forms of retailing begin as low-cost, cut-price and narrow-margin operations and then trade up until they mature as high-price operators, vulnerable to a new influx of low-cost operators

World Wide Web a collection of computer files that can be accessed via the Internet, allowing organizations to include documents containing text, images, sound and video

Companies and Brands Index

Page numbers in **bold** refer to main entries and those in *italics* refer to illustrations.

3G services **152**, 624–5
3M 341, 348, 464
5pm.co.uk 721
20th Century Fox 617

A

AAMS 134
Abbey National 576
Absolut Vodka **76**
ACE *see* Air Catering Enterprises
Action Cancer 144
Advanced Passenger Train (APT) 340
Advantage card (Boots) **513**
Air Catering Enterprises (ACE) 206–8
Air Products *108*
Airtours 134, 476
Alpen *270*
Amazon.com 565
America Online (AOL) 142, 718
American Express 417
Anadin 281
Andy Thornton Ltd 326–7
AOL *see* America Online
Apple Computer 70, 359–60, **693–4**, *695*
APT *see* Advanced Passenger Train
Arcadis 288–9
Argos 534
Ariel 284
ASDA (Associated Dairies) 39, 384, 435, **703–5**, **770**
Associated Marketing Services 825
Audi 236
Austin-Trumans (steel) 380
Australian Homemade 667
Avon *673*, **673–4**

B

B&Q 861
Bacardi Breezer 348, *349*
Bacardi Rum *220*
Baileys liqueur 282–3
Bang & Olufsen 234, **694**
Barclays bank 539
Beck's *239*, 239
Ben & Jerry's 144–5
Benetton 432, **646**, 699, 862, 864
Bird's Eye Walls 599

Black Diamond products **740–8**
Black Magic chocolates 215
Bluetooth Technology 551–2, *553*
BMW 12, 15, 75, **229**, 236, 269, 274, **368–70**, 436, 609
Boddingtons 269, *270*, *424*
Boden 534
Body Shop 132, 149, 159, 664, 773
Bofors 146
Boots **513**
Bosch 384, *387*
Branson, Richard *755*
    see also Virgin, Virgin Atlantic, Virgin Trains
Brightnoil (anti-spam technology) 578
British Aerospace 147
British Airways 21, 713, 716, *794*
British Airways World Cargo **879–82**
British Rail 340, 660–1
British Telecom (BT) **261**, 276
Britvic 644
Brylcreem 730
BT *see* British Telecom
Buccleuch Scotch Beef 721
Budweiser **239, 246–52**, *612*
Burberry **304–6**
Burger King 403
Burton Group 234

C

Cadbury **531**, 596, 715
Cadbury Schweppes 326
Caffé Nero **95–6**
CamRA *see* Real Ale
Canon 43, *218*, 361, *362*
Capital One (credit cards) 536–7
Carbery (cheese) 202–5
Carling *611*
Carlsberg 434, 444
Carnation 326
Casio watches 720
Caterpillar 717
Cathay Pacific *313*
Channel 4 216
Cherokee 69
Chinon brand 824
Christie's 148
Cisco Corporation **118**
Cisco Systems 132, **715**
Clarks shoes 217
Classic FM 10, 214
Clubcard (Tesco) **513**, *521*, 522
Co-op 664
Coca-Cola 77, 221, 263–4, 397, 722, 856, 862

Coco Pops 577
Coffeemate 326
Compaq Computers 132, 689
Consignia 289
Coors Brewers Ltd (Bass) **555–6**
Corn Flakes 716
Corolla 865
Corus Engineering Steels **253–6**
Cosmopolitan **20**
Costa Coffee **95**, 664
Costa Republic **95–6**
Covisint online marketplace **115**
Currys 824

D

Dabs.com 314
Daewoo 495
Daimler Chrysler 115
Dell Computers Corporation 123, 153, 269, **309**, 465, **566**, 568
Delta Airlines 814
DHL 635, *656*
Diet Coke 264–5
Diet Pepsi 265
Direct Line 384, 386, 507, 536
Disney 284–5
Distillers 727
Dixons 824
Doritos Dippas snack 217
DPD service *103*
Drambuie *430*
Dream Works 617
Dual System Deutschland 149
Dunhill 608, 609
Duplo 276
Dyson 269, *325*, *634*, **687**, 700

E

easyCar 832
easyJet **408–10**, 567
eBay 314, *557*
echoecho.com 691
Egg financial services **275**, 576
Electrolux 135
Elle magazine 283
Elsevier 135
EMI Group 143, 638
Emirates (airline) *424*
Enjoy! frozen foods 599
Envirosell 201
Ethical Consumer 97

Euromonitor GMID Database 183
Eurosport 216
Eurotunnel 712

F

Family Hostel 235
Fanta Icy Lemon 221
Federal Express 567, 656
Femidom **197**
Fiat 163–7, 397
Firebox 58
First Choice 134
Fisons 728
5pm.co.uk 721
Flora margarine 608
Fokker 147
Ford 115, 283, 314, 343, 355, 393, 466, 759
France Télécom **551**
Freedom Foods 97
Friends Reunited.com *562*
Fruitibix 339

G

Gael Software 852
General Motors (GM) 115, 265, 688, 759
Gerber baby food 235
gettyimages *194*
Gillette 346
Glaxo SmithKline 861
Glaztex plc **502–3**
GM *see* General Motors
GNER 104
Google 142, 437, **583–5**
Grandtravel 235
Greenhouse Fund 752
Grundig 725
Guinness *436*

H

H&M *see* Hennes & Mauritz
Häagen-Dazs 282–3
Halifax *759*
Hansen Bathrooms **411**, **790**
Harley-Davidson (motorcycles) 12
Heineken 440
Heinz 431, 523
Hennes & Mauritz (H&M) **28–30**, 653
Heron Engineering **59–61**
Hewlett Packard 349, 423, 654
Highland Distillers 512
Hilton Hotels **291**

Index

Holsten Pils **239**
Honda 327
Hoover 601
Hope Community Resources, Inc. **837–42**
HP Foods 462
HSBC *872*
Hutchison 3g **624–5**

I

IBM 39, 76, 428, 695, 718–19, 728
ICI 152
ICL 123
IKEA 87
iMac computers 693, 694, *695*
    see also Apple Computer; Macintosh computers
IMP group 118
Intel 132, *282*, 283

J

Jaguar 654
Jambo Records **787–9**
JamCast 638
Johnson's Baby Lotion 716

K

Kahn Research 201
Kellogg's 262, 326, 577, 716
Kiss 100 (radio) **531**
KLM (airline) *522*
Kodak 725
KPMG 143
Kwik-Fit 16

L

Ladbrokes **291**
Laker Airlines 21
Land Rover *260*
Lastminute.com 814
Legal & General Direct 537
Lego 276
Legoland 31–4
Leith Agency **833–6**
Lettuseat advertising campaign **453–60**
Lever Brothers 287, 686
Lever GmbH 149
Levi Strauss 221, 274, 281, **301–3**, 395, 856, 867, **868**
Levitt 285
Linux **354**
Little Chef 85, *600*

L'Oréal **673–4**, 875
Lucozade 271, 279–80, *597*
Lufthansa 723

M

Macallan whisky 512
McCain's 426, 599
McDonald's 85, 237, 284–5, **403–4**, 794, 810, 856, 859, 862, **876–8**
McDonnell Douglas 724
Macintosh computers 70, 238, 359–60
    see also Apple Computer; iMac computers; Rowntree Macintosh
McVitie's 349, 862
Manchester United **611**
Marathon 859
MarketMind Brand Tracking System **453–60**
Marks & Spencer 81, **160–2**, 266, 377, 691, 715, 844–5
Marlboro 418, 420
Marriott hotels 802, 803
Mars (confectionery) *432*, 719, 859, 862
Marsh-McBirney Inc **615**
Matsui 824
Matsushita 725
Mercedes 12, *858*
MGTF *238*
Microsoft **331–4**, **354**, **718**
Millenniuim Dome 31–4
MindGenius 852
Mini (BMW) 236, **368–70**
Minitel **551**
Mitsubishi Ireland **740–8**
Moben Kitchens 445
Model T (Ford) 759
Mondeo (Ford) 355
Morris Services **130**
Morrisons **735–9**
Motorola 725
Müller yoghurt 396, 634
MyTravel 277, 476

N

Napster software **578**, 638
National Lottery (UK) **371–4**
Navigator browser 718
NCR 397
Nectar loyalty card 513, *514*, **544–7**
Nestlé 134–5, 147, **496**, 596, *598*, 786, 863
Next 132, 534
NFO WorldGroup **453–60**
Nike 295, 418

Nokia **9**, **40**, 312, 800, *801*
Norsk Hydro 727–8
Norsk Kjem 654
Northern Foods **27**
Norway advertisement *814*

O

Octavia cars 241
Oldsmobile cars 688
Orange **110**, 614, **829**
Overture 437

P

P&O Cruises *812*
Pampers *435*, 858
Panasonic *695*
Parceline **103**
Pears soap 595
Pearson 135
Pentium computers 69–70, 71
PeopleSoft Supply Management *657*
Pepsi 265, 274, 573, 722
Perpetual Calendar *720*
Perrier 134–5
Peugeot 123
Philips 135, **363**, 377, 864
Pilkington 135
Pizza Magic 13, 14
PlayStation 221
Polo (VW) 74
Polycell 349
Post Office 289
Pret A Manger 269, 664
Priceline.com 556–7, 572
PricewaterhouseCoopers 143
Procter & Gamble 18, 186, 197, 428–9, *435*, 609, 755, 777, 858, 870–1
Prudential **275**, 576
Psion 153
Puissance 7 279

Q

Qualcast 355
Quantum International 533

R

Radio 3 10
Radisson SAS hotel 21
Raider 279
Range Rover 17, 19
Reader's Digest 525
Real Ale (CamRA) 215
Reebok *18*, 418
Reemtsma Cigarettenfabriken 398
Renault 123
Reuters **752**
Roche (pharmaceuticals) 397
Rover 74, 397
Rowntree Macintosh 715
Royal Society for the Prevention of Cruelty to Animals (RSPCA) 97
Royal Society for the Protection of Birds (RSPB) 521
RPM consultancy 816
RSPB *see* Royal Society for the Protection of Birds
RSPCA *see* Royal Society for the Prevention of Cruelty to Animals
Ryanair **408–10**, 696

S

Saab 17, 77, *524*
Safeway **735–9**
Sainsbury 237, *597*, 737–9
The Samaritans *826*
Samsung *310*
Scandinavian Airlines System (SAS) 809
Scania 134
Schering 605
Schweppes 81, 644, 647
Seiko 699, *720*
Senior Citizen foods 235
Sensor razors 346
Shell *151*, 279, 522
Siemens *106*, 724
Silhouette (sunglasses) 395
Ski yogurt 81
Skoda **241**, *523*
Sky (television) 216, 434
SmithKline Beecham 730
   see also Glaxo SmithKline
SNCF railway company 661
Sony 123, 221, 267, *268*, 327, 864
Sony Walkman 340, 359, 689
Sotheby's 148
Southwest Airlines 696
SPA Marketing Systems 824
Speedlink rail service 660–1
Star Alliance 723
Starbucks **95**
StoraEnso **706–9**
Sun Microsystems 350
Sunderland of Scotland **51**
Survey Monkey **191**
Swatch 210, 267, 269

T

Talking Newspapers 721
Tango 13, **75**
Target Group Index 216
Tesco 16, **395**, 571, 572, 634, 737–9, 867, **868**
  Clubcard **513**, *521*, 522
Tetley Bitter 609
Texas Instruments 351, 386–7
Thin Red Line **586–92**
3G services **152**, 624–5
3M 341, 348, 464
Time Out 238
Tio Pepe *425*
Toshiba *282*, 283
Toughbook PC *695*
Toyota 7, *150*, 232, 264–5, 274, **525**, 865
Travelworld 715
TVR cars 234
TWA 21, 713, 716
20th Century Fox 617
Twix 279

U

UK National Lottery **371–4**
Unilever 320, **335–6**, 342, 602, 608, 719, 776, 777
United Airlines 723
United Parcel Service (UPS) *107*, 769
Usenet 142

V

Vauxhall 418
Virgin 280, 638
Virgin Atlantic *693*
Virgin Trains 654, 803, **804**

Visa credit cards 610
Vodafone 152, 607, **611**, 654, **669–72**
Volkswagen 74, **241**
Volvo 134, 613

W

Wal-Mart 435, **554**, **703–5**
Walkers (snacks) 217
Walkman 340, 359, 689
Walls 719
Wash & Go shampoo 609
Weatherpruf Shoe Waxes **62–3**
Weetabix 339, *598*
Whirlpool 284
White Horse Whisky **450–2**
WHSmith 651
Winters Company Ltd **129**

X

Xbox **331–4**
Xerox 107, 728, **763**

Y

Yahoo! 724
Yamaha 350–1
Yoplait 354

Z

Zantac 724, 861
Zara 646, **653**
ZDNet *572*
Zovirax 861

Subject Index

A

AC²ID test 289, 291–3
acceptance
    change 755, 756, 758
    gaining 769
accessibility improvement 637
account information systems 512
ACORN targeting classification 223
acquisitions 276, 721
ad hoc research 175–6
adaptation 856–60
    marketing mix 858
additions, product lines 339
adoption factors 557–8
advertising 413–60
    affordability 427
    agencies 441–4
    budgets 427–8
    campaigns 439, 440–4, 453–60
    direct response 532–3
    ethics 444–6
    evaluation 439–40
    expenditure 419
    media decisions 433–9
    positioning brands 864
    strategies 422–40
    taboos 863
    theories 421–2
age
    consumer behaviour 85–7
    demographic variables 220–1
    distribution 139–40
agencies
    advertising 441–4
    client relationships 176
    industrial customers distribution 640
    marketing research 175
air freight 661–2
Ajzen model 71–2
alliances 309
allowances 601
alternatives evaluation 71–3
analysis
    competitors 677–710
    cost 782–3
    market share 781–2
    profitability 782–3
    sales 781–2
analytical techniques 509

Ansoff Matrix 325–6
anti-social behaviour 618–19
application and implementation 749–882
art sponsorship 829
Asia 823
    see also China; Japan
attack strategies 717
attitudes, consumer behaviour 83–4
attractive conditions
    divest objectives 731
    harvest objectives 730
    hold objectives 726–9
    niche objectives 729
audiences
    advertising strategies 422–3
    direct marketing campaigns 519–20
audits
    external 41–2
    internal 42
    marketing 41–4, 569
    retail 177
    websites 691
automatic vending 820
awareness, advertising 423

B

BCG growth-share matrix 320–1
B2B *see* business-to-business
bargaining power
    buyers 680
    supplier 680
    target marketing 231
barriers
    brand development 859
    implementation 758–61
    service quality 804, 805
    standardization 859
base, brand extensions 265
behavioural forces 462–4
behavioural segmentation 214–18
    benefits 214–15
    purchase occasion 215
    usage 216–17
beliefs 83–4, 217–18
benefits
    e-commerce 558–62
    Internet 558–62
    organizations 797–8
    unquantifiable 760
blending marketing mix 21
blockbuster movies 626–31
blocking marketing reports 762

bonding 800–1
bonus packs 595
boosting sales 601
brainstorming 347–8
brands
    building 266–73
    definition 260–1
    developing economies 294
    extensions 265, 279–81
    identities 258–306
    key decisions 273–5
    managers 343–6
    naming strategies 273–5
    personality 431–2
    positioning 864
    product life cycle 308–10
    sponsorship associations 609–10
    tracking 453–60
    types 262–4
bribery 495
briefs, research 179–80
browsers 718
budget airlines 696
budgets, advertising 427–8
build objectives
    attractive conditions 714–16
    competitive marketing strategies 714–25
    strategic alliances 723–5
business
    analysis 352
    marketing orientation 23
    marketing philosophy 23–5
    mission 39–40
    new products analysis 352
    organizational buying 110
    performance 22–5
    planning 39–40
business-to-business (B2B)
    communication 104
    markets 516
buy class
    microsegmentation 227
    organizational buying 110–12
buy-response method 388–9
buyers
    bargaining power 680
    behaviour 66–7, 475
    powers 463–4
    seller negotiations 463
    seller relationship 119–20, 123
buying
    see also purchase

behaviour 99–130
    building relationships 122–4
    complexity 100–1
    organizational 100–13
    purchasing practice 113–17
    relationship management 117–22
organizations 99–130

C

call objectives 474–5
campaigns
    advertising 439, 440–4, 453–60
    direct mail 523–6
    direct marketing 519–38
canvassing 470
capability
    companies 684, 849–50
    profiles 684, 849–50
    target marketing 232
capacity utilization 698–9
car companies 391, 525
cartels 148
cash cows 320
catalogue marketing 533–5
catalogue stores 819
category killers 819
category manager growth 776
cause-related principles 144
central Europe 137–8
    see also eastern Europe
centralization
    purchasing 114
    vs decentralization 870–1
change management
    acceptance 758
    agents 752
    commitment 758
    compliance 758
    implications 757
    marketing implementation 754–8
    pricing 397–401
    resistance 761
    search for meaning 756
channel intermediaries
    conflict management 650–2
    consumers 637–40
    conventional 645
    efficiency 636
    evaluation 649–50
    franchising 645–7
    functions 635–7

industrial 640–1
  integration 645–7
  management 647–52
  motivation 648–9
  ownership 647
  selection 642–3, 648
  services 641
  strategies 641–7
  training 649
  types 637–41
children 445–6, 577, 578
China
  consumers 219
  marketing to 861
  personal selling 479
choice criteria
  consumer behaviour 74–7
  microsegmentation 227
  organizational buying 107–12
cinema 436
class decisions, media 433–8
classical conditioning 82
classics, product life cycle 315
client-agency relationships 176, 442
closing sales, personal selling 477–8
clothing 28–30
  costs 30
  lead times 30
co-branding 281–5
co-existence 713
co-operation 713
co-ordinated marketing systems 509
codes of practice 147
coffee wars 95–6
cognitive learning 82
cold canvassing responsibilities 470
collusion 713
combination brand names 274
commercialization 357–63
commitment, change management 758
committees 344
communications
  brand building 271–2
  co-branding 284–5
  employees 814
  faux pas 848
  integrated marketing 416–18
  processes 418–20
  rebranding 279
community relations 610, 624–5

companies
  capability profiles 684, 849–50
  values 264
comparative advantages, Internet 558
compensation 490–2
competencies, Internet marketing 563–6
competition 675–748
  see also competitive...
  advertising budgets 428
  analysing 677–710
  external marketing audits 42
  going international 845
  information gathering 197–8
  marketing strategies 711–48
  new product development 363
  personal selling 474
  policies 134–5
  positioning products 426
  price changes 399–401
  pricing strategies 394–5
  strategies 711–48
  strong brands 264
  target marketing 231–2
  undermining 867
competitions 601
competitive advantage 49, 677, 687–91
  building 696
  cost leadership 697–700
  differentiation 687, 688, 691–7
  industry structure analysis 678–86
  Internet use 566–8, 696
  marketing mix 19–21
  sources 689–91
  strategies 687–9
  value chain 690–1
competitive behaviour 712–13
competitive bidding 381–2
competitive industry structure 678–86
  buyer bargaining power 680
  strategy implications 684
  success factors 683–4
  supplier bargaining power 680
competitive marketing strategies 711–48
  build objectives 714–25
  competitive behaviour 712–13
  development 714
  direct objectives 731
  harvest objectives 730
  hold objectives 725–9
  niche objectives 729
  strategic triangle 712

Index

competitive shakeout 309
competitive strength 322
competitors
    analysis 681–6
        objectives 685
        strategies 685–6
    defining 682–3
    identification 683–8
    industry 681
    orientated pricing 380–2
    strengths 683–5
    targets 49
    weaknesses 683–5
    who are they 682–3
complaints
    handling 804
    sales responsibilities 471
compliance, change 758
concept testing 351–2
conflict
    competitive behaviour 713
    management 650–2
conjoint analysis *see* trade-off analysis
consolidation, brands 277
consultation, experts 185
consumer behaviour 65–98
    alternatives evaluation 71–3
    brand strength 264–5
    buyer behaviour 66–74
    choice criteria 74–7
    decision-making process 79, 97–8
    emotions 76
    ethics 97–8
    extended problem-solving 77–9
    influences 77–89
    information search 70–1
    perceived risk 78
    personal influences 79–87
        age 85–7
        attitudes 83–4
        beliefs 83–4
        information processing 79–82
        life cycle 85–6
        lifestyle 84–5
        motivation 82–3
        personality 84
    post purchase evaluation 73–4
    purchase situation 71–3
    rebranding 279
    social influences 87–9
    strong brands 264–5
    who buys? 67–8

consumers
    benefits and limitations 559
    brand personality 431–2
    channels 637–40
    China 219
    consumer movement 145
    direct producer distribution 637–8
    ethnographic research 186
    Internet benefits/limitations 559
    market segmentation 212–25
    panels 177
    positioning products 424–6
    producer distribution 639
    producers
        direct sales 637–8
        reconciliation 635–6
    promotions 596
    protection 539
    segmentation methods 214
continuous research 177–8
control
    see also marketing control
    core strategies 51–2
convenience stores 819
copycatting 263
core strategies
    see also strategies
    control 51–2
    effectiveness tests 49
    implementation 50–1
    marketing mix decisions 50
    organization 50–1
    planning 48–52
    target markets 48
corporate identities
    management 288–93
    products 258–306
corporate resources 21
corporate strategy changes 277
cost leadership
    see also direct cost pricing; marginal cost pricing
    capacity utilization 698–9
    competitive strategies 688
    creation 697–700
    economies of scale 697–8
    integration 699
    interrelationships 699
    learning 698
    linkages 699
    policy decisions 699–700
    timing 699

Index

costs
  analysis 782–3
  clothing 30
  focus 688
  going international 845
  Internet marketing 567
  orientated pricing 378–80
  pricing strategies 396–7
coupons 598, 618
creative decisions 536–7
creative leadership 342
CRM *see* customer relationship management
culture
  forces 138–45
  problems 54
  social influences 87–8
customer relationship management (CRM) 514–18, 796–804
  success factors 518
  systems 177–8
  value creation 548
customers
  buyer-seller negotiations 463
  database information 510–11
  distribution services 640, 656–7
  expectations 462–3, 806
  going international 845
  marketing service benefits 798–9
  nature 100
  needs matching 19
  organizational buying 100, 110
  orientation 5
  pricing new products 386
  producer distribution 640
  product value 388–92
  production involvement 808
  prospecting 470
  psychology 81
  records 470
  retention strategy development 799–804
  satisfaction 15–16, 781
  size, organizational buying 100
  value 13–16
customized marketing 236–9
customized products 568
cycle of motivation 490

D

data-collection
  quantitative stage 186–94
  questionnaires 191–4
  survey methods 188–91
data warehousing (data mining) 568

databases
  e-marketing 217
  marketing
    direct 509–14, 527–8
    information 183
    market research 177
    uses 512–14
decentralization vs centralization 870–1
deception
  packaging 294
  pricing 402
  sales management 495
decision-making process
  consumer behaviour 79
  media vehicle 438–9
  organizational buying 102–7, 110–11
  retailing 821–6
decision-making units (DMUs)
  cultural forces 141
  microsegmentation 227–8
  organizational buying 102–7, 110–11
defence strategies 727
delivery companies online 635
delivery salespeople 468
demand curves 376
demography
  forces 138–40
  psychographic segmentation 220–2
demonstrations 476
denial 755, 756
department stores 819
departments, new product development 344
derived demand 101–2
descriptive research 187
design
  clothing 29–30
  salesforce 482–7
developing economies 294
development
  advertising campaigns 440–4
  advertising strategies 422–40
  buyer-seller relationships 119–20
  competitive marketing strategies 714
  customer retention strategies 799–804
  European markets 133–7
  marketing implementation 762–72
  marketing mix 828
  new products 337–74
  products 352–5
  relationship management 119–20
differential advantage
  creation 691–7
  distribution 694

eroding 697
price 695–6
products 693
promotion 694–5
sales management 481
style 694
sustaining 697
differential marketing strategies 211
differentiation 234
competitive advantage 687, 688
focus 688
retailing 822
service quality 811–12
target marketing 827–8
diffusion
innovations 357
products 359
the digital divide 576
direct cost pricing 379–80
see also marginal cost pricing
direct exporting 851–2
foreign-based agents 851
sales representatives 851–2
direct investment 855–6
direct mail
campaigns 523–6
ethics 538
direct marketing 414–15, 505–48
campaigns 519–38
definitions 507–8
ethics 538–9
growth in activities 508–9
techniques 466
direct response advertising 532–3
directors' roles 345
disbelief 755, 756
discount houses 819
discounts 600
discrimination, pricing 404
display support 770
distortion 80
distribution 633–74, 851
accessibility improvement 637
air 661–2
channels
consumers 637–40
intermediaries 635–41
types 637–41
consumers 637–40
customer services 656–7
differential advantages 694
e-commerce marketing mix 574–5
efficiency 636

ethics 662–4
exclusive 644
human elements 654
intensity 643–4
intermediaries 635–41
inventory control 658–9
materials handling 662
order processing 657–8
physical 652–62
pipelines 662
pricing strategies 396
rail 660–1
rebranding 279
road 661
selective 644
specialist services 637
transportation 660–2
types 637–41
warehousing 659–60
water 662
diversification 327
divest objectives 731
DMUs see decision-making units
doing versus saying 760–1
domestic markets 845
dullness sources 12–13
dumping products 404

E

e-business
environment 146
hotel industry 808
e-commerce
benefits 558–62
Internet marketing 551, 553–6
limitations 558–62
market exchanges 556–7
marketing mix 569–75
productivity 566
terms 552
e-mails 573
e-marketing
audience segmentation 217
branding by association 261
change agents 752
consumer research 67
customer relationship management 516, 518
databases 217
delivery companies 635
e-business 146
e-commerce 551
e-mails 573

Index

e-procurement systems 555–6
export 852
fast food 14
financial services 805
growth market building 715
guerrilla marketing 721
hotel industry 808
information technology 821
integrated Internet business 118
Internet survey tool 191
low-cost airlines 696
measuring competitiveness 691
music industry 638
network communities 562
new product development 343, 354
online
    consumer research 67
    financial services 805
    product development 344
    services 565
planning 51
pricing new products 386
product development 344
product life cycle 314
productivity 566
retailing 821
sales management 465, 473
services 565
success story 554
technology use 229, 554
telemarketing 530
website analysis 178
e-procurement systems 555–6
early stage, relationship management 119
eastern Europe 137–8
    see also central Europe
ecological forces 148–51
economic environment 132
economic forces 132–8
economic growth 132–3
economic value to the customer (EVC) analysis 392
economies of scale 697–8
economists 376–8
EDI *see* electronic data interchange technology
effectiveness
    core strategies 49
    marketing mix 16–19
    vs efficiency 7–8
efficiency
    channel intermediaries 636
    distribution 636
    vs effectiveness 7–8

Ehrenberg and Goodhart model 72
electronic data interchange (EDI) technology 553
electronic sales channels 465–6
emotions 76
employees 814
endorsements, ethics 618
energy conservation 150–1
enquiries 470
entertainment opportunities 609
environmental issues 131–68
    change responses 155–7
    cultural forces 138–45
    e-business 146
    ecological forces 148–51
    economic forces 132–8
    energy conservation 150–1
    environmental change responses 155–7
    environmental scanning 153–5
    ethics 157
    forces 462–6
    friendly ingredients 148
    Internet marketing 557
    legal forces 145–8
    physical forces 148–51
    political forces 145–8
    sales 462–6
    social forces 138–45
    target marketing 232
    technological forces 151–3
environmental scanning 153–5, 171–2
erosion, differential advantages 697
ethics 11
    advertising 444–6
    consumer decision-making 97–8
    dilemmas 157, 198
    direct marketing 538–9
    distribution 662–4
    environmental issues 156
    Femidom case 197
    Internet marketing 575–8
    marketing research 196–8
    personal selling 495–7
    pricing strategies 401–4
    products 293–5
    public relations 618–19
    reciprocal buying 497
    sales management 495–7
    sales promotions 618–19
    social responsibility 142–5
ethnographic research 186

Europe
see also central Europe; eastern Europe
advertising
agencies 442
expenditure 419
agencies 442
branding 285–8
direct marketing 506
market development 133–7
single market 135–7
strategic alliances 723
top advertisers 429
European Union (EU) 133
cartels 148
information sources 184
licensing 853
movement into 138
population 140
statistics sources 184
evaluation
advertising 439–40
channel intermediaries 649–50
direct marketing campaigns 537–8
e-commerce marketing mix 575
exhibitions 616
market factors 229–31
market segments 229–32
marketing implementation 772
sales promotions 602–3
salesforce 492–4
sponsorship 612–13
total sales operation 494–5
EVC see economic value to the customer analysis
event sponsorship 610–13
exchanges, e-commerce 556–7
exclusion, Internet marketing 576
exclusiveness, distribution 644, 663
exhibitions 613–16
existing product pricing 387–8
expectations, customers 462–3, 806
expected profits 381
expenditure
advertising 419
direct marketing 506
sponsorship 610–12
experience curve effects 386
experimentation 187, 390–2
expertise, relationship building 122
experts, consultation 185
explicability, pricing 394
exploratory research 181–6

export
direct 851–2
e-marketing 852
indirect 850–1
extended problem-solving 77–9
determinants 78–9
external marketing audits 41–2

F

face-to-face interviews 189
fads, product life cycle 315
fair trading 663–4
family brand names 273
fast food
online 14
youth obesity 402–4
fast reaction-times 696–7
feedback, information 470
fighter brands 262
film industry see movie industry
financial competencies 564
financial services online 805
fiscal barriers 133–4
Fishbein and Ajzen model 71–2
fixing prices 401–2
focused marketing 234–6
follow-ups 478–9
foreign based agents 851
foreign investment 137
foreign markets
see also international marketing
direct investment 855–6
entry strategies 850
'how to enter' decisions 850–6
joint ventures 854–5
selection 846
'which to enter' decisions 846–50
foundations, brand extensions 265
4-P's 16
criticism 21–2
fragmentation
markets 464, 508
media 508
franchising
channel strategy 645–7
foreign markets 853–4
international 646
free samples 597–8, 599
friendly ingredients, environmental 148
full cost pricing 378–9

Index

functional cost allocation 782
functional organization 773–4
fundamentals 1–256
    consumer behaviour 65–98
    information systems 168–208
    market segmentation 209–56
    marketing environment 131–68
    marketing research 168–208
    modern firms 2–34
    organizational buying behaviour 99–130
    overview 35–64
    planning 35–64
    positioning 209–56

G

gaining acceptance 769
GAM *see* global account management
gender 222
genetically modified (GM) ingredients 144
geodemographics
    consumer behaviour 89
    database information 512
geographic factors 560–1
geographic information systems (GIS)
    segmentation 224
    store location 823, 824
geographic variables 222–4
Germany 391
global account management (GAM) 486–7
global branding 285–8
globalization
    markets 464
    organization 869–70
    process management 871
glossary 905–16
GM *see* genetically modified ingredients
goal achievements 5
going international 844–6
going-rate pricing 380
Goodhart model 72
goods-service continuum 793
gradual strategic repositioning 156
green marketing 143
grey jeans case 868
grey markets 235, 663
growth
    category managers 776
    direct marketing 508–9
    life cycle 311
    market building 715
    products
        life cycle 311
        placement 617
        strategies 325–7
    projections 311
    strategies 325–7, 335–6
    Unilever 335–6
Growth-Share Matrix 318–22
guerrilla marketing 720–1

H

habitual problem-solving 79
'happy hours' 619
the hard sell 495
harvest objectives 730
hedonistic influences 79
high-cost solutions 758–9
high-involvement situations 72–3
hold objectives 725–9
    attractive conditions 726–9
hotel industry 808
households
    classification 89
    two-income 140

I

idea generation, new products 347–9
ideology 11
implementation 749–882
    see also marketing implementation
    core strategies 50–1
imports
    lager market 239
    pricing strategies 395
indirect exporting 850–1
individual brand names 273
inducements 618
industry
    channels 640–1
    competitors 681
        see also competitive industry structure
    customers 640, 641
    direct distribution to 640, 641
    structure analysis 678–86
infant formula, ethics 496–7
information
    see also marketing research
    competition 197–8
    consumer behaviour 70–1, 79–82
    databases 510–12
    EU 184

feedback 470
gathering 197–8
online services 185
problems 54
processing 79–82
searches 70–1
sources 183–5
systems 169–208
   definitions 170–2
   market research 172–4
   online competence 566
   use of 195–6
use of 195–6
websites 185
information technology
   price setting 397
   retailing 821
ingredient co-branding 282–3, 285
innovations
   commercialization 357–8, 363
   constraints 12
   creative leadership 342
   culture creation 340–1
   Internet marketing 564
   keys to success 339
   organizations 228
   pricing 383
   radicalization 350–1
inseparability, marketing services 795
inside order-takers 467–8
intangible marketing services 792–5
intangible repositioning 241–2
integration
   cost leadership 699
   efforts 5
   Internet business 118
   marketing communications 416–18
   media campaigns 535–6
   public relations 608
intensity, distribution 643–4
interactive television (ITV) advertising 434
internal ad hoc data 171
internal continuous data 170–1
internal factors, Internet marketing 557, 571
internal market segmentation 764
internal marketing
   audits 42
   brand building 273
   Internet 557, 571
   mix programmes 765
   services 801–2
internalization 755, 756–7

internally orientated businesses vs market-driven businesses 8–10
international franchising 646
international marketing 843–82
   adaptation 856–60
   advertising taboos 863
   deciding to go international 844–6
   macroenvironmental issues 846–8
   market entry method 857
   microenvironmental issues 849–50
   mix decisions 861–9
   organizing operations 869–70
   place 869
   price 865–9
   products 861–2
   promotion 862–5
   rebranding 277
   standardization 856–60
   strategy development 856–69
   which market to enter 846–50
international salesforce motivation 492
Internet
   benefits 558–62
   building competitive advantages 696
   business integration 118
   consumer benefits/limitations 559
   integrated business 118
   international marketing 852
   limitations 558–62
   media class decisions 437
   new product development 343
   pricing new products 386
   product life cycle 314
   sales management 465
   survey comparisons 189
   survey tools 191
   terms 552
Internet marketing 549–92
   adoption factors 557–8
   advertising 414–15
   comparative advantages 558
   competencies 563–6
   competitive advantages 566–8
   costs 567
   e-commerce 551, 553–6
   environmental factors 557
   ethics 575–8
   exclusion 576
   innovations 564
   internal factors 557
   price 567
   privacy issues 576–7

productivity 565–6
quality 565, 567
services 567
websites 550–3
interrelationships, cost leadership 699
intrusions 196
inventory control 658–9
investment
    see also return on capital investment
    direct 855–6
    foreign 137
iTV *see* interactive television advertising

J

Japan 639–40
job specification 779
job types 528
joint ventures 854–5
just-in-time purchasing 113–14

K

key account management (KAM) 484–6
key branding decisions 273–5
knowledge lack 54

L

ladder of support 757–8
launch strategies 384
launching theme parks 32–3
lead times, clothing 30
leadership 342
    see also cost leadership
leasing 116–17
legal issues 145–8, 277
licensing 853
life cycle
    consumer behaviour 85–6
    costs 109
    demographic variables 222
    organizational buying 109
    products *see* product life cycle
    stages 86
lifestyle
    consumer behaviour 84–5
    psychographic segmentation 218
    segmentation 219
limited problem-solving 79
linkages, cost leadership 699
listening to customers 16
lists, direct marketing 509
low-cost airlines 696
low-involvement situations 72–3
loyalty schemes 544–7
    cards 600

M

MA–CP *see* Market Attractiveness-Competitive Position Model
macroenvironmental issues
    international marketing 846–8
    political-legal influences 847–8
    socio-cultural influences 847
macrosegmentation 225–6
mail
    direct marketing campaigns 523–6
    ethics 538
    orders 820
    surveys 190
maintenance, repair and operation (MRO) 112
major store types 818–20
malredemption of coupons 618
management
    see also change...; customer relationship...; key account...; relationship...
    channel intermediaries 647–52
    client-agency relationship 442
    direct marketing campaigns 519–38
    forces, sales 462–6
    globalization process 871
    marketing implementation 751–90
    marketing services 796–817
    new products 346–63
    products and brands 343–6
    QCi customer models 517
    sales 461–504
    salesforce 487–94
    self 471
    services
        productivity 806–9
        quality 804–6
        staff 809–10
manager job specification 779
manufacturers
    brands 262
    selection 173
marginal cost pricing *see* direct cost pricing
margins
    negotiation 396
    retailers 667–72
market attractiveness 849
Market Attractiveness-Competitive Position (MA–CP) Model 322–4
market centred organization 777–8
market factor evaluation 229–31

Index

market research *see* marketing research
market segmentation 209–56
   advantages 210
   behavioural 214–18
   consumers 212–25
   geographic information systems 224
   methods 228
   organizational markets 225–8
   process 212
   psychographic segmentation 218–24
   purpose 210–11
   target marketing 228–36
   variable combination 224–5
market-driven businesses vs internally orientated
   businesses 8–10
marketing concept 4–5
   approaches 24
   effects 315
   ideology 11
   limitations 10–13
marketing control 751, 779–80
marketing ethics
   see ethics
marketing implementation 749–882
   barriers 758–61
   change management 754–8
   developing strategies 762–72
   evaluation 772
   execution 765–72
   good ideas 770
   managing 751–90
   negotiation 772
   objectives 757–8, 762–4
   operational control 781–3
   performance 753–4
   politics 769–71
   resistance 761
   strategic control 781
   strategies 753–4, 764–5
   successful 770
   time 771–2
   unquantifiable benefits 760
marketing mix
   adaptation 858
   blending 21
   characteristics 19–21
   competitive advantages 19–21
   core strategy decisions 50
   corporate resources 21
   customer needs matching 19
   decisions 257–674
   development 828
   differential advantages 692

   e-commerce 569–75
   effectiveness 16–19
   internal programmes 765
   international marketing 861–9
   place 137
   price 136
   products 136
   promotion 136–7
   services 813–17
   standardization 858
marketing orientation
   business performance 23
   pricing 382–400
   vs production orientation 5–7
marketing report blocking 762
marketing research
   agencies 175
   approaches 174–5
   continuous 177–8
   DIY approaches 174
   environmental scanning 171–2
   ethics 196–8
   findings misuse 196–7
   importance 172–4
   information systems 169–208
   process stages 178–95
   selling under guise of 198
   types 175–8
   use of 195–6
   validity 173
marketing services 791–842
   customer benefits 798–9
   inseparability 795
   intangibility 792–5
   management 796–817
   nature 792–6
   organizational benefits 797–8
   people 816
   perishability 796
   place 815–16
   price 815
   process 816–17
   retailing 817–25
   variability 795–6
marketing-orientated pricing 382–400
markets
   attractiveness 849
   exchanges 556–7
   fragmentation 508
   going international 845
   international entry methods 846–50, 857
   microenvironmental issues 849
   new product development 355–6

Index

niching 309
  penetration 46–7
  sales 464
  share analysis 781–2
  testing 355–6
Maslow's hierarchy of needs 83
masts, mobile phones 624–5
matching competition, advertising budgets 428
materials handling 662
matrix organization 778
mature markets 312
measurement
  competitiveness 691
  satisfaction 781
  service quality 806
  success 827
  website audits 691
media
  advertising 433–9
  decisions 433–9
  direct marketing campaigns 522
  fragmentation 508
  integrated campaigns 535–6
  neutral planning 417–18
  press 434, 470
  vehicle decisions 438–9
merchandisers 469
mergers
  or acquisitions 721
  legal forces 147
  rebranding 276
message decisions 428–32
microenvironmental issues 849–50
microsegmentation 225
  decision-making units 227–8
  purchasing organization 227–8
misconception elimination 768
misleading advertising 444–5
missionary salespeople 468
misuse, research findings 196–7
mobile marketing 530–2
mobile phones
  community relations 624–5
  markets 312
  masts 624–5
modern firms 3–34
  see also companies
Mole survey 141
money-off promotions 595
monopolies and mergers 147
motivation 82–3
  channel intermediaries 648–9
  salesforce management 490–2

movie industry
  blockbusters 626–31
  product placement 616–17
MRO *see* maintenance, repair and operation
multinational organization 870
music industry 638

N

national boundaries 277
needs
  identification 475–6
  Maslow's hierarchy 83
  recognition 68–70
negotiation
  buyer-seller 463
  margins 396
  marketing implementation 766, 772
network communities 562
new entrants, threats 678–80
new product development (NPD) 337–74
  definitions 339–40
  departments and committees 344
  management 346–63
  organization structures 341–6
  pricing 383–7
news releases 606–7
niche markets
  catalogue marketing 534
  shakeout survival 309
niche objectives 729
non-profit organizations 826–9
  characteristics 826–7
  procedures 827–8
non-store types 818–20
non-wasteful packaging 149
NPD *see* new product development
numbness, change 755, 756

O

obesity 402–4
objections, personal selling 476–7
objectives
  advertising budgets 428
  advertising strategies 423–7
  direct marketing campaigns 520–2
  e-commerce marketing mix 569–70
  exhibitions 614–15
  market penetration 46–7
  marketing 46–8
  personal selling 481–2
  pricing strategies 387–8
  sales promotions 601–2

salesforce management 487
   strategic 46, 47–8
   and tasks 428
obsolescence, products 294
office politics, organizational buying 109
omnibus studies 176
on-the-go consumption 85
online...
   see also e-business; e-commerce; e-marketing
   communities 142
   consumer research 67
   delivery companies 635
   financial services 805
   food service 14
   marketing 414–15
      see also Internet marketing
      advantages 566–8
      competencies 563–6
      information 185
   performance 178
   product development 344
   purchasing 114–15
   services 185, 635
   social responsibility 142
   website analysis 178
openings, personal selling 475
operant conditioning 82
operational issues
   control 781–3
   international marketing 869–70
   service 807
opportunities 211
   see also SWOT analysis
   strength matching 46
opportunity cost 53–5
opportunity to see (OTS) 438
opposition interaction 770–1
order-creators 468
order-getters 468–9
order-processing 657–8
order-takers 467–8
organization
   campaign development 440–4
   core strategies 50–1
   functional 773–4
   market-centred organization 777–8
   marketing 773–9
   matrix organization 778
   new product development 341–6
   reorganization 135
   salesforce 483–7
   structures 341–6

organizations
   benefits of services 797–8
   buying behaviour 99–130
      building relationship 122–4
      business customers 110
      buy class 110–12
      centralized purchasing 114
      characteristics 100–2
      choice criteria 107–12
      customer nature/size 100
      decision-making process 102–7, 110–11
      derived demand 101–2
      dimensions 102–10
      how they buy 104–6
      influences 110–13
      just-in-time purchasing 113–14
      life-cycle costs 109
      online purchasing 114–15
      perceived risk 109
      personal likes/dislikes 109
      price 109
      product types 112–13
      purchase practice developments 113–17
      reciprocal buying 101
      risks 101
      specific requirements 101
      supply continuity 109
      who buys? 102–4
   innovativeness 228
   market segmentation 225–8
   segmentation methods 228
   services benefits 797–8
   structures 751, 773–9
OTS *see* opportunity to see
outside order-takers 468
overpowering, product life cycle 314
overseas sales
   see also foreign markets; international marketing
   offices 852
own-label brands 262
   copycatting 263
ownership, channels 647
ozone layer protection 149

P

packaging
   products 294
   recyclable 149
pan-European
   branding 285–8
   marketing 136–7

Index

parallel co-branding 283, 285
parallel importing 395
payment systems, advertising agencies 443–4
peer-to-peer technology 638
penetration
    markets 46–7
    pricing 402–4
people, marketing services 816
perceived risk
    consumer behaviour 78
    organizational buying 109
percentage of sales 427
perception 80
performance
    controls 575
    e-commerce marketing mix 575
    marketing implementation 753–4
perishability 796
perpetual mapping 239–40
personal ambitions 760
personal criteria 75–6
personal likes/dislikes 109
personal selling 414–15, 461–504
    ethics 495–7
    objectives and strategies 481–2
    preparation 474
    skills 472–9
personalities
    brands 431–2
    consumer behaviour 84
    problems 54
    segmentation 219
persuasion 766
philosophy
    marketing 23–5
    visitor attractions 31–2
physical barriers 133
physical distribution 655–62
physical forces 148–51
pipeline distribution 662
place
    international marketing 869
    marketing mix 19, 137
    marketing services 815–16
planned obsolescence 294
planning
    business mission 39–40
    core strategy 48–52
    e-marketing 51
    flow chart 38
    fundamentals 36–7
    key questions 52
    overview 35–64
    problems 53–4
    processes 37–46
    research 179–80
    rewards 52–3
    stages 52
PLC *see* product life cycle
policies
    competition 134–5
    cost leadership 699–700
    decisions 699–700
political factors
    forces 145–8
    implementation strategies 766–7
    legal influences 847–8
    macroenvironmental issues 847–8
    marketing implementation 769–71
    pricing strategies 396
    problems 53
    target marketing 232
pollution 150
poorly worded questions 193
population growth 138–9
Porter model 679
portfolio management
    balance 845–6
    BCG Growth-Share Matrix 320–1
    Market Attractiveness-Competitive Position (MA–CP)
        Model 322–4
    planning 308–27
positioning 209, 236–42
    brand building 268–71
    co-branding 283
    imported lager market 239
    intangible 241–2
    perpetual mapping 239–40
    products 424–6
    repositioning 240–2
    retailing 822
    services 810–12
    strategies 383
    tangible 242
post purchase evaluation 73–4
post-testing research 603
posters 434–6
power application 767
powers, buyers 463–4
pre-opening, theme parks 32–3
pre-relationship stage 118–19
pre-testing research 602
predatory pricing 402
premiums 596–7
presentation, reports 194–5
presentations, personal selling 474, 476

press
    see also media
    media class decisions 434
    prospecting 470
price 825
    changes 397–401
    differential advantages 695–6
    discounts 600
    e-commerce marketing mix 571–2
    ethics 401–4
    existing products 387–8
    information technology 397
    international marketing 865–9
    Internet marketing 567
    marketing mix 18, 136
    marketing orientation 382–400
    marketing services 815
    new products 383–7
    organizational buying 109
    parallel importing 395
    product lines 393
    quality relationships 393, 425
    sensitivity 230
    strategies 375–411
    undermining competitors 867
privacy issues
    direct marketing 538–9
    Internet marketing 576–7
    market research 196
prize promotions 599
problem handling 54–5
problem identification 475–6
problem solving 79
processes
    globalization 871
    management 871
    marketing services 816–17
    personal selling 474
    planning 37–46
producer distribution
    to agents to industrial customers 640
    consumer reconciliation 635–6
    direct to consumers 637–8
    to distributors to industrial customers 641
    to industrial customers 640
    to retailers to consumers 639
    to wholesalers to retailers to consumers 639–40
product life cycle (PLC)
    limitations 314–17
    management 308–10
    uses 310–14
production
    customer involvement 808
    orientation, vs marketing orientation 5–7

productivity
    Internet marketing 565–6
    service management 806–9
products
    assortment 823–4
    BCG Growth-Share Matrix 320–1
    brand and corporate identities 258–306
    co-branding 281–4
    customization 568
    database information 511
    definition 260–1
    development 352–5
    differential advantages 693
    diffusion 359
    dumping 404
    e-commerce marketing mix 571
    ethics 293–5
    functional cost allocation 782
    growth strategies 325–7
    international marketing 861–2
    knowledge 474
    life cycle 310–17
    lines 262, 393
    management 307–36
    managers 343–6
    Market Attractiveness-Competitive Position (MA–CP) Model 322–4
    marketing mix 16–18, 136
    mix 262
    new 337–74
    organizational buying 112–13
    personal selling 474
    placement 616–18
    planning 308–37
    portfolios 320–1, 324–5
    positioning 424–6
    pricing 383–8, 393
    product-based organization 774–7
    profitability 783
    replacements 360–1
    types 112–13
    variety 567
professional qualifications 466
profitability
    analysis 782–3
    competitive bidding 381
    products 783
    strong brands 264–5
project teams 342–3
promise fulfilment 802–3
promotional mix 414–15
    methods 593–631

Index

promotions
    see also sales promotions
    database information 511
    differential advantages 694–5
    e-commerce 572–4
    international marketing 862–5
    marketing mix 18–19, 136–7, 572–4
    sponsorship 610
proposals, research 180
prospecting 470
prospects, database information 510–11
psychographic segmentation 218–24
    demographic variables 220–2
    lifestyle 218
    personality 219
psychology, customers 81
public relations
    ethics 618–19
    integration 608
    promotional mix 603–7, 608
public scrutiny 827
publicity 414–15, 603–7
    see also advertising
    characteristics 605–6
    sponsorship 608–9
purchase
    see also buying
    behaviour 215–16
    behavioural segmentation 215
    consumer behaviour 79
    importance, organizations 113
    involvement levels 79
    microsegmentation 227–8
    occasion 215
    organizations 227–8
    practice developments 113–17

Q

QCi customer management model 517
QSCV *see* quality, service, cleanliness and value
qualifications, sales management 466
qualitative research 182
quality
    see also total quality management
    brand building 268–9
    certification 265–6
    Internet marketing 565, 567
    management 804–6
    pricing 425
quality, service, cleanliness and value (QSCV) 13, 810
quantitative data-collection stage 186–94
questionnaire design 191–4
    poorly worded questions 193

R

radical innovation 350–1
radical strategic repositioning 156
radio 436–7
rail distribution 660–1
reasoning, personal influences 82
rebranding 276–9
reciprocal buying
    ethics 497
    organizations 101
records, customers 470
recruitment 487–9
recycling 149
reference groups 89
reference selling 470
rejections, sales people 480
relational development model 484–6
relationship management 117–22, 471–2
    account relationships 484–7
    customers 177–8, 514–18, 548
    development stage 119–20
    early stage 119
    final stage 120–2
    long-term stage 120
    managing service relationships 796–804
    pre-relationship stage 118–19
    relationship building 122–4
    systems 177–8
reorganization 135
replacement products 339, 360–1
reports
    blocking 762
    presentation 194–5
    social 143
    writing 194–5
repositioning 156, 240–2
    advertising 450–2
    brand building 271
research
    see also marketing research
    brief 179–80
    exploratory 181–6
    planning 179–80
    proposals 180
    qualitative 182
    sales promotions 602–3
    secondary 181–2
resistance to change 761
resource support 124
response patterns 686
responsibilities, sales 469–72
restrictions, supply 663
restrictive practices 147

Index

retailing 817–25
   Asia 823
   audits 177
   customer psychology 81
   databases 513
   differentiation 822
   e-marketing 821
   evolution 820–1
   key decisions 821–6
   margins 667–72
   marketing databases 513
   positioning 822
   pricing strategies 396, 825
   producer distribution 639
   rebranding 279
   store location 822–3
   technology 807–8
   theory 820–1
retention strategy development 799–804
return on capital investment (ROI) 24
reverse marketing 115–16
rewards
   planning 52–3
   systems 760
      problems 54
risk
   organizational buying 101
   perceived risk 78
   product placement 617–18
   reduction 124
   relationship building 124
road distribution 661
ROI *see* return on capital investment

S

safety 293
sales
   advertising 414–15
   advertising budgets 427
   analysis 781–2
   ethics 495–7, 618–19
   job types 528
   management 461–504
      ethics 495–7
      problems 480
   marketing conflict 775
   objectives 601–2
   presentations 474
   promotions 594–603
      advertising 414–15
      ethics 618–19
      evaluations 602–3
      major types 595–601
      objectives 601–2
   representatives 851–2
   responsibilities 469–72
   volume 327
salesforce
   automation 464
   design 482–7
   management 487–94
   positioning products 427
samples, sales promotions 597–8, 599
sampling processes 188
satisfaction
   customers 13–16, 781
   measurement 781
saying versus doing 760–1
scale building 135
screening new products 349, 351
search for meaning concept 756
secondary research 181–2
segmentation *see* market segmentation
selection
   advertising agencies 443
   channel intermediaries 642–3, 648
   foreign markets 846
   manufacturers 173
   salesforce management 487–9
   suppliers 106
selective distortion 80
selective distribution 644
selective retention 81
self-doubt 755, 756
self-image 78
self-management 471
sellers
   buyer relationships 119–20, 123
   skills 472–9
   types 466–9
selling under guise of research 198
senior management roles 345–6
sensitivity, price 230
served markets 350
services
   see also marketing services
   barriers 804, 805
   channel intermediaries 641
   differential advantage 811–12
   Internet marketing 567
   levels 124
   management 804–6
   marketing mix 813–17
   measurement 806
   online 635

Index

positioning 810–12
productivity 806–9
provision 471
quality 567, 804, 805
recovery strategies 803
sales responsibilities 471
scales 806
staff management 809–10
setting budgets 427–8
shakeout survival 309
SIC *see* Standard Industrial Classification
simulated market testing 356
simultaneous engineering 343
single European market 135–7
skills
    lack 54
    personal selling 472–9
    problems 54
'slack' packaging 294
slotting allowances 663
social...
    class 88
    engineering 11
    exclusion 576
    factors 232
    forces 138–45
    grade 88
    influences
        consumer behaviour 87–9
        culture 87–8
        reference groups 89
        social class 88–9
    marketing 11
    reporting 143
    responsibility
        ethics 142–5
        online communities 142
    values 445
society and marketing 11–12
socio-cultural influences 847
socio-economic variables 222
sources
    competitive advantage 689–91
    dullness 12–13
    information 184
    marketing information 183–5
    statistics 184
specialist distribution services 637
speciality shops 819
sponsorship 607–13
    arts 829
    associations 609–10

evaluation 612–13
expenditure 610–12
selection 612–13
sport sponsorship 611
Standard Industrial Classification (SIC) codes 226
standardization
    development barriers 859
    global brands 859
    international marketing 856–60
    marketing mix 858
statistics sources 184
stores
    atmosphere 825
    location 822–3, 824
strategic alliances 309
strategic competencies 563–4
strategic focus
    divest objectives 731
    harvest objectives 730
    niche objectives 729
strategic objectives
    BCG Growth-Share Matrix 319–20
    MA–CP Model 323–4
    sales management 481
strategic thrust
    generic options 47
    marketing objectives 46
strategic triangle 712
strategies
    see also competitive marketing strategies
    advertising 422–40
    alliances 723–5
    attack 717
    build objectives 723–5
    channels 641–7
    clothing 28
    competitive advantage 687–9
    competitive industry structure 684
    competitor analysis 685–6
    control 781
    defence 727
    e-commerce marketing mix 569–70
    growth 325–7, 335–6
    implementation combination 753–4
    international marketing 856–69
    Internet marketing 566–8
    marketing implementation 753–4, 764–5, 781
    marketing orientated pricing 382–8
    personal selling 481–2
    planning 48–52
    pricing 375–411
    product growth 325–7

sales 480–1
target marketing 233–8
target markets 48
strengths
see also SWOT analysis
competitors 683–5
opportunity matching 46
stretching brand extensions 279–81
strong advertising theories 421–2
strong brands 264–6
style 694
substitutes, threats 680–1
success
competitive industry structure 683–4
factors 683–4
marketing implementation 770
measurement 827
supermarkets 818–19
see also stores
suppliers
bargaining power 680
continuity 109
organizational buying 106, 109
selection 106
supply and demand balancing 808–9
supply restrictions 663
support online 635
surveys
comparisons 189
data-collection 188–91
Internet tools 191
methods 188–91
SWOT analysis 44–6
e-commerce marketing mix 569
strategic development 45
symbols, positioning products 426

T

taboos, advertising 863
tactics
implementation 767–8
price changes 398–9, 401
tailored marketing mix 211
tangible repositioning 242
target audiences
advertising strategies 422–3
direct marketing campaigns 519–20
target marketing 810–11
bargaining power 231
capability 232
competitive factors 231–2
customized 236–9

differentiation 827–8
evaluation 229–32
grey markets 235
market segmentation 228–36
process 212
strategies 233–8
target markets
core strategy 48
sales management 480–1
selection 211
targeting classification 223
tasks, advertising budgets 428
teams 342–5
technical barriers 134
technical support 122
technology 807–8
see also information technology
commercialization 361–2
direct marketing 509
e-marketing 229
forces 151–3
peer-to-peer 638
sales forces 464–6
sales management 473
use 229
telemarketing 526–36
applications 528–36
databases 527–8
ethics 538
television
media class decisions 433–4
viewership panels 177
termination of products 310–11
test marketing see market testing
testing
AC^2ID test 289, 291–3
change management 756
theme parks 31–4
theories
advertising 421–2
retailing 820–1
weak 421–2
third-generation mobile phones 624–5
third-party endorsements 618
threats
see also SWOT analysis
new entrants 678–80
and opportunities 211
substitutes 680–1
time, implementation 771–2
total quality management (TQM) 108
total sales operation evaluation 494–5
TQM see total quality management

tracking brands 453–60
trade directories 470
trade inducements 618
trade marketing 818
trade promotions 596
trade-off analysis
    German car companies 391
    value to customers 389–90
training
    channel intermediaries 649
    salesforce management 489
transactions, database information 511
transfer pricing 868–9
transition curves 755
transnational organization 870
transportation 660–2
trials
    advertising strategies 423–4
    sales promotions 601
trust
    building 803
    strong brands 266
two-income households 140

U

umbrella branding 273
undermining competitors 867
undifferentiated marketing 233–4
unemployment 132–3
unpredictability, product life cycle 315
unquantifiable benefits 760

V

validity, marketing research 173
value chain 690–1
value creation 548
values
    advertising 445
    and beliefs 217–18
    companies 264
    customers 13–16, 388–92, 548

variability, marketing services 795–6
vicarious learning 82
videoconferencing 472, 473
videotext systems 551
viral marketing
    exhibitions 615
    tools 572–3
virtual sales office 464
visitor attractions 31–2

W

warehousing 659–60
waterways 662
weak theories, advertising 421–2
weaknesses
    see also SWOT analysis
    competitors 683–5
web technologies 530
websites
    analysis 178
    audits 691
    Internet marketing 550–3
    marketing information 185
    measuring competitiveness 691
    online performance 178
weighting systems 323
well-blended communications 271–2
word of mouth 814
workforce 564
workload approach 482–3
world population growth 138–9

Y

youth markets 87, 221, 301–3
youth obesity 402–4